Praise for *The Third Reich in Power*

"Heir to a British tradition of dons who write engagingly for a broad public, Evans has done a great service simply in digesting the mountain of recent scholarship on the Nazis for the general reader."
—*The New York Times Book Review*

"A wonder of synthesis and acute judgment, this work when completed will be the definitive study for at least a generation . . . [A] magnificent achievement . . . When his game is on, as it usually is, few can rival his ability to write crisply argued history. Evans's coolly precise, profoundly disquieting history gives the most thorough answer yet to the question that will nag humanity for a thousand years: What accounts for the German people's support—at times passive, at times fervent—for the vicious and often ridiculous thugs who ruled over them for nearly twelve years?"
—Benjamin Schwartz, *The Atlantic Monthly* (editor's choice)

"Evans' new book is a masterly and exhaustive account . . . a most impressive study."
—*Foreign Affairs*

"There seems to be nothing Mr. Evans does not cover. What sets [his trilogy] apart . . . is the narrative command Mr. Evans exercises over the innumerable components of the history and the breadth and depth of his synthesis."
—*The Washington Times*

"Evans' masterly account blends narrative with the discussion of important themes. . . . Brilliantly told."
—*The Globe and Mail* (Toronto)

"Mr. Evans' latest book has been lauded as a definitive, authoritative English-language account, blending narrative, description, and analysis."
—*Embassy*

"A work drawn from a mountain of scholarship . . . As a readable, compelling synthesis of the period, [*The Third Reich in Power*] . . . is a major achievement."
—*The Boston Globe*

"A major achievement. No other recent synthetic history has quite the range and narrative power of Evans's work. . . . When complete, Evans's trilogy will take its place alongside Ian Kershaw's monumental two-volume biography of Hitler as the standard works in English."
—*Publishers Weekly* (starred review)

"A superb account of the growth and day-to-day functioning of the Nazi state."
—*Kirkus Reviews* (starred review)

ABOUT THE AUTHOR

Richard J. Evans is one of the world's leading historians of modern Germany. He was born in London in 1947. From 1989 to 1998 he was Professor of History at Birkbeck College, University of London. Since 1998 he has been Professor of Modern History at Cambridge University. In 1994 he was awarded the Hamburg Medal for Art and Science for cultural services to the city, and in 2000 he was the principal expert witness in the David Irving libel trial. His books include *The Feminist Movement in Germany, 1894–1933, Death in Hamburg* (winner of the Wolfson Literary Award for History), *In Hitler's Shadow, Rituals of Retribution* (winner of the Fraenkel Prize in Contemporary History), *In Defence of History* (which has so far been translated into eight languages), *Telling Lies About Hitler* and *The Coming of the Third Reich* (shortlisted for the *Los Angeles* Times Book Prize).

RICHARD J. EVANS

The Third Reich in Power

PENGUIN BOOKS

PENGUIN BOOKS

Published by the Penguin Group

Penguin Group (USA) Inc., 375 Hudson Street, New York, New York 10014, U.S.A.

Penguin Group (Canada), 90 Eglinton Avenue East, Suite 700, Toronto,
Ontario, Canada M4P 2Y3 (a division of Pearson Penguin Canada Inc.)

Penguin Books Ltd, 80 Strand, London WC2R 0RL, England

Penguin Ireland, 25 St Stephen's Green, Dublin 2, Ireland (a division of Penguin Books Ltd)

Penguin Group (Australia), 250 Camberwell Road, Camberwell,
Victoria 3124, Australia (a division of Pearson Australia Group Pty Ltd)

Penguin Books India Pvt Ltd, 11 Community Centre, Panchsheel Park, New Delhi – 110 017, India

Penguin Group (NZ), cnr Airborne and Rosedale Roads, Albany,
Auckland 1310, New Zealand (a division of Pearson New Zealand Ltd)

Penguin Books (South Africa) (Pty) Ltd, 24 Sturdee Avenue,
Rosebank, Johannesburg 2196, South Africa

Penguin Books Ltd, Registered Offices:
80 Strand, London WC2R 0RL, England

First published by Allen Lane 2005
First published in the United States of America by The Penguin Press,
a member of Penguin Group (USA) Inc. 2005
Published in Penguin Books (UK) 2006
This edition published in Penguin Books (USA) 2006

5   7   9   10   8   6   4

Copyright © Richard J. Evans, 2005
All rights reserved

Maps drawn by Andras Bereznay

THE LIBRARY OF CONGRESS HAS CATALOGED THE HARDCOVER EDITION AS FOLLOWS:
The Third Reich in power, 1933–1939 / Richard J. Evans.
p.   cm.
Includes bibliographical references and index.
ISBN 1-59420-074-2 (hc.)
ISBN 0 14 30.3790 0
1. Germany—History—1933–1945.   2. National socialism—History.   I. Title.
DD256.5.E924 2005
943.086—dc22   2005052128

Printed in the United States of America

For Matthew and Nicholas

Contents

List of Illustrations

ILLUSTRATION CREDITS

List of Maps

Preface

This book tells the story of the Third Reich, the regime created in Germany by Hitler and his National Socialists, from the moment when it completed its seizure of power in the summer of 1933 to the point when it plunged Europe into the Second World War at the beginning of September 1939. It follows an earlier volume, *The Coming of the Third Reich*, which told the story of the origins of Nazism, analysed the development of its ideas and recounted its rise to power during the years of the ill-fated Weimar Republic. A third volume, *The Third Reich at War*, will follow in due course, covering the period from September 1939 to May 1945 and exploring the legacy of Nazism in Europe and the world in the rest of the twentieth century and on to the present. The general approach of all three volumes is set out in the Preface to *The Coming of the Third Reich* and does not need to be repeated in detail here. Those who have already read that book can go straight to the beginning of the first chapter of this one; but some readers might like to be reminded of the central arguments of the earlier volume, and those who have not read it may wish to turn to the Prologue, which sketches the main lines of what happened before the end of June 1933, when the story told in the following pages begins.

The approach adopted in the present book is necessarily thematic, but within each chapter I have tried, as in the previous volume, to mix narrative, description and analysis and to chart the rapidly changing situation as it unfolded over time. The Third Reich was not a static or monolithic dictatorship; it was dynamic and fast-moving, consumed from the outset by visceral hatreds and ambitions. Dominating everything was the drive to war, a war that Hitler and the Nazis saw as leading to the German racial reordering of Central and Eastern Europe and the re-emergence of Germany as the dominant power on the European Continent and beyond that, the world. In each of the following chapters, dealing in turn with policing and repression, culture and propaganda, religion and education, the economy, society and everyday life, racial policy and antisemitism, and foreign policy, the overriding imperative of preparing Germany and its people for a major war emerges clearly as the common thread. But that imperative was neither rational in itself, nor followed in a coherent way. In one area after another, the contradictions and inner irrationalities of the regime emerge; the Nazis' headlong rush to war contained the seeds of the Third Reich's eventual destruction. How and why this should be so is one of the major questions that run through this book and bind its separate parts together. So too do many further questions: about the extent to which the Third Reich won over the German people; the manner in which it worked; the degree to which Hitler, rather than broader systematic factors inherent in the structure of the Third Reich as a whole, drove policy onwards; the possibilities of opposition, resistance, dissent or even non-conformity to the dictates of National Socialism under a dictatorship that claimed the total allegiance of all its citizens; the nature of the Third Reich's relationship with modernity; the ways in which its policies in different areas resembled, or differed from, those pursued elsewhere in Europe and beyond during the 1930s; and much more besides. A narrative thread is provided by the arrangement of the chapters, which move progressively closer to the war as the book moves along.

Inevitably, however, while separating out the many different aspects of the Third Reich into different themes makes it easier to present them coherently, it also comes at a price, since these aspects impinged on each other in a variety of different ways. Foreign policy had an impact on racial policy, racial policy had an impact on educational policy, propaganda went hand-in-hand with repression, and so on. So the treatment of a theme in a particular chapter is necessarily incomplete in itself, and the individual chapters should not be treated as comprehensive accounts of the topics with which they deal. Thus, for example, the removal of the Jews from the economy is dealt with in the chapter on the economy, rather than in the chapter on racial policy; Hitler's formulation of his war aims in the so-called Hossbach memorandum in 1937 is covered in the section on rearmament rather than in the chapter on foreign policy; and the impact of the German takeover of Austria on antisemitism in the Third Reich is discussed in the final chapter, rather than in the section on antisemitism in 1938. I hope that these decisions about the structure of the book make sense, but their logic will only be clear to those who read the book consecutively, from start to finish. Anyone who wants to use it simply as a work of reference is recommended to turn to the index, where the location of the book's principal themes, characters and events is laid out in detail.

In the preparation of the present work I have once more benefited from the incomparable resources of Cambridge University Library, the Wiener Library and the German Historical Institute London. The Staatsarchiv der Freien- und Hansestadt Hamburg and the Forschungsstelle für Zeitgeschichte in Hamburg kindly permitted consultation of the unpublished diaries of Luise Solmitz, and Bernhard Fulda generously supplied copies of key issues of German newspapers. The advice and support of many friends and colleagues has been crucial. My agent, Andrew Wylie, and his staff, particularly Christopher Oram and Michal Shavit, gave their time to the project in many ways. Stephanie Chan, Christopher Clark, Bernhard Fulda, Christian Goeschel, Victoria Harris, Robin Holloway, Max Horster, Valeska Huber, Sir Ian Kershaw, Scott Moyers, Jonathan Petropoulos, David Reynolds, Kristin Semmens, Adam Tooze, Nikolaus Wachsmann and Simon Winder read early drafts, saved me from many errors and made many useful suggestions: I am indebted to them for their help. Christian Goeschel also kindly checked the proofs of the Notes and Bibliography. Simon Winder and Scott Moyers have been exemplary editors, and their advice and enthusiasm have been essential throughout. Conversations with, or suggestions from, Norbert Frei, Gavin Stamp, Riccarda Tomani, David Welch and many others have been invaluable. David Watson was an exemplary copy-editor; Alison Hennessy took immense pains over the picture research; and it was extremely instructive to work with András Bereznáy on the maps. Christine L. Corton read the entire manuscript and beyond the application of her professional expertise, her practical support over the years has been indispensable to the whole project. Our sons Matthew and Nicholas, to whom this book, like its predecessor, is dedicated, have provided welcome relief from its grim subject-matter. I am grateful to them all.

Richard J. Evans
Cambridge, May 2005

PROLOGUE

I

The Third Reich came to power in the first half of 1933 on the ruins of Germany's first attempt at democracy, the ill-fated Weimar Republic. By July, the Nazis had created virtually all the fundamental features of the regime that was to govern Germany until its collapse almost twelve years later, in 1945. They had eliminated open opposition at every level, created a one-party state, and co-ordinated all the major institutions of German society with the exceptions of the army and the Churches. Many people have tried to explain how they managed to achieve such a position of total dominance in German politics and society with such speed. One tradition of explanation points to long-term weaknesses in the German national character that made it hostile to democracy, inclined to follow ruthless leaders and susceptible to the appeal of militarists and demagogues. But when one looks at the nineteenth century, one can see very little evidence of such traits. Liberal and democratic movements were no weaker than they were in many other countries. More relevant, perhaps, was the relatively late creation of a German nation-state. After the collapse in 1806 of the Holy Roman Reich created by Charlemagne a millennium before – the famous thousand-year Reich that Hitler sought to emulate – Germany was disunited until the wars engineered by Bismarck between 1864 and 1871, which led to the formation of what was later called the Second Reich, the German Empire ruled by the Kaiser. In many ways this was a modern state: it had a national parliament that, unlike its British counterpart for example, was elected by universal manhood suffrage; elections attracted a voter turnout of over 80 per cent; and political parties were well organized and an accepted part of the political system. The largest of these by 1914, the Social Democratic Party, had over a million members and was committed to democracy, equality, the emancipation of women and the ending of racial discrimination and prejudice, including antisemitism. Germany's economy was the most dynamic in the world, rapidly overtaking the British by the turn of the century, and in the most advanced areas like the electrical and chemical industries, rivalling even the Americans. Middle-class values, culture and behaviour were dominant in Germany by the turn of the century. Modern art and culture were beginning to make their mark in the paintings of Expressionists like Max Beckmann and Ernst Ludwig Kirchner, the plays of Frank Wedekind and the novels of Thomas Mann.

Of course, there was a down-side to the Bismarckian Reich. Aristocratic privilege remained entrenched in some areas, the national parliament's powers were limited and the big industrialists, like their counterparts in the USA, were deeply hostile to unionized labour. Bismarck's persecution, first, of the Catholics in the 1870s, then of the fledgling Social Democratic Party in the 1880s, got Germans used to the idea that a government could declare whole categories of the population 'enemies of the Reich' and drastically curtail their civil liberties. The Catholics responded by trying to integrate more closely into the social and political system, the Social Democrats by sticking rigidly to the law and repudiating the idea of violent resistance or violent revolution; both behavioural traits that were to resurface to disastrous effect in 1933. In the 1890s, too, small extremist political parties and movements emerged, arguing that Bismarck's work of unification was incomplete because millions of ethnic Germans still lived outside the Reich, especially in Austria but also in many other parts of Eastern Europe. While some politicians began to argue that Germany needed a large overseas Empire like the British already possessed, others began to tap lower-middle-class feelings of being overtaken by big business, the small shopkeeper's fear of the department store, the male clerk's resentment of the growing presence in business of the female secretary, the bourgeois sense of disorientation when confronted by Expressionist and abstract art and many other unsettling effects of Germany's headlong social, economic and cultural modernization. Such groups found an easy target in Germany's tiny minority of Jews, a mere 1 per cent of the population, who had mostly been remarkably successful in German society and culture since their emancipation from legal restrictions in the course of the nineteenth century. For the antisemites the Jews were a source of all their problems. They argued that the civil liberties of the Jews had to be restricted and their economic activities curtailed. Soon political parties like the Centre Party and the Conservatives were losing votes to these fringe parties of antisemites. They responded by incorporating into their own programmes the promise to reduce what they described as the subversive influence of the Jews in German society and culture. At the same time, in a very different area of society, Social Darwinists and eugenicists were beginning to argue that the German race needed to be strengthened by discarding the traditional Christian respect for life and by sterilizing or even killing the weak, the handicapped, the criminal and the insane.

These were still minority strands of thought before 1914; nor did anyone weld them together into any kind of effective synthesis. Antisemitism was widespread in German society, but overt violence against Jews was still rare. What changed this situation was the First World War. In August 1914 cheering crowds greeted the outbreak of war on Germany's main town squares, as they did in other countries too. The Kaiser declared that he recognized no parties any more, only Germans. The spirit of 1914 became a mythical symbol of national unity, just as the image of Bismarck conjured up a mythical nostalgia for a strong and decisive political leader. The military stalemate reached by 1916 led to the German war effort being put in the hands of two generals who had won major victories on the Eastern Front, Paul von Hindenburg and Erich Ludendorff. But despite their tight organization of the war effort, Germany was unable to withstand the might of the Americans when they entered the war in 1917, and by early November 1918 the war was lost.

Defeat in the First World War had a disastrous effect on Germany. The peace terms, though no harsher than those which Germany planned to impose on other countries in the event of victory, were bitterly resented by almost all Germans. They included the demand for massive financial reparations for the damage caused by the German occupation of Belgium and northern France, the destruction of the German navy and air force, the restriction of the German army to 100,000 men and the banning of modern weapons like tanks, the loss of territory to France and above all to Poland. The war also destroyed the international economy, which did not recover for another thirty years. Not only were there huge costs to pay, but the collapse of the Habsburg Empire and the creation of new independent states in Eastern Europe fuelled national economic egotism and made international economic co-operation impossible. Germany in particular had paid for the war by printing money in the hope of backing it by annexing industrial areas of France and Belgium. The German economy could not meet the reparations bill without raising taxes, and no German government was willing to do this because it would have meant its opponents would have been able to accuse it of taxing the Germans to pay the French. Inflation was the result. In 1913 the dollar had been worth 4 paper marks; by the end of 1919 it was worth 47; by July 1922, 493, by December 1922, 7,000. Reparations had to be paid in gold and in goods, and at this rate of inflation the Germans were neither willing nor able to manage it. In January 1923 the French and Belgians occupied the Ruhr and began to seize industrial assets and products. The German government announced a policy of non-cooperation. This sparked a decline of the mark's value against the dollar that was unprecedented in scale. An American dollar cost 353,000 marks in July 1923; in August four and a half million; in October 25,260 million; in December four million million, or four followed by twelve noughts. Economic collapse stared Germany in the face.

Eventually the inflation was halted. A new currency was introduced; passive resistance to the Franco-Belgian occupation ended; the foreign troops withdrew; reparations payments resumed. The inflation fragmented the middle classes, by pitting one interest group against another, so that no political party was able to unite them. The post-inflation stabilization, retrenchment and rationalization meant massive job losses, both in industry and in the civil service. From 1924 onwards there were millions of unemployed. Business resented the failure of government to help it in this deflationary situation and began to look for alternatives. For the middle classes in general, the inflation meant a moral and cultural disorientation that was only worsened for many by what they saw as the excesses of modern culture in the 1920s, from jazz and cabaret in Berlin to abstract art, atonal music and experimental literature such as the concrete poetry of the Dadaists. This sense of disorientation was present in politics too, as defeat in war had brought about the collapse of the

Reich, the flight of the Kaiser into exile, and the creation of the Weimar Republic in the revolution of November 1918. The Weimar Republic had a modern constitution, with female suffrage and proportional representation, but these were not instrumental in its downfall. The real problem of the constitution was the independently elected President, who had wide-ranging emergency powers under article 48 of the constitution to rule by decree. This was already used extensively by the Republic's first President, the Social Democrat Friedrich Ebert. When he died in 1925, his elected successor was Field Marshal Paul von Hindenburg, a staunch monarchist who had no deep commitment to the constitution. In his hands, article 48 would prove fatal to the Republic's survival.

The final legacy of the First World War was a cult of violence, not just in the hands of veterans such as the radical right-wing Steel Helmets, but more particularly in the younger generation of men who had not been old enough to fight, and now tried to match the heroic deeds of their elders by fighting on the home front. The war polarized politics, with Communist revolutionaries on the left and various radical groups emerging on the right. The most notorious of these were the Free Corps, armed bands who were used by the government to put down Communist and far-left revolutionary uprisings in Berlin and Munich in the winter of 1918–19. The Free Corps attempted a violent coup d'état in Berlin in the early spring of 1920, which led to an armed left-wing uprising in the Ruhr, while there were further left- and right-wing uprisings in 1923. Even in the relatively stable years from 1924 to 1929, at least 170 members of various political paramilitary squads were killed in street fighting; in the early 1930s the deaths and injuries escalated dramatically, with 300 killed in street and meeting-room clashes in the year from March 1930 to March 1931 alone. Political tolerance had given way to violent extremism. The parties of the liberal centre and moderate left suffered dramatic electoral losses in the mid-1920s, as the spectre of Communist revolution retreated and the middle classes voted for parties further to the right. Those parties that actively supported the Weimar Republic never had a parliamentary majority after 1920. Finally, the Republic's legitimacy was further undermined by the bias of the judiciary in favour of right-wing assassins and insurgents who claimed patriotism as their motive, and by the neutral stance taken by the army, which became steadily more resentful at the Republic's failure to persuade the international community to lift the restrictions placed on its numbers and equipment by the Treaty of Versailles. German democracy, hastily improvised in the aftermath of military defeat, was by no means doomed to failure from the start, but the events of the 1920s meant that it never had much of a chance to establish itself on a stable footing.

II

There was a huge variety of extremist, antisemitic groups on the far right in 1919, especially in Munich, but by 1923 one of them stood out above the rest: the National Socialist German Workers' Party, led by Adolf Hitler. So much has been written about the power and impact of Hitler and the Nazis that it is important to point out that his party was out on the far margins of politics until the very end of the 1920s. Hitler, in other words, was not a political genius who raised mass support for himself and his party single-handedly. Born in Austria in 1889, he was a failed artist with a Bohemian lifestyle who possessed one great gift: the ability to move crowds with his rhetoric. His party, founded in 1919, was more dynamic, more ruthless and more violent than other extreme-right-wing fringe groups. In 1923 it felt confident enough to try a violent coup d'état in Munich as a prelude to a march on Berlin along the lines of Mussolini's successful 'march on Rome' the previous year. But it failed to win over the army or the forces of political conservatism in Bavaria, and the coup was dissipated in a hail of gunfire. Hitler was convicted and put into Landsberg prison, where he dictated his autobiographical political tract, *My Struggle*, to his dogsbody Rudolf Hess: not a blueprint for the future, to be sure, but a compendium of Hitler's ideas, above all antisemitism and the idea of a racial conquest of Eastern Europe, for all who cared to read it.

By the time he came out of prison, Hitler had assembled the ideology of Nazism from disparate elements of antisemitism, pan-Germanism, eugenics and so-called racial hygiene, geopolitical expansionism, hostility to democracy, and hostility to cultural modernism, which had been floating around for some time but had not so far been integrated into a coherent whole. He gathered around him a team of immediate subordinates – the talented propagandist Joseph Goebbels, the decisive man of action Hermann Göring and others – who built up his image as leader and reinforced his sense of destiny. But despite all this, and despite the violent activism of his brownshirt paramilitaries on the streets, he got nowhere politically until the very end of the 1920s. In May 1928 the Nazis only won 2.6 per cent of the vote, and a 'Grand Coalition' of centrist and leftist parties led by the Social Democrats took office in Berlin. In October 1929, however, the Wall Street crash brought the German economy tumbling down with it. American banks withdrew the loans on which German economic recovery had been financed since 1924. German banks had to call in their loans to German businesses in response, and businesses had no option but to lay off workers or go bankrupt, which indeed many of them did. Within little more than two years more than one German worker in three was unemployed, and millions more were on short-term work or reduced wages. The un-employment insurance system broke down completely, leaving increasing numbers destitute. Agriculture, already under strain because of a fall in world demand, collapsed as well.

The political effects of the Depression were calamitous. The Grand Coalition broke up in disarray; so deep were the divisions between the parties over how to deal with the crisis that a parliamentary majority could no longer be found for any kind of decisive action. Reich President Hindenburg appointed a cabinet of experts under the Catholic politician Heinrich Brüning, an avowed monarchist. It proceeded to impose savagely deflationary cutbacks, only making the situation worse still. And it did so by using the Presidential power of rule by decree under article 48 of the constitution, bypassing the Reichstag altogether. Political power was diverted from parliament upwards, to the circle around Hindenburg, who could use his power of ruling by decree, and downwards, onto the streets, where violence escalated exponentially, pushed on by Hitler's brownshirted stormtroopers, now numbering hundreds of thousands. For the thousands of young men who joined the brownshirts, violence quickly became a way of life, almost a drug, as they launched against the Communists and the Social Democrats the fury their elders had vented on the enemy in 1914–18.

Many brownshirts were without a job in the early 1930s. It was not unemployment, however, that drove people to support the Nazis. The unemployed flocked above all to the Communists, whose vote rose steadily until it reached 17 per cent, giving the party 100 seats in the Reichstag, in November 1932. The Communists' violent revolutionary rhetoric, promising the destruction of capitalism and the creation of a Soviet Germany, terrified the country's middle classes, who knew only too well what had happened to their counterparts in Russia after 1918. Appalled at the failure of the government to solve the crisis, and frightened into desperation by the rise of the Communists, they began to leave the squabbling little factions of the conventional political right and gravitate towards the Nazis instead. Other groups followed, including many Protestant small farmers, and manual workers from areas where the culture and traditions of the Social Democrats were weak. While all the middle-class parties collapsed completely, the Social Democrats and the Centre Party managed to restrict their losses. But by 1932 they were all that was left of the moderate centre, squashed helplessly between 100 uniformed Communist and 196 brownshirted deputies in the Reichstag. The polarization of politics could hardly be more dramatic.

The Nazis, then, as the elections of September 1930 and July 1932 showed, were a catch-all party of social protest with particularly strong middle-class support and relatively weak, though still very significant, working-class backing at the polls. They had broken out of their core constituency of the Protestant lower middle classes and farming community. Other parties, appalled at their losses, tried to beat them at their own game. This had nothing to do with specific policies, much more with the image of dynamism that the Nazis projected. The hated, calamitous Weimar Republic had to be got rid of, and the people united once more in a national community that knew no parties or classes, just as it had been in 1914; Germany had to reassert itself on the international scene and become a leading power again: that was more or less what the Nazis' programme amounted to. They modified their specific policies according to their audience, playing down their antisemitism where it met with no response, for example, which is to say in most parts of the electorate after 1928. Besides the Nazis and the Communists battling it out on the streets, and the intriguers around President Hindenburg vying for the old man's ear, a third major player now entered the political game: the army. Increasingly alarmed by the rise of Communism and the growing mayhem on the streets, the army also saw the new political situation as an opportunity to get rid of Weimar democracy and impose an authoritarian, military dictatorship that would repudiate the Treaty of Versailles and rearm the country in preparation for a war of reconquest of Germany's lost territories, and perhaps more besides.

The army's power lay in the fact that it was the only force that could effectively restore order in the shattered country. When President Hindenburg's re-election in 1932 was achieved only with the help of the Social Democrats, who backed him as a less unacceptable choice than his main rival, Hitler, Chancellor Brüning's days were numbered. He had failed in almost everything he had undertaken, from solving the economic crisis to restoring order to Germany's towns and cities, and he had now offended Hindenburg by failing to secure his re-election unopposed and by proposing the break-up of the kind of landed estate Hindenburg himself owned in Eastern Germany to help the destitute peasantry. The army was anxious to get rid of Brüning because his deflationary policies were preventing rearmament. Like many conservative groups it hoped to enlist the Nazis, now the largest political party, as legitimation and support for the destruction of Weimar democracy. In May 1932 Brüning was forced to resign and replaced by the Catholic landed aristocrat Franz von Papen, a personal friend of Hindenburg's.

Papen's advent to power sounded the death-knell of Weimar democracy. He used the army to depose the Social Democratic state government in Prussia and prepared to reform the Weimar constitution by restricting voting rights and drastically curtailing the legislative powers of the Reichstag. He began to ban critical issues of daily newspapers and to restrict civil freedoms. But the elections he called in July 1932 only registered a further increase in the Nazi vote, which now reached 37.4 per cent of the poll. Papen's attempt to enlist Hitler and the Nazis in support of his government failed when Hitler insisted that he and not Papen had to head the government. Lacking almost any support in the country, Papen was forced to resign when the army lost patience with him and put its own man into office. The new head of government, General Kurt von Schleicher, did no better at restoring order or co-opting the Nazis to give the semblance of popular backing to his policy of creating an authoritarian state. After the Nazis had lost two million votes in the Reichstag elections of November 1932, their evident decline and their obvious lack of funds created a serious division in the Party's ranks. The Party's organizer and effective second man after Hitler, Gregor Strasser, resigned from the Party in frustration at Hitler's refusal to negotiate with Hindenburg and Papen. The moment seemed right to take advantage of the Nazis' weakness. On 30 January 1933, with the agreement of the army, Hindenburg appointed Hitler as head of a new government in which all the other posts bar two were held by conservatives, with Papen as deputy Chancellor at their head.

III

In reality, 30 January 1933 marked the beginning of the Nazi seizure of power, not of a conservative counter-revolution. Hitler had avoided the mistakes he had made ten years previously: he had achieved office without formally destroying the constitution, and with the support of the conservative establishment and the army. The question now was how to convert his position in yet another Weimar coalition cabinet into a dictatorship in a one-party state. First, all he could think of doing was to intensify the violence on the streets. He persuaded Papen to appoint Hermann Göring as Prussian Minister of the Interior, and in this capacity Göring promptly enrolled the brownshirts as auxiliary police. They went on the rampage, smashing trade union offices, beating up Communists, and breaking up Social Democratic meetings. On 28 February chance came to the Nazis' aid: a lone Dutch anarcho-syndicalist, Marinus van der Lubbe, burned down the Reichstag building in protest against the injustices of unemployment. Hitler and Göring persuaded a willing cabinet effectively to suppress the Communist Party. Four thousand Communists including virtually the entire party leadership were immediately arrested, beaten up, tortured and thrown into newly created concentration camps. There was no let-up in the campaign of violence and brutality in the weeks that followed. By the end of March the Prussian police reported that 20,000 Communists were in prison. By the summer over 100,000 Communists, Social Democrats, trade unionists and others had been arrested, with even official estimates putting the number of deaths in custody at 600. All of this was sanctioned by an emergency decree signed by Hindenburg the night after the fire suspending civil liberties and allowing the cabinet to take any necessary measures to protect public safety. Van der Lubbe's lone act was portrayed by Joseph Goebbels, soon to become Reich Propaganda Minister, as the result of a Communist conspiracy to stage an armed uprising. This convinced many middle-class voters that the decree was right.

Yet the government did not ban the Communists in a formal, legal sense, because it feared that the party's voters would all desert to the Social Democrats in the elections Hitler had called for 5 March. Amidst massive Nazi propaganda, paid for by an inflow of fresh funds from industry, and violent intimidation, in which most rival political meetings were banned or broken up, the Nazis still failed to achieve an overall majority, peaking at 44 per cent and only getting over the 50 per cent barrier with the help of their conservative Nationalist coalition partners. The Communists still won 12 per cent and the Social Democrats 18 per cent, with the Centre Party holding firm at 11 per cent of the vote. This meant that Hitler and his cabinet colleagues were still far short of the two-thirds majority they needed to alter the constitution. But on 23 March 1933 they still managed to get it by threatening civil war if they were frustrated, and by winning over the Centre Party deputies with the promise of a comprehensive Concordat with the Papacy guaranteeing Catholics' rights. The so-called Enabling Act passed by the Reichstag that day gave the cabinet the right to rule by decree without reference either to the Reichstag or to the President. Together with the Reichstag Fire Decree it provided the legal pretext for the creation of a dictatorship. Only the ninety-four Social Democratic deputies present voted against it.

The Social Democrats and Communists between them had won 221 seats in the Reichstag elections of November 1932 as against 196 for the Nazis and another 51 for the Nazis' allies the Nationalists. But they failed completely to mount any concerted resistance to the Nazi seizure of power. They were bitterly divided. The Communists, under orders from Stalin in Moscow, labelled the Social Democrats 'Social Fascists' and argued that they were worse than the Nazis. The Social Democrats were reluctant to co-operate with a party whose deviousness and unscrupulousness they rightly feared. Their paramilitary organizations fought hard against the Nazis on the streets, but they would have been no match for the army, which backed the Hitler government all the way in 1933, and their numbers were also well below those of the stormtroopers, who numbered more than three-quarters of a million in February 1933. The Social Democrats wanted to avoid bloodshed in this situation, and stayed true to their law-abiding traditions. The Communists believed that the Hitler government was the last gasp of a moribund capitalist system that would quickly collapse, opening the way to a proletarian revolution, so they saw no need to prepare for an uprising. Finally, a general strike was out of the question when unemployment stood at 35 per cent; striking workers would quickly have been replaced by unemployed people desperate to rescue themselves and their families from destitution.

Goebbels got the agreement of the trade union leaders to support the creation of a new national holiday on Mayday, a long-held demand of the unions, and turned it into a so-called day of national labour, with hundreds of thousands of workers gathering on Germany's public squares under the swastika to listen to speeches by Hitler and the other Nazi leaders broadcast over loudspeakers. The next day stormtroopers all over Germany raided trade union and Social Democratic offices and premises, looted them, carried off the funds, and closed them down. Within a few weeks, mass arrests of union officials and Social Democratic leaders, many of whom were beaten up and tortured in makeshift concentration camps, had broken the spirit of the labour movement. Other parties were now targeted in turn. The liberal and splinter parties, reduced by electoral attrition to being small groups on the fringes of politics, were forced to dissolve themselves. A whispering campaign began against Hitler's Nationalist coalition partners, coupled with the harassment and arrest of Nationalist officials and deputies. Hitler's chief Nationalist ally, Alfred Hugenberg, was forced to resign from the cabinet, while the party's floor leader in the Reichstag was found dead in his office in suspicious circumstances. Protests by Hugenberg met with a hysterical outburst from Hitler, in which he threatened a bloodbath if the Nationalists resisted any longer. By the end of June the Nationalists too had been dissolved. The remaining big independent party, the Centre, suffered a similar fate. Nazi threats to sack Catholic civil servants and close down Catholic lay organizations combined with the Papacy's panic fear of Communism led to a deal, concluded in Rome. The party agreed to dissolve itself in return for the finalization of the Concordat already promised at the time of the Enabling Act. This supposedly guaranteed the integrity of the Catholic Church in Germany along with all its assets and organizations. Time would show that this was not worth the paper it was written on. In the meantime, however, the Centre Party followed the others into oblivion. By the middle of July 1933, Germany was a one-party state, a position ratified by a law formally banning all other parties apart from the Nazis.

It was not just parties and trade unions that were abolished however. The Nazi assault on existing institutions affected the whole of society. Every state government, every state parliament in Germany's federal political system, every town and district and local council was ruthlessly purged; the Reichstag Fire Decree and the Enabling Act were used to dismiss supposed enemies of the state, meaning enemies of the Nazis. Every national voluntary association, and every local club, was brought under Nazi control, from industrial and agricultural pressure-groups to sports associations, football clubs, male voice choirs, women's organizations – in short, the whole fabric of associational life was Nazified. Rival, politically oriented clubs or societies were merged into a single Nazi body. Existing leaders of voluntary associations were either unceremoniously ousted, or knuckled under of their own accord. Many organizations expelled politically leftish or liberal members and declared their allegiance to the new state and its institutions. This whole process ('co-ordination' in Nazi jargon) went on all over Germany from March to June 1933. By the end, virtually the only non-Nazi associations left were the army and the Churches with their lay organizations. While this was going on, the government passed a law that allowed it to purge the civil service, a vast organization in Germany that included schoolteachers, university staff, judges and many other professions that were not government-controlled in other countries. Social Democrats, liberals and not a few Catholics and conservatives were ousted here too. To save their jobs, at a time when unemployment had reached terrifying dimensions, 1.6 million people joined the Nazi Party between 30 January and 1 May 1933, when the Party leadership banned any more recruiting, while the number of brownshirt paramilitaries grew to over two million by the summer of 1933.

The proportion of civil servants, judges and the like who were actually sacked for political reasons was very small. The major reason for dismissal, however, was not political but racial. The civil service law passed by the Nazis on 7 April 1933 allowed dismissal of Jewish civil servants, though Hindenburg had succeeded in getting a clause inserted protecting the jobs of Jewish war veterans and those appointed under the Kaiser, before 1914. The Jews, Hitler claimed, were a subversive, parasitical element who had to be got rid of. In fact most Jews were middle-class, and liberal-to-conservative in their politics, insofar as they had any. Nevertheless Hitler believed that they had deliberately undermined Germany during the First World War and caused the revolution that created the Weimar Republic. A few socialist and Communist leaders had been Jewish, it is true, but the majority were not. For the Nazis this made no difference. The day after the March election, stormtroopers rampaged along the Kurfürstendamm, a fashionable shopping street in Berlin, hunting down Jews and beating them up. Synagogues were trashed, while all over Germany gangs of brownshirts burst into courthouses and dragged off Jewish judges and lawyers, beating them with rubber truncheons and telling them not to return. Jews who were amongst those arrested as Communists or Social Democrats were particularly harshly treated. Over forty Jews had been murdered by stormtroopers by the end of June 1933.

Such incidents were widely reported in the foreign press. This formed the pretext for Hitler, Goebbels and the Nazi leadership to put into action a long-mulled-over plan to stage a nationwide boycott of Jewish shops and businesses. On 1 April 1933 stormtroopers stood menacingly outside such premises warning people not to enter them. Most non-Jewish Germans obeyed, but not with any enthusiasm. The biggest Jewish firms were untouched because they contributed too much to the economy. Realizing it had failed to arouse popular enthusiasm, Goebbels called the action off after a few days. But the beatings, the violence and the boycott had their effect on the Jewish community in Germany, 37,000 of whose members had emigrated by the end of the year. The regime's purge of Jews, whom it defined not by their religious adherence but by racial criteria, had a particular effect in science, culture and the arts. Jewish conductors and musicians such as Bruno Walter and Otto Klemperer were summarily dismissed or prevented from performing. The film industry and radio were rapidly purged of both Jews and political opponents of the Nazis. Non-Nazi newspapers were closed down or brought under Nazi control, while the journalists' union and the newspaper publishers' association both placed themselves under

Nazi leadership. Left-wing and liberal writers, such as Bertolt Brecht, Thomas Mann and many others, were stopped from publishing; many left the country. Hitler reserved his particular enmity for modern artists like Paul Klee, Max Beckmann, Ernst Ludwig Kirchner and Vassily Kandinsky. Before 1914 he had been rejected from the Vienna Art Academy because his painstakingly representational drawings of buildings had been thought talentless. Under the Weimar Republic, abstract and Expressionist artists had gained wealth and reputation with what Hitler thought were ugly and meaningless daubs. While Hitler railed against modern art in his speeches, gallery and museum directors were sacked and replaced with men who enthusiastically removed modernist works from exhibition. The many modernist artists and composers, like Klee or Schoenberg, who held positions in state educational institutions, were all fired.

Altogether about 2,000 people active in the arts emigrated from Germany in 1933 and the following years. They included virtually everyone with an international reputation. Nazi anti-intellectualism was underlined still further by events in the universities. Here too Jewish professors in all fields were dismissed. Many, including Albert Einstein, Gustav Hertz, Erwin Schrödinger, Max Born and twenty past or future Nobel prize winners, left the country. By 1934, some 1,600 out of 5,000 university teachers had been forced out of their jobs, a third because they were Jewish, the rest because they were political opponents of the Nazis. Sixteen per cent of physics professors and assistants emigrated. In the universities it was above all the students, helped by a small number of Nazi professors such as the philosopher Martin Heidegger, who drove the purges on. They forced Jewish and leftist professors out by violent demonstrations, and then, on 10 May 1933, they organized demonstrations in the main squares of nineteen university towns and cities in which huge numbers of books by Jewish and left-wing authors were piled up and set alight. What the Nazis were trying to achieve was a cultural revolution, in which alien cultural influences – notably the Jews but also modernist culture more generally – were eliminated and the German spirit reborn. Germans did not just have to acquiesce in the Third Reich, they had to support it with all their heart and soul, and the creation of the Propaganda Ministry under Joseph Goebbels, which soon acquired control over the whole sphere of culture and the arts, was the main means by which the Nazis sought to achieve this end. Nevertheless, Nazism was in many respects a thoroughly modern phenomenon, keen to use the latest technology, the newest weapons, and the most scientific means of reshaping German society to its will. Race, for the Nazis, was a scientific concept, and by making it the basis of all their policies, they were taking their stand on what they conceived of as the application of scientific method to human society. Nothing, neither religious beliefs, nor ethical scruples, nor long-hallowed tradition, was to get in the way of this revolution. Yet in the summer of 1933, Hitler felt constrained to tell his followers that it was time for the revolution to come to a stop. Germany needed a period of stability. This book begins at that moment, the moment when the destruction of the remnants of the Weimar Republic had been completed and the Third Reich was finally in power.

I

THE POLICE STATE

'NIGHT OF THE LONG KNIVES'

I

On 6 July 1933 Hitler gathered leading Nazis together for a stock-taking of the general situation. The National Socialists' revolution had succeeded, he told them; power was theirs, and theirs alone. It was now, he said, time to stabilize the regime. There should be no more talk, of the kind that had been circulating amongst senior members of the brown-shirted paramilitary wing of the Party, the Storm Division (*Sturmabteilung*, or SA), of a 'second revolution' to follow the 'conquest of power':

Revolution is not a permanent condition. It must not develop into a permanent condition. The stream of revolution has been undammed, but it must be channelled into the secure bed of evolution . . . The slogan of the second revolution was justified as long as positions were still present in Germany that could serve as points of crystallization for a counter-revolution. That is not the case any longer. We do not leave any doubt about the fact that if necessary we will drown such an attempt in blood. For a second revolution can only direct itself against the first one.[1]

This declaration was followed by numerous similar, if less overtly threatening, statements by other Nazi leaders in the following weeks. Pressure was mounting from the Reich Justice and Interior Ministries to deal with arbitrary violence, and the Reich Economics Ministry was worried that continuing unrest would give the international financial community the impression of continuing instability in Germany and so discourage economic investment and recovery. The Interior Ministry complained about arrests of civil servants, the Justice Ministry about arrests of lawyers. Brownshirt violence was continuing all over the country, most notoriously in the 'Köpenick blood-week' in June 1933, when a raiding party of stormtroopers had encountered resistance from a young Social Democrat in a Berlin suburb. After the Social Democrat shot three stormtroopers dead, the brownshirts mobilized *en masse* and arrested more than 500 local men, torturing them so brutally that ninety-one of them died. Amongst them were many well-known Social Democratic politicians, including the former Minister-President of Mecklenburg, Johannes Stelling.[2] Clearly, this kind of violence had to be checked: it was no longer necessary to beat the opponents of the Nazis into submission and establish a one-party state. Moreover, Hitler was beginning to be concerned about the power that the rampages of the ever-expanding SA gave to its leader Ernst Röhm, who had declared on 30 May 1933 that its task of completing the National Socialist Revolution 'still lies before it'. 'Whether declarations of loyalty come every day from "co-ordinated" beekeeping or bowling clubs makes no odds,' Röhm added, 'nor whether a town's streets get up-to-date names.' Others might celebrate the Nazi victory, but the political soldiers who had fought it, he said, had to take matters in hand and carry it further.[3]

On 2 August 1933, worried by such declarations, Hermann Göring, acting in his capacity as Minister-President of Prussia, rescinded an order of the previous February enrolling the brownshirts as auxiliary officers of the Prussian police. The Ministries of other federated states followed suit. The established police force now had more room for manoeuvre in dealing with the stormtroopers' excesses. The Prussian Ministry of Justice set up a central Public Prosecutor's Office to deal with murders and other serious crimes in the concentration camps, though it also ordered the end of ongoing prosecutions of SA and SS men for crimes of violence, and the pardoning of those few who had actually been sentenced. Strict regulations were issued about who was entitled to place people in protective custody, and what procedures were to be observed in doing so. An indication of what had been the practice to date was provided by the prohibitions contained in the consolidated regulations issued in April 1934: no one was to be taken into protective custody for personal reasons such as slander, or because they had dismissed employees, or acted as legal representatives of people subsequently imprisoned, or had brought an objectionable legal action before the courts. Deprived of its initial *raison d'être* as the street-fighting, saloon-brawling arm of the Nazi movement, and removed from its position in charge of many small improvised prison camps and torture centres, the SA found itself suddenly without a role.[4]

Elections were now no longer seriously contested, so the stormtroopers were robbed of the opportunity that the constant electioneering of the early 1930s had given them to parade through the streets and break up the meetings of their opponents. Disillusion began to set in. The SA had expanded hugely in the spring of 1933, as sympathizers and opportunists from many quarters flooded in. In March 1933 Röhm had announced that any 'patriotically minded' German man could join. When recruitment to the Nazi Party had been halted in May 1933, because the Party leadership feared that too many opportunists were joining, and their movement was being swamped by men who were not really committed to their cause, many people had seen enrolment in the brownshirts as an alternative, thus weakening the links between the Party and its paramilitary wing. The incorporation of the huge veterans' organization, the Steel Helmets, into the brownshirt organization, in the second half of 1933, further boosted SA numbers. At the beginning of 1934 there were six times as many stormtroopers as there had been at the beginning of the previous year. The total strength of the 'Storm Division' now stood at nearly three million men; four and a half million if the Steel Helmets and other incorporated paramilitary groups were counted in. This completely dwarfed the size of the German armed forces, which were legally restricted to a mere 100,000 by the Treaty of Versailles. At the same time, however, despite restrictions imposed by the Treaty, the army was by far the better equipped and better trained fighting force. The spectre of civil war that had loomed so ominously at the beginning of 1933 was beginning to raise its head once more.[5]

The discontents of the stormtroopers were not confined to envy of the army and impatience with the stabilization of politics after July 1933. Many 'old fighters' resented the newcomers who jumped onto the Nazi bandwagon early in 1933. Tension was particularly high with the former Steel Helmets who came into the organization. It increasingly found an outlet in fights and scuffles in the early months of 1934. In Pomerania the police banned former Steel Helmet units (now organized as the National Socialist German Front-Fighters' League) after a stormtrooper leader was murdered by an ex-Steel Helmet member.[6] But the resentment of old brownshirts could also be felt on a wider scale. Many had expected rich rewards on the elimination of the Nazis' rivals, and were disappointed when established local politicians and conservative partners of the Nazis took many of the best pickings. One brownshirt activist, born in 1897, wrote in 1934:

After the seizure of power, things changed dramatically. People who had hitherto scorned me were now overflowing with praises. In my family and among all the relatives I was now considered number one, after years of bitter feuding. My Storm Division grew by leaps and bounds from month to month so that (from 250 in January) by 1 October 1933, I had 2,200 members – which led to my promotion to Senior Storm Division Leader at Christmas time. The more the philistines lauded me, however, the more I came to suspect that these scoundrels thought they had me in the bag . . . After the incorporation of the Steel Helmets, when things came to a stop, I turned on the reactionary clique which was sneakily trying to make me look ridiculous before my superiors. There were all kinds of denunciations against me at the higher SA offices and with the public authorities . . . Finally, I succeeded in being appointed local mayor . . . so that I could break the necks of all the prominent philistines and the reactionary leftovers of the old times.[7]

Such feelings were even stronger amongst the many veteran stormtroopers who failed to manoeuvre themselves into positions of power as successfully as this man did.

As the young brownshirts found their violent energies deprived of an overtly political outlet, they became involved in increasing numbers of brawls and fights all over Germany, often without any obvious political motive. Gangs of stormtroopers got drunk, caused disturbances late at night, beat up innocent passers-by, and attacked the police if they tried to stop them. Matters were made still worse by Röhm's attempt to remove the brownshirts from the jurisdiction of the police and the courts in December 1933; henceforth, the stormtroopers were told that all disciplinary matters had to be handled by the organization itself. This was a licence for inaction, even though prosecutions still took place. Röhm found more difficulty in establishing a separate SA jurisdiction that would deal retroactively with more than 4,000 prosecutions of SA and SS men for crimes of various kinds that were still before the courts in May 1934, mostly resulting from the early months of 1933. Many others had been quashed, and more offences still had never been prosecuted in the first place, but this was still a considerable number. Moreover, the army had its own courts-martial; by so setting up a parallel system within the SA, Röhm would obtain a large measure of equal status to it for his own organization. Privately, he had announced the previous July that an SA leader with jurisdiction over the murder of an SA man would be able to sentence to death up to twelve members of 'the enemy organization which initiated the murder'. This gave a grim indication of the nature of the justice system he hoped to create.[8] Clearly, some means had to be found of diverting all this excess energy into useful channels. But leadership of the SA only made matters worse by seeking to direct the movement's violent activism into what a regional leader in the East, Edmund Heines, publicly described as 'the continuation of the German revolution'.[9] As head of the SA, Ernst Röhm spoke at numerous rallies and marches in the first months of 1934, emphasizing in similar fashion the revolutionary nature of Nazism and launching open attacks on the Party leadership and in particular the German army, whose senior officers the brownshirts blamed for their temporary banning by order of former Reich Chancellor Heinrich Brüning in 1932. Röhm caused considerable alarm in the army hierarchy when he declared that he wanted the stormtroopers to form the basis of a national militia, effectively bypassing and perhaps eventually replacing the army altogether. Hitler attempted to fob him off by making him Minister without Portfolio with a seat in the cabinet in December 1933, but given the increasing redundancy of the cabinet by this stage, this meant very little in practical terms, and was no substitute for Röhm's real ambition, which was to occupy the Ministry of Defence, held at the time by the army's representative General Werner von Blomberg.[10]

Deprived of real power at the centre, Röhm began to build up a cult of his own leadership within the SA and continued to preach the need for further revolution.[11] In January 1934, stormtroopers gave practical expression to their radicalism when they burst into the Hotel Kaiserhof in Berlin and broke up a celebration of the ex-Kaiser's birthday being held there by a number of army officers.[12] The next day, Röhm sent Blomberg a memorandum. Perhaps exaggerating its import for effect, Blomberg said that it demanded that the SA should replace the army as the country's main fighting force and the traditional military should be restricted to training the stormtroopers to assume this role.[13] To the army leadership, the brownshirts now appeared an increasingly serious threat. Since the summer of 1933, Blomberg had brought the army round from its previous formal political neutrality towards increasingly open support for the regime. Blomberg and his allies were seduced by Hitler's promises of a massive expansion of German military strength through the resumption of conscription. They had been won over by Hitler's assurance that he would conduct an aggressive foreign policy that would culminate in the recovery of the territories lost by the Treaty of Versailles and the launching of a new war of conquest in the east. Blomberg in turn ostentatiously demonstrated his loyalty to the Third Reich by adopting the 'Aryan Paragraph', which banned Jews from serving in the army, and incorporating the swastika into the army's insignia. Although these were largely symbolic gestures – at the insistence of President Hindenburg, for example, Jewish war veterans could not be dismissed, and only some seventy soldiers were actually cashiered – they were still important concessions to Nazi ideology that indicated just how far the army had come to terms with the new political order.[14]

At the same time, however, the army was still by no means a Nazified institution. Its relative independence was underpinned by the close interest taken in its fortunes by Reich President Paul von Hindenburg, its formal Commander-in-Chief. Hindenburg indeed had refused to appoint Walther von Reichenau, the pro-Nazi choice of Hitler and Blomberg, to succeed the conservative and anti-Nazi Kurt von Hammerstein as head of the army when he retired. Instead, he had enforced the appointment of General Werner von Fritsch, a popular staff officer of strong conservative views, with a passion for horsemanship and a strict Protestant outlook on life. Unmarried, workaholic and narrowly military in outlook, Fritsch had the Prussian officer's arrogant contempt for the vulgarity of the Nazis. His conservative influence was backed by the head of the Troop Office, General Ludwig Beck, appointed at the end of 1933. Beck was a cautious, shy and withdrawn man, a widower whose main recreation was also horse-riding. With men such as Fritsch and Beck occupying two of the senior posts in the army leadership, there was no chance of the army yielding to pressure from the SA. Blomberg secured a meeting with Hitler and the leadership of the SA and SS on 28 February 1934 at which Röhm was forced to sign an agreement that he would not try to replace the army with a brownshirt militia. Germany's military force of the future, declared Hitler emphatically, would be a professional and well-equipped army, for which the brownshirts could only act in an auxiliary capacity. After the army officers had left the following reception, Röhm told his men that he was not going to obey the 'ridiculous corporal' and threatened to send Hitler 'on leave'. Such insubordination did not go unnoticed. Indeed, aware of his attitude, Hitler had already had him put under covert surveillance by the police.[15]

Competition with the SA led Blomberg and the military leaders to try and win Hitler's favour in a variety of ways. The army regarded the SA as a potential source of recruits. But it was worried by the prospect that this might lead to political infiltration, and scornful of the fact that the SA leadership included men who had been dishonourably discharged from the military. It preferred therefore to agitate for the reintroduction of conscription, embodying this in a plan drawn up by Beck in December 1933. Hitler had already promised that this would happen when he had talked to army leaders the previous February. He had told the British Minister Anthony Eden, indeed, that it would be a mistake to allow a 'second army' to exist, and that he intended to bring the SA under control and to reassure foreign opinion by demilitarizing it.[16] Yet despite this, stories of local and regional brownshirt commanders prophesying the creation of an 'SA state' and a 'night of the long knives' began to multiply. Max Heydebreck, an SA leader in Rummelsburg, was reported as saying: 'Some of the officers of the army were swine. Most officers were too old and had to be replaced by young ones. We want to wait till Papa Hindenburg is dead, and then the SA will march against the army. What can 100,000 soldiers do against such a greatly superior force of SA-men?'[17] SA men began stopping army supplies in transit and confiscating weapons and supplies. Yet on the whole, such incidents were local, sporadic and uncoordinated. Röhm never devised any concerted plan. Contrary to later allegations by Hitler, he had no immediate intention of launching a putsch. Indeed Röhm announced at the beginning of June that he was going on a rest cure, on doctor's orders, to Bad Wiessee, near Munich, and sent the SA on leave for the whole of July.[18]

II

The continued disturbances and radical rhetoric were enough to worry not just the army leaders, but also some of Hitler's conservative colleagues in the cabinet. Up to the passage of the Enabling Act, the cabinet had continued to meet regularly in order to pass draft decrees for forwarding to the President. From the end of March, however, it started to be bypassed by the Reich Chancellery and the individual Ministries. Hitler did not like the extensive and sometimes critical discussions that a cabinet meeting involved. He preferred decrees to be worked out as fully as possible before they came to the full meeting of Ministers. Increasingly, therefore, the cabinet met only to rubber-stamp previously decided legislation. Up to the summer recess of 1933, it still met four or five times a month, and there were also relatively frequent meetings in September and October 1933. From November 1933, however, a distinct change could be noted. The cabinet met only once that month, three times in December, once in January 1934, twice in February and twice in March. Then it failed to convene in April 1934, met only once in May and had no sessions at all in June. By this time it had long since ceased to be dominated even numerically by the conservatives, since the Nazi propaganda chief Joseph Goebbels had joined it as Reich Propaganda Minister in March 1933, to be followed by Rudolf Hess and Ernst Röhm on 1 December and another Nazi, the Education Minister Bernhard Rust, on 1 May 1934. The Nationalist Alfred Hugenberg had resigned on 29 June 1933 and been replaced as Agriculture Minister by the Nazi Walther Darré. The cabinet appointed by Hindenburg on 30 January 1933 had contained only three Nazis – Hitler himself, Wilhelm Frick, the Interior Minister, and Hermann Göring as Minister without Portfolio. Of the seventeen cabinet Ministers in office in May 1934, however, a clear majority – nine – were long-term members of the Nazi Party. It had become clear, even to a man as prone to self-deception and political blindness as the conservative Vice-Chancellor Franz von Papen, that the original expectations with which he and his conservative colleagues had entered the cabinet on 30 January 1933 had been completely dashed. It was not they who were manipulating the Nazis, but the Nazis who were manipulating them, and intimidating and bullying them as well.[19]

Yet, astonishingly, Papen had by no means abandoned his dream, articulated openly during his period of office as Chancellor in 1932, of a conservative restoration brought about with the mass support of the Nazi Party. His speechwriter Edgar Jung continued to argue in the summer of 1933 for a vision of the 'German revolution' that would involve 'the depoliticization of the masses, their exclusion from the running of the state'. The rampant populism of the SA seemed a serious obstacle to the anti-democratic and elitist regime that Papen desired. Around the Vice-Chancellor there gathered a group of young conservatives who shared these views. Meanwhile the Vice-Chancellery became the destination of an increasing number of complaints from people of all kinds about Nazi violence and arbitrary behaviour, giving Papen and his staff an increasingly negative view of the effects of the 'national revolution' which they had so far backed, and turning his group rapidly into a focus for all kinds of discontent.[20] By May 1934 Goebbels was complaining in his diary about Papen, who was rumoured to have his eye on the Presidency once the aged Hindenburg was dead. Other conservative members of the cabinet were not exempt from the Nazi propaganda chief's scorn either ('there has to be a real clear-up there as soon as possible', he wrote).[21] There was an obvious danger that the Papen group, already under close police surveillance, would make common cause with the army. Indeed Papen's press secretary Herbert von Bose was beginning to establish active contact with critical generals and senior officers worried about the activities of the SA. Hindenburg, long a buffer between the army and the conservatives on the one hand, and the leading Nazis on the other, was known to have become seriously ill in April 1934. It was soon clear that he was not going to recover. He retired to his landed estate in Neudeck, East Prussia, at the beginning of June, to await the end. His passing would clearly create a moment of crisis for which the regime had to be prepared.[22]

The moment was all the more critical for the regime because, as many people were aware, the enthusiasm of the 'national revolution' in 1933 had discernibly fallen off a year later. The brownshirts were not the only section of the population to feel disappointed at the results. Social Democratic agents reported to the exiled party leadership in Prague that people were apathetic, constantly complaining, and telling endless political jokes about the Nazi leaders. Nazi meetings were poorly attended. Hitler was still widely admired, but people were even beginning to direct criticisms in this quarter too. Many of the Nazis' promises had not been kept, and fears of a new inflation or a sudden war were leading to panic buying and hoarding in some places. The educated classes feared that the disorder caused by the stormtroopers might spill over into chaos or, worse, Bolshevism.[23] The leading Nazis were aware that such mutterings of discontent could be heard beneath the apparently smooth surface of political life. In answer to questions from the American journalist Louis P. Lochner, Hitler went out of his way to stress the unconditional loyalty he required of his subordinates.[24]

Matters were coming to a head. The Prussian Minister-President Hermann Göring, himself a former leader of the SA, was now so concerned at the drift of events that he agreed to hand over control of the Prussian political police to Heinrich Himmler on 20 April 1934, enabling the ambitious young SS leader, already in charge of the political police in all other parts of Germany, to centralize the police apparatus in his own hands. The SA, of which the SS was at this point still nominally a part, was an obvious obstacle to the achievement of Himmler's aims.[25] On a four-day cruise in the navy vessel *Deutschland* off Norway in mid-April, Hitler, Blomberg and top military officers seem to have reached an agreement that the SA should be curbed.[26] May passed, and the first half of June, without Hitler making an open move. Not for the first time, Goebbels began to feel frustrated at his master's seeming indecision. By late June, he was recording, 'the situation is getting ever more serious. The Leader must act. Otherwise Reaction will become too much for us.'[27]

Hitler's hand was finally forced when Papen gave a public address at Marburg University on 17 June 1934 in which he warned against a 'second revolution' and attacked the personality cult surrounding Hitler. It was time for the permanent upheaval of the Nazi revolution to come to an end, he said. The speech, written by Papen's adviser Edgar Jung, mounted a strong attack on the 'selfishness, lack of character, insincerity, lack of chivalry, and arrogance' at the heart of the so-called 'German revolution'. It was greeted with thunderous applause from his listeners. Shortly afterwards, appearing at a fashionable horse-racing meeting in Hamburg, Papen was greeted by cheers and shouts of 'Hail, Marburg!' from the crowd.[28] Back from a frustrating meeting with Mussolini in Venice, Hitler vented his spleen at Papen's activities before he had even learned of his Vice-Chancellor's speech in Marburg. Addressing the Party faithful in Gera, Hitler attacked the 'little pygmies' who were trying to stop the victory of the Nazi idea. 'It is ridiculous when such a little worm tries to fight such a powerful renewal of the people. Ridiculous, when such a little pygmy fancies himself capable of obstructing the gigantic renewal of the people with a few empty phrases.' The clenched fist of the people, he threatened, would 'smash anyone who dares to make even the slightest attempt at sabotage'.[29] At the same time, the Vice-Chancellor's complaint to Hitler, coupled with a threat to resign, met with a promise that the SA's drive towards a 'second revolution' would be stopped and a suggestion, which Papen too readily accepted, that the whole situation should be discussed in due course with the ailing President.[30] Not for the first time, Papen was lulled into a false sense of security by Hitler's disingenuous promises and a misplaced faith in Hindenburg's influence.

Hitler rushed off to consult with Hindenburg. Arriving at Neudeck on 21 June, he was confronted by Blomberg, who had been discussing Papen's speech with the President. The army chief made it clear that if the brownshirts were not immediately brought to heel, Hindenburg would be prepared to declare martial law and put the government in the hands of the army.[31] Hitler had no option but to act. He began planning Röhm's overthrow. The political police, in collaboration with Himmler and his deputy Reinhard Heydrich, head of the SS Security Service, began to manufacture evidence that Röhm and his stormtroopers were planning a nationwide uprising. Leading officers in the SS were presented with the 'evidence' on 24 June and given instructions on how to deal with the supposed putsch. Lists of 'politically unreliable' people were drawn up and local SS leaders informed that they would be called upon to kill a number of them, particularly any who resisted, when the day of action came on 30 June. The army put its resources at the disposal of the SS for the eventuality of a serious conflict.[32] Woe betide anyone, warned Rudolf Hess in a radio broadcast on 25 June, who thought to betray their loyalty to the Führer by carrying out revolutionary agitation from below.[33]

On 27 June, Hitler met with Blomberg and Reichenau to secure the army's co-operation; they responded by expelling Röhm from the German Officers' League the next day, and by putting the army on full alert.

Blomberg published an article in the Nazis' flagship daily, the *Racial Observer*, on 29 June declaring the army's absolute loyalty to the new regime. Meanwhile, it seems, Hitler learned that Hindenburg had agreed to give an audience to Papen, scheduled for 30 June, the day of the planned action against the SA. This confirmed the leading Nazis in their belief that the opportunity must be used to strike against the conservatives as well.[34] Nervous and apprehensive, Hitler sought to allay suspicions by going to a wedding reception in Essen, from where he telephoned Röhm's adjutant in his vacation hotel at Bad Wiessee ordering the SA leaders to meet him there on the morning of 30 June. Hitler then organized a hurried conference in Bad Godesberg with Goebbels and Sepp Dietrich, the SS officer who commanded his personal bodyguard. He would act against Röhm the next day, he told the astonished Goebbels, who had been expecting merely a blow against the 'reactionaries' and had hitherto been kept in the dark about everything else.[35] Göring was sent off to Berlin to take charge of the action there. Fantastic rumours began to circulate, and the SA itself began to be alarmed. Some 3,000 stormtroopers rampaged through the streets of Munich on the night of 29 June, shouting that they would crush any attempt to betray their organization and denouncing the 'Leader' and the army. Calm was eventually restored by Adolf Wagner, the Regional Leader of Munich; but there had been other, similar demonstrations elsewhere. When Hitler learned of these events on flying into Munich airport at 4.30 on the morning of 30 June 1934, he decided that he could not wait for the planned conference of SA leaders at which he was going to launch the purge. Now there was not a minute to lose.[36]

III

Hitler and his entourage drove first to the Bavarian Interior Ministry, where they confronted the leaders of the previous night's brownshirt demonstration in the city streets. In a rage, he shouted at them that they would be shot. Then he tore off their epaulettes with his bare hands. As the chastened stormtroopers were taken off to Munich's state prison at Stadelheim, Hitler assembled a group of SS bodyguards and police and drove off in a convoy of saloon cars and convertibles to Bad Wiessee, where they entered the Hanselbauer Hotel. Accompanied by his head chauffeur Julius Schreck, and followed by a group of armed detectives, Hitler marched up to the first floor. The brownshirts were still sleeping off a major drinking bout from the night before. Erich Kempka, who had driven Hitler to Wiessee, described what happened next:

Taking no notice of me, Hitler enters the room where SA-Senior Group Leader Heines is lodging. I hear him shout: 'Heines, if you are not dressed in five minutes I'll have you shot on the spot!' I take a few steps back and a police officer whispers to me that Heines had been in bed with an 18-year-old SA Senior Troop Leader. Eventually Heines comes out of the room with an 18-year-old fair-haired boy mincing in front of him. 'Into the laundry room with them!' orders Schreck. Meanwhile, Röhm comes out of his room in a blue suit and with a cigar in the corner of his mouth. Hitler looks at him grimly but says nothing. Two detectives take Röhm to the vestibule of the hotel where he throws himself into an armchair and orders coffee from the barman. I stand in the corridor a little to the side and a detective tells me how Röhm was arrested. Hitler had entered Röhm's bedroom alone with a whip in his hand. Behind him had stood two detectives holding pistols with the safety catch removed at the ready. He had spat out the words: 'Röhm, you are under arrest.' Röhm had looked up sleepily out of the pillows on his bed. 'Hail, my Leader.' 'You are under arrest', Hitler had bawled for the second time. He had turned on his heel and left the room. Meanwhile, upstairs in the corridor things have become very lively. SA leaders are coming out of their rooms and being arrested. Hitler shouts at each one: 'Have you had anything to do with Röhm's machinations?' Of course, none of them says yet, but that doesn't help them. Hitler mostly knows the answer himself; now and then he turns to Goebbels or Lutze with question. And then comes his decision: 'Arrested!'[37]

The brownshirts were locked in the hotel's linen cupboard and shortly afterwards taken off to Stadelheim. Hitler and his party followed them back to Munich. Meanwhile leading brownshirts arriving at Munich's main railway station en route for the planned meeting were arrested by the SS as they got off the train.[38]

Back in Munich, Hitler drove to Nazi Party Headquarters, which he had had sealed off by regular troops, and ranted against Röhm and the brownshirt leaders, announcing that they were dismissed and would be shot. 'Undisciplined and disobedient characters and asocial or diseased elements' would be annihilated. A senior brownshirt, Viktor Lutze, who had been informing on Röhm for some time and had accompanied Hitler to the Bad Wiessee hotel, was named as the new leader of the SA. Röhm, Hitler shouted, had been in the pay of the French; he was a traitor and had been conspiring against the state. The Party faithful who had gathered to hear his diatribe yelled their assent. Ever obliging, Rudolf Hess volunteered to shoot the traitors personally. Privately, Hitler was reluctant to have Röhm, one of his longest-serving supporters, put to death; eventually on 1 July he sent word to him that he could have a revolver with which to kill himself. When Röhm failed to make use of the opportunity, Hitler sent Theodor Eicke, the commandant of Dachau, and another SS officer from the camp, to Stadelheim. Entering Röhm's cell, the two SS officers gave him a loaded Browning and told him to commit suicide; if not, they would return in ten minutes and finish him off themselves. On re-entering the cell after the time was up, they encountered Röhm standing up, facing them with his chest bared in a dramatic gesture designed to emphasize his honour and loyalty; without uttering a word they immediately shot him dead at point-blank range. In addition, Hitler ordered the Silesian brownshirt Edmund Heines, who in 1932 had led an uprising against the Nazi Party in Berlin, to be shot, along with the leaders of the Munich demonstration the night before, and three others. Other SA men were driven off to the concentration camp at Dachau, where they were badly beaten by SS guards. At six in the evening Hitler flew off to Berlin to take charge of events in the capital city, where Hermann Göring had been implementing his orders with a ruthlessness that belied his widespread reputation as a moderate.[39]

Göring had not confined himself to carrying out the action against the brownshirt leaders. The atmosphere in Göring's office, where the Prussian Minister-President was closeted with Heydrich and Himmler, was later described as one of 'blatant bloodthirstiness' and 'hideous vindictiveness' by a policeman who looked on as Göring shouted orders for people on the list to be killed ('shoot them down . . . shoot . . . shoot at once') and joined in bouts of raucous laughter with his companions as news of successful murder operations came in. Striding up and down the room in a white tunic, white boots and grey-blue trousers, Göring ordered the storming of the Vice-Chancellery. Entering with an armed SS unit, Gestapo agents gunned down Papen's secretary Herbert von Bose on the spot. The Vice-Chancellor's ideological guru Edgar Jung, arrested on 25 June, was also shot; his body was dumped unceremoniously in a ditch. Papen himself escaped death; he was too prominent a figure to be shot down in cold blood. The assassination of two of his closest associates had to be warning enough. Papen was confined to his home for the time being, under guard, while Hitler pondered what to do with him.[40]

Other pillars of the conservative establishment did not fare so well. General von Schleicher, Hitler's predecessor as Reich Chancellor, and a man who had once described Hitler as unfit to hold office, was shot dead by the SS in his home, together with his wife. He was not the only army officer to be killed. Major-General Kurt von Bredow, who was thought to have published criticisms of the regime abroad, was killed at his home, shot, the newspapers reported, while resisting arrest as a partner to Röhm's infamous conspiracy. Apart from anything else, these killings served as a warning to the army leadership that they too would have to face the consequences if they did not toe the Nazi line. The former police chief and leader of 'Catholic Action' Erich Klausener, now a senior civil servant in the Transport Ministry, was shot down on Heydrich's orders as a warning to another former Chancellor, Heinrich Brüning, who had been tipped off about the purge and had left the country. Klausener's murder sent a clear message to Catholics that a revival of independent Catholic political activity would not be tolerated. Subsequent claims by the Nazi leadership that men such as these had been involved in the Röhm 'revolt' were pure invention. Most of these men had been listed by Edgar Jung as possible members of a future government, without actually having agreed to it or even known about it. Their mere inclusion on the list amounted to a death-warrant for most of them.[41]

Gregor Strasser, the man whom many thought of as a possible figure-head for the Nazi Party in a restored conservative government, was targeted as well. A short time before Hitler's appointment as Reich Chancellor in January 1933, Strasser, the head of the Nazi Party's admin-istration and the architect of many of its principal institutions, had resigned in despair at Hitler's refusal to enter any coalition govern-ment except as its head. Strasser had been negotiating at the time with Schleicher and there had been rumours that he had been offered a position in Schleicher's cabinet late in 1932. Although he had lived in retirement since his resignation, Strasser continued to pose in the minds of the leading Nazis a potential threat as an acceptable coalition partner for the conservatives. He was also a long-time personal enemy of Himmler and Göring, and he had not been sparing in his criticism of them while he had been a member of the senior Party leadership. Göring had him arrested and taken to police headquarters, where he was shot dead. Strasser's friend and collaborator Paul Schulz, a former top official in the SA, was also sought out by Göring's emissaries and taken into a forest to be shot; on getting out of the car at the chosen place of execution, he made a dash for it and feigned dead when he was shot, though he was only lightly wounded. He made good his escape while his attackers went back to the car to get a sheet to wrap his body in, and later managed to negotiate his exile from Germany with Hitler personally. Another target who escaped was Captain Ehrhardt, the Free Corps leader in the Kapp putsch of 1920, who had helped Hitler in 1923; he fled as the police entered his home and eventually managed to cross the border into Austria.[42]

In Berlin, the 'action' took on a different character from the events in Munich, where SA leaders from all over the country had been gathering on Hitler's orders. In Munich the brownshirts were the principal target, in Berlin the conservatives. The action was carefully planned in advance. Ernst Müller, the head of the SS Security Service in Breslau, was given a postdated sealed letter in Berlin on 29 June and sent back home on a private plane supplied by Göring. On the morning of 30 June Heydrich ordered him by telephone to open it; it contained a list of brownshirt leaders to be 'eliminated', along with instructions to occupy the police headquarters and summon the leading SA men to a meeting. Further orders included the seizure of SA arms stores, the securing of airports and radio transmitters, and the occupation of SA premises. He followed his instructions to the letter. By the early evening not only were the police cells at Breslau full, but also numerous other rooms were packed with bewildered brownshirted prisoners as well. Heydrich phoned Müller repeatedly to demand the execution of those men on the list who had not already been disposed of in Munich. The men were taken to SS headquarters, their epaulettes were removed, and they were driven out to a nearby forest and shot in the middle of the night.[43]

There were further arrests and shootings the next morning, on 1 July. In the general climate of violence, Hitler and his underlings took the opportunity to settle old scores or eliminate personal rivals. Some, of course, were too grand to touch, notably General Erich Ludendorff, who had been causing some headaches for the Gestapo with his far-right, anti-Freemasonry campaigns; the hero of the First World War was left alone; he was to die peacefully on 20 December 1937 and to be granted respectful obsequies by the regime. But in Bavaria, the former Minister-President Gustav Ritter von Kahr, who had played a key part in quelling the Hitler putsch in 1923, was cut to pieces by SS men. The music critic Wilhelm Eduard Schmid was also killed, in the mistaken belief that he was Ludwig Schmitt, a former supporter of Gregor Strasser's radical brother Otto, who had been forced to resign from the Party because of his revolutionary views and had maintained a constant barrage of criticism of Hitler from the safety of exile ever since. The conservative Bavarian politician Otto Ballerstedt, who had successfully prosecuted Hitler for breaking up a political meeting at which he had been speaking in 1921, resulting in the Nazi Leader spending a month in Stadelheim, was arrested and shot in Dachau on 1 July. One senior SS officer, Erich von dem Bach-Zelewski, chose the moment to get rid of a hated rival, the SS Cavalry leader Anton Baron von Hohberg und Buchwald, who was duly gunned down in his home. In Silesia, the regional SS boss Udo von Woyrsch had his former rival Emil Sembach shot despite a prior agreement with Himmler that Sembach should be sent to Berlin to be dealt with. The violence spilled over into another unconnected area too. Four Jews were arrested in Hirschberg and 'shot while trying to escape'. The leader of the Jewish veterans' league in Glogau was taken out to a wood and shot dead.[44]

Despite such obviously personally motivated actions, the Nazis lost no time in pumping out propaganda justifications for the murders. Goebbels broadcast a lengthy account of the 'action' the next day, alleging that Röhm and Schleicher had been conspiring to bring about a 'second revolution' that would have plunged the Reich into chaos. 'Every clenched fist that is raised against the Leader and his regime', he warned, generalizing the action potentially to every kind of opposition, 'will be prised open, if necessary by force.'[45] Despite this, Hitler still had a lot of explaining to do, not least to the army, two of whose senior officers he had had killed during the purge. Addressing the cabinet on 3 July, Hitler alleged that Röhm had been plotting against him with Schleicher, Gregor

Strasser and the French government for over a year. He had been forced to act as these plots threatened to culminate in a putsch on 30 June. If there were legal objections to what he had done, then his answer was that due process was not possible in such circumstances. 'If a mutiny broke out on board a ship, the captain was not only entitled but also obliged to crush the mutiny right away.' There was to be no trial, therefore, just a law to legalize the action retroactively, backed enthusiastically by Reich Justice Minister Gürtner. 'The example that he has given would be a salutary lesson for the entire future. He had stabilized the authority of the Reich government for all time.'[46] In the press, Goebbels concentrated on underlining the breadth and depth of support for the action, in order to reassure the public that order had been restored rather than undermined. The formal gratitude of Blomberg and Hindenburg was recorded in banner headlines, while other stories recorded 'declarations of loyalty from all over Germany' and 'everywhere veneration and admiration for the Leader'. The events were generally described as a clean-up of dangerous and degenerate elements in the Nazi movement. Some of the brownshirt leaders, the press reported, had been found with 'catamites' and one 'was startled from his sleep in the most disgusting situation'.[47]

When the Reichstag was convened on 13 July, Hitler elaborated on these remarks in a speech broadcast on the radio and blared out to the population in pubs, bars and town squares across the land. Surrounded by steel-helmeted SS men, he presented his audience with an elaborate and fantastic web of claims and assertions about the supposed conspiracy to overthrow the Reich. There were four groups of malcontents who had been involved, he said: Communist street-fighters who had infiltrated the SA, political leaders who had never reconciled themselves to the finality of 30 January 1933, rootless elements who believed in permanent revolution, and upper-class 'drones' who sought to fill their empty lives with gossip, rumour and conspiracy. Attempts to curb the excesses of the SA had been frustrated, he now knew, by the fact that they were all part of the mounting plot to overthrow public order. He had been forced to act without recourse to the law:

If anyone reproaches me and asks why we did not call upon the regular courts for sentencing, my only answer is this: in that hour, I was responsible for the fate of the German nation and was thus the Supreme Justiciar of the German people! . . . I gave the order to shoot those parties mainly responsible for this treason . . . The nation should know that no one can threaten its existence – which is guaranteed by inner law and order – and escape unpunished! And every person should know for all time that if he raises his hand to strike out at the State, certain death will be his lot.[48]

This open confession of the complete illegality of his action in formal terms did not run into any criticism from the judicial authorities. On the contrary, the Reichstag enthusiastically applauded Hitler's justification and passed a resolution thanking him for his action. State Secretary Meissner sent a telegram in the name of the ailing President Hindenburg giving his approval. A law was quickly passed giving the action retro-active legality.[49]

Social Democratic agents reported that the events had initially created considerable confusion in the population. Anyone who openly criticized the action was immediately arrested. The press reported that the police had issued a 'sharp warning to subversives and malicious agitators'. 'Concentration camp is threatened' for 'rumour-mongering and offering slanderous insults of the movement itself and its Leader'. This wave of repression, which continued in the early part of August, left people apprehensive about the future, fearful of arrest. Many suspected that there was more to the events of 30 June than met the eye, and local police authorities reported an atmosphere of widespread rumour and speculation, 'grumbling' and 'carping'. The Propaganda Ministry noted with alarm in an internal memorandum, the 'innumerable nonsensical rumours that are in circulation'. The orchestrated press campaign that followed had little effect in countering such feelings. The divisions exposed by the conflict led to optimistic talk among former Social Democrats and German Nationalists that 'Hitler will soon be finished'.[50] Most people, however, were at least relieved that Hitler had acted against the 'brown bigwigs' and that the streets, as it seemed, would now be safe from the excesses of drunken and disorderly stormtroopers.[51]

Not untypical was the reaction of the conservative Hamburg school-teacher Luise Solmitz, who had been so enthusiastic for the coalition cabinet and the Day of Potsdam in 1933 ('that great, unforgettably beautiful German day!'), only to become worried about the possible socialist tendencies of the regime when it began to confiscate the assets of émigré Jews like Albert Einstein ('They should not do that. Don't confuse the concept of property; Bolshevism without it'). Like many others, she described the 30 June 1934 as 'a day that has shattered all of us right down to our innermost heart'. Half persuaded by the 'moral transgressions' of some of the murdered men ('a disgrace for the whole of Germany'), she spent her time swapping rumours with friends and listening breathlessly to the radio in a friend's house for the latest news. As details began to emerge, she found herself overcome with admiration for Hitler's conduct. 'The personal courage, the decisiveness and effectiveness he showed in Munich, the decisiveness and effectiveness, that is unique.' She compared him to Frederick the Great of Prussia or Napoleon. The fact that, as she noted, there was 'no trial, no drumhead court-martial' seemed only to increase her admiration. She was fully persuaded that Röhm had been planning an uprising together with Schleicher.

This was the last of the widely mistrusted former Chancellor's many political adventures, Luise Solmitz noted. Her credulity and relief were typical of the majority of middle-class Germans after the initial hours of confusion. They had supported Hitler not least because by the middle of 1933 he had restored order on the streets and stability to the political scene, and now he had achieved this a second time. The day after the action, crowds gathered in front of the Reich Chancellery and the Propaganda Ministry, singing the Horst Wessel Song and protesting their loyalty to the Leader, though whether it was enthusiasm, nervousness or relief that prompted them to do this is uncertain. Hitler's own standing was widely agreed to have been strengthened by his swift and decisive action. It contrasted even more sharply than before in the minds of many with the disorder and radicalism of the Party.[52] Some, like the former Social Democrat Jochen Klepper, were shocked by the murder of Schleicher's wife, who could not possibly have been suspected of anything.[53] Only the more disaffected commented sourly that the only thing wrong with the purge was that too few Nazis had been executed.[54]

The scale of the purge had been considerable. Hitler himself told the Reichstag on 13 July 1934 that seventy-four people had been killed, while Göring alone had had over a thousand people arrested. At least eighty-five people are known to have been summarily killed without any formal legal proceedings being taken against them.[55] Twelve of the dead were Reichstag deputies. The SA leaders and their men had been almost wholly unsuspecting; many of them, indeed, went to their deaths believing their arrest and execution had been ordered by the army and swearing eternal loyalty to the 'Leader'. In the following days and weeks, arrests and dismissals continued, directed in particular against the rowdiest and most corrupt elements amongst the brownshirts. Heavy drinking, homosexuality, embezzlement, riotous behaviour, all the things that had lent the brownshirts such public notoriety over the previous months, were ruthlessly purged. Drunken brawls involving Nazi stormtroopers still occurred thereafter, but no more on the dangerous scale of the months before 30 June 1934. Disillusioned, without a role, and unable to assert themselves any more, the brownshirts began leaving the organization *en masse* – 100,000 in August and September 1934 alone. From a total membership of 2.9 million on August 1934, the SA declined to 1.6 million in October 1935 and 1.2 million in April 1938. Strict entry requirements and quotas limited recruitment. The decline of unemployment and, from 1935, the introduction of conscription, also took away many of the young men who might otherwise have joined.[56]

Yet although they no longer threatened the army or the state, the brownshirts' potential for violence and aggression survived. A report by one SA leader of events in the brownshirts' camp during a single night at the Nuremberg Rally in 1934 indicates this very clearly. Everyone was drunk, he noted, and a large fight between two regional groups at one in the morning left several men with knife-wounds. On their way back to the camp, stormtroopers attacked cars, threw bottles and stones at the windows and beat up their occupants. The entire Nuremberg police force was mobilized to try and stop the mayhem. A brownshirt was hauled out of the camp latrine, into which he had fallen in a drunken stupor, but he died of chlorine gas poisoning shortly afterwards. The camp was not quiet until four in the morning, by which time six men had been killed and thirty wounded, as well as another twenty who had been injured by jumping on or off cars and trucks, hanging onto the sides, or falling off the back while the vehicle was moving. Such incidents repeated themselves on other occasions. Chastened, reduced in numbers, deprived of its autonomy and – so the Nazi leaders claimed – purged of its most extreme, violent and corrupt elements, the SA nevertheless remained a source of violence whenever the regime chose to make use of it and sometimes even when it did not.[57]

Meanwhile, the army breathed a sigh of relief. General Blomberg expressed his gratitude and assured Hitler of the complete devotion of the army. He congratulated Hitler on his 'soldierly decision' to deal with 'traitors and murderers'. General von Reichenau quickly explained away the cold-blooded murder of one of the army's most senior and publicly prominent officers, Kurt von Schleicher, in a communiqué that claimed he had been conspiring with Röhm and with foreign powers to overthrow the state and had been shot when he had offered armed resistance to his arrest. Whether his wife, also shot, had been involved, he did not say. Army officers uncorked bottles of champagne in the mess to celebrate. From young firebrands like Lieutenant Claus von Stauffenberg, who described the action as the lancing of a boil, to senior officers like Major-General Erwin von Witzleben, who told his fellow officers he wished he had been there to see Röhm shot, all of them rejoiced to a degree that even Blomberg found unseemly. Only one man, a retired captain and former senior civil servant in the Reich Chancellery, Erwin Planck, thought the army's jubilation misplaced. 'If you look on without lifting a finger,' he told General von Fritsch, 'you will meet the same fate sooner or later.'[58]

REPRESSION AND RESISTANCE

I

While these events had been in progress, Reich President Hindenburg's condition had been steadily deteriorating. When Hitler visited him on 1 August in Neudeck, the Head of State and former First World War military leader, in a confusion that graphically symbolized the shift in the balance of power and authority between the two men that had taken place over the previous eighteen months, addressed him as 'Majesty', evidently thinking he was talking to the Kaiser.[59] Noting the old man's physical and mental dissolution, Hindenburg's doctors told Hitler that the President only had twenty-four hours to live. Flying back to Berlin, Hitler convened a cabinet meeting the same evening. Without waiting for the old man to die, the cabinet agreed a decree merging the offices of President and Chancellor and transferring all the powers of the former to the latter, to come into effect at the moment of Hindenburg's passing. Hitler did not have long to wait. At 9 a.m. on 2 August 1934, the President finally gave up the ghost. Many conservative Germans felt this was the end of an era. He was, noted Luise Solmitz in her diary, 'a real fighter and blameless human being and has carried his, our, era with him into the grave'. He took his office with him to the grave, too. The title of Reich President, Hitler announced, was 'inseparably united with the name of the great deceased'. It would be wrong for it to be used again. In future, Hitler would be known as the 'Leader and Reich Chancellor'. A law was put forward to this effect and ratified by a nationwide plebiscite held on 19 August.[60]

With this act, Hitler became Head of State in every sense of the term. The most important attribute of this office was the fact that it was to the

Head of State that the armed forces swore allegiance. On 2 August 1934, troops all over the land were summoned and made to swear a new oath, devised by General von Reichenau without any consultation with Hitler himself. The old oath had pledged allegiance to the abstract entity of the Weimar Constitution and the unnamed person of the President. The new one was very different: 'I swear by God this holy oath, that I will render unconditional obedience to the Leader of the German Reich and people, Adolf Hitler, the supreme commander of the armed forces, and as a brave soldier am willingly prepared to risk my life for this oath at any time.'[61] Nor was this a merely formal pledge. For the oath of allegiance was of far more importance in the German army than in most of its equivalents elsewhere. It was the subject of specific training and education sessions, in which duty and honour were emphasized and examples given of the consequences of breaking it. Most important of all, perhaps, was the novel inclusion of the pledge to *unconditional* obedience to Hitler, whether or not his commands might have been considered legal, in contrast to the primacy given by the previous oath of allegiance to the constitution and the 'lawful establishments' of the German nation.[62]

A few officers in the military were fully aware of what the oath meant. Some had doubts. The evening after swearing the oath, Major-General Ludwig Beck, the conservative, hard-working, middle-class artillery officer who had risen by 1934 to become a senior staff officer at the head of the Troop Office (renamed the Army General Staff in 1935), described 2 August as 'the blackest day of my life'. But most were either in favour, given the way in which Hitler had fulfilled the army's wishes over the previous eighteen months, or remained unaware of the oath's potential significance. Hitler himself had no doubt as to the importance of what had been done. After promulgating a law on 20 August 1934 giving retroactive legal validity to the new oath, he wrote a fulsome letter of thanks to Werner von Blomberg, the Minister of Defence, expressing his gratitude and promising that the army's loyalty would be reciprocated. Gratified in his turn, Blomberg ordered that the armed forces would now address Hitler as 'My Leader' instead of the civilian appellation of 'Mr Hitler' which they had previously used.[63] The military oath provided the model for a similar oath ordered in the law of 20 August to be sworn by civil servants. Once more it was to the 'Leader of the German Reich and

People', an office unknown in any constitution, a form of authority derived from Hitler's person rather than from the German state.[64]

These events cemented Hitler's power as 'the Leader'. As the young constitutional lawyer Ernst Rudolf Huber explained in 1939, this was not a governmental office, but derived its legitimation from 'the united will of the people':

The authority of the Leader is total and all-embracing: within it all resources available to the body politic merge; it covers every facet of the life of the people; it embraces all members of the German community pledged to loyalty and obedience to the Leader. The Leader's authority is subject to no checks or controls; it is circumscribed by no private preserves of jealously guarded individual rights; it is free and independent, overriding and unfettered.

Hitler's opinion, Huber declared, in his treatment of the *Constitutional Law of the Greater German Reich*, which quickly became a standard work, represented the 'objective' will of the people, and in this way he could counter 'misguided public opinion' and override the selfish will of the individual. Hitler's word, as another commentator, Werner Best, a Nazi intellectual who had been the central figure in the 'Boxheim affair' in 1931, noted, was thus law, and could override all existing laws. He was not given his powers by the state, but by history. In time, therefore, his merely constitutional secondary title of Reich Chancellor was quietly dropped.[65]

Not just Hitler personally but also the Nazi movement in general had always held the letter of the law and the institutions of the state in contempt. From the very beginning, they had operated extra-legally, and this continued even after they had abandoned the idea of a direct putsch as the way to power. For the Nazis, the bullet and the ballot-box were complementary tools of power, not alternatives. Votes and elections were treated cynically as instruments of formal political legitimation; the will of the people was expressed not through the free articulation of public opinion, but through the person of Hitler and the Nazi movement's incorporation of the historical destiny of the Germans, even if the Germans themselves disagreed with this. Moreover, widely accepted legal norms such as the notion that people should not commit murder or acts of violence, destruction and theft, were disregarded from the outset by the Nazis because they believed that history and the interests of the German ('Aryan') race justified extreme measures in the crisis that followed Germany's defeat in the war.[66]

At the same time, at least in the early years of the Third Reich, the massive apparatus of state bureaucracy, judiciary, police, penal and welfare systems inherited from the Weimar Republic and ultimately to a large extent from the Bismarckian Reich could not simply be brushed aside or overridden at will. There existed what the exiled political scientist Ernst Fraenkel called *The Dual State*, to quote the title of his famous book, published in the USA in 1941. On the one hand was the 'normative state', bound by rules, procedures, laws and conventions, and consisting of formal institutions such as the Reich Chancellery, the Ministries, local authorities and so on, and on the other there was the 'prerogative state', an essentially extra-legal system that derived its legitimation entirely from the supra-legal authority of the Leader.[67] Theorists like Huber distinguished carefully between 'the authority of the state and the authority of the Leader', and made it clear that the latter always had precedence over the former. Thus formally illegal acts such as the murders committed in the 'Night of the Long Knives' were sanctioned by the Leader's authority and so in fact were not illegal at all. The arrests, imprisonments and murders had been carried out not by the police or the regular law enforcement agencies but by the SS, and the formal apparatus of the law and the state almost fell over itself in the rush to give these acts of violence the approval of the law. This was a graphic demonstration of the fact that there was increasingly little serious conflict between the 'normative' and 'prerogative' systems in Nazi Germany. The former had to defer more and more to the latter, and as time went on it became increasingly permeated by its spirit; rules were relaxed, laws dispensed with, scruples abandoned. Already at the beginning of July 1933, Hans-Heinrich Lammers, head of the Reich Chancellor's office, was beginning to sign his letters 'Hail, Hitler! (*Heil Hitler!*)'.[68] Towards the end of the month, all civil servants, including university teachers, lawyers and other state employees, were instructed to use the 'German greeting' when conducting official business. Not to say 'Hail Hitler' or give the Nazi salute when the occasion seemed to demand it was from this point on an overt sign of dissidence.[69] These were only the outward signs of a compliance that increased rapidly in intensity as the regime settled down into power.

Ministers such as Franz Gürtner, who had been Reich Justice Minister in the last two cabinets before Hitler's and continued in office under the Third Reich, still made strenuous efforts to try and get the arbitrary authority of the Leader mediated through formal acts of law. This required the repeated invention of phrases and concepts designed to make it look retrospectively as if Hitler's orders were in conformity with existing legal rules and regulations. In some cases, as with the 'Night of the Long Knives', it also meant the passing of legislation giving retroactive legality to the regime's most blatantly illegal acts. On 1 December 1933, the supremacy of the prerogative over the normative state was formally proclaimed in a Law for Guarantees of the Unity of Party and State, though the vague terms in which the legislation was couched meant that it had little real effect in practice. In reality, this situation meant that there was continual skirmishing between the organs of Party and state, with Nazi bosses interfering with state policy and decision-making at every level from local authorities upwards. Hitler tried to control the interference by Nazi Party Regional Leaders and other Party officials in the business of the state in 1934 in particular, as they threatened to disrupt economic policy in some areas. He declared the Party to be mainly an instrument of propaganda now that the state was in Nazi hands. But this too in the end meant very little.[70]

To begin with, Hitler also introduced a number of measures to make the Party more effective. The decentralization of its organization after the resignation of Gregor Strasser at the end of 1932 was creating problems. Constant faction fighting and struggles for power within the Party organization allowed clever civil servants to reduce the Party's influence by playing off the factions against one another. Anxious to centralize the Party again without putting power in the hands of a potential rival, Hitler first made the ever-faithful Rudolf Hess 'Leader's Deputy for Party Affairs', but without control over the organizational apparatus. Then, on 1 December 1933, he appointed him to a cabinet post. On 27 July 1934, Hitler decreed that all laws and decrees proposed by Reich Ministries had to pass through Hess's office. In 1935 Hess got the power to vet senior civil service appointments and promotions as well. All this gave the Party very extensive influence over the state. Hess himself was scarcely capable of wielding it. He had no serious ambitions apart from abnegating himself to Hitler's will. His powers were increasingly used, however, by the undoubtedly ambitious Martin Bormann, Chief of Staff in Hess's office since 1 July 1933. Bormann created an elaborate apparatus of the 'Staff of the Leader's Deputy', organized into different departments and manned by loyal supporters who shared his determination to centralize the Party and use it systematically to create policy and push it through the civil service. In 1935 Bormann took over the management of Hitler's rural headquarters on the Obersalzberg, in Bavaria. He used his presence there to act as Hitler's private secretary and exert growing control over access to the Leader. It was typical of the way the Third Reich was run that Bormann's office now rivalled the official, state institution of the Reich Chancellery, run by the top civil servant Hans-Heinrich Lammers. When Hitler was in Berlin, Lammers had more access and thus more influence; but the Leader spent increasing amounts of time on the Obersalzberg, where Bormann could deny access even to Lammers himself.[71]

This kind of duality was repeated at every level. As the chaos of the seizure of power in the first half of 1933 subsided, the Third Reich was left with a mass of competing institutions across the board. Reich Governors, Minister-Presidents and Regional Leaders all competed for supremacy in the federated states, and in Prussia, which covered over half the land surface of Germany, with the regional state governors as well. These clashes were partly solved by the appointment of the top Regional Leader of every federated state as Reich Governor in his particular area in April 1933. Another step was taken on 30 January 1934 when, under pressure from the Reich Interior Ministry under the Nazi Wilhelm Frick, a new law abolished all the federated states, from Prussia downwards, along with their governments and parliaments, and merged their Ministries into the corresponding Reich Ministries. Thus the federal constitution which in one form had characterized the German political system for over a thousand years, and was to do so again after 1945, was swept away. Characteristically, however, some elements of federalism remained, so the process of dissolution was incomplete. The Party Regional Leaders retained their position as regional Reich Governors, and continued to occupy powerful positions within the Party hierarchy. They wielded considerable influence over local and regional affairs, though here the Reich Local Government Law of 1935, in abolishing local elections, placed the appointment of mayors largely within the

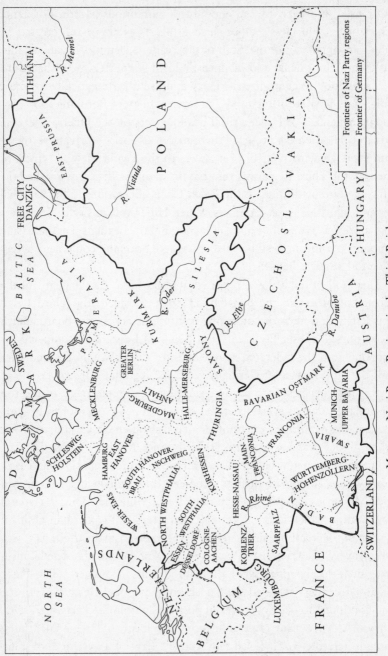

Map 1. Nazi Party Regions in the Third Reich, 1935

competence of the Interior Ministry in Berlin. This in turn aroused the hostility of the District Leaders (*Kreisleiter*) of the Party, who often exploited the right of participation accorded them by the law in the appointment of local officials to interfere in local government and place their cronies and clients in offices for which they were often quite unsuited.[72]

None of this infighting, needless to say, involved any real opposition to the Nazi leadership or its policies. After the purges of 1933, the vast majority of state bureaucrats were themselves either Nazi Party members or broadly sympathetic to the movement. The heads of some of the key Ministries in Berlin were the same. Their position was reinforced by such leading figures in the movement as Hermann Göring, who managed characteristically to prevent most of the proposed changes in the administration of the Prussian state from being put into effect. Indeed, the opposition of the Regional Leaders among others ensured that the whole reform never went as far as the Reich Interior Ministry intended, so that the administrative structures of the federated states remained largely intact even after most aspects of their autonomy, and all remaining vestiges of their representative institutions, had been abolished.[73] There was nothing neat about the administration of the Third Reich, and the idea that it was a smoothly functioning, completely centralized state has long since been abandoned by historians. Instead, the mess of competing institutions and conflicting competencies effectively prevented the 'normative' state machine from asserting itself against the arbitrary interventions of the 'prerogative' apparatus and doomed it to a slow decline in its power and autonomy.

Meanwhile, after the upheavals of the summer and early autumn of 1934, Hitler moved quietly to make arrangements for the eventuality that he himself might be incapacitated or struck down unexpectedly. It was not Hess, nor was it Himmler, who had played the key role in the 'Night of the Long Knives', but the redoubtable, ruthless and decisive figure of Hermann Göring. On 7 December 1934, Hitler issued a decree making Göring 'his deputy in all aspects of national government' should he be unable to carry out his duties himself. Göring's position as the second man in the Third Reich was cemented a few days later by another law, issued on 13 December, in which Hitler named Göring as his successor, and instructed the civil service, the army, the SA and the SS to swear an oath of personal allegiance to him immediately after his own death. Göring was to use this position in the next few years to build up a position for himself in the Third Reich so powerful, it has been said, as to amount to a state within the state. What his designation as Hitler's deputy and successor also showed, however, was how quickly after Hindenburg's death the real and formal distribution of power within the Third Reich had become a matter of personalities rather than constitutional rules and regulations. This was now a fully fledged dictatorship, in which the Leader could do as he wished, including naming his own successor without reference to anyone else.[74]

II

Nowhere was the personal nature of Hitler's authority clearer than in the rise to prominence and power of the SS. Originating as Hitler's private bodyguard and 'Protection Squad' (*Schutzstaffel*, hence the abbreviation 'SS'), it owed allegiance solely to him and obeyed no laws apart from its own. Heinrich Himmler, its leader since 1929, had built it up rapidly, until it reached a strength of over 50,000 by the spring of 1933. From this large force Hitler once more selected an elite to form a new 'Headquarters Guard', renamed 'Adolf Hitler's Bodyguard' in September 1933; other elite groups of SS men were put into special detachments to be placed at Hitler's disposal for particular tasks of policing, terror and operations such as the 'Night of the Long Knives'.[75] Already by 1934, Himmler was thinking of the SS in more ambitious terms than just a special force of loyal troops to be used by Hitler whenever he needed them. He conceived the ambition of turning the SS into the core elite of the new Nazi racial order. In deliberate contrast to the plebeian disorder of the brownshirts, Himmler intended his SS to be strictly disciplined, puritanical, racially pure, unquestioningly obedient, incorporating what he regarded as the best elements in the German race. Bit by bit, the older generation of SS men, with histories of violence often going back to the Free Corps of the early years of the Weimar Republic, were pensioned off, to be replaced by a younger, better-educated generation of officers.[76]

Himmler created an elaborate hierarchy of SS officers, each level with its own grandiose-sounding title – Senior Group Leader, Standard Leader (*Obergruppenführer*, *Standartenführer*) and so on – and its own subtle indications of status in the insignia borne on the smart, military-style uniforms all the officers wore. These redesigned uniforms included now not only the original silver death's head badge of the organization but also a pseudo-runic version of the letters 'SS', shaped like a double bolt of lightning; SS typewriters were soon supplied with a special key carrying the runic title to use in official correspondence and memoranda. More grades and insignia followed. Himmler even raised money for his organization by doling out honorary ranks and titles such as 'Sponsoring Member' to donors, and money duly began to flow in from industrialists, bankers and businessmen. The 'Friends of the Reich Leader-SS', another source of funds, included men like the banker Friedrich Flick, the I.G. Farben Director Heinrich Bütefisch, and representatives of firms like Siemens-Schückert, the Deutsche Bank, Rheinmetall-Borsig and the Hamburg-America Shipping Line. Many of these men received honorary SS titles as a reward. This, as they no doubt realized, was more than an empty gesture, since their association with the SS could protect them from interference by over-zealous members of the Party in their business. Not surprisingly, the magazine started by Himmler for his 'Friends' had a circulation of 365,000 by September 1939, and the collective financial contributions of the Friends ranged between half a million and a million Reichsmarks a year.[77]

All this threatened to dilute the close-knit, elite character of the SS, so between 1933 and 1935 Himmler expelled no fewer than 60,000 men from its swollen ranks. In particular he purged homosexuals, alcoholics and men who had obviously joined out of opportunism and were less than fully convinced Nazis. Above all, from 1935 he required proof of pure Aryan ancestry, as he termed it, going back to 1800 for the rank and file, 1750 for officers. Serving and aspirant SS men combed the parish registers for proof of their racial purity, or hired professional genealogists to do it for them. Recruits now had to undergo a physical examination to confirm their 'Aryan' qualities; Himmler considered that in time, with suitably directed racial evolution, only blond men would be accepted. Already since 1931 every SS man had to receive special permission from Himmler or his office to get married; it would only be granted if his fiancée was racially suitable as well.[78] But these plans fell far short of the ideal. For example, out of 106,304 SS men who applied for marriage certificates issued from 1932 to 1940, only 958 were turned down, despite the fact that all the requirements were satisfied only by 7,518. The few hundred men who were expelled for contravening the marriage rules were subsequently reinstated. The new racial elite would clearly be a long time in coming.[79]

The elite formed by the SS gradually came to acquire a different characteristic from the racial supremacy originally intended by Himmler. It was above all, and in sharp contrast to the SA, highly educated.[80] Leading SS figures like Werner Best, Otto Ohlendorf, Walter Schellenberg and Franz Six possessed university degrees, even doctorates; born in the run-up to the First World War, they were too young to have fought at the front, but were imbued instead with the compensatory nationalist fanaticism that was so prevalent in the universities they attended during the 1920s. Coming to maturity in an era of uncertainty, in which the political system was in flux, money, for a time at least, had lost its value, and a steady job or a stable career seemed out of the question, they had lost their moral compass, perhaps even never acquired one in the first place. To such young men, only the Nazi movement appeared to offer a solid identity, moral certainties and a perspective on the future. Typical of this generation was Otto Ohlendorf, who was born in 1907 into a well-off Protestant farming family of conservative, Nationalist political inclinations. Ohlendorf joined the brownshirts in 1925 while still attending grammar school, and was transferred to the SS in 1927, when he also joined the Nazi Party. From 1928 to 1931 he studied Law and Political Science at the Universities of Leipzig and Göttingen, then he spent a year at the University of Pavia in order to learn about Italian Fascism. The experience left him disillusioned with the rigidities of the 'Corporate State' but also directed his attention towards economics, which he began to study seriously, although his attempts to take a doctorate and build an academic career for himself failed. From 1936 onwards he concentrated on developing his ideas within the SS, where he became Director of the economics section of the SS Security Service (*Sicherheitsdienst* or SD), where his attacks on Nazi economics for damaging the middle classes got him into trouble, but also won him a reputation for intelligence and assertiveness. It was probably these abilities, denoting a willingness to digest and articulate unpalatable truths, that in September 1939 secured him the position of Director of the German-speaking areas covered by Security Service operations.[81]

The Security Service itself had its origins in reports early in 1931 that the Nazi Party had been infiltrated by its enemies. Himmler established the Security Service to investigate the claims, and put the business in the hands of a man who subsequently became perhaps more universally and cordially feared and disliked than any other leading figure in the Nazi regime – Reinhard Heydrich. Born in 1904 into a highly cultured middle-class family – his father was an opera singer, his mother an actress – Heydrich was an accomplished violinist, who, contemporaries reported, played with feeling, often weeping as he did so. Tall, slim, blond, his striking good looks marred for some only by his narrow face and small, close-set eyes, he also became an expert swordsman who excelled at fencing. Joining a Free Corps at the age of sixteen, he enlisted as an officer cadet in the navy in 1922 and had become a lieutenant by 1928, working in the signals department. His future in the armed forces had seemed assured.[82] But Heydrich also found it easy to make enemies. The sailors disliked his abrupt, overbearing manner and mocked his high, almost falsetto voice. His numerous affairs with women got him into trouble with his superiors when the father of one of his girlfriends, a director of I.G. Farben and a friend of Admiral Raeder, head of the navy, complained; not only was the girl pregnant, but at the naval court of honour summoned to hear the case, Heydrich tried to pin the blame for the conception on her, causing general outrage amongst the officers and leading to his being cashiered from the navy in April 1931. Marrying his new girlfriend, Lina von Osten, who held strong Nazi convictions and had family connections with the SS chief in Munich, Karl Baron von Eberstein, Heydrich found new employment in the SS and was immediately set to work rooting out infiltrators. So thorough was he at this task that he convinced Himmler that the Security Service needed to widen the scope of its activities to become the core of a new German police and surveillance force. His intrusive investigations aroused the hostility of a number of old Nazis, including the Regional Leader of Halle-Merseburg, who riposted with the malicious allegation that Heydrich had Jewish ancestry in his blood. An investigation ordered by Gregor Strasser, Reich Organization Leader of the Nazi Party at the time, came to the conclusive finding that the allegations were untrue, though they continued to dog Heydrich for the rest of his career and have surfaced periodically since his death as well.[83]

None of this stopped Heydrich's meteoric rise to power within the SS. Unsentimental, cold, efficient, power-hungry and utterly convinced that the end justified the means, he soon won Himmler over to his ambitious vision of the SS and its Security Service as the core of a comprehensive new system of policing and control. Already on 9 March 1933, the two men took over the Bavarian police service, making the political section autonomous and moving SS Security Service personnel into some of the key posts. They went on to take over the political police service in one federated state after another, with the backing of the centralizing Reich Interior Minister Wilhelm Frick. At this point they ran into a major obstacle to their plan to create a unified national political police system, however, in the formidable shape of Hermann Göring, the Prussian Minister-President, who on 30 November 1933 established a separate political police service for Prussia. This was based on the political police section of the Berlin police presidium, which had acted as an information-gathering centre on Communists during the Weimar Republic and was staffed by professional policemen, headed by the career police officer Rudolf Diels. Göring's new, independent force was known as the Secret State Police, *Geheime Staatspolizei*, or Gestapo for short.[84]

The conflicts that rumbled on through the early months of 1934 were eventually resolved by the need felt by Göring to counter what he saw as the growing menace of Röhm's brownshirts. Diels had implemented Nazi policy with gusto in the course of 1933, but his professional detachment was unsuited to the task of fighting the brownshirts by fair means or foul. On 20 April 1934 Göring replaced Diels with Himmler at the head of the Gestapo.[85] Himmler and Heydrich now played off Göring and Frick against one another, and gained further room for manoeuvre thanks to the cutting of the formal ties that bound the SS to the SA after the 'Night of the Long Knives'. Göring and Frick were forced to recognize that they were unable to control the Gestapo, whatever the formal powers they might claim to possess over it. While Göring effectively abandoned his efforts in November 1934, Frick and the Interior Ministry continued the bureaucratic struggle. It was finally resolved in Himmler's favour in 1936. A new law, passed on 10 February, took the Gestapo out of the jurisdiction of the courts, so that there could henceforth be no appeal to any outside body against its actions. Then a decree, issued by Hitler on 17 June, made Himmler Chief of the German Police. In this capacity, Himmler put Heydrich in charge of the Gestapo and the Criminal Police, as well as the SS Security Service, while the uniformed police were also run by an SS man, Kurt Daluege. Police and SS began, in effect, to merge, with professional policemen now joining the SS in increasing numbers, and SS men taking up an increasing number of posts within the police force. Thus a key law enforcement agency in the Reich began to move decisively from the 'normative' to the 'prerogative' state, a transition symbolized in 1939 by the subordination of the SS Security Service and the security police to the Reich Security Head Office, controlled from the top by Himmler and Heydrich.[86]

III

The Third Reich's elaborate apparatus of policing and repression was directed in the first place at hunting down and apprehending Nazism's enemies within Germany. Organized opposition to Nazism was offered only by the Communists and the Social Democrats in the early years of the dictatorship. The left-wing political parties had won 13.1 million votes in Germany's last fully free election, in November 1932, to the Nazis' 11.7 million. They represented a huge chunk of the German electorate. Yet they had no effective means of standing up to Nazi violence. Their entire apparatus, along with that of their paramilitary wings, the 'Red Front-Fighters' League' and the Reichsbanner, and associated organizations such as the trade unions, was ruthlessly swept aside in the first months of 1933, their leaders exiled or imprisoned, their millions of members and supporters, many of them looking back on a lifetime's commitment to the cause, isolated and disoriented. Former activists were placed under more or less permanent surveillance, shadowed, their correspondence and contacts monitored. Divided, mutually hostile and taken by surprise at the speed and ruthlessness of the Nazi seizure of power, they were initially helpless and uncertain how to act. Reorganizing to form an effective resistance movement seemed out of the question.[87]

Yet in some ways the Social Democrats and Communists were better prepared for resistance than any other groups in Nazi Germany. The labour movement had been repeatedly banned or suppressed in the past, under Metternich's police repression of the early nineteenth century, in the post-revolutionary reaction of the 1850s and early 1860s, and most notably during Bismarck's Anti-Socialist Law of 1878–90. Going underground was nothing new. Indeed some veterans of the Anti-Socialist Law, when the Social Democrats had developed a whole network of secret contacts and communications, were still active forty-odd years later, under the Nazis. Fuelled by their stories of heroism and derring-do in the 1880s, and disillusioned with the compromises the party had made in the later years of the Weimar Republic, many younger Social Democrats relished the prospect of returning to the party's revolutionary traditions. Where the international statesman Bismarck had failed to crush them, surely the beer-hall demagogue Hitler was unlikely to succeed. Social Democratic activists quickly began cyclostyling illegal broadsheets, pamphlets and newspapers and distributing them secretly amongst sympathizers to try and strengthen their resolve to resist the new regime's attempts to win them over. Many were sustained by the belief, rooted in the Marxist theory that still dominated the thinking of the Social Democrats in this period, that the Nazi regime was unlikely to last. It was a final, desperate attempt at self-preservation by a capitalist system plunged into its deepest ever crisis by the crash of 1929. All that was needed was to stick together and prepare for the Third Reich to self-destruct. By spreading clear and accurate information about the true state of affairs in Germany, it would be possible to destroy the ideological foundations of the regime and get the masses poised to remove it.[88]

In many parts of Germany, above all in its industrial heartlands, with their decades-old traditions of labour movement solidarity, clandestine groups quickly organized and sprang into action. Even in less secure cultural environments, Social Democrats managed to regroup and continue their activities in secret. In Hanover, for instance, the young Werner Blumenberg, later to make a name for himself as a Marx scholar, set up a 'Socialist Front' that counted some 250 members and produced a series of mimeographed newsletters, the Socialist Flysheets (Sozialistische Blätter), in editions of 1,500 that were distributed to contacts throughout the region.[89] Similar, smaller groups were established in the Bavarian towns of Augsburg and Regensburg, and even in the 'capital' of the Nazi movement, Munich. Their activities included such actions as pasting up posters in the streets at night and urging people to vote 'no' in the plebiscite of 19 August 1934. Leaflets were left in workplaces with slogans or brief news items criticizing the Nazi propaganda machine's portrayal of events. All over Germany, thousands of former activists in the Social Democratic Party were engaged in this kind of work. They concentrated in particular on maintaining contacts with the party's leadership in exile, in Prague. Their aim was not just to rouse the masses, but to keep old party and trade union loyalists within the fold and wait for better times. Most of them lived a double life, maintaining outward conformity with the regime but engaging in resistance activities in secret, in their spare time. Some collected the leaflets and newspapers the exiled party organization printed, such as the *New Forwards* (*Neue Vorwärts*) on journeys across the border, smuggled them into Germany and distributed them to the remnants of the party's membership. And they fed detailed information to the exiled leadership about the situation in Germany in turn, providing it month by month with a remarkably sober and increasingly realistic assessment of the chances of staging a revolt.[90]

Yet these activities stood little chance even of achieving the most basic of their aims, that of maintaining solidarity amongst former Social Democrats, let alone of spreading the resisters' message to the masses. For this there were many reasons. The resisters lacked leadership. The most prominent Social Democrats had mostly gone into exile. Even those who wanted to stay on were too well known to escape the attention of the police for long: the Silesian Reichstag deputy Otto Buchwitz, for example, had a number of narrow escapes while travelling around Germany distributing illegal party literature, before he finally bowed to the inevitable and allowed the underground movement to smuggle him into Denmark at the beginning of August 1933.[91] By this time, almost all the other leading Social Democrats who had remained in Germany were in prison, in a concentration camp, silenced or dead. The leadership in exile proved to be an unsatisfactory substitute. Its uncompromising position had already alienated many of those comrades who had elected to stay in Germany in 1933, and it made matters worse in January 1934 by issuing the 'Prague Manifesto', which called for a radical policy of expropriation to destroy big business and the big landed estates once

Hitler had been overthrown.[92] This was unpalatable to many local opposition groups, while failing to convince others that the party leadership had really shaken off the passivity and fatalism that had hampered its will to resist in 1932–3.[93] Dissatisfied with what they saw as the party's feebleness, small, more radical groups acted independently, taking a variety of names such as the International Socialist Fighting League, the Revolutionary Socialists of Germany or the Red Shock-Troop (a purely Berlin organization). These in turn quarrelled with other underground groups that remained loyal to the exiled leadership in Prague, disagreeing not only over policies but also over tactics.[94]

In such circumstances, any idea of rousing the masses to outright opposition to the regime, the traditional goal pursued by underground movements in European history, was doomed to failure from the start. Finding a basis in the masses was almost impossible. The tattered remnants of labour movement culture that remained under the Third Reich were few and usually unimportant. The Nazi 'co-ordination' of local associational life of all kinds had simply been too thorough. Rabbit-breeding circles, gymnastic clubs and similar groups that changed their names by dropping Social Democratic terms from their titles but kept the same leadership and membership as before were quickly recognized for what they were and closed down by the police or the municipal authorities. The Social Democratic resistance was thus never able to expand beyond small, locally organized elite groups of activists. Moreover, the Nazi regime could not be convincingly portrayed, like the regimes of Metternich or Bismarck, as the representative of a tiny, authoritarian elite; on the contrary, its rhetoric announced from the start that it intended to represent the people as a whole, mobilizing them in support of a new kind of state that would overcome internal divisions and create a new national community for the whole German race. This was a dispiriting fact with which Social Democratic activists quickly came to terms.[95]

It was probably loyalty to the memory of the Social Democratic-oriented trade unions that lay behind the mass abstentions that met the annual elections legally required of shop-floor representatives in 1934 and 1935. There were so many blank or spoiled ballots that the results were kept secret in 1934 and 1935 and the process was abandoned thereafter.[96] The Gestapo tracked down many of the 'Marxists' who distributed leaflets urging a 'no' vote in the plebiscite of 19 August 1934, arresting over 1,200 of them in the Rhine-Ruhr area alone. Massive waves of arrests of Social Democrats rolled over other parts of Germany such as Hamburg. The issue of a special leaflet by the Social Democratic resistance on 1 May 1935 prompted a further series of arrests. By the end of the year, the formal underground organization of the Social Democrats had been effectively destroyed. Yet the sheer size of the party's former membership and the enduring power of its former cultural milieu and traditions ensured that hundreds of thousands of old Social Democrats remained loyal in their hearts to the fundamental values of their party. Loosely organized, informal, decentralized groups of Social Democrats continued throughout the rest of the Third Reich to keep these values and ideals alive, even though they could do nothing to put them into effect.[97]

A small number of radical Social Democrats, gathered since 1929 in a group that called itself New Beginning (*Neu-Beginnen*), took the view that the main prerequisite for a successful workers' resistance was the reunification of the German labour movement, whose bitter division between Social Democrats and Communists they thought had opened the way to the rise of fascism. Its hundred or so members, backed by a rather larger number of sympathizers, expended a great deal of effort in trying to bring the parties together, using tactics such as infiltrating Communist cells and working to change the party's line from within. The organization's manifesto, written by its leader Walter Loewenheim and published in Karlsbad in August 1933 in an edition of 12,000, aroused some debate in resistance circles when it was secretly distributed in Germany. But Loewenheim concluded in 1935 that the prospects for success were so small that there was no point in carrying on. Although some members, like the future historian Francis Carsten, tried to continue, waves of arrests by the Gestapo soon crippled the remnants of the movement; Carsten himself went into emigration and began a doctorate on the early history of Prussia. Other small groups in exile and within the country worked along similar lines, including the International Socialist Fighting League and the Socialist Workers' Party of Germany, one of whose leading members was the young Willy Brandt, who left Germany for exile in Scandinavia and became Mayor of West Berlin and then Federal Chancellor of West Germany after the war. All these groups, however, rejected the politics of both the major working-class parties as divisive and outmoded, without really developing any coherent political concept to put in their place.[98]

The hardline attitude of the Communists made any idea of creating a united front quite impossible to fulfil. Since the end of the 1920s the Communist Party of Germany had been following the 'ultra-left' party line in Moscow, which damned the Social Democrats as 'social fascists' and regarded them, indeed, as the main obstacle to a proletarian revolution. Nothing that happened in 1933 or 1934 changed this. In May 1933 the German Communist Party's Central Committee reaffirmed what the Cominterm praised as the party's 'absolutely correct political line' against 'social fascism'. 'The complete exclusion of the Social Fascists from the state apparatus, the brutal suppression of the Social Democratic party organization and its press as well as our own, do not alter the fact that now as before they constitute the main social support of the dictatorship of capital.' Critics of the ultra-left line and advocates of co-operation with the Social Democrats, such as Hermann Remmele and Heinz Neumann, had already been removed from the party leadership in 1932, leaving the ever-faithful Ernst Thälmann at least nominally in charge, though he had in effect been out of action since his arrest and imprisonment immediately after the Reichstag fire in February 1933. 'For the working class,' trumpeted the leading German Communist Fritz Heckert at the end of 1933 despite all the evidence, 'there is only one real enemy – that is the fascist bourgeoisie and Social Democracy, its principal social support.'[99]

Such grotesquely unrealistic views were not simply the result of uncon-ditional obedience to Moscow. They also reflected the long legacy of bitterness between the two major working-class parties since the Revol-ution of 1918 and the murder of the Communist leaders Karl Liebknecht and Rosa Luxemburg by Free Corps units raised at the behest of the Social Democrats. In their turn, Social Democrats knew that the Bol-shevik regime in Russia had murdered some thousands of its opponents, and that their counterparts there, the Mensheviks, had been among the first victims. Unemployment, which affected Communists more than Social Democrats, had driven a further wedge between the two parties. Nobody raised the prospect of united action within either the Social Democratic Party or the Communist Party with any success in 1931–4. The Social Democrats could boast a much larger membership than the

Communist Party – over a million at the beginning of 1933, as against only 180,000 or so for the Communists – and their members tended to stay loyal to their party for longer than Communists did to theirs. However, years of purges and the repeated disciplining of internal dissidents had left the Communists well disciplined and united, while a tradition of clandestine work and secret organization more recent and more effective than that of the Social Democrats ensured that illegal Communist cells were quickly set up all over Germany once the shock of the first months of 1933 had passed. The party's lack of realism about the situation was, ironically, another positive factor. Believing fervently that the final collapse not only of Nazism but also of capitalism as a whole was now only just a matter of months away, Communists saw every reason to risk their freedom and their lives in a struggle that would surely end before long in total victory for the proletarian revolution.[100]

Yet what did that struggle consist of? For all the Nazis' alarmist propaganda in 1933 about the imminence of a violent Communist revolution, the fact was that the reconstituted German Communist Party could do little more than its Social Democratic counterpart. There were a few acts of sabotage, and a handful of Communists tried to obtain military information to feed to the Soviet Union. But the vast majority of the scores of thousands of Communists active in the resistance could only concentrate on keeping the movement alive underground, ready for the day when Nazism fell, along with the capitalist system they thought sustained it. They held secret meetings, distributed illicit imported political propaganda, collected membership dues and produced and circulated crude mimeographed flysheets and newsletters, sometimes in quite large numbers, in pursuit of their aim of reaching as many people as possible and rousing them to oppose the regime. They set up clandestine distribution networks for magazines and leaflets produced by the Communist apparatus outside Germany and smuggled into the country by couriers. There was also extensive co-operation between the resistance within Germany and the leadership outside: the newspaper *The Red Flag*, for instance, was edited in exile but printed in a number of centres within the country, including for example at an illegal press in Solingen-Ohligs, which produced about 10,000 copies of each edition once or twice a month. In a few places, the Communists staged secret demonstrations on Mayday, running up red flags, or the hammer and sickle banner, on high buildings, and daubing slogans on railway stations. Like the Social Democrats, the Communists leafleted for a 'no' vote in the plebiscite of 19 August 1934.[101]

There is no doubt that the Communists were more active and more persistent than the Social Democrats in organizing resistance in the early years of the Third Reich. Apart from the greater commitment – some would say fanaticism – of its members, the Communist Party was also under instructions from its leadership in exile to maintain as visible a presence in Germany as possible. Couriers and agents came and went from Paris, Brussels, Prague and other outside centres, often under assumed identities, constantly attempting to keep the movement going or to revive it where it had been destroyed. Raids and arrests were frequently followed by jauntily assertive mass leafleting to expose the brutality of the police and demonstrate the regime's failure to destroy the resistance. But such tactics proved the party's undoing, since they inevitably rendered it visible not just to workers but also to the Gestapo.[102] The party's bureaucratic structure and habits also helped the police identify and track down its members, as branch treasurers and secretaries like Hans Pfeiffer, in Düsseldorf, for example, meticulously continued to keep copies of letters, minutes of meetings, records of subscriptions and lists of members, all of which proved invaluable to the regime when they fell into the hands of the police.[103] The same problems that afflicted the Social Democrats also plagued the Communists – difficulty of communication with the exiled leadership, destruction of the social and cultural infrastructure of the labour movement, exile, imprisonment or death of the most experienced and talented leaders.[104]

Despite the legendary discipline of the party, too, serious divisions soon emerged within the exiled leadership, between an ultra-left majority that continued to pour venom on the Social Democrats and the Communist International, which recognized the scale of the defeat the party had suffered and eventually began to urge collaboration with Social Democrats in a 'popular front' against fascism. In January 1935 the Communist International openly condemned the party's former policy as 'sectarian' and began to tone down its revolutionary rhetoric. Sensing the way the wind was blowing, a growing minority amongst the German Communists went along with the new Moscow line. They were led by Walter Ulbricht, the former Berlin Communist leader, and Wilhelm

Pieck, a long-term Reichstag deputy and companion of Liebknecht and Luxemburg in their final days, before their murder by the Free Corps during the 'Spartacus uprising' of 1919. Alongside this ideological reorientation, the centralized structure of the party in Germany, so helpful to the Gestapo, was now dismantled and replaced with a looser organization in which the different parts were kept largely separate. The way finally seemed open to a united and effective working-class resistance against the Nazis.[105]

But it was all far too late. The local organizers and many of the rank and file of the Communist resistance had spent too long fighting the Social Democrats to abandon their hatred now. When 7,000 workers paraded in Essen in the middle of 1934 to demonstrate at the grave of a Communist who had died in prison, the local Communist leadership made it clear that Social Democrats, 'against whom the deceased had always fought', would not be welcome. Moreover, Ulbricht, charged with bringing about a Popular Front of Communists and Social Democrats in Germany from his position of exile in Paris, had a talent for antagonizing people. Some thought that he was being deliberately abrasive so as to put the blame on the Social Democrats for the failure of a policy that he did not really support anyway. It also proved impossible to communicate the new party line to many activists within Germany, given the vigilance over couriers exercised by the Gestapo. The German Social Democrats for their part remained as suspicious of the Popular Front, which really did lead to genuine, if uneasy co-operation in France and Spain, as they had been of the 'United Front', a well-known tactic of the Communists to undermine them during the Weimar Republic. The legacy of bitterness sown in 1919–23 proved too powerful for any real co-operation to come about in Germany.[106]

In any case, by the time the Popular Front policy was in full swing, both Communist and Social Democratic resistance organizations had been severely damaged by the Gestapo. The mass arrests carried out in June and July 1933 obliged the resistance movement to regroup, but the Gestapo was soon on the track of the new organizations and began to arrest their members too. The experience of the Düsseldorf branch of the illegal Communist resistance was probably not untypical. A great industrial centre with a tradition of radicalism, Düsseldorf was a stronghold of the Communist Party, which won 78,000 votes in the Reichstag election of November 1932, 8,000 more than the Nazis and more than twice as many as the Social Democrats. The mass arrests that followed the Reichstag Fire Decree on 28 February 1933 severely damaged the local party, but under the leadership of the 27-year-old Hugo Paul, it regrouped and put out a steady stream of leaflets and propaganda. In June 1933, however, the Gestapo seized the party's records and arrested Paul himself at the home of the man who printed the leaflets. Brutal interrogation revealed the names of further activists, and over ninety had been arrested by the end of July. The party's clandestine leadership in Berlin sent a series of replacements for Paul, changing them frequently to avoid discovery, and by the spring of 1934 the local organization had a membership of around 700, producing an internal newsletter in editions of 4–5,000 copies and distributing leaflets by pushing them through letter-boxes at night, or scattering them from the top of high buildings such as the railway station, banks, cinemas and hotels, by means of a device known as a 'jumping jack' (*Knallfrosch*). The party regarded the distribution of a bitingly sarcastic commentary on the 'Night of the Long Knives' as a particular success.

However, the Gestapo was able to turn a clandestine Communist functionary, Wilhelm Gather, into a double agent, and when he re-entered the local Communist Party after his release in 1934, arrests soon followed – sixty in the town's central ward, followed by fifty in the working-class district of Friedrichstadt. Other Communists who were arrested and tortured committed suicide rather than betray their comrades. Yet despite the repression, the murder of Röhm led to renewed optimism about the imminent collapse of the regime, and membership actually increased, reaching about 4,000 in the Lower Rhine and Ruhr districts combined. This did not last long. The growing centralization and efficiency of the Gestapo under Himmler and Heydrich soon led to further arrests; most crucially, the entire secret national leadership of the Communist Party in Berlin was taken into custody on 27 March 1935. This left local and regional groups disoriented and leaderless, their morale further damaged by growing disillusion with the ultra-left policy pursued by the party since the late 1920s. Desertions and further arrests left the clandestine party organization in the Ruhr and Lower Rhine in tatters. It consisted of no more than a few isolated groups by the time the new District Leader, Waldemar Schmidt, arrived in June 1935. He had little time to make his report to the exiled party leadership, however, since he too was very quickly arrested in his turn.[107]

A similar story could be told in virtually every other part of Germany. In Halle-Merseburg, for example, a police spy led the Gestapo to a meeting of the district leadership early in 1935; those arrested were tortured to force them to reveal the names of other members; documents were seized, there were more arrests, more torture; and eventually over 700 people were arrested, totally destroying the regional Communist Party organization and leaving the few remaining members completely demoralized. The party cadres were now politically paralysed, not without justification, by mutual suspicion.[108] Through careful information-gathering, house-searches, ruthless interrogation and torture of suspects, and the use of spies and informants, the Gestapo had succeeded in destroying the organized resistance of the Communist Party by the end of 1934, including its welfare organization the Red Aid (*Rote Hilfe*), which was dedicated to helping the families of prisoners and members who had fallen on hard times. From now on, only small, informally organized groups of Communists could continue to meet, and in many places not even these existed.[109] They more or less abandoned their earlier ambition of rousing the masses, and focused instead on preparing for the time when Nazism would eventually fall. Of all the groups who held out against Nazism in the early years of the Third Reich, the Communists were the most persistent and the most undaunted. They paid the greatest price as a consequence.[110]

Those Communists who had sought refuge from repression in the Soviet Union fared little better than their comrades who remained in Germany. The gathering threat of fascism across Europe, the failures of agricultural collectivization in Russia and the Ukraine, and the travails and tribulations of forced industrial growth, all induced a growing sense of paranoia in the Soviet leadership, and when one of the most prominent and popular of the younger generation of Bolshevik leaders, Sergei Kirov, was murdered with the obvious complicity of Bolshevik Party officials in 1934, the Soviet leader Josef Stalin began to organize the mass arrest of Bolshevik Party functionaries, sparking a massive purge that quickly gained its own momentum. Soon, leading Communist functionaries were being arrested and shot in their thousands, and made to confess fantastic crimes of subversion and treachery in widely publicized show trials. The purge spread rapidly down the party's ranks, where officials and ordinary members vied with each other in denouncing supposed traitors and subversives among their own number. The 'Gulag archipelago' of labour camps strung across the less hospitable parts of the Soviet Union, above all in Siberia, swelled to bursting with millions of prisoners by the late 1930s. From Stalin's acquisition of supreme power at the end of the 1920s to his death in 1953, it has been estimated that over three-quarters of a million people were executed in the Soviet Union, while at least two and three-quarter million died in the camps.[111]

In this atmosphere of terror, fear and mutual recrimination, anything out of the ordinary could become the pretext for arrest, imprisonment, torture and execution. Contact with foreign governments, even previous residence in a foreign country, began to arouse suspicion. Soon the purges began to suck the German Communist exiles into their vortex of destruction. Thousands of German Communists who had sought refuge in Stalin's Russia were arrested, sent to labour camps, or exiled to Siberia. Over 1,100 were condemned for various alleged crimes, tortured by Stalin's secret police, and imprisoned in grim conditions in the labour camps for lengthy periods of time. Many were executed. Those killed included several members or former members of the party's Politburo: Heinz Neumann, the former propaganda chief whose advocacy of violence in 1932–3 the Politburo had vehemently rejected; Hugo Eberlein, a former friend of Rosa Luxemburg, whose criticisms of Lenin had not found favour in the Soviet Union; and Hermann Remmele, who had been incautious enough to say in 1933 that the Nazi seizure of power marked a defeat for the working class. Of the forty-four Communists who belonged to the Politburo of the German party between 1920 and 1933, more were killed in Stalin's purges in Russia than died at the hands of the Gestapo and the Nazis in Germany.[112]

'ENEMIES OF THE PEOPLE'

I

In custody after his arrest for setting fire to the Reichstag on 27–8 February 1933, the young Dutch anarchist Marinus van der Lubbe must have known that he would never leave prison alive. Hitler indeed had said as much. The culprits, he declared, would be hanged. But in saying so, he immediately ran into difficulties with the law. Hanging was the favoured method of execution in his native Austria, but not in Germany, where decapitation had been the only method used for almost a century. Moreover, the German Criminal Code did not make arson punishable by death, unless it had led to someone being killed, and nobody had died as a direct result of van der Lubbe's deed. Brushing aside the scruples of legal advisers and bureaucrats in the Reich Justice Ministry, the cabinet persuaded President Hindenburg to issue a decree on 29 March 1933 applying the death penalty provisions of the Reichstag Fire Decree of 28 February retroactively to offences, including treason and arson, committed since 31 January, Hitler's first full day in office. As some newspaper commentators still dared to point out, this violated a fundamental principle of the law, namely that laws should not apply punishments retroactively to crimes that had not carried them when they were committed. If the death penalty had been prescribed for arson at the time of van der Lubbe's offence, then he might have been deterred from committing it in the first place. Now nobody committing an offence could be sure what the punishment would be.[113]

Hitler and Göring were not just determined to see van der Lubbe executed; they also wanted to pin the arson attack on the German Communist Party, which they had effectively outlawed on the basis of the claim that it was behind the attempt. So on 21 September 1933 it was not only van der Lubbe but also Georgi Dimitrov, the Bulgarian head of the Western European Bureau of the Communist International in Berlin, two of his staff, and the German Communist Reichstag floor leader Ernst Torgler, who stood in the dock at the Reich Court in Leipzig to answer the charges of arson and high treason. Presiding over the proceedings was the conservative judge and former People's Party politician Wilhelm Bünger. But Bünger, for all his political prejudices, was a lawyer of the old school, and stuck to the rules. Dimitrov defended himself with ingenuity and skill, and made Hermann Göring look a complete fool when he was called to the witness box. Combining forensic ability with impassioned Communist rhetoric, Dimitrov managed to secure the acquittal of all the accused apart from van der Lubbe himself, who was guillotined shortly afterwards. Immediately rearrested by the Gestapo, the three Bulgarians were eventually expelled to the Soviet Union; Torgler survived the war, and subsequently became a Social Democrat.[114]

The court's judgment was careful to conclude that the Communist Party had indeed planned the fire in order to start a revolution, and that therefore the Reichstag Fire Decree had been justified. But the evidence against Dimitrov and the other Communists, it concluded, was insufficient to justify a conviction.[115] The Nazi leadership was humiliated. The Nazi daily newspaper, the *Racial Observer*, condemned it as a miscarriage of justice 'that demonstrates the need for a thoroughgoing reform of our legal life, which in many ways still moves along the paths of outmoded liberalistic thought that is foreign to the people'.[116]

Within a few months Hitler had removed treason cases from the competence of the Reich Court and transferred them to a special People's Court, set up on 24 April 1934. It was to deal with political offences speedily and according to National Socialist principles, and the two professional judges in charge of cases were to be assisted by three lay judges drawn from the Nazi Party, the SS, the SA and other, similar organizations. After a period of rotating chairmanship, it was presided over from June 1936 by Otto-Georg Thierack, a long-time Nazi, born in 1889, who was appointed Saxon Minister of Justice in 1933 and Vice-President of the Reich Supreme Court two years later.[117] Thierack was to prove a figure of major significance in the undermining of the judicial system during the war. He introduced a new, sharply ideological note into the court's already highly politicized proceedings.

Meanwhile, preparations had been under way for the trial of the Communist Party leader Ernst Thälmann, which would set the seal on the regime's conviction of the Communists for trying to start a revolutionary uprising in 1933. A dossier of charges was compiled, alleging that Thälmann had planned a campaign of terror, bombing, mass poisoning and the taking of hostages. Yet the trial had to be postponed because of the lack of hard evidence. Thälmann's high profile as the former leader of one of Germany's major political parties ensured that over a thousand foreign journalists applied for admission to the trial. This already gave the regime pause for thought. There was a distinct possibility that Thälmann might try to turn the trial to his advantage. A death sentence had been agreed in advance. Yet the experience of the Reichstag fire trial made the Nazi leadership, above all Goebbels, wary of putting on another big show trial. So in the end the Nazi leadership considered it safer to keep Thälmann in 'protective custody', manacled and isolated, in the obscurity of a cell in the state prison at Moabit, in Berlin, then later in Hanover and later still in Bautzen, without a formal trial. The Communist Party made the most of his imprisonment, retaining him indefinitely in the formal position of Chairman. An attempt to spring him from gaol in 1934, by Communists dressed as SS men, was foiled at the last minute by the action of a Gestapo spy who had infiltrated himself into the rescue group. Under close observation, his correspondence with his family censored, Thälmann did not stand a chance of escape. He never came before a court, and was never formally charged with any offence. He remained in prison, the object of repeated international campaigns for his release organized by Communists and their sympathizers across the world.[118]

Deprived of the chance to stage a show trial of Thälmann, the People's Court preferred initially at least to deal with less conspicuous offenders. Its aim was to judge speedily and with a minimum of rules, which in this case meant a minimum of guarantees of the rights of the defendants. In 1934 the Court passed 4 death sentences; in 1935 the figure rose to 9; in 1936, to 10; all but one of these sentences were carried out. Once Thierack had taken over in 1936, however, the People's Court became much harsher in its approach, condemning 37 defendants to death in

1937, with 28 executions, and 17 in 1938, all but one of whom were executed.[119] From 1934 to 1939, roughly 3,400 people were tried by the People's Court; nearly all of them were Communists or Social Democrats, and those who were not executed received sentences averaging six years' penitentiary each.[120]

The People's Court stood at the apex of a whole new system of 'Special Courts' established to deal with political offences, often of a fairly trivial nature, such as telling jokes about the Leader. In this, as in so many other areas, the Nazis were not being particularly inventive, but drew on earlier precedents, notably the 'People's Courts' set up in Bavaria during the White Terror after the defeated revolution of 1919. There was no appeal from their summary jurisdiction.[121] But the People's Court and the Special Courts had nothing like a monopoly over political cases. Nearly 2,000 people were condemned for treason between 18 March 1933 and 2 January 1934 by the regular courts; twice as many were still in remand custody at that point. They included many prominent and less prominent Communists and Social Democrats. Thus the new courts, all of which had a formal juridical status, ran alongside the courts of the established legal system, which were also engaged in dealing with political offences of many kinds. Indeed, it would be a mistake to imagine that the regular courts continued more or less unaltered by the advent of the Nazi dictatorship. They did not. Already in the first full year of Hitler's Chancellorship, a total of 67 death sentences were passed on political offenders by all the different kinds of court combined. Capital punishment, effectively abrogated in 1928 then reintroduced, though only on a small scale, in 1930, was now applied not only to criminal murders but even more to political offences of various kinds. There were 64 executions in 1933, 79 in 1934, 94 in 1935, 68 in 1936, 106 in 1937 and 117 in 1938, the great majority of them widely publicized by garish scarlet posters that Goebbels ordered to be put up around the town where they took place. Previous ceremonial accompaniments to executions, which took place inside state prisons, were abolished, and in 1936 Hitler personally decreed that the hand-held axe, traditional in Prussia but the object of a good deal of criticism from the legal profession, including prominent Nazi jurists, should be replaced everywhere with the guillotine.[122]

The death penalty was reserved above all for Communists and was applied both to activists in the 'Red Front-Fighters' League' who had attracted the hostility of the Nazis in the street violence of the early 1930s and to Communist cadres who continued to try and fight the Nazis under the Third Reich, usually by doing no more than printing and spreading critical leaflets and holding supposedly secret meetings to plot the downfall of the regime. The first batch of Communists to be beheaded consisted of four young men arrested for their supposed part in the events of the Altona 'Bloody Sunday' in June 1932, when a number of brownshirts had been shot dead – supposedly by Communists, in reality by panicking units of the Prussian police – during a march through a heavily Communist district of the Prussian town. Condemned by a Special Court in Altona on trumped-up charges of planning an armed uprising, the four men appealed for clemency to Hermann Göring. The local state prosecutor advised him to turn the appeal down: 'Carrying out the sentences will bring the whole seriousness of their situation graphically before the eyes of people of Communist inclinations; it will be a lasting warning for them and have a deterrent effect.'[123] The sentences were duly carried out and the executions were widely publicized in the press.[124] A spirit of pure revenge was what informed the decision to force forty Communists sentenced in another mass trial to witness the beheading by hand-held axe of four of their fellow 'red marines' in the yard of a Hamburg prison in 1934 at a ceremony also attended by brownshirts, SS men and the male relatives of Nazi activists who had died in street fighting in 1932. The defiant reaction of the Communists, who shouted political slogans and physically resisted the executioners, ensured that this would not happen again.[125]

II

The vast majority of judges and prosecutors expressed few doubts about such acts, although one of the conservative bureaucrats in the Reich Ministry of Justice was concerned enough to make a special marginal note in the draft statistics on capital punishment that one man, beheaded on 28 September 1933, was only nineteen years of age, and international concern was expressed in a number of campaigns for clemency for condemned Communists such as the former Reichstag deputy Albert

Kayser, executed on 17 December 1935. Women too were now coming under the axe, as they had not done under the Weimar Republic, starting with the Communist Emma Thieme, executed on 26 August 1933. They and others fell foul of a whole new set of capital offences, including a law of 21 March 1933 prescribing death for anyone found guilty of threatening to destroy property with the intention of causing panic, a law of 4 April 1933 applying the death penalty to acts of sabotage, a law of 13 October 1933 making the planned assassination of any state or Party official punishable by death, and another law, of 24 April 1933, perhaps the most far-reaching of all of these, laying down beheading as the punishment for anyone planning to alter the constitution or detach any part of Germany from the Reich by threat of force or conspiring to do so; thus anyone distributing leaflets ('planning') critical of the dictatorial political system ('the Constitution') could now be executed; and so too, on the basis of a law of 20 December 1934, under particular circumstances, could someone convicted of making 'hateful' statements, including jokes, about leading figures in the Party or the state.[126]

Presiding over this resumption and extension of the application of capital punishment was Reich Justice Minister Franz Gürtner, not a Nazi but a conservative who had been Bavarian Justice Minister in the 1920s and had already served as Reich Justice Minister in the cabinets of Papen and Schleicher. Like most conservatives, Gürtner applauded the crackdown on disorder in 1933 and 1934. After the 'Night of the Long Knives', he arranged for legislation to sanction the murders retrospectively, and nipped in the bud the attempts of some local state prosecutors to initiate proceedings against the killers. Gürtner believed in the use of written laws and procedures, however draconian, and he quickly appointed a committee to revise the Reich Criminal Code of 1871 in accordance with the new ethos of the Third Reich. As one committee member, the criminologist Edmund Mezger, put it, the aim was to create a new synthesis of 'the principle of the individual's responsibility to his people, and the principle of the racial improvement of the people as a whole'.[127] The committee sat for many hours and produced lengthy drafts, but it was unable to keep up with the pace at which new criminal offences were being created, and the legalistic pedantry of its recommendations was wholly unwelcome to the Nazis, who never put it into effect.[128]

Meanwhile the judicial system was coming under growing pressure from leading Nazis, who complained, as Rudolf Hess did, about the 'absolutely un-National Socialist tendency' of some judicial decisions. Above all, as Reinhard Heydrich complained, the regular courts were continuing to pass sentences on 'enemies of the state' that were 'too low according to the normal popular feeling'. The purpose of the law, in the eyes of the Nazis, was not to apply long-held principles of fairness and justice, but to root out the enemies of the state and to express the true racial feeling of the people. As a manifesto issued in 1936 under the name of Hans Frank, now Reich Commissioner for Justice and head of the Nazi Lawyers' League, stated:

The judge is not placed over the citizen as a representative of the state authority, but is a member of the living community of the German people. It is not his duty to help to enforce a law superior to the national community or to impose a system of universal values. His role is to safeguard the concrete order of the racial community, to eliminate dangerous elements, to prosecute all acts harmful to the community, and to arbitrate in disagreements between members of the community. The National Socialist ideology, especially as expressed in the Party programme and in the speeches of our leader, is the basis for interpreting legal sources.[129]

However harshly they sentenced Communists and other political offenders, the regular courts, judges and prosecutors were never likely to live up to this ideal, which in effect demanded the abrogation of all rules of justice and the translation of the Nazi street violence of the pre-1933 period into a principle of state.

Far from objecting to the police and SS taking offenders out of the judicial system, or complaining about the Gestapo's habit of arresting prisoners on their release from custody and putting them straight into concentration camps, the judiciary and legal and penal administrators were happy to co-operate in this whole process of subversion of the rule of law. State prosecutors handed over offenders for confinement in the camps when they lacked the evidence to prosecute or when they could not be brought before the courts for some other reason, such as their youth. Judicial officials issued guidelines ordering prison governors to recommend dangerous inmates (especially Communists) for 'protective custody' on their release, which they did in thousands of cases. In one prison, in Luckau, for example, 134 out of 364 in a sample of prisoners studied by one historian were handed over to the Gestapo on completing their sentence, on the explicit recommendation of the prison administration.[130] How the practice worked was shown by the governor of the Untermassfeld prison, who wrote to the Thuringian Gestapo on 5 May 1936 about Max K., a printer who had been sentenced to two and a quarter years' custody in June 1934 for his involvement in the Communist underground. K. had behaved well in prison, but the governor and his staff had investigated his family and connections and did not believe he had turned over a new leaf. He told the Gestapo:

K. did not attract any special attention in the institution. But in view of his past life, I cannot believe that he has changed his mind and I believe that he has, just like most leading Communists, only kept out of trouble now through cunning calculation. In my view it is absolutely essential that this active leading Communist is taken into protective custody after the end of his sentence.[131]

K. was in fact only a foot-soldier of the Communist movement, not one of its leaders. But the letter, sent twelve weeks before he was due to be released, had its effect, and the Gestapo were waiting for him at the prison gate when he came out on 24 July 1936: by the next day he had been delivered to a concentration camp. Some prison officials tried to stress the good conduct and reformed character of such inmates on occasion, but this had little effect where the police considered that they remained a threat. Before long, this system of prison denunciations was extended to other categories as well. Only in 1939 did the Reich Justice Ministry call for an end to explicit demands for prisoners to be taken into police custody on their release, a practice that seemed to undermine the very basis of the judicial system's independence. This had no effect. Prison officials continued to inform the police of prisoners' release dates, and indeed to make cells or even whole wings of state prisons available to the police to house thousands of prisoners in 'protective custody' without any formal process of prosecution or trial at all, and not only in the chaotic period of mass arrests in March–June 1933.[132]

The efforts of the judicial apparatus to preserve some degree of autonomy for itself seldom had much effect on the eventual outcome as far as offenders were concerned. Gürtner managed to block police and SS efforts to secure the transfer of prisoners to concentration camps before the end of their prison term, but he had no principled objection to their transfer at the end of it, only to the penal authorities' formal involvement in such transfers. The constant barrage of SS criticism of judicial leniency did not lead to the dismissal or forced retirement of a single judge. The legalistic pointlessness of Gürtner's attitude, and the hollowness of the judicial apparatus's resistance to SS interference, were neatly illustrated by the Ministry of Justice's campaign against the brutality of police interrogations. From the very beginning of the Third Reich, interrogation sessions by the police and the Gestapo often resulted in prisoners being returned to their prison cells beaten, bruised and badly injured to a degree that could not escape the attention of defending lawyers, relatives and friends. The Justice Ministry found these practices objectionable. They did not reflect well on the reputation of the law enforcement apparatus in Germany. After a good deal of negotiation, a compromise was found at a meeting held on 4 June 1937, when police and Justice Ministry officials agreed that such arbitrary beatings should cease. Henceforth, the meeting ruled, police interrogators were to be limited to administering twenty-five lashes to interviewees in the presence of a doctor, and they had to use a 'standard cane' to do so.[133]

III

The regular judicial and penal system also continued under the Third Reich to deal with ordinary, non-political crime – theft, assault, murder and so on – as well as implementing the new repression of the police state. Here too, there was a rapid expansion of capital punishment, as the new system moved to implement death sentences passed on capital offenders in the late Weimar Republic but not carried out because of uncertainty about the political situation in the early 1930s. The Nazis promised that there would be no more lengthy stays of execution while petitions for clemency were being considered. 'The days of false and mawkish sentimentality are over', declared a far-right newspaper with satisfaction in May 1933. By 1936, some 90 per cent of death sentences passed by the courts were being carried out. Prosecutors and courts were now encouraged to charge all homicides with murder rather than the non-capital offence of manslaughter, to reach a guilty verdict and to pass the harshest sentence, resulting in an increase of the number of murder sentences per 1,000 of the adult population from 36 in 1928–32 to 76 in 1933–7.[134] Criminals, the Nazis argued, drawing on the work of criminologists over the previous few decades, and brushing aside all the qualifications and subtleties with which their central theses were surrounded, were essentially hereditary degenerates and must be treated as outcasts from the race.[135]

The consequences of such doctrines for ordinary offenders against the criminal law were serious in the extreme. Already under the Weimar Republic, criminologists, penal experts and police forces had reached a large degree of consensus on proposals to confine 'habitual criminals' indefinitely for the protection of society. On 24 November 1933, their wishes were granted with the passing of a Law against Dangerous Habitual Criminals, which allowed the courts to sentence any offender convicted of three or more criminal acts to 'security confinement' in a state prison after their formal sentence had been served out.[136] More than 14,000 offenders had received such a sentence by October 1942. They included existing inmates of prisons recommended by prison governors for retroactive sentencing – in some prisons, as in Brandenburg penitentiary, over a third of the inmates were proposed for this treatment. These were not major or, in general, violent criminals but overwhelmingly petty offenders – bicycle thieves, pilferers, shoplifters and the like. Most of them were poor people without steady employment who had taken to stealing during the inflation and resumed it during the Depression. Typical, for example, was the case of a carter, born in 1899, who had served a large number of prison sentences for minor theft in the 1920s and early 1930s, including eleven months for stealing a bicycle and seven months for the theft of a coat. Each time he was released, he was sent out into society with a handful of marks as payment for his prison work; and with his record he could neither get a job during the Depression nor persuade the welfare authorities to give him benefits. In June 1933 he was sentenced for stealing a bell, some glue and a few other knick-knacks during a bout of drinking, and after serving out his time he was retroactively sentenced to security confinement in the Brandenburg penitentiary; he was never released. His fate was shared by many others.[137]

Within the prisons where they were held, conditions rapidly worsened under the Third Reich. Nazis habitually accused the Weimar prison service of being soft on criminals, pampering inmates with food and entertainment far better than they were likely to have experienced outside. This was hardly surprising, when so many of them, from Hitler and Hess to Bormann and Rosenberg, had done time under Weimar and been treated with conspicuous leniency because of their nationalist politics. In fact, conditions in Weimar's prisons had been quite strict, and a military approach to prison life dominated many institutions.[138] However, attempts had also been made to introduce a more flexible system of administration in some places, with an emphasis on education, rehabilitation and rewards for good conduct. These now came to an abrupt end, much to the relief of the majority of prison warders and administrators who had resented them from the outset. Reformist governors and senior staff were summarily sacked, and a new, harsher regime was introduced. The rapid expansion of numbers soon created further problems of hygiene, nutrition and general welfare for the prisoners. Food rations deteriorated until prisoners were complaining of weight loss and gnawing hunger. Verminous infestation and skin diseases became commoner even than they had been in the far from perfect conditions of Weimar. Hard labour was initially not a major priority, since it was thought to undermine job-creation schemes on the outside, but this policy was soon reversed, and up to 95 per cent of inmates were engaged in forced labour in many prisons by 1938. Many of the prisoners were held in specially built labour camps run by the state prison service, most notoriously on moorland clearance and cultivation in the barren North German area of the Emsland, where nearly 10,000 prisoners were engaged in backbreaking work, digging and draining the barren soil. Conditions here were worse even than in the regular state prisons, with constant beatings, whippings, deliberate attacks by warders' dogs and even murders and shootings. Many of the guards were ex-brownshirts who had staffed the main moorland camp before the Justice Ministry took it over in 1934. Their attitude had an influence on the regular state prison staff who gradually moved in over the following years. Here, unlike in the other camps, the brutal and arbitrary conditions of the early concentration camps of 1933 continued well into the middle and late 1930s with little interference from above.[139]

In the regular state prisons and penitentiaries, new regulations imposed on 14 May 1934 codified local and regional changes, removed privileges and introduced novel punishments for refractory inmates. Expiation, deterrence and retribution were now the declared aims of imprisonment. Education programmes were slashed and thoroughly Nazified. Sports and games were replaced by military drill. Prisoners' complaints were dealt with much more harshly. The long-term criminal with whom the Communist political prisoner Friedrich Schlotterbeck shared a prison cell was in no doubt about the degree to which conditions had deteriorated. As the old lag told his new cell-mate:

First of all they sawed off the backs of the forms in the eating-hall. That was supposed to be too comfortable. Spoiled us. Later on they abolished the eating-hall altogether. Sometimes there used to be a concert or a lantern-slide lecture on Sundays. There never is now. Lots of books have been taken out of the library, too ... The food got worse. New punishments were introduced. Seven days solitary on bread and water for instance. When you've had that you don't feel so good at the end of it. And then you get solitary in chains, hand and foot. But the worst is when you get chained hands and feet behind your back. You can only lie on your belly then. The rules haven't really changed. It's only that they're stricter in carrying 'em out.[140]

Punishments, Schlotterbeck himself observed during his few years in prison, became steadily more frequent and more severe, despite the fact that most warders were old professionals rather than newly appointed Nazis.[141] Many prison officers were not satisfied with the removal of Weimar's reforming practices. They still wanted a return to the old days of the Imperial period, when corporal punishment in prisons had been widespread. Yet their desire for a reinstatement of what they conceived of as the proper order of things in the state prisons was frustrated in many institutions by massive overcrowding. Things were not improved by the employment by 1938 of over 1,000 Nazi street-fighting veterans as assistant warders. These men were grateful for the employment but proved impossible to discipline. They were contemptuous of state authority and all too inclined to exercise casual brutality against inmates with weapons hitherto unfamiliar in the state prison system such as rubber truncheons.[142]

The 'security confined' had a particularly hard time. They were sentenced to nine hours' hard labour a day and subjected to strict military discipline. Since they were permanently in prison, these conditions weighed ever more heavily on them as they grew older. By 1939 more than a quarter of them were in their fifties or above. Cases of self-mutilation and attempted suicide increased rapidly. 'I won't do another 3 years here,' wrote one inmate to her sister in 1937: '. . . I have stolen, but I will rather do myself in, my dear sister, than be buried alive for that in here.'[143] New laws and greater police powers drove the number of inmates of all kinds in state prisons on an average day up by 50 per cent in 1933, until it reached a peak of 122,000 at the end of February 1937, compared to a mere 69,000 ten years earlier.[144] Nazi policy towards crime was not directed by any rational attempt to reduce ordinary offences of theft and violence, although it was common to hear older Germans in the postwar years claiming that whatever Hitler's faults, he had at least made the streets safe for the honest citizen. In fact, amnesties were declared for minor, non-political, criminal offences in August 1934 and April 1936, quashing no fewer than 720,000 prosecutions that would have led to short prison sentences or fines. This was not the kind of offender whom the Nazis were interested in pursuing. So-called habitual criminals, however, were not included in such amnesties, a further indication of the arbitrariness of Nazi penal practice.[145]

Meanwhile large numbers of new offences were created by a series of new laws and decrees, some of them with retroactive effect. They were designed not least to serve the ideological and propaganda interests of the regime. Thus, for instance, in 1938, Hitler ordered a new law making highway robbery on a motorway retroactively punishable by death after two men had been found guilty of this offence in 1938 and sentenced to a term of imprisonment. They were duly sent to the guillotine.[146] Offences of all kinds were given a political or ideological slant, so that even pilfering or picking pockets became evidence of hereditary degeneracy, and vaguely defined activities such as 'grumbling' or 'idling' became grounds for indefinite imprisonment. Punishments increasingly no longer fitted the crime, but were designed to assert the supposed collective interest of the 'racial community' in the face of deviance from the norms set by the Nazis. Whole categories of people were increasingly defined by police, prosecutors and courts as inherently criminal and caught up in their thousands in the process of arbitrary arrest and confinement without trial.

Deviant and marginal, but hitherto socially more or less tolerated, professions like prostitution also began to be defined as 'asocial' and subject to the same sanctions. Vague and wide-ranging laws and decrees gave the police almost limitless powers of arrest and detention, virtually at will, while the courts did not lag far behind in applying the policies of repression and control, for all the regime's continual attacks on them for their supposed leniency. All this was cheered on, with only small and often quite technical reservations, by considerable numbers of criminologists, penal specialists, lawyers, judges, and professional experts of one kind and another – men like the criminologist Professor Edmund Mezger, a member of the committee charged with preparing a new Criminal Code, who declared in a textbook published in 1933 that the aim of penal policy was 'the elimination from the racial community of elements which damage the people and the race'.[147] As Mezger's phrase indicated, crime, deviance, and political opposition were all aspects of the same phenomenon for the Nazis, the problem, as they put it, of 'community aliens' (*Gemeinschaftsfremde*), people who for whatever reason were not 'racial comrades' (*Volksgenossen*) and therefore one way or another had to be removed from society by force. A leading police expert of the period, Paul Werner, summed this up in 1939 when he declared that only those who completely integrated themselves into the 'racial community' could be given the full rights of a member; anyone who was just merely 'indifferent' towards it was acting 'from a criminal or asocial mentality' and was thus a 'criminal enemy of the state', to be 'combatted and brought down' by the police.[148]

INSTRUMENTS OF TERROR

I

The systematization of the Nazi mechanism of repression and control under the aegis of Heinrich Himmler's SS had a marked effect on the concentration camps.[149] At least seventy camps had been hastily erected in the course of the seizure of power in the early months of 1933, alongside an unknown but probably even larger number of torture cellars and small prisons in the stormtroopers' various branch headquarters. Around 45,000 prisoners were held in them at this time, beaten, tortured and ritually humiliated by their guards. Several hundred died as a result of their maltreatment. The vast majority were Communists, Social Democrats and trade unionists. However, most of these early concentration camps and unofficial torture centres were closed down in the second half of 1933 and the first two or three months of 1934. One of the most notorious, the illegal concentration camp set up in the Vulkan shipyard in Stettin, was closed in February 1934 on the orders of the State Prosecutor. A number of the SA and SS officers who had taken the lead in the torture of prisoners there were put on trial and given lengthy sentences. Well before this time, however, a series of official and unofficial amnesties had led to the release of large numbers of chastened and browbeaten inmates. A third of the camp population was released on 31 July 1933 alone. By May 1934 there were only a quarter as many prisoners as there had been a year before, and the regime was beginning to regularize and systematize the conditions of internment of those who remained.[150]

Some time before, in June 1933, the Bavarian State Prosecutor had charged camp commandant Wäckerle of Dachau, together with the camp physician and the camp administrator, with being accessories to the murder of prisoners.[151] Himmler, who had taken a hand in drawing up the camp regulations enforced, though not very consistently, by Wäckerle, was obliged on 26 June 1933 to sack him and appoint a new commandant. This was Theodor Eicke, an ex-policeman with a distinctly chequered past. Born in 1892, Eicke had been an army paymaster and security guard who had risen through the ranks of the SS to become a battalion leader, in command of over 1,000 men, by the end of 1931. The following year, however, he had been forced to flee to Italy after being convicted of preparing bomb outrages. After running a refugee camp on behalf of the Fascist government, Eicke had returned to Germany in February 1933 to take part in the Nazi seizure of power. But he soon quarrelled violently with Josef Bürckel, the Regional Leader of the Palatinate, who committed him to a mental hospital; the alarmed Himmler had him psychiatrically examined and found sane.[152] One of his subordinates in Dachau, Rudolf Höss, described him as 'an inflexible Nazi of the old type' who regarded the mainly Communist prisoners in the early concentration camps as 'sworn enemies of the state, who were to be treated with great severity and destroyed if they showed resistance'.[153]

In June 1933 Himmler remembered that Eicke had organized a camp in Italy with some success, and appointed him to run Dachau. The new commandant reported later that he had found corruption amongst the guards, poor equipment and low morale in the camp administration. There were 'no cartridges or rifles, let alone machine guns. Of the entire staff only three men could handle a machine gun. My men were billeted in draughty factories. Everywhere there was poverty and misery' – everywhere, that is, among the guards; he did not mention any possible poverty and misery among the prisoners. Eicke sacked half the complement of 120 staff and appointed replacements. He issued a comprehensive set of regulations in October 1933, which, unlike the previous ones, also laid down a code of conduct for the guards. These imposed the appearance of order and uniformity where previously there had been arbitrary brutality and violence. They were draconian in the extreme. Prisoners who discussed politics with the aim of 'incitement', or spread 'atrocity propaganda', were to be hanged; sabotage, assaulting a guard, or any kind of mutiny or insubordination was punishable by the firing squad. Lesser infringements met with a variety of lesser punishments. These included solitary confinement on a diet of bread and water for a period of time varying with the offence; corporal punishment (twenty-five strokes of the cane); punishment drill; tying to a post or a tree for a period of hours; hard labour; or the withholding of mail. Additional punishment of this kind also carried with it a prolongation of the inmate's sentence.[154]

Eicke's system was intended to rule out personal and individual punishments and to protect officers and guards from prosecution by the local law officers by setting up a bureaucratic apparatus to provide written justification for the punishments inflicted. Formal regulation could thus claim to have replaced arbitrary violence. Beatings for example were to be carried out by several SS men, in front of the prisoners, and all punishments had to be recorded in writing. Strict rules were laid down governing the behaviour of the SS guards. They had to conduct themselves in a military fashion. They were not to engage in private conversations with the prisoners. They had to observe minutely detailed procedures for conducting the daily roll-call of the inmates, the supervision of prisoners in the camp workshop, the issuing of commands, and the implementation of punishments. Prisoners were issued with regular uniforms and prescribed exact duties in keeping their living quarters tidy. Arrangements were made for basic sanitary and medical provisions, notably absent in some of the camps in the early months of 1933. Work details outside the camp, consisting mainly of hard, unremitting physical labour, were also introduced. Eicke established a systematic and hierarchical division of labour among the staff, and issued guards with special insignia to be worn on their collars: the death's head, after which the concentration camp division of the SS, given a separate identity after the end of 1934, was soon to be known. This symbolized Eicke's doctrine of extreme severity towards the prisoners. As Rudolf Höss later recalled:

It was Eicke's intention that his SS-men, by means of continuous instruction and suitable orders concerning the dangerous criminality of the inmates, should be made basically ill-disposed towards the prisoners. They were to 'treat them rough', and to root out once and for all any sympathy they might feel for them. By such means, he succeeded in engendering in simple-natured men a hatred and antipathy for the prisoners which an outsider will find hard to imagine.[155]

Höss himself, after signing up with the SS in September 1933, had been asked by Himmler, whom he knew from their contact through the 'blood-and-soil' Artamen League, to join the 'Death's Head Formation' of SS concentration camp guards at Dachau. Here his habitual discipline and industriousness won him rapid promotion. He received his officer's commission in 1936 and was put in charge of the stores and of prisoners' property.

A former inmate of a state prison himself, Höss later wrote that most concentration camp inmates found the uncertainty of the duration of their sentence the hardest psychological burden to bear. While an offender sentenced to a term in prison knew when he was going to get out, release for the concentration camp inmate was determined by the whim of a quarterly review board, and could be delayed by the malice of any of the SS guards. In the world of the camps created by Eicke, the rules gave untrammelled power to the guards. The detailed and elaborate rules gave the guards multifarious possibilities of inflicting serious violence on inmates for real or alleged infringements at every level. The rules were designed not least to provide legally defensible excuses for the terror they vented upon the inmates. Höss himself protested that he could not bear to watch the brutal punishments, the beatings and the whippings, inflicted on the inmates. He wrote disparagingly of the 'malicious, evil-minded, basically bad, brutal, inferior, common creatures' amongst the guards, who compensated for their sense of inferiority by venting their anger on the prisoners. The atmosphere of hatred was total. Here, Höss, like many other SS guards, believed, were two hostile worlds fighting it out, Communists and Social Democrats on the one side, the SS on the other. Eicke's rules made it certain the latter would win.[156] Not surprisingly, Eicke's reorganization of Dachau won the approval of Himmler, who appointed him inspector of the concentration camps throughout the Reich on 4 July 1934. On 11 July, Eicke was given the top rank of SS Group Leader alongside Heydrich, the head of the Security Service.[157] Eicke's systematization of the concentration camp regime became the basis for all camps right across Germany. In view of the continued interventions of State Prosecutors in cases of murder committed by camp guards, Eicke confidentially ordered that the rules invoking capital punishment for serious infringements of discipline were not to be applied; they were to remain principally as a means of 'intimidation' for the prisoners. The number of arbitrary killings began to decline sharply, though the main reason for this was the continued fall in the overall number of inmates. After some 24 deaths in Dachau in 1933, the number fell to 14 in 1934 (not counting those shot as part of the Röhm purge), 13 in 1935 and 10 in 1936.[158]

Just as Himmler was taking over and centralizing police forces across Germany, so too he took the concentration camps into the control of the SS in 1934 and 1935, aided by the growth in the power and influence of the SS after the Röhm purge. By this time there were only 3,000 inmates left, a sign that the dictatorship had established itself on a more or less stable basis. Along with the process of systematization went a parallel process of centralization. Oranienburg and Fuhlsbüttel camps were wound up in 1935, Esterwegen in 1936, and Sachsenburg in 1937. By August 1937 there were only four concentration camps in Germany: Dachau, Sachsenhausen (where Höss was transferred the following year), Buchenwald and Lichtenburg, the last-named a camp for women. This reflected to a degree the regime's growing sense of security and its successful crushing of left-wing opposition. Social Democrats and Communists thought to have learned their lesson were released in the course of 1933–6. Those kept in custody were either too prominent to be released, like the former Communist leader Ernst Thälmann, or were regarded as a hard core who would continue resisting the Third Reich if released. The relatively small numbers were also an indication that the regime had succeeded in bending the state judicial and penal systems to its will, so that the official state prisons, after the closing of the small camps and torture centres set up by the SA in 1933, now played the major role in the incarceration of the real and supposed political enemies of the Third Reich. In the summer of 1937, for instance, the overall number of political prisoners in the camps paled into insignificance in comparison with the 14,000 officially designated political offenders who were held in state prisons. After the initial period of violence and repression in 1933, it was the state rather than the SA and SS that played the major part in dealing with those who offended against the Third Reich's political norms.[159] Here too there was a decline in number as political offenders were released into the community. The effective smashing of the Communist resistance in the mid-1930s was reflected in a decline of high treason convictions from 5,255 in 1937 to 1,126 in

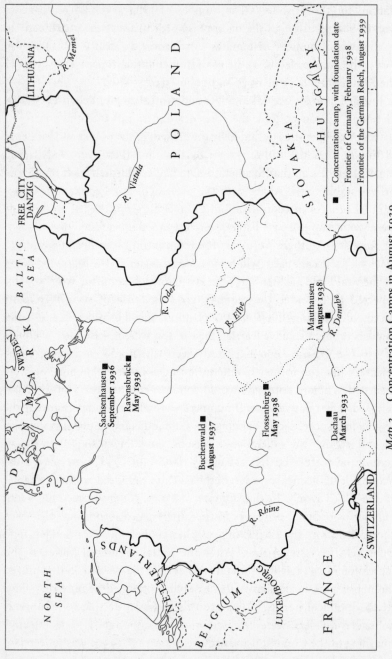

Map 2.   Concentration Camps in August 1939

1939, and a corresponding fall in the number of state prison inmates classified as political offenders from 23,000 in June 1935 to 11,265 in December 1938.[160] But this was still more than the concentration camps held, and the police, the courts and the prison system continued to play a more important role in political repression under the Third Reich than the SS and the concentration camps did, at least until the outbreak of war.

By February 1936, Hitler had approved a reorientation of the whole system, in which Himmler's SS and Gestapo were charged not only with preventing any resurgence of resistance from former Communists and Social Democrats, but also – now that the workers' resistance had been effectively crushed – with purging the German race of undesirable elements. These consisted above all of habitual criminals, asocials and more generally deviants from the idea and practice of the normal healthy member of the German racial community. Jews, so far, did not form a separate category: the aim was to purge the *German* race, as Hitler and Himmler understood it, of undesirable and degenerate elements. Thus the composition of the camp population now began to change, and the numbers of inmates began to increase again. By July 1937, for instance, 330 of Dachau's 1,146 inmates were professional criminals, 230 had been sentenced, under welfare regulations, to labour service, and 93 had been arrested as part of a Bavarian police action against vagrants and beggars. Fifty-seven per cent of the prisoners by this time were thus not classified as political at all, in sharp contrast to the situation in 1933–4.[161] A dramatic change in the nature and function of the camps was in progress. From being part of a concerted effort, involving also the People's Court and the Special Courts, to clamp down on political opposition and, above all, resistance from members of the Communist Party, the concentration camps had become instead an instrument of racial and social engineering. The concentration camps were now dumping-grounds for the racially degenerate.[162] And the change of function, coupled with Himmler's success in securing immunity from prosecution for the camp guards and officials for anything they did behind the perimeter fence, soon led to a sharp increase in inmate deaths once more after the relative hiatus of the mid-1930s.[163] In 1937, there were 69 deaths in Dachau, seven times more than in the previous year, out of a camp population that had remained more or less unchanged at around

2,200. In 1938 the number of deaths in the camp jumped again, to 370, out of a greatly increased camp population of just over 8,000. In Buchenwald, where conditions were a good deal worse, there were 48 deaths among the 2,200 inmates in 1937, 771 amongst 7,420 inmates in 1938, and no fewer than 1,235 deaths amongst the 8,390 inmates in 1939, these last two figures reflecting not least the effects of a raging typhus epidemic in the camp in the winter of 1938–9.[164]

The crackdown on 'community aliens' in fact had begun immediately in 1933, when several hundred 'professional criminals' had been arrested by the police in the first of a number of concerted actions, concentrating among others on organized criminal gangs in Berlin.[165] In September 1933, as many as 100,000 vagrants and mendicants were arrested in a 'Reich beggars' week' staged to coincide with the launch of the first Winter Aid programme, in which voluntary contributions were collected for the destitute and the unemployed – a neat illustration of the interdependence of welfare and coercion in the new Reich.[166] Offenders such as these did not on the whole end up in the camps, but on 13 November 1933, criminals, along with sex offenders, had been made subject in Prussia to preventive police custody in concentration camps, and there were nearly 500 of them incarcerated there by 1935. After the centralization of the police and its takeover by the SS, this policy became far more widespread and systematic. In March 1937, Himmler ordered the arrest of 2,000 so-called professional or habitual criminals, that is, offenders with several convictions to their name, however petty the offences might be; unlike the 'security confined', whose fate had to be determined by the courts, these were put straight into concentration camps without any legal process at all. A decree issued on 14 December 1937 allowed for the arrest and confinement in concentration camps of everyone whom the regime and its various agencies, now working in closer co-operation with the police than before, defined as asocial. Shortly afterwards, the Reich and Prussian Ministries of the Interior extended the definition of asocial to include anyone whose attitude did not fit in with that of the racial community, including gypsies, prostitutes, pimps, tramps, vagrants, beggars and hooligans. Even traffic offenders could be included under some circumstances, as were the long-term unemployed, whose names were obtained by the police from labour exchanges. By this time, the reasoning went, there was no need to be unemployed, so they must be congenitally work-shy and therefore in need of correction.[167]

In April 1938 the Gestapo launched a nationwide series of raids. The raids also covered doss-houses of the sort where Hitler had once found shelter in his days of poverty and unemployment in Vienna before the First World War. By June 1938 there were some 2,000 such people in Buchenwald concentration camp alone. At this point, on 13 June, the Criminal Police, acting under orders from Heydrich, launched another series of raids, targeting beggars, tramps and itinerants. The police also arrested unemployed men with permanent places of residence. In many areas they went well beyond Heydrich's instructions and took all the unemployed into custody. Heydrich had ordered 200 arrests in every police district, but the Frankfurt police arrested 400 and their Hamburg colleagues 700. The total number of arrests across the country was well in excess of 10,000.[168] The economic considerations that played such an important role in these actions could be read in the documents justifying preventive detention for these men. The papers on one 54-year-old man arrested in Duisburg in June 1938 as part of this wider action against people classified as asocials noted for example:

According to information from the welfare office here, C. is to be classified as a work-shy person. He does not care for his wife and his 2 children, so that these have to be supported from the public purse. He has never taken up the work duty assigned to him. He has given himself over to drink. He has used up all his benefit payments. He has received several warnings from the welfare office and is described as a classic example of an asocial, irresponsible and work-shy person.[169]

Taken to the concentration camp at Sachsenhausen, the man lasted little more than eighteen months before dying, so the camp records claimed, from general physical weakness.[170]

People classified as asocial now swelled the depleted concentration camp population across Germany, causing massive overcrowding. More than 6,000 were admitted to Sachsenhausen in the summer of 1938, for example; the effects of this on a camp where the total number of inmates had not been more than 2,500 at the beginning of the year were startling. In Buchenwald, 4,600 out of the 8,000 inmates in August 1938 were classified as work-shy. The influx of new prisoners prompted the opening of two new camps, at Flossenbürg and Mauthausen, for criminals and 'asocials', run by the SS but linked to a subsidiary organization founded on 29 April 1938, the German Earth- and Stoneworks Company. Under the aegis of this new enterprise, the prisoners were forced to work in quarries blasting and digging out granite for the grandiose building schemes of Hitler and his architect Albert Speer.[171] The asocials were the underclass of camp life, just as they had been the underclass of society outside. They were treated badly by the guards, and almost by definition they were unable to organize self-help measures of the sort that kept the political prisoners going. The other prisoners looked down on them, and they played little part in camp life. Death and sickness rates among them were particularly high. An amnesty on the occasion of Hitler's birthday on 20 April 1939 led only a few of them to be released. The rest were there indefinitely. Although their numbers declined, they still formed a major part of the camp population on the eve of the war. In Buchenwald, for instance, 8,892 of the 12,921 preventive detainees counted on 31 December 1938 were classified as asocial; a year later the comparable figure was 8,212 out of 12,221. The raids had fundamentally changed the nature of the camp population.[172]

II

By the eve of the war numbers in the concentration camps had grown again, from 7,500 to 21,000, and they now had a much more varied population than in the early years of the regime, when the inmates had overwhelmingly been sent there for political offences.[173] The camp population was concentrated in a small number of relatively large camps – Buchenwald, Dachau, Flossenbürg, Ravensbrück (the women's camp, which had replaced Lichtenburg in May 1939), Mauthausen and Sachsenhausen. Already, the search by the SS for building materials had led to the opening of a sub-camp (*Aussenlager*) of Sachsenhausen, in the Hamburg suburb of Neuengamme, where bricks for Hitler's planned transformation of the Elbe port were to be manufactured. More were to follow in due course. Labour was becoming an increasingly important function of the camps.[174] Yet labour was expendable, and conditions in the new camps were harsher even than they had been in their predecessors in the mid-1930s. From the winter of 1935-6 some camp authorities began to require the different categories of inmates to carry appropriate designations on their uniforms, and in the winter of 1937-8 this was standardized across the system. From now on, every prisoner had to wear an inverted triangle on the left breast of his or her striped camp uniform: black for an asocial, green for a professional criminal, blue for a returning Jewish emigrant (a rather small category), red for political, violet for a Jehovah's Witness, pink for a homosexual. Jewish prisoners were assigned to one or other of these categories (usually, they were classed as political) but had to wear a yellow triangle underneath their category badge, sewn in the right way up so that the corners were showing, making the whole ensemble into a star of David. These categories were of course often very rough, inaccurately applied or even quite arbitrary, but this did not matter to the camp authorities. By granting limited privileges to political prisoners, they were able to arouse the resentment of the others; by putting criminals in charge of other prisoners, they could stir up divisions between the different types of inmate even further.[175]

The brutality of camp life in the later 1930s is well conveyed in the memoirs of some of those who managed to survive the experience. One such was Walter Poller, born in 1900, a Social Democratic newspaper editor under the Weimar Republic. Poller became active in the Social Democratic resistance after his dismissal in 1933. He was arrested at the beginning of November 1934 for high treason after the Gestapo had identified him as the author of oppositional leaflets, the third time he had been arrested since early 1933. At the end of his four years in prison he was immediately rearrested and taken to Buchenwald. His experience there testified to the extreme brutality that had now become the norm in the camps. As soon as they arrived, Poller and his fellow prisoners were subjected to a violent and completely unprovoked beating by the SS guards, who drove them into the camp, hitting them with rifle butts and rubber truncheons as they ran. Arriving, dirty, bruised and bloody, in the main barracks for political prisoners, they were read a version of the camp rules by an SS officer, who told them:

Here you are, and you're not in a sanatorium! You'll have got that already. Anyone who hasn't grasped that will soon be made to. You can rely on that ... You're not prison inmates here, serving a sentence imposed by the courts, you're just 'prisoners' pure and simple, and if you don't know what that means, you'll soon find out. You're dishonourable and defenceless! You're without rights! Your fate is a slave's fate! Amen.[176]

Poller soon found that although the political prisoners received superior quality camp uniforms and were housed separately from the others, the heavy work to which he was assigned on daily marches outside the camp was too much for him. The Social Democratic and Communist camp inmates, who were well organized and had an elaborate system of informal mutual aid, managed to get him assigned to a job as clerk to the camp doctor. In this position, Poller was able not only to survive until his eventual release in May 1940, but also to observe the daily routine of camp life. It involved a necessary degree of self-government by the prisoners, with senior inmates made responsible for each barracks and *Kapos* in charge of mustering and presenting the inmates at roll-call and on other occasions – a task which many of them carried out with a brutality that rivalled that of the guards. But all the prisoners, whatever their position, were completely at the mercy of the SS, who did not hesitate to exploit their position of absolute power over life and death whenever they pleased.[177]

Every day, Poller reported, the inmates were roused at four or five in the morning, according to the season, and had to wash, get dressed and make their beds, military-style, eat and get out onto the parade-ground for roll-call in double-quick time. Any infringement, such as a poorly made-up bed or a late arrival for roll-call, would call forth a rain of curses and blows from the *Kapos* or the guards, or placement on a punishment detail, where conditions of work were especially harsh. Roll-call provided another opportunity for beatings and assaults. On one occasion in 1937, Poller saw how two political prisoners were roughly hauled out of the ranks, taken out through the camp gates and shot, for reasons that nobody ever discovered. SS men had no problem in using the painstakingly detailed regulations to convict prisoners they did not like of infringements – including such vague offences as laziness at work – and ordering them to be whipped, a procedure that had to be officially recorded on a two-page yellow form. Prisoners were frequently forced to watch as the offender was tied hand and foot to a bench, face down, and beaten by an SS guard with a cane. Not one beating, Poller reported, ever followed the rules laid down on the form. Prisoners sentenced according to regulations to five, ten or twenty-five strokes were required to count them out aloud, and if they forgot, the beating would start all over again. The prescribed cane was frequently replaced by a dog-whip, a leather strap or even a steel rod. Often the beatings continued until the offender lost consciousness. Frequently the camp authorities tried to drown out the screams of the prisoners undergoing a beating by ordering the camp band, consisting of prisoners with proven musical abilities, to play a march or a song while it lasted.[178]

For more serious infringements of the rules, prisoners could be put into 'arrest', kept in a tiny, darkened, unheated cell for days or weeks on end, living only on bread and water. In winter, this could often be as good as a death sentence. More common was the punishment of being suspended from a pole for hours on end by the wrists, causing long-lasting muscular pain and damage, and sometimes, if it went on for long enough, loss of consciousness and death. Escape attempts aroused the particular rage of the SS guards, who realized that in view of their small numbers in comparison to those of the inmates, a determined mass escape attempt was more than likely to succeed. Those caught were savagely beaten, sometimes to death, in front of the others, or publicly hanged on the camp square as the commandant issued a warning to the whole camp that this was the fate of all who tried to get away. On one occasion at Sachsenhausen, a prisoner found trying to escape was dragged onto the camp parade-ground, severely beaten, nailed into a small wooden box and left there for a week in full view of all the inmates until he was dead.[179] Faced with such threats, the vast majority of camp inmates concentrated on simply staying alive. During the day, they worked in the camp in small workshops if they had some particular handicraft skill; most of them, however, were marched out of the camp on work-details to carry out labour-intensive tasks such as digging up stones for the camp roads, quarrying chalk or gravel, or clearing away rubble. Here too, guards beat those they thought were not working hard, or quickly, enough and shot without warning anyone who strayed too far from the main group. In the late afternoon the prisoners were marched back into the camp for yet another lengthy roll-call, standing to attention sometimes for hours on end, wet, dirty and exhausted.

Sometimes in winter men would collapse in the cold, dead from hypo-thermia. As the lights were turned out in the barracks, the camp guards warned that anyone seen walking around outside would be shot.[180]

The arbitrary and sometimes sadistic brutality of the guards reflected not least the brutality and sadism of their own training as SS men. By the late 1930s about 6,000 SS men were stationed in Dachau, and 3,000 in Buchenwald. The (much smaller) daily details of camp guards were drawn from these units, which consisted mostly of young men from the lower classes – farmers' sons in Dachau, for example, with some young men from the lower middle and working classes in addition at Buchen-wald. Mostly poorly educated and already used to physical hardships, they were schooled to be tough, showered with bellowed curses and verbal abuse by their officers during training, and given humiliating punishments if they failed to make the grade. One SS recruit later recalled that anyone who dropped a cartridge during weapons training was required to pick it up off the ground with his teeth. Such ideological indoctrination as they received mostly emphasized the need for hardness in the face of the enemies of the German race such as they were to encounter in the camps. On arrival at the camp, they lived in their barracks largely cut off from the outside world, with few amusements, few opportunities to meet girls or take part in local everyday life, con-demned to the daily tedium of surveillance. Under such circumstances it was not surprising that they were rough towards the prisoners, showered them with obscene abuse, strengthened their own feelings of importance by condemning them to harsh punishments on the slightest pretext, relieved their boredom by subjecting them to every kind of brutal trick or avenged the physical humiliation and hardship of their own training by visiting the same upon them; it was, after all, the only kind of drill and discipline they knew themselves. Those who joined the SS after 1934 at the latest generally knew, of course, what they were letting themselves in for, so they already came with a high degree of ideological commit-ment; still, anyone who did not want to take part in the daily infliction of pain and terror in the camps had every opportunity to resign, and many in fact did so, especially in 1937 and 1938, as the camp regime became notably harsher. In 1937, for instance, nearly 8,000 men were released from the SS, including 146 from the Death's Head Squads, 81 of these at their own request. Eicke ordered on 1 April 1937 that any member of these squads 'who is incapable of obedience and looks for compromise *must* go'. One guard who took up his duties around Easter 1937 asked his commandant for release from the service after seeing prisoners being beaten and hearing screams coming from the cells. He wanted to be a soldier, he said, not a prison warder. He was forced to do punishment drill and even interviewed by Eicke himself to try and make him change his mind, but he stood firm, and was granted his request on 30 July 1937. Those who remained were therefore, it can safely be assumed, committed to their job and without scruples or qualms about the sufferings to which the prisoners were subjected.[181]

Many thousands of inmates were released from the camps, especially in 1933-4. 'I know', a senior camp official told Walter Poller as he was given his release papers, 'that you've seen things here that the public perhaps doesn't wholly understand yet. You must keep absolute silence about them. You know that, don't you? And if you don't do that, then you'll soon be back here, and you know what'll happen to you then.'[182] Communication between inmates and their relatives or friends was restricted, officers and guards were banned from talking about their work to outsiders. What happened in the camps was meant to be shrouded in mystery. Attempts by the regular police and prosecution authorities to investigate murders that took place there in the early years were generally rebuffed.[183] By 1936 the concentration camps had become institutions beyond the law. On the other hand, however, the regime made no secret at all of the basic fact of their existence. The opening of Dachau in 1933 was widely reported in the press, and further stories told how Communist, Reichsbanner and 'Marxist' functionaries who endangered state security were being sent there; how the numbers of inmates grew rapidly into the hundreds; how they were being set to work; and how lurid atrocity stories of what went on inside were incorrect. The fact that people were publicly warned in the press not to try and peer into the camp, and would be shot if they tried to climb the walls, only served to increase the general fear and apprehension that these stories must have spread.[184] What happened in the camps was a nameless horror that was all the more potent because its reality could only be guessed at from the broken bodies and spirits of inmates when they were released. There could be few more frightening indications of what would happen to people who engaged in political opposition or expressed political dissent, or, by 1938–9, deviated from the norms of behaviour to which the citizen of the Third Reich was supposed to adhere.[185]

III

Nazi terror was nowhere more apparent than in the emerging power and fearsome reputation of the Gestapo. The role of the police in hunting down and apprehending political and other types of offenders had become more central to the repressive apparatus of the regime once the first wave of mass violence by the brownshirts had ebbed away. The Gestapo in particular quickly attained an almost mythical status as an all-seeing, all-knowing arm of state security and law enforcement. People soon began to suspect that it had agents in every pub and club, spies in every workplace or factory, informers lurking in every bus and tram and standing on every street corner.[186] The reality was very different. The Gestapo was a very small organization with a tiny number of paid agents and informers. In the shipbuilding city of Stettin, there were only 41 Gestapo officers in 1934, the same number as in Frankfurt am Main; in 1935 there were only 44 Gestapo officers in Bremen, and 42 in Hanover. The district office for the Lower Rhine, covering a population of 4 million people, had only 281 agents in its headquarters in Düsseldorf and its various sub-branches in the region, in March 1937. Far from being the fanatical Nazis of legend, these men were generally career policemen who had joined the force under the Weimar Republic or in some cases even earlier. Many of them thought of themselves in the first place as trained professionals. In Würzburg, for example, only the head of the Gestapo office and his successor had joined the Nazi Party before the end of January 1933; the others had kept their distance from political involvement. All told, of the 20,000 or so men who were serving Gestapo officers across the whole of Germany in 1939, only 3,000 were also members of the SS, despite the fact that their organization had been run by the head of the SS, Heinrich Himmler, from early on in the Third Reich.[187]

The professional policemen who staffed the Gestapo included its head, Heinrich Müller, of whom a local Nazi Party official wrote in 1937 that 'we can hardly imagine him as a member of the Party'. An internal Party memorandum from the same year, indeed, could not understand how 'so odious an opponent of the movement' could become head of the Gestapo, especially since he had once referred to Hitler as 'an immigrant unemployed house-painter' and 'an Austrian draft-dodger'. Other Nazi Party officials noted, however, that Müller was 'incredibly ambitious' and would be 'bent on recognition from his superiors under any system'. The key to his durability under the Nazi regime was his fanatical anti-Communism, imbibed when he had been assigned his first case as a policeman at the age of nineteen – the murder of the hostages by the 'Red Army' in revolutionary Munich after the end of the First World War. He had run the anti-Communist department of the Munich political police during the Weimar Republic and put the crushing of Communism above everything else, including what the Nazi regime liked to refer to as 'legal niceties'. Moreover, Müller, who had volunteered for war service at the age of seventeen and subsequently been decorated several times for bravery, was a stickler for duty and discipline, and approached the tasks he was set as if they were military commands. A true workaholic who never took a holiday and was hardly ever ill, Müller was determined to serve the German state, irrespective of what political form it took, and believed that it was everyone's duty, not least his own, to obey its dictates without question. Impressed with his exemplary efficiency and dedication, Heydrich kept him on and indeed enrolled him in the Security Service with his entire team.[188]

Most of the leading Gestapo officials were office workers rather than field operatives. They spent much of their time in compiling and updating elaborate card indices, processing floods of incoming instructions and regulations, filing masses of papers and documents and disputing competence with other agencies and institutions. Building on the already very detailed indices of Communists and their sympathizers drawn up by the political police under the Weimar Republic, the Gestapo aimed to keep a comprehensive register of 'enemies of the state', broken down into a host of different categories who were to be subject to different kinds of treatment. Tabs on the index cards showed the category to which each individual belonged – dark red for a Communist, light red for a Social Democrat, violet for a 'grumbler' and so on. Bureaucratized policing had a long tradition in Germany. It was largely information-gathering and processing systems such as these, and the clerks needed to maintain them, that accounted for the increase in the Berlin Gestapo headquarters budget from one million Reichsmarks in 1933 to no less than forty million in 1937.[189]

Fewer than 10 per cent of the cases with which the Gestapo dealt came from investigations it had begun itself. Some derived from paid informers and spies, most of them casually employed amateurs. Other agencies in which people's identity could be checked, such as population registration offices and the local criminal police, the railways and the Post Office, contributed their part as well. Sometimes, the Gestapo asked known Nazi Party activists to help them track down oppositional elements. No particular disadvantage seems to have resulted to most of these people if they refused. The League of German Girls activist Melita Maschmann was contacted by the Gestapo and asked to spy on the family of a former friend whose brothers were active in a Communist youth resistance group. When she refused, she wrote later, 'I was harassed daily and finally my National Socialist convictions were called into question.' Beyond this, however, nothing happened to her. In any case, she eventually came round. A senior member of the League of German Girls convinced her that the resistance group was 'endangering the future of Germany'. So she complied, only to find that she was unable to convince her friend's family of her *bona fides*, so the house was empty when she arrived there on the day on which the resistance group was scheduled to meet. 'The Gestapo official', she remembered, 'was waiting for me outside the house and dismissed me with a curse.' It was only because she was valued as a propagandist, she thought, that she was kept on in the League of German Girls after this.[190]

Most frequently, information on labour movement resistance activities came from Communists or Social Democrats whose will had been broken by torture and who had agreed in consequence to inform on their former comrades. Gestapo agents may have spent most of their time in the office, but their duties there included brutal interrogations, with the dirty work being done by SS thugs employed for the purpose. A graphic portrayal of Gestapo questioning was provided by the Communist sailor Richard Krebs, who remained in Germany after the Reichstag fire as a secret courier for the Comintern. Krebs was arrested in Hamburg in 1933 and subjected to weeks of merciless beatings and whippings, completely cut off from the outside world, allowed neither a lawyer nor any kind of communication with his family or his friends. In between interrogations, he was kept chained to a cot in a tiny cell, not allowed to wash, his thumb, broken in one of the sessions with the Gestapo, untreated save for having a bandage wrapped around it. A Gestapo officer fired detailed questions at him, clearly based on information received, and on a bulky police file on him that had been compiled from the early 1920s onwards. Kept in the local prison at Fühlsbüttel for most of the time, Krebs continued to be driven at intervals to Hamburg's Gestapo headquarters to be questioned by police officers who looked on while SS men beat him up. After several weeks of this, Krebs's back was a bloody mess, his kidneys were seriously damaged through carefully targeted beating, and he had lost the hearing in one ear. Despite such treatment, he refused to reveal any details of the organization for which he worked.[191]

Transported to the central office of the Gestapo in Berlin, Krebs was impressed by the more refined and less brutal methods employed there. These depended more on tiring prisoners out by prolonged standing or kneeling in awkward positions than on direct brutality and physical abuse. But the atmosphere was the same as in Hamburg:

Grimy corridors, offices furnished with Spartan simplicity, threats, kicks, troopers chasing chained men up and down the reaches of the building, shouting, rows of girls and women standing with their noses and toes against the walls, overflowing ash-trays, portraits of Hitler and his aides, the smell of coffee, smartly dressed girls working at high speed behind typewriters – girls seemingly indifferent to all the squalor and agony about them, stacks of confiscated publications, printing machines, books, and pictures, and Gestapo agents asleep on tables.[192]

Before long, the Gestapo's tactics with the recalcitrant Communist sailor reverted to their old brutality again. Krebs later claimed that he was again subjected to hours of continuous beating with rubber truncheons, and confronted by a series of former comrades whose will had been broken by the same means. A more serious impact was made on his morale, however, when the Gestapo revealed to him that they had arrested his wife when she returned to Germany from exile to look for their son, who had been taken from them and had disappeared into the welfare network. Desperate to stop the Gestapo from doing anything worse to his wife, he approached his fellow Communists in the prison and suggested he offer to work for the Gestapo, while in fact functioning for the Communist Party as a double-agent. Successfully concealing from them the fact that his wife had left the party shortly after his own arrest, he presented his stratagem as a means of rescuing a dedicated comrade from the clutches of the regime. They agreed, and the ruse worked. In March 1934 he gave in to the Gestapo, who, initially at least, accepted his feigned conversion as genuine.[193] Now the tables were turned. Krebs was quickly released under an amnesty and resumed contact with the Comintern. Much of the information he gave the Gestapo seems to have been either false, or – as far as he was aware – already known to them from other sources. Their suspicions aroused, the Gestapo refused to allow his wife's release, and she died in custody in November 1938. Convincing the Gestapo that he would be more use in the international arena, Krebs obtained permission to leave for the USA. He did not return.[194] His history illustrated the close co-operation that quickly grew up between the Gestapo, the SS, the courts and the camps. It also showed the unremitting zeal with which the Nazi regime pumped Communist agents for information about the resistance, and the ruthlessness with which they pursued the goal of turning them to work for the Third Reich instead of the Communist International.[195]

I V

Information supplied by Communists and Social Democrats under torture in the prison cells of the Gestapo was mainly important in tracking down organized political opposition. Where casual remarks, political jokes and individual offences against various Nazi laws were concerned, denunciations sent in by Nazi Party agents of one kind and another, and also by members of the general public, were more important. In Saarbrücken, for instance, no fewer than 87.5 per cent of cases of 'malicious slander against the regime' handled by the district Gestapo office originated in reports sent in by innkeepers or people sitting in their bars, by work colleagues of the accused, by people who had overheard suspicious remarks in the street, or by members of the accused person's family.[196] So many denunciations were sent in to the Gestapo that even fanatical leading Nazis such as Reinhard Heydrich complained about them and the district Gestapo office in Saarbrücken itself registered its alarm at the 'constant expansion of an appalling system of denunciation'. What dismayed them was in particular the fact that many denunciations appeared to be made from personal rather than ideological motives. Leading figures in the Party might have encouraged people to expose disloyalty, grumbling and dissent, but they wanted this practice to be a sign of loyalty to the regime, not a means of offloading personal resentments and gratifying personal desires. Thirty-seven per cent of 213 cases subsequently studied by one historian arose out of private conflicts, while another 39 per cent had no discernible motive at all; only 24 per cent were clearly made by people acting primarily out of political loyalty to the regime. Neighbours denounced noisy or unruly people living in the same building, office workers denounced people who were blocking their promotion, small businessmen denounced inconvenient competitors, friends or colleagues who quarrelled sometimes took the final step of sending in a denunciation to the Gestapo. School or university students even on occasion denounced their teachers. Whatever the motive, the Gestapo investigated them all. If the denunciation was without foundation, they usually simply relegated it to the files and took no further action. But in many cases, denunciation could lead to the arrest of the person denounced, torture, imprisonment and even death.[197]

In prosecuting 'malicious gossip', the police, the Gestapo and the courts tended to be fairly lenient where middle-class offenders were concerned, and much tougher if the offender was a worker, though the largest group of offenders came from the lower middle class, reflecting not least the fact that denunciation seems to have been most common in this social group. Basing themselves on this law, the Special Courts cracked down hard on the kind of casual dissent that would go unremarked in a normal democratic political system, sentencing over 3,700 people in 1933, and sending the majority of them to prison for an average of six months each. Two-thirds of the defendants tried under this law in the Frankfurt Special Court had been denounced in pubs and bars by fellow drinkers for their remarks. Most offenders were working-class men, who, probably because the courts suspected them of being closet Communists or Social Democrats, received much harsher treatments than Nazi Party members or members of the middle and upper classes.[198]

A study of several thousand malicious gossip cases brought before the Munich Special Court has shown, however, that the proportion of cases where the accused acted from party-political motives fell from 50 per cent in 1933 to an average of only 12 per cent in 1936–9. From breaking the will of Communists and Social Democrats to resist in 1933–4, the Court had moved to the new function of preventing any kind of open criticism of the regime, and indeed there was a mild increase in the proportion of ex-Nazis and conservatives and a substantial increase in the proportion of Catholics amongst the accused in the late 1930s.[199]

Among the statements that landed offenders in gaol under the Malicious Gossip Law were allegations that the Nazis were suppressing the people's freedom, that civil servants were overpaid, that Julius Streicher's sensationalistic antisemitic paper *The Stormer* brought shame on culture, that prisoners were being beaten up in Dachau, that Hitler was an Austrian deserter, that the brownshirts were all ex-Communists (this was a favourite accusation of conservative Catholics), and that Hermann Göring and other leading figures in the Third Reich were corrupt. The offenders were hardly radical, principled or sophisticated critics of the regime, then, and their offending statements were often little more than inarticulate and uninformed expressions of discontent, put into a personal form.[200] Some officials felt uneasy at the fact that, as a regional administrator put it in 1937, 'the sentencing of chatterboxes makes up a very large proportion of the activities of the Special Courts'. Most of those arrested and tried under the Malicious Gossip Law, he thought, were just grumblers who did not oppose the regime in any serious way at all. 'Necessary though it is to crack down hard on treasonable verbal propaganda,' he went on, 'there is also a considerable danger that the excessively harsh punishment of basically harmless chatter will lead to bitterness and incomprehension among the friends and relatives of those who are condemned for it by the courts.' But this was to miss the point. Jokes and rude remarks about the Nazi leaders never amounted to opposition or resistance on principle; it was in most cases little more than blowing off steam. But the regime was not just concerned to suppress active opposition; it sought to eliminate even the tiniest signs of discontent, and to suppress anything that might suggest that the population was not massively and wholeheartedly behind everything it did.

From this point of view, malicious gossip and political jokes could be just as objectionable as outright criticism and resistance.[201]

Offenders often landed before the courts as the result of mere chance. An actor, for example, sat down at a table in a restaurant near the railway station in Munich one spring day in 1938; the table was already occupied by a married couple, whom he had not met before, and they fell into conversation. As he began to criticize the regime's foreign policy, he noticed from their reaction that he had gone too far; he hurriedly rose from the table to catch his train, or so he claimed. The couple followed him, but could not find him, so they gave his description to the police, who tracked him down and arrested him two days later. Others landed before the court as a result of personal quarrels that got out of hand, as when a drunken postal worker began insulting Hitler in the presence of two minor Party functionaries whom he knew. When they tried to shut him up, he made matters worse by insulting one of the two men in his capacity as a Party official, so that the latter felt he could only restore his authority amongst the pub regulars by denouncing the postal worker to the police. Whatever the way in which a denunciation occurred, it was obviously dangerous to speak freely in public; people could never be sure who was listening. It was the unpredictability of denunciation, rather than its frequency, that mattered. It caused people to believe that agents of the Gestapo, paid or unpaid, were everywhere, and that the police knew everything that was going on.[202]

Denunciations from ordinary people were important. By far the largest proportion of them came in from men; the places in which denouncers overheard suspicious statements, like pubs and bars, were frequently socially barred to women, and even when it was a woman who overheard a statement, perhaps in the stairway of a block of flats or in some similar domestic environment, she often left it to her husband or father to bring the matter to the attention of the police. The proportion varied from place to place, but on average about four out of five denouncers were male. The same domination of men obtained among the denounced. Politics in the Third Reich, even at this very basic level, was predominantly a man's business.[203] Denunciations, however, were only one of many different means of repression and control available to the Gestapo, and, of course, the proportion of ordinary people who actually sent in denunciations was extremely small when set against the population as a whole. A study of the Düsseldorf Gestapo office has shown that out of 825 Gestapo investigations in the historian's random sample from the period 1933 to 1944, 26 per cent began with information sent in from members of the general population, 17 per cent from the criminal police and other agencies of law enforcement and control such as the SS, 15 per cent from the Gestapo's own officers or informers, 13 per cent from persons under interrogation in the Gestapo's cells, 7 per cent from local authorities and other agencies of the state, and 6 per cent from Nazi Party organizations of one kind and another.[204] Some of these too may have been initiated in the first place by members of the population, for example sending in a denunciation to a Party agency or local government office. But Party agencies were undoubtedly very important in the whole process of bringing dissent before the Special Courts. In the Bavarian town of Augsburg, it was noted that areas with a strong tradition of labour movement solidarity and the presence of organized opposition to the regime produced fewer denunciations than districts with a high degree of support for the Nazis. Forty-two per cent of denouncers belonged to the Nazi Party or one of its organizations, and 30 per cent of these had joined before 1933.[205]

The role of active Nazis in denouncing critical or nonconformist statements was particularly prominent in 1933, 1934 and 1935. Not surprisingly, 54 per cent of those denounced in Augsburg were former Communists or Social Democrats, though as many as 22 per cent were actually Nazis, showing that the regime was not immune from criticism from within its own ranks at this time. As in other parts of Germany, many statements picked up by denouncers were made in the town's pubs and bars, reflecting the long tradition of political discourse that existed in these social institutions. Most strikingly, however, while three-quarters of all critical remarks prosecuted by the courts were overheard in Augsburg's pubs and bars in 1933, the proportion sank to two-thirds in 1934 and little more than a half in 1935. A few years later it was only one in ten. Clearly, fear of being overheard rapidly inhibited free conversation in pubs, destroying yet another aspect of social life that had hitherto existed free from Nazi control.[206] Knowledge of the ever-present danger of denunciation for an incautious word or expression spoken in a public place was important in spreading general fear and anxiety among the population. 'Everyone cringes with fear,' wrote the Jewish professor Victor Klemperer in his diary on 19 August 1933: 'No letter, no telephone conversation, no word on the street is safe any more. Everyone fears the next person may be an informer.'[207] What counted was not whether or not there really were informers everywhere, but the fact that people thought there were. The disillusioned writer and journalist Friedrich Reck-Malleczewen recorded his friends' and his own hatred of Hitler in the privacy of his diary and wondered on 9 September 1937 if anyone outside Germany had 'any idea of how completely without legal status we are, of what it is to be threatened with denunciation at any time by the next hysteric who comes along'. How, he asked rhetorically, could foreigners comprehend the 'deathlike loneliness' of those who did not support the Nazis?[208]

People could, of course, try to relieve their fear by joking about the situation, preferably in private. 'In future', so one joke went, 'teeth in Germany will be extracted through the nose, since nobody is allowed to open their mouth any more.' Some began to speak of 'the German glance', a counterpart to 'the German greeting' when two friends happened on one another in public: it meant looking round to make sure nobody was within earshot. On ending a possibly subversive conversation, one might say to one's companion instead of 'Hail, Hitler!', 'You've said some things as well!'[209] Humour could be anecdotal too, of course:

In Switzerland a Nazi bigwig asks the purpose of a public building. 'That's our Ministry of Marine,' says the Swiss man. The Nazi laughs and mocks him. 'You with your two or three ships, what do you need a Ministry of Marine for?' The Swiss man: 'Yes, – so what do you still need a Ministry of Justice in Germany for then?'[210]

Political jokes themselves might have been irresistible as a release from tension, but everyone knew they could also be dangerous. 'In the wintertime, two men are standing in the tram making strange movements with their hands under their coats,' began another one. ' "Look at those two", says one passenger to his fellow, "what are they up to?" "Ah, I know those two, they're deaf-mutes, they're telling political jokes to each other!" '[211] Of course, in practice people often told each other political jokes in the open, in pubs, on trams, or when meeting on the street, as the files of the Gestapo agents who arrested them reveal. The authorities themselves realized that humour was usually a way people found to live with the regime; it seldom indicated real opposition to it. As one local police official noted in March 1937:

For some time the devising and telling of political jokes has grown to become a real nuisance. So long as these jokes are the expression of a sound spirit and are harmless in character, there will be, as has been repeatedly underlined at the top level of government, nothing to object to in them. But if they are slanderous in content, then for security reasons we can and must not tolerate their being spread around.[212]

The journalist Jochen Klepper agreed with this assessment: 'For all their political jokes and private disappointments, the people are still living in the illusion of the "Third Reich",' he concluded resignedly in the summer of 1934.[213] Those arrested for disrespectful humour were often released without charge if they had no previous convictions. Only where they had an oppositional record were matters taken further, often ending in a short spell in prison. What mattered in the end was the identity of the joker rather than the nature of the joke, and it is not surprising that the vast majority of those imprisoned under the relevant law (for 'malicious gossip') were working-class former Communists or Social Democrats.[214] Yet it was the arbitrariness of the police and the defencelessness of those whom they arrested that struck people most. As another joke had it: 'At the Belgian border crossing, huge numbers of rabbits appear one day and declare that they are political refugees. "The Gestapo wants to arrest all giraffes as enemies of the state." – "But you're not giraffes!" – "We know that, but try explaining that to the Gestapo!"'[215]

Fear of being denounced, overheard or arrested extended even to private conversations, letters and telephone calls. As early as March and April 1933, Victor Klemperer was complaining in his diary: 'Nobody dares to say anything any more, everyone's afraid.'[216] The Reichstag Fire Decree of 28 February 1933 allowed the Gestapo to open people's letters and tap their telephones, so, reported Klemperer: 'People don't dare write letters, people don't dare to phone each other, they visit each other and calculate their chances.'[217] In Berlin, the journalist Charlotte Beradt heard a Social Democratic friend confide to her early in February 1933 a dream he had had, in which Goebbels had visited his workplace, but the dreamer had found it almost impossible to raise his arm in the

Nazi salute, and when he finally managed it after half an hour, Goebbels said coldly: 'I don't want your salute.' Alienation from himself, loss of identity, isolation, fear, doubt, all the feelings expressed here were so striking that Beradt decided to make a collection of people's dreams. By the time she finally left for England in 1939, her unobtrusive inquiries among friends and acquaintances, particularly doctors, who were unlikely to arouse their patients' suspicions by asking about their dreams, had amassed a collection large enough to fill a book even after all the dreams with no discernible political significance had been weeded out.[218]

Many of the dreams Beradt collected bore witness to people's fear of surveillance. One doctor dreamed in 1934 that the walls of his consulting-room and of all the houses and flats in the neighbourhood suddenly vanished, while a loudspeaker blared forth the announcement that it was 'according to the Decree for the Abolition of Walls, passed on the 17th of this month'. A woman dreamed that when she was at the opera, watching a performance of Mozart's The Magic Flute, a troop of policemen marched into her box immediately after the line 'That's surely the Devil' had been sung, because they had noted that she had thought of Hitler in connection with the word Devil. As she looked around for help, the old gentleman in the next box spat on her. A girl reported that in a dream she had seen the two pictures of angels that hung over her bed move their eyes downwards from their accustomed heavenward gaze so that they could keep her under observation. A number of people dreamed of being imprisoned behind barbed wire, or having their telephone conversations interrupted, like one man who, after telling his brother over the telephone 'I can't enjoy anything any more', dreamed the same night that his phone had rung and an expressionless voice had announced itself as 'Office for the Surveillance of Telephone Conversations': the dreamer immediately realized that being depressed in the Third Reich was a crime, and had asked for forgiveness, but met with nothing but silence. A few dreamed of carrying out small acts of resistance that always turned out to be futile, like the woman who dreamed that she removed the swastika from the Nazi flag every night, but it reappeared every morning all the same.[219] In recounting and analysing all these dreams, Charlotte Beradt recalled a claim by the Labour Front leader Robert Ley: 'The only person in Germany who still has a private life is a person who's sleeping.' The dreams she collected showed, she concluded gloomily, that even this was not true.[220]

V

The Gestapo, the Nazi Party and the stormtroopers turned their attention not just to opponents, dissenters and malcontents, but also to those who failed to show sufficient enthusiasm for the Third Reich and its policies. Every group of houses had a 'Block Warden', the popular name for a variety of officials on the lowest rung of the Nazi hierarchy, whose task it was to ensure that everybody hung out bunting and Nazi flags on special occasions and went along to Nazi rallies and parades. Every local branch of the Nazi Party had an average of eight cells, each organized into roughly fifty blocks containing around fifty households each. The Political Leaders of the Nazi Party, as these low-ranking local officials were generally known, looked after one block each and in turn appointed helpers to cover each block of flats or small group of houses. Already by 1935 there were perhaps 200,000 of these Political Leaders; including their helpers there were almost two million 'Block Wardens' by the beginning of the war. Over two-thirds of the Political Leaders were of middle-class origin according to the 1935 Party statistics, and they were particularly hated in working-class districts with a strong Communist or Social Democratic past. They were often the first port of call for denouncers, and they exercised close surveillance over known dissenters, Jews and those who maintained contact with them, and 'politically unreliable' people, usually former opponents of the Nazis. Known derisively as 'golden pheasants' from their brown-gold uniforms with red collar epaulettes, they were required to report 'rumour-mongers' and anyone who failed to conform to the district Party organization, which would pass on their names and their misdemeanours to the Gestapo. Those who fell foul of the Block Wardens could also be denied state benefits and welfare payments. Other branches of the huge Nazi Party apparatus had similar local officials, ranging from the welfare service to the Labour Front and the women's organization, and all of them carried out similar functions of surveillance and control.[221] In factories and workplaces, officials of the Labour Front, the employers, the foremen and the Nazi Security Service took over the functions of the Block Warden. Those workers who did not toe the line were singled out for discriminatory treatment, denial of promotion, transfer to less congenial duties, or even dismissal.[222] 'You couldn't say anything,' recalled one worker in the Krupp engineering factory later: 'the foreman was always standing behind you, nobody could risk it.'[223] The Nazi terror machine reached down even to the smallest units of everyday life and daily work.

Intimidation was particularly evident during the national plebiscites and elections that Hitler held from time to time to provide the appearance of legitimacy to his actions, especially in foreign policy. The tightening of the regime's grip can be read from the growing proportion of votes it secured at these propaganda events, which were legitimized by a law of 14 July 1933, passed at the same time as the law turning Germany into a one-party state. The new law allowed the government 'to consult the people' on particular policies on its own initiative, a stark difference from the situation under the Weimar Republic, when the power to initiate plebiscites lay with the people. Under the Third Reich, plebiscites and elections became propaganda exercises in which the regime mobilized the electorate, by all the means at its disposal, to provide the appearance of popular legitimacy for controversial measures.[224] The first opportunity for using these methods came with the Reichstag election of 12 November 1933. The decree dissolving the Reichstag also permanently abolished the regional state parliaments, whose collective assembly, the Reichsrat, the upper house of the national legislature, was abolished early in 1934. In the Reichstag election, voters were presented with a single party list against which they could record a 'yes' or a 'no'. To placate middle-class electors, the list included a number of non-Nazi conservatives such as Papen and Hugenberg, and even a few former representatives of the Centre Party and the People's Party. A massive propaganda campaign, including a radio broadcast by Hindenburg, was backed up by confidential instructions from the Reich Interior Ministry allowing returning officers wide latitude to interpret spoiled ballot papers as 'yes' votes. Some critical spirits suspected that this was what would happen anyway. Victor Klemperer for example noted in his diary on 23 October that 'no one will dare *not* to vote, and no one will respond with a No in the vote of confidence. Because 1) Nobody believes in the secrecy of the ballot and 2) a No will be taken as a Yes anyway.'[225] Few people dared to complain openly of manipulation, but those who did revealed malpractices such as the violation of ballot secrecy through the numbering of ballot papers, the filling-in of blank papers by returning officers, the removal of opponents of the regime from the electoral register and much more besides. Those who demonstratively refused to vote were arrested; and the presence of Nazis and brownshirts in the polling stations put pressure on people to show their loyalty to the regime by voting openly instead of in the secrecy of the polling booths. With the help of such methods, the regime obtained a 'yes' vote of 88 per cent, although almost three and a half million spoiled ballots were cast. Nearly 5 per cent of the voters put a cross against the 'no' in the accompanying plebiscite.[226]

The methods used to obtain such results were made clear in the plebiscite held on 19 August 1934 to set the seal of popular approval on Hitler's self-appointment as Head of State after Hindenburg's death. Clandestine reports from Social Democratic agents to their party headquarters in exile noted that the polling stations were surrounded by brownshirts, creating a 'terror-atmosphere, which did not fail to have an effect even where terror was not directly employed'. In many places, the polling booths had been removed, or access to them was barred by brownshirts, or they were labelled 'Only traitors enter here'. Clubs and societies were marched *en masse* by groups of stormtroopers to the polling stations and forced to cast their votes in public. In some polling stations all the ballot papers were already marked 'yes', while in others spoiled papers were counted as 'yes' votes. So many 'no' votes were replaced with one or more forged 'yes' votes that the number of votes cast actually exceeded the number of electors in some constituencies. The degree of terror varied from area to area, so that in the Palatinate, where the Social Democratic agents reported record levels of intimidation and falsification, the 'yes' votes were well above average, at 94.8 per cent of the electorate, while in a few less heavily policed Rhenish constituencies, by contrast, up to half the votes were recorded as 'no' votes or spoiled ballots. In Hamburg only 73 per cent of the electorate voted yes, in Berlin only 74 per cent, and in some former Communist strongholds like Wilmersdorf and Charlottenburg the vote was below 70 per cent. Remarkably, under such circumstances, the regime only managed to secure the votes of 85 per cent of the electors. Five million electors refused to endorse the law, either by voting 'no' or by spoiling their ballot papers.[227] Despite the massive pressure to vote 'yes', many Germans still thought the vote had been free: Luise Solmitz called it on polling day 'a plebiscite of which one cannot predict the result, at least I could not'.[228] Victor Klemperer was less sanguine. 'One-third said yes out of fear,' he wrote, 'one-third out of intoxication, one-third out of fear and intoxication.'[229]

Four years later, the regime had perfected its techniques of electoral terror and manipulation to the extent that it achieved a 'yes' vote of more than 99 per cent in the April 1938 plebiscite on the union with Austria, which was coupled with a personal vote of confidence in Hitler and his actions to date. The conflation of these two issues alone muddied the waters by making it clear that anyone who voted against the union was also voting against Hitler and could thus fall under the provisions of the treason laws. Gangs of brownshirts toured every street at regular intervals, forcing people out of their homes and carting them off to the polling stations. The sick and bedridden were made to cast their votes at mobile polling stations that visited them at home. People who refused to vote, or threatened to vote 'no', were beaten up, forced to parade through the streets with a placard round their neck with words such as 'I am a traitor to the people', dragged round pubs to be shouted at and spat upon, or consigned unceremoniously to lunatic asylums. In many places, known opponents of the regime were arrested in advance and kept in custody until polling day had passed. In others, they were given specially marked ballot papers, with a number typed on them by a typewriter without a ribbon and the same number placed by the name on the list of electors. On 7 May 1938, the Koblenz branch of the SS Security Service reported that in this way it had been able 'to discover the persons who had voted "no" or spoiled their papers. Skimmed milk', it reported in pedantic and humourless detail, 'was used to bring out the numbers.' In many towns, the overwhelming majority of electors were forced to cast their votes in public, at long tables manned by groups of brownshirts; in some, they were simply handed ballot papers already marked 'yes' by the officiating brownshirts. Even where the appearance of a secret ballot was maintained, rumours were deliberately circulated in advance that the ballot papers would be marked so that all voters if necessary could be identified during the count, and in some places indeed

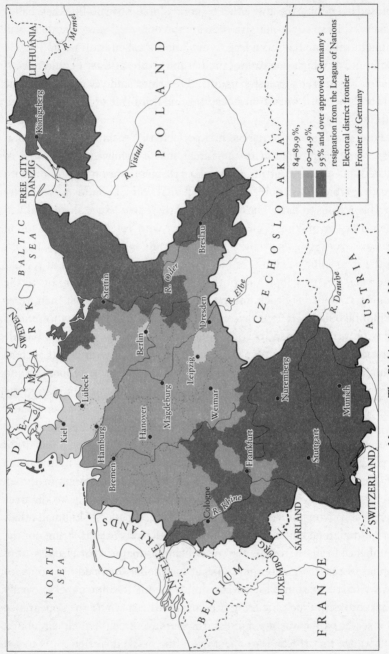

Map 3.   The Plebiscite of 12 November 1933

they were. Where, despite all these precautions, a substantial number of spoiled ballot papers or 'no' votes appeared at the count, they were simply discounted. And when a voter took the unusual step of publicly announcing his abstention, as the Catholic bishop Joannes Sproll did in protest against the inclusion of Alfred Rosenberg and Robert Ley on the Nazi Party list, the reaction was severe; Bishop Sproll's action called forth raucous demonstrations by brownshirts outside his church, and led to his expulsion from his diocese, though the regime regarded him as too prominent to be arrested.[230] Despite such incidents, many Germans who supported the Nazis in such plebiscites glowed with pride at the results. '99 per cent for the Leader,' noted Luise Solmitz triumphantly, 'that must make an overwhelming impression on foreign countries.'[231]

VI

How far, then, did terror and intimidation penetrate into German society under the Nazis? Blatant intimidation and manipulation at election time may have rendered the results completely unreliable as an indicator of popular attitudes, but they undoubtedly concealed a good deal of support for the regime as well as stifling criticism and opposition, and on some issues at least – the remilitarization of the Rhineland and the annexation of Austria, for instance – it is more than likely that a majority would have voted 'yes' even had the election been completely free. Moreover, for most Germans, Nazi terror, as we have seen, rapidly evolved from a reality, as it was in the near-universal violence of the first half of 1933, into a threat that was seldom translated into action. In 1933 a huge apparatus of surveillance and control was rapidly brought into being to track down, arrest and punish anyone who opposed the Nazi regime, including a good third of the electorate who had voted for the parties of the left in the last free German elections. By the end of 1935 organized opposition had been completely crushed. The 'Night of the Long Knives' was also a lesson to dissenters within the Nazi movement, above all of course to the millions of men who belonged to the turbulent brownshirt paramilitary movement. Politicians in many other parties, from the Democrats to the Nationalists, had been arrested, threatened, even murdered as a warning to others to fall into line. But from 1936 onwards, overt terror was directed increasingly against relatively small minorities such as persistent or committed Communists and Social Democrats, the asocial and work-shy, petty criminals and, as we shall see later in this book, Jews and homosexuals. For the vast majority of Germans, including millions of former Communists and Social Democrats, provided they kept their noses clean, the threat of arrest, imprisonment and concentration camp receded into the background.[232]

Recently, indeed, some historians have built upon these facts to argue that the Nazis did not rule by terror at all. Violence and intimidation rarely touched the lives of most ordinary Germans. After 1933 at least, terror was highly selective, concentrating on small and marginal groups whose persecution not only met with the approval of the vast majority of Germans, but was actually carried out with the co-operation and often voluntary participation at the local level of the broad mass of ordinary German citizens. German society under the Nazis was, in this view, a society engaged in 'self-surveillance'.[233] This went beyond denunciations for personal motives to include a good degree of ideological input, as was clear, for example, in the case of Augsburg. Statistics of denunciations that include, for example, reports to the Gestapo by customers in inns and bars or 'colleagues at work' make no mention of how many of these were in fact loyal Nazi Party members or officials of organizations like the Labour Front; a good many of them are likely to have been, given the huge numbers of people who had joined the Nazi Party by the mid-1930s or belonged to ancillary organizations like the stormtroopers, the Hitler Youth and so on. If we look at the composition of the inmate population of concentration camps at any time in the Third Reich, we do indeed find overwhelmingly members of minorities who were generally regarded with suspicion by a large part of the German population.

Yet to speak of a self-policing society understates the element of top-down terror and intimidation in the functioning of the Third Reich.[234] Those cases that landed up on the Gestapo's desks constituted only a tiny proportion of criminally liable statements in any given year. The vast majority were never denounced by anybody. Denunciation was the exception, not the rule, as far as the behaviour of the vast majority of Germans was concerned. In Lippe, for instance, a district with 176,000 inhabitants, the total number of denunciations sent in to Party agencies from 1933 to 1945 was a mere 292; the maximum submitted in any single year was only 51, the minimum was three denunciations.[235] In 1937, moreover, only 17,168 cases of contravention of the Law on Malicious Gossip were reported by the Gestapo in the whole of the German Reich. The actual number of contraventions is likely to have been many hundred times greater. Thus, from whatever motive, the overwhelming majority of witnesses to such contraventions declined to become denouncers. Particularly in working-class districts, the fear of ostracism or counter-denunciation, even of revenge attacks, must have been considerable. Moreover, it was not ordinary German people who engaged in surveillance, it was the Gestapo; nothing happened until the Gestapo received a denunciation, and it was the Gestapo's active pursuit of deviance and dissent that was the only thing that gave denunciations meaning. After they had broken labour movement resistance, the Gestapo turned to suppressing a far broader range of less ideological forms of dissent, and the consequences for those whom it brought in for questioning and prosecution could be serious indeed, beginning with brutal violence and torture meted out by Gestapo officers themselves, or under their supervision, in the course of interrogation, and ending in the courts, the prisons and the camps.[236] In this process, the Gestapo called on a network of local officials of the regime, from the Block Warden upwards, and the very existence of such a network, with the Gestapo at its centre, was in itself an incentive to denunciation. Nazi officials knew that failure to pursue dissent could easily land them in trouble themselves; they also knew that bringing it to the Gestapo's attention could earn them approbation as true servants of the Third Reich. Ultimately, it was the Gestapo and the agencies it employed, exploited or worked alongside, who kept Germans under surveillance, not the Germans themselves.[237]

In defence of the argument that the overwhelming majority of Germans approved of the repressive policy of the regime, it has been pointed out, correctly, that the Nazis, far from concealing the existence of repressive institutions and practices, regularly announced executions, prison sentences, court verdicts against dissent, 'malicious gossip' and so on, in the newspapers and other propaganda organs of the regime. Therefore, the argument continues, the vast majority of ordinary people who read the newspapers had no objection to these practices. But such publicity cut more than one way, and a major function of advertising the terror imposed by the regime on deviants and dissenters was to deter millions of ordinary Germans from going down the same road. The open threat of concentration camp for people who spread rumours about the Röhm purge only made explicit what was implicit in every report of this kind. In a similar way, the fact that top police and SS officials like Reinhard Heydrich and Werner Best saw the Gestapo as working on behalf of the German people and with its co-operation in a kind of ethnic and political purification, encompassing the whole of society, should not simply be taken at face value: Nazi ideology constantly reiterated the belief that the regime in all its aspects enjoyed the support of all the people, but in fact the openly proclaimed vastness of the Gestapo's ambition was yet another instrument of terror in itself, fostering the belief amongst the broad mass of Germans that its agents were everywhere and knew everything that was going on.[238]

Despised minorities were, to be sure, put in the concentration camps; but to focus exclusively on this ignores the much larger number of political and other deviants condemned by the courts and put in state prisons and penitentiaries. The further in time we get from Nazi Germany, the more difficult it becomes for historians living in democratic political systems and in cultures which respect the rights of the individual to make the leap of imagination necessary to understand people's behaviour in a state such as Nazi Germany, where imprisonment, torture or even death might await anyone who dared to voice the slightest criticism of the regime and its leaders. Those who approved of such repression were in all likelihood a minority, active supporters and functionaries of the Party like the Block Wardens, and a good number of middle- and upper-class, conservative Germans who thought the best place for Marxists to be was in prison anyway. Even they, however, knew well enough that they had to be careful about what they said and did, and the dangers of not doing so became abundantly clear once opposition began to spread among these groups too. The shots that killed Kurt von Schleicher, Herbert von Bose, Edgar Jung, Gustav von Kahr, Erich Klausener and Kurt von Bredow at the beginning of July 1934 were also a warning to upper- and middle-class conservatives to keep their heads down if they did not want them to be blown off.[239]

Ordinary conservative citizens like Luise Solmitz, who harboured no thoughts of political activism, may have turned aside from the bleak fact of the regime's willingness to murder its opponents, revealed so starkly in late June and early July 1934, in their relief that the order they craved had been restored; to such people, Röhm's stormtroopers seemed as great a menace as the Reichsbanner or the Red Front-Fighters' League of the Weimar years. Yet behind closed doors they cannot have been oblivious to the fate of the conservative clique around Vice-Chancellor von Papen. It was not only the third or so of the population who had been committed to the Marxist left before 1933 that was subject to massive intimidation. Indeed, scarcely had the murderous violence of the 'Night of the Long Knives' receded, than an even larger minority than the Marxists, that of the German Catholics, began to be prosecuted and imprisoned as they gave vent to their increasingly critical views of the regime in public. More general still were measures such as the Law on Malicious Gossip, which clamped down on the most trivial expressions of dissent and put people who told jokes about Hitler and Göring in prison. These were mainly members of the German working class, it is true, but the working class after all made up around half the entire population, and middle- and even upper-class offenders in this respect were brought before the Special Courts as well. Successful prosecutions under this law were a further instrument of mass intimidation, adding to the general climate of fear and helping to create the spiral of silence in which the regime could commit ever greater crimes without fear of public censure or opposition.[240]

The truth is that far from Nazi terror being levelled exclusively against small and despised minorities, the threat of arrest, prosecution and incarceration in increasingly brutal and violent conditions loomed over everyone in the Third Reich, even, as we have seen in the cases brought before the Special Courts, over members of the Nazi Party itself. The regime intimidated Germans into acquiescence, visiting a whole range of sanctions upon those who dared to oppose it, systematically disorienting people, and depriving them of their traditional social and cultural milieux, such as the pub or the club or the voluntary association, above all where these could be seen as a potential source of resistance, as in the case of the labour movement. Fear and terror were integral parts of the Nazis' armoury of political weapons from the very beginning.[241] The state and the Party could use them because within a few months of

Hitler's appointment as Reich Chancellor, they had systematically deprived all Germans of virtually every basic human and civil right they had enjoyed under the Weimar Republic. The law was no protection against the state if the state or any of its agencies suspected that a citizen was disinclined to demonstrate approval of its policies and purposes. On the contrary, vast numbers of new, often draconian laws were decreed that gave the police, the Gestapo and the SS a virtual *carte blanche* to deal with anyone suspected of deviating from the norms of human behaviour laid down by the Third Reich for its citizens. In this situation, it was not surprising that ordinary people and lower-level officials of the Nazi Party began to reinforce the atmosphere of pervasive terror and intimidation by sending their own unsolicited denunciations of deviants to the Gestapo.

At the same time, the Gestapo was only one part of a much wider net of surveillance, terror and persecution cast by the Nazi regime over German society in the 1930s; others included the SA and SS, the Criminal Police, the prison service, the social services and employment offices, the medical profession, health centres and hospitals, the Hitler Youth, the Block Wardens and even apparently politically neutral organizations like tax offices, the railway and the post office. All of these furnished information about deviants and dissidents to the Gestapo, the courts and the prosecution service, forming a polymorphous, uncoordinated but pervasive system of control in which the Gestapo was merely one institution among many.[242] Everything that happened in the Third Reich took place in this pervasive atmosphere of fear and terror, which never slackened and indeed became far more intense towards the end. 'Do you know what fear is?' an elderly worker asked an interviewer some years after it was all over: 'No. The Third Reich was fear.'[243] Yet terrorism was only one of the Third Reich's techniques of rule. For the Nazis did not just seek to batter the population into passive, sullen acquiescence. They also wanted to rouse it into positive, enthusiastic endorsement of their ideals and their policies, to change people's minds and spirits and to create a new German culture that would reflect their values alone. This meant propaganda, and here too, as we shall now see, they went to unprecedented lengths to achieve their aims.

2

THE MOBILIZATION OF
THE SPIRIT

ENLIGHTENING THE PEOPLE

I

'The revolution we have made', declared Joseph Goebbels, on 15 November 1933, 'is a total one. It has encompassed every area of public life and fundamentally restructured them all. It has completely changed and reshaped people's relationship to each other, to the state, and questions of existence.' This was, he went on, a 'revolution from below', driven on by the people, because, he said, it had brought about 'the transformation of the German nation into one people'. Becoming one people meant establishing a unity of spirit across the nation, for, as Goebbels had already announced in March: 'On 30 January the era of individualism finally died ... The individual will be replaced by the community of the people.' 'Revolutions', he added, 'never confine themselves to the purely political sphere. From there they reach out to cover all other areas of human social existence. The economy and culture, science and scholarship, and art are not protected from their impact.' There could be no neutrals in this process: no one could stand aside under false claims of objectivity, or art for art's sake. For, he declared: 'Art is no absolute concept, it only gains life from the life of the people.' Thus: 'There is no art without political bias.'[1]

The revolution of which Goebbels was speaking was not a social or economic revolution along the lines of the French Revolution of 1789 or the Russian Revolution of 1917. Nor was it a revolution of permanent upheaval such as Röhm and the stormtroopers had seemed to envisage before they were crushed in 1934. It was a cultural revolution. It envisaged the deepening and strengthening of the Nazis' conquest of political power through the conversion of the whole German people to their way of thinking. Not 37 per cent of the people, as Goebbels said on 25 March 1933, referring to the highest proportion of the vote the Nazis had ever succeeded in winning in a free German election, but 100 per cent of the people must be behind them.[2] It was to this end that Hitler had created a new Ministry of Popular Enlightenment and Propaganda on 13 March 1933 and put Goebbels himself into the Ministry, with a seat in the cabinet.[3] On 25 March, Goebbels defined the Ministry's task as the 'spiritual mobilization' of the German people in a permanent re-creation of the spirit of popular enthusiasm that had, so the Nazis claimed, galvanized the German people on the outbreak of war in 1914. The Nazis' belief in the positive power of propaganda also owed a great deal to the experience of the First World War, when, they felt, the British had succeeded in purveying damaging myths about Germany. Goebbels's Ministry, staffed by young, committed Nazi ideologues, sought not just to present the regime and its policies in a positive light, but to generate the impression that the entire German people enthusiastically endorsed everything it did. Of all the things that made the Third Reich a modern dictatorship, its incessant demand for popular legitimation was one of the most striking. The regime put itself almost from the very start in a state of permanent plebiscitary consultation of the masses. It went to immense trouble to ensure that every aspect of this consultation delivered a resounding and virtually unanimous endorsement of its actions, its policies and above all, its Leader. Even if it knew, as it must have done, that this endorsement was in reality far from genuine, the mere appearance of constantly renewed mass enthusiasm for the Third Reich and hysterical mass adulation of its Leader would surely have an effect in persuading many otherwise sceptical or neutral Germans to swim with the tide of popular opinion. It would also intimidate opponents of the regime into silence and inaction by persuading them that their aim of gaining the support of their fellow citizens was a hopelessly unrealistic one.[4]

Goebbels was quite open about the fact that this popular legitimation of the Third Reich was manipulated by the regime. It was the Propaganda Ministry's job to co-ordinate and run the entire public presentation of the regime and its policies. 'All that goes on behind the backcloth', he said, 'belongs to stage management.'[5] This included ceremonies and rituals such as the torchlit parades held to mark the appointment of

Hitler as Reich Chancellor on 30 January 1933, the formal state opening
of the Reichstag at Potsdam on 21 March 1933, the annual Nazi Party
Rally in Nuremberg every autumn, the 'Day of National Labour' on
1 May, and much more besides. New holidays and festivals were added
to the traditional calendar, including Hitler's birthday on 20 April
and the commemoration of the 1923 putsch on 9 November. All over
Germany, street names were altered to remove suddenly unwanted, or
inconvenient, reminders of the democratic past and to celebrate Hitler,
or other leading Nazis, or sacrificial heroes of the movement such as
Horst Wessel, after whom the working-class district of Friedrichshain in
Berlin was now called. A street was also renamed in Hamburg after the
seventeen-year-old Otto Blöcker, a member of the Hitler Youth shot in
an armed Communist raid on a local branch headquarters of the Nazi
Party on 26 February 1933.[6] There were many similar examples.

But it was Hitler who was celebrated above all else. The cult of Hitler
had already reached major proportions within the Party by the early
1930s, but now it was propagated in the nation with the full resources
of the state and projected not just in words and images, but also in
countless small, symbolic ways.[7] From March 1933 onwards, towns
rushed to appoint Hitler an honorary citizen. In almost every town across
Germany the main square was renamed Adolf-Hitler-Platz by the end of
1933. Already on 20 April 1933 the Leader's forty-fourth birthday saw
flags and banners in every German town, garlands hung outside houses
in villages all over the land, shop windows carrying special displays to
mark the occasion and even public transport decorated with celebratory
bunting. Parades and torchlit processions brought the celebrations into
the streets, while the churches held special services to wish the Leader
well. Goebbels's propaganda machine pumped out rhetoric comparing
Hitler to Bismarck, while the Bavarian Minister of Education, Hans
Schemm, went still further, describing him as 'the artist and master-
builder whom the Lord God has given to us', creating 'a new face of
Germany' that gave the people its 'final shape' after 'the events of two
thousand years': 'In the personality of Hitler, a millionfold longing of the
German people has become reality.'[8] Posters and magazine illustrations,
newsreels and films proclaimed Hitler as the man from the trenches,
with the common touch, not only a many-sided genius with a sense of
destiny, but also a humble, even simple human being who had few needs,

spurned wealth and display, was kind to children and animals and dealt compassionately with old comrades fallen on hard times. Soldier, artist, worker, ruler, statesman, he was portrayed as a man with whom all sectors of German society could identify. Many ordinary Germans were overwhelmed by the scale and intensity of this propaganda. The emotion that overcame Luise Solmitz when she stood on the street awaiting Hitler's arrival in her home town of Hamburg was typical: 'I shall never forget the moment when he drove past us in his brown uniform, performing the Hitler salute in his own personal way . . . the enthusiasm [of the crowd] blazed up to the heavens . . .' She went home, trying to digest the 'great moments I had just lived through'.[9]

The embedding of the Hitler cult in everyday life was nowhere more obvious than in the introduction of the German greeting – 'Hail, Hitler! (*Heil Hitler*)' – to be used on all official correspondence by state employees from 13 July 1933. It was reinforced by the Hitler salute, the upstretched right arm, sometimes accompanied by the barking-out of the same German greeting, which was also compulsory, this time for all citizens, when the national anthem or the Horst Wessel Song were being sung. 'Anyone not wishing to come under suspicion of behaving in a consciously negative fashion will therefore render the Hitler greeting', the decree proclaimed.[10] Such rituals not only cemented the formal solidarity of the regime's supporters but also isolated those who stood apart from the regime. And they gave a further boost to Hitler's standing.[11] After the death of Hindenburg and the subsequent plebiscite on the headship of state on 19 August 1934, accompanied by the slogan 'Hitler for Germany – the whole of Germany for Hitler', the Leader-cult knew no more limits. Goebbels's rapid propaganda spin on the 'Night of the Long Knives' only won the Leader more backing, as the man who had supposedly saved Germany from disorder yet again, crushed excessive ambition amongst the Party 'big-shots' and restored decency and morality to the Nazi movement.[12] From now on, whatever popular criticism there was of the regime was likely to be directed against Hitler's satraps; the Leader himself was largely immune.[13]

The Hitler cult achieved its grandest stage-management yet at the Party Rally held in Nuremberg in 1934, the second to be held under the new regime. Five hundred trains carried a quarter of a million people to a specially built railway station. A vast city of tents was constructed to house the participants, and gargantuan quantities of supplies were brought in to feed and water them. At the Rally itself, an elaborate series of rituals commenced. Extending over a whole week, it celebrated the unity of the movement after the alarums and excursions of the preceding summer. Outside the city, on the huge Zeppelin Field, the serried ranks of hundreds of thousands of uniformed brownshirts, SS men and Nazi Party activists took part in ritual exchanges with their Leader. 'Hail, my men,' he would shout, and a hundred thousand voices would answer back in unison: 'Hail, my Leader.' Speeches, choruses and march-pasts gave way after dusk to torchlit parades and dramatically choreographed ceremonies, with over a hundred searchlights beaming up into the sky, enclosing participants and spectators in what the British ambassador described as a 'cathedral of ice'. Spotlights in the arena picked out thirty thousand red, black and white swastika standards as their bearers moved through the brownshirted ranks. At the most hushed moment of the ritual, the 'blood-banner', the flag carried in the beer-hall putsch of 1923, was ceremonially rededicated and touched on the new flags to pass on to them its nimbus of violent struggle and bloody sacrifice for the cause.[14]

The American correspondent William L. Shirer, attending his first Nazi Party Rally, was suitably impressed. 'I'm beginning to comprehend, I think, some of the reasons for Hitler's astonishing success,' he confided to his diary on 5 September 1934:

Borrowing a chapter from the Roman church, he is restoring pageantry and colour and mysticism to the drab lives of twentieth-century Germans. This morning's opening meeting in the Luitpold Hall on the outskirts of Nuremberg was more than a gorgeous show; it also had something of the mysticism and religious fervour of an Easter or Christmas Mass in a great Gothic cathedral.

As Hitler entered, followed by his entourage, walking slowly down the centre aisle, 'thirty thousand hands were raised in salute'. Standing on the podium beneath the 'blood-flag', Hess read out the names of those killed in the 1923 putsch, and silent tribute was paid. 'In such an atmosphere', wrote Shirer, 'no wonder, then, that every word dropped by Hitler seemed like an inspired Word from on high.' Shirer saw for himself the emotion that Hitler's presence could inspire amongst his supporters, as the Leader rode into Nuremberg from the nearby airfield on the eve of the Rally in an open-topped car, greeting with raised hand the shouting crowds lining the old city's streets. Shirer went on:

I got caught in a mob of ten thousand hysterics who jammed the moat in front of Hitler's hotel, shouting: 'We want our Leader.' I was a little shocked at the faces, especially those of the women, when Hitler finally appeared on the balcony for a moment. They reminded me of the crazed expressions I saw once in the back country of Louisiana on the faces of some Holy Rollers who were about to hit the trail. They looked up at him as if he were a Messiah, their faces transformed into something positively inhuman. If he had remained in sight for more than a few moments, I think many of the women would have swooned from excitement.[15]

One 'great pageant' followed another, wrote Shirer, culminating in a mock battle fought by army units on the Zeppelin Field. The whole event closed with a seemingly endless march-past of military and paramilitary units through the streets, giving Shirer a strong impression of the 'sheer disciplined strength' of the Germans under the Nazi regime. To convey a choreographed image of new-found spiritual unity through a series of gargantuan displays of huge masses of men moving and marching in unison, arranged four-square in rank and file, or standing patiently in huge geometrical blocks on the field, was the primary purpose of the Rally; and it was Hitler and Goebbels's intention to convey it not just to Germany, but to the world.[16]

It was in pursuit of this aim that Hitler had indeed arranged for the entire 1934 Rally to be filmed, commissioning a young actress and film director, Leni Riefenstahl, to do the job, and issuing orders that she should be provided with all the resources she needed to carry it out. With thirty cameras at her disposal, operated by sixteen cameramen, each with an assistant, and four sound-equipment trucks, Riefenstahl made a documentary like none before it. A crew of 120 deployed new techniques such as telephoto lenses and wide-angle photography to achieve an effect that many found mesmerizing when the film was released in 1935 under the title – chosen by Hitler himself – of *Triumph of the Will*. The 'will' in question was, as Riefenstahl later explained, not only that of the German people but also and above all that of Hitler, whom her cameras almost invariably portrayed alone, descending through the clouds into Nuremberg in his aeroplane; standing in his open car as it drove through the city to the cheers of the crowds lining the streets; stopping to accept a bouquet from a small girl; speaking to his followers against a backdrop of empty sky; ritually touching the new Party banners with the 'blood-flag'; and finally, in the Luitpold Hall, working himself up into a frenzy in a speech that had the crowd shouting repeated unison cries of 'Hail, Victory' like the worshippers in a revivalist chapel, and Rudolf Hess, his face glowing with fanatical devotion, shouting: 'The Party is Hitler! But Hitler is Germany, just as Germany is Hitler! Hitler! Hail, Victory! (*Sieg, heil!*)'[17]

Triumph of the Will was striking for its monumentalism and its presentation of vast, disciplined masses moving in perfect co-ordination as if they were one body, not thousands. The light relief it presented through interludes of young brownshirts indulging in rough masculine horseplay elided into the glorification of the male body, as much a product of Riefenstahl's own predilections as it was an expression of Nazi ideology, as they stripped off their clothes to jump into a nearby lake. All of this concealed a less glorious reality of drunkenness, brawling, mayhem and murder that went on behind the scenes.[18] But Riefenstahl's film altered reality in more subtle ways than this, not only depicting the events of the Rally in a different order from the one in which they took place, but also, backed by Hitler's licence to interfere in proceedings as she wished, rehearsing and staging some of them deliberately for cinematic effect. Some scenes, indeed, only made sense when seen from the camera's eye. One of the film's most breathtaking moments, as Hitler paced slowly up the broad, blank aisle between the still, silent ranks of more than 100,000 uniformed paramilitaries, with Himmler and the new brownshirt leader Lutze following, to lay a wreath in memory of the movement's dead, cannot have made a visible impact on more than a handful of those taking part. In the final stages of the film, the screen was filled with columns of marching stormtroopers and black-shirted, steel-helmeted SS men, leaving audiences no room for doubt not just about the disciplined co-ordination of the German masses, but also, more ominously, about the primacy of military models in their organization. Presented as a documentary, it was a propaganda film designed to convince Germany and the world of the power, strength and determination of the German people under Hitler's leadership.[19] This was the only film made in the Third Reich about Hitler; it said all that needed to be said, and did not need to be followed by another. It was released in March 1935 to widespread acclaim, not only at home but also abroad. It won the National Film Prize, presented to Riefenstahl by Joseph Goebbels, who described it as 'a magnificent cinematic vision of the Führer', and was also awarded the Gold Medal at the Venice Film festival in 1935 and the Grand Prize at the Paris Film Festival in 1937. It continued to be shown in cinemas, and, though banned in Germany after the war, remains one of the great classics of documentary propaganda of the twentieth century.[20]

Ironically, *Triumph of the Will* had originally been commissioned and shot in the teeth of fierce opposition from the Reich Propaganda Minister following the failure of a first attempt by Riefenstahl the year before, filmed under the title *Triumph of Faith*. Riefenstahl was not a Nazi Party member, indeed she never became one, and Goebbels resented the fact that she had been directly commissioned by Hitler, bypassing what he regarded as the proper channels for works of propaganda.[21] Moreover, *Triumph of the Will* went against every precept that Goebbels had ordered the film industry to observe. Addressing representatives of the film industry on 28 March 1933, Goebbels condemned crude propaganda films that were 'out of touch with the spirit of the times': 'The new movement does not exhaust itself with parade-ground marching and blowing trumpets,' he said. Praising the Soviet director Sergei Eisenstein's film *Battleship Potemkin*, he declared that 'it is not only a film's convictions that make it good, but also the abilities of the people making it'. Films had to conform to the new spirit of the age, he said, but they also had to cater to popular taste.[22] Propaganda, Goebbels said, was most effective when it was indirect:

That is the secret of propaganda: to permeate the person it aims to grasp, without his even noticing that he is being permeated. *Of course* propaganda has a purpose, but the purpose must be concealed with such cleverness and virtuosity that the person on whom this purpose is to be carried out doesn't notice it at all.[23]

In pursuit of this policy, Goebbels sanctioned, perhaps even wrote, a scathing review of an early Nazi film set in the early 1930s, *SA-Man Brand*, with its crude, fictional and obviously propagandistic depiction of a sixteen-year-old working-class schoolboy who defied his Social

Democrat father to join the brownshirts, is victimized at work with the collusion of the Jewish-dominated trade union and is eventually shot dead by Communists, a martyr for the Nazi cause. Goebbels considered the film unlikely to win over any new adherents to the Nazi cause: it was addressed to the already converted. In October he sharply criticized another film glorifying the life and death of the brownshirt Horst Wessel, shot dead by a Communist in 1930. The film told a similar story to *SA-Man Brand*, but with a far stronger antisemitic content. It portrayed the Communists who eventually killed the hero as dupes of Jewish criminals and intellectuals. Goebbels declared that the film was not equal to Wessel's memory. 'We National Socialists', he said, 'see no value in our SA marching on the stage or screen; their place is on the streets. Such an ostensible show of National Socialist ideology is no substitute for real art.'[24]

On the morning of the Horst Wessel film's première, which was to have been attended by a wide variety of prominent figures in Berlin society, including the Hohenzollern Crown Prince, eldest son of the last Kaiser and a noted supporter of the Nazis, Goebbels issued a formal prohibition on its screening. His high-handed action aroused a furious reaction from the film's backers. These included Putzi Hanfstaengl, one of Hitler's old friends, who had composed the music for the film and had personally raised a good deal of the money needed to finance it. Complaining in person to Hitler and Goebbels, Hanfstaengl eventually managed to get enough support in the Party hierarchy to have the ban reversed, though only under the condition that the film's title was changed to *Hans Westmar: One of Many*. In this guise, the film won widespread approbation in the press and public, who rose to their feet in many cinemas as the Horst Wessel Song rang out in the final scene.[25] But Goebbels had made his point. The row convinced Hitler that the Propaganda Minister should have more effective control over the film industry in future. And he used it to ensure that straightforward propaganda films of this kind, which might have been popular amongst committed 'Old Fighters', but were no longer appropriate to the period when the Nazi Party had consolidated its rule, were not made again.[26]

II

The 1930s were a golden age of cinema worldwide, with the advent of sound and in some films colour too. Audiences in Germany increased, with the average number of visits per person per year almost doubling from four to nearly eight between 1932–3 and 1937–8, and tickets sold increasing over the same period from 240 million to almost 400 million a year.[27] Many leading film stars and directors had emigrated from Germany in the early-to-mid-1930s, some, like Marlene Dietrich, following the lure of Hollywood, others, like Fritz Lang, leaving for political reasons. But the majority remained. One of the most famous was Emil Jannings, who in his Hollywood days in the late 1920s had won the first ever Oscar for his performance in *The Last Command*. Back in Germany, Jannings soon found himself starring in overtly political films such as *The Ruler* (*Der Herrscher*), a celebration of strong leadership based loosely on a well-known play by Gerhart Hauptmann and set in a monied middle-class family of industrialists modelled on the Krupps. The script-writer, Thea von Harbou, who had worked on silent films such as Fritz Lang's *Metropolis* and *Dr Mabuse*, now made a new career for herself in the talkies during the 1930s. New stars such as the Swedish-born Zarah Leander achieved huge popularity among the cinema-going public, while others, like the German actor Theodor Loos, seemed to be an almost permanent presence on screen. A fresh generation of directors, among whom Veit Harlan was perhaps the most prominent, emerged to put across the Nazi message on film.[28] Not all those who played a part in the film industry of the Third Reich escaped hostile scrutiny, however. In 1935 and 1936 the Party encouraged cinemagoers to send in inquiries about the racial and political affiliations of leading screen actors. There were repeated inquiries about one of Germany's best-loved stars, Hans Albers, who was rumoured to have a Jewish wife. The rumour was true: his wife Hansi Burg was indeed Jewish; but Albers made sure she stayed in Switzerland for the duration of the Third Reich, out of harm's way. Goebbels, who knew this, felt unable to take any action, given Albers's extraordinary popularity, and the Propaganda Ministry's officials steadfastly denied Hansi Burg's existence.[29]

Actors such as Albers and Jannings played their part in boosting the extraordinary popularity of German cinema in the 1930s. Yet such successes were balanced out by the rapidly growing isolation of the German film industry. Foreign sales of German films plummeted. This was due partly to their increasing political content and declining quality, but above all to the hostility of foreign distributors, particularly if they were Jewish or had political objections to the controls which were now imposed on their colleagues in Germany. More serious still from the industry's point of view was the virtual cessation of imports of foreign films into Germany. The problems that faced foreign films can be illustrated through the unlikely figure of Mickey Mouse, who achieved enormous popularity in Germany in the early 1930s, spawning a huge range of merchandizing from model figures to comic books. One Pomeranian Nazi newspaper declared stridently in 1931: 'Micky Maus is the shabbiest, miserablest ideal ever invented.' But this was very much the exception. So popular was Mickey with the German cinema-going public that Nazi film censors were more or less forced to pass all of Disney's *Silly Symphonies* for exhibition. Disney's cartoon of *The Three Little Pigs* had a particular appeal to the censors, since it contained a scene, later excised by Disney, in which the big bad wolf appeared at the door of one of the pigs' houses disguised as a travelling brush salesman, with a cartoon-caricature false nose that the Nazis had no difficulty in interpreting as Jewish. *The Mad Doctor*, in which a crazed scientist tried to cross-breed the dog Pluto with a chicken, was a solitary exception, possibly banned because it could be taken as a satire on Nazi eugenic ideas, more likely because it was thought to be too frightening for children.[30]

Yet Disney's cartoons, enormously popular though they were in Germany, soon ran into difficulties all the same. The basic reason was financial. Roy Disney, who handled the financial side of his brother's business, concluded a new contract on 20 December 1933 with UFA to distribute Walt's films in Germany, but on 12 November 1934 the German government quadrupled import duties on films, forcing distributors to pay 20,000 Reichsmarks in tax for every foreign film they bought. The government also imposed stringent controls on currency exports, making it virtually impossible for American companies to take any income out of Germany at all. As a result, Universal and Warner Brothers closed their businesses in Germany, while Disney never made a profit from its massive German success. The situation was hardly eased by a change in the regulations on 19 February 1935. From this point, imported films had to be paid for by exchanges with the export of German films; but the Germans no longer made films that foreign distributors wanted to show. The hostility of American distributors and the American public to Nazi antisemitism would have made it difficult to show them even had this not been the case. In the autumn of 1937 the Disney contract with UFA ran out, and to make matters worse, Disney's accumulated assets in Germany were written off, partly to cover the bankruptcy of a major distributor. A visit to Berlin by Roy Disney failed to produce a solution, and by 1939 hardly any Disney cartoons were being shown in Germany at all. Adolf Hitler, who was given eighteen Mickey Mouse films by his Propaganda Minister Joseph Goebbels as a Christmas present in 1937, was a lucky exception to the rule.[31]

By the second half of the 1930s, state control over the German film industry had become even tighter, thanks to the Film Credit Bank created in June 1933 by the regime to help film-makers raise money in the straitened circumstances of the Depression. By 1936 it was funding nearly three-quarters of all German feature films, and was not afraid to withhold support from producers of whose projects it did not approve. Meanwhile, the Propaganda Ministry's control over the hiring and firing of people in all branches of the film industry had been cemented by the establishment of the Reich Film Chamber on 14 July 1933, headed by a financial official who was directly responsible to Goebbels himself. Anyone employed in the film industry was now obliged to become a member of the Reich Film Chamber, which organized itself into ten departments covering every aspect of the movie business in Germany.[32] The creation of the Reich Film Chamber in 1933 was a major step towards total control. The next year, Goebbels's hand was further strengthened by a crisis in the finances of the two biggest film companies, UFA and Tobis, which were effectively nationalized. By 1939, state-financed companies were producing nearly two-thirds of German films.[33] A German Film Academy, created in 1938, now provided technical training for the next generation of film-makers, actors, designers, writers, cameramen and technicians, ensuring that they would work in the spirit of the Nazi regime. Financial control was backed by legal powers, above all through the Reich Cinema Law, passed on 16 February 1934. This made pre-censorship of scripts mandatory. It also merged the existing film censors' offices, created in 1920, into a single bureau within the Propaganda Ministry. And as amended in 1935 it gave Goebbels the power to ban any films without reference to these institutions anyway. Encouragement was to be provided, and cinemagoers' expectations guided, by the award of marks of distinction to films, certifying them as 'artistically valuable', 'politically valuable', and so on.[34]

As Goebbels intended, there were plenty of entertainment films produced in Nazi Germany. Taking the categories prescribed by the Propaganda Ministry, fully 55 per cent of films shown in Germany in 1934 were comedies, 21 per cent dramas, 24 per cent political. The proportions fluctuated year by year, and there were some films that fell in practice into more than one category. In 1938, however, only 10 per cent were classed as political; 41 per cent were categorized as dramas and 49 per cent as comedies. The proportion of political films had declined, in other words, while that of dramas had sharply risen. Musicals, costume dramas, romantic comedies and other genres provided escapism and dulled people's sensibilities; but they could carry a message too.[35] All these films of whatever kind had to conform to the general principles laid down by the Reich Film Chamber, and many of the movies glorified leadership, advertised the peasant virtues of blood and soil, denigrated the Nazi hate-figures such as Bolsheviks and Jews, or depicted them as villains in otherwise apparently unpolitical dramas. Pacifist films were banned, and the Propaganda Ministry ensured that the correct line would be taken in genre movies of all kinds. Thus for example in September 1933, the *Film-Courier* magazine condemned the Weimar cinema's portrayal of 'a destructive, subversive criminal class, built up through fantasies of the metropolis into a destructive gigantism' – a clear reference to the films of Fritz Lang, such as *Metropolis* and *M* – and assured its readers that in future, films about crime would concentrate not on the criminal 'but on the heroes in uniform and in civilian dress' who were serving the people in the fight against criminality.[36] Even entertainment, therefore, could be political.[37]

Overt political propaganda was supplied by the newsreels, above all the *Weekly Review* (*Wochenschau*), which had to be shown at every commercial film programme from October 1938 onwards, and which devoted on average half its coverage to political issues alongside the usual fare of sport, society gossip and the like. Stylized, cliché-ridden, couched in a thoroughly Nazified language of combat and struggle, delivered by the voice-over speaker in a tone of unrelenting aggressiveness, and often portraying events especially staged for the purpose of being filmed, the newsreel's relation to reality was at best only intermediate. By 1939 all the newsreels, originally owned by a variety of companies, one of them American (the *Fox Talking Weekly Review*), were speaking with one voice, co-ordinated by a special office in the Propaganda Ministry and backed by a Newsreel Law passed in 1936. Like many other visual sources for the history of Nazi Germany, therefore, newsreel footage has to be used by the historian with a considerable degree of caution.[38] As far as contemporaries were concerned, the propaganda intent was obvious to all but the most obtuse of cinemagoers.

III

Newsreels were not the principal means by which most Germans learned about what was going on in their country and the rest of the world: of far more importance was radio, which had grown rapidly in popularity under the Weimar Republic. Everyone involved in the industry, from broadcasters to engineers and salesmen, had to belong to the Reich Radio Chamber, established in the autumn of 1933. This gave the Propaganda Ministry complete power over the hiring and firing of staff. German broadcasting had already been brought under government control earlier in the year; and regional stations were eventually incorporated into the Reich Radio Company on 1 April 1934 and subordinated directly to the Propaganda Ministry. The Nazis extended their grasp to the production of wireless sets as well, paying large subsidies to manufacturers to make and sell cheap radios known as People's Receivers (*Volksempfänger*), available for 76 Reichsmarks or in a smaller version at only 35. This was no more than the average weekly wage of a manual worker, and it was payable if required in instalments. One and a half million of these sets were already made in 1933. In 1934 over six million radio sets were in use in Germany, and by the middle of 1939 over 70 per cent of households in Germany owned a wireless, the highest percentage of any country in the world, including the USA. Many country people were

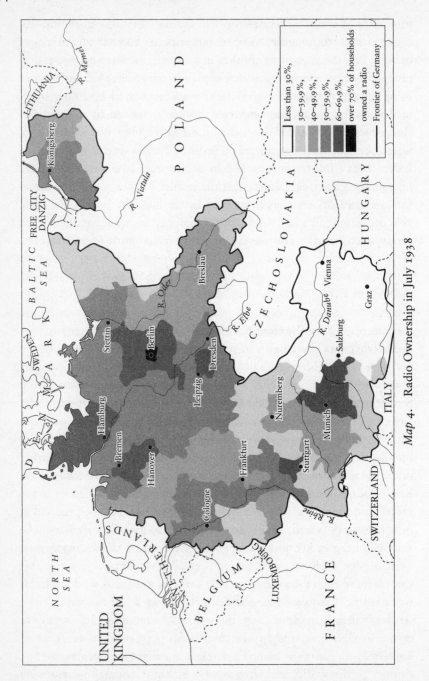

Map 4.   Radio Ownership in July 1938

brought within reach of government propaganda on a regular basis for the first time by this means. The spread of the radio enabled the regime to bring its message to parts of the nation that had hitherto been relatively remote from the political world. Altogether, over seven million People's Receivers were manufactured; by 1943 every third radio set in Germany's homes was a People's Receiver. A particular feature of the People's Receiver was that it only had a limited range, so that away from border areas, listeners were unable to tune in to foreign radio stations. On special occasions, radio wardens would arrange for a speech by Hitler to be broadcast over loudspeakers in public places, on factory shop-floors, in offices, schools and restaurants. On the sounding of a siren, people were supposed to stop whatever they were doing and gather round the radio set or within hearing distance of the loudspeaker for a session of communal listening. They were also meant to listen to 'Hour of the Nation', broadcast every evening on all stations from seven to eight o'clock. Plans were even laid for a nationwide network of 6,000 loudspeaker pillars to facilitate public listening; their implementation was interrupted only by the outbreak of war in 1939.[39]

Already on 25 March 1933, Goebbels had told broadcasters and radio managers that 'radio will be purged' of nonconformists and leftists, and asked them to undertake this task themselves, otherwise he would do it for them. By the summer, the airwaves had indeed been purged. Often this could mean real hardship for the dismissed. One of many affected was the novelist, poet and journalist Jochen Klepper. Born in 1903, he was not Jewish, but his wife was, a fact that aroused suspicion in itself. And though he was a deeply religious Protestant, he had a Social Democratic past. An anonymous denunciation brought about his dismissal from the state-controlled radio in June 1933. Like many such people, he now feared for his economic future. Publishing novels and poems was no substitute for his radio job, and in any case he thought it quite likely that he would be banned from publishing too. 'I can't really believe that the German Publishing Institution will stand by me', he wrote despairingly. 'How is a publishing house to keep an author afloat these days if he does not explicitly represent the "nation's hope"?' Finally he was rescued by an appointment to work on the staff of the Ullstein Publishing Company's radio magazine.[40] Many others had to emigrate, or go into an impecunious early retirement. But Goebbels was not content with mere personnel changes. In the same address to radio executives and producers, he went on to state, with remarkable candour:

There is nothing at all that is without political bias. The discovery of the principle of absolute objectivity is the privilege of German university professors – and I do not believe that university professors make history. We make no bones about the fact that the radio belongs to us and to no one else. And we will place the radio in the service of our ideology, and no other ideology will find expression here . . .[41]

But just as in film, so in radio, Goebbels knew that people would not tolerate a diet of unremitting propaganda. Already in May 1933 he began turning down requests from Nazi Party bosses keen to hear their voices on the radio, and limited broadcasts of political speeches to two a month.[42]

Radio, said the Propaganda Minister, had to be imaginative, modern, up-to-date. 'The first law', he told radio managers on 25 March 1933: 'Don't become boring!' They were not to fill their programmes with martial music and patriotic speeches. They had to use their imagination. Radio could bring the whole people behind the regime.[43] Despite this warning, the radio network was initially used for broadcasting large quantities of political propaganda, with fifty speeches by Hitler being transmitted in 1933 alone. On 1 May 1934 broadcasts of the Mayday celebrations, with their speeches, songs, marches and the rest, took up no fewer than seventeen hours of radio time. No wonder that there were reports that listeners were growing blasé in the face of such excesses and listening, when they could, to foreign radio stations. Only gradually was Goebbels's oft-repeated advice heeded. From 1932 to 1939 the proportion of broadcasting time devoted to music grew steadily. By 1939 the total broadcasting hours devoted to 'literature' and 'talks' had been cut to around 7 per cent; two-thirds of broadcasting time was now taken up by music, seven-eighths of it popular rather than classical. Particularly successful was the regular request concert, introduced in 1936 and purveying hit songs and entertainment music whose style remained generally unchanged from that of the Weimar years. But some still complained that even the music was boring, and they missed the radio plays that had been so popular under the Weimar Republic.[44] As the Security Service of the SS complained in 1938, the 'dissatisfaction of radio listeners' was demonstrating itself in the fact that 'almost all kinds of German radio listeners ... now as before regularly listen to German-language broadcasts from foreign stations'.[45]

IV

Goebbels's multi-faceted campaign to mobilize the spirit of the German people in the service of the Third Reich and its ideas did not run entirely smoothly. For, in a manner characteristic of so many areas of the regime, he was far from enjoying a monopoly over the territory he claimed as his own. Already in the course of the discussions leading up to the creation of the Propaganda Ministry, his original intention of including education under its aegis had been frustrated by Hitler, who had passed education over to a separate ministry headed by Bernhard Rust. More seriously, however, Goebbels had to battle for supremacy over the cultural sphere against the self-designated Party ideologue Alfred Rosenberg, who saw it as his duty to propagate Nazi ideology, and in particular his own elaborate version of it, throughout German culture. At the end of the 1920s, Rosenberg had become leader of the Fighting League for German Culture (Kampfbund für deutsche Kultur), one of many specialist organizations established within the Party at the time. In 1933, the League moved swiftly to take 'co-ordinate' German theatrical institutions under its control.[46] Rosenberg was also keen to impose ideological purity on many other aspects of German culture, including music and the visual arts, the Churches, and university and intellectual life, all areas that Goebbels had originally envisaged falling under the control of the Ministry of Propaganda.[47] The Fighting League for German Culture was small but very active. Its membership increased from 2,100 in January 1932 to 6,000 a year later, 10,000 in April 1933, and 38,000 by the following October. Many of the assaults on Jewish and left-wing musicians that took place in the spring and early summer of 1933 were organized or inspired by the Fighting League for German Culture, to which a substantial number of far-right music critics and writers belonged. In addition, Rosenberg had a powerful propaganda weapon at his disposal in the shape of the Racial Observer, the Nazi daily newspaper, of which he was the editor-in-chief. To make matters worse for Goebbels, Rosenberg's views on art and music were much more in tune with Hitler's than were his own, and on more than one occasion, Goebbels's penchant for cultural innovation threatened to give Rosenberg the upper hand.[48]

Goebbels himself had little time for Rosenberg, whose magnum opus, *The Myth of the Twentieth Century*, he is said to have called a 'philosophical belch'.[49] While Rosenberg's office was a purely Party institution, Goebbels had the advantage of combining his Party strength as Reich Propaganda Leader with the power of a fully fledged Ministry of State that was at the same time politically unimpeachable because it was staffed by committed Party members. Hitler did not think very highly of Rosenberg's political abilities, perhaps as a result of the mess Rosenberg had made of things when put in charge of the Party after the abortive beer-hall putsch in Munich in 1923. So he refused to give him a government appointment. Moreover, while he shared many of his cruder prejudices, Hitler had almost as low an opinion of Rosenberg's pretentious, pseudo-philosophical theorizing as Goebbels did. He never admitted him to the inner circle of his friends and companions. Already by the summer of 1933 the disruption caused by the Fighting League for German Culture had begun to become politically inconvenient.[50] On 22 September 1933, Goebbels succeeded in getting a decree passed to establish the Reich Culture Chamber, with himself as President. It contained seven designated sub-sections, also known as Chambers – literature, theatre, music, radio, film, fine arts, and the press, corresponding to the divisions already established in his Ministry. Some of these specialized Chambers already existed, as with the Reich Film Chamber, or were in the process of formation; now they became monopoly state institutions. Goebbels was able to recapture German theatre from Rosenberg in this way. The legal requirement that anyone who wished to work in any of these areas had to be a member of the appropriate Chamber gave Goebbels the power to exclude anyone whose views were unacceptable to the regime and effectively marginalized Rosenberg in the cultural sphere. Goebbels also used the Reich Culture Chamber to establish better pension rights and to crack down on the untrained and unqualified, though this latter policy was softened from 1935 onwards. At the same time, he took care to present the Reich Culture Chamber and its specialist sub-Chambers as a form of cultural self-administration. The Propaganda Ministry would manage them with a light touch while the real power supposedly lay with the senior artists, musicians and writers who presided over them and ran them on a day-to-day basis. In these ways, the Propaganda Minister won the support of the overwhelming majority of those Germans who depended on culture in one form or another for their living – and their numbers were considerable: 35,000 in the Reich Chamber for Visual Arts in 1937, for example, 95,600 in the Reich Music Chamber, 41,100 in the Reich Theatre Chamber at the same date.[51]

The Reich Culture Chamber was inaugurated in a grand ceremony presided over by Hitler himself at the Berlin Philharmonic Hall on 15 November 1933, with music from the hall's prestigious resident orchestra conducted first by Wilhelm Furtwängler and then by Richard Strauss, followed by a speech from Goebbels and a chorus ('Awake! Full soon will dawn the day!') from Wagner's *The Mastersingers of Nuremberg*. Rosenberg was subsequently fobbed off with the grandiloquent but essentially empty title of 'Representative of the Leader for the Overall Philosophical and Intellectual Training and Education of the National Socialist Party', granted to him on 24 January 1934. His Fighting League for German Culture, renamed in more neutral terms as the National Socialist Cultural Community in 1934, struggled on, a kind of cultural counterpart to the brownshirts, deprived of a role now that the battle against Nazism's opponents had been won, until it was finally dissolved in 1937.[52] Rosenberg continued to make trouble for Goebbels from time to time, but in the end he was not effective enough seriously to trouble the Propaganda Minster's dominance of the cultural scene, once Goebbels had abandoned his toleration of cultural modernism in the face of Hitler's obdurate hostility to it.[53]

Rosenberg was not the only senior figure with whom Goebbels had to contend. Hitler, who had at one time earned a living from painting postcards, took an intense personal interest in the visual arts. He was an enthusiast for the music of Richard Wagner, developed an obsession with architecture, and spent much of his time watching films in his private cinema. Then there was Hermann Göring, whose position as Prussian Minister-President put him in control of many major cultural institutions run and financed by the Prussian state, though he made no attempt at influencing cultural policy in a wider sense. The Education Minister Bernhard Rust was also heavily involved in cultural policies, particularly where they affected the young. He established a panel of senior musicians, including the conductor Wilhelm Furtwängler, the pianist Wilhelm Backhaus and others, to control and in effect censor the programmes of all concerts and other musical events in Berlin. He oversaw institutions such as music conservatories and art academies. His main concern seems to have been to keep the Propaganda Ministry from encroaching on his sphere of influence, an ever-present danger given the original claim of the Ministry to include education in its remit. Finally, the Nazi Labour Front, led by Robert Ley, absorbed a large number of artists and musicians and their organizations during its takeover of the trade unions in May 1933 and seemed determined to defend the position it had thereby gained in musical life against all comers. Demarcation disputes between these various organizations and their leaders became so violent that the Education Ministry actually attempted to ban public discussion of artistic issues on 15 July 1933, though without success.[54]

Whatever their differences, and however much they varied on points of detail, all the Nazi cultural organizations and their leaders were agreed that Jews and political opponents of the Nazi regime had to be removed from cultural life as quickly as possible, and that 'cultural Bolshevism' had to be destroyed, though they disagreed frequently about the particular individuals and works to which the concept could be applied. In the course of 1933 and the following years, some 2,000 artists, writers, musicians, film actors and directors, journalists, architects and others active in the cultural sphere left Germany, some of them because they disagreed with Nazism, many because they were Jewish and so had been deprived of the work that gave them their livelihood. Removing Jews from the Reich Chamber of Culture took some time partly because of objections from the Economics Ministry, which thought it would be economically damaging. By the middle of 1935, however, it was done.[55] Purged of dissidents and nonconformists, and those whom the regime regarded as racially undesirable, German culture and the German mass media now faced a future of growing regimentation and control. The many quarrels between the leading Nazi contenders for supremacy in these areas did little or nothing to hinder its arrival.

WRITING FOR GERMANY

I

In the 1920s and early 1930s there was no doubt which newspaper in Germany had the widest national and international reputation. The *Frankfurt Newspaper* (*Frankfurter Zeitung*) was renowned the world over for its thorough and objective reporting, its fair-minded opinion columns and its high intellectual standards. If there was one German newspaper to which foreigners who wished to know what was going on in the country turned, this was it. Although its readership was not large, it was highly educated and included many key formers of opinion. Politically liberal, the paper had long remained independent of the great press empires that had grown up around figures such as Alfred Hugenberg or the Mosse and Ullstein families. Its editorial and personnel policy was determined not by a chief executive but by the collective decision of an editorial board. Under the Weimar Republic, however, it got into financial difficulties and had to make over a controlling interest to the massive I.G. Farben chemical concern, which soon began to compromise its editorial independence, above all in questions of economic policy. By 1932 its editorials were arguing that it was time to bring Hitler and the Nazis into a coalition government and to rescue Germany from the crisis by reforming the Weimar constitution in an authoritarian direction.[56]

The newspaper's staff bent with the wind in the early months of 1933, editorializing in favour of the suppression of the Communist Party after the Reichstag fire and abandoning their previous criticisms of the Nazis. But their liberal reputation prompted the invasion of the paper's offices by an armed squad of stormtroopers on 11 March 1933 and the threat that the paper would be banned if it did not toe the line in every respect.

Soon editorial staff began to resign, and the board bowed to pressure from the Propaganda Ministry to dismiss Jews; by the end of 1936 there was none left in its employ, though two half-Jews and two spouses of Jews still remained. Seeing which way things were moving, the Jewish family of the paper's founder, Leopold Sonnemann, sold its shares on 1 June 1934 to I.G. Farben, who now possessed a 98 per cent stake in the paper's parent firm. At this stage, the Nazi regime could not afford to offend the giant chemical combine, whose help it needed in its programmes of rearmament and job creation. I.G. Farben had originally bought into the paper in order to generate more favourable publicity for itself at home and abroad among those whose opinions counted, but its leading figures such as Carl Bosch were also political and cultural conservatives who did not want to see the paper's central features disappear. Quite apart from this, too, Hitler and Goebbels valued the paper's reputation abroad and did not want to alarm foreign opinion by forcing it to change too radically. All this meant that the paper had rather more freedom of action under the Third Reich than the rest of the press did.[57]

Thus the paper's foreign correspondents continued to file stories on foreign criticism of the Nazis well into the mid-1930s. And its editors, particularly in the cultural pages of the *Feuilleton* section of the paper, not uncommonly failed to print stories emanating from the Propaganda Ministry, even when they were ordered to do so by Goebbels. They attempted, sometimes successfully, to carry articles emphasizing the humane values which they considered the Nazis to be trampling on. Many of the forty new members of the editorial staff appointed between 1933 and 1939 came from parts of the press that had fared badly under the Nazis, including Social Democrats, Nationalists and Catholics. Many of them, such as Walter Dirks, or Paul Sethe, became famous West German journalists in the postwar years. Two other well-known writers, Dolf Sternberger and Otto Suhr, who had Jewish wives, were also able to remain in their posts.[58] Staff writers printed ostensibly historical articles about Genghis Khan or Robespierre whose parallels with Hitler were obvious to the average intelligent reader. They became adept at conveying facts and reports that were unpalatable to the regime with formulae such as 'there is no truth in the rumour that' and headlines that denounced as lies stories which were then expounded in considerable detail. The paper soon acquired a reputation as virtually the only organ in which such things could be found, and its circulation actually began to increase once more.[59]

The Gestapo was well aware of the fact that the *Frankfurt Newspaper* in particular contained articles that 'must be described as malicious agitation' and thought that 'now as before the *Frankfurt Newspaper* dedicates itself to the representation of Jewish interests'.[60] Until 1938, indeed, the paper continued to carry Leopold Sonnemann's name on its masthead, dropping it only when directly ordered to by the government.[61] 'The virtuosity with which attempts are made to alter National Socialist principles and trains of thought and to change their meaning', the Gestapo complained on another occasion, 'is sometimes astounding.'[62] Yet with time, and especially after 1936, the regime forced the paper more and more onto the defensive. Innumerable compromises with the Propaganda Ministry's instructions were unavoidable. Direct resistance was barely possible. Already in August 1933 the English journalist Henry Wickham Steed noted that the once-proud liberal newspaper had become a 'tool of unfreedom' under the new regime.[63] The foreign press quickly stopped citing stories carried in the paper, taking the view that they had now become mostly indistinguishable from the torrent of misinformation and propaganda pumped out on a daily basis by Goebbels's Ministry.[64] In 1938, realizing that it no longer needed to influence public opinion, since there was effectively no public opinion left in Germany, I.G. Farben secretly sold the firm to a subsidiary of the Nazi Party's Eher Publishing House without even troubling to inform the paper's editors or staff. On 20 April 1939 the Nazi Party's publishing mogul, Max Amann, formally presented the newspaper to Hitler as a birthday present. Its function as a vehicle for free, if disguised, comment was over; its readership declined further, and it was eventually closed down altogether in 1943.[65]

That it had managed to retain even a vestige of independence for so long was remarkable. As with other areas of propaganda and culture, central control over newspaper personnel was established in the autumn of 1933, with the creation of the Reich Press Chamber under Max Amann. Working in the publishing industry was impossible for non-members of the Chamber. Amann was able to take over an increasing number of papers as head of the Eher Publishing House, by exploiting the weak financial position of the press in the Depression and by depriving rival papers of revenue by switching government advertising contracts to the Nazi press. Readers anxious not to be stigmatized by subscribing to a liberal paper switched their allegiance. By the beginning of 1934 the circulation of the liberal *Berlin Daily News-Sheet* (*Berliner Tageblatt*) had fallen from 130,000 to less than 75,000, and that of the venerable *Vossian Newspaper* (*Vossische Zeitung*) from 80,000 to just under 50,000. The Nazis expanded their press empire from 59 daily newspapers with a combined circulation of 782,121 at the beginning of 1933 to 86 papers with a total circulation of over three million by the end of the year. In 1934 they bought the large Jewish publishing firm of Ullstein, responsible for some of Germany's most respected dailies. Fortified by new regulations of the Reich Press Chamber issued in April 1935, banning confessional or 'special interest group' papers, debarring business corporations, foundations, societies and other organizations from press ownership, and enabling him to close papers that were financially unsound or owned by non-Aryans, Amann was able to close down or buy up between 500 and 600 more newspapers in 1935–6. By 1939 the Eher Publishing House owned or controlled over two-thirds of German newspapers and magazines.[66]

While Amann was busy buying up the German press, Goebbels and his ally Otto Dietrich, the head of the Nazi press bureau, were extending their own controls over its contents. Dietrich secured the promulgation on 4 October 1933 of a new Editors' Law, which made editors personally responsible for the content of their papers, removed the proprietors' powers of dismissal and laid down rules governing the content of newspapers, which were not to print anything 'which is calculated to weaken the strength of the German Reich abroad or at home, the community will of the German people, German defence, culture or the economy, or to injure the religious sensibilities of others'. Membership in the Reich Association of the German Press was now compulsory by law and subject to revocation if a journalist contravened a code of conduct enforced by professional courts. As a result, within two years of Hitler's appointment as Chancellor, 1,300 Jewish, Social Democratic and left-liberal journalists had been barred from working. Thus Goebbels ensured control through the editors and journalists, while Amann established it through the Press Chamber and the proprietors.[67] At a regional and local level, however, as middle-ranking Nazi officials took the initiative in assuming control over the press, both means were often used at once, particularly where a regional newspaper publishing house was established. Enforcing by one means or another the closure of rival papers not only eliminated ideological alternatives to local Nazi papers but also turned them from often struggling small businesses into thriving and profitable enterprises.[68]

Towering over all other newspapers in the Nazi era was the Party's own daily, the *Racial Observer*. Alone amongst German dailies, it was a national paper, published in Munich and Berlin at the same time. The mouthpiece of the Party leadership, it became essential reading for the party faithful and indeed anyone else who wanted to be told what to think and believe. Teachers in particular subscribed to it so that they could use it in their classes and on occasion check out their pupils' essays to see if they were lifted from its pages, before daring to criticize them for either style or content. The paper's circulation shot up from 116,000 in 1932 to 1,192,500 in 1941, the first German paper to sell more than a million copies a day. Its editor, Wilhelm Weiss, injected a stronger factual content into its pages after 1933, but he also encouraged writers to employ a hectoring, threatening, triumphalist tone in their articles, advertising on a daily basis the arrogance of Nazi power and the Party's determination to destroy anyone who could be considered a threat to it. He was unable, however, to persuade the Party to fund a permanent staff of full-time foreign correspondents, and had to rely largely on press agency reports for foreign news instead. The *Racial Observer* was followed by a whole range of other newspapers and magazines, notably Julius Streicher's sensationalist *The Stormer*, which achieved a circulation of something like 500,000 by 1937 compared to 65,000 three years before, largely thanks to block orders from Nazi organizations of one kind and another. It was widely sold on the streets, its front page displayed in advertising boxes for all to see. So obviously untrue were many of its stories of ritual murder and similar atrocities supposedly committed by Jews, and so clearly pornographic were its regular reports of sex scandals involving Jewish men and non-Jewish German girls, that many people refused to have copies in their houses; the Party leadership was even forced to withdraw it from circulation on occasion. On the other hand, numerous readers wrote in to the paper to denounce in its pages neighbours and acquaintances who failed to give the Hitler salute, or mixed with Jews, or uttered statements critical of the regime, and a notable feature of the paper was its organization of public petitions for the closure of Jewish businesses and similar antisemitic actions. Block orders also accounted for the high circulation figures of less sensationalist Party magazines such as *The SA Man*, which sold 750,000 copies a week to the stormtrooper movement in the middle of the 1930s. Individual subscriptions tended to go instead to the illustrated weekly magazines, which concentrated on less overtly political articles and pictures.[69]

Goebbels was clear that control over the press should mean that all newspapers and magazines should follow the same line. To help steer their content from the centre, the Propaganda Ministry took over the two main press agencies, Hugenberg's Telegraph Union and the rival Wolff's Telegraph Office, in December 1933 and merged them into the German News Office. This supplied not only much of the national and international news content for all papers but also commentaries and instructions as to how the news was to be interpreted. Editors were banned from taking their news from any other source except from their own correspondents. Goebbels's instructions to editors, issued at regular press conferences and conveyed over the wire to regional press offices for the benefit of the local press, included frequent bans as well as orders about what to print. 'Pictures which show Ludendorff together with the Leader or at the same time must under no circumstances be published', said one such instruction issued on 6 April 1935. 'Ambassador von Ribbentrop suffered a car accident yesterday. His oldest daughter was severely injured in this accident. The ambassador himself is unhurt. This incident must not be reported in the German press,' ran another sent out on 14 April 1936. 'In future the names of leading Soviet officials and politicians will only be cited with the prefix "Jew" and their Jewish name, insofar as they are Jewish', the German press was told on 24 April 1936. 'The visit of SA-leaders of the Central Group to the Freemasonry Museum during their presence in Berlin may not be reported,' editors were instructed on 25 April 1936. 'Reports on Greta Garbo may be positive,' they learned, perhaps to their relief, on 20 November 1937.[70] The detail was astonishing, and was intended to leave little room for initiative on the part of editors.[71]

The results of these measures were not wholly successful. As the example of the *Frankfurt Newspaper* showed, an intelligent and determined editor or correspondent could still convey news that the regime did not want people to read, or engage in veiled criticism of the regime's actions in the guise of writing about subjects such as dictatorships in Ancient Greece or Rome. On 20 April 1935, a local paper, the *Schweinitz District News-Sheet* (*Schweinitzer Kreisblatt*), printed a large photograph of Hitler on the front page in such a way that part of his head covered the letters '*itzer*' in the title, leaving the letters '*Schwein*', the German for 'pig', to provide what the Gestapo, who promptly banned the paper for three days, thought of as an insulting description of the Leader. It is unlikely that the offending layout was an accident.[72] Nevertheless, whatever the journalists of the *Frankfurt Newspaper* might have been able to achieve, the majority of editors and journalists lacked the ability or the inclination to vary the propaganda they were required to serve up to their readers with any touch of independence or originality. The number of newspapers declined from 4,700 to 977 between 1932 and 1944, and the number of magazines and periodicals of all kinds from 10,000 to 5,000 between 1933 and 1938. And the contents of those that remained became increasingly homogeneous. Moreover, the rapid increase in the importance of radio as a purveyor of instant, up-to-the-minute news confronted daily newspapers with a problem that they still face today, namely how to retain readers when the news they print is not new any more.[73] The result was a crescendo of dissatisfaction amongst the newspaper-reading public, relayed through the regular surveillance reports of the Gestapo. 'The uniformity of the press', noted the Gestapo office in Kassel in its monthly report for March 1935, 'is felt to be unbearable by the people and also in particular by those who are National Socialist in their views.' Furthermore, the report went on, people did not understand why they could not read any reports in the press about things that were everyday current knowledge but were evidently thought too sensitive by the authorities to print. That was the way, the Gestapo considered, to allow rumours to take hold or, just as bad, to prompt people to get their news from the foreign press, particularly German-language newspapers printed in Switzerland, which were selling increasing numbers of copies even in small communities well outside the big cities.[74]

But the regime had taken steps to deal with this problem too, and not merely by exercising the power of confiscation of foreign press imports.

The Reich Press Chamber controlled the Reich Association of German Railway Station Booksellers, and this body made sure that 'it must be the first duty of station booksellers to spread German ideas. The leaseholders of station bookshops must be instructed to desist from everything that could promote the distribution of foreign papers.' And what applied to railway station kiosks also applied to high street news-agents as well.[75] With such restrictions in place, it is not surprising that the public became even more distrustful of what they read in the newspapers, as Gestapo reports indicated in 1934–5. They turned instead to other sources. In the course of 1934 alone the circulation of the Party press decreased by over a million all told, and it would have fallen still further in this and subsequent years but for bulk orders by Nazi Party organizations. In Cologne, the circulation of the local Nazi paper dropped from 203,000 in January 1934 to 186,000 in January 1935, while that of the local Catholic paper rose from 81,000 to 88,000 over the same period. Similar developments could be observed in other parts of Germany too. It was therefore less than surprising that 24 April 1935 saw the introduction of the 'Amann regulations', which allowed for the revocation of the licence of any paper if it was deemed to be offering 'unfair competition' or doing 'moral harm' to the readership. The Party press did do a bit better after this; but only because competition was being eliminated, and people were being forced by threats and intimidation to subscribe to Party newspapers instead.[76]

Control over the press therefore was gradually tightened as the regime found a variety of ways to stamp out dissent. Journalists, editors and other staff constantly had to make difficult decisions as to how far they could follow the regime's dictates without wholly abandoning their professional integrity. As time went on, however, they had little choice but to surrender it almost entirely, and all who did not were ousted from their posts. Despite his loudly proclaimed injunction to broadcasters and pressmen not to be boring, Goebbels ended up, therefore, by imposing a political straitjacket on radio and the press that led to widespread popular complaints about the monotonous conformity of these two key opinion-forming mass media and the dull subservience of those who worked in them. Already in 1934 he was telling newspapermen how pleased he was that the press was now reacting to current events correctly without necessarily being told how to.[77] But with his customary cynicism, he concluded a few years later that 'any man who still has a residue of honour will be very careful not to become a journalist'.[78]

II

When he wrote *Little Man – What Now?*, published in June 1932, Hans Fallada created the last best-selling serious novel of the Weimar Republic. It sold over 40,000 copies in the first ten months, it was serialized in no fewer than ten daily papers, it was turned into a film, and it rescued the book's publisher Ernst Rowohlt from almost certain bankruptcy. The title itself seemed to sum up the predicament of so many Germans in the desperate last months of 1932, when there seemed no way out of economic depression and political impasse. Many readers could identify with the novel's protagonist, the humble clerk Johannes Pinneberg, who went through one humiliation after another. He had to come to terms with the fact that his girl-friend was pregnant. He had to marry her despite the hostility of her father. He had to go through numerous travails in order to find a flat for the couple to live in. And then he had to adjust himself to family life when the baby arrived. Inevitably, after many anxious moments, Pinneberg lost his job and joined the swelling ranks of the unemployed. But unlike other characters in the book, he did not take to crime to make ends meet. He remained upright and decent in the face of adversity. That he was able to do so was possible above all because of his wife, who after overcoming her initial inexperience, managed to create a home life that became a refuge from the cruelties and hardships of the world outside. In the end, indeed, it was the wife, 'Lambkin', who became the novel's central character and whose portrayal was generally agreed to be the key element in the novel's popularity.[79]

'Hans Fallada', the pen-name of Rudolf Ditzen, born in Greifswald in 1893, was not a great writer or a major literary figure. His novels and short stories achieved popularity above all because of their gritty realism and their close attention to the humdrum detail of everyday life. He was a very German figure, who would have found it difficult to make a living from his writing in any other country. Emigration, therefore, was scarcely an option, and in any case, as a largely unpolitical writer and a non-Jew,

Rudolf Ditzen did not see why he should leave.[80] A member of no political party, and too popular an author to have been elected to august bodies like the Prussian Academy of Arts, he was not considered particularly objectionable by the regime. His books were not amongst those burned on the funeral pyres of literary freedom in Germany's university towns on 10 May 1933. But he had no other means of making a living apart from his writing, and he had an expensive drinking habit to maintain. During the Weimar Republic, nervous breakdowns and bouts of drug addiction, alcoholism and delinquency had landed him for considerable periods of time in prisons and asylums. These provided the basis for a new novel, *Once a Jailbird*, completed in November 1933.[81]

In order to get the book published, Ditzen felt it necessary to write a preface claiming that the appalling criminal justice system the book depicted was a thing of the past, an assertion which he must have known was the reverse of the truth. Even his publisher, Ernst Rowohlt, considered this 'too ingratiating'. But Rowohlt himself had been obliged to make his own compromises. Half the books he had previously published were now banned, and to keep his firm going he replaced them with more acceptable titles, as well as engaging well-known right-wing figures, though not out-and-out Nazis, like Ernst von Salomon, a nationalist author who had been implicated in the murder of Walther Rathenau, the liberal, Jewish-born Foreign Minister of the early Weimar Republic. Behind the scenes, too, Rowohlt had worked to get American visas to enable his Jewish authors to emigrate, though as a private employer he was not obliged to dismiss his Jewish staff until 1936, and he kept on key figures such as Ditzen's Jewish editor Paul Mayer. Income from the sale of foreign rights fell sharply as a result of Rowohlt's enforced slashing of his list. Rowohlt became a Nazi Party member to try and ease his situation, while he employed Jewish typists and proof-readers and ex-Communist illustrators on a freelance basis behind the scenes. None of this saved him, however; his firm was taken over by the giant Ullstein Publishing House, itself now a part of the Nazis' Eher Publishing House, and in July 1938 he was expelled from the Reich Literary Chamber and banned from publishing. His firm was passed over to the German Publishing Institution, which eventually wound it up. He left for Brazil, returning somewhat surprisingly in 1940 because he thought the Hitler regime by this time was on its last legs.[82]

All this made life increasingly difficult for Ditzen, who relied a good deal on the close personal support of his publisher. Retreating to his modest and remote country home in Mecklenburg, he hoped to continue to make a living by writing fairy-tales and children's books. In his serious social novels, he aimed at making enough concessions to the regime to keep it happy, while preserving the essence of his work intact and avoiding being co-opted into the regime's violent antisemitism. This was not easy for someone whose novels were all about contemporary German life. In 1934, Ditzen tried to strike a balance by removing all references to the brownshirts from a new edition of *Little Man – What Now?* He turned a violent SA man into an aggressively inclined goal-keeper, while retaining the novel's positive depiction of its Jewish characters. He refused to modify its description of the Communist sympathies of its heroine, 'Lambkin'. But his most recent novel, *Once a Jailbird*, was fiercely attacked in the Nazi press for its supposedly sympathetic attitude to criminal 'degenerates'. Ditzen riposted with a new novel set in the rural world of North Germany, *Once We Had a Child* (1934), which he hoped could appeal to Nazi ideas of 'blood and soil'. In practice lacked most of the genre's key features such as earth-mothers, racism, anti-intellectualism and above all the view of contact with the land as a source of national renewal (the main character in fact was a failure in life and remained so to the end).[83]

Under growing pressure from the regime, Ditzen's balancing act began to wobble ever more violently. His next novel, *Old Heart Goes A-Journeying*, not one of his best, ran into trouble because it depicted Christianity rather than Nazism as the basis for uniting the people. It led to his being classified by the Reich Literary Chamber as an 'unwanted author'. Although the classification was soon revoked, Ditzen began to suffer from renewed bouts of depression serious enough to require hospitalization. However, another novel, *Wolf among Wolves*, set in the inflation of 1923, met with a more favourable response from the Nazis ('a fantastic book', Goebbels noted in his diary for 31 January 1938). They approved of its sharply critical portrayal of the Weimar Republic, and the book sold well on its publication in 1937. Its success led to *Iron Gustav*, a family saga centred around a conservative coachman who refused to compromise with the motor car. Intended from the start to be filmed, with Emil Jannings in the starring role, it attracted the attention of Goebbels himself, who insisted against the author's original intentions that Ditzen bring the story up to 1933, when he had to show how the hero became a Nazi and the villain a Communist. Despite the fact that Ditzen went along with this humiliating compromise, the film was never made, because Alfred Rosenberg raised serious objections to any filming of a novel by 'Hans Fallada', and the book was quickly withdrawn from the bookshops after being criticized as destructive and subversive. *Iron Gustav* turned out in fact to be Ditzen's last serious novel published under the Third Reich. The next one, *The Drinker*, a graphic portrayal of one man's descent into alcoholism, written in the first person, ran counter to everything the Third Reich thought should be dealt with in works of literature. Interwoven with it on the pages of the manuscript, written upside-down, between the lines, and across the page, so as to make the whole extremely difficult to decipher, was a lengthy account of Ditzen's own life under the Nazis, shot through with sharp criticism of the regime and suffused with guilt about the compromises he had made. Neither saw the light of day until after Ditzen's death in 1947. At the time he was writing the manuscript, he was incarcerated in a prison for the criminally insane. 'I know I'm weak,' he wrote to his mother shortly after the war, 'but not bad, never bad.'[84]

III

Rudolf Ditzen's travails showed how limited the possibilities were for authors who remained in Germany. Nearly all of the country's internationally famous writers were in exile, including Thomas and Heinrich Mann, Lion Feuchtwanger, Bertolt Brecht, Arnold Zweig, Erich Maria Remarque and many others. Here they quickly organized publishing ventures, refounded banned magazines, mounted lecture and reading tours, and tried to warn the rest of the world about the menace of Nazism. Many of the now-classic fictional accounts of the Nazi rise to power and the first years of the Third Reich came from this exile milieu in the mid-to-late 1930s, from Feuchtwanger's *The Oppermanns* to Zweig's *The Axe of Wandsbek*. Some, like Brecht's *The Resistible Rise of Arturo Ui*, asked why no one had stopped Hitler coming to power; others, like Klaus Mann's *Mephisto*, explored the personal and moral motivations of those who had stayed on to work with the regime. None of these, needless to say, found any distribution within Germany itself. Any writer who had been associated with the anti-fascist movement in the Weimar Republic and had remained in Germany was either under constant surveillance or already in prison.[85]

Probably the most prominent of these was the pacifist journalist and essayist Carl von Ossietzky, the editor of the famous left-wing periodical *The World Stage* (*Die Weltbühne*), who had been unsparing in his ridiculing of Hitler before 30 January 1933. Imprisoned in concentration camps since the beginning of the Third Reich and badly maltreated by the guards, Ossietzky became the focus of an international campaign for the award of the Nobel Peace Prize among other things, for his work in exposing clandestine German rearmament in the late 1920s. The campaign succeeded in drawing attention to Ossietzky's fragile state of health and in persuading the International Red Cross to put pressure on the regime for his release. Continual bad publicity in the foreign press over the beatings and insults Ossietzky had had to endure achieved the desired effect, and the journalist was transferred to a hospital in Berlin in May 1936 in order, as the Propaganda Ministry declared, 'not to give foreign media the opportunity to accuse the German government of causing Ossietzky's death in prison'. Despite all the efforts of the German government to stop it, Ossietzky was awarded the Nobel Peace Prize in November 1936. The writer was prevented from going to Oslo to accept it. His representative at the ceremony embezzled the prize money and Ossietzky never received a penny. Shortly afterwards, Hitler banned German citizens from receiving Nobel prizes, and founded a German National Prize for Art and Science instead. Ossietzky's health never recovered from his maltreatment in the camps and he died, after two years in hospital, on 4 May 1938. Only his widow and his physician were allowed to attend the cremation, and the regime saw to it that his ashes were buried in an unmarked grave.[86]

Ossietzky had become a symbol of opposition without actually publishing a word since the end of the Weimar Republic. Open criticism of the regime while remaining in Germany rapidly became impossible; the most active literary opposition came from exiled Communist writers like Bertolt Brecht, Jan Petersen or Willi Bredel, whose work was smuggled into Germany from outside in clandestine pamphlets and periodicals. Such activities ceased once the Gestapo had smashed the underground Communist resistance, which is to say, from 1935 onwards.[87] Less politically active writers who stayed in Germany were faced with the kind of choices that had so troubled Rudolf Ditzen. Many chose 'inner emigration', retreating from human subjects by writing about nature, replacing description of external events by introspection, or distancing themselves from the realities of the present by writing about far-distant times or topics tied to no particular time at all. Under this guise they could sometimes engage in veiled criticism of the regime, or at least write novels that could be taken as such. Werner Bergengruen's novel *The Great Tyrant and the Law-Court*, for example, published in 1935, was praised by Nazi reviewers as 'the Leader novel of the Renaissance age' and its author obtained a special permit from the Reich Literary Chamber to continue publishing despite the fact that his wife was classified as three-quarters Jewish. Yet it was read by many for its critical portrayal of tyranny, terror, the abuse of power and the eventual remorse of the guilty tyrant. When it was serialized, the censors in the Ministry of Propaganda changed its title to *The Temptation*, cut obvious parallels with Hitler, such as the tyrant's love of architecture, and excised all allusions to political life. The author was careful to disclaim any critical or satirical intent and indeed he had begun the book before 1933, intending it to be a broad meditation on the problem of power rather than a direct attack on the Nazi dictatorship. Nevertheless, issued as a single volume, unabridged, with the cuts made by the censors of the serialized version restored, and, once more under its original title, it became a major best-seller. The political circumstances of the Third Reich lent its message a sharp edge that its author seemed never to have intended.[88]

Critiques such as Bergengruen's came from the conservative end of the political spectrum, and were perhaps easier to smuggle through because they were written by authors who had never aroused suspicion as men of the left would have done. The disillusioned journalist and theatre critic Friedrich Reck-Malleczewen managed to publish a historical study of the sixteenth-century reign of terror unleashed in the city of Münster by the Anabaptists under their leader Jan Bockelson, with the title *Bockelson. History of a Mass Hysteria* (Berlin, 1937) in which the parallels with Hitler and the mass enthusiasm he seemed to generate were obvious. Reck-Malleczewen was a more or less unknown author, whose pseudo-aristocratic contempt for the mob won him few friends; Ernst Jünger, one of Germany's most prominent right-wing writers, was a different case altogether. Already a best-selling writer for his graphic and heroic depiction of the soldier's experience of the First World War, he had been close to the Nazis during the 1920s but was ill at ease under the Third Reich. In his short novel *On the Marble Cliffs*, Jünger depicted a vague, symbolic world, sometimes located in the past, sometimes in the present, centred on a tyrant who has come to power by undermining a decaying democracy and now rules by force and terror. Jünger always denied, even after 1945, any political intentions in writing the novel, and the vague, pre-industrial setting for its story certainly bore few resemblances to Nazi Germany. The book, published in 1939, sold 12,000 copies within a year, and was frequently reprinted. And yet, many readers understood it to be a powerful attack on the Nazi regime, a clear act of literary resistance. In the circumstances of the Third Reich, context could condition a book's reception far more than its author's intentions did.[89]

Jünger was protected from interference, perhaps, because he was a war hero, much admired by Hitler and Goebbels. Others never had any need of protection. There were plenty of journeymen writers prepared to turn out 'blood-and-soil' novels set in an idyllic and mythical world of German peasant farmers, to celebrate heroes of the Nazi pantheon such as the murdered brownshirt Horst Wessel, or to pen fawning lyrics praising the greatness of Germany's Leader.[90] Speaking to the Reich Chamber of Culture on 15 November 1933, Goebbels – himself the author of a novel – recommended writers to depict Germany's reawakening in a positive light. He advocated a 'steely Romanticism' as the basic approach to take.[91] Versifiers celebrated Nazi values and the reawakening of the German spirit: 'Germany lies not in parliaments and government palaces', wrote Kurt Eggers in 1934, but:

Where the brown earth bears its fruits,
Where the lord's hand holds the reins, there lies Germany.
Where columns march and battle-cries sound, there lies Germany.
Where poverty and self-sacrifice build themselves memorial sites
And where defiant eyes blaze towards the enemy,
Where hearts hate and fists are raised:
There germinates, there grows new life for Germany![92]

Under the Weimar Republic, Nazi songs and verses had concentrated on raising the spirits of Party members in their struggle against everything they hated – the Republic, the Jews, 'reaction', parliamentarism. From 1933 onwards, however, such sentiments gave way to a broader appeal to the entire German nation to mobilize against the country's enemies within and without. Violent hatred was still present, but it was overlaid now with cloying encomia to the new Germany, the new Reich and above all, the new Leader. Speaking, in his imagination, for the German people, the lyricist Fritz Sotke addressed Hitler in 1934:

> Lead us home.
> Be your path uneven,
> And leading over the abyss,
> Over rock and iron wastes,
> We will follow you.
>
> If you ask us for all we have,
> We will give it to you, because we believe in you.
>
> We swear allegiance to you,
> None can break this oath –
> Even you – only death can break it!
> And that is the fulfilment of our being.[93]

Death was often close to the surface in such lyrics, generalizing the Nazi myth of sacrifice and martyrdom into a general principle for the entire German people.[94]

Authors of such verses were hardly well-known literary figures. One of the leading German literary and artistic movements of the 1920s and early 1930s was Expressionism, whose exponents were mostly on the left, though a few, like the playwright Hanns Johst, did lend their services to the Nazis from 1933 onwards; Johst indeed became head of the Reich Literary Chamber and wielded considerable power under the new regime.[95] The values of Expressionism did in fact bear a superficial resemblance to those of the National Socialists, emphasizing emotional self-expression, the virtues of youth, the evils of the industrial world, the banalities of the bourgeoisie, and the remaking of the human spirit in a revolt against the intellect. On the other hand, Expressionism gained much of its originality from a very un-Nazi rejection of naturalism in favour of the direct communication of emotion from the soul, often avoiding the realistic depiction of outward appearances. The Expressionists' radical, often unconventional style rendered them on the whole unacceptable to the Nazi cultural apparatus. The most celebrated literary convert from Expressionism to National Socialism, the writer Gottfried Benn, was a case in point. Already an established poet in the 1920s, Benn had another life as a medical practitioner that drew him into the orbit of the racial hygienists. He saw the coming to power of the Nazis as an opportunity for his profession to put the principles of eugenics into effect at last. Previously unpolitical, he now proclaimed his allegiance to the new Reich. He threw himself energetically into purging the Academy of dissident writers. When he was taken to task for this by Klaus Mann, the exiled son of the novelist Thomas Mann, and himself a prominent writer, Benn replied that only those who stayed on in Germany could understand the release of creative energy which the coming of the Third Reich had brought about.[96]

Although his poetry was pure, elevated and far removed from the struggles of everyday life, Benn none the less praised the regime's re-vivification of faith in German nature and rural life. He regarded Hitler as the great restorer of German dignity and honour. But after the initial purges of the Academy, Benn fell rapidly out of favour with the regime. As the Nazi cultural establishment turned its guns on Expressionism in music, art and literature, Benn made things worse for himself by attempting to defend it. The fact that he did so in terms he thought would appeal to the Nazis, as anti-liberal, primal, Aryan, born of the spirit of 1914, did not impress those who denounced it as unpatriotic, over-intellectual, perverse and immoral. 'If anyone is to be named as the moving spirit of the bolshevistic delight in the disgusting that celebrates its orgies in degenerate art,' one of his critics told him, 'then *you* have a right to be the first to be put in the pillory.' Poems with titles such as *Flesh, Whores' Crusade, Syphilis Quadrille* and similar 'pornopoetry' proved it, he said.[97] Benn was expelled from the Reich Chamber of Literature in March 1938. Banned from publishing any more verse, he had already taken up a post in the War Ministry in July 1937. In January 1934 he had written: 'As far as the future is concerned, it seems natural to me that no book should be allowed to appear in Germany that holds the new state in contempt.' When his own books were put into this category, because their aesthetic spirit was considered alien to the new state's culture, he had no response.[98]

As the problems encountered by Rudolf Ditzen and Gottfried Benn showed, the regime had multifarious ways of controlling the literary output of its citizens. Membership of the Reich Chamber of Literature was compulsory not only for all writers, poets, screenwriters, dramatists, critics and translators, but also for publishing houses, booksellers first- and second-hand, lending libraries and anything connected with the book trade, including scientific, academic and technical publications. Jews were excluded, as were any dissidents or people with a politically suspect past. Backing this up was a plethora of different censorship institutions. They based their activities on a decree issued almost immediately after the appointment of Hitler as Reich Chancellor, on 4 February 1933, which allowed the seizure by the police of any books that 'tended to endanger public security and order'. Armed with this weapon, censors scarcely needed the additional powers granted by the Reichstag Fire Decree on 28 February 1933. In addition, the Criminal Code had long contained provisions for the seizure and suppression of allegedly dangerous books, and there was a lengthy and legally legitimate tradition of confiscating and banning 'dirty and trashy literature (*Schund- und Schmutzliteratur*)'.[99]

Soon libraries and bookshops were being raided, often in rapid succession, by agents of the Criminal Police, the Gestapo, the Interior Ministry, the courts, local authorities and the Supreme Censorship Authority for Dirty and Trashy Literature, based in Leipzig. The Hitler Youth, the brownshirts and the Nazi students' organization were equally vigilant in rooting out books by Jews, pacifists, Marxists and other proscribed authors. Rosenberg's Fighting League for German Culture played its part too, as did the Official Party Censorship Commission, which had to vet publications produced by the Party itself. By December 1933 over a thousand titles had been banned by these various institutions. After the book-burning in university towns on 10 May 1933, the book trade journal issued a blacklist of 300 titles from 139 authors in the field of literature, following this up with 68 authors and 120 works in the fields of politics, and further lists covering other areas. Not only German books were affected. Banned foreign works ranged from Charles Dickens's *Oliver Twist* to Sir Walter Scott's *Ivanhoe* and virtually anything else either written by a Jewish author, dealing with a Jewish theme or featuring a Jewish character. Foreign books were not banned as such, and popular non-German authors in the Third Reich ranged from the blood-and-soil novelist Knut Hamsun to the social critic John Steinbeck and the adventure story writer C. S. Forester, creator of the fictional naval captain Horatio Hornblower. The confusion and overlap of different censoring bodies may have been a nuisance to the tidy-minded, but it achieved the removal of objectionable literature many times over.[100] Four thousand one hundred different printed works were banned by a total of forty different censorship bodies in 1934 alone.[101] In the first two to three years of the Third Reich, literature by Jewish writers disappeared from public bookshelves, and Jewish poets such as Heinrich Heine were now condemned as superficial imitations of true German writing. The works of non-Jewish classic writers like Goethe and Schiller were reinterpreted in a manner suitable to the regime's ideology. Inconveniently philosemitic plays such as Lessing's *Nathan the Wise* were dropped from theatre repertories.[102]

Control over the theatre was in some ways easier than control over books, since all performances were basically public events. It was entrusted to the Propaganda Ministry by a Theatre Law passed on 15 May 1934, which enabled Goebbels to license all theatres and performances, including amateur dramatic societies, and limited the prerogatives of other institutions such as the police in this respect. The Reich Theatre Chamber for its part licensed actors, directors and stage and theatre staff, excluding Jews and the politically unreliable in the usual way. The Chamber's President, Reich Literary and Artistic Theatre Director Rainer Schlösser, ordered that there should be a four-to-one ratio of German plays to foreign plays in the programme of every theatre, and censored new plays in advance. More controversially, the Theatre Chamber harassed and in some cases closed down amateur theatre companies in the economic interests of the professionals, who were still plagued by underemployment as a result of the Depression. Complaints from irate local amateur dramatic societies flooded in to the Propaganda Minister, who overruled the Chamber in March 1935.[103] As in other areas, Goebbels was careful not to carry his cultural revolution to such lengths that the popular demand for entertainment was stifled by ideological correctness. Theatres across Germany continued to offer high-quality performances of the classics, and people who felt alienated from the regime could take refuge in the thought that here, at least, German culture was still alive and flourishing. A great actor such as Gustav Gründgens claimed after 1945 that his theatre, like others, had remained an island of cultural excellence amidst the surrounding barbarities under the Third Reich. However, he lived in a villa that had been 'Aryanized' from its former Jewish owner, and cultivated close relations with Hermann Göring and his wife. Institutions such as the Munich Chamber Theatre did not become pure instruments of Nazi propaganda, and the number of Party members on the staff remained extremely low.[104] Not all theatres were able to resist the pressure to conform. While fewer than 5 per cent of the plays performed by the Munich Chamber Theatre under the Third Reich – roughly 8 per cent – could be described as openly or implicitly Nazi, the proportion at the Düsseldorf Theatre, at 29 per cent, was far higher. A study of four theatres in Berlin, Lübeck and Bochum has shown that only 8 per cent of the 309 plays they put on between 1933 and 1945 purveyed Nazi ideology in any kind of recognizable form. Yet even the least conformist theatres could not mount new, critical or radical plays, or plays banned by the regime. They had to follow the dictates of the regime in outward appearance at least, in the language and presentation of their programmes for example, or in their relationship with Party leaders in Munich. Their flight into the classics was a form of escapism to which Goebbels, who was always alive to the political advantages of allowing people to get away temporarily from the incessant demands of political mobilization and propaganda, was never likely to object.[105]

Goebbels tolerated mainstream theatre's presentation of the classics, even where, as in some of Shakespeare's plays, they dealt with themes such as tyranny and rebellion (though *The Merchant of Venice* told a story far more congenial to Nazi cultural arbiters). But he was not slow to clamp down in another area, namely a radical movement to create a truly Nazi form of theatre, in the self-styled *Thingspiel*, or 'meeting-play' (after the Old Norse for 'meeting'), which flourished briefly in the early years of the Third Reich. Performing specially written political and pseudo-Nordic dramas in purpose-built open-air theatres, these ritualistic plays put into dramatic form the Nazi cult of hero-worship and celebration of the glorious dead. But they also involved audience participation, speech-choruses and other elements of the Communist-inspired workers' theatre movement of the Weimar period. And some of their techniques had too close an affinity with the revolutionary aspects of Expressionist drama for even Goebbels to find them comfortable. Nor, despite the construction of over forty *Thing* theatres and the mounting of several hundred performances, were they particularly popular or financially successful. Goebbels banned the use of the word *Thing* in connection with the Party in October 1935 and went on to outlaw the use of speech-choruses in May the following year. This effectively killed the movement off, and it quickly went into a decline from which it never recovered.[106]

Goebbels thought that dramatists, novelists and other writers should aim to capture the spirit of the new times, not its outer manifestations.[107] This left at least some room for manoeuvre. Those who were careful not to offend could meet with a considerable degree of success in such circumstances, amongst a book-buying and book-reading public that remained avid for new work. Nevertheless, it was undeniable that many of the best-selling books in Germany during the 1930s often treated themes close to the Nazi heart. Kuni Tremel-Eggert's novel *Barb*, published in 1933, sold 750,000 copies within ten years; it did little more than purvey in fictionalized form the key Nazi tenets about women's place in society. Perhaps the most successful author of the period, Paul Coelestin Ettighofer, sold 330,000 copies of *Verdun, the Supreme Judgment*, between 1936 and 1940. Ettighofer's novels were self-conscious responses to Remarque's grimly realistic view of the First World War in *All Quiet on the Western Front*: they glorified combat and were full of ideologically driven portrayals of heroism and self-sacrifice on the battle-front. Even more explicitly Nazi was Karl Aloys Schenzinger's novel *Hitler Youth Quex*, published in 1932, which sold 244,000 copies by 1940, probably helped by the fact that the story had been filmed and shown in cinemas across Germany. Among 'blood-and-soil' novels, Theodor Kröger's *The Forgotten Village* sold 325,000 copies between 1934 and 1939, and Gottfried Rothacker's *The Village on the Border* 200,000 from 1936 to 1940. Some extremely popular books, like Hans Zöberlein's *Conscience's Command*, which sold 480,000 copies from 1936, the year of its publication, to 1943, purveyed a spirit of anti-semitism that was hardly less virulent than that of Hitler himself, with frequent references to Jewish 'vermin' and similar biological terms inviting readers implicitly to regard extermination as the only way to deal with the Jews. With other previously popular authors often banned, such literature had less competition than it would otherwise have done.[108] Moreover, as in the case of newspapers and periodicals, overtly political novels and histories also benefited from mass orders by Nazi Party organizations. Given the massive propaganda effort that went into boosting sales of such works, it would have been surprising if they had not sold well. What the Nazis wanted from books was demonstrated in propaganda events such as the German Book Week, held annually from 1934 onwards. 'Sixty million people will be roused at the end of October by the drumbeat of book promotion,' declared one of the leading organizers of the 1935 event. These 'days of mobilization' would 'implement inner military preparedness from the spiritual angle in the cause of building up our people'.[109] Speaking beneath a huge banner advertising 'The Book: A Sword of the Spirit', the Vice-President of the Reich Chamber of Literature declared on one such occasion: 'Books are weapons. Weapons belong in the hands of fighters. To be a fighter for Germany means to be a National Socialist.'[110]

Yet, as in other areas of culture, Goebbels realized that entertainment was important to keep people contented and take their minds off the problems of the present. He managed to fend off Rosenberg's attempt to prioritize overtly ideological literature, and from 1936 onwards, the best-seller lists were dominated by popular literature with only an indirect political relevance. The comic novels of Heinrich Spoerl, such as *Burnt Rum and Red Wine Punch*, which sold 565,000 copies from 1933 to 1944, were extremely popular; they satirized the 'little man' of the Weimar years, unable to readjust to the new climate of the Third Reich.

Even more widely read were Schenziger's scientific novels, which balanced out the nostalgia purveyed by 'blood-and-soil' literature by celebrating modern inventions, scientific discoveries and industrial growth: his *Anilin* was the most popular of all novels published in the Third Reich, selling 920,000 copies from 1937 to 1944, and he followed this up with *Metal*, which sold 540,000 copies between 1939 and 1943. Foreign writers continued to be published in Nazi Germany if they did not overtly offend the Nazis' ideological susceptibilities; Trygve

Gulbranssen's romances, with titles like *And the Woods Sing for Ever* and *The Legacy of Björndal*, published in German in 1934 and 1936 respectively, both sold over half a million copies by the time the Third Reich was over, and another world best-seller, Margaret Mitchell's *Gone with the Wind*, found 300,000 German purchasers within four years of its publication in German in 1937 and was only the most popular of a wide variety of American cultural offerings imported into Germany during the 1930s.[111] Many that had been published before 1914 and were still thought by the regime to be more or less acceptable continued to sell in their hundreds of thousands. They offered to those who sought it a return in the imagination to a sane and stable world. Just as popular were the reliable pleasures of a well-known author such as Karl May, whose turn-of-the-century stories of the Wild West some have seen as adumbrating Nazi values before their time; certainly, they were enjoyed by many committed Nazis, including Hitler himself.[112] Ordinary Germans did not swallow Nazi literature whole; on the contrary, they chose for themselves what they wanted to read, and from the mid-1930s onwards, much of this was not overtly Nazi at all. The success of the Nazi ambition of creating a new human being permeated by Nazi values was as limited here as it was in other areas of German culture.[113]

PROBLEMS OF PERSPECTIVE

I

Alongside the 'new objectivity' (*Neue Sachlichkeit*), Expressionism was in many ways the dominant movement not only in German literature but also in German art during the Weimar Republic.[114] Its most widely acceptable face was represented by the sculptor Ernst Barlach, whose work was heavily influenced by the primitive peasant art he encountered on a visit to Russia before the First World War. Barlach produced solid, stumpy, stylized, self-consciously folksy sculptures of human figures, first of all carved in wood, later in other media such as stucco and bronze. The figures were usually given a monumental, immobile quality by being depicted draped in stylized robes or cloaks. They were popular, and he received numerous commissions after 1918 for war memorials in many parts of Germany. Elected to the Prussian Academy of Arts in 1919, he had become an establishment figure by the mid-1920s, and was known for his hostility to abstraction, his critical distance from the rest of the Expressionist movement itself, and his steadfast refusal to engage in party politics. His art might have been expected to appeal to the Nazis, and indeed Joseph Goebbels recorded his admiration for one of Barlach's sculptures in a diary entry in the mid-1920s and was said later to have displayed two small figures by Barlach in his house.[115] The Propaganda Minister invited Barlach, along with some other Expressionist artists including Karl Schmidt-Rottluff, to the opening ceremony of the Reich Chamber of Culture, and his inclination to support them was backed by a campaign launched by members of the Nazi Students' League in Berlin for a new kind of Nordic modernism, based on an Expressionism purged of Jewish artists and abstract images.[116]

THE MOBILIZATION OF THE SPIRIT

But these efforts foundered on the hostility of Alfred Rosenberg on the one hand, and the refusal of Barlach himself to compromise with the regime on the other. Rosenberg denounced Barlach and the Expressionists in the pages of the *Racial Observer* and branded the Berlin students as outmoded revolutionaries along the lines of the disgraced Nazi leftist Otto Strasser. For his part, Barlach refused the invitation to the opening of the Reich Chamber of Culture. He had come to feel the hostility of the regime at a local level, and commissions for war memorials, plans for exhibitions and publications of his writings started to be cancelled soon after the appointment of Hitler as Reich Chancellor in January 1933. His monuments to the war dead had already run into criticism in the early 1930s from right-wing veterans' associations such as the Steel Helmets for their refusal to portray German soldiers of the First World war as heroic figures dying in a noble cause. Germanic racists accused Barlach of showing German soldiers with the features of Slavic subhumans. Living in the strongly National Socialist province of Mecklenburg, Barlach began to be exposed to anonymous letters and insults posted on the front door of his house. He felt obliged to withdraw his acceptance of a commission for a new war memorial in Stralsund under this pressure.[117] Barlach had stayed in Germany partly because he hoped that the Third Reich would respect the creative freedom of the artist, partly because, given the kind of work he did, it would not have been easy for him to make a living elsewhere.[118] By the beginning of May 1933 he was already disillusioned. 'The fawning cowardice of this magnificent era', he wrote bitterly to his brother, 'makes one go red up to the ears and beyond to think that one is German.'[119]

Barlach's unacceptability to the regime became clearer in 1933–4. The most controversial of his war memorials was a large wooden sculpture located in Magdeburg Cathedral. It showed three figures – a helmeted skeleton, a veiled woman pressing her fists together in agony and a bare-headed man with a gas mask between his arms, closing his eyes and clutching his head in despair – rising from the ground in front of the stylized forms of three soldiers, draped in greatcoats and standing side by side. The soldier in the middle has a bandage on his head and rests his hands on a large cross with the dates of the war on it, thus forming the centrepiece of the whole ensemble. Soon after Hitler's appointment as Chancellor, the press began to carry petitions for its removal, encouraged by Alfred Rosenberg, who described its figures as 'little half-idiotic, morose-looking bastard variations of indefinable human types with Soviet helmets' in the *Racial Observer* in July 1933.[120] While negotiations dragged on between the Propaganda Ministry, the Church and the Party about its removal, the press campaign against Barlach escalated. Allegations that he was Jewish prompted Barlach to respond that he did not want to issue a public rebuttal since he did not feel insulted by the claim. His friends researched his ancestry and published evidence that he was not Jewish. It filled his heart with sadness, he wrote, to think that such a thing was necessary.[121] The memorial was eventually taken down towards the end of 1934 and placed in storage.[122] Barlach defended himself from widespread attacks on his art as 'un-German' by pointing to the fact that its roots lay among the North German peasantry amongst whom he lived. Now in his mid-sixties, he found it difficult to understand how his sculptures could arouse such venomous hostility. In an attempt to deflect it, he signed a declaration in support of Hitler's assumption of the headship of state after the death of Hindenburg in August 1934. But this did nothing to assuage the Nazi Party leadership in Mecklenburg, and the regional government began to remove his works from the state museum.

Many of Barlach's admirers, including enthusiastic supporters of the Nazi movement, found such treatment difficult to accept. The Nazi girls' organization official Melita Maschmann, for example, admired his work and could not understand why he had been branded by the Nazis as 'degenerate'.[123] In the end, however, Barlach fell foul of the regime because his work went against the Nazi glorification of war, because he refused to compromise his art, because he responded assertively to criticism and because he made no secret of his dislike of Nazi Germany's cultural policies. In 1936, the Bavarian police seized all the copies of a new book of his drawings from the publisher's warehouse in Munich. They were acting on the orders of Goebbels: 'Have banned a crazy book by Barlach,' he wrote in his diary: 'It isn't art. It is destructive, incompetent nonsense. Disgusting! This poison must not enter our people.'[124] The Gestapo added insult to injury by describing the drawings as 'art-bolshevik expressions of a destructive concept of art not appropriate to our age'. The book was placed on the index of forbidden literature. Despite his continued protests at the injustices to which he was being

subjected, Barlach became progressively more isolated. He was forced
to resign from the Prussian Academy of Arts in 1937. 'When day after
day one has to expect the threatened, deadly blow, work stops by itself,'
he wrote. 'I resemble someone driven into a corner, the pack at his
heels.'[125] His health underwent a serious decline, and he died in hospital
of a heart attack on 24 October 1938.[126]

The kind of sculptor for whom the Nazis could feel a genuine enthusiasm was Arno Breker. Born in 1900, Breker belonged to a younger
generation than Barlach. During his student days he had produced a
number of sculptures that clearly showed the older man's influence. A
lengthy stay in Paris, from 1927 to 1932, put him firmly under the aegis
of Aristide Maillol, whose figurative style now shaped his own. During
a sojourn in Rome early in 1933, when he was working on the restoration
of a damaged sculpture by Michelangelo, he met Goebbels, who recognized his talent and encouraged him to return to Germany. After winding
up his affairs in Paris, Breker duly obliged. Previously unpolitical, indeed
as an expatriate not very well informed about German politics at all, he
quickly fell under the spell of the Nazis. Breker's style was framed mainly
by non-German influences – Classical Greek sculpture, Michelangelo,
Maillol. Some of his busts, like one of the Impressionist painter Max
Liebermann, completed in 1934, were penetrating, subtle and full of
illuminating detail. But soon he was smoothing over the rough edges of
his work, rendering it more impersonal, and giving it a more monumental, less intimate quality, projecting toughness, hardness and aggression
in his figures rather than the softer human qualities with which he had
endowed them in the 1920s. By the mid-1930s, Breker was producing
massive, musclebound, superdimensional male nudes, Aryan supermen
in stone.[127]

This soon paid dividends. Prizewinning entries in a competition
mounted in 1936 on the theme of sporting achievement won him an
increasing number of official commissions. In 1937 he joined the Nazi
Party to smooth the way for further official patronage. Breker became
personally acquainted with Hitler, who put his bust of Wagner in his
private quarters in Berchtesgaden. He was nominated 'Official State
Sculptor' on Hitler's birthday in 1937 and given a huge studio with
forty-three employees to help him with his work. He became an influential figure, lionized by Göring and other leading Nazis and protected by

them from any criticism. In 1937 his work was given a prominent place in the German pavilion at the Paris World Exposition. In 1938 he designed two massive male nudes to be placed at the entrance to the newly built Reich Chancellery – *Torch Bearer* and *Sword Bearer*. Others followed, notably *Readiness*, in 1939, a muscly male figure frowning in hatred at an unseen enemy, his right hand about to draw a sword from its scabbard to begin the fight. Breker became a wealthy man, enjoying a huge variety of favours and decorations, including several houses, massive subsidies and of course large fees for his public work. Lifeless, inhuman, striking contrived poses of unbridled menace, and embodying the empty, declamatory assertion of an imagined collective will, Breker's sculptures became the hallmark of the public artistic taste of the Third Reich. Their almost machine-like quality placed them unmistakeably in the twentieth century; they looked forward to the new type of human being whose creation was one of the primary aims of Nazi cultural policy, unthinkingly physical, aggressive, ready for war.[128]

II

By the time Breker came to public prominence, the cultural managers of the Third Reich had effectively disposed of abstract, modernist art of the kind they were accustomed to describe as 'degenerate'. Hitler's own tastes played a role here greater perhaps than in any other area of cultural policy apart from architecture. He himself had once attempted to make a career as an artist, but from the very beginning he had rejected modernism in all its varieties.[129] Once in power, he turned his prejudices into policy. On 1 September 1933 Hitler told the Nuremberg Party Rally that it was time for a new, German art. The coming of the Third Reich, he said, 'leads ineluctably to a new orientation in almost every area of the people's life'. The effects 'of this spiritual revolution' must be felt in art too. Art must reflect the racial soul of the people. The idea that art was international must be rejected as decadent, and Jewish. He condemned what he saw as its expression 'in the cubist-dadaist cult of primitivism' and in cultural Bolshevism and announced in its stead 'a new artistic Renaissance of the Aryan human being'. And he warned that modernist artists would not be forgiven their past sins:

In the cultural sphere, too, the National Socialist movement and leadership of the state must not tolerate mountebanks or incompetents suddenly changing their colours and thus, as if nothing had happened, taking a place in the new state so that they can talk big about art and cultural policy ... Either the monstrous products of their production at that time reflected a genuine inner experience, in which case they are a danger to the healthy sense of our people and belong in medical care, or they were just done to make money, in which case they are guilty of fraud and belong in the care of another appropriate institution. In no way do we want the cultural expression of our Reich to be distorted by these elements; for this is not their state, but ours.[130]

Nineteen thirty-three had seen, accordingly, a massive purge of Jewish artists, abstract artists, semi-abstract artists, left-wing artists and indeed almost all the artists in Germany at the time who had any kind of international reputation. Declarations of support for the new regime, even Nazi Party membership since the earliest days, as in the case of the primitivist painter and sculptor Emil Nolde, failed to save those of whose earlier work Hitler disapproved. The few artists of distinction who remained in the hope of better times to come, like Ernst Barlach, were quickly disillusioned.[131]

In 1933, Jewish, Social Democratic, liberal and leftist art museum directors had been summarily removed from their posts and replaced with people deemed by the Nazis to be more reliable. The Folkwang Museum in Essen was even put into the hands of an SS officer, Klaus Graf Baudissin, who had the museum's famous murals by Oskar Schlemmer, an artist closely associated with the Bauhaus, painted over. Yet art museum directors continued to show works of which the more extreme wing of the Nazi Party disapproved. Even Baudissin, a trained art historian, kept works by Oskar Kokoschka, Franz Marc and Emil Nolde on show well into 1935. The Director of the Bavarian State Painting Collections, Ernst Buchner, a Nazi Party member since 1 May 1933, fought for the right to exhibit the work of a Jewish-German artist such as the Impressionist Max Liebermann and in 1935 successfully resisted attempts by the Reich Education and Religion Minister Bernhard Rust to force him to sell off works by Van Gogh and the French Impressionists, to whom the Nazis objected not least because they were not German. When Hitler personally removed the long-term and pro-modernist Director of the National Gallery, Ludwig Justi, from his post in 1933, his successor, Alois Schardt, organized a spectacular new exhibition of German art that included works by Nolde and a variety of Expressionists. Visiting the gallery for a preview, Education Minister Bernhard Rust was outraged. He immediately fired the new director and ordered the exhibition to be dismantled; Schardt emigrated to the United States after presiding at a small Berlin gallery over an exhibition of work by Franz Marc that was closed down by the Gestapo the day it opened in May 1936. Schardt's successor Eberhard Hanfstaengl, previously a gallery director in Munich, fared no better; he fell foul of Hitler when the Leader paid a surprise visit and saw some Expressionist works on the walls. On 30 October 1936 the new wing of the National Gallery was closed after it had housed an exhibition that included paintings by Paul Klee.[132] Similar closures now followed elsewhere. Over the period since the middle of 1933, gallery and museum directors, including those appointed by the Nazis themselves, had fought a cultural guerrilla war against the demands of local Nazi bosses to remove paintings of one kind or another from exhibition. A few, like Hanfstaengl, had continued to purchase modern art, though he discreetly left it out of the museum's published catalogue. But the time for such compromises and evasions was now over.[133]

From the very beginning, some of the most fanatical of the Nazi art gallery and museum directors organized shows of the modernist works they had withdrawn from exhibition, under titles such as 'Chamber of Art Horrors', 'Images of Cultural Bolshevism', 'Mirrors of Decadence in Art' or 'The Spirit of November: Art in the Service of Decay'. Those exhibited included Max Beckmann, Otto Dix and George Grosz, Ernst Ludwig Kirchner, Franz Marc, August Macke, Karl Schmidt-Rottluff and Emil Nolde. German-based foreign artists such as Alexei Jawlensky and Vassily Kandinsky also featured, alongside the inevitable Cubists and avant-garde artists from other countries.[134] The inclusion of Macke and Marc caused particular controversy because they had both been killed on the front in the First World War, and veterans' associations objected to the insult their proscription did to their memory.[135] Some of the earliest of these exhibitions, held already in 1933, had aroused strong protests on the part of art-loving visitors, leading in some cases to their arrest. But within a very short space of time, such opposition became impossible. By the mid-1930s exhibitions of this kind had been mounted in sixteen different cities. Hitler visited the most important of them, in Dresden, in August 1935. Close inspection of the offending works prompted him to deliver another lengthy diatribe against them at the Nuremberg Party Rally shortly afterwards, the third time he had used this occasion to lecture his followers on the subject. Clearly, Goebbels needed to fall into line if he was to prevent Rosenberg, Rust and the other anti-modernists from taking over the lead in cultural policy. So, in June 1936, he acted. 'Horrible examples of art Bolshevism', he wrote in his diary, 'have been brought to my attention', as if he had not seen them before; 'I want to arrange an exhibit in Berlin of art from the period of degeneracy. So that people can see and learn to recognize it.' By the end of the month he had obtained Hitler's permission to requisition 'German degenerate art since 1910' (the date of the first abstract painting, by the Munich-based Russian artist Vassily Kandinsky) from public collections for the show. Many in the Propaganda Ministry were reluctant to go along with the project. Its political opportunism was cynical even by Goebbels's standards. He knew that Hitler's hatred of artistic modernism was unquenchable, and so he decided to gain favour by pandering to it, even though he did not share it himself.[136]

The exhibition's organization was entrusted to Adolf Ziegler, President of the Reich Chamber for the Visual Arts, and a painter of classical nudes whose pedantic realism earned him the popular nickname of the 'Reich Master of Pubic Hair'.[137] Armed with commissions from Goebbels and Hitler, Ziegler and his entourage toured German galleries and museums and picked out works to be taken to the new exhibition. Museum directors, including Buchner and Hanfstaengl, were furious, refused to co-operate, and pleaded with Hitler to obtain compensation if the confiscated works were sold abroad. Such resistance was not tolerated, and Hanfstaengl lost his job at the Berlin National Gallery as a result. One hundred and eight works were seized from the Munich collections, and comparable numbers from museums elsewhere.[138] When the Degenerate Art show opened in Munich, long recognized as Germany's art capital, on 19 July, 1937, visitors found that the 650 or so works it contained were deliberately badly displayed, hung at odd angles, poorly lit, and jammed up together on the walls, higgledy-piggledy, under general titles such as 'Farmers Seen by Jews', 'Insult to German

Womanhood' and 'Mockery of God'.[139] Ironically, the diagonal lines and the graffitoid slogans on the walls owed something to the design techniques of the Dada movement, one of the exhibition's prime targets. Here, however, they were intended to express a congruity between the art produced by mental asylum inmates, a major point of discussion amongst liberal psychiatrists under the Weimar Republic, and the distorted perspectives adopted by the Cubists and their ilk, a point made explicit in much of the propaganda surrounding the assault on degenerate art as the product of degenerate human beings.[140]

Hitler toured the exhibition before it opened to the public, and devoted a major part of a speech on the eve of its inauguration to a ferocious denunciation of the works it showed:

Never has the human race been closer in appearance and temperament to Antiquity than today. Sporting, competitive and combative games are steeling millions of youthful bodies and they are increasingly taking on a form and constitution that have not perhaps been seen for a thousand years, indeed have scarcely been dreamed of . . . This type of human being, my art-stutterer gentlemen, is the type of the new age. And what do you knock together? Malformed cripples and cretins, women who can only arouse repulsion. Men who are nearer to animals than to humans, children who, if they lived so, would virtually have to be regarded as curses of God![141]

He even instructed the Reich Interior Ministry to investigate the defective visual capacities he thought had partly led to such distortion. They were, he thought, inherited. Cubists and others who did not stick to slavishly accurate representations of their human subjects were to be sterilized.[142]

In fact, the most important criteria for the selection of works to be displayed in the exhibition were not aesthetic, but racial and political. Of the nine sections into which it was divided, only the first and the last were based on aesthetic criteria. The others pilloried the subjects chosen rather than the manner in which they were depicted. The first section covered 'barbarism of representation', 'garish-coloured blobs of paint' and 'deliberate contempt for all the basic skills of the visual arts'. The second showed work deemed to be blasphemous, and the third political art advocating anarchism and the class struggle. A fourth section displayed paintings showing soldiers as murderers or, alternatively, as war cripples. According to the catalogue, in these pictures 'the deeply ingrained respect for every soldierly virtue, for courage, bravery and readiness for action is to be driven out of the people's consciousness'. A fifth section was devoted to immoral and pornographic art (most too disgusting to be shown, it was claimed). A sixth part of the exhibition showed the 'destruction of the last remains of racial consciousness' in pictures supposedly presenting negroes, prostitutes and the like as racial ideals. In a similar way, a seventh section was devoted to paintings and graphic works in which 'the idiot, the cretin und the paraplegic' were depicted in a positive light. Section eight was given over to the work of Jewish artists. The last and biggest section covered the '"isms", that Flechtheim, Wollheim and their Cohnsorts [sic] have hatched up, pushed and sold at knockdown prices over the years', from Dadaism to Cubism and beyond. All of this, declared the catalogue, would show the public that modern art was not just a fad: Jews and cultural bolshevists were mounting a 'planned attack on the existence and continuation of art altogether'. Five out of the brochure's ten illustrated recto pages carried antisemitic messages just to underline the point.[143] Modernist art, as many Nazi polemics of the time claimed, was above all the product of international, foreign influences. Art had to return to the German soul. As for modernism, one writer concluded with the fervent wish: 'May the degenerate suffocate in its own filth, without anybody sympathizing with its fate.'[144]

The exhibition was enormously popular and attracted over two million visitors by the end of November 1937. Entry was free, and massive press publicity drew people's attention to the horrors it contained.[145] The exhibits were, the papers proclaimed, 'shoddy products of a melancholy age', 'ghosts of the past', from the era when 'bolshevism and dilettantism celebrated their triumphs'. Lurid descriptions and illustrations showed readers what they could expect to see when they went to the exhibition.[146] In its first few weeks, at least, it was visited mainly by people from the Munich lower middle classes, many of whom had never been to an art exhibition before, and by the Party faithful, eager to imbibe a new form of antisemitic hatred. The stipulation that children and young persons were not to be allowed in because the exhibits were too shocking added an element of titillation to entice the eager public. Despite this, some young people did attend, among them the seventeen-year-old Peter Guenther, who went in July. The son of a liberal art journalist who had been expelled from the Reich Chamber of Literature in 1935, Guenther knew a fair amount about paintings. He found the atmosphere at the exhibition frightening and intimidating. The visitors, he reported later, commented loudly on how incompetently executed the works displayed were, and how there had been a conspiracy of art critics, dealers and museum directors to fool the public, a sentiment encouraged by the fact that a number of the exhibits had price tags attached to them indicating how much they had cost ('paid from the pennies paid in tax by the German working people'). One painting by Erich Heckel came with a price-tag of a million Marks; the exhibitors did not say that this had been paid in 1923, towards the height of the hyperinflation, and was in fact worth very little in real terms. Some Party groups who visited the exhibition telegrammed the Propaganda Ministry with messages such as: 'The artists should be tied up next to their pictures so that every German can spit in their faces.' Carola Roth, a friend of the artist Max Beckmann, noted how while older visitors went round the exhibition shaking their heads, younger Party activists and brownshirts laughed and jeered at the exhibits. The atmosphere of hatred and loudmouthed ridicule allowed no dissent; indeed it was an essential part of the exhibition itself, turning it into yet another mass propaganda exercise for the regime. Later on, however, when young Peter Guenther paid a second visit, the atmosphere was, he reported, much quieter, with some visitors lingering in front of artworks they clearly enjoyed and which they had come to see for what they suspected might be the last time. Yet overall, the exhibition was clearly a success. Like much else in Nazi culture, it allowed ordinary conservative citizens the opportunity to voice out loud prejudices that they had long held but previously been hesitant to reveal.[147]

Many of the artists whose work was on display were either foreigners, like Pablo Picasso, Henri Matisse, or Oskar Kokoschka, or had emigrated, like Paul Klee or Vassily Kandinsky. But some of the artists who featured in the exhibition had stayed on in Germany, in the hope that the tide would turn and they would be rehabilitated. Max Beckmann, whose last solo exhibition had been as recently as 1936, in Hamburg, left for exile in Amsterdam the day after the opening of the Degenerate Art exhibition. Though far from well off, Beckmann was still painting. He was supported by sympathetic dealers and foreign admirers in the following, difficult years.[148] Others were not so fortunate.[149] The Expressionist artist Ernst Ludwig Kirchner, who at this time, like Beckmann, was in his fifties, had already been living for most of the time in Switzerland since the 1920s, but he depended far more than Beckmann did on the German art market for his livelihood. Until 1937 he did not give up hope. But in July 1937 he was finally expelled from the Prussian Academy of Arts, and many of his works were confiscated from German collections by the Ziegler commission, which exhibited no fewer than thirty-two of them in the Degenerate Art show. Kirchner was already ill, and for some years he had lost his way as an artist, never really recapturing the greatness of his period in Berlin from 1910 to the mid-1920s. For him this was the last straw. 'I had always hoped that Hitler was for all Germans,' he wrote bitterly, 'and now he has defamed so many and really serious, good artists of German blood. This is very sad for those affected, because they – the serious ones among them – all wished to, and did, work for Germany's fame and honour.' A fresh round of confiscations of his work only deepened his despair. On 15 June 1938 he destroyed many of the works he kept in his rural retreat in Switzerland, stepped outside the house, and shot himself in the heart.[150]

III

Meanwhile, the regime, in a way that was characteristic of its decision-making in other areas too, took the opportunity of the exhibition to pass legislation generalizing the policy it represented. Hitler declared the day before the exhibition opened that the time for tolerance was at an end:

From now on we shall wage a remorseless war of cleansing against the last elements of the subversion of our culture . . . But now – I will assure you here – all those cliques of chatterers, dilettantes and art-frauds who puff each other up and so keep each other going, will be caught and removed. As far as we're concerned, these prehistorical, antediluvian cultural stone-agers and art-stutterers can go back to their ancestral caves to carry on their international scrawlings there.[151]

The 'chatterers' indeed had already been silenced by an order issued by Goebbels on 27 November 1936 banning art criticism, which, he said, had been 'elevated into a court of judgment over art in the era of foreign, Jewish domination of art'. In its place came 'art reporting', which was to limit itself to simple description. In an art world where everything exhibited in public museums and galleries was there with the approval of the Propaganda Ministry and the Reich Chamber of the Plastic Arts, art criticism could seem too much like criticism of the regime.[152] To ensure that modernist works could no longer to be put on public display, Ziegler declared in his opening address that the country's galleries would soon be stripped of such excrescences altogether.[153] Goebbels told the Reich Culture Chamber shortly afterwards that the 'frightening and horrifying forms of the "Exhibition of Degenerate Art" in Munich' showed 'botched art works', the 'monstrous, degenerate creations' of men of 'yesterday', 'senile representatives . . . of a period that we have intellectually and politically overcome'. On 31 May 1938 a Law for the Confiscation of the Products of Degenerate Art was promulgated. It retrospectively legalized the seizure of degenerate artworks not only from galleries and museums but also from private collections, without compensation save in exceptional cases 'to avoid hardship'.[154] The confiscation programme was centralized in the hands of a commission headed by Adolf Ziegler and including the art dealer Karl Haberstock and Hitler's photographer Heinrich Hoffmann.[155]

The commission increased the number of artworks seized to around 5,000 paintings and 12,000 graphic works, drawings, woodcuts and watercolours from a total of 101 art galleries and museums all over Germany.[156] Some non-German works were returned to foreign institutions and individuals who had loaned them to German museums, some forty were eventually given back, and some were exchanged. In addition, Hermann Göring reserved fourteen of the most valuable pieces for himself: four paintings by Vincent Van Gogh, four by Edvard Munch, three by Franz Marc and one each by Paul Cézanne, Paul Gauguin and Paul Signac. He sold them off to raise money to buy tapestries to adorn Carinhall, the palatial hunting lodge he had built in memory of his first wife; an illegal piece of profiteering which hinted strongly at how he would behave when the art of other European countries was at his disposal.[157] Moreover, as artists in exile and their supporters abroad quickly organized counter-exhibitions of 'Twentieth-Century German Art', most notably in London, Paris and Boston, they drew attention to the reputation many of the banned artists enjoyed abroad. The Nazi regime simply could not ignore the demand for modernist German art in other countries in its search for badly needed hard currency. Goebbels began negotiations with Wildenstein and other dealers outside Germany and remodelled Ziegler's commission into a body more closely under his control. Set up within the Propaganda Ministry in May 1938, it included three art dealers and was charged with the disposal of the confiscated works. Over the next few years, up to 1942, over a million Reichsmarks from the sale of up to 3,000 confiscated artworks were deposited in a special account in the Reichsbank. The most public transaction was a sale of 125 works by Ernst Barlach, Marc Chagall, Otto Dix, Paul Gauguin, Vincent Van Gogh, George Grosz, Ernst Ludwig Kirchner, Paul Klee, Max Liebermann, Henri Matisse, Amadeo Modigliani, Pablo Picasso, Maurice Vlaminck and others at the Galerie Fischer in Lucerne on 30 June 1939. All but thirty-one of them found a buyer. Some of the proceeds went to the museums and galleries from which the works had been seized, but most of them were put into a London account to enable Hitler to buy paintings for his personal collection. In this way, a good number of the confiscated artworks survived.[158]

The great majority, however, did not. The total sum realized from the Lucerne auction, just over half a million Swiss francs, was disappointing even by the standards of the day. The knowledge that the regime was confiscating and offloading large quantities of modern art caused prices to plummet in behind-the-scenes sales as well. One painting by Max Beckmann, *Southern Coast*, went for only $20. It seemed that big profits were not to be made from them after all. A million Reichsmarks was little enough in the end. Although two further auctions were planned, another small sale was held in Zurich in August 1939, and private transactions took place all the way up to 1942, the looming threat of war made the transport of large quantities of artworks abroad increasingly inadvisable.[159] Their disposal was made more difficult by the fact that Hitler had personally inspected the collection of 12,167 remaining pieces in a warehouse in Berlin and forbidden their return to the collections from which they had been removed. There seemed little alternative but to destroy those that had not been sold. After all, in the eyes of Ziegler and his commission they were artistically worthless anyway. On 20 March 1939, therefore, some 1,004 oil paintings and 3,825

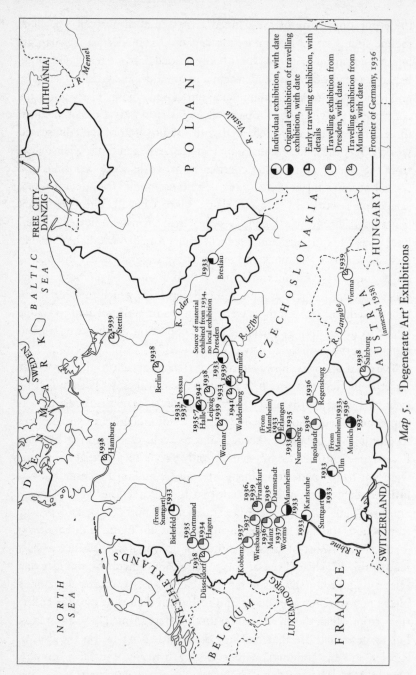

Map 5. 'Degenerate Art' Exhibitions

watercolours, drawings and graphic works were piled up in the courtyard of the central fire station in Berlin and set alight. The bonfire was not attended by the public or accompanied by any formal ceremony or public announcement. None the less, it bore strong reminiscences of the earlier book-burnings of 10 May 1933 that had consumed the works of Jewish, left-wing and modernist writers on the public squares of Germany's university cities.[160]

Modernist art in Germany had finally been destroyed in the most physical possible way. Modernist works had now been removed from German collections and thrown onto a bonfire. The only ones to be seen were displayed in the Degenerate Art exhibition, which now went on tour in a reduced form, and attracted substantial numbers of visitors in other cities such as Berlin, Düsseldorf and Frankfurt in the following two years.[161] Modernist artists had been forced into exile or prevented from selling or exhibiting their work in public. Yet they had not disappeared altogether. On the contrary, as the Security Service of the SS reported in 1938, 'cultural bolshevist' and 'Expressionist' works were still being exhibited at private galleries and shows, especially in Berlin. In a competition held in Berlin in 1938, the SS complained, 'the exhibition of young artists offered for the most part a picture of degeneracy and incompetence, so that this part of the artistic younger generation has opposed itself to the National Socialist conception of art'.[162] It seemed, then, that Nazi views of art had not triumphed after all, except by the brutal physical suppression of the alternatives. Nor was this all. The SS also complained in 1938 that 'opposition to the National Socialist view of art was present amongst wide sections of the German artistic community itself . . . insofar as they are not to be regarded as markedly National Socialist by inclination'. Particularly unpopular was the Reich Chamber for the Visual Arts, which, according to the SS report, almost all German artists disliked.[163] It exercised extensive powers over its 42,000 members, who included architects, garden designers, interior decorators, copyists, antiques dealers, potters, and indeed almost anyone who had any connection with the visual arts. To qualify for membership it was necessary to fill in an elaborate questionnaire listing the applicant's previous political affiliations and giving the racial background of family members.[164] Anyone who did not qualify could not practice. Unable to make a living any more from selling their work, some turned to humiliatingly menial alternatives. By 1939, for instance, Oskar Schlemmer was painting camouflage on military buildings.[165]

In the meantime, 'German' artists like Arno Breker prospered as never before. They were encouraged by the Propaganda Ministry, which instituted a whole series of prizes, awards and titles for artists whose work conformed to the Nazi ideal.[166] Art exhibitions all over Germany now carried titles such as 'Blood and Soil' or 'Basic Forces of the German Will to Form', and devoted themselves to subjects such as portraits of National Socialist leaders, above all, of course, Hitler himself.[167] Moreover, the Degenerate Art Exhibition was not mounted in isolation, but was in fact the pendant to a 'Great German Art Exhibition' opened in Munich the day before.[168] The huge show, which was renewed annually thereafter and preceded by a massive pageant of German culture in the streets of Munich, contained landscapes, still life paintings, portraits, allegorical statues and much more besides. Its themes included animals and nature, motherhood, industry, sport, and peasant life and rural trades, though not, perhaps surprisingly, soldiers or warfare. Massive, impersonal nudes provided prominent, untouchable, superhuman images of permanence and timelessness to contrast with the human dimension of the art now branded as degenerate.[169] Hitler himself inspected the exhibits in advance and personally threw out one in ten from the list of works chosen for display. Dissatisfied with the lack of rigour shown by Ziegler's commission, he appointed his photographer Heinrich Hoffmann to make the final selection.[170] The relatively low attendance at the exhibition – little over 400,000 compared to almost three million who attended the Degenerate Art exhibition in Munich and on tour – was probably due mainly to the fact that visitors had to pay.[171] But it too was a success. According to Peter Guenther, visitors praised the craftsmanship and the realistic, lifelike quality of the statues and paintings (even those intended as allegories) and were generally impressed by the exhibits. Once more, many visitors, in the view of young Guenther, had not been to an art exhibition before.[172] Nazi art policy, above all, was for people such as these.[173]

IV

The Great German Art exhibition was housed in a purpose-built museum, designed in the style of an antique temple by the architect Paul Ludwig Troost. Its heavy, squared-off columns marching in front of a solid rectangular block of a building were a long way away from the delicate and subtle neo-Classical architecture that Troost sought to imitate. Like other Nazi buildings, it was first and foremost a statement of power.[174] The House of German Art was only one of a large number of prestigious projects Hitler had begun as soon as he took power in 1933. Indeed, he had been thinking about them since the early 1920s. Hitler imagined himself an architect even more than he thought of himself as a painter, and paid more attention to architecture than to any other of the arts. 'Every great era finds the concluding expression of its values in its buildings,' he declared in 1938: 'When peoples inwardly experience great times, they also give these times external expression. Their word is then more convincing than when it is spoken: it is the word in stone!'[175]

The new public buildings of the Third Reich were all conceived in this massive, pseudo-Classical, monumental style. Like the public buildings Hitler had observed and drawn on Vienna's Ringstrasse in his younger days, they were intended to project permanence and durability. All of them were influenced by Hitler's own personal architectural and design plans. Hitler spent hours working with architects on refining their ideas, poring over models and discussing the finer points of style and decoration. Already in 1931–2 he had collaborated with Troost on redesigning the Königsplatz in Munich, and when he came to power, these plans were put into effect. The old Party headquarters at the Brown House were replaced by a gigantic Leader Building and a huge Administration Building, housing vast reception halls and decorated with swastikas and eagles on the façade. There was a balcony on each one from which Hitler could speak to the crowds who were expected to gather below. Despite their appearance, the new buildings incorporated advanced technology in their construction and equipment, including air-conditioning. Adjoining were two characteristic expressions of the Nazi cult of the dead: temples of honour dedicated to the Nazis who had been killed in the 1923 beer-hall putsch. In each of them, an atmosphere of reverent sacrality prevailed, with the bodies of the recently exhumed martyrs displayed in sarcophagi mounted on a dais, open to the elements, and flanked by twenty limestone pillars lit by flaming braziers. The huge grass arena of the Königsplatz itself was paved over with 24,000 square feet of granite slabs. 'Something new has been created here,' remarked a commentator, 'the deepest meaning of which is a political one.' Here the organized and disciplined masses would gather to swear allegiance to the new order. The whole ensemble was, he concluded, 'ideology become stone'.[176]

As in other fields, Nazi cultural managers took some time to impose their views. The Reich Chamber of Architects soon expelled Jewish practitioners from the profession, but despite Nazi hostility to ultra-modern architecture, it was slower to move against the modernists, some of whom, such as Mies van der Rohe, remained in Germany for a while, though finding it increasingly difficult to practise. By 1935, however, the more experimental types of modernism had been effectively routed; Mies soon emigrated to New York.[177] By the mid-1930s, constructions of the Weimar era such as modernist apartment blocks were no longer in fashion. Instead, the Nazi ideal of domestic architecture favoured a vernacular, pseudo-peasant style such as that practised by the leading proponent of racial theories of modern art, Paul Schultze-Naumburg. These were only showcases for the suburbs; necessity meant that blocks of flats still had to be constructed in the inner cities, where pitched roofs, however, were now preferred over flat roofs because they were believed to be more German.[178] But it was into public buildings that Hitler put his real passion. In Munich, the foundations were laid for a gigantic new central railway station that was designed to be the largest steel-frame structure in the world, with a dome higher than the twin towers of Munich's signature landmark, the Frauenkirche. Not only Munich, but other cities too were to be transformed into massive stone statements of the power and permanence of the Third Reich. Hamburg was to be graced with a new skyscraper for the Nazi Party's regional headquarters higher than the Empire State Building in New York, crowned by an enormous neon swastika to act as a beacon for incoming ships. Down-river, the suburb of Othmarschen was to be demolished to make way for the ramps and piles of a gargantuan suspension bridge across the Elbe. The bridge was to be the largest in the world, larger by far than the Golden Gate Bridge in San Francisco, on which it was modelled.[179]

In Berlin, a huge new airport terminal was built at Tempelhof, with over 2,000 rooms. A grandiose new Ministry of Aviation incorporated lavish, marble-floored halls, swastikas and memorials to famous German aviators. A vast Olympic Stadium, costing 77 million Reichsmarks, held 100,000 spectators, attending not only sporting events, but also major Nazi rallies. Here too, in adjoining towers, there were memorials for the fallen, in this case German soldiers of the First World War. By 1938 Hitler had also commissioned a new Reich Chancellery, since he now found the existing one too modest. It was even bigger and more imposing than the Munich buildings. The main gallery was nearly 500 feet long; twice as long, as Hitler noted, as the Hall of Mirrors at Versailles.[180] Inaugurated in 1939, the new Reich Chancellery, one commentator recorded, advertised 'the eminence and richness of a Reich which has become a super-power'.[181] In fact, the gigantism of all these projects, planned for completion by the early 1950s – a remarkably short space of time – was intended to signify Germany's arrival by that date not just as a super-power but as the dominant power in the world.[182]

The new Reich Chancellery was designed not by Hitler's favourite architect, Paul Troost, who had died in January 1934, but by a newcomer who was to play a central role in the Third Reich's later years, Troost's young collaborator Albert Speer. Born in Mannheim in 1905, Speer belonged to a generation of professionals whose ambitions were framed by the bitter and chaotic experiences of the First World War, the Revolution and the hyperinflation. The son of an architect, and thus a member of Germany's educated upper middle class, Speer trained with the architect Heinrich Tessenow in Berlin, and formed close friendships with a number of Tessenow's other pupils. Their teacher imbued them with an open approach to architecture, espousing neither modernism nor its antithesis, but emphasizing simplicity of form and the importance of rooting their style in the experience of the German people. As in every university in the mid-to-late 1920s, the atmosphere among the students was strongly right-wing, and despite his liberal background, Speer succumbed. In 1931, Hitler addressed Berlin's students at a beer-hall meeting. Speer, in the audience, was, he later confessed, 'carried away on the wave of the enthusiasm which, one could almost feel this physically, bore the speaker along from sentence to sentence. It swept away any scepticism, any reservations.'[183]

Overwhelmed, Speer joined the Nazi Party and threw himself into its work, volunteering for the National Socialist Drivers' Corps and exploring, though not taking up, the possibility of joining the SS. By 1932 he was practising architecture independently, and began to use his Party contacts to get commissions. Goebbels asked him to help with the conversion and refurbishment of the Propaganda Ministry, a building by the great nineteenth-century architect Friedrich von Schinkel which Goebbels had vandalized with the help of a gang of brownshirts on moving in. Not surprisingly, Goebbels scorned Speer's attempt to preserve what was left of Schinkel's Classical interiors, and had the work redone in a more grandiose style a few months after Speer had completed his task. The young architect's next project was more successful, however. Seeing the plans developed in the Propaganda Ministry for the celebration of the Day of National Labour on the Tempelhof Field in Berlin on 1 May 1933, Speer complained about their unimaginative quality and was commissioned to improve them. His successful innovations, including massive banners, swastikas and searchlights, led Goebbels to commission him to design the surround for the Nuremberg Rally later that year. It was Speer who, in 1934, created the 'cathedral of light' effect produced by upward-beamed searchlights that so impressed foreign visitors. Soon he was refurbishing Nazi Party offices and remodelling the interior of Goebbels's new house on the Wannsee, just outside Berlin. Speer felt himself energized by the purposeful atmosphere surrounding the Nazi leaders. He worked extremely hard and got things done quickly. In no time at all, still only in his late twenties, he had made a name for himself amongst the Nazi leadership.[184]

The death of Troost, whom Hitler had revered, catapulted Speer into the Leader's personal entourage, as Hitler co-opted the young man as his personal architectural adviser, someone to whom he could talk about his favourite hobby without the deference he had felt was owed to Troost. Speer was overwhelmed by this attention, and moved his family and home to be near to Hitler's Bavarian retreat above Berchtesgaden. A frequent guest at Hitler's mountain lodge, Speer was carried along by the Leader's desire to construct huge, monumental buildings in a style ultimately derived from Classical antiquity. Soon he was being entrusted with schemes of rapidly increasing ambition, many of them based on sketches Hitler had himself made in the early-to-mid 1920s. Speer was commissioned to rebuild and extend the Nuremberg Party Rally grounds in a series of imposing new buildings constructed at vast expense from the late 1930s, including a stadium that would hold 405,000 people, a Congress Hall seating 60,000 and two huge parade-grounds, the Zeppelin Field and the Mars Field, flanked by rows of columns and providing standing room for 250,000 and 500,000 people respectively.[185] Meanwhile he designed and built the German Pavilion at the 1937 World Exposition in Paris, another huge, bombastic structure, the largest in the entire exhibition. It was dominated by a massive pseudo-Classical tower of ten fluted piers joined by a cornice at the top, towering over all the nearby structures, including the Soviet pavilion, and outdone only by the Eiffel Tower, which stood at the end of the avenue on which the pavilions were located. Red swastikas glowed at night from the spaces between the piers. Next to the tower, the long, rectangular, windowless main hall projected a monolithic sense of unity to the outside world. Its interior was compared by an exiled German art critic, Paul Westheim, in a macabre, prophetic image, to a crematorium, with the tower taking the place of the chimney.[186]

Speer's success as the architect of propaganda constructions such as these led to his appointment by Hitler on 30 January 1938 as the General Building Inspector for the National Capital, charged with putting into effect the Leader's megalomaniac plans for the transformation of Berlin into a world capital, Germania, by 1950. A huge axis of wide boulevards designed for military parades was to be cut through Berlin. In the middle would stand a triumphal arch 400 feet high, more than twice as big as its counterpart in Paris, the Arc de Triomphe. The main avenue would lead up to a Great Hall, whose dome was to be 825 feet in diameter, the largest in the world. At the end of each of the four boulevards there would be an airport. Hitler himself had drawn up the plans many years before and discussed them with Speer many times since they had first met. Now, he decided, was the time to begin to put them into effect.[187] They would last for all eternity, a monument to the Third Reich when Hitler had long since departed the scene. Evictions and the bulldozing of houses and apartment blocks levelled the ground for the new boulevards, and part of the scheme was eventually opened to traffic. Meanwhile, fresh buildings were added, including the new Reich Chancellery, and soon Speer had built a scale model which Hitler spent many hours in the following years poring over in his company, making adjustments, and bemoaning the fact that he himself had never become an architect.[188]

By the mid-1930s, Speer was heading a large firm of architects and gaining managerial experience that would stand him in good stead when he was suddenly catapulted into a much larger and more important role during the war. Many of his most striking designs were not purely his own but were worked out in a team whose members, notably Hans Peter Klinke, a fellow student of Tessenow's, played a role at least as creative as his own. Moreover, the firm's designs were far from original or even particularly Nazi in style: the civic architecture of the era drew on Classical models in other countries too, and the idea of remodelling cities along geometrical lines, with broad boulevards and great public buildings, was hardly new either; in many ways, for instance, Speer's plans for Berlin bore a striking resemblance to the centre of the Federal capital of the United States in Washington, D.C., with its wide central mall surrounded by large colonnaded neo-Classical structures all in gleaming white stone. What distinguished Nazi civic architecture and city planning was not the Classical derivation of its style but the maniacal gigantism of its scale. Everything might not be very different from civic structures elsewhere, but it certainly was going to be vastly bigger than anything the world had so far seen. This was already apparent in the models of Berlin that Speer spent so much time inspecting with his master. On one occasion, he showed them in a private session to his 75-year-old father, himself a retired architect. 'You've all gone completely crazy,' the old man said.[189]

FROM DISCORD TO HARMONY

I

When Propaganda Minister Joseph Goebbels established the Reich Music Chamber in November 1933, he pulled off something of a coup by persuading Richard Strauss to act as the Chamber's President. Well before his appointment, Strauss had won the plaudits of the regime by taking over at short notice a conducting engagement originally assigned to the Jewish conductor Bruno Walter. Strauss disliked Walter, and was persuaded that if he did not step in, the orchestra – the Berlin Philharmonic – would lose vital earnings because the public would stay away. The regime, predictably, exploited the event for its own purposes.[190] Not long after, Strauss also stepped in to replace another banned conductor, Fritz Busch, and the anti-fascist Italian conductor Arturo Toscanini, who had refused on political grounds to conduct at the Bayreuth Festival.[191] Of his loyalty to the new regime, therefore, there could be little doubt. Strauss was at this time nearly seventy years of age. Over the preceding decades he had established an international reputation as Germany's leading composer, far outdoing all others in eminence and popularity. He was very conscious of his pre-eminence and his historic role. Writing in a lush, late-Romantic style, he was not an admirer of modernist and atonal music; when he was once asked what he thought of the atonal music of the serialist composer Arnold Schoenberg, Strauss said he would have been better off shovelling snow.[192]

Despite his huge reputation, Strauss was acutely conscious that he ultimately failed to achieve the standing of his great predecessors like Bach, Beethoven, Brahms or Wagner ('I may not be a first-class composer,' he is once said to have remarked with resigned self-deprecation, 'but I am a first-rate second-class composer'). His father, the illegitimate son of a Bavarian court clerk, had risen through his own musical talents to become a famous horn player, but the knowledge of his origins gave Strauss a sense of social insecurity that he was never quite able to shake off. Born in 1864, the composer had achieved conspicuous social and financial success in the Wilhelmine Reich, and during the Weimar Republic, not surprisingly, he was very much a political conservative. He was recorded by one observer at a private lunch in 1928 – the aesthete Count Harry Kessler – as condemning the Weimar Republic and calling for the establishment of a dictatorship, though Kessler, somewhat charitably, thought the remark may have been made ironically.[193] Strauss grasped the chance to become the leader of the musical profession in Germany. He accepted the Presidency of the Reich Music Chamber as his birthright. For many years, he had been campaigning and organizing on behalf of musicians over issues such as copyright, which had become more acute than ever in the age of the radio and the gramophone. Frustrated by the Weimar Republic's seeming inability to defend the position of the German musical tradition against the flood of popular music, operettas, musicals and jazz on the one hand, and the emergence of atonal and modernist music on the other, Strauss thought that the Third Reich would cut through the delays and confusions of the legislative process and deliver him, and his profession, what they wanted.[194]

Strauss was an experienced cultural politician, therefore, and expected something from Goebbels in return for his loyalty. The Propaganda Minister duly obliged, creating a central state agency for the protection of music copyright in 1934 and acceding to the Berne Copyright Convention, which extended protection over musical compositions from thirty to fifty years after the composer's death. But Goebbels was less enamoured of Strauss's attempts to use the Reich Music Chamber to enforce his own detestation of cheap operettas, jazz and light entertainment music, and Strauss's appointees to the Chamber were no match for Goebbels's men in the black arts of bureaucratic in-fighting and political intrigue. Soon the Ministry's representatives were complaining that the Chamber was not being run properly. Strauss was unable to defend himself because he was often away composing. He did not get on with his Vice-President, the eminent conductor Wilhelm Furtwängler. And, crucially, both men were soon at odds with the regime over the employment of Jewish musicians. During his younger years, Strauss had made many derogatory remarks about Jews, and Furtwängler too accepted commonplace right-wing shibboleths about 'Jewish-Bolshevism' and Jewish 'rootlessness'. But, as with many casual rather than fanatical antisemites, this did not prevent either of them from working with Jews if it suited them.[195]

In Strauss's case this meant the librettists Hugo von Hofmannsthal, who died in 1929, and Stefan Zweig, a best-selling author with whom he collaborated happily on a new opera, *The Silent Woman* (*Die schweigsame Frau*), in 1933–4. Alfred Rosenberg saw this as an opportunity to undermine Goebbels's control of the musical establishment, and pointed out that not only was the librettist of *The Silent Woman* Jewish, but the director of the opera house where the première was to be held had a Jewish wife. When Strauss insisted on Zweig's name being included in the programme, the director, who was held responsible, was forced into retirement. For his part, Zweig, who lived in Austria, had already signed a protest against the regime's policies, along with the novelist Thomas Mann, one of the Third Reich's most vociferous critics. He now declared himself unwilling to continue the collaboration with Strauss on the grounds that he could not approve of his work being produced in a Germany that subjected his fellow Jews to such persecution. Attempting to dissuade him, Strauss wrote to Zweig on 17 June 1935 claiming that he had not become President of the Reich Music Chamber because he supported the regime, but 'simply out of a sense of duty' and 'in order to prevent worse misfortunes'. By this time, the Gestapo had Zweig under observation and were opening his mail. They intercepted the letter, copied it and sent it to the Reich Chancellery. Strauss was already under attack from various quarters in the regime not only for his collaboration with Zweig, but also for using a Jewish-owned music house to print his works and commissioning a Jewish musician to make the piano reduction of the opera. Under growing pressure, and disappointed by the composer's inefficient management of the Reich Music Chamber, Goebbels decided that Strauss finally had to go. The composer was persuaded on 6 July 1935 to hand in his resignation as President of the Reich Music Chamber 'on account of a deterioration in his health'. Meanwhile, *The Silent Woman* was withdrawn after the second performance and banned for the duration of the Third Reich.[196]

Attempting to rescue something from the débâcle of *The Silent Woman*, Strauss wrote a personal letter to Hitler on 13 July 1935 asking for an audience. The intercepted letter which had led to his dismissal had, he protested, been 'misinterpreted ... as if I had ... little understanding for antisemitism or for the concept of the people's community'. Hitler did not even bother to reply. Attempts to obtain an interview with Goebbels were also brusquely rejected. Privately, Strauss noted bitterly: 'But it's a sad day when an artist of my standing has to ask a little lad of a Minister what he may compose and perform. I too just belong to the nation of "servants and waiters" and I almost envy my racially persecuted fellow Stefan Zweig.'[197] This did not stop him from trying to make a comeback. He composed the official hymn for the 1936 Berlin Olympics, but it was commissioned by the International Olympic Committee, not by the German government. The commission, and the hymn's success, did make Goebbels realize that Strauss's international prestige could be useful to the regime, and he was permitted to travel abroad as a cultural ambassador for Germany and to receive once more the plaudits of the international music-loving public. Goebbels arranged for him to conduct his work at the Reich Music Festival of 1938 in Düsseldorf, and with his blessing Strauss served on prize juries, received awards and birthday congratulations from the regime. The composer continued to launch new operas, including *The Day of Peace* (*Der Friedenstag*, 1938), designed to be acceptable to the regime, with libretti written by the safely Aryan Joseph Gregor, whom Strauss regarded as greatly inferior to his previous collaborators. But these were poor compensations for his removal from the centre of power, where other, more up-to-date composers were now finding favour with the regime.[198]

I I

Who those composers were, however, was by no means clear in 1933. Mere adherence to the Nazi Party in a political sense was only a matter of secondary importance. What really counted was, first of all, the racial affiliation of a given composer, living or dead. Jews, according to Nazi precept, were superficial, imitative, incapable of genuine creativity; worse still, they were subversive, degenerate, destructive of true music in the

German tradition. The composer Felix Mendelssohn, for instance, was alleged to have been a successful imitator of genuine German music, not the real thing; Gustav Mahler was the composer of degeneracy and decay; Arnold Schönberg's atonal music disrupted the idea of a harmonious German racial community with its dissonance. The Propaganda Ministry encouraged the publication of anything that helped to undermine the reputation of such composers with the concert-going public, from pseudo-scholarly tomes such as Richard Eichenauer's *Music and Race*, published in 1932, to dictionaries like *Musical Jews A-B-C*, which appeared in 1935. Regular articles in the specialist musical press and the cultural sections of the newspapers reinforced the message carried by such books.[199] And Nazi musicologists did not rest content with words alone.

In May 1938, inspired by the 'Degenerate Art' exhibition in Munich, Hans Severus Ziegler, manager of the national theatre in Weimar, organized an exhibition of 'Degenerate Music' in Düsseldorf as part of the first Reich Music Rally. Assisted by staff from Rosenberg's office, Ziegler hurriedly gathered a staff of cartoonists, technicians, designers and others and mounted a large exhibition, with sections on Jewish composers and conductors, music critics and teachers, modernist and atonal music and much more besides. 'What's been gathered together in the exhibition "Degenerate Music"', he thundered at the opening ceremony, 'constitutes the portrayal of a true witches' sabbath and the most frivolous spiritual-artistic cultural bolshevism and a portrayal of the triumph of subhumanity, of arrogant Jewish insolence and total spiritual senile dementia.' The exhibition dealt with the problem of how to show people what such music was actually like by installing six audio-booths where visitors could listen to specially cut gramophone records with extracts from music by Arnold Schönberg, Ernst Křenek and others. One, featuring excerpts from Kurt Weill's *Threepenny Opera*, was particularly sought after. Long queues formed in front of it, testifying to the music's enduring popularity amongst a public that had been deprived of the opportunity to hear it for half a decade. Yet there is good reason to believe that many of the other exhibits confirmed the prejudices of a conservative musical public that had never much liked the modernists anyway.[200] This action, and the radical intent behind it, were not wholly to the liking of Goebbels, who preferred instead to use the Reich Music Chamber as a means of regulating performances. 'Dr Ziegler's exhibition "Degenerate Music", he noted in his diary, 'is getting a lot of criticism. I get the objectionable parts removed.'[201] The exhibition closed after a mere three weeks.[202]

Meanwhile, a Reich Music Censorship Office had been established within the Chamber and issued lists of banned composers and works, including those of Irving Berlin, who was Jewish. Not only performances, but also records and broadcasts of anything or anyone on the list were banned. Mendelssohn posed a particular problem because many of his works were very popular. Individual conductors continued on occasion to perform his work – Furtwängler, for example, conducted the Berlin Philharmonic in three movements from Mendelssohn's *A Midsummer Night's Dream* in February 1934 to celebrate the 125th anniversary of the composer's birth – but when this happened, the newspapers simply did not mention it, so the impact was confined to those who attended the concert. In November 1936, when the British conductor Sir Thomas Beecham arrived with the London Philharmonic Orchestra for a guest performance at the Leipzig Gewandhaus, he obtained the permission of the city's conservative Lord Mayor, Carl Goerdeler, to lay a wreath at the memorial to Mendelssohn, who had done so much for Anglo-German musical relations in the nineteenth century. But when they looked for the memorial the morning after the concert, it was no longer there; the local Party boss, taking advantage of Goerdeler's absence on holiday, had removed it during the night and had it smashed to pieces. Furious, Goerdeler resigned as mayor shortly after his return and became increasingly hostile to the Nazi regime. As far as Mendelssohn was concerned, this also proved the turning-point. If Mendelssohn's music was still performed, it was from now on without attribution. By 1938 Mendelssohn's name had finally been removed from music publishers' and record company catalogues, and public performances of his music had virtually ceased. No fewer than forty-four different attempts were made between 1933 and 1944 by a whole variety of composers to provide an alternative to Mendelssohn's incidental music to *A Midsummer Night's Dream*; every one of them was inferior, as critics reviewing these performances were frequently forced to confess.[203]

Well-known works by non-Jewish composers were also subject to disapproval when they involved lyrics by Jewish writers such as Heinrich Heine, whose poem *The Lorelei* was so widely known that the regime decided to try and convince the general public that it was a folk-song rather than a poem written by a Jew. Problems of a different kind were posed by the operas of Wolfgang Amadeus Mozart. Three of the best-loved, Così fan tutte, The Marriage of Figaro and Don Giovanni, not only used libretti written by his Jewish collaborator Lorenzo da Ponte but were usually performed in German translations by the Jewish conductor Hermann Levi. By commissioning new translations from a non-Jewish author, Siegfried Anheisser, which were soon in use all over Germany, Rosenberg's office managed to distract attention from the inescapable fact that the original version had been written by a Jew. Rosenberg's encouragement of the 'Aryanization' of Handel's oratorios, which included a good deal of Old Testament material, aroused the hostility of Goebbels's Reich Music Chamber, which banned changes to their texts on 19 September 1934. This did not, however, prevent performances of Handel's Judas Maccabeus going ahead with the Jewish names and biblical references removed, and the whole oratorio appearing under the title The Commander.[204]

Non-Jewish composers were likely to incur the wrath of Rosenberg's office if they were in any way modernist or atonal or had aroused controversy in some way. If they were not German, then whether or not their music was performed was a matter of secondary importance as far as the Reich Music Chamber was concerned. This was why attacks on the music of Igor Stravinsky, one of the major butts of ridicule at the Degenerate Music Exhibition, failed to prevent it from being performed throughout the 1930s. Performances in Germany were encouraged by the composer himself, whose legendary business acumen even extended to obtaining special permission for royalties to be sent to him in Paris, where he had lived since before the First World War. Diplomatic considerations were never far from the mind of the Propaganda Ministry when dealing with foreign composers, so the modernist compositions of Béla Bartók were not banned because he was Hungarian, and Hungary was an ally of Germany. Bartók himself, an ardent anti-fascist, changed his German publishers when they were Aryanized, declared his solidarity with banned composers and protested to the Propaganda Ministry when he discovered that he had not featured in the Degenerate Music Exhibition, but all to no avail; his music continued to be performed in Germany, like that of Stravinsky.[205]

Where the composer in question was German, or even Austrian (which in the eyes of the Nazis was the same thing), matters stood quite differently. The pupils of Arnold Schönberg were singled out by the regime for their adherence to twelve-note atonality. Anton von Webern's music was banned from the beginning, while a performance of an orchestral concert suite from Alban Berg's as yet unfinished opera *Lulu* under the conductor Erich Kleiber in Berlin in November 1934 created a major uproar, with cries of 'Hail, Mozart!' from outraged members of the audience. The leading critic Hans-Heinz Stuckenschmidt, who had given the work a positive review in a Berlin newspaper, was expelled from the German Music Critics' Association (part of the Reich Chamber of Literature) and denied further employment as a result. The critic had already made enemies through his stubborn insistence on the virtues of composers like Stravinsky. They successfully blocked his subsequent attempts to find work for himself in Germany, and he was forced to leave for Prague. The work's conductor Erich Kleiber, dismayed at the hostility his performance had aroused, emigrated to Argentina two months later. Berg's music was not performed again in public under the Third Reich.[206] Doubtless the sensational character of *Lulu*, which included depictions of prostitution and featured Jack the Ripper as a character, also had something to do with the scandal. Another non-Jewish pupil of Schönberg's, Winfried Zillig, continued to use twelve-tone techniques, though in a relatively tonal way, but he escaped censure and continued to get work as a conductor and composer. His works included scenes from peasant life, the depiction of self-sacrificing heroism, and similar themes close to Nazi ideology. Here, as in the work of one or two other composers, the message triumphed over the medium.[207]

In one notorious case, however, neither the medium nor the message proved acceptable to the authorities, despite the fact that both appeared superficially to be reconcilable with Nazi aesthetics. Paul Hindemith, perhaps Germany's leading modernist composer under the Weimar Republic, had earned a reputation in the 1920s as an *enfant terrible* but changed his style to a more accessible neo-Classicism around 1930. This transition was recognized by some influential figures on the Nazi cultural scene in 1933, including Goebbels, who was keen to keep him in Germany as he was widely recognized as the country's second-most important composer after Strauss. At the beginning of the Third Reich,

Hindemith was engaged in writing to his own libretto an opera, *Matthias the Painter*, which centred on the medieval German artist Matthias Grünewald, a figure much beloved of Nazi art historians. The opera told of the painter's rebellious struggle to establish himself as a German artist, and its culmination in his acceptance of patronage from a state that finally recognized his talents. A new element of Romanticism in the score testified to its composer's continuing efforts to render his somewhat academic style more accessible to a wider public. Although he had made no secret of his opposition to fascism before the Nazi seizure of power, Hindemith had evidently decided to stay on and take his chances. He was duly appointed to the governing council of the Composers' Section of the Reich Music Chamber in November 1933. A three-movement symphony drawn from the music to *Matthias the Painter* was premièred by Furtwängler and the Berlin Philharmonic on 12 March 1934 and further performances were scheduled, together with a gramophone record. All seemed set for Hindemith's acceptance as the leading modern composer of the Third Reich.[208]

But Goebbels had not reckoned with the continuing machinations of his rival on the cultural-political scene, Alfred Rosenberg. Largely inspired by Rosenberg, a series of vitriolic attacks on Hindemith's past musical style and previous political affiliations appeared in the musical press in the course of 1934, and pressure was put on radio stations and concert agencies to ban performances of his work. In response to this campaign, the conductor Wilhelm Furtwängler wrote a stout defence of the composer in a daily newspaper on 25 November. Unfortunately, in doing so, the conductor chose to generalize his attack on the denunciations of Hindemith's work in the Nazi musical press. 'Where would we be,' he asked rhetorically, 'if political denunciations in the broadest sense were applied to art?' The affair escalated when Furtwängler's appearance on the rostrum at a performance of Wagner's *Tristan and Isolde* in the Berlin State Opera on the day of publication of his article was met by noisy demonstrations of support from the audience, who clearly felt that the conductor was defending artistic freedom against interference from the regime. Both Goebbels and Göring were present in the theatre to witness the demonstration. This put the whole affair onto a new level. Goebbels now closed ranks with Rosenberg in the face of this open opposition to the regime's cultural policies. On 4 December,

Goebbels forced Furtwängler to resign from all his posts in the Berlin State Opera, the Berlin Philharmonic, and the Reich Music Chamber. From now on, he would have to earn his living as a freelance. In a speech delivered to representatives of the creative arts in the Sports Palace on 6 December, the Propaganda Minister noted that Furtwängler had declared that Hindemith's days as a musical *provocateur* were over. But: 'ideological derailments cannot be excused by dismissing them as juvenilia'. That Hindemith was 'of pure Germanic origin' merely showed 'how deeply the Jewish-intellectual infection has already eaten into our own racial body'.[209]

Shocked by the suddenness of his downfall, Furtwängler met Goebbels on 28 February 1935 and told the Minister of his regret at the political implications that some had drawn from his original article. He had in no way intended, he assured the Minister, to criticize the artistic policies of the regime.[210] By 27 July 1936 Goebbels was noting a 'long conversation with Furtwängler in the garden at Wahnfried. He tells me all his concerns', noted the Propaganda Minister, 'sensibly and cleverly. He has learned a lot and is completely with us.'[211] Already in April 1935 Furtwängler was performing in his new capacity as guest conductor of the Berlin Philharmonic. In his absence, the orchestra's last remaining Jewish players, whom he had insisted on retaining while he had still been conductor-in-chief, had been fired. Furtwängler did very well in his new position. In 1939 he earned well over 200,000 Reichsmarks from this job and other sources, roughly a hundred times the annual income of the average manual labourer. He still considered leaving Germany, and early in 1936 he was offered the post of chief conductor of the New York Philharmonic. But Göring made it clear that, if he accepted, he would not be allowed back. And Furtwängler's capitulation to Goebbels the year before had aroused fierce criticism in the United States. He had since then conducted Wagner's *The Mastersingers of Nuremberg* at the Nuremberg Party Rally of 1935, where harsh discriminatory laws were promulgated against Germany's Jewish community. Not only the New York Philharmonic's Jewish supporters, but also many others, voiced their concern and threatened to boycott the orchestra if he was appointed. If Furtwängler had ever wanted to leave Germany for a top job in the USA, then he had simply left it too late. So he stayed on, to the plaudits of the regime.[212]

Hindemith himself went on indefinite leave of absence from his teaching position in Berlin, but stayed on in Germany for a while, trying to retrieve the situation by publicly distancing himself from atonal music and swearing an oath of allegiance to Hitler. His efforts on behalf of musical education might also have recommended him to the regime. His work continued to be performed in small concerts on the fringes of national musical life, and he received a commission for a new piece from Göring's air force. But attacks on him continued in the press, and opera directors and concert organizers were generally too nervous after the débâcle of *Matthias the Painter* to include his works in their repertoire. Most decisively of all, Hitler himself had never forgotten the notoriety that Hindemith had gained with his opera *News of the Day* in the 1920s. In 1936, Hitler used a speech at the annual Nuremberg Rally to urge the Party to redouble its efforts to purify the arts. The Propaganda Ministry promptly banned any more performances of Hindemith's music. The composer's treatise on harmony was exhibited at the Degenerate Music show in 1938, and Hindemith emigrated to Switzerland, where the first performance of his opera *Matthias the Painter* took place in May. From there he eventually left for the United States. In the end, what counted most was not his attempt to ingratiate himself artistically with the regime, but the fact that the controversy stirred up by his radical compositions of the 1920s was still remembered by leading Nazis a decade later. The fact that his wife was half-Jewish had not helped his cause. An earlier collaboration with Bertolt Brecht was still held against him, as was his work with a number of Jewish artists over the years. All of this made it easy for Rosenberg and his supporters to use him as a means of trying to loosen Goebbels's grip on music and the arts. They succeeded in this instance, but on the wider front of cultural politics they met with little success. By 1939 Rosenberg had all but abandoned his interest in the cultural scene, and had turned to foreign policy instead.[213]

III

If it was by no means easy for the Nazis to decide what kinds of music they did not like, and what kinds of conductors and composers they did not want, it was even more difficult reaching any kind of consistent policy on what kind of music they did wish to encourage. No real body of genuinely Nazi music emerged under the Third Reich, for all the theorizing of Nazi musicologists.[214] Those composers who flourished did so partly because they were not Jewish, partly because they made their style more accessible than it might otherwise have been, and partly because they turned to themes and topics that were acceptable to the regime, such as peasant life or national heroes. But it is impossible to bring the music they actually wrote down to any obvious common denominator. Moreover, few if any of them remained completely immune to the influence of the modernist style the Nazis so abhorred. Werner Egk, for example, wrote in a distinctly Stravinskyan mode, often putting the Bavarian folk tunes he employed into a context of spiky dissonance. Egk's opera *The Magic Fiddle*, first performed in 1935, won the plaudits of the regime, however, for its portrayal of the charm and tranquillity of peasant life. Its plot centred on the evil machinations of a villain, Guldensack (Money-bags), who in the context of the Third Reich was very obviously a Jew. The rumblings of a few critics from the Rosenberg camp were quickly subdued, and Egk cemented his triumph by declaring that no piece of German music should be so complicated that it could not be performed at a Nazi Party rally. Egk's next opera, *Peer Gynt*, also featured a quasi-Jewish villain, or rather villains, in the form of deformed and degenerate trolls, a somewhat loose interpretation of Ibsen's original play; Hitler himself, on attending a performance, which included not only Egk's usual Stravinskyan dissonances but also tango music and even a hint of jazz, was none the less so taken with the performance that he hailed Egk afterwards as a worthy successor to Richard Wagner.[215]

Stravinsky's influence was also to be found in the music of Carl Orff, who detested dissonance and had savagely attacked modernist composers such as Hindemith during the Weimar Republic. Orff first won the support of the regime through devising a large-scale project of musical

education in the schools, and successfully defended it against obscur-
antist criticisms from some of Rosenberg's supporters who disliked its
use of unconventional musical instruments. Although the project relied
heavily on folk music, however, it was too complex and too ambitious
to have much influence in the institutions for which it was designed,
such as the Hitler Youth. Orff shot to real prominence with the first
performance of his cantata *Carmina Burana* in June 1937. Based on
secular medieval poems, the cantata featured strong, simple rhythms
and monodic singing over a strongly percussive accompaniment. Its
primitivism, its use of often ribald verses and its preference in many parts
for Latin over German, aroused the suspicion of conservative critics
from the Rosenberg stable; but Orff had gained influential supporters
through his educational activities and Rosenberg's influence was on the
wane. *Carmina Burana*, powerful and original, yet simple and easy to
comprehend, was an immediate success and was performed all over
Germany. His further compositions may never quite have matched this,
but Orff's income and reputation were now secure. If any one musical
work of distinction composed under the Third Reich fitted the Nazi idea
of culture, then *Carmina Burana* was surely that work: its crude tonality,
its brutal, repetitious rhythms, its medieval texts and folksy tunes, its
numbing, insistent pulse, its absence of anything to engage the mind,
seemed to sweep away all the excrescences of modernity and intellectual-
ism that Nazism so detested and take culture back to the supposed
primitive simplicities of the distant, peasant past.[216]

In the end, however, compositions such as *Carmina Burana*, for all
their popularity, took second place in the musical pantheon to the work
of the great composers of previous ages most admired by Hitler. Chief
among these was Richard Wagner. Hitler had been a devotee of his
operas since his youth in Linz and Vienna before the First World War.
They filled his head with mythical pictures of a heroic Germanic past.
Wagner was also the author of a notorious pamphlet attacking *Jewry in
Music*. Yet the composer's influence on Hitler has often been exaggerated. Hitler never referred to Wagner as a source of his own antisemitism,
and there is no evidence that he actually read any of Wagner's writings.
He admired the composer's gritty courage in adversity, but did not
acknowledge any indebtedness to his ideas. If Wagner did have an influence on the Nazis, it was less direct, through the antisemitic doctrines of

the circle that his widow Cosima gathered after his death, and through the mythical world portrayed in his operas. In this area at least, they inhabited the same cultural space, filled with mythic Germanic nationalism. Hitler's devotion to Wagner and his music was obvious. Already in the 1920s he had become friendly with Wagner's English daughter-in-law Winifred and her husband Siegfried Wagner, guardians of the composer's shrine at the great opera house he had built in Bayreuth. They were staunch supporters of the far right. In the Third Reich they became something very like cultural royalty.[217]

From 1933 onwards, Hitler attended the Bayreuth festival of Wagner's music-dramas for a ten-day period every year. He poured money into the opera house, which he had subordinated directly to himself rather than to the Propaganda Ministry. He inaugurated monuments and memorials to Wagner, and tried to ensure packed houses at Wagner performances by instructing his underlings to make block bookings for their men. He even proposed rebuilding the opera house in a more grandiose style, and was only dissuaded by Winifred Wagner's insistence that the unique acoustics of the existing building, purpose-designed by the composer for performances of his own work, could not be reproduced in a larger space. His interference in productions was frequent, but it was also erratic. Hitler's personal patronage meant that neither Goebbels nor Rosenberg nor any of the other cultural politicians of the Third Reich could bring Bayreuth under their aegis. Paradoxically, therefore, Winifred Wagner and the managers of the Festival were granted an unusual degree of cultural autonomy. They were not even members of the Reich Theatre Chamber. They used their freedom, however, in a way that was entirely in keeping with the spirit of the Third Reich. The annual Bayreuth Festival became a Hitler festival, with Hitler greeting the audience from a balcony, his portrait on the frontispiece of the programme, Nazi propaganda in all the hotel rooms, and the streets and walkways surrounding the theatre bedecked with swastika flags.[218]

Goebbels and other leading Nazis grumbled about Hitler's passion for Wagner, which they thought rather eccentric. On Hitler's insistence the Nuremberg Party Rally opened every year with a gala performance of Wagner's *The Mastersingers of Nuremberg*. In 1933 Hitler issued a thousand free tickets to Party officials, but when he entered his box he found the theatre almost empty; the Party men had all chosen to go off to drink the evening away in the town's numerous beer-halls and cafés rather spend five hours listening to classical music. Furious, Hitler sent out patrols to haul them out of their drinking-dens, but even this could not fill the theatre. The next year was no better. Under strict orders to attend, many roughnecked Party officials could be seen dozing off during the interminable performance, waking up only at the end, to render rather half-hearted applause for an opera they had neither appreciated not understood. After this, Hitler gave up and the seats were sold to the public instead.[219] Yet despite this lack of interest on the part of almost everyone in the Party leadership except Hitler himself, the influence of Wagner's music was everywhere in the cultural scene. Journeymen composers churned out vast quantities of sub-Wagnerian sludge to order on any occasion when it was desired. Film, radio, newsreels were saturated with music of this kind. Over-exposure may have been one reason why Wagner actually became less popular with opera houses and the public during the Third Reich. Performances of his work declined from 1,837 in the 1932–3 opera season to 1,327 in 1938–9, while those of Verdi rose from 1,265 to 1,405 in 1937–8 and Puccini from 762 to 1,013 the following year. And while the list of the fifteen most popular operas in 1932–3, headed by Bizet's *Carmen*, contained four works by Wagner, in third, fourth, fifth and sixth place respectively, the same list in 1938–9, headed this time by Leoncavallo's *I Pagliacci*, included only one, at number twelve.[220] In the orchestral repertoire, the conventional late-Romantic music of the curmudgeonly, conservative and deeply anti-semitic Hans Pfitzner replaced that of the second most frequently performed twentieth-century composer after Richard Strauss, the now-banned Gustav Mahler, after 1933. At the same time, performances of foreign composers such as Sibelius, Debussy and Respighi continued alongside growing numbers of such now forgotten luminaries of the Nazi musical pantheon as Paul Graener and Max Trapp. In all of this, there was an obvious series of compromises between the political and racial imperatives of the regime, the continued, basically conservative taste of the musical public and the commercial requirements of keeping concert halls and opera houses afloat.[221]

Control over classical concerts and operas was relatively easy. But what went on in people's homes was more difficult to monitor. Musical culture ran very deep in Germany, and there was a long tradition of playing and singing within the family or groups of friends. Doubtless, where there were no sharp-eared neighbours or Block Wardens listening, people still continued to play Mendelssohn's much-loved *Songs without Words* on their piano at home despite their condemnation in the Nazi press as 'prattling chatter'.[222] Musical clubs, choirs, amateur chamber music groups and all the other small-scale, local institutions of Germany's rich musical tradition had all been Nazified in 1933, but even so, small groups of people could gather in private to play and listen to whatever chamber music they wanted, provided they were careful enough about whom they invited. Pre-censorship of sheet music by the Reich Chamber of Music only covered new work, after all. Playing Mendelssohn at home was hardly an act of resistance to the regime, and did not in any case constitute an offence against the law.[223] Even in public, however, there was at least some latitude. The Reich Music Censorship Office's list of banned works mainly covered jazz, and even in its second edition, published on 1 September 1939, it contained only fifty-four entries.[224]

Music is the most abstract of the arts, and therefore the most difficult to monitor and control under a dictatorship. The cultural arbiters of the Third Reich thought they knew what they wanted: ideological conformity in opera and song, tonal simplicity and the absence of dissonance in music where there were no words to betray the writer's ideological leanings. According to their cultural ideology, the spirit of tonality and simplicity was Aryan, that of atonality and complexity Jewish. Yet firing and banning Jewish musicians and composers had no effect on musical life apart from depriving it of many of its most distinguished and exciting figures. For what, in the end, was tonal music, what was dissonance? Technical definitions got nowhere, since all composers since before the days of Bach and Mozart have made liberal use of dissonance in the technical sense. Of course the extremes of atonality, above all the twelve-tone method developed by Arnold Schönberg and his pupils, were anathema; and tonal Romanticism such as that purveyed by Hans Pfitzner or Richard Strauss was unlikely to raise any objections. But most composers worked in the area between these two extremes. They had to tread a fine line between acceptance and rejection, often dependent on the patronage of powerful figures in the Party, either at national or local level, to ward off criticism from others. In this way, figures like Paul Hindemith or

Werner Egk became to some extent pawns in the power-games of Goeb-bels, Rosenberg and the other Nazi satraps. And where a composer or musician overstepped the mark and entered into the political realm, even Goebbels's sympathy for modernity could not save him.[225]

As in other areas of German culture, Goebbels in particular was conscious that music too could provide people with a refuge from the turmoil of everyday life. Just as he encouraged entertainment films and light music on the radio, so too he realized that performances of well-loved classical music could soothe and distract, and help people reconcile themselves to living in the Third Reich. Audiences for their part may, as many people claimed, have found in Furtwängler's concerts a source of alternative values to those propagated by the Nazis, but if this was indeed the case, then those values remained locked in their private souls, and it was indeed difficult, given music's abstraction from the real world, to see how it could have been otherwise. Music, in any case, like the other arts, had in Goebbels's view to be a sphere of relative autonomy for the creative artist. It could be purged and censored, and was, but it also had to be encouraged and supported, and in the main, the musicians had to run their own show; the state certainly was not competent to do it for them. The Propaganda Ministry was keen to nurture musicians through competitions, subsidies and improved arrangements for royalties. In March 1938 a thorough reorganization of salaries and pensions helped bring new musicians into a profession that had suffered financially in the economic depression. So many musicians had left the country, or been purged, or quit the profession, that a shortage was now threatening, exacerbated by the expansion of big organizations like the army, the SS, and the Labour Front, with their growing employment of military bands and orchestras. All of this continued to ensure the vitality of musical life in Germany, and great orchestras continued to perform great music under the baton of great conductors, although the range of music per-formed, and the number of prominent conductors who directed it, were both smaller than before 1933. Yet many considered that there were no new great composers. Strauss himself took this view. If anything, it even increased his already unshakeable sense of his own importance as the heir of the great tradition of German composers. 'I am the last mountain of a large mountain range,' he said: 'After me come the flatlands.'[226]

IV

Alfred Rosenberg's declining influence in the cultural sphere during the mid-1930s could not rescue the most excoriated and most defamed form of music under the Third Reich, namely jazz. Regarded by the Nazis as degenerate, foreign to German musical identity, associated with all kinds of decadence, and produced by racially inferior African-Americans and Jews, jazz, swing and other forms of popular music were stamped on as soon as the Nazis came to power. Foreign jazz musicians left or were expelled, and in 1935 German popular musicians were banned from using the foreign pseudonyms that had been so fashionable under the Weimar Republic. Jazz clubs, tolerated to a degree in the first year or so of the regime, began to be raided more frequently, and by larger numbers of agents from the Gestapo and the Reich Music Chamber, who intimidated the musicians by calling to see the papers that certified their membership of the Chamber, and by confiscating their scores if they were playing music by blacklisted Jewish composers such as Irving Berlin. Tight control over radio broadcasts made sure that light music did not swing too much, and the newspapers announced with a fanfare of publicity that 'Nigger music' had been banned from the airwaves altogether. Brownshirts patrolled summer beaches frequented by young people with portable wind-up gramophones and kicked their fragile shellac jazz records to smithereens. Classical composers whose music made use of jazz rhythms, such as the young Karl Amadeus Hartmann, found their music totally proscribed. Unable to make a living in Germany, but unwilling to leave, Hartmann depended for an income entirely on concerts and recordings abroad, where his identification with critics of the Third Reich put him in a situation of considerable potential risk. His wealthy and influential friends and relatives, mostly alienated from the regime, kept him afloat. His music made no compromises with the Third Reich's demands for simplicity and straightforwardness, and he went out of his way to distance it still further by taking composition lessons with the most extreme of Schönberg's modernist pupils, Anton von Webern. Hartmann took great care to avoid publicity, and his outward conformity with the regime in matters such as the Hitler salute warded off suspicion. When he dedicated a symphonic poem to his friends, dead and alive, who had been imprisoned in the concentration camp at Dachau, he made sure that the dedication was only visible on the original score, seen only by the conductor, a personal friend, at its first performance in Prague in 1935; it never became known to the Nazis.[227]

Jazz rhythms in classical music could easily be spotted and damned as inappropriate. But much if not most popular music was neither classical nor jazz, but existed somewhere in between, whether in the form of operettas – much favoured by Hitler himself – or the music of café crooners, palm-court orchestras or dance bands. The kind of popular music that was played in dance-halls, nightclubs, hotel bars and similar venues, above all in Berlin, was far more difficult to control, not least because of the extreme difficulty of drawing a clear line between what was jazz or swing, and what was not. The often wealthy and upper-class young people who patronized many such places were usually able to ward off hostile attention from agents of the Gestapo or the Reich Music Chamber. Imported jazz records could always be purchased discreetly from back-street shops, while even Goebbels was conscious enough of the popularity of jazz and swing to allow some to reach the airwaves in late-night broadcasts. And if it could not be heard on German radio stations, then jazz could always be found on Radio Luxemburg, where, Goebbels feared, listeners might also encounter factual broadcasts of a politically undesirable kind. Goebbels himself was a long-time patron of the variety shows at Berlin's Scala, where an audience of 3,000 not only gazed at the famous, high-kicking chorus line but also listened to the music of proscribed composers such as the Jewish-American George Gershwin. Goebbels was taken aback when criticisms of this programme appeared in Julius Streicher's *The Stormer* in May 1937, and with good reason. The managers had been changing the programme whenever Goebbels's staff telephoned in advance to say that he would be in the audience, so that it would not contain anything to offend Nazi taste after he arrived. He went ahead and purged the management all the same, enforcing on it a programme his deputy was soon describing as 'tame'.[228]

Jazz and swing were suspect to the regime not least because it thought they encouraged sexual licentiousness among the young. It also came under pressure from professional ballroom dancing instructors, who wanted to scotch the threat of swing-dancing, a new fad that had come into fashion in the summer of 1937. The Hitler Youth frowned on swing too, preferring to champion German folk dancing. Local authorities soon began to impose bans on this new fashion. Pouring scorn on such stuffiness, the gilded youth of Hamburg's wealthy mercantile and professional elite quickly began to flaunt their disdain in public, dressing up in the latest and most elegant British fashion clothes, sporting Union Jacks, carrying copies of The Times under their arms and greeting each other in English with phrases such as 'Hallo, Old Swing Boy!' In clubs and bars, and at private parties, they danced to swing music and played jazz records banned by the regime. They did not intend to mount a political protest. But under the Third Reich, everything was political. The young swingers crossed a significant line when, in 1937, they decided to defy the Hitler Youth Leader Baldur von Schirach's ordinance of 1 December 1936 proclaiming that all young Germans should join his organization. More seriously, the free-and-easy social mixing of Jews, half-Jews and non-Jews in the social scene of the swingers was crassly at odds with the dictates of the regime's racial policy. What had begun as an act of adolescent cultural wilfulness was rapidly becoming a manifestation of political protest. It would take on more serious dimensions during the war.[229]

The confusion and irrationality of Nazi policy towards music, where definitions were often arbitrary and acceptance or rejection frequently a matter of whim, can be neatly illustrated by the history of the humble mouth-organ, an instrument in whose world production Germany was absolutely dominant in the 1920s. In the mid-to-late 1920s, German exports of mouth-organs, or harmonicas, accounted for 88 per cent of the world export trade in the instrument as a whole. Within this trade, the Hohner company, in the small Swabian town of Trossingen, had the lion's share, producing between 20 and 22 million mouth-organs a year in this period, more than half the total. Almost all of these went to the United States. By this time, many markets had been virtually saturated, and the world economic crisis was depressing demand. So the company had to look to boosting its sales within Germany as a substitute. Unfortunately, the conservative classical music establishment took a very dim view of the instrument, considering it vulgar and amateurish. Their representatives succeeded in getting the harmonica banned from Prussian schools in 1931. The Hohner family riposted with an American-style advertising campaign, with pictures of the German heavyweight boxer Max Schmeling blowing away on his harmonica, and combined this with a counter-attack to try and persuade the musical world that their instrument was not subversive. After the Nazi seizure of power, Ernst Hohner, though in no way a convinced National Socialist, joined the Party to try and gain influence, and campaigned for the harmonica on the basis that it was an important part of folk music, played by ordinary, simple folk, and ideal for brownshirts and Hitler Youth parties to play as they sat swapping patriotic reminiscences round the camp fire.[230]

But this tactic was not successful. For one thing, folk music only took up 2.5 per cent of broadcasting time anyway. Then the Reich Music Chamber, still in many ways dominated by traditionalists, took the view that the harmonica was a modern instrument and not traditionally German at all, and pointed to its use by some jazz groups, surely damning evidence of its unsuitability. The Hitler Youth banned harmonica groups, though it still allowed individuals to play the instrument. A total ban in the long run seemed to be more than likely. But in the end, nobody seemed to know quite how to categorize the instrument, or perhaps even to care very much about it. Hohner and his firm were able to continue in existence, even running a school for mouth-organists in their home-town of Trossingen, in the ultimately vain hope that the harmonica would eventually gain the status of other, more conventional musical instruments. Here too, therefore, regulation, control, and in-fighting within the world of music ended by producing a stalemate. In the end, even the humble mouth-organ defied easy categorization within the world of Nazi ideology.[231]

V

Of all modern regimes that of the Third Reich defined itself most clearly by its art and mass culture. Hitler devoted more space in his speeches to these subjects than did any other twentieth-century dictator.[232] Of course, the Nazis borrowed a great deal from the rituals and symbols of Fascist Italy; and the disciplining of individual human bodies into a single, monolithic mass was a characteristic of Stalin's Russia as much as it was of Franco's Spain. All these regimes reduced the arts to instruments of propaganda and eliminated any sign of creative dissent, or at least tried to. They cracked down on complex and elitist aspects of modernist cultural productions and attempted to force on artists, writers and musicians a simple style that could communicate itself easily to the masses. Socialist realism in the Soviet Union was in many ways a parallel to what one might call racist and nationalist realism in the Third Reich. As the propaganda campaigns of the early 1930s had shown, well before Hitler came to power, the appeal to the emotions in sight and sound was a potent political weapon, and all political groupings, even the staid Social Democrats, had sought to exploit it, believing that in the age of the masses, the rational, verbal, intellectual appeal of previous ages was no longer enough. Under the Third Reich, the weapon of cultural propaganda was made into an instrument of state power, just as it was in Stalin's Russia. Artists and writers are by their nature individualistic, and both the Soviet Union and Nazi Germany waged an unremitting war on individualism, proclaiming art's only acceptable function to be the expression of the soul of the masses. Music proved the most difficult of the arts to control in both regimes, with composers such as Prokoviev and Shostakovich continuing to produce works in a very personal idiom despite occasional attempts to discipline them and periodic gestures of compromise on their part towards the cultural dictates of their political masters. In architecture, the style favoured by Troost, Speer and their ilk did little more than repeat the common features of the public building design of the age across Europe and the United States, only on a larger scale. Hitler's hostility to cultural modernism was extreme and contrasted with the more relaxed attitude of the Italian Fascists, one of whose main ideological sources had been the artistic politics of the Futurists. An Italian Futurist exhibition held in Berlin in 1934 aroused the disapproval of Nazi art commentators, who were bold enough to comment that they did not want to see such 'art bolshevism' again, despite the fact that the artists had declared themselves for Fascism. But looking back on the buildings of Speer, the sculptures of Breker, the music of Egk, or the films of Riefenstahl, it is clear that Nazi culture was recognizably part of the culture of its time. It belonged unmistakably to the 1930s; it was not a throwback to some earlier age.[233] In all these respects, the Third Reich's approach to culture and the arts was far from unique.[234]

And yet there was also something special about it. Of course, it was not surprising, in view of his early life and ambitions, that Hitler took a personal interest in the visual arts. His constantly repeated diatribes against modernism were surely the key factor in swinging policy away from Goebbels's relatively relaxed point of view and towards the effective suppression of modernism in all its varieties from 1937 onwards. But it would be illegitimate to conclude from this that he personally dictated cultural policy in every other area as well.[235] Apart from a passion for Wagner, he had little real interest in or understanding of music, whose essential abstraction in any case resisted easy classification into the acceptable and the unacceptable from the Nazi point of view; even the enthusiasm he developed towards the end of the 1930s for the music of Anton Bruckner was in the end rather half-hearted. Despite his penchant for watching old movies late at night, and his commissioning of Leni Riefenstahl to shoot *Triumph of the Will*, he did not intervene much in the film business, which was largely left to Goebbels, as were radio and literature. In all these areas, Goebbels had to contend with many rivals, most notably of course Alfred Rosenberg, but despite all the in-fighting, he achieved effective control for his Propaganda Ministry fairly early on in the regime, by the first months of 1935 at the latest. It would be easy to emphasize the complexities and contradictions of cultural life under the Third Reich, and indeed there were always marginal cases with whom the Nazis found it difficult to deal, and other cases where their decisions seemed almost entirely arbitrary and in retrospect might have gone either way. Artists, writers, musicians and others adopted a variety of strategies to deal with Nazi cultural dictatorship, ranging from total compliance through what they conceived of as necessary, minimal compromises in the interest of their art, to inner emigration and even complete silence, which was not always forced by the regime. Normal cultural life was not, despite the fears of many, totally extinguished under the Third Reich. People could still listen to symphonies by Beethoven, view the paintings of the Old Masters in state-funded art galleries, read the literature of the classics, even in some places visit jazz clubs and dance-halls where the latest swing numbers were played. For his part, Goebbels was a subtle enough politician to realize that people needed to escape from their everyday troubles in these ways, and allowed them the latitude to do so.[236]

For all this, however, the situation of the arts in the Third Reich was still determined by a cultural dictatorship imposed from above. As the

Degenerate Art exhibition showed, aesthetic and stylistic considerations were only a relatively minor determining factor in Nazi cultural policy. More important were political and ideological imperatives. Whatever the arts of the past had done, the Nazis wanted to ensure that what was produced in the present did not oppose their fundamental values and wherever possible worked to support them. Antisemitism, the removal of Jews from cultural life, the furthering of militarism and the crushing of pacifism and social criticism were basic tenets of Nazi cultural policy. So too were the improvement of the Aryan race and the suppression of the unfit and the weak, the re-creation of a mythical world of 'blood-and-soil' peasant life, the destruction of creativity that was personal and independent and the furthering of an impersonal cultural production that served the collective needs of the nation and the race. Above all, perhaps, Nazi culture glorified power, most obviously in architecture. Racial and political discrimination, implemented from the outset, resulted in the emigration from Germany of the country's best and most internationally acclaimed writers, painters and musicians. Those who were left were silenced, driven into irrelevance, forced to compromise, or enlisted in the service of the Nazis' overriding purpose: to make the nation and the country fit and ready for war.[237] To this end, the Nazis made an unprecedented effort to bring what they understood as culture to the masses, distributing cheap radios, holding concerts in factories, taking films to remote villages in mobile cinemas, bussing people to view the horrors of the Degenerate Art exhibition and much more besides. Culture in the Third Reich was no longer the privilege of an elite; it was intended to penetrate every area of German society and German life.[238]

Nazi cultural policy was ultimately of a piece with Nazi policy in other areas, and shared its contradictions. Hitler's own appreciation and understanding of the arts was fundamentally a political one. Art was in the end to be reduced to little more than a celebration of power and an instrument of propaganda. Ever alive to possible accusations of this kind, Goebbels declared on 17 June 1935:

The National Socialist movement . . . takes the view that politics is actually the greatest and noblest of the arts. For just as the sculptor chisels out of dead stone a form that breathes life, and just as the painter transforms pigment into life, and just as the composer translates dead notes into melodies that will charm

Heaven, so the politician and statesman has no other task than to convert an amorphous mass into a living people. Thus art and politics belong together.[239]

Nazism aestheticized politics; but it also politicized the arts.[240] 'We have often been accused', said Goebbels, 'of dragging German art down to the level of a mere matter of propaganda – how is this? Is propaganda something to which one can drag something else down? Isn't propaganda as *we* understand it also a kind of art?' Art and propaganda were one, he went on: and their purpose was to bring about a spiritual mobilization of the entire German people:

National Socialism is not only a *political* doctrine, it is a *total* and *all-encompassing* general perspective on all public matters. So our entire life has to be based on it as a matter of natural assumption. We hope that the day will come when nobody needs to *talk* about National Socialism any more, since it has become the air that we breathe! Thus National Socialism cannot be content with mere lip-service – it must be acted upon with hand and heart. People must get used *inwardly* to this way of behaving, they must make it into their *own* set of attitudes – only then will it be recognized that a new will to culture has arisen from National Socialism and that this will to culture determines our entire national existence in an organic manner. One day, the spiritual awakening of our own time will emerge from this will to culture.[241]

Nazi emblems, signs, words and concepts permeated everyday life as part of this campaign. Not only were film, radio, newspapers, magazines, sculptures, painting, literature, poetry, architecture, music and high culture increasingly informed by Nazi ideals, or confined within the boundaries they set, but everyday culture was as well. Between the flag-waving and swastika-bedaubed days of ideological mobilization such as Hitler's birthday or the anniversary of his appointment as Reich Chancellor, ordinary life was permeated by the principles and precepts of Nazism too. From 1935, as Victor Klemperer noted, the regime encouraged people to use new, pseudo-Germanic names of the months. Ever enthusiastic, Luise Solmitz began using them immediately in her diary, instead of the traditionally Latinate ones: *Julmond*, *Brechmond* and so on.[242]

Advertising and design began to incorporate Nazi symbols and to adopt approved Nazi style.[243] Foreign advertising agencies were banned, and the usual mechanisms were set up to ensure that posters and advertisements would be 'German' in origin and style. Consumer products were now advertised in a manner that conformed to the regime's requirements as much as high art did.[244] Everyday objects quickly acquired a political veneer. Already in March 1933 the sharp-eyed Victor Klemperer noticed that the toothpaste tube he purchased in the pharmacy was labelled with a swastika.[245] Before long, people could buy eggcups, hairpins, pencils or tea services decorated with swastikas, or give their children presents like toy models of stormtroopers, music boxes that played the Horst Wessel Song, or a puzzle that asked them to 'put the letters together correctly to make the name of a great leader: L-I-T-R-E-H.'[246] The tubular steel furniture so beloved of the Bauhaus in the 1920s used up valuable metal badly needed for armaments, so in a convenient marriage of ideology and economics, it now gave way to lacquered wood and a pseudo-natural style – pseudo because it was increasingly delivered by industrial mass production, despite the appearance of being made by hand.[247] Even a seemingly neutral area such as landscaping and garden design was not immune from this process: formality and foreign plants were out and a natural look based on native German species was in.[248] Those who enjoyed collecting cigarette cards could now stick them into an album depicting 'the struggle for the Third Reich'. Among cards available to smokers were portrayals of Hitler talking to a blonde child ('Leader's eyes – Father's eyes'), Hitler and Technology, Hitler and Hindenburg and of course Hitler and the Workers.[249] As a leading Nazi art magazine remarked in 1937: 'It is everyday things, not great individual works, that give an era its cultural atmosphere.'[250]

The aestheticization of politics created the illusion that social, economic and national problems were immediately being solved by acts of will. It directed people's attention away from many of the hard realities of life in a Germany that was still suffering from a severe economic depression in the early-to-mid-1930s, and towards fantasy-worlds and myths, stage-managed enthusiasm for the government and its policies, a feeling of living in a new world much of which, in fact, was illusion. In an advanced industrial culture such as that of Germany in the 1930s, these illusions depended to a degree on the resurrection of pseudo-archaic certainties such as 'blood and soil', Classical artistic models, traditional tonal music, and massively solid public buildings; but the means used were the most modern available, from radio and film to novel print techniques and the latest methods of construction. Much of this must have seemed startlingly new to the average person in rural or small-town Germany. Above all, Nazi culture, driven on by the Propaganda Ministry, aimed to crush individual thought and feeling and mould Germans into a single, obedient, disciplined mass, much as they appeared on the screen in Riefenstahl's *Triumph of the Will*.[251] It implemented this aim only gradually, partly because of initial uncertainty about the direction of cultural policy, partly because of intra-party rivalries; but in the notable radicalization that occurred in 1937–8, the contours of Nazi cultural policy finally became clear to all. By this time, virtually all the organs of opinion-formation in German society had been taken over by Goebbels and his Propaganda Ministry, co-ordinated, purged of real and potential dissenters, Aryanized and brought under ideological, financial and administrative control. 'Public opinion' as such had effectively ceased to exist; the opinions that were purveyed on the screen, broadcast over the radio, or printed in newspapers, magazines and books were with few and very partial exceptions the opinions of the regime. Regular reports from the Gestapo and local and regional administrators kept Goebbels, Himmler and the other Nazi leaders informed on the state of opinion of the people and allowed the Propaganda Ministry to run specifically targeted propaganda campaigns in order if necessary to correct it. Nazi propaganda was the essential accompaniment to Nazi terror and intimidation in suppressing open dissent and creating mass support for the regime. In this respect, the Propaganda Ministry was one of the regime's most obvious successes.[252]

So deep was the penetration of Nazi propaganda, so all-encompassing its permeation of the German mass media, that it affected the very language Germans wrote and spoke. In his home in Dresden, Victor Klemperer began compiling a dossier of Nazi language – *LTI* – *Lingua Tertii Imperii*, the language of the Third Reich. Words that in a normal, civilized society had a negative connotation acquired the opposite sense under Nazism, he noted; so that 'fanatical', 'brutal', 'ruthless', 'uncompromising', 'hard' all became words of praise instead of disapproval. The German language became a language of superlatives, so that everything the regime did became the best and the greatest, its achievements unprecedented, unique, historic and incomparable. Government statistics underwent an inflation that took them far beyond the limits of the plausible. Decisions were always final, changes were always made to last for ever. The language used about Hitler, Klemperer noted, was shot through and through with religious metaphors; people 'believed in him', he was the redeemer, the saviour, the instrument of Providence, his spirit lived in and through the German nation, the Third Reich was the eternal and everlasting Kingdom of the German people, and those who had died in its cause were martyrs. Nazi institutions domesticated themselves in the German language through abbreviations and acronyms, until talking about them became an unthinking part of everyday life. Above all, perhaps, Nazism imbued the German language with the metaphors of battle: the battle for jobs, the struggle for existence, the fight for culture. In the hands of the Nazi propaganda apparatus, the German language became strident, aggressive and militaristic. Commonplace matters were described in terms more suited to the battlefield. The language itself began to be mobilized for war.[253]

If language structures sensibility, and the words available to a society set the limits to what is thinkable, then the Third Reich was well on the way to eliminating even the possibility of thinking about dissent and resistance, let alone acting it out in reality. Yet the minds of most Germans, of course, had been formed well before Hitler came to power, and powerful cultural traditions such as those shared by millions of Catholics, Social Democrats and Communists could not be wiped from the face of Germany overnight. Even amongst the millions who had voted for Hitler in 1932 and 1933, there were many, probably indeed the majority, who did not vote for the full package of Nazi ideology. Many middle-class voters had supported the Nazi Party at the polls not least because in the election campaigns of the early 1930s the Nazis had been deliberately vague about what they proposed to do once they had achieved power. The Nazi vote in 1932 was above all a protest vote, more negative than positive. Powerful, sophisticated and all-pervasive though it was, therefore, Goebbels's propaganda machine could not persuade people that all their most dearly held values and beliefs had to be abandoned in the brave new world of Hitler's Third Reich. Moreover, many people soon found the regime's untiring demands for constant popular acclamation of its policies and leaders wearisome. 'The huge hyperactivity in the field of cultural politics', reported the Gestapo in the Potsdam district as early as August 1934, 'is partly felt to be a burdensome compulsion and for this reason it is either rejected or sabotaged.' Local cultural initiative had been stifled by the creation of huge mass organizations in the process of 'co-ordination'. The introduction of the leadership principle everywhere only made things worse. 'It is schematized, and thus nothing produces success, which is always individual.'[254]

The mass acclamation which the regime demanded on occasions such as Hitler's birthday, plebiscites and elections, Mayday and other festivals, was rendered as much out of fear as out of enthusiasm, and people were getting tired of constantly having to go to meetings and demonstrations, the Potsdam district Gestapo office reported two months later in October 1934.[255] In radio, cinema, literature and the arts, as we have seen, all that Goebbels's efforts to make propaganda interesting did was to make people bored, because individual creative initiative was stifled, the variety of cultural life was drastically reduced by censorship, and the monotony of Nazism's cultural offerings quickly became tedious. Even the Nuremberg Rallies soon lost much of their power to inspire, despite the fact that those who attended were by definition the most fanatical and the most enthusiastic of Hitler's supporters. As Social Democratic agents in Germany reported to the exiled party headquarters in Prague in 1937, with just a hint of exaggerated optimism:

In the first two or three years one saw the Nazis' morale at a high point, and the population still paid attention to the Leader's announcements, which usually provided surprises. When the columns of Party activists marched to the railway stations, one saw in the streets not infrequently groups of women and men, and particularly young people, who cheered on the soldiers of the Party with enthusiasm. All that has gone. Even the greatest demonstration of power becomes boring in the long run. The hackneyed speeches have become familiar to the point of excess. Hitler's former voters see in the Party no longer a redemptive force but instead the all-oppressing power-apparatus of a ruthless organization that is capable of anything. People let the Party divisions ordered to Nuremberg march past in silence. Here and there one hears a cry of 'hail!' from a persistent admirer, but it trails shyly away because nobody echoes it. As far as the population is concerned, this propaganda business is like everything else, just a way of getting money from them, nothing more. Always the same picture: the military, marching columns and groups bearing flags. Sometimes fewer, sometimes more. People cast a glance at them and go on their way.[256]

Goebbels seemed, therefore largely to have failed in his aim of bringing about a genuine, long-term spiritual mobilization of the German people. What he had mostly achieved, except in a relatively small group of fanatical Nazi activists, was the kind of dull conformity he had seen as so unsatisfactory in 1933.[257]

Nazi propaganda was most effective at the points where it hit the area of overlap between Nazi ideology and other ideologies. This was greater among some groups and areas than others. In the conservative, nationalist upper classes, the overlap was so considerable that men such as Vice-Chancellor Franz von Papen, Defence Minister Werner von Blomberg, Justice Minister Franz Gürtner or Finance Minister Lutz Schwerin von Krosigk willingly entered into a coalition with the Nazis in 1933 and stayed there, whatever their reservations, through the following years. Some of them, like Papen, gradually realized that the differences between their own beliefs and those of the Nazis were greater than they had at first thought; others, like Gürtner, gradually came round to a greater degree of conformity under the impact of propaganda and the pressure of events. Amongst middle-class Germans, the regime's propaganda offensive against 'Marxism' and Communism met with widespread support, helped by revulsion at the violent revolutionary rhetoric of the Communist champions of a 'Soviet Germany' and at the continuing ideological allegiance paid by the Social Democrats to Marxist theories of the socialist overthrow of existing institutions of capitalist society. Far more widespread was nationalist resentment at the 1919 Peace Settlement, a belief in the need to unite Germany in a rebirth of the spirit of 1914 after the deep and damaging divisions of the Weimar years, and a longing for a strong leader in the tradition of Bismarck. Similarly, antisemitism had become widespread in German culture during the Weimar Republic, though it never had much purchase on the organized working class, belief in the backwardness of Slavs was shared by almost everyone right of the Communists, and the conviction in the racial inferiority of black Africans was virtually universal.

In all these areas, Nazi propaganda was able to build on existing beliefs and values and create a new consensus that may well have encompassed a majority of the German people, though it hardly ever reached universal acceptance in any of the areas it touched upon. Moreover, the Nazi spin on specific events could usually convince people if it appealed to their existing fears and prejudices. On the face of it, for instance, the regime's explanation of the Reichstag fire in 1933 was not particularly plausible, and was indeed publicly falsified by the subsequent trial. Yet people already infused with fear of the Communists could easily be persuaded that van der Lubbe had been acting as a tool of a revolutionary conspiracy when he burned down the nation's legislature. Similarly, the murders committed on Hitler's and Göring's orders in the 'Night of the Long Knives' were quite blatantly outside the law; yet the German tradition of treating law as a creation of the state, and the widespread fear of further revolutionary violence of the kind the brownshirts seemed to be preparing, combined to convince most people of the legitimacy of Hitler's actions. Indeed, the regime succeeded within a remarkably short space of time in elevating Hitler to a status of almost mythical impregnability, deflecting criticism and discontent onto his subordinates and projecting on to him all kinds of unrealistic hopes and desires. Hitler became the Leader who was above party, almost above politics. For the great majority of Germans, including millions in the otherwise recalcitrant Catholic and working-class communities, Hitler was the Leader who could do no wrong.[258]

Where Nazi propaganda ran up against deeply ingrained attitudes, however, it found it far less easy to make an impact. Correspondingly, it was most successful with people whose opinions were not strongly formed, which meant above all the young. Moreover, whatever propagandists might claim, people had a clear idea of the realities of the economic and social situation on the ground. They did not find it difficult to disbelieve the grandiose claims of the Propaganda Ministry. The proclamation of the abolition of class differences, the creation of a unified national community, or the miraculous recovery of the economy meant little to them if their own situation continued to show few improvements over the dire straits of the early 1930s. Propaganda depended for its effect, in other words, not least on the extent to which it bore at least some relation to the truth, when it came to specific issues like the economy, or Germany's place in the world. Success bred support for the regime and belief in its purposes, failure created scepticism about its claims and doubts about its policies.[259] Yet, the Nazis claimed, time was on their side. The permeation of the thought and actions of all Germans did not depend simply on the power and sophistication of propaganda in the present. In the longer term, remoulding the educational system would create a new generation of young Germans who had known no alternative source of values to Nazism. Yet there was of course one area in which such values did persist, long after Marxism, socialism and all the other political and social creeds had been swept away. That was religion. For reasons of political expediency and caution, the Third Reich had stopped short in 1933 of attacking the Churches and their dependent secular institutions. As it became more self-confident, however, it began to turn its attention to Christianity too, and to seek a means of either converting it to a form more suitable to the new Germany, or, if that did not work, of doing away with it altogether.

3

CONVERTING THE SOUL

MATTERS OF FAITH

I

The Nazis abhorred the confessional division of Germany, and, in an obvious parallel to their policy of co-ordination in secular areas of politics, culture and society, many of them wanted a single national religion with a single national Church. The division, they believed, had deepened under the Weimar Republic during bitter conflicts over issues such as education, welfare, mixed marriages and local religious processions, undermining the national will.[1] The German Evangelical Church seemed to the Nazis to offer an almost ideal vehicle for the religious unification of the German people. Uniting the Lutheran and Calvinist faiths since the early nineteenth century, the Evangelical Church, unlike its Catholic counterpart, owed no real allegiance to any worldwide body or any institution, such as the Papacy, outside Germany itself. It had long been politically extremely conservative. In the days of the Bismarckian Reich it had been effectively an arm of the state; the King of Prussia, who also served as German Emperor, was Head of the Evangelical Church in Prussia, and he made no secret of the fact that he expected it to show loyalty to established institutions. German nationalists saw the German Reich as a Protestant state, a belief expressed in many ways over the decades, from the persecution of Catholics by Bismarck in the 1870s to the widespread and sometimes murderous hostility shown to Catholic priests by German troops during the invasion of France and Belgium in 1914. Germany's Protestant clergy had presented the First World War as a religious crusade against the Catholic French and Belgians and the Orthodox Russians, and it was clear that, for many, nationalism and Protestantism had become two sides of the same ideological coin.[2]

A characteristic personal example of the fusion of patriotism, militarism and religiosity in the mainstream tradition of German Protestantism was provided by the Berlin pastor Martin Niemöller, born in 1892, and himself the son of a Lutheran pastor, though one who had been baptized as a Calvinist. Niemöller became an officer-cadet in the German navy and then served on board submarines in the First World War, taking command of one in June 1918. His war reminiscences were no literary masterpiece, but they exuded a gung-ho spirit comparable to that of Ernst Jünger's *Storm of Steel*, celebrating the sinking of enemy merchant ships with gusto. Docking at Kiel in late November 1918 after hearing over the radio the news of the war's end and the monarchy's collapse, he found himself, as he later wrote, 'a stranger in my own country'. There was 'no rallying-point for nationally-minded men' who opposed 'the wirepullers of this "Revolution"'.[3] A period working on a farm convinced him that he had to take a hand in rescuing his nation from the spiritual catastrophe he thought had overwhelmed it, and he began training as a pastor in Westphalia. Active in the students' league of the German Nationalists, he supported the abortive Kapp putsch that attempted the overthrow of the Republic in March 1920. He helped found a 750-man student Free Corps unit to fight against the Red Army that had been formed by left-wing groups in the region. Later on, he was involved in another far-right paramilitary group, the Organization Escherich. In 1923, Niemöller and his brothers acted as pallbearers to the nationalist saboteur Albert Leo Schlageter, shot by French troops in Düsseldorf during their occupation of the Ruhr.[4]

Of Niemöller's opposition to the Weimar Republic, as of his rejection of the 1919 Peace Settlement, there could be no doubt. Yet his recipe for national renewal was as much spiritual as political. After taking on government-sponsored emergency relief work as a railway ganger to keep his family afloat during the great inflation of 1923, he joined the Protestant Church's social welfare division, the Inner Mission, learning a great deal about Germany's social problems, gaining valuable administrative experience and building up a network of contacts in the Protestant community across Germany. In 1931, he became third pastor of the plush villa suburb of Dahlem, in Berlin. Characteristically he paid as much attention to the servants and estate workers who formed the district's lower class as he did to the wealthy and cultivated families who inhabited its large and elegant villas. Committed right-wing but populist pastors like Niemöller were particularly susceptible to the appeal of the Nazis, and Niemöller voted for Hitler in March 1933. In 1931 he had already delivered a radio broadcast calling for the emergence of a new national leader, and in 1933 he thought one had at last arrived in the shape of Adolf Hitler. His sermons of this period took up the Nazi call for a united, positive Christianity that would overcome the religious divisions that had plagued Germany for so many years. And he echoed the Nazi claim that the Jews had been unduly influential in the Weimar Republic. In 1935 he sermonized about the poisonous influence of the Jews in world history, the outcome, he thought, of the curse that had lain on them since the Crucifixion.[5]

For nationalist Protestants like Niemöller, the enemy was Marxism, in both its Communist and Social Democratic variants. Its atheistic doctrines had been dechristianizing the working class since well before the end of the nineteenth century.[6] Many Protestants, including senior figures such as the Lutheran bishop Theophil Wurm, saw the advent of the Third Reich as an opportunity finally to reverse this trend, especially since point 24 of the Nazi Party programme presented the movement in terms of 'positive Christianity' and announced its fight against 'Jewish materialism'. And indeed, in the first months of the Third Reich, enthusiastic Protestant pastors staged a number of spectacular mass baptisms of children who had been left unbaptized during the Weimar years, and even mass simultaneous weddings of brownshirts and their brides who had only undergone a secular marriage under the old regime.[7] The Protestant population, numbering about 40 million, almost two-thirds of the population of the Reich as a whole, had also provided the broadest and deepest reservoir of support for the Nazi Party in all social groups during its electoral triumphs of the early 1930s. A substantial number of Nazi voters were former supporters of the quintessential Protestant party, the Nationalists. The Nazis capitalized on this. In 1933 they organized massive celebrations for the 450th anniversary of Martin Luther's birth, reworking his memory to convert him into a precursor of themselves.[8] Pseudo-restorationist events, such as the Day of Potsdam in March 1933, deliberately held in the Garrison church in order to underline the symbiosis of Protestant religion and Prussian tradition, exerted a strong appeal to many Protestants.[9]

In the light of all this, and particularly of the long history of state control, it was not surprising that there were serious moves to Nazify the Evangelical Church in 1933. Hitler seems to have had the ambition of converting it into a new kind of national Church, purveying the new racial and nationalist doctrines of the regime and eventually winning over the mass of Catholics to the Nazi cause as well.[10] The key role was to be played here by the 'German Christians', a pressure-group organized by Nazi supporters amongst the clergy in May 1932. These were by no means a negligible minority. By the mid-1930s they numbered some 600,000 members of the Evangelical Church. As early as November 1932 they won a third of the seats in the Prussian Church elections. This put them in a strong position to take over the whole Church, an intention they announced at a mass meeting in Berlin in early April 1933. Just as the government were centralizing the federal structure of Germany through the 'co-ordination' of the federated states, so the German Christians now pressed for the abolition of the federal structure of the Evangelical Church, with its 28 autonomous regional Churches, and its replacement by a centralized 'Reich Church' under Nazi control. With Hitler's public support, this Church was duly created, the majority candidate for the post of Reich Bishop, Fritz von Bodelschwingh, was overthrown after only a few weeks in office, and Ludwig Müller, a Nazi nominee, was appointed to the new post. Backed by a massive outpouring of propaganda from Goebbels's Ministry and the press, the German Christians won a sweeping victory in the Church elections of 23 July 1933.[11]

These moves brought to dominance Protestants whose declared aim since well before the Nazi seizure of power had been to oppose the 'Jewish mission in Germany', to reject 'the spirit of Christian cosmopolitanism' and to fight 'racial mixing' as part of its mission to establish a 'belief in Christ appropriate to our race'.[12] Such views had wide support amongst Protestant clergymen and theologians. Already in April 1933 the Bavarian Protestant Church ordered flags to be flown from all its buildings on Hitler's birthday. By the summer, congregations were becoming used to seeing their German Christian pastors preaching in SA or even SS uniforms instead of surplices, and holding special services to dedicate flags and other emblems of the stormtroopers, whose uniformed presence at services now added a clear element of intimidation to the deliberations of the Evangelical Church at every level. Nevertheless, the German Christians were in no sense opportunists driven by fear; on the contrary, they represented the culmination, in an extreme form, of a long-term identification of German Protestantism with German nationalism. They proceeded with enthusiasm to hang swastika flags in their churches, carve the Nazi symbol into new church bells, and mount rituals and ceremonies to celebrate the symbiosis of the Protestant faith and the Third Reich.[13]

The co-ordination of the Protestant Church was driven forward, among other factors, by the appointment of the lawyer August Jäger as State Commissioner for the Evangelical Churches in Prussia. Jäger declared that Hitler was completing what Luther had begun. They were 'working together for the salvation of the German race'. Jesus represented 'a flaring-up of the Nordic species in the midst of a world tortured by symptoms of degeneracy'.[14] In conformity with the 'leadership principle', Jäger dissolved all elected bodies in the Prussian Church and replaced many existing officials with German Christians. Meanwhile, Reich Bishop Ludwig Müller had taken over the administrative headquarters of the Evangelical Church with the aid of a band of stormtroopers. By September, pressure was growing within the Reich Church to dismiss all Jews from Church employment.[15] Much of the pressure came from ordinary pastors. Prominent here were young pastors from lower-middle-class backgrounds or non-academic families, men for whom war service had often been a life-defining experience, and racially conscious pastors from areas near Germany's eastern borders for whom Protestantism represented German culture against the Catholicism of the Poles or the Orthodox faith of the Russians. Such men desired a Church militant based on the aggressive propagation of the Gospel, a crusading Church whose members were soldiers for Jesus and the Fatherland, tough, hard and uncompromising. Muscular Christianity of this kind appealed particularly to young men who despised the feminization of religion through its involvement in charity, welfare and acts of compassion. The traditional Pietist emphasis on sin and repentance, which dwelt on images of Christ's suffering and transfiguration, was anathema to such men. They demanded instead an image of Christ that would set a heroic example for German men in the world of the here and now. For them, Hitler took on the mantle of a national redeemer who would bring about the rechristianization of society along with its national reawakening.[16]

II

On 13 November 1933, to mark their triumph within the Protestant Church, 20,000 German Christians assembled at the Sports Palace in Berlin demanded the sacking of all pastors who had not yet declared in favour of the new regime. At the same meeting, the regional Church administrator Reinhold Krause called for the removal of the 'Jewish' Old Testament from the Christian Bible and the purging of the New Testament of the 'Rabbi Paul's theology of inferiority'. He declared that the spirit of Christ was closely related to the Nordic spirit. The cross, too, he added, was a Jewish symbol, unacceptable in the new Reich.[17] But his speech did not go without contradiction. Politically conservative though they were, a substantial number of Protestant clergy believed that religion, not race, should be the touchstone of Church membership. They were becoming increasingly worried about the rapid Nazification of the Church and its consequent loss of autonomy. The 27-year-old Berlin theologian Dietrich Bonhoeffer spoke out in April 1933 in defence of equal status for Jewish converts. He took a hand in organizing the unsuccessful opposition to the German Christians in the Church elections. Oppositional pastors soon began to organize in groups, then in regional synods. Among them was Martin Niemöller, who, for all his sympathy with the regime, now considered that the racist politicization of the Church was a threat to his traditionalist conception of Protestant Christianity. On 11 September 1933, with a group of colleagues, he set up the Pastors' Emergency League. Led by Bonhoeffer and Niemöller, the Emergency League won the allegiance of nearly 6,000 pastors by the end of 1933. Autonomous diocesan organizations began to re-establish themselves in the wake of this protest too, reversing their previous co-ordination into a centralized national body.[18]

The rebel movement was propagated above all by middle-class pastors from academic backgrounds. A quarter of the core group of Berlin parish priests who joined and stayed with the rebels were from theologians' or pastors' families; for them, war service had not in general been a transforming experience, and, nationalists though they were, religion came first. Only 5 per cent of them were members of the Nazi Party, as against 40 per cent of German Christian pastors in Berlin. Many of the rebels came from the central Prussian provinces, far from Germany's contested ethnic borderlands. They rejected the unscriptural theological innovations of the German Christians, and founded their movement above all on Bible study groups, where women were very much in the majority, in contrast to the male-dominated movement of the German Christians. The rebels' basic beliefs were formed by a piety that veered increasingly towards biblical fundamentalism, a factor which repelled those few pastors who were former liberals or Social Democrats and who therefore stayed well clear of the movement themselves.[19]

Reich Bishop Müller tried to undermine the rebels by banning any mention of the dispute from sermons, disciplining some of the dissidents, and merging the Protestant youth organizations, with over a million members, into the Hitler Youth. At the same time he also demonstratively resigned from the German Christian movement, in an attempt to show his even-handedness. But it was all to no avail. Oppositional pastors defied his rulings and spoke out against 'Nazified Christianity' from their pulpits. They now rejected the Reich Church altogether and founded a rival body, the Confessing Church, which adopted a declaration of principles, inspired by the theologian Karl Barth, at its meeting in Barmen in May 1934, repudiating the 'Aryan Paragraph' and expressing its faith in the Bible. Barth, who was Swiss, but based in Bonn, was soon afterwards forced to leave Germany for his native country, from where his writings, calling Protestants to resist the encroachments of the regime and return to a pure religion based on the Bible, continued to exert a considerable influence on his followers.[20]

As a result of these events, Reich Bishop Müller felt obliged to sack Krause shortly after the Sports Palace rally and abandon the disciplinary measures he had launched to curb the rebels, throwing the German Christian movement into disarray and inaugurating a period of internal disputes that lasted for well over a year. Soon, Müller's position as Reich Bishop was rendered more or less meaningless by the Confessing Church's creation of a central, co-ordinating 'Provisional Management of the German Evangelical Church' on 22 November 1934.[21] One preacher who joined the Confessing Church now proclaimed that: 'The men who now rule speak only of their own deeds and their own egos; there's never any talk of the fear of God, and for this reason the Third Reich won't be able to keep going for very long.' A Franconian pastor was recorded as saying in his Sunday sermon 'that a proper Christian cannot be a National Socialist at the same time, and a proper National Socialist cannot be a Christian at the same time'. Martin Niemöller in particular delivered a series of sermons whose hostility to the regime was unmistakable. To packed congregations in his parish of Dahlem, numbering 1,500 on at least one occasion, Niemöller publicly named Goebbels, Rosenberg and Gürtner as the men responsible for the imprisonment of refractory pastors; he read out lists of the names of pastors who had been arrested or barred from speaking; on 30 January 1937, the fourth anniversary of Hitler's appointment as Reich Chancellor, he preached on a text describing the apostle Paul's imprisonment; and he led prayers for non-Aryans who had been deprived of their jobs. The Gestapo noted with concern that 242 churches in the Potsdam district had failed to fly swastika flags on 9 November 1935, the anniversary of the 1923 Nazi beer-hall putsch.[22] Political regimes would come and go, proclaimed another preacher; only God remained eternal. The Gestapo noted that the congregation in such sermons often consisted of all kinds of enemies of National Socialism, not just 'old officers who can't adapt themselves', large landowners and the like, but also Freemasons 'and even some former Communists who have suddenly discovered they are churchgoing people at heart'.[23] A song was doing the rounds in Marburg, noted another Gestapo report:

> Once we were Communists
> Steel Helmets and SPD
> Today we're Confessing Christians
> Fighters against the NSDAP.[24]

Oppositional elements were beginning to gravitate towards the Confessing Church. The threat to the Nazi regime seemed very real to some.[25]

Yet the Confessing Church never became a general centre of opposition in the way that the Protestant Church was to become in the German Democratic Republic in the late 1980s. Hitler and the leading Nazis still considered religion too sensitive an area to back Müller's policies with real force. Jäger's attempt to dismiss the Lutheran bishops Wurm and Meiser from their posts, for example, had led to mass public demonstrations among which Party members were prominent, and was clearly alienating many of the Nazis' supporters amongst the farming population of Württemberg and Franconia. The bishops were reinstated.[26] The Nazi leaders were obliged therefore to accept the failure of the German Christians' attempt to co-ordinate the Evangelical Church from within. Still, many leading figures in the Confessing Church protested their loyalty to the Third Reich and denied that they were doing anything political. Even in 1934, at the height of the conflict, Dietrich Bonhoeffer, one of the Confessing Church's more radical thinkers, was unusual in taking the critical line that 'dreamers and the naïve like Niemöller still believe they are the true National Socialists'. Few members of the Church, he thought, would develop their commitment into the broader resistance to Nazism that would eventually become necessary.[27] In any case, by 1937 the Protestant Church was either deeply divided between the German Christians and the Confessing Church, as in Berlin, Westphalia or the Rhineland, or still dominated by the German Christians, as in most other parts of North Germany. Many ordinary Protestants wearied of the bitter internal struggles and simply gave up involvement in the Church altogether; for this silent majority, biblical fundamentalism and Nazified Christianity were equally repellent.[28]

Moreover, the most important cause of the quarrel, the demand of the German Christians to expel racially defined non-Aryans from the Church, drew from some not a principled rejection of antisemitism from the Confessing pastors, but merely a different version of it. They believed that baptized Jews were by definition no longer Jews, and they cared little about the unbaptized. Niemöller himself declared publicly in 1935 that the Jews had been eternally cursed because they had caused Christ's crucifixion. Yet he went on to use this argument to urge a stop to their persecution in the Third Reich: if God had judged them, it was not for humans to intervene with their own hatred, and in any case, had not Jesus told Christians to love their enemies? In this way, Niemöller sought to turn the Nazis' arguments against themselves. The Jews, he declared, had been too proud of their racial identity as 'Abraham's seed' to heed the gospel of Jesus; now racial pride was causing the Germans to tread the same road, thus opening up the possibility that they too might be cursed for all eternity. Such arguments may themselves seem antisemitic in retrospect; but in the context of the time they had practical consequences of a very different kind.[29] Pastors who baptized Jewish children or preached on the virtues of the Old Testament were defamed by

German Christians as 'Jew-pastors' and had to bear the brunt of repeated invective and insults from their opponents. The difference between the German Christians and the Confessing Church was real enough in the 1930s.[30]

The Evangelical Church, as a state institution, had been obliged to adopt the 'Aryan Paragraph' in 1933 and to dismiss the eighteen pastors to whom it applied (eleven others were exempt because they had fought in the First World War). For many decades it had devoted some attention to converting Jews to Christianity, but these efforts now encountered growing disapproval in the Church. The Confessing Church had indeed come into existence partly around a protest against this measure, which aroused strong hostility amongst some local pastors. Many Protestant laymen were also disturbed by the overt racial antisemitism of the German Christians. The novelist, poet and broadcaster Jochen Klepper, whose wife was Jewish, was already complaining about the regime's antisemitism in March 1933. The 'national revolution' was creating nothing less than a 'pogrom atmosphere', he noted in his diary. For Klepper, a devout Protestant, antisemitism, far from being a natural accompaniment of Christianity, was a denial of Christianity's biblical heritage: 'I'm not an antisemite,' he wrote, 'because no Believer can be one. I'm not a philosemite, because no Believer can be one – But I believe in God's Mystery, that he has manifested through the Jews, and for this reason I can do nothing but suffer because of the fact that the Church tolerates what is going on at present.'[31]

Yet political considerations among those who were taking responsibility for resisting the German Christians on an institutional level dictated caution. Even Niemöller urged 'restraint' on non-Aryan pastors.[32] Reflecting a common tendency to blame anyone but Hitler, another pastor from the Confessing Church coupled his criticism of the leadership principle in the Church with a reminder that God had given them the Leader; it was not Hitler but the Reich Bishop who was responsible for the troubles.[33] Moreover, if some rural congregations went over to the Confessing Church *en masse*, this was generally because, as a Gestapo report on the Potsdam district noted, 'farming people seem to want to celebrate their Church festivals in the traditional form; as far as they are concerned, they are a part of rural custom and to do away with them would be unthinkable'. What applied to rural districts could equally well apply to the dwindling congregations in the towns and cities, long since deserted by the working class but still popular in conservative artisan, bourgeois and aristocratic circles. The Gestapo report added that the regime had not done enough to overcome such inbred tradition-alism.[34] But it was difficult to see what more it could do in reality. The German Christians' attempt to create a synthesis between German Protestantism and Nazi racism had effectively collapsed.[35]

III

Meanwhile, leading figures in the Confessing Church, such as Niemöller, were placed under surveillance, and acts of official harassment against Confessing pastors began to multiply, augmented by sometimes violent attempts to wrest back control of particular churches by the German Christians, who continued to hold the allegiance of many Protestants all the way up to 1945.[36] The failure of the regime to bring the Church to heel was not to be borne lightly. Hitler reluctantly abandoned his ambition of converting it into the official state Church of the Third Reich. Instead, he ordered the creation of a new Ministry for Church Affairs, established in July 1935 under the 48-year-old Hanns Kerrl, a Party member since 1925 and Prussian Minister of Justice from 1933 until the Ministry's dissolution the following year. The new Ministry was given wide-ranging powers, which Kerrl did not hesitate to deploy in order to bring refractory pastors to heel.[37] Kerrl launched serious repressive measures against the Confessing Church, and in particular its Berlin-Brandenburg section, where the dissenters were strongest. Pastors were banned from preaching, or had their pay stopped. They were forbidden to teach in schools. All theological students were ordered to join Nazi organizations. An important Protestant publishing house was confiscated and a Protestant church in Munich demolished. Niemöller was arrested, and by the end of 1937, over 700 Protestant pastors in the country had been imprisoned. Their offence was to have disobeyed government gagging orders on their sermons, government bans on fund-raising for the Confessing Church, or other official decrees and regulations. One hundred and two pastors were arrested in the Postdam district in 1935 for reading out the declar-ations of the Confessing Church's synod, though all of them were subsequently released. In some places they were welcomed home by triumphant demonstrations of members of the Steel Helmets, breaking free momentarily from their incorporation into the brownshirts. 'All the measures taken so far against the Confessing Church', the Gestapo was forced to confess, 'have so far proved to be inadequate, and only made the pastors more insubordinate still.'[38]

Niemöller's trial was a fiasco, and he was acquitted of all serious charges. A series of witnesses appeared to testify to his patriotism, and Niemöller himself said that he was far from being a political opponent of the Nazis. He was immediately released. However, when Niemöller was freed on 2 March 1938, he found the Gestapo waiting for him at the prison gates. Hitler had personally ordered him to be rearrested. Niemöller was placed in solitary confinement in Sachsenhausen concentration camp. On the outbreak of war in September 1939, he offered to join the navy again, but the offer was rejected. His rebellion was, he still insisted, purely religious. Nevertheless, his arrest and incarceration aroused widespread condemnation. He was remembered daily in prayers not just in the Confessing Church but in Protestant congregations in many other countries, where he was regarded as a martyr for Christian principles. His continued imprisonment, after having been acquitted by a court of law, caused international embarrassment for the regime. In order to blunt the edge of this worldwide criticism, Hitler gave him day release to see his dying father. The fact that Niemöller was the Leader's personal prisoner also gave him a limited number of special privileges on certain occasions to placate world opinion. He was allowed occasional visits from his wife, and when news of his poor health became public after one such meeting, the resulting protests led to an improvement in his rations. Nevertheless, when Niemöller's wife asked Hitler directly for his release in 1939, the Nazi Leader replied that if he was set free he would only gather round him an oppositional group that would endanger the state.[39]

Niemöller was in no way immune from the daily humiliations and brutalities which the SS camp guards visited on the inmates. In view of his patient suffering of such maltreatment, and his constantly reiterated faith in God, he gained a considerable degree of moral authority over the other inmates, all of whom he treated undifferentiatingly as victims of an evil regime. It was at this time, seeing the sufferings of the camp's

Jewish inmates, that he came to repudiate his earlier antisemitic views. Jews, he told a fellow inmate, should be treated exactly like other Germans: his earlier advocacy of restrictions on their civil rights had been wrong. Although Niemöller was given relatively light work duties such as chopping wood, he was frequently beaten on the slightest pretext. On one occasion in the late 1930s, ordered to give his name, he replied that he was Pastor Niemöller. Viciously beaten by the camp guards, he then had to say, 'I am the swine Niemöller.' On numerous occasions, the guards, according to the memoir of a fellow inmate, written shortly after the event,

made him hop on one foot between them, sometimes crouch and hop. They beat him at the same time to make him more agile. One day he evidently used the name of God (though I could not catch it), for I heard one of the guards shout, 'The *Schweinhund* is calling his *Drecksgott* (dirty god). I would like to see if He will help him out of here.' Sometimes the Commandant or other officers would stop to watch the play. Then the guards would outdo themselves as they received approving laughs.[40]

In 1941, when it seemed possible for a while that Niemöller would convert to Catholicism, Hitler had him moved with three Catholic priests to Dachau, where he was kept in considerably improved conditions almost to the end of the war. But there was never any prospect that he would set him free, particularly when Niemöller decided that he would not convert to Catholicism after all.[41] And in the meantime, in his parish in the plush Berlin suburb of Dahlem, the German Christians had won the upper hand again, as his rival, the senior pastor Eberhard Röhricht, previously eclipsed by Niemöller's charisma, seized the initiative and drove out the core group of the Confessing Church's supporters from the parish altogether.[42]

Looking back on his arrest and imprisonment later in life, Niemöller came to regret the compromises he had made with the regime, and blamed himself for pursuing narrowly religious interests. In the statement that more than anything else has caused his memory to live on across the world, he said:

First they took the Communists, but I was not a Communist, so I said nothing. Then they took the Social Democrats, but I was not a Social Democrat, so I did nothing. Then it was the trade unionists' turn, but I was not a trade unionist. And then they took the Jews, but I was not a Jew, so I did little. Then when they came and took me, there was no one left who could have stood up for me.[43]

For all its power in projecting Niemöller's retrospective remorse, this famous statement also illustrated the continuing narrowness of his confessional outlook, and the continuing depth of the confessional divide in Germany; for there was one group about which he said nothing at all: the Catholics.[44]

CATHOLICS AND PAGANS

I

Hitler both admired and feared the Catholic Church, which at the time of his appointment as Reich Chancellor claimed the allegiance of about 20 million Germans, or one-third of the population, mostly in the South and West. Like Bismarck before him, he considered Catholics less than totally committed to the national cause because their Church owed its institutional allegiance not to the German state but to Rome. Other leading Nazis who had come from a Catholic background, such as Joseph Goebbels, also stood in some awe of the Church's powerful and elaborate organization and its ability to convince its members of the rightness of its creed. Hitler admired the commitment that celibacy gave its priests, and the closeness of its links with the common people.[45] Himmler's deputy, Reinhard Heydrich, reacted against a strict Catholic upbringing with a hatred of the Church that can only be called fanatical. In 1936, Heydrich classified the Jews and the Catholic Church, acting above all through political institutions such the Centre Party, as the two principal enemies of Nazism. As an international body, he argued, the Catholic Church was necessarily subversive of the racial and spiritual integrity of the German people.[46] Moreover, the Catholics, unlike the Protestants, had been largely represented by a single political party, the Centre, whose voters, again unlike those of most other parties, had mostly remained loyal and resisted the appeal of Nazism during the elections of the early 1930s. Much of the blame for this could be laid in the Nazis' view at the feet of the clergy, who had preached vehemently against the Nazi Party, in many cases ruled that Catholics could not join it, and strongly urged their congregations to continue voting for the Centre or its

Bavarian equivalent, the Bavarian People's Party.[47] For many if not most leading Nazis, therefore, it was vitally important to reduce the Catholic Church in Germany as quickly as possible to total subservience to the regime.

The Catholic community had already agreed in 1933 to abandon the Centre Party, which duly wound itself up along with a few other obviously political organizations such as the Catholic Trade Unions, but it expected the vast majority of other lay organizations within the Catholic confession to be allowed to maintain their independence. This expectation seemed reasonable enough to many Catholics in view of the formal Concordat concluded between the Nazi regime and the Papacy in July 1933, which had promised to protect Catholic lay institutions in return for the Church's commitment to abstain from any involvement in politics.[48] The Concordat's provisions on this point were extremely vague, however, and during the summer of 1933 the regime began seizing the property of Catholic lay organizations and forcing them to close down if they did not do so voluntarily. On 20 July newspapers were forbidden to call themselves 'Catholic' (all newspapers were to be 'German'), and on 19 September 1933, the Bavarian political police, under Heinrich Himmler, banned 'all activities on the part of Catholic organizations' apart from youth groups, church choirs meeting for rehearsal, and charitable organizations considering applications for support. Alarmed, Cardinal Bertram, in Breslau, told Pope Pius XI on 4 October of the problems he foresaw with the Nazi ambition to exert total control over society, the banning of Catholic periodicals, the state's interference in Church charities, and the banning or 'co-ordination' of Catholic voluntary associations. Another leading figure in the Church, Cardinal Michael Faulhaber, objected publicly to attacks on non-Aryan Catholics, although he made no criticism of the regime's moves against non-Catholic Jews. In the Vatican, Cardinal Pacelli, former Papal Nuncio to Germany and now Secretary of State under Pope Pius XI, complained to the German Foreign Ministry and threatened to issue a public letter of protest. But in practice nothing was done. The Catholic hierarchy in Germany considered it more effective to issue general declarations of support for the regime in the hope that they would stem the tide of anti-Catholic actions. Thus Archbishop Gröber in Freiburg declared publicly on 10 October 1933 'that I am placing myself completely behind

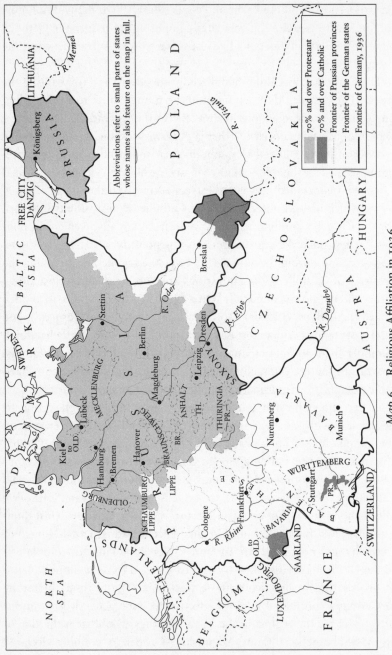

Map 6. Religious Affiliation in 1936

the new government and the new Reich', and then used his open loyalty to the regime to try to persuade the Nazi authorities in Baden to stop attacks on the Church. Yet the hierarchy could not protest too force-fully against measures it disliked because that was to enter the realm of politics, from which it had explicitly excluded itself by agreeing to the Concordat.[49]

In practice, the leading Nazis were aware of the dangers inherent in attacking deep-rooted institutions and traditions in the Catholic com-munity. So they proceeded slowly. Even Himmler insisted in an order issued on 2 November 1933 that no anti-Catholic measures were to be taken without his instructions. The Gestapo began surveillance of Cath-olic activities, including church services, and paid particular attention to laymen formerly prominent in the Centre Party and the Bavarian People's Party, drawing up lengthy lists of Catholics thought still to be opposed to the regime.[50] Leading Nazis were particularly concerned at the continued refusal of Catholic youth organizations to dissolve themselves, which meant that the Hitler Youth was unable to make much progress in strongly Catholic areas. Control over the younger generation was vital for the building of the future. On 15 March 1934 the Hitler Youth leader Baldur von Schirach condemned the divisive influence of Catholic youth groups and urged parents to enrol their children in his own movement. He also started to encourage Hitler Youth units to pick fights with members of rival Catholic youth groups, thus beginning to apply the kind of coercion on the streets that had proved so effective on a wider scale in the first half of 1933.[51] The hierarchy was given a sharp reminder when the SS shot dead Erich Klausener, General Secretary of Catholic Action, an important lay body, in his office in Berlin during the 'Night of the Long Knives' in 1934, along with Adalbert Probst, National Director of the Catholic Youth Sports Association. In Munich those shot included Fritz Gerlich, editor of the Catholic weekly *The Strait Way* (*Der gerade Weg*) and a well-known critic of the regime. It was also strongly rumoured that the former Centre Party leader and ex-Reich Chancellor Heinrich Brüning had been on the death-list, but he happened fortuitously to be on a visit to London and so escaped. The import of these events, which took place in the middle of personal negotiations between Hitler and the Catholic hierarchy on the future of Catholic lay organizations, could hardly have been clearer. Yet the same hierarchy made no protest about the murders. Instead, it joined with the Evangelical Church in a shared sense of relief at the defeat of supposedly immoral brownshirt radicals such as Röhm and appeared outwardly satisfied with the explanation that the murdered men had committed suicide or been shot while trying to escape.[52]

II

These events were swiftly followed by the death of Hindenburg, who was strongly identified as a representative of a conservative, Protestant, Christian faith, and the ending of the Nazi project of creating a national Church united around the German Christian idea. All this opened the way to a sharp escalation of anti-Catholic policies. It was at this time that a fierce debate began over the anti-Christian writings of the Nazi ideologue Alfred Rosenberg, who publicly rejected such central doctrines as the immortality of the soul and Christ's redemption of humankind from original sin. In his book *The Myth of the Twentieth Century*, Rosenberg excoriated Catholicism as the creation of Jewish clericalism, and he elaborated these ideas further in a series of books published in the mid-1930s.[53] Even the German Christians were appalled. They asked Hitler to repudiate these ideas, though without success. Rosenberg's publications were immediately placed on the Catholic Church's Index of Prohibited Books, and elicited a furious response from the German Catholic clergy. A variety of pamphlets, books, meetings and sermons condemned Rosenberg's teachings, and anathematized his supporters within the Nazi Party. Rosenberg's works were officially treated by the regime as nothing more than expressions of his own private views, however. It felt no need to disown them. But the regime recognized at the same time that the controversy was building up the resistance of the Catholic community to further penetration by Nazi ideology and institutions. As a Gestapo report noted in May 1935: 'Numerous clerics are now taking a very critical position from the pulpit towards Rosenberg's *Myth* and his new work *To the Obscurantists of Our Day*. They curse the spirit of the new age, the Godless and the heathen, by which they mean National Socialism.'[54]

The controversy over Rosenberg's ideas soon began to take on what the Nazi leadership regarded as more dangerous forms as the German bishops issued public rebukes to the Nazi ideologue and called on the faithful to reject his ideas.[55] In his Easter message, written on 19 March 1935, Clemens von Galen, the Bishop of Münster, launched a fierce attack on Rosenberg's book. 'There are heathens again in Germany,' he noted in alarm, and he criticized Rosenberg's idea of the racial soul. 'The so-called eternal racial soul', declared Galen, 'is in reality a nullity.' Early in July 1935, Rosenberg took the opportunity to criticize Galen at a rally in Münster, and in response, the Catholic faithful in Münster appeared in unprecedented numbers at the annual July procession through the streets held to commemorate the local Church's survival of Bismarck's persecution half a century before and – on this occasion – the 400th anniversary of the defeat of the Anabaptists who had instituted a reign of terror in the town during the Reformation. Nineteen thousand Catholics, double the usual number, came out to cheer their bishop, who issued a ringing declaration that he would never give in to the enemies of the Church. In response, the local Party put up notices denying any intention of renewing the Bismarckian attempt to suppress the Church's independence, while local officials reported to Berlin that Galen was stirring up discontent and accused him of meddling in politics.[56] Galen wrote personally to Hitler complaining about attacks on the clergy by leading Nazis such as Baldur von Schirach.[57] Compromise was clearly not in the air. Tightening the screws on the Church, Himmler and the Gestapo now began to introduce tougher measures against Catholic lay organizations and institutions, limiting public meetings, censoring the remaining Catholic newspapers and magazines and banning particular issues, and putting proven Nazis into editorial positions in the Catholic press. Both Hermann Göring and Wilhelm Frick, the Reich Interior Minister, spoke out against 'politicizing Catholicism', declaring that the continued existence of Catholic lay organizations was incompatible with the spirit of the age.[58] Towards the end of 1935, Goebbels and the Propaganda Ministry took a hand in the controversy, releasing a flood of accusations against Catholic organizations for financial corruption, just as they had done in 1933 with the trade unions.[59]

These new tactics failed altogether to have the desired effect in weaning the Catholic community away from its faith. The Gestapo reported that the priesthood, through the confessional and through a whole programme of house visits, was so successful in countering the allegations that the laity, especially in rural areas, 'regards what stands written in the newspapers as a falsehood, or at least a great exaggeration'.[60] The drive to recruit young people to the Hitler Youth and its female equivalent, the League of German Girls, ran up against tough opposition from Catholic priests, who were reported in some areas to be refusing absolution to girls who joined the League instead of a Catholic girls' organization.[61] Incidents began to multiply. Catholic congregations reacted with undisguised fury at the attempts of local Party bosses to remove religious statuary from public buildings such as mortuaries, and demonstratively flew Church flags instead of swastika banners to welcome visiting Catholic dignitaries. The brownshirts staged public demonstrations such as one in Rosenheim, where they demanded the sacking of a teacher who had been disciplining his pupils for failing to attend Church ('to Dachau with him!' was the cry).[62] The Church, complained the regional government in Upper Bavaria in July 1937, was becoming a 'state within a state', and local Nazis were angry 'that the Church is propagating an ongoing opposition in the most public way from its pulpits'.[63] The regime's policy even had repercussions near the centre of government: when Hitler held a ceremony to pin the golden party badge on the remaining non-Nazis in the cabinet on 30 January 1937, the Postal and Transport Minister, Peter Baron von Eltz-Rübenach, a staunch Catholic, refused to accept it and told Hitler to his face to stop repressing the Church. Furious at the embarrassment, Hitler stormed out of the room without saying a word, while the quick-witted Goebbels secured the refractory Minister's resignation on the spot.[64]

In one area the conflict erupted into open protest. Villagers in a rural, deeply Catholic part of southern Oldenburg had already been upset by a reduction of religious education in the schools and the regional Education Minister's defence of Rosenberg's anti-Catholic diatribes. On 4 November, the Minister made matters far worse by banning the religious consecration of new school buildings and ordering the removal of religious symbols such as crucifixes (and, for that matter, portraits of Luther) from all state, municipal and parish buildings, including schools. The local Catholic clergy protested from the pulpit. On 10 November, 3,000 war veterans assembled to celebrate Remembrance Day heard a priest swear never to tolerate the removal of crucifixes from the schools.

He would, he told the crowd, fight the decree and if necessary die for the cause, just as the veterans had in the First World War. Parish bells were rung everywhere in the morning and evening as a further sign of protest. Mass petitions were handed in ceremoniously to the regional Education Ministry. Crosses on people's houses and in the schools were decorated, and large crosses were affixed to church towers and lit up at night with electric light bulbs. Parishioners began to resign from the Nazi Party and one branch of the brownshirts dissolved itself in protest. At a meeting attended by 7,000 ordinary citizens, the Party's Regional Leader was forced to announce the decree's withdrawal. It was followed by the renewed ringing of church bells all over the district, services of thanksgiving and the publication in the whole diocese, far beyond the immediate locality, of a pastoral letter by Bishop von Galen recounting the affair, celebrating the victory, and vowing to have no truck with enemies of Christ. The affair did lasting damage to the standing of the Nazi Party in southern Oldenburg, where despite massive manipulation and intimidation it gained a strikingly low vote in the Reichstag election of 1938 – 92 per cent as against 99 per cent in the same district in the election of March 1936.[65]

Already since even before the Concordat had been ratified, Cardinal Pacelli, the Vatican Secretary of State in Rome, had been sending a steady stream of lengthy and circumstantially detailed complaints to the German government about such violations, listing hundreds of cases in which the brownshirts had closed down Catholic lay organizations, confiscated money and equipment, engaged in anti-Christian propaganda, banned Catholic publications, and much more. In response, the German government repeatedly told the Vatican that its fight against Marxism and Communism demanded the unity of the German people through the ending of confessional divisions. Catholic priests were hindering this struggle, publicly branding the swastika as the 'Devil's cross', refusing to use the Hitler greeting, expelling brownshirts from church services and continuing to violate the Concordat by including political attacks on the regime in their sermons. The regime therefore continued the war on the cultural infrastructure of the Catholic community on many fronts. Catholic youth organizations, which in May 1934 numbered 1.5 million members, and ranged from the Catholic equivalent of the Boy Scouts to Catholic sports clubs of many kinds, were an obvious target, especially since there were frequent clashes with the Hitler Youth, though these were mostly confined to the shouting of insults. Catholic youth organizations in the eyes of the regime were 'anti-nationalist and anti-National Socialist' and had to be suppressed. Members of these organizations came under growing pressure to resign and join the Hitler Youth instead.[66] The Reich Theatre Chamber began from 1935 onwards to ban Church-sponsored musical and also theatrical events, arguing that they were competing financially and ideologically with Nazi-sponsored concerts and plays. By 1937 it was banning Nativity plays, arguing they were a form of Catholic political propaganda and so contrary to the provisions of the Concordat.[67]

In these as in many other areas, Pacelli continued to remonstrate with the German government in a stream of lengthy, detailed and strongly worded memoranda. After the beginning of Goebbels's campaign against alleged financial corruption in the Church, the tone of the exchanges between Berlin and Rome became much sharper. Relations seemed to be plunging into open hostility.[68] Church services and sermons in Germany were now, the Vatican complained, being subjected to constant surveillance by the authorities: 'The repellent phenomenon of informers hovers around every step, every word, every official act.'[69] In many parts of the country, Catholic priests were engaging in a largely spontaneous war of words with local Party leaders and officials over continuing Party attempts to co-ordinate denominational schools and Catholic youth organizations. These struggles were indeed, regional state officials reported, the only cause of open political dissent within Germany by the mid-1930s.[70] Matters came to a head when, alarmed at the escalating conflict, a delegation of senior German bishops and cardinals, including Bertram, Faulhaber and Galen, went to Rome in January 1937 to denounce the Nazis for violating the Concordat. Meeting with a favourable response from the Pope, Faulhaber drafted a Papal Encyclical which was considerably extended by Pacelli, drawing on his lengthy correspondence with the German government and summing up the complaints that the Vatican had now been making for several years. The document was approved by the Pope, smuggled into Germany, secretly printed at twelve different locations, distributed to parish priests by boys on bicycles or on foot, and read out from virtually every Catholic pulpit in the land on 21 March 1937.

Written in German and entitled *Mit brennender Sorge*, 'with burning concern', it condemned the 'hatred' and 'calumny' poured on the Church by the Nazis.[71] Although much of the document was cast in theological language not easily comprehensible to laypeople, some of it at least was clear enough. When it came to the regime's policies towards the Church, Pope Pius XI, using language supplied to him by Cardinal Pacelli, certainly did not mince words. 'Anyone', he thundered,

who unties the race, or the people, or the form taken by the state, the bearers of state power or other basic values of human social construction – which claim a significant and honourable place within the earthly order of things – from this, its temporal scale of values, makes it the highest norm of all, including religious values, and deifies it with an idolatrous cult, overturns and falsifies the order of things created and commanded by God.[72]

For the faithful, the eternal values of religion had to be paramount. In order to undermine them, however, the Encyclical went on, the German government, was conducting an 'annihilatory struggle' against the Church:

With measures of compulsion both visible and concealed, with intimidation, with threats of economic, professional, civic and other disadvantages, the doctrinal faithfulness of Catholics and in particular of certain classes of Catholic civil servants are being placed under a pressure that is as illegal as it is inhumane.[73]

Enraged at this condemnation, and alarmed at the evidence it provided of the Catholic Church's ability to organize a nationwide protest without arousing the slightest suspicion in advance even from the Gestapo, Hitler ordered all copies of the Encyclical to be seized, anyone found in possession of it to be arrested, any further publication of it to be banned and all the firms who had printed it closed down.[74]

Armed since 1936 with his new powers as Head of the German Police, Himmler now stepped up the campaign against the Church. Together with his deputy Reinhard Heydrich, he placed secret agents in Church organizations, and escalated police harassment of clerics. There was a further clamp-down on the diocesan press, restrictions were placed on pilgrimages and processions, even Catholic marriage guidance and parenthood classes were banned because they did not convey the National Socialist view of these things. By 1938 the majority of Catholic youth groups had been closed down on the grounds that they were assisting in the dissemination of 'writings hostile to the state'. Catholic Action, whose leaders in Germany allegedly maintained communications with Prelate Kaas, the former leader of the Centre Party, was also banned in January 1938.[75] State subsidies for the Church were cut in Bavaria and Saxony, and monasteries were dissolved and their assets confiscated. House-searches and arrests of 'political' priests underwent a sharp increase, with a steady stream of well-publicized cases of 'abuse of the pulpit' brought before the court. The arrest and trial of one Jesuit priest, Rupert Mayer, led to angry public demonstrations in court by his supporters and special prayers for him being defiantly said in Munich's St Michael's church. Some priests continued to refuse to knuckle under, and there were reports of priests refusing to give the Nazi salute and telling children to say 'Praised be Jesus Christ' instead of 'Hail, Hitler'.[76] In the course of this struggle, more than a third of Catholic priests in Germany were subject to some form of disciplining by the police and state authorities, up to and including imprisonment, over the whole course of the Third Reich.[77] The Encyclical had clearly failed to have any immediate effect apart from further worsening relations between the Church and the regime.

The campaign was not confined to the police and the judicial administration. Reich Propaganda Minister Goebbels also played his part. After the Encyclical, he intensified the publicity campaign against alleged sexual scandals involving Catholic priests that had already begun in the middle of 1935. Fifteen monks were brought before the courts in November 1935 for offences against the law on homosexuality in a home for the mentally ill in western Germany, revealing, as the press put it, a state of affairs that was 'worse than Sodom and Gomorrah'.[78] They received severe prison sentences and the attention of endless column-inches in the press. Other priests were soon being tried for alleged sexual offences against minors in Catholic children's homes and similar institutions. By May 1936 the press was reporting the trial in Koblenz of over 200 Franciscans for similar crimes.[79] Such stories meshed with the Nazi disapproval of homosexuality. They often took up the whole of the front page of national newspapers. Less publicity was given to incidents of Catholic priests and monks arrested for sexual offences against girls. Focusing on allegations of pederasty, the press claimed that the monasteries were 'breeding-grounds of a repulsive epidemic' which had to be stamped out. By April 1937 over a thousand priests, monks and friars were said – with what degree of truth is uncertain – to be awaiting trial on such charges.[80] The tabloid press had no hesitation in leading these stories with headlines such as 'Houses of God degraded into brothels and dens of vice', and demanding of the Catholic Church 'off with the mask!', more than hinting that homosexuality and paedophilia were endemic in the Church as a whole, and not merely in isolated instances.[81] These trials were created above all by the Propaganda Ministry, which supplied detailed reports to the Reich Justice Ministry and pressed for the supposed culprits to be brought before the courts in such a way that would allow it to draw the maximum publicity.

Particularly offensive, declared the press, was the fact that the Church stood behind the accused and treated them as martyrs.[82] As more trials followed, the Propaganda Ministry built up a steady campaign to portray the Church as sexually corrupt and unworthy of being entrusted with the education of the young. Reporting on other sexual offences was largely suppressed, in order to convey the impression that such things only went on in the Church, where, it was suggested, they were an inevitable by-product of the celibacy that was required of the priesthood by the Church. The Catholic Church was a 'sore on the healthy racial body' that had to be removed, declared one article in the Nazi press.[83] The campaign culminated in a furious speech by the Reich Propaganda Minister himself, delivered to an audience of 20,000 of the Party faithful, and broadcast on national radio, on 28 May 1937, denouncing Catholic 'corrupters and poisoners of the people's soul' and promising that 'this sexual plague must be exterminated root and branch'.[84] These were not show trials on trumped-up charges, as the Catholic Church had complained, he told his audience, but a necessary 'reckoning', as the press put it, with the 'hereditarily diseased wearers of the monk's habit in monasteries and brotherhoods' in the name of the moral rectitude that was inborn in the true German. The state was confronting a systematic undermining of the morality of the German people. And if the bishops continued to dispute the facts, they too would be brought before the courts. 'It is not the law of the Vatican that rules here amongst us,' he warned the Church, 'but the law of the German people.'[85]

The campaign was a typical product of the Propaganda Ministry –

drawing on what may have been an element of truth in some of the allegations, but then blowing it up out of all proportion in the service of a political aim that had little or nothing to do with the cases at issue. Goebbels's intention was to convince ordinary Catholics that the Church was corrupt and immoral as an institution. More specifically, however, the trials provided a constant backdrop of propaganda, backed by police harassment and intimidation, against which the Nazis now launched a sustained campaign to close denominational schools and replace them with non-religious 'community schools', backed by votes from parents that followed the familiar pattern of elections organized by the Nazis. Parents were forced to sign prepared statements declaring that they 'did not want the education of my child at school to be misused by stirring up religious unrest' and supported the slogan 'One Leader, One People, One School'. Already at the beginning of 1936, Cardinal Bertram had complained directly to Hitler of the 'unheard-of terror' which was being practised 'in Bavaria, Württemberg and elsewhere. Those who vote for the denominational school are branded as enemies of the state.' His appeal fell on deaf ears. The campaign, backed up by massive local propaganda, continued.[86] 'We don't want to let the chaplain teach us any more!' children were reported as saying by the leading Nazi daily paper on 25 May 1937 under the headline: 'Entire school class defends itself against sex offender in priest's clothing'.[87]

The campaign was not long in bringing results. In 1934, 84 per cent of children were still registered in denominational schools in Munich; but by the end of 1937, the proportion had fallen to a mere 5 per cent, a result achieved, as the Munich Diocesan Administration complained, 'by means that were entirely unjust and illegal' and involved 'indescribable terrorism that contravened every principle of law and justice', including the withdrawal of welfare support for those who refused to vote for the schools' abolition. By the summer of 1939, all denominational schools in Germany had been turned into community schools, and all private schools run by the Churches had been closed down or nationalized, and the monks and priests who staffed them dismissed. Pastors and priests were prevented from teaching in primary schools in increasing numbers. At the same time, religious instruction classes were reduced in number. Later the same year, the Nazi teachers' organization told its members not to take over religious instruction classes from the now-banned clergy, though not all obeyed. By 1939 religious instruction in vocational schools had been reduced to half an hour a week, and in many areas it had to follow guidelines that described Jesus as non-Jewish. Parents who objected to these moves – and there were many of them, Protestant as well as Catholic – were obliged by the local authorities to withdraw their objections, summoned to special meetings at the school to pressure them to sign their children up for ideological instruction instead of religious education, or even threatened with dismissal from their jobs if they refused. In similar vein, the Education Ministry drew up plans to merge or close down many of the theological faculties in the universities, while from 1939 theology posts in teacher training colleges that fell vacant were no longer filled, by order of the Education Ministry in Berlin. In a few areas, notably in Württemberg, where the Education Minister Mergenthaler was strongly anti-Christian, there were attempts to abolish religious instruction and replace it with classes on the Nazi world-view. The regime did not succeed in abolishing religious education altogether by 1939, but its long-term intentions had become abundantly clear by this date.[88]

The power and influence of the Catholic Church in Germany, like that of its Protestant counterpart, had been severely dented by 1939. It had been intimidated and harassed until it began to scale down its criticisms of the regime for fear that even worse might follow. Widespread threats of imprisonment, reported a local government official towards the end of 1937, had produced a 'cautious restraint on the part of the clergy'.[89] In some areas, the Gestapo took over the anti-Church campaign and rapidly succeeded in driving the Catholic Church out of public life.[90] Elsewhere, there were reports by mid-1938 of a general 'pacification in the area of Church affairs'.[91] From Rome, Cardinal Pacelli continued to send interminable letters of complaint to the German government charging it with continued violations of the Concordat.[92] Yet although he contemplated doing so in September 1937, Hitler in the end refrained from openly repudiating the Concordat. It was not worth the risk of arousing the hostility of the Vatican and the protests of Catholic states, particularly Austria, in the increasingly delicate state of international relations in the late 1930s. Privately, however, the Foreign Ministry made no bones about the fact that it regarded the Concordat as 'out of date' because many of its provisions, particularly concerning education, were 'fundamentally opposed to the basic principles of National Socialism'.[93] It was easier to proceed piecemeal and by stealth and avoid all mention of the Concordat. In public, Hitler continued to call for the Church's loyalty and to point out that it still received substantial state support. In the long run, however, he made it clear in private that it would be completely separated from the state, deprived of income from state taxes, and become a purely voluntary body, along with its Protestant equivalent. Catholics by and large were unaware of such intentions. For all the bitterness of the conflict, it did not result in any general alienation of the Catholic community from the Third Reich. Many Catholics were highly critical of the Nazi Party, and especially of zealots such as Rosenberg, but Hitler's standing even here was only mildly affected. The deep-seated desire of the Catholic community since Bismarck's time to be accepted as a full part of the German nation blunted the edge of its hostility to the anti-Christian policies of the regime, which many imagined were being pushed by radicals without the knowledge or approval of Hitler himself. This was an illusion. In the long run, as Rosenberg declared in September 1938, since young people were now almost completely under the control of the Hitler Youth and the Nazified education system, the hold of the Church over its congregation would be broken and the Catholic and Confessing Churches would disappear from the life of the people in their present form. It was a sentiment from which Hitler himself did not dissent.[94]

III

Dramatic though the escalation of this conflict may have appeared, it was in fact neither new in kind nor exclusive to Germany. Like the older generation of Social Democrats in the 1930s, older Catholic priests at the same time had experienced persecution before. In the 1870s, Bismarck had launched a determined assault on the Catholic Church in Germany that had resulted in the arrest and imprisonment of hundreds of Catholic priests and the imposition of a wide range of secular checks and controls over the clergy. Similar policies were pursued at around the same time by secularizing governments in Italy and France, where the newly created states – the unified Italian monarchy and the French

Third Republic – had wrested control of education from the clergy and placed it in the hands of state-appointed teachers in state-funded schools. Such policies were justified, too, by massive secularist propaganda against the supposed sexual immorality of the Catholic priesthood, above all in the use of the confessional to discuss the intimate secrets of young Catholic women. Pope Pius IX had partly sparked these conflicts, partly fuelled them, by issuing his denunciation of secularism and modernity through the Syllabus of Errors (1864) and by claiming first call on the allegiance of his flock through the Declaration of Papal Infallibility (1871). In the twentieth century, secularist persecution of the Christian Church had reached a new intensity in Mexico and Russia in the wake of the two countries' respective revolutions. Crushing an international organization like the Church, which downgraded the state in its thinking, could form part of the process of building a new nation or a new political system. At a local level, village schoolteachers and village priests were engaged in a battle for supremacy over the minds of the young all across western Europe in the late nineteenth and early twentieth centuries. Bitter Church–state struggles were nothing new, therefore, in the 1930s. What was new, perhaps, was the Nazi rejection of rationalistic secularism. In all these other cases the persecution of the Church was not tied to the promotion of an alternative religion. However powerful the claim of the state's ideology might be, it was the claim of a secular, earthbound ideology. In the case of the Third Reich, however, the matter was not so clear.[95]

What would replace the Churches in Germany when they finally disappeared? Leading Nazis took a variety of positions on this issue. Hitler and Goebbels's religious beliefs retained a residual element of Christianity, albeit an eccentric one that became notably weaker after the failure of the German Christian project in 1934–5. Even Rosenberg qualified his anti-Christian stance with support for the German Christians until their failure to take over the Evangelical Church had become clear. Initially at any rate, he admired Luther, adapted doctrines from the medieval mystic Master Eckhart and thought that a racially amended Christianity could be merged into a new Germanic religion, which would dispense with the services of priests and dedicate itself to the interests of the Aryan race. Still, by publicly advocating such a new religion in the mid-1930s, Rosenberg became the most prominent spokesman for the anti-Christian tendency within the Nazi Party.[96] *The Myth of the Twentieth Century* sold over a million copies,[97] though Hitler subsequently rejected any idea that it was an official statement of Party doctrine. 'Like many Regional Leaders', he remarked, 'I have myself only read a little bit of it.' It was, he said 'written in a style too difficult to understand'. It only began to sell, he claimed, when it was publicly condemned by Cardinal Faulhaber and placed on the Church's Index of Prohibited Books.[98] Yet leading Nazis, despite having failed to plough all the way through the *Myth*, were not averse to using its ideas in support of their policies, as when Baldur von Schirach, urging young people in 1934 to leave Catholic youth organizations and join the Hitler Youth, declared that 'Rosenberg's path is the path of German youth'.[99] In July 1935, at the height of the controversy over Rosenberg's attacks on the Churches, a speaker told a meeting of the Nazi Students' League in Bernau: 'One is either a Nazi or a committed Christian.' Christianity, he said, 'promotes the dissolution of racial ties and of the national racial community . . . We must repudiate the Old and the New Testaments, since for us the Nazi idea alone is decisive. For us there is only one example, Adolf Hitler and no one else.'[100]

Such anti-Christian ideas were widespread in the Hitler Youth and formed an increasingly important part of the Party's programme for the indoctrination of the young. Children receiving lunches from the National Socialist welfare organization in Cologne, for example, were obliged to recite a grace before and after the meal which substituted the Leader's name for God's when thanks were given.[101] At one training camp for schoolchildren in Freusberg, the inmates were told that the Pope was 'a half-Jew' and that they had to hate the 'oriental-Jewish, racially alien teaching of Christianity', which was incompatible with National Socialism. The mother of a twelve-year-old Hitler Youth found the following text in his pocket when he came home one evening; it was also sung in public by the Hitler Youth at the 1934 Nuremberg Party Rally:

> We are the jolly Hitler Youth,
> We don't need any Christian truth
> For Adolf Hitler, our Leader
> Always is our interceder.

Whatever the Papist priests may try,
We're Hitler's children until we die;
We follow not Christ but Horst Wessel.
Away with incense and holy water vessel!

As sons of our forebears from times gone by
We march as we sing with banners held high.
I'm not a Christian, nor a Catholic,
I go with the SA through thin and thick.

Not the cross, they sang, but 'the swastika is redemption on earth'.[102]

Such propaganda emerged at least in part out of the drive to abolish Catholic youth organizations and enrol their members in the Hitler Youth instead. Yet it also propagated a fiercely anti-Christian ethic whose virulence and potency should not be underestimated. Watching a young Hitler Youth member enter a Munich classroom in August 1936, Friedrich Reck-Malleczewen

observed how his glance fell on the crucifix hanging behind the teacher's desk, how in an instant his young and still soft face contorted in fury, how he ripped this symbol, to which the cathedrals of Germany, and the ringing progressions of the *St Matthew Passion* are consecrated, off the wall and threw it out of the window into the street . . . With the cry: 'Lie there, you dirty Jew!'[103]

And there were other outspokenly anti-Christian figures within the Nazi leadership besides Schirach. Open paganism in the Party, championed by Erich Ludendorff in the mid-1920s, did not disappear with Ludendorff's foundation of the Tannenberg League in 1925 and his expulsion from the Party two years later. Robert Ley, leader of the Labour Front, went even further than Rosenberg in his disdain for Christianity and his rejection of the Divinity of Christ, though he did not follow him down the road of creating a substitute religion.[104] A more consistently paganist figure in the Nazi elite was the Party's agricultural expert Richard Walther Darré, whose ideology of 'blood and soil' made such a powerful impression on Heinrich Himmler. Darré believed that the medieval Teutons had been weakened by their conversion to Christianity, which he claimed had been foisted on them by the effete Latins from Southern Europe.[105] Himmler in his turn abandoned his early Christian faith under Darré's influence. In Himmler's plans for the SS after 1933, the black-shirted racial elite was to become a kind of quasi-religious order, modelled to some extent on the Jesuits. The ideas that were to cement it together were drawn from supposed Germanic pagan rituals and beliefs of the Dark Ages. As an SS plan put it in 1937: 'We live in the age of the final confrontation with Christianity. It is part of the mission of the SS to give to the German people over the next fifty years the non-Christian ideological foundations for a way of life appropriate to their own character.' These were to be a mixture of bits of Viking or Teutonic pagan religion with Wagnerian symbols and pure invention. The SS devised its own marriage service, with runes, a bowl of fire, Wagnerian music playing in the background and symbols of the sun presiding over the whole bizarre ceremony. The families of SS men were ordered by Himmler not to celebrate Christmas, but to mark Midsummer instead. Christianity, Himmler was to declare on 9 June 1942, was 'the greatest of plagues'; true morality consisted not in exalting the spirit of the individual but in abnegating oneself in the service of the race. Moral values could be derived only from consciousness of one's place in, and duty to, the chain of 'valuable' heredity.[106]

Once it became clear that there was no real possibility of fulfilling the Nazis' early ambition of creating a unified state Church along German Christian lines for the whole of the Third Reich, leading Nazis began to encourage Party members to declare their formal renunciation of Church membership. Rosenberg, predictably, had already left the Church in 1933; Himmler and Heydrich resigned in 1936, and a growing number of Regional Leaders now followed suit. The Interior Ministry ruled that people leaving their Church could declare themselves to be 'Deists' (*gottgläubig*), and the Party decreed that office-holders could not simultaneously hold any office in the Catholic or Protestant Church. In 1936, stormtroopers were forbidden to wear uniforms at Church services, and early in 1939 the ban was extended to all Party members. By 1939, over 10 per cent of the population in Berlin, 7.5 per cent in Hamburg, and between 5 and 6 per cent in some other major cities were registered as Deists, a term which could encompass a variety of religious beliefs including paganism. The great majority of these are likely to have been Party members; the proportion of Deists in the SS had reached over 25 per cent by 1938, for instance. This process was accelerated by an escalating series of measures pushed by the energetic and strongly anti-

Christian head of Rudolf Hess's office, Martin Bormann, banning priests and pastors from playing a part in Party affairs, or even, after May 1939, from belonging to it altogether. Still, there was a long way to go before the population as a whole took part in this movement. 'We won't let ourselves be turned into heathens,' one woman in Hesse was heard to say by a Gestapo agent.[107] The German Faith Movement, which propagated a new, racial religion based on a mishmash of Nordic and Indian rites, symbols and texts, never won more than about 40,000 adherents, and other neopagan groups, like Ludendorff's esoteric Tannenberg League, were even smaller.[108] Nevertheless, for all the general unpopularity of the movement, it remained the case that the Nazi Party was on the way to severing all its ties with organized Christianity by the end of the 1930s.[109]

Whether this process was leading in the direction of a heavily amended form of 'German Christianity' or out-and-out paganism was the subject of an ongoing struggle between Rosenberg, whose office repeatedly tried to clamp down on publications sympathetic to the old idea of a Reich Church based on a synthesis of Nazism and Christianity, and Goebbels, who, as so often, took a more relaxed view. Goebbels teamed up with the head of the Leader's Chancellery, Philipp Bouhler, who ran the 'Official Party Examination Commission for the Protection of National Socialist Literature'. Its task, endorsed by Goebbels, was to check Nazi Party publications for their ideological correctness. Rosenberg's Office for Ideological Information repeatedly tried to take over Bouhler's commission, which it considered ideologically lax, but without success, despite the occasional tactical victory in getting Hitler to intervene against particular publications.[110] Another, far less adept player in these complicated games, the Church Minister Hans Kerrl, tried to propagate the idea of a reconciliation of Protestantism and Nazism, but this had already had its day by the time of his appointment in 1935, and the obdurate refusal of the Confessing Church to go along with his plans made him seem weak and rendered him vulnerable to the attacks of more radical figures like Himmler and Rosenberg. His Ministry's attempt to get the Concordat with the Catholic Church annulled met with similar failure, as Hitler considered it diplomatically inadvisable. By 1939, Kerrl's influence was on the wane. He had proved quite unable to assert the monopoly over policy towards the Churches that his Ministry had ostensibly been set up to exercise.[111]

IV

Nazi policy towards the Churches was thus in a state of some confusion and disarray by the eve of the war. The ideological drift was clearly away from Christianity, though there was a long way to go before the neopaganist alternative found general acceptance even within the Party. Yet for all the ideological in-fighting, one objective had remained clear from the very outset: the regime was determined to reduce, and if possible eliminate, the Churches as centres of real or potential alternative ideologies to its own.[112] The primacy of this objective was nowhere clearer than in the regime's treatment of one small but close-knit sect, the 'Earnest Bible Researchers', or Jehovah's Witnesses. Since the members of this sect had sworn to obey only Jehovah, they refused absolutely to render an oath of loyalty to Hitler. They did not give the 'German greeting', go to political demonstrations, take part in elections or agree to be conscripted into the armed forces. Although their humble social background in the lower middle and working classes did bring them into contact with former Communists and Social Democrats, Gestapo claims that they were merely a front for labour movement resistance groups had no basis in fact whatsoever. Indeed, the Witnesses' movement had some resemblances to that of the small, anti-liberal political sects of the immediate postwar years from which Nazism itself had sprung. Just as important for the police was the fact that their organization was directed from outside Germany, in the United States; the movement's headquarters in Brooklyn was one of the earliest public critics of European fascism, and supported the Republican side in the Spanish Civil War. Predictably enough, Nazi Party organizations and Gestapo officers used crude intimidation and bullying to try to bring the Jehova's Witnesses into line. But this only made them more stubborn. Fortified by a resolution passed at their international conference in Lucerne in 1936 strongly criticizing the German government, they began distributing what the regime regarded as seditious leaflets. The police responded with arrests and prosecutions, and by 1937 Jehovah's Witnesses accounted for well over half of all cases brought before the Special Court in Freiberg, Saxony, and a substantial proportion elsewhere as well.[113]

Inside the prisons, the Witnesses steadfastly refused to abandon their faith and compromise with the secular state. While some prison governors and officials considered them no more than harmless fools, others, such as the governor of the Eisenach prison in Thuringia, made strenuous efforts to brainwash them, subjecting them to regular sessions of indoctrination. After a year, however, his experiment, begun in 1938, had made no real progress and was abandoned. Punishment and persecution for the Witnesses were simply tests of their faith, imposed on them, as they saw it, by God. Many of them refused to work in prison despite repeated punishments. Others went even further. The Jehovah's Witness Otto Grashof, sentenced to four years in the Wolfenbüttel gaol for refusing to serve in the army and trying to convince another young man to do the same, went on hunger strike when his family was evicted from their home and his children taken into care. Brutal force-feeding had little effect, and he died early in 1940, weighing less than forty kilos.[114]

Legal repression had no effect on the Jehovah's Witnesses, therefore. They were strengthened not least by the close family and community ties that bound many of them together. Frustrated at their refusal to knuckle under, the police and the SS began taking them straight into the concentration camps on their release from prison. Even a senior official at the Justice Ministry criticized the judiciary for failing to take the threat posed by the Jehovah's Witnesses with sufficient seriousness. There were, he claimed, nearly two million of them in Germany – a gross exaggeration, since there were in reality fewer than 30,000 – and they were acting as a Communist front, an assertion for which, needless to say, there was not a shred of evidence. Nevertheless, the Gestapo unleashed a fresh wave of arrests. By the end of the Third Reich about 10,000 Witnesses had been imprisoned, 2,000 of them in the camps, where some 950 died.[115] Here too, however, their sufferings only spurred them on to fresh acts of pious self-sacrifice and martyrdom. In some respects they were model prisoners, clean, orderly and industrious. Yet the SS man Rudolf Höss, a senior official in the Sachsenhausen camp in the late 1930s, reported later that Witnesses refused to stand to attention, take part in drill parades, remove their caps, or show any sign of respect to the guards, since respect, they said, was due only to Jehovah. Flogging only made them ask for more, as a sign of their devotion. Forced to watch the execution of fellow Witnesses who had refused to carry out military-related work or obey orders conscripting them into the armed forces, they only begged to be allowed to be martyred themselves. Höss reported that Himmler was so impressed by their fanaticism that he frequently held it up to his SS men as an example.[116]

The Jehovah's Witnesses were, however, alone amongst religious groups in their uncompromising hostility to the Nazi state. For all the courage of many leading figures in the mainstream Churches, and many ordinary members of their congregations, none of them opposed the Third Reich on more than a narrowly religious front. The Gestapo might allege that Catholic priests and Confessing pastors hid out-and-out opposition to National Socialism under the cloak of pious rhetoric, but the truth was that, on a whole range of issues, the Churches remained silent. Both the Evangelical and Catholic Churches were politically conservative, and had been for a long time before the Nazis came to power. Their fear of Bolshevism and revolution, forces that showed their teeth once more in reports of the widespread massacre of priests by the Republicans at the beginning of the Spanish Civil War, strengthened them in their view that if Nazism went, something worse might well take its place. The deep and often bitter confessional divide in Germany meant that there was no question of Catholics and Protestants joining forces against the regime. The Catholics had been anxious to prove their loyalty to the German state since the days when it had been doubted by Bismarck during the 1870s. The Protestants had been an ideological arm of the state under the Bismarckian Empire and strongly identified with German nationalism for many years. Both broadly welcomed the suppression of Marxist, Communist and liberal political parties, the combating of 'immorality' in art, literature and film, and many other aspects of the regime's policies. The long tradition of antisemitism amongst both Catholics and Protestants ensured that there were no formal protests from the Churches against the regime's antisemitic acts. The most they were prepared to do was to try and protect converted Jews within their own ranks, and even here their attitude was at times extremely equivocal.

Yet the Nazis regarded the Churches as the strongest and toughest reservoirs of ideological opposition to the principles they believed in. If they could win the ideological battle against them, then it would be easy to mould the whole German people into a unanimous Nazi mass. Despite the many setbacks they encountered in their confrontation with the Churches, they did indeed seem to be winning this battle by 1939. Many lower officials in the regime concluded that the only way to combat the Churches was to develop an attractive alternative to Christian ritual. 'It is necessary to effect a kind of mysticism', a Gestapo report urged as early as 1935, 'that exerts an even stronger effect on the masses than that which the Christian Church has built up through the objects of a – dusty – tradition, surrounding them with an atmosphere of foreign magic and covering them with the patina of age.'[117] Yet despite the prevalence of such views amongst the more committed Nazis, most notably Heinrich Himmler, Hitler and Göring remained deeply sceptical about such attempts to revive what Göring referred to as the 'ridiculousness' of 'Wotan and Thor' and the 'Germanic wedding'. The Nazi Education Minister Bernhard Rust inveighed against attempts to propagate 'Valhalla as a substitute for a Christian heaven'.[118] And on 6 September 1938, Hitler himself weighed in with a speech attacking attempts to turn Nazism into a religion:

National Socialism is a cool, reality-based doctrine, based upon the sharpest scientific knowledge and its mental expression. As we have opened the people's heart to this doctrine, and as we continue to do so at present, we have no desire to instil in the people a mysticism that lies outside the purpose and goals of our doctrine . . . For the National Socialist movement is not a cult movement; rather, it is a racial and political philosophy which grew out of exclusively racist considerations. Its meaning is not that of a mystic cult; but rather the cultivation and command of people determined by its blood. Therefore we do not have halls for cults, but exclusively halls for the people. Nor do we have places for worship, but places for assembly and squares for marches. We do not have cult sites, but sports arenas and play areas . . . In the National Socialist movement subversion by occult searchers for the Beyond must not be tolerated.

Nazism, he concluded, was based on respect for the laws of nature, which themselves were given by God; at its centre was the creature whom God had created to rule the earth, namely the human being, and it was by serving the interests of humanity that Nazism served God. 'The only cult we know is that of a cultivation of the natural and hence of that which God has willed.'[119]

Many observers over the years have seen in Nazism a kind of political religion.[120] Its use of religious language, ritual and symbolism, its unquestionable and unalterable dogma, its worship of Hitler as a messiah come to redeem the German people from weakness, degeneracy and corruption, its demonization of the Jew as the universal enemy, its promise that the individual, racked by doubt and despair in the wake of Germany's defeat in 1918, would be born again in a shining new collectivity of the faithful – all these were strongly reminiscent of a religion, shorn of its supernatural elements and applied to the world people really lived in. The Nazis had no hesitation about adapting the Ten Commandments or the Creed to the purposes of a nationalistic catechism of belief in Germany or its Leader, nor did they shrink from using language that portrayed Hitler's gathering of his early supporters such as Göring and Goebbels in the same terms as the Bible portrayed Jesus gathering His early disciples.[121] 'Once you heard the voice of a man,' Hitler told his followers on 11 September 1936 at the Nuremberg Party Rally, 'and that voice knocked at your hearts, it wakened you, and you followed that voice.'[122] Clearly much of this was calculated to have an appeal to disoriented people searching for a solution to the terrible problems they confronted in the chaotic times they lived in. Equally clearly, the more the Third Reich moved away from the attempt to co-ordinate the Churches and towards the drive to destroy them, the more the regime began to take on quasi-religious qualities of its own.[123] But one must be careful about pushing the religious metaphor too far. It would be just as easy to interpret Nazism by means of a military image: the promise of turning defeat into total victory, the image of a nation marching in step, annihilating its enemies and merging the doubting individual into the motivated military mass, the hierarchical command structure dominated by the great military leader, and so on; and though religion and militarism have often been connected, in essence they have also frequently been two quite different and mutually hostile forces.[124]

Nazism as an ideology was no religion, not just because Hitler said it was not, nor because it had nothing to say about the hereafter or eternity or the immortal soul, as all genuine religions do, but also, more importantly, because it was too incoherent to be one. Leading Nazis did not spend time disputing the finer points of their ideology like medieval scholastics or Marxist-Leninist philosophers, their modern equivalents. There was no sacred book of Nazism from which people took their texts for the day, like the bureaucrats of Stalin's Russia did from the works of Marx, Engels and Lenin: Hitler's *My Struggle*, though everyone had to have it on their bookshelf, was too verbose, too rambling, too autobiographical to lend itself to this kind of use. Nor in the end did Nazism promise any kind of final victory to be followed by a Heaven-like stasis; rather, it was a doctrine of perpetual struggle, of conflict without end. There was nothing universal about its appeal, as there is with the great world religions, or with major political ideologies such as socialism and Communism: it directed itself only to one small segment of humanity, the Germans, and ruled everyone else ineligible for its benefits. Conservative philosophers of the mid-twentieth century commonly argued that Nazism as a political religion filled the need for religious faith felt by millions of Germans who had been left bereft by the secularism of modernity. But its appeal cannot be reduced in this way. Millions of Catholics opposed it or remained relatively immune. Millions of Protestants, including many of the most committed, such as the German Christians, did not. Millions more people resisted its ideological blandishments despite having grown up in the atheistic and anticlerical political traditions of the German labour movement.[125]

Religion does not necessarily imply a rejection of democracy, rationality or toleration; some historians have pointed out that the labour movement too had its banners, its rituals, its dogma and its eschatology, though none of this prevented the Social Democrats from embracing democracy, rationality and toleration. Nor, finally, are dogmatism, faith in a great leader, intolerance or belief in future redemption from present ills confined to religious modes of thought and behaviour. Nazism's use of quasi-religious symbols and rituals was real enough, but it was for the most part more a matter of style than substance. 'Hitler's studied usurpation of religious functions', as one historian has written, 'was perhaps a displaced hatred of the Christian tradition: the hatred of an apostate.'[126] The real core of Nazi beliefs lay in the faith Hitler proclaimed in his speech of September 1938 in science – a Nazi view of science – as the basis for action. Science demanded the furtherance of the interests not of God but of the human race, and above all the German race and its future in a world ruled by ineluctable laws of Darwinian competition between races and between individuals. This was the sole criterion of morality, overriding the principles of love and compassion that have always formed such an important element in the beliefs of the world's great religions.[127] A conceptualization of Nazism as a political religion, finally, is not only purely descriptive but also too sweeping to be of much help; it tells us very little about how Nazism worked, or what the nature of its appeal was to different groups in German society. The failure of the Third Reich to find a substitute for Christianity, indeed the feebleness of such attempts as it did make, was nowhere more apparent than in its policy towards the youth of the country, Germany's future.

WINNING OVER THE YOUNG

I

A picture of Adolf Hitler is hanging on the wall in almost every classroom. Next to the memorial plaque in the stairwell a particularly valuable portrait of the Leader, acquired from funds of the Nölting Foundation, holds a place of honour. Teachers and pupils greet each other at the beginning and end of every lesson with the German greeting. The pupils listen to major political speeches on the radio in the school hall.

Thus reported the headmaster of a state secondary school in Wismar at the end of the school year 1933–4, a year, as he noted, of 'growing into the thought-world of the new National Socialist state'.[128] The process of adjustment had been made easier, he noted, through the membership of the staff in the National Socialist Teachers' League and of the pupils in the Hitler Youth. It was also pushed on by a stream of new regulations and directives from the government in Berlin and the state authorities in other parts of Germany. Already on 30 July 1933 a central decree laid down 'Guidelines for History Textbooks' according to which history lessons had from now on to be built around the 'concept of heroism in its Germanic form, linked to the idea of leadership'. Soon students were being set essays on topics such as 'Hitler as the accomplisher of German unity', 'the nationalist revolution as the start of a new era', 'the film "Hitler Youth Quex" as a work of art' and 'I am a German (a word of pride and duty)'. One school student's imagination ran riot in an essay on 'Adolf Hitler as a boy', written in 1934:

The boy Adolf Hitler was no stay-at-home. He liked to rough-and-tumble with other boys in the open. Why was he staying out so long today? His mother went restlessly from the cooker to the table, shook her head, looked at the clock, and began to think the worst about what Adolf was up to again. A few hours before she had seen from the window how he took off with a dozen other boys, who were almost all a head taller than slight Adolf and if it came to it could give him a real thrashing.

Then the door burst open and her Adolf stormed in, with bumps on his head and scratches on his face, but also with shining eyes, and shouted: 'Mother, the boys have made me their General today.'[129]

Another child, pupil at a primary school, given the question 'Were our Germanic ancestors barbarians?', knew immediately how to draw a parallel with the recent past: 'The allegation that our Germanic ancestors were barbarians', he wrote, 'is just as much a lie as for example the lie that Germany alone was to blame for the world war. It has been proved that the Germanic tribes stood on a high cultural plane even in the stone age.'[130] The Nazi cult of death found its way into lessons too, as schoolchildren were asked to write about Horst Wessel and other martyrs for the Nazi cause. 'We must not forget either, those who fell for the movement,' wrote a fourteen-year-old in 1938, and added: 'in thinking about all that we must also think of our own death'.[131]

Numerous essay questions also required school students of all ages to regurgitate the antisemitic bile the regime poured into them. Erna, a primary school pupil, sent her essay for publication in Streicher's *The Stormer*, of which she readily confessed to being a reader. Set the topic of 'The Jews are our misfortune', she wrote: 'Unfortunately many people still say today: "The Jews are also God's creatures. So you must respect them too." But we say: "Vermin are also animals, but despite this we exterminate them."' On occasion, particularly in working-class districts, schoolchildren could take a different view. In 1935, for example:

In a lesson that was devoted to those who had fallen for their country in the war, the teacher said that very many Jews had fallen as well. Straight away a young Nazi exclaimed: 'They died of fright! The Jews don't have any German Fatherland!' At this, another pupil said: 'If Germany isn't their Fatherland and they died for it despite that, that even goes beyond heroism.'[132]

A student essay written in 1938, however, registered the effects of years of indoctrination on the opinions of the young. 'Jews', it claimed, 'do not constitute a race in itself, but are a branch of the Asiatic and Oriental race with a negroid mixture.' Jews, it went on, had made up 60 per cent of the higher civil service under the Weimar Republic (an estimate many times higher than the true figure) and 'the theatre was completely Jewified too', an equally drastic, vulgar overestimation. Despite this, 'You'll never have seen a Jew working, because they only want to trick their fellow men, non-Jews, out of their hard-earned money.' Jews, it concluded, 'had driven the German people into the abyss. This time is now over.'[133]

These student essays reflected a sharp change in the direction of teaching, ordained from above. History, ruled a directive issued on 9 May 1933 by the Reich Minister of the Interior, Wilhelm Frick, had to take a commanding position in the schools. The idea that history should be objective, added the General German Teachers' Paper (Allgemeine Deutsche Lehrerzeitung) on 9 August 1933, was a fallacy of liberalism. The purpose of history was to teach people that life was always dominated by struggle, that race and blood were central to everything that happened in the past, present and future, and that leadership determined the fate of peoples. Central themes in the new teaching included courage in battle, sacrifice for a greater cause, boundless admiration for the Leader and hatred of Germany's enemies, the Jews.[134] Such themes found their way into the teaching of many other subjects too. Biology was transformed to include 'the laws of heredity, racial teaching, racial hygiene, teaching about the family, and population policy' from the latter part of 1933 onwards.[135] Basic reading primers acquired a picture of Hitler, often in the company of children, on their cover or as a frontispiece, or sometimes both. Tiny children learned to recite verses like the following:

> My Leader!
> I know you well and love you like my mother and father.
> I will always obey you like I do my father and mother.
> And when I grow up, I will help you like I will my father and mother,
> And you will be pleased with me.[136]

Reading books such as the German Reading Book, issued in 1936, were filled with stories about children helping the Leader, about the healthy virtues of peasant life, or about the happiness of Aryan families with lots of children. A favourite was a story by Hitler's press chief Otto Dietrich, recounting Hitler's bravery in flying by aeroplane through a massive storm during the Presidential election campaign of April 1932. The Leader's serenity conveyed itself to Dietrich and the other Nazis on the plane and calmed the terror they felt as the winds tossed the plane about the sky.[137] By the mid-1930s there was scarcely a reading primer which did not mention one Nazi institution or another in a positive way.[138] Picture-books for the very young portrayed Jews as devilish figures lurking in dark places, ready to pounce on the unsuspecting blond-haired German child.[139]

Some textbooks from the Weimar era remained widely in use for a while, though they were increasingly frequently censored at a local or school level, and already in 1933 the state committees that checked school textbooks were purged and staffed with committed Nazis. A steady stream of directives flowed from the education authorities in the regions, while additional teaching materials were also issued by Nazi teachers' organizations in different parts of the country. Thus teachers knew within a few months of the Nazi seizure of power the basic outlines of what they had to teach. A directive issued in January 1934 made it compulsory for schools to educate their pupils 'in the spirit of National Socialism'.[140] In order to help achieve this aim, the Breslau regional chapter of the Nazi Teachers' League for instance had issued more than a hundred extra pamphlets by the beginning of 1936 on subjects from '5,000 Years of the Swastika' to 'The Jew and the German Person'. They were sold to pupils for 11 pfennigs each. In some schools the teachers added to the education of their pupils in such matters by reading out loud to them articles from Julius Streicher's *The Stormer*.[141] All this was backed up by a whole battery of central government requirements, ranging from forced attendance in every school hall in the land to listen to Hitler's speeches when they were broadcast on the radio, to the compulsory requirement to watch films issued by the school film propaganda division of Goebbels's Propaganda Ministry from 1934, including movies thought to have an appeal to the young such as *Hitler Youth Quex* and *Hans Westmar*. In every school, libraries were combed for non-Nazi literature and Nazi books stocked instead. Increasingly, classes were interrupted in order for the teachers and pupils to celebrate a whole variety of Nazi festivals, from Hitler's birthday to the commemoration of fallen martyrs of the Nazi movement. School noticeboards were covered in Nazi propaganda posters, adding to the general atmosphere of indoctrination from very early on in the Third Reich.[142]

From 1935 onwards, regional initiatives were augmented by central directives covering the teaching of a whole variety of different subjects in different years. By 1938, these directives covered every school year and most subjects, even those without any directly ideological content.[143] The teaching of the German language had to focus on speech patterns as the product of racial background, German words as instruments of German national consciousness and modes of speech as expressions of character.[144] Even physics teaching was reoriented towards military-related topics such as ballistics, aerodynamics and radiocommunication, though necessarily a good deal of the teaching of basic principles had no clear political point of reference.[145] Biology was redirected towards the study of race.[146] Basic arithmetic textbooks compiled under the Education Ministry's direction also began to appear from 1935. A central feature of these books was their inclusion of 'social arithmetic', which involved calculations designed to achieve a subliminal indoctrination in key areas – for example, sums requiring the children to calculate how much it would cost the state to keep a mentally ill person alive in an asylum.[147] 'The proportion of nordic-falian blood in the German people is estimated as 4/5 of the population,' went one such question: 'A third of these can be regarded as blond. According to these estimates, how many blond people must there be in the German population of 66 million?'[148] Geography was recast in terms of Nazi ideology to stress 'the concepts of home, race, heroism and organicism', as the chapter headings of one handbook for teachers put it. Climate was linked to race, and teachers were advised that studying the Orient was a good way into the 'Jewish question'.[149] Innumerable geography textbooks propagated concepts such as living-space and blood and soil, and purveyed the myth of Germanic racial superiority.[150] World maps and new textbooks emphasized the importance of geopolitics, implicitly underpinned the concept of 'one people, one Reich', or traced the expansion of Germanic tribes across East-Central Europe in the Middle Ages.[151]

II

Despite all these developments, teachers in some situations did retain a little room for manoeuvre. Many village schools were tiny, and the majority of all elementary schools still had only one or two classes in 1939. Teachers here could exercise a degree of freedom in interpreting the materials they were fed by the regime. Moreover, some textbook writers seem to have colluded implicitly with officials in the Ministry of Education to include a good dose of ideologically neutral material in their publications, enabling teachers whose priorities were educational rather than ideological to exercise a degree of choice.[152] One handbook for primary schoolteachers, issued by the National Socialist Teachers' League in 1938, insisted that the three Rs had to remain at the core of the curriculum. Children would serve the nation better, its author declared, if they mastered basic skills of literacy and numeracy before going on to secondary tasks.[153] The more intelligent pupils, such as the artist Joseph Beuys, who went to school in a Catholic area of western Germany during this period, later remembered how they could spot which teachers were 'opponents of the regime beneath the surface'; sometimes they distanced themselves by easily deniable gestures such as adopting an unorthodox stance or attitude when rendering the Hitler salute.[154] One teacher in a Cologne school greeted his class ironically every morning with the salute: 'Hail, You Ancient Germanic Tribesmen!' Many made it clear that they were paying no more than lip-service to Nazi ideology.[155] Yet such ambiguities could have a damaging effect on teaching. As one girl who left Germany at the age of sixteen in 1939 reported, the children were well aware that many of the teachers

had to pretend to be Nazis in order to remain in their posts, and most of the men teachers had families which depended on them. If somebody wanted to be promoted he had to show what a fine Nazi he was, whether he really believed what he was saying or not. In the last two years, it was very difficult for me to accept any teaching at all, because I never knew how much the teacher believed in or not.[156]

Really open dissent in the schools had become virtually impossible long before the eve of the war.[157]

As employees of the state, teachers fell under the provisions of the Reich Law for the Re-establishment of a Professional Civil Service, passed on 7 April 1933, and politically unreliable pedagogues were soon being identified by a network of investigative committees established by the Prussian Minister of Education, Bernhard Rust, who was himself a schoolteacher and a Nazi Regional Leader. Packed with active Nazis and controlled by the Regional Leaders and local Nazi officials, these committees brought about the removal of 157 out of 1,065 male second-ary school heads in Prussia, 37 out of 515 male senior teachers and 280 out of 11,348 tenured male teachers. No fewer than 23 out of 68, or 32 per cent, of all women heads of secondary schools in Prussia were sacked.[158] In some areas the proportion was higher. In the Social Demo-cratic and Communist stronghold of Berlin, for instance, 83 out of 622 head teachers were fired, and progressive institutions such as the Karl Marx School in the working-class district of Neukölln were reorganized under Nazi auspices, in this case with the loss of 43 out of 74 teachers.[159] Those Jewish teachers who were not fired in April 1933 were compul-sorily pensioned off in 1935; two years later, Jews and 'half-Jews' were formally banned from teaching in non-Jewish schools.[160] Yet in general the proportion of dismissals was relatively low. The fact that so few non-Jewish teachers had been purged suggests powerfully that the great majority of schoolteachers were not unsympathetic to the Nazi regime. Indeed, they had been one of the better represented professional groups in the Party and its upper echelons before 1933, reflecting among other things a widespread discontent at salary cuts, sackings and job losses as the Weimar Republic reduced state expenditure during the Depression.[161]

The National Socialist Teachers' League, founded in April 1927 by another schoolteacher-become-Regional-Leader, Hans Schemm, in-creased its membership rapidly from 12,000 at the end of January 1933 to 220,000 by the end of the year, as teachers scrambled to secure their positions by this obvious manifestation of their loyalty to the new regime. By 1936, fully 97 per cent of all schoolteachers, some 300,000 in all, were members, and the following year the League belatedly succeeded in merging into itself all the remaining professional associations. Some, like the Catholic Teachers' League, were forcibly closed down, in this case in 1937. Others, such as specialist groups of teachers in particular subjects, continued to exist as separate entities or sub-groups of the National Socialist Teachers' League. The League initially had to contend with a rival organization, the German Educationalists' Community, backed by a rival Nazi boss, the Interior Minister Wilhelm Frick. But it emerged victorious. From 6 May 1936 the League was formally responsible for the political indoctrination of teachers, which it carried out by setting up political education courses, usually lasting for between one and two weeks, in its own special camps. Of the teachers employed in German schools in 1939 215,000 had undergone this training, which, like the fare offered at other Nazi camps, also included a large dose of military drill, physical jerks, marches, songs and the like, and required all the inmates to wear a military-style uniform for the duration of their stay.[162]

The pressures on teachers to follow the Nazi line were not just exerted from above. An incautious word in class could result in a teacher being arrested. On one occasion, a 38-year-old teacher in the Ruhr district told a joke to her class of twelve-year-olds that she immediately realized could be given an interpretation critical of the regime; despite her entreaties to the children not to pass it on, one of them, who had a grudge against her, told his parents, who promptly informed the Gestapo. Not only the teacher, who denied any intention of insulting the state, but also five of the children were interrogated. They had liked their previous teacher better, one of them said, adding that this was not the first time that the woman under arrest had told a political joke in class. On 20 January 1938 she was brought before the Special Court in Düsseldorf, found guilty and ordered to pay a fine; her three-week imprisonment on remand was taken into account. She had already been dismissed from her job at the beginning of the affair several weeks before. In everyday schoolroom situations, which were saturated with political obligations of one kind and another, fears of denunciation must have been widespread. Teachers under suspicion were likely to receive frequent visits from the inspectors, and every teacher, it was reported, who tried to reduce the impact of the increasingly Nazified teaching he was required to give, 'had to consider every word before he said it, since the children of the old "Party comrades" are constantly watching out so that they can put in a denunciation.'[163]

Pressures to conform worked both ways; children who failed to give the required 'Hail, Hitler' greeting, for example, could be disciplined; in one instance, where Catholic schoolgirls were found greeting each other with the formula 'H.u.S.n.w.K', which a pro-Nazi girl learned, under a promise of strict secrecy, meant '*Heil und Sieg, nie wieder Krieg*', 'Hail and Victory, War Never Again', a full-scale police investigation was launched. The new emphasis of the regime on physical education and military discipline played into the hands of traditionalist disciplinarians and martinets as well as newly fledged Nazis among the teaching staff. Corporal punishment and beatings became more common in schools, as the military spirit began to permeate the educational system. 'In his lessons', wrote a headmaster admiringly of one of his teachers, 'a sharp Prussian wind blows, that does not suit the slack and idle students.' Correspondingly, children who failed to show the required upright posture, who did not stand to attention smartly when addressed, or who showed any kind of 'softness and slackness' were in for trouble from Nazis and authoritarians on the staff.[164]

Yet teachers had to endure a barrage of criticism from adult Nazi activists at every level, starting with Hitler himself, and going on to what one group of teachers called 'a tone of contempt for the teaching profession' in the speeches of the Reich Youth Leader Baldur von Schirach. The result of such open contempt was, they went on, 'that nobody wants to take up the teaching profession any more, since it is treated in this way by top officials and is no longer respected'.[165] This observation was no idle complaint. Continuing pressure by the government to keep pay down in order to make money available for other aspects of state expenditure, such as armaments, added to the deterrent effect. In small village schools, teachers found it increasingly difficult to make ends meet as they were deprived of their traditional sources of additional income as village scribes, while many found it impossible to function as paid church organist and choirmaster at a time of growing conflict between the Church and the Party.[166] Increasing numbers of teachers took early retirement or left the profession for other jobs. In 1936, there were 1,335 unfilled posts in elementary schools; by 1938 the number had grown to nearly 3,000 while the annual number of graduates from teacher training colleges, at 2,500, was nowhere near adequate to the estimated need of the school system for an additional 8,000 teachers a year.[167] The result was that by 1938, class sizes on average in all schools had increased to 43 pupils per teacher as compared to 37 in 1927, while less than one-fourteenth of all secondary schoolteachers were now under the age of forty.[168]

Those teachers who remained in the profession soon lost much of the enthusiasm with which so many of them had greeted the coming of the Third Reich. The militarization of educational life caused increasing disillusion. 'We're nothing more than a department of the Army Ministry,' teachers were reported to be saying in 1934.[169] The training camps they were required to attend were particularly unpopular.[170] More and more time had to be spent away on officer training courses and military exercises.[171] The lives of school heads and administrators were made a misery by endless regulations and decrees poured down from a whole variety of different agencies, one often contradicting the other. A Social Democratic observer described the situation in drastic terms towards the end of 1934:

Everything that has been built up over a century of work by the teaching profession is no longer there in essence. Only the outer shell is still standing; the school houses and the teachers and the pupils are still there, but the spirit and the inner organization has gone. They have been wilfully destroyed from above. No thought any more of proper working methods in school, or of the freedom of teaching. In their place we have cramming and beating schools, prescribed methods of learning and apprehensively circumscribed learning materials. Instead of freedom of learning, we have the most narrow-minded school supervision and spying on teachers and pupils. No free speech is permitted for teachers and pupils, no inner, personal empathy. The whole thing has been taken over by the military spirit, and by drill.[172]

In every school there were likely to be two or three fanatical Nazis amongst the teachers, willing at any point to report colleagues if they expressed unorthodox views. The more considerate ones even warned their colleagues openly that they would be obliged to inform on them if they said anything out of line. The common room became a place to avoid instead of a place for lively intellectual debate. When one head teacher, as was reported in Bremen, 'criticizes in sharp terms the breach of confidentiality of decisions and the writing of anonymous letters that are even sent to the political police', and called for a stop to 'this attack on our honour and these reprehensible denunciations', he was painting a grim picture of the changed atmosphere in the nation's school common rooms; he was also a rare exception to the norm.[173] School management committees and parents' associations were turned from democratic institutions into agencies of control; from 1936, head teachers were no longer allowed to be appointed from the school's own staff but had to be brought in from outside.[174] This further reinforced the leadership principle that had already been introduced in 1934, with the head now the 'Leader' of the school and the teachers his 'retinue', who no longer had any input into the running of the school, but simply had to accept orders from above.[175] In many schools, teachers also had to put up with the presence of old brownshirts who were found jobs as caretakers or even in positions of authority over them.[176] Two or three 'school assistants' were appointed to help the teachers in each school; their continual presence in the classroom was resented by many teachers, who saw them, correctly, as political spies. Most of them were untrained and many were not even particularly well educated. Their ideological interventions became notorious. 'The school assistants', teachers joked amongst themselves, 'are like the appendix: useless and easily inflamed!'[177]

III

As time went on, the Nazi Party, impatient with the inbuilt inertia of the state educational system, began to bypass it altogether in its search for new means of indoctrinating the young. Chief among these was the Hitler Youth, a relatively unsuccessful branch of the Nazi movement before 1933 when compared to, for example, the National Socialist German Students' League. At that time, the Hitler Youth could not compete with the massive numbers of youth groups gathered together in Protestant or Catholic youth organizations, the youth wings of the other political parties, and above all the free youth movement that carried on the tradition of the *Wandervogel* and similar, loosely organized groups from before the First World War. Non-Nazi youth organizations simply dwarfed the Hitler Youth, a mere 18,000-strong in 1930 and still numbering no more than 20,000 two years later. By the summer of 1933, however, as in other areas of social life, the Nazis had dissolved almost all the rival organizations, with the exception of the Catholic youth organizations, which, as we have seen, took rather longer to close down. Boys and girls came under massive pressure to join the Hitler Youth and its affiliated organizations. Teachers were obliged to set selected pupils essays with titles such as 'Why am I not in the Hitler Youth?' and students who did not join had to endure continual taunting from their teachers in the classroom and their fellow students in the playground; as a last resort, they could even be refused the school-leaving certificate when they graduated, if they had not become members by this time. Employers increasingly restricted their apprenticeships to members of the Hitler Youth, thus bringing a particularly powerful material pressure to bear on school students nearing graduation.[178]

From July 1936 the Hitler Youth had an official monopoly on the provision of sports facilities and activities for all children below the age of fourteen; before long, sports for 14–18-year-olds were subjected to the same monopoly; in effect, sports facilities were no longer available to non-members. Hitler Youth members were given special days off school for their activities. The results of such pressure soon became apparent. By the end of 1933 there were 2.3 million boys and girls between the ages of ten and eighteen in the Hitler Youth organization. By the end of 1935 this figure was approaching four million, and by the beginning of 1939 it had reached 8.7 million. With a total population of 8.87 million Germans aged ten to eighteen by this time, this gave the Hitler Youth and its associated groups a near-total claim on the allegiance of the younger generation, especially when the fact that Jewish children were barred from joining is taken into account. From 1 December 1936 the Hitler Youth was given the status of an official educational institution and taken away from its previous subordination to the Reich Interior Ministry. From this point on it was an autonomous organization directly accountable through its leader Baldur von Schirach to the Leader alone. After 25 March 1939, membership was legally binding from the age of ten, and parents could be fined if they failed to enrol their children, or even imprisoned if they actively tried to stop them joining.[179]

It was above all through the Hitler Youth and its associated affiliates that the Nazis sought to build the new Germans of the future. Already in *My Struggle*, Hitler devoted a considerable amount of space to outlining his views on the nature and purpose of education in the racial state he wanted to build in Germany.[180] 'The folkish state', he proclaimed, 'must not adjust its entire educational work primarily to the inoculation of mere knowledge, but to the breeding of absolutely healthy bodies. The training of mental abilities is only secondary.' Character-building came next, then the promotion of will-power, then the training of joy in responsibility. 'A people of scholars, if they are physically degenerate, weak-willed and cowardly pacifists, will not storm the heavens.' An academic education was useless. 'The youthful brain should in general not be burdened with things ninety-five per cent of which it cannot use.' Academic subjects would be taught only through 'an abridgement of the material', and they should be geared to the interests of the race: history teaching for example should cut out pointless detail and concentrate on encouraging patriotism. Physical education and character-building would culminate in military service, the last stage of education. The overriding purpose of the school was 'to burn the racial sense and racial feeling into the instinct and the intellect, the heart and brain of the youth entrusted to it'.[181]

These nostrums were applied to the German schools, as we have already seen, after the Nazis came to power, backed by the pedagogic doctrines of Nazi educational theorists like Ernst Krieck, now standard fare in the teacher training institutions.[182] But even when it had been centralized and taken completely under state control, the traditional primary and secondary education system was still only of limited use in achieving these ends. As Hitler proclaimed at the Nuremberg Party Rally in 1935:

In our eyes the German boy of the future must be slender and supple, swift as greyhounds, tough as leather and hard as Krupp steel. We must bring up a new type of human being, men and girls who are disciplined and healthy to the core. We have undertaken to give the German people an education that begins already in youth and will never come to an end. It starts with the child and will end with the 'old fighter'. Nobody will be able to say that he has a time in which he is left entirely alone to himself.[183]

Members of the Hitler Youth were required to learn this speech by heart and proclaim it when the swastika flag was raised.[184]

The indoctrination which young Germans received through the Hitler Youth was ceaseless. Although it borrowed the style of existing youth organizations, with hikes, camping, songs, rituals, ceremonies, sports and games, it was emphatically a top-down organization, run not by young people themselves, as the old youth movement had been, but according to the leadership principle, by the Reich Youth Leadership under Schirach. The organization issued strict guidelines on the activities to be carried out. All those who joined had to swear a personal oath of allegiance to Hitler. Their training was compulsory and legally binding. Every age-cohort of the Hitler Youth had a set syllabus to get through each year, covering topics such as 'Germanic gods and heroes', '20 Years' fight for Germany', 'Adolf Hitler and his fellow-fighters', or 'The people and its blood-heritage'. The songs they sang were Nazi songs, the books they read were Nazi books. Specially prepared information packs told the leaders what to say to the assembled children and young people and provided further material for their indoctrination.[185] As time went on, military training increasingly came to the fore. Candidates for admission even to its most junior levels had to pass a medical and fitness test and only then could they become full members. On 20 February 1938 Hitler's listing of its key divisions claimed:

The Naval-Hitler-Youth comprises 45,000 boys. The Motor-Hitler-Youth comprises 60,000 boys. 55,000 members of the Junior Hitler Youth are serving in aerial training through learning gliding. 74,000 Hitler Youths are organized in the Flying Units of the Hitler Youth. In 1937 alone, 15,000 boys passed their gliding tests. Today 1,200,000 Hitler Youths are receiving regular instruction in small-calibre shooting, led by 7,000 shooting instructors.[186]

By this time, training sessions were concentrating on parade-ground marching, learning the morse code, map-reading, and similar activities for boys, while girls focused on military nursing and air-raid protection.[187] The result was that, as agents reporting secretly to the exiled Social Democratic Party leadership in Prague noted, even if the older boys retained something of the beliefs their Social Democratic, Communist or Catholic parents had passed on to them, the younger ones were 'from the beginning onwards fed exclusively on the National Socialist spirit'.[188] The possibility of holiday trips with the Hitler Youth, the sporting facilities, and much else, could make the organization attractive to children from poor working-class families who had not previously had the opportunity to enjoy these things. Some could find excitement and a sense of self-worth in the Hitler Youth.[189] Idealism undoubtedly played a role in committing many young people to the cause in defiance of their parents' wishes. Melita Maschmann joined the League of German Girls on 1 March 1933, secretly, because she knew her conservative parents would disapprove. Her attempts to read through ideological tomes such as Hitler's *My Struggle* or Chamberlain's *Foundations of the Nineteenth Century* came to nothing.[190] She later claimed that, like many of her upper-middle-class friends, she discounted the violence and antisemitism of the National Socialists as passing excesses which would soon disappear. The League of German Girls offered her a sense of purpose and belonging, and she devoted herself to it night and day, to the neglect of her schooling and the distress of her parents. Yet, she wrote later, she was 'only secondarily interested in politics, and even then often only under duress'.[191] For boys, the constant emphasis on competition and struggle, heroism and leadership, in sport as in other things, had its effect. There must have been many incidents like this one reported by a Social Democratic agent in the autumn of 1934:

The son of a comrade in my house is 13 years old and in the Hitler Youth. Recently he came home from a training evening and asked his father: 'Why didn't you defend yourselves then? I despise you because you didn't possess a shred of heroism. Your Social Democracy is worthy of nothing more than to be beaten to a pulp because you didn't have a single hero!' His father said to him: 'You don't understand any of that.' But the boy laughed and believed what his leader had told him.[192]

Old Social Democrats despaired. A whole generation was growing up, as one of them said, 'that has no concept of the labour movement, that hears nothing all the time but "heroes and heroism". This generation of young people doesn't want to hear anything from us any more.'[193]

Yet despite this massive programme of military training and ideological indoctrination, the effect of the Hitler Youth on the younger generation was mixed. The more it evolved from a self-mobilizing movement fighting for a cause into a compulsory institution serving the interests of the state, the less attractive it became to the younger generation. Ideological indoctrination was often superficial, since the leaders of the Hitler Youth groups were more often men in the brutal, anti-intellectual tradition of the brownshirts than educated thinkers along the lines of the leaders of the old youth movement.[194] Thus the majority of their charges had no very firm grasp of 'the idea of National Socialism'. If there was a regime change, one of the more reflective youth leaders thought, for example through defeat in a war, then most of them 'would adjust themselves to the new situation without particular inner complications'.[195] The emphasis on sporting activities that was such an attraction to many to join the Hitler Youth also hindered a full-scale indoctrination, since the interest of many boys and girls went no further than using the facilities to play games. Physical exercise was not to every child's taste. Particularly unpopular was the obligation to go round with a collecting-box for donations, especially since this was increasingly a feature of school life too. With hikes sometimes beginning at 7.30 in the morning on a Sunday and lasting all day (not coincidentally obliging the religious amongst the participants to miss church) or compulsory gymnastics at eight o'clock on a Wednesday evening, it was not surprising that some young people began to long for time to spend on their own private pursuits. Yet unorganized hiking and spontaneous activities organized by the young people themselves, notable features of the pre-1933 youth movement, were expressly forbidden.[196]

In September 1934 the Hitler Youth leadership in a working-class district of Hamburg sent a lengthy memorandum to Hitler Youth members, with copies to their parents, complaining:

You are not turning up to do your duty and are not even giving any excuses for your absence. Instead you are pursuing private pleasures. The 'liberal Marxist I' counts amongst you once more, you are denying the National Socialist 'we'. You are sinning against the interests of the nation. You are excusing yourselves from service because you want to go to an acquaintance's wedding feast, you are excusing yourselves because you are overburdened with school homework and want to go for a spin on your bicycle. When you get to school you use your Hitler Youth service as an excuse for not finishing your homework.[197]

Most hated of all was the military discipline, which became more pronounced as time wore on.[198] Schirach proclaimed that 'the principle of self-leadership' would apply as it had in the old youth movement,[199] but in practice the organization was effectively run by grown-ups. Hitler Youth members were drilled by adult brownshirts, plunged into ice-cold water to toughen them up, forced to go on lengthy exercises in winter with inadequate clothing to teach them physical endurance and subjected to increasingly brutal punishments if they disobeyed orders. There were reports of boys being forced to run the gauntlet for minor misdemeanours, or even being beaten with spring-hooks. Doctors complained that long hours of drill, night marches with full packs and military exercises without proper nourishment were ruining young people's mental and physical health.[200]

Social Democratic agents reported that young people absented themselves from training evenings, or failed to pay their dues, so that they were excluded from the organization, rejoining only when they needed to show their membership card to get a job or enter university. One agent in Saxony reported in 1938: 'The boys are past-masters in telling the latest jokes about Nazi institutions. They fritter away their hours of service whenever they can. In their spare time, when they meet to play in a school-friend's home, they talk contemptuously of "the plan of service".'[201] Children quickly got bored with long evenings sitting around a camp fire singing patriotic songs: 'Most of them', reported one Social Democratic agent, 'want to go home already after the first song.'[202] Weekly parades lasting from 7.30 to 9.30 in the evening were notable for their poor attendance. There was little that the organization could do to punish those who stayed away. As long as they paid their dues, they could not be expelled, and many a young person was, as one member of the League of German Girls noted, 'more or less only a paying member', since a fifteen-year-old 'had all kinds of other interests'. Young people who were already at work in their teens found the hours of training particularly wearisome.[203] Camping, once a favourite activity in the youth movement, became increasingly unpopular as it became more militarized. As one young man returning from a camp complained:

We hardly had any free time. Everything was done in a totally military way, from reveille, first parade, raising the flag, morning sport and ablutions through breakfast to the 'scouting games', lunch and so on to the evening. Several participants left the camp because the whole slog was too stupid for them. There was no kind of fellow-feeling between the camp inmates. Comradeship was very poor, and everything was done in terms of command and obedience . . . The camp leader was an older Hitler Youth functionary of the drill sergeant type. His entire educational effort amounted to barking orders, holding scouting exercises, and general slogging . . . The whole camp was more hyperactivity and an exaggerated cult of the muscular than a spiritual experience or even an active and co-operatively shaped leisure time.[204]

Another, remembering his time in the Hitler Youth some years later, confessed that he had been 'enthusiastic' when he had joined at the age of ten – 'for what boy is not roused to enthusiasm when ideals, high ideals like comradeship, loyalty and honour, are held up before him?' – but soon he was finding the 'compulsion and the unconditional obedience . . . exaggerated'.[205] The 'endless square-bashing' was boring and the punishments for the tiniest infringements could lead to bitterness, remembered another, but nobody complained, since proving your toughness was the only way to get on, and it had its effects too: 'Toughness and blind obedience were drilled into us from the moment we could walk.'[206]

Even young Nazis were 'disappointed and discontented'. Under the surface, the old tradition of the youth movement lived on, as rebellious boys learned old, now forbidden, hiking songs and hummed the tunes to one another at Hitler Youth camps as a sign of recognition; they clubbed together at camp and organized their own activities where they could.[207] But a good number of other Social Democratic observers curbed their desire to seek light at the end of the tunnel and reported gloomily that the younger generation were losing touch with the values of their elders and falling prey to Nazi ideology under the impact of the Hitler Youth and indoctrination in the schools. For all their deficiencies, the Hitler Youth movement and the increasingly Nazified school system were driving a wedge between parents who still retained some loyalty to the beliefs and standards they had grown up in themselves, and their children who were being indoctrinated at every stage of their lives. As one such agent ruefully observed:

It is extremely difficult for parents who are opponents of the Nazis to exercise an influence on their children. Either they ask the child not to talk at school about what is said at home. Then the children get the feeling, aha, the parents have to hide what they think. The teacher permits himself to say everything out loud. So he's bound to be right. – Or the parents express their opinion without giving the child a warning. Then it's not long before they are arrested or at the very least called up before the teacher, who shouts at them and threatens to report them. – 'Send your father to the school!' That is the normal answer to suspicious doubts and questions on the part of the child. If the father is quiet after such a visit, then he gives the child the impression that he has been convinced by what the teacher has told him, and the effect is far worse than if nothing had ever been said.[208]

There were even more disturbing reports of children whose membership in the Hitler Youth was disapproved of by their parents threatening to report them to the authorities if they tried to stop them going to meetings. For adolescents, it was only too easy to annoy parents who were former Social Democrats by greeting them at home with 'Hail, Hitler!' instead of 'good morning'. 'Thus war is taken into every family', one wife of an old labour movement activist observed. 'The worst is', she added apprehensively, 'that you've got to watch yourself in front of your own children.'[209]

Thus state and Party were both undermining the socializing and educating functions of the family. Baldur von Schirach was aware of this criticism and sought to counter it with the allegation that many poor and working-class children did not have a proper family life anyway. The middle-class parents who were most vociferous in complaining about the time their children were forced to spend outside the home in activities organized by the Hitler Youth or the League of German Girls should remember, he said, 'that the Hitler Youth has called up its children to the community of National Socialist youth so that they can give the poorest sons and daughters of our people something like a family for the first time'.[210] But such arguments were only liable to increase resentment among working-class parents. Bringing up children, many of them complained, was no longer a pleasure. The costs of providing uniforms and equipment for their children in the Hitler Youth was considerable, and they got nothing back in exchange. 'Nowadays, childless couples are often congratulated by parents on their childlessness. These days parents have nothing more than the duty to feed and clothe their children; educating them is in the first place the task of the Hitler Youth.'[211] One 'old soldier' was heard complaining about his son, a Hitler Youth activist, in bitter terms: 'The lad has already been completely alienated from us. As an old front-soldier I'm against every war, and this lad is just mad about war and nothing else. It's awful, sometimes I feel as if my lad is the spy in the family.'[212]

The overall effect of Hitler Youth membership, some Social Democratic observers complained, was a 'coarsening' of the young. The suppression of any discussion or debate, the military discipline, the emphasis on physical prowess and competition, led boys to become violent and aggressive, especially towards young people who for whatever reason had not joined the Hitler Youth.[213] Hitler Youth groups travelling by train amused themselves by insulting and threatening guards who failed to say 'Hail, Hitler!' every time they asked a passenger for his ticket. Camps held in rural districts were liable to give rise to a flood of complaints from local farmers about thefts of fruit from their orchards. So rough was the training to which the children were subjected that injuries of one kind and another were a frequent occurrence. Training in 'boxing' made a point of dispensing with rules or precautions: 'The more blood the lads saw flowing on such occasions, the more enthusiastic they became.' In the Hitler Youth, as in the SA, the army and the Labour Service, one Social Democratic agent noted, a process of brutalization was setting in. 'The kind of leader they have and the way they treat everyone degrades human beings to animals there, turns everything sexual into smut. There are many who get venereal diseases.' 'Once a month, in many divisions of the Hitler Youth, they carry out the kind of "sex parade" that we all remember from the war'.[214] The Hitler Youth refused to provide sex education, declaring it a matter for parents. Cases of homosexual behaviour by Hitler Youth leaders in the camps were hushed up; there was no question of bringing them to the attention of the press, as had happened in the campaign of allegations brought against Catholic priests working in care institutions. In one particularly serious case in 1935, just as Goebbels was beginning his exposure of sex scandals in the Church, a boy was sexually assaulted by several others at a Hitler Youth camp then knifed to death to stop him talking. When his mother found out what had happened and reported it to Reich Commissioner Mutschmann, he immediately had her arrested and imprisoned to prevent the scandal from coming out into the open. Parents who complained about any aspect of their children's treatment in the camps, or took their children out of the organization for their own good, were liable to be accused of undermining the Hitler Youth and could even on occasion be silenced by the threat that, if they continued, their children would be taken into care.[215] An attempt by no less a personage than Heinrich

Himmler, in collaboration with Schirach, to impose discipline through an internal Hitler Youth police force, established in July 1934, was effective mainly in providing a recruiting mechanism for the SS.[216]

The indiscipline of the Hitler Youth had a particularly disruptive effect in the schools. Its teenage activists, showered by the regime with assurances of their central importance to the nation's future and accustomed to commanding groups of younger children considerably larger than the classes their teachers taught, behaved with increasing arrogance towards their elders in school. 'By continually whipping up their self-confidence,' one Hitler Youth leader himself admitted, 'the leadership encourages amongst many boys a kind of megalomania that refuses to recognize any other authority.'[217] In the struggle between the Hitler Youth and the schools, the former was gradually getting the upper hand.[218] The Hitler Youth wore their own uniforms in school, so that increasingly the teachers faced classes dressed to advertise their primary allegiance to an institution run from outside. A regulation of January 1934 giving the Hitler Youth equal status with the schools as an educational institution further boosted their self-confidence.[219] Adolescent rebelliousness was being channelled against socializing institutions such as the school, as well as parents, the family and the Churches. Former Hitler Youth members recalled in interviews after the war how they had gained more power in school through their membership.[220] Even the Security Service of the SS expressed its concern in 1939 at the deteriorating relations between teachers and Hitler Youth.[221] In 1934, one Social Democratic agent reported that a Hitler Youth 'school leader' told a sixty-year-old teacher who had put his hat on in the bitter winter cold of the weekly Monday-morning collective drill, when the whole school sang the national anthem and greeted the raising of the Nazi flag with doffed caps, that if he did this again he would be reported.[222] Only rarely were teachers ingenious enough to find a way of reasserting their control without running the risk of denunciation, as in the case of one mathematics teacher at a Cologne secondary school, who addressed particularly knotty arithmetical questions to two Hitler Youth leaders who appeared in his class in uniform, with the words: 'As Hitler Youth leaders you must surely set a good example; surely you can solve this question!'[223]

IV

The school system of the Third Reich was formally under the aegis of Bernhard Rust, who was appointed Prussian Minister of Education and Religion (*Kultusminister*) in 1933. A schoolteacher himself, Rust had joined the Nazi Party early on and became District Leader of Southern Hanover and Brunswick in 1925. He was fifty years of age when Hitler was appointed Chancellor, somewhat older than the other leading Nazis, who were mostly in their thirties or early forties. On 1 May 1934 Rust secured his own appointment to the new Reich Ministry of Science and Education, which took over the Prussian Ministry and, in effect, the regional Ministries, at the beginning of 1935, while responsibility for religion and the Churches passed to the new Reich Church Ministry led, as we saw earlier in this chapter, by Hans Kerrl. On 20 August 1937 the Reich Education Ministry took central control over the appointment of all established teachers, and in 1939 it set up a Reich Examination Office to oversee all educational examinations. Meanwhile, it had also acted on 20 March 1937 to rationalize the secondary school system, a long-standing demand of teachers, already planned under the Weimar Republic, into three basic types of school, concentrating on modern languages and the humanities, on science and technology, or on a classics-based curriculum.[224] And on 6 July 1938 the regime issued another law extending the Prussian school structure established in 1927 to the whole of Germany, laying down a minimum requirement for all children of eight years at school – a step forward for Bavaria, which had hitherto only had required seven, but a step backward for Schleswig-Holstein, where the minumum had traditionally been nine. It was this law that also laid down a centrally determined curriculum, including 'racial education' for all.[225]

On Hitler's birthday, 20 April 1933, Rust founded three National Political Educational Institutions or 'Napolas', boarding schools set up in the premises of former Prussian military cadet schools (rendered defunct by the Treaty of Versailles) and designed to train a new elite to rule the future Third Reich.[226] The need to please President Hindenburg, who had been a student at one of these cadet schools, may have played a role as well. By 1939 there were 16 Napolas in existence.[227] They were intended to provide a military training and were equipped with riding stables, motor-bikes, yachts and the like, all signs that the sports the students were trained in had a distinctly aristocratic tinge that would reinforce their elitist self-image. On graduating, the pupils usually went into the armed forces, the SS or the police as officers.[228] The students were selected in the first place according to racial criteria, decided by a medical examination carried out by a qualified doctor, and then by character traits, displayed during an entrance test that consisted above all of competitive sports in which the applicants were required to demonstrate their courage and aggression.[229]

At the same time, however, at the insistence of the officials in Rust's Ministry, the Napolas continued to teach the regular state school curriculum with its academic subjects, as befitted state educational institutions. At the Party Congress in 1934, and again in 1935, Hitler insisted that political education was a matter for the Party and not for state-run institutions or state-appointed teachers. In conformity with this view, the Napolas were run by SS and SA officers without any previous educational experience. The administration appointed a parallel staff of 'educators' from the same background to work alongside the trained teachers who provided the pupils with normal school lessons. All the staff had to undergo regular special training, and the students also had to spend time several weeks a year working on a farm or a factory to maintain contacts with the people. Under these circumstances it was not surprising that it soon proved difficult to find enough qualified teachers. Those who did serve in many cases did so because they themselves had had previous experience of the Prussian cadet schools, and some of the heads consciously revived some of the old Prussian cadet school traditions. It was apparent to some in the Nazi leadership by 1934 therefore that the Napolas were more reactionary throwbacks to the old Prussian tradition than modern institutions dedicated to the creation of a new elite for the Third Reich. They seemed to be more interested in supplying the army with officers than the state with leaders.[230] The man in charge of the day-to-day management of the schools was Joachim Haupt, a professional educationalist who had published a number of writings under the Weimar Republic urging the foundation of a new educational system devoted to racial and political training. But in the wake of the 'Night of the Long Knives', Haupt came under attack from the SS, who

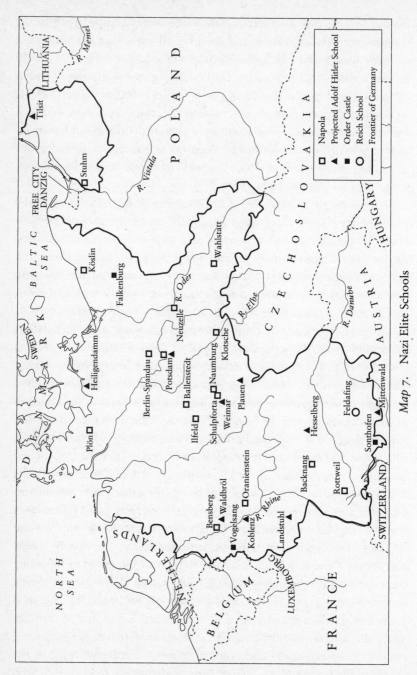

Map 7. Nazi Elite Schools

more than hinted that he was homosexual and claimed that Rust wanted to be rid of him because he was too reactionary. As a consequence, Haupt was sacked in 1935 and the overall management and inspection of the Napolas transferred to a senior SS officer, August Heissmeyer; eventually, the administration of the Napolas was turned over to the SS altogether. As a new type of state educational institution, they had not been much of a success. Nor were their standards really high enough to provide the regime with a new elite cadre of leaders for the future.[231]

As these events illustrated, Rust was less than effective when it came to dealing with the big hitters in the Nazi power structure. He was subject to bouts of depression, alternating with periods of manic optimism and aggression, which made it difficult for him to carry out a consistent policy line; his civil servants distrusted him and often obstructed his orders and he was often in no shape to stand up to the predatory aggression of his rivals in the top echelons of the Party. Rust also suffered from a progressive paralysis of the facial muscles that caused him increasing pain as time went on, which further limited his ability to stand up to opposition.[232] His Napolas were soon outflanked by two far more ideological institutions, run not, as the Napolas were, by the state, but controlled from the outset by organs of the Party. On 15 January 1937, Reich Youth Leader Baldur von Schirach and German Labour Front Leader Robert Ley issued a joint announcement reporting that Hitler, at their request, had ordered the founding of 'Adolf Hitler Schools', secondary schools run by the Hitler Youth, which would determine the curriculum and be supervised by Nazi Party Regional Leaders.[233] Overriding Rust's furious objections, the two leaders set up the first Adolf Hitler School on 20 April 1937. The intention was, as Ley declared, that nobody in future would be able to take on a leading position in the Party without first having undergone an education in these institutions. Two-thirds of the pupils at the Adolf Hitler Schools were boarders. The Hitler Youth determined the curriculum, which focused even more strongly than the Napolas on physical and military education. Like the Napolas, the Adolf Hitler Schools did not provide any religious instruction. There were no examinations but instead a regular 'Achievement Week' at which the students had to compete against each other in every area.[234] Drawing on the Hitler Youth across Germany, these schools, which provided an education from the age of twelve free of charge, became something of a vehicle of upward social mobility, with 20 per cent of their pupils coming from backgrounds that could broadly be defined as working-class.[235] Initially only physical criteria were applied to select students for admission, but by 1938 it had become clear that the neglect of intellectual abilities was causing serious problems, since a large proportion of the pupils could not grasp even the fairly basic political ideas that the teachers were trying to transmit to them. From this time onwards, therefore, academic criteria were added to the other elements in the admission process. The teachers appointed in the first couple of years, all leaders of the Hitler Youth, were not very competent either, and from 1939 onwards they were required to undergo proper teacher training at a university before taking up their posts. Ley's idea was that there should be one of these schools in each Nazi Party Region, under the general management of the Party Regional Leader; but the Nazi Party management successfully objected that the costs would be too great for the Party to bear, and the full complement of schools was never reached. In 1938 only 600 pupils were taken on nationwide, far fewer than the original plan had envisaged. The buildings under construction to house the schools were never completed, and until 1941 the schools depended overwhemingly on rented premises in the Order Castle at Sonthofen.[236]

The Order Castles (*Ordensburgen*) were the next stage in the system of Party-based education dreamed up by Schirach and Ley. They were intended exclusively to teach graduates of the Adolf Hitler Schools, though before being admitted the students had to undergo vocational training or university education and prove their personal and ideological soundness. Not only did the students not pay any fees, they even received pocket-money from the schools. There were three Order Castles, located high up in remote country districts. They were designed by leading architects on a lavish scale. Construction began in March 1934 and the buildings were opened two years later. They were intended to form an interconnected system of education and training. Students were to spend the first year at the Falkenburg, on the Crössin Lake in Pomerania, being educated in racial biology and undertaking various sporting activities; in their second year the students were supposed to move to Vogelsang Castle, in the Eifel hills above the Rhine, which concentrated more exclusively on sport; and in their third year they were to move to Sonthofen Castle, in the mountainous district of Bavaria Allgäu, where they were to undergo further ideological training and to engage in dangerous sports such as mountaineering. The regime intended to build a fourth Order Castle, at Marienburg, to focus on instruction about Eastern Europe, and ultimately a 'High School' on the Chiem Lake, in Bavaria, to carry out research and to train teachers for the Order Castles and the Adolf Hitler Schools. In the meantime, however, the elite pupils of the Order Castles had to spend three separate monthly periods every year working in Party organizations in the regions, so that they had experience of practical politics; and the Order Castles in turn functioned as training centres for numerous Nazi Party officials on short courses, as well as teacher training centres for the Adolf Hitler Schools.[237] As the name suggested, the aim of the Order Castles was to create a modern version of the medieval knightly and monastic orders of old: disciplined, united and dedicated to a cause; to underline this intention, the students were known as 'Junkers'. Together with the Adolf Hitler Schools, they were the means by which the Party planned to secure its future leadership in the long term.[238]

Measured by normal academic standards, the level of education provided by the Order Castles was not high. The overwhelming emphasis on physical training and the ideologically driven curriculum made them poor substitutes for a conventional higher education, and the criteria on which the students were selected left intellectual ability more or less out of account. In July 1939 Vogelsang Castle was the subject of withering criticism by an internal Nazi Party report, which pilloried the low intellectual level of the graduates and expressed serious doubts about their ability to give a coherent account of Nazi ideology and added: 'Only in the smallest number of cases does blooming health and strength also vouch for a pronounced intellectual capacity.' As early as 1937, Goebbels's paper *The Attack* had raised doubts about the institution's effectiveness after a reporter had heard one of the earliest graduates 'give an ideologically coloured lecture, but he didn't say much to the point. Have the right people been selected at all?' it asked pointedly. Two years later, the situation in Vogelsang Castle descended into chaos when its commander, Richard Manderbach, whose main claim to distinction was that he had founded the first branch of the stormtroopers in the Siegerland district in 1924, was discovered to have had his youngest child secretly baptized in a Catholic church. Although Manderbach denied any knowledge of this, the Junkers greeted him in the dining hall and the teaching room with rude choruses, songs and shouts demanding to know why he had been consorting with 'Pope and priest'. Order was only restored with his dismissal on 10 June 1939.[239] As one of the students of the Adolf Hitler School housed in the Order Castle at Sonthofen, the future Hollywood movie actor Hardy Krüger, later noted, the students were constantly told that they were going to be the leaders of Nazi Germany in the future, so it was not surprising that they did not tolerate ideological backsliding. In an atmosphere that encouraged physical toughness and ruthlessness, he added, bullying and physical abuse of the younger by the older boys was inevitably widespread, the general spirit brutal and rough.[240]

The same ideas that inspired the Adolf Hitler Schools, the Order Castles and to a more limited extent the Napolas were also evident in yet another elite school, founded under the aegis of Ernst Röhm and the SA: the National Socialist High School on the Starnberger Lake. A private school owned by the brownshirt organization, opened in January 1934, it had only been in existence for a few months when Röhm was shot dead on Hitler's orders. In desperation, the school's head sought to preserve it by putting it under the protection first of Franz Xaver Schwarz, the Party Treasurer, then of Rudolf Hess's office, where Martin Bormann was the key functionary. On 8 August 1939 Hess renamed it the Reich School of the NSDAP Feldafing, by which time it had already become the most successful of the Nazi elite schools. Housed in forty villas, some of them confiscated from their Jewish owners, the school was under the academic control of the Nazi Teachers' League, and all the pupils and teachers were automatically members of the SA. With its powerful patrons in the top ranks of the Party, the school managed without too much difficulty to obtain lavish funding and first-rate equipment, and, with its connections to the teaching profession, it provided a much better academic education than the other elite schools, although it shared with them a common emphasis on sport, physical training and character-building. Yet critics maintained that the pupils, often the scions of high-ranking Party officials, learned only how to be playboys.[241] All in all, none of the elite schools could match the standards of Germany's long-established academic grammar schools. Eclectic and often contradictory in their approach, they lacked any coherent educational concept that could serve as the basis for training a new functional elite to rule a modern technological nation like Germany in the future. On the eve of the war, with a mere 6,000 male and 173 female pupils in the sixteen Napolas, the ten Adolf Hitler Schools and the Reich School combined, they formed only a small part of the boarding school system: at the same point in time, September 1939, other residential schools were educating 36,746 pupils of both sexes, or six times as many.[242]

Nevertheless, the low academic standards evident in the Napolas, the Adolf Hitler Schools and the Order Castles had also begun to become apparent in the state school system by the eve of the Second World War. At every level, formal learning was given decreased emphasis as the hours devoted to physical education and sport in the state schools were increased in 1936 to three a week, then in 1938 to five, and fewer lessons were devoted to academic subjects to make room for indoctrination and preparation for war.[243] Children still learned the three Rs, and in grammar schools and other parts of the secondary education system much more than this, but there can be little doubt that the quality of education was steadily declining. By 1939 employers were complaining that school graduates' standards of knowledge of language and arithmetic were poor and that 'the level of school knowledge of the examinees has been sinking for some time'.[244] Yet this did not cause any concern to the regime. As Hans Schemm, the leader of the Nazi Teachers' League up to 1935, declared: 'The goal of our education is the formation of character', and he complained that too much knowledge had been crammed into children, to the detriment of character-building. 'Let us have', he said, '. . . ten pounds less knowledge and ten calories more character!'[245] The progressive demoralization of the teaching profession, the growing shortage of staff and the consequent increase in class sizes also had their effects. As we have seen, the Hitler Youth proved a thoroughly disruptive influence on formal education. 'School', one Social Democratic report already noted in 1934, 'is constantly disrupted by Hitler Youth events.' Teachers had to allow pupils time off for them almost every week.[246] The abolition of the compulsory ceremonies attached to the State Youth Day, which on one reckoning had taken up 120 hours of out-of-school preparation each year, in 1936, made little real difference in this respect.[247] Despite the military-style discipline in the schools, there were numerous reports of indiscipline and disorder, violent incidents between pupils, and insubordination towards teachers.[248] 'One can't speak of the teacher having authority any more,' noted one Social Democratic agent in 1937: 'The snotty-nosed little brats of the Hitler Youth decide what goes on at school, they're in charge.'[249]

In the same year, the teachers of one district in Franconia complained in the half-yearly report of their branch of the National Socialist Teachers' League that the attitude of pupils towards education was giving

repeated cause for justified complaints and to concern about the future. There is a widespread lack of zeal for work and feeling for duty. Many school pupils believe that they can just sail through their school-leaving examinations by sitting tight for eight years even if they fall way below the required intellectual standard. In the Hitler Youth and Junior Hitler Youth units there is no kind of support for school; on the contrary, it is precisely those pupils who serve in leading positions there who are noticeable for their disobedient behaviour and their laziness at school. It is necessary to report that school discipline is noticeably declining and to a worrying degree.[250]

Educational standards had declined markedly by 1939. What really mattered was, as one Social Democratic observer noted ruefully in June 1937: 'Whether one observes young people playing or working, whether one reads what they write or visits their homes, whether one looks through the school timetable or even follows what goes on at camp, there is only one will that rules the entire carefully devised and ever more efficiently operating machine: the will to war.'[251]

'STRUGGLE AGAINST THE INTELLECT'

I

While the Nazis concentrated a great deal of effort on turning the school system to their own purposes after 1933, they were somewhat less vigorous in imposing their views on Germany's universities. Only in 1934, with the founding of the Reich Education Ministry, did the regime really began to get a grip on higher education from the centre. Even then, the grip was but a feeble one. Not only was the Education Minister Bernhard Rust weak and indecisive, he was also fundamentally uninterested in universities. His incurable tendency to vacillation soon became the butt of mocking humour amongst university professors, who joked that a new minimum unit of measurement had been introduced by the government: 'One Rust', the time that elapsed between the promulgation of a decree and its cancellation. Nor were the other Nazi leaders particularly concerned about higher education. When Hitler spoke to a student audience on the tenth anniversary of the founding of the Nazi Students' League in January 1936, he barely mentioned student affairs; he never addressed a student audience again. In a fashion only too typical of the Third Reich, higher education became the focus of intra-Party rivalries, as the Office of the Leader's Deputy, nominally under Rudolf Hess but in reality spurred on by his ambitious chief of staff, Martin Bormann, began to take an interest in academic appointments. Research funding fell under the aegis of the Interior Ministry. Regional Leaders interfered in university affairs too. The SA tried to enlist students. And the Nazi Students' League took the lead in the Nazification of university life. The Ministry took the view that the main function of the Students' League should be to further the political indoctrination of the undergraduates and graduates; but running the university was the job of the Rector, whom the guidelines issued by the Education Ministry on 1 April 1935 defined as the leader of an institution; the duty of the rest of the staff and students was to follow him and obey his commands.[252]

In practice, however, the weakness of the Education Ministry made it impossible for this principle to be applied with any consistency. Academic appointments became the object of struggles between the Ministry, the Rector, the Nazi Students' League, the professors and the local Nazi Party bosses, all of whom continued to claim the right of political control within the universities. Like the Hitler Youth in the schools, the Nazi Students' League and its members did not fight shy of naming and shaming the teachers they thought were not toeing the Nazi line. In 1937 a Hamburg professor complained that no student meeting had been held in the previous few years 'in which the professoriate has not been dismissed in contemptuous terms as an "ossified" society that is not fit to educate or lead young people in the universities'.[253] From 1936 the Students' League had a new leader, Gustav Adolf Scheel. As a student before 1933 he had led a successful campaign of harassment and intimidation against the pacifist professor Emil Julius Gumbel at Heidelberg University. He strengthened the League's position with the incorporation of all student unions and the formal recognition of its right to appoint its own leaders and run its own affairs. Scheel cultivated excellent relations with Hess's office and was thereby able to ward off all attempts by the Education Ministry to curb his growing influence. With a seat on the academic senate of every university, the student organization was now able to gain access to confidential information about prospective appointments. It did not hesitate to make its wishes and objections known. Since it was clear that if the students did not like a new Rector they could – and would – make life very difficult for him, from 1937 onwards the Education Ministry felt obliged to consult the students' representatives in advance, giving Scheel and his organization yet more say in how the universities were run.[254]

Yet in the end, the influence of the Nazi Students' League was limited. Although it had swept the board in student union elections all over Germany well before 1933, it was in fact a comparatively small organization, with a membership that fell just short of 9,000 on the eve of Hitler's appointment as Reich Chancellor. Since many of these belonged to the League's female affiliate or studied in non-university higher education institutions, and others were located in German-speaking universities outside the Reich, the number of male students in German universities who were members actually fell just short of 5,000, or less than 5 per cent of German university students as a whole.[255] During and after the seizure of power, this figure grew rapidly, helped by the mixture of terror and opportunism characteristic of the process of social and institutional co-ordination in 1933. Beyond this, the overwhelmingly nationalist German student body was swept by enthusiasm for the spirit of 1914 unleashed by the new regime in the initial period of its power. Yet the Nazi Students' League was not without competition in the student world at this time. Many students joined the stormtroopers in the spring of 1933, and following Hitler's instruction in September 1933 that the task of politicizing the student body was to be undertaken by the SA, the brownshirts set up their own centres in the universities and put pressure on students to join. By the end of the year, over half the students at Heidelberg university, for example, had enrolled as stormtroopers. Early in 1934 the Interior Ministry made military training organized by the brownshirts compulsory for male students. Soon they were spending long hours training with the SA. This had a serious effect on their studies. University authorities began to note a drastic fall in academic standards as students spent days or even weeks away from their studies, or appeared at lectures in a state of exhaustion after training all night. Nor was that all. As the Rector of Kiel University complained to the Education Ministry on 15 June 1934:

There is now a danger that under the title 'struggle against the intellect', a struggle against the intelligentsia is being waged by the SA University Office. There is further the danger that under the motto 'rough soldierly tone' students in the first three semesters adopt a tone that must frequently be labelled no longer rough but positively coarse.

Some brownshirt leaders even told their student members that their first duty was to the stormtroopers: their academic studies were leisure pursuits, to be conducted in their spare time. Such claims encountered rapidly rising resistance amongst the majority of students. In June 1934 the national student leader Wolfgang Donat encountered 'howling, trampling and whistling' when he tried to address a meeting at Munich

University, while some university teachers who dared to include a pinch of criticism of the regime in their lectures met with outbreaks of wild applause. Open fights broke out in some universities between Nazi activists and other students.[256]

That these events coincided with the first great crisis of the regime in June 1934 was not coincidental. The decapitation of the SA leadership in the 'Night of the Long Knives' at the end of the month opened the way for a thoroughgoing reform of the Nazi presence in the student body. The Office of the Deputy Leader, Rudolf Hess, took over the running of the Nazi Students' League and reshaped its leadership, while at the end of October the SA was effectively removed from the universities, and training with the brownshirts replaced with less demanding sports education. Membership in the Nazi Students' League began to rise sharply, reaching 51 per cent of male university students by 1939, and 71 per cent of female.[257] By this time, the League had managed to overcome the stubborn resistance of the traditional student fraternities, which in 1933 had encompassed more than half the entire male student body. Like other conservative institutions, the fraternities had vehemently opposed the Weimar Republic and gone along with the Nazi seizure of power; most of their members had probably joined the Party by the summer of 1933. At the same time, however, they had been obliged to introduce the leadership principle in their previously collective management, to appoint Nazis to top posts, and to expel any even remotely Jewish members and Jewish 'old gentlemen', the ex-members whose financial clout gave them a major say in how the fraternities were run. The aristocratic tone and traditional independence of the fraternities were still not to the liking of Nazi leaders, however, and when members of one of the most exclusive Heidelberg duelling fraternities were seen interrupting one of Hitler's radio broadcasts in a drunken state and, a few days later, loudly speculating during a riotously bibulous meal at an inn on whether the Leader ate asparagus 'with his knife, his fork or his paw', Hitler Youth leader Baldur von Shirach unfolded a massive press campaign against them and ordered that no Hitler Youth member was to join such a disgracefully reactionary organization in future. Since this went against the known views of the head civil servant of the Reich Chancellery, Hans Heinrich Lammers, himself a prominent and influential 'old gentleman', the matter landed with Hitler. In a two-hour monologue before assembled Nazi dignitaries on 15 June 1935 the Leader made it clear that he expected the fraternities to wither away in the Nazi state as remnants of a bygone aristocratic age. In May 1936 Hitler and Hess openly condemned the fraternities and barred Party members from belonging to them. Seeing the writing on the wall, Lammers had already abandoned his defence of the fraternities, and by the end of the academic year the fraternities had either dissolved themselves or merged into the Nazi Students' League.[258]

I I

Thus the Nazi Students' League had achieved supremacy in the student body by the mid-1930s, effectively pushing other institutions of student representation aside. But it had done so in the context of a rapid decline in student numbers overall. One of the many factors that had fuelled student dissatisfaction with the Weimar Republic had been the drastic overcrowding that the universities had experienced as a result of the large birth-cohorts of the pre-1914 years entering the higher education system. Under the Third Reich, however, the number of students in universities plummeted, from a high of almost 104,000 in 1931 to a low of just under 41,000 in 1939. In the Technical Universities, numbers underwent a similar if slightly less precipitous decline, from just over 22,000 in 1931 to slightly more than 12,000 eight years later.[259] Within this overall decline, some subjects fared worse than others. Law was particularly badly affected. Law students, making up 19 per cent of the total student body in 1932, only constituted 11 per cent by 1939. A similar decline was experienced by the humanities, where 19 per cent of students were enrolled in 1932 but only 11 per cent seven years later. The natural sciences suffered a decline too, though of less dramatic proportions, from 12 per cent to 8 per cent of the student body over the same period. Theology, perhaps surprisingly, held its own in pro-portional terms, at around 8 to 10 per cent, and economics even experi-enced a modest rise, from 6 to 8 per cent. But the real winner was medicine, which already accounted for a third of the student body in 1932 and reached nearly half, at 49 per cent, by 1939. The true dimen-sions of these changes become apparent when it is recalled that the total

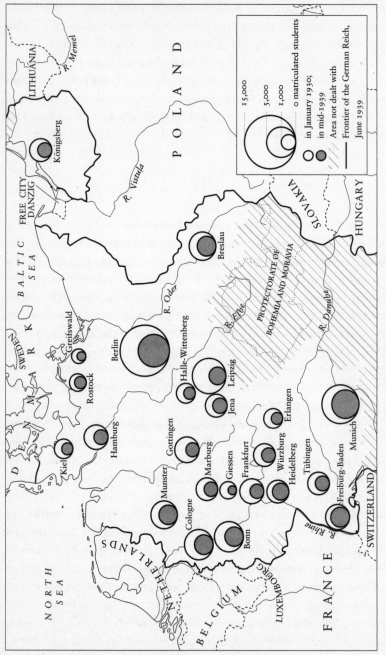

Map 8. The Decline of German Universities, 1930–39

numbers of university students fell by more than half during these years, so that it is reasonable to speak of a genuine crisis above all in the humanities and law by the eve of the Second World War. There were a number of reasons for this. Both the humanities and the law were the object of continual criticism by the regime, reducing their attractiveness to applicants. Similarly, the civil service, a traditional destination of law graduates, was under heavy fire from 1933 onwards, and its influence and prestige sharply declined as those of the Party grew. Teaching, the main source of employment for humanities graduates, similarly declined in attractiveness in the mid-1930s, as we have seen. By contrast, the social and political standing of the medical profession rocketed during these years, as the regime placed racial hygiene at the centre of its domestic policy, and the removal of Jewish doctors from the profession created a large number of vacancies for Aryan graduates to fill.[260]

The decline of the humanities, by far the most popular choice of female students, was in part a consequence of the restrictions placed on women entering university by the regime in these years. Hitler took the view that the main purpose of educating girls should be to train them to be mothers. On 12 January 1934, the Interior Ministry under Wilhelm Frick ordered on the basis of the Law against the Overcrowding of German Higher Education Institutions and Schools (25 April 1933) that the proportion of female grammar school graduates allowed to proceed to university should be no more than 10 per cent of that of the male graduates. In Easter the same year, roughly 10,000 female grammar-school students passed the university entrance examination; as a result of this directive, only 1,500 were allowed to go on to university, and by 1936 the number of female university students had been halved as a consequence. The Nazi elite educational institutions, the Adolf Hitler Schools and the Order Castles, did not admit female students, though a small number of the state elite schools, the Napolas, did. Moreover, the reorganization of German secondary schools ordered in 1937 abolished grammar-school education for girls altogether. Girls were banned from learning Latin, a requirement for university entrance, and the Education Ministry did its best instead to steer them into domestic education, for which a whole type of girls' school existed; the only other secondary education available to girls was a language-based girls' school, where domestic science was also now compulsory. From April 1938, all girls who still managed to graduate with the university entrance examination despite all these obstacles were obliged to have a 'domestic year'; only after this would they be given the school-leaving certificate and allowed to proceed to university, provided the quota had not already been exceeded.[261] The number of female students in higher education fell from just over 17,000 in 1932–3 to well under 6,000 in 1939, faster than that of male students: the proportion of female students fell from just under 16 per cent to just over 11 per cent over the same period. Attempts to reverse this trend in order to satisfy growing demand for skilled and qualified female professionals as rearmament took a grip on the economy had no discernible effect, since they ran counter to all the other measures taken to push women out of the universities since 1933.[262]

The Law against the Overcrowding of German Higher Education Institutions and Schools of 25 April 1933 affected only Jewish students at first, but in December 1933 the Reich Interior Ministry announced that only 15,000 of the 40,000 grammar-school students who were expected to pass the school graduation examination in 1934 would find places at Germany's universities. Unemployment was still at seriously high levels, and it would be wrong for students to go to university if they had no prospect of a job at the end. However, this measure only lasted for two semesters, since the Reich Interior Ministry lost its competence over universities when the Education Ministry was founded in May 1934, and the new Ministry quickly abandoned the restrictions, even allowing those denied entry in that year to reapply, provided that they were unemployed and counted as politically reliable.[263] More influential than such measures was perhaps the oft-expressed contempt of the Nazi leadership for the universities and those who taught and studied in them. In November 1938 Hitler launched a furious attack on intellectuals, amongst whom there was little doubt that he included university teachers and professors. He declared that intellectuals were fundamentally unreliable, useless and even dangerous, and contrasted their irreducible individualism and their constant critical carping with the instinctive and unquestioning solidarity of the masses. 'When I take a look at the intellectual classes we have – unfortunately, I suppose, they are necessary; otherwise one could one day, I don't know, exterminate them or something – but unfortunately they're necessary.'[264] How long for, he did not say. Anyone who had read *My Struggle* would be aware of his contempt for intellectuals, whom he blamed in large part for the disaster of 1918. This inevitably had the effect of producing disillusion amongst academics and a reluctance to enrol amongst potential students. In Germany before 1933, a university degree had been the way to social prestige and professional success. Now, for many, it was no longer. Under the Third Reich, there could be no doubt that Germany's universities were in decline. Student numbers were falling, leading scientists and scholars had been dismissed and in many cases replaced by the second-rate. Chairs and teaching positions remained unfilled.[265]

The decline had already begun before Hitler came to power, as mass unemployment had deterred young people and especially young women from entering university when the prospects of obtaining a job afterwards were minimal. In addition to this, the very small birth-cohort of the First World War years, when the birth rate had plunged to half its prewar level, began in 1934 to reach the age at which university entrance was an option. Far from acting to counter the effects of this demographic decline on student numbers, the regime did everything to magnify them. Finally, the huge expansion of the professional army with the introduction of conscription in 1935 opened up a very large number of prestigious and well-paid posts in the officer corps, so that while fewer than 2 per cent of male high-school graduates joined the army in 1933, no fewer than 20 per cent did in 1935, and 28 per cent in 1937. By this time, too, prospective students were having to wait for two years and more after graduating from high school before they could enter university, since much of the intervening time was now taken up with obligatory military service. By their mid-twenties, many young men had no stomach for yet more years without a job. The banning of Jews from universities, it has been calculated, reduced student numbers by another 3 to 4 per cent, while, as we have been, Nazi measures against women students also had the effect of reducing numbers overall.[266]

The attractiveness of university study was further undermined by the decision of the Nazi Students' League that all high-school graduates should carry out a period of labour service for the Reich before being allowed to begin their studies at university. From Easter 1934, six months' labour service was obligatory for all successful university applicants, while first- and second-year students already at university were forced to serve a ten-week period in a labour camp. The purpose was to instil into university students the kind of character-building was also becoming so important in the schools: as Bernhard Rust told Berlin students in June 1933: 'Anyone who fails in labour camp has forfeited the right to seek to lead Germany as a university graduate.' Students were the first in the Third Reich to be subjected to these measures. Not only were they intended to give practical expression to their commitment to building the new Germany, they were also meant to help overcome the class snobbery and intellectual arrogance of the highly educated; in order to bring this about, the organizers of the Labour Service made sure that students did not make up more than 20 per cent of the inmate population of any labour camp into which they were drafted.[267]

Yet the policy signally failed to achieve its aim of helping to build a new, classless racial community. The vast majority of students who served in the camps hated the way in which, as a memorandum of the student organization itself complained in November 1933, 'the bawling NCO type' of the old army, 'always putting on airs', who ran the camps offloaded their social resentments on the young inmates. Strict military discipline, verbal abuse and bullying were common tactics employed by the uneducated camp leaders to humiliate the students. One inmate later remembered of these men that

They get bored, drink themselves silly every evening and then play tricks on us ... We were hauled out of bed three, four hours after the Last Post, and had to parade outside in our night-clothes, then run round the barracks, and back in the barracks crawl under our beds and then climb up onto the cupboards and sing ditties that seemed appropriate to our actions.[268]

Long hours of unskilled physical labour, building roads or draining marshes, carried out on meagre rations, exhausted many of the largely middle-class students. They were also the butt of continual practical jokes, tricks and verbal abuse from the majority of camp inmates, who were mainly from a rural or working-class background and were far more accustomed to tough and unskilled manual work than they were. For the students this was a world turned upside down, which created not solidarity with other social classes but hatred, bitterness and resentment towards them.[269]

Nor was pre-university labour service the end of such activities for students. Once they had entered university, they came under increasing pressure to spend several weeks every year, in the vacation, working without pay in a factory or on the land. This was not popular with university students, and participation rates remained low – only 5 per cent of the student body in 1936. Himmler also ordered that 25,000 students should help with the harvest in 1939, because the tense international situation at the time meant that the Polish seasonal labourers who usually performed this function were unavailable. This measure caused widespread unrest and open protests at several universities. The Gestapo were called in and a number of students were arrested. All the same, only 12,000 students actually materialized for the harvest; the others had found one way or another of avoiding it. Other attempts to carry the spirit of the labour camp life into the universities were equally unsuccessful. The Nazified student unions wanted to establish 'comradeship houses' in which students would live collectively instead of lodging in private accommodation as they had done up to 1933. This was intended not least as a takeover bid for the duelling and other fraternities, whose premises were to be used for the comradeship houses. The fraternities used their influence in the Ministries, many of whose senior civil servants were old members, to block this initiative, and the Nazi Students' League also opposed the move. Finally, Hitler himself also intervened, declaring in November 1934 that the comradeship houses would encourage homosexuality.[270] The collapse of the fraternities in 1936 gave the idea a second chance, however, this time under the aegis of the Nazi Students' League, and by 1939 there were no fewer than 232 comradeship houses, which made themselves more attractive to students by abandoning their earlier insistence on waking their inmates at 6.15 a.m. for a vigorous bout of gymnastics. At the same time, however, the equally unpopular institution of three evenings a week spent on political indoctrination had not been abolished. Many students had been pressured to join a comradeship house in one way or another, and saw them mainly as social institutions. After going through years of incessantly repeated and intellectually vapid indoctrination at school and in the Hitler Youth, the last thing they wanted when they got to university was more of the same. Those responsible for the comradeship houses in Hamburg, for instance, complained in 1937 of 'fatigue with every kind of political education', while a keen Nazi student in Marburg declared his disappointment in 1939 'that in the comradeship houses of the

National Socialist German Students' League, basically it is only the way of life of the former student fraternities that continues to be cultivated'. 'Nowadays,' concluded the Nazi student leader in Würzburg in 1938, 'there are very few politically fanatical people in the university. They are either hardened or satiated.'[271]

III

The Nazi Students' League was not content with attempting to change the student experience through the institution of compulsory work camps, labour service and comradeship houses. It also tried to influence what was taught in the universities themselves. It made clear in 1936

that we . . . will intervene where the National Socialist view of the world is not made into the basis and the starting-point of scientific and scholarly research and the professor does not of his own initiative lead his students to these ideological points of departure within his scientific or scholarly material.[272]

Nazi Party bosses never tired of repeating this view with varying degrees of emphasis – brutally open in the speeches of a rhetorical thug like Hans Frank, seemingly moderate and flexible in the addresses of a vacillating character like Bernhard Rust. The universities, it was clear, had to pursue the same aims as the schools and put Nazi ideology at the centre of their teaching and research. New chairs and institutes were founded at a number of universities in racial studies and racial hygiene, military history and prehistory, while additional chairs in German Folklore were founded at half of all German universities between 1933 and 1945. Most of these new positions were the result of initiatives from the university rectors rather than the Education Ministry. In 1939, Institutes for Racial Studies existed at twelve out of the twenty-three universities of Germany (in its boundaries of 1937). The new foundations involved a considerable investment of money and prestige in subjects that had not been well represented at the top level in German universities before 1933.[273]

These new areas of teaching and research were backed up in many universities by special lecture courses in these subjects, and in the political ideas of National Socialism, which in some universities were made compulsory for all students before they took their exams. In Heidelberg,

1. Hitler keeps the workers at a safe distance: speaking at the Mayday celebrations on the Tempelhof field in Berlin, 1935, the Nazi leader is protected by a security cordon of SS bodyguards.

2. Brownshirt leader Ernst Röhm, posing as a bureaucrat, seated at his desk at home in 1933. The artwork on the wall behind him gives a good idea of his taste.

3. Heinrich Himmler, Reich Leader of the SS, tries his skill with a pistol at the police shooting range in Berlin-Wannsee in 1934.

4. Hitler taking the salute at a march-past of the Order Police during the Nuremberg Party Rally in September 1937.

5. Reinhard Heydrich, head of the SS Security Service, poses for a portrait photo.

6. Prisoners of the Flossenbürg concentration camp, reserved especially for 'asocials' and 'criminals', working at the quarry that supplied stones for Albert Speer's public buildings.

7. Leni Riefenstahl tries out a camera angle for her film *Triumph of the Will* at the Nuremberg Party Rally in 1934.

Ganz Deutschland
hört den Führer

mit dem Volksempfänger

8. 'The whole of Germany hears the Leader with the People's Receiver': advertisement for cheap radio sets that could only receive broadcasts from domestic stations.

9. Actor Emil Jannings (*right*) towers over 'the little doctor', Propaganda Minister Joseph Goebbels (*left*), during a break at the Salzburg Festival in 1938.

10. Ernst Barlach's Magdeburg War Memorial, 1929; it was removed from display in the Cathedral by the Nazis as unpatriotic.

11. The preferred style of Nazi art: Arno Breker's 'Readiness', shown at the Great German Art Exhibition in 1938.

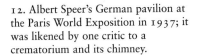

12. Albert Speer's German pavilion at the Paris World Exposition in 1937; it was likened by one critic to a crematorium and its chimney.

13. 'Degenerate Music: A Reckoning by State Counsellor Dr H. S. Ziegler'. Front cover of the booklet accompanying the exhibition, attempting to portray jazz as both Jewish and black, and therefore racially degenerate: the exhibition was not a success.

14. Monsignor Caccia Dominioni, the Papal *Maestro di Camera*, flanked by German and Vatican officials, about to take Hermann Göring into an audience with Pope Pius XI on 12 April 1933, as part of negotiations for the Concordat.

15. 'Adolf Hitler's Young People enrol in the Non-Denominational School'. Placard urging parents to take their children out of Church-run education.

16. 'If all young Germans looked like this, we would have no need to fear for the future.' Children in a primary school class in 1939.

Jugend dient dem Führer

ALLE ZEHNJÄHRIGEN IN DIE HJ.

17. Education Minister Bernhard Rust, photographed on 3 August 1935, attempting in vain to look decisive.

18. 'Young People serve the Leader: All ten-year-olds into the Hitler Youth.' The Party intensifies its campaign to make all young Germans join the organization, 1936.

19. Hitler Youth camp in Nuremberg, 8 August 1934: the vast scale and military organization of such camps did not satisfy young people looking for freedom, adventure, communion with nature, and other traditional goals of the youth movement.

20. The modernism of the *Autobahn*: a motorway bridge in the 1930s.

21. Fritz Todt, the Nazis' chief engineer, rewards workers on the West Wall fortifications. Many workers were drafted into the project against their will.

the leading Nazi professor, Ernst Krieck, who became Rector in 1937, lectured on the National Socialist world-view. Similar lectures were held elsewhere. After the first flush of enthusiasm, however, most of the special lecture courses on Nazi ideology were dropped from university teaching, and by the mid-1930s, fewer than 5 per cent of lectures at German universities were overtly Nazi in their title and contents. Most professors and lecturers who had not been purged in 1933 – the great majority – continued to teach their subjects as before, with only marginal concessions to Nazi ideology, leading to repeated complaints by the Nazi students. These were echoed on many occasions by Nazi Party officials: the accusation levelled in 1936 by Walter Gross, head of the Racial Policy Office of the Nazi Party, of the 'often extremely embarrassing efforts of notable scientists and scholars to play at National Socialism', was far from untypical. After 1945, many former students of this period recalled that their teachers had overwhelmingly been professors of the old school, who had adapted to Nazi ideology only superficially.[274] The Nazi Students' League had attempted to force changes by creating an alternative to the existing teaching syllabus in the form of student-run, subject-specific groups (*Fachschaften*) that would provide a thoroughly Nazi education outside regular academic lectures and classes. But these had not been popular with students, not least since they could not really afford to miss regular classes and so had to work twice as hard as before if they went along. They aroused the antagonism of lecturers and had been largely neutralized by the need to incorporate the teaching staff into their work, since the students mostly lacked the necessary knowledge.[275] In many regular classes, too, relatively open discussion was still possible, and the lecturers were able to avoid Nazi ideology easily enough when they dealt with highly technical subjects, even in subjects like philosophy, where discussion of Aristotle or Plato allowed basic questions of morality and existence to be debated without recourse to the concepts and terminology of National Socialism.[276]

The success of the Nazis in turning the universities to their own ideological purposes was thus surprisingly limited.[277] Teaching continued with only relatively superficial changes in most areas. Studies of doctoral dissertations completed during the Nazi era have shown that no more than 15 per cent of them could be said to be Nazi in their language and approach.[278] Snobbish and elitist professors of the traditional sort openly despised the carpetbaggers brought into the universities by the regime, while most of the latter were so taken up with university administration that they had little time for the propagation of their own ideas to the students. On the other hand, the anti-intellectualism of the Nazi movement made sure that many senior figures in the Party, from Hitler down, ridiculed many of these ideas and thought them too abstruse to have any real political relevance. Neither Bernhard Rust nor Alfred Rosenberg, the two leading senior Nazis in the field of education and ideology, was politically skilled or determined enough to outmanoeuvre wily professors whose abilities to intrigue and dissemble had been honed in decades of in-fighting on university committees. The foundation of a new institute dedicated to the pursuit of a favourite obsession of the Nazis could be welcomed by conservative professors as a way of shunting off an unpopular colleague into an academic byway, as it was for example when the cantankerous far-right historian Martin Spahn was given his own Institute for Spatial Politics at the University of Cologne in 1934. This killed two birds with one stone, since it got Spahn out of the History Department, where he was deeply unpopular, into an area where he did not have to come into contact with his colleagues, and demonstrated at the same time the university's commitment to the geopolitical ideas of the new regime.[279]

In general, however, Nazi ideology itself was too meagre, too crude, too self-contradictory and in the end too irrational to have any real impact on teaching and research at the sophisticated level at which they were pursued in higher education. Attempts to corral university teaching staff into a National Socialist German Lecturers' Association in December 1934 – very late, compared to similar organizations in other professions – failed not least because of the ineptitude of its leader, Walter 'Bubi' Schultze, who had earned Hitler's gratitude by fixing the shoulder the Leader had dislocated during the failed putsch of 1923. Schultze made enemies everywhere by ill-concealed intrigues. He rubbed the Education Ministry up the wrong way. His organization was also regarded by the professors as constituting an unwarranted interference with their power over the profession at large. Its parent body, the Higher Education Commission of the Nazi Party, founded in July 1934, fared no better, since it was led by men who had no standing in the academic community. There could be no question of requiring German professors to go on indoctrination courses in labour camps like their schoolteacher colleagues. Secure within their own bailiwick, they took a dim view of the anti-intellectualism of the Nazis. The initial enthusiasm of nationalist academics like the philosopher Martin Heidegger for the Nazi cultural revolution soon faded as it became clear that the new regime had no interest in the renewal of German science and scholarship as an end in itself. By 1939 even a convinced and determined Nazi academic like Ernst Krieck was asking: 'Has the professor changed? No! The spirit of 1933 has departed from him once more, or at least from his scholarship, even if he is otherwise at least partially well-disposed.'[280]

Such a sweeping generalization needs to be qualified, of course; in some universities, Nazism made greater inroads among the professoriate than in others. Jena, Kiel or Königsberg, for example, counted as relatively strong centres of Nazi teaching and research, while universities in Catholic regions remained less strongly affected; Bonn University, indeed, became something of a dumping-ground for unwanted professors compulsorily relocated from other centres of higher education, while the student body here remained dominated by Catholic and conservative groupings until their dissolution by the Nazis in the mid-1930s. In Bonn, only a minority of posts – about 5 per cent in this case – was ever occupied by fanatical Nazis, another 10 per cent by committed supporters of the Party, and the rest by either superficial sympathizers, by the indifferent, or by academics who were opposed to the regime; the fact that nearly a quarter of Bonn's 380 professors were hostile to Nazism was unusual, but the dominance of scholarly and scientific criteria in the majority of faculty appointments even after 1933 was not, nor was it in most other German universities either.[281] Surveying the field in 1938, the Security Service of the SS drew understandably gloomy conclusions. 'In almost all universities', it complained, 'there are complaints about the passive attitude of the lecturers, who reject any political or ideological work that breaks the narrow bounds of their specialisms.'[282]

IV

The difficulties experienced by the Nazis in turning traditional academic subjects into expressions of their political ideology were nowhere clearer than in physics. Here there was a thoroughgoing attempt to Nazify the discipline, led by the physicist Philipp Lenard, an elder statesman of German science who had retired from his Chair in Heidelberg in 1931. Born in 1862, the son of a wine merchant, Lenard had studied with Heinrich Hertz, the discoverer of radio waves, and been awarded the Nobel Prize himself for path-breaking experiments on cathode rays in 1905. Despite his Nobel Prize, Lenard was full of bitterness and resentment at being pipped to the post by his pupil Wilhelm Röntgen in the discovery of x-rays, and accused the British physicist J. J. Thomson, who established the nature of cathode rays, of stealing and then suppressing his own later work in the field. A charismatic and popular lecturer who achieved widespread fame in Germany through his work, Lenard emphasized careful and precise experimentation and had no time for theory. His hatred of Thomson intensified into a general dislike of the British, while the German nationalism he had imbibed in his birthplace, in Bratislava, in the multinational Habsburg monarchy, spilled over into chauvinism in 1914, and into antisemitism at the end of the First World War. All of this caused him to act with undisguised fury when the general theory of relativity was empirically validated in May, 1919, bringing Albert Einstein worldwide fame.[283]

A pacifist, a Jew, a theoretician and a supporter of the Weimar Republic, Einstein represented everything Lenard hated most. Moreover, the scientists who had validated his theory were British. In the ensuing debate over relativity, Lenard took the lead in rejecting Einstein's theory as a 'Jewish fraud' and in mobilizing the physics community against it. He was driven into the arms of the Nazis when his refusal to join in official mourning for the murdered Foreign Minister Rathenau – whose assassination he himself had openly advocated not long before – sparked trade union demonstrations against him in 1922, in which he had to be taken into police custody for his own protection. Banned from returning to work by his own university, Lenard was reinstated as a result of pressure from right-wing students, into whose orbit he now gravitated.

In 1924 he openly praised Hitler's beer-hall putsch of the previous year, and although he did not formally join the Nazi Party until 1937, he was now to all intents and purposes a follower of the movement and participated actively in the work of groups such as Rosenberg's Fighting League for German Culture. He greeted the coming of the Third Reich with unbridled enthusiasm, celebrated the removal of Jewish professors from the universities, and published a four-volume textbook on *German Physics* in 1936–7 which he clearly hoped would provide the foundation for a new, racially based 'Aryan physics' that would eliminate the Jewish doctrine of relativity from German science altogether.[284]

Lenard's relatively advanced age by this time, however, prevented him from taking the lead in the struggle for an Aryan physics. This role fell to his friend and close associate Johannes Stark, another gifted but extremely quarrelsome experimentalist whose discoveries included the splitting of spectral lines in an electric field, a phenomenon that became known as the Stark effect. Like Lenard, he was a German nationalist and he was driven into opposition to Einstein not least by the latter's pacifism and internationalism in 1914–18. His growing hostility to modern physics, and particularly to the predominance achieved in Einstein's wake by theoretical physics, hampered the advancement of his career in the 1920s; his failure to find a job led him to blame the Weimar Republic for his misfortunes and to form close connections with leading Nazi ideologues like Hans Schemm and Alfred Rosenberg. As a result, the Minister of the Interior, Wilhelm Frick, appointed Stark as President of the Imperial Institute of Physics and Technology on 1 May 1933, and a year later he was given the post of President of the Emergency Association of German Science (later the German Research Community), in charge of disbursing large sums of government research money. From these positions of power, Stark launched a concerted campaign to position the supporters of Aryan physics in academic posts, and to reshape the funding and management of research in the field in such a way as to cut off support from the proponents of modern theories such as relativity and quantum mechanics.[285]

But Stark was too effective at making enemies for his own good. Before long he had aroused the hostility of leading civil servants within the Education Ministry, of the SS (whose own racial and genealogical research he had brusquely dismissed as unscientific) and of the Party

Regional Leader of Bavaria, Adolf Wagner. Moreover, the 'German physicists' themselves were divided, with Lenard championing pure research while Stark embraced the application of physics to technology. Above all, however, when the political polemics and antisemitic diatribes were taken out, there was not much of use left in Aryan physics, whose ideas were muddled, confused and contradictory. Quantum mechanics and relativity were just too useful to be ignored, and other physicists got round Lenard's criticisms by arguing that such theories embodied key Nordic concepts, and constituted a rejection of Jewish materialism. The majority of physicists therefore repudiated Lenard and Stark's ideas, and the Aryan physicists' progress was slow. By 1939 they had only managed to fill six out of the eighty-one physics chairs in Germany, and these mainly with their own students. Nevertheless, their influence did not disappear. A characteristic triumph was the campaign they mounted against Werner Heisenberg, who had won a Nobel Prize for his pioneering of quantum mechanics in 1932. Born in 1901, Heisenberg had studied with such luminaries of modern physics as Niels Bohr and Max Born, and had been appointed Professor of Theoretical Physics at Leipzig in 1927. A conservative nationalist, though not politically active, Heisenberg like many of his colleagues felt strongly that the damage done to German science by the dismissal of Jewish researchers could only be repaired if men like himself stayed in Germany.[286]

But the Aryan physicists had other ideas. They mobilized a vigorous campaign against his appointment to a prestigious Chair of Theoretical Physics at Munich in 1937. Stark's open attack on Heisenberg in the Nazi press as a follower of the detested Einstein was pure polemic: in fact, Einstein rejected quantum mechanics altogether. The attack, however, clearly threatened mainstream physics as a whole. It called forth a public response drafted by Heisenberg and signed by seventy-five leading physicists, an almost unprecedented public intervention under the circumstances of the Third Reich. The physicists reaffirmed the principle that no progress in experimentation was possible without the theoretical elucidation of the laws of nature. The actions of the Aryan physicists, they declared, were damaging the subject and putting students off. There were already too few physicists of the younger generation in Germany. After this, open attacks ceased, but behind the scenes, the Aryan physicists enlisted the support of Reinhard Heydrich's SS Security

Service and of the Munich branch of the National Socialist German University Teachers' League to block Heisenberg's appointment. To counter this, Heisenberg capitalized on his family's acquaintance with the family of Heinrich Himmler, whose father had been a schoolteacher in Munich at the same time as his own. He sent his mother to intercede with Himmler's mother, with the gratifying result that the head of the SS cleared his name in July 1938. Yet in the end the outcome was still a victory for Stark and his supporters. With effect from 1 December 1939, the Munich chair was filled not by Heisenberg but by Wilhelm Müller, who was not even a physicist, but an aerodynamics expert whose main recommendation was the fact that he had published a small book entitled *Jews and Science* in 1936, attacking relativity as a Jewish con-trick. After this, the teaching of theoretical physics at Munich University ceased altogether, a result wholly congenial to the Aryan physicists, whose greatest triumph this represented so far.[287]

Apart from physics, no other traditional scientific subject was quite so convulsed by an attempt by some of its most eminent practitioners to turn it into a specifically Nazi form of knowledge, with the possible exception of biology. There was a rather feeble attempt to create a 'German mathematics', stressing geometry rather than algebra because it was supposedly more closely related to the ideal human form as expressed in the Aryan racial type, but it was ignored by most mathematicians as abstruse and irrelevant, and came to nothing.[288] In a similar way, the attempt to create a 'German chemistry', which, like its parallels in other disciplines, was launched by scientists themselves rather than emanating from the regime or the Nazi authorities, was too vague and diffuse to have any real impact. Less antisemitic than Aryan physics, it preferred to direct its attacks against 'Western' rationalism and to base its theories on a recovery of the organic concepts of nature favoured by the German Romantics; but the results were even less impressive, not least because the Aryan chemists could boast nobody among their ranks of the stature of Lenard or Stark.[289] What united all these attempts to Nazify science was a characteristically National Socialist suspicion of abstraction and formalism, comparable to that demonstrated so graphically in official diatribes against 'degenerate art'. But 'degenerate science' was both less easy to identify and less obviously connected to liberal and leftist trends in cultural politics.[290] In the end, it survived, but not unscathed. The Third Reich saw a marked decline in the standard of scientific teaching and research in German universities between 1933 and 1939. This was not just because of the enforced emigration of so many distinguished Jewish scientists, but also because German science gradually became cut off from the international conferences, visiting professorships, research exchanges and other contacts with the world-wide scientific community that have always played such a vital role in stimulating new developments. Numbers of scientists from leading countries in the international research community visiting German universities fell sharply after 1933. Already in 1936, Heisenberg was complaining to his Danish colleague Niels Bohr of his growing isolation. Foreign academics and institutions began to reduce their contacts with German colleagues in protest against the dismissal of Jewish scientists, foreign travel was increasingly restricted or turned to political purposes, and university library subscriptions to leading international journals were cancelled if – like the British periodical *Nature*, for example – they contained any hint of criticism of the Third Reich.[291]

Yet despite these developments, scientific research did not atrophy or collapse altogether in Nazi Germany. While standards in the universities might have fallen, the universities had never enjoyed a monopoly over research in Germany. Ever since the nineteenth century, large, modern companies in areas like the electrical, engineering and chemical industries had depended heavily on their own research and development sections, staffed by highly trained and well-paid scientists, for the technological innovations on which they relied to keep at the forefront of world markets. Even more importantly, perhaps, the state itself had instituted massive investment in scientific research institutes not only inside but, more importantly, outside the universities through a variety of bodies, notably the German Research Community and the Kaiser Wilhelm Society. Not surprisingly, the Third Reich directed its funding heavily towards investment in military or war-relevant technology, from new weaponry to synthetic fuels. Medicine and biology benefited from the Nazis' encouragement in areas such as the improvement of crop yields, chemical fertilizers and synthetic fibres. As the drive to rearm and prepare for war became more urgent, so those parts of the scientific community that contributed to it were able to direct increasing amounts of funding towards themselves. It was symptomatic of this development that Heisenberg and his colleagues were able not only to secure the acceptance of their argument that theoretical physics was necessary for the development of sophisticated military technology, but also to secure the removal of Johannes Stark from the Presidency of the German Research Community in 1936 because his obdurate hostility to theoretical physics was hampering the funding of war-relevant research.[292]

The government sharply increased the funding of the German Research Community and the Kaiser Wilhelm Society, making its grants conditional on the ability of the recipients to demonstrate the relevance of their work to the preparation of Germany for war. Other governments in other states and at other times, of course, have directed their research support towards what they have considered useful to the state, a tendency that has seldom been of much comfort to the arts and humanities. But the scale, intensity and single-mindedness of the Third Reich in this respect far outdid most parallels elsewhere. The scientific research community in Germany was immensely strong; measured by the country's overall population, it was probably the strongest in the world in 1933. Especially in government-funded research institutes and company research and development departments, it continued to pioneer many scientific and technological innovations under the Third Reich. These included the discovery of nuclear fission by Otto Hahn and Lise Meitner in 1938, the creation of important drugs such as methadone and Demerol, and the nerve gas sarin, technological developments like the jet propulsion engine, electron microscopes and the electronic computer, and major inventions such as cold-steel extrusion, aerial infrared photography, power circuit breakers, tape recorders, x-ray tubes, colour film processing, diesel motors and intercontinental ballistic missiles. It has even been claimed that the first television broadcast strong enough to reach out beyond the planet Earth was of a speech by Hitler, delivered at the opening of the 1936 Olympic Games. Thus while the Third Reich tended to prioritize military training in the schools and the universities, to the detriment of other kinds of learning, it fully backed the most modern, most advanced scientific and technological research elsewhere if it could be shown to have even the remotest possibility of relevance to the war the regime was preparing to launch on Europe in the medium-term future.[293]

V

Traditional approaches to academic subjects survived in German universities not least because their complexity and sophistication defied easy assimilation into the crude categories of Nazi ideology.[294] In history, for example, established professors obdurately resisted attempts by the Nazis to introduce a new, racial, 'blood-and-soil' approach to the past in the first years of the regime. In the universities, as in the schools, ideologues like Alfred Rosenberg demanded that history should become a form of political propaganda and indoctrination, abandoning traditional ideas of objectivity based on scholarly research. Since the middle of the nineteenth century, German academic historians had been accustomed to try and view the past in its own terms and consider the state as the driving force in history. Now they were being told that Charlemagne, for example, was a German, in an era when many historians believed that it was anachronistic to think that Germans existed at all, and asked to affirm that race was the foundation of historical change and development. Some went along willingly with the idea of Charlemagne's Germanness. In the case of the Eastern European specialist Albert Brackmann, this even included the attempt to minimize the extent to which Charlemagne had been motivated by Christian belief. But traditionalists such as Hermann Oncken insisted that history was in the first place a search for the truth, irrespective of its ideological implications. Another historian, Johannes Haller, who had publicly supported the Nazis in the elections of July 1932, declared in November 1934 that historians who adopted a 'mythical view of the past' were committing 'hara-kiri': 'For', he proclaimed, 'where myth had the word, history has nothing more to say.' Thus many university historians resisted the regime's attempt to revolutionize their subject through new foundations like the Reich Institute for the History of the New Germany, led by the Nazi Walter Frank. The new institute was not a success. It largely failed to produce any research, except from its section for the Jewish question, led by Karl Alexander von Müller, whose association with Hitler went back to his time in Munich at the end of the First World War.[295]

Müller took over the editorship of the profession's flagship periodical, the *Historical Journal* (*Historische Zeitschrift*), from the liberal Friedrich

Meinecke in 1935. But apart from a few brief articles and reports on the 'Jewish question', the history of Germans abroad, and one or two other political topics, the journal continued as before to publish specialized articles on academic themes based on detailed archival research.[296] The leadership principle was introduced into historical organizations and research institutes, but this made little difference in reality; the profession was already extremely hierarchical, with enormous power resting in the hands of the senior professors. The national organization of historians first incorporated a couple of prominent Nazis onto its executive committee in 1933, then was itself taken under the control of the Education Ministry in 1936. This led to a more politically motivated selection of German delegates to international historical conferences, and to the domination of the organization's annual congresses by Nazi historians from Walter Frank's Reich Institute. The main consequence of this, however, was that university-based historians did not bother to go any more, and the apathy of the majority was now such that the 1937 national congress proved to be the last.[297] As the Security Service of the SS noted the following year, historians were mostly content 'to carry on compiling old scholarly encyclopedias and to deliver new scholarly contributions to the illumination of individual epochs'. There was not much sign of any advance of National Socialist concepts and methods to record.[298] It seemed, therefore, that the historical profession was relatively unaffected by the Nazi regime and successfully preserved its custodianship of the legacy of the great German historians of the past against the onslaught of the new anti-intellectualism.

Yet when historians, particularly of the older generation, protested that history was an unpolitical subject, they meant, as so many conservatives had done under the Weimar Republic, that it should not be tied to party politics, not that it was devoid of any political content. From their point of view, patriotism was unpolitical, a belief in the historical rightness and inevitability of the Bismarckian unification of Germany in 1871 was unpolitical, the assertion that Germany had not been responsible for the outbreak of war in 1914 was unpolitical. A scholarly, objective approach to the past dovetailed miraculously with the nationalist prejudices and preconceptions of the educated German bourgeoisie in the present. For almost all, for example, it was axiomatic that the eastward Germanic migration in the Middle Ages had brought civilization to the Slavs. The German right to conquer Slavic nations like Poland and Czechoslovakia in the present grew in this way of seeing things out of the objective facts of Germany's historic mission to civilize this part of Europe. Nobody gave a thought to the possibility that they were reading history backwards rather than forwards.[299] Thus although no full professor of history had been a member of the Nazi Party before 1933, hardly any resigned his chair on grounds of political belief or conscience when the Nazis took over the universities, because hardly any saw the need to.[300]

The traditional Rankean concept of objectivity was not shared by all historians, particularly in the younger generation. One of them, Hans Rothfels, openly rejected what he called the 'tendentious misconception of objectivity without a standpoint' in favour of a conscious 'unification of scholarship and life' in the present.[301] Even younger scholars who rejected the notion of objectivity in such terms, however, still insisted on the need for scholarly standards of research to be maintained and the open conversion of history into propaganda to be resisted. Hard-line ideologues like Rosenberg and Himmler thus met with considerable opposition when they attempted to foist racial interpretations of history, 'blood-and-soil', paganist anti-Christian views and the like onto the historians. Hitler himself preferred to praise German military prowess and great national heroes in the past. This point of view was far more congenial to the professors. Despite the interest of some younger historians in a populist-oriented history of the common people, under Nazi or quasi-Nazi ideological auspices, diplomatic and military history were still dominant in Germany, as in many other European countries, at this time, and writing biographies of great men was widely thought of as central to the historian's business.[302]

A not untypical example of the academic historian in this respect was the Freiburg professor Gerhard Ritter, who became during the 1930s one of the most prominent representatives of the profession. Born in 1888 into an educated middle-class family, Ritter had been marked for life by his experience as an army officer in the Battle of the Somme in 1916. His patriotism gained a strong dose of sober realism in these circumstances, and though he never ceased to argue for the revision of the Treaty of Versailles and against the thesis of German war guilt in 1914, he also warned repeatedly against irresponsible warmongering and empty patriotic rhetoric. Unusually, perhaps, Ritter never had any truck with antisemitism and he mistrusted the populism of the Nazis, preferring an elitist conception of politics that excluded the irresponsible and uneducated masses from full political participation. After Hitler came to power, Ritter's attitude towards the regime fluctuated ambivalently between conditional support and limited opposition. Combative and courageous, he did not hesitate to support Jewish pupils and colleagues dismissed or persecuted by the regime. On the other hand, he vigorously supported a whole variety of Hitler's policies at home and abroad, while at the same time hoping continuously for the reform of the regime in a less radical direction. As he wrote in his biography of Frederick the Great in 1936, the Germans had rightly learned 'to make sacrifices of political freedom' for the 'advantage of belonging to a leading nation-state'. In private, he was critical of many aspects of the Nazi regime, but in public, his books and articles served its educational purposes in broad terms by emphasizing the historians' usual themes of German nationhood and the lives of great Germans of the past, even if some of the standpoints they took were not wholly shared by the Nazi leadership.[303]

In a similar fashion, other disciplines too found little difficulty in fitting in with the regime's broader requirements while preserving at least some of their scholarly or scientific autonomy. At Heidelberg University, for example, the Social and Economic Sciences Faculty focused its research on population, agricultural economics and the vaguely named 'spatial research' which in fact was focused on accumulating knowledge relevant to the proposed future expansion of the Reich in the pursuit of 'living-space'. The sociologists put their faith in detailed empirical work and cold-shouldered the rabid Nazi ideologues who tried to use their own fanaticism to gain promotion. A similar development could be observed in other universities too.[304] In university-level teaching and research on German language and literature, professors and lecturers in the Nazi period focused on literary and linguistic history as a field in which the German spirit and expressions of German racial identity could be traced back through the ages. They contrasted this tradition with the threat posed by foreign influences such as Romance literature and American popular culture. This seemed a Nazi view, but it had been held by the great majority of scholars in this area since even before the First World War.[305]

Theology faculties, divided institutionally between Protestant and Catholic institutions, were in a more difficult position. Protestant theology faculties became the sites of bitter quarrels between supporters of the German Christians and the Confessing Church. At Bonn University, for instance, where Karl Barth, the chief theologian of the Confessing Church, was the guiding spirit, a new dean, the German Christian Emil Pfennigsdorf, was elected in April 1933. Within three years he had fired or transferred ten out of the faculty's fourteen members and replaced them with his own supporters, with the result that before long the faculty was virtually without any students. The hostility of the Nazi Party to the Catholic Church found its expression in the refusal of the state authorities to sanction the filling of posts in Bonn's Catholic theology faculty made vacant by retirements. Eight out of the faculty's twelve chairs were unfilled in 1939; only the forcible transfer of two professors from the faculty in Munich, which the Nazis had closed down altogether, allowed teaching to continue. Similar upheavals occurred in other universities too.[306]

The contrast with what rapidly became the most important of all university faculties under Nazism, medicine, could not have been more stark. Teachers of medicine made up roughly a third of all university faculty members by 1935, and the absolutely dominant position of medicine in universities was reflected in the fact that, from 1933 to 1945, 59 per cent of university rectors were drawn from the medical profession. The close interest of the regime in the teaching of medicine was signalled right away in 1933, as Hitler appointed Fritz Lenz to the first full Chair in racial hygiene at any German university, in Berlin; this was quickly followed by chairs in the subject in other universities or, where this did not happen, in the institution of regular lecture courses in the subject. Unfortunately, not only was the subject itself poorly developed in intellectual terms, but those who rushed to teach it were often more noted for their ideological fanaticism than for their scientific competence. The abler students mocked such teachers behind their backs, but even they were often unable to pass the simplest tests in the subject, identifying as Aryan, for example, Nordic-looking individuals who were in fact Jews. The absurdity of such tests did not deter Nazi professors from investing a good deal of time and energy into racial studies. At the University of Giessen, for instance, an Institute for Hereditary Health and Race Preservation, partly sponsored by the Nazi Party in 1933, became a full university department in 1938 under its founder, the 'old fighter' Heinrich Wilhelm Kranz, who as a medical student had taken part in the cold-blooded shooting of fifteen workers by a Free Corps Unit in Thuringia in the wake of the Kapp putsch in 1920. Kranz was actually an ophthalmologist, with no scientific expertise in physical anthropology at all, but this did not prevent him using his connections in the Party to further his own empire-building in the field of racial research.[307]

If the quality of its teachers was often poor and the content of what they taught dubious in scientific terms, racial hygiene was at least accepted in principle by most medical faculties in the 1930s. But this was not all that the Nazis tried to foist onto the universities in this field. The head of the Nazi Physicians' League from before 1933, and from 1936 leader of the Reich Physicians' Chamber, was Gerhard Wagner, a close associate of Rudolf Hess and an enthusiast for alternative medicine.[308] Wagner backed the Nazi radicals who championed a holistic approach based on herbs and other natural remedies, known as the New German Healing. He did not conceal his disdain for the mechanistic, scientific approach of conventional university medicine, and rejected its dependency on synthetic pharmacology. Wagner set up a teaching hospital in Dresden in June 1934 with the aim of disseminating the naturopathic ideas of the New German Healing. He followed this up with a variety of special training courses. Racial hygiene was an integral part of the teaching of the new academy for state public health officials that Wagner established in Munich in 1933. Soon 'people's health' was a feature of teaching in university medical schools too. Wagner backed this up with persistent and often successful interventions with the Education Ministry in appointments to university medical chairs, many of which had become vacant as a consequence of the dismissal of their Jewish occupants in 1933–4. At Bonn University, for example, twelve out of seventeen chairs in medicine became vacant in the years from 1933 on; ten of the fourteen new professors appointed up to 1945 were active Nazis, who then formed the dominant group within the faculty. Often the new incumbents were not up to their predecessors either as researchers or as practitioners. Even so, by 1938 there was such a shortage of qualified candidates for medical chairs that the Ministry of Education started to ask retiring incumbents to stay in office. In Berlin, for example, the 67-year-old Walter Stoeckel, an eminent gynaecologist, was given another two years in post because no replacement could be found. The fact was that for competent physicians and surgeons there were already greater rewards, and more freedom as researchers, to be had in industry or the armed forces. And the burden of student numbers in areas such as racial hygiene was now so great that non-specialists from other fields were being drafted in to do the teaching.[309]

Everywhere in the educational system, therefore, the Third Reich had an impact that was ultimately disastrous. 'Scholarship is no longer essential,' noted Victor Klemperer in his diary in October 1933 as he recorded the cancelling of lectures on two afternoons a week in his university to make time for military sports.[310] In a regime that was built on contempt for the intellect, this should hardly have been a cause for surprise. The Nazis saw the educational system in the first place as a means for inculcating the young with their own view of the world, still more as a means of training and preparing them for war. Anything that stood in their way, including traditional educational values such as freedom of inquiry, critical intelligence or the ideal of pure research, was to be sidelined or swept aside. As preparations for war became more extensive, so the demands of the armed forces for doctors became more urgent; and in 1939 the course of university study for medical students was shortened. The quality of teaching had already been diluted by a reduction of the time taken up in mainstream medical training to make room for new subjects such as racial hygiene, not to mention the students' multifarious obligations to the Party, from attendance at labour camps to participation in the activities of the stormtroopers. Already in 1935 the surgeon Ferdinand Sauerbruch was complaining about the poor quality of the new intake of medical students, many of whom had, he claimed, been picked because they or their parents were Party members. There was even some evidence that examination standards were being lowered to enable them to get through. When a dissertation on racial hygiene could serve as the final qualification for medical practice, it was not surprising that traditionalists like Sauerbruch were concerned for the future of the medical profession in Germany.[311]

Nevertheless, in medicine as in other areas, established professors largely carried on teaching and researching as they had done before. For all his diatribes against academic medicine, Wagner realized that the doctors were essential for the implementation of many of the Nazis' eugenic plans. He balked at the idea, pushed by the proponents of the New German Healing, of abolishing the medical faculties altogether. Besides, the achievements of German medical research over the previous decades had won worldwide recognition, and there were powerful nationalist arguments for attempting to continue this proud tradition. Serious medical research in a variety of fields had an obvious relevance to the protection of German troops from infectious diseases and the improvement of the health of the German population in general. So it did indeed carry on under the Third Reich. The pathologist Gerhard Domagk even won the Nobel Prize in 1939 for his development of sulfa drugs for combating bacterial infection (he was not allowed by the regime to accept it). In trying to improve the health and fecundity of the racially acceptable part of the German population, the Nazis gave strong support to preventive medicine and research into major killers. It was a Nazi epidemiologist who first established the link between smoking and lung cancer, establishing a government agency to combat tobacco consumption in June 1939. Party and government agencies actively pursued bans on carcinogenic substances like asbestos and dangerous pesticides and food colouring agents. Already in 1938 the air force had banned smoking on its premises, to be followed by other workplace smoking bans imposed by the post office and offices of the Nazi Party itself, in April 1939. Books, pamphlets and posters warned of the dangers of smoking, and pointed out repeatedly that Hitler himself never put a pipe, cigar or cigarette to his lips. Nor did he imbibe alcohol, and the Nazis were equally active in combating excessive consumption of beer, wines and spirits. The fact that tobacco manufacturers, brewers, distillers and wine merchants were more than likely to be members of the Party and give it substantial financial support cut little ice here: the overriding imperative was to improve the health of the Aryan race.[312]

Such policies helped dull the minds of medical researchers to the negative side of Nazi health policy. Improving the race included not only research and prevention of this kind, but also, as we shall see, eliminating supposed negative influences on the race and its future by forcible sterilization and, eventually, murder, dressed up in the neutral-sounding rhetoric of preventive medicine.[313] The intrusion of racial hygiene and eugenics into medical education under the Third Reich had its own influence on medical ethics too, as medical researchers in other fields also succumbed to the idea that racially inferior or subhuman people could legitimately be used as the objects of medical experimentation.[314] The immense power and prestige of medicine and allied subjects in the Third Reich gave some medical researchers the belief that anything was justified in the name of the advancement of science, not only if it could be directly linked to the fortunes of the nation in the struggle for power, but even in far-removed realms of pure research. In this belief, they were encouraged by the regime's contempt for conventional morality. The deep-rooted Christian beliefs that underpinned medical ethics and were held more broadly by many millions of Germans appeared to the Nazis in the end as yet another obstacle to the mobilization of the Aryan racial spirit. Nowhere was there any clear evidence that the Nazis had succeeded in their ambition of sweeping away alternative sources of moral and cultural identity amongst the great mass of Germans and replacing it with unqualified enthusiasm for their own world-view. Yet allegiance to a political system, even one as extreme as that of the Third Reich, never depends wholly on ideological identification. In conventional politics at least, material factors are even more important. The Nazis came to power in the midst of, and in large measure also as a consequence of, the most calamitous economic depression of modern times. If they could manage to pull Germany out of the morass of mass unemployment and economic despair into which it had fallen at the end of the 1920s, that alone might be enough to secure people's assent to the Third Reich even when they remained indifferent to its more ambitious religious, cultural and educational purposes.

4

PROSPERITY AND PLUNDER

'THE BATTLE FOR WORK'

I

On 27 June 1933 Hitler's government issued a law authorizing the building of a new type of road, the motorway (*Autobahn*). The dual-carriageway roads would link Germany's major cities with one another, establishing a communications network that would allow citizens and freight to be transported with unprecedented speed and directness across the land. The idea originally came from Italy, where a prototype had been built as early as 1924. A private enterprise scheme had already been proposed to link Hamburg, Frankfurt and Basel and planned in some detail from 1926 onwards, but in the circumstances of the Depression it had come to nothing. Almost as soon as he was appointed Reich Chancellor, Hitler took it up again. Speaking at the Berlin International Motor Show on 11 February 1933, Hitler declared that the state of the nation's highways would in future be the chief yardstick by which its prosperity would be measured. An enthusiastic devotee of the automobile, he had travelled the length and breadth of the land by car during the election campaigns of the previous years, and regarded driving – or at least being driven – as an aesthetic experience far superior to that provided by flying or travelling by train. Thus the new motorways were going to be built along scenic routes, with lay-bys for travellers where they could get out of their vehicles, stretch their legs and admire the German countryside. For Fritz Todt, the man whom Hitler appointed on 30 June 1933 to oversee the building of the motorways, they even fulfilled a racial purpose, linking the motor-borne German soul to the authentic woods, mountains and fields of its native land, and expressing the Nordic race's delight in the adventure, speed and excitement provided by modern technology.[1]

It was Todt who had been largely responsible for persuading Hitler to adopt the idea. A civil engineer by training and background, he had worked on tar and asphalt roads for the Munich firm of Sager and Woerner and had been a member of the Nazi Party since the beginning of 1923. Born in the Swabian town of Pforzheim in 1891, he had received a technical education and served in the air force during the First World War. His commitment to the Party was in the first place the product of his personal admiration for Hitler. After the failure of the Munich putsch, Todt avoided active political engagement and concentrated instead on his career, but by 1932 he had become a member of the stormtrooper reserve, and at this point he assumed the leadership of the engineers' division of the Party's Fighting League of German Architects and Engineers, founded the previous year. Like other professionally qualified men in the Party, he saw it as a decisive, energetic, modern movement that would do away with the dithering of the Weimar Republic and impel Germany into a new future based on the centralized application of science and technology to society, culture and the economy in the interests of the German race. Within the Party, he tried to counter the hostility of economic thinkers like Gottfried Feder to mechanization and rationalization, which they considered to be destroying jobs, by proposing ambitious new construction schemes such as the motorways, on which he submitted a report to the Party leadership in December 1932. By this time he had gained important backing for his ideas through his appointment as chief technological adviser in the office of Hitler's deputy, Rudolf Hess. When Hitler announced the initiation of the motorway construction programme, it was largely Todt's ideas that he proposed to put into action.[2]

On 23 September 1933, Hitler turned the first sod on the long-planned Hamburg-to-Basel motorways; by May 1935 the first stretch, from Frankfurt to Darmstadt, was open; 3,500 kilometres were completed by the summer of 1938. The motorways were perhaps the most durable of the propaganda exercises mounted by the Third Reich; they survive to the present day. Hitler took a close personal interest in the routes the motorways followed, intervening on occasion to redirect them when he thought they were not going by the most picturesque route. He also insisted on personally approving the design of bridges and service stations. Many of these were bold examples of modernism, and Hitler

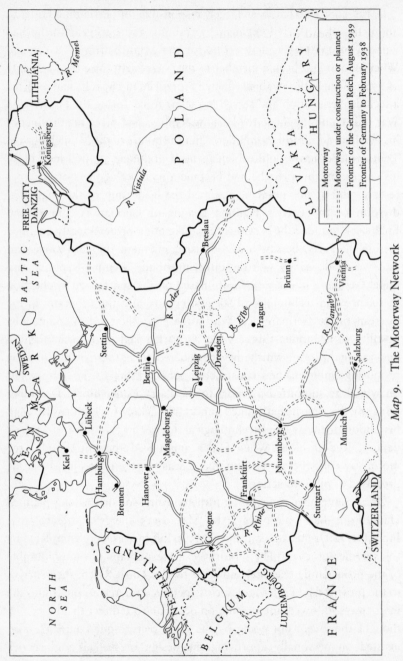

Map 9. The Motorway Network

gave the task of designing them to architects rather than to engineers; the former head of the Bauhaus, Mies van der Rohe, even submitted plans for two of the service stations. The modernity of the motorways, the vast, simple bridges striding across rivers and gorges, the elegant dual carriageways cutting through hills and sweeping across the plains, made them one of the Third Reich's most striking creations. Todt instructed the planners to merge embankments and cuttings into the landscape, to use native varieties of plants for the verges, and to construct the roads so that the landscape was clearly visible to all drivers and their passengers.[3] But in fact they signified not the German soul's merging with the landscape, but technology's mastery over it, an impression strengthened in the propaganda that celebrated them as the modern age's equivalent of the pyramids of Ancient Egypt, outdoing the Gothic cathedrals of the Middle Ages or the Great Wall of China in the grandiosity of their conception. 'Clear the forest', declared the bold slogan on Carl Theodor Protzen's illustration of a motorway bridge, '– blow up the rock – cross the valley – overcome distance – drive a path through German land.'[4]

There were other respects in which Todt's plans failed to work out as he had predicted. Only 500 kilometres in addition to the 3,500 kilometres completed by 1938 were finished by 1945, since building resources were soon diverted to construction programmes more directly related to the war; the Reich Defence Ministry even vetoed strategically unimportant routes and insisted on priority being given to military roads in sensitive areas like East Prussia. As a result of such interventions and further postwar delays, the motorway linking Hamburg to Basel was not actually completed until 1962.[5] Moreover, few people had the means to enjoy them before 1939, since Germany was one of the least motorized societies in Europe. In 1935, only 1.6 per cent of the population in Germany owned motor vehicles, compared to 4.9 per cent in France, 4.5 per cent in Britain, and 4.2 per cent in Denmark. Even Ireland had a higher proportion of vehicle-owners, at 1.8 per cent. All of these figures were dwarfed by vehicle ownership in the USA, which stood at 20.5 per cent, or one in five of the population.[6]

In his speech at the Berlin motor show, Hitler announced not only the inauguration of the motorway building programme but also the promotion of motor sports and the reduction of the tax burden on car ownership.[7] The result was a 40 per cent increase in the number of workers in the motor vehicle industry from March to June 1933 alone. Motor car production doubled from 1932 to 1933 and again by 1935. Well over a quarter of a million cars were now being produced every year, and prices were much lower than they had been at the end of the 1920s. Foreign car sales in Germany had fallen from 40 per cent of all car sales in 1928 to below 10 per cent six years later.[8] The number of passenger cars on the roads increased from just over half a million in 1932 to just under a million in 1936.[9] Even Victor Klemperer bought himself a car at the beginning of 1936 despite his growing financial worries, though he soon came close to regretting his decision: 'The car', he wrote on 12 April 1936, 'gobbles up my heart, nerves, time, money. It's not so much my wretched driving and the occasional agitation it causes,' he added, 'not even the difficulty of driving in and out, it's that the vehicle is never right, something's always going wrong.'[10]

Even he, however, had to admit that the new motorways were 'magnificent'. Driving down one on 4 October 1936, he noted with enthusiasm that he and his wife enjoyed a 'glorious view' and he even 'dared a speed of 80 km an hour a few times'.[11] Despite the spread of car ownership, however, the motorization of German society had still not got very far by 1939, and to describe it as the powerhouse behind Germany's economic recovery in these years is a considerable exaggeration.[12] By 1938, to be sure, Germany's vehicle production was growing faster than that of any other European country, but there was still only one motor vehicle there per forty-four inhabitants, compared with one for every nineteen in Britain and France.[13] The vast majority of personal travel and the movement of bulk goods was still accounted for by Germany's railway system, Germany's largest employer at this time, which was brought under centralized administration and provided with enough additional funds to produce a 50 per cent increase in the (very small) stock of electrically powered locomotives and a quadrupling of the number of small shunting engines between 1932 and 1938.[14] However, in general the railways suffered from chronic under-investment during this period. The railway management, jealous of its leading position in goods traffic, succeeded in delaying the removal of taxes on commercial vehicle sales until January 1935, though as soon as this happened, production of commercial vehicles increased much faster than that of passenger cars – 263 per cent in 1934–5 as compared to 74 per cent for cars.[15]

None the less, even after this, the motor-car embodied an important part of Hitler's technological vision of Germany's future, which encompassed car ownership on an almost universal scale. Already in the 1920s he had come across an article on the 'motorization of Germany' as he whiled away his leisure time in Landsberg prison, and by the early 1930s he was drawing rough sketches of a small family vehicle that would sell for less than a thousand Reichsmarks and so be within reach of the vast majority of the population. Meeting with scepticism from the mainstream motor industry, Hitler secured the collaboration of the racing-car engineer Ferdinand Porsche, whose prototype design was ready by the end of 1937. At Hitler's personal insistence, the car's production was funded by the German Labour Front, the Nazi Party's successor to the trade unions, which built a vast new factory to produce the car. In this way, the dominance of the American-owned Opel and Ford works over the small-car market in Germany would finally be broken. Dubbing the vehicle the 'People's Car' or 'Strength Through Joy car', Hitler envisaged up to a million models a year rolling off the production line, and a huge advertising campaign was launched to persuade workers to put aside part of their wages to save up for one, with the slogan 'a car for everyone'.[16]

The campaign met with a good deal of success. In April 1939 a Social Democratic agent in Rhineland-Westphalia reported:

For a large number of Germans, the announcement of the People's Car is a great and happy surprise. A real Strength-Through-Joy car-psychosis developed. For a long time the car was a main topic of conversation in all sections of the population in Germany. All other pressing problems, whether of domestic or foreign policy, were pushed into the background for a while. The grey German everyday sank beneath notice under the impression of this music of the future. Wherever the test models of the new Strength-Through-Joy construction are seen in Germany, crowds gather around them. The politician who promises a car for everyone is the man of the masses if the masses believe his promises. And as far as the Strength-Through-Joy car is concerned, the German people do believe in Hitler's promises.[17]

Hitler proudly presented one of the first models in person to the International Motor Show in Berlin on 17 February 1939, and gave another one to his partner Eva Braun for her birthday. Although no production models came off the assembly-line during the Third Reich, the car stood the test of time: renamed the *Volkswagen*, or People's Car, after the war, and popularly known as the 'beetle' from the rounded shape Hitler gave it in his original design, it became one of the world's most popular passenger vehicles in the second half of the twentieth century.[18]

II

Creating a motorized society was not just a grand technological vision for the future. It was also intended to produce more immediate benefits. Fritz Todt calculated that building the motorways would provide employment for 600,000 men, not just on the roads themselves but also in all the industries that supplied the basic materials for their construction. By June 1935 there were some 125,000 men working on motorway construction alone, so the programme did indeed create jobs, though fewer than many supposed.[19] The Nazis had gained their stunning electoral successes of the early 1930s not least on the strength of their promise to pull Germany out of the catastrophic economic depression into which it had fallen. Six million people were registered as unemployed in January 1933, and three million more had disappeared from the employment statistics altogether, many of them women. Twenty million Germans had been in work in mid-1929; by January 1933 the number had fallen to 11.5 million. Many more were in short-time work, or had been forced to accept cuts in their hours, their wages or their salaries. Mass unemployment had robbed the labour movement of its principal bargaining lever, the strike, and made things easier for the new regime to destroy it in the first few months of 1933. Nevertheless, getting Germany back to work was the most immediate priority announced by the coalition government that took office under Hitler's Chancellorship on 30 January 1933.[20] Already on 1 February 1933 Hitler declared in his first-ever radio broadcast that the 'salvation of the German worker in an enormous and all-embracing attack on unemployment' was a key aim of his new government. 'Within four years', he declared, 'unemployment must be finally overcome.'[21]

Hitler's government was able to use work-creation schemes already set in motion by its predecessors. Germany's effective departure from the Gold Standard in the summer of 1931 had allowed the state to pump money into the economy to try and revive it. Under pressure from the trade unions, General Kurt von Schleicher's short-lived government in particular had made a significant beginning of this process late in 1932, building on plans already drafted under his predecessors Franz von Papen and Heinrich Brüning. While Papen had made 300 million Reichsmarks available in tax vouchers for road-building, agricultural improvement and housebuilding, Schleicher put 500 million directly into the economy for such purposes; this was increased to 600 million by the Nazis in the summer of 1933. This programme only started coming into effect on 28 January 1933, enabling the Nazis to take the credit for it. The plans were in large measure the brainchild of Günter Gereke, an economist who had become Reich Commissioner for Work Creation on 15 December 1932 and continued in this position in 1933. By 27 April 1933 the Labour Minister Franz Seldte was able to announce that the number of jobless had fallen by over half a million. Some of this was doubtless the result of seasonal factors as employment picked up after the winter slump. The beginnings of economic recovery that had already made themselves noticeable in the last months of 1932 also played a role. Hitler's government was lucky in its timing.[22]

Nevertheless, the Nazi Party was not entirely without its own ideas in this field. The Party Programme of 1920 had presented leftish-sounding ideas for economic reform, including widespread state takeovers of private firms, so that when gaining power had begun to seem a real possibility ten years later, Hitler and the leadership had been forced to work hard to convince industrialists and financiers that they had grown up a good deal in the meantime. In 1930 the Party's chief administrator Gregor Strasser had set up an Economic Policy Division which cultivated close contacts with business and devoted itself to working out job-creation schemes for the future. By July 1932 the Nazis were making great play in their electioneering with a proposal to use state credits for public works as a means of reducing unemployment, through schemes such as draining marshes, building canals, bringing moorland under cultivation and the like. Germany, they declared, needed to pull itself up out of the Depression by its own boot-straps; it could no longer afford to wait for international trade to recover.[23]

Seldte presented further, more ambitious proposals based on a new issue of treasury bonds for labour-intensive public works projects. These were accepted by the cabinet, and on 1 June 1933, the government promulgated the first Law on the Reduction of Unemployment, which made an additional 1,000 million Reichsmarks available for public works in the so-called 'First Reinhardt Programme', named after the State Secretary in the Reich Finance Ministry, Fritz Reinhardt. A second Law on the Reduction of Unemployment, also known as the 'Second Reinhardt Programme', issued on 21 September 1933, made 500 million Reichsmarks in credits available for private businesses, particularly in the construction industry, to take on new projects and employ new workers.[24] Taking these schemes all together and adding other, minor interventions to them, it has been calculated that the government had placed more than 5,000 million Reichsmarks at the disposal of job-creation schemes by the end of 1933, of which some 3,500 million were spent by early 1936. In this way, it hugely expanded the modest dimensions of the programme it had taken over from the Schleicher government at the beginning of the year.[25] In addition, the regime developed a scheme for subsidizing house purchases, conversions and repairs started under the Papen government in September 1932 to stimulate the construction industry. Finally, it steered substantial funds towards areas of special deprivation, above all mainly agrarian provinces; at the back of its mind was also the thought that when war broke out, the more industries that were relocated out of the big cities, the less damage would be done to industrial production by enemy bombing.[26]

The new regime also acted quickly to take people out of the labour market as well, thereby reducing the number of economically active persons against whom the proportion of unemployed were measured. The most notable scheme in this area was the issuing of marriage loans, begun as part of the Law on the Reduction of Unemployment issued on 1 June 1933 and backed up by subsequent regulations. Young couples intending to get married could apply in advance for an interest-free loan of up to 1,000 Reichsmarks provided that the prospective wife had been in employment for at least six months in the two years up to the promulgation of the law. Crucially, she had to give up her job by the time of the wedding and undertake not to enter the labour market again until the loan was paid off, unless her husband lost his job in the meantime. That this was not a short-term measure was indicated by the terms of repayment, which amounted to 1 per cent of the capital per month, so that the maximum period of the loan could be as much as eight and a half years. In practice, few loans were made at the maximum rate – the average was 600 Reichsmarks, amounting to roughly a third of the average annual earnings of an industrial worker. However, the loans were made more attractive, and given an additional slant, by a supplementary decree issued on 20 June 1933 reducing the amount to be repaid by a quarter for each child born to the couple in question. With four children, therefore, couples would not have to repay anything. Of course, the loans were only made to couples recognized as Aryan, so that like so much else in the Third Reich they became an instrument of racial policy in addition to their primary functions. Not only did all applicants have to undergo a medical examination to prove their fitness, as laid down in a supplementary decree on 26 July 1933, but they were likely to be turned down if they had any hereditary diseases, or were asocial, or vagrants, or alcoholics, or connected with oppositional movements like the Communist Party. Moreover, to stimulate production and ensure that the money was well spent, the loans were issued not in cash but in the form of vouchers for furniture and household equipment.[27]

The idea of reducing unemployment amongst men by taking women out of the labour market was not new in 1933. Indeed as part of government retrenchment measures in the stabilization of 1924 and the crisis of 1930–32, so-called double earners, that is, married women who augmented their husband's income by engaging in waged or salaried labour themselves, had been fired from the civil service, and were also under pressure in the private sector.[28] All political parties in the Weimar Republic, despite the advent of female suffrage, agreed that a woman's place was primarily with her family, at home.[29] The Nazis were only saying what others were saying, but more loudly, more insistently, and more brutally. Here, as in so many other areas, Hitler gave the lead. The idea of women's emancipation, he told a meeting of National Socialist women on 8 September 1934, was the invention of 'Jewish intellectuals' and un-German in its essence. In Germany, he proclaimed, the man's world was the state, the woman's 'her husband, her family, her children, and her home'. He went on:

We do not consider it correct for the woman to interfere in the world of the man, in his main sphere. We consider it natural if these two worlds remain distinct. To the one belongs the strength of feeling, the strength of the soul. To the other belongs the strength of vision, of toughness, of decision, and of the willingness to act.[30]

Goebbels had already put it in more homely terms in 1929: 'The mission of the woman is to be beautiful and to bring children into the world . . . The female bird pretties herself for her mate and hatches the eggs for him. In exchange, the mate takes care of gathering the food, and stands guard and wards off the enemy.'[31] This demonstrated among other things Goebbels's extreme ignorance of ornithology: there are of course many species, such as peacocks or birds of paradise, where it is the male who is the gaudy one, and others, like the emperor penguin, where it is the male who keeps watch over the eggs. It was also characteristic of Goebbels that he should lay some emphasis on women's duty to be beautiful, something that never seems to have concerned Hitler very much. However, the point was clear, and the analogy from the natural world telling. 'The German resurrection', as a primer of Nazi ideology put it in 1933, 'is a male event.' Women's place was in the home.[32]

The marriage loans scheme and the declaration of war on women working outside the home were thus central to Nazi ideology as well as useful for the reduction of unemployment figures. And as soon as the scheme was launched, Nazi propagandists greeted it as an outstanding success. In the first full year of the scheme, 1934, nearly a quarter of a million loans were issued. The number fell to just over 150,000 in 1935, but increased to over 170,000 in 1936, by which time about a third of all newly contracted marriages were assisted by a state loan.[33] These were impressive figures. Yet the effects of the measure on unemployment were less than the Nazis claimed. For women on the whole were not competing with men for the same jobs, so that taking a woman out of the labour market would seldom in practice mean freeing up a job for a man. The gender balance in the economy was shifting during the 1920s and 1930s. Still, the same basic pattern of gender differences remained as in the late nineteenth century. Less than a quarter of those classed as workers were female. Within this category they were concentrated above all in textiles, clothing and food and drink. Most domestic servants were also women, as were the greater proportion of 'family assistants'. By contrast, there were very few women in the major industrial employment sectors. The main difference the marriage loans made, therefore, was to overall employment statistics; they did not in reality create space for unemployed men to get back to work, for no unemployed steelworker or construction labourer was likely to take up household cleaning or weaving, no matter how desperate his situation might be. Moreover, the take-up of the marriage loans has to be viewed in the context of the economic recovery that began tentatively in the second half of 1932 and gathered pace thereafter. During the Depression, previously unregistered women had come onto the labour market as their fathers or partners had lost their jobs, and as men began to find work again, above all in the heavy industrial sector that was so crucial to rearmament, so these women gave up their jobs, glad to be rid of the double burden of housekeeping and childcare on the one hand and working outside the home on the other. Many had delayed getting married and having children because of the economic crisis. The very high take-up of loans in the first year suggests that a large proportion of those who received them belonged in this category. Their decisions were taken largely independently of government incentives, therefore.[34]

None the less, the Nazis soon began loudly to proclaim that with measures such as these, they had drastically reduced the catastrophic unemployment levels that had devastated the German economy and society since the end of the 1920s. By 1934 the official statistics showed that unemployment had fallen to less than half the levels of two years before; by 1935 it stood at no more than 2.2 million, and by 1937 it had dropped below the million mark. Hitler's boast that he would solve the unemployment problem within four years of taking office seemed to have been triumphantly justified. Incessant Nazi propaganda boasting that the 'battle for work' was being won gained widespread credence. It helped win over many doubters and sceptics to the government's side from May 1933 onwards, and pumped new euphoria into the Third Reich's supporters. Belief that Hitler really was reconstructing the German economy was a major factor in underpinning popular acceptance of his regime in its early months.[35] Was this, then, 'Hitler's economic miracle', as some have suggested, involving the conquest of unemployment, a Keynesian kick-starting of the economy by a bold policy of deficit spending, a huge increase in investment, and a general recovery of prosperity and the standard of living from the depths to which they had sunk in the Depression? Did this sow the seeds from which, after the destruction of the war, the West German economic miracle of the 1950s sprang?[36]

To some extent, of course, worldwide economic recovery was already under way, though slowly; in Germany it was helped by rapidly growing business confidence as a result of the political stability that the Third Reich seemed to guarantee, in contrast to its immediate predecessors, and in consequence of the suppression of the labour movement, which gave employers the feeling they had far more room for manoeuvre than before. Moreover, while the unemployment problem of the Depression years from 1929 to 1931 had been made worse by the fact that the large birth-cohorts of the years immediately before the First World War were flooding onto the labour market after leaving school, the situation was reversed from 1932 onwards, as the small birth-cohorts of the war years entered adulthood. Indeed, over two million births expected according to observable statistical trends did not take place in 1914–18, while the death-rate amongst children in the war years, strongly affected by food shortages during the war, was 40 per cent above normal. So the labour market benefited from the consequent fall in people's overall demand for jobs as well.[37]

The impression that the Nazis were extremely lucky in coming to power when the economy was already starting to recover is strengthened when it is realized that some of their much-trumpeted measures did little more than restore the status quo of the pre-Depression years. In housing, for instance, the numbers of newly built or converted dwellings looked impressive at 310,490 in 1936; but this was still below the figure of 317,682 which had been achieved by the despised Weimar Republic in 1929. The government had in fact cut public subsidies for housebuilding back from a billion Reichsmarks in 1928 to almost nothing by 1934 and concentrated its resources on subsidizing repairs. Beyond this, too, the figures of additional workers in the construction industry were mostly derived from employment, much of it compulsory, on large earth-moving projects that had no connection with housing at all.[38] The regime was indeed far from averse to cooking the books. Not only men drafted into labour service but also previously unregistered family and other effectively unpaid farm helpers, most of whom were women, were now counted as employed. None of these people could be considered as active participants in the labour market; none of them received a regular wage with which they could support themselves, let alone support a family. On this reckoning there were at least one and a half million 'invisible unemployed' in Germany at this time, and the total number of unemployed, which Nazi statisticians put at just over two million, was in fact much nearer four.[39] As late as January 1935, a contemporary observer reckoned that there were still over four million unemployed people in Germany.[40] There were subtler methods of statistical manipulation too. Occasional workers were now counted as permanently employed. Between January 1933 and December 1934 the number of long-term unemployed dependent on welfare fell by over 60 per cent in cities with more than half a million inhabitants, an impressive achievement, at least on paper. Yet this was not least because the figures of 'welfare unemployed' were now drawn from those registered with labour exchanges for job applications rather than, as previously, those who had signed on at welfare offices for receipt of benefits. In Hamburg, for example, the labour exchange counted 54,000 welfare unemployed at the end of March, 1934, in contrast to the welfare office's figure of close on 60,000.[41]

In addition, new regulations were introduced cutting working hours in some branches of trade and industry, making it necessary to employ more workers but cutting the wages of those already in employment quite substantially. Labour exchanges were usually able only to provide short-term employment; permanent jobs were still in short supply. Young men and some women too came under massive pressure to enrol in the so-called Voluntary Labour Service or to be drafted into agricultural work, where the peasants often resented their lack of experience and regarded them as simply more mouths to feed. Deprivation of welfare payments, forced labour or even imprisonment threatened those who resisted. In some areas all unemployed young men between the ages of eighteen and twenty-five were rounded up and given the choice of serving on the land or losing all benefits forthwith. Yet the payment for such work was so poor that in many instances it actually fell below welfare benefit levels, and if workers had to live away from home on these schemes they still needed benefits to meet the additional expenditure this involved.[42] Even on the prestigious motorway projects, working conditions were so poor, food rations so low and hours so long that there were frequent protests, all the way to the burning down of the workers' barracks. Many of those drafted onto the projects, such as hairdressers, white-collar workers or travelling salesman, were wholly unsuited to hard physical labour. Accidents were frequent, and repeated, acts of protest on one construction site led to the arrest of thirty-two out of the 700 workers in the space of a few months; the most vociferous complainers were sent to Dachau for 're-education' and to intimidate the others into silent acquiescence.[43] Such measures also helped, along with strict labour controls and the abolition of the unions, to keep net real wages down.[44]

The so-called Voluntary Labour Service was not in fact a creation of the Nazis; it had already been in existence before the seizure of power, with 285,000 men enrolled already in 1932. By 1935 the number had increased to 422,000, but many of these were city-dwellers employed as short-term agricultural labourers for jobs, such as bringing in the harvest, which would otherwise have been carried out by rural workers anyway. So while these schemes led to a reduction of the numbers of the unemployed that figured in the official statistics, they did not bring about a general increase in the purchasing power of the population. Informed observers pointed out that the recovery had not affected consumer goods, where production in May 1935 was still 15 per cent below the level of seven years previously. Retail trade actually declined in quantity between 1933 and 1934, as wages continued to be pegged down while prices of food and clothing rose. The classical Keynesian theory of job creation, adopted at least in theory by the Papen government, envisaged a kick-start to the economy as state loans and job-creation schemes put money into workers' pockets and fuelled consumer demand, thus stimulating production, leading to more employment, and so on, until the process of recovery became self-sustaining. Two and a half years after Hitler had come to power, there was still little sign of this happening.[45]

III

In fact, the Nazi job-creation programme was about something quite different than starting a general economic recovery. Its real aims were explained by Hitler to the Ministers on 8 February 1933:

The next 5 years in Germany must be devoted to the rearmament of the German people. Every publicly supported job creation scheme must be judged by the criterion of whether it is necessary from the point of view of the rearmament of the German people. This principle must always and everywhere stand in the foreground . . . Germany's position in the world will be decisively conditioned by the position of Germany's armed forces. Upon this, the position of Germany's economy in the world also depends.[46]

The motorways, he added, were also to be built 'on strategic principles'.[47] When Hitler presented the motorway construction plan to industrialists on 29 May 1933 he even suggested that the motorways should be roofed over with reinforced concrete to protect them against enemy attacks from the air while tanks and armoured troop-carriers rumbled along beneath them on their way to the front. In the end, the routes they followed were too far from any possible front lines in a war, and the road surface was too thin to carry tanks and heavy military equipment. Their gleaming white surfaces were to provide enemy aircraft with such an easy means of orientation that they had to be covered in camouflage paint during the war. Still, for all the importance given to their ideological, aesthetic and propaganda functions, the intention behind them, not only in Hitler's mind but also in the mind of their architect, Fritz Todt, was primarily strategic.[48] Hitler called attention to what he believed was the vital, if indirect importance of the motor industry for Germany's military future. 'Automobiles and airplanes have a common basis in the motor industry,' he declared: 'Without the development of, for instance, the diesel engine for motor traffic, it would have been practically impossible to lay the necessary groundwork for its utilization in aviation.'[49] The build-up of automobile production would allow factories to be converted to military production at short notice, while the profits from motor manufacture could be used to finance the development of aero engines by the same companies.[50]

The 'motorization of Germany' turned out to be another false Nazi vision, as the diversion of resources to military production from the mid-1930s put a brake on the manufacture of cars, which began to level off and was in no way keeping pace with demand by 1938. The scheme by which workers, under the influence of a massive advertising campaign, parted with a portion of their wages each week to put towards buying a 'Strength Through Joy car' turned out to be no more than a means of getting them to put in more overtime so that they could contribute to the financing of rearmament. By the end of 1939, 270,000 people had lent 110 million Reichsmarks to the state in this way. In the end, no fewer than 340,000 people invested their money in the scheme. Not one of them ever got a Volkswagen in return. The factory was converted to war production in September 1939.[51] The army itself considered that the expansion of motor vehicle manufacture was an essential precondition for the later rapid motorization of the armed forces. More generally, basic industries like iron and steel, manufacturing and engineering were to be given priority over the consumer goods industries because they would provide the basic infrastructure for rearmament. And getting Germans, especially German men, back to work would toughen them up and turn them from unemployed layabouts into potential fighters: hence it was more important to discipline them than to pay them well. From Hitler's point of view, the camps and barracks in which young men toiled for wages below the benefit level in voluntary labour schemes that in reality were not voluntary at all were important not least because they trained them for the privations of a future war.[52]

More immediately, Hitler also wanted to get arms production under way again after the many years in which it had effectively been banned by the limitations imposed on Germany's armed forces by the Peace Settlement of 1919. Addressing leading figures from the armed forces, the SA and the SS on 28 February 1934, Hitler said that it would be necessary in about eight years' time to create 'living-space for the surplus population' in the East, because the economic recovery would by then have run out of steam. Since the 'Western Powers would not let us do this . . . short, decisive blows to the West and then to the East could be necessary'. Rearmament thus had to be complete by 1942.[53] There was a long way to go. In 1933 Germany was more or less without an air force, without capital ships, without tanks, without most basic items of military equipment, and restricted to an army of no more than 100,000 men. Already in early February 1933 Hitler set a programme of rearmament in motion, where possible disguised as job creation (the revamped Schleicher programme, he said on 9 February, 'facilitates in the first place the disguising of work for the improvement of national defence. Particular stress must be laid on this concealment in the immediate future').[54] The army itself asked for 50 million Reichsmarks from the Schleicher programme to fund the initial phase of expansion, along lines it had already drafted in 1932, while the commissioner for aviation asked for just over 43 million. These sums were far too modest for Hitler, who thought that rearmament would require 'billions' of marks and had to be done as quickly as possible in order to get over the difficult period when Germany's enemies began to realize what was going on before it had reached a stage where any serious German resistance to, say, a Polish invasion was possible. The military eventually convinced Hitler that more was not possible in the initial stage of rearmament. He ordered that priority in the allocation of resources from the economic recovery programme was to be given to the military, and he gave the armed forces control over their own rearmament budget in April 1933.[55]

The army drew up a register of 2,800 firms to which arms orders could be sent; in 1934 these accounted for over half of all iron and steel, engineering and motor vehicle production. The effects of the Depression included a massive under-utilization of productive capacity, so initial arms orders were in many cases just taking up the slack, and did not require major new investment. Investment in German industry in 1932 had been less than 17 per cent of its 1928 level, but it now began to increase, reaching just over 21 per cent in 1933, 40 per cent in 1934 and 63 per cent in 1935. Work began almost immediately in preparation for the creation of a German air force. In March 1934 a production schedule was drawn up aiming at 17,000 aircraft by 1939; many of these were disguised as passenger planes though intended for conversion to bombers when the time was ripe. Fifty-eight per cent of them were listed, somewhat implausibly, as 'trainers'. By 1935 there were 72,000 workers employed in aircraft construction, compared to fewer than 4,000 at the beginning of 1933. Similarly, Krupps embarked on the large-scale production of what were coyly described as 'agricultural tractors' in July 1933; in reality they were tanks. In 1934, the Auto Union company

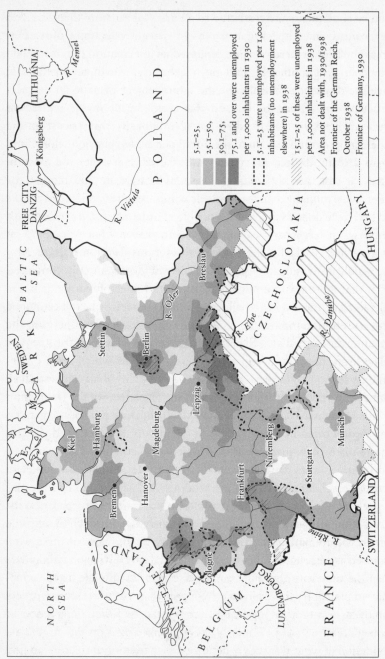

5.1–25,
25.1–50,
50.1–75,
75.1 and over were unemployed
per 1,000 inhabitants in 1930

5.1–25 were unemployed per 1,000
inhabitants (no unemployment
elsewhere) in 1938

15.1–25 of these were unemployed
per 1,000 inhabitants in 1938

Area not dealt with, 1930/1938

Frontier of the German Reich,
October 1938

Frontier of Germany, 1930

Map 10. The Fall in Unemployment, 1930–38

launched another military vehicle production department, disguised in its accounts under the vague name of 'Central Office'. In November 1933 the navy ordered over 41 million Reichsmarks' worth of military equipment and another 70 million Reichsmarks' worth of ships. Major firms such as Borsig, in Berlin, and the Bochumer Association, in Hanover, started up production of rifles and guns. All this had an immediate effect on employment. Already in January 1933 the Mauser rifle factory increased its workforce from 800 to 1,300; in the first four months of 1933, the Rhine Metal Company, which made howitzers and machine guns, took on 500 new workers too. Similar developments could be observed in hundreds of companies across Germany. All this feverish activity inevitably had a knock-on effect on industry more broadly, as iron and steel, engineering, coal and mining companies stepped up production and hired additional labour to cope with the new and rapidly rising demand from the arms and arms-related sector. By the end of 1934, the government, noting the reduction of unemployment figures to less than half the level at which they had been when it had taken office, suspended specific job-creation programmes. From now on, it did not need to rely on such measures to absorb the remaining German unemployed.[56]

The final step in the reduction of the unemployment figures was taken by the introduction of compulsory military service in May 1935. Already in October 1933, Hitler had asked the British Ambassador if his government would agree to a trebling of the size of the German army to 300,000; and the army itself soon took advantage of an international agreement signed on 11 December 1932 that proposed to replace the disarmament clauses of the Treaty of Versailles by a convention that gave Germany equal rights within a new system of international security. Massive recruitment drives in the course of 1934, initially launched to replace the drafting of thousands of troops into the newly formed German air force, resulted in an increase of the army's strength to 240,000 by 1 October. But this was not enough. Hitler had already promised the army on 3 February 1933 that he would reintroduce conscription. Taking a proposed increase in the length of French military service as a pretext, Hitler made the formal announcement to the Reich Defence Council on 15 March, taking many of the officers present by surprise. From now on, all able-bodied, non-Jewish German men would have to serve for one year in the armed forces – extended to two in August 1936 – once they reached the age of eighteen and served the required six months in the Reich Labour Service. By 12 June 1936, the General Staff was estimating that the total personnel strength of the army stood at just over 793,000 men, including reservists and non-combatants; by the eve of the war, there were nearly three-quarters of a million men on active army service, and more than a million in the reserve. In the spring of 1935, too, the German government formally announced the existence of an air force (Luftwaffe), which by this time had 28,000 officers and men serving in it; by August 1939 this number had grown to 383,000.[57] Naval rearmament began more slowly, initially based on plans drawn up in November 1932, but here as well, expansion eventually reached a headlong pace. There were 17,000 naval officers and seamen in service in 1933, an increase of only 2,000 on the previous year, but by the beginning of the war in 1939 the number had grown to almost 79,000.[58] Taken together, these increases soaked up any remaining unemployment amongst the young. After 1936, Hitler and the leading Nazis did not trouble to mention the 'battle for work' again; the fact that it had been won had long since been accepted by the overwhelming majority of the German people.[59]

IV

Germany's government was in a parlous financial state when Hitler became Reich Chancellor in January 1933. More than three years of the most catastrophic economic depression in German history had forced his predecessors to cut back sharply on state expenditure. Bankruptcies, business failures and mass unemployment had led to a huge drop in the gross domestic product and a precipitate fall in tax revenues. This situation did not change overnight. In 1938, for example, state expenditure took up 35 per cent of national income. The 17,700 million Reichsmarks that came into the state's coffers from taxation was only sufficient to cover little over half the money that the state actually spent – 30,000 million Reichsmarks in all. How did the regime manage to pay for its massive programme of rearmament and job creation? It could only pay for it by what it called 'creative credit production.' Such a policy was anathema to traditional economic managers in view of the danger of inflation that such a policy threatened to bring. Nobody wanted a repeat of the uncontrollable hyperinflation of 1923. The President of the Reichsbank, Hans Luther, was unsympathetic to the regime's aim of deficit-financed rearmament. A high priest of monetary orthodoxy, he also had a political past, as a former Reich Chancellor. His concern to maintain the neutrality of the internationally guaranteed Reichsbank led him to protest to Hitler in person when brownshirts ran up the swastika over the bank building on 30 January 1933. All this made him an uncomfortable bedfellow for the Nazis. So Hitler replaced him in the middle of March 1933 with Hjalmar Schacht, the financial wizard who had been largely responsible for bringing the inflation under control at the end of 1923.[60]

Schacht was an anomalous figure in the leadership of the Third Reich. On official occasions, while other ministers appeared in jackboots and uniforms, Schacht stood out in his grey civilian suit, high white collar, shirt and tie, dark overcoat and bowler hat. His thin, somewhat unassuming physical presence and his rimless glasses lent him a slightly withdrawn, academic air which was equally at odds with the rough energy of other leading figures in the regime. Nor was his background in any way similar to theirs. Born in January 1877 into a family of modest means, he was christened Horace Greeley Hjalmar Schacht; his father had spent seven years in the United States and so admired the founder of the *New York Herald Tribune* and coiner of the phrase 'Go west, young man' that he named his son after him. 'Hjalmar', the name by which he was generally known in Germany, was a traditional name in the Hamburg and Schleswig-Holstein family from which his mother descended. Educated at a famous grammar school in Hamburg, he studied political economy under Lujo Brentano at Munich University, then, after gaining practical experience as a cub journalist, learned French in Paris and wrote a doctorate on British economics. Schacht's background was thus both varied and cosmopolitan, and he went on to work with major economists and commentators of the Wilhelmine period such as Hans Delbrück and Gustav Schmoller. He gravitated naturally towards the National Liberal Party, and wrote for the Trade Treaty Association, which brought him into contact with Georg von Siemens, founder of the Deutsche Bank. Through this connection, he entered the real world of finance, and rose rapidly through the ranks. Schacht played a part in the economic management of the German war effort in 1914–18, but he was in no sense a right-wing nationalist, and indeed, if he is to be believed, he eventually separated from his first wife in 1938 because of her radical, pro-Nazi views. Schacht's allegiance during the Weimar years lay rather with the Democrats.[61]

Schacht shot to fame towards the end of 1923 through his role as Commissioner for National Currency, a post to which he had been appointed by Hans Luther, at that time Finance Minister. He probably owed this preferment to the extensive connections in financial circles he had built up over the previous few years as director of a succession of major banks. His role in ending the hyperinflation brought him appointment as President of the Reichsbank after the previous incumbent died suddenly on 20 November 1923. Here he cemented his reputation as a financial miracle-worker by successfully maintaining the stability of the Rentenmark and then – to a chorus of disapproval from the far right – playing a key role in the renegotiation of reparations under the Young Plan. When early in 1930 the government renegotiated parts of the Plan that Schacht considered should have been retained, he resigned and went into temporary retirement. This suggested he had now moved to the nationalist far right politically; and indeed by this time, he had left the Democratic Party, though without transferring his allegiance anywhere else. Introduced to Hitler at a dinner-party thrown by Hermann Göring early in 1931, he was favourably impressed by the Nazi Leader. Like many other Establishment figures, he thought Hitler's radicalism could be tamed by associating him with more conservative and more experienced figures such as himself.[62]

From Hitler's point of view, Schacht was simply the best financial manager around. He needed him to provide the money for his rearmament programme, and to ensure that the rapid growth in state expenditure would not create any problems. Schacht did not even have to become a member of the Nazi Party. He later claimed, like many others, that he had accepted a position in the regime in order to prevent anything worse from happening. In fact, however, by this time Schacht's political views had moved much closer to Hitler's own. He may not have been a rabble-rousing apostle of violence, but he had certainly become enough of a radical nationalist to approve wholeheartedly of the regime's primary aim of rearming Germany at maximum speed. By the end of May 1933 he had come up with an ingenious scheme for deficit financing. A Metallurgical Research Institute (*Metallurgisches Forschungsinstitut*), set up by four big companies with a capital of a million Reichsmarks, was authorized to issue so-called 'Mefo bills', which were guaranteed by the state and discounted by the Reichsbank. The bank in turn simply met the bills presented to it by printing banknotes. Fifty per cent of arms purchases by the military were made in these bills between 1934 and 1936. Since the Reichsbank covered the bills by printing money, the notes in circulation increased by 6,000 million by the end of March 1938, by which time about 12,000 million Mefo bills had been spent. Schacht was already worried about the inflationary effects of these measures, and he stopped the issue of Mefo bills in 1937, after which point tax vouchers and non-interest-bearing treasury notes were used instead. In the meantime, gross Reich debt had spiralled almost out of control. But neither Hitler nor his economic managers considered this very important. For deficit financing was only a short-term measure in their view; the debts would be paid by territorial expansion in the near enough future. And besides rapid rearmament, Hitler was busily taking other steps to ensure that this would not only be possible but would also, as he saw it, bring the maximum economic benefit.[63]

From the outset, Hitler wanted Germany to be economically self-sufficient. In preparation for the coming war, the German economy had to be freed from its dependence on foreign imports. Hitler had seen the effects of the Allied blockade of Germany in the First World War for himself: a malnourished and discontented population; arms production hamstrung by lack of basic raw materials. He did not want this to happen again. 'Autarky', the Nazi term for self-sufficiency, was a basic precept of Nazi economics from the early 1920s on. It took up a large part of the economic discussion, such as it was, in Hitler's politico-autobiographical tract *My Struggle*. It was intimately connected with another basic idea of Nazi policy, that of the conquest of 'living-space' in Eastern Europe, which Hitler believed would secure food supplies for Germany's urban population. Thus from the outset, Nazi policy focused on withdrawing trade from international markets and reorienting it towards countries, for example in South-eastern Europe, which one day would be part of the Nazi empire. Given the current depressed state of the world economy,

Hitler told military leaders in early February 1933, it was pointless trying to boost exports; the only way to a long-term, secure recovery of the German economy was through the conquest of 'living-space' in the East, and preparations for this now had to take priority over everything else.[64]

At home, the Third Reich pursued the objective of autarky in food supplies through the Reich Food Estate, promulgated on 13 September 1933. Headed by the 'blood-and-soil' ideologue Richard Walther Darré, now adorned with the title of Reich Farmers' Leader, this was a characteristic Nazi organization, hierarchically structured on the basis of the leadership principle, with Farmers' Leaders appointed at every level through to districts and localities. The idea, long advocated by farming lobbyists, was to unite producers, wholesalers, retailers and consumers in a single chain that would eliminate the exploitation of one by another and ensure a fair deal for all. Thus in the fishing industry, for example, fishermen, fish processors, fish wholesalers, fish distributors and fishmongers were organized into a single association run from Berlin, and the same was done for other branches of agriculture, from fruit farmers to grain producers. These elaborate structures were backed up by import agencies to protect the domestic producers of particular products, and enforced by sanctions including hefty fines and even imprisonment for contravention of the regulations. In this way, the whole national production and supply of foodstuffs could be controlled, prices fixed, and quantities and quotas determined in the interests of the producers. In some ways, the Reich Food Estate, which was intended to function as an independent corporation, was seen by Darré as the vehicle through which peasant farmers would strengthen their economic interests and claim their rightful place in the new Germany. It was also an imitation of the institutions of the Corporate State in Fascist Italy, binding together everybody in a particular area of society and the economy in a structure that, theoretically at least, would replace mutual antagonism with mutual co-operation and generate a sense of community through removing real and potential sources of conflict.[65]

But the Reich Food Estate proved a problematical institution.[66] Very soon, Darré's ideological vision of a future Germany based on a healthy and stable community of peasant farmers began to be pushed aside by the more immediate imperatives of autarky and rearmament. In line with general economic policy, the Reich Food Estate had to keep prices down, restrict imports (including animal fodder) and ration consumption. Price controls squeezed farmers' profits and meant they could not compete with the big industrial firms in the level of wages they paid their workers. The shortage of iron and steel and the prioritizing of the armaments industry in allocating them meant severe restrictions on the manufacture of agricultural machinery that might have been an acceptable substitute for their vanishing labour force, assuming that farmers could afford to pay for it. Already in September 1934 Schacht launched a 'production battle' aimed to make Germany self-sufficient in food supplies, a goal that the Reich Food Estate had to play its part in fulfilling. Yet success proved elusive. Subsidies for the construction of grain stores, silos and the like had some effect. But this was more than counteracted by the requisitioning of large quantities of agricultural land for motorways, airfields, barracks and camps, and army training areas, and the drafting of agricultural labourers into arms-related industries in the towns and cities. Between 1933 and 1938, 140 villages were broken up and 225 rural communities disrupted or displaced by compulsory army land purchases, while in the last two years of peace, the building of the defensive emplacements known as the 'West Wall' caused the abandonment of 5,600 farms with 130,000 hectares of land. Grain yields generally failed even to reach the levels of 1913, while there was a shortfall in domestic production against demand of between 10 and 30 per cent in pork and fruit, 30 per cent in poultry and eggs, around 50 per cent in fats, butter, and margarine, up to 60 per cent in legumes and over 90 per cent in vegetable oils.[67] In this as in other areas, the diversion of production to armaments and associated industries from consumer goods manufacture and the clampdown on non-military-related imports had created a shortage of consumer goods by the autumn of 1936, as demand began to outstrip supply. Prices therefore began to rise. A Price Commissioner – the conservative politician Carl Goerdeler, Mayor of Leipzig – had already been appointed late in 1934, but his advocacy of a slow-down in rearmament as the remedy had been brusquely rejected, and his office was little more than a propaganda show. To prevent a resurgence of the dreaded inflation of the early 1920s, the government imposed a compulsory freeze on prices on 26 October 1936. On 1 January 1937 it introduced rationing of butter, margarine and fat. Thus consumers began to feel the pinch as well as producers.[68]

As Darré was also Minister of Agriculture, he had to go along with these measures. Every time the interests of the state clashed with those of the Reich Food Estate, it was the latter that had to yield. Moreover, by 1936, therefore, it was clear that the goal of self-sufficiency in food was as far away as ever. The Reich Food Estate was caught between the Party and the state. Formally an institution belonging to neither, it lost its functions as each of the two asserted its own interests. Darré's star was now waning rapidly. His deputy, Herbert Backe, persuaded Göring and Himmler that Darré was an ideologue who lived in a dream-world and the practical goal of achieving self-sufficiency in food production could only be achieved by an expert such as himself. In addition, a war of attrition with Robert Ley over the interests of agricultural labourers had led to further inroads into the position of the Reich Food Estate in rural society. Ley was also able to use his role as Reich Organization Leader of the Party to remove a variety of functions, for example in education and training, away from Darré's organization as a prelude to incorporating it into the Labour Front. Attempting to shore up his waning power, Darré had in fact already yielded to the demands of autarky, for example sponsoring a law of 26 June 1936 that allowed the state to merge farms together compulsorily to create larger and more efficient units. Moreover, he was also compelled to cede the care of the social and cultural welfare of its members to the Party and its subordinate organizations. The unpopularity of his schemes amongst the peasantry sealed his fate.[69]

Göring and Backe devoted considerable energy to boosting the country's home-produced food supply: measures taken included cheap loans to farmers for the purchase of machinery, price cuts for fertilizers, price incentives for producing grain, eggs and the like, and the requirement in some cases to cultivate crops that would provide the raw materials for textile fibres, such as flax, or vegetable oils and fats. They also tried to remedy the growing labour shortage on the land. From the outset of the Third Reich, hundreds of thousands of young people had been drafted onto the land to try and offset a long-term shortage of agricultural manpower, although many of them were too young, lacked the physical strength, or were too ignorant of the countryside and its ways to be of much use. Even concentration camp inmates were roped into clearing moorland for cultivation. This was not what Darré had imagined when he had set up the Reich Entailed Farms and the Reich Food Estate. On the eve of the war, his original vision had all but disappeared.[70]

Germany did indeed become self-sufficient in some basic foodstuffs like bread, potatoes, sugar and meat by 1939, but there were still many products, notably fat, pulses (except lentils), and even eggs where imports were still necessary on a considerable scale to meet demand. The number of rural workers dropped by 1.4 million between 1933 and 1939, partly because of the removal of foreign workers, partly because of a continuing drift to better-paid jobs in the towns.[71] The land brought under cultivation was not enough to make a significant difference. Thirty per cent of fodder for horses, still a vital component of the army transport system in 1938, had to be imported. Crop yields for cereals in 1939 were not much better than they had been in 1913. On the eve of war, roughly 15 per cent of Germany's food supplies still came from abroad.[72] All this pointed yet again in the minds of the Nazi leaders to the need for 'living-space' in the East to make up the deficit. On the other hand, the fact that the trade agreements Schacht had negotiated brought in cheap agricultural produce from South-eastern Europe allowed Hitler and Göring to avoid taking yet more draconian measures to subordinate peasant farmers completely to the dictates of autarky, which would have alienated them even more. The peasants were not going to be militarized or dragooned into a new kind of serfdom to satisfy the demands of the state. Some of the measures introduced by Darré early on thus remained, and the farming community could look back in 1939 to an improvement in its situation during the previous six years, in which the overall proceeds of agriculture had grown by 71 per cent in comparison to 1933, far less than those of industry but still, by the eve of the war, better than the situation of the late 1920s.[73]

German consumers did not do so well. More and more foodstuffs were subject to official rationing as the government stockpiled supplies in preparation for war and requisitioned agricultural workers and craftsmen for arms-related industries. Butter and fat had long been restricted; fruit and coffee were also rationed from the early spring of 1939. Apples remained unpicked because workers had been drafted into the towns. People were urged to grow their own fruit and to make preserved fruit for use in the winter months. Food supplies were not helped by a series of poor harvests in the mid-1930s caused by bad weather, a cold snap in the spring of 1938 that froze a lot of fruit blossoms off the trees and a bad outbreak of foot-and-mouth disease among the nation's cattle the same year. Coffee imports fell as the shortage of hard currency in Germany began to limit the ability of importers to pay for it. The shortage of wheat and rye meant official controls on bakers, who were instructed to bake only 'homogenized bread' made from an amalgam of inferior flours. White bread could be purchased only on presentation of a medical certificate. To prevent people evading controls on the purchase of milk by going directly to the producer, dairy farmers were obliged from 1 January 1939 to deliver all their supplies to central milk depots. Later the same year, it was reported that no eggs were to be had in Munich for the whole of Easter Week, while in Elberfeld people were unable to bake Easter cakes for lack of fat. Training courses were put on for Saxon housewives to show them how to cook 'Hungarian fish gulash' since meat for the real thing was so hard to come by. On 28 March 1939, the meat counter at the Hertie department store on the Dönhoffplatz in Berlin was opened only to sell registered customers their weekly ration of fat; there was no fresh or frozen meat available at all. Shortages inevitably led to a flourishing black market in scarce foodstuffs. Berlin's markets were already cleared out of fruit by seven in the morning, before the price commissioners came in to check that stallholders were adhering to the official price limits. Imported fruit, such as bananas and oranges, was particularly hard to come by. Only well-off early risers could afford to circumvent the regulations in this way, though at a price well over the official maximum. In the Ruhr, many workers were only able to eat meat once a week. 'The people', reported a Social Democratic agent in May 1939, 'are suffering a great deal from the shortage of all kinds of foodstuffs and respectable, solid clothing. Still,' he added, 'this has not led to any kind of unrest, apart from queueing in front of shops, which has become a daily occurrence.'[74]

BUSINESS, POLITICS AND WAR

I

Despite interventionist institutions like the Reich Food Estate, Hitler and the Nazi leadership generally sought to manage the economy by tough control of the market economy rather than by nationalization or direct state takeovers.[75] Thus, to take one example, the regime pressed the giant chemicals combine I.G. Farben into developing and producing synthetic fuel for motor vehicles and aeroplanes through the hydrogenation of coal, so as to reduce Germany's dependence on oil imports; an agreement was signed on 14 December 1933, committing the combine to produce some 300,000 tons a year in return for a guaranteed ten-year purchase order from the state.[76] Where a company refused to go along with demands of this kind, however, the regime stepped in to bring it to heel, as in the case of Hugo Junkers, the aircraft manufacturer, who was forced to sell his majority interest in his two companies to the Reich at the end of 1933 after attempting to resist the government's calls to convert them from civil to military purposes. On his death in April 1935, indeed, both companies were nationalized, although only briefly.[77] Moreover, the Economics Ministry actively insisted on the creation of cartels in key areas so as to make it easier for the state to direct and monitor increases in war-related production.[78] Yet despite this increase in state intervention, as Nazi economic spokesmen repeatedly insisted, Germany was to remain a free-market economy, in which the state provided leadership and set the primary goals. For this purpose, at least early on, when the 'battle for work' and the reorientation of the economy towards rearmament were the main aims, Hitler needed the willing co-operation of business.

It was not surprising, therefore, that he chose a leading representative of the business community as his Reich Economics Minister after the enforced departure of the cantankerous German Nationalist Alfred Hugenberg.[79] This was the general director of the Allianz Insurance Company, Kurt Schmitt. Born in 1886 into the modest bourgeois family of a doctor, Schmitt had been an enthusiastic duelling corps member at university, where he had studied commercial law, then worked briefly in the Bavarian civil service under Gustav Ritter von Kahr, later to become notorious on the far right in Bavaria. Shortly before the outbreak of war, Schmitt entered the Munich branch of the Allianz. Immensely hard-working, he was none the less no cold pen-pusher. He developed a human approach to insurance, personally mediating between claimants and insured, and thus reducing substantially the number of expensive lawsuits which the company had to handle. Not surprisingly, this led to his rapid promotion through the managerial ranks, a rise that was not seriously interrupted by the war, from which he was invalided out early on with a minor wound that became repeatedly reinfected and so prevented him from returning to the front. He became general director at the age of thirty-four. Soon, encouraged by his subordinates, Schmitt was wearing expensive, tailor-made suits and hobnobbing with the great and the good in the gentlemen's clubs of Berlin. Under Schmitt's leadership, Allianz expanded rapidly in the kind of mergers and takeovers that characterized other sectors of the business world in the 1920s as well. Like other businessmen, Schmitt was dissatisfied with the conditions under which private enterprise had to labour during the Weimar era, and he lobbied for a reform of the law affecting insurance through the Reich Association for Private Insurance. This brought him into contact with leading politicians, many of whom were impressed by his competence, his decisiveness and his obvious financial acumen. By the early 1930s he had become a public figure of some repute. He enhanced his reputation with his performance on the Economic Advisory Council set up by Brüning. Both Brüning and Papen offered him the post of Finance Minister. He turned the offers down in the belief that the prevailing economic situation would not allow him to do the job with any degree of success.[80]

By this time, Schmitt had taken up contacts with the Nazi Party. In November 1930, like Schacht a little later on, he had met Göring at a dinner and been extremely impressed by his political advocacy. Soon

Schmitt was indulging Göring's impressive appetite for food and wine in regular lunchtime meetings in a Berlin restaurant, held at his company's expense. Before long, he had met Hitler too. The Nazis' promise to defeat the menace of Communism and end the party-political bickering of the Weimar years won him over to their cause. A self-made man who had risen by his own abilities, Schmitt was less wedded to traditional conservative politics than were colleagues from old-established business or civil service backgrounds. As the Nazis seized power in Germany, Schmitt abandoned his previous discretion and signed up as a Party member in the spring of 1933, leading company celebrations of Hitler's birthday on 20 April. Schmitt shared the common elite prejudice that regarded Jews as too prominent in public and intellectual life, banking, finance and the law; the most common adjective he used when referring to them was 'unpleasant'. He agreed with Göring's proposal, made to him at one of their private meetings, to deprive Jews of the vote and ban them from holding positions of authority over Germans. By the summer, his contacts with Göring had borne spectacular fruit. Seeking to replace Hugenberg as Reich Economics Minister, Hitler was persuaded by Göring that it would be politic to have a leading representative of the business community in the post. Hitler offered it to Schmitt, who was sworn in on 30 June 1933, believing that he had a role to play now that the political situation had been stabilized.[81]

Despite attempting to strengthen his position by, for example, becoming an officer in the SS, Schmitt proved no match for the big beasts in the Nazi power jungle like Goebbels, Ley or even Darré, all of whom had removed substantial areas of the economy from the purview of his Ministry within a few months. Underlings such as the Nazi economic theorist Gottfried Feder, who had written the abolition of 'interest slavery' into the Party programme in 1920, were a continual source of trouble. Schmitt's announcements and instructions to state and regional officials not to endanger the economic recovery by countenancing actions against Jewish businesses were omitted from press reports and generally disregarded by 'old fighters'. Most seriously of all, Schmitt was opposed to what he considered as unproductive expenditure on rearmament and of spectacular but, as he argued, useless ideas such as the motorways. Here too he was ignored. Schmitt disapproved of the Nazis' extravagant propaganda claims about an economic recovery, the end of unemployment and the like. He increasingly thought of himself as a failure. Under increasing stress on all sides, he suffered a serious heart attack on 28 June 1934 and eventually resigned with effect from 30 January the following year. Before long, he had returned to the insurance business. He had realized his incompetence as a politician and refused all subsequent invitations to leave the walk of life he knew best.[82]

Schmitt was replaced on 3 August 1934 as Acting Economics Minister, then from 30 January 1935 on a permanent basis, by Hjalmar Schacht, who had already made it clear privately to Hitler that, unlike his predecessor, he would regard rearmament as a top priority irrespective of the economic situation. Schacht was given dictatorial powers of economic management. He began by promptly sacking Feder from his post in the Ministry and purged other Party figures who, the army had complained, were trying to impose their ideas on the management of the economy. In the next four months, Schacht established a new structure under the aegis of his Ministry, in which all firms were compulsorily enrolled in one or other of seven Reich Groups (industry, trade, banking, and so on), further subdivided into specialist and regional sub-groups. This enabled the Ministry to take a stronger lead in implementing rearmament policy on the existing basis of private enterprise rather than on the kind of anti-capitalist ideas favoured by Feder.[83]

Already by this time, however, the nascent armaments boom was beginning to have some unwelcome effects. By boosting domestic industrial production, the state and the army caused industry to switch away from export-oriented, mostly consumer products. Added to a continuing slump in world trade and the imposition of trade sanctions by Britain and the United States in protest against the regime's persecution of the Jews, this caused a fall in exports from 1,260 million Reichsmarks in the last quarter of 1933 to 990 million in the second quarter of 1934. Simultaneously imports grew rapidly in volume, as demand in Germany for products like rubber, oil and cotton all increased. Imports of raw materials rose by 32 per cent from the middle of 1932 to the beginning of 1934, while the prices obtained for German exports fell by 15 per cent. The situation was made worse by the fact that Britain and the USA had allowed their currencies to depreciate, while the Nazi government, like its predecessors, was unwilling to devalue the Reichsmark for fear that it would encourage inflation. Thus German goods became more expensive on the world market, encouraging other economies to turn elsewhere for their sources, while imports to Germany became cheaper, prompting German firms to buy more of them. In 1934, Germany's balance of payments went into deficit.[84] Germany's foreign debt rose, while its gold and foreign exchange reserves fell by more than half between January and September.[85] Piecemeal foreign currency quotas and restrictions failed to have any real effect on the rapidly deteriorating situation.[86] On 14 June 1934 the Reichsbank imposed a six-month stop on the repayment of all long-term and medium-term foreign debts.[87]

On 19 September 1934, to try and counter these mounting problems, Hjalmar Schacht, the newly anointed 'economic dictator' of Germany, announced a 'New Plan' according to which trade would from now on be on a bilateral basis: a kind of barter between Germany and other states, in which imports would only be permitted from states to which Germany exported substantial quantities of goods. 'Implementation of the rearmament programme', he declared on 3 May 1935, was '*the* task of German policy.' In order to pay for it, imports had to be restricted as far as possible, to arms-related raw materials and foodstuffs that could not be grown in Germany.[88] South-eastern Europe seemed a particularly favourable area for bilateral trade arrangements. A focus on the Balkans might well open up a perspective on a future Greater German trade area in East-Central Europe, the long dreamed-of *Mitteleuropa* (Central Europe) project. It would be safer in the event of war than existing trade links to the north and the west. Besides this, cutting back on overseas trade would lessen Germany's dependence on the British merchant marine, which might prove severely damaging in the event of a future war between the two nations.

Too many raw materials came from far-flung parts of the globe, and the New Plan sought to reduce Germany's dependence on such sources. Enforced by twenty-five Surveillance Officers, the new plan helped cut German imports from the rest of Europe from 7.24 billion Reichsmarks in 1928 to 2.97 billion ten years later; by the latter date, imports from South-eastern Europe, which had made up 7.5 per cent of the total in 1928, had risen to 22 per cent of the whole.[89] Yet the army was soon complaining that while Schacht was managing to find the money to pay for the initial stages of rearmament, he had not succeeded in making the economy ready for war. In particular, import restrictions had

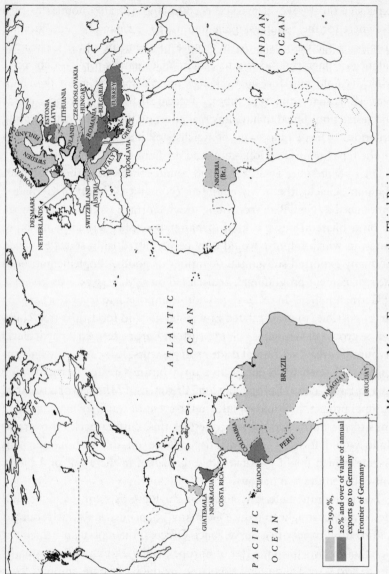

Map 11. Major Exporters to the Third Reich

dangerously depleted Germany's domestic reserves of raw materials, ore and metals, while attempts to find substitutes – home-grown textiles, synthetic rubber and fuel, locally drilled oil and so on – had so far made only a very limited impact. The time had come, in Hitler's view, for a far more radical intervention in the economy – one which Schacht, who made no secret of the fact that he thought the German economy had reached the limits of its ability to sustain rearmament and war mobilization by 1936, could no longer be trusted to manage.[90]

II

On 4 September 1936, Hermann Göring read out to the cabinet a lengthy memorandum that Hitler had drawn up in the light of the mounting evidence of the New Plan's bankruptcy. In typical fashion, it ranged widely over history and politics before coming to the point at issue: preparing the economy for war. Politics, Hitler declared, was 'a struggle of nations for life'. In this struggle, the Soviet Union was now becoming a threat. 'The essence and goal of Bolshevism is the elimination of those strata of mankind which have hitherto provided the leadership and their replacement by worldwide Jewry.' Germany had to take the lead in the struggle against it, since Bolshevism's victory would mean 'the annihilation of the German people'. Preparing for the coming battle, Hitler declared, was an absolute priority. All other issues were of secondary importance. 'The German armed forces must be operational within four years.' 'The German economy', he added, 'must be fit for war within four years.' Hitler went through his familiar litany of economic beliefs: Germany was overpopulated and could not feed itself from its own resources; the solution lay in extending living-space to obtain new raw materials and foodstuffs. Raw materials could not be stockpiled for a war, since the quantity needed was simply too great. The production of fuel, synthetic rubber, artificial fats, iron, metal substitutes and so on had to be ratcheted up to a level that would sustain a war. Savings had to be made in food supplies; potatoes for example were no longer to be used for making schnapps. The people had to make sacrifices. An economic plan had to be drawn up. The interests of individual businesses had to be subordinated to those of the nation. Businessmen who kept funds abroad had to be punished by death.[91]

In presenting this memorandum to the cabinet, Göring launched a fierce attack on the view, propagated by Schacht and his ally the Price Commissioner Goerdeler, that the solution to the economic blockage of 1936 lay in scaling down the rearmament programme. On the contrary, since 'the showdown with Russia is inevitable', it had to be speeded up. There had to be much tighter controls on the economy and on the export of currency. Göring revealed that it was he who had been entrusted by the Leader with the execution of the Four-Year Plan that Hitler went on to proclaim at the Party Rally on 9 September. Schacht had begun to outlive his usefulness. On 18 October 1936 a decree made Göring's supremacy official. He used it to establish a whole new organization dedicated to preparing the economy for war, with six departments dealing with the production and distribution of raw materials, the co-ordination of the labour force, the control of prices, foreign exchange and agriculture. Göring appointed the top civil servants in the Ministries of Labour and Agriculture to run the relevant two departments in the Four-Year Plan organization. In this way he began to bring the two Ministries under the aegis of the Plan, bypassing Walther Darré and Franz Seldte, the two responsible Ministers. Göring's operation also undercut Schacht, who had been sent on compulsory leave on the day that the Plan had been unveiled to the cabinet. Schacht soon found that the Four-Year Plan operation was taking policy decisions without reference to his Economics Ministry. His protests had no effect. Increasingly frustrated at this loss of power, and increasingly worried by the rapid expansion of military and raw material production on what he regarded as an inadequate financial basis, Schacht wrote to Hitler on 8 October 1937 reaffirming his view that there could only be one head of economic affairs in the Third Reich, and making it clear he thought that person should be himself. The threat of resignation was clearly implicit.[92]

By this stage, however, Hitler had lost all confidence in Schacht, whose economic realism was now a serious irritation to him. On 25 October 1937, the head of the navy, Admiral Erich Raeder, had formally asked Reich War Minister General Werner von Blomberg to get Hitler to step in personally to arbitrate between the different interests – army, navy and air force – that were competing for the inadequate supplies of iron, steel, fuel and other raw materials. Hitler responded by getting Blomberg to call a meeting in the Reich Chancellery on 5 November 1937, at which the Nazi Leader outlined his overall strategy to a small group consisting of Raeder, Blomberg, the Commander-in-Chief of the army General Werner von Fritsch, the head of the air force Hermann Göring and Foreign Minister Konstantin von Neurath. Notes were taken by Hitler's military adjutant Colonel Friedrich Hossbach, and these were subsequently used as evidence that Hitler was already planning a war in the not-too-distant future. In fact, there was no concrete plan, although there were certainly intentions. Hitler was mainly concerned to impress on his audience the need for urgency in rearmament and the imminence of armed conflict, particularly in East-Central Europe. Much of what he had to say would already have been familiar to his listeners from earlier statements of this kind. 'The aim of German foreign policy', Hitler began, according to Hossbach's memorandum of the meeting, 'was to make secure and to preserve the racial stock (*Volksmasse*) and to enlarge it. It was therefore a question of space.' By this he meant, as he had always done, the conquest of East-Central and Eastern Europe, which would solve the German race's need for expansion 'only for a foreseeable period of about one to three generations' before further expansion, probably overseas, became necessary and indeed, with the probable collapse of the British Empire, possible. After a detailed survey of the shortages in raw materials and foodstuffs, Hitler concluded that 'autarky, in regard both to food and to the economy as a whole, could not be maintained'. The solution especially in terms of food supplies was to be found in 'gaining space for agricultural use' in Europe, by conquest and, implicitly, the removal or reduction of the people who lived there. 'Germany's problem', he declared, 'could be solved only by the use of force.'[93]

Hitler went on to warn that other nations were catching up in armaments, and the domestic food crisis would soon reach breaking point. Hossbach noted that Hitler's speech sounded a new note of anxiety about his own health: 'If the Leader was still living, it was his unalterable determination to solve Germany's problem of space by 1943-5 at the latest.' Indeed, he would take military action earlier if France was weakened by a serious domestic crisis or became involved in a war with another state. In either case, if war came, Germany's first priority would be to overthrow Austria and Czechoslovakia to reduce the threat on its south-eastern flank. The forced removal of two million people from Czechoslovakia and one million from Austria would free up additional food supplies for the Germans. The British and the French, he added, were unlikely to intervene, while the Poles would remain neutral as long as Germany was victorious.[94] Thus Hitler's response to the supply bottleneck was not to reduce the pace of rearmament but to accelerate the pace of proposed conquest of 'living-space'. Despite the doubts of some of those present at the meeting, Hitler thus pressed on with rearmament at an ever more frenetic tempo. The caution of Schacht and his allies – who included some of those present at the meeting – was brushed aside. The solution of Germany's economic problems was reserved until the creation of 'living-space' in the East. With Hitler in such a mood, Schacht's position had now become wholly untenable. On 26 November 1937 Hitler accepted his resignation as Minister of Economics. The management of the economy now passed effectively to Hermann Göring. The discussion earlier in the month made it clear that it was Goring's job to make sure that the brakes were taken off rearmament whatever the economic problems this might cause.[95]

The results of these changes could soon be seen. The pace of rearmament quickened still further. As Schacht had predicted, by 1938 expenditure on preparations for war was clearly spiralling out of control: 9,137 million Reichsmarks were spent on the army, compared to 478 million in 1933; 1,632 million on the navy, compared to 192 million five years earlier; and 6,026 million on the air force, compared to 76 million in 1933. Including expenditure on administration, and on the redemption of Mefo bills, rearmament costs had risen from 1.5 per cent of national income in 1933 to 7.8 per cent in 1934, to 15.7 per cent in 1936 and 21.0 per cent two years later, where national income itself had almost doubled in the same period. The Reich's finances, which had recorded a modest surplus in 1932, recorded a deficit of 796 million Reichsmarks in 1933, rising to nearly 9.5 billion in 1938. Acting now in his capacity as President of the Reichsbank, Schacht wrote a personal letter to Hitler on 7 January 1939, signed by all the other directors of the Reichsbank, in which he warned that 'overstretching public expenditure' was rapidly leading to the 'looming danger of inflation'. 'The limitless expansion of state expenditure', they told Hitler, 'is destroying every attempt to put the budget in order. Despite an enormous tightening of the screw of taxation, it is bringing the finances of the state to the edge of ruin and from this position it is wrecking the bank of issue and its currency.' Hitler's response was to sack him along with the entire board of directors a few days later, on 20 January 1939. He no longer fitted into the general National Socialist scheme of things, Hitler told Schacht.[96]

Schacht went on a long holiday to India and retired from public life on his return. After the death of his first wife, he married a member of the staff at the Munich House of German Art, a woman thirty years his junior, and after a honeymoon in Switzerland in 1941 they lived quietly in the countryside, though Schacht retained a variety of more or less meaningless titles including that of Minister without Portfolio. His successor was the former state secretary in the Propaganda Ministry, Walther Funk, whom Göring had shoehorned into the position of Reich Minister of Economics on 15 February 1938. Funk now took over the running of the Reichsbank as well, thus subordinating both institutions to the Four-Year Plan. Unsurprisingly, what Schacht and his fellow directors, some of whom were subsequently reinstated, had called the 'unrestrained spending habits of the public finances' continued unabated, at an even more frenetic tempo than before. On 15 June 1939 a new law removed all limits on the printing of money, thus realizing Schacht's worst fears. But Hitler and the Nazi leadership did not care. They were counting on the invasion and conquest of Eastern Europe to cover the costs. In February 1934, Hitler had stated that rearmament had to be complete by 1942. By the time of the Four-Year Plan, the date had been moved forward to 1940. Germany's economic problems, as Hitler had always said, could only be definitively solved by war.[97]

III

The switch from the New Plan to the Four-Year Plan in 1936 testified to the growing sense of urgency with which Hitler was now pursuing this goal. But neither could really be called a plan in the normal sense of the word. At least Schacht, as economic supremo in the early years of the Third Reich, had retained a firm conceptual grasp of the economy and state finances as a whole. But Göring, for all his undoubted energy, ambition and intuitive grasp of how power worked, possessed no such overview. He had very little understanding of economics or finance. He did not set clear priorities, nor could he, since Hitler kept changing his mind as to which arm of the services – air force, navy, army – should come top of the allocation list. New blueprints kept being produced and then superseded by more ambitious ones. The chaos of overlapping and competing competencies in the management of the economy was characterized subsequently by one senior official as the 'organizational jungle of the Four-Year Plan'. There was a fundamental contradiction between the drive to autarky in anticipation of a long war and reckless rearmament in preparation for an imminent conflict. It was never resolved. Nor was the statistical information available which was necessary for the provision of a rational planning system. Despite its elaborate structure, which included a General Council that was supposed to coordinate operations and harmonize the activities of the various government Ministries involved, the Four-Year Plan consisted in reality of little more than a series of piecemeal initiatives. Yet these met with some success. Coal production, for instance, increased by 18 per cent from 1936 to 1938, lignite by 23 per cent, and coke by 22 per cent. By 1938, Germany was producing 70 per cent more aluminium than two years before and had overtaken the USA as the world's largest producer. In 1932 Germany had only been able to meet 5.2 per cent of demand for textiles, essential among other things for military uniforms. Increased production of rayon and other artificial fibres raised this to 31 per cent in 1936 and 43 per cent by 1939. The goal of abolishing Germany's reliance on imported fuel moved nearer to fulfilment as petroleum production went up by 63 per cent and output of synthetic fuel by 69 per cent between 1937 and 1939. In 1937 Hitler announced the establishment of 'two gigantic buna [i.e. synthetic rubber] factories' which would soon produce enough to meet all Germany's requirements.[98]

Yet these impressive figures masked a failure of the Four-Year Plan to produce the desired result of making Germany entirely self-sufficient by 1940. To begin with, the Plan failed to solve Germany's chronic balance of payments problem. Although exports did rise in 1937, they fell again in 1938 as German manufacturers put their faith in safe and lucrative domestic contracts instead of risking their products on the world market. And in both years, they were exceeded in value by imports, further reducing Germany's already seriously depleted foreign currency reserves.

It was this issue more than any other, perhaps, that occasioned Schacht's growing alienation from the regime he had served so faithfully from the beginning.[99] Imports continued to be vital in a number of fields after he had departed the scene. Despite massively increasing their output, Germany's aluminium factories, for instance, relied almost entirely on imported raw materials. High-grade steel was similarly reliant on metals not to be found in Germany. Buna production amounted to no more than 5 per cent of Germany's domestic consumption of rubber in 1938; only 5,000 tonnes had been produced, as against a planned target of 29,000. Germany still depended on imports for half its mineral oil in 1939. Expansion to the East might bring new sources of oil within Germany's reach, but it would certainly do nothing to alleviate the shortage of rubber. Above all, these increases in domestic production had to be set against massive growth in demand, above all from the armed forces. Initially, the armed forces had conceived of rearmament as a means of strengthening Germany's defences; but the long-term goal was always the mounting of an offensive war against the East, and already on 30 December 1935 General Ludwig Beck, Chief of the General Staff, built on the experience of successful armoured manoeuvres the previous summer to demand the creation of a more mobile kind of army, increasing the number of tank brigades and motorized infantry units. By the middle of 1936 the army was planning to include three armoured divisions and four motorized divisions in its peacetime force of thirty-six. All of these would require huge quantities of steel to build and massive amounts of fuel to drive.[100]

Building naval strength was less urgent, since Hitler's main aim in the short to medium term was the conquest of Europe, and above all Eastern Europe. But in the long term, as he had indicated in his unpublished second book, he envisaged a titanic transcontinental clash with the United States, and for this a large navy would be necessary. In the spring of 1937 he increased the number of battleships to be constructed from four to six, to be completed by 1944. In addition there were to be four pocket battleships (changed in 1939 to three battle cruisers), and the pace of construction increased sharply as the threat of war with Britain loomed ever closer. Expenditure on the navy rose from 187 million Reichsmarks in 1932 to 497 two years later, 1,161 million in 1936 and 2,390 million in 1939. In 1936 ship construction accounted for nearly half of all naval expenditure, though this had sunk to under a quarter by the eve of the war, as men were drafted in to crew the new fleet and munitions were manufactured for the new guns to fire. Even in 1938 the planned fleet was thought to require six million tonnes of fuel oil a year and two million of diesel oil, in a situation in which total German consumption of mineral oils stood at six million, of which less than half was produced at home. Plans for the expansion of the air force were even more ambitious, and came up rapidly against very similar constraints. Overriding the objections of the army and navy, which saw airplanes as little more than support forces, Hitler created a Reich Aviation Ministry on 10 May 1933 under Hermann Göring, himself a former fighter pilot. Göring, aided by his talented and energetic state secretary Erhard Milch, a former director of the Lufthansa airline, immediately adopted a plan drawn up by another Lufthansa director, Robert Knauss, that envisaged an independent air force designed to fight a two-front war against France and Poland. Long-range bombers were the key to success, argued Knauss. By 1935 aircraft production had been reorganized, with many firms making components, thus saving the time of the big manufacturers such as Junkers, Heinkel or Dornier. Defensive fighters were soon added to the Ministry's targets. In July 1934 a long-term programme envisaged the manufacture of more than 2,000 fighters, another 2,000 bombers, 700 dive-bombers, over 1,500 reconnaisance aircraft and thousands more training aircraft by the end of March 1938. By 1937, however, iron and steel shortages were beginning to have a serious effect on these ambitious plans. Constant changes in the design of bombers slowed things down further. Aircraft production actually fell from 1937 to 1938, from around 5,600 to 5,200.[101]

Meanwhile, iron ore imports increased from just over 4.5 million tonnes in 1933 to almost 21 million tonnes in 1938; the drive to rearm was negating the drive for autarky. Nevertheless, restrictions on foreign currency severely limited the extent to which shortfalls could be made good by imports. By 1939 the army was imposing what an American survey later described as 'drastic restrictions on the use of motor vehicles in order to save rubber and fuel'. Already in 1937 it only received half the steel it wanted. Ammunition was in short supply, and too few barracks were being constructed to house the rapidly growing numbers of troops. The navy was unable to obtain the steel it needed to fulfil its shipbuilding programme.[102] In 1937 the air force only received a third of the steel it required to meet its production targets. In October 1938, however, Göring announced a fivefold increase in the size of the air force to a size so enormous that it would have required the import of 85 per cent of known world production of aircraft fuel to keep it going. Nearly 20,000 front and reserve aircraft were to be ready for action at the beginning of the coming war in late 1941 or early 1942. In the event, when war actually did break out, the air force had just 4,000 aircraft ready for action. This was an impressive number, especially when compared to the situation six years before, but it was far below the target envisaged by Göring.[103]

By 1939, shortages of raw materials were leading to grotesque consequences for the everyday life of ordinary Germans. From 1937 onwards, the regime began to encourage the collection of scrap metal in order to feed the insatiable demands of the iron and steel industry. It became people's patriotic duty to surrender any old or unused metal objects to the authorities. A Reich Commissioner, Wilhelm Ziegler, was appointed to organize the collection and, increasingly, the forced requisition of scrap. In 1938 he ordered the removal of all metal garden fences throughout the Reich. Uniformed brownshirts forcibly uprooted iron railings around factories, churches, cemeteries and parks. Iron lampposts were replaced by wooden ones. Iron railings around family graves were torn down by gangs of stormtroopers, who also combed factories and workplaces for wire, tubing and other disused metal objects. Boys from the Hitler Youth searched people's cellars and attics for discarded tin plates, disused metal radiators, old keys and the like. Everywhere, local committees were formed to organize the hunt for scrap. Metal for non-military purposes was strictly rationed, and heavy fines were meted out to building contractors who installed central heating with metal piping in their houses instead of the more old-fashioned tiled stoves. When a toilet was put into a house, its outlet pipes had to be made of clay rather than iron. Homeowners and town councils tried to replace confiscated iron lampposts and railings with wooden ones, but there was a shortage of wood as well, also leading to a shortage of paper. Building projects were instructed to cut back their use of wood by 20 per cent, while country-dwellers were told to burn peat instead of usable wood. Coal for domestic use was rationed. Official limits were placed on the use of gold by watchmakers. A black market began to grow up in metal spare parts for washing machines and other domestic appliances. There were instances of copper and other metals being stolen and sold to arms manufacturers, who were by now so desperate that they did not ask too many questions about where it all came from.[104]

IV

In addition to shortages of raw materials, the rearmament programme also created bottlenecks in the labour supply that became steadily tighter as time went on. As coal, iron and steel production, engineering, manufacturing, armaments and munitions factories sucked in all the available skilled and semi-skilled labour, the regime was forced to rethink its attitude towards women's work. Women might not be able to work in heavy industry, but surely they would be able to take over more jobs in clerical work, and in assembly-lines in modern sectors of the economy like chemicals and electrotechnics and more generally in consumer goods production. Already in a series of decrees in 1936–7, the government withdrew the requirement that a woman receiving a marriage loan would have to give up her job and not take another one. This led to an immediate increase in the number of applications for loans, as might have been expected, and heralded a general reorientation of policy towards women's work across the board. Only in one area, largely by chance, did restrictions become tighter: Following a conference in the Reich Justice Ministry in August 1936, at which participants raised among other things the issue of women in the judicial system, Martin Bormann asked Hitler whether women should be allowed to practise as lawyers. Hitler's response was comprehensively negative: women, he told Bormann, could not become judges or lawyers; if they were legally qualified, then jobs should be found for them in the civil service.[105] Apart from this area, however, women were returning to employment in larger numbers already. The number of women physicians increased from 2,814, or 6 per cent of the profession, in 1934, to 3,650, or 7 per cent of the profession, in early 1939, by which time 42 per cent of them were married. More significantly, women workers in industry grew in number from 1,205,000 in 1933 to 1,846,000 in 1938. The growing labour shortage in the countryside also led to an increased use of female family labour on the farms. Aware of the need to provide welfare and other kinds of support particularly for married women workers with children, the German Labour Front, the Nazi successor to the old trade unions, put increasing pressure on employers to provide day-nurseries for the young children of female workers and to regulate hours and conditions of women workers so that their health would not suffer.[106]

In February 1938 the Four-Year Plan organization announced that all women under twenty-five who wanted to work in industry or the service sector had first to complete a year of duty on a farm (or in domestic work for married women workers). Extended ten months later, the scheme mobilized 66,400 young women by July 1938, and another 217,000 by July 1939. This was far more successful than the voluntary labour service promoted by the various Nazi women's organizations with much the same purpose; by 1939 there were only just over 36,000 young women working, mainly on farms, as part of these programmes.[107] One young woman who took part in such a scheme was the League of German Girls activist Melita Maschmann, who did her labour service in rural East Prussia. Here she encountered a degree of poverty and backwardness wholly alien to her comfortable background in the upper middle class of Berlin. Long hours of hard physical work were relieved only by short periods of sport, political instruction or singing. Nevertheless, despite all the hardships, as a committed member of the League of German Girls, she found the experience uplifting, even inspiring. She later confessed:

Our camp community was a model in miniature of what I imagined the National Community to be. It was a completely successful model. Never before or since have I known such a good community, even where the composition was more homogeneous in every respect. Amongst us there were peasant girls, students, factory girls, hairdressers, schoolgirls, office workers and so on . . . The knowledge that this model of a National Community had afforded me such intense happiness gave birth to an optimism to which I clung obstinately until 1945. Upheld by this experience, I believed, despite all the evidence to the contrary, that the pattern of our camp would one day be magnified on an infinite scale – if not in the next then in future generations.[108]

For farmers themselves, untrained city girls were often of little use, however. Moreover, in the economy as a whole, two-thirds of married women were still not registered as employed on the eve of the war in 1939. If they did work, it was often as unregistered, part-time cleaners or family assistants, above all in the countryside.[109]

By contrast, more than 90 per cent of unmarried adult women had jobs in 1939. Yet the increase since 1933 in the number of female industrial workers had not kept pace with the corresponding increase in the number of male industrial workers: between 1933 and 1939 the percentage of women working in industry actually fell, from just over 29 per cent to just over 25. The Labour Front's attempts to persuade firms to provide facilities for working mothers had largely run into the sands. The mobilization of the potential female labour force also ran up against the continuing insistence of the regime and its leaders that women's most important role was to bear and bring up children for the Reich. Marriage loans, with their continuing bonuses for every child born, and the general recovery of male employment in the course of rearmament made it seem unnecessary for mothers to endure the hardships of factory work while bringing up a family. Towards the end of 1937, indeed, the government even attempted to make girls leaving school get training in domestic science and childcare before they entered the labour market. In reality, neither working men, nor their womenfolk, nor the regime itself really thought it appropriate for women to work in heavy industry, iron and steel or other arms-related industries in what were generally agreed to be men's jobs. Despite pressure from the armed forces for the mobilization of what one senior labour official described in June 1939 as a huge potential labour supply of some 3.5 million women currently without paid employment, the contradiction between economic interest and ideological belief ensured that nothing was done to draft women into war production before 1939.[110]

Behind the scenes, too, Hitler and the leading Nazis were concerned about another potential problem. Believing, as they did, that Germany had lost the First World War on the home front, not in the trenches, they were almost obsessively concerned to avoid what they thought of as a repetition of the poverty, privation and hardship suffered between 1914 and 1918 by the families of serving soldiers at home. Knowledge of this, they thought, had demoralized the troops and made the population in general susceptible to the blandishments of subversives and revolutionaries. The spectre of 1918 haunted all the Nazis' preparations for war in the late 1930s. Drafting women into factory work would have given it concrete shape. With the outbreak of a new war, the men called up to fight would fight harder if they knew their wives were not having to slave long hours on assembly-lines producing munitions, but were instead being cared for, together with their children, by the Third Reich.[111] All this meant that the regime had to look elsewhere for labour as rearmament began to intensify demand for particular kinds of workers from 1936 onwards. This meant above all foreign labour. Recruitment and virtually every other aspect of the control of workers from other countries had already been centralized under the Labour Ministry in 1933, building on previous laws and regulations that gave German workers priority and reduced foreign workers to the status of second-class citizens. Up to the summer of 1938 foreign workers were mostly unskilled and were recruited to alleviate the desperate shortage of labour on farms and to work on construction sites. Seasonal Polish workers, along with Italians, made up the bulk of this workforce. Between 1936/7 and 1938/9 the number of foreign workers increased from 274,000 to 435,000. Yet foreign workers were a drain on the economy because they sent much-needed hard currency back home. Thus their numbers had to be kept in check unless some means could be found of stopping them damaging Germany's balance of payments. By 1938–9, a solution was beginning to appear, predicated, as so much else in the economy, on foreign conquest through war. Foreign workers would be recruited as forced labour, from prisoners of war and other groups in countries like Poland and Czechoslovakia once the Germans had taken control of them. And they would be subject to a particularly harsh police regime that would ensure they would do as they were told. Regulations along these lines were already introduced in August 1938 and toughened up in June 1939. They were to reach draconian extremes during the war.[112]

Meanwhile, however, all these measures did little to alleviate the immediate problems they were intended to address. The difficulties which the German economy was experiencing in 1938–9 were a testimony to the fundamental contradictions inherent in the Four-Year Plan. Its basic aim was to render Germany self-sufficient in foodstuffs and raw materials in preparation for a lengthy war along the lines of 1914–18, a precedent that was never far from the forefront of Hitler's mind. A general European war, focused on the invasion of the East but encompassing the traditional enemy, France, and perhaps Great Britain as well, was expected to begin some time in the early 1940s. Yet by accelerating the pace of rearmament, the Plan created tensions and bottlenecks that could only be resolved by bringing the date of military action forward in order to obtain fresh supplies of raw materials and foodstuffs from conquered countries such as Austria and Czechoslovakia. This meant in turn that a general war might break out when Germany was less than fully prepared for it. The war that came would have to be swift and decisive because the economy was clearly in no shape to sustain a prolonged conflict in 1938–9.[113] This solution was already becoming clear to Hitler in 1937, when, at the meeting recorded by Friedrich Hossbach, he told his military chiefs that the forthcoming 'descent upon the Czechs' would have to be carried out 'with lightning speed'.[114] The state of preparedness of the economy simply would not allow for a long-drawn-out conflict. The concept of the 'lightning war', the *Blitzkrieg*, was born. Yet neither economic planning, nor military technology and arms production, was doing anything to help prepare for putting it into effect.

V

The Four-Year Plan marked a massive escalation of state intervention in the economy. The priorities were being set by the regime, not by industry, and mechanisms were being put in place to make sure that business fulfilled them whatever the consequences to itself. The senior staff of the Plan were all hard-line National Socialists, from Göring at the top through the Regional Leaders Walter Köhler and Adolf Wagner, the 'old fighter' Wilhelm Keppler and others, who had largely displaced the traditionalist economic bureaucrats who had worked with Schacht. At the same time, however, given the focus of the Plan on synthetic fuel and synthetic rubber, as well as chemical fertilizers for agriculture and synthetic fibres for clothing and uniforms, it was not surprising that senior managers of I.G. Farben, the mammoth firm that was being commissioned to manufacture these products, played a key role in the Plan's administration. Most prominent amongst them was one of the firm's directors, Carl Krauch, in charge of research and development under the Plan, but there were others too, notably Johannes Eckell, head of the chemical division. Clearly these men were there above all for their expertise; but they also took on these jobs not least in the interests of their own company. This has led some historians to describe the Four-Year Plan as an 'I.G. Farben Plan' and to ascribe a good deal of the impetus behind the armaments and autarky programmes to the profit-making greed of big business. After the war, indeed, twenty-three leading figures in the firm were put on trial at Nuremberg for conspiring to prepare and launch a war. Although they were in fact acquitted of this charge, a large literature, not all of it Marxist, ascribed to I.G. Farben in particular and German big business in general a large part of the responsibility in driving Europe and the world to war in 1933–9.[115] More generally, a huge mass of Marxist and neo-Marxist writing both at the time and subsequently, particularly in the 1950s and 1960s, sought to present the economic and ultimately too the foreign and military policy of the Third Reich as driven by capitalist interests.[116]

Yet already in the 1960s, some Marxist historians were beginning to argue that in Nazi Germany at least, the economy was subjected to a 'primacy of politics' in which the key parameters were set by ideology rather than by capitalist self-interest.[117] The truth is, the economic system of the Third Reich defied easy categorization. To some extent its sheer irrationality undermines any attempt to portray it as a system at all. Superficially, the Four-Year Plan in Germany was more than reminiscent of Stalin's Five-Year Plan in the Soviet Union. But Nazi economic planning was clearly not designed to further the interests of the working class, as its Soviet counterpart was, at least officially. While Soviet planning under Stalin more or less eliminated free markets and free enterprise, Nazi planning left business intact, from great firms like I.G. Farben all the way down to small retailers and backstreet artisanal workshops. On the other hand, Nazi rhetoric, especially in the 1920s, had a strongly anti-capitalist flavour, so it is not surprising that business only swung round to support the Party after Hitler became Chancellor in January 1933. The destruction of the labour movement in the following months convinced many businessmen that they were right to back the new regime. But as time went on, businessmen found that the regime had its own objectives that increasingly diverged from their own. Chief of these was the ever more frenetic drive to rearm and prepare for war. Initially, business was happy to accommodate itself to this objective, which brought it renewed and then increased orders. Even consumer goods producers benefited from the armaments-driven economic recovery. But within a few years, as the regime's demands began to outstrip German industry's capacity to fulfil them, industrialists' doubts began to grow.[118]

Few industrialists' reactions to this process were as sharp as those of the steel boss Fritz Thyssen, whose support of the Nazi Party before 1933 was as extreme as the extent of his disillusion with the movement six years later. In 1939 Thyssen bitterly condemned the state's direction of the economy and prophesied that the Nazis would soon start shooting industrialists who did not fulfil the conditions prescribed by the Four-Year Plan, just as their equivalents were shot in Soviet Russia. He fled abroad after the outbreak of the war, his property was confiscated by the Gestapo, and he was subsequently arrested in France and put into a concentration camp.[119] His alarm at the state's growing interference in the economy was shared by many others, however. At the centre of their concerns was the Four-Year Plan. In his attempt to increase supplies of domestic raw materials, Göring had first of all berated industrialists for their egotism in exporting their products for profit instead of using them to further German rearmament, then taken matters into his own hands, nationalizing private deposits of iron ore, taking over control of all privately owned steelworks and setting up a new company, known as the Hermann Göring Works.

Founded in July 1937, this state-owned and state-run enterprise, based at Salzgitter, was designed to produce and process low-grade German iron ore at an uneconomic price, something private industry had been unwilling to do. The Hermann Göring Works would use the state's money to pay over the odds for coking coal and other raw materials, and for labour too, forcing private firms to compete. The effect would be to push up the price of German iron and steel and make it more difficult to export; yet exports at this time were where the biggest profits lay. Worse still, the Hermann Göring Works soon began taking over small firms in the same area, then in April 1938 the Rheinmetall-Borsig armaments company. The nationalization of the large Thyssen concern was in fact part of a wider process in which Göring was getting industry into line to serve the interests of autarky and rearmament. Heavy industrialists in firms such as the United Steelworks, backed behind the scenes by Schacht while he was still in office, objected furiously to this increase in state ownership and control and to state-subsidized competition with their own enterprises. They began intriguing against the Four-Year Plan and talking about ways of getting state controls reduced. Göring had their secret meetings bugged and their telephone conversations tapped and even summoned the two leading conspirators to his office to play back recordings of their conversations. Faced with such pressure, and the more than implicit threat of arrest and consignment to a concentration camp, the industrialists, intimidated, disillusioned and divided, caved in.[120]

Typical of such men in many respects was the steel magnate and arms manufacturer Gustav Krupp von Bohlen und Halbach, who had presided over the Krupp firm in the company town of Essen, in the Ruhr, since marrying into the family in 1906. The Krupps had a long and close association with the Prussian state, which they supplied with arms. Kaiser Wilhelm II himself had given formal permission to Gustav to add the Krupp name to his own on his marriage to the family heiress Bertha. From that point on, Gustav, previously a career diplomat (although from an industrial family), regarded the preservation of the firm as his principal task in life. Stiff, formal, cold and unbending, he worked long hours to further the company's interests, and was rewarded by huge armaments orders which ensured that by 1917, 85 per cent of Krupp's output consisted of war-related products. Although not active in politics, Gustav was, like most industrialists, a conservative nationalist; Alfred Hugenberg was the chairman of the company's supervisory board from 1909 on, and the two men shared many of the same views. A paternalist who supplied his workers with housing, welfare and other benefits in return for their agreement not to join trade unions or engage in political activity, Gustav thought the state should behave in much the same way, looking after the masses so long as it retained their loyalty. This became more difficult for the firm during the postwar inflation and even more so during the French occupation of 1923, during which Gustav was imprisoned for seven months for allegedly encouraging German resistance. However, the company survived, reorienting itself successfully towards peacetime production until it was hit by the world economic crisis in 1929. By 1933 its output of steel and coal had virtually halved since 1927, and its workforce at Essen had been reduced from 49,000 to little over 28,000.[121]

These events did not turn Gustav Krupp into a supporter of Nazism. On the contrary, he regarded its demagogy with considerable distaste, preferring to lend his support to the radical-conservative government of Franz von Papen. Krupp's importance was enhanced by his position as head of the Reich Association of German Industry, the national organization of employers, on behalf of whom he lobbied against the idea of autarky and promoted the idea of a strong state which would repress the unions, cut welfare expenditure, and provide the political stability necessary for a recovery of the economy. Like many others, he did not at first see Hitler's appointment as Reich Chancellor on 30 January 1933 as much more than the creation of yet another short-lived Weimar government. In the subsequent election campaign he gave funds to Papen and the German People's Party in the forlorn hope of a conservative victory. Under pressure from Thyssen and other supporters of the new regime, he was forced to agree to the 'co-ordination' of the Reich Association. When Paul Silverberg, a Cologne industrialist and one of the Association's most prominent figures, was deprived of his positions in 1933 and forced into exile because he was Jewish, Krupp made a point of going to visit him in his new Swiss home. He did not join the Nazi Party in its first years of rule, and although he became director of the 'Adolf-Hitler Donation from the German Economy', which regularly supplied the Nazi Party with large sums of money from June 1933 onwards, this was not least undertaken in order to fend off the numerous and rapacious demands made to industrialists and employers for *ad hoc* donations by Regional Leaders, brownshirt gangs and local Party officials. A visitor who met Krupp in Berlin towards the end of 1934 found him in despair at the arbitrary nature of Party rule. 'Believe me', he said, 'we are worse off here than the natives in Timbuctoo.'[122]

Nevertheless, Krupp on balance was not dissatisfied with the Third Reich in the early years of its rule. He was reassured by the presence in government of men like Papen and Schacht, the continuing domination of the armed forces by officers like Blomberg and Fritsch, the relatively orthodox financial policies pursued by the Economics Ministry, and above all the swelling order books that resulted in a virtual doubling of Krupp's profits by 1935 and an increase in the workforce at Essen from 26,360 at the beginning of October 1932 to 51,801 two years later. Before long, however, Krupp began to find that the new regime did not allow his company the freedom of action he wanted for it. An important part of the firm's growth lay in exports, including major arms contracts in Turkey and Latin America, and Krupp was sufficiently concerned about the regime's growing drive for autarky to speak out against it in public in 1935. He continued to maintain a mixed portfolio of products, in which armaments were only part of a wider whole. From 1937 he began to become alarmed at the Four-Year Plan's downgrading of basic heavy industry, its hostility to international trade and its promotion of state ownership, above all in the Reich Works. The growth in the firm's profits had slowed down considerably. The independence Krupp had sought for his business had become severely restricted by the regime's manic concentration on preparations for a European war, in which the Krupp firm's name marked it out for a significant part. The government provided it with interest-free loans to expand capacity, but only at the price of putting the state in charge of determining what it was used for. Things had not turned out at all as Krupp had hoped, and already in 1937 he was beginning to put his business in the hands of younger men who, he hoped, would press his company's interests more aggressively than he himself now felt able to do. In 1941 he suffered the first of a series of strokes that forced him to relinquish his part in the business altogether. Incapacitated, he lived on until 1950, largely oblivious of what was going on around him.[123]

Ostensibly, a concern like I.G. Farben, whose products were at the centre of the regime's plans for an autarkic economy, was better placed to profit from the Third Reich. From 1933 onwards its influence on the formation and implementation of government economic policy in this area grew rapidly. The concern began preparing for war as early as 5 September 1935, when it established an Army Liaison Office to co-ordinate preparation for a war economy. Yet the combine's role should not be exaggerated, for its share of expenditure under the Plan amounted in all to no more than a quarter, and the share of the chemical industry in the German economy overall did not markedly increase under the Third Reich. Metal processing, iron, steel and mining were always more central to the rearmament programme. At the same time, I.G. Farben was forced to reorient its own production increasingly to meet the military demands of the regime. Complex and seemingly interminable negotiations over the financial conditions under which the combine would produce the much-desired buna (synthetic rubber) illustrated only too clearly the gulf between the primacy business placed on profits and the disregard the Four-Year Plan had for anything except accelerating rearmament and the drive towards autarky. I.G. Farben dragged its feet in the process because of its concern to minimize costs. By the autumn of 1939, national output of buna was only just in excess of two-thirds of the targeted 30,000 tons, while production and stockpiles of rubber in September 1939 were only sufficient for two months of warfare.[124] Such caution ensured that the giant combine did well out of the Four-Year Plan, though growth rates were still slower than they had been in the initial years of recovery. From 1933 to 1936, net profits grew by 91 per cent, and between 1936 and 1939 by another 71 per cent. The five most important branches of the combine under the Plan – fuel oil, metal, rubber, plastics and nitrogen for explosives – increased their share in I.G. Farben's turnover from 28 per cent in 1936 to almost 33 per cent in 1939; during this period they accounted for more than 40 per cent of the combine's sales. But the contribution made to the total turnover of I.G. Farben by product lines fostered by the Four-Year Plan only grew from 28.4 per cent in 1936 to 32.4 per cent in 1939, and the combine in effect had to pay for the development of these products itself. Thus neither was the Plan mainly dependent on I.G. Farben, nor I.G. Farben on the Plan.[125]

Big business undoubtedly benefited from rearmament and more generally from the economic recovery that occurred, partly in the natural form of the economic upswing that had already begun before the Nazis came to power, and then increasingly from the knock-on effects of rearmament for the rest of the economy. The financial policies pursued by Schacht were bold and ingenious but in the end financially relatively orthodox. By 1938 they had run their course, and the regime, running up against the limits imposed on rearmament by the profit motive that was always the central feature of free enterprise, began to take matters into its own hands. Hitler's unrelenting drive to rearm had already brought vastly increased interference by the regime in the economy with the Four-Year Plan. By 1938 the Nazi Party and various affiliated organizations such as the Labour Front, under Hitler's direction, were creating huge economic enterprises that aimed to bypass conventional capitalist operations in the pursuit of the regime's power-political goals. The automobile industry was to be outflanked by the Volkswagen company; iron and steel by the Hermann Göring Works. A rapidly swelling flood of laws and regulations aimed at setting limits on prices, forcing the rationalization of businesses, diverting investment into war-related branches, imposing production quotas, steering foreign trade, and much more.

Promises made in the Party programme and subsequently to nationalize the banks and stock exchanges of Germany had quietly been forgotten as the realities of the financial world became clear to Hitler and his lieutenants. They needed money, and banks were needed to supply it.[126] Nevertheless, here too the regime gradually imposed tighter and more comprehensive controls on financial institutions in order to steer capital into the rearmament programme. By 1939 a series of laws on credit, mortages, loans and banks had ensured that freedom to invest in anything apart from rearmament had been severely curbed.[127] Businessmen spent increasing amounts of time dealing with the mass of regulations and requirements imposed on them by the state. These involved increasingly detailed interference in production and trade. On 2 March 1939, for instance, Colonel von Schell, Plenipotentiary for the Automobile Industry, issued a series of orders restricting the number of different models that could be manufactured. Thus the production of spare parts could be rationalized and made less expensive, and military vehicles could be repaired more quickly and efficiently. Instead of 113 different kinds of truck and van, for example, only nineteen were allowed to be manufactured in future, and by specifically nominated companies. 'Private property has remained in industry, to be sure,' concluded a critical observer, but very little initiative remained 'for entrepreneurial initiative, which is being pushed back by the power of the state in giving orders.'[128] No wonder that some thought that the socialism in National Socialism was coming to the fore once more.

ARYANIZING THE ECONOMY

I

'Socialism' in the Nazis' ideology had involved a real element of hostility to big business in the early 1920s, usually mixed with a strong dose of antisemitism. In the last years of the Weimar Republic, Hitler had done his best to play this down. What was left was, predictably, a continuing hatred of Jews' role in the German economy, which the Nazis exaggerated for their own purposes. The economic history of the Third Reich is indeed inseparable from the history of the regime's expropriation of the Jews, a vast campaign of plunder with few parallels in modern history. In keeping with those ideological imperatives, one of the prime targets of Nazi propaganda before 1933 had been the department store (*Warenhaus*), where since the late nineteenth century people had been able to go to buy cheap, mass-produced goods of all kinds. Many of the founders of such stores were Jewish, reflecting perhaps the existing concentration of Jews in drapery and similar branches of the retailing trade.

The most famous of these enterprises had been founded by members of the Wertheim family after 1875, when Ida and Abraham Wertheim opened a small shop in Stralsund selling clothes and manufactured goods. Soon their five sons joined them, and introduced a new system of retailing based on high turnover, low profit margins, fixed prices for goods, a broad selection of merchandise, a right to return or exchange goods and payment strictly in cash. The firm grew quickly, and in 1893–4 it constructed a large new building on the Oranienstrasse in the Berlin district of Kreuzberg, followed by three more stores in the capital. Wertheim offered a new concept of shopping, in bright, airy and well-designed stores with helpful shop assistants and a mixture of cheap and luxury goods to encourage impulse buying. It also displayed an advanced attitude towards labour relations and employee welfare; the company was the first in Germany, for example, to make Sunday a compulsory rest day for all those who worked for it. The Wertheims were not the only Jewish family to found a chain of department stores; in 1882, for instance, Hermann Tietz and his nephew Oscar founded a small shop in Gera, on similar principles. This too flourished, and by 1930 the Tietzes owned fifty-eight department stores, including the famous KaDeWe (*Kaufhaus des Westens*, or Department Store of the West) in Berlin. Compared to the annual sales of the Tietz stores, which stood at 490 million Reichsmarks in 1928, and their massive workforce of more than 31,450 employees, Wertheim by this stage, with a mere seven stores and 10,450 employees and sales of 128 million Reichsmarks, was a relatively modest enterprise.[129]

Despite their popularity, these department stores accounted for less than 5 per cent of total retail sales in Germany up to the late 1920s.[130] Anti-semitic attacks on them remained muted before 1914, even among small retailers' associations.[131] This situation changed with the economic problems of the early Weimar Years. Point 16 of the Nazi Party programme appealed directly to small shopkeepers in 1920 when it demanded the 'immediate nationalization of the big department stores and their renting out at low prices to small businessmen'.[132] In 1932, a local election pamphlet in Lower Saxony urged retailers and small tradesmen to join the Party to oppose the opening of new branches of 'the vampire business' of Woolworth's, which would supposedly ruin them in the name of 'finance capital'.[133] In March 1933 stormtroopers broke into a branch of Woolworth's in Gotha and trashed the entire store; violent attacks were launched on a number of department stores irrespective of their ownership. In Braunschweig the restaurant in a local department store was shot to pieces by brownshirts armed with pistols. Less dramatically, there were many demands in the first months of the Third Reich to close down the department stores or tax them out of existence. But the Ministry of Economics and the Nazi leadership quickly realized that closing down enterprises that employed so many scores of thousands of people would seriously damage the 'battle for work'. Hess stepped in to protect the department stores, and the nationwide boycott of Jewish-owned shops on 1 April 1933 had no impact beyond the day itself.[134]

Nevertheless, the department stores soon began to experience discrimination in less obvious ways. When the Ministry of Finance began to issue marriage loans from the summer of 1933 onwards, for instance, the purchase coupons through which the loans were made were not allowed to be redeemed in department stores, whether or not they were Jewish-owned, or in Jewish businesses of any kind. One official report estimated that those shops and businesses affected lost at least 135 million Reichsmarks in sales in 1934. Department stores, irrespective of their ownership, and Jewish businesses of all kinds were also banned from advertising in the press from the middle of 1933 onwards. Coming on top of a decline in sales that had begun already with the onset of the Depression in 1933, this got them into serious difficulties. Sales figures for the Hermann Tietz stores fell by up to 41 per cent in 1933. The company was forced to seek a loan of 14 million Reichsmarks from the banks. Brokered by Economics Minister Schmitt, who wanted to avoid a spectacular bankruptcy involving the loss of 14,000 jobs, serious damage to suppliers and financial problems for the banks, the loan was made conditional on the 'Aryanization' of the management, or in other words the removal of Jewish owners, board members and other senior officials. The remaining Tietz brothers were forced out in 1934 after a lengthy audit, with a compensation of 1.2 million Reichsmarks. Covering his back, Schmitt made sure to obtain Hitler's approval for these arrangements. From now on the stores were known under the name *Hertie*, which ingeniously kept the link to their founder's name while at the same time advertising to everyone that the business had been placed on a new footing; Leonard Tietz's stores were renamed with the neutral-sounding title of *Kaufhof*, or 'shopping court'.[135]

These events prompted the remaining members of the Wertheim family to take action to preserve their own interests. A family friend, the banker Emil Georg von Stauss, who knew Hitler and Göring personally and supported the Nazi Party in various ways, was brought onto the board. His protection ensured that attempts by stormtroopers to close down the Wertheim store in Breslau were frustrated. But Nazi Party activists, especially those connected with its trade union branch, the Factory Cell Organization, barred Georg Wertheim from going into his own stores. He never ventured into one after 1934 and stopped taking part in meetings of the company's supervisory board. To avoid a repetition of the

problems that had assailed the Tietz family, he transferred his shares
and some of his late brother's to his wife Ursula, who was not Jewish.
She now became the majority shareholder. However, this did not get the
firm out of difficulties. As Hertie and other chains successfully neutralized the Nazi assault on department stores by making it clear that
they were not Jewish-owned, the hostility of both local Nazis and the
central government and Party organizations was directed more precisely
towards the chains, like Wertheim, that still were. The Propaganda
Ministry ordered all Wertheim's book departments to be closed early in
1936 following a denunciation by a former employee in Breslau, though
the firm had already withdrawn at least 2,500 banned books from its
shelves. Stauss managed to reverse the order, though only at the price of
a donation of 24,000 Reichsmarks from the firm to the German Schiller
Foundation. Complaining about such pressures in an interview with
the Minister of Economics, Georg Wertheim and his son were told by
Schacht: 'You have to howl with the wolves.'[136]

The howling increased noticeably in 1936. Wertheim's sales had in
fact grown while those of its rivals had fallen. This may have been
because the removal of Jewish managers and employees from rival chains
had led to the appointment of inexperienced personnel in their stead, or
because only Wertheim had retained its well-known and trusted image,
name and style intact. Nevertheless, Stauss, who now held Ursula
Wertheim's shares in trust while she spent her income on expensive
holidays, first forced the smaller family shareholders to transfer their
shares to non-Jewish shareholders at well below their value, then made
it clear to Georg and Ursula Wertheim that Hess's office demanded that
they must divorce if she was to be allowed to keep her shares; they did
so in 1938. Charged by Hitler with buying land in Berlin on which the
new Reich Chancellery was to be built, Stauss selected a site occupied
by a number of properties owned by Wertheim, had the banks undervalue
them to save money, then pressured Wertheim into selling them to pay
off some of the debts that creditor banks were now calling in. By 1938
there were no more Jewish shareholders, both Jewish managers had been
forced out, and the last thirty-four Jewish employees had been fired;
there is no evidence that they received any severance pay, in contrast to
their colleagues in the other chains. In consultation with the Ministry of
Economics, Stauss agreed to change the stores' name from Wertheim to

AWAG. This was a similar though less obvious compromise to the renaming agreed on for Tietz. Most people thought the new name was an acronym for A. Wertheim AG (*Albrecht Wertheim Aktien-Gesellschaft*, or Albrecht Wertheim Company). But it actually stood for *Allgemeine Warenhaus Aktien-Gesellschaft*, or General Department Store Company, thus severing it from any association with the family at all. Georg Wertheim, now over eighty years old and nearly blind, died on 31 December 1939. A year later, his widow married Arthur Lindgens, a non-Jewish member of the supervisory board of the new company.[137]

II

The fate of the department stores illustrated in microcosm how the Nazi Party's priorities had changed since 1920. Starting off with a pronounced anti-capitalist message, they had first soft-pedalled it under the influence of economic necessity, then substituted for it a determined drive to remove the Jews from the German economy. The department stores themselves did not disappear; indeed, the campaign against Jewish owners opened up new opportunities for non-Jewish companies to expand their operations. If, as the Nazis claimed, the country's economic ills in the 1920s and early 1930s had originated with the Jews, then would they not be solved by, among other things, getting rid of the Jewish economic influence on business rather than by attacking business itself? The boycott of 1 April 1933 had already advertised the Party's intentions in this respect. Although the boycott itself had met with relatively little public support, local Party groups continued to harass and attack Jewish shops and businesses, as the example of the Wertheim store in Breslau indicated. Stormtroopers continued to paint slogans on the display windows of Jewish-owned shops, to discourage people from patronizing such establishments, or to pressure local authorities into placing their orders elsewhere. Alarmed at the economic effects of such actions, the government and the Party issued a series of official warnings. Hitler himself issued a declaration at the beginning of October 1933 expressly permitting civil servants to buy goods in Jewish-owned shops and department stores. Yet in 1933's Christmas shopping season, gangs of stormtroopers were again standing outside Jewish-owned shops in many localities with placards proclaiming anyone who went inside to be a traitor to the German race. Increasing numbers of local markets barred Jewish traders, no Jewish firms were permitted to advertise any more, local authorities broke off all business relations with Jewish-owned companies, and there were further, quite widespread boycott actions again in the spring of 1934. Violence often accompanied such events, ranging from the smashing of Jewish shop windows to a bomb attack on the synagogue in Ahaus, Westphalia. It culminated in a mass demonstration of up to 1,500 inhabitants of the town of Gunzenhausen, in Franconia – a town whose entire population numbered no more than 5,600. Inflamed by a vehemently antisemitic speech from a local Nazi leader, the demonstrators broke into the houses and flats of Jews in the town, and dragged thirty-five people off to the local prison, where one was subsequently found hanged.[138]

German consumers gave little support to boycott actions. Under threat of reprisals if they patronized Jewish shops in their own small town, people in Falkenstein, noted the diarist Victor Klemperer in June 1934, travelled to nearby Auerbach to shop in a Jewish establishment there, where they would not be recognized; the inhabitants of Auerbach in turn visited the Jewish shop in Falkenstein.[139] Even Hermann Göring was seen as late as 1936 paying a lengthy visit to Bernheimer's carpet store in Munich, which ended with the purchase of two carpets for the impressive sum of 36,000 Reichsmarks. The February sales at Sally Eichengrün's textile house in Munich in the same year were said by the local police to be attracting queues of customers. Both enterprises were Jewish-owned. The following year, the Security Service of the SS complained that – especially in Catholic areas – people were still ignoring the Party's exhortations not to buy from Jewish businesses.[140] Nevertheless, Party activists were not deterred. Many of them were motivated by the personal desire to get rid of business rivals at a time when the consumer economy was in the doldrums.[141] Violent boycott campaigns continued throughout 1934 and reached a new high point in the Christmas shopping season. In November, for example, the district Party leadership of Baden-Baden sent the following threatening letter to a Jewish-owned toyshop, informing the owner:

That we will in no way tolerate you, as a non-Aryan toyshop, selling models of SA and SS men. People are already upset by this and complaining to us about it. So we urgently request you to take these SA and SS model figures out of your Jew-shop, otherwise we will not be in any position to guarantee public order and tranquillity.[142]

On 23 and 24 December 1934, Party members in civilian clothing blocked the entrances to Jewish-owned shops and department stores in Frankfurt am Main, and shouted insults at customers, beating up those who persisted in trying to go in. They smashed the shop windows, and when police arrived to arrest them, they became so threatening that the officers had to draw their weapons.[143] This campaign proved the prelude to a much wider wave of economic terror, in which local Party organizations threatened to withdraw welfare payments from anyone seen entering a Jewish-owned shop. Civil servants and municipal employees in many localities were ordered to stay clear of such establishments. Such actions were particularly common in small-town Pomerania, Hesse and Central Franconia. In Marburg a large group of students entered a Jewish-owned shoe shop, drove out the customers and looted or destroyed the contents. In Büdingen almost all the shop windows of Jewish-owned retailers were smashed in the night of 18–19 April 1935. Similar incidents took place elsewhere. As these actions died down, a new wave of antisemitic attacks on Jewish-owned shops rolled across the country in the summer of 1935, including a total boycott in the centre of Munich on 25 May, carried out mainly by SS men in civilian clothes, some of whom burst into the shops and beat up the assistants. The action only came to an end after the boycotteers tried to storm a police station to release one of their number who had been arrested.[144]

The reaction of government ministers to these actions was mixed. Foreign Minister von Neurath for example told his colleagues that the antisemitic incidents would have no effect on foreign opinion; stopping them was not going to lead to any improvement in Germany's international position. On the other hand, Economics Minister Hjalmar Schacht declared himself extremely worried about their effect on the economy, including economic relations with other countries. Indeed, when the Party organization in the town of Arnswalde, in Brandenburg, put up a picture of the wife of the local branch manager of the

Reichsbank in a display cabinet as a 'traitor' because she had been seen shopping at a Jewish-owned establishment, Schacht closed the branch in protest. On 18 August 1935 he spoke out in a public address held in Königsberg. 'Lord', he said, 'preserve me from my friends. That is,' he went on, 'from the people who heroically daub shop windows under cover of darkness, branding every German who buys goods in a Jewish shop as a traitor to the people . . .' Nevertheless, Schacht, despite his later claims to the contrary, was not opposed in principle to driving the Jews out of economic life. He believed, as he explained to a group of ministers and senior officials two days later, 'that letting this lawlessness take its course among other things puts a question mark under rearmament. His remarks', the minutes of the meeting reported, 'culminated in the statement that the programme of the NSDAP must be carried out, but only on the basis of legal decrees.' Schacht agreed with the Gestapo and Party representatives that the way forward lay in an orderly, legal restriction of the ability of Jews to engage in business, the public marking of Jewish shops as such, and the exclusion of Jewish businesses from public contracts.[145] Indeed, Schacht shared in full measure the antisemitic prejudices of many bourgeois Germans, remarking as late as 1953 that Jews had brought an 'alien spirit' into German culture in the Weimar Republic, and had been too prominent in many areas of public life.[146] He co-operated fully in the dismissal of Jewish officials from the Reichsbank under the so-called Law for the Re-establishment of a Professional Civil Service and publicly defended the antisemitic laws passed by the regime in the years 1933 and 1935; it was only open violence that he rejected.[147]

Yet there were less violent means of putting pressure on Jewish firms, and these were often more effective. The huge size of Nazi organizations like the SA, the Labour Front or indeed the Party itself gave them a great deal of economic power through the placing of bulk orders for constructions, furnishings, flags, uniforms and supplies of all kinds. They used these from the outset to discriminate against Jewish-owned businesses. The shoe industry was a case in point. Under the Third Reich, not surprisingly, it profited enormously from a tremendous rise in demand for jackboots. But these orders went of course to non-Jewish companies. Jewish-owned firms, however, dominated the industry, so that there was an immediate pressure on them to Aryanize. Almost as soon as Hitler became Reich Chancellor, for example, a campaign began against the Salamander shoe company, which was half Jewish-owned and had contracts with about 2,000 individually owned branches, some 500 of which were also Jewish-owned. Stormtroopers had already burst into some of these shops and closed them down by the end of March 1933, while the Nazi press organized a boycott campaign against the firm itself, accusing it (without any justification) of fleecing its customers and ensuring that it did not receive any bulk orders from Party organizations. Sales began to plummet. Seeing a crisis looming, the Jewish family that owned half of the shares sold its holding for a million Reichsmarks to the non-Jewish family that owned the other half. The company then fired its Jewish employees, removed its Jewish board members, and cancelled its contracts with its Jewish-owned branch stores, 20 per cent of which had already passed into non-Jewish hands in any case by the end of 1934. The press campaign, the boycotts and the closures ceased forthwith, and turnover grew again. Yet there was no evidence in this instance of any overtly ideological antisemitism on the part of the firm's owners or managers; they had simply bowed to the economic realities of the situation imposed on them by local Party and brownshirt organizations.[148]

Where economic considerations of a different kind played a role, local and regional Party organizations could urge restraint too. In Hamburg, for example, a port city whose interests did not coincide with the rearmament and autarky priorities of the regime, the local economy was a good deal slower to recover from the Depression than elsewhere. Continuing economic problems, which contributed to a startling 20 per cent 'no' vote in the plebiscite of 19 August 1934 on Hitler's self-appointment as head of state, made Regional Leader Karl Kaufmann particularly sensitive to any disruption of the city's economy. There were over 1,500 Jewish-owned companies in Hamburg, and they mostly lasted a good deal longer than their counterparts in the rest of the Reich. Hamburg's mercantile elite was less than enthusiastic about the antisemitic policies of the regime, and leading institutions such as the Chamber of Commerce refused to provide information about which firms were Jewish and which were not. As late as November 1934 it was still using a Jewish printer to produce its information sheets. Older merchants and businessmen had a traditionally allergic reaction to any interference by the state in the business world, and saw Aryanization as a portent of a larger state takeover of business.[149] Yet attitudes had changed by 1938. By this time it seemed clear to even the most diehard Hanseatic merchant that the Nazi regime was going to last. Economic recovery had reached a point where the removal of Jewish businesses no longer seemed such a threat to economic stability. Most important of all, growing restrictions on foreign currency dealings in 1936–7 had forced the closure of a substantial number of Jewish-owned import and export companies in the city. A raft of investigative bodies, including the Foreign Currency Search Office (*Devisenfahndungsamt*) established under the aegis of Reinhard Heydrich on 1 August 1936, and a local equivalent, allowed the authorities to take companies into administration if they were suspected of assisting the flight of capital from Germany. Officials working for these bodies forged confessions, invented interrogation records and denounced solicitors acting for Jewish companies to the Gestapo. As a result, 1,314 securing orders were granted against Jewish businessmen in Hamburg between December 1936 and October 1939.[150]

Such policies were justified in memoranda and other internal documents in strongly antisemitic language, replete with references to 'Jewish unscrupulousness', 'Jewish black marketeers' and the like. The President of the Hamburg Regional Finance Office described one Jewish suspect in 1936 as a 'parasite upon the people.'. While the state played its part in this way, the Regional Economic Consultant of the Nazi Party asserted himself in 1936 as another co-ordinating agent for the Aryanization of Jewish businesses. More than in some other parts of Germany, the Consultant's office took the lead in the process, although it did not in fact have any legal right to do so. It appointed trustees to Jewish firms, and insisted that all remaining Jewish employees be fired. It also set the purchase price for these firms deliberately low, not least by demanding that they be sold without any 'goodwill' being taken into account, since (it was argued) as Jewish firms they had none. The occupants of the office were all young men from an academic background; convinced Nazis with little business experience, such as Dr Gustav Schlotterer (aged twenty-six), Carlo Otte (twenty-four) and Dr Otto Wolff (twenty-five). The economist in charge of the Aryanization Department in Hamburg, Karl Frie, was just nineteen when he joined the Consultant's office. Their ruthlessness, characteristic of the generation that had been born just before the First World War and grown up in the years of inflation, revolution, political instability and economic depression, brooked no opposition. Soon the Hamburg Chamber of Commerce had abandoned its previous reluctance to go along with the Aryanization programme and was ordering that all purchases of Jewish firms made before 1938 be reinvestigated and refunds made for any goodwill element included.[151]

What was striking about this process was not so much the way that it was pushed forward by the Party's economic officials, but the extent to which agencies of the state were involved as well; and the latter were, if anything, even more unscrupulous than the former. Here too, as in the legal system, the idea of a 'dual state', in which legal norms were being upheld by the traditional institutions of the 'normative' state and undermined by the new, only quasi-legal apparatus of Hitler's 'prerogative state', must be heavily qualified if not altogether abandoned.[152] A whole range of state offices was involved in driving Jews out of economic life. This was hardly surprising, in a sense, because those civil servants who staffed them had participated in the dismissal of Jews from their own departments in 1933-4. A tax reform on 16 October 1936, for instance, required all tax laws to reflect the National Socialist world-view and to use National Socialist principles in assessing individual cases. The result was that Jewish companies were now frequently faced with new demands for supposedly unpaid back-taxes, as tax regulations were freely interpreted to disadvantage them. This process of Aryanization had thus begun already in 1933; it did not commence simply when, less still because, Schacht was ousted from his position as economic supremo in 1936. Schacht himself signed an order on 26 November 1935 banning Jewish stockbrokers from plying their trade, and he pressed repeatedly for the promulgation of laws restricting Jewish economic activity in the last two months of 1935. The foreign currency restrictions that were so important in the case of Jewish firms in Hamburg were largely Schacht's own doing, and the Reichsbank ordered its branches on 14 October 1936 to inaugurate investigations of foreign currency dealings if others failed to do so.[153] Aryanization was thus a continuous process, sometimes creeping, sometimes galloping, but always on the go.[154]

III

From 1936, the Four-Year Plan undoubtedly accelerated the whole process. Hitler's own memorandum setting up the Plan identified in his usual fashion 'international Jewry' as the hidden force behind the Bolshevik menace and demanded laws making all Jews in Germany financially responsible for any damage caused by any Jew to the German economy, for example by accumulating currency reserves abroad, an offence for which Hitler demanded the death penalty.[155] The foreign currency investigation apparatus which played such a baleful role in Hamburg was a creation of the forerunner of the Plan, Göring's Raw Materials and Currency Staff established in the spring of 1936. Ministerial discussions on further anti-Jewish economic measures continued through 1936, leading to laws passed at the end of the year making the transfer of Jewish-owned funds abroad illegal. A number of prosecutions followed, leading to numerous prison sentences, though not to execution. The mere suspicion that someone was about to transfer funds was enough under these laws to cause their confiscation. It provided the legal pretext for a growing number of expropriations over the following months and years. The powers that accompanied the Plan, notably the rationing of key raw materials, were deliberately used to disadvantage Jewish firms. The government now amended an emergency decree first passed under Heinrich Brüning to prevent the flight of large amounts of capital from Germany by lowering the sum at which the decree became operative from 200,000 Reichsmarks to 50,000 and basing it on the estimated taxable value of the property rather than on the sum it realized on sale. As a consequence, Jews who emigrated were subject in practice to the loss of far more than the 25 per cent tax provided for by the Brüning decree. In 1932–3 this tax had brought in less than a million marks in revenue to the state; by 1935–6 this income had risen to just under 45 million; in 1937–8, more than 80 million; in 1938–9, 342 million. In addition, transfers of capital abroad were subject to a fee of 20 per cent levied by the German Gold Discount Bank, through which the transfers had to be handled; in June 1935 this fee was raised to 68 per cent, in October 1936, 81 per cent, and in June 1938, 90 per cent. Thus Jewish companies and individuals were being systematically plundered not just by other businesses and by the Nazi Party, but also by the state and its dependent institutions as well.[156]

At the same time, sporadic local boycotts and attacks continued, most notably in the run-up to Christmas, while laws and regulations promulgated from Berlin made life progressively more difficult for Jewish businesses. Increasingly, forced sales were made at well below the market price and under threat of arrest and imprisonment on trumped-up charges that had nothing to do with the conduct of the business itself. In the town of Suhl, for example, Regional Party Leader Fritz Sauckel arrested the Jewish owner of the arms manufacturing company Simson and put him in prison in 1935 after he had refused to sell his company at a knockdown price; citing Hitler's explicit authorization, he then transferred ownership to a specially created foundation, in the alleged interests of national defence. Supposed debts were given as the reason for denying the owner compensation of any kind.[157] By 1 January 1936, many Jewish bankers had been squeezed out of business, or decided that enough was enough and closed down in order to emigrate. About a quarter of Germany's 1,300 private bankers had given up banking; the great majority of the 300 private banks closed had been Jewish-owned.[158] Only a few major banks, like M. M. Warburg of Hamburg, clung on stubbornly until 1938, not least out of a sense of duty to the Jewish community and to the company tradition.[159] Banking was in no way exceptional. A quarter of all Jewish enterprises of all kinds had been Aryanized or closed down by this point.[160] By July 1938, only 9,000 Jewish-owned shops were left in Germany out of an estimated 50,000 in existence in 1933. At the beginning of the Third Reich there had been about 100,000 Jewish-owned firms in Germany all told; by July 1938 about 70 per cent of these had been Aryanized or closed down.[161] Regulations of various kinds put even the humblest Jewish private enterprises out of business. In the summer of 1936, for instance, the introduction of an official registration system for rag-and-bone men led to between 2,000 and 3,000 Jewish dealers being banned from carrying out this trade.[162]

Aryanization had been more or less continuous since 1933 in most localities. In Marburg, for example, eleven out of the town's sixty-four Jewish-owned businesses had already been Aryanized or gone into liquidation in 1933; seven in 1934; eight in 1935; nine in 1936; six in 1937;

and five in the first three quarters of 1938. In Göttingen, fifty-four of the ninety-eight Jewish-owned businesses operating in the town in 1933 had been Aryanized or gone into liquidation by the beginning of 1938.[163] At this point, it was clear to everyone involved that the final stage was now commencing. To expedite matters, Göring and the Interior Ministry issued a decree on 26 April 1938 forcing every Jew or non-Jewish spouse of a Jew to declare all assets held at home and abroad over the value of 5,000 Reichsmarks, following this up with internal discussions on the ultimate exclusion of the Jews from the economy altogether. Further orders barred Jews from acting as auctioneers, from possessing or selling arms, and – a particularly serious blow – from signing legal contracts. By this time, pressures on Jewish-owned companies had become well-nigh irresistible. Since the autumn of 1937, local authorities had been ordering the erection of signs outside Jewish businesses designating them publicly as such – a clear invitation to harassment, boycott and attack. There were nearly 800 Aryanizations in January–October 1938, including 340 factories and twenty-two private banks. The pace was now increasing. In February 1938 there were still 1,680 independent Jewish tradesmen in Munich, for example; by 4 October this number had fallen to 666, and two-thirds of these were in possession of a foreign passport. The final removal of the Jews from the German economy was clearly within sight, and many German businesses and individuals were ready to reap the rewards.[164]

DIVISION OF THE SPOILS

I

On 16 April 1938, a Munich businessman who had been working as an expert consultant in Aryanization cases wrote a strongly worded letter to the local Chamber of Commerce and Industry. He was, he noted, a 'National Socialist, member of the SA, and admirer of Hitler'. Nevertheless, he went on, he was

so disgusted by the brutal ... and extortionate methods employed against the Jews that, from now on, I refuse to be involved in any way with Aryanizations, even though this means losing a handsome consultancy fee ... As an experienced, honest, and upstanding businessman, I [can] no longer stand idly by and countenance the way many Aryan businessmen, entrepreneurs and the like ... are shamelessly attempting to grab up Jewish shops and factories etc. as cheaply as possible and for a ludicrous price. These people are like vultures, swarming down with bleary eyes, their tongues hanging out with greed, to feed upon the Jewish carcass.[165]

Aryanization did indeed offer many opportunities to non-Jewish businesses and businessmen to enrich themselves. Many eagerly grasped them. At the very least, when Jewish businesses went into liquidation, non-Jewish businesses in the same branch of the economy could congratulate themselves on losing some of the competition. This was true at all levels. In January 1939, for instance, 2,000 shops were said to be standing empty in Hamburg as a result of the Aryanization process, a fact singled out for favourable mention by the leader of the Nazi Traders' Association in the city. Since the majority of Jewish business enterprises were small-scale, it was predominantly modest-sized non-Jewish enterprises that benefited from their closure. Indeed, to a degree the regime actually tried to ensure that this was so, as when Jewish chain stores in Hamburg like Bottina shoes or Feidler's stocking shops were broken up and the individual shops sold off separately.[166]

To be sure, this was not widely recognized at the time. Particular resentment was caused among small shopkeepers by the regime's failure to keep its promise to close down the department stores and break up the big chains. 'Department stores,' complained one in 1938, 'whether they are Jewish or Aryan, are still firms that compete unfairly against small businesses.'[167] A Berlin businessman, writing to the exiled Social Democratic leadership while on a trip outside Germany in 1939, claimed indeed that it was overwhelmingly large companies that were snapping up Jewish businesses. 'This process has led to an enormous concentration of industrial and financial power in every branch of the economy, a power that is wielded without compunction by the leaders of the big concerns.'[168] But large firms initially hesitated before moving in too aggressively. Large-scale Jewish enterprises and conglomerates were less susceptible to local boycotts and attacks than smaller, independent businesses and shops were, and at least in the early years of the Third Reich, the regime was careful not to put too much pressure on them because it needed them for economic recovery and rearmament, and many of them were internationally well known.[169]

Thus, Jews remained on the boards of firms such as Mannesmann and I.G. Farben for some time after 1933. The Deutsche Bank still had a Jewish member of the supervisory board as late as July 1938, though he had been abroad since the previous year. Nevertheless, these were exceptions. Most firms bowed earlier to pressure to dismiss Jewish directors, board members and employees. In the Dresdner Bank, internal Aryanization continued a policy of slimming down the workforce begun when the bank took over the Danat Bank in 1931 after it had crashed; the difference now was that it was mainly directed against Jewish employees. The Dresdner Bank was obliged to do this because on 9 May 1933 the Law of 7 April was extended to 'legally recognized public bodies and equivalent institutions and undertakings', which covered a very wide range of institutions indeed. The bank's employees now had to fill out forms detailing their religious and racial background, their war service and other relevant factors. The regulations allowed institutions to claim 'urgent need' as a reason for retaining employees, so the bank was able to avoid the chaos that would have resulted from mass, simultaneous dismissals; but after 30 June 1934 no more such permits were issued by the Economics Ministry. By the end of the year, all Jews had left the bank's supervisory board; 80 per cent of unprotected Jews had left the bank's service by October 1935, and all remaining Jewish employees were gone a year later. These measures were no doubt welcome to the younger non-Jewish men who worked for the bank since they cleared paths to promotion that would probably have stayed blocked for some time. The seven top managers who were forced to resign in 1933–4 because they were Jewish were replaced by men in their thirties and early forties who might not otherwise have been promoted. Those who took over showed little compassion for those who had left. Only in some instances, such as, notably, I.G. Farben, were Jewish employees transferred to positions in foreign subsidiaries instead of having to lose their livelihoods altogether.[170] Whatever their fate, the removal of Jewish managers from German businesses assisted the rise of a new, young managerial elite that was already beginning to take over from the older generation by the time the war came.[171]

The Allianz insurance company, whose chief Kurt Schmitt had been Schacht's predecessor as Economics Minister, was another firm that did not actively pursue a policy of dismissal. It treated its two Jewish directors well when they were forced to resign. On the other hand, the firm offered no serious resistance when it came under pressure from the Nazi press and the Reich Supervisory Office for Insurance to dismiss Jewish employees and sever connections with Jewish salespeople and agents. In 1933, for instance, the company extended the contract of its agent Hans Grünebaum, who had worked for its Stuttgart branch since 1929, for five years, then in 1936 extended it again until 1941. However, this attracted hostile comment from the local press and then a threatening letter from the Nazi Party Regional Leader's office. The company riposted by arguing that Jewish agents were needed to deal with Jewish customers. But this cut no ice with the Nazis. Grünebaum's contract was terminated at the beginning of June 1938; the company agreed to pay him his full annual commission of 35,000 Reichsmarks, covering the period to the end of 1939, though how much of this he was able to take with him when he emigrated to America is uncertain. By this time, government bans on Jews acting as travelling salesmen, estate agents and the like had effectively put an end to this particular kind of business relationship in any case.[172]

In a number of instances, large firms seem to have offered fair prices for Jewish businesses in the early years of the Third Reich, as in the case of the acquisition of the Jewish-owned North German Hop Industry Company by the Henkel Company.[173] Reflecting this, the Regional Economic Consultants' Offices of the Party frequently sent contracts back even when they had assured themselves that the purchasers had the necessary money, were expert in the area concerned, and were racially and politically acceptable. In southern Westphalia, indeed, the great majority of contracts were referred back for renegotiation because the price offered was considered too high.[174] However, as Aryanization gathered pace, big business, especially where it was relatively recent in origin, began to drop any scruples it might have had to begin with, and to join in the profiteering.[175] As in the case of the Wertheim department stores, it could in some cases be managed internally, with Jewish directors making way for non-Jewish ones; of the 260 large firms that had passed from Jewish into non-Jewish hands by the end of 1936, indeed, relatively few had done so through a takeover by another company.[176] From 1936 onwards, however, given the number of Jewish enterprises now coming onto the market, large firms began to keep a look-out for business opportunities. By 1937 many were seizing them with alacrity. Thus the engineering firm Mannesmann took over the Wolf, Netter and Jacobi company in the metal industry, with a turnover of more than 40 million Reichsmarks in 1936–7; it also participated in a consortium that absorbed the Stern scrap metal company in Essen, which had been forced to sell up after the cancellation of contracts.[177] In some cases, Aryanization offered a way out of economic difficulties brought on by the policies of the regime, particularly in the consumer industries. The Salamander shoe company, for instance, which had Aryanized itself in 1933, came under heavy pressure under the Four-Year Plan to export leather shoes for much-needed foreign currency, and use leather substitutes for the shoes it sold on the home market. Leather itself, however, was strictly rationed as early as 1934. It made sense for Salamander to create a series of vertically integrated combines by buying up Jewish-owned leather companies and tanneries like Mayer and Son in Offenbach, which it purchased in 1936; working in the opposite direction, the leather processing company of Carl Freudenberg bought up the Jewish-owned shoe firm Tack, which was already suffering from boycotts and attacks by the local Nazis in 1933.[178]

By 1937, virtually every large company in Germany was joining in the division of the spoils. A big company like Allianz abandoned any reluctance it had previously felt and participated with increasing cynicism in taking advantage of the plight of Jewish insurance agencies now forced to abandon their businesses. While it was still possible, Allianz also offered mortgage loans to the purchasers of Jewish properties and their assets.[179] Banks in their turn stood to make a good deal of money on commission from such sales; in 1935, for instance, when the Jewish owner of the Aron Works Electricity Company in Berlin, a major manufacturer of radios, finally gave in after several spells in a concentration camp and agreed to sell his company to Siemens-Schuckert and another company, the Deutsche Bank made 188,000 Reichsmarks on the transaction. Soon the major banks were competing with each other for this lucrative business. The Deutsche Bank charged a commission of 2 per cent for brokering such transfers, and between 1937 and 1940 made several million Reichsmarks in this way.[180] In a similar way, the Commerzbank acted as an agent for purchasers of Jewish businesses, acting out of commercial logic when it refused new loans to the latter. No help or advice was offered to Jewish vendors; on the contrary, since it was competing in an obviously growing market against other banks doing the same thing, at a time when its freedom to invest in industry or foreign trade was becoming increasingly restricted, the Commerzbank actively sought out companies from which it could gain a commission on such transactions. By 1938, Aryanization actions had become an integral part of the everyday business of the big banks.[181]

Direct participation in the Aryanization of Jewish-owned businesses brought far greater rewards. The chain-store empire of Helmut Horten, for example, was largely built up through the process of Aryanization.[182] Of course, some purchases – perhaps a fifth of such transactions altogether – were carried out by personal friends or sympathizers of Jewish businesspeople who persuaded them to buy their enterprises for inflated prices (to disguise the banned inclusion of goodwill) or for sums including secret bonuses, or, where this was not possible, to hold them in trust until the Third Reich came to an end, whenever that would be. Paying a fair price under the Third Reich, particularly in the later 1930s, and thereby maintaining basic business ethics, was in effect a criminal offence; indeed, to get round the rules and regulations governing Aryanization by this time, some sympathetic businessmen even gave the Jewish vendors secret and illegal monthly payments not mentioned in the transfer documents, or, in one case, smuggled Swiss watches and gold chains to Amsterdam to be collected by the Jewish vendor when he emigrated. Others, like the Degussa chemical company, acting more from commercial logic than from moral principle, kept the Jewish bosses of the Aryanized firms in office for some time because they valued their expertise and their contacts in the business.[183]

A far larger proportion of buyers – perhaps 40 per cent – made no attempt to circumvent the regulations. They paid the minimal price that had become customary, taking advantage of the devaluation of inventory and stocks to get themselves a bargain. There is every indication that they regarded these transactions as entirely legitimate; indeed, after the war, many of them reacted with outrage when faced with demands for compensation to the former Jewish owners of the businesses they had taken over in this way. A third category, also about 40 per cent, and including many active Nazi Party members, encouraged Aryanization and drove down the price as hard as they could. In Hamburg, for instance, business rivals campaigned against the Beiersdorf company, which made Nivea hand cream, by paying for advertisements in the local press and issuing stickers notifying customers that 'Whoever buys Nivea articles is helping to support a Jewish company'.[184] Some did not scruple to use threats and blackmail, or to bring in the Gestapo. A characteristic incident occurred in the summer of 1935, in the town of Fürstenwalde, when the Jewish owner of a shop agreed after lengthy negotiations to sell it to a non-Jewish purchaser who had repeatedly attempted to beat the price down. As he took the money from the purchaser during the final meeting in his lawyer's offices, the door opened and two Gestapo officers came in and declared the money confiscated on the basis of a law covering the property of 'enemies of the state'. Seizing it from the Jewish vendor, they arrested him for resisting authority, while the purchaser banned him and his family from returning to their business and to their home above the shop, although the contract allowed them to do so.[185]

Foreign-owned businesses were also active in the Aryanization of their workforces. Concerned about their status under an obviously nationalistic regime, some of them moved particularly quickly to divest themselves of their Jewish employees when the Nazis seized power in 1933. The managing director of Olex, the German subsidiary of what subsequently became British Petroleum, fired its Jewish employees, or limited their contracts, as early as the late spring of 1933. Later on the same year, the Swiss chemical company Geigy sought official certification as an Aryan concern so that it could continue selling dyes to the Nazi Party to make 'symbols of the national movement'.[186] Major foreign-owned firms, like the car manufacturer Opel, a subsidiary of General Motors, and the German branch of the Ford Motor Corporation, went along with the Aryanization policy and rid themselves of Jewish employees. Both these companies also allowed their factories to be converted to war production, although of course foreign currency restrictions did not permit them to export their profits to their headquarters in the USA. There was little point, therefore, given these restrictions, in foreign-owned companies joining the scramble to take over Jewish businesses.[187]

That scramble degenerated all too easily in the hands of some of those involved into a morass of blackmail, extortion, corruption and plunder. True, Göring, in his capacity as head of the Four-Year Plan, and Hess, the Leader's Deputy, had ordered that Aryanization had to be carried out legally and that Party office-holders were not to obtain any financial advantage from the process, an order repeated by other senior Nazis such as Heinrich Himmler and the Regional Leader of Baden, Robert Wagner. But it was already clear from the frequency and insistence of such warnings that Party officers were all too prepared to exploit the expropriation of Jewish businesses to their own personal gain. Middle- and lower-ranking Nazi activists were simply not prepared to let the despised organs of the state and the law get in the way of the struggle against the Jews, and frequently regarded the plunder they stood to make as a just reward for the sacrifices they had endured in the 'time of struggle' under the Weimar Republic. In any case, they reasoned, Jewish-owned property and funds had been stolen from the German race. The mass, nationwide and largely uncoordinated violence that underpinned the Nazi seizure of power in the first half of 1933 provided the context for brownshirts to purloin gold and jewellery from Jewish houses and flats, on occasion torturing the owners until they got the keys to the safe. It was not uncommon for arrested Jews to be released on provision of a large amount of 'bail' money, which disappeared immediately into the pockets of the SA or SS men who had taken them into custody. Party officials in Breslau who had threatened Jews with violence if they did not pay up were first arrested for obtaining money with menaces, then amnestied as the state prosecutor excused their action as 'excessive National Socialist zeal'.[188]

After the 'Night of the Long Knives' at the end of June 1934, such actions more or less ceased, although a few more did occur in the summer of the following year. The Aryanization of Jewish businesses, however, especially where it was driven forward by the Party's Regional Economic Consultants' offices, provided opportunities for gain on a much larger scale. In Thuringia, for instance, the Party's Regional Economic Adviser took a 10 per cent commission on the purchase price of Aryanization actions, in order, he said, to cover office costs; in the end he was able to bank more than a million Reichsmarks from this procedure, opening a special Party account from which funds were then disbursed to favoured Party members to buy further Jewish businesses when they came up for sale. Thus 'Party Comrade Ulrich Klug' was provided with a 'loan' of 75,000 Reichsmarks to help him buy a cement works, while 'Party Comrade Ignaz Idinger' was supplied with 5,000 Reichsmarks for the Aryanization of the Hotel Blum in Oberhof. Similar practices could be found in other regions too. The money was never expected to be repaid. Senior Nazi Party officials could enrich themselves very substantially by such means. The Regional Leader of the Party in Hamburg, Karl Kaufmann, demanded 'Aryanization contributions' from vendors and purchasers alike, using them for example to buy up all the shares of the Siegfried Kroch Company, a chemicals factory. The Regional Educational Leader of the Party in Württemberg-Hohenzollern managed to buy a slate quarry in Metzingen which increased his annual income tenfold.[189]

On a smaller scale, many humble Party activists were able to get the money from Aryanization actions to buy up lottery concessions, tobacco stalls and the like. Given the official ban on direct profiteering, it was not surprising that close relatives of leading local Party officials got in on the act instead, as with Gerhard Fiehler, who bought a Jewish shoe and leather goods shop for himself through the good offices of his brother, the Mayor of Munich. In many such instances it was clear that the family of the Nazi official in question was acting in concert. Such actions, circumventing the law rather than openly flouting it, shaded off into clearly criminal activities when Nazi Party officials obtained money from Jews by deception through fraudulent offers of help or protection, or took bribes to help them get round the financial regulations that made emigration so hard. Businessmen who wanted to be well placed to buy up Jewish firms on the cheap were even more generous in their bribes. 'To do business under the Nazis', an Aachen estate agent who had profited considerably from the Aryanization of Jewish property told an American agent, 'you had to have a friend in every government office, but it was too dangerous to bribe openly. You had to work it indirectly.' Inviting the key Party functionary out for an expensive meal with fine wines, or buying rounds of drinks in the pubs and bars frequented by the local party elite, were his favoured methods. 'It cost me plenty of money,' he admitted, 'but in the end I made his acquaintance.'[190]

II

Aryanization was only one part of a vast and rapidly growing system of plunder, expropriation and embezzlement under the Third Reich. It started at the very top, with Hitler himself. To begin with, when Hindenburg died, Hitler was able to lay his hands on the President's official funds. Expenditure from these had previously been subject to internal audit in the Finance Ministry and the ultimate approval of the Reichstag, as had also been the case with the Reich Chancellor's personal budget. With the effective emasculation of the Reichstag and the removal of any element of critical investigation of government actions by the press and the mass media, not to mention the overwhelming personality cult that surrounded Hitler himself, a cult that brooked no criticism of the Leader in any respect, the way was now open for the expenditure of these funds for any purpose Hitler desired. Despite some misgivings in the higher ranks of the civil service, Hitler now began to dole out money to all and sundry with increasing liberality. Aware of this, leading Nazis now began to suggest to the Chancellor objects deserving of his largesse. Already in the autumn of 1933, at the suggestion of the Reich Interior Minister and one of his officials, Hitler had granted from the Reich Chancellor's funds a monthly pension of 300 Reichsmarks to seventeen individuals who were designated as 'racist and antisemitic precursors' of the Nazi movement. The writer Richard Ungewitter, from Stuttgart, author of numerous books with titles such as *From Serving the Jews to Freedom* and *The Undermining of the Race by Jews*, was included on the list along with other, similar individuals. By 1936 Hitler's generosity in this manner had extended to people who had been imprisoned in the Weimar Republic for treasonable activities of one kind and another. Over a hundred men and women received pensions of between 50 and 500 Reichsmarks a month for their special services to the Party. By issuing such grants, Hitler made it clear he was compensating racist and antisemitic propagandists and Party activists for the sacrifices they had made before the seizure of power, thus underlining the self-image of the brownshirts and the 'old fighters' as selfless martyrs in a great cause and binding them to the new regime in a symbolic as well as a material sense.[191]

Nor did Hitler neglect the army, whose regimental headquarters were the frequent recipients of presents of oil paintings with military themes donated by the Leader. Moreover, from July 1937 onwards, Hitler's official funds were used to pay out 100,000 Reichsmarks a year 'for officers of the armed forces to go on rest cures'. Keeping the armed forces happy was certainly an important matter, particularly in the wake of the assassination of General von Schleicher during the 'Night of the Long Knives', and Hitler also paid out considerable sums of money to increase the pensions of retired officers such as Vice-Admiral von Reuter, who had ordered the sinking of the surrendered German fleet at Scapa Flow on 21 June 1919. August von Mackensen, by the mid-1930s the last surviving Field-Marshal of the Kaiser's army, and thus a significant symbolic figure for the army, received a large tax-free gift of a landed estate in the Prenzlau district, together with 350,000 Reichsmarks to cover the costs of renovation. As a monarchist, Mackensen felt it necessary to write to the former Kaiser Wilhelm II in exile excusing himself for accepting the gift, since in his view only the Kaiser himself was actually entitled to make such donations. Predictably, the ex-Kaiser was not amused, and regarded the Field-Marshal from this point on as a traitor to his cause. Hitler made generous subventions to a number of other aristocratic landowners to help them with their debts and keep them conspiring with the ex-Kaiser.[192]

In order to facilitate such generosity, the funds allocated in the state budget for Hitler's personal disposal increased steadily until they reached the astonishing sum of 24 million Reichsmarks in 1942.[193] Hitler could add to these sums the royalties derived from sales of *My Struggle*, purchased in bulk by Nazi Party organizations and a virtually compulsory item on the ordinary citizen's bookshelf. These amounted to 1.2 million Reichsmarks in 1933 alone. From 1937 Hitler also claimed royalties on the use of his portrait on postage stamps, something Hindenburg had never done; one cheque alone handed over by the Minister of Posts was for 50 million Reichsmarks, as Speer, who was present on the occasion, reported later. The annual Adolf Hitler Donation of German Business added a further sum, along with fees and royalties paid every time one of Hitler's speeches was published in the papers. Hitler also received considerable sums from legacies left to him in the wills of the grateful Nazi dead. When all this was taken into account, it was clear that Hitler had little use for the modest salary of 45,000 Reichsmarks he earned as Reich Chancellor, or for the annual expense allowance of 18,000 Reichsmarks; early on in his Chancellorship, therefore, he publicly renounced both salary and allowance in a propagandistic gesture designed to advertise the spirit of selfless dedication in which he ruled the country. Nevertheless, when the Munich tax office reminded him in 1934 that he had never paid any income tax and now owed them more than 400,000 Reichsmarks in arrears, pressure was brought to bear on the tactless officials and before long they had agreed to write off the whole sum and destroy all the files on Hitler's tax affairs into the bargain. A grateful Hitler granted the head of the tax office, Ludwig Mirre, a pay supplement of 2,000 Reichsmarks a year for this service, free of tax.[194]

Hitler's personal position as the Third Reich's charismatic Leader, effectively above and beyond the law, gave not only him but also others immunity from the normal rules of financial probity. His immediate subordinates owed their position not to any elected body but to Hitler alone; they were accountable to no one but him. The same personal relationships replicated themselves all the way down the political scale, right to the bottom. The result was inevitably a vast and growing network of corruption, as patronage, nepotism, bribery and favours, bought, sold and given, quickly assumed a key role in binding the whole system together. After 1933, the continued loyalty of the Party faithful was purchased by a huge system of personal favours. For the hundreds of thousands of Nazi Party activists who were without employment, this meant in the first place giving them a job. Already in July 1933 Rudolf Hess promised employment to all those who had joined the Party before 30 January 1933. In October the same year, the Reich Office for Unemployment Insurance and Jobs in Berlin centralized the campaign to provide jobs for everyone with a Party membership number under 300,000, all those who had held a position of responsibility in the Party for over a year and anyone who had been in the SA, the SS or the Steel Helmets before 30 January 1933. This caused some resentment, since the Party membership had already passed the number 300,000 at the end of 1930, so many who had joined since were ineligible. In practice, however, these regulations counted for little, as anyone with a claim to be an old Nazi was likely to be included, while ambitious Nazis who already had jobs used the scheme to get better ones. By 1937 the Reich Postal Service had given jobs to more than 30,000 'deserving National Socialists', while only 369 out of 2,023 Nazis who had been given permanent and well-paid state employment in the Ministry of War by the end of 1935 had actually been previously without a job.

This system of 'jobs for the boys' was in fact modelled on a long-held practice in Prussia and elsewhere, whereby retiring non-commissioned officers in the army automatically received employment in the state service, notably in the police but also in other branches of the public sector. The application of this principle to members of the SA and the Nazi Party was a different matter, since they were being rewarded as members of a political party, not former servants of the state. Its scale and suddenness were also new. The Nazi Party in Berlin found jobs for 10,000 members by October 1933, while 90 per cent of all white-collar jobs in the public sector went to 'old fighters'. When a candidate for a job was proposed by the local stormtroopers, it was a brave employer who refused, however poor his qualifications might be. Many of those who obtained state employment found that their previous service in the Party, the SA or the SS was counted in calculating their seniority in their new positions, giving them a clear advantage over their colleagues when it came to promotion to the next grade up. Some of these jobs were obvious sinecures. In July 1933, for instance, the brownshirt Paul Ellerhusen, commandant of the concentration camp in Fuhlsbüttel, and an unqualified clerk who had been unemployed since 1929, was appointed personal secretary to the Reich Commissioner for Hamburg with the title of State Councillor; not long afterwards he was transferred to a better-paid job in the city's Youth Office, though he seldom turned up for work, it was reported, because he was almost permanently drunk.[195]

There were many similar cases all over Germany. Municipal utilities, such as gasworks, waterworks and the like, offered ample opportunity for SA men to find employment, often surplus to requirements. An audit of the Hamburg Sickness Fund office found that it had employed 228 more administrators than it actually needed. Thousands of old Party men found comfortable jobs in the transport system; the Hamburg local railways took on over a thousand in 1933–4, though whether they really needed them was another matter. The Hamburg Regional Farmers' Leader Herbert Duncker, for instance, was paid 10,000 Reichsmarks a year as 'agricultural adviser to the Hamburg Electricity Works' without ever once turning up even to see what the job might involve. In this way, public corporations were in effect required to subsidize the Nazi Party and its ancillary organizations. Similar pressures were brought to bear on a wide variety of private enterprises. Meanwhile, laws passed in 1934 and 1938 indemnified Party members against claims for damages as a result of the destruction they had meted out to trade union and other offices in 1933, and allowed them to clear their debts without penalty if they had got into financial difficulties before 1 January 1934.[196] By contrast, former activists in the Communist or Social Democratic Party found their attempts to get a job repeatedly rebuffed, until the demand for labour in the arms industry became so insistent that their previous political activity could conveniently be forgotten. The experience of Willi Erbach, a skilled engineering worker who had been a member of the Reichsbanner, the paramilitary wing of the Social Democrats, cannot have been unusual: sacked for his political activities in 1933, he did not find a job again until three years later, in 1936, when the labour exchange suddenly assigned him to the Krupp factory in Essen. Meanwhile, less skilled workers found getting a job easy enough if they were members of the Nazi Party.[197]

The opportunities for self-aggrandizement went all the way down the scale, right down to the ordinary brownshirts who helped themselves to the cash-boxes, the furniture, the bed-linen and the equipment they found in the trade union premises they raided on 2 May 1933, and in the homes of the men and women they arrested. Not untypical was the case of the leader of the Munich Student Union, Friedrich Oskar Stäbel, victor in a bout of in-fighting that resulted in his appointment as head of the national German Students' Union in September 1933. Stäbel celebrated his climb to the top by using student union fees for personal expenditure, clothes, cars and the like, and to finance and equip a marching band for his own entertainment. The local student union in Berlin spent its members' contributions on the purchase of no fewer than seven automobiles for the personal use of its officers.[198] The quantity of money and property flowing into the Party from early 1933 onwards was so vast that few proved able to resist the temptation to squirrel some of it away for themselves. The Party Treasury did not take kindly to embezzlement from its own funds, and between 1 January 1934 and 31 December 1941 it brought no fewer than 10,887 prosecutions for misappropriation of Party funds before the courts; they involved ancillary organizations of the Party as well as the Party itself. The auditing of accounts and the control of finances in general were almost bound to be chaotic in a situation like that of 1933, when the Nazi Party and its myriad subordinate groups were growing almost exponentially. It was hardly surprising that among the 1.6 million people who joined the Party in the first few months of 1933 there were many who hoped to make their fortune by doing so.[199]

III

With such money flowing into their accounts, it was small wonder that Nazi officials at every level of the hierarchy were soon enjoying a lifestyle they had not even dreamed of before 1933. This included the men at the very top. Reich Propaganda Minister Joseph Goebbels, for instance, had declared an annual income of no more than 619 Reichsmarks to the tax authorities in 1932. Within a few years, however, he was earning 300,000 Reichsmarks a year in fees for his weekly leading articles for the Nazi magazine *The Reich*, a sum that was out of all proportion to standard journalistic rates and represented in practice a huge annual bribe from the magazine's publisher Max Amann. For his part, Goebbels wrote off 20 per cent of his earnings as business expenses, although in fact he had none. With this money, The Propaganda Minister bought among other things a villa on the Berlin island of Schwanenwerder, which its previous owner, the Jewish physician Charlotte Herz, had been forced to sell. In 1936 the city of Berlin placed another property at his lifelong disposal, on Lake Constance: he then spent 2.2 million Reichsmarks on extending and refurbishing it. In 1938 he sold the Schwanenwerder property to the industrialist Alfred Ludwig, who then let it to him rent-free. Yet Goebbels counted in popular opinion as one of the less corrupt of the Nazi leaders, as did Albert Speer, whose architectural fees, augmented by the usual Christmas presents from the Labour Front Leader Robert Ley and the tax concessions commonly made to leading Nazis, made him a millionaire already before the war.[200]

Most notorious of all was Hermann Göring, whose hunting lodge Carinhall was extended and refurbished at a cost of more than 15 million Reichsmarks in taxpayers' money. The upkeep and administration of these palatial premises cost not far short of half a million marks, again paid for by the taxpayer; and beyond this, Göring also owned another hunting lodge in East Prussia, a villa in Berlin, a chalet on the Obersalzberg, a castle, Burg Veldenstein, and five further hunting lodges, not to mention a private train whose coaches accommodated ten automobiles and a working bakery, while Göring's private quarters on the train, taking up two whole carriages, cost the state 1.32 million Reichsmarks in 1937 even before the extravagantly luxurious furnishings and fittings had been installed. In the same year, the Reich Association of Automobile Manufacturers donated to him a yacht worth three-quarters of a million Reichsmarks for his personal use. In all these locations Göring displayed a large and ever-growing collection of artworks, though his real chance for building it up would not come until the war. Like the other leading Nazis, he also managed to conceal much of his income from the tax authorities and obtain massive concessions on the rest; tax evasion was made easier by a ruling in 1939 that the tax affairs of Reich Ministers and Nazi Party Reich Leaders were to be dealt with exclusively by the finance offices of Berlin Central and Munich North, where they could be sure of a sympathetic handling.[201]

Such conspicuous consumption was not just a mark of the personal corruption that affects every dictatorship, but also expressed a widespread desire among the higher Nazi officials to demonstrate symbolically that they were the new masters of Germany. Hunting became a favourite pastime of many Regional Leaders, who bought themselves hunting grounds even where they had shown no previous interest in this most aristocratic of pastimes. Faced with the need to keep up with his colleagues in this respect as in others, the Regional Leader of Hamburg, Karl Kaufmann, was unable to do very much initially, since his urban fiefdom had no hunting land. With the creation of Greater Hamburg in 1937, however, the incorporation of a wooded area to the north of the city gave him the chance; he immediately declared it a nature reserve, stocked it with game, enclosed it from the public with eleven kilometres of fencing, and then leased it from the city for his own use. In a similar way, most of the leading Nazis followed Hitler's example and purchased Old Masters and new works from the Great German Art exhibition to put on the walls of their grandiose villas and hunting lodges, not because they were particularly fond of art, but because this was an obvious symbol of their status in the Nazi hierarchy.[202]

Not surprisingly, corruption allied itself to theft and extortion when Nazi leaders and their underlings came into contact with the helpless and the powerless. The hatred that Nazi activists felt for Jews, Communists, 'Marxists' and other 'enemies of the Reich' gave them free rein to plunder them at will. In the course of the violent seizure of power in 1933, brownshirt gangs enrolled as auxiliary police carried out 'house-searches' that were little more than pretexts for robbery. In the concentration camps, officers and commanders treated the workshops staffed by inmates as their personal possessions, taking furniture for their quarters, pictures and paintings for their walls, and so on. The commandant of the concentration camp at Lichtenburg had inmates make new bindings for his books, shoes and boots for himself and his family, letterboxes and ironing-boards for his household, and much more besides. Lower camp officials forced inmates to steal asparagus and strawberries for them from the camp vegetable garden, they 'organized' food for themselves from the camp kitchen, and embezzled money from the camp canteen. Theft of personal possessions and money brought into the camps by those unfortunate enough to be sent to them was the rule, not the exception. In 1938 the commandant of Buchenwald, Karl Koch, confiscated no less than 200,000 Reichsmarks' worth of goods and currency from Jews brought into the camp, dividing some of it amongst his subordinates but depositing most of the money in his personal account.[203]

If anyone at a relatively senior level was prosecuted for such offences then it was more likely to be as a result of carelessness than of any sense of rectitude on the part of his superiors. When Robert Schöpwinkel, a senior official of the Reich Association of German Hoteliers and Innkeepers, was tried and sentenced with his two most senior officials for embezzling 100,000 Reichsmarks, this was mainly because their corruption had become so notorious in the trade that the innkeeper of the Rheinhotel Dreesen, in Bad Godesberg, where Hitler frequently stayed, approached the Leader and told him that if nothing was done to bring Schöpwinkel to book, the whole innkeeping trade in the Rhineland would become disaffected from the regime.[204] A few court cases such as this enabled the leaders of the regime to portray themselves as resolute in the combating of corruption, unlike their predecessors under the Weimar Republic. In fact, corruption of this kind was more often concealed from the media. It was encouraged by the lack of any press or public control over the government and the Party, by the personal nature of power in the regime, and by the general distaste of the Nazis for formal administrative structures and rules. In the depressed economic climate of the early and mid-1930s, power seemed a quick way to riches, and there were few in any position of responsibility in the Nazi Party who could resist the temptation to take it. Rumours and stories about corruption spread rapidly amongst the population. In September 1934 Victor Klemperer recorded a conversation with a Hitler Youth member, the son of a friend, who described how Group Leaders embezzled the members' contributions for excursions and used them to buy luxuries as expensive as motorbikes for themselves. All this was common knowledge, he said.[205]

The morass of corruption into which the economy rapidly sank after 1933 was the source of a good deal of bitter humour amongst the population. The definition of a 'reactionary' was said to be 'someone who has a well-paid post that a Nazi likes the look of'. Göring's taste for uniforms and titles was a particular butt of popular humour. A 'Gör' was popularly said to be 'the quantity of tin that one man can carry on his chest'. On a visit to Rome to negotiate with the Vatican, Göring wired back to Hitler: 'Mission accomplished. Pope unfrocked. Tiara and pontifical vestments are perfect fit.' At night, according to another joke, Göring's wife woke up to find her naked husband standing next to the bed waving his marshal's baton around. What was he up to, she asked. 'I am promoting my underpants to overpants,' came the reply. Jokes about corruption even made it onto the stage: in 1934 the cabarettist Wilhelm Finck, doing a stand-up comic routine at Berlin's *Catacomb*, posed holding up his right arm in the Nazi salute while a tailor measured him for a new suit. 'What sort of jacket should it be?' asked the tailor: 'With chevrons and stripes?' 'You mean', said Finck, 'a straitjacket?' 'How would you like your pockets?' 'Wide open, in the current fashion,' came Finck's reply. Not long afterwards, the cabaret was closed down on Goebbels's orders and Finck taken off to a concentration camp. Hitler was usually exempt from jibes about corruption, whether public or private. Complaints about corruption were directed against his subordinates, above all the 'little Hitlers' who ruled the roost in the regions. A typical joke had the Goebbels children invited to tea in turn to the houses of Göring, Ley and other leading Party figures. After each visit they came home raving about the wonderful cream cakes, treats and other goodies they had been given. After a visit to Hitler, however, in which they had only been given malt coffee and tiny cakes, they asked: 'Daddy, isn't the Leader in the Party?'[206]

Yet alongside such humour was a widespread feeling that the Nazi regime had achieved a good deal in the economic sphere by 1939. After all, the economy had recovered from the Depression faster than its counterparts in other countries. Germany's foreign debt had been stabilized, interest rates had fallen to half their 1932 level, the stock exchange had recovered from the Depression, the gross national product had risen by 81 per cent over the same period, and industrial investment and output had once more attained the levels they had enjoyed in 1928. The two greatest economic bugbears of the Weimar years, inflation and unemployment, had been conquered.[207] All this had been achieved by a growing state direction of the economy which by 1939 had reached unprecedented proportions. Whatever the propaganda messages about the battle for work might claim, Nazi economic policy was driven by the overwhelming desire on the part of Hitler and the leadership, backed up by the armed forces, to prepare for war. Up to the latter part of 1936, this was conducted in a way that aroused few objections from business; when the Four-Year Plan began to come into effect, however, the drive for rearmament began to outpace the economy's ability to supply it, and business began to chafe under a rapidly tightening net of restrictions and controls. More ominously, private enterprise started to be outflanked by state-run enterprises founded and funded by a regime increasingly impatient with the priority accorded by capitalism to profit. Yet none of this, whatever critics suspected, represented a return to the allegedly socialist principles espoused by the Nazis in their early days. Those principles had long been left behind, and in reality they were never socialist anyway. The Third Reich was never going to create total state ownership and centralized planning along the lines of Stalin's Russia. The Darwinian principles that animated the regime dictated that competition between companies and individuals would remain the guiding principle of the economy, just as competition between different agencies of state and Party were the guiding principles of politics and administration.[208]

What Hitler wanted to ensure, however, was that firms competed to fulfil the overall policy aims laid down by himself. Yet those aims were fundamentally contradictory. On the one hand, autarky was designed to prepare Germany for a lengthy war; on the other hand, rearmament was pursued with a headlong abandon that paid scant regard to the dictates of national self-sufficiency. Measured by its own aims, the Nazi regime had only succeeded partially at most by the summer of 1939. Its preparations for a large-scale war were inadequate, its armaments programme incomplete; drastic shortages of raw materials meant that targets for the construction of tanks, ships, planes and weapons of war were not remotely being met; and the situation was exacerbated by Hitler's own inability to set stable and rational priorities within the rearmament programme. The answer was plunder. The corruption, extortion, expropriation and downright robbery that became the hallmarks of the regime and its masters and servants at every level in the course of the Aryanization programme put plunder at the heart of the Nazi attitude towards the property and livelihood of peoples they regarded as non-Aryan. The enormous stresses and strains built up in the German economy between 1933 and 1939 could, Hitler himself explicitly argued on several occasions, ultimately only be resolved by the conquest of living-space in the east. The 'old fighters' of the Party had been rewarded for their sacrifices during the 'years of struggle' under the Weimar Republic with money, jobs, property and income after the seizure of power. Now, writ large, the same principle was applied to the German economy and the economies of the rest of Europe: sacrifices were demanded of the German people in the build-up to war, but once war came, they would be rewarded with a vast new domain in Eastern Europe that would deliver wealth on an unprecedented scale, supply the nation with food for the foreseeable future, and solve all Germany's economic problems at a stroke.[209]

Meanwhile, the German people had to make the sacrifices. The regime bent all its efforts towards building up production while keeping the lid firmly on consumption. Shortages of fat, butter and other consumables, not to mention luxury items such as imported fruit, had become a standard part of daily life by 1939. People were constantly exhorted to make contributions to savings schemes of one kind and another. Savings were directed into government bonds, loan certificates and tax credits, so that the vast bulk of them became available for spending on arms. People were remorselessly exhorted to save, save, rather than spend, spend, spend. Compulsory pension schemes were introduced for the self-employed that forced them to invest funds in insurance companies which the government could then draw upon to help finance rearmament. At the same time, government departments and the military often delayed paying contractors for well over a year, thus extracting from them what was in effect a kind of hidden loan. In many small and medium-sized enterprises engaged on arms production or arms-related projects, this created cash-flow problems so serious that they were sometimes unable to pay their workers' wages on time.[210] The regime justified all this with its customary rhetoric of sacrifice for the greater good of the German racial community. But did people accept the reality of that community? Did the Third Reich, as the Nazis had promised, sweep away the class antagonisms and hostilities that had rendered Weimar democracy unworkable and unite all Germans in a rebirth of national unity and struggle for the common cause? On the fulfilling of this promise a great deal of the regime's popularity and success would surely depend.

5

BUILDING THE
PEOPLE'S COMMUNITY

BLOOD AND SOIL

I

For Friedrich Reck-Malleczewen, the Third Reich represented the coming to power of the mob and the overthrow of all social authority. Although Reck lived in aristocratic style in Upper Bavaria, where he had an old country house with eleven hectares of land, he was in fact North German; he owed his origins and his allegiance, he explained to a Munich newspaper in 1929, not to the Bavarian but to the ancient Prussian aristocracy. Deeply conservative, snobbish, steeped in nostalgia for the days before the Junkers were dragged screaming into the modern world by Bismarck, Reck loathed Nazi Germany with a rare intensity. From the comparative safety of his rural retreat, he poured into his diary all the distaste he felt at the new order of things. 'I am the prisoner of a horde of vicious apes,' he wrote. Hitler was a 'piece of filth' whom he should have shot when he had had the opportunity when, carrying a revolver to protect himself against the raging mob violence of the times, he had encountered him in the Osteria restaurant in Munich in 1932. Listening to Hitler speak, Reck's overwhelming impression was one of the Leader's 'basic stupidity'. He looked 'like a tram-conductor'; his face 'waggled with unhealthy cushions of fat; it all hung, it was slack and without structure – slaggy, gelatinous, sick'. And yet people worshipped this 'unclean . . . monstrosity', this 'power-drunk schizophrenic'. Reck could not bear to witness the 'bovine and finally moronic roar of "*Hail!*" . . . hysterical females, adolescents in a trance, an entire people in the spiritual state of howling dervishes'. 'Oh truly,' he wrote in 1937, 'men can sink no lower. This mob, to which I am connected by a common nationality, is not only unaware of its own degradation but is ready at any moment to demand of every one of its fellow human beings the same mob roar . . . the same degree of degradation.'[1]

The Nazi leaders, Reck thought, were 'dirty little bourgeois who . . . have seated themselves at the table of their evicted lords'.[2] As for German society in general, he wrote bitterly in September 1938:

Mass-man moves, robotlike, from digestion to sleeping with his peroxide-blonde females, and produces children to keep the termite heap in continued operation. He repeats word for word the incantations of the Great Manitou, denounces or is denounced, dies or is made to die, and so goes on vegetating . . . But even this, the overrunning of the world with Neanderthals, is not what is unbearable. What is unbearable is that this horde of Neanderthals demands of the few full human beings who are left that they also shall kindly turn into cavemen; and then threatens them with physical extinction if they refuse.[3]

Wisely, perhaps, Reck hid his diary every night deep in the woods and fields on his land, constantly changing the hiding place so that it could not be discovered by the Gestapo.[4]

Reck was particularly distressed at what had happened to the younger generation of the aristocracy. Visiting a fashionable Berlin nightclub early in 1939, he found it filled with 'young men of the rural nobility, all of them in SS uniforms':

They were having a fine time dropping pieces of ice from the champagne coolers down the décolletages of their ladies and retrieving the pieces of ice from the horrible depths amidst general jubilation. They . . . communicated with each other in loud voices that must certainly have been understandable on Mars, their speech the pimps' jargon of the First World War and the Free Corps period – the jargon which is what the language has become during the last twenty years . . . To observe these men meant looking at the unbridgeable abyss that separates all of us from the life of yesterday . . . The first thing is the frightening emptiness of their faces. Then one observes, in the eyes, a kind of flicker from time to time, a sudden lighting up. This has nothing to do with youth. It is the typical look of this generation, the immediate reflection of a basic and completely hysterical savagery.[5]

These men, he wrote prophetically, 'would turn the paintings of Leonardo into an ash heap if their Leader stamped them degenerate'. They 'will perpetrate still worse things, and worst, most dreadful of all, they will be totally incapable of even *sensing* the deep degradation of their existence'. Aristocrats of ancient and honourable lineage, he raged, accepted meaningless titles and honours from a regime that had degraded them and so brought disgrace on their famous names. 'This people are insane. They will pay dearly for their insanity.' The traditional moral and social order had been turned upside-down, and the man he blamed more than any other was Hitler himself. 'I have hated you in every hour that has gone by,' he told the Nazi leader in the privacy of his own diary in August 1939, 'I hate you so that I would happily give my life for your death, and happily go to my own doom if only I could witness yours, take you with me into the depths.'[6]

Reck was unusual in the vehemence of his disdain for what he saw as the Nazified masses. The sharpness and percipience of some of his observations perhaps owed something to his extreme marginality. For the claims to noble lineage made in his 1929 article in the Munich newspaper were as false as the details of his supposed origins in the Baltic aristocracy that he provided in his elaborately constructed family tree. He was, in truth, just plain Fritz Reck. His grandfather had been an innkeeper, and though his father had acquired enough wealth and standing to get himself elected to the Prussian Chamber of Deputies in 1900, it was in the lower house that he sat, as befitted a commoner, not in the upper house, where the hereditary nobility belonged. Reck himself was a qualified physician who devoted most of his time to writing – novels, plays, journalism, film scripts and much more. He constructed a whole fantastic past for himself, involving military service in many different theatres of war, and even service in the British colonial army. All of it was invented. Yet Reck's claim to be an aristocrat seems to have aroused no suspicion or animosity in the circles in which he moved. It was underpinned by his notoriously superior and arrogant bearing in public. Reck took on in his social and personal life all the attributes of the Prussian Junker. His belief in his own aristocratic character and in the virtues of the social elite of the titled and the cultured seems to have been absolutely genuine.[7] And however many of the details in his diary were invented, Reck's hatred for Hitler and the Nazis was unquestionably authentic.[8]

Reck's conservatism was far more extreme than that of most of the genuinely old Prussian aristocracy. As he astutely recognized, it was scarcely shared by the younger generation at all. The German aristocracy had undergone an unusually sharp generational divide during the Weimar years. The older generation, deprived of the financial and social backing they had enjoyed from the state under the Bismarckian Reich, longed for a return to the old days. They regarded the Nazis' pseudo-egalitarian rhetoric with suspicion and alarm. But the younger generation despised the old monarchies for giving up without a fight in 1918. They saw in the Nazi Party in the early 1930s the potential vehicle for the creation of a new leadership elite. They regarded the aristocracy to which they belonged not as a status group based on a shared sense of honour, but as a racial entity, the product of centuries of breeding. It was this view that had prevailed in the 17,000-strong German Nobles' Union (*Deutsche Adelsgenossenschaft*) in the early 1920s as it had banned Jewish nobles (about 1.5 per cent of the total) from becoming members. But it was not universally held. Catholic nobles, overwhelmingly concentrated in the south of Germany, stayed aloof from this process of racialization, and many took the side of their Church when it began to come under pressure in the Third Reich. Relatively few even of the younger Bavarian aristocracy followed their North German Protestant counterparts into the SS, although many had opposed the Weimar Republic. They felt instead more comfortable in other right-wing organizations such as the Steel Helmets. Older nobles in all German regions were usually monarchists, and indeed an open commitment to the restoration of the German monarchies was a precondition of belonging to the Nobles' Union until it was dropped under the Third Reich. Yet many of them were attracted by the Nazis' hostility to socialism and Communism, their emphasis on leadership, and their rhetorical attacks on bourgeois culture. For the younger generation, the rapid expansion of the armed forces offered new opportunities for employment in a traditional function in the officer corps. The Nazi prioritizing of the conquest of living-space in Eastern Europe appealed to many in the Pomeranian and Prussian nobility who saw it as reviving the glorious days in which their ancestors had colonized the East. Conscious of the need to win votes from the conservative sectors of the population, the Nazis frequently brought scions of the nobility along to stand with them on electoral platforms in the early 1930s. The younger members of the Hohenzollern family took the lead in supporting the Nazis: Prince August Wilhelm of

Prussia was an officer in the stormtroopers well before 1933, and Crown Prince Friedrich Wilhelm urged people to vote for Hitler against Hindenburg in the Presidential elections of 1932.[9]

Although the brownshirts and a good number of 'old fighters' continued to pour scorn on what they saw as the effete degeneracy of the German nobility, Hitler himself recognized that its younger generation would be indispensable in staffing his new, vastly expanded officer corps and in giving a continued veneer of respectability to the foreign service. He even allowed the German Nobles' Union to continue in existence, duly co-ordinated under Nazi leadership. However, as soon as he felt it was no longer necessary to treat the conservatives with kid gloves, Hitler made it clear he was not going to contemplate the restoration of the monarchy. Aristocratic celebrations of the ex-Kaiser's birthday in Berlin early in 1934 were broken up by gangs of brownshirts and a number of monarchist associations were banned. Any remaining hopes amongst the older generation of German nobles were finally dashed with Hitler's assumption of the headship of state on the death of Hindenburg, when many had hoped for a restoration of the monarchy. But if Hitler's treatment of the aristocracy became cooler, this was more than compensated for by the growing enthusiasm shown towards them by Heinrich Himmler, Reich Leader of the SS. Bit by bit, the older generation of SS men, with histories of violence often going back to the Free Corps of the early years of the Weimar Republic, were pensioned off, to be replaced by the highly educated and the nobly born. Nazi populists might have castigated the German aristocracy as effete and degenerate, but Himmler was convinced he knew better; centuries of planned breeding, he thought, must have produced a steady improvement in its racial quality. Soon he was conveying this message to receptive audiences of German aristocrats. Figures such as the Hereditary Grand Duke of Mecklenburg and Prince Wilhelm of Hesse had already joined the SS before 30 January 1933; now young aristocrats fell over themselves to enrol, including many from the Prussian military nobility such as the Barons von der Goltz, von Podbielski and many more.[10]

By 1938 nearly a fifth of the senior ranks of SS men were filled by titled members of the nobility, and roughly one in ten among the lower officer grades. To cement his relations with the aristocracy, Himmler persuaded all the most important German horse-riding associations, preserves of upper-class sportsmanship and snobbish socializing, to enrol in the SS, irrespective of their political views, much to the disgust of some of the older generation of SS veterans, so that SS riders regularly won the German equestrianism championships, hitherto the preserve of privately run riding clubs. But some, especially those who had come down in the world under the Weimar Republic, took a more active and committed role. Typical here was Erich von dem Bach-Zelewski, who had volunteered for service in the war at the age of fifteen, joined a Free Corps, then been cashiered from the army in 1924 because of his proselytizing for the Nazis. He had made a living running a taxi firm, then a farm, before joining the Nazi Party and the SS in 1930; by the end of 1933 he was already moving rapidly up the hierarchy. Other young noblemen with similar careers included Ludolf von Alvensleben, who had also served in a Free Corps, lost his Polish estate at the end of the war and his compensation for the loss during the inflation, and made an unsuccessful attempt to run a car firm, which eventually went bankrupt; or Baron Karl von Eberstein, who had tried to eke out his existence in the 1920s as a travel agent. Reck-Malleczewen's observation in the Berlin nightclub had been shrewd and percipient: many of the younger members of the Junker aristocracy had indeed joined Himmler's new German elite. Others, especially those who had enrolled in the army or the foreign service, enthusiastic though they may have been to begin with, were in time to become bitterly disillusioned with the regime.[11]

I I

Germany's aristocracy had traditionally made its living from the land. Although over the years nobles had come to play a significant and in some areas more than significant role in the officer corps, the civil service, and even industry, it was the land that still provided many of them with the main source of their income, social power and political influence in the 1920s and 1930s. Reich President Paul von Hindenburg had been particularly susceptible to the influence of the Prussian landed aristocrats with whom he socialized when he was down on his estate in East Prussian Neudeck, and a great deal of public comment had been aroused by the special concessions the government had made to landowners like him, in the form of aid for agricultural producers in the rural East. As far as the Nazis were concerned, however, it was not the large landowner but the small peasant farmer who constituted the bedrock of German society in the countryside. Point 17 of the Nazi Party programme of 1920 indeed demanded 'a land reform suited to our national needs' and the 'creation of a law for the confiscation of land without compensation and for communally beneficial purposes'. Following on point 16, which demanded the abolition of the department stores, this clause seemed on the face of it to be directed against the great estates. But Nazism's critics made it look as if the Party was threatening peasant farms with expropriation as well, so on 13 April 1928, Hitler issued a 'clarification' of this clause in what had in the meantime been repeatedly trumpeted as a fixed, unalterable and non-discussable list of demands. Point 17 of the Party programme simply referred, he said, to Jewish land speculators who did not control land in the public interest but used it for profiteering. Farmers need not worry: the Nazi Party was committed in principle to the sanctity of private property.[12]

Reassured by this statement, and driven to despair by the deep economic crisis into which agriculture had fallen even before the onset of the Depression, the North German peasantry duly voted for the Nazi Party in large numbers from 1930 onwards. The landowning aristocracy stayed aloof, preferring to support the Nationalists. On the face of it, Nazism seemed to have little to offer them. Nevertheless, their interests were well represented in the coalition that came to power on 30 January 1933. Alfred Hugenberg, the Nationalist leader, was not only Minister of Economics but Minister of Agriculture too, and in this capacity he swiftly introduced a series of measures designed to pull his supporters, and German farmers more generally, out of the economic morass into which they had sunk. He banned creditors from foreclosing on indebted farms until 31 October 1933, he increased import duties on key agricultural products, and on 1 June he introduced measures providing for the cancellation of some debts. To protect dairy farmers, Hugenberg also cut the manufacture of margarine by 40 per cent and ordered that it should include some butter amongst its constituents. This last measure led in a very short space of time to an increase of up to 50 per cent in the price of fats, including butter and margarine, and caused widespread popular criticism. This was yet another nail in Hugenberg's political coffin. By late June the process of co-ordination had long since overwhelmed the key agricultural pressure-groups and was reaching Hugenberg's own Nationalist Party. By the end of the month, Hugenberg had resigned all his posts and disappeared into political oblivion.[13]

The man who replaced him was Richard Walther Darré, the Party's agricultural expert and inventor of the Nazi slogan 'blood and soil'. For Darré, what mattered was not improving the economic position of agriculture but shoring up the peasant farmer as the source of German racial strength. In his books *The Peasantry as the Life-Source of the Nordic Race*, published in 1928, and *New Aristocracy from Blood and Soil*, which appeared the following year, Darré argued that the essential qualities of the German race had been instilled into it by the peasantry of the early Middle Ages, which had not been downtrodden or oppressed by the landowning aristocracy but on the contrary had essentially formed part of a single racial community with it. The existence of landed estates was purely functional and did not express any superiority of intellect or character on the part of their owners.[14] These ideas had a powerful influence on Heinrich Himmler, who made Darré the Director of his Head Office for Race and Settlement. Himmler's idea of a new racial aristocracy to rule Germany had many aspects in common with Darré's, at least to begin with. And Darré's ideas appealed to Hitler, who invited him to join the Party and become head of a new section devoted to agriculture and the peasantry in 1930. By 1933 Darré had built up a large and well-organized propaganda machine that spread the good news amongst the peasantry about their pivotal role in the coming Third Reich. And he had successfully infiltrated so many Nazi Party members into agricultural pressure-groups like the Reich Land League that it was relatively easy for him to organize their co-ordination in the early months of the new regime.[15]

By the time of Hugenberg's resignation, Darré already effectively controlled the Nazified national farmers' organization, and his appointment as Minister of Agriculture cemented his existing position as leader of some nine million farmers and agricultural workers, who with their dependants made up something like 30 per cent of the population of Germany as a whole.[16] Within a couple of months of his appointment he was ready to introduce measures which aimed to put his ambitions into effect. Apart from the Reich Food Estate, these focused on new inheritance laws through which Darré sought to preserve the peasantry and build it into the foundation of a new social order. In some parts of Germany, notably the South-west, partible inheritance customs and laws meant that when a farmer died, his property and assets were divided up equally between his sons, thus leading to morcellization (the creation of farms so small as to be unviable) and thus to the proletarianization of the small peasant farmer. Darré's ideal was a Germany covered by farms that were big enough to be self-sufficient. Instead of being inherited by all the heirs equally, or, as in most of North Germany, the eldest son, farms should pass, he thought, to the strongest and most effective of the heirs alone. Keeping them in the family in this way would also isolate them from the market. Over the years, encouraged by this new rule, natural selection would strengthen the peasantry until it fulfilled its destiny of providing a new leadership caste for the nation as a whole. On 29 September 1933, in pursuit of this ambitious goal, Darré's Reich Entailed Farm Law was passed. It claimed to revive the old German custom of entailment, or inalienable inheritance. All farms of between 7.5 and 125 hectares were to fall under the provisions of the Law. They could not be bought or sold or split up, and they could not be foreclosed because of debt. Nor could they be used as security on loans. These were extremely draconian restrictions on the free market in land. But they were not very realistic. In practice, they owed most to Darré's abstract and ideal image of the solid and self-sufficient peasant farmer. Yet Germany was a country where centuries of partible inheritance had already created thousands of very small farms at one end of the scale, while the accumulation of property by landowners had led to the development of large numbers of estates far bigger than 125 hectares at the other. Only 700,000 farms, or 22 per cent of the total, were affected by the Law, making up about 37 per cent of the area covered by agricultural land and forests in Germany. Of these, some 85 per cent were at the lower end of the scale, between 20 and 50 hectares in size. In some areas, notably in Mecklenburg and estate-dominated parts of the East Elbian plain on the one hand, and in the heavily morcellized South-west on the other, the Law applied to relatively few properties and had little effect. But in parts of central Germany its impact was potentially considerable.[17]

Darré hoped to get round the problem of what to do with the heirs who were disinherited by the Law by encouraging them to start new farms in the East. This revived the tradition, much hallowed by German conservatives, of the 'colonization' of the East, but with one crucial difference: the area that was now to be colonized to create a new society of small and self-sufficient peasant farms was already occupied by large and middling Junker estates. On 11 May 1934, Darré spoke out bluntly against the estates' current owners who, he said, had destroyed the peasantry of East Elbia over the centuries and reduced many small farmers to the status of landless labourers. It was time, he declared, to return to the peasants the land that the Junkers had stolen from them. Of course, since the abandonment of the idea, originally mooted in point 17 of the Nazi Party programme, of expropriating the large estate-owners and dividing up their land between small peasant farmers, it was not possible even for Darré to urge compulsory measures in order to carry out his proposals. Instead, therefore, he urged that the state should do nothing to help estate owners who got into financial difficulties, a position not far from that of Hitler himself, who had declared on 27 April 1933 that large estates that failed should be 'colonized' by landless German peasants.[18]

Darré's ambitious plans were only partially fulfilled. They made him deeply unpopular in many sections of the population, including large parts of the peasantry. Moreover, for all his willingness to let failing estates be divided up, Hitler basically saw the conquest of living-space in the East as the main solution to Germany's agrarian problems. Colonization in his view thus had to wait until Germany had extended its dominion across Poland, Belarus and the Ukraine. In any case, for all his verbal egalitarianism, Hitler did not want to destroy the economic basis of the Prussian landed aristocracy. Many economic experts realized that the Junker estates, many of which had successfully rationalized and modernized their production and management since the late nineteenth century, were far more efficient as food producers than small peasant farmers, and the maintenance of food supplies in the present could not be mortgaged to the creation of a racial utopia in the future. In practice, therefore, the number of new small farms created east of the river Elbe did not significantly increase over what it had been in the last years of the Weimar Republic. Reich Entailed Farmers' sons disinherited by the Law did not, by and large, manage to find new properties under the scheme, and in any case, many Catholic peasants from the South German

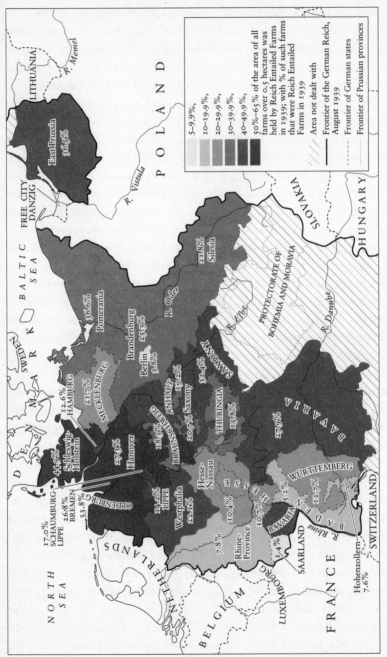

Map 12.   Reich Entailed Farms

hills were less than enthusiastic about being uprooted to the distant shores of Pomerania or East Prussia, far from their families, surrounded by alien Protestants speaking strange dialects in an unfamiliar, flat and featureless landscape.[19]

Under the debt clearance scheme initiated by Darré's predecessor Alfred Hugenberg, 650 million Reichsmarks were paid out by the government to make peasant farmers and estate owners solvent. This compared well with the 454 million paid out under Weimar between 1926 and 1933. Indebted farmers who fell under the aegis of the Reich Entailed Farm Law suddenly found that the threat of foreclosure had disappeared. However, the owners of entailed farms were frequently refused credit on the grounds that they could no longer use their farm as collateral. The fact that some used their new status to refuse to pay their existing debts only reinforced the determination of suppliers and merchants to make them pay cash for everything they bought. The Law thus made it more difficult than before for farmers to invest in expensive machinery, or to buy up small pieces of agricultural land adjoining their own farms. 'What use to us is a hereditary farm that's going to be debt-free in about 30 years' time,' one said, 'when we can't raise any money now, because nobody's giving us anything?'[20] There was bitterness and resentment amongst the sons and daughters of farmers who now saw themselves suddenly disinherited: many of them had worked hard all their lives as unpaid family assistants in the expectation of inheriting a portion of their father's land, only to have this prospect brusquely removed by the provisions of the new law. Farmers sympathetic to their children's plight could no longer follow the custom, common in areas of primogeniture, of remortgaging the farm to raise money for dowries or cash sums to be made over to their disinherited offspring in their last will and testament. In the practice of one notary alone, it was reported in the spring of 1934, twenty engagements had been called off since the Law's introduction since the brides' fathers could no longer raise the money for the dowries.[21] Moreover, it was now more difficult for the disinherited to buy their own farms even if they did possess some cash, since by taking 700,000 farms out of the property market the Law increased prices for non-entailed farmland. Ironically, therefore, the Reich Entailed Farm Law left the unsuccessful sons and daughters of farmowners no option but to leave the land and migrate to the cities, the very opposite of what Darré had intended. So onerous were the restrictions it imposed that many entailed farmers no longer felt they really owned their property at all; they were merely trustees or administrators for it.[22]

The removal of automatic inheritance rules created serious tensions in the family. Farmers thought the Law would be 'the occasion for an embittered sibling war', it was reported, 'and see as the consequence the introduction of a system of one-child families' – another respect in which the effects of the Law promised to be the reverse of what Darré had expected. In Bavaria towards the end of 1934 one such farmer, the longest-serving Party member in his district, was sent to prison for three months for saying in public that Hitler was not a farmer and did not have any children himself, or he would not have passed the Law. In court he repeated these sentiments, though without the earthy obscenities that had accompanied them in his original statement. Peasant farmers even brought court cases challenging the decision to designate them as Reich entailed farmers.[23] By the summer of 1934 peasant farmers had turned against the Nazis' agrarian policies everywhere; in Bavaria the atmosphere on market-days was said to be so hostile to the Party that local gendarmes did not dare intervene, and well-known Nazis avoided the farmers for fear they would be subjected to a barrage of aggressive questions. Even in areas like Schleswig-Holstein, where the rural population had voted in overwhelming numbers for the Nazi Party in 1930–33, the peasants were said by July 1934 to be depressed, particularly about the prices they were getting for their pigs. In addition, a Social Democratic agent reported at this time from North-west Germany:

Formerly the middling and large landowners of Oldenburg and East Friesia were very enthusiastic for the Nazis. But nowadays they are almost unanimously rejecting them and returning to their old conservative tradition. A particular contribution to this change had been made amongst East Friesian cattle-breeders and rich polder-farmers by the Entailed Farm Law, and amongst the middling farmers and land-users above all by the compulsory regulation of milk and egg production.[24]

The problem here was that instead of selling their milk and eggs direct to consumers, as they had done previously, the farmers were now having to go through the elaborate structure of the Reich Food Estate, which meant that they were only getting 10 pfennigs a litre of milk instead of the previous 16, since the wholesalers raked off 10 pfennigs and the price maximum was fixed at 20. Not surprisingly, a black market in eggs and milk soon emerged, to the irritation of the authorities, who responded with police raids, the mass seizure of contraband eggs and arrests of those people involved.[25]

Older peasants remembered the grand promises made by Darré in 1933 and continued to grumble more openly and unrestrainedly than almost any other sector of the population, because the regime felt unable to crack down on them hard in view of their indispensability. Nazi speakers continued to encounter heckling at farmers' meetings; at one such assembly, in Silesia in 1937, when the speaker lost his temper and told his audience that the Gestapo would soon teach them how to be National Socialists, most of the listeners simply got up and walked out. Farmers complained not only about low prices, the flight of their labourers from the land, the cost of machinery, fertilizer and the rest, but also about the high salaries of Reich Food Estate officials who did nothing but interfere. Many, like other Germans, resented the continual demands of the Party and affiliated organizations for donations and contributions.[26] Particularly vociferous were the owners of Reich Entailed Farms, who felt so secure in their tenure that they could afford to speak with a sometimes astonishing openness. Asked by a young Nazi whether the peasants in a particular Bavarian village could really be supporters of the Party when they were so ready to curse it, one such farmer replied, 'Nah, we're no Hitlerites, they only have those in Berlin.' When the young man then said he thought he should enlighten them and bring them to their senses, the farmer, applauded by the others present, told him: 'We don't need any enlightening, you scamp! You ought to be still at school!' Peasant farmers felt they had lost their freedom to buy and sell their goods, and in the cases of the Reich Entailed Farms their property too, on the open market, and had gained nothing in return. Yet many observers remembered 'that farmers have always cursed every government through the ages'. Grumbling at the Nazi regime was no different. Moreover, younger farmers and farmers' sons saw opportunities in the regime as well, in many cases in terms of jobs in the administration of the Reich Food Estate itself. The Nazi ideology of 'blood and soil' had more appeal to them than to cynical old peasant farmers who thought they had seen it all before and who paid more attention in the end to material factors. But even the older farmers were aware that their situation by 1939 was not so bad as it had been six or seven years earlier.[27]

III

Despite the many and often contradictory pressures to which they were subjected under the Third Reich, village communities did not change fundamentally between 1933 and 1939. In rural areas of Protestant North Germany, the Nazi Party had been able to unite local opinion, often backed by leading figures in the community such as the village pastor and schoolteacher, the more prosperous farmers and even sometimes the local estate owner, behind the promise to keep the class struggle that was raging in the towns and cities from disturbing the relative peace of the countryside. Here as elsewhere, the promise of a united national community was a potent slogan that won Nazism many supporters before 1933.[28] Leading peasant families in many villages slipped effortlessly into leading roles in the new Reich. In rural Bavaria, the Nazi Party was wary of upsetting local opinion by parachuting 'old fighters' into village councils or mayors' offices if they did not already have the respect of the villagers by virtue of their family or their place within the traditional hierarchy of the farming community. Particularly where Catholicism was strong, and villagers had continued to vote for the Centre Party or its Bavarian equivalent, the Bavarian People's Party, up to 1933, the Nazis trod warily. Generating consensus and neutralizing potential opposition were the priorities. For their part, villagers were mostly quite happy to adapt to the new regime if this preserved existing social and political structures.[29]

In the Bavarian village of Mietraching, for example, village treasurer Hinterstocker, who had held office since 1919, was persuaded by other members of the Bavarian People's Party to join the Nazi Party in 1933 so that he could keep his post and prevent a rabid 'old fighter' from getting his hands on the community purse-strings. When a particularly disliked Nazi threatened to take over the mayoralty in 1935, the village elders once more persuaded the popular and ever-obliging Hinterstocker to do the decent thing and become mayor himself. In this position, Hinterstocker was said to have done everything he could in subsequent years to keep the most unpopular measures of the regime from impacting on the village, and he made a point of taking part every year without fail in the village's religious processions, much to the satisfaction of the other villagers. On 12 December 1945, as the regional administrator told the American occupation authorities, 90 per cent of the villagers were reported to be in favour of his reappointment.[30] In another Bavarian village, when the local Party tried to put an 'old fighter' into a key post, the local administrator's office registered its alarm:

The district office is not in a position to agree to the suggestion that the master tailor S. should be appointed mayor of the commune of Langenpreising. In discussion with the councillors, the latter have unanimously expressed a wish to leave the existing mayor Nyrt in office, since as a farmer he is better suited to this post than the master tailor S . . . The district office is also of the opinion that the appointment of a respected farmer is a better guarantee for the smooth running of communal business.[31]

Village council members even had to be reminded from time to time that mayors were appointed and not elected under the Third Reich, when the minutes of their meetings reached higher authority.[32] In parts of rural Lippe, things could be even more disconcerting for the Party, as in the case of Mayor Wöhrmeier in the village of Donop, who refused to take part in Nazi Party functions or to use the 'Hail, Hitler!' greeting when signing off his letters, never possessed a swastika flag and organized successful economic boycotts against village artisans and tradespeople who backed the efforts of the local Party Leader to oust him. Despite repeated denunciations, Wöhrmeier successfully held on to his post all the way up to 1945.[33]

The solidarity of village communities in many parts of Germany had been created over centuries through a dense network of customs and institutions, which governed common rights such as gleaning, wood-collecting and the like. Villages often consisted of intertwined groups of family and kin, and the role of unpaid family assistants, who might include at times of particularly heavy demand for labour cousins, uncles and aunts from nearby farms as well as the family itself, was similarly governed by long-hallowed tradition. The precariousness of everyday life on the land had generated an economy based on a system of mutual obligations that could not easily be disturbed – hence the resentment in many parts of the countryside against the Reich Entailed Farm Law, even among those it ostensibly benefited. At the same time, there were also considerable inequalities of class and status within village communities, not only between farmers on the one hand and millers, cattle dealers, blacksmiths and the like on the other, but also amongst the farmers themselves. In the Hessian village of Körle, for instance, with roughly a thousand souls around 1930, the community was split into three main groups. At the top were the 'horse-farmers', fourteen substantial peasant farmers with between 10 and 30 hectares each, producing enough of a surplus for the market to be able to keep horses and employ labourers and maids on a permanent basis and more temporarily at harvest-time. In the middle were the 'cow-farmers', sixty-six of them in 1928, who were more or less self-sufficient with 2 to 10 hectares of land apiece but depended for labour on their own relatives and occasionally employed extra labourers at time of need, though they generally paid them in kind rather than in money. Finally, at the bottom of the social heap, there were the 'goat-farmers', eighty households with less than 2 hectares each, dependent on the loan of draught animals and ploughs from the horse-farmers, and paying for their services by working for them at times in return.[34]

By the 1920s, the economic situation of this last group had become precarious enough for a number of the menfolk to have to earn a living during the week by working as industrial labourers in nearby towns, to which the village was linked by a good railway connection. This brought them into contact with Communism and Social Democracy, which soon became the political preference of many of the poorer families in Körle. Nevertheless, the network of mutual dependencies and obligations helped unite the community and cement the role of the horse-farmers as its natural and generally accepted leaders; political differences worried the village elite, but they were still expressed largely outside the traditional structures of the village. The horse-farmers and cow-farmers were mostly Nationalist by political conviction, and cannot have been very pleased when the existing mayor was ousted in 1933 to make way for a leading local Nazi. Yet the rhetoric of Nazism had a powerful social appeal to the community at all social levels. Villagers, suitably encouraged by the outpourings of the Propaganda Ministry and its numerous organs, could readily identify with the image of Hitler as head of a national household based on a network of mutual obligations in the organic national community. If propaganda had its limitations in the countryside, with only one radio set for every twenty-five inhabitants compared with one in eight in the towns even in 1939, and no direct access to cinemas, then the Ministry did its best to get its message across through encouraging the purchase of 'People's Receivers' and sending mobile cinemas round the villages. The message they conveyed, of the new People's Community in which the peasantry would occupy a central place, was not unwelcome and helped reassure the older farmers that not a lot would change; perhaps the new regime would even restore the hierarchical community structures that had been undermined by the drift of young men from poor families into the towns and the spread of Marxist ideology amongst the goat-farmers.[35]

Given such cohesive social structures, it is not surprising that village communities remained largely intact during and after the Nazi seizure of power. There was little resistance to the takeover; the local Communists were subject to house-searches and threatened with arrest, and in social terms the suppression of the labour movement in Körle, such as it was, clearly represented the reassertion of the dominance of the horse-farmers and cow-farmers over the village lower class, the goat-farmers. However, using the rhetoric of community to crush opposition to the new regime also had implications in the village as to how far the process of co-ordination could go. The goat-farmers and their sons were too valuable to the village elites to be crushed altogether. Thus the monarchist father of the local Nazi who led the police and brownshirt raids on the homes of the local Communists in 1933 threatened to disinherit him if any of those affected were taken out of the village, and thus he limited the effects of the action. When stormtroopers were brought in to the village from outside to confiscate the bicycles of the local cycling club, which was close to the Communist Party, the local innkeeper, a long-established Nazi Party member, presented them with a fictitious deed purporting to show that the club owed him so much money that he was entitled to seize the bicycles in lieu of payment. The stormtroopers withdrew, and the innkeeper stowed the bicycles away in his loft, where they remained until they were retrieved by their former owners after the war. Village solidarities were often more important than politics, particularly when they were threatened from outside.[36]

Nevertheless, the Third Reich did not leave them wholly untouched. In Körle, for example, as in other parts of rural Germany, the Nazi regime opened up generational tensions as most fathers of all social groups remained opposed to Nazism while many sons saw membership and activity in the Party as a means of asserting themselves against an authoritarian older generation. By joining a variety of Nazi Party organizations they found a new role that was not dependent on their elders. Interviewed after the war, villagers said the early years of the Third Reich brought 'war' into every household.[37] As the demand for industrial labour grew, more young men, and, increasingly, young women from the goat-farmer households spent more time working for wages in the towns, bringing new prosperity into the home but also getting exposed to new ideas and new forms of social organization. The Hitler Youth, the Labour Service, the army and a whole variety of women's organizations took boys and girls, young men and women out of the village and showed them the wider world. The escalating Nazi attack on the Churches also began to undermine another central village institution, both as an instrument of socialization and as a centre of social cohesion. At the same time, however, these changes had their limits. The older generation's belief in the community and the farmers' dependence on the labour and other obligations of the young meant that the arrogance of the younger generation was tolerated, the tensions it generated dispelled by humour, and the household and community preserved intact. And the younger generation's involvement in Nazi Party organizations did not bring them much new independence as individuals; it mainly meant they extended their community allegiance to a new set of institutions.[38]

The fact that village social structures were not fundamentally affected by the regime perhaps helps explain why in the end, for all their grumbling, the peasants were not driven into outright opposition. The major bones of contention – labour shortages, the unwelcome side-effects of the Reich Entailed Farm Law, the low prices for their produce set by the Reich Food Estate – presented the peasantry with obstacles they did their best to circumvent with their traditional cunning, adulterating flour to make it go further, selling produce directly on the black market and so on. They could also have recourse to the law, and many did so. The effects of the Reich Entailed Farm Law, for example, were mitigated by the inclusion of provisions for legally removing entailed farmers who refused to pay their debts, or failed to run their farms in an orderly manner. Special local courts, on which the local farming community was well represented, were not afraid to disbar such miscreants, since it was clearly in the interests of efficient food production as well as of peace and stability in the countryside that they do so.[39] On the whole, indeed, these courts took their decisions on a practical rather than an ideological basis, and they went some way towards assuaging the anger of the farming community at the deleterious consequences of the Entailed Farm Law.[40]

In the rural Protestant district of Stade, on the North German coast, where the Nazis had already won far more votes than average in the elections of the early 1930s, peasant farmers were basically in favour of a system of fixed prices and quotas, since that made life less uncertain, and the whole ethos of peasant society there, as in other parts of Germany, had never been wholly attuned to free market capitalism in any case. What they did not like were prices that were fixed too low. The lower the prices, the more they grumbled. As might be expected from people whose whole lives, like those of their forebears, had been constructed around the need to eke a precarious living from the land, their dissatisfaction with the regime was limited to the instances in which it had an adverse effect on their livelihood. Moreover, evasion of the production quotas laid down by the Reich Food Estate or the Four-Year Plan often sprang more from the contradictory and irrational ways in which the agrarian economy was managed than from any objection to the quotas in principle. Thus, for example, when small farmers refused to meet their grain quotas, as they often did, this was in many cases so that they could use the withheld grain to feed their livestock and so meet their milk and cattle quotas. The solidarity of rural communities also meant that farmers felt relatively safe in evading the quotas or indeed in voicing their dissatisfaction over the regime's agrarian politics: in contrast to the situation in urban Germany, it was rare for anyone in the countryside to be denounced to the Gestapo or the Party for uttering criticism of the regime, except where really severe conflicts emerged between the old village elites and the aspiring but politically frustrated younger generation. Despite the exhortations of the Reich Food Estate and the Four-Year Plan administration, peasant farmers often remained suspicious of agricultural modernization, new techniques and unfamiliar machinery, quite apart from the practical difficulties of obtaining these things, and the Third Reich did little in consequence to push on the modernization of small-farm agriculture. Instead, grandiose nationwide pageants like the annual Harvest Thanksgiving Festival, which drew more participants than any other ceremony or ritual occasion in the Third Reich, confirmed the peasants in their stubbornness through the uncritical celebration of their contribution to the national community. In the end, therefore, Darré's promise of a new rural utopia was no more realized by 1939 than was the contrary ambition of the regime to achieve national self-sufficiency in food supplies; but few peasants were really interested in these things, however flattered they might have been by the accompanying propaganda. What really mattered to them was that they were making a decent living, better than they had done in the Depression years, and they could live with that.[41]

THE FATE OF THE MIDDLE CLASSES

I

The peasantry were generally assigned in German political discourse in the late nineteenth and early twentieth century to that peculiar and amorphous social group known by the untranslatable German appellation of the *Mittelstand*. This term expressed in the first place the aspirations of right-wing propagandists that the people who were neither bourgeois nor proletarian should have a recognized place in society. Roughly equivalent to the French *petite bourgeoisie* or the English lower middle class, they had come by the early 1930s to embody much more than a mere social group: in German politics they stood for a set of values. Located between the two great antagonistic classes into which society had become divided, they represented people who stood on their own two feet, independent, hard-working, the healthy core of the German people, unjustly pushed to the side by the class war that was raging all about them. It was to people like these – small shopkeepers, skilled artisans running their own workshops, self-sufficient peasant farmers – that the Nazis had initially directed their appeal. The Nazi Party programme of 1920 was indeed among other things a typical product of the far-right politics of the German *Mittelstand*; the support of such people was among the factors that had got the Party off the ground in the first place.[42]

The resentments of such groups were many, their perceived enemies legion. Small shopkeepers resented the big department stores, artisans hated the mass production of the big factories, peasants grumbled about unfair competition from the big estates. All of them were susceptible to the appeal of political rhetoric that blamed scapegoats such as the Jews for their problems. Representatives of all these groups saw an opportunity in the coming of the Third Reich to realize their long-held aspirations. And initially, indeed, they met with some success. The locally based attacks on the department stores, the boycotts and discriminations driven in many cases by artisans and small shopkeepers themselves, acting through the Nazi Party and the SA, were quickly backed by a Law for the Protection of Individual Trade passed on 12 May 1933. From now on, chain stores were forbidden to expand or open new branches, to add new lines, or to house within their walls self-contained departments such as barbers' shops or shoemaking and shoe-repair sections. Restaurants in department stores, widely believed to be undercutting independent innkeepers and restaurateurs, were ordered to be closed. In August 1933 a new decree imposed further bans on baking, sausage-making, watch-repairing, photo-developing, and car-servicing by department stores. Three months later, department and chain stores were prohibited from offering a discount of more than 3 per cent on prices, a measure also extended to consumer co-operatives. Mail-order firms were reined in; Party organizations did their best to ensure that contracts for uniforms and equipment went to small businesses. From September 1933 the government's housing repair and reconstruction subsidies provided a boost for many carpenters, plumbers, masons and other craftsmen.[43] Artisans' pressure-groups, frustrated by their failure to get what they wanted during the Weimar years, pressed for better qualifications and recognition of their corporate status through compulsory membership in trade guilds, and got them: from June 1934 artisans had to belong to a guild (*Innung*), which was required to regulate their particular branch of trade, from January 1935 under the supervision of the Economic Ministry. After 1935 it was compulsory for artisans to pass a master's examination in order to be officially registered and thus to receive permission to open a workshop. These were long-held ambitions which went some way towards restoring the status many artisans felt they had lost in the course of industrialization and the rise of factory-based mass production. They were strongly backed by Schacht, who felt that small workshops and their owners made a useful contribution to the economy and deserved defending against the attempts of the Labour Front to degrade their status to that of workers by incorporating them into its organization.[44]

But for all the rhetoric and for all the pressure applied on the ground by local Party and brownshirt activists whose own background in many cases lay in the world of the small shopkeeper, trader or artisan, the initial flurry of practical action and legislative intervention in favour of small businesses soon died away as the economy began to be driven by the overwhelming imperatives of rearmament. Headlong rearmament necessarily favoured big business. Despite all the Nazis' promises to rescue the lower middle class and the small businessman, the number of artisan enterprises, which had increased during the economic recovery by around 18 per cent between 1931 and 1936, declined by 14 per cent between 1936 and 1939.[45] Between 1933 and 1939 the number of cobblers' workshops decreased by 12 per cent, of carpenters' by 14 per cent. The total turnover of artisanal trade had not recovered to its 1926 levels by 1939. Many artisans indeed were actually poorer than industrial workers. The shortage of raw materials, the competition of larger enterprises, the prohibitive expense of purchasing the machinery needed to process, for example, artificial leather, were some of the factors involved in bringing about these problems. Some traditional handicrafts like violin-making in Mittenwald or clock-making in the Black Forest were progressively undercut by factory production and went into a steep decline. Moreover, small business, like its bigger rivals, was increasingly beset by government regulations. Compulsory guild membership and the requirement to take an examination before receiving a formal certificate of competence that would allow them to go into business proved to be decidedly mixed blessings; many master artisans had to take the examinations all over again, and the paperwork involved in this was too much for many of them, particularly when in 1937 they were required to keep records of their income and expenditure. Instead of self-governing corporations, artisans found themselves drafted into guilds organized on the leadership principle and directed from above. The promise of enhanced status in a new corporate state had proved to be illusory. The Four-Year Plan, in addition, demanded rapid training rather than the thorough preparation and high standards which had been the idea behind compulsory examinations, so the Artisanal Chambers lost the exclusive right to award mastership qualifications.[46]

Small business was squeezed in another way, too, by the loss of labour through conscription and the better wages offered to employees in directly war-related industries. The concentration of business was suggested strongly by a 7 per cent decline in the number of owners and managers in trade, communications and transport in the official statistics between 1933 and 1939. True, some of this was accounted for by the closure of Jewish-owned workshops; between 1933 and 1938 the number of Jewish-owned artisanal businesses fell from 10,000 to 5,000, and by the end of 1938 all the rest had disappeared as well. Almost all of them were too small to be worth taking over, and indeed the grand total Aryanized rather than driven to closure was no more than 345. But there was more to the decline than this. Over the same period, the number of unpaid family employees grew by 11 per cent in commercial establishments as it became more difficult to find paid employees. Increasingly, as young men drifted away from this sector of the economy to other, more attractive ones, or were drafted into the armed forces, businesses were run by older men and their womenfolk. A survey of soap and brush shops at the beginning of 1939, for instance, showed that 44 per cent were run by women, and over 50 per cent of the male owners were over the age of fifty; nearly 40 per cent of the male owners also had to supplement their earnings from other sources of income.[47]

A further financial burden was imposed from December 1938, when artisans were required to insure themselves without government assistance. By 1939 the Four-Year Plan, with its fixed quotas and prices, had drastically circumscribed the independence of small businessmen, from butchers, greengrocers, sweet-shop owners, bakers and corner-shops to cobblers, tobacco-stall proprietors and stallholders on Germany's markets. Regulations and auditing took up time, while new taxes and compulsory donations cut into profits. The drastic shortage of labour in armaments and arms-related industries had led to growing official pressure on small businesses and workshops to swell the nation's industrial workforce; by 1939 even independent artisans had to carry a work-book with dates of their training, qualifications and experience; thus registered, they could be drafted into a compulsory labour scheme at any moment; master shoemakers, for example, were drafted into the Volkswagen factory to retrain and work as upholsterers. In order to facilitate this redeployment of artisanal labour into war-relevant production (as the Volkswagen factory indeed was), the Artisanal Chambers were required in 1939 to 'comb through' their trades and pick out unviable enterprises in the consumer industries; perhaps 3 per cent of artisanal businesses were wound up as a consequence, almost all of them one-man workshops in which the owner was so poor that he had to rely on welfare payments for part of his income.[48]

Characteristic of the disappointment of many such groups in the Third Reich was the experience of the pharmacists, a branch of retailing based overwhelmingly on small independent drug stores. Many pharmacists saw in the coming of the Third Reich the chance to realize their long-term ambition of having their profession formally put on a par with medicine, to push back the growing might of the big drug companies, and to restore the integrity of the apothecary as a skilled, trained expert – a professional, indeed – who produced most medicinal remedies and treatments himself and was guaranteed against competition from herbalists and other unqualified rivals by the establishment of a legal monopoly. But this vision quickly turned out to be a mirage. Although the training of pharmacists was reformed in 1934 and Aryanized, with few objections, in 1935, the apothecaries themselves could not agree on how best to assert their monopolistic claims, and their organizations were absorbed into the Labour Front in 1934. The regime's priorities soon took over, and pharmacists found themselves involved in the search for home-grown drugs to render Germany independent of pharmaceutical imports, and helping to prepare the medicaments that would be needed when war came. In this game, the big drug companies were the major players, and military priorities soon rendered the pseudo-medieval idea of the independent, small-town apothecary producing his own drugs and approved remedies almost entirely obsolescent.[49] The same tale could be told in many other parts of the independent business sector. In the veterinary profession, for example, the same processes of co-ordination took place, with existing organizations dissolving themselves, and 4,000 out of Germany's 7,500 vets already members of the new Reich Association of German Veterinary Surgeons by January 1934. Here as elsewhere, the voluntary professional associations largely co-ordinated themselves, and their reward was their formal incorporation into a Reich Chamber of Veterinary Surgeons in 1936. But early attempts by one wing of the profession to impose a backward-looking corporate form on their national organization gave way very quickly to the standard institutional structures of the Third Reich, centralized, hierarchical, and easily subject to central government control, as in other areas of small business as well.[50]

Social Democratic observers in Germany reported the dissatisfaction of artisans and small shopkeepers with their situation in the Third Reich. Already in May 1934, small businessmen and retailers were complaining that the economic situation had not improved enough for people to be spending more on the consumer goods and services they mainly produced and sold, while the Party was constantly badgering them for contributions of one kind and another which they had no choice but to pay. Among their many grievances was the fact that promises to curb consumer co-operatives, in many cases institutions formerly close to the Social Democratic labour movement, had not been kept. Co-ordinated into the Labour Front and used as a convenient means of rewarding 'old fighters' by putting them in executive positions, the co-ops lost little more than the subsidies and tax privileges they had been granted under the Weimar Republic. A law of May 1935 arranged for the winding-up of financially weak co-ops, but attempts to ban civil servants from membership were quashed by Hess in 1934; and while around a third of the country's 12,500 co-op stores did close down by 1936, often under pressure from local Party groups, there were still some two million co-op members at the latter date, and small shopkeepers still felt cheated because they had not disappeared altogether.[51] In Silesia, according to the report of a Social Democratic agent, there was great 'bitterness' in these circles:

The ceaseless collections are leading people to grasp the beggar's staff. Turnover has fallen rapidly. Because of poor wages, workers can only buy the cheapest articles, and of course they flock to the department stores and one-price shops. People are cursing like fishwives, and their disappointment has already made itself publicly apparent in meetings ... At a recent meeting in Görlitz a shop-keeper spoke up in the discussion and said: 'What didn't they promise us before?! – The department stores were going to be closed, the co-operative societies were going to be destroyed, the one-price shops were going to disappear. Nothing has happened! We've been lied to and betrayed!' The next day the man was arrested. This caused a great deal of bitterness.[52]

Not only was consumer demand slow to recover, but the regime had, in this sense, not been National Socialist enough.[53]

In 1935, even some shopkeepers and artisans who had been zealous Nazis in previous times were reported to be voicing their disappointment that their situation had not improved. One master artisan from Aachen was heard to say that all his colleagues were opponents of Hitler, but only three out of fifty he knew would actually dare to open their mouths; the rest remained silent.[54] One could not say that the Nazis had done nothing for them, a Social Democratic report noted later, but almost all the measures they had taken had been double-edged. Credit had become difficult to obtain, demand was slow to recover, price controls had a damaging effect on profits, guild contributions were burdensome, the guilds were badly run, and taxes were being ratcheted upwards and collected with far greater zeal than before.[55] Yet in the end, even the Social Democrats were forced to conclude in 1939 that: 'For the moment, the artisans' discontent against their increasingly oppressive situation scarcely has a political point.' They grumbled about shortages of raw materials, complained about the loss of their workers to the armed forces or the munitions industry, and cursed the requirement placed on them to keep elaborate business records, but none of this came together into any generalized criticism of the regime itself. The Social Democrats concluded that these were 'social strata for whom political thinking has always been alien'. This was dubious. Disappointment created disillusion, even dissent; but as in other areas of society, there were good reasons why this did not spill over into outright opposition to the regime. Those artisans and small businessmen who did keep their heads above water – the great majority – found for all their troubles and travails that their economic situation was at least better than it had been in the Depression. The small-business sector remained deeply divided, between producers and retailers, services and manufactures, and in many other ways. Finally, of all the sectors of German society this had been the most favourable to right-wing nationalism, antisemitism, and anti-democratic sentiment since the late nineteenth century. It would take more than economic discontent to turn it against the regime altogether.[56]

I I

Artisans and shopkeepers were not the only social group who hoped for an improvement in status with the coming of the Third Reich. White-collar workers and salaried employees of private businesses had long looked enviously at the superior pay, status and privileges of civil servants. Known popularly as the 'new *Mittelstand*', they were, however, deeply divided politically, with liberal and Social Democratic organizations rivalling those of the far right, and their votes for the Nazi Party in the Weimar years had not been above the average for the country as a whole. Many hoped that the Third Reich would once more set up the barriers of status between white-collar workers and manual labourers that the previous years had torn down. Fear of 'proletarianization' had been a major driving force in the white-collar unions, whether on the left, the centre or the right. But they were bitterly disappointed when Hitler came to power. The leaders of all three political wings of the white-collar unions were arrested and put into concentration camps, and the unions themselves, along with all other white-collar organizations, were amalgamated into the German Labour Front.[57] Moreover, the fact that the workers and their organizations were formally integrated into the national community dismantled a further barrier. White-collar workers did not possess the close-knit traditions or distinctive culture that organized labour had enjoyed in the Social Democratic and to a lesser extent Communist movement, so they were more vulnerable to atomization and terrorization and less capable even of passive resistance.[58] It was not surprising, therefore, that a Social Democratic agent in a life insurance business in central Germany reported in 1936 that most were politically apathetic, apart from a few former supporters of the Steel Helmets and the Nationalists, who might not have been fanatical adherents of Hitler but were none the less pleased with the way in which he had crushed 'Marxism' in 1933. 'The majority of the male employees are dully accepting of the political compulsion and all the various regulations,' he admitted. Most of them came from the lower middle class. They blamed problems on the 'little Hitlers' of the regime and continued to admire the Leader himself. The chances of any kind of critical thinking about the regime were fairly remote here.[59]

More complicated was the position of university-trained professionals, of lawyers, doctors, teachers, engineers, university professors and the like. As we have seen, the Third Reich had a variable impact on the status of these groups, downgrading lawyers, civil servants, schoolteachers and professors on the one hand, and upgrading doctors in particular on the other. The Nazis' anti-intellectualism and populism had an obviously damaging effect on the social prestige of such groups overall, and the changes that came about in university training reflected this, with the drastic fall in student numbers, the requirement to spend long periods of time in labour camps and the abolition of autonomous student institutions like the corporations. The rapidly growing power and prestige of the armed forces opened up new careers for bright and ambitious young men from the upper and middle classes in the officer corps, and made the professions seem dull and unrewarding in comparison. The oft-repeated and openly expressed Nazi contempt for the law made a career in it unappealing, and it is not surprising that by 1939 there were widespread complaints about the lack of suitable recruits for the judiciary and the legal profession. Even where a profession did relatively well out of the Third Reich, like the engineers, their situation did not improve that much. Rearmament, with its requirement for technical expertise in the design of tanks, ships, planes and weaponry; fortifications like the West Wall and public projects like the motorways; prestigious building projects in Berlin, Munich and elsewhere: these and other factors even led the Ministry of Labour to exempt engineers from labour mobility restrictions in 1937, especially if they changed jobs to further their professional training and development. None of this made much difference to their pay, however: in a company like Siemens, for example, the starting salary of a qualified engineer was still less than that of a first-year schoolteacher in 1936, while the engineers' organization, led by Fritz Todt, was still complaining in 1939 that humanities graduates enjoyed greater social prestige than engineers. The award at the 1938 Nuremberg Party Rally of the second German Prize for Art and Science (the substitute for the now-banned Nobel Prizes) to Fritz Todt, the car designer Ferdinand Porsche and the aircraft engineers Wilhelm Messerschmidt and Ernst Heinkel in explicit and much-trumpeted recognition of the achievements of German technology did not seem to compensate much in the eyes of most engineers.[60]

All professional groups, however, had lost substantially in autonomy through the process of co-ordination in the early months of the Third Reich, when their various professional associations were closed down, merged and brought under Nazi leadership. All had acquiesced in the process, as they had also in the purging of Social Democrats and Communists and the removal of Jewish members from the professional associations and in the end from the professions themselves. The dumbing-down of university education and professional training, with its emphasis on ideological indoctrination and military preparedness rather than on the traditional acquisition of knowledge and skills, added to this regimentation of professional activities to produce a palpable demoralization amongst many professionals. Even the doctors, probably the most favoured of the traditional professions under the Third Reich, lost some of their old privileges without gaining new ones. When in 1935 the government introduced a Reich Physicians' Ordinance, for example, supplemented by a Professional Statute in November 1937, the doctors found themselves tightly bound by a set of rules imposed from above with penal sanctions threatened to anyone who infringed them. Disciplinary courts quickly became active in issuing warnings, meting out fines and even suspending doctors who transgressed. Not only did the doctors themselves now have to keep the Reich Physicians' Chamber, founded in 1936, informed of any changes in their own circumstances, and submit to it any new contractual arrangements they entered into for approval; they also had to breach patient confidentiality by reporting serious cases of alcoholism, hereditary or congenital disabilities and sexually transmitted diseases to the authorities. Indeed the 1935 Ordinance, while affirming the principle of confidentiality in theory, explicitly said it could be overridden in practice if required by the 'common sense of the people', which of course, as ever, was defined by the regime and its servants. Doctors, no matter how senior they might be, were also required to undergo new training courses in racial hygiene and hereditarian biology. Five thousand physicians had to attend such courses in 1936 alone: many of them resented having to listen to interminable lectures by Nazi ideologues whose qualifications they frequently regarded as inferior to their own and whose ideas many of them treated with justified scepticism and suspicion.[61]

An even worse blow to their collective pride was the regime's failure

to concede the medical profession's long-held demand for the suppression of 'quacks', or non-university-trained healers, of whom there
were at least 14,000 in Germany in 1935, or three for every ten qualified
doctors. The National Socialist Physicians' League, to which about a
third of doctors belonged, lacked influence and prestige and was generally thought to be rather ineffective. The position of the Reich Physicians'
Chamber, to which all doctors had to belong, was stronger, but the basic
problem was that leading Nazis, from Hitler downwards, were quite
sympathetic to alternative medicine. The head of the Reich Physicians'
Chamber, Gerhard Wagner, as we have already seen, supported what he
called the 'New German Healing' and tried to foist courses in it on
university medical faculties.[62] In the face of contradictory pressures from
the doctors' organization on the one hand and its own leaders on the
other, the regime dithered for years until in February 1939 it finally
announced that all lay healers had to be registered with the German
Natural Healers' Union, and that henceforth there were to be no new
recruits into the occupation. Not only did this give the lay healers professional status, but from now on, those who could show the required
degree of competence could get the title 'physician of natural healing',
thus counting as doctors, while university-trained physicians could now
be required to assist registered nature healers if the latter asked for their
help. Particularly talented lay healers could even gain admittance to
medical faculties in the universities without the usual qualifications.
Finally, the whole set of rules and regulations was not backed up by any
kind of sanctions against unregistered lay healers, who could continue to
practise so long as they did not charge fees. Thus the German medical
profession had to endure loss of professional status, increased government
interference, and the erosion of traditional ethical positions.[63]

Yet all this was more than balanced out by the enormous increase in
the power doctors wielded over the individual in the Third Reich, bolstered by state policies such as sterilization and health screening for a
whole variety of purposes, from military service to marriage. Health was
central to a regime whose main priority was racial fitness, and the vast
majority of doctors were more than willing to go along with the state's
new requirements in this respect; indeed, the idea of racial hygiene had
been widely popular in the medical profession well before 1933. Doctors'
pay increased sharply after 1937, with average gross earnings rising from

just over 9,000 Reichsmarks in 1933 to nearly 14,000 four years later; by 1939 it was said to be in the region of 20,000. The removal of so many Jewish physicians from the profession had led to a growth in the practices of those who remained, the economic recovery had increased people's willingness to contribute to health insurance funds, and the funds themselves had been reformed so as to make it less expensive for patients to visit the surgery and less complicated for doctors to get the fees. This put doctors comfortably ahead of lawyers in the earning stakes, and, incidentally, amounted to around twice the income of dentists, whose role in racial hygiene and its associated health policies was more or less minimal. Outside the surgery, the rapid growth in the armed forces opened up new opportunities to doctors to serve in the medical corps. Doctors were recruited to provide medical services for many branches of the Nazi Party and its affiliated organizations, from the brownshirts to the Hitler Youth. The most ambitious could join the SS, where they could obtain prestige and promotion more easily than in civilian life. Himmler set up an SS medical academy in Berlin to provide them with ideological training, and the doctors within the SS were headed by the grandly titled SS Reich Doctor, parallel to Himmler's own title of SS Reich Leader. Altogether, it has been estimated that over two-thirds of physicians in Germany had a connection with the Nazi Party and its affiliates. The doctors' key role in the imagined Nazi future was marked out by institutions such as the Leadership School of German Physicians, a training camp located in a picturesque part of rural Mecklenburg, where members of the Nazi Physicians' League underwent a two-week training programme in Nazi ideology to prepare them for a political role in the Third Reich in years to come. Younger doctors thus found scope for their ambition in the highly ideologized area of racial hygiene, while older, established members of the profession were able to carry on their traditional work, and even be paid better than before for it, at the price of an unprecedentedly high level of interference in it from the state. It was an implicit bargain that most medical men were willing to accept.[64]

III

Other professional groups were somewhat less satisfied, in particular Germany's vast and ramified state civil service. Despite Hitler's attempt in 1934 to try and sort out a division of labour between the traditional state service and the Party, tensions and struggles between the normative and prerogative arms of the 'dual state' continued and if anything got worse as time went on. While institutions like the Interior Ministry felt obliged to warn civil servants not to accept instructions from Nazi Party agencies or individuals without any formal capacity in the state, Hitler himself, notably in a proclamation read to the Nuremberg Party Rally on 11 September 1935, insisted repeatedly that if state institutions proved ineffective in implementing the Party's policies, then 'the movement' would have to implement them instead. 'The battle against the inner enemy will never be frustrated by formal bureaucracy or its incompetence.'[65] The result was that the civil service soon began to seem very unattractive to ambitious young graduates eager to make their way in the world. As the SS Security Service noted in a report in 1939:

The development of the sphere of the civil service has in general again been in a negative direction. Well-known, threatening phenomena have in the period under review once more increased in dimension, such as the shortage of personnel, negative selection and absence of younger recruits because of the poor pay and public defamation of the civil service, failures in personnel policy because of the lack of any unity of approach, and so on.[66]

There were serious problems of recruitment already by 1937. The law faculties of Germany's universities, upon which the civil service largely depended for recruits, had shrunk dramatically in size since 1933, as students went into more fashionable subjects like medicine. On the other hand, the bureaucratization of Nazi Germany – a term actually used in 1936 by the Reich Statistical Office – had led to a 20 per cent growth in public employment in federal, state and local administration between 1933 and 1939. But better-paid administrative posts were still to be had in the Party and its affiliated organizations. By 1938 there were serious staff shortages in state offices at all levels. Yet it was not until the summer of 1939 that the salary cuts imposed by Brüning's austerity programme during the Depression were at least partially reversed. Interior Minister Wilhelm Frick painted a drastic picture of civil servants' chronic indebtedness and predicted that the civil service would soon be unable to carry out its tasks any more. For the sharp decline in the prestige and position of civil servants, however, the Party and its leaders, who constantly poured scorn upon the state apparatus and those who staffed it, only had themselves to blame.[67]

In view of these developments, it was not surprising that a thoughtful civil servant, Count Fritz-Dietlof von der Schulenburg, himself a member of the Nazi Party since 1932, voiced his despair at the way things were going in September 1937. He drew Ministers' attention to the new Reich Civil Service Law, which described the civil service as the main pillar of the state. Without it, he pointed out, the Four-Year Plan could not be properly implemented. Yet its efficient functioning was being blocked by a sharp decline in strength as a result of repeated political and racial purges, while the proliferation of Party and state institutions had led to a chaos of competing competences that made proper administration virtually impossible. He went on:

Although it has considerable achievements to its credit since the take-over of power, it is publicly *ridiculed* as a 'bureaucracy' either by the Leader or by the community and decried as alien to the people, disloyal, without anyone being prepared to reject officially this disparagement of a class on which the state depends. Civil servants, especially leading ones, are *exposed to attacks* on their work, *which in fact are directed against the state as such* . . . The consequences of this treatment of the civil service are that the civil service feels increasingly *defamed, without honour, and in some degree of despair. Recruitment is beginning to dry up* . . . The civil service is largely reduced to the economic status of the proletariat . . . By comparison, business offers many times the salary . . .[68]

Among senior civil servants such as Schulenburg, disappointment at the dashing of the high hopes they had held in 1933 was palpable. Things, he declared, were even worse than they had been under Weimar. The long and honourable tradition of the civil service was being destroyed.[69]

Schulenburg's disillusion was to lead him rapidly into a position strongly hostile to the regime. As far as the great majority of civil servants were concerned, however, the forces of tradition and inertia proved superior. The civil service had held a special place in German society and politics since its formation in eighteenth-century Prussia. Some of the ideals of duty to the nation, contempt for politics, and belief in efficient administration, survived into the twentieth century and informed civil servants' reaction to the Nazis. Rigid bureaucratic procedures, formal rules, a plethora of grades and titles, and much more besides, marked out the civil service as a special institution with a special consciousness. It was not easily displaced. Some decided to soldier on in the interests of the nation they thought the civil service had always represented. Others were attracted by the authoritarian style of the Third Reich, its emphasis on national unity, on the removal of overt political conflict, and particularly, perhaps, its effective removal of a whole range of constraints on bureaucratic action. Efficiency replaced accountability, and that too was attractive to many civil servants. In every Ministry in Berlin, every regional and local government office, civil servants obeyed the laws and decrees handed down to them by Hitler, Göring and other Ministers to implement because, above all, they considered it their duty to do so. Dissenters, of course, had been weeded out in 1933; but the vast majority of German bureaucrats were in any case arch-conservatives who believed in an authoritarian state, considered Communists and even Social Democrats traitors, and favoured renewed national expansion and rearmament.[70]

One such bureaucrat, typical in many ways, whose voluminous family correspondence has by chance survived to give us a detailed view of a middle-class perspective on the Third Reich, was Friedrich Karl Gebensleben, City Planning Officer in Braunschweig. Born in 1871, the year of German unification, Karl Gebensleben had trained as an engineer and worked for the German railway system in Berlin before taking up his post in 1915. He was obviously a man of integrity who was trusted by his colleagues, and by the early 1930s he was combining his administrative post with the office of deputy mayor of the city. His wife Elisabeth, born in 1883, came from a prosperous farming background, as did her husband. The couple were pillars of Braunschweig society, frequented concerts and patronized the theatre, and were to be seen together at all major public celebrations, receptions and similar events. Their daughter Irmgard, born in 1906, had married a Dutchman, and her presence in Holland was the occasion for most of the family's letter-writing; their son Eberhard, born in 1910, studied law at a series of universities, as was normal at the time, including Berlin and Heidelberg, and aimed to take up work in the Reich civil service as a career. This was a solid, conventional, bourgeois family, therefore. But in the early 1930s it was clearly in a deep state of anxiety, plagued above all by fears of a Communist or socialist revolution. Elisabeth Gebensleben expressed a widely held view when she wrote to her daughter on 20 July 1932 that Germany was in mortal peril from the Communists, aided and abetted by the Social Democrats. The country was swarming with Russian agents, she thought, and the violence on the streets was the beginning of a planned destabilization of the country. Thus any measures to ward off the threat were justified.[71]

Well before the Nazi seizure of power, Elisabeth Gebensleben had become an admirer of Hitler and his movement: 'This readiness to make sacrifices, this burning patriotism and this idealism!' she exclaimed in 1932 on witnessing a Nazi Party demonstration: 'And at the same time such tight discipline and control!'[72] Not surprisingly, she was full of enthusiasm for the coalition government headed by Hitler and appointed on 30 January 1933 – in the nick of time, she thought, as she witnessed a Communist demonstration against the appointment ('Has Hitler grasped the tiller too late? Bolshevism has taken far, far deeper anchor in the people than one suspected').[73] The mass, brutal violence meted out by the Nazis to their opponents in the following months did not, therefore, cause her many sleepless nights: 'This ruthless, decisive action by the national government', she wrote on 10 March 1933, 'may put some people off, but first there surely has to be a root-and-branch purge and clear-out, otherwise it won't be possible to start reconstruction.'[74] The 'purge' included the Social Democratic Mayor of Braunschweig, Ernst Böhme, who had been elected in 1929 at the age of thirty-seven. On 13 March 1933 Nazi stormtroopers burst into a council session and hauled him roughly out onto the street. Within a few days he had been forced under duress to sign a paper resigning all his offices in the town. A band of SS men took him to the offices of the local Social Democratic newspaper, stripped him naked, threw him onto a table and beat him unconscious, after which they threw a bucket of water over him, dressed him again as he was, paraded him through the streets and put him in the town gaol, from which he was eventually released some time later, to return to private life. As his deputy, Karl Gebensleben took over temporarily and without demur as the city's new mayor. Although he was upset by the dramatic and unexpected scene he had witnessed in the council chamber, Karl nevertheless took strong exception to newspaper reports that he had wept as the mayor was carried off to his fate. He had indeed worked closely with Böhme over the past few years, but his probity as a civil servant would not have allowed him such an unrestrained show of emotion. His wife Elisabeth, though disapproving ('I would have wanted Böhme to have a somewhat less ignominious send-off'), consoled herself with the thought that in the Revolution of 1918 the conservative mayor of the time had himself been humiliated by the 'Reds'.[75]

Like other conservatives, the Gebenslebens were reassured by the obeisance to tradition paid in the opening ceremony of the Reichstag at Postdam on 21 March. They dusted off their black-white-red imperial flag and hung it out in triumph, while Karl took part in a celebratory march through the streets of Braunschweig.[76] Anything the Gebenslebens disliked, especially acts of violence committed by the stormtroopers and SS, they dismissed as the work of Communist infiltrators.[77] They believed implicitly the trumped-up charges of peculation brought by the Nazis against trade union officials and others.[78] As Elisabeth reported to her daughter Hitler's speeches over the radio, what shone through in her words was a strongly reawakened national pride: Germany now had a Chancellor to whom the whole world paid attention.[79] A staunch Protestant, she joined the German Christians ('So, reform in the Church. I'm pleased') and listened excitedly as her pastor compared Hitler to Martin Luther.[80] The family's illusions were as significant as their enthusiasms. Karl Gebensleben applauded the 'strict discipline' introduced into public life and the economy by 'the leadership principle, which alone has validity' and the 'co-ordination down to the tiniest institutions', but thought that in time a moderate opposition along English lines would be permitted to exist. Towards the end of May, he and his wife finally joined the Nazi Party, not out of self-preservation, but out of a positive sense of commitment to the new Germany. As he wrote proudly if somewhat self-consciously to his daughter:

So your 'old' dad has also had to procure for himself a brownshirt, peaked cap, belt, tie and party badge as fast as possible. Mum thinks the uniform fits me fantastically and makes me look decades (?) younger!!! Oh!!! Well, well, my dear, if only someone had told me before! But it's a grand feeling to see how everyone is trying through discipline to do the best for the Fatherland – strictly according to the motto: *The public interest comes first*.[81]

As an administrator, Karl welcomed the decision to exclude the city council from most future issues and to decide them instead in a small committee. 'By this means, time and energy are made available for useful work.'[82] Before him, he saw a new time of efficiency and coherence in administration. Things, of course, did not quite turn out that way.

This was not the only point on which the Gebenslebens deceived themselves. There were illusions too in the family's attitude to the regime's posture towards the Jews. Antisemitism initially played little part in the family's support for Nazism. When Elisabeth Gebensleben saw the shattered display windows of Jewish-owned shops in the town in mid-March 1933, she ascribed this to '*provocateurs* . . . who, as has been ascertained, have smuggled themselves into the NSDAP in order to discredit the nationalist movement at home and abroad . . . Communists and fellow travellers'. If any Nazis were involved, it was clear that Hitler disapproved, she thought.[83] She found antisemitic speeches by Goebbels and Göring 'terrible' and was alarmed by the Nazis' disruption of Fritz Busch's work as a conductor in Leipzig (she thought this was because he was Jewish, although in fact he was not). Such attacks on Jewish artists were 'catastrophic', she wrote, and added: 'There are rogues amongst the Jews too, but one mustn't forget all the great men amongst the Jews, who have achieved such an enormous amount in the fields of art and science.'[84]

Yet she was soon taking a different view, following the boycott of Jewish shops on 1 April 1933 and the accompanying massive propaganda. 'The era in which we are now living', she wrote to her daughter with unintentionally prophetic force on 6 April 1933, 'will only be judged fairly by posterity.' She went on:

It's world history that we're experiencing. But world history rolls over the fate of the individual, and that makes this epoch, which is so pure and elevated in its *aim*, so difficult, because side-by-side with the joy we are experiencing, there is also sympathy with the fate of the individual. That applies to the fate of the individual Jew too, but does not alter one's judgement of the Jewish question as such. The Jewish question is a worldwide question just like Communism, and if Hitler intends to deal with it, just as he does with Communism, and his aim is achieved, then perhaps Germany will one day be envied.[85]

She considered the boycott justified in view of the 'smear campaign against Germany' that the regime claimed was being mounted by Marxists and Jews abroad. All stories of antisemitic atrocities in Germany were '*pure invention*', she roundly declared to her daughter in Holland, following Goebbels's injunction to anyone who had contacts with foreigners to take this line; either she had forgotten the incidents she had found so shocking only three weeks before, or she had decided deliberately to suppress them. Germany had been robbed of the 'possibility of life' by the Treaty of Versailles, she reminded her daughter: 'Germany is protecting itself with the weapons it has. That the Jews are partly being shown the door of their offices in the legal system, in medicine, is *also* correct in economic terms, as hard as it hits the individual, innocent person.' She believed, wrongly of course, that their number was merely being reduced to the same proportion as that of Jews in the population as a whole (though this principle, she failed to reflect, did not apply to other groups in Germany society, for example Protestants, whose share of top jobs was proportionately far higher than that of Catholics). In any case, she said, demonstrating how far she had taken Nazi propaganda on board in the space of a mere few weeks, perhaps because it built on prejudices already latent in her mind, the Jews were 'cunning': 'The Jews want to rule, not to serve.' Her husband Karl told her stories of Jewish ambition and corruption that seemed to justify the purge.[86] By October 1933 she had slipped effortlessly into the use of Nazi language in her letters, describing the Communist-front *Brown Book* of Nazi atrocities as a work of 'lying Jewish smears'.[87]

As far as Karl was concerned, the achievement of the Third Reich was to have replaced disorder with order. 'When the National Socialist government took power,' he said in a speech welcoming the new Nazi mayor of Braunschweig as he took up his office on 18 October 1933, 'it found chaos.' The removal of the endlessly quarrelling political parties of the Weimar years had paved the way for orderly municipal improvements. Beyond this, Germany's pride had been restored.[88] When disorder seemed to raise its head once more at the end of June 1934, in the shape of Ernst Röhm and the brownshirts, Elisabeth breathed a sigh of relief as Hitler acted. Unlike her daughter, she expressed no doubts about the rightness of the murders committed at Hitler's behest. 'One feels absolutely insignificant in the face of the greatness, the truthfulness and the openness of such a man,' she wrote.[89] After these events, the family had little more to say to each other about politics. Their concerns turned inwards, to the birth of grandchildren, and to Karl and Elisabeth's son Eberhard, who was planning to study for a doctorate with the conservative, pro-Nazi jurist Walter Jellinek in Heidelberg; after much discussion, Jellinek suddenly disappeared from their correspondence: it turned out that he was Jewish and he therefore lost his job.[90]

Eberhard signed on for paramilitary training with the brownshirts, did his military service, then entered the Reich Economics Ministry as a junior civil servant, joining the Nazi Party on 29 November 1937. The family's interest in politics did not revive. Nazi Germany for the Gebenslebens provided the stability they had longed for, a kind of return to normality after the upheavals of the Weimar years. In comparison with this, small doubts and niggles about the way in which it had been done seemed insignificant, hardly worth bothering about. The defeat of Communism, the overcoming of political crisis, the restoration of national pride were what the Gebenslebens wanted. Everything else they ignored, explained away, or, more insidiously, gradually took on board as the propaganda apparatus of the Third Reich incessantly hammered its messages home to the population. The conformity of middle-class families like the Gebenslebens was bought at the price of illusions that were to be rudely shattered after 1939. Karl and Elisabeth did not live to see this happen. Karl died on the day he retired, 1 February 1936, of a heart attack; his widow Elisabeth followed him on 23 December 1937. Eberhard's career in the civil service did not last long: by 1939 he had been drafted into the army.[91]

THE TAMING OF THE PROLETARIAT

I

By far the largest social class in Germany in 1933 was the proletariat, comprising roughly 46 per cent of the economically active population. The occupational census of 16 June 1933, long planned and carried out largely free of Nazi interference, showed that a further 17 per cent could be classed as civil servants, white-collar workers or soldiers, 16.4 per cent as self-employed, the same proportion, 16.4 per cent, as unpaid family assistants (mostly on small farms), and 3.8 per cent as domestic servants. Looking at the adult population by economic sector, the census-takers reckoned that 13.1 million were active in industry and artisanal trades in 1933, 9.3 million in agriculture and forestry, 5.9 million in trade and transport, 2.7 million in public and private service, and 1.3 million in domestic service. German society, in other words, was a society in which the industrial working class was large and growing, agriculture was still significant but in decline, and the service sector, which dominates the advanced economies of the twenty-first century, was only relatively small in scale, though expanding rapidly. Modern industries, like chemicals, printing and copying, and electrical products, pointed to the future with between a quarter and a fifth of their workers being women, and women were prominent in some areas of the service sector too. In the traditional and still immensely powerful industries such as mining, metalworking, construction and the like, however, it was still a man's world. Roughly a quarter of all economically active people in industry were concentrated in metallurgy and engineering in their broadest sense. More than three million people were active in these industries in 1933,

and over two million in building and construction; to these, in the core
of the traditional industrial working class, could be added 867,000 in
the timber and woodworking industries, just over 700,000 in mining,
saltworking and turf-digging and 605,000 in quarrying and stone-
working. Only a tiny proportion of those active in these fields were
women – less than 2 per cent in mining and construction, for example.
And it was these classic areas of male employment – or, in the early
1930s, unemployment – that gave the tone to the working class and the
labour movement as a whole.[92]

Mass unemployment had undermined the cohesion and morale of the
working class in the early 1930s. It had destabilized Germany's large
and well-organized trade union movement. In the search for a solution,
the major working-class parties had either lost the capacity for independent action, like the Social Democrats, or deceived themselves with futile
and self-destructive revolutionary fantasies, like the Communists. In
1933 they paid the price. Between March and July 1933 the Nazis
destroyed the long-established German labour movement, closed down
the trade unions and banned the two main parties of the working class.
Organized resistance by remnants of the old labour movement continued
for a while but it too was eventually suppressed.[93] In the meantime, the
Nazis moved to create a new labour organization that would co-ordinate
the workers under the control of the state. The existing Nazi trade
union, the National Socialist Factory Cell Organization, was viewed
with suspicion by employers, who saw its potential for militancy as a
threat. Business did not want to get rid of the old trade unions only
to see another, more powerful form of unionism taking their place.
Industrialists and bankers were dismayed by the disorder in the factories,
as brownshirts and Factory Cell Organization agents attacked and
expelled elected union and workers' council representatives and took
over the representation of employees themselves. Employers soon began
complaining that these agents were interfering in the running of their
businesses, making unreasonable demands, and generally disrupting
things by throwing their weight around. In Saxony, for example, the
Nazi Party Regional Leader Martin Mustchmann even arrested the President of the State Bank, Carl Degenhardt, and held him in custody for a
month. Such actions were not welcomed by the business community.[94]

The disruption was a consequence not least of the radical ambitions

of the Factory Cell Organization, whose influence in this period was out
of all proportion to its relatively weak membership of a mere 300,000
employees. Backed by the muscle of the stormtroopers and the co-
ordinating will of the new regime, its agents had already moved in to
trade union offices and were beginning to run their affairs well before
the unions were effectively abolished on 2 May 1933. The Factory Cell
Organization's leading figure, Reinhard Muchow, not yet thirty years of
age at the time of the Nazi seizure of power, had cut his teeth in a series
of bitter labour disputes in the final years of the Weimar Republic, most
notably in the Berlin transport workers' strike of 1932, when the Nazis
had fought side by side with the Communists. As propaganda assistant
to Goebbels in the latter's capacity as Party Regional Leader for Berlin,
Muchow had directed his appeal to the capital city's working class,
to which indeed he himself belonged. In his vision, the Factory Cell
Organization would grow into a gigantic trade union organization representing every employed person in the Third Reich. In this capacity it
would form a crucial element in the new corporate state; it would
determine wages and salaries, present the government with new labour
protection measures, and take over the unions' social functions.[95]

But the Nazi leadership did not want class conflict imported from the
Weimar Republic into the new Reich. Already on 7 April, Hess had
ordered the Factory Cell Organization not to interfere in the running of
businesses, or, indeed, to disrupt the work of the trade unions, whose
role in paying benefits to unemployed members was crucial during the
Depression. The takeover of the unions on 2 May was in some respects
a classic example of the Nazi leadership's tendency to try to channel
uncoordinated activism into institutional forms when it began to become
a nuisance.[96] The unions were immediately replaced by the German
Labour Front, officially celebrated at a ceremony attended by Hitler and
the cabinet on 10 May 1933. The man appointed to lead the Labour
Front was one of the Third Reich's more colourful characters, Robert
Ley. Born in 1890 as the seventh of eleven children of a West German
farmer, Ley had suffered a life-shaping trauma as a child when his father
had got deeply into debt and tried to raise insurance money to repay it
by setting fire to his farm. To judge from Ley's later autobiographical
writings, the poverty and disgrace that ensued for the family after his
father's conviction for arson left the boy with a permanent sense of

social insecurity and resentment against the upper classes. Intelligent and ambitious, he chose to rebound by working hard at his studies, and, unusually for someone of his background, entered university. Partly supporting himself through part-time work, he studied chemistry from 1910 onwards. In 1914, however, the war put a temporary halt to all this; Ley volunteered immediately and served in an artillery unit on the Western Front until 1916, when, bored with the constant pounding and the bloody stalemate of trench warfare, he trained as a pilot and began to fly spotter-planes. On 29 July 1917 his aircraft was shot down; almost miraculously, his co-pilot managed a crash-landing. But they landed behind enemy lines. Ley was captured, and spent the rest of the war as a prisoner of the French. The incident left Ley with serious injuries, including not just damage to his leg, which was saved only after six operations, but also to the frontal lobe of his brain, which seems to have gradually deteriorated over the years. He spoke with a stammer, and became increasingly prone to bouts of alcoholism and unrestrained behaviour of all kinds.[97]

Ley returned to university at the end of the war and completed his studies, gaining a doctorate in 1920 for his dissertation in food chemistry, part of which was published in a scientific journal. With this training, it is not surprising that he secured a good job in the Bayer chemical company, in Leverkusen. This enabled him to marry and start a family. Yet he remained discontented and insecure, his dissatisfaction with the humdrum routine of everyday life fired by his reading of romantic and utopian literature. The French occupation of the Rhineland, where he lived, fuelled his nationalist beliefs, which turned into admiration for Hitler when Ley read reports of the Nazi Leader's speech at the trial of the Munich putschists early in 1924. Ley joined the Nazi Party and soon became a leading local campaigner, rising to become Regional Leader for the Southern Rhineland in June 1925. As with many other prominent early Nazis, Ley was won over by Hitler's oratory on first hearing it. He conceived a boundless admiration for the Nazi Leader, perhaps, as psychohistorians have suggested, finding in him a substitute for the father whose disgrace had cast such a pall over Ley's childhood. Ley backed Hitler in the disputes that divided the Rhineland branches of the Party from the leadership in the mid-1920s, and helped Hitler to take the reins of power in the Party back into his hands again after his enforced inactivity following the failure of the 1923 Munich putsch. It was for this reason, and because Ley, despite his stutter, proved to be an effective, rabble-rousing speaker, that Hitler repeatedly overlooked complaints from Ley's colleagues about his financial mismanagement, his high-handed attitude towards subordinates, and his administrative incompetence. Ley was soon running a regional Nazi newspaper, full of antisemitic propaganda whose virulence yielded little to that of the more notorious *The Stormer*, published by Julius Streicher, the Party Regional Leader in Nuremberg. The paper, the *West German Observer*, ran repeated allegations of ritual murder by Jews, and carried pornographic stories about the supposed seduction of Aryan girls by their Jewish employers. Such claims led to several prosecutions and fines being imposed on Ley, which did nothing to deter him from repeating them.[98]

Brought by Hitler to Munich Party headquarters in 1931, Ley stepped into Gregor Strasser's shoes on the latter's sudden resignation as Reich Organization Leader of the Party in December, 1932, though he did not inherit the immense administrative power his predecessor had possessed. Ley's experience in trying to win over the voters of the strongly working-class areas of the Rhineland, coupled with his utopian idealism and his social resentments, gave his Nazism a discernibly collectivist tinge. It made him Hitler's obvious choice to work out plans for the remodelling of Germany's labour organizations early in April 1933. In formal political terms, Ley's task was to fulfil Hitler's vision of integrating the working class into the new Germany, to win over perhaps the most recalcitrant, most anti-Nazi part of Germany's population to enthusiastic support of the new order. But Ley lacked the expertise to do this on his own initiative. He was quick to install the Labour Front in the old trade union offices and to incorporate the Factory Cell Organization. But he had little alternative but to make use of the Organization's officials in setting up the Labour Front's internal structures. Initially, these just placed existing union institutions under new management with new names and arranged them into five large sub-groups. Thus the old trade union organization became one sub-group, with all its subordinate divisions such as its press bureau and its newspaper, while the white-collar unions formed another sub-group, retailers a third, the professions a fourth and business the fifth. The way for the Labour Front to become the nucleus of a Corporate State on the Italian Fascist model, reconciling the interests of all the different sectors of the economy in the service of the new political order, seemed to be open.[99]

But these ideas, pushed by Muchow and the Factory Cell Organization leaders, did not last very long. Neither the professions nor business were enthusiastic about them, the retailers never had much influence, and Muchow and his friends were by far the most dynamic force in the new structure. Before long, the Labour Front had become what they had wanted the Factory Cell Organization to be, a sort of super-union representing above all the interests of the workers. In this capacity it issued orders regulating paid vacations, wage agreements, equal pay for women, health and safety and much more besides. At a local level, agitation continued, with some officials threatening to send employers to concentration camp if they did not give in to their demands. Muchow declared that ex-Social Democrats and even some ex-Communists were responsible, and instituted an investigation of the political past of all the functionaries of the Labour Front with a view to purging 100,000 of them from the organization. But complaints continued to multiply, from the Minister of Labour, the Interior Minister, even the Transportation Minister, all worried that their authority was being eroded by the unilateral actions of lower-level Labour Front functionaries. Things seemed to be getting out of hand, and it was time to bring the situation under control.[100]

II

On 19 May 1933, acting under pressure from the employers and from government Ministries in Berlin, the cabinet promulgated a Law on Trustees of Labour. This established twelve state officials whose job it was to regulate wages, conditions of work and labour contracts in each of their respective districts, and to maintain peace between workers and employers. The Trustees were officials of the Reich Ministry of Labour. Only two of them belonged to the Factory Cell Organization; five of them were corporate lawyers and four were civil servants. The rather vague terms of the Law were filled out in detail in a further measure, the Law for the Ordering of National Labour, issued on 20 January 1934 and drafted by a civil servant who had previously been employed by an industrial pressure-group.[101] The new Laws swept away the framework of bilateral collective bargaining and regulation between employers and unions that had been one of the great achievements of Weimar labour policy and replaced it with a new structure that incorporated the National Socialist 'leadership principle'. They stressed that there was no need for antagonism between workers and employers in the new National Socialist state; both would work together in harmony as part of the newly unified German racial community. To underline this, the Laws were couched in a neo-feudal language of reciprocity which, like the real feudalism of the Middle Ages, concealed the fact that real power lay predominantly in the hands of one side: the employers. The powers of the Trustees of Labour included the appointment of Councils of Trust for individual plants, the arbitration of disputes, the confirmation of redundancies, the regulation of working hours and the basis for calculating piece-rates, and the referral of abuses of authority, provocation, disruption, breach of confidence and similar misdemeanours to Courts of Honour which would have a quasi-judicial function and include judges appointed by the Ministry of Justice among their members. The employer was now called the 'plant leader' (*Betriebsführer*) and the workers his 'retinue' (*Gefolgschaft*). Replacing Weimar's system of elected works councils and legally binding contracts of employment, the new system put all the cards into the hands of the bosses in collaboration with the Trustees of Labour. In fact, the Courts of Honour were virtually a dead letter; only 516 cases were brought before them in 1934–6, mostly concerning the physical abuse of apprentices by master-artisans. They might have looked fair and just on paper, but in practice they had little real effect.[102]

This new system of industrial relations represented a major victory for the employers, backed by Hitler and the Nazi leadership, who badly needed the co-operation of industry in their drive to rearm. While the new Trustees of Labour poured open scorn upon the idea of a corporate state, the chances of the Factory Cell Organization's ideas gaining wider influence were struck a fatal blow by the shooting of Reinhard Muchow in a tavern brawl on 12 September 1933. This took the driving force out of the radical wing of the Labour Front, and opened the way for Ley, now more versed in the complexities of labour relations than he had been the previous spring, to re-establish his authority. On 1 November 1933, Ley told workers at the Siemens factory in Berlin:

We are all soldiers of labour, amongst whom some command and the others obey. Obedience and responsibility have to count amongst us again . . . We can't all be on the captain's bridge, because then there would be nobody to raise the sails and pull the ropes. No, we can't all do that, we've got to grasp that fact.[103]

Ley now reorganized the Labour Front, getting rid of the remnants of trade union culture and attitudes, abolishing the last separate functions of the Factory Cell Organization, and acceding to the insistence of the Labour Ministry and the new labour laws that it had no role to play in the negotiation of wage agreements. The Labour Front was restructured along the same lines as the Party, with a top-down organization replacing the previous parallel representation of workers, white-collar employees and the rest. It now had a number of central departments – propaganda, law, education, social affairs, etc. – whose orders went down to the corresponding departments at the regional and local level. The old Factory Cell Organization officials did their best to obstruct the new system, but after the 'Night of the Long Knives' they were summarily dismissed *en masse*. Behind these political manoueverings lay the recognition of Hitler and the other regime leaders that rearmament, their principal economic priority, could only be achieved smoothly and rapidly if the workforce could be kept under control. This involved clearing away the more revolutionary elements in the Labour Front, just as it involved clamping down on any ideas of a 'second revolution' pushed by the brownshirts and their leaders. By the autumn of 1934 it was clear that in the battle to control labour relations, the employers had come out on top. Yet the struggle had not left them in the situation they really wanted. The organization and structure of the shopfloor under National Socialism certainly had a lot in common with the kind of management and industrial relations system desired by many employers in the 1920s and early 1930s, but it also introduced massive interference in labour relations by the state, the Labour Front and the Party, in areas where management had traditionally sought exclusive control. The trade unions were gone, but despite this, the employers were not masters in their own house any more.[104]

In the meantime, the huge apparatus of the German Labour Front quickly began to gain a reputation as perhaps the most corrupt of all the major institutions of the Third Reich. For this, Ley himself had to shoulder a large part of the blame. His position as head of the Labour Front made him comfortably off, with a salary of 4,000 Reichsmarks, to which he added 2,000 Reichsmarks as Reich Organization Leader of the Party, 700 Reichsmarks as a Reichstag deputy, and 400 Reichsmarks as a Prussian State Councillor. But this was only the beginning. His books and pamphlets, which Labour Front officials were encouraged to buy in bulk for distribution to the members, brought in substantial royalties, while profits from his newspaper – 50,000 Reichsmarks a year – went straight into his pocket. Ley made free personal use of the substantial funds confiscated by the Labour Front from the former trade unions, and in 1940 he benefited from a one-off gift of a million Reichsmarks bestowed on him by Hitler. With such funds, he bought a whole series of grand villas in the most fashionable districts of Germany's towns and cities. The running costs, which in his villa in Berlin's Grunewald included a cook, two nannies, a chambermaid, a gardener and a housekeeper, were met by the Labour Front up to 1938, and even after that it paid all Ley's entertainment expenses. He was fond of expensive automobiles and gave two to his second wife as presents. Ley also had a railway carriage refitted for his personal use. He collected paintings and furniture for his houses. In 1935 he bought a landed estate near Cologne and promptly began to turn it into a Nazi utopia, demolishing the old buildings and hiring the architect Clemens Klotz, designer of the Nazi Order Castles, to construct a new house in a grandiose style, confiscated land to increase the acreage of his own, drained marshes, introduced new machinery and set up a training scheme for apprentice farmhands. Here Ley played the neo-feudal landlord, with the staff lined up, standing to attention, to greet him when he flew in from Berlin, and secured the farm's official designation as a hereditary entailed estate.

Ensconced within such pretentious residences, surrounded by expensive paintings and furniture, Ley spent his leisure hours in womanizing and increasingly heavy drinking, both of which often led to embarrassing scenes in public. The drinking bouts he indulged in with his entourage often ended in violence. One such occasion in Heidelberg ended with the Minister-President of Baden being beaten up. In 1937 Ley was visibly drunk while hosting a visit by the Duke and Duchess of Windsor, and after driving them in his Mercedes straight through a set of locked factory gates, was hurriedly replaced on Hitler's orders by Herman Göring for the rest of the visit. Two years earlier, after a string of affairs, Ley had begun a liaison with the young soprano Inge Spilker, whom he married in 1938 immediately after divorcing his first wife. His infatuation with her physical charms led to him commissioning a painting of her, naked from the waist up, which he proudly showed to visiting dignitaries, while on one occasion he was even said to have torn her clothes off in the presence of guests in order to show them how beautiful her body was. Subjected to such pressure, and unable to cope with Ley's growing alcoholism, Inge herself took to the bottle, became a drug addict, and shot herself dead on 29 December 1942 after the last of many violent rows with her husband. Hitler warned the Labour Front leader about his behaviour on more than one occasion, but he carried on regardless. As so often, the Nazi Leader was prepared to forgive almost anything of a subordinate so long as he remained loyal.[105]

Corruption within the Labour Front by no means ended with Ley himself; indeed he could be said to have set an example to his subordinates in how to milk the organization for personal gain. A huge variety of business enterprises of one kind and another operated by the Labour Front offered multifarious opportunities for making money on the side. The Labour Front's construction companies, led by a senior official, Anton Karl, a man with previous convictions for theft and embezzlement himself, paid out more than 580,000 Reichsmarks in bribes in 1936–7 alone in order to secure contracts. Sepp Dietrich, the leader of Hitler's SS bodyguard, took due note of the gifts showered over him by Karl, including a gold cigarette-case, hunting-weaponry, silk shirts and a holiday in Italy for his wife, and issued Karl's Labour Front construction firm with a contract to rebuild his unit's barracks in Berlin. In return for favour and influence, Karl used the Labour Front's bank to grant leading Nazis cheap credit or even to buy houses for them at well below their market price. Hitler's adjutants, Julius Schaub and Wilhelm Brückner, his photographer Heinrich Hoffmann and anyone else thought to possess the Leader's ear were the frequent recipients of bribes from the Labour Front; Ley gave them 20,000 Reichsmarks each as a 'Christmas present' in 1935 alone.[106] Social Democratic observers gleefully chronicled a whole mass of corruption and embezzlement cases involving officials of the Labour Front every year. In 1935, for example, they noted that Alois Wenger, a Labour Front official in Konstanz, had been condemned for pocketing funds intended for workers' leisure activities and forging receipts to try and deceive the auditors. Another official, an 'old fighter' of the Nazi Party, embezzled his colleagues' Labour Front contributions and obtained 2,000 Reichsmarks – probably with menaces – from his employer to cover the missing money. He spent it all on drink. What was done with Labour Front contributions, reported another Social Democratic agent, could be seen in front of the organization's headquarters in Berlin:

2 to 3 private cars used to be parked in front of the old Trade Union House up to 1932. They belonged to the Workers' Bank or the Trade Unions. Nowadays you ought just to see them waiting there in a rank, it's 50 or 60 cars a day, and sometimes even more. The Labour Front chauffeurs have got blank cheques for petrol, they can fill their tanks as much as they like, and they do it often because they don't have to account for it. The corruption in the Labour Front is vast, and the general standard of morals correspondingly low.[107]

Ley was far from the only beneficiary of the Labour Front's funds; his open and obvious corruption was only the tip of an enormous iceberg of peculation. Such goings-on did not endear the Labour Front to the millions of workers who were forced to sustain it with compulsory contributions from their wages.

III

The Nazi regime was all too aware that the closure of the trade unions and the regimentation and subordination of workers in the corrupt and authoritarian Labour Front might cause discontent in the ranks of Germany's largest social class, a class which until 1933 had given powerful support to Nazism's bitterest enemies, the Communists and the Social Democrats. Along with its constant propaganda trumpeting of victories in the 'struggle for work', therefore, it also sought to provide alternative means of reconciling the working class with the Third Reich. Chief among these was the extraordinary organization known as the 'National Socialist Community Strength Through Joy', founded as a subsidiary of the German Labour Front on 27 November 1933. Strength Through Joy aimed to organize workers' leisure time rather than allow them to organize it for themselves, and thus to make leisure serve the interests of the racial community and reconcile the divergent worlds of work and free time, factory and home, production line and recreation ground. Workers were to gain strength for their work by experiencing joy in their leisure. Above all, Strength Through Joy would bridge the class divide by making middle-class leisure activities available to the masses. Material prosperity, declared Robert Ley in his inaugural address on 27 November, would not make the German nation happy; that was the vulgar error of the 'Marxists' of the Weimar years. The National Socialist regime would use spiritual and cultural means to achieve the integration of the workers into the national community. Borrowing from the Italian Fascist organization 'After Work' (*Dopolavoro*), but extending its tentacles into the workplace as well, Strength Through Joy rapidly developed a wide range of activities, and quickly mushroomed into one of the Third Reich's largest organizations. By 1939 it had over 7,000 paid employees and 135,000 voluntary workers, organized into divisions covering such areas as sport, education and tourism, with wardens in every factory and workshop employing more than twenty people.[108]

'Strength Through Joy', proclaimed Robert Ley in June 1938, 'is the shortest formula to which National Socialism for the broad masses can be reduced.'[109] It would insert an ideological content into every kind of leisure. In attempting to fulfil this task, it commanded very considerable resources. By 1937 Strength Through Joy was being subsidized by the Labour Front to the tune of 29 million Reichsmarks a year, while its incorporation of the huge leisure and cultural apparatus of the Social Democratic labour movement brought in further assets, including premises such as hiking hostels and sports grounds. With such resources, Strength Through Joy was able to offer heavily discounted leisure activities that were within the financial reach of many workers and their families. By 1934–5, over three million people were taking part in its physical education and gymnastics evenings, while many others took advantage of the cheap coaching it offered in tennis, sailing and other hitherto quintessentially upper-middle-class sports. In the cultural field, the organization purchased blocks of theatre tickets to make available cheaply to its members, accounting for over half of all theatre bookings in Berlin by 1938. It laid on classical music concerts in factories, creating several touring orchestras to play at them; it built theatres, formed travelling troupes of actors, and arranged art exhibitions. In 1938, over two and a half million people attended its concerts and over thirteen and a half million its 'folk performances'; more than six and a half million went to opera and operetta evenings under its auspices, and nearly seven and a half million to plays. One and a half million visited its exhibitions, and over two and a half million participated in 'entertainments' mounted on the Reich motorways. Membership came automatically with membership of the Labour Front, so that 35 million people belonged to it by 1936. It advertised intensively both at home and abroad, winning many enthusiastic supporters amongst those in Britain, the USA and elsewhere who admired its energy in civilizing the masses.[110]

Strength Through Joy's most striking activity was undoubtedly the organization of mass tourism for the workers. 'For many', it was reported in February 1938, '"Strength Through Joy" is nothing more than a kind of travel organization.'[111] Already in 1934, some 400,000 people participated in package tours provided by Strength Through Joy within Germany itself; by 1937 the number had grown to 1.7 million, while nearly seven million took part in shorter weekend excursions and 1.6 million in organized hikes. Although these numbers fell slightly in 1938–9, there could be no doubt about the success of these operations. Bulk ordering made it possible to put on package tours at a heavy discount – 75 per cent in the case of rail fares, for example, and 50 per cent in the case of hotel and bed-and-breakfast rooms. This could have a major effect on the economies of tourist regions; already in 1934, for example, Strength Through Joy tourists brought in 175,000 people to southern Bavaria, spending a total of five and a half million Reichsmarks on their vacations. Most striking of all were the foreign trips that the organization mounted, whether rail journeys to destinations in friendly Fascist Italy or cruises to Madeira, which was governed by the favourably disposed Portuguese dictatorship of Dr Salazar. In 1939 alone, 175,000 people went to Italy on such organized trips, a good number of them travelling on cruises. By 1939 the organization owned eight cruise ships (two of which it had had specially constructed) and rented four more on a more or less permanent basis, to carry its members to such exotic places as Libya (an Italian colony), Finland, Bulgaria and Istanbul, celebrating Germany's solidarity with real or potential allies and advertising the contours of a future German-dominated European empire. That year

140,000 passengers travelled on these cruises. Wherever they called, delegations from the local German consulates were ready to greet them and arrange onshore visits and tours, while friendly governments frequently arranged lavish receptions for the tourists.[112]

Strength Through Joy cruises were carefully arranged so as to combine pleasure with indoctrination. They were intended to represent the new Germany to the rest of the world, or at least the friendlier parts of it. Traditional passenger liners were divided into different classes of cabin and other facilities, according to the ability to pay, but Strength Through Joy disdained such relics of the past, and celebrated the unity of the German racial community by building its new ships on a one-class basis and converting others to the same model. Once on board, passengers were reminded that they were not there to have fun, or to show off, like traditional bourgeois cruise passengers, but to participate in a serious cultural enterprise. They were exhorted to dress modestly, to avoid excessive drinking, to eschew shipboard affairs and to obey unconditionally the orders of the tour leaders. A new liner such as the *Robert Ley* included a gymnasium, a theatre and a swimming pool to ensure that participants engaged in regular healthy exercise and partook of serious cultural offerings. Tour brochures advertised the achievement of the cruises and land-based tours in bringing Germans of different classes and regional backgrounds together in a common enterprise to help build the organic racial community of the Third Reich. Participants had to travel to foreign parts above all to educate themselves about the world, and in so doing to remind themselves of the superiority of Germans over other races. Within Germany, a prime purpose of the tours was to help bind the nation together by familiarizing people with regions of their native land which they had never previously visited, especially if, as in some of the more remote rural areas, they could be presented as centres of ancient German folk traditions.[113]

Yet, as so often in Nazi Germany, the reality did not really match up to the propaganda claims. Often the facilities provided for Strength Through Joy tourists were poor, involving mass dormitories with little or no privacy, or accommodation without proper sanitation. Classical music concerts were not always to the workers' taste, especially when they had to pay for them. One concert laid on for the organization in Leipzig had to be cancelled when only 130 out of the 1,000 tickets were sold.[114] Some theatres, like the 'Theatre of the West' in Berlin, put on cheaply staged operettas exclusively for Strength Through Joy, while the mainstream theatres continued to be patronized largely by the middle classes; even when Strength Through Joy bought up blocks of seats for particular performances and made them available to members at a discount, these were generally snapped up by middle-class theatre-goers.[115] The vision of a classless society rapidly receded when Strength Through Joy parties descended noisily upon quiet rural resorts. Far from increasing feelings of national solidarity, package tours in Germany itself led to serious objections from local tourist industries, inns and spas who saw their prices being heavily undercut by the discounted block bookings of the new organization. Well-heeled tourists of the traditional sort, appalled at having their favourite holiday spots invaded by hordes of the socially inferior, whose often rowdy behaviour aroused frequent complaints from innkeepers and hoteliers as well as private holiday-makers, rapidly took their custom elsewhere.[116]

Undeterred, the organization set about building its own model resort on the Baltic island of Rügen, at Prora. Construction began under the supervision of Albert Speer on 3 May 1936 and was scheduled for completion in 1940. The resort spanned eight kilometres of the Baltic shore, with six-storey residence blocks interspersed with refectories and centred on a huge communal hall designed to accommodate all 20,000 of the resort's holidaymakers as they engaged in collective demon-strations of enthusiasm for the regime and its policies. It was consciously designed for families, to make good the lack of tour facilities for them in other Strength Through Joy enterprises, and it was intended to be cheap enough for the ordinary worker to afford, at a price of no more than 20 Reichsmarks for a week's stay. The resort was provided with the most up-to-date facilities available, including centrally heated rooms with hot and cold running water, a heated swimming pool, a cinema, bowling alleys, a pier for cruise liners to moor alongside, a large railway station and much more besides. Designed by Clemens Klotz, the architect of the Order Castle at Vogelsang, it represented pseudo-Classical Nazi modernism at its most monumental. Like everything else in the Strength Through Joy organization, it emphasized gigantism, collectivism, the sinking of the individual in the mass. Unlike the contemporary British holiday camps set up by the entrepreneur Billy Butlin, which provided vacationers with individual holiday chalets and thus freed them from the intrusive supervision of widely feared figures such as the Blackpool landlady, Prora's massive six-storey accommodation blocks lined up its small guestrooms along endless, anonymous corridors and regimented the visitors whenever they ventured outside, even regulating the amount of space each family was allowed to occupy on the beach. At its height employing almost as many construction workers as the motorways, the resort never opened for business: the outbreak of war led to an immediate suspension of work, though some buildings were later quickly finished to house evacuees from the bombed-out cities. Looted extensively by local people and by the occupying Russians after the war, it was subsequently used as a barracks and training centre by Communist East Germany and today lies in ruins.[117]

IV

Strength Through Joy thus never got round the difficulties that the Prora resort was intended to solve. But there were worse failures than this. For the people who travelled with Strength Through Joy obstinately refused to do so in the spirit in which the regime intended. Concerned at the possible influence of ex-Social Democrats who participated in the tours, and worried about illicit contacts between arms workers and foreign agents, the organization arranged for the Gestapo and the SS Security Service to send along undercover agents disguised as tourists to spy on the participants. The picture their reports revealed almost as soon as they started work, in March 1936, was a disturbing one. Far from overcoming the social divide in the interests of the racial community, Strength Through Joy tours often brought to light social differences that might otherwise have remained merely latent. Because the income they gained from the tours was so low, hoteliers and restaurateurs frequently served inferior food and drink to the package trippers, who took it ill that the private tourists at the next table were getting something better. Theatre tickets sold to the organization were often for the worst seats in the house, adding to class resentments as those who were allotted them were forced to look down from the gods at the fur-clad bourgeois in the stalls. On cruises, where no amount of internal restructuring of the ships could entirely abolish the differences in quality between cabins on the upper decks and those on or below the water-line, Party officials, civil servants and others took the best berths. Such people indeed took the lion's share of the best cruises anyway, so much so that the Madeira cruise was popularly known as the 'bigwigs' trip' (*Bonzenfahrt*). Surveys of passenger lists of Strength Through Joy's cruise liners revealed that salaried employees were the largest single group, just as they were in ordinary tourism. Only 10 per cent of the thousand passengers on a Strength Through Joy cruise to Norway in 1935 were said to be from the working class; the rest were Party officials, who drank the ship dry long before it reached its home port again. 'These chaps are stuffing themselves with food and slurping up the drinks like pigs,' complained a crew member. Single women and young, unmarried men predominated amongst the workers, or in other words, wage-earners with disposable incomes rather than family men or mothers. Most of the workers on the trip were skilled and relatively well paid. The less well-off were usually heavily subsidized by their employers. The cost of the trips was still beyond the pockets of most wage-earners, who could only increase their income by working longer hours, thus reducing the opportunity to go on vacation. In many cases they could not afford the extra expenses that travel inevitably involved, such as holiday clothing.[118]

On cruises and other trips, while Party officials and middle-class passengers spent lavishly on presents, souvenirs and expensive meals and entertainments onshore, the workers were unable to afford even the simplest additions to the basics provided by the tour itself. There were many complaints from working-class participants about the ostentatious behaviour of their bourgeois fellow tourists, and little real social mixing on most of the trips. Class antagonism was paralleled by regional rivalries; on one cruise to Italy, discord between the Rhinelanders and Silesians on board reached such a pitch that the two groups refused to stay in the same room with each other. On a later Italian trip on the same ship, a group of Westphalians insulted their Silesian fellow passengers, calling them 'Polacks', and only the intervention of the crew stopped the quarrel from degenerating into a brawl.[119] Moreover, the behaviour of many participants on the tours often signally failed to match up to the standards set by the organizers. Like tourists everywhere, what most of them really wanted was to let their hair down. Instead of being restrained and committed to the racial community, they turned out to be pleasure-seeking and individualistic. Gestapo agents reported frequent mass drunkenness and riotous behaviour. On some ships, the lifeboats were said to be filled with writhing couples every night. Especially shameless, the Gestapo complained, were the young, single women who travelled on the cruise ships in considerable numbers. One agent thought they had only come along for 'erotic purposes'. Flirtations, dalliances and affairs with men on board or, worse, with dark-skinned young Italian, Greek or Arab men on shore, aroused frequent critical comment from the Gestapo spies. The passengers in general showed a distressing lack of interest in political lectures and meetings. Worst of all were the Party functionaries, whose drunkenness and riotous behaviour became notorious. On one cruise organized for Party Regional Leaders, for example, the Gestapo dis-covered two known prostitutes on the passenger list. Predictably enough, the very worst was Robert Ley himself, who frequently went on Strength Through Joy cruises, where he spent much of the time so drunk that the captain had to have him flanked by two sailors when he went on deck to ensure that he did not fall overboard. Strength Through Joy wardens arranged for him also to be accompanied by a group of blonde, blue-eyed young women to provide him with 'companionship' on the voyage.[120] No wonder a popular nickname for Strength Through Joy was the 'bigwigs' knocking-shop' (*Bonzenbordell*).[121]

Yet while it largely failed to achieve its ideological aims, Strength Through Joy was still one of the most popular of the regime's cultural innovations. By providing holidays and other activities that otherwise would have been beyond the means of many of the participants, the organization became widely appreciated amongst workers.[122] Much of what Strength Through Joy offered was new to those whom it targeted. Early in 1934, for instance, a poll of 42,000 workers at the Siemens factory in Berlin revealed that 28,500 of them had never taken a holiday outside Berlin and its surrounding countryside; they grasped the opportu-nity provided by Strength Through Joy. 'If you get it so cheaply then it's worth raising your arm now and then!' said one of them to a Social Democratic agent in 1934.[123] 'The Nazis really have created something good,' was often the reaction, noted another such report.[124] Another agent reported from Berlin in February 1938:

'Strength Through Joy' is very popular. Its programmes meet the humble man's longing to get out for once and participate in the pleasures of the 'great'. It's a clever speculation built on the petty-bourgeois inclinations of the unpolitical worker. For such a man it's really something if he goes on a Scandinavian cruise or even just travels to the Black Forest or the Harz. He imagines that this has moved him up a rung on the social ladder.[125]

So widespread was the use of Strength Through Joy's offerings that a popular joke maintained that the people were losing their strength through too much joy.[126] Some despairing Social Democratic commentators concluded, therefore, that the programme did in the end have an important function in reconciling people, especially formerly oppositional elements, to the regime. 'The workers', as one commented in 1939, 'have a strong feeling that sand is being thrown in their eyes with Strength Through Joy, but they take part in it all the same, and in this way its propagandistic aim is still achieved in the end.'[127]

Strength Through Joy, indeed, had a symbolic effect that went far beyond its actual programmes. Its tours and cruises stood out in retrospect amongst the experiences of the peacetime years when workers came to reminisce about the Third Reich after it was over.[128] Even – or, as some former Social Democrats sourly asserted, especially – those who had never been on its organized mass tours or cruises admired its enterprise and initiative, and its concern to bring hitherto unattainable pleasures within the reach of the ordinary man's pocket.[129] A Social Democratic observer summed up its purposes and effects as early as December 1935:

Atomization and the loss of individuality, occupational therapy and surveillance for the people. There is to be no room for individual leisure, physical exercise and cultural activities, there is to be no space for voluntary get-togethers or for any independent initiatives that could arise from them. And something is to be 'offered' to the masses ... At the very least, Strength Through Joy distracts people, contributes to the befogging of their brains, and has a propagandistic effect on behalf of the regime.[130]

People who took part in Strength Through Joy activities might have taken their ideological content with a pinch of salt, but at the same time these activities brought them still further away from the edifying and improving traditions of Social Democratic and Communist mass culture. This no doubt was one reason why some Social Democratic observers looked down on them ('"Strength Through Joy"', sniffed one in 1935, 'lacks any cultural foundation. Its events remain at the level of village beer festivals in peasant inns').[131] At the same time, however, they brought about a further, and in the end fatal, undermining of labour movement cultural traditions by the growth of commercialized leisure activities. The vast cultural apparatuses of the Social Democrats and the Communists, built up since the nineteenth century, had been strongly educative, and were linked to a variety of core values of the labour movement. The Nazis not only took all this over, but also reoriented it in a more populist direction, dovetailing with the emergence of popular, unpolitical culture under the Weimar Republic. Partly as a consequence, when working-class culture re-emerged after 1945, it was to be in a far less ideological form than before.[132]

These effects have to be kept in proportion, however. Most of the people who went to plays and concerts continued to do so as private citizens. Strength Through Joy attracted a good deal of attention, but it never accounted for more than 11 per cent of annual overnight stays in German hotels.[133] The annual turnover of the largest commercial tourist agency, the Central European Travel Office, was 250 million Reichsmarks in 1938 compared to 90 million for the tourism department of Strength Through Joy.[134] Moreover, while Strength Through Joy was drastically scaled down on the outbreak of war, its cruise ships converted into troop transports, its hostels into hospitals and its resorts into convalescent homes, commercial tourism, despite a few disapproving noises from the authorities, continued to flourish. From the beginning, however, the regime had sought to mould it to its own purposes, encouraging people to travel within Germany rather than abroad (for both patriotic and economic reasons), and attempting to direct tourists to countries abroad where their presence as ambassadors for the new Germany would be most useful. New tourist sites emerged, from grandiose structures such as the Reich Chancellery to sites of mourning and memory for the Nazi dead; guidebooks were rewritten to conform to the ideological dictates of the regime, giving greater emphasis to continuities with the remote Germanic past at one end, and mentioning wherever possible the association of Hitler and other Nazi leaders with tourist spots at the other. The leadership of the Third Reich was aware of the tensions that arose between the growing commercial tourist industry and the organized tourism of Strength Through Joy, but far from clamping down on the former in the interests of the latter, Propaganda Minister Joseph Goebbels and the boss of the tourist industry, Gottfried Feder, realized that people needed to get away from the stresses and strains of everyday work even if they did so in an unpolitical environment. A consumer society was emerging in Nazi Germany, and for all its prioritization of rearmament in its economic policy, the regime was not only unable, but also unwilling, to stop it.[135]

Consumer assertion was perhaps one reason for the failure of the department of Strength Through Joy that went under the name of 'Beauty of Labour'. The basic intention was still to compensate for low wages and long hours, but here it was to be implemented not through the provision of leisure facilities, but through improvements in the workplace. Beauty of Labour campaigned energetically for the provision of washing facilities and toilets, changing rooms and lockers, showers, and generally improved hygiene and cleanliness in factories, for more air, less noise, proper work clothing, tidiness and order. Healthy workers in a clean workplace would work better and be happier in their jobs, and to reinforce all this, Beauty of Labour arranged concerts and similar events on the shopfloor, encouraged the building of onsite sports and recreation facilities and pressured employers to provide decent canteens for their workers and clean up debris and waste lying about on the shop floor. By 1938 it claimed that nearly 34,000 companies had improved their performance in many of these respects, repainting and decorating their shops, building recreation areas and improving sanitation. Tax incentives helped encourage employers to do this, and Beauty of Labour also staged competitions and awarded prizes for the most improved firm, issuing the winners with certificates signed by Hitler declaring them to be 'model firms'. The benefits both to employers and the regime in terms of the increased productivity that could be expected were obvious. But all these improvements were bought at the workers' own expense, since many firms expected their employees to do the painting, cleaning and building themselves after hours for no extra pay, docked their wages to cover the costs, and threatened those who did not 'volunteer' with dismissal or even the concentration camp.[136]

Workers were not fooled by the inflated rhetoric of the scheme, least of all if they had been influenced by Communist or Social Democratic ideas before 1933, as millions of them had. If, despite all this, Strength Through Joy as a whole was popular, it was not because of its ostensible aim of motivating people to work harder, but because it allowed them a means of escape from the tedium and repression of everyday life on the shop-floor. People took its offerings of amusement and diversion because for the great mass of them there was nothing else on offer. Many calculated that they were paying for the organization anyway through their compulsory contributions to the Labour Front, so they might as well get their money's worth. In time, it even overcame the reluctance of former Social Democrats who did not want to be seen taking anything on offer from the hated Labour Front.[137] Strength Through Joy events, a Social Democratic report noted in 1935, 'offer, to be sure, cheap opportunities to find simple relaxation. Old friends can meet each other there in a very casual environment and over a glass of beer they can discuss the very opposite of what the organizers want them to.'[138] It was not only old Social Democrats who recognized the compensatory function of such events. A memorandum circulating in the Reich Labour Ministry in 1936 noted soberly: 'Tourist trips, plays and concerts are not going to clear away any poverty-ridden slums or fill hungry mouths.' 'A relaxing cruise on a luxury steamer', concluded an official of the Labour Front in 1940, 'does not really bring relaxation, if the tourist has to go back at the end to the material oppressiveness of his everyday existence.'[139]

SOCIAL PROMISE AND SOCIAL REALITY

I

That Strength Through Joy and associated programmes were a substitute for real economic improvements was a view that was widely shared, and had a good deal of basis in fact. Most statistical investigations are agreed that the economic situation of the mass of working-class wage-earners did not markedly improve between 1933 and 1939. Nominal hourly wages in 1933 were 97 per cent of what they had been in 1932, and they had still not recovered in 1939, by which time they had risen only by one percentage point, to 98.[140] The German Institute for Business Research conceded on 24 February 1937 that rearmament had entailed 'a large economic sacrifice for the German people' even as it attempted to refute the claim that living standards had actually declined.[141] Calculating real wages has always been a tricky business, more so in the Third Reich than in most economies. Price Commissioner Goerdeler took the business of keeping consumer prices low very seriously; but even the Reich Economics Ministry admitted in 1935 that official statistics underestimated price rises, not to mention rents and other factors. Recent estimates have put average industrial real wages below their levels for 1928 (admittedly a particularly good year) until 1937, rising to 108 per cent in 1939; in practice, however, this meant that many workers in the consumer goods industries continued to earn less than they had done before the Depression; only those in arms and arms-related industries earned substantially more.[142] Moreover, shortages of many kinds also entered the equation, along with the declining quality of many goods in consequence of the growing use of substitutes for basic raw materials like leather, rubber and cotton. *Per capita* consumption of many basic foodstuffs actually declined in the mid-1930s. In addition, wage increases were achieved above all by longer hours. In July 1934, Trustees of Labour were given the right to increase working time to more than the legal norm of eight hours a day and, particularly in arms-related industries, they used it. In machine engineering, for example, average weekly hours, after falling during the Depression from 49 in 1929 to 43 in 1933, rose to over 50 in the first half of 1939.[143] Despite this, however, wages as a percentage of national income fell by 11 per cent between 1932 and 1938. Inequality actually increased between 1928, when the top 10 per cent of earners took 37 per cent of total national income, and 1936, when they took 39 per cent.[144] The numerous deductions made from pay packets, for Strength Through Joy, Labour Front membership and the like, not to mention the endless collections held on the streets, in effect reduced income still further, in some cases by as much as 30 per cent. Under such circumstances, it was not surprising that by 1937–8 workers were having to put in longer hours just to maintain their existing, very modest standard of living.[145]

Overtime, generally paid at time and a quarter, was the only realistic way of increasing wages for most workers, since the closure of the trade unions had taken away their role in formal wage bargaining processes. Whether or not to work overtime was a matter for the individual employee. The result was a rapid atomization of the workforce, as each worker was pitted against his fellow workers in the struggle to increase wages and improve performance. It was not rationalization, but simple extra work, that led to increased production: the great period of rationalization and mechanization had been the mid-1920s; these trends did continue in many industries under the Third Reich, but at a much slower pace.[146] And of course overtime, frowned on by the regime and its agencies in consumer goods industries, was strongly encouraged in war-relevant production. This was not least because the frantic pace of rearmament led not only to serious bottlenecks in the supply of raw materials but also to an increasingly serious shortage of suitably skilled and qualified workers. In the early days of the Third Reich, the government had concentrated on trying to direct labour into agriculture, where the shortage was obvious, particularly through labour service and labour camps of one kind and another. Laws passed on 15 May 1934 and

26 February 1935 required all workers to carry work-books, containing details of their training and qualifications and employment; these were kept on file at labour exchanges, where they could be consulted when the government was looking for workers to draft into new jobs. If a worker wanted to go abroad on holiday, he had to get permission from the labour exchange to do so. Employers could put critical remarks in the book, making things difficult for the employee in future posts. And as rearmament gathered pace, the government began to use the work-books to direct labour towards arms-related industries. On 22 June 1938 Göring issued a Decree on the Duty of Service, permitting the President of the Reich Institute for Labour Exchange and Unemployment Insurance to draft workers temporarily into particular projects where labour was in short supply. In February 1939 these powers were extended to make labour conscription indefinite in duration. Before long, over a million workers had been drafted in to munitions factories, defensive works like the so-called West Wall, better known as the Siegfried Line, a vast system of fortifications guarding Germany's western borders, and other schemes judged vital for the coming war. Only 300,000 of these were conscripted on a long-term basis, but a million was still a sizeable chunk of a workforce that totalled 23 million by this time.[147]

These measures did not just deprive workers of the power of changing jobs, transferring to a better-paid position or moving to a different area. They also in many cases put them into situations where they found it difficult to cope. In February 1939, for example, Social Democratic observers reported that the workers forcibly removed from their jobs in Saxony to work on fortifications near Trier, on the other side of Germany, included a 59-year-old accounts clerk who had never wielded a pick and shovel before, and similarly unsuitable characters. Forced labour was being used as a punishment: 'Anyone who in any way lets slip an incautious word is sent there, when the labour shortage means that he is not arrested.' Textile workers were made to undergo compulsory medical examinations to see whether they were fitted for manual labour on the fortifications. There were reports that people who refused to go were arrested and transported by the prison authorities to their new place of work, where they were given the most exhausting jobs to do. Travelling by train to Berlin, one observer was surprised when:

In Duisburg a group of about 80 people stormed onto the train, shouting loudly, poorly dressed, in some cases in their work-clothes, their luggage mostly the poor man's suitcase in the Third Reich, the Persil carton. In my compartment the travel guide sits down with a few women and girls. It soon becomes clear that they are unemployed textile workers from the area around Krefeld and Rheydt, who are to be resettled in Brandenburg, the men to work on motorway construction, the women in a new factory in Brandenburg. The people turn up in our compartment one after another, to get their 2 Reichsmarks money for the journey from the travel guide. A short while later some of them are drunk; they have spent their money in the restaurant car, on beer.[148]

Such groups, the reporter was told, were taken by train to new places of work week after week. The married men had the right to visit their families four times a year.

Even this did not solve the problem, which was made still worse by the insatiable appetite of the armed forces for new recruits. In April 1939 the Hanover labour exchange district reported a shortage of 100,000 workers for a variety of jobs, about half of them in construction; the building of the West Wall had drained the industry of large numbers of employees. In August 1939 there were said to be 25,000 vacancies in the metalworking industry in Berlin. Shortly afterwards the air force administration complained that there was a shortage of 2,600 engineers in the aircraft construction industry. So desperate were the labour administrators in the government that they even suggested releasing 8,000 state prisoners who happened to be qualified metalworkers; since a good number of these were probably in prison for political offences, the suggestion was never actually taken up. All this put a new bargaining power in the hands of workers in the key industries. On 6 October 1936 the Ministries of Economics and Labour pointed out in a letter sent directly to Hitler that labour shortages were leading to late fulfilment of contracts and delaying the whole rearmament programme. Employers were taking matters into their own hands and enticing workers away from rivals with higher wage offers, thus increasing the price of the goods they produced. In some factories employees were working as much as fourteen hours a day, or up to sixty hours a week.[149] Workers at Daimler-Benz averaged fifty-four hours a week by the late 1930s, as against forty-eight in the last pre-Depression years.[150] In a number of cases the Labour Front, concerned about the goodwill of the workforce, took a more flexible line towards wage increases than the government wished, bringing down a fiercely worded directive from Rudolf Hess, in the name of the Leader, on 1 October 1937, urging all Party institutions not to curry popularity by giving in to wage demands. Things would get better eventually, he promised; but for the moment, it was still necessary to make sacrifices.[151]

On 25 June 1938 Göring allowed Trustees of Labour to fix maximum wages in an effort to keep costs under control. The economic logic of rearmament's effects on the labour market was against him. By this time even work stoppages – in effect, informal strikes – were being used by factory employees to try and improve their wages; the pressure to work longer hours was leading workers to go slow or call off sick to a degree that some officials even began to speak of 'passive resistance' on the shop-floor. Labourers drafted into projects such as the West Wall faced arrest and imprisonment if they left without permission; early in 1939, for example, it was reported that one such worker, Heinrich Bonsack, had been sentenced to three months in prison for leaving the West Wall without permission twice to visit his family in Wanne-Eickel. That workers ran away from the West Wall was not surprising: construction was carried out round the clock in twelve-hour shifts, living conditions were primitive, the pay was poor, safety measures non-existent, accidents frequent, and if work got behind schedule, labourers were forced to work for double or even treble shifts to catch up, with a break only once every twelve hours. Another worker, a turner, was refused permission by his employer in Cologne to leave his job for a better-paid one else-where, and when he signed off sick, the company doctor forced him back to his workplace. When his workbench was found shortly afterwards to be damaged, he was arrested and sentenced to six months' imprisonment for sabotage, an offence that was being used by the authorities increas-ingly at this time. Conscription to jobs away from home led to so many incidents that in November 1939 Hitler ordered that workers where possible be conscripted into schemes or factories in the district where they lived, a measure that seems to have had little effect in practice.[152]

In characteristic fashion, the regime increasingly sought to enforce its measures by terror. A favourite measure on the part of employers was to threaten alleged troublemakers with sacking and immediate transfer to work on the West Wall. This had little impact. At their wits' end, some employers began to call in the Gestapo to place agents on the shop-floor to spy out cases of loafing and slacking. From the second half of 1938, labour regulations had included increasingly severe penalties for contraventions such as refusing to work as ordered, or even smoking and drinking on the job, but these were relatively ineffective, and the courts were getting clogged with cases that were taking far too long to resolve. In August 1939 the Labour Front administration in the I.G. Farben factory at Wolfen wrote to all workers warning them that slackers would be handed over to the Gestapo without trial in future. Already in April, four companies in Nuremberg had called in the Gestapo to catch out under-performing employees. In the railway engineering works at Dresden, the Gestapo even carried out twice-weekly searches of the workforce without giving any reason. Munitions and war production factories were frequently convulsed by management fears of espionage or sabotage. Former Communists and Social Democrats were particularly vulnerable to arrest, even if they had long since ceased to be politically active. In the autumn of 1938, at the Heinkel aircraft works in Rostock and Warnemünde, where workers were relatively privileged and well paid, the works police were said to be arresting employees virtually every day, acting on denunciations from the spies they kept in the workforce. In many factories, workers were arrested for sabotage when they protested against the lowering of piece-rates or the worsening of working conditions. So intrusive did the Gestapo become in some factories that even the employers started to object. After the arrest of 174 employees at a munitions factory in Gleiwitz in 1938, the employers obtained their release after twenty-four hours, explaining to the Gestapo that a bit of criticism of the regime by the workers had to be tolerated, otherwise production would be disrupted, and that was surely not in the national interest.[153]

The suppression and fragmentation of political and organizational life directed people towards private pleasures and purposes: getting a steady job, marrying, having children, improving living conditions, going on holiday. It was for this reason that Strength Through Joy was so fondly remembered by many Germans after the war. Yet when people recalled this period, they found it difficult not just to remember public events, but even to recount their memories in chronological order. The years from 1933 to 1939 or even 1941 became a retrospective blur, in which the routines of private life made one day difficult to distinguish from the next. Economic achievement became the only real meaning in life for many: politics was an irrelevant irritation, a life in which it was impossible to participate with any kind of autonomy or independence and so not worth participating in at all, except insofar as one was obliged to. From this point of view, 1939 attracted a kind of nostalgic glow, the last year of relative peace and prosperity before plunging into a maelstrom of war and destruction, destitution and ruin that lasted until 1948. It was in the mid-to-late 1930s, indeed, that the foundations were laid for the hard-working, relatively unpolitical German society of the years of the 'economic miracle' in the 1950s. By the end of the 1930s, the great mass of German workers had reconciled themselves, often with varying degrees of reluctance, to the Third Reich. They might be unpersuaded by its core ideological tenets, irritated by its constant appeals for acclamation and support and annoyed by its failure to deliver a greater degree of prosperity. They might grumble about many aspects of life and privately pour scorn on many of its leaders and its institutions. But at least, most people reflected, it had given them a steady job and overcome, by whatever means, the economic hardships and catastrophes of the Weimar years, and for that alone, the vast majority of German workers seem to have thought it was worth tolerating, especially since the possibility of organized resistance was so minimal and the price of expressing dissent so high. There was widespread informal and individual refractoriness in Germany's factories and workplaces on the eve of the Second World War, but it did not really amount to anything that could be called opposition, let alone resistance, nor did it create any real sense of crisis in the Third Reich's ruling elite.[154]

II

How did the Third Reich deal with the unemployed and the destitute who suffered in their millions under the Depression and were still suffering when they came to power? Nazi ideology did not in principle favour the idea of social welfare. In *My Struggle*, Hitler, writing about the time he had spent living amongst the poor and the destitute in Vienna before the First World War, had waxed indignant about the way in which social welfare had encouraged the preservation of the degenerate and the feeble. From a Social Darwinist point of view, charity and philanthropy were evils that had to be eliminated if the German race was to be strengthened and its weakest elements weeded out in the process of natural selection.[155] The Nazi Party frequently condemned the elaborate welfare system that had grown up under the Weimar Republic as bureaucratic, cumbersome and directed essentially to the wrong ends. Instead of giving support to the biologically and racially valuable, Weimar's social state, backed by a host of private charities, was, the Nazis alleged, completely indiscriminate in its application, supporting many people who were racially inferior and would, they claimed, contribute nothing to the regeneration of the German race. This view was in some respects not too far from that of the public and private welfare bureaucracy itself, which by the early 1930s had become infused with the doctrines of racial hygiene, and also advocated the drawing of a sharp distinction between the deserving and the degenerate, although putting such a distinction into effect was not possible until 1933. At this point, welfare institutions, whose attitudes towards the destitute had become increasingly punitive in the course of the Depression, moved rapidly to bring criminal sanctions to bear on the 'work-shy', the down-and-out and the socially deviant. Nazi ideas on welfare were thus not wholly alien to the thinking of welfare administrators in the later stages of the Weimar Republic.[156]

Faced with ten million people in receipt of welfare assistance at the height of the Depression, however, it would have been political suicide for the Nazis to have written off the mass of the unemployed and destitute as not worth helping. However much the employment situation improved, or was made to look as if it improved, in the spring, summer and autumn of the Nazis' first year in office, Propaganda Minister Joseph Goebbels recognized that the economic situation would still be serious enough for many people to be living below the poverty line in the first full winter of the Third Reich in power. To boost the regime's image and convince people it was doing everything it could to foster solidarity between the better-off and the worst-off amongst the Germans, he announced on 13 September 1933 that he was setting up a short-term relief programme which he called the Winter Aid Programme of the German People. This built on, formalized, co-ordinated and carried further a number of emergency relief schemes already launched by Regional Party Leaders; more importantly, it continued and expanded similar schemes that had already been mooted under the Weimar Republic and formally established in 1931 under Reich Chancellor Brüning.[157] Soon, some 1.5 million volunteers and 4,000 paid workers were ladling out soup to the poor at emergency centres, taking round food parcels to the destitute, collecting and distributing clothes to the unemployed and their families, and engaging in a wide variety of other centrally directed charitable activities. When Hitler, in a widely publicized speech, urged people to contribute, two million Reichsmarks were pledged by a variety of institutions, including Nazi Party headquarters in Munich, the very next day. Donations received during the winter of 1933–4 eventually totalled 358 million Reichsmarks. Goebbels's Propaganda Ministry blared forth its satisfaction at this evidence of a new spirit of community solidarity and mutual help amongst the German people.[158] This was not charity, therefore, or state welfare, even though it was in fact run by the state, by the Propaganda Minister and by a specially appointed Reich Commissioner for Winter Aid. It was, on the contrary, Goebbels declared, a form of racial self-help run by the German people for the German people.[159]

Yet again the reality was different from the propaganda. For contributions to the Winter Aid were virtually compulsory for everyone from the outset. When a burly, brown-uniformed stormtrooper appeared at the door demanding a donation, few were brave enough to refuse, and those who did faced the prospect of escalating threats and intimidation until they relented and put their money in the collection box. In Bavaria it was announced that those who did not contribute would be regarded as enemies of the Fatherland; some were publicly paraded through the streets with placards round their necks advertising their sin of omission; others were even dismissed from their jobs as a result. The experience of a Reich Entailed Farmer in Franconia who had refused to contribute in 1935 can hardly have been untypical: he was informed by Party District Leader Gerstner 'that you are not worthy to bear the honourable title of farmer in National Socialist Germany' and warned that it would be necessary 'to take measures to prevent public disorder being created by your attitude' – in other words, that he could expect either removal to 'protective custody' in a concentration camp or face physical violence from the local SA. In one cinema in Breslau in December 1935, eight armed SS men appeared on the stage at the end of the performance and announced that the exits had all been sealed; there were enemies of the state in the auditorium, and everyone had to make a donation to the Winter Aid to prove that they were not amongst their number. As the brief announcement ended, the doors burst open and fifty stormtroopers poured in, armed with collection boxes. Across the land, workers came under pressure to allow their contributions to be automatically deducted from their wage packets at a rate of 20 per cent of the basic income tax (later reduced to 10 per cent). Those who earned too little to pay tax still had to contribute 25 pfennigs from each pay packet. In one factory in 1938, workers were told that if they did not agree to a deduction, the sum they should be paying would be added to the sums deducted from the pay packets of their fellow employees.[160]

Crucially, regular, automatic contributions entitled the donor to receive a plaque which he could nail to the front door of his home, which brownshirts, Hitler Youth members and other Party members knocking on doors to collect donations were instructed to take as an instruction to move on without disturbing him. In some factories, however, workers were asked for additional contributions even if they had agreed to have Winter Aid deducted from their wage packets. And this still did not protect such donors from the importunities of brown-uniformed men standing on the streets with their collecting-boxes, or the pressure exerted by shopkeepers and customers to put loose change into the Winter Aid receptacles that were placed on the counters of most retail outlets. Winter Aid vendors also offered opportunities to collect various sets of illus- trated cards, including a set of photographs of Hitler. Children were sometimes given part of a day off school and provided with knick-knacks to sell on the street for the Winter Aid collection. Purchase of a Winter Aid badge might help ward off the importunities of street-collectors; better still was to buy a Winter Aid nail, evidence that one possessed a Winter Aid shield, into which the nails, costing 5 pfennigs each, could be hammered, until the entire surface was covered with an estimated 1,500 of them. Wearing a Winter Aid badge on the street might have been a form of self-protection, but it also had the effect of advertising to others one's solidarity with the regime. Nearly 170 million badges were sold in the winter of 1938–9. It became popular to use them as a decoration for Christmas trees in the home.[161]

As with so many other emergency measures in the Third Reich, the Winter Aid soon became a permanent feature of the sociopolitical landscape. The action was underpinned legislatively on 5 November 1934 by a Collection Law which allowed the Interior Minister and the Nazi Party Treasurer to suspend any charities or funds that competed with the Winter Aid, thus forcing all other philanthropic activities into the summer months and ensuring that demands for contributions would be addressed to the German people all the year round. On 4 December 1936 this was backed up by a Winter Aid Law that formally put the scheme on a permanent basis. The statistics were impressive. By the winter of 1938–9, 105 million Reichsmarks were coming in from wage deductions, with collections and donations, the largest from industry and big business, making up the rest of the total of 554 million. Winter Aid donations thus accounted for nearly 3 per cent of the average worker's income at this time. Some changes had taken place since 1933, of course: after the winter of 1935–6, Jews were no longer included in the ranks of either donors or receivers. And the economic recovery had brought about a halving of the number of those in receipt of Winter Aid, from 16 million in 1933–4 to 8 million in 1938–9. Notable additions to the scheme included a 'Day of National Solidarity' every 1 December, when prominent members of the regime appeared in public to solicit donations on the streets, netting 4 million Reichsmarks in 1935 and no less than 15 million in 1938. By this time, too, it had become more or less compulsory for every family, indeed every German, to eat a 'one-pot meal' or cheap stew, with ingredients costing no more than 50 pfennigs in all, on the first Sunday of each month, 'one-pot Sunday'; in the evening, stormtroopers or SS men or a representative of the Nazi People's Welfare would appear at the door to demand the difference between 50 pfennigs and the normal cost of a family meal as a contribution. The same policy was implemented in restaurants as well. Hitler ostentatiously followed suit, passing round the Sunday dinner-table a list for his guests to pledge a donation of suitable grandeur. Every such meal, Albert Speer later complained, 'cost me fifty or a hundred marks'. Under such pressure, the number of Hitler's guests on the first Sunday of every month soon shrank to two or three, 'prompting', Speer reported, 'some sarcastic remarks from Hitler about the spirit of sacrifice among his associates'.[162]

In the meantime, however, the Nazi Party had also been active in reshaping the private charity sector. The leading figure here was Erich Hilgenfeldt, a Saarlander, born in 1897 and an officer in the First World War. A former Steel Helmet activist, Hilgenfeldt had joined the Nazi Party in 1929 and become a District Leader in Berlin; he was thus close to Joseph Goebbels, who was his immediate Party boss as Berlin's Regional Leader. Hilgenfeldt had co-ordinated and centralized a variety of internal brownshirt and Party welfare groups in the capital into the National Socialist People's Welfare. With Magda Goebbels, the Propaganda Minister's wife, as its patron, and with the backing of Hitler himself given on 3 May 1933, Hilgenfeldt extended his grip on Party self-help groups across the entire country, against considerable opposition from Robert Ley and Baldur von Schirach, who wanted welfare to be run by their own respective organizations. Hilgenfeldt successfully argued that welfare was not the first priority for either the Labour Front or the Hitler Youth, so a separate, comprehensive institution was needed that would put welfare at the top of its agenda. In the turbulent months from March to July 1933, he successfully took over virtually all the private welfare and philanthropic organizations in Germany, above all the massive welfare arms of the Social Democrats and the Communists. From 25 July 1933 there were just four non-state welfare organizations in Germany: the Nazi People's Welfare, the Protestant Inner Mission, the Catholic Caritas Association and the German Red Cross. However, only the Nazi organization now received state funding; a good number of welfare institutions such as church kindergartens were passed over to it by the Inner Mission during the brief hegemony of the German Christians over the Protestant Church; and despite formal permission to collect contributions during the summer months, the other organizations, especially the Caritas, were increasingly disrupted in their work by physical attacks from brownshirt gangs, and then from 1936 onwards they were required to run their street and house-to-house collections at the same time as those of the Nazi organization, putting them at a severe disadvantage against this powerful competitor.[163]

Interior Minister Wilhelm Frick left people in no doubt as to where their contributions should go: it was, he declared in October 1934, 'indefensible to allow the population's charitable impulses and sense of sacrifice to be used for purposes whose implementation is not in the interests of the National Socialist state and thus not for the common good'. As this suggested, Christian charity was now to be displaced by the desire for self-sacrifice that Nazi ideology placed so high on its list of supposed attributes of the German race. There was another point to this, too: unlike the Winter Aid and other organizations like the Red Cross, the Nazi Party restricted its donations from the very beginning exclusively to people of 'Aryan descent'.[164] The National Socialist People's Welfare enshrined in its constitution the statement that its aim was to promote 'the living, healthy forces of the German people'. It would only assist those who were racially sound, capable of and willing to work, politically reliable, and willing and able to reproduce. Those who were 'not in a condition completely to fulfil their communal obligations' were to be excluded. Assistance was not to be extended to alcoholics, tramps, homosexuals, prostitutes, the 'work-shy' or the 'asocial', habitual criminals, the hereditarily ill (a widely defined category) and members of races other than the Aryan. People's Welfare officials were not slow to attack state welfare institutions for the indiscriminate way in which they allegedly handed out their charity, thus pushing them still further down the racial hygiene road they had in fact already begun to tread. The Christian concept of charity was if anything even more reprehensible in Nazi eyes, and the pushing aside of Caritas and the Inner Mission by the Nazi welfare organization was in part designed to limit as far as possible what were seen as the racially undesirable effects of Church philanthropy.[165]

Despite these limitations, the National Socialist People's Welfare was, alongside Strength Through Joy, probably the most popular Party organization in the Third Reich. With 17 million members by 1939, it projected a powerful image of caring and support for the weaker members of the German racial community, or at least, those who were judged to have got into difficulties through no fault of their own. By 1939, for example, it was running 8,000 day-nurseries, and it was providing holiday homes for mothers, extra food for large families and a wide variety of other facilities. Yet it was feared and disliked amongst society's poorest, who resented the intrusiveness of its questioning, its moral judgments on their

behaviour and its ever-present threat to use compulsion and bring in the
Gestapo if they did not fulfil the designated criteria for support. Many
others were dismayed at the way it brusquely elbowed aside the Church
welfare institutions upon which they had traditionally relied in time of
need. It was also impossible to ignore the widespread irritation, even
anger and fear, aroused more widely by the ubiquity of street collections
which, a Social Democratic agent reported in 1935, had 'completely
assumed the character of organized highway robbery'. 'The importunity
is so great', reported another agent, 'that nobody can escape it.' 'Last
year one could still speak of it as a nuisance,' one informant complained
of the Winter Aid in December 1935, 'but this winter it has become a
plague of the first degree.' There were not only Winter Aid collections
but also Hitler Youth collections for the building of new youth hostels,
collections for the support of Germans abroad, collections for air-raid
shelters, collections for needy 'old fighters', a lottery for the benefit of
job creation, and many more collections for local schemes. There were
pay deductions for the Volkswagen car and workplace contributions for
Strength Through Joy and Beauty of Labour, and much, much more.
Such contributions, whether in kind or in money or in the form of unpaid
voluntary work, amounted in effect to a new, informal tax. People
grumbled and cursed, but all reports agree that they paid up anyway.
There was no organized boycott of any of the collection actions, despite
a few individual incidents of refusal to pay. People got used to the
perpetual demands for money, clothing and other contributions; it
became a normal part of everyday life. It was widely believed that old
Nazis were amongst the most frequent and most favoured recipients of
the aid dispensed in this way, and there were many stories of preferential
treatment to Party members over ex-Communists or Social Democrats.
This was not surprising, since political reliability was indeed a prime
criterion for the receipt of support. Those who benefited were indeed
most frequently Party members and their hangers-on. It was equally
unsurprising that there were also many jokes about the corruption that
was said to be inherent in the whole operation. One joke had two Party
officials discovering a 50-Reichsmark note in the gutter as they were
walking along the street. Picking it up, one of the two men announced
he was going to donate it to the Party's Winter Aid relief scheme. 'Why
are you doing it the long way round?' asked the other.[166]

By devolving welfare spending onto the (allegedly) voluntary sector, the regime was able to save official tax-based income and use it for rearmament instead. Conscription, marriage loans and other schemes to take people out of the labour market led to further reductions in the burden of benefit payments on the state and so to further savings in state expenditure that could then be turned to the purposes of military-related expenditure. Unemployment benefits had already been severely cut by governments and local authorities before the Nazis took power. The new regime lost little time in cutting them even more sharply. Voluntary Labour Service and other, similar schemes to massage the unemployment statistics downwards also had the effect of reducing the amount of unemployment benefits that had to be paid out. Unemployment, of course, as we have seen, had by no means vanished from the scene by the winter of 1935–6, but local authorities continued to drive down the level of benefit payments by whatever means they could. From October to December 1935, when the official figure of welfare unemployed rose from 336,000 to 376,000, the total benefits paid to them across the Reich actually fell from 4.7 to 3.8 million Reichsmarks. Everywhere, welfare authorities were calling in the unemployed for questioning and examination as to whether they were fit to work; those who were deemed fit were drafted into the Reich Labour Service or emergency relief schemes of one kind or another; those who failed to appear were taken off the register, and their payments stopped. Rent supplements were cut, payments to carers for the old and the sick for medication were slashed. In Cologne, a working-class woman who asked the welfare officer for help in paying for medication for her 75-year-old mother, whom she cared for at home, was told that the state would no longer pay for such people, who were nothing but a burden on the national community.[167]

Cutting back on welfare payments was only part of a wider strategy. Urging the German people to engage in self-help instead of relying on payouts from the state carried with it the implication that those who could not help themselves were dispensable, indeed a positive threat to the future health of the German people. The racially unsound, deviants, criminals, the 'asocial' and the like were to be excluded from the welfare system altogether. As we have seen, by 1937–8 members of the underclass, social deviants and petty criminals were being arrested in large numbers and put into concentration camps since they were regarded by the Nazis as being of no use to the regime. In the end, therefore, as soon as rearmament had soaked up the mass of the unemployed, the Nazis' original scepticism about the benefits of social welfare reasserted itself in the most brutal possible way.

III

The National Socialist Welfare organization, Winter Aid and Strength Through Joy were by far the most popular schemes mounted by the Third Reich at home. For many, they were tangible proof that the regime was serious about implementing its promise to create an organic national community of all Germans, in which class conflict and social antagonisms would be overcome, and the egotism of the individual would give way to the overriding interests of the whole. These programmes explicitly aimed to obliterate distinctions of class and status, to involve the better-off in helping their fellow Germans who had suffered in the Depression and to improve the lives of the mass of ordinary people in a variety of different ways. Paradoxically, it was the better-off who were most attracted to the ideology of the people's community; workers were often too deeply imbued with Marxist ideas of class conflict to yield directly to its appeal. Not untypical was the reaction of Melita Maschmann, a young woman brought up in a conservative, upper-middle-class household, where her nationalist parents instilled in her a conception of Germany that she later described as 'a terrible and wonderful mystery'.[168] Conversation in her parents' home in the early 1930s frequently turned to matters such as the humiliation of Germany's defeat in the First World War, the divisions and squabbles of the political parties in the Reichstag, the constantly escalating violence and mayhem on the streets, and the poverty and desperation of the growing numbers of unemployed. Nostalgic for the Kaiser's day, when, her parents said, Germans had been proud and united, Melita herself found it impossible to resist the lure of the Nazis' promise to stop internal dissension and unite all social classes in a new national community in which rich and poor would all be treated as equals.[169] Her experience was echoed by that of many others. Yet although reactions to the welfare and leisure schemes that the Nazis deployed to give effect to such unifying ideas were often favourable, especially in retrospect, there was a down-side too. The element of compulsion in all of them could hardly be ignored. Despite the regime's constant trumpeting of the virtues of self-sacrifice, these did not possess a universal appeal; on the contrary, many people were fixated on the achievement of material improvements in their own situation – hardly surprising after all they had been through in the war, the inflation and the Depression. Class distinctions seemed as alive as ever, and were compounded by a newly emerging distinction between 'old fighters' and local Party bosses, who were widely perceived as the principal beneficiaries of these schemes, and the rest. Deeply held beliefs among wide sections of the population, possibly even the majority, ranging from faith in the Christian idea of universal charity to an ingrained habit amongst many workers of viewing everything through the lens of a Marxist-influenced idea of class struggle, proved extremely difficult for the regime to eradicate.

By 1939, therefore, disillusion was widespread even with some of the most popular schemes implemented by the Third Reich. The first flush of enthusiasm for the regime had already begun to fade in 1934, and by early 1936 it had reached such a low level that even Hitler's popularity was beginning to wane.[170] How far did this disillusion reach, how general was it, and why did it fail to translate into a wider and more principled opposition to the regime? A good picture of how ordinary people regarded the Third Reich, the ways in which society changed between 1933 and 1939, and the extent to which the promise of a united, organic national community was realized, can be derived from the experience of a provincial town during this period. In the Lower Saxon town of Northeim, the most obvious outward and visible sign of change in the eyes of the inhabitants was the return of prosperity and order after the poverty and disorder of the last years of the Weimar Republic. Street clashes and meeting-room brawls, which had caused so much anxiety among the citizenry, were now a thing of the past. The town's Nazi mayor, Ernst Girmann, after ousting his rivals within the local Party in September 1933, ruled Northeim alone, unfettered by any democratic controls, a position confirmed in January 1935 when a new, nationwide law came into effect giving mayors untrammelled power over the communities they ran. Girmann put out a substantial propaganda campaign unveiling elaborate plans for a revival of the job market in the town.

These plans were never taken up by Northeim's hard-headed businessmen; but after the unemployed had been taken off the streets into labour camps and public works schemes, the general revival of the economy that had already begun before the Nazi seizure of power started to have a real impact. Workers drafted into the Reich Labour Service were engaged on highly visible municipal improvements such as the extension of the town's parkland, or the repainting of some of the town's old houses.[171]

The most notable construction project involved the building of a *Thingplatz* or Nazi cultic meeting-place, an open-air theatre in a nearby forest, on land purchased by the city at an extremely high price from one of Girmann's friends. A large number of new houses and apartment blocks were built in the town with subsidies made available by the government, though the most widely trumpeted construction project, a settlement of forty-eight new houses on the outskirts of the town, had been conceived already in the early 1930s and had in fact been delayed by objections raised by the local Nazis themselves in 1932. Only Aryan families who belonged to the Party or an ancillary organization could move in, and only if they were sponsored by the local Party. Still, the propaganda surrounding the 'battle for work' had the effect in Northeim of convincing most people that the Third Reich had indeed brought about a miraculous economic recovery. The sense of everyone pulling together to get Germany out of the economic rut was strengthened by the hyper-activism of the local National Socialist Welfare organization, with its collection boxes, benefit evenings, stewpot Sundays and mass rallies. However, the Third Reich's most significant benefit to the local economy was brought by the army's reoccupation of a local barracks, whose refurbishment triggered a mini-boom in Northeim's construction industry. A thousand soldiers and ancillary staff meant a thousand new consumers and customers for local shops and suppliers.[172]

Yet according to regional Gestapo reports, none of this convinced the town's many former Social Democrats and Communists, who were still unreconciled to the regime at the end of 1935, and were continuing to spread negative propaganda by word of mouth. Hostility was also noted amongst local Catholics; people still shopped in Jewish stores; conservatives were disillusioned and forging contacts with the army; and Girmann's attempt to crush the local Lutheran congregation and make the town the first town in Germany without Christians foundered on the passive resistance of both clergy and laity. In conformity with national policy, Girmann did manage to force the closure of the town's Catholic school, achieved mainly through a series of personal interviews with its pupils' parents in which an undertone of intimidation must have been clearly audible to them. But higher authority would not allow him to employ overt violence against the Lutherans, and getting the Hitler Youth to throw snowballs at the crucifix on the town church was not really very effective, and so his campaign failed. Girmann was not above threatening people he observed failing to conform. People who did not turn up to meetings or left them early were confronted and asked for an explanation, and in one case, Girmann personally wrote to a young woman who had neglected to raise her arm in the Nazi salute, telling her she would be in danger of physical assault if she did the same again. Faced with such threats, local people were generally careful to conform, at least outwardly. All the same, there was no denying a widespread loss of enthusiasm for the regime in the town after the first months of euphoria.[173]

The local Party found it difficult to counter such disillusionment. By the end of 1935 it had lost its dynamism; its leaders, Mayor Girmann included, had become comfortable, well-off even, drawing high salaries and reaping the rewards of their earlier struggles. Even Girmann did little in the later 1930s except rebuild the town's horse-riding facilities, which he proceeded to use himself on regular occasions. Nazi festivals and celebrations became empty rituals, with people participating more out of fear than commitment. The few open incidents of antisemitic violence in the town met with reactions from the townsfolk ranging from indifference to outright disapproval; this was, after all, the kind of disorder they had supposed the Third Reich had come into being in order to suppress. Former Social Democrats were grudgingly tolerated if they abstained from oppositional activities, which on the whole they did after 1935, when the last remaining resistance groups had been suppressed. Block Wardens visited the households in their charge on a regular basis, to extract Winter Aid payments and to check on their political reliability. They had to submit reports on anyone from their block who was applying for social welfare, seeking a position in any of the town's numerous guilds and clubs, or looking for a government job.

They had to fill in a form to this end, giving details of the applicant's attendance at meetings, contributions to charity and so on. Yet of the thousands of such reports stored in the local archives, hardly a single one after 1935 classified the subject as politically unreliable; only for a brief while, at the height of the Church struggle, did the reports contain negative comments along these lines, usually concerning active Catholics. Many of the Block Wardens' notes were vague or said little that was meaningful, but on one point, they were all specific, and that was whether or not their subjects contributed to Winter Aid and similar schemes. Failure to do so earned the person in question a black mark and a designation as 'selfish' or 'unfriendly'. Such an individual had made the Block Warden's job more difficult, and held the potential to get him into trouble if he did not deliver his designated quota of payments. Nothing much else mattered, except on occasion a rare failure of someone to hang out a flag on Hitler's birthday or forgetting to give the Hitler greeting. Some kind of political stability had been achieved, and most Block Wardens now seemed to want little more than to carry out their regular duties unhindered and without trouble. They no longer cared very much about people's political beliefs, so long as they conformed in outward appearance and kept their beliefs to themselves. No doubt they were somewhat more vigilant in former Communist strongholds in Berlin or the Ruhr than in a small provincial town like Northeim. Still, by 1939, a kind of *modus vivendi* had been reached: townspeople, whatever their views, participated in public rituals as required, though generally without much enthusiasm; the local Party was careful to leave it at that and not push people too far. Acquiescence and lip-service were all, in the end, that it had been able to achieve; but it was realistic enough to admit that this would have to do, and that was probably the situation elsewhere as well.[174]

The situation in Northeim reflected that of many other parts of Germany. Germans had not all become fanatical Nazis by 1939, but the basic desire of the vast majority for order, security, jobs, the possibility of improved living standards and career advancement, all things which had seemed impossible under the Weimar Republic, had largely been met, and this was enough to secure their acquiescence. Propaganda may not have had as much effect in this regard as the actual, obvious fact of social, economic and political stability. The violence and illegality of the

Röhm purge had been widely accepted, for example, not because people supported Hitler's use of murder as a political tool, but because it appeared to restore the order that had been threatened by Röhm's storm-troopers over the preceding months. There was a broad consensus on the primacy of orderliness that the Nazis recognized, accepted and exploited. In the long run, of course, it was to prove illusory. But for the moment, it was enough to take the wind out of the sails of any oppositional movements that tried to convert rumblings of dissatisfaction with one or the other aspect of daily life under the Third Reich into a broader form of opposition.[175]

IV

The social promises made by the Third Reich's leaders were far-reaching indeed. Nazism had won support at the polls in the early 1930s not least because of its incessantly reiterated promise to overcome the divisions of the Weimar Republic and unite the German people in a new national, racial community based on co-operation not conflict, mutual support not mutual antagonism. Class differences would disappear; the interests of the Germanic race would be paramount. The two great symbolic propaganda demonstrations choreographed by Goebbels and the Nazi leadership in the opening months of the Third Reich, the 'Day of Potsdam' and the 'Day of National Labour', had both been intended to demonstrate how the new Germany would unite the old traditions of the Prussian Establishment on the one hand and the labour movement on the other. Interviewed by the Nazi playwright Hanns Johst on 27 January 1934, Hitler declared that Nazism 'conceives of Germany as a corporate body, as a single organism'. 'From the camp of bourgeois tradition', he told Johst, National Socialism 'takes national resolve, and from the materialism of the Marxist dogma living, creative socialism.' He went on:

People's Community: that means a community of all productive labour, that means the oneness of all vital interests, that means overcoming bourgeois privatism and the unionized, mechanically organized masses, that means unconditionally equating the individual fate and the nation, the individual and the people ... The bourgeois must become a citizen of the state; the red comrade must become a racial comrade. Both must, with their good intentions, ennoble the sociological concept of the worker and raise the status of an honorary title for labour. This patent of nobility alone puts the soldier and the peasant, the merchant and the academician, the worker and the capitalist under oath to take the only possible direction in which all purposeful German striving must be headed: towards the nation ... The bourgeois man should stop feeling like some sort of pensioner of tradition or capital and separated from the worker by the Marxist concept of property; rather, he should strive, with an open mind, to become integrated in the whole as a worker.[176]

Hitler underlined these points by projecting himself as a worker by origin, a humble man of the people who had risen through the ranks without ever losing touch with his lowly origins.

Hitler frequently reminded his audiences that, as he told an audience of over a million people assembled in Berlin's Pleasure Gardens on Mayday 1937, he 'did not issue from some palace: I came from the worksite. Neither was I a general: I was a soldier like millions of others.' The camaraderie of the front line in 1914–18, when social barriers were wiped away in the heat of commitment to the national cause, was to live again in the spirit of the Third Reich:

It is a miraculous thing that, here in our country, an unknown man was able to step forth from the army of millions of German people, German workers and soldiers, to stand at the fore of the Reich and the nation! Next to me stand German people from every class of life who are today Regional Leaders etc. Though, mind you, former members of the bourgeoisie and former aristocrats also have their place in this movement. To us it makes no difference where they come from; what counts is that they are able to work for the benefit of our people.[177]

As Hitler's use of the word 'former' on this occasion suggested, the Third Reich sedulously propagated the notion that all class distinctions had been abolished in the new Germany. 'We are', declared Robert Ley in 1935, 'the first country in Europe to overcome the class struggle.'[178] In token of this, many institutions of the Nazi Party made a point of elevating members of the lower classes into positions of authority over members of the bourgeoisie, as in the Hitler Youth, or of subjecting the scions of the elites to the authority of their supposedly former social inferiors, as when university students were sent to labour camps, or schoolteachers were disciplined by 'old fighters' from humble backgrounds in their compulsory training sessions. The Nazi students' attack on the traditional student duelling corps was only one instance of a widespread assault on Germany's most publicly prominent bastions of social privilege, and – to the disgust of traditionalists like Reck-Malleczewen – it was accompanied by a good deal of egalitarian rhetoric and verbal assaults on the reactionary nature of the class discrimination that the duelling corps so openly practised.[179]

Crucially, the rhetoric was accompanied by actual deeds. The decline in status, autonomy and power of the academically trained professions in the first six years of the Third Reich was real. Traditional institutions like the universities had been downgraded as part of the life-experience of young Germans, and far fewer went to them in 1939 than had done six years before. Small businessmen and white-collar workers saw the social divisions between them and the working class eroded by more than just Nazi speechifying. Aristocrats found themselves elbowed aside in the corridors of power by brash young Nazis from social classes far below theirs. Old-established figures of authority, from doctors to pastors, large landowners to village elders, found themselves under attack. Everywhere, the young, or at least a significant minority among them, seized their chance and asserted themselves against their elders: in the aristocracy, in the village, in the schoolroom, in the university. A new political elite had undeniably taken over. From the top rank of Nazis such as Goebbels and Göring, Schirach and Ley, down through the Regional Leaders to the bottom level of the Block Wardens and Hitler Youth commanders, new men, mostly young, often from unorthodox social backgrounds, sometimes, like Rosenberg for example, even from outside Germany itself, took over the reins of power. Moreover, a whole range of traditional social values had been downgraded: the professor's prioritization of learning for its own sake, the doctor's Hippocratic ethic of putting the patient's interests before everything else, even the businessman's enshrinement of profit as the ultimate measure of success – all these were swept aside by the Third Reich's prioritization of war, race and the national community.

Yet the equality of status so loudly and so insistently proclaimed by the Nazis did not imply equality of social position, income or wealth. The Nazis did not radically revise the taxation system so as to even up people's net incomes, for example, or control the economy in the way that was done in the Soviet Union, or later on in the German Democratic Republic, so as to minimize the differences between rich and poor. Rich and poor remained in the Third Reich, as much as they ever had. In the end, the aristocracy's power over the land remained undisturbed, and younger nobles even found a new leadership role in the SS, Germany's future political elite. Peasant families that had run their village communities for decades or even centuries managed for the most part to retain their position by reaching a limited accommodation with the new regime. Businessmen, big and small, continued to run their businesses for the usual capitalist profit motive. Professors shunted the most obviously unscientific and unscholarly excrescences of Nazi ideology into little institutes on their own, where they could be isolated from the mainstream of teaching and research, and continued much as before. Judges and lawyers still judged and pleaded, still fought cases, still sent people to prison. Doctors had more power over their patients, employers over their workers. The Churches undeniably lost ground in areas such as education, but all reports agree that the priest and the pastor by and large retained the loyalty of their flock despite all the efforts of the regime to undermine it. The rhetoric of the national community convinced many, perhaps even most Germans on the political level: party rivalries had gone, everyone seemed to be pulling together under Hitler's leadership. 'No more class struggle', as Luise Solmitz noted in her diary on 27 April 1933, 'or Marxism, religious antagonisms, – only Germany, – in Hitler.'[180] But far fewer were convinced that the social utopia promised by the Nazis in 1933 ever really arrived.

A society cannot be totally transformed in a mere six years without huge, murderous violence of the kind that occurred in Russia, from the 'red terror' of the civil war years (1918–21) to the massive purges carried out by Stalin in the 1930s. The leadership of the Third Reich did, as we have seen, carry out a limited killing action against dissidents, or supposed dissidents, within its own ranks at the end of June 1934, and it also killed some thousands of its own real or supposed opponents within Germany, but its major violence was reserved for people outside the country and was carried out in wartime. There was no parallel to the

Soviet regime's killing of some three million of its own citizens, mostly in time of peace, nor to its imprisonment of many more millions in labour camps, nor to the violent upheavals that brought about the state ownership of industry and the collectivization of agriculture in Stalin's Russia. Similarly, while the Third Reich restricted wages and consumption, this was not as part of a deliberate attempt to narrow the gap between rich and poor, as with the far more drastic restrictions imposed in Soviet society, but simply as a means of saving money to pay for rearmament. Nazism did not try to turn the clock back, for all its talk of reinstating the hierarchies and values of a mythical Germanic past. As we have seen, the groups who hoped for a restoration of old social barriers and hierarchies were as disappointed as were those who looked to the Third Reich to carry out a radical redistribution of land and wealth.[181]

The problem was that any programme of social change that the Nazis might have desired was in the end ruthlessly subordinated to the over-riding determinant of preparation for war. Whatever helped get Germany ready for the conquest of Eastern Europe was good; whatever got in the way was bad. The realization of any social or racial utopia was postponed until Germany had acquired its much-vaunted living-space in the East, just as economic prosperity for the masses was ultimately made dependent on the same thing. Yet any assessment of what might have been then becomes increasingly speculative, the more so since there is every indication that Hitler would not have stopped with the conquest of the East but would have transformed the war from one waged for European supremacy to one fought for world domination. Still, something of the nature of the utopian character of the future Third Reich imagined by its leaders and ideologues could already be discerned by 1939. Nazism's romance with technology, though driven by rearmament, went beyond the merely military. Here was a regime that wanted the latest machinery, the latest gadgets, the latest means of communication. All these things implied big factories, large businesses, modern cities, elaborate organizations. The principles on which the Nazi future would be based were scientific: the appliance of racial hygiene and Darwinist selectionism to human society without regard for any traditional morality or religious scruples, directed by an elaborate, hierarchical state apparatus that would brook no dissent. At times, Nazi rhetoric might seem to envision a Europe of peasant farmers, of Germans united by ties of 'blood and soil', enslaving and exploiting members of inferior races in a pseudo-feudal world shorn of the complexities and ambiguities of industrial society; de-industrialization and de-urbanization would be the essentials of the final incarnation of the Third Reich on a European scale.[182] But the fiercest proponents of this view, such as Darré, were outflanked by those who believed that the new European racial order had to combine the most advanced industry, technology and communications with the reordering of agriculture and the countryside in a new balance between the two.[183]

In the real world of twentieth-century Germany, Nazism's moderniz-ing effects impacted on a context where rapid social and economic change had already been going on since the industrial revolution of the mid-nineteenth century. Here too there were ultimately fatal contradic-tions. Preparation for war, for example, undoubtedly speeded up already existing processes of concentration and rationalization in industry, and accelerated technological developments of many kinds. Military and medical technology and research, as we have seen, forged ahead in government-funded institutes and company research and development departments. On the other hand, the educational policies of the Third Reich moved rapidly towards reducing the professional, scientific and intellectual competence of Germany's future professional elites, which were already beginning to decline in strength and numbers by 1939. If a future elite was beginning to emerge from the SS and from the new elite schools and Order Castles, then it was a dumbed-down elite that would find difficulty in managing a complex, modern industrial and technologi-cal social and economic system of a kind that would be capable of waging and sustaining a complex, modern, industrial and technological war. Traditional social institutions such as the trade unions were cleared away to make room for a total identification of the individual with state and race; yet the result was the exact opposite, a retreat of ordinary people into their private worlds of the home and family, a prioritization of consumer needs that the Third Reich was neither willing nor able wholly to satisfy. The destruction of the traditional institutions of the labour movement can plausibly be seen as a blow for modernity, paving the way for a very different, less antagonistic structure of labour relations after 1945. In the longer run, however, the decline of the traditional industrial working class and the rise of the service sector in a post-industrial society would have achieved this result by other means.

The problem with arguing about whether or not the Third Reich modernized German society, how far it wanted to change the social order and in what ways it succeeded in doing so, is that society was not really a priority of Nazi policy anyway. True, social divisions were to be, if not abolished altogether, then at least bridged over, social discord was to be replaced by social harmony, and status, though not class, was to be equalized as far as possible in new Reich. But much of this was to be achieved by symbols, rituals and rhetoric. Above all, what Hitler and the Nazis wanted was a change in people's spirit, their way of thinking, and their way of behaving. They wanted a new man, and for that matter a new woman, to emerge out of the ashes of the Weimar Republic, re-creating the fighting unity and commitment of the front in the First World War. Their revolution was first and foremost cultural rather than social. Yet it was underpinned by something more concrete, that had real physical consequences for thousands, and in the end millions of Germans, Jews and others: the idea of racial engineering, of scientifically moulding the German people into a new breed of heroes, and its corollary, of eliminating the weak from the chain of heredity and taking those who were seen as the Germans' enemies, real and potential, out of the reforged national community altogether. This meant a concerted attempt to improve the physical quality of the German race on the one hand: and a comprehensive drive to remove elements the Nazis considered undesirable, including above all the Jews, from German society on the other, as we shall now see.

6

TOWARDS THE RACIAL UTOPIA

IN THE SPIRIT OF SCIENCE

I

Racial hygienists greeted the coming of the Third Reich with unalloyed anticipation. Since the 1890s they had been campaigning for social policies that put the improvement of the race at the centre of their concerns and targeted those whom they identified as weak, idle, criminal, degenerate and insane for elimination from the chain of heredity. At last, as Fritz Lenz, a long-time advocate of such measures, remarked, Germany had a government that was prepared to take such issues seriously and do something about them.[1] His enthusiasm was not misplaced. From 1924 at the latest, when Hitler had read some racial-hygiene tracts during his period of enforced leisure in Landsberg prison, the future Leader considered that Germany and the Germans could only become strong again if the state applied to German society the basic principles of racial hygiene and racial engineering. The nation had become weak, corrupted by the infusion of degenerate elements into its bloodstream. These had to be removed as quickly as possible. The strong and the racially pure had to be encouraged to have more children, the weak and the racially impure had to be neutralized by one means or another.[2]

Seeing that Hitler offered them a unique opportunity to put their ideas into practice, leading racial hygienists began to bring their doctrines into line with those of the Nazis in areas where they had so far failed to conform. A sizeable minority, to be sure, were too closely associated with political ideas and organizations on the left to survive as members of the Racial Hygiene Society, which was taken over by the Nazis and purged in 1933. Jewish doctors, of whom more than a few were enthusiastic racial hygienists, were similarly ousted. Even Lenz found that some of his ideas, such as, for example, the theory that illegitimate children were racially degenerate, ran into heavy criticism from Nazi ideologues like Heinrich Himmler. Very quickly, leading racial hygienists in the medical profession were outflanked by a younger generation, who led the key political institutions in the field, from the Racial-Political Office of the Nazi party, headed by Walter Gross (born 1904), the National Socialist Welfare organization, the Nazi Doctors' League, and, increasingly, the SS, all of which had their own ideas about breeding and selection that rode roughshod over the scientific and medical niceties debated in the learned journals of the racial hygiene movement. Nevertheless, the leading figures in the movement were not disappointed by the new regime. Writing personally to Hitler in April 1933, Alfred Ploetz, the moving spirit of the eugenics movement for the past forty years, explained that since he was now in his seventies, he was too old to take a leading part in the practical implementation of the principles of racial hygiene in the new Reich, but he gave his backing to the Reich Chancellor's policies all the same.[3]

Practical policies were not long in coming. At the beginning of the Third Reich, Interior Minister Wilhelm Frick announced that the new regime was going to concentrate public spending on racially sound and healthy people. It was not only going to reduce expenditure on 'inferior and asocial individuals, the sick, the mentally deficient, the insane, cripples and criminals', it was also going to subject them to a ruthless policy of 'eradication and selection'. On 14 July 1933, this policy took legislative form in the Law for the Prevention of Hereditarily Diseased Offspring.[4] This prescribed compulsory sterilization for anyone who suffered from congenital feeble-mindedness, schizophrenia, manic-depressive psychosis, hereditary epilepsy, Huntingdon's chorea, hereditary deafness, blindness or severe physical deformity, or severe alcoholism. These conditions were subject to further definition by the large bureaucracy set up by the Reich Interior Ministry to administer the Law, while decisions on individual cases were taken by 181 specially established Hereditary Health Courts and appeal courts consisting of a lawyer and two doctors, acting on referrals from public health officers and the directors of institutions such as state nursing homes, clinics, old-age homes, special schools and the like, as well as social workers in the welfare system. This Law had long been an ambition of Germany's

influential racial hygiene movement, led by senior physicians such as
Alfred Ploetz and Fritz Lenz, and had become a more insistent demand
during the Depression. The enormous burden of welfare on the national
finances had greatly increased the number and boldness of those in the
welfare and medical professions who believed that many aspects of social
deviance, poverty and destitution were the results of the hereditary
degeneracy of those who suffered from them. Already in 1932 on the
advice of the German Medical Association, a law had been proposed to
allow voluntary sterilization. Now, suddenly, it was reality.[5]

There was nothing voluntary about the Law of 1933. Doctors were
required to register every case of hereditary illness known to them, except
in women over forty-five, and could be fined for failing to do so; at the
same time the arbitrary and vague criteria used to define these cases left
them with a good deal of latitude. Some patients agreed to be sterilized,
but most did not. In 1934, the first year of the Law's operation, nearly
4,000 people appealed against the decisions of the sterilization authorities; 3,559 of the appeals failed. As these figures indicate, the scale on
which sterilization was carried out was very considerable. In 1934 alone
the courts received over 84,500 applications for sterilization, roughly
half for men and half for women. Of these, nearly 64,500 received
rulings the same year; over 56,000 were in favour of sterilization. Thus
an application from a doctor, social worker or other legitimate source
was over 90 per cent likely to be approved and extremely unlikely to be
overturned on appeal. In each of the first four years of the Law's operation, over 50,000 people were sterilized in this way; by the time the
Third Reich was over, the total number sterilized had reached over
360,000, almost all of them treated before the outbreak of war in
September 1939.[6]

Three-quarters of the orders were made in respect of 'congenital feeble-
mindedness', an extremely vague and elastic concept that placed great
power in the hands of doctors and the courts: it became common, for
example, to define many kinds of social deviance, such as prostitution, as
forms of 'moral feeble-mindedness'. The inclusion of alcoholism affected
mainly members of the underclass. The techniques employed – vasectomy
for men and tubal ligation for women – were often painful, and sometimes led to complications: the overall death-rate, overwhelmingly
among women rather than men, ran at 0.5 per cent, or a total of about

2,000 people. Before long, the scale of the programme had transformed the medical profession, as all doctors had to undergo training in recognizing hereditary degeneracy (for example, through the shape of the patient's earlobes, the patient's gait, or the configuration of the half-moon at the base of the patient's fingernails). University medical faculties spent much of their time writing expert reports for the courts and devised 'practical intelligence tests' to sort out the sheep from the goats ('What form of state do we have now? Who were Bismarck and Luther? Why are houses higher in the city than in the countryside?'). These ran into trouble when tests in rural areas revealed an equal degree of ignorance amongst allegedly normal schoolchildren as amongst supposedly feeble-minded ones. The possibility that rank-and-file members of the brown-shirts from country districts might fail the tests was enough in itself to discredit the whole process of testing in the eyes of some senior Party doctors.[7]

Roughly two-thirds of those sterilized were the inmates of mental hospitals, many of whose directors zealously combed through their patient files for candidates for the courts. The proportion of alleged schizophrenics was higher here; in the asylum at Kaufbeuren-Irsee, indeed, some 82 per cent of the 1,409 patients were ruled to fall within the provisions of the Law, though elsewhere a proportion of about a third was more usual. Sterilization was attractive to asylum directors because it meant that the patients could in many cases be discharged into the community afterwards. This affected particularly the younger, less severely disturbed patients, so that the better their chances of recovery were thought to be, the more likely they were to be sterilized. At the Eglfing-Haar asylum, two-thirds of the patients sterilized in 1934 were released within a few months; at the Eichberg asylum, nearly 80 per cent of those sterilized in 1938 were also rapidly discharged. This reduced running costs at a time when asylums, like the rest of the welfare system, were under heavy pressure to cut expenditure. Indeed some young women were clearly sterilized mainly in order to prevent them bearing illegitimate children who would be a burden on the community.[8]

The reasons given for sterilization were frequently concerned more with social deviance than with any demonstrably hereditary condition. As one doctor wrote in putting forward a candidate for the operation on the basis of 'moral feeble-mindedness':

In his social worker's files he is described as a beggar or vagrant who has come down in the world. He is in receipt of a fifty per cent war injury pension because of TB of the lungs and intestine. He spends his money very irresponsibly. Smokes a lot and sometimes gets drunk. He has repeatedly been an inmate at Farmsen. He usually leaves the institution to go tramping. He has previous convictions for resisting arrest, breach of the peace, public slander and grievous bodily harm. In his welfare files it is reported that he has often disturbed the operation of the service and physically attacked officials, so that he was banned from entering the welfare office. According to Dr [. . .], C. is 'a mentally seriously inferior individual who is totally without value for the community'.[9]

In cases such as this, sterilization appeared principally as a punishment or a measure of social control. The prospect of the man in question having children seemed to be remote indeed. Sterilizing the inmates of asylums and similar institutions was in many cases an excuse for discharging the public purse from the responsibility of maintaining them.

These were not, therefore, seriously ill people, still less those whose ailments condemned them to a life of perpetual institutionalization. Those who were too ill, too helpless or too dangerous to be let out into society were unlikely to have children and so did not require sterilization. In essence, therefore, the regime was using sterilization to crush those areas of society that did not conform to the Nazi ideal of the new man or the new woman: overwhelmingly, members of the underclass, beggars, prostitutes, vagrants, people who did not want to work, graduates of orphanages and reform schools, the slum and the street: people who could not be expected to join the Hitler Youth, give money to the Winter Aid, enlist in the armed forces, hang out flags on the Leader's birthday or turn up at work every day on time. The new Law gave the regime the power to reach into the most intimate sphere of human existence, sexuality and reproduction, a power that it would subsequently extend to its dealings with the Jews and indeed, potentially at least, every adult German. To back up these measures, a regulation issued on 26 July 1933 blocked access to marriage loans for people who suffered from hereditary mental or physical ailments; another regulation issued a couple of months later extended this ban to child benefits. It was only a small step from here to ban racially undesirable marriages altogether.[10]

Against the background of reasoning such as this, it was not surprising that 'habitual criminals' were also one of the groups whose enforced sterilization had long been thought desirable by psychiatrists and criminologists. Local health officers, most notoriously Gerhard Boeters, in Zwickau, were vigorous in campaigning for such a measure under the Weimar Republic. The prison doctor in Straubing, Theodor Viernstein, considered that 'enemies of the race, enemies of society' had to be removed from the chain of heredity as fast as possible.[11] Even Social Democrats such as Wilhelm Hoegner urged at least the voluntary sterilization of persistent offenders, though the Communists and the Centre Party, for very different reasons, were strongly opposed.[12] Hitler and leading Nazis such as the legal expert Hans Frank were strongly in favour of including 'habitual criminals' in the list of those to be sterilized. But Reich Justice Minister Franz Gürtner successfully blocked such a move, both in the Sterilization Law and in the Habitual Criminals Law. He continued to do so despite pressure from eugenicists such as Ernst Rüdin, partly because officials were not convinced that it would be possible to separate hereditarily determined criminality cleanly from environmentally conditioned deviance, but mainly because they considered it unnecessary anyway because 'habitual criminals' were now incarcerated for life under the new rules for 'security confinement' and therefore could not reproduce. Nevertheless, state prisoners could be sterilized if they fell under any of the other grounds specified in the law, and prison doctors were energetic in identifying them amongst the inmates. The criteria for sterilization were extremely elastic and included the 'congenitally feeble-minded' and 'alcoholics', amongst whom a large proportion of prison inmates could be counted by a determined prison doctor. Hans Trunk, Viernstein's successor at Straubing, for instance, proposed to have up to a third of the prison's inmates sterilized, a figure considered too high even by the local Hereditary Health Court. It was hardly surprising that prisoners were over-represented amongst the compulsorily sterilized, with nearly 5,400 subjected to this procedure by December 1939. It was equally unsurprising that the threat of a vasectomy or hysterectomy spread fear amongst prison inmates, who often told each other the correct answers to the intelligence tests administered by the doctors and learned them off by heart.[13]

On the other hand, the physically handicapped were considerably less severely affected. True, one of the conditions laid down by the 1933 Law was 'serious hereditary physical deformity', which it declared included anyone who suffered from 'deviations from the norm that more or less strongly prevent normal functioning', so long as these could be demonstrated to be inherited. Whether or not they were also mentally handicapped was completely irrelevant from this point of view. State support for such people was to be effectively abolished since they were of no use to the community. Already in the Depression, Germany's residential care facilities for the physically handicapped, which provided 11,000 beds in 1927, had been forced by financial constraints to accept only children, and even there only those whom they considered capable of recovery through treatment. Well before 1933, therefore, the distinction between the 'valuable' and the 'inferior', or people suffering from curable physical handicaps on the one hand, and severe or multiple disabilities on the other, had become commonplace in care institutions. In the light of the massive propaganda attacks launched by the Nazis against the physically handicapped in connection with the sterilization law in 1933, many families withdrew their handicapped children or relatives from these institutions, fearing the worst for them.[14]

But by the mid-1930s, the atmosphere was beginning to change. Doctors pointed out that at least three-quarters of physical handicaps developed after birth, and that the vast majority were in any case extremely unlikely to be passed on to the next generation. Conditions such as a dislocation of the hips were regarded as perfectly treatable. So too was club-foot, which must have come as a relief to the Reich Propaganda Minister Joseph Goebbels, Germany's best-known sufferer from the condition. It was of course already too late to propose him for sterilization, and the futility of the idea that his disability was hereditary was amply demonstrated by the sound and healthy physical constitution of his own numerous offspring. Possibly the obvious embarrassment of dismissing the club-footed as a danger to the future of the race was a factor in bringing about a change of policy towards physical disabilities in the Third Reich. But the major factor was economic. Orthopaedic surgeons and physicians, fearful for their jobs should a policy of sterilization and effective abandonment of treatment be adopted, pointed out that so long as the physically handicapped were of sound mind, they could be employed in a whole variety of appropriate jobs, especially if their treatment had met with some success. They noted that successful therapy required early treatment, yet the attitude of the Nazis was causing mothers to conceal their children's disabilities from the medical profession for fear of what would happen to them.

Local officials met on 12 October 1937 and agreed that the growing shortage of labour made it advisable to integrate the physically handicapped into the economy. Otto Perl, the founder in 1919 of the League for the Advancement of Self-Help for the Physically Handicapped, successfully lobbied for the pejorative official designation of 'cripple' (*Krüppel*) to be replaced in official documents by the more neutral 'physically handicapped' (*Körperbehinderte*), as indeed it increasingly was from 1934 onwards. Many of those he represented were of course war-wounded; but his campaigns had implications for younger handicapped people too. The result was that the proportion of the forcibly sterilized who suffered from exclusively physical disabilities remained throughout the Nazi period below 1 per cent. In 1934 Perl's organization was officially recognized, incorporated into the National Socialist People's Welfare under the name of the Reich League of the Physically Handicapped (*Reichsbund der Körperbehinderten*) and charged with the task of integrating its members into the productive economy. Those with disabilities such as haemophilia, severe progressive rheumatoid arthritis, serious spasmodic muscular contractions or chronic deformities of the hands or the spine were consigned to institutions with the instruction that they had to be given a miminal level of care. But even here, the idea of compulsory sterilization was dropped; in a land where many thousands of severely physically handicapped war veterans could be seen on the streets every day, it would have been difficult to justify such a policy to the general public.[15] Still, this change of heart had its limits. The physically handicapped might be useful to the regime, but they were in no way to be full or equal members of the racial community. The emphasis placed on physical health and vitality by the Nazis already discriminated against them at school, where from 17 March 1935 onwards they were banned from progressing to secondary education, along with students who had showed 'persistent failure in physical training' and 'young people who exhibit a persistent unwillingness to look after their bodies'. The way to preferment at school, university, the Hitler Youth and virtually all the other institutions of the Third Reich was not least through the demonstration of fitness to fight. Those who were not in a position to show it remained second-class citizens.[16]

Some doctors outside Germany also held the view that many social ills were the result of the hereditary degeneracy of certain sections of the population. Even before the Nazis came to power in Germany, twenty-eight states in the USA had passed sterilization laws resulting in the compulsory sterilization of some 15,000 people; the total had more than doubled by 1939. German racial hygienists such as Gerhard Boeters pointed to the American example in justifying their own stance; others also incidentally pointed to anti-miscegenation laws in the southern states of the USA as another example that could usefully be followed in Germany. The American eugenicist Harry Laughlin, who in 1931 put forward a programme to sterilize some 15 million Americans of inferior racial stock over the next half-century, received an honorary doctorate from Heidelberg in 1936. US eugenicists admired the German Laws in turn; and Laughlin himself proudly claimed that his own ideas had in part inspired it.[17] Sterilization laws of one kind and another were passed by Switzerland in 1928, by Denmark in 1929, by Norway in 1934 and by a variety of other European countries, both democratic and authoritarian in their political structures. Six thousand Danes were sterilized, and no fewer than 40,000 Norwegians. Even more remarkably, nearly 63,000 sterilizations were performed in Sweden between 1935 and 1975. It has been argued that the Swedish sterilizations were carried out to remove non-productive people from the chain of heredity and targeted the socially rather than the racially deviant; and certainly, the welfare state constructed by Swedish Social Democracy in these decades was not racially based in the way that the Nazi state was. Still, the Swedish National Institute for Racial Biology did establish physical characteristics among the criteria for forced sterilization, and Gypsies were targeted as a supposedly racially inferior group. Moreover, in the first six years of the Third Reich, sterilization, although carried out on a scale far greater than anywhere else, was not primarily racial in character, in the sense of being based on the identification of inferior races: the people who were being sterilized were overwhelmingly 'Aryan' Germans, and they were being sterilized for reasons not very different from those given by the Swedish authorities and eugenicists elsewhere at around the same time.[18] The real difference was to emerge only later, when the war began, as the Nazi regime turned from sterilizing social deviants to murdering them.

II

Applying the principles of racial hygiene to society meant sweeping away traditional Christian morality and replacing it with a system of ethics that derived good and bad solely from the imagined collective interests of the German race. This did not stop some Protestant welfare officials from agreeing with this policy, but when the Catholic Church objected to measures such as forcible sterilization, Nazi ideologues like the doctors' leader Gerhard Wagner portrayed this as another episode in the long struggle between religious obscurantism and scientific enlightenment, a struggle which science was bound to win.[19] In few areas, indeed, were the differences between conservative traditionalism and Nazi modernism more apparent than in the regime's attitude to women, marriage and the family, all of which appeared to Nazi ideologues in the light not of conventional Christian morality but of the scientific principles of racial policy. Any overlap there might have appeared to be between conservative and National Socialist views of women's place in society was purely superficial. Alarmed by the long-term decline in Germany's birth-rate that had set in around the turn of the century, conservative nationalists and Nazis alike preached women's return to the home; but while conservatives saw the key to the decline's reversal in the revival of traditional marriage patterns, the Nazis were willing to take up even the most radical ideas in the pursuit of more children for the Reich, adding on to this the insistence that such children had to be racially pure and hereditarily untainted, principles that traditional conservatives abhorred. Abortion, deeply repugnant to Catholic morality, provided a case in point. The Third Reich tightened up and enforced more rigorously the existing laws banning abortion except on medical grounds, thereby reducing the number of officially sanctioned abortions from nearly 35,000 a year in the early 1930s to fewer than 2,000 a year by the end of the decade. But it also allowed abortion on eugenic grounds from 1935 onwards and in November 1938 a Lüneburg court created a significant precedent when it legalized abortion for Jewish women.[20] At the same time, contraceptives, another bugbear of the Catholic Church, continued to be available throughout the 1930s, although birth-control clinics were closed down because of the association of the birth-control movement with left-wing, libertarian politics.[21]

Given their Darwinian view of world politics, the Nazis considered a high birth-rate essential for a nation's health. A declining birth-rate meant an ageing population, and fewer recruits for the armed forces in the longer term. A rising birth-rate meant a young, vigorous population and the promise of ever-expanding military manpower in the future. Racial hygienists had pointed with alarm to the decline in Germany's birth-rate, from thirty-six live births per 1,000 population in 1900 to a mere fifteen per 1,000 population in 1932. As early as 1914, Fritz Lenz had opined that women's emancipation was to blame and advocated putting a ban on women going into higher education. He was critical of other racial hygienists who argued modestly that a healthy woman should give birth to eight or nine children during her life. A woman, he thought, could continue to give birth over a period of thirty years; with one birth possible at least every other year, this meant, he declared, a minimum of fifteen. Anything else was due to 'unnatural or pathological causes'.[22] The Nazis could not have agreed more. As soon as they came to power, they moved into action to eliminate what they thought of as the causes of the declining birth-rate and to provide incentives to women to have more children. Their first target was Germany's large and active feminist movement, which was swiftly closed down and its constituent associations dissolved or incorporated into the Party's national women's organization, National Socialist Womanhood (NS-Frauenschaft). The leading radical feminists, including Anita Augspurg and Lida Gustava Heymann, pioneers of the campaign for women's suffrage, and Helene Stöcker, advocate of sexual liberation for women, went into exile; apart from anything else, their pacifist convictions put them at the risk of arrest and imprisonment in the new regime. The more conservative feminists, like Gertrud Bäumer, who had dominated the movement in the 1920s, retreated into self-imposed 'inner exile', leaving the field open to women of openly Nazi convictions.[23]

The National Socialist Womanhood was led, after a fierce internal power-struggle that lasted until the beginning of 1934, by Gertrud Scholtz-Klink, a proud mother (eventually) of eleven children; her devotion to the idea of the family was unquestionable. The Womanhood was intended to provide the active leadership for a comprehensive mass organization of German women, called the German Women's Bureau (*Deutsches Frauenwerk*), which would convert the entire female sex in Germany to the Nazi way of thinking.[24] Once appointed to head these two organizations, as Reich Women's Leader, in February 1934, Scholtz-Klink sprang into action, setting up a range of schemes to persuade women to have more children and to take better care of those they already had. One of the most ambitious was the Reich Mothers' Service. This drew on the experience of old-established women's welfare groups. It ran courses on childcare, cooking, sewing and of course racial hygiene; they had reached more than 1.7 million women by March 1939 and were funded by the sale of badges on Mother's Day, supplemented by a small fee for taking part. Mother's Day itself became a major propaganda event, and was made into a national holiday in 1934. Goebbels ordered all brownshirts, Hitler Youth and other Nazi Party organizations to give their members the day off so that they could be with their families; theatres were to stage relevant plays on the day and give out free tickets to mothers and families; priests and pastors were to preach sermons on motherhood. On Mother's Day in May 1939, three million women who had given birth to four or more children each were invested with the title of 'Mother of the Reich' in special ceremonies held all over Germany. Their new status was signalled by the award of specially minted Mother's Honour Crosses – bronze for four children, silver for six and gold for eight or more, an achievement considered sufficiently noteworthy for the crosses to be pinned on by Hitler himself. Wearers were allowed to jump queues in food stores, and Hitler Youth members were instructed to salute them in the street. Mothers whose performance exceeded even this, and who gave birth to ten children, were given the additional honour of having Hitler as godfather of the tenth child, which in the case of boys meant naming the infant 'Adolf', something which Catholic families who resented Hitler's persecution of their Church must have found somewhat distressing.[25]

The involvement of Goebbels in this propaganda exercise pointed to the fact that Scholtz-Klink's women's organizations by no means had a monopoly over policy and its implementation in this area. As a mere woman, Scholtz-Klink enjoyed a low status in the Nazi hierarchy and was therefore no match even for relatively unsuccessful male Nazi leaders in the turf wars that were such a constant feature of the regime's internal politics. Soon the Labour Front, the Reich Food Estate and the National Socialist Welfare organization had all taken over major areas of women's welfare, while the Labour Front and its ancillary organizations also ran a wide range of women's leisure activities. At the same time, the limited resources available to Scholtz-Klink meant that her women's organizations failed to achieve the ambitious aims she had set them: they did not reach far beyond the middle-class women who had provided the main constituency for the old women's movement of the Weimar years, and housewives were resistant to being mobilized in the service of the nation in the ways that Scholtz-Klink intended. Husbands and children were spending increasing amounts of their time outside the home in Party-related activities, in camps, or at evening training sessions. German women, as one contributor to a remarkably critical collection of addresses from women to Hitler published in 1934 complained, were falling into a 'shadow of loneliness' as a result.[26]

Moreover, government pronatalism meant in itself interference by the regime in the family, sexuality and childbirth, as pressures of all kinds were exerted on women to get married and have lots of children. The Nazi regime propagated the interests of large families by taking over the already-extant Reich League of Child-Rich Families, an organization that also became an instrument of racial engineering, since many socially disadvantaged large families were excluded from it, and the privileges it conferred, on the grounds that they were asocial or degenerate. For those that made the grade, with four or more children under the age of sixteen, there were many advantages, including priority in training, work for the father and better housing for the family as a whole, and single child supplements introduced in October 1935 and averaging 390 Reichsmarks per family. By July 1937 400,000 such families had received them. 240,000 families also received ongoing family support, and one-off grants to the maximum of 1,000 Reichsmarks per child were made for the parents to buy household goods, bed-linen and so on. From April 1936 the government added a supplementary grant of 10 Reichsmarks a month for the fifth and each subsequent child in every family. In 1938 these benefits were extended from children aged sixteen and under to those under the age of twenty-one. Tax reforms introduced improved allowances for large families on a national basis, while local governments took their own steps by reducing gas, water and electricity charges, providing free Hitler Youth uniforms, subsidizing the costs of schooling, supplementing the wages of municipal employees with four or more children, or (as in Leipzig) publishing monthly 'honour tables' of large families. The costs of all these measures were borne by single people and childless couples and constituted a clear incentive to have more children, especially for the worse off: a poor family with three young offspring could improve its position dramatically by having a fourth. Yet there were limits, especially in housing, where the priority that was supposed to be given to large families counted for little in the face of a continued housing shortage. Landlords still preferred to let to single people or childless couples because they used less gas, water and electricity in a situation where there was a freeze on rents. State investment in new housing actually fell from one and a third billion marks in 1928 to a quarter of a billion in 1938.[27]

Such problems were reflected in the fact that the decline in the percentage of marriages with four or more children continued unabated. Nearly half of all couples married in 1900–1904 had four or more children, but for those married in 1926–30 the proportion was only 20 per cent; in 1931–5 it fell further to 18 per cent, and in 1936–40 again to 13 per cent.[28] The regime's efforts counted for little in the face of a secular decline in family size that had begun decades before and was to continue long afterwards. The economic, social and cultural costs of having more than one or two children were simply too great for the Third Reich to counteract.[29] Superficially, at least, it seemed to enjoy more success in reversing the associated long-term decline in the birth-rate that so concerned racial hygienists. From a low of 14.7 live births per thousand inhabitants in 1933 the birth-rate increased to 18.0 in 1934 and 18.9 in 1935. It then levelled off at 19.0 in 1936 and 18.8 in 1937 before rising slightly again to 19.6 in 1938 and 20.4 in 1939.[30] By the beginning of the 1940s a commentator could claim that an extra three million Germans had been born as a direct result of policies introduced by the Third Reich.[31] Yet the leap in the number of marriages, by nearly a quarter between 1932 and 1938, was mainly due to the economic recovery. People had been postponing getting married and having children because of the Depression: with well over a third of the working population

unemployed, this was understandable enough. Even without the marriage loan scheme, therefore, a majority of the marriages and births that
happened from 1934 onwards would have happened anyway. Other
additional births reflected the greater difficulty women had in obtaining
abortions after 1933; only relatively few could be ascribed directly to
policies introduced by the Third Reich.[32]

III

Those policies impinged ever more closely on marriage and the family
as time went on. In 1938, a new Marriage Law made it possible for a
fertile husband or wife to file for divorce on grounds of 'premature
infertility' or the refusal of the other partner to procreate. Three years'
separation and the irretrievable breakdown of a marriage were also
introduced as grounds for divorce. In this way, completely disregarding
the traditional Christian view of marriage as a divinely sanctified partner-
ship for life, the Third Reich hoped to make it easier for people to marry
for the purposes of having children. By 1941 nearly 28,000 people had
filed for divorce on the basis of breakdown and separation, while 3,838
divorces had been granted because of premature infertility and 1,771
because of refusal to procreate. These were not very impressive figures,
and made only a small impact on the birth-rate, if they made any at all.
Still, in a society where divorce was still something rather unusual and
generally frowned-on, they made up a good fifth of all divorces. The
Vatican duly registered its disapproval with the German Ambassador. It
was disregarded.[33] Potentially far more intrusive was the Law for the
Protection of the Hereditary Health of the German People, promulgated
on 18 October 1935. This provided for the banning of a marriage where
one of the engaged couple suffered from an inherited disease, or from a
mental illness. As a consequence, anyone who wanted to get married
would have to provide written proof that they qualified according to the
Law. Local Health Offices would have been overwhelmed with requests
for medical examinations had there been any question of implementing
these requirements comprehensively. So in practice it was up to registry
offices to demand an examination if they had any doubts about the
fitness of the prospective marriage partners. Indeed some had already

done so even before the Law had been passed. The demand for written proof was postponed indefinitely, and in the following years the Law was watered down by a series of amendments. None the less, it made it markedly more difficult for people to get married if they were classified as asocial or morally feeble-minded – diagnoses which had already disqualified them for the marriage loan scheme; in practice, those who fell foul of it were also likely to fall foul of the sterilization programme as well.[34]

Finally, illegitimacy, a persistent stigma in socially and morally conservative circles, was wholly irrelevant to the Nazi view of childbirth. If the infant was racially pure and healthy, it did not matter at all whether its parents were legally married. The logical consequences of prioritizing breeding in this morally neutral way were carried to an extreme by Heinrich Himmler, who founded a series of maternity homes from 1936 under an SS-run association called the 'Well of Life' (*Lebensborn*). These were intended for racially approved unmarried mothers, who otherwise might not receive the facilities he thought they deserved: infant mortality rates amongst illegitimate children were notoriously far higher than the national average. But Himmler's bizarre attempt to encourage his elite to breed a future master-race was not very successful: the homes were quickly used by prominent married couples in the SS and later in the Nazi Party more generally, because of their low charges, good facilities and (especially during the war) favourable rural locations. In peacetime, under half the mothers in the homes were unmarried, though this in itself was enough to attract criticism from Catholics and conservatives. Altogether, some 8,000 children were born in the homes, hardly sufficient to inaugurate a new master-race. Nor did he have much more luck with SS officers who actually were married. An investigation carried out in 1939 showed that the 115,690 married SS men had an average of only 1.1 children each.[35]

Beyond all this, the Nazis also went to considerable lengths to propagate and indeed enforce an image of women that expressed their intended function of becoming mothers for the Reich. Rejecting French fashions became a patriotic duty; eschewing make-up and lipstick, widely marketed by big American firms, advertised commitment to the Germanic race; giving up smoking became a badge of femininity, as well as improving the health of the potential mother and unborn child – a result of which Nazi medical experts were already convinced in the 1930s. Parents were encouraged to present their female offspring in pigtails and dirndls, especially if they were blonde. The German Fashion Institute put on shows of new German *haute couture*, fighting the international dominance of Paris fashion. All this was more than mere propaganda. The district leadership of the Party in Breslau, for instance, banned women from attending Party meetings if they 'painted' themselves with make-up. Notices were put up in cafés requesting women customers to refrain from smoking, while the police chief in Erfurt admonished citizens 'to remind women they meet smoking on the streets of their duty as German wives and mothers'. There were reports of stormtroopers snatching cigarettes from the lips of women whom they saw smoking in public, or giving a dressing-down to women with plucked eyebrows and strongly coloured lipstick. Newspapers and journals polemicized on the one hand against the androgynous 'new woman' of the Weimar years, with her cropped hair and mannish clothing, and against the sexually seductive 'vamp' on the other, with her fashionable allure and permanently waved hair. Physical exercise was touted as the best way for women to achieve the healthy, glowing look that the future of the German race required.[36]

Yet here too the Nazis ultimately failed to get their way. It proved impossible to curb the cosmetics industry, which soon found new ways of making profits. Magazines were soon full of advice to German women on how to achieve a natural look by artificial means. Shampoo companies quickly marketed new products enabling women to achieve a much-desired head of blonde hair. German-Jewish clothing firms were Aryanized, and supposedly cosmopolitan Jewish fashion designers were excluded from the trade, but international fashion was too strong to resist. Women's magazines continued to feature the look of Hollywood stars and to explain how they achieved it. Prominent women in Nazi high society scorned the attack on fashion: Magda Goebbels often appeared in public smoking through a cigarette-holder, Winifred Wagner went to opera galas dressed in Parisian silk, and even Hitler's partner Eva Braun smoked when he was not around and made regular use of Elizabeth Arden cosmetics. The German Fashion Institute lacked the energy to make much of an impact, and the regime's attempt to help the autarkic economy and boost national pride by encouraging women to wear homespun clothes ran into increasing difficulty because of the cheapness of mass-produced, off-the-peg dresses made out of artificial fibres – another product of the drive to autarky. Anxious to counter the widespread perception abroad that German women were frumpish and dowdy, women's magazines, under instructions from the Propaganda Ministry, tried to persuade them to be elegant in appearance, especially when foreign visitors were around. The dirndl did indeed make something of a comeback during the later 1930s, but often in forms so heavily modified in the direction of international fashion styles that it was hardly recognizable any more. German women could in the end no more be persuaded to present themselves merely as actual or potential mothers than they could be persuaded to behave as such.[37] This was scarcely surprising, given the extent to which the Nazis undermined traditional distinctions between public and private, the home and the wider world. While government policy penetrated and politicized the domestic sphere, Party organizations took women and children out of the home and socialized them in camps, expeditions, and meetings. The result was a blurring of distinctions that made it impossible for women to conform to the domestic and maternal roles for which Nazi propaganda was attempting to fit them. In few areas, indeed, were the contradictions and irrationalities of the Third Reich more crass than this.[38]

How different was all this from the situation elsewhere in Europe? Almost all major European countries adopted policies to try and boost their birth-rate in the 1930s, since almost all governments were concerned about the potential effects of the declining birth-rate on future military effectiveness. Mussolini's Italy and Stalin's Russia both imposed restrictions on child limitation and offered rewards to fecund mothers, and pronatalist propaganda in France, where the decline in the birth-rate had been particularly severe over a very long time, almost reached fever-pitch in the interwar years. Fascist Italy also saw an attack on women's work and an attempt to reduce women to the status of childbearers and childrearers, and in Soviet Russia the relatively liberal sexual atmosphere of the 1920s gave way under Stalin to a much more prudish and repressive regime. Everywhere, autonomous feminist movements declined, lost support or were crushed by authoritarian governments. Yet at the same time there were differences too. The power of the Catholic Church in Italy meant that Mussolini could not include the kind of amoral racial engineering that was the cornerstone of population policy in Nazi Germany. In Russia, while there may have been racist undertones to Moscow's policies towards other nationalities in the Soviet empire, racism was not a central part of the regime's ideology and there was no equivalent to the Nazi sterilization, marriage or race legislation. Moreover, while Soviet Russia frowned on make-up and high fashion, it was largely because these were 'bourgeois' and detracted from women's role as workers, which – unlike in Nazi Germany – was assiduously propagated through posters featuring female tractor-drivers and steel-workers. Aside from all this, too, in Nazi Germany, marriage and population policy, like almost every other social policy, had a negative as well as a positive impact and further disadvantaged those racial and other minorities who did not conform to the Third Reich's image of the new Aryan human being.[39] And there were many of these.

IV

One particular group which the Third Reich considered a danger on racial grounds were the so-called Gypsies, of whom some 26,000 were living in Germany in the early 1930s.[40] These consisted of extended family groups that assigned themselves to one or other of a variety of larger tribes – the Romanies, the Sinti, the Lalleri – and lived a nomadic lifestyle. They had arrived in Central Europe in the late fifteenth century, some thought via Egypt (hence the English word 'Gypsy'); in fact they originally hailed from India. Dark-skinned, speaking a different language, living largely apart from the rest of German society and relying on itinerant trades of one sort and another, they had attracted social stigma and harsh repressive legislation as territorial states emerged in the period of social and political consolidation following the end of the Thirty Years' War in 1648. Early nineteenth-century Romantics had idealized them as both primitive and exotic, the repository of occult knowledge such as fortune-telling. But with the emergence of criminal biology towards the end of the century, legislators and administrators had begun to assign them once more to the criminal classes. Gypsies were increasingly subjected to petty police harassment because of their refusal to conform to the modern ideal of the citizen – attending school, paying taxes, registering a domicile – and their disregard for conventional notions of private property, work, regularity, sanitation and the like. Contraventions of the increasingly close net of regulations that bound society in these and other areas meant that the majority of Gypsies had criminal records, which simply confirmed law enforcement agencies in their view that they were hereditarily disposed to criminality. In 1926, the Bavarian government passed a particularly severe law against Gypsies, coupling them with travellers and the work-shy, and founded a Central Office to collect information on them systematically. Ten years later it had compiled an index of nearly 20,000 files.[41]

The coming of the Third Reich did not at first mean major changes for German Gypsies, except insofar as they fell into other categories of people targeted by the regime, such as criminal, asocial or work-shy. A number of regional and local authorities stepped up their harassment of itinerants, raiding their camps, moving them on from their resting-places and arresting those thought to be engaged in activities such as begging. On 6 June 1936 these efforts were co-ordinated in a decree issued by the Reich Interior Ministry, and a number of cities began to set up special camps for Gypsies, on the lines of one started in Frankfurt am Main. These were not exactly concentration camps, since the Gypsies were at least nominally entitled to come and go as they wished, and there was no attempt to impose discipline or inflict punishments. However, conditions were often very poor: the camp in the Berlin suburb of Marzahn, which held 600 Gypsies who were forcibly removed from the city in July 1936, had only two latrines, three sources of water, no electricity and too few barracks for those who did not have caravans. Disease was rife, and in March 1939 some 40 per cent of the inmates were said to have scabies. Brutal guards set their dogs on inmates who refused to obey orders. By this time there were well over 800 inmates, and the camp had its own school. Nevertheless, the majority of Gypsies continued to live in society, particularly since there was a high intermarriage rate with Germans, and many of them rented their own rooms or apartments rather than pursuing their traditionally nomadic lifestyle.[42]

As part of the intensified crime prevention measures he undertook in 1938, Himmler moved the Bavarian Central Office for Gypsy Affairs to Berlin and turned it into a Reich authority. His police round-ups of the supposedly work-shy netted a substantial number of Gypsies, but they were still not specifically targeted on racial grounds. It was only on 8 December 1938 that Himmler issued a decree on the Gypsies as such, although it had been in preparation for several months. The decree consolidated existing measures and centralized them under the control of the Criminal Police in Berlin. It ordered all Gypsies and itinerants to be registered and to undergo racial-biological examination. The resulting identity card would state whether the holder was a Gypsy, a mixed-race Gypsy, or a non-Gypsy itinerant; only on presentation of the card could the holder obtain a job, a driving licence, benefits and so on. The registration was carried out on the basis of police records and with the assistance of a special research institute set up in the Reich Health Office in 1936 under the leadership of Dr Robert Ritter, a young physician who quickly became the government's favoured special adviser on the Gypsies. Born in 1901, Ritter was a criminal biologist who organized a team of researchers to visit Gypsy camps, measure and register the inhabitants, and take blood tests: those who refused to co-operate were threatened with consignment to a concentration camp. Ritter and his team combed parish records, assimilated the files of the Munich Central Office for Gypsy Affairs and compiled an index of over 20,000 people. Soon, Ritter boasted, he would have complete records on every Gypsy or part-Gypsy in Germany.[43]

Ritter argued that Gypsies were a primitive, inferior race who were constitutionally unable to pursue a normal lifestyle. Pure Gypsies posed no threat to society, therefore, and should be allowed to make their living in their traditionally nomadic way. There were, however, he warned, very few of them left. The vast majority of so-called Gypsies had intermarried with Germans living in the slums where they had found a home, and so had created a dangerous substratum of criminals and layabouts. Thus he arbitrarily reversed the Nazi dogma of antisemitism, according to which pure Jews were more of a threat to Germany than part-Jews. Such theories provided a pseudo-scientific justification for the police measures now undertaken by Himmler. They enjoyed widespread support amongst social workers, criminologists, police authorities, municipalities and ordinary German citizens. The decree of 8 December 1938 banned Gypsies from travelling in 'hordes' (groups of several families), ordered the expulsion of foreign Gypsies and gave the police power to arrest itinerants classified as asocial. It applied already existing racial legislation to Gypsies, who now had to provide a certificate of suitability before being allowed to marry. This was unlikely to be granted. In March 1939 Himmler ordered that racial mixing between Gypsies and Germans was to be prevented in future. Every regional office of the Criminal Police was to set up a special office dealing with Gypsies. It was to ensure that once Gypsies had undergone racial examination, they were to be issued with special identity cards, coloured brown for pure Gypsies, brown with a blue strip for mixed-race Gypsies and grey for non-Gypsy itinerants. By the time the war broke out, Himmler had gone a long way down the road to preparing what he called in his decree of 8 December 1938 'the final solution of the Gypsy question'.[44]

V

While the regime approached the 'Gypsy question' gradually, and initially at least on the basis of existing police practices that were only partially racist in character, and not much different to those enforced in other European countries, the same could not be said of its dealings with another, much smaller minority in German society, the so-called 'Rhineland bastards'. The term itself was a polemical piece of nationalist terminology, referring to black or mixed-race Germans who, it was almost universally believed, were the result of the rape of German women by French African colonial troops during the occupation of the Rhineland after 1919 and above all the Ruhr in 1923. There had in fact been very few rapes; most of the children were the offspring of consensual unions, and there were, according to a later census, no more than five or six hundred of them; other African-Germans, though often regarded as the product of the French occupation, were the children of German settlers and African women in the colonial period before 1918 or in the years afterwards, when many Germans returned from the former colonies such as Cameroon or Tanganyika (the mainland part of present-day Tanzania). Such had been the nationwide publicity given to the allegations of rape, however, that they remained in the public eye throughout the 1920s. African-Germans were regarded by nationalists as the living embodiment of Germany's shame.[45]

Already in 1927, proposals were circulating in the Bavarian Ministry of the Interior for their forcible sterilization, lest African characteristics should enter the German bloodstream, and these were revived almost as soon as the Nazis came to power, when Göring ordered the collection of information on the children, many of whom were now in their teens. Investigations of some of them by racial experts had reported, predictably enough, that they were inferior in every respect. But the legal basis for dealing with them on the grounds provided for in the sterilization law of 1933 was still extremely dubious, so after lengthy deliberations within the bureaucracy, it was decided in 1937, almost certainly with Hitler's explicit backing, that the children should be sterilized on the basis of the Leader's authority alone. A special commission was set up within the Gestapo, staffed with racial hygienists and anthropologists; branches were opened in the Rhineland; the young people in question were located and examined; and the sterilization programme, organized in secret by Ernst Rüdin, Fritz Lenz and Walter Gross, among others, went ahead.[46]

How it impinged on the individuals most directly affected can be seen in the case of what the Gestapo filed as 'number 357', a boy born in 1920 to a consensual union between a German mother and a French colonial soldier from Madagascar, who willingly acknowledged his paternity, confirmed by the mother. A medical-anthropological examination conducted in 1935 concluded that the boy's facial features were un-German and probably negroid. By the time the sterilization policy had been decided on, he had begun work on a Rhine barge; the Gestapo tracked him down and he was arrested at midnight on 29 June 1937. Purely on the basis of the earlier confirmation of his paternity by the mother, and the medical examination of 1935, the branch commission in Cologne ordered that he should be sterilized; his mother, who had in the meantime married a German, gave her approval, as did her husband, and the boy was subjected to a vasectomy in the Evangelical Hospital in Cologne on 30 June, the day after his arrest. He was discharged on 12 July and went back to his job. Legally German, he was given no opportunity to protest or appeal against the decision because he was a minor, and it is more than likely that his parents had given their consent only under considerable pressure from the Gestapo. Many of those sterilized were younger. Girls as young as twelve were forced to undergo tubal ligation. It is questionable whether many of them really knew what they were being subjected to, or why, or what the eventual consequences for their lives would be. The actual number of those treated in this way is not known but was probably in the region of 500. After this, however, nothing much more happened to them, unless they fell foul of the regime for some other reason. A substantial number of African-Germans, indeed, managed to make a living for themselves in circuses and fairgrounds, or as extras in German movies set in the African colonies. The effects of their sterilization, physical and psychological, would remain with them for the rest of their lives.[47]

VI

At the same time as they pursued these racial minorities, the Nazis also launched an increasingly intensive persecution of a much larger group of Germans. Homosexual behaviour among men, though not among women, had long been outlawed in Germany, as in most other European countries. Paragraph 175 of the Reich Criminal Code prescribed imprisonment for any man who indulged in 'activity similar to sexual intercourse' with another man. In other words, to secure a conviction it was necessary to show that penetration had occurred. This restrictive definition was difficult to prove and allowed many other kinds of homosexual sex to exist unpunished. Homosexual culture flourished in the free-and-easy atmosphere of Berlin and one or two other great cities in the Weimar Republic, so much so that it formed something of a magnet for homosexuals from other, more repressive countries, the most famous of them being, perhaps, the British writer Christopher Isherwood. Still, on coming to power, the Nazis were not really doing much more than enforcing the law when they raided well-known homosexual bars and meeting-places in Berlin and clamped down on the movement to abolish Paragraph 175, though the violence that accompanied these actions could certainly not be justified by any existing legal code.[48]

For the Nazis, homosexuals were degenerate, effeminate and perverted: they were undermining the strength of the Aryan race by refusing to have children, and they were subverting the masculine idea which so much of Nazi politics propagated. For Heinrich Himmler, whose narrow-minded bourgeois upbringing had imbued him with more than the usual social prejudices in this area, homosexuality was a 'symptom of dying races'; it caused 'every achievement, every attempt to achieve things in a state, to collapse'. There were millions of homosexuals in the Weimar Republic, he told SS officers in 1937, so it was no wonder that it was weak, chaotic and incapable of restoring Germany to its proper place in the world. Himmler's pathological fear of homosexuality derived further strength from his belief that only tightly knit groups of Aryan men were fit to rule Germany and the world. Bound by close ties of comradeship, living together in barracks and camps, and spending most of their time in their own company rather than that of the opposite sex, they could all too easily fall prey to sexual urges from each other, as homoeroticism crossed the fatal boundary into homosexuality. Himmler was not only inclined to lecture the SS on the dangers of male homosexuality, he also wanted to impose the severest sanctions on any officer or man found guilty of indulging in it, all the way up to the death penalty.[49]

By contrast, the Nazis paid little attention to female homosexuality. In Germany, as in most other European countries, it was not against the law, and no reference was made to it in the Criminal Code. None the less, in Nazi Germany lesbians were still likely to be arrested and placed in concentration camps if they overstepped the mark in the eyes of the authorities. Prosecutions were brought before the courts under Paragraph 176 of the Criminal Code, which outlawed the sexual exploitation of subordinates by superiors in organizations like the Hitler Youth and the League of German Girls. In addition, because of their unconventional lifestyle and frequent refusal to undertake what the regime regarded as women's principal natural obligation to the race, namely to have children, lesbians were also in some cases classified as asocial. Marrying gay men as a cover (for both partners), an increasingly common practice in these circles after 1933, did not necessarily help, since the fact that such couples rarely had children also attracted the hostile scrutiny of the authorities. Lesbian clubs and bars were closed down by the police in 1933 and it was clear there was no chance of their being revived. Yet on the whole there was no systematic persecution of lesbians like there was of homosexual men. Lesbian society continued to function, especially in big cities like Berlin, though behind closed doors. Given the Nazi view of women as essentially passive and subordinate, it was not really seen as much of a threat.[50]

Male homosexuality on the other hand received a great deal of alarmed attention, and not just from the obsessive Heinrich Himmler. SS publications sometimes echoed Himmler's view that what was needed was the 'eradication of the degenerate for the purposes of maintaining the purity of the race'. But this had its limits. Medical and scientific opinion certainly treated homosexuality as a perversion. Yet as with other kinds of deviance, it tended to distinguish between a hard core of incorrigibles, which Himmler himself reckoned at about 2 per cent of the general homosexual population, or some 40,000 men, and the rest, who could be cured of their perversion by re-education. Since this was in his view best carried out in concentration camps, it was bound to consist mainly of harsh punishments, conceived of as a deterrent to further homosexual activity, a position not very different from that taken by the courts. And it was to the courts that Himmler initially had to leave the subject; for in 1933 the SS was still a relatively small organization, almost completely overshadowed by the far larger and very different SA. Led by Ernst Röhm, whose homosexuality was an open secret, the brownshirts took no action at all against homosexuals within their own ranks. Not only Röhm's enemies, the Social Democrats, but also his rivals within the Nazi movement itself brought up his homosexuality, and that of some other leading brownshirts, as an issue on a number of occasions, notably on Röhm's recall to the leadership of the stormtroopers at the beginning of 1931. Yet Hitler dismissed such concerns. The SA was, he said, 'not a moral institution for the education of nice young girls, but a band of rough fighters'. The private life of its leaders and members was their own concern unless it 'seriously contravened the basic tenets of National Socialism'. Meanwhile, anyone who attacked Röhm and his comrades for their sexuality would be expelled from the movement. This did not stop debate, either within the Party or without, over Röhm's sexuality. But as long as Hitler considered the SA chief indispensable, it had no practical effect.[51]

All this changed dramatically on 30 June 1934 when Hitler struck at the SA leadership and used the homosexuality of Röhm and other figures murdered on his orders, notably Edmund Heines, to gain understanding for his actions. This gave Himmler his chance. Addressing leading members of the SS, he claimed that Röhm had intended to establish a homosexual dictatorship and bring the country to ruin, a view also expressed by Alfred Rosenberg. Homosexuality would now lead to immediate exclusion from the movement. A wave of homophobia swept across the Nazi Party and its affiliated organizations. Police forces all over Germany carried out a fresh series of raids on homosexuals and their meeting-places. Forty-eight men with previous convictions for pederasty were rearrested and sent to the concentration camp at Dachau. In December 1934, 2,000 men were reported to have been arrested in a series of police raids on homosexual bars and clubs. A new department was created within the Gestapo after the Röhm action, and given the task of compiling a card-index of homosexuals, above all within the Party. Here was another area where unsolicited denunciations began to play a role, since the behaviour in question mostly took place in private, behind closed doors. By the middle of 1935 a whole series of prosecutions of Hitler Youth leaders under Paragraph 175 was under way. Dozens of them were hauled off secretly to Gestapo headquarters in Berlin for interrogation. Once confessions had been extracted, a good number of them were sent to concentration camps for an indefinite period of time. Himmler also used the new climate to get rid of awkward opponents, such as the Silesian Regional Party Leader Helmut Brückner, who had complained of the numerous murders carried out by the SS officer Udo von Woyrsch in his area in the course of the Röhm purge. Himmler managed to get Brückner arrested for gross indecency with an army officer, sacked from his office and sentenced to eighteen months' imprisonment. Brückner's protestations that nobody had bothered about his bisexuality at the time he had had the relationship, before 30 June 1934, went unheard.[52]

Brückner was sentenced, as had become all too common in the legal practice of the Third Reich, retroactively, under a new Law passed on 28 June 1935. It amended Paragraph 175, providing harsher punishments for homosexual behaviour and redefining the latter in far vaguer terms than before, as an 'unnatural sexual act' (*Unzucht*). The requirement to prove that penetration had taken place was dropped. In February 1937, Himmler devoted a lengthy speech to the subject, telling SS leaders that any homosexuals found in the organization would henceforth be arrested, tried and sentenced, sent on their release to a concentration camp and there 'shot while trying to escape'.[53] Police forces all over Germany received fresh instructions on how to recruit informers in places frequented by homosexuals, while efforts to compile dossiers on all possible suspects were redoubled. It was not surprising that convictions under the Criminal Code now rocketed. In the years 1933 to 1935, nearly 4,000 men were convicted under Paragraph 175 in its unamended and amended forms; in the years 1936 to 1938, however, the number reached more than 22,000. The raids and arrests were co-ordinated from 1 October 1936 by a new Reich Central Office for the Combating of Homosexuality and Abortion, building on the Gestapo department created to deal with the same area in the wake of the Röhm purge, which gave fresh impetus to the wave of persecutions.

Altogether under the Third Reich, no fewer than 50,000 men were arrested under Paragraph 175, nearly half of them in 1937-9; some two-thirds of them were convicted and sent to prison. These figures need to be seen in the perspective of the general criminalization of homosexuality in advanced industrial societies until the last third or quarter of the twentieth century, however. They appear less striking when compared with the fact that nearly 100,000 men were tried for violations of Paragraph 175 of the Criminal Code in West Germany in the twelve years from 1953 to 1965, of whom roughly a half were convicted.[54] It was not until Paragraph 175 was amended in 1959 and again in 1965 that homosexual acts between consenting adult males in private were effectively legalized in West Germany; the fact that homosexuals imprisoned during the Third Reich were condemned by the regular courts under a regular paragraph of the Criminal Code has since then proved a major obstacle to their receiving recognition of their sufferings.[55] These figures were also far from exceptional by international standards, though the peak of prosecutions in 1937-9 perhaps was. In Britain, gross indecency between adult males had been punishable since the nineteenth century by two years' imprisonment; in this sense, the 1935 German amendment to Paragraph 175 was doing little more than catching up with the legal position across the North Sea. In the early 1950s around 1,000 cases of sodomy and bestiality were filed by the police in England and Wales every year, and 2,500 cases of gross indecency. These figures marked a dramatic increase over the statistics for the 1930s, when there had been fewer than 500 a cases a year of both offences combined – a jump largely attributable to the appointment of rabidly homophobic senior law enforcement officials in the intervening years.[56]

Yet even at this stage there was still at least one major difference between Nazi Germany and other modern states in the persecution of gay men. For on their release from prison, a substantial minority of offenders against the German Law were immediately rearrested by the Gestapo or the SS and taken straight to a concentration camp, a practice that became markedly more common from 1937 onwards. Altogether between 5,000 and 15,000 homosexuals were imprisoned in the camps over the whole period from 1933 to 1945.[57] Here they were distinguished by a pink triangle sewn onto their camp uniform, identifying them as homosexuals in contrast to political prisoners (red), asocials (black), criminals (green) and so on. Homosexuals were well down the hierarchy of prisoners, subjected to brutal and contemptuous treatment by the guards, their life-span significantly shorter than that of most other categories. One investigation has reached the conclusion that their death-rate in the camps was around 50 per cent over the whole period of the Third Reich, compared to about 40 per cent for politicals and 35 per cent for Jehovah's Witnesses. That would put the total number who died in the camps at between 2,500 and 7,500 all told.[58] There was no parallel to this deliberately murderous policy in other countries, however severe discrimination may have been, or however free homophobes were to beat up homosexuals without fear of reprisal.

For those who escaped death, the alternative was sometimes hardly more palatable. A significant number of homosexuals were also subject to 'voluntary' castration to 'cure' them of their 'degeneracy'. The legally dubious nature of this procedure did not prevent pressure being brought on inmates of prisons and concentration camps to have themselves castrated. Homosexuals in state prisons were sometimes told that they would be handed over to the Gestapo on their release if they refused consent, or put in security confinement. Some 174 men were 'voluntarily' castrated in state penal institutions as a result up to 1939. The number castrated in the camps is likely to have been considerably higher and probably exceeded 2,000.[59] The scale of these operations put those carried out in other countries into the shade, and compulsory castration was in any case only carried out in Finland and a few states in the USA. In addition, the German Habitual Criminals Law of 24 November 1933 allowed sex offenders of all kinds to be castrated, even against their will, as advocated by leading criminologists and penal experts. Two serious sex offences were needed for this, and up to the end of 1939 just over 2,000 men had been subjected to this punishment.[60] They included not only rapists and paedophiles, but also a large number of exhibitionists, who may have been offensive and irritating to the public but posed little direct physical threat to anyone. Many first-time offenders were castrated immediately and given no chance to mend their ways. The physical after-effects of the operation included constant pain, loss of body hair and growth of breasts, tiredness and obesity. To add to all this, the operation did not necessarily eliminate sexual desire. Homosexuals were not formally allowed to be castrated against their will, but for a good number of them there was in effect very little choice: the alternative to castration was perpetual confinement and probable death in a concentration camp.[61] The persecution of homosexuals under the Third Reich probably only directly affected a fraction of Germany's gay men; but the knowledge of what might happen to them if they were denounced, arrested and convicted must have struck fear into them all.[62]

THE NUREMBERG LAWS

I

Discrimination against minorities such as homosexuals, Gypsies, asocials, the mentally ill or handicapped or African-Germans was designed in the first place to purify the German race and render it fit for a war of world conquest. German society was to be rid in the long term of its social ballast, of categories of people who would not or could not play their part in working towards war, through joining the armed forces, toiling away in armaments factories or toughening themselves up for the coming conflict. Seen in this light, they were burdens on Germany's state and society that posed a long-term threat to the future. Removing them by imprisoning them, and, just as crucially, taking them out of the chain of heredity, would eventually save the nation money, therefore, by reducing the numbers of unproductive people who, as the Nazis saw it, had to be supported by all the rest. One minority in German society, however, appeared to the Nazis as something entirely different: not a tiresome burden, but a vast threat, not merely idle, or inferior, or degenerate – although Nazi ideology held them to be all these things too – but actively subversive, engaged in a massive conspiracy to undermine and destroy everything German, a conspiracy moreover that was not just organized from within the country, but operated on a worldwide basis. This minority, no more than 1 per cent of the population, was the Jewish community in Germany.[63]

Antisemitism was intimately connected with other aspects of Nazi racial policy. The Law for the Prevention of Hereditarily Diseased Offspring was originally conceived as part of a package that included laws removing citizenship from the Jews and banning marriage and sexual relations with Aryans. These latter laws were temporarily withdrawn, however, mainly because of the bad effect it was thought that they would have had on public opinion abroad. In the early years of the regime, the state's eugenic policies against minorities such as the asocials, criminals, gypsies and homosexuals were a good deal more radical than they were against the Jews. When Jews fell into one or other of these groups, of course, they were more harshly treated than most; yet the *general* policy of the regime to Germany's Jewish minority did not include sterilization or castration solely and simply because the person in question was Jewish. Such policies, however, demonstrated to the Nazis how much they could get away with, and inured them to state-sponsored violence against the body on a systematic scale. It was an experience that was to prove useful to them as their antisemitic actions began to become more radical with time. In the meantime, however, the contrast was clear enough. After the promulgation of the Law of 7 April 1933 banning Jews from occupying posts in the civil service, the universities, the teaching profession, the judiciary and other state-funded institutions, the government put a brake on antisemitic violence for a while. As we have seen, it was concerned to dampen down the violent activism of the brownshirts. It was worried about the effects of antisemitic actions on the fragile economic recovery. It was apprehensive about the economic and diplomatic consequences that the law and the preceding, government-sponsored boycott of Jewish shops were bringing in the reaction of foreign states and foreign businesses. Finally, it was anxious to placate its increasingly restive conservative partners, who – for example – had insisted, in the person of Reich President Hindenburg, on exempting former front-line soldiers from the law.[64]

It took some time for the effects of the law of 7 April 1933 to work their way through the institutions, but by the end of 1933 the purge was for the moment more or less complete. The cooling-down of the leadership's ardour was not welcome to many Party activists, least of all within the paramilitary Storm Divisions, who organized repeated local boycotts of Jewish businesses during this period, reaching renewed and often violent heights in the spring of 1934. The stormtroopers' activism was muted for a while following the purge of 30 June 1934, but by the Christmas period at the end of the year, boycott actions were in full swing again. Moreover, local Party organizations also pushed forward the economic marginalization of Jewish businesses in other ways too, as we have seen, and in this area they were encouraged by the Party leadership as well.[65] In the spring and summer of 1935, however, antisemitic violence broke out afresh in many parts of the country. Antisemitic propaganda became more widespread than ever. The circulation of the sensationalist antisemitic paper *The Stormer* soared in 1935 when its editor, Julius Streicher, the Party Regional Leader of Franconia, secured a contract with the Labour Front for copies to be placed in every factory and workplace in the land. From now on, the paper was omnipresent and inescapable. The deal made Streicher into a millionaire: the paper had always been his personal property rather than the organ of the Nazi-owned Eher Publishing House.[66] More immediately, its new-found wealth and power enabled it to advertise more widely than before, with posters seemingly on every street corner. Other Regional Leaders besides Streicher held public meetings and gave speeches to harangue people, and especially Party members, about the evils of the Jew. Behind all this were more general ideological influences, ranging from increased sales of Hitler's *My Struggle* to frequent attacks on the Jews in the Party press. Many local groups took all this as giving the green light to go on the offensive once more.[67]

The reasons for this recrudescence of attacks on Germany's Jews by Party groups and stormtroopers in 1935 lay above all in the growing unpopularity of the regime. As we have seen, whatever public euphoria had accompanied the Nazis' establishment of the Third Reich in 1933 wore off in the course of 1934, and the brief fillip given the regime by Hitler's decisive action in crushing Röhm's supposed putsch attempt at the end of June 1934 had dissipated by the end of the year. During the first months of 1935, Gestapo, Security Service and other agents reported a sharp increase in popular discontent, as material conditions remained miserable, real levels of unemployment stayed high, prices of food and other basic necessities rose sharply, and people became wearied of the regime's constant demands for acclamation, support and money. Rumours and jokes about the corruption of local and regional Nazi bosses multiplied, and all the efforts of the Propaganda Ministry to generate positive popular enthusiasm for the Third Reich seemed to have failed.[68] Within the Nazi movement itself, too, the crushing of any remaining hopes for a 'second revolution' in June–July 1934 had created a good deal of bitterness. The desire for violent action, ingrained in many parts of the SA, needed a fresh outlet. How could the brownshirts justify their existence, either to themselves or to the Party, except by violent action? That after all was what they had been created for. But the desire to resume a policy of struggle was not confined to disgruntled stormtroopers. The Nazi Party more generally was well aware of the fact that it had not only failed to sustain the enthusiasm of the broader public but was actually losing what support it had ever enjoyed amongst it. Action was needed.

Not only the Nazi Party but also significant parts of the state and civil service had wanted since the middle of 1933 to introduce measures banning marriage and sexual relations between Jews and non-Jews, creating a special category of citizenship for Jews, and accelerating the removal of the Jews from economic life. Point 4 of the Nazi Party programme stated unequivocally that in the Third Reich, Jews were not to be citizens, and a number of Hitler's early meetings, not to mention *My Struggle*, had made it clear that he was viscerally intolerant of sexual relations between Aryans and Jews. Acting on this principle, the Party's Reichstag delegation had already unsuccessfully tried to pass a bill to outlaw racial miscegenation in March 1930, with sanctions up to and including the death penalty. Such provisions would also have the effect of extending the Party's sphere of influence still further, into the most intimate areas of private life. A new citizenship law would, moreover, not just give rights as an automatic consequence of racial identity, but would also apply political criteria, with refractory elements denied civil rights too. Driving the Jews out of economic life would placate the Party's many lower-middle-class supporters and give them much-desired opportunities to improve their own situation. A fresh campaign of anti-semitic propaganda, terror and legislation would divert popular hostility to the regime, it was thought, by putting the blame for the people's miserable situation firmly onto the Jews.[69]

The antisemitic actions carried out in the spring and summer of 1935 took many forms. In May there were, as we have seen, numerous boy-cotts of Jewish shops organized by stormtroopers and SS men, often accompanied by violence. It was also at about this time that antisemitic street signs were put up by the roadside on the boundaries of many towns and villages. These were not new in principle, for many had already been erected in Julius Streicher's fiefdom of Franconia, but they were erected in many more places in the spring and summer of 1935, including in southern Bavaria. The commonest slogan painted on them was 'Jews are not wanted here', but some essayed ironic understatement ('Our demand for Jews has been sufficiently supplied'), uttered threats ('Jews enter this locality at their own peril!') or tried an appeal to religious sentiment ('The Jew's Father is the Devil').[70] In a number of municipalities, including Weimar, local authorities banned Jews from going to the cinema; in Magdeburg all the trams acquired signs placed over the entry doors bearing the words 'Jews not wanted!' The same town also stopped Jews from using the city library. Inns and restaurants in Stralsund and other places closed their doors to Jewish customers. Swimming pools and public baths, reported a Social Democratic agent in August, were barred to Jews 'in innumerable communities'. Jewish cemeteries and synagogues were desecrated. Non-Jews who had relationships with Jews were publicly paraded as 'race defilers' and frequently had to be taken into custody by the Gestapo, for once in truth for their own protection. The atmosphere on the streets of many towns in the Rhineland, Westphalia, Hesse, Pomerania and East Prussia was so threatening that many Jewish inhabitants scarcely dared leave their houses any more.[71]

Actions such as these were encouraged not only by the general atmosphere of antisemitism but also explicitly by leading figures in the Party. 'Some people think', Goebbels told a rally of the Berlin Region of the Nazi Party on 30 June 1935, 'that we haven't noticed how the Jews are trying once again to spread themselves over all our streets. The Jews ought please to observe the laws of hospitality and not behave as if they were the same as us.' Reporting on 15 July that an antisemitic film had been jeered at by 'troops of Jewish trouble-makers' on its first performance three days previously, Goebbels's Berlin Party paper *The Attack* urged Party members to take violent action: the Jews, it declared, must 'ever and again feel the flat of our hand'. In fact, the Jewish 'demonstration', whether real or invented, was the excuse by which Goebbels sought to justify the antisemitic violence that now inevitably followed, with Party activists beating up Jews on the main shopping street, the Kurfürstendamm, or pursuing them into nearby pubs and bars and physically attacking them. This incident in turn sparked a fresh wave of violent boycott actions in other parts of the country.

Goebbels was not the only Nazi leader who whipped up his followers in this way. On 30 August 1935, Julius Streicher held a rally in Hamburg. The day before, two lorryloads of stormtroopers drove through streets known to be inhabited by Jews, throwing blazing torches onto the road with chants of 'Let the Jews perish!' Party comrades were told that attendance at the rally was compulsory; a massive advertising campaign offered tickets at 10 Reichsmarks apiece to the unemployed. Twenty thousand people attended, many of them in SA, SS, Hitler Youth, Labour Service or other uniforms, strategically placed in the audience to lead the applause at preordained points in Streicher's speech. Working his voice up to a deafening bellow, Streicher inveighed against foreign correspondents who criticized Nazi antisemitism. 'I say here', he shouted, 'that we do what we want with the Jews in Germany!' As his speech went on, so a listener reporting secretly to the exiled Social Democrats in Prague observed, he became more and more obscene, not only declaring that hundreds of German women had been raped by Jews, but also giving graphic details of these supposed crimes. When one girl gave birth to a baby nine months after marrying a Jew, he went on, 'what lay there in the crib, comrades?! A little ape!' Some of the listeners walked out at this; others, drafted in from the Labour Service, had apparently long since fallen asleep. Nevertheless, although ordinary people in the audience seem to have been either indifferent or repelled, such rantings must have had an effect on the committed Nazis amongst them; and they were repeated, if in less extreme form, by other Nazi leaders across the country. Most local and regional Party leaders took Streicher's insistence that antisemitic actions should be legal and non-violent as nothing more than an attempt to assuage public opinion at home and abroad.[72]

II

Neither this wave of terroristic actions nor the accompanying campaign against the Catholic Church had the desired revitalizing effect on public support for the regime. Indeed, the coincidence of these campaigns caused many Catholics to sympathize with the Jews and to feel, as the Gestapo in Münster reported, 'that the measures taken against the Jews are going too far'. They were in any case hostile to the idea that race rather than religion should be the guiding principle of social action. Boycotts and, still more, violence, inspired 'rejection rather than approval' in the wider population, as another Gestapo agency reported. In Mannheim-Neckarau shoppers even engaged in fisticuffs with storm-troopers who tried to stop them from patronizing Jewish retailers. The middle classes were particularly upset at such open disorder on the streets and feared its impact on foreign opinion. Some took the cynical view that petty-bourgeois Nazi activists were just trying to drive out competition.[73]

A Social Democratic agent in Bavaria reported, however, in more nuanced terms:

The persecution of the Jews is not meeting with any active support from the population. But on the other hand it is not completely failing to make an impression. Unnoticed, racial propaganda is leaving its traces. People are losing their impartiality towards the Jews, and many are saying to themselves that the Nazis are actually right to fight them; people are only against this fight being exaggerated. And when people shop in Jewish department stores they do so in the first place not to help the Jews but to cock a snook at the Nazis.[74]

The Nazi leadership had no objection to the violence in principle, but there was a growing feeling that, whatever Streicher might say, it was having a damaging effect on foreign opinion when the regime still needed sympathy abroad. In the last week of August 1935 it was reported that brownshirts had staged a violent demonstration against the Jews in Breslau and beaten up the Swedish consul in the city in the process. Göring, Bormann and Hess, speaking for Hitler himself, all put the police on notice in late July and early August that uncoordinated terror actions against Jews had to be stopped. As Göring told the Gestapo, general regulations for dealing with the Jews would soon be issued. These were indeed already in the air. Debate had been conducted in a desultory fashion within the Interior and Justice Ministries since July 1934 without getting beyond what were seen as formidable legal obstacles to a new law governing citizenship and interracial sexual relations. On 21 May 1935, however, a new Defence Law included in its provisions the banning of 'mixed marriages' between German soldiers and non-Aryan women.

Local registry offices had already begun to refuse applications for mixed marriages on a wider basis. On 19 July representatives of the Justice and Interior Ministries and Hess's office proposed a law to prevent such marriages altogether. The matter had become urgent not least because of the numerous attacks on 'race traitors' and a wave of arrests of such people by the Gestapo. In May 1935 a new law governing citizenship applications by foreigners already ruled out Jews and other non-Aryans. A consensus on legislative action thus seemed to have been achieved; and as this became clear to local and regional Party organizations at the beginning of September, the wave of violent antisemitic actions finally began to subside, though it did not stop altogether.[75]

Not only the idea of a new citizenship law but also a considerable number of concrete proposals for its formulation were therefore familiar to state and Party officials by the time the annual Party Rally began in Nuremberg on 9 September. At this point dock workers in New York who had torn down a swastika flag from a German ship were released by a magistrate with a lengthy denunciation of Nazism and all its works. This so enraged Hitler that he decided on the spot that the time had come to declare the swastika Germany's national flag. As he told the Party Rally on 11 September 1935, the recent congress of the Communist International in Moscow, which had declared an international war on fascism, demonstrated that it was time to tackle the Bolshevik menace, which he regarded as the product of an international Jewish conspiracy. Hitler summoned the Reichstag to a session in Nuremberg on 15 September, the final day of the Rally; the fact that he could simply command it to attend in this way showed how insignificant it had now become. The Reichstag session, he now decided, would be the opportune moment to introduce the citizenship, miscegenation and state flag laws all in one go. After some hurried, last-minute drafting of the detailed Laws in collaboration with an Interior Ministry official, Hitler introduced them on 15 September 1935. The Jews in Germany, he said, had been using the tense international situation to stir up trouble. 'Vehement complaints are coming in from innumerable places about the provocative behaviour of individual members of this people,' he claimed: indeed, Jewish provocations had been organized and thus had to be answered with decisive action if they were not to lead to 'individual, uncontrollable defensive actions carried out by the outraged population'. Here was a

characteristic mixture of lies and threats, capped by an equally characteristic assurance that the new laws would be 'a once-and-for all, secular
solution'.[76]

Hitler left the detailed justification of the Laws to Göring, whose
speech to the Reichstag left little doubt that he was no less rabid an
antisemite than Goebbels, Streicher or indeed the Leader himself. The
swastika, he told the assembled, brown-uniformed Reichstag deputies,
was a 'symbol of our struggle for our own, species-specific race, it was a
sign to us of the struggle against the Jews as racial wreckers'. When 'an
impudent Jew, in his bottomless hatred' for Germany had insulted the
flag in New York, he had insulted the whole nation. Thus Jews were not
to be allowed to fly the flag. The new Laws, indeed, would go much
further, and protect German blood against pollution by Jews and other
alien races. They were, he declared,

a declaration of faith in the strengths and blessings of the Germanic-Nordic
spirit. We know that to sin against the blood is to sin against the inheritance of
a people. We ourselves, the German people, have had to suffer greatly because
of this hereditary sin. We know that the final root of all Germany's decompo-
sition came in the last analysis from these sinners against heredity. So we have
to try to make a connection again to the chain of heredity that comes to us from
the greyness of prehistory . . . And it is the duty of every government, and above
all it is the duty of the people themselves, to ensure that this purity of the race
can never again be made sick or filled with rottenness.[77]

The parliament naturally passed all three laws with acclamation, and
they were printed in full in prominent positions in the daily newspapers
the following day. But they were not all as simple and straightforward
as they might at first sight have seemed.[78] The Reich Citizenship Law
defined citizens of the Reich exclusively as people of 'German or kindred
blood'. Just as crucially, it declared that only someone who, 'through
his conduct, shows that he is both desirous and fit to serve the German
people and Reich faithfully' was entitled to be a citizen of the Reich.
Only citizens could enjoy full political rights. All other people, notably
the Jews, but also potentially all opponents of the regime, or even those
who silently distanced themselves from it by their lack of enthusiasm for
its policies, were merely 'subjects of the state'. They had 'obligations
towards the Reich' but were given no political rights in return. Details

of implementation were left to the Interior Ministry, in conjunction with Hess's office, to work out, and in due course two officials in the Ministry, Dr Wilhelm Stuckart and Dr Hans Globke, issued a commentary justifying its provisions and outlining its implications. Within a fortnight, Interior Minister Frick had ordered the dismissal of any civil servants of Jewish ancestry who had remained in post as a result of the special provisions of the civil service law of 7 April 1933.

But who exactly was a Jew? Frick's decree applied to people with at least three out of four grandparents who were Jewish and, naturally, to all those who practised the Judaic religion. According to contemporary estimates, which varied widely, there were in addition some 50,000 Jews in Germany in 1935 who had converted to Christianity or were the children of Jewish parents who had converted, and 2,000 three-quarter Jews who had converted. The high rate of intermarriage between Jews and Christians over the previous decades had produced between 70,000 and 75,000 people who had only two Jewish grandparents and 125,000 to 130,000 who had only one. In addition, many of these were married to non-Jews, as were anything up to about 20,000 people who fell into the Nazis' category of full Jews, and many of these, again, had children. The Nazis themselves reckoned in 1939 that there were 20,454 racially mixed marriages in the Greater German Reich (including, by this time, Austria and the Sudetenland). The same census, the first to define Jews by racial criteria, also counted 52,005 half-Jews and 32,669 quarter-Jews living in the old German Reich. Over 90 per cent of people defined as mixed race belonged to a Christian Church. As with any racist legislation, the devil lay in the detail, and in these circumstances reaching a hard-and-fast definition of who was Jewish and who was not was nigh impossible. An insoluble ideological dilemma faced Nazi legislators: was the poison they thought Jewish blood carried with it into the bloodstream of the German race so virulent that only a small admixture would be enough to turn a person into a Jew, or was German blood so strong and healthy that it would overcome all but the most powerful admixture of Jewishness in a person's hereditary constitution? To such questions there was no rational answer, because there was from the beginning no rational basis to the assumptions on which they rested. All solutions the Nazis arrived at in the question of mixed-race Germans and mixed marriages were thus in the end entirely arbitrary.[79]

The niceties of racial classification kept civil servants busy in endless meetings and internal memoranda over the following weeks. The more cautiously inclined warned that defining half-Jews as fully Jewish would add a substantial number of previously loyal Germans to the tally of Nazism's internal enemies. Their counsels prevailed, and such people were classified in a supplementary decree issued on 14 November 1935 as mixed-race of the first degree, unless they practised the Judaic faith, or were married to a full Jew, in which case they were counted as fully Jewish (*Geltungsjuden*, in official jargon), with all the consequences this entailed. People with only one fully Jewish grandparent counted as mixed-race of the second degree. There were further provisions dealing with anyone born out of wedlock, or born after the promulgation of the Nuremberg Laws in 1935 (they were more likely to be classified as fully Jewish). The legislators recognized the arbitrariness of these measures by including a final provision for Hitler to grant exemptions whenever and to whomsoever he pleased. In due course, he did indeed do this, or others did it in his name through the application of a stamp bearing his signature to a document known as a Declaration of German Blood. Meanwhile, all the authorities had to go on in establishing Jewish ancestry was whether or not someone's grandparents had practised the Judaic religion, a fact which rather made a nonsense of scientific claims about the importance of race and blood in determining Jewish or German identity. Genealogists suddenly became the most sought-after experts in the whole country, as Germans scrambled to find evidence in parish registers and other sources of their racial purity to include in their so-called Ancestry Proof (*Ahnennachweis*), a document that now formed the essential prerequisite for a career in the civil service or indeed virtually any other kind of job.[80]

III

The Nuremberg Laws were presented in the press as a stabilizing measure that would help the Jewish minority in Germany to settle down to living its own life. Goebbels's Propaganda Ministry was careful to ban triumphant or gloating articles in the press, forbidding 'leading articles in the tone "go to it!"'[81] Nevertheless, the Laws opened the way for further, massive discrimination against anyone who counted as a Jew. Two weeks after the decree of 14 November 1935, Hitler retroactively annulled its provision banning any extension of measures to ensure the purity of German blood beyond those contained in legislation. This effectively authorized non-governmental organizations to apply the Aryan paragraph to their members and employees, not only Jews but also those of mixed race as well. Further measures placed more restrictions on the admittance of Jews to state-regulated professions. People with two Jewish grandparents now had to get official permission from a Reich Committee for the Protection of German Blood if they wanted to marry a non-Jew. But the Party representatives on the Committee voted down such applications with such regularity that it was wound up in 1936 and the applications passed to a single official to deal with. Mixed-race people could still study, they were not banned from sexual or other kinds of relationship with non-Jews, and in many respects they lived a relatively unrestricted life. This included, for men, the performance of military service. The army leadership was naturally exercised by the fact that banning men of mixed race from doing military service would deprive them of thousands of potential recruits. Writing to Hitler's army adjutant, Colonel Friedrich Hossbach, on 3 April 1935, an official in the Interior Ministry estimated that there were 150,000 male half-Jews and quarter-Jews of military age in the country – a considerable exaggeration that further fed the army's concern.[82]

The army leadership certainly had good cause for concern. By the end of 1935 it had cashiered virtually all remaining fully Jewish officers and men, and in the early summer of 1936 the army reached an agreement with Hitler that while male half- and quarter-Jews had to perform military service, they should no longer be allowed to hold positions of authority in the armed forces unless granted a specific, personal exemption on Hitler's own authority. The Nazi Party's Genealogy Office bombarded the military with information about officers who were 'not purely Aryan' and ought in its view to be removed from their posts. However, many senior officers in 1936–7 still resented political interference in military affairs and ignored these demands. In addition, checking up on the ancestry of tens of thousands of men was a well-nigh impossible task, and quite a few officers managed successfully to conceal their part-Jewish ancestry at least until the outbreak of the war and in some cases even longer. From the point of view of the military, of course, what mattered was whether or not they were good soldiers, or sailors, or airmen.[83]

The army's attitude mirrored precisely the debatable and uncertain status of Germany's many part-Jewish inhabitants after 1935. Nevertheless, on the whole, mixed-race people, indeed even Jews, were to some extent relieved by the passage of the Nuremberg Laws because they seemed to remove the major elements of uncertainty in their position and promise an end to the violent antisemitic campaigns of the preceding months. Party activists were understandably enthusiastic about the Nuremberg Laws, and rightly saw them as a major step along the road to the complete removal of Jews from German society. However, both Gestapo and Social Democratic agents reported a critical, even hostile, attitude to the Nuremberg Laws even amongst groups in society that were normally far from favourably inclined towards the Jews. Four-fifths of the population in the Palatinate were said to disapprove of the Laws, the working class was almost unanimous in its rejection of Nazi antisemitism, and the petty-bourgeoisie disliked the Laws because small businessmen feared they would lead to renewed boycotts of German goods in other countries. Even the Social Democrats, however, admitted that most people were feeling so intimidated after the violence of the summer and the propaganda surrounding the Nuremberg Laws that they no longer patronized Jewish shops. Indifference and passivity characterized the reactions of the majority of the population.[84]

Gradually, the never-ending violence, the incessant propaganda and the legal endorsement of Nazi policies by the state were having an effect. As one Social Democratic agent reported from Berlin in January 1936:

The campaign against the Jews is not without influence on people's opinions either. Very slowly, views are being filtered into it that they used to reject. First people read the 'Stormer' out of curiosity, but then in the end something from it sticks. At the same time one has to admit: it says a lot for the German people that despite years of campaigns against the Jews it is still possible at all for Jews to live in Germany. If the German people were not naturally good-natured, this propaganda would have led to Jews simply being beaten to death on the streets . . . In general one can conclude that the National Socialists really have brought about a deeper gulf between the people and the Jews. The feeling that the Jews are another race is general nowadays.[85]

The effect that the constant barrage of antisemitism had on a thought-ful young person can be gauged from the memoirs of Melita Maschmann. She had plenty of contact with Jews, who made up about a third of her class in the secondary school she attended in a well-to-do part of Berlin in the early 1930s. Here the non-Jewish girls instinctively dissociated their Jewish classmates from 'the Jews', who 'were and remained some-thing mysteriously menacing and anonymous'. 'The anti-semitism of my parents', Maschmann went on in the open letter she wrote to a former Jewish schoolmate after the war,

was a part of their outlook which was taken for granted ... One was friendly with individual Jews whom one liked, just as one was friendly as a Protestant with individual Catholics. But while it occurred to nobody to be ideologically hostile to *the* Catholics, one was, utterly, to *the* Jews ... In preaching that all the misery of the nations was due to the Jews or that the Jewish spirit was seditious and Jewish blood compelled you to think of old Herr Lewy or Rosel Cohn: I thought only of the bogey-man, '*the* Jew'. And when I heard that the Jews were being driven from their professions and homes and imprisoned in ghettos, the points switched automatically in my mind to steer me round the thought that such a fate could also overtake you or old Lewy. It was only *the* Jew who was being persecuted and 'made harmless'.[86]

After joining the Nazi League of German Girls, however, she felt an 'open breach' with her Jewish schoolfriend '. . . to be my duty, because one could only do one or two things: either have Jewish friends or be a National Socialist'.[87]

Constantly exposed to antisemitic propaganda, Maschmann later remembered that she and her upper-middle-class friends had considered it rather vulgar, and often laughed at attempts to convince them that the Jews performed ritual murders and similar crimes. As educated people they looked down on the antisemitic scandal-sheet *The Stormer*. Yet although she did not take part in violent actions or boycotts, Maschmann accepted that they were justified, and told herself: 'The Jews are the enemies of the new Germany ... If the Jews sow hatred against us all over the world, they must learn that we have hostages for them in our hands.' Later on, she suppressed the memory of the violence she had seen on the streets, and 'as the years went by I grew better and better at switching off quickly in this manner on similar occasions. It was the only way. Whatever the circumstances, to prevent the onset of doubts about the rightness of what had happened.'[88] A similar process of rationalization and moral editing must have taken place with many others, too.

IV

From September 1935, antisemitism became a principle governing private life as well as public. Enshrined as the cornerstone of Nazi ideology since the beginning, it was now penetrating larger areas of German society more deeply than ever before. The whole of the civil service was now engaged in applying the Nuremberg Laws and others besides. Judges, prosecutors, policemen, Gestapo and other law enforcement agencies spent increasing amounts of their time on enforcing antisemitic legislation. Town councils and their employees in libraries, swimming pools and all other kinds of municipal establishments carried out antisemitic regulations. Innkeepers, shopkeepers (many of whom protected themselves by putting up signs advertising themselves as a 'purely Aryan establishment'), traders, businessmen, people in every walk of life were aware of laws against the Jews and had little hesitation in complying with them. Of course, the Social Democrats' secret reports were filled with examples of individual landlords and restaurant-owners who turned a blind eye to notices they were forced to put up banning Jewish customers. Nevertheless, all of this was having an effect. Together with the progressive economic marginalization of the Jews, the Nuremberg Laws marked a significant step in the direction of the removal of Jews from German society. Their isolation was considerably greater after September 1935 than before.[89]

The third of the measures promulgated at the Nuremberg Party Rally of 1935, dubbed by the Nazis the Law for the Protection of German Blood and German Honour, was perhaps the most significant of all of them in bringing Nazism into the private sphere. It forbade marriages between Jews and Germans 'or kindred blood' and banned sexual relations outside marriage between the two categories as defined by the Citizenship Law as well. Jews were not allowed to employ female domestic servants under the age of forty-five if they were Germans, in an allusion to a sexual fantasy that often made its appearance in the pages of *The Stormer*. These laws were to be administered by the regular courts. Cases were brought under the loaded heading of 'racial defilement' (*Rassenschande*, literally 'racial shame' or 'racial disgrace'). By their very nature such cases were difficult to identify, and prosecution depended heavily from the beginning on denunciation by neighbours, acquaintances and sometimes family members of those involved. From 1936 to 1939 the annual average of convictions for racial defilement under the Nuremberg Laws ran at about 420, two-thirds of them Jewish men. Under continuous pressure from the Gestapo and the Reich Justice Ministry, the courts became steadily harsher; in 1938, for example, a majority of racial defilement sentences passed by the Hamburg Regional Court involved lengthy periods of imprisonment in a penitentiary rather than an ordinary prison. The definition of illicit sexual relations was extended until it covered almost any kind of bodily contact between Jews and 'Aryans', including socially conventional embraces and kisses.[90] Eleven sentences were passed for racial offences in the remaining months of 1935, then in the first full year of the law's effect, 1936, the number jumped to 358, increasing to 512 in 1936 and falling back to 434 in 1938, 365 in 1939 and 231 in 1940. The increasing emigration of young and middle-aged Jews may have been a factor in the decline. It is possible, too, that the law's deterrent effect had an influence, as sentences grew steadily harsher over time.[91]

Inside prison, offenders were frequently exposed to antisemitic abuse from warders; in some institutions they were routinely put on short commons, and even good behaviour was often regarded as 'typical of the racial character which understands how to conform even in a position of powerlessness', as one Bavarian prison official noted in 1939. 'I suffer very much because of the hatred of Jews', wrote a young Jewish inmate to his mother, in a letter confiscated by the prison authorities in June 1938: 'One official calls me Moses, even though he knows exactly what I am called . . . Another one called me a damn Jewish swine this lunchtime.' Their sufferings did not end there. Following an order issued by the Reich Minister of Justice on 8 March 1938, Jews who were sent to prison for race defilement were rearrested by the Gestapo when they completed their sentence and taken off to concentration camps.[92] Here they were frequently singled out because of the nature of their alleged offence. In the Buchenwald concentration camp, the twenty-year-old Julius Meier, a well-educated, middle-class Jew, serving a two-year prison sentence after being denounced by a neighbour who had observed him being intimate with his family's non-Jewish domestic servant, was marked down by the camp doctor for castration. Refusing to sign the consent form, on the grounds that his emigration papers were about to be completed, Meier was repeatedly punched in the face by an SS guard on the doctor's orders, kicked, denied medical assistance for his injuries, and put in the camp's punishment bunker for twelve days. Using what influence they had, Meier's parents completed his emigration papers and obtained an order from Reich Security Head Office – not to release him, however, but to countermand the castration order. The telegram thus went not to the commandant, who would have arranged his immediate release, but to the camp doctor, for whom breaking Meier's will had by now become a matter of personal pride: on his orders, Meier was put back into the punishment bunker and murdered by an SS guard.[93]

The law offered many new opportunities for the harassment and persecution of German Jews, especially men. In December 1935, a 43-year-old Jewish clerk was condemned to one year and three months in gaol for race defilement. He had lived together with his non-Jewish partner for a year and they had a nine-month-old baby. But prosecutions were often brought on the flimsiest of pretexts. In Bad Dürkheim, for example, a 66-year-old Jewish man, Hermann Baum, was condemned to a year in prison in November 1935 on the evidence of a fifteen-year-old girl who testified that he had tried to kiss her. The Gestapo called in domestic servants who worked in Jewish households to inform them that they had to leave, and plied them with leading questions ('but he's touched you sometimes on the shoulder hasn't he?') in the hope of making an arrest, threatening them with imprisonment themselves if they did not incriminate their masters.[94] In November 1935, a fifty-year-old Jewish businessman, Ludwig Abrahamson, was denounced to the Gestapo for carrying on sexual relations with a non-Jewish employee, Wilhelmina Kohrt. Under interrogation he admitted that he had forced his attentions on her (whether in fact this was true may, in view of the methods used by the Gestapo to extract confessions, be doubted). He was sentenced to two years in prison and on his release was taken by the Gestapo to Buchenwald concentration camp, from which he only secured release on 6 October 1938 by providing proof that he would emigrate.

An even more striking case was that of Hannelore Krieger, a worker in a factory producing alcoholic beverages, who was denounced anonymously in April 1938 for carrying on sexual relations with her boss, Julius Rosenheim. He had, she said, demanded sexual favours in return for money; but at her trial, she changed her testimony and said the relationship had ended in 1934, before the Law was passed. The court agreed to acquit both of them, but the Gestapo arrested Rosenheim at the end of the trial and took him off to a concentration camp anyway.[95]

If Krieger's conduct perhaps bordered on prostitution, then real prostitutes were particularly vulnerable to denunciation from hostile neighbours for entertaining Jewish clients. Jewish men and women who had more committed relationships with non-Jewish partners took considerable precautions to conceal them after September 1938, but inevitably many fell victim to denunciations from prying neighbours or zealous Nazi snoopers. As time went on, people were denounced simply for being 'friendly to Jews': innkeepers for incautiously telling someone that Jews were still welcome in their establishments, German citizens for maintaining friendly relations with Jews of an entirely non-sexual kind, or even non-Jews for shaking hands with Jews in the street. On occasion the behaviour for which such people were denounced could denote a principled opposition to Nazi antisemitism; more often it was the product of indifference to official rules and regulations, or even simply long-maintained habit. Many such denunciations were false, but this in a sense was beside the point; false denunciations contributed as much as truthful ones to a general atmosphere in which Germans gradually cut off all their ties to Jewish friends and acquaintances, much as Melita Maschmann had done. By going well beyond what the Nuremberg Laws prescribed, and by pursuing all the denunciations they received, however frivolous or self-interested, the Gestapo and other agencies of law enforcement and control dismantled piece by piece the elaborate networks of social contacts which had been built up between German Jews and their fellow Germans over the decades. They were backed by the whole range of Party institutions, from the Block Warden upwards, who were similarly dedicated to preventing any further social intercourse between Aryans and Jews.[96]

Only occasionally did a Block Warden turn a blind eye, as in the case of the young lawyer and aspiring journalist Raimund Pretzel and his partner, a Jewish woman whom he met on his return from Paris in 1934. Pretzel had originally left Germany because of his dislike of the Third Reich's repression and racism, and also in pursuit of a girl; when she married another man, he went back to Germany and began to make a living writing unpolitical articles for the arts pages of newspapers and magazines. His new partner had been sacked from her library job because of her race, and her marriage had also recently broken up. Her son, Peter, was blond and blue-eyed, and was even photographed as an ideal Aryan child. When Pretzel moved into her flat, they were contravening the Nuremberg Laws, but the Block Warden liked the family and protected them from interference. However, in 1938 she became pregnant, and the danger of denunciation became too great. Taking Peter with her, she went to an emigration office and obtained leave to join her brother in England. Pretzel himself got permission to go to England separately, using the pretext that he was writing a series of articles about English life; viewed with suspicion by the British authorities when he overstayed, he found great difficulty in making ends meet, and was rescued only by Frederic Warburg, head of the publishers Secker and Warburg, who was sufficiently impressed by the synopsis of a book he had submitted to offer him a contract. This satisfied the Home Office, who gave Pretzel a year's extension to his visa. In the meantime, he had married his partner, and they had had a son. The future for both of them, however, seemed anything but certain, as it did for thousands of others who emigrated at this time.[97]

'THE JEWS MUST GET OUT OF EUROPE'

I

Jews in particular emigrated from Germany if they were young enough to start a new life abroad and wealthy enough to finance it. This was not voluntary or free emigration, of course; it was flight into exile to escape conditions that for many were becoming wholly intolerable. We do not really know how many Jews left Germany during these years. The official statistics, which continued to classify Jews by religion alone, are all we have to go on. Given the very high rates of conversion to Christianity over the decades before 1933, the official figures might have under-represented by 10 per cent or more the number of people who fled the country because the Nazi regime classified them as Jewish whatever their religion. According to the official statistics, there were 437,000 Germans of Jewish faith in Germany in 1933. By the end of 1937, the figure had dropped to around 350,000. Thirty-seven thousand members of the Jewish faith left Germany in 1933, under the impact of the boycott of 1 April and the Law of 7 April; a fall in the number of emigrants to 23,000 the following year reflected the absence of any similar nationwide actions or laws in 1934. The number stayed relatively low in the follow-ing years too – 21,000 in 1935, 25,000 in 1936 and 23,000 in 1937. As Europeans, most of them preferred to stay in another country on the same continent – 73 per cent of 1933's Jewish emigrants remained within Europe – while only 8 per cent travelled overseas, to destinations such as the United States. In 1933, despite the relative weakness of Zionism in Germany, no fewer than 19 per cent settled in Palestine. Altogether, 52,000 German Jews went there between 1933 and 1939. A significant reason for this surprisingly high number lay in the fact that

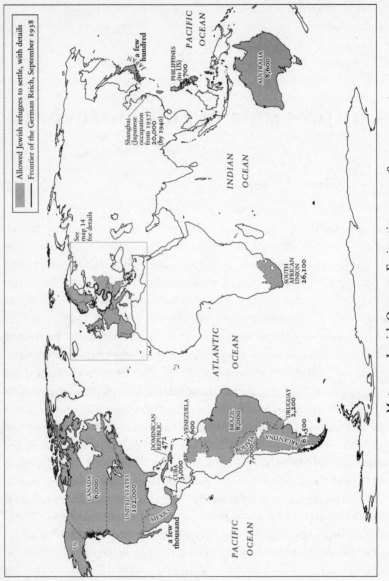

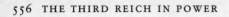

Allowed Jewish refugees to settle, with details

Frontier of the German Reich, September 1938

PACIFIC OCEAN

a few hundred

PHILIPPINES (to US) 700

Shanghai (Japanese occupation from 1937) 20,000 (by 1940)

AUSTRALIA 8,600

INDIAN OCEAN

See map 14 for details

SOUTH AFRICAN UNION 26,100

ATLANTIC OCEAN

CANADA 6,000

UNITED STATES 102,000

US

MEXICO

a few thousand

CUBA 3,000

DOMINICAN REPUBLIC 472

VENEZUELA 600

BRAZIL 8,000

BOLIVIA 7,000

ARGENTINA 63,500

URUGUAY 2,200

PACIFIC OCEAN

Map 13. Jewish Overseas Emigration, 1933–8

representatives of the Zionist movement in Germany and Palestine had signed a pact with the Nazi government on 27 August 1933. Known as the Haavara Transfer Agreement, it was personally endorsed by Hitler and committed the German Ministry of Economics to allowing Jews who left for Palestine to transfer a significant portion of their assets there – about 140 million Reichsmarks all told – while those who left for other countries had to leave much of what they owned behind.[98]

The reasons for the Nazis' favoured treatment of emigrants to Palestine were complex. On the one hand, they regarded the Zionist movement as a significant part of the world Jewish conspiracy they had dedicated their lives to destroying. On the other, helping Jewish emigration to Palestine might mitigate international criticism of antisemitic measures at home. Moreover, and crucially, the principal aim of the Nazis in these years was to drive the Jews out of Germany and preferably out of Europe too; for all the murderous violence they meted out to them, they did not at this stage intend, still less plan, to exterminate all Germany's Jews. A Germany free of Jews would, in Nazi eyes, be a stronger Germany, fit to take on the rest of Europe and then the world. Only when that happened would the Nazis turn to solving what they thought of as the Jewish problem on a world scale. The Zionists were prepared to do a deal with the Nazis if the result was a strengthening of the Jewish presence in Palestine. German Jews would bring much-needed skills and experience with them; they would also, many leading Zionists thought, bring money and capital for investment. In return, the Haavara Transfer Agreement, which formalized these arrangements, provided for the export of much-needed goods such as citrus fruit from Palestine to Germany as part of the exchange. On both sides, therefore, this was above all a marriage of convenience. But it was increasingly disputed within the Nazi regime itself. This was not least the consequence of the establishment of the Jewish Affairs Division of the SS Security Service in 1935. One of the principal sections of the organization, it was led by an increasingly radical group of young officers, including Dieter Wisliceny, Theodor Dannecker and Adolf Eichmann. These men became progressively more anxious that encouraging Jews to go to Palestine would accelerate the formation of a Jewish state there, with dangerous consequences for Germany in the long run, or so they thought.[99]

For Zionists, the cloud of persecution and discrimination, above all in

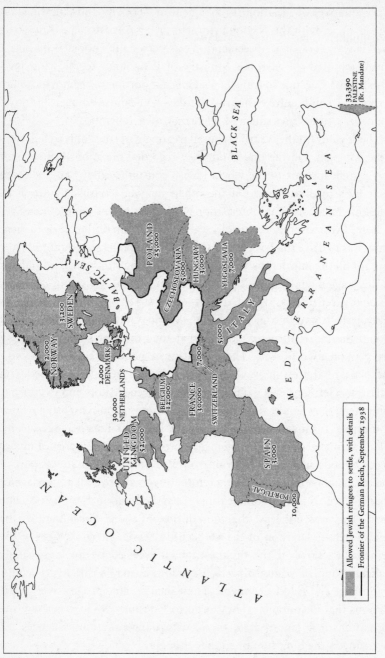

Map 14. Jewish Emigration within Europe, 1933–8

the shape of the boycott of 1 April 1933 and the subsequent civil service law, had a certain silver lining, for it brought Germany's deeply divided Jews closer together. Already in 1932, in the light of mounting antisemitic attacks, regional Jewish associations had decided to establish a national organization, which was set up on 12 February 1933. It did little apart from protesting that it had nothing to do with what the Nazis described as the international campaign for the boycott of German goods. It was not until September 1933 that this organization, together with others, including the German Zionists, set up an umbrella organization in the shape of the Reich Representation of German Jews under the chairmanship of the Berlin rabbi Leo Baeck. Its purpose was to regroup and defend Jewish life in the new Germany. Its leaders urged a dialogue with the Nazis, perhaps with a view to reaching a Concordat like the one the Third Reich had concluded with the Catholics. They emphasized the patriotic service many Jews had rendered the Reich at the front during the First World War. Jews were not the only Germans to believe that the violence that accompanied the seizure of power would soon dissipate, leaving a more stable, ordered polity. Leo Baeck even encouraged the preparation of a large dossier illustrating the Jewish contribution to German life.

But the dossier was banned before it could be published.[100] The financial penalties imposed on German Jews, the Aryanization of Jewish businesses and the tightening of restrictions on the export of currency and chattels ensured that German Jews found it increasingly difficult to obtain refuge in countries whose governments did not want immigrants if they were going to be a burden on the welfare system. Even finding the money to pay for a passage out of Germany had become a problem. The fact that an increasing proportion of German Jews was now near or over retirement age made things worse. Jewish immigrants of working age were often resented because unemployment remained high in many countries as a result of the Depression. Jewish organizations in receiving countries did their best to help by providing funds and opportunities for work, organizing visas and the like, but the extent to which they were able to influence government policy was very restricted, and they were hampered in addition by their own fear of arousing antisemitism at home.[101]

On 6 July 1938, a conference of thirty-two nations met at Evian, on the French shore of Lake Geneva, to discuss the growing international phenomenon of migration. The conference made an attempt to impose generally agreed guidelines, especially in the light of the possible expulsion of hundreds of thousands of destitute Jews from Poland and Romania. But it was careful not to upset German sensibilities at a time when international relations were becoming increasingly fraught. The German government did not take part, declaring Jewish emigrants to be an internal matter. One delegation after another at the conference made it clear that it would not liberalize its policy towards refugees; if anything, it would tighten things up. Britain and the European states saw themselves mainly as countries of transit, from which Jewish migrants would quickly disperse overseas. Anti-immigrant sentiment in many countries, complete with rhetoric about being 'swamped' by people of 'alien' culture, contributed further to this growing reluctance.[102]

At the same time, of course, the situation offered new opportunities for corrupt German officials, who frequently demanded money or goods in return for their agreement to apply the all-important rubber stamp to the papers of would-be emigrants. The temptation to enrich oneself was all the greater since the emigrants had to leave virtually everything behind. One Jew who applied for emigration papers was told by an official after preliminary formalities had been completed:

'Well, give me a thought when you emigrate, won't you?' I told him to say what he wanted, and I'd see what I could do. A few hours later, as I was having supper at home, the doorbell rang, and there was the official himself (in his uniform with a coat over it), and as I opened the door and was obviously surprised to see him there, he said he only wanted to tell me that he would very much like to have a round table and a rug about 2 metres by 3. And indeed our emigration permits were issued in an amazingly short time.[103]

To get round currency and other problems the Gestapo eventually organized illegal transports of Jewish emigrants, chartering boats to Palestine down the Danube via the Black Sea, and charging, as might be expected, hugely inflated prices for tickets.[104]

II

For those who stayed in Germany, the leaders of the Jewish community organized new institutional structures to try and alleviate the situation. A central Committee for Aid and Reconstruction was founded on 13 April 1933, following on a similar Central Institution for Jewish Economic Aid the previous month. These organizations raised loans for Jews who found themselves in economic difficulties, tried to find employment for Jews who had lost their jobs and ran retraining courses for Jews who wanted to go into agriculture or handicrafts (many of these subsequently emigrated). Increasingly, Jewish organizations rendered logistical, bureaucratic and sometimes financial assistance to those who wanted to emigrate. Until 1938 Jews were still entitled to public welfare benefits, so Jewish charities acted more in the way of a supplement than a substitution when it came to aiding the really destitute; however, as the Jewish community grew steadily more impoverished, so the work of the charities became increasingly important.[105]

The process of segregation had a particularly stark impact on Jewish children. In 1933 there were about 60,000 Jewish children aged from seven, the starting age for formal schooling, to fourteen, the age at which it ceased to be compulsory, in Germany, and a substantial further number who were enrolled in secondary schools. Emigration, particularly amongst Jews of child-bearing and child-rearing age, reduced the number of young Jewish people between six and twenty-five years of age from 117,000 in 1933 to 60,000 in 1938. The children had to face a concerted effort by the Nazis to drive them out of German schools. The Law Against the Overcrowding of German Schools and Universities, promulgated on 25 April 1933, together with its implementation orders, set a maximum for new admissions to all schools above the primary level of 1.5 per cent of non-Aryan children. At the same time, the rabid hostility of the Nazi Students' League drove most Jewish students out of the universities within a short space of time, so that only 590 were left in the autumn semester of 1933 compared to 3,950 in the summer semester of the previous year. In a similar way, the hostility of fanatical Nazi teachers and, increasingly, Hitler Youth activists in the schools had a powerful effect in driving Jewish children out. In Württemberg, for instance, while 11 per cent of Jewish pupils were forced to abandon their secondary education because of the Law, some 58 per cent broke it off as a result of the hostility of some teachers and children at their schools. So fierce was the pressure that even Education Minister Rust complained about it in May 1933, and repeated his strictures in July.

In some schools, Jewish children were made to sit on a special 'Jewish bench' in the classroom, and they were banned from German lessons. They had to listen to their teachers describing Jews as criminals and traitors. And they were not allowed to take part in ceremonies and festivals, concerts and plays. Teachers deliberately humiliated them and gave them bad marks for their work. Of course, the atmosphere varied strongly from school to school; in some working-class areas, the other children showed considerable solidarity with their Jewish classmates, while in small-town Germany, local bullies made their life a misery and caused them to live in permanent fear of being beaten up. The result of such pressure was that in Prussia the number of Jewish children in state secondary schools fell from 15,000 in May 1932 to 7,000 in May 1935 and just over 4,000 the following year; figures that almost certainly underestimate the scale of the decline, since they only include the children of parents of Jewish faith, not children classified as Jewish on racial grounds by the regime. By 1938, a mere 1 per cent of state secondary school pupils in Prussia was Jewish, and from January that year these young people were in any case officially excluded from sitting the common university entrance examination. The remaining Jewish school pupils were all summarily expelled at the end of the year.[106]

The expulsion of Jewish children from German state schools urgently demanded the provision of replacement educational facilities by the Jewish community. Parents from the acculturated Jewish middle class looked down on Germany's Jewish schools in 1933; many considered their standards low and did not share their religious stance. This applied particularly, of course, to the many parents of Christian faith who now suddenly found themselves classified by the regime as Jewish by race and thrown together with a community they had up to now studiously avoided. Many local Jewish communities had no educational facilities at all. Concerned parents, appalled at the isolation into which their children were being driven by the hostility they encountered in state schools, often took the lead in providing them. By 1935 over half of the

30,000 Jewish children of primary-school age were attending Jewish community schools, funded mostly by Jewish organizations. Finding trained teachers was difficult, and classes were often very large, with up to 50 children each, in cramped and inadequate accommodation. Especially in the secondary schools, children from widely varying backgrounds, abilities and educational experience were suddenly thrown together. Transport and travel were major problems for many parents and children. There were bitter quarrels between different ideological factions, Orthodox, liberal and secular, right and left, about the curriculum, which only died down as increasing discrimination and repression made them seem less important. By early 1937 there were 167 Jewish schools in Germany, attended by nearly 24,000 pupils out of a total of 39,000 in all. Emigration soon reduced their number; by October 1939 there were fewer than 10,000 Jewish schoolchildren left in Germany, and a number of Jewish schools had closed down. Their achievement was above all, perhaps, to provide an educational environment free from the ethos of race hatred, militarism and brute physical prowess that had come to dominate the vast majority of German schools by this time.[107]

Jewish self-help played a role in other areas too. Jewish sportsmen and women set up their own organization after Jews were expelled from mainstream sports clubs in 1933; in 1934 its members numbered no fewer than 35,000. An even more notable achievement was the Jewish Culture League, set up by the Jewish ex-deputy director of the Berlin City Opera, Kurt Singer. Eight thousand Jewish artists, musicians, performers and writers belonged to the Jewish Culture League, which catered exclusively for the Jewish community; 180,000 Jews eventually joined to take advantage of its offerings. Its foundation was officially approved by Hermann Göring. From the Nazi point of view, it was welcome because it marked the complete separation of Jewish cultural life from that of the nation as a whole, and at the same time reassured other Germans that Jews were not banned from writing, painting or performing. Singer was quickly elbowed aside, however, and the Culture League was run by a Nazi, Hans Hinkel, for most of its existence. Hinkel, working under the aegis of Göring, was responsible for the elimination of Jews from cultural institutions in Prussia, so it seemed to Göring obvious that he should run the Culture League as well. Hinkel soon began to ban the Culture League and its members from performing

German works, starting with medieval and romantic German plays and moving on to Schiller (1934) and Goethe (1936). Jewish musicians were not allowed to perform music by Richard Wagner or Richard Strauss; Beethoven was added to the list in 1937 and Mozart in 1938.[108]

In 1933–4 alone, however, the League put on sixty-nine opera performances and 117 concerts. But although some leading members saw such activities as an opportunity to show the contribution that Jewish artists and performers could make to German cultural life, many more must have been aware that they were evidence of a creeping ghettoization of Jewish culture in Germany. By gradually restricting what the Culture League could do, the Nazis were pushing it inexorably towards a situation where it provided nothing but 'Jewish' culture to audiences consisting of Jews alone. The cultural ghettoization of Germany's Jews was completed after 10 November 1938, when Jews were banned from attending German theatres, cinemas, concerts, lectures, circuses, cabarets, dances, shows, exhibitions and all other cultural events. Following this, all Jewish cultural institutions of whatever kind were merged into the centralized Jewish Culture League on 1 January 1939, including the remaining Jewish publishing houses. There were plenty of works to perform for Jewish audiences, including those of Jewish writers and composers banned by the Nazis on racial grounds. There were exhibitions of Jewish painters and readings from Jewish writers. Non-Jewish Germans, of course, were not allowed to go to these functions. Whether there really was a Jewish-German culture independent and separate from non-Jewish-German culture many, if not most, doubted; most Jewish writers, artists and composers had not really considered the possibility, but had regarded themselves simply as Germans.[109]

Paradoxically, perhaps, many Jews found the process of cultural ghettoization rather reassuring as they came to terms with the new restrictions on their life. As one of them remarked critically later: 'The Jews were left more or less undisturbed within the bounds that had been drawn for them. In the Jewish Culture League, in the Jewish school, in the synagogues, they could live as they pleased. It was only interference in the Aryans' sphere that was a taboo and a danger.'[110] This attitude was in many cases a psychological necessity for those who remained. Increasingly, these were the old and the poor. In 1933, 20 per cent of German citizens of the Jewish faith who had been born in Germany were aged 50 or over; by 1938, the proportion of the Jewish community in Germany aged 50 and above had risen to over 48 per cent; a year later, it was over half.[111] Many Jews were German patriots, their families deeply linked to their home towns and communities by decades, indeed centuries, of residence, work, culture and tradition. Breaking with all this was too hard for some to bear. Many left Germany in tears, vowing to come back when things got better. It was not surprising that many German Jews refused to emigrate, or indeed saw no need to do so. 'Why should I emigrate?' one middle-aged German Jew answered the entreaties of his anxious son in 1937. 'Not everything will be eaten as hot as it's cooked. After all, we live under the rule of law. What can happen to me? – I'm an old soldier, I fought for four years for my Fatherland on the Western Front, I was an NCO and was awarded the Iron Cross, First Class.'[112]

III

One particular group of Jews who stayed were those who were married to partners classified by the regime as Aryan. There were 35,000 couples living in mixed marriages in 1933 – that is, in marriages where the partners had come respectively from the Jewish and Christian faiths. Most such marriages were between Jewish men and Christian women. The Nuremberg Laws, of course, redefined the mixed marriage in racial terms. Mostly, by this time, both partners were Christian in religion. Non-Jewish spouses came under increasing pressure from the Gestapo to bring divorce proceedings. The courts had quickly begun to allow divorce petitions brought by non-Jewish spouses on the grounds, for instance, that only since National Socialism had come to power had they realized the dangers of race defilement. Because of the removal of Jews from virtually every area of public and social life by this time, Jewish husbands in mixed marriages had been forced to cede power over their children, their financial affairs, their assets, their businesses, their property and almost everything else to their non-Jewish wives. Increasingly, as economic opportunities were closed off to the husband, the wife became the principal breadwinner in the family. On 28 December 1938, acting on orders from Hitler, Göring issued new regulations governing the status of mixed marriages. In order to assuage the potential wrath of Aryan relatives, he declared that mixed marriages where the husband was Jewish and the children had been brought up as Christians, or where the wife was Jewish but there were no children, should be classified as 'privileged' and exempted, in a piecemeal way, from some of the discriminatory acts of the regime in the following years.[113]

In mixed marriages where the husband was Jewish and there were no children, or where the wife had converted to Judaism or the children had been brought up in the Jewish faith, then, there were no privileges. The pressure on non-Jewish wives caught in this situation to bring divorce proceedings was considerable and mounted steadily. Nazi marriage laws, enshrined above all in the Marriage Law of 6 July 1938, defined marriage as a union between two people of healthy blood, the same race and opposite sexes, concluded for the common good and the purpose of procreating children of healthy blood and raising them to be good German racial comrades. Mixed marriages clearly did not fall under this definition, and indeed new ones had been banned since September 1935. The new Law codified recent court decisions on existing mixed marriages and pushed them further. German-blooded people, as the Law put it, who were married to a Jewish spouse could now apply to have the marriage annulled purely on racial grounds. In addition, a Jewish man who had lost his livelihood could be sued for divorce by a non-Jewish wife on the grounds that he was failing in his duty to support his family. Separation for three years was now also a ground for divorce, so that if a Jewish husband had been in a concentration camp, or in exile abroad, for this period, his non-Jewish wife could divorce him without any problem. Increasing economic and other difficulties inevitably placed a huge strain on such marriages, and even without direct pressure being brought to bear by the Gestapo or various Party agencies, as it often was, breakdown was frequently the result. It took a good deal of courage, loyalty and love to maintain a mixed marriage in such circumstances.[114]

By 1938, however, people were becoming aware of the fact that divorce would mean not just additional hardship for a Jewish spouse, but also quite possibly violence, imprisonment, and death. When a non-Jewish spouse died, the Gestapo now customarily appeared within a day of the death being reported to the authorities and arrested the surviving Jewish husband or wife. The Gestapo, indeed, began a regular campaign of inviting Aryan women married to Jewish men into police headquarters for a friendly chat. Why would a good-looking blonde German woman want to carry on being married to a Jew in present circumstances? Surely life would be better divorced? She only had to say that National Socialism had dispelled her previous ignorance about the Jewish threat for the divorce to go through. Promises were mingled with threats. Divorce would bring glittering careers for her children, who would be reclassified as German, and economic improvement for her family, which would now be rid of the dependent spouse. Refusal would condemn the children to a shadowy existence, deprived because of their mixed race of many of the benefits and privileges that went with being purely German. If she did not divorce, the state would confiscate her property. Driven to desperation, a few German women in mixed marriages without children divorced in order to cling to their material assets and continued seeing their husbands in secret even after they had moved out of the family home. Many, however, resisted such pressure and reacted with outrage at the suggestion that they should divorce out of base pecuniary motives: what, they asked, did that imply about the reasons they had got married for in the first place?[115]

One such woman was Eva, wife of Victor Klemperer, who stood by him through all the vicissitudes of the 1930s. As a war veteran and the husband of an Aryan, he was still entitled to keep his job as a professor of French literature at Dresden's Technical University, but he was removed from examining, he was unable to find a publisher for his latest book, and his teaching was so severely restricted that attendance at his lectures fell to single figures and he felt in danger of being made redundant. He was dismayed still further by some of his Jewish friends' continuing illusions about the regime; all around him, Jewish colleagues were being dismissed and young Jewish families he knew were emigrating to Palestine. As a German nationalist, he was shocked by the extent to which other Jewish friends were taking on a more Jewish identity and losing their Germanness. He considered Zionism little better than Nazism. He saw his Jewish friends emigrating to Palestine, but had no thought of going there himself – 'anyone who goes there is exchanging nationalism and narrowness for nationalism and narrowness' – and in any case he felt that he could not adapt to another life at his age. He was, he wrote, a 'useless creation of excessive culture'.[116]

At the beginning of October 1934, he and his wife moved into the house they had long been having built for themselves at Dölzschen, a quiet suburb of Dresden.[117] They had scarcely put the house in order when Klemperer's situation began seriously to deteriorate further. In March 1935 the non-Nazi Saxon Minister of Education was dismissed and his duties taken over by the Nazi Party Regional Leader Martin Mutschmann. 'In all aspects of the destruction of culture, Jew-baiting, internal tyranny', Klemperer confided to his diary, 'Hitler rules with ever worse creatures.'[118] On 30 April 1935 he received his dismissal notice through the post, signed by Mutschmann. None of his colleagues did anything to help him; the only sympathy came from a secretary. Klemperer wrote to a number of colleagues abroad in search of a new job, but nothing materialized, and in any case he did not feel that his wife Eva, who was frequently ill, was strong enough to withstand the rigours of exile. Now in his mid-fifties, he had to live off a pension fixed at just over half his previous salary. He was saved by his older brother Georg, a successful surgeon, aged seventy and now retired, who had left Germany and made Victor a loan of 6,000 Reichsmarks, not the last such help he rendered to his distressed relatives. Meanwhile, however, antisemitic outrages became more frequent and more noticeable. In the middle of Dresden, Klemperer noticed a man shouting repeatedly, 'Anyone who buys from a Jew is a traitor to the nation!' On 17 September 1935 he noted the passage of the Nuremberg Laws. 'Disgust makes one ill.'[119] Deprived of his teaching, Klemperer doggedly continued to write his history of French literature in the eighteenth century, though the prospects of publishing it were minimal. In the meantime he spent a good deal of time going on expeditions in his new car and discussing with his friends the possibility – remote, he concluded – of the Third Reich collapsing. Everybody grumbled, he said, but nobody was prepared to do anything, and many saw the Third Reich as a necessary bulwark against Communism. Klemperer began to feel his views changing. 'No one can take my Germanness away from me,' he wrote, 'but my nationalism and patriotism are gone for ever.'[120]

Yet some found it easier to separate their enthusiasm for the Third Reich's nationalistic policies from their dismay at its antisemitism. When retired Major Friedrich Solmitz took on the position of Air Raid Protection League Block Warden soon after the Nazis came to power, he and his wife seemed all set to move comfortably into the Third Reich. Early in 1934, however, he had to write to Peter Schönau, the local Nazi Party Leader, resigning as Block Warden because of the latter's persistent hostility towards him. In all his dealings, Solmitz protested, he had followed the Party's orders, including the implementation of the Aryan Paragraph, meaning the exclusion of all Jews from positions of responsibility in preparing for air raids. He could not comprehend why he was being singled out for criticism. Yet, amazingly, the reason why Solmitz was coming under pressure was because he himself was Jewish.[121]

As far as their religion was concerned, the family were Christians and had no contact with the Jewish community, which no doubt explains why his wife, Luise Solmitz, in the privacy of her diary, noted in 1933 that in Hamburg 'no brownshirt is doing anything to the Jews, no curses fly after them, everyday life in Hamburg is just the same, everyone is going about his own business as always'.[122] Luise Solmitz had no Jewish ancestry. Yet even she found the Nazi boycott of Jewish shops carried out on 1 April 1933 a cause for concern, 'a bitter April Fool's joke'. 'Our entire soul', she complained, 'was oriented towards the rise of Germany, not towards this.' Nevertheless, she reflected, at least the Eastern European Jews were no longer in evidence ('the underworld creatures from East Galicia really do seem to have disappeared for the moment').[123] A year later she was becoming bitter about the discrimination from which her Jewish husband and half-Jewish daughter had to suffer. She was depressed to see

how Fr[iedrich] is at the mercy of every dishonourable rogue, how he is excluded from the SA and Steel Helmets, the National Socialist War Officers' Association, and the Academic Association. To know how every avenue of happiness, whether it is in professional or married life, will also be closed off for Gis[ela]! To tremble at every chance word, at every visit, every letter: what do people want of us?[124]

In 1935 Solmitz lost his citizenship rights as a consequence of the Nuremberg Laws, although he and his non-Jewish wife were subsequently classified as living in a privileged mixed marriage because they were bringing up their daughter in the Christian religion. The Nuremberg

Laws, she wrote on 15 September 1935, were 'our civil death sentence'. They meant that as in 1918 the family would now be banned from flying the Imperial flag (now adorned with the swastika), and much more:

Our black-white-red flag is lowered for the second time. – Any man who marries my daughter will land up in the penitentiary, and she with him. – The serving-maid has to be sacked ... Our child is cast out, excluded, despised, worthless. Who is really aware of the isolation from the people, the rootlessness, of the 'Jewish-related' woman, insofar as she does not draw on her own resources with a defiant 'despite everything I'm always with you', my people, my Fatherland? Most people, or many, will still reject Jewry, like I do; they have no relation to that side, and they don't want any. Have never had any, don't know any Jewish people. – And when we're together with our own racial comrades, every chance word terrifies us, every one shows the gulf.[125]

Outraged at their treatment, the Solmitzes wrote a personal letter to Hitler. It was referred to the local police and the Interior Ministry, who informed the couple that they could under no circumstances be exempted from the provisions of the Law.[126] Despite this, Luise Solmitz remained optimistic. The growing isolation of her daughter, and her bitterness at not being able to join the League of German Girls, continued to give her concern, but the family was comfortably off, and the family's national pride in Germany's achievements under the Third Reich more than compensated for any minor worries, which she dismissed in 1937 as 'biting midges on the summer lakes'.[127]

IV

And indeed, beginning late in 1935, the situation of the Jews in Germany eased a little for a while. The reason for this was unexpected, and in one sense at least, beyond the control of the Nazi regime. For in 1936 Germany was scheduled to hold the Olympic Games, a decision that had been taken by the International Olympic Committee well before the Nazis had come to power. The Winter Games were due to be held at the ski resort of Garmisch-Partenkirchen, the Summer Games in Berlin. Hitler was initially sceptical. Sport for its own sake had no appeal to Nazi ideology, and he found the internationalism of the event highly suspect. But when a boycott campaign was mounted, particularly in the United States, over the Third Reich's treatment of the Jews, he realized that the transfer of the Games elsewhere would be extremely damaging, and that the staging of the Games in Germany would provide an unmissable opportunity to influence world opinion in favour of the Third Reich. Preparations duly got under way. The German team contained no Jews: under pressure to avoid a US boycott, the German team managers had attempted to recruit Jewish athletes, but the denial of top-class training facilities to Jews in Germany since 1933 meant that none made the grade. Three half-Jews were called into the team, all of them living outside Germany, including the blonde fencer Helene Mayer. This seemed to be enough, along with the Germans' assurances that they would abide by the Olympic spirit, to ward off the threat of an international boycott.[128]

Elaborate preparations were made to show Germany's best face to the world. Goebbels's Berlin paper, *The Attack*, told Berliners: 'We must be more charming than the Parisians, more easygoing than the Viennese, more vivacious than the Romans, more cosmopolitan than London, and more practical than New York.'[129] Just to ensure the right impression, people with criminal records were arrested and expelled or imprisoned for the duration. A massive new stadium was constructed, with seats for 110,000 spectators, at the centre of a vast sporting complex on the north-western side of Berlin. The Games were broadcast across the world on radio and, for the first time, they were also televised, although only on an experimental basis, since hardly anyone possessed a set. Leni Riefenstahl, employing the saturation camera coverage that had been so effective in filming the 1934 Nuremberg Rally for *Triumph of the Will*, directed what is still the classic Olympic film, a celebration of human physical prowess that sat easily with both the Olympic ideal and Nazi ideology. Nazi and Olympic flags were hung out everywhere in the capital city, and at the opening ceremony a choir of 3,000 was directed by Richard Strauss in a performance of his newly written Olympic Hymn, following a rendition of the Horst Wessel Song. The Olympic flame was lit, Hitler declared the Games open and 5,000 athletes began the competitions.[130]

Hitler was only a guest at the Games, of course, which were staged by the International Olympic Committee, and when he began calling victorious German athletes to his box to receive his personal congratulations, he was sternly reminded by the Committee that he should not offend against the international spirit of the Games by discriminating between victors from different countries. Either he should congratulate them all without exception, or he should desist from congratulating anybody at all. Not surprisingly, he chose the latter course, though he continued to offer his felicitations to German victors in private; but this incident, and the fact that he left the stadium during the high-jump competition when the last German competitor had been eliminated, gave rise to the later legend that Hitler had snubbed the undoubted star of the Games, four-times gold medal winner Jesse Owens, by refusing to shake his hand because he was black, and walking out of the stadium when he came first in a race. Even Hitler, however, knew better than to ruin the impression the Games were making on international opinion by engaging in a petulant demonstration of this kind. As Albert Speer later reported, Hitler was indeed none too happy about Owens's victories, which he put down to the superior physical strength of primitive man: in future, he said in private, such unfair competition should be eliminated, and non-whites barred from taking part. Taken with the success of the Games, Hitler ordered Speer to design a new stadium many times larger than the existing one. In 1940 the Games would take place in Japan as planned, he conceded, but after that they would be permanently located in Berlin.[131]

'I'm afraid the Nazis have succeeded with their propaganda,' William L. Shirer wrote on 16 August 1936, as the Games ended. 'First, they have run the games on a lavish scale never before experienced, and this has appealed to the athletes. Second, they have put up a very good front for the general visitors, especially the big businessmen,' some of whom told the American correspondent that they had been 'favourably impressed by the Nazi "set-up"'. The story had been the same at the Winter Olympics earlier in the year, though Shirer had got into trouble with the Propaganda Ministry for filing a report that 'Nazi officials had taken all the good hotels for themselves, and had put the press in inconvenient bed-and-breakfast accommodation, which was true'. Shirer had also reported to his American readers that the Nazis at Garmisch had 'pulled down all the signs saying that Jews were unwanted (they're all over Germany) and that the Olympic visitors would thus be spared any signs of the kind of treatment meted out to Jews in this country'.[132] This was also true. Hitler explicitly distanced himself from *The Stormer* in June 1936 as a sop to international opinion, and copies of the paper were withdrawn from display in the Reich capital while the Games were on.[133] His major speeches in 1936 barely mentioned the Jews at all.[134] On 13 August 1936 Victor Klemperer noted that for the Nazi regime, the Olympics were

a through-and-through political undertaking. 'German Renaissance through Hitler', I read recently. People at home and abroad are constantly being told that they are here witnessing the revival, the blossoming, the new mind, the unity, the steadfastness and glory, of course also the peacefulness of the spirit of the Third Reich, that lovingly embraces the entire world. The slogan-chanting mobs are banned (for the duration of the Olympics), campaigns against the Jews, warlike speeches, everything disreputable has vanished from the newspapers until 16 August, and still, day and night, the swastika flags are flying everywhere.[135]

Nevertheless, despite all this, Hess's deputy Martin Bormann had reminded Party officials in February 1936 that 'the aim of the NSDAP, to shut out Jewry bit by bit from every sphere of life of the German people, remains irremoveably fixed'. That this aim had in no way been modified or abandoned became clear almost as soon as the Summer Olympics were over.[136]

V

Meanwhile, several thousand Jews who had left the country in 1933 had actually returned in the following years as the situation on the streets seemed to calm down in comparison to the mass violence of the seizure of power and the leading figures in the regime seemed to soft-pedal their antisemitic rhetoric. Restrictions placed by the French government on the employment of foreign workers as the Depression began to hit France severely in 1934 drove many German-Jewish exiles there back to their homeland. Noting the arrival of such 'elements who are to be looked upon as undesirable' in the early months of 1935, the Bavarian political police decreed:

It can basically be taken that non-Aryans have emigrated for political reasons, even if they have said that they went abroad to start a new life for themselves. Returning male emigrants will be sent to the Dachau concentration camp; returning women will go to the concentration camp at Moringen.[137]

Much worse was to come.[138] Moreover, whatever the cosmetic adjustments the Nazis made to their antisemitic policies in the course of 1936, the Aryanization of Jewish businesses continued unabated throughout the year, and indeed the promulgation of the Four-Year Plan in the autumn, as we have seen, brought with it a sharp acceleration of the programme's pace. It was accompanied by a fresh wave of intimidatory boycotts in many parts of the country, a fact that suggested strongly that many German shoppers were still patronizing Jewish businesses and that the Nazi leadership at every level was becoming increasingly frustrated at this situation. The Gestapo launched a concerted action to break the long-established custom of peasants in many parts of Germany using Jewish cattle-dealers to buy and sell their livestock. Peasant farmers who stubbornly kept up their links were threatened with the withdrawal of their hunting licences, the denial of Winter Aid and other measures, while Jewish cattle-dealers were arrested or physically expelled from markets and slaughterhouses, and their record-books confiscated and handed over to non-Jewish rivals. By the end of 1937, they had largely been driven out of business as a result.[139]

It was not until 1938, however, that violent action began again on a really large scale. Once again, the leadership of the Third Reich drove it on, Hitler to the fore. As the regime went over to a more aggressive military and foreign policy, it felt less need than previously to worry about possible foreign reactions to antisemitic violence. Carried out in a piecemeal way, the Aryanization of the economy was now within sight of its goal, and no economic disaster had occurred as a result of the removal of Jews from economic life. War was now looming, and it was essential from the regime's point of view to reduce the number of Jews in Germany faster so as to minimize the possibility of a replay of the 'stab-in-the-back' that had cost Germany the First World War – not the last time this fantasy was to play a key role in guiding the policies of Hitler and his leading associates. In the shadow of the coming war, portraying Germany's Jews once more as the enemy within would provide a significant means of preparing public opinion for the conflict. This new phase of antisemitic violence, the third following those of 1933 and 1935, was inaugurated by Hitler himself at the Party Rally on 13 September 1937, when he devoted a large part of his speech to attacking the Jews as 'inferior through and through', unscrupulous, subversive, bent upon undermining society from within, exterminating those cleverer than themselves and establishing a Bolshevik reign of terror. The speech was followed by antisemitic disturbances in Danzig, and then by a fresh wave of intimidatory boycotts of Jewish shops during the Christmas season. Recording a long private conversation with Hitler on 29 November 1937, Goebbels noted in his diary: 'The Jews must get out of Germany, indeed out of Europe altogether. That will take some time yet, but it will and must happen. The Leader is firmly resolved on it.'[140]

The new phase of persecution brought with it a whole new raft of laws and decrees that together significantly worsened the position of Germany's Jews. On 25 July 1938 all but 709 of the remaining 3,152 Jewish doctors lost their licence to practise; the 709 were denied the right to call themselves doctors but could continue treating Jewish patients, who would otherwise be deprived of medical care altogether. A decree of 27 September applied the same principle to Jewish lawyers; 172 out of 1,753 were allowed to continue working, only with Jewish clients; Jewish dentists, vets and apothecaries followed on 17 January 1939. On 28 March 1938 a new law on Jewish cultural associations deprived them of their previous status as public corporations with effect from the previous first of January, thus removing an important legal protection and opening them up to increased taxation. Other measures accelerated the Aryanization of the economy by banning Jews from further professions, removing tax concessions for Jews with children, forcing the registration of Jewish assets and more besides. The Interior Ministry began working out a new law, promulgated on 17 August, which made it compulsory for all Jews to bear a Jewish name, or if they did not, to add the name 'Israel' or 'Sara' to their existing names from 1 January 1939. Thus Jews could now be automatically identified from the personal identity papers which every German, by long custom, had been obliged to carry on his or her person and show to the authorities on demand. To many Jews, this law also made it humiliatingly clear that they were now in every respect inferior, marked out as a race apart. Faced with the unavoidable prospect of seeing her Jewish husband Friedrich carry the name Israel, Luise Solmitz worried about his depressed state of mind, which must have been typical for many in his position: 'The shame that is unavoidably coming with the 1. 1. 39 is gnawing at him, the dishonouring, depressing additional name.'[141]

Total separation from the rest of society, indeed, was what Berlin's Regional Party Leader, Joseph Goebbels, had in mind in the summer of 1938, as he reacted to complaints by visiting Regional Leaders from other parts of Germany about what they saw as the large number of Jews visible on the streets of the Third Reich's capital city. Goebbels commissioned a report from the Berlin police chief, Count Helldorf, which recommended a special identifying mark for Jews and for their shops, a special identity card for Jews, their removal from a whole range of professions, special compartments for them in trains, their confinement in a special quarter of the city and more. These ideas were now clearly becoming common currency. Heydrich's Security Service pointed out that it would be inadvisable for Berlin to go ahead on its own, even though fully a third of Germany's Jewish population now lived there; and in any case these measures were not linked to any coherent scheme of Jewish emigration. So they was not acted upon. Nevertheless, these proposals did not go away, and in the meantime the Berlin police raided a large, well-known café on the Kurfürstendamm and arrested 300 Jewish customers, including numerous foreigners. They included, the police announced, many criminal elements. This did not go nearly far enough for Goebbels, who called Helldorf in for a discussion. 'Aim – drive the Jews out of Berlin', he wrote in his diary on 4 June 1938, '. . . and without any sentimentality' – a purpose he also revealed to an audience of 300 senior police officers from Berlin on 10 June 1938. Goebbels was not acting on his own in this matter. A few days later, over 1,500 Jews were arrested on Hitler's personal orders in the course of a large-scale police action against 'asocials', beggars, down-and-outs and the like. These Jews – who were known to the police because of their previous criminal convictions, including of course contraventions of the race laws – were not intended, as the much greater numbers of 'asocials' arrested in this action were, for conscription as labourers. Their arrest was meant, rather, to put pressure on them to emigrate. Indeed, they were only released when arrangements had been made, through Jewish agencies, for their emigration. Beyond this, the action was also intended to equate Jews with criminality in the mind of the general public, an impression sedulously reinforced by reports in the daily press.[142]

All these speeches, laws, decrees and police raids signalled clearly to the Nazi Party rank and file that it was time to take violent action on the streets once more. The example of the mass scenes of violence in Vienna following the Nazi annexation of Austria in March 1938 was a further incentive.[143] Berlin's Nazis were encouraged by Goebbels and police chief Helldorf; they daubed the star of David on Jewish shops, doctors' surgeries and lawyers' chambers all over the city, looted a good number of them, and demolished three synagogues. The violence spread to other cities, including Frankfurt and Magdeburg. Hitler reined in this violence on 22 June, not least because it had affected many foreign Jews caught in the city at the time and relations with other countries were at a delicate point. This action was purely tactical, however. On 25 July 1938, Goebbels recorded a conversation in which Hitler had given his general approval to his actions in Berlin. 'The main thing is that the Jews are driven out. In 10 years they must be out of Germany.' How this was to be done was a matter of secondary importance. Foreign policy considerations currently forbade open violence, but it was not ruled out in principle.[144] Changing their tactics, the Berlin police issued a confidential 76-point list of ways in which Jews could be harassed without the law being broken in the process – by summoning them to police stations on the Sabbath, by pedantically applying health and safety regulations to Jewish premises, by delaying the processing of legal documents (unless they concerned emigration), and so on. Nevertheless, violence continued, sometimes with a legal pretext, sometimes without. After the local authorities in Nuremberg and Munich ordered the demolition of the main synagogues in their respective cities, Nazis trashed synagogues in at least a dozen other towns. In parts of Württemberg there were renewed attacks on Jewish premises, and Jewish inhabitants were pulled out of their homes, beaten and spat upon, and driven out of the towns in which they lived. Thanks to the officially sponsored actions of the previous few months, all Jewish shops and premises had been clearly marked, Jewish men, women and children issued with special identity papers and their domiciles specially registered with the police. They were all easy enough, therefore, to locate.[145] In the SS Security Service, plans began to be discussed for the arrest of all remaining Jews in the event of war breaking out. Finally, under ever-increasing pressure from Hitler to finance and deliver more armaments, the Four-Year Plan organization, with Hermann Göring in the lead, eyed the remaining Jewish property and assets in Germany with an increasing sense of urgency.[146]

The situation was building up to a pogrom-like atmosphere once more, as in the summer of 1935. Meanwhile, the regime began to take steps to expel all non-German Jews from the Reich. Aryan employers were ordered to dismiss all such employees in the autumn of 1937, following which up to a thousand Russian Jews were expelled from the country, although the process took longer than planned because of the unco-operative attitude of the Soviet authorities.[147] The following year, the SS Security Service turned its attention to the 50,000 Polish Jews resident in Germany. Forty per cent had actually been born in Germany, but from Heydrich's point of view they were all an irritation, since none of them was subject to German anti-Jewish laws. Worried that they might be returned, the antisemitic military dictatorship that ruled Poland passed a new law on 31 March 1938 that allowed it to remove Polish citizenship from these unfortunate people, who would then became stateless. Negotiations between the Gestapo and the Polish Embassy in Berlin got nowhere, and on 27 October the German police began arrest-ing Polish workers, sometimes together with their entire families, putting them on sealed trains under close guard and taking them to the Polish border. Eighteen thousand people were transported in this way, without any proper notice, without anything but the most minimal and basic luggage, and often without food or drink on the journey. Arriving at the border, they were driven out of the trains by the accompanying police and forced, often under blows, to the other side. Very quickly the Polish authorities sealed their side of the border so that the expellees were left to wander about aimlessly in no-man's land until the Polish government eventually relented and set up refugee camps for them just inside the border. When the Polish authorities ordered the expulsion of German citizens across the border in the other direction, the German police brought the action to a close, on 29 October 1938. Negotiations between the two governments finally led to the deportees being allowed back to Germany to collect their belongings before returning to Poland for good.[148]

THE NIGHT OF BROKEN GLASS

I

On 7 November 1938, a seventeen-year-old Pole, Herschel Grynszpan, who had grown up in Germany but was currently living in Paris, discovered that his parents were amongst those who had been deported from Germany to Poland. Grynszpan obtained a revolver and marched into the German Embassy, where he shot the first diplomat he came across: a junior official called Ernst vom Rath, who was seriously wounded and taken to hospital. The political atmosphere of early November 1938 was already heavy with antisemitic violence, as the regime and its most active supporters continued to step up the pressure on Germany's Jews to emigrate. It was not surprising that Goebbels decided to make the incident into a major propaganda exercise. That same day, the Propaganda Ministry instructed the press to give the incident a prominent place in its reporting. It was to be described as an attack by 'world Jewry' on the Third Reich that would entail the 'heaviest consequences' for Germany's Jews. This was a clear invitation to the Party faithful to act. Goebbels instructed the regional propaganda chief in Hesse to launch violent attacks on the synagogues and other buildings of the Jewish community to see whether a more widespread pogrom was feasible. While the stormtroopers swung into action, the SS and Gestapo were roped in to support the action as well. In Kassel the local synagogue was trashed by brownshirts. In other Hessian towns, as well as in parts of adjacent Hanover, there were also attacks and arson attempts on synagogues and on the houses and apartments of the local Jewish population. These acts of violence expressed, the orchestrated press declared on 9 November, the spontaneous rage of the German people against the outrage in Paris and its instigators. The contrast with the murder of a regional official of the Party, Wilhelm Gustloff, by David Frankfurter, a Jew, in February 1936, which did not elicit any kind of violent verbal or physical reaction from the Party, its leaders or its members because of Hitler's concern to keep international opinion sweet in the year of the Olympics, could not have been greater. It showed that the assault was the pretext for what followed, not the cause of it.[149]

By chance, when Grynszpan fired his shot on 7 November 1938, Hitler was due to address Nazi Party Regional Leaders and other senior members of the movement in Munich the next day on the eve of the anniversary of his failed putsch in 1923. Conspicuously, he did not mention the Paris incident in his speech; he was clearly planning action to follow vom Rath's death, which would surely not be long in coming. On the evening of 9 November, while the Party leaders were making their way to the main hall of the Munich town hall, Hitler was informed by his personal doctor, Karl Brandt, whom he had sent to keep watch by vom Rath's Parisian bedside, that the embassy official had died of his wounds at half-past five, German time. Thus the news reached not only him but also Goebbels and the Foreign Office late in the afternoon of 9 November. Hitler immediately issued instructions to Goebbels for a massive, co-ordinated, physical assault on Germany's Jews, coupled with the arrest of as many Jewish men as could be found and their incarceration in concentration camps. This was the ideal opportunity to intimidate as many Jews as possible into leaving Germany, through a terrifying, nationwide outburst of violence and destruction. Vom Rath's death would also provide the propagandistic justification for the final, total expropriation of Germany's Jews and their complete segregation from the rest of German economy, society and culture. Having taken these decisions, Hitler agreed with Goebbels that they should be presented to the Party faithful, in a calculated act of theatrical deception, as a spur-of-the-moment reaction to the assassination of vom Rath, taken in a spirit of sudden shock and anger.[150]

Over dinner at the town hall, where they could be observed by many of the participants, Hitler and Goebbels were accosted at around nine o'clock by a messenger, who announced to them what they had in fact already known since late afternoon, namely that vom Rath had succumbed to his wounds. After a brief, intense conversation, Hitler left for his private apartment, earlier than usual. Goebbels now spoke to the Regional Leaders, at around ten o'clock, announcing that vom Rath was dead. A subsequent report by the Party's Supreme Court took the story up at this point:

On the evening of 9 November 1938 the Reich Propaganda Leader Party Comrade Dr Goebbels informed the Party leaders who had gathered at the Old Town Hall in Munich for an evening of comradeship, that there had been demonstrations against the Jews in the regions of Electoral Hesse and Magdeburg-Anhalt, in the course of which Jewish shops had been destroyed and synagogues set alight. The Leader had decided on hearing his report that such demonstrations should neither be prepared nor organized by the Party, but that no obstacles should be placed in their way if they took place spontaneously . . . The Reich Propaganda Leader's verbal instructions were understood by the Party leaders who were present to mean that the Party should not appear publicly as the organizer of the demonstrations, but that it should in reality organize them and carry them out. The instructions were immediately – i.e. a good time before the sending of the first telegram – relayed by telephone in this sense by a large part of those Party comrades who were present to the offices in their regions.[151]

In the regional Party headquarters, officials telephoned stormtrooper commanders and Party activists in the localities, passing down the chain of command the order to burn down synagogues and wreck Jewish shops, houses and apartments. When Hitler and Himmler met in Hitler's rooms shortly before the traditional swearing-in of SS recruits at midnight, they briefly discussed the pogrom. As a result, another central command was issued, this time more formally, by telex at five minutes to midnight. It came from Heinrich Müller, Himmler's subordinate and head of the Gestapo, and it transmitted Hitler's personal order, also recorded by Goebbels in his private diary the following day, for the arrest of a large number of German Jews, to German police commanders across the country:

Actions against Jews, in particular against their synagogues, will very shortly take place across the whole of Germany. They are not to be interrupted. However, measures are to be taken in co-operation with the Order Police for looting and other special excesses to be prevented . . . The arrest of about

20–30,000 Jews in the Reich is to be prepared. Propertied Jews above all are to be chosen.[152]

A further telex sent by Heydrich at twenty past one in the morning ordered the police and the SS Security Service not to get in the way of the destruction of Jewish property or to prevent violent acts being committed against German Jews; it also warned that looting was not to be allowed, foreign nationals were not to be touched even if they were Jewish, and care was to be taken to ensure that German premises next to Jewish shops or synagogues were not damaged. As many Jews were to be arrested as there was room for in the camps. At 2.56 in the morning, a third telex, issued at Hitler's instigation from the office of his deputy, Rudolf Hess, reinforced this last point by adding that it had been ordered 'at the very highest level' that no fires were to be raised in Jewish shops because of the danger to nearby German premises.[153]

By this time, the pogrom itself was in full swing. The initial orders telephoned from Munich to the Regional Leaders' officers were rapidly transmitted further down the chain of command. A typical example was that of the SA leader for the Northern Mark, Joachim Mayer-Quade, who was in Munich to hear Goebbels's speech, and telephoned his chief of staff in Kiel at 11.30 in the evening. He told him:

A Jew has fired a shot. A German diplomat is dead. In Friedrichstadt, Kiel, Lübeck and elsewhere there are completely superfluous meeting-houses. These people still have shops amongst us too. Both are superfluous. There must be no looting. There must be no manhandling. Foreign Jews must not be touched. The action must be carried out in civilian clothing and be concluded by 5 a.m.[154]

Mayer-Quade had got Goebbels's message. His subordinates had no difficulty in understanding what this meant. Nor did others who received similar orders elsewhere. All over Germany, stormtroopers and Party activists were still celebrating the anniversary of the 1923 putsch in their headquarters when the orders arrived; many of them were drunk, and not inclined to take the warnings against looting and personal violence particularly seriously. Gangs of brownshirts sallied forth from their houses and headquarters, mostly in mufti, armed with cans of petrol, and made for the nearest synagogue. Soon virtually every remaining Jewish house of prayer and worship in the country was in flames. Alerted by the brownshirts, local policemen and fire services did nothing except protecting adjacent buildings from damage. Social Democratic agents later estimated that 520 synagogues were destroyed in this orgy of violence, but their information is likely to have been incomplete, and the true figure well over a thousand. After 10 November 1938 it was virtually impossible for Germany's remaining Jews to carry out their normal religious acts of public worship any more.[155]

Along with the synagogues, stormtroopers and SS men also targeted Jewish shops and premises. They smashed the display windows, leaving the pavements outside covered in a deep layer of broken glass. With their characteristically bitter, ironically understated humour, people in Berlin soon came to refer to 9–10 November as the 'Reich Crystal Night', or night of broken glass. But the stormtroopers smashed more than shop windows; everywhere, they broke into Jewish premises, trashed the contents, and looted what they could.[156] And then they made for the homes and apartments of Jewish families, with the same intent. In Düsseldorf, it was reported that ordinary Jews were awakened by the feared knock on the door from the Gestapo in the early hours of the morning:

While the Gestapo were searching the house, the SA men outside occupied themselves by demolishing the window-panes and the doors. Then the SS turned up, and went inside to carry out their work. Almost everywhere, every piece of furniture was smashed to smithereens. Books and valuables were thrown around, the Jewish inhabitants were threatened and beaten. Scenes of genuine horror were played out. Only now and again was there a decent SS-man who let it be clearly known that he was only doing his duty, because he had received an order to break into the flat or house. Thus we have been told that two students in SS uniform smashed one vase each and then reported to their superior: 'Orders carried out!'[157]

In many towns, gangs of stormtroopers broke into Jewish cemeteries and dug up and smashed the gravestones. In some, groups of Hitler Youth also took part in the pogrom. In Esslingen, brownshirts dressed in everyday clothes and armed with axes and sledgehammers broke into the Jewish orphanage at between midnight and one in the morning and destroyed everything they could, throwing books, religious insignia and anything else combustible onto a bonfire they lit in the yard. If they did not leave immediately, one stormtrooper told the weeping children, they too would be thrown onto the fire. Some of them had to walk all the way to Stuttgart to find accommodation.[158] All over Germany, shops and homes were looted, jewellery, cameras, electrical goods, radios and other consumer goods stolen. Altogether at least 7,500 Jewish-owned shops were destroyed, out of a total of no more than 9,000 altogether. The insurance industry eventually put the damage at 39 million Reichsmarks' worth of destruction caused by fire, 6.5 million Reichsmarks' worth of broken windows, and 3.5 million Reichsmarks' worth of looted goods. Only in the course of the morning of 10 November 1938 did policemen appear and stand guard before the ransacked premises to ensure there were no further thefts.[159]

What happened in the town of Treuchtlingen was not untypical of events in antisemitic Franconia. Just after midnight on 10 November 1938, the district SA commander, Georg Sauber, received a phone call instructing him to destroy the local synagogues in his area and arrest all male Jews. By 3 a.m. he had driven to Treuchtlingen and ordered the town's stormtroopers to be hauled out of bed and report to the fire station. Some of them went to the nearby synagogue, where they gathered outside the door of the adjacent house, shouting at its occupant, the synagogue's cantor Moses Kurzweil, to open up or be burned to death. Breaking down his door, they went from his house into the synagogue and set it alight. Within a short space of time it had been completely destroyed. The fire brigade arrived and began spraying water on the adjacent, Aryan-owned houses. Some local people gathered at the scene and, shouting encouragement to the brownshirts, went with them to a series of Jewish-owned shops, where they helped smash the windows and loot the contents. They moved on to Jewish homes, breaking and entering them and rampaging at will. One local Jewish man, Moritz Mayer, later reported that he was woken up between four and five in the morning of 10 November by the sound of footsteps in his garden: looking out of the window, he saw eight or ten stormtroopers, armed with axes, hatchets, daggers and revolvers, who broke into the house and were already smashing washbasins, mirrors, doors, cupboards and furniture by the time he had woken his family. Mayer was hit in the face and his glasses were broken; he was thrown into a corner and pelted with pieces of furniture. In the kitchen, the brownshirts smashed all the crockery, then, descending into the cellar, where Mayer's family were cowering in terror, they forced the women to break all the wine-bottles and preserving-jars. No sooner had they gone than local inhabitants and youths arrived on the scene, looting everything they could. Mayer and his family packed some clothes quickly and fled, accompanied by the derisive laughter of the mob, to the local train station, where they boarded a train to Munich, along with most of the rest of the town's ninety-three Jewish inhabitants.[160]

II

The extreme violence and deliberate, demeaning humiliation meted out to the Jews during the progrom was familiar from the behaviour of the brownshirts in the early months of 1933. But this time it went much further, and was clearly more widespread and more destructive. It demonstrated that visceral hatred of the Jews had now gripped not only the stormtroopers and radical Party activists but was spreading to other sectors of the population as well, above all, but not only, to the young, upon whom five years of Nazism in the schools and the Hitler Youth had clearly had an effect.[161] Going out onto the streets of Hamburg the morning after the pogrom, Luise Solmitz found 'silent, astonished and approving people. A hateful atmosphere. – "If they shoot our people dead over there, then this action has to be taken" decided an elderly woman.'[162] In the Saarland Jews were said to have been too frightened to go out onto the street in the days following the pogrom:

As soon as one appears in public, swarms of children run after him, spit after him, throw dirt and stones at him or make him fall over by "pecking" at his legs with bent sticks. A Jew who is persecuted in this way dare not say anything or he will be accused of threatening the children. The parents lack the courage to hold the children back, because they fear this will cause difficulties.[163]

Children, the report added, had often been taught at school to regard the Jews as criminals, and had no compunction about looting their property.[164] Nevertheless, while young Germans in the particularly antisemitic region of Franconia and some other areas willingly took part in the pogrom, the story in some parts of Germany was often rather different. 'Man', a Berlin transport worker was overheard telling a friend the day after the pogrom, 'no one can tell me that the people have done that. I've slept the whole night through and my workmates have slept as well and we belong to the people, don't we?'[165]

In Munich, Friedrich Reck-Malleczewen found himself revolted by 'all this misery and this immeasurable shame' after witnessing the events of 9–10 November 1938 in Munich. He admitted he was unable to understand it.[166] Elswhere, there were isolated reports that policemen had warned Jews in advance in a few places and so enabled them to go into hiding to avoid the violence. The Social Democrats, while conscientiously recording incidents in which local people had participated in the pogrom, concluded on balance that the popular reaction in many places had been one of horror. In Berlin, it was reported, popular disapproval 'ranged from a contemptuous glance and attitude of repulsion to open words of disgust and even dramatic abuse'.[167] The writer and journalist Jochen Klepper, whose wife was Jewish, reported in his diary on 10 November 1938:

We hear from the various 'Jewish' quarters of the city how the people are rejecting such organized actions. It is as if the antisemitism that was still plentifully present in 1933 had to a large degree disappeared since the excesses of the Nuremberg Laws. But it's probably different with the Hitler Youth, which includes, and educates, all young Germans. I don't know how far the parental home can supply a counterweight there.[168]

Melita Maschmann later remembered that she had been taken aback by the damaged shops and the mess on the streets when she had gone into Berlin on the morning of 10 November 1938; asking a policeman what had happened, she had learned that the wrecked premises were all Jewish. 'I said to myself: The Jews are the enemy of the new Germany. Last night they had a taste of what this means.' And with that, she 'forced the memory of it out of my consciousness as quickly as possible'.[169] There were many who thought like her. Institutions that claimed to give a moral lead remained silent too. Some individual pastors criticized the violence and destruction, but the Confessing Church took no stand, and when it came some time later to allude to the situation of the Jews, it was only for the Jews of Christian faith that it asked its members to pray.[170] A number of Catholic priests cautiously and rather obliquely hinted at their disapproval of the pogrom by giving particular emphasis

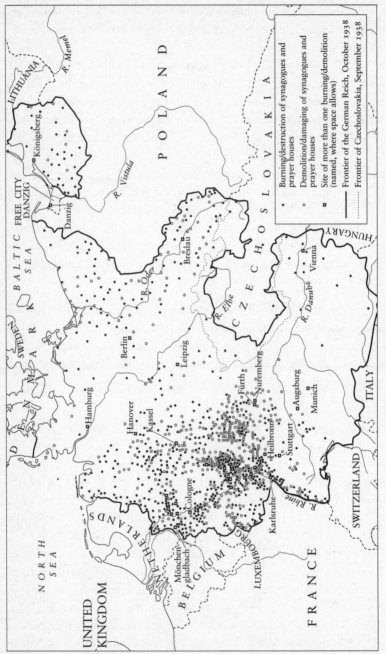

Map 15. Synagogues Destroyed on 9–10 November 1938

to the 'Jewish components in Christian teaching and history' in their sermons, as regional authorities in Bavaria noted.[171] One priest, Provost Bernhard Lichtenberg of Berlin, declared on 10 November 1938 that the synagogue that had been burned down during the night was also a house of God. But the time when, as in 1933, senior dignitaries of the Catholic Church like Cardinal Faulhaber had spoken out openly against pride in one's own race degenerating into hatred of another seemed to be long gone.[172] Some ordinary Catholics at least feared they might be next. A passer-by in Cologne on the morning of 10 November 1938 encountered a crowd standing in front of the still-smouldering synagogue. 'A police-man came up. "Move along, move along!" Upon this a Cologne woman said: "Are we not allowed to think about what we're supposed to have done?"'[173] Nevertheless, the Third Reich had passed a milestone in the persecution of the Jews. It had unleashed a massive outbreak of unbridled destructive fury against them without encountering any meaningful opposition. Whether people's sensibilities had been dulled by five years of incessant antisemitic propaganda, or whether their human instincts were inhibited by the clear threat of violence to themselves should they express open condemnation of the pogrom, the result was the same: the Nazis knew that they could take whatever further steps against the Jews they liked, and nobody was going to try to stop them.[174]

In Munich, meanwhile, Goebbels had been thoroughly enjoying the looting and destruction vented upon the city's Jewish community. 'The Hitler shock-troop gets going immediately to clear things out in Munich,' he noted in his diary recording the events of the night of 9–10 November 1938. 'That then happens straight away. A synagogue is battered into a lump ... The shock-troop carries out frightful work.' Led by Julius Schaub, a long-time Nazi who had taken part in the failed beer-hall putsch of 1923 and had served as Hitler's personal adjutant ever since 1925, the violence clearly reflected the atmosphere present in Hitler's immediate entourage during the night. 'Schaub is completely worked up,' Goebbels noted: 'His old shock-troop past is waking up.'[175] On receiving a phone call at about 2 a.m. with the news of the first Jewish death, Goebbels replied 'that the man reporting it should not get upset because of one dead Jew; thousands of Jews were going to cop it in the coming days.'[176] He could scarcely conceal his glee:

In Berlin 5, then 15, synagogues burn down. Now the people's anger is raging. Nothing more can be done against it for the night. And I don't want to do anything either. Should be given free rein . . . As I drive to the hotel, windows shatter. Bravo! Bravo! The synagogues are burning in all big cities. German property is not endangered.[177]

As dawn broke, however, he began to consult with Hitler, probably over the phone, on how and when the action should be brought to an end. 'New reports rain down all morning,' he wrote in his diary entry for 10 November 1938. 'I consider with the Leader what measures should be taken now. Let the beatings continue or stop them? That is now the question.' Following this conversation, he drafted an order to halt the pogrom and took it to Hitler, who was lunching at the Osteria, his favourite Munich restaurant. 'I report to the Leader at the Osteria,' he wrote. 'He agrees with everything. His views are totally radical and aggressive. The action itself has taken place without any problems.' Hitler approved the draft decree; it was read out over the radio the same afternoon and printed on the front pages of the newspapers the following morning. The pogrom was finally over.[178]

Many Jews had been seriously injured in the course of the violence. Even the official report on the pogrom by the Nazis estimated ninety-one Jewish deaths. The true number will probably never be known, but it was certainly many times greater, above all when the maltreatment of the Jewish men after they were arrested is taken into consideration, along with at least 300 suicides caused by the despair it engendered; deaths undoubtedly ran into the hundreds and probably numbered between one and two thousand.[179] Moreover, for many Jewish men, the violence continued well after the pogrom itself was over. As the police, storm-troopers and SS units, following Hitler's orders, arrested all the Jewish men they could find, terrible scenes took place on the streets and squares of every German town. In Saarbrücken the Jews were made to dance and kneel outside the synagogue and sing religious songs; then most of them, wearing only pyjamas or nightshirts, were hosed down with water until they were drenched. In Essen stormtroopers manhandled Jewish men and set their beards alight. In Meppen, Jewish men had to kiss the ground in front of SA headquarters while brownshirts kicked them and walked over them. In many places they were forced to wear placards round their necks with slogans such as 'We are the murderers of vom Rath'. In Frankfurt am Main, the arrested men were greeted at the train station by a crowd which shouted and jeered at them and attacked them with clubs and sticks. In some places, whole classes were taken out of school to spit on the Jews as they were being led away.[180]

Altogether about 30,000 Jewish men were arrested between 9 and 16 November and transported to Dachau, Buchenwald and Sachsenhausen. The camp population of Buchenwald doubled from around 10,000 in mid-September 1938 to 20,000 two months later. Moritz Mayer was picked up in Munich along with most of the other Jewish men from Treuchtlingen and taken to Dachau, where he had to stand to attention for hours in the November cold along with the others, dressed only in a shirt, socks, trousers and jacket. Anyone who moved was beaten by the SS guards. The beds had been removed from the camp barracks in preparation and the men were packed in, sleeping on straw on the hut floors. Washing was out of the question, and there were only two makeshift latrines. With the new, mass arrival of Jews in the camps, arrested for no other reason, or even pretext, than that they were Jews, the atmosphere changed, and the SS guards forgot the rules that had been established by Theodor Eicke a few years before. Mayer saw SS guards at Dachau beat an old man to the ground when he forgot to add the title 'prisoner in protective custody' to his name at roll-call; his injuries were so severe that he died. Another old man with a weak bladder was beaten to death on the spot when he asked the SS at roll-call for leave to use the latrines. The death-toll at Dachau had been running at between twenty-one and forty-one a year from 1933 to 1936; in September 1938, twelve prisoners died, in October, ten. After the arrival of the Jewish prisoners, the death-toll rose to 115 in November and 173 in December, making 276 for the year overall.[181]

Goebbels's Propaganda Ministry lost no time in presenting these events to the world as a spontaneous outburst of righteous anger on the part of the German people. 'The blow struck at us by international Jewry', the *Göttingen Daily News-Sheet* (*Göttinger Tageblatt*) told its readers on 11 November 1938, 'was too powerful for our reaction to be only verbal. A fury against Judaism pent up for generations was unleashed. For that the Jews can thank their racial fellow member Grünspan [i.e. Grynszpan], his spiritual or actual mentors and themselves.' Yet, the paper assured readers, 'the Jews themselves were treated quite well in the course of what happened'.[182] In similar vein, the flagship Nazi daily, the *Racial Observer*, reported, with a disregard for the truth that went beyond even what was normally to be found in its pages:

All over the west side of Berlin, as in other parts of the capital where Jews still swagger and strut, not a single storefront window of a Jewish business has remained intact. The anger and fury of the citizens of Berlin, who maintained the greatest discipline despite everything, was kept within definite limits, so that excesses were avoided and not a single hair was touched on a Jewish head. The goods on display in the store windows, some of which were decorated in a quite magnificent manner, remained untouched.[183]

Even more brazenly, the Propaganda Ministry instructed the papers on 10 November to claim that 'here and there window-panes had been smashed; synagogues had set themselves alight or burst into flames in some other way'. The stories, Goebbels insisted, should not be given too much prominence in the press, which of course was read outside Germany as well as within, and there were to be no pictures of the damage.[184]

On 11 November 1936, in the *Racial Observer*, Goebbels attacked the 'hostility to Germany of the mostly Jewish foreign press' for over-reacting to the pogrom. In a widely syndicated article, replete with headlines such as 'Last Warning to the Jewry of the World', he dismissed such reports as lies. The spontaneous reaction of the German people to the cowardly murder of vom Rath came from a 'healthy instinct'. 'The German people', he declared proudly, 'are an antisemitic people. They take no pleasure or delight in allowing themselves to be restricted in their rights or allowing themselves to be provoked as a nation by the parasitic Jewish race.' The government, he concluded, had done all in its power to stop the demonstrations, and the people had obeyed. Germany and the Germans had nothing to be ashamed of.[185] This was not the view taken by the international press, however, who reacted with a mixture of shock and disbelief. For many foreign observers, indeed, the events of 9–10 November 1938 came as a turning-point in their estimation of the Nazi regime.[186]

III

At their lunchtime meeting in the Osteria restaurant in Munich on 10 November 1938, Hitler and Goebbels, besides finalizing the draft of the decree bringing the pogrom to an end, also discussed what was to be done next. Hitler now took up once more the idea he had mooted in his memorandum on the creation of the Four-Year Plan back in 1936: a law making Germany's Jews collectively liable for any damage caused to the German people 'by individuals from this criminal element'.[187] 'The Leader', confided Goebbels to his diary, 'wants to take very tough measures against the Jews. They must themselves put their businesses in order again. The insurance companies will not pay them a thing. Then the Leader wants a gradual expropriation of Jewish businesses.'[188] Such measures indeed were already in train; on 14 October 1938, Goebbels had announced to a confidential meeting that the time had come to drive the Jews out of the economy altogether. Two weeks later, on 28 October, the banks had noted that Heydrich's Foreign Currency Control Office was preparing measures to restrict the Jews' power of disposal over their own assets. Since these assets had recently been registered, Hitler's 'compensation' order of 10 November 1938 could be implemented immediately. The responsibility for taking these steps lay with Hermann Göring, as head of the Four-Year Plan, and Hitler telephoned him on 11 November 1938 ordering him to call a conference to this effect. It met on 12 November 1938. Göring took the chair, and the hundred or so participants included Goebbels, Heydrich, Finance Minister Schwerin von Krosigk, Economics Minister Walther Funk and representatives of the police, the Foreign Ministry and the insurance companies. Elaborate minutes were taken. They were very revealing of the attitude of the Nazi leadership towards the Jews in the aftermath of the pogrom.[189]

Göring began by reporting to the assembled participants that Hitler had ordered him in writing and on the phone to co-ordinate the final expropriation of the Jews. He complained, with a touch of irony, that the 'demonstrations' of 9–10 November had harmed the economy; consumer goods made by, and belonging to, the people had been destroyed. 'I would have preferred it', he said, 'if you had beaten 200 Jews to death and hadn't destroyed such valuable property.' Goebbels added that the economy was not the only area from which the Jews now had to be removed. It was still possible, for example, he said, for them to share a compartment with Germans on a train. The minutes continued:

Goebbels: . . . They will be given a separate compartment only after all Germans have secured seats. They are not to mix with Germans, and if there is no more room, they will have to stand in the corridor.

Göring: In that case I think it would be more sensible to give them separate compartments.

Goebbels: Not if the train is overcrowded!

Göring: Just a moment. There will be only one Jewish coach. If that is full up, the other Jews will have to stay at home.

Goebbels: Suppose, though, there aren't many Jews going to the express train to Munich, suppose there are two Jews in the train and the other compartments are overcrowded. These two Jews would then have a compartment all to themselves. Therefore, Jews may claim a seat only after all Germans have secured one.

Göring: I'd give the Jews one coach or one compartment. And should such a case as you mention arise and the train be overcrowded, believe me, we won't need a law. We'll kick him out and he'll have to sit alone in the lavatory all the way![190]

Goebbels also wanted Jews banned from all remaining public facilities such as parks and gardens, beaches and resorts, insofar as they were not already. The separation of the Jews from the rest of German society was to be complete: and indeed an order was duly issued the same day by the Reich Chamber of Culture banning Jews from going to the cinema, the theatre, concerts and exhibitions. The Interior Ministry ordered them to surrender all firearms and forbade them to carry offensive weapons. Municipalities were given the right to ban them from certain streets or districts at specified times. Himmler withdrew their driving licences and vehicle registration documents. Another order, effective from 6 December 1938, prohibited Jews from using sports or playing fields, public baths and outdoor swimming pools.[191]

However much they may have disagreed on minor details, Göring,

Goebbels and the others present at the meeting held on 12 November 1938 agreed unanimously to issue a string of decrees giving concrete form to the various plans for the expropriation of the Jews that had been discussed over the previous weeks and months. The murder of vom Rath, which Goebbels's propaganda apparatus had already blamed on a Jewish conspiracy, provided an ideal opportunity, but if it had not occurred, then something else would doubtless have served as a pretext instead. The issue of railway compartments was solved by Hitler, with whom Göring discussed the matter in December. The Leader decreed that no special compartments for Jews should be allowed, but they should be barred from using sleeping compartments or dining cars on long-distance expresses. He confirmed that Jews could be banned from well-known restaurants, luxury hotels, public squares, much-frequented streets and smart residential districts. Meanwhile, Jews were also barred from attending university. On 30 April 1939 they were stripped of their rights as tenants, thus paving the way for their forcible ghettoization. They could now be evicted without appeal if a landlord offered them alternative accommodation, no matter how poor. Municipal authorities could order Jews to sublet parts of their houses to other Jews. From the end of January 1939, all tax concessions were also removed from the Jews, including child benefits; they were now taxed at a single rate, the highest one.[192]

As an immediate result of the meeting on 12 November, the Jews were ordered the same day to pay a collective fine of 1 billion Reichsmarks as atonement for the murder of vom Rath. All Jewish taxpayers were ordered on 21 November to pay a fifth of all their assets, as declared the previous April, in four tax instalments by 15 August 1939. In October 1939 the proportion was raised to a quarter on the grounds that the total sum of a billion Reichsmarks had not been reached, although in fact the total collected was no less than 1.127 billion. In addition, they were commanded to clear up the mess left by the pogrom at their own expense, and to pay for the repair of their own properties even though it had everywhere been damaged by the stormtroopers and they themselves were entirely blameless. All insurance payments to Jewish property-owners for the damage caused by the stormtroopers and their helpers were confiscated by the state. This last sum amounted to 225 million Reichsmarks, so that if it is added to the fine and to capital flight taxes, the total sum plundered from the Jewish community in Germany in 1938–9 reached well over 2 billion Reichsmarks, even before profits gained from Aryanization are taken into account.[193]

Another measure promulgated on 12 November, the First Decree on the Exclusion of Jews from German Economic Life, banned Jews from almost all remaining gainful occupations in Germany and ordered any still engaged in them to be dismissed without compensation or pensions. A few weeks later, on 3 December 1938, a Decree on the Utilization of Jewish Assets ordered the Aryanization of all remaining Jewish businesses, allowing the state to appoint trustees to complete the process if necessary. Already on 1 April 1939, nearly 15,000 of the 39,000 Jewish businesses still in existence in April 1938 had been wound up, some 6,000 had been Aryanized, just over 4,000 were undergoing Aryanization, and just over 7,000 were under investigation for the same purpose.[194] All these, the press trumpeted in anticipation on 12 November, were 'justified retributive measures for the cowardly murder of Ambassadorial Counsellor vom Rath'.[195]

On 21 February 1939, all Jewish cash, securities and valuables, including jewellery (except for wedding rings), were ordered to be deposited in special blocked accounts; official permits were required for any withdrawals from them. Permits were rarely if ever issued, and the Reich government eventually seized these accounts without compensation. In practice, therefore, almost all Jews who stayed in Germany were virtually penniless and had increasingly to depend for support on the charitable activities of the Reich Association of Jews in Germany, which had been created on 7 July 1938 as a more pliant and subordinate successor of the Reich Representation. Hitler explicitly ordered it to be kept in existence so that the Reich was not faced with the obligation to give support to Jews who had become utterly destitute. Other leading Nazis, however, argued that the now destitute and frequently unemployed Jews who had not yet reached retirement age – about half the remaining population – should be put to work for the Reich rather than being allowed to remain idle. Plans had already begun in October 1938, well before the pogrom, and were firmed up at a meeting called by Göring on 6 December 1938. On 20 December 1938, the Reich Unemployment Agency instructed regional labour exchanges to ensure that, since the number of unemployed Jews had increased substantially, such people should be put to work, freeing up Germans for armaments production.

On 4 February 1939, Martin Bormann repeated this instruction. Jewish workers were to be kept separate from the others. Firms that employed them would not suffer any disadvantage. Some were drafted into farm work, others in menial tasks of one kind or another. Labour service became the favoured means of keeping destitute Jews off the streets after they had been removed from the public welfare system. By May 1939, around 15,000 unemployed Jews were already employed on forced labour schemes, carrying out tasks such as rubbish collection, street-sweeping, or road construction; the ease of separating them from other workers meant that the last-named quickly became the main area into which they were drafted, and by the summer of 1939 some 20,000 were employed on heavy construction work for the motorways, work for which many of them were physically totally unprepared. Jewish forced labour remained on a relatively small scale in 1939, but already it was clear that it would reach much greater dimensions once war came, and plans were drawn up early in the year for the creation of special labour camps in which Jewish work draftees would be housed.[196]

IV

When, on 16 November 1938, Heydrich finally ordered the arrests of Jewish men in the wake of the pogrom to stop, he did not do so with the purpose of simply releasing them back into society to continue their life in the Third Reich, such as it was. All Jews over sixty, sick or handicapped Jews and Jews involved in Aryanization processes were to be freed immediately. The release of others was made conditional in many cases on their promise to leave the country. Moritz Mayer's wife was told that he would not be released until his brothers and sisters, who had already emigrated, made over their share in his property to him; he was released on condition that he sell his house and business. Turning over the negotiations to a local non-Jewish businessman, Mayer left for Palestine with his brother Albert and their families in February 1939, never to return.[197] As his example makes clear, the pogrom can only be understood in the context of the regime's drive to force Jews to emigrate and thereby bring Jewish life in Germany to an end. The SS Security Service reported shortly afterwards that Jewish emigration had

considerably declined and . . . almost come to a standstill as a consequence of the defensive posture of foreign countries and the lack of sufficient currency reserves in their possession. A contributory factor was the absolute resignation of the Jews, whose organizations only carried on performing their task under increased pressure from the authorities. In this situation, the November-action brought about a fundamental change.

The 'radical procedure against the Jews in the November days', continued the report, had 'increased the Jewish community's will to emigrate . . . in the highest degree'. In the following months, measures were taken to try and translate this will into action.[198]

In January 1939, Heydrich took the further step of ordering police authorities all over Germany to release all Jewish concentration camp prisoners who had emigration papers in their possession, and to tell them that they would be returned to the camp for life if they ever came back to Germany. There were still many Jewish men in the camps at this point, following the mass arrests of 9–10 November the previous year, and they were given three weeks to leave the country after their release.[199] Yet at the same time, Nazi policies within Germany were actually making it more difficult for Jews to leave. The bureaucratic formalities that accompanied the application process for emigration were so complicated that they made it impossible for all but a few of those arrested in November 1938 to meet the three-week deadline. Jewish agencies worked reasonably well with officials in the Reich Interior Ministry, often former Nationalists or Centre Party members, in organizing emigration up to 30 January 1939, but at this point Göring, as head of the Four-Year Plan, passed the task of arranging Jewish emigration over to the Reich Centre for Jewish Emigration, founded on 24 January 1939 under Heydrich's control. Jews' funds were blocked so that they could not pay their passage to America. One of the aims of the Centre was 'to take care that the emigration of poorer Jews is given preferential treatment' since, as a Foreign Ministry circular noted in January 1939, 'it would increase antisemitism in the western countries, in which Jews have found refuge . . . It is emphasized that it is in the German interest to pursue the Jews as beggars over the borders, for the poorer the immigrant, the greater the burden on the receiving country.'[200]

Despite all these obstacles there was a sharp rise in Jewish emigration from Germany after the pogrom and the arrests. Panic-stricken Jews crowded foreign embassies and consulates in their desperation to obtain entry visas. The numbers who succeeded in getting them are almost impossible to estimate, but according to Jewish organizations' own statistics, there were about 324,000 Germans of Jewish faith still in the country at the end of 1937, and 269,000 at the end of 1938. By May 1939 this figure had fallen again to just under 188,000, and it fell again to 164,000 by the outbreak of war in September 1939. The official census taken at this time showed that there were 233,646 racially defined Jews left in Germany. Of them, 213,930 adhered to the Judaic faith, leaving around 20,000 Jewish members of the Christian Churches. Roughly 26,000 of the total were foreign Jews, however, so according to the official figures there were around 207,000 German Jews left in the 'old Reich' by this time, about 187,000 of whom practised the Judaic faith. In effect, therefore, the figures supplied by Jewish organizations were roughly correct, since Christian Jews and foreign Jews more or less cancelled each other's numbers out.[201]

According to one estimate, 115,000 Jews left Germany in the ten months or so between 10 November 1938 and 1 September 1939, making a total of around 400,000 who had fled the country since the Nazi seizure of power. Most were now fleeing to countries outside the mainland of Europe: in all, 132,000 to the USA, around 60,000 to Palestine, 40,000 to the United Kingdom 10,000 each to Brazil and Argentina, 7,000 to Australia, 5,000 to South Africa, and 9,000 to the free port of Shanghai, which was to prove an unexpectedly accommodating refuge well into the war. Many more Germans who were classified as Jewish even though they did not practise the Jewish faith joined the flood of emigrants. So many people fled in terror without even a passport or a visa that neighbouring states began to set up special camps for them. Before the pogrom, the question of whether or not to emigrate had been a topic of continual and impassioned debate among Germany's Jews; afterwards, there was no doubt left. There was no pretence any more on the part of the regime that Jews would be protected by law; they were, in effect, fair game for any Nazi activist or official to exploit, beat,

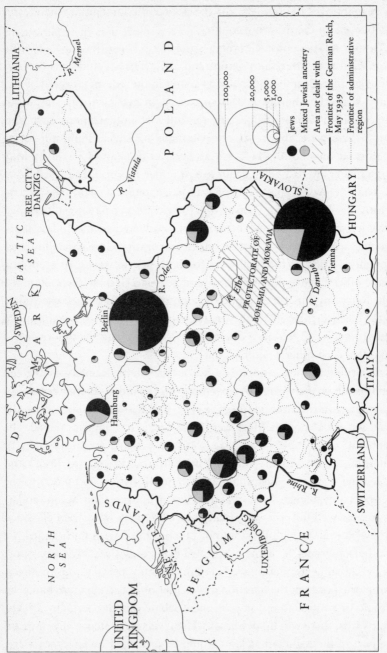

Map 16. Jews in the Nazi Racial Census of 1939

arrest or kill. For many Jews, the shock of the pogrom was profound, destroying any last illusion they might have had that their patriotism, their war service, their skills, their education, or even the fact that they were human beings would protect them from the Nazis.[202]

Already at the Evian conference it had been clear that nativists and xenophobes in a number of countries were pressuring their governments to halt Jewish immigration from Germany in case their native culture became 'swamped' – hardly a likely prospect when the overall numbers of German Jews were so small, even leaving aside other considerations. By the same token, however, Jewish children could be acculturated into their host nations relatively easily; and the shock that went round the world at the events of 9–10 November 1938 and the subsequent drastic deterioration of the situation of the remaining Jews in Germany prompted a range of schemes to provide Jewish children with new homes abroad. Seventeen hundred children were sent to Holland, and more than 9,000 to the United Kingdom. But an attempt by Protestant and Catholic clergy to obtain entry for 20,000 children into the United States foundered on the rock of public opinion. A bill to this effect was withdrawn by its sponsor, Senator Robert F. Wagner, when Congress insisted that the 20,000 places be accommodated in existing immigration quotas, which would have meant refusing entry to 20,000 adults.[203] Emigration was becoming more difficult than ever as the war drew near: another example of the increasingly irrational and contradictory nature of the policies of the Nazi regime on a wider scale.

Remaining in Germany was anything other than an easy option, however, as the experience of Victor Klemperer showed. As the antisemitic atmosphere became thicker in the spring and summer of 1938, Klemperer had to endure repeated harassment by the local authority over petty details of the construction and maintenance of his house and garden at Döltzschen, on the outskirts of Dresden. In May 1938 the Klemperers' non-Jewish charlady resigned after the local authorities had threatened to dismiss her daughter from her job if she continued to work with them. Living outside town, the Klemperers escaped the violence of 9–10 November 1938, but on 11 November two policemen subjected their house to a thorough search (allegedly for hidden weapons): Klemperer's wartime sabre was discovered in the attic and he was taken into custody. Although he was treated courteously and released after a few hours without being charged, it was nevertheless a considerable shock. A more severe blow came when Klemperer, already banned from using the reading room of the local library the previous year, was officially barred from entering the library at all. The librarian in charge of the lending section, Klemperer reported, wept as he issued the ban; he wanted to kill the Nazis, he said ('not simply kill, – torture, torture, torture').[204] The sharp increase in the tempo of antisemitic legislation after the pogrom began to restrict Klemperer's life in other ways too. On 6 December 1938 he noted Himmler's new decree withdrawing driving licences from all Jews and the ban on Jews visiting public cinemas. Unable to continue his work on eighteenth-century French literature because he could no longer use the library, Klemperer was now deprived of his two main leisure activities as well. He was faced with a large tax bill as part of the aftermath of the pogrom and feared that his house would soon be confiscated. Further attempts to emigrate came to nothing, though his friends and acquaintances were leaving the country in ever-growing numbers. A compulsive writer, Klemperer now turned to composing his memoirs, and his diary entries became ever more voluminous. He remained convinced that German Jews were Germans first and Jews second and continued to think of Zionism as little better than Nazism. But life was becoming rapidly harder, and he looked forward with foreboding to the future.[205]

A similar atmosphere of gloom spread through the household of Luise Solmitz and her Jewish husband. Immediately after the pogrom, the Gestapo called on them and were only dissuaded from arresting Friedrich Solmitz when he showed them his war medals. Nevertheless, he had to surrender his old war weapons ('touched in honour, surrendered in shame'). The fine levied on German Jews came as a further shock. 'Now Freddy admits it too: we are annihilated.' Once again, however, Solmitz's war service protected him. Asked by finance officials whether he wanted to emigrate he replied: 'I am an old officer, born in Germany, and will die in Germany too.' The officials allowed him to make over his property and assets to his wife so that they escaped confiscation. But the ban on Jews attending the theatre and other public events, and the looming threat of destitution, weighed heavily on their minds. 'One doesn't dare enjoy one's possessions any more,' wrote Luise Solmitz. 'Today the house is no refuge, no protection any more.'[206]

V

By the summer of 1939, as these experiences indicated, the remaining Jews in Germany had been completely marginalized, isolated and deprived of their main means of earning a living. This was not enough for Heydrich, however. At the meeting of 12 November 1938, Heydrich had admitted that it would not be possible to force all of them to emigrate within a short space of time. He suggested that those Jews who stayed in Germany in the meantime should be made to wear a special badge. 'But, my dear Heydrich,' Göring had protested, 'you won't be able to avoid the creation of ghettoes on a very large scale in all the cities. They will have to be created.'[207] For the moment, as Göring reported on 6 December 1938, Hitler himself vetoed the proposal to concentrate Jews in specific houses and to oblige them to wear a yellow badge in public, out of consideration for international opinion, which had reacted critically to the pogrom and the consequent legislation; and he also limited measures against mixed marriages and people of mixed race as defined by the Nuremberg Laws, in case harsh treatment would arouse discontent amongst their non-Jewish relatives. In practice, however, Jewish society in Germany was fast retreating into a ghetto anyway, almost completely cut off from mainstream everyday life, fast slipping beyond the consciousness of most Germans altogether.[208]

It was at this time, following the unopposed mass violence of 9–10 November and the imprisonment in concentration camps of 30,000 Jewish men, if only for a few weeks, without any serious opposition being offered, that Hitler began for the first time to threaten their complete physical annihilation. Over the course of the previous two years, he had held back with public statements of hostility towards the Jews, partly out of foreign policy considerations, partly out of a desire to distance himself personally from what he knew was one of his regime's less popular aspects amongst the great majority of the German people. It was fully in line with this approach that he withdrew from the Party meeting on 9 November once he had taken the decision to launch the pogrom.[209] But this relative abstention from public justification of anti-semitic policy in rhetoric did not mean that Hitler had withdrawn from the implementation of antisemitic policy in practice. He discussed it on a number of occasions in private during 1936 and 1937, and there is little doubt that his Party Rally speech in September 1937 provided the deliberate stimulus for the intensification of antisemitism that began again at that point.[210] In characteristic fashion, he presented the pogrom as the expression of a universal and fanatical hatred of the Jews amongst the German population, which he himself was doing his best to rein in. 'What do you think, Mr Pirow,' he asked the South African Defence Minister on 24 November, 'would happen in Germany, if I took my protecting hand away from the Jews? The world could not imagine it.'[211] The scarcely veiled threat here was palpable. Hitler was keen to pressure the Evian powers into accepting more refugees, and he did this not least by making it clear what would happen to Germany's Jews if they were refused entry to other countries. On 21 January 1939 he told the Czecho-slovakian Foreign Minister: 'The Jews among us will be annihilated. The Jews had not carried out 9th November 1938 in vain; this day will be avenged.'[212]

On 30 January 1939, Hitler repeated these threats in public, and broadened them onto a European scale. Speaking to the Reichstag on the sixth anniversary of his appointment as Reich Chancellor, he said:

I have often been a prophet in my life and I was mostly laughed at. In the time of my struggle for power it was in the first place the Jewish people who received with nothing but laughter my prophecy that one day I would take over the leadership of the state and with it the whole people and then among many other things bring the Jewish problem to its solution. I believe that the roars of laughter of those days may well have suffocated in the throats of the Jews in the meantime.

I want to be a prophet again today: if international finance Jewry in Europe and beyond should succeed once more in plunging the peoples into a world war, then the result will not be the Bolshevization of the earth and thus the victory of Jewry, but the annihilation of the Jewish race in Europe.[213]

This threat, broadcast on the weekly newsreel in its entirety, could not have been more public. It was to remembered and cited on numerous subsequent occasions. It deserves, therefore, the closest consideration.

The pogrom of November 1938 reflected the regime's radicalization in the final stages of preparation for war.[214] Part of this preparation in Hitler's mind had to consist of the neutralization of what he conceived of as the Jewish threat. With a disdain for reality characteristic of paranoid antisemites, he assumed that 'international finance' was working together with international Communism, both steered from behind the scenes by the Jews, to broaden out this European war, which they knew Germany would win, onto a world scale, which could only mean by bringing the United States into it. This would be the only way they would stand any chance of success. By the time it happened, Germany would be master of Europe and have the vast majority of the continent's Jews in its grasp. Anticipating this moment, therefore, Hitler was announcing that he would hold Europe's Jews hostage as a means of deterring America from entering the war. If the USA did come in on the side of Germany's enemies, then the Jews, not just in Germany, but in all Europe, would be killed. Nazi terrorism had now acquired an additional dimension: the practice, on the largest possible scale, of hostage-taking.[215]

VI

The radicalization of antisemitism that took place in 1938 thus formed part of what everybody knew was the final run-up to the long-prepared war for the German domination and racial reordering of Europe. Expelling or, failing that, isolating Germany's Jewish population was, in the Nazis' paranoid racist ideology, an essential prerequisite for establishing internal security and warding off the threat from within – a threat that, in reality, existed only in their own imaginations. Radicalization occurred in 1938 not least because, indeed, this process of conquest and reorganization had already begun, starting with the annexation of Austria. Germany's Jewish population had been, by and large, prosperous, and its expropriation by the state, and by numerous private businesses, was accelerated at this time not least because of the increasingly desperate need for hard cash to pay Germany's rapidly growing armaments bill. It is tempting to describe anti-Jewish violence in the Third Reich as a 'regression into barbarism', but this is fundamentally to misunderstand its dynamics. Boycotts and expropriations of Jewish shops and businesses were driven on in particular by lower-middle-class small businessmen who may have been disappointed by the regime's failure to better their economic position by more conventional means. But the social and economic extinction of Germany's Jewish community was also ordered from above, as part of a general preparation for war. It was justified by a radical nationalist ideology that was linked, not to a vague vision of Germany's return to some quiet medieval backwater, but on the contrary to a technologically advanced war of European domination, predicated on what counted at the time as the most modern, scientific criteria of racial fitness and racial supremacy.

That antisemitism in its racist guise was a fundamentally modern ideology can also be seen from its manifestations in other East-Central European countries at this time. In Poland, too, there was a rabidly antisemitic party in the form of Roman Dmowski's Endeks, who attracted a broad coalition of the middle classes behind an increasingly fascist ideology during the 1930s. Poland was ruled by a military junta after 1935, and the Endeks were in opposition; nevertheless, they organized widespread boycotts of Jewish shops and businesses, which were often accompanied by considerable violence: one estimate claims that 350 Polish Jews were killed and 500 injured in violent antisemitic incidents in over 150 Polish towns and cities between December 1935 and March 1939. The Endeks pressed for the disfranchisement of the Jews, the banning of Jews from the army, the universities, the business world, the professions and much more besides. Poland's Jews – 10 per cent of the population, some 3.5 million people – were to be herded into ghettoes and then forced to emigrate. Such pressure forced the increasingly weak government, disoriented by the death of the Polish dictator Piłsudski in 1935, to consider antisemitic measures to try and stop its support seeping away to the Endeks. Already since the 1920s, Jews had been effectively excluded from employment in the public sector and from receiving government business contracts. Now strict limits were set on Jewish access to secondary and higher education and medical and legal practice. Jewish students in Poland's universities fell from 25 per cent in 1921–33 to 8 per cent in 1938–9.[216]

By this time, Polish students had succeeded in forcing their Jewish fellow students to occupy separate 'ghetto-benches' in lectures. In addition, increasingly severe restrictions were imposed on Jewish export businesses and artisanal workshops – a mainstay of Jewish economic life in a country where the Jews were on the whole not among the better-off sections of society. In 1936 the government outlawed the ritual slaughter of animals according to Judaic prescription, a direct attack not only on

Judaic religious tradition but also on the livelihood of the numerous Jews who made a living from it. A ban on Sunday shopping struck at Jewish retailers, who now either had to open on the Jewish Sabbath or lose customers by staying closed two days a week. In 1938 the government party adopted a thirteen-point programme on the Jewish question, proposing a variety of new measures to underline the Jews' status as aliens in the Polish national state. By 1939 the professions had barred Jews from joining them even if they had managed to obtain the requisite qualifications at university. Increasingly, the government party was thus taking on board policies first advanced by the Nazis in Germany: in January 1939, for example, some of its deputies put forward a proposal for a Polish equivalent of the Nuremberg Laws.

Nevertheless, there was one crucial difference. The vast majority of Poland's Jews spoke Yiddish rather than Polish and adhered strongly to the Judaic religion. They appeared to Polish nationalists, as they did to the Polish Catholic Church, as a major obstacle to national integration. They were in effect treated as a national minority in the new Polish state. Polish antisemitism was thus by and large religious rather than racist, although the boundaries between the two inevitably became more than blurred in the violence of antisemitic rhetoric and following the Nazi example.[217] By the late 1930s, the Polish government was pressing the international community to allow massive Jewish emigration from the country – a major reason for the summoning of the Evian conference, as we have seen. One idea, a commonplace of antisemites in many parts of Europe since the late nineteenth century, was to send the Jews to the French island of Madagascar, off the east African coast. Lengthy but inconclusive negotiations took place between the Polish and French governments on this issue in the late 1930s.[218]

Similar ideas and policies could be found in other countries in East-Central Europe that were struggling to build a new national identity at this time, most notably Romania and Hungary.[219] These countries had their own fascist movements, in the form of the Iron Guard in Romania and the Arrow Cross in Hungary, that yielded little or nothing to the German National Socialists in the virulence of their hatred of the Jews; as in Germany, antisemitism here too was linked to radical nationalism, the belief that the nation had not achieved its full realization and that it was above all the Jews who were preventing it from doing so. In

Romania, there were around 750,000 Jews in the early 1930s, or 4.2 per cent of the population, and as in Poland they counted as a national minority. Under increasing pressure from the radical fascist Iron Guard in the later 1930s, King Carol appointed a short-lived right-wing regime that began to enact antisemitic legislation which the King continued to enforce when he took over as dictator in 1938. By September 1939, at least 270,000 Jews had been deprived of their Romanian citizenship; many had been expelled from the professions, including the judiciary, the police, teaching and the officer corps, and all were coming under heavy pressure to emigrate.[220]

The situation of the 445,000 or so Jews in Hungary was closer to that of Jews in Germany than to that of Jews in Poland: that is, they spoke Hungarian and were strongly acculturated. Most of them lived in Budapest, the capital, and regarded themselves as Hungarians in every respect. The prominence of Jews in the short-lived, radical Communist regime of Béla Kun in 1919 fuelled antisemitism on the right. The state's counter-revolutionary ruler, Admiral Miklós Hórthy, allied Hungary to Nazi Germany in the late 1930s in the hope of winning back territory lost to Czechoslovakia and Romania in the Peace Settlement of 1919. This in turn brought new supporters to the Arrow Cross, whose popularity the government tried to undercut in May 1938 by passing the First Jewish Law, which imposed detailed restrictions on the proportion of Jewish employees in businesses, in the professions and other walks of life. Later in the same year a Second Jewish Law was passed, coming into effect in May 1939, tightening these quotas from 20 per cent to 6 per cent and barring Jews altogether from running newspapers, cinemas and theatres, from teaching, from buying land, from serving as officers in the army, and from joining the civil service. These laws, clearly reflecting the influence of Nazi Germany, were to a large extent racial in character, affecting for example Jews who had converted to Christianity after 1919. Hórthy himself disliked this fact, but was unable to prevent the racial clauses of these laws from coming into force.[221]

On a broader scale, all the states created or refounded in East-Central Europe at the end of the Second World War on the principle, enunciated by US President Woodrow Wilson, of national self-determination, contained large national minorities, which they attempted with a greater or lesser degree of force to assimilate to the dominant national culture. But the Jews in nearly all of them bore the additional burden of being regarded by nationalist extremists as agents of a worldwide conspiracy, allied to Russian Communism on the one hand and international finance on the other, and so posing a threat to national independence many times greater than that of other minorities within their borders. Seen in the context of other countries in East-Central Europe, therefore, the policies adopted and enforced by the Nazis against the Jews between 1933 and 1939 do not seem so unusual. Germany was far from the only country in the region at this time that restricted Jewish rights, deprived Jews of their economic livelihood, tried to get Jews to emigrate in large numbers, or witnessed outbursts of violence, destruction and murder against its Jewish population. Even in France there was a strong current of antisemitism on the right, fuelled by bitter hostility to the Popular Front government of Léon Blum, himself a Jew and a socialist and supported in the Chamber of Deputies by the Communist Party, that came to power in 1936.

Yet there were obviously also real differences, which arose partly out of the fact that Germany was far larger, more powerful and, despite the economic crisis of the early 1930s, more prosperous than other countries in the region, partly out of the fact that Germany's Jewish minority was far more acculturated than Jewish minorities in Poland or Romania. Only in Germany was racial legislation actually introduced and enforced in the area of marriage and sexual relations, although a law along these lines was proposed in Romania; only in Germany were the Jews systematically robbed of their property, their jobs and their livelihood, although restrictions on all of these were certainly imposed elsewhere; only in Germany did the government organize a nationwide pogrom, although there were certainly pogroms in their hundreds elsewhere; and only in Germany did the country's rulers succeed in driving more than half the entire Jewish population into exile, although there were certainly powerful political groups who dearly wanted to do this elsewhere. Above all, only in Germany did nationalist extremists actually seize power in the 1930s rather than wield influence; and only in Germany was the elimination of Jewish influence regarded by the state and its ruling party as the indispensable basis for a rebirth of the national spirit and the creation of a new, racially pure human society. The antisemitic policies of the Third Reich became something of a model for antisemites in other countries during these years, but nowhere else was there a regime in power that regarded it as crucial that they should be implemented all the way down the line and extended to the whole of Europe. The time for the Third Reich to take such steps had not yet arrived. It would only come with the outbreak of the Second World War.

7

THE ROAD TO WAR

FROM WEAKNESS TO STRENGTH

I

Hitler's working habits were irregular. He had always been a stranger to routine. His Bohemianism was still evident in his lifestyle after he came to power. He often stayed up well into the small hours watching movies in his private cinema, and he was often very late to rise the next day. Generally, he would start work at about ten in the morning, spending two or three hours hearing reports from Hans Heinrich Lammers, head of the Reich Chancellery and Hitler's principal link with his Ministers, and Walther Funk, Goebbels's deputy in the Propaganda Ministry. After covering the administrative, legislative and propaganda issues of the day, he would sometimes take time for urgent consultations with individual Ministers, or with State Secretary Otto Meissner, who ran what had once been the President's office. Lunch was routinely prepared for one in the afternoon, but sometimes had to be postponed if Hitler was delayed. Guests would generally consist of Hitler's immediate entourage, including his adjutants, his chauffeurs and his photographer, Heinrich Hoffmann. Göring, Goebbels and Himmler attended with varying degrees of frequency, and later on Albert Speer, but most senior Ministers were seldom to be seen. If they were out of favour, indeed, they were never admitted to Hitler's presence at all: Agriculture Minister Walther Darré for instance tried without success for more than two years to see Hitler in the late 1930s to discuss the worsening food supply situation. After lunch, Hitler would hold discussions on foreign policy issues and military matters with a variety of advisers, or pore over architectural plans with Speer. Rather than spend hours wading through mountains of paperwork, Hitler always preferred to talk to people, which he did at great length, and usually without interruption from his sycophantic listeners, over lunch or dinner.[1]

When Hitler was in residence at his retreat at the Obersalzberg in the Bavarian Alps his lifestyle was even less regular. Originally a small hilltop chalet, this was reconstructed after 1933 to form a large complex of buildings known collectively as the Berghof ('mountain court' or 'mountain farm'), with stunning views across the mountains from a terrace and further buildings down the hill for members of his entourage. Here, he would sometimes fail to emerge from his private quarters until the early afternoon, go for a walk down the hill (a car was waiting at the bottom to take him back up again), greet the streams of ordinary citizens who toiled up the mountain to file silently past him and removed pieces of his fence as souvenirs and take refreshments on the terrace if the weather was good. After dinner there would be more old movies, and he seldom went to bed before two or three in the morning. He was often accompanied here by Eva Braun, an attractive young woman, twenty-three years his junior, and a former employee of Heinrich Hoffmann. Hitler's sex life, the subject of much lurid speculation then and later, appears to have been completely conventional, except for the fact that he refused to marry or to admit to any relationships to the wider public, for fear that doing so would compromise the aura of lonesome power and invulnerability with which propaganda had surrounded him. Earlier on, in 1931, his niece Angela ('Geli') Raubal was killed in an accident, giving rise to unsavoury, but unfounded, rumours about their relationship. Eva Braun, a naive and submissive young woman, was clearly in awe of Hitler, and felt overwhelmed by his attention. The relationship was quickly accepted by Hitler's entourage, but kept secret from the public. Living in luxury, with few duties, Eva Braun was present at the Berghof as Hitler's private companion, not his official consort.[2]

The absence of routine in Hitler's style of leadership meant that he paid little attention to detailed issues in which he was not interested, such as the management of the labour force, or the details of financial management, which he happily left to Schacht and his successors. This could mean on occasion that he put his signature to measures which had to be shelved because of opposition from powerful vested interests, as in a decree on the Labour Front issued in October 1934.[3] It also meant that those who had, or controlled, direct personal access to him could wield considerable influence. Access became an increasingly important key to power. Hitler's Bohemian lifestyle did not mean, however, that he was lazy or inactive, or that he withdrew from domestic politics after 1933. When the occasion demanded, he could intervene powerfully and decisively. Albert Speer, who was with him often in the second half of the 1930s, observed that while he appeared to waste a great deal of time, 'he often allowed a problem to mature during the weeks when he seemed entirely taken up with trivial matters. Then, after the "sudden insight" came, he would spend a few days of intensive work giving final shape to his solution.'[4] Hitler, in other words, was erratic rather than lazy in his working habits. He wrote his own speeches, and he frequently engaged in lengthy and exhausting tours around Germany, speaking, meeting officials and carrying out his ceremonial functions as head of state. In areas where he did take a real interest, he did not hesitate to give a direct lead, even on matters of detail. In art and culture, for instance, Hitler laid down the policy to be followed, and personally inspected the pictures selected for exhibition or suppression. His prejudices – against the composer Paul Hindemith, for example – invariably proved decisive. In racial policy, too, Hitler took a leading role, pushing on or slowing down the implementation of antisemitic and other measures as he thought circumstances dictated. In areas such as these, Hitler was not merely reacting to initiatives from his subordinates, as some have suggested. Moreover, it was Hitler who laid down the broad, general principles that policy had to follow. These were simple, clear and easy to grasp, and they had been drummed into the minds and hearts of Nazi activists since the 1920s through his book *My Struggle*, through his speeches and through the vast and ceaselessly active propaganda machine built up by the Party before 1933 and the Propaganda Ministry after that. Hitler's underlings did not have to imagine what he would want in any given situation: the principles that guided their conduct were there for all to grasp; all they had to do was to fill in the small print. Beyond this, too, at decisive moments, such as the boycott action of 1 April 1933 or the pogrom of 9–10 November 1938, Hitler personally ordered action to be taken, in terms that necessarily, from his point of view, avoided specifics, but were none the less unmistakeable in their general thrust.[5]

The area in which Hitler took the most consistent and most detailed interest, however, was undeniably that of foreign policy and preparation for war. It was without question Hitler, personally, who drove Germany towards war from the moment he became Reich Chancellor, subordinating every other aspect of policy to this overriding aim and, as we have seen, creating a growing number of stresses and strains in the economy, society and the political system as a result. The war he envisaged was to be far more extensive than a series of limited conflicts designed to revise the territorial provisions of the Treaty of Versailles. On one of many similar occasions, he announced on 23 May 1928 that his intention was 'to lead our people into bloody action, not for an adjustment of its boundaries, but to *save it into the most distant future* by securing so much land and ground that the future receives back many times the blood shed'.[6] He did not modify this intention after he came to power. In early August 1933, for instance, he told two visiting American businessmen that he wanted to annex not only Austria, the Polish corridor and Alsace-Lorraine but also the German-speaking parts of Denmark, Italy, Czechoslovakia, Yugoslavia and Romania as well. This meant total German domination over Europe.[7] In the long run, indeed, he intended Germany to dominate the world.[8] But to begin with, of course, Hitler had to contend with the problem that Germany was extremely weak internationally, its armed forces severely limited by the Treaty of Versailles, its economy depressed, its internal constitution, as he thought, chaotic and divided, beset by enemies within. Hitler's initial aim, therefore, which guided his foreign policy for the first two years and more of the Third Reich, was to keep Germany's potential enemies at bay while the country rearmed.[9]

It was in practice not difficult to do this. Germany enjoyed a great deal of sympathy internationally in the early-to-mid-1930s. The idealism that had played such a huge part in the creation of the Peace Settlement of 1918–19 had long turned round to work against it. The principle of national self-determination, invoked to give independence to countries like Poland, had manifestly been denied to Germany itself, as millions of German-speakers in Austria, in the Czech Sudetenland, in parts of Silesia (now part of Poland), and elsewhere had been refused the right for the lands they lived in to become part of the Reich. A widespread feeling amongst British and French elites that the First World War had been the disastrous result of a chapter of accidents and poor decisions fuelled a sense of guilt at the harshness of the peace terms and a general

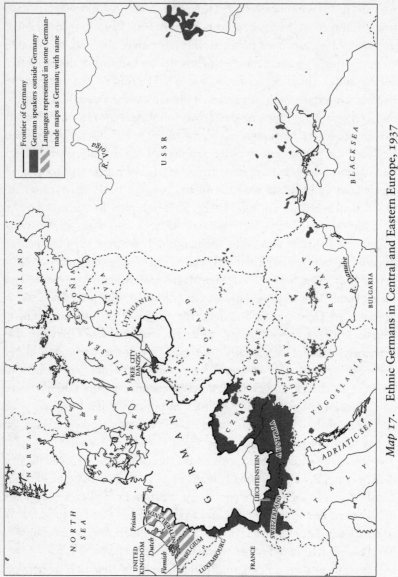

Map 17. Ethnic Germans in Central and Eastern Europe, 1937

disbelief in the war guilt clause that pinned the blame on Germany. Reparations had been brought to a premature end in 1932, but the continued restrictions on Germany's armaments seemed unfair and absurd to many, especially in the face of belligerently nationalist and authoritarian governments in countries like Hungary and Poland. For Britain and France the Depression meant financial retrenchment, and a huge reluctance to spend any more money on arms, especially in view of the perceived need to defend and maintain their far-flung overseas empires in India, Africa, Indo-China and elsewhere. In France, the late onset of the Depression, in the mid-1930s, made rapid rearmarment extremely difficult anyway. Most of the postwar generation of politicians in Britain and France were second-rate figures. Having seen the best and brightest of their generation killed on the front in the First World War, they were determined to avoid a repetition of the slaughter if they were humanly able to. Their reluctance to prepare for, still less to go to, war, over problems of European politics that seemed eminently soluble by other means, with a modicum of goodwill on all sides, was compounded, finally, by a nagging fear of what such a war would bring: not only renewed carnage in the trenches but also massive aerial bombardment of the great cities, huge destruction and loss of civilian life, and possibly even social revolution as well.[10]

Thus in effect all Hitler had to do to get through the initial, dangerous phase of rearmament was to appease international opinion by assuring everybody that all he wanted to do was to redress the wrongs of the Peace Settlement, achieve an acceptable degree of national self-determination for the Germans and restore his country to its rightful, equal place in the world of nations, complete with adequate means with which to defend itself against potential aggressors. And this, essentially, is what he did up to the middle of 1938, with the backing not only of the Nazi Party's Foreign Policy Office under Alfred Rosenberg but also of the conservative bureaucrats who still dominated the German Foreign Office under Baron Konstantin von Neurath. Nationalists to a man, the officials had chafed at the policy of fulfilment pursued by Foreign Minister Gustav Stresemann in the 1920s, and welcomed the change of tack brought about by Reich Chancellor Heinrich Brüning, who had replaced Stresemann's senior aide with the more aggressively inclined Bernhard von Bülow as State Secretary in 1930. The diplomats welcomed the new regime in January 1933, especially since Neurath, who continued as Foreign Minister from the previous government at the express wish of President Hindenburg, was one of their own. On 13 March 1933 Bülow submitted a memorandum to Neurath and Defence Minister Blomberg in which he stressed that the medium-term aims of foreign policy, now that reparations had been wound up and the French, British and Americans had ended their military occupation of the Rhineland, should be to get back the territory lost to the Poles in 1918–19, and to incorporate Austria into the Reich. In the immediate future, however, he advised, Germany should avoid any aggressive moves until rearmament had restored its strength.[11]

But the road to achieving this was a rocky one. International disarmament negotiations begun in Geneva early in 1932 had run into the sands because the British and French had been unwilling to allow parity to Germany either by running down their own armed forces or permitting the Germans to build up theirs. Increasingly keen to introduce conscription, particularly in view of the growing threat of Ernst Röhm's brownshirts as an *ersatz* army, Defence Minister Blomberg, with the support of the Foreign Ministry, bypassed Hitler and encouraged the German representatives in Geneva to take a hard line in the face of continuing Anglo-French objections to the removal of limitations on German arms. As negotiations reached deadlock, Blomberg persuaded Hitler to pull out on 14 October 1933, and to underscore the significance of this move by withdrawing Germany from the League of Nations, the main sponsor of the negotiations, at the same time.[12] The move was made, Hitler declared, 'in view of the unreasonable, humiliating and degrading demands of the other Powers'. Protesting his desire for peace and his willingness to disarm if the other Powers did the same, Hitler declared, in a lengthy speech broadcast on the radio the same evening, that the deliberate degradation of Germany could no longer be tolerated. Germany had been humiliated by the Peace Settlement and plunged into economic disaster by reparations; to add insult to injury by refusing to grant equality in disarmament talks was too much to bear. The decision, he announced, would be put to the German people in a plebiscite.[13] Held a few weeks later, it delivered the predictably overwhelming majority in favour of Hitler's decision, thanks not least to massive intimidation and electoral manipulation. Although it is impossible to say with certainty, it is likely that a majority of the electors would have backed withdrawal in a free vote; only former Communists and left-wing Social Democrats would have been likely to have voted 'no' if voting had been free.[14]

Departure from the League of Nations was the first decisive step in the foreign policy of the Third Reich. It was followed rapidly by another move that caused general astonishment both within Germany and without: a ten-year non-aggression pact with Poland, signed on 26 January 1934, forced through by Hitler personally over serious reservations on the part of the Foreign Office. For Hitler, the pact's advantage was that it covered Germany's vulnerable eastern flank during the period of secret rearmament, improved trade relations, which were extremely poor at the time, and provided some security for the free city of Danzig, which was now run by a Nazi local government under League of Nations suzerainty but was cut off from the rest of Germany by the corridor to the Baltic granted to Poland by the Peace Settlement. The pact could be used to demonstrate to Britain and other powers that Germany was a peaceful nation; even the much-admired Gustav Stresemann, Foreign Minister during the Weimar Republic, had not concluded an 'Eastern Locarno', only managing to settle matters in the West through the treaty of that name. For the Poles, it served as a substitute for the security formerly provided by the League of Nations, and replaced the alliance concluded in 1921 with France, whose internal political and economic situation was making it look increasingly unsatisfactory as a defensive support against German aggression (undermining French influence was another bonus for Hitler, of course). The pact was, however, a purely temporary expedient on Hitler's part: a piece of paper, serving its purpose for the moment, to be torn up without ceremony when it was no longer of any use. There were to be many more like it.[15]

II

For most of 1934, Hitler's attention was directed towards internal politics, particularly with the tensions that led up to and followed the purge of the SA carried out at the end of June. Just before the purge, Hitler paid his first visit abroad as German Chancellor, to the Fascist leader Mussolini, in Venice, to try and secure his understanding for the events that were about to unfold. Hitler's admiration for Mussolini was patently sincere. However, the atmosphere at the meeting was distinctly frosty. Mussolini was deeply suspicious of the Nazis' intentions in Austria, which he felt lay within his own sphere of influence. A small, landlocked country half in the Alps bordering Italy, German-speaking Austria had experienced repeated political turbulence since the international rejection of the proposal to merge it into Germany after the collapse of the Habsburg monarchy in 1918–19. Few Austrians had much confidence in the viability of their state. Massive inflation in the early 1920s had been followed by deflation, and then came the Depression, much as in Germany. The country was divided politically into two great political camps, the Socialists, based mainly in the working class of 'Red' Vienna, where nearly a third of the country's seven million inhabitants lived, and the Catholic-oriented Christian Social Party, which drew its strength from the Viennese middle classes and from conservative farmers and small-town voters in the provinces. Tension between them had broken out into open hostility in 1933, when the Christian Social Chancellor, Engelbert Dollfuss, permanently dissolved parliament and established an authoritarian regime. Increased police harassment of the Socialists provoked an armed uprising in the working-class districts of Vienna in February 1934. It was put down with brutal force by the Austrian army. Leading Socialists, including their most influential ideologue, Otto Bauer, fled to safety through Vienna's famous underground sewers. Dollfuss now outlawed the Socialists altogether. Thousands were arrested and put in prison. On 1 May 1934 the Austrian dictator pushed through a new constitution for his country. It abolished elections and established, at least on paper, a pale version of the Corporate State based on the model devised by Mussolini.[16]

For all their seeming decisiveness, these moves left Dollfuss looking distinctly shaky. The economic situation was worse than ever. The large Viennese working class was seething with resentment. On the right, the paramilitary Home Defence Brigades, who wanted a more radical kind of fascism, based more clearly on the Italian model, were causing unrest. The previously tiny Austrian Nazi Party was growing rapidly in size and ambition. Its formal banning by Dollfuss in July 1933 had little effect. Bringing together tradesmen and small shopkeepers in Vienna and the Austrian hinterland, lower civil servants, army veterans, recent university graduates and significant elements of the police and gendarmerie, the Party counted nearly 70,000 members at the time of its banning. It gained a further 20,000 in the following months. Held together, though always somewhat precariously, by a violent, vicious brand of antisemitism, fortified by anticlericalism and anti-Catholicism, it looked back to the pan-Germanism of Georg Ritter von Schönerer, whose ideas had so powerfully influenced the young Adolf Hitler in Linz and Vienna before 1914. Its main aim was immediate unification with the Third Reich. As its members listened to the constant stream of Nazi propaganda poured out by radio stations across the border, they became ever more convinced that unification was imminent. Violence and terror became their favoured means of undermining the Austrian state so as to leave it easy prey for the Third Reich.[17]

By the early summer of 1934, the moment seemed ripe for action. Fridolin Glass, leader of the SS Standard 89 in Vienna, decided to overthrow the Austrian government. On 25 July 1934, 150 of his men, mostly unemployed workers and soldiers who had been cashiered from the army because of their Nazism, dressed themselves in borrowed Austrian army uniforms and entered the Austrian Chancellery. The cabinet had already left the building, but the SS men caught Dollfuss trying to leave by a side-entrance and shot him dead on the spot. Rushing into the neighbouring headquarters of the Austrian broadcasting corporation, the putschists commandeered a radio microphone and announced to the country that the government had resigned. Sympathizers in the police had probably made it easy for them to enter the buildings. But this was about the extent of the backing they got from anybody. The Austrian SA, whose leaders were gathered in a nearby hotel, pretended they had known nothing of the putsch at any stage, and refused to intervene. Less than four weeks after the German SA leaders had been shot by the SS, they could not bring themselves to let bygones be bygones. Uprisings in many parts of the country, triggered off, as arranged, by the putschists' radio broadcasts, were put down by the Austrian army, aided in places by the Home Defence Brigades. There were several hundred deaths and injuries. Where the SA did stage an uprising, the SS refused to support them. Even Nazi officers in the army and police in many places took part willingly in the suppression of the revolt. The Austrian Nazis turned out to be poorly trained and ill prepared for such a venture, over-confident, internally divided and incompetent. In Vienna, the Minister of Justice, Kurt von Schuschnigg, formed a new government and after brief negotiations with the putschists had them all arrested. Hitler abandoned them to their fate. The two men who had fired the fatal shots at Dollfuss were hanged in the yard of the Vienna Regional Court. Their last words were 'Hail, Hitler!' The German Ambassador in Rome, who had been implicated in the plot, tried unsuccessfully to commit suicide. Even before these events, an Austrian Nazi had complained that 'the Austrian on average is incapable as an organizer. In the organizational field he needs Prussian help! . . . Without the Prussian power of organization there will always be chaos at decisive moments.' The bloody but farcical putsch seemed to bear him out. From now on, Schuschnigg was able to reconstruct the clerico-fascist dictatorship on a firmer basis, curbing the Home Defence Brigades and sending the Nazis underground, from where they continued to commit acts of violence and sabotage against state institutions, for the moment without much effect.[18]

Hitler undoubtedly knew about these events in advance. The Austrian SS had undergone training for the putsch at the Dachau concentration camp. After the banning of the Austrian Nazi Party in June 1933 Dr Theo Habicht, a German Reichstag deputy whom Hitler had appointed to lead the Austrian Nazis, had organized its underground activities from exile in Munich. He poured clandestine antisemitic propaganda into Austria, accusing Dollfuss of presiding over a regime run by Jews. It was in Habicht's flat in Munich that leading Austrian Nazis met shortly before the putsch to finalize preparations. He told Hitler what was being planned, and Hitler gave his blessing for a general uprising – though in the belief, evidently inspired by Habicht's exaggerated optimism on the occasion, that the Austrian army would back the putsch. From his exile in Munich, Habicht in reality was less than well informed about the true state of affairs in Austria. Not only did the putsch fail, and the army stick by the government, but Mussolini moved his troops to the Brenner Pass and made it abundantly clear that he would intervene on the side of the Austrian government if the situation got out of control. Hitler was beside himself with rage and embarrassment. Amidst assurances of disapproval that convinced nobody, he dismissed Habicht and closed down the Munich office of the Austrian Party.[19]

In one respect, however, the catastrophe provided an opportunity.

22. The Daimler-Benz automobile company boasts of its success under the Third Reich, 1936.

23. 'Your Strength Through Joy car': a young German couple, the man at the wheel, going for a spin in a Volkswagen beetle, built by Ferdinand Porsche from an original design by Adolf Hitler.
In fact, no production models came off the assembly-line until after the war.

24. 'If this happened, one would not have to fear any measures of self-defence on the part of Germany.' Cartoon in a once-independent satirical magazine, 11 March 1934, designed to advertise Germany's defensive weakness but also testifying to widespread fears about the effects of aerial bombardment.

25. 'A people helps itself: Gertrud's understood it.' A family eating the obligatory Sunday stew or 'one-pot meal', as shown in a school reading primer in 1939.

26. The hall at Hermann Göring's modest rural hunting-lodge, Carinhall.

27. The ideal of peasant family life: 'Harvest', by Karl Alexander Flügel, shown at the Great German Art Exhibition in 1938.

28. Workers refuse to conform: clad in traditional full-dress uniforms, the coalminers at Penzberg, in Bavaria, show their disdain for Nazi ceremonial by failing to render the Hitler salute in the approved manner; a formation of Hitler Youth near the back shows how it should be done, but the miners pay no attention.

29. 'Here you are sharing the load. A hereditarily sick person costs on average 50,000 Reichsmarks up to the age of 60.' A poster of 1935 shows a healthy German bearing the burden of keeping the mentally ill in institutions such as the one in the background. Such propaganda aimed to persuade people of the need to sterilize the mentally handicapped, and eventually to kill them.

30. 'The decline in marital fertility: of married women aged 15–45, every third one had a live-born child in 1900, every fourth in 1910, every seventh in 1925, and every eighth in 1930.' Propaganda illustration from 1933, urging Germans to have more children.

31. Parading of a couple accused of 'race defilement': the placard around the woman's neck reads: 'I am the biggest swine in town and choose/only ever to go with Jews.' The man's placard reads: 'As a Jewish boy I'm always sure/to let only German girls through my door.' Such scenes, staged by brownshirts like those in the background, were commonplace before the passage of the Nuremberg Laws in 1935.

32. Racial research in a Gypsy camp in 1933: Eva Justin, an assistant of Robert Ritter, the leading Nazi expert in the field, measures a woman's head as part of a survey of the supposed racial characteristics of the Gypsies,

33. 'Jews enter the place at their own peril!' Banner over the road leading to Rottach-Egern, on Lake Tegern, in Bavaria, in 1935. Many towns and villages put up similar notices around this time, removing them for a while in 1936 to avoid bad publicity during the Winter and Summer Olympic Games.

34. The morning after the pogrom of the 'Reich Night of Broken Glass', 10 November 1938: a passer-by surveys the damage to a Jewish-owned shop in Berlin while the owners try to clear up the mess.

35. Hitler's deputy Rudolf Hess, on the right, with his increasingly influential subordinate Martin Bormann, in Berlin, 1935.

36. The aftermath of the Saarland plebiscite, 1935: children give the Nazi salute beneath a canopy of swastikas.

37. Rhinelanders greet the German army as it enters the demilitarized zone on 7 March 1936. Amidst the rejoicing, some of them are rendering the Nazi salute.

38. Members of the Condor Legion at Gijo harbour, leaving Spain on their way to Germany, 3 June 1939, after successfully intervening on behalf of Generalissimo Franco in the civil war.

39. A German soldier is overwhelmed by the euphoric welcome given to his armoured car unit by Austrian girls when it reaches Vienna, 21 March 1938.

40. The other side of the picture: Viennese Jews are forced to scrub pro-Austrian graffiti off the street in March 1938, in front of cheering crowds, including many children.

41. The handshake that sealed the fate of Poland: Stalin and Ribbentrop agree on the country's partition of 24 August 1939. Ten days later, the Second World War began.

Such was the gravity of the breach in relations with Germany's neighbour, Hitler told Deputy Chancellor von Papen, who was still under
effective house arrest after the 'Night of the Long Knives', that it required
a senior statesman to smooth things over: as a personal friend of the
murdered Austrian Chancellor, and a well-known Catholic statesman,
Papen was the man to pour oil on the troubled waters of Austro-German
relations. So Hitler appointed him ambassador in Vienna. Realizing he
had little choice, Papen accepted. At his request, his secretary, Günther
von Tschirschky-Bögendorf, was released from the prison where he had
been held since the action of 30 June and accompanied him to Austria.
The last remaining independent-minded conservative politician in the
government was finally out of the way – an unexpected by-product of
the mismanaged putsch.[20]

III

Germany's diplomatic isolation in the winter of 1934–5 seemed complete.[21] The only light in the gloom was provided by the results of a
plebiscite held in the small territory of the Saarland, on the western side
of the Rhineland on 13 January 1935. At the peace negotiations in 1919
the French, who clearly hoped they would be able to detach it from
Germany, given enough time, had the Saarland mandated to them by
the League of Nations, with the commitment that a referendum would
be held after fifteen years to give the area's inhabitants a final choice as
to which country they wanted to belong to. The fifteen years were up at
the end of 1934. The Saarland's mainly German-speaking citizens had
never wanted to be separated from Germany in the first place: 445,000
Saarlanders, nearly 91 per cent of those who cast their ballots, duly
expressed their desire to become citizens of the Third Reich. They did so
from a number of motives. The prospect of living as a German-speaking
minority in France was not an enticing one: in Alsace-Lorraine, the
French authorities had gone to great lengths to try and suppress the
German language and culture of the inhabitants and discriminated
heavily against those who remained loyal to their heritage. In the
Saarland too, the French rulers had been tactless and exploitative. They
were almost universally seen not as democrats but as imperialists. In

Germany, relations between Nazis and Catholics had not deteriorated at this stage to such a point where the Catholic Church, representing the vast majority of Saarlanders, would have felt it necessary to advise a continuation of the *status quo*, still less adherence to France, where the Communist Party seemed to be gaining steadily in strength. To encourage priests to advise their flocks to vote for Germany, the Nazis toned down their anti-Catholic propaganda in the run-up to the plebiscite. The clergy duly obliged with their support.[22]

Moreover, when the Centre Party had voluntarily dissolved itself in Germany in 1933 as a *quid pro quo* for the Concordat, it had done the same in the Saarland too, though it was not strictly necessary. Throughout the 1920s it had vigorously campaigned for a return of the Saarland to Germany – indeed, every political party in the Saarland had done the same – and in June 1934 it joined forces with the Nazis and the remnants of the Nationalists and other parties to fight for a 'yes' vote in a unified 'German Front' which projected itself to voters as being above politics. Only the Communists and Social Democrats remained outside, but since they too had fought for reunification for many years, their sudden *volte-face* confused their supporters and was accepted by few as sincere. Up to this point, indeed, patriotic rituals, war memorials to the German dead, national festivals and much more besides, supported financially and in other ways by nationalist enthusiasts within Germany, had worked to strengthen German national consciousness in the Saar. Their effect was not going to be undone in a couple of years. The Nazi Party in Germany also offered a variety of material inducements to the Saarlanders, sending Winter Aid over the border to help the needy, pointing out to teachers and other state employees the superior pension and other financial arrangements for them that could be obtained in Germany, and contrasting the economic recovery in the Reich with the rapidly deepening Depression in France. Goebbels's Propaganda Ministry blared out propaganda on German radio and exported large numbers of cheap 'People's Receivers' into the Saar to help the population receive the message. Rhenish printing presses rolled off millions of leaflets that were soon being read all over the Saarland; 80,000 posters went up in the region urging people to vote for Germany. Fifteen hundred public meetings were held to help convince people of the rightness of reunification. For the vote itself, 47,000 Saarlanders living in the Reich were brought in to cast their ballots, further strengthening the nationalists' support. The campaign against reunification scarcely existed in comparison, and was hamstrung by internal divisions over whether to campaign for a continuation of the *status quo* or for absorption into France.[23]

In many parts of the Saarland, the local Nazi Party exerted massive intimidation and violence behind the scenes to deter the opposition from voting against reunification with Germany. The terror it unfolded was reminiscent of the early months of 1933 in Germany. Social Democratic meetings were broken up by brownshirts wielding steel bars. People distributing propaganda against reunification were beaten up with rubber truncheons or even shot. Anti-fascist pubs were attacked and their windows shattered in a hail of bullets. Opposition meetings were turned into riots. The atmosphere resembled that of a civil war, as one local inhabitant remarked. The local police stood by while all this went on. While German SS units were sent into the area to help escalate the terror, rumours put about by the 'yes' campaign encouraged voters to believe that the ballot would not be secret, a plausible enough suggestion in view of what had been going on in plebiscites and elections in Germany itself. Strong hints were dropped that those known to have voted 'no' would be carted off to concentration camps once the Germans came in. Especially in small communities, the identity of the local Communists and Social Democrats was generally known anyway, so anti-Nazis were aware that this was no empty threat. The international monitors appointed to oversee the plebiscite admitted that the campaign was violent and called for the terror to stop, but their soldiers on the ground were commanded by officers strongly hostile to the Communists and Social Democrats, and so took no action.[24] It was not surprising that a majority of former Communist and Social Democratic voters decided that unity with Germany was the best course; they had not experienced the reality of life in the Third Reich, and their national identity as Germans was strong. The labour movement had always been weak in the Saarland, where, one German trade unionist noted, the Prussian state had been a major employer, putting miners in uniform and disciplining dissidents, and the big industrialists had wielded huge influence. 'The population of the Saar', he concluded resignedly, 'belongs among the politically most backward population in Germany.'[25] How far it was possible to draw general conclusions from the plebiscite about the attitude of the majority of Germans to the Third Reich must remain in doubt, particularly given the small size of the population and its peculiar political culture as a border region. For most Saarlanders, the vote was a 'yes' for Germany irrespective of Hitler and the Nazis.[26]

Under pressure, the government in Berlin had been obliged to promise that German laws and practices would only be introduced gradually into the Saar, and that Jews in particular would not be exposed to the kind of violence that had been common in the Reich since the end of January 1933. However, it was not long before the Saarlanders began to experience the realities of life in the Third Reich. 'Prussian' carpet-baggers moved in to take over offices and jobs, the Gestapo set up its headquarters in the old trade union building, and people suspected of pro-French sympathies were unceremoniously sacked from their jobs. Prominent Communists and Social Democrats fled the country without delay. The mass of ordinary Saarlanders doubtless never wished they had voted otherwise than for reunification, but all the same, it failed to bring them the immediate improvements they had been promised. Unemployment did not vanish overnight, and food shortages quickly began to affect the region. The region's Jews were initially allowed to emigrate on more favourable terms than those on offer in the rest of Germany, but from September 1935, with the promulgation of the Nuremberg Laws, they were exposed to the full rigours of Nazi antisemitism. There were mutterings, even strikes, but no real resistance; conditions in this largely rural and small-town society, with its weak labour movement traditions, made it virtually impossible.[27] It was not until 1938 that economic recovery, fuelled by rearmament, began to reconcile the Saarlanders to their lot, and the continuing propaganda barrage from Berlin, the Nazification of education, and compulsory enrolment in the Hitler Youth, began to spread acceptance of the Third Reich amongst young Saarlanders in particular.[28]

All this was still to come when, on 1 March 1935, the day of formal incorporation, Hitler spoke in Saarbrücken of his joy at the Saarlanders' decision. It was a great day for Germany, he said, and a great day for Europe. It showed the power and popularity of the Third Reich and its ideas for all Germans. 'In the end', he proclaimed, 'blood is stronger than any documents of mere paper. What ink has written will one day be blotted out by blood.' The implications for German-speaking minorities in other European countries, notably Poland and Czechoslovakia, were unmistakeable.[29] The Hamburg schoolteacher Luise Solmitz celebrated the 'Day of the Saar's Homecoming' by hoisting up her old black-white-red Imperial banner for the last time, before raising her new one, decorated with the swastika, over her house.[30] All over Germany, flags were flown to celebrate the event. Correspondingly, the vote spread despondency among the clandestine Social Democratic and Communist opposition in Germany and gave a boost to the self-confidence of the Nazi rank and file.[31]

It also injected a new boldness in foreign affairs into the German Leader. Hitler was increasingly unable to conceal the pace or extent of rearmament from the world, and indeed the Saar plebiscite provided the spur to fresh demands from the military which would be completely impossible to keep from prying eyes abroad if they were carried out. The success of the Saar plebiscite seems to have prompted his announcement of the existence of a German air force and the introduction of conscription, on 16 March 1935. The army would be expanded to more than half a million men, five times the size permitted by the Treaty of Versailles, he said. The following day saw a grandiose military parade in Berlin, at which Defence Minister General Werner von Blomberg announced that Germany was about to take up its rightful place in the world of nations once again.[32] Naturally Hitler assured everyone that all Germany wanted was peace. Many of his middle-class sympathizers believed him. 'We've got general conscription again!' wrote Luise Solmitz triumphantly in her diary:

The day that we have longed for since the disgrace of 1918 . . . In the morning France had its much-fought-over two-year period of military service in its pocket, in the evening we had general conscription as an answer to it. We would never have experienced Versailles if such actions had always been taken, such answers always given . . . General conscription is to serve not war but the maintenance of peace. For a defenceless country in the midst of heavily armed people must necessarily be an invitation and encouragement to maltreat it as territory to march into or to plunder. We haven't forgotten the invasion of the Ruhr.[33]

As the formal announcement came over the radio, Luise Solmitz reported, 'I rose to my feet. It overcame me, the moment was too great. I had to listen standing.'[34]

But the announcement sparked widespread anxiety amongst many Germans too, particularly those who had experienced the First World War. Many young men groaned at the prospect of being conscripted after they had already spent many months doing labour service. At the same time, however, some older workers welcomed the relief that would be given to the unemployment situation by the move. And accompanying what one report called a general 'really particularly strong war psychosis', often in the very same people, was also a widespread feeling of satisfaction that Germany was at last achieving international respect again. 'There is no doubt', reported a Social Democratic agent in Rhineland-Westphalia, 'that the perpetual banging-on about equality of honour and German freedom has had an effect far into the ranks of the formerly Marxist working-class and caused confusion there.'[35]

International reaction was sobering. The British, French and Italian governments responded by meeting at Stresa, in Italy, on 11 April 1935, and declaring their determination to defend the integrity of Austria against the German threat that had been obvious since July 1934 and now seemed to be looming once again. Less than a week later, the League of Nations formally censured Germany's rearmament programme. Shortly after this, France concluded an agreement with the Soviet Union. These moves had more rhetorical effect than real clout. Continuing the policy of bilateral negotiations with individual countries begun with the Polish pact. Hitler had been discussing a naval agreement with the British since November 1934. He realized that it would be a very long time before the renascent German fleet could hope to match the size of Britain's enormous navy, and for the time being at any rate he wanted to reassure the British so that they would not interfere with Germany's achievement of Continental hegemony. Later on, as he told the head of the navy, Admiral Raeder, in June 1934, the fleet could be built up to its full strength and turned against Britain, as Raeder and his fellow officers envisaged; but not now. Hitler accompanied his reassurances to the British with threats. He warned British negotiators that German rearmament was far advanced, particularly in air power (more so, indeed, than it actually was). In the long run Germany needed colonies to expand its living-space (a scarcely veiled threat to the far-flung British Empire). But Hitler declared that his preferred choice was to take the first step along this road with Britain rather than against, in the hope of smoothing things over later on. The British, realizing they were not going to get Germany to rejoin the League of Nations, and worried about the growing naval strength of Japan, agreed to what seemed perfectly reasonable terms, and on 18 June 1935 a joint Anglo-German Naval Agreement was signed, allowing the Germans to build up their navy to 35 per cent of the strength of the British navy and to reach parity with the British in the number of submarines. This rode a coach and horses through the Stresa agreement, concluded only a few months before, and was a major diplomatic triumph for Hitler.[36]

The German negotiating team in London was led by a man who was soon to join the top rank of Nazi leaders: Joachim von Ribbentrop. Born in 1893 in the Rhineland, son of a professional soldier of bourgeois origin, Ribbentrop had graduated from grammar school, but instead of going to university he spent time in a variety of jobs in Britain, Canada and Francophone Switzerland, gaining a good command of English and French, and making a number of contacts that were to prove useful later on. He served on both the western and eastern fronts in the First World War, and was awarded the Iron Cross for bravery. At the end of the war, he was at the Prussian military mission in Constantinople, after which he was assigned to a military team preparing for the Peace Conference. By the time he left the army in 1919, therefore, Ribbentrop's travels and diplomatic activities had given him a strong interest in foreign affairs. But it was business to which he initially returned – first cotton, then the drinks trade, through his marriage to Annelies Henkell, the daughter of a well-known manufacturer of *Sekt*, German sparkling wine. The marriage gave him financial security and an *entrée* into high society. By getting himself adopted by an aunt from the aristocratic branch of his family, he was able to add the noble prefix 'von' to his name. But the move backfired. It was rumoured that he had paid his aunt for this service. Moreover, some noted that while the complicated adoption legislation governing his choice treated the 'von' as part of the adoptive parent's name and therefore transferable with it to the adopted children, it insisted at the same time that the transfer of the noble prefix did not in any way transfer noble status to the adoptee. The incident was characteristic as much of Ribbentrop's social pretentiousness as it was of his social ineptitude: in London, in the 1930s, he was sometimes known as 'von Ribbensnob'.[37]

Ribbentrop was far from being a Nazi of the first hour. For most of the Weimar Republic he shared the hatred of most middle-class Germans for the Peace Settlement, despised the parliamentary system, and was considerably alarmed by the menace of Communism, but he did not gravitate towards the far right until 1932. As a member, inevitably, of the fashionable *Herrenclub*, the gentlemen's club in Berlin patronized by the aristocracy, including Papen and his friends, Ribbentrop met Hitler and became involved in the complex negotiations that eventually led to his appointment as Reich Chancellor in January 1933. To the provincial Hitler, Ribbentrop, rather like the Nazi Leader's old intimate Putzi Hanfstaengl, seemed a man of the world, experienced in foreign travel, multi-lingual, socially adept. Hitler began to use him for special diplomatic missions, bypassing the conservative, routine-bound Foreign Ministry. Doubtless with Hitler's approval, Ribbentrop set up his own independent office, along the lines of Alfred Rosenberg's, to develop and influence policy on foreign affairs. Before long it had a staff of 150, who were engaged in a kind of institutional guerrilla warfare with the mandarins of the Foreign Ministry. Ribbentrop's success in negotiating the Anglo-German Naval Agreement brought him the reputation of getting on with the British, and in the late summer of 1936 Hitler appointed him ambassador to London, his mission to improve relations still further and if possible deliver a formal Anglo-German alliance.[38]

Unfortunately, all of this was something of a misapprehension. Ribbentrop's style of diplomacy – brusque, peremptory, authoritarian – may have appealed to Hitler, but it did not go down well with diplomats, and in London the new ambassador soon acquired another derisive nickname: 'von Brickendrop'. Soon he was burning with resentment at imagined slights by British high society. Many of these were of his own making. A low point was reached at a reception at court in 1937, when he startled the shy, stuttering King George VI by greeting him with clicked heels and a Nazi salute. Ribbentrop did not in fact like Britain and the British at all. When Sir John Simon, the British Foreign Secretary, expressed his pleasure during the naval negotiations at Ribbentrop's unusual frankness, he probably did not mean it as a compliment. Ribbentrop did not want the London posting, delayed taking it up for three months, and went home to Berlin so often that the humorous London magazine *Punch* called him 'the Wandering Aryan'. Hated and despised by the 'old fighters' in the Nazi leadership, including Goebbels and Göring, who resented the influence wielded by this Johnny-come-lately, Ribbentrop needed to maintain a presence in Berlin if he was not to be marginalized. But he was not without influence on Hitler himself. He bombarded Hitler with dispatches from London proclaiming the total incompatibility of British and German aims in the world and forecasting war between the two powers in the end. At the same time, however, he also considered the British effete and vacillating and so he repeatedly told Hitler not to take the possibility of British intervention in Europe too seriously. Hitler listened to him. But this too proved in the end to be bad advice.[39]

IV

Initally, however, it seemed all too plausible. For, towards the end of 1935, the international situation in Europe had begun to undergo a dramatic series of changes. First of all, Mussolini launched an invasion of Abyssinia, the last major uncolonized African state remaining, in October 1935, in pursuit of his dream of creating a new Roman Empire, and revenge for the humiliating defeat of an Italian army by Ethiopian forces at the battle of Adowa in 1896. The motley feudal armies of the Ethiopian Emperor Haile Selassie were no match for the mechanized legions of the Italians. The brief war demonstrated perhaps for the first time the murderous potential of supremacy in the air. Without any serious opposition, Italian planes obliterated the Ethiopian forces by bombing them incessantly, using not only high explosives to destroy the gaudily arrayed cavalry but also poison gas to wipe out the poorly disciplined foot-soldiers. It was no contest. But Abyssinia was a vast country, and it took time for the Italian forces to penetrate to its interior and place it under occupation. Haile Selassie made a dramatic journey to Geneva, where he earned widespread sympathy with a moving appeal for help to the League of Nations. For his part, Mussolini had supposed that the French and British would not intervene, but public opinion forced the hand of the new British Foreign Secretary, Anthony Eden, who lent his support to the imposition of economic sanctions on Italy by the League. Suddenly isolated, the Italian dictator, urged on by his pro-German son-in-law Galeazzo Ciano, turned to Hitler for help.[40]

Hitler saw this as an opportunity to break out of Germany's diplomatic isolation. The murder of Dollfuss had marked a low point in his relations with Mussolini, from whom he had taken so many ideas, and whom he still greatly admired.[41] Things now began to improve. The German Foreign Ministry was still deeply suspicious of the Italians' motives, however. Summoning the German Ambassador in Rome, Ulrich von Hassell, to Berlin, Hitler told him in the presence of Foreign Minister Neurath that it was time to regard the tensions of 1934 as 'a closed chapter' and to come to Italy's aid. 'We must do everything', he said, 'to prevent the various opponents throughout the world of the authoritarian system of government from concentrating upon us as their sole object.' If Italian Fascism were destroyed, Germany would be alone. Accordingly, Germany, while remaining formally neutral on the Abyssinian issue, refused to impose sanctions on Italy, and carried on business as usual. Grateful for this support, Mussolini let Hitler know that as far as he was concerned, from now on, Austria lay within the German sphere of influence. Stresa, he told von Hassell, was dead.[42] Sanctions in any case proved totally without effect. The Italians pressed the war on to a successful conclusion in May, 1936, while Britain, France and the League continued to bicker and dither. These events sealed the fate of the League, whose ineffectiveness was now palpable. They also convinced Hitler and Mussolini that they had nothing to fear from Britain and France. More immediately, the Italian victory seemed to provide concrete evidence that air supremacy was the key to military success. The British, who had hitherto dominated the Mediterranean by virtue of their naval power, now seemed suddenly vulnerable. To cement his new friendship with Germany, Mussolini sacked his pro-French Foreign Minister and replaced him on 9 June 1936 with Ciano.[43]

By this time, too, France's position in Europe had been dramatically weakened, making an alliance seem less attractive to the Italians anyway. The British and French had not seen eye to eye over the response to the Ethiopian War. Internal political upheavals in France that culminated in the electoral victory of the Popular Front in May 1936 seemed to have focused the attention of French politicians on the domestic scene. The international community had displayed a complete inability to curb Italian imperialism. And the Italian *rapprochement* with Germany had increased Germany's freedom of action. All these factors came together to convince Hitler that France and Britain would not try to prevent the German army marching into the Rhineland. The western part of Germany still remained a demilitarized zone according to the provisions of the Treaty of Versailles even after the departure of the Anglo-French occupying forces at the end of the 1920s. Hitler had got away with quitting the League of Nations. He had got away with announcing German rearmament. And the domestic situation in Germany was so bad in the spring of 1936, with food shortages, worsening conflict with the Catholic Church and general grumbling and discontent, that a diplomatic coup was badly needed to cheer people up. Hitler had already obtained assurances from the army leadership that it could be done. They agreed that it was necessary to establish proper defences in the West. Nevertheless, Blomberg and the leading generals were extremely nervous, realizing that the army was still no match for the French should they choose to act. Even Hitler hesitated, knowing full well the risk he was taking. By the beginning of March, encouraged at every juncture by Ribbentrop, he had made up his mind. The forthcoming ratification of the Franco-Soviet Pact by the French Chamber of Deputies would provide the pretext. The German army units who marched into the Rhineland would be reinforced by police units to make them seem more numerous than they really were. The whole operation would be prepared in the utmost secrecy, with troops moving into their pre-arranged positions overnight. Even the cabinet would not be told until the last minute.[44]

On Saturday 7 March 1936, Hitler appeared in the Reichstag, summoned at short notice to a noontide session in the Kroll Opera House. As he rose to speak, unknown to the deputies, German troops had already been marching into the demilitarized zone since dawn; at one o'clock in the afternoon they reached the river itself. Hitler began with a tirade against Bolshevism. Yet, he went on, the French had recently signed a pact with the Soviet Union, and ratified it on 4 March. In view of this, he told the Reichstag, Germany no longer felt bound by the Locarno Pact of 1925, which had regulated its relations with France. The American journalist William L. Shirer, who was present, observed the hysterical scenes that followed:

Now the six hundred deputies, personal appointees all of Hitler, little men with big bodies and bulging necks and cropped hair and pouched bellies and brown uniforms and heavy boots, little men of clay in his fine hands, leap to their feet like automatons, their right arms upstretched in the Nazi salute, and scream 'Heil's' ... Hitler raises his hand for silence ... He says in a deep, resonant voice: 'Men of the German Reichstag!' The silence is utter. 'In this historic hour, when in the Reich's Western provinces German troops are at this minute marching into their future, peace-time garrisons, we all unite in two sacred vows.' He can go no further. It is news to this hysterical 'Parliamentary' mob that German soldiers are already on the move into the Rhineland ... They spring, yelling and crying, to their feet ... Their hands are raised in slavish salute, their faces now contorted with hysteria, their mouths wide open, shouting, shouting, their eyes, burning with fanaticism, glued on the new god, the Messiah.[45]

The two pledges Hitler made were, characteristically, that Germany would never yield to force on the one hand, but would strive for peace on the other. As before, he declared that Germany had no territorial demands in Europe. And he offered a series of peace pacts to reassure Germany's neighbours. All of this was merely rhetorical. To underline the importance of the moment, he also dissolved the Reichstag and called elections, coupled with a plebiscite on his action, for 29 March 1936. His first speech of the campaign, on 12 March, was delivered in Karlsruhe, on the banks of the Rhine, a stone's throw away from France.[46]

German propaganda films and press reports showed pictures of ecstatic Rhinelanders welcoming the troops with Hitler salutes and strewing their path with flowers. Luise Solmitz wrote:

I was completely overpowered by the events of this moment ... delighted by our soldiers marching in, by the greatness of Hitler and the power of his language, the force of this man ... We've been longing for this language, this firmness, as subversion reigned over us, together with the Entente. But we hadn't dared think of such deeds. Again and again the Leader puts a *fait accompli* before the world ... If the world had heard us use such language for 2,000 years – we would have needed to use it only sparingly, would always have been understood and would have been able to spare ourselves much blood, many tears, loss of land and humiliation ... Reports of the mood in every town speak of unprecedented jubilation.[47]

Social Democratic observers, however, told a different story. 'The occupation of the Rhine zone,' one agent reported, 'has allegedly been greeted by the entire population with huge jubilation. But reports from the whole of the West are agreed that it was only the Nazis who celebrated.'[48]

Some businessmen were admittedly pleased because they thought things would now improve for them. Most people indeed quietly approved of the remilitarization. Young people in particular were enthusiastic in some places. 'It's our country, after all,' declared one worker. 'Why shouldn't we be allowed to have any military there?'[49] But there were also widespread fears that the action would lead to war. Many active Nazis responded to them by pointing to Hitler's professions of pacific intent. Only a few boasted that they would welcome a war.[50] People were proud of the recovery of national sovereignty, but at the same time, they were desperately worried about the dangers of a general war, about the prospect of mass bombing of German cities and about a repeat of the death and destruction of 1914–18.[51] The fears of the great majority were not diminished by the extensive air-raid precautions that accompanied the remilitarization action. 'The people', one Social Democratic agent summed up, 'are very worked-up. They're afraid of war, since everyone is clear that Germany will lose this war and then will go to its downfall.'[52]

In March 1936, Germans held their breath while 3,000 troops marched deep into the Rhineland, backed by another 30,000 who remained on or near the eastern bank of the river. Had the French chosen to send their own troops in, the Germans would have been driven out within a few hours despite Hitler's orders for them to resist. But they did not. Believing that the German military presence was ten times greater than it really was, and hamstrung by public anxiety about war at a time when a general election was looming, the French government chose inaction. Their position was bolstered by the British, who moved quickly to restrain any precipitate response. What had happened, after all, was only a recovery of Germany's sovereignty over its own territory, and no one thought that was worth risking a general war. Nobody at this stage thought of Hitler as different from previous German statesmen, and these had never hidden their desire to move troops back into the Rhineland. Indeed, such was the public indifference to the issue in Britain that the government even refused to support the idea of imposing League

Map 18.   The Saarland Plebiscite and the Remilitarization of the
Rhineland, 1935–6

of Nations sanctions on Germany for what was in fact a breach of international treaty agreements. Hitler had taken his biggest gamble yet, and got away with it.[53] The experience, confirmed by another rigged election and plebiscite held on 29 March 1936, which delivered the inevitable 98.9 per cent for the Nazi Party and the government's actions, confirmed Hitler in the belief that he could not fail. Convinced in the myth of his own invincibility, he now began to quicken the pace of Germany's march towards European domination and world conquest. 'Neither threats nor warnings', he declared in Munich on 14 March 1936, 'will prevent me from going my way. I follow the path assigned to me by Providence with the instinctive sureness of a sleepwalker.'[54]

CREATING GREATER GERMANY

I

The remilitarization of the Rhineland profoundly altered the balance of international relations in Europe. Up to this point, as had been made abundantly clear in 1923, the French were potentially able to enforce Germany's obligations by marching across the Rhine and occupying the country's biggest industrial region, the Ruhr. From now on, they were no longer able to do so. The French position from 1936 onwards was a purely defensive one. It left the Third Reich a free hand in moving against the small countries of Eastern Europe. Shocked by a development that left them dangerously vulnerable, many of them, previously allied to France, moved to try and improve relations with the Third Reich. Austria now felt particularly at risk, given the new-found friendship between Germany and Italy.[55] Before long, too, Hitler and Mussolini's relationship drew even closer. For, following a left-wing victory in the Spanish elections held in February 1936, right-wing army officers in various parts of the country launched a concerted uprising on 17 July 1936 to overthrow the Republic and create a military dictatorship. The uprising failed to achieve its objectives in most parts of the country, and soon Spain was plunged into a desperate and bloody civil war. German officials and businessmen in Spain urged on Hitler the support of the rebels, and one of the leading figures in the uprising, General Francisco Franco, appealed directly to Hitler for help. It was not long in coming.[56]

Even before the end of July 1936, German planes were in Spain ferrying rebel forces to the key fronts and thus helping to ensure that the uprising did not fizzle out. From this modest beginning, German intervention was soon to reach startling proportions. The main reasons were both military and political. As the political situation in Spain polarized with unprecedented intensity, Hitler began to be concerned about the possibility that a Republican victory would deliver the country into the hands of the Communists at a time when a Popular Front government, backed by the Communist Party, had just come to power in France. A union between the two countries might create a serious obstacle in Western Europe to his plans for expansion and war in the East, particularly when this encompassed the Soviet Union, as it eventually would. Beyond this, he soon realized that the war would provide an ideal proving-ground for Germany's new armed forces and equipment.[57] Soon, Werner von Blomberg, the German Minister of War, freshly promoted to Field-Marshal, was in Spain telling Franco that he would get German troops and *matériel* provided he agreed to prosecute the war with more vigour than he had displayed to date. In November 1936, 11,000 German troops and support staff, supplied with aircraft, artillery and armour, landed at Cadiz. By the end of the month, the Nationalist regime had been officially recognized as the government of Spain by the Third Reich, and the German forces had been organized into an effective unit under the name of the Condor Legion.[58]

Hitler and his generals were clear that German assistance to Franco could not expand indefinitely without attracting the hostility of the other European powers. Britain and France had agreed on a policy of non-intervention. This did not stop supplies from the United Kingdom in particular from reaching the Nationalist side, but it did mean that if the fiction of general neutrality was to be preserved, other powers would have to be careful about the extent to which they intervened. Mussolini's assistance to the rebels was far greater than Hitler's, but both were countered by the aid that the Soviet Union gave to the Republican side. Volunteers from many countries flocked to the Republican banner to form an International Brigade; a rather smaller number went to fight for the Francoists. In this situation, preventing the conflict from escalating into a wider war seemed to be in everybody's interest. The stakes scarcely seemed overwhelming. So Hitler kept the Condor Legion as a relatively small, though highly trained and professional, fighting force.[59]

Under the command of General Hugo Sperrle, however, it played a significant part in the Nationalist war effort. Soon the Legion was testing its new 88-millimetre anti-aircraft guns against Republican planes. But its most effective contribution was made through its own bombers, which took part in a concerted advance, undertaken at Sperrle's behest, on the Basque country. On 31 March 1937 the Legion's Junkers aircraft bombed the undefended town of Durango, killing 248 inhabitants, including several priests and nuns, the first European town to be subjected to intensive bombing. Far more devastating, however, was the raid they carried out, in conjunction with four new fast Heinkel 111 bombers and some untried Messerschmitt Bf-109 fighters, on the town of Guernica on 26 April 1937. Forty-three aircraft, including a small number of Italian planes, dropped 100,000 pounds of incendiary, high-explosive and shrapnel bombs on the town, while the fighters strafed the inhabitants and refugees in the streets with machine-gun fire. The town's population, normally not more than 7,000, was swollen with refugees, retreating Republican soldiers and peasants attending market-day. Over 1,600 people were killed and more than 800 injured. The centre of the town was flattened. The raid confirmed the widespread fear in Europe of the devastating effects of aerial bombing. Already a symbol of the assault on Basque identity, it gained a worldwide significance through the exiled, pro-Republican Spanish artist Pablo Picasso, who dedicated the mural he had been commissioned to produce for the Paris World Exposition a large painting, *Guernica*, depicting with unique and enduring power the sufferings of the town and its people.[60]

The international furore that greeted the raid led the Germans and the Spanish Nationalists to deny any responsibility. For years afterwards it was claimed that the Basques had blown their own town up.[61] Privately, Colonel Wolfram von Richthofen, who had organized the raid, concluded with satisfaction that the new planes and bombs had proved their effectiveness, though he was less than satisfied with the failure of the Spanish Nationalist generals to follow up the raid with an immediate knock-out blow to their Basque opponents.[62] But the Condor Legion did not repeat this murderous experiment. Later on, its bid to use fast-moving tanks in the concluding phase of the war was vetoed by the traditionalist Franco. Nevertheless, thanks to German and Italian help, superior resources and generalship, internal unity and international neutrality, the Francoists completed their victory by the end of March 1939. On 18 May 1939, led by Richthofen, the Legion marched proudly past in Franco's final victory parade in Madrid.[63] Once more, international inaction had allowed Hitler free rein. The Spanish Civil War was one more example for him of the supine pusillanimity of Britain and France, and thus an encouragement to move faster in the fulfilment of his own intentions. In this sense, at least, the Spanish conflict accelerated the descent into war.[64]

More immediately, however, it cemented the alliance between Hitler and Mussolini. Already in September 1936 Hans Frank visited Rome to begin negotiations, and the next month, the Italian Foreign Minister Ciano went to Germany to sign a secret agreement with Hitler. By November 1936 Mussolini was referring openly to a 'Rome–Berlin Axis'. Both powers had agreed to respect each other's ambitions and ally themselves against the Spanish Republic. At the same time, behind the backs of the Foreign Ministry, Hitler arranged for Ribbentrop's office to conclude an Anti-Comintern Pact with Japan, pledging both to a defensive alliance against the Soviet Union. For the moment, it was of little value, but together with the Rome–Berlin Axis, it completed the line-up of revisionist, expansionist powers that was to take such devastating shape during the Second World War.[65] The attempt to bring Britain into the Anti-Comintern Pact, spearheaded by Ribbentrop's appointment as Ambassador in London in August 1936, was never likely to succeed; it foundered almost immediately on the new envoy's tactlessness and his use of the threat of undermining Britain's overseas empire as an instrument of blackmail – a threat taken all too seriously by the British. As far as Hitler was concerned, moreover, nothing less than a global arrangement with the United Kingdom would by this stage have been worth the price of alienating the Italians, given the substantial British presence in the Mediterranean. He did not abandon the idea of some kind of arrangement with the British and continued to believe that the United Kingdom would stand aside from events in Europe, however they unfolded. For the moment, however, such calculations took second place to the pursuit of his immediate aims on the European Continent.[66]

II

Those aims were moving appreciably closer to fulfilment by the second half of 1936. The Four-Year Plan, designed to build up Germany's military power fast enough to undertake a general war by the early 1940s, was under way. The Rome–Berlin Axis, the Anti-Comintern Pact, the successful prosecution of the Spanish Civil War and the ascendancy of appeasement in the British government all helped convince Hitler that he could accelerate the pace of his foreign policy even in the absence of a British alliance. It was in this mood that Hitler held the conference with Blomberg, Fritsch, Göring, Neurath and Raeder on 5 November 1937 where Colonel Hossbach recorded the Nazi Leader's intention of taking military action against Austria and Czechoslovakia in the not-too-distant future.[67] But by this time, Hitler had begun to feel that he was being hamstrung by obstructionism and lack of enthusiasm from some of his underlings. In the winter of 1937–8, he began to replace them with men who would be more willing to go along with an accelerated pace towards war. For a number of top military leaders, backed by sympathizers in the Foreign Office, had become extremely alarmed by Hitler's increasingly impatient drive towards war. Germany might be able to take over Austria and possibly Czechoslovakia, but the country's state of military preparedness meant that it was in their view far from ready for a war with Britain and France should military action in East-Central Europe ignite a general conflagration. War Minister Field-Marshal Werner von Blomberg, Foreign Minister Konstantin von Neurath and Army Commander-in-Chief Werner von Fritsch all expressed serious doubts after the meeting of November 1937. Chief of the Army General Staff General Ludwig Beck was even more alarmed and expressed his dismay at Hitler's irresponsibility. All these men believed that a general war was both inevitable and desirable, but they were also convinced that to launch it now would be dangerously premature.[68]

Early in 1938 the opportunity to move presented itself to Hitler in the form of an unexpected scandal. On 12 January 1938, Blomberg, a lonely widower, married a woman thirty-five years younger than himself. He had met her while walking in the Tiergarten in Berlin. Blomberg's new wife, Margarethe Gruhn, was a simple young woman from a humble background. Hitler approved of the match because it showed the irrel-evance of social distinction in the Third Reich. So he agreed to act as a witness in the wedding ceremony. But Gruhn's background was in reality far from simple. An anonymous phone-call informed Fritsch that she had once registered with the police as a prostitute, posed for pornographic photographs and been convicted of stealing from a client. The police confirmed her identity. On 24 January Göring felt obliged to show her police file to Hitler. Alarmed at the ridicule he would suffer if it became known that he had been a witness to the marriage of an ex-prostitute, Hitler plunged into a deep depression, unable to sleep. The situation was made worse for him, characteristically, by the revelation that the pornographic photographs had been taken by a Jew with whom Gruhn had been living at the time. It was, wrote Goebbels in his diary, the worst crisis in the regime since the Röhm affair. 'The Leader', he reported, 'is completely shattered.' Goebbels thought the only honourable way out for Blomberg was to shoot himself. Blomberg turned down Göring's offer of an annulment of the wedding, and was forced to resign as Defence Minister. On 27 January Hitler saw him for the last time; the next day the Field-Marshal and his wife departed for a year's holiday in Italy.[69]

But this was by no means the end of the affair. Brooding on the possibility that other senior officers might also be tainted by moral scandal, Hitler suddenly recalled a file he had been shown on Colonel-General Fritsch in the summer of 1936, containing allegations of homo-sexual conduct levelled at him by a Berlin male prostitute, Otto Schmidt. At the time, Hitler had dismissed the allegations out of hand and ordered the file to be destroyed. But the meticulous Heydrich had kept it locked away, and on 25 January 1938 he submitted it to Hitler. Horrified, Hitler's military adjutant Colonel Hossbach told Fritsch, who declared that the allegations were completely false. Perhaps, Fritsch told a hastily summoned meeting the next day with Hitler, Göring and Otto Schmidt, hauled out of prison by the Gestapo for the occasion, they referred to a time in 1933–4 when he had regularly lunched alone with a member of the Hitler Youth whom he had provided with free meals. If so, he could assure everybody that the relationship had been entirely innocent. Previously unaware of this relationship, Hitler was now even more alarmed. Fritsch's lack of indignation as he coolly dismissed Schmidt's story did not help him either. Interrogated on 27 January by the Gestapo,

Schmidt added further circumstantial details of his own supposed relationship with Fritsch. The Army Commander had little difficulty in proving these to be false. But the damage was done. Hitler did not trust him any more. Justice Minister Gürtner, consulted on the matter, opined that Fritsch had failed to clear his name. Plunged into even deeper gloom, Hitler cancelled his annual speech on the anniversary of his appointment as Reich Chancellor on 30 January. On 3 February 1938 he asked Fritsch to resign.[70]

At Gürtner's insistence, Fritsch was tried by a military court on 18 March 1938. He was unambiguously cleared of all charges, which rested, the court concluded, on mistaken identity: the Fritsch in question had been someone else altogether. Barred from further access to high military office, he volunteered for service on the Polish front and was killed in battle on 22 September 1939; Blomberg survived the war in retirement, dying in an Allied prison in March 1946.[71] In the meantime, Hitler still had to find a way out of the crisis. After intensive discussions with Goebbels, however, Hitler finally acted. The fall of the two top army men could be usefully disguised as part of a much wider reshuffle. Hitler dismissed no fewer than fourteen generals, including six from the air force; they included many men who were known to be lukewarm about National Socialism. Forty-six other senior officers were redeployed. Fritsch was replaced as commander-in-chief of the army by Walther von Brauchitsch, an artillery officer who was now promoted to the rank of colonel-general. Brauchitsch was not a Nazi, but he was an admirer of Hitler, and he was far more subservient to him than his predecessor had been. Hitler brushed aside the claims of Göring for appointment as War Minister. His existing military rank (retired captain) was too junior for this to be acceptable to the generals, and in any case the post might have made him too powerful. Hitler fobbed him off with the title of Field-Marshal.[72]

The War Ministry remained unoccupied. From now on, Hitler would carry out its functions himself as supreme commander, creating subordinate Ministries for each of the three branches of the armed forces, co-ordinated by a new High Command of the Armed Forces (*Oberkommando der Wehrmacht*, or OKW), under General Wilhelm Keitel, the top military administrator under the old structure. At the same time, he took the opportunity to replace Neurath as Foreign Minister with his own man, Joachim von Ribbentrop, who could be trusted far more to do his bidding. The conservative Ulrich von Hassell was recalled from the embassy in Rome and replaced with a more pliant ambassador. Hitler also announced the appointment of the loyal Walther Funk as a replacement for Schacht at the Ministry of Economics, from which Schacht had resigned on 26 November 1937. The official explanation for these changes was that Blomberg and Fritsch had retired on health grounds, but Hitler told the real story to both the cabinet, meeting for its last ever time on 5 February 1938, and the senior generals, earlier the same day. The army officers, convinced by the circumstantial details that Hitler enumerated, were aghast. The moral integrity of the army leadership had been destroyed. It was now completely at Hitler's mercy. On 20 February Hitler addressed the Reichstag for several hours. The armed forces, he declared, were now 'dedicated to this National Socialist state in blind faith and obedience'.[73]

These changes left Hitler in unfettered command of German foreign, military and economic policy. Surrounded by acolytes who constantly reiterated their admiration for him, he now had nobody who was willing to restrain him. By this time, too, he had shed the few personal friends who retained anything like a mind of their own. One of them, Ernst 'Putzi' Hanfstaengl, who had supported Hitler in his early days, had been granted the somewhat empty title of Foreign Press Chief of the Nazi Party in 1932. But he had never been able to challenge Goebbels's domination of this area of propaganda, and Hitler himself had no more real use for him. Gone were the undignified days when Hitler had strode around Hanfstaengl's drawing-room waving his arms about while his host played Wagner on the piano. Vain, self-centred, never one of Hitler's slavishly adoring followers, Hanfstaengl caused mounting irritation in the Nazi leadership with exaggerated stories of his bravery in staying in New York during the First World War after America entered the war in 1917, at a time when several of them had been fighting on the front. When he coupled this with disparagement of the courage of the German troops fighting on Franco's side in the Spanish Civil War, Hitler and Goebbels decided to teach him a lesson. In February 1937 Hitler ordered Hanfstaengl to go to Spain to liaise with German war correspondents behind the front. In mid-air, the pilot, following Hitler's instructions, informed Hanfstaengl that he was in fact being sent on a secret mission behind enemy lines. Not the bravest of men, Hanfstaengl panicked. Eventually the pilot set him down on an airstrip near Leipzig, claiming there was something wrong with the engine. Every part of the episode was caught on film by Goebbels's cameramen. The resulting footage, Goebbels later noted in his diary, was enough to make him die laughing. Hanfstaengl did not see the joke. Convinced he had been the subject of an assassination attempt, he fled to Switzerland and did not return.[74]

III

At the beginning of 1938, Hitler's attention turned once more to Austria. He had concluded a formal agreement with the Austrian government on 11 July 1936 in which Austria had accepted the principle that it was a German state and the Austrian dictator, Kurt von Schuschnigg, had complied with Hitler's request to give the 'national opposition', or in other words the Austrian Nazi Party, a share in government. But while Schuschnigg regarded this as settling the difficulties that had emerged in Austo-German relations with the coup attempt of two years before, Hitler saw it only as the thin end of a political wedge that would eventually prise open Austrian sovereignty and deliver complete union with Germany.[75] Yet for a long time, Hitler did not think the moment was appropriate for a move. Throughout 1936, he urged caution on the Austrian Nazis, not wanting to cause international alarm while the rest of Europe was digesting the remilitarization of the Rhineland and its consequences. He continued in this vein through much of 1937 as well. The leadership of the Austrian Nazis obeyed, downplaying the hostility to the Catholic Church that was creating such a furore in their neighbour to the north. Austria was an overwhelmingly Catholic state, and it was vital to keep the Church hierarchy at worst neutral, at best sympathetic, towards the idea of a reunion with Germany. The movement's rank and file chafed at the restrictions this policy imposed on their activism, and the underground Party was seriously divided. Another source of tension was supplied by Schuschnigg's appointment of Arthur Seyss-Inquart, a pro-Nazi lawyer, to the government. So great was the Austrian Nazi Party's resentment at this seeming co-optation of one of its leading figures into the governmental political machine that it formally expelled one of

Seyss-Inquart's team, Odilo Globocnik, in October 1937. The Austrian SS, led by Ernst Kaltenbrunner, was particularly forceful in propagating illegal activities against the wishes of the Party leadership. In the light of these divisions, any hope that Austrian independence could be overthrown from within had to be abandoned.[76]

While Hitler was urging caution, however, Hermann Göring was taking a somewhat bolder line. As head of the Four-Year Plan, he was becoming increasingly anxious about the rapidly growing shortfalls of raw materials and skilled industrial labour in the drive to rearm and prepare for war. Austria possessed both in abundance. Göring was particularly keen to grasp rich iron-ore deposits in Styria. Making his intentions clear, he showed a specially made map of Europe, with Austria already incorporated into Germany, to Mussolini in September 1937, and to the top official in the Austrian Foreign Ministry two months later. He took Mussolini's silence for assent. The incorporation of Austria fitted well into Göring's geopolitical idea of a broad, German-led economic sphere in Central Europe – the traditional idea, familiar since the early 1900s, of *Mitteleuropa*. So he also pressed for a currency union between the two countries. The idea met with a lukewarm response from the Austrian government, which suspected that this would lead inexorably to political union, given the vastly greater economic strength of Germany. This aggressive policy was too tough, Hitler told Mussolini during the Italian leader's visit to Germany in September 1937. Nevertheless, he did nothing to stop Göring's initiatives. For in practice he was already moving towards Göring's position and beginning to think that the incorporation of Austria should come sooner rather than later.[77]

The heightened sense of urgency that began to grip Hitler early in 1938 had several different causes. German rearmament was progressing at a headlong pace, but other countries were beginning to rearm too, and soon the advantage that Germany had built up would be lost. At the moment, too, experience seemed to show that Britain and France were still reluctant to take firm action against German expansion. This reluctance was underlined by the replacement on 21 February 1938 of Anthony Eden by the more conciliatory Lord Halifax as British Foreign Secretary. But how long would the will for appeasement last? Moreover, around 1937–8, Hitler himself began to feel that his own time was running out. He was nearing his fiftieth birthday, and he was becoming concerned about his health; in May 1938, he even suspected for a while that he had cancer. More immediately, and most crucially, one way of distracting attention from the crisis in the army leadership was to undertake some spectacular move in foreign policy. And here, for neither the first nor the last time, events played into Hitler's hands. The growing rapprochement between Germany and Italy had resulted among other things in Mussolini's withdrawal of all his previous objections to a German takeover of Austria, an aim that Hitler, as a native Austrian, had entertained since the beginning of his political career. Moreover, Schuschnigg, encouraged by Hitler's special ambassador in Vienna, Franz von Papen, was anxious to meet Hitler to try and curb the violence of the Austrian Nazis, who, he feared, were planning a coup along the lines of the failed putsch that had resulted in the death of his predecessor in 1934. The meeting was to be a momentous one.[78]

Schuschnigg's government had grown steadily weaker since 1936. It had made almost no headway at all in trying to improve the economic situation, which remained sunk in the depths of the Depression. Years of grinding poverty and mass unemployment had left the majority of the population not only disillusioned with the government but also more convinced than ever that the small Austrian Republic would never become economically viable on its own. Throughout the 1920s all the major political parties had been committed to reunifying Austria – part of Germany in its various incarnations all the way up to 1866 – with the Reich. Although the Nazi seizure of power had led the Marxist-oriented Austrian Socialists to drop this particular demand from their programme in 1933, there was no doubt that many of them continued to believe it was the best solution to their country's problems; after all, they thought, by joining the Third Reich they would only be leaving an unsuccessful dictatorship for a successful one. Moreover, many Socialists, embittered by their violent suppression by the government and the army in February 1934, were under no circumstances prepared to lend their support to the hated Schuschnigg, whom they held partly responsible for the killing of hundreds of their comrades during the conflict. More generally, Austrian antisemitism, a government report noted in 1936, was 'continuously growing' as people cast about for someone to blame. It was encouraged not only by the Austrian Nazis but also by the small but increasingly popular monarchist movement, led by the Archduke Otto von Habsburg, heir to the Habsburg throne. Schuschnigg's attempt to rally support by founding his own fascist-style Fatherland Front had completely failed; fascist movements in Europe gained their power from harnessing popular discontent, and a government-sponsored imitation convinced nobody. In 1936, Schuschnigg banned the turbulent Home Defence Leagues. This deprived him of the only remaining paramilitary force that might have helped him resist a German invasion; the paramilitary division of the Austrian Socialists had already been outlawed under his predecessor Dollfuss. Thousands of disgruntled paramilitaries gravitated towards the underground Austrian Nazi Party, also banned under Schuschnigg.[79]

Brokered by Papen, a meeting took place between Hitler and Schuschnigg at Berchtesgaden on 12 February 1938. In order to intimidate the Austrian dictator, Hitler had arranged for senior German military figures to be present at his mountain retreat, including the commander of the Condor Legion in Spain, Hugo Sperrle. Hitler had already been fully informed by Seyss-Inquart about Schuschnigg's position. Giving him no chance to put his arguments, Hitler launched into a furious tirade. 'The whole history of Austria', he ranted, 'is just one uninterrupted act of high treason. That was so in the past and remains so today. This historical paradox must now reach its long-overdue end.' For two hours he lectured Schuschnigg on his own invincibility ('I have achieved everything that I set out to do and have thus perhaps become the greatest German of all history') and made clear that military action would follow, unimpeded by foreign intervention, if the Austrians did not bow to his demands ('The German Reich is a major power, and no one can or will try to interfere when it puts things in order at its borders').[80] When Schuschnigg demurred, and asked for time for consultation, Hitler called General Keitel into the room, where he sat for ten minutes, full of implicit menace, before being sent away again. The following morning, to underline the threat, Keitel was ordered to Berlin to make the arrangements for intimidatory military manoeuvres on the Austrian border.[81]

On 15 February, Schuschnigg, thoroughly browbeaten, complied with all Hitler's demands, agreeing formally to conduct a joint foreign policy with Germany, to legalize the Austrian Nazi Party within the Fatherland Front, to release imprisoned Nazis and revoke all measures taken against them and to embark on programmes of military and economic collaboration. On Hitler's demand, Seyss-Inquart was appointed Austrian

Minister of the Interior. Many Austrian Nazis hated Seyss-Inquart, whose willingness to compromise with the government they regarded as treason, and their response was to smash all the windows in the German Embassy in Vienna. On 21 February 1938, Hitler summoned five top leaders of the Austrian Nazis to Berlin and effectively sacked them, forbidding them to return. From now on, he said, their Party had to take a legal course. Evolution, through a forced takeover of the Austrian government, not revolution by violence from below, was the way forward, he told them. But even this failed to quell the radicalism of some elements in the Austrian Nazi Party, who staged public demonstrations that far outweighed those of the Fatherland Front. More and more people, it was reported, were using the Hitler salute and the swastika emblem in public despite Seyss-Inquart's attempts to ban them in pursuit of his policy of taking over the government from within. The police were now refusing to enforce these regulations and the army was clearly going over to the National Socialists as well. A familiar dialectic was emerging of official pressure from above, coupled with the rhetoric of restraint, and matched by rapidly mounting pressure from below. Schuschnigg's agreement to Hitler's terms had turned Austria into a German satellite state; now, amidst mounting expectations that this would lead to a rapid union between the two countries, his support, and the already fragile legitimacy of the Austrian state, was disappearing before his very eyes.[82]

On the morning of 9 March 1938, in response to this increasingly desperate situation, Schuschnigg suddenly announced that a referendum was to be held on 13 March to ask Austrian voters whether they were in favour of 'a free and German, independent and social, Christian and united Austria; for freedom and work, and for the equality of all who declare for people and fatherland'. To ensure that this heavily loaded question got a resounding 'yes' from the Austrian electorate, voting was restricted to people over twenty-four years of age, thus disenfranchising a large part of the Nazi movement, whose supporters were predominantly young. Moreover, under the repressive conditions of Schuschnigg's clerico-fascist dictatorship, there was no guarantee that voting would be free or secret, nor did the Chancellor provide any assurances that it would be; the lack of a proper electoral register opened the way to potentially massive electoral fraud. Hitler was outraged at what he saw as a betrayal of the Berchtesgaden agreement. Summoning Göring and Goebbels, he began feverish discussions on what could be done to stop the vote. While the army was hastily organizing invasion plans based only on a study prepared earlier for the eventuality of a Habsburg restoration, Hitler sent an ultimatum to Schuschnigg at ten in the morning on 11 March 1938: the referendum had to be postponed for a fortnight and the wording changed to one similar to that of the Saar plebiscite, in other words, implicitly asking people to approve union rather than oppose it. Schuschnigg had to resign and be replaced by Seyss-Inquart. Schuschnigg agreed to postpone the vote but refused to resign. Seizing the initiative, Göring telephoned the nervous and reluctant Seyss-Inquart and told him to inform the Austrian Head of State, Wilhelm Miklas, that if he did not appoint him Chancellor 'then an invasion by the troops already mobilized on the border will follow tonight and that will be the end of Austria'. And, he added, 'you must let the National Socialists loose throughout the whole country. They are now to be allowed to go on the streets everywhere.'[83]

By the evening of 11 March, Austrian Nazis were demonstrating all over the country, while an SS contingent occupied the headquarters of the Tyrolese provincial government. The Nazi Regional Leader of Upper Austria announced to an ecstatic crowd of 20,000 on the main square in Linz that Schuschnigg had resigned, as indeed he had at 3.30 in the afternoon under the impact of Göring's second ultimatum. The plebiscite was summarily cancelled. In Vienna by chance, William L. Shirer was 'swept along in a shouting, hysterical Nazi mob'. The police, he reported, were 'looking on, grinning'. Some were already wearing swastika armbands. 'Young toughs were heaving paving blocks into the windows of the Jewish shops. The crowds roared with delight.' As the demonstrations spread, Göring told Seyss-Inquart to send a formal request for German troops to restore order. Not yet appointed Chancellor, he hesitated; the request had to be sent by Wilhelm Keppeler, the head of the Nazi Party's Austrian bureau, who was now in Vienna, instead. It went off at ten past nine on the evening of 11 March 1938. Meanwhile, Hitler had sent Prince Philip of Hesse to Mussolini to secure his neutrality. At 10.45 p.m., the prince telephoned Hitler personally to say that everything was all right. 'Please tell Mussolini I will never forget him for this,' Hitler said. 'Never, never, never, whatever happens.' The British signalled their neutrality. At midnight, the Austrian President finally

yielded and appointed Seyss-Inquart Chancellor. It was all too late anyway; spurred on by Göring, who told him that he would seem weak if
he did not act, whether or not the Austrians accepted the ultimatum
Hitler had given Keitel the invasion order already, at a quarter to nine.
Earlier in the evening, Schuschnigg had made an emotional broadcast to
the Austrian people, outlining the terms of the ultimatum and denying
that there was any disorder. 'We are not prepared even in this terrible
situation to shed blood,' he said. At 5.30 in the morning of 12 March
1938, German troops, mustered in Bavaria over the previous two days,
crossed the Austrian border. They met with no resistance.[84]

IV

As they drove and marched slowly towards Austria's main towns in the
course of the morning, the German troops were greeted by ecstatic
crowds shouting 'Hail' and throwing flowers at their feet. Everywhere,
clandestine members of the banned Austrian Nazi Party were openly
revealing their allegiance, ostentatiously turning over the swastika but-
tons they had hitherto kept hidden behind their lapels.[85] Assured by
army commanders that he would be safe, Hitler flew to Munich and was
driven towards the border in an open-topped car, accompanied by a
motorized column of his SS bodyguard. Arriving at 3.50 in the afternoon
at his birthplace, Braunau am Inn, he was greeted by jubilant crowds,
who cheered him on his way. Later in the evening, after a four-hour
journey by road, constantly slowed down by the enthusiastic crowds
that lined the streets, he reached Linz, where he joined a group of leading
Nazis including Himmler and Seyss-Inquart. As the church bells rang
out, Hitler addressed a huge crowd from the balcony of the town hall,
repeatedly interrupted by shouts of 'hail!' and chants of 'one people, one
Reich, one Leader'. 'Any further attempt to tear this people asunder', he
warned, 'will be in vain.'[86] After laying flowers on his parents' grave at
Leonding, and visiting his old home, Hitler returned to his hotel to
consider how the formal union of Austria with Germany could best be
achieved. Initially he had thought merely of becoming President of
Austria himself and holding a plebiscite on union, which would keep most
of Austria's existing institutions intact. But the rapturous reception he

had received now convinced him that a full incorporation of Austria into the Reich could be achieved immediately without any serious opposition. 'These people here are Germans,' he told a British journalist.[87]

By the evening of 13 March 1938 a Law providing for the annexation of Austria, drafted by a senior Interior Ministry official flown in from Berlin, had been approved by the reconstituted Austrian cabinet and signed by Hitler. The union of the two countries created 'Greater Germany' (*Grossdeutschland*). Initially, Austria as a whole became a province by itself, headed by Seyss-Inquart; but Hitler was now determined to erase Austrian identity and downgrade Vienna, the capital, which he had always disliked, in favour of the regions. By April 1939, the Rhenish Nazi Party Regional Leader Josef Bürckel, flown in to become Reich Commissioner for the Reunification of Austria with the Reich, had abolished the regional assemblies and merged regional with Party administration, though retaining, with some modifications, the identity of the regions themselves. Austria became the Eastern March (*Ostmark*); its identity was to be obliterated conclusively in 1942 when it was divided into the Reich Regions of the Alps and Danube.[88] This was not what many Austrians, and especially Viennese, had expected; even the leaders of the Austrian Nazi Party were bitterly disappointed at being sidelined in favour of administrators imported from Germany. Yet initially at least their enthusiasm was overwhelming. On 14 March 1938, Hitler's motor cavalcade drove from Linz to Vienna, again slowed down by cheering crowds; he was obliged to address them from his hotel balcony after his arrival, since they would not quieten down until they had heard him speak. The delay in his arrival had given the Viennese Nazis time to prepare: schools and workplaces were closed for the occasion, and Nazis and Hitler Youth members has been bussed in from the countryside. On 15 March, Hitler addressed a vast, delirious crowd of perhaps a quarter of a million people in Vienna, announcing that Austria's new historic mission was to provide a bulwark against the threat from the East.[89]

Austrians' acceptance of the reunification was assured not merely by the long-term disillusion of the country's citizens with their tiny, barely viable state, but also by careful preparation on the part of the Nazis. The Socialists had long been in favour of reunification, allowing doubts to creep in only because of the form the German government took from 1933, not because of any matter of broader national principle. The party

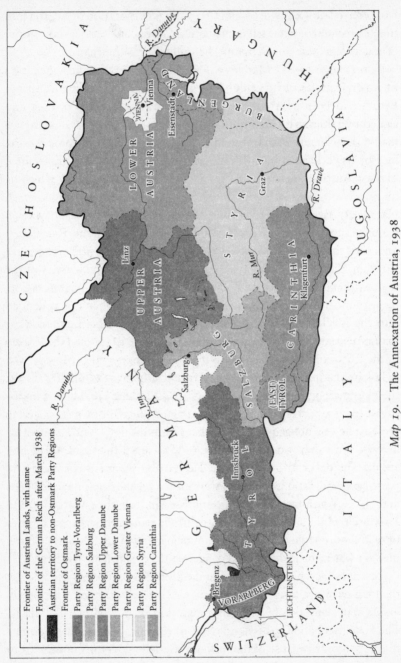

Map 19.   The Annexation of Austria, 1938

had in any case been crushed by Dollfuss in the brief civil conflict of February 1934. Its leaders were mostly in exile, in prison, in the underground opposition, such as it was, or politically quiescent. The Nazis carefully wooed the moderate wing of the party, persuading its leading figure Karl Renner to declare openly on 3 April that he would vote yes in the forthcoming plebiscite. And in a meeting brokered by the indefatigable Franz von Papen, Cardinal Innitzer, leader of Austria's Catholics, accepted Hitler's personal assurances that the Church and its institutions, including schools, would not be affected. Already inclined to see in Nazism the best defence against the threat of Bolshevism, Innitzer recruited other leading prelates to issue a joint declaration in favour of the reunion on 18 March, affixing a personal 'Hail, Hitler!' to the foot of the page.[90] Organized by Josef Bürckel, who had masterminded the Saar vote, the plebiscite was coupled with an election in which voters were presented with the Leader's list of candidates for the Greater German Reichstag. It was held on 10 April amidst massive manipulation and intimidation. A predictable 99.75 per cent of Austrian voters supported the annexation, although probably, to judge at least from some Gestapo reports, only a quarter to a third of Viennese voters were genuinely committed to the idea of union.[91]

Austrians soon found out what being incorporated into the Third Reich meant in practical terms. The postal service, the railways, the banking system, the currency and all other economic institutions were obliterated by their German equivalents; the taxation systems were merged with effect from January 1940. Within two days of the takeover, the Austrian economy had been subsumed into the Four-Year Plan. German firms moved in to take over Austrian businesses, which the Plan's economic managers considered slow and inefficient. Parts of Austrian business were already German-owned, of course, but the takeover spurred a new wave of purchases. A huge new Hermann-Göring-Works was set up in Linz to take advantage of Austria's large iron ore deposits. Petroleum and iron production increased substantially as a result of the takeover. Austria's very considerable gold and foreign currency reserves also accrued to the Reich, giving a temporary boost to Germany's reserves. The extension of the German border to the southeast made trade with the Balkans easier. Austria also supplied manpower to the Four-Year Plan. Absorption into the already overheated German economy brought many benefits for Austrians; unemployment fell rapidly, and the influx of German soldiers and administrators into Austria increased local demand. But Austria's economic problems did not disappear overnight, and higher wages in Germany proved insufficient as an incentive to bring unemployed skilled industrial workers in from the Austrian provinces. To relieve the manpower shortage in Germany and help reduce Austrian unemployment statistics, therefore, Göring decided to draft workers by force. A decree to this effect was issued on 22 June 1938 and by the following year, 100,000 Austrian workers had been compulsorily taken off to work in what was now known as the 'Old Reich', including 10,000 skilled engineering workers. Their removal, the provision of new jobs in Austria itself, and the enrolment of all Austrian workers into the German Labour Front and the Strength Through Joy organization, had a further dampening effect on workers' opposition.[92]

But the Nazis were not taking any chances. Among the earliest arrivals in Vienna were Himmler and Heydrich, who brought in a team of Gestapo officers to eliminate the opposition. While many leading men in the former regime fled into exile, ex-Chancellor Schuschnigg refused to leave and was arrested; he spent the rest of the Third Reich in custody. Papen's secretary, Wilhelm von Ketteler, was picked up by the Gestapo; shortly afterwards his lifeless body was found in a canal. The former leader of the Home Defence Brigades, Major Fey, who had played a leading role in putting down the Nazi uprising in 1934, killed himself with his entire family; 2,555 officers were compulsorily retired from the Austrian army, and an even larger number were transferred to administrative duties. These measures affected over 40 per cent of the officer corps. The rest of the troops were dispersed throughout the German army, obliterating the military identity of Austrians altogether. The State Secretary for Security, in overall charge of the police, was replaced by the head of the Austrian SS, Ernst Kaltenbrunner, while the new Vienna chief of police was Otto Steinhäusl, who had played a significant role in the abortive 1934 putsch. Six thousand ordinary German policemen were drafted in as reinforcements, along with a substantial number of Gestapo agents. But in general the Austrian police needed no thorough purge. Many of them were secret Nazis. They willingly made over the elaborate and extensive lists of oppositional elements compiled under Dollfuss and Schuschnigg. The Gestapo moved swiftly into action, arresting everyone thought to pose a threat to Nazi rule – 21,000 in all – in the night of 12–13 March. Special new facilities were made available in the Dachau concentration camp to accommodate them. Most of those imprisoned were released later in the year; only 1,500 were left by the end of 1938. There was to be no significant resistance in Austria until near the end of the war. Meanwhile, Himmler set up an entirely new camp, at Mauthausen, close to Linz, where prisoners from across the Reich would quarry stone for use in Speer's building projects. It was to prove the harshest of all the camps within the territory of Greater Germany before the invasion of the Soviet Union in 1941. The Vienna City Council made the land available on condition that some of the stone was used for cobbling the city's streets.[93]

The harshest repression of all fell on Austria's Jews, the overwhelming majority of whom – 170,000 out of nearly 200,000 – lived in Vienna. After living for years in the frustration of illegality, Austria's Nazis had accumulated a degree of pent-up aggression that now outstripped anything seen so far in the Old Reich. Hard-line Nazis were jubilant at what one called 'the liberation of Vienna and the East March from alien Jewish rule' and proclaimed a 'general cleansing of jewified Austria'.[94] All the various stages of antisemitic policy and action that had been developing over the years in Germany now happened in Austria at the same time, telescoped into a single outburst of rabid hatred and violence. The country's new Nazi rulers rapidly introduced all the Old Reich's antisemitic legislation, including the Aryan Paragraph and (in May 1938) the Nuremberg Laws. Jews were summarily ousted from the civil service and the professions. An elaborate bureaucracy – the Property Transfer Office, with a staff of 500 – was set up to manage the Aryanization of Jewish-owned businesses. A great deal of Jewish assets and property found its way into the hands of old Austrian Nazis, who demanded it as compensation for the years of repression they had suffered under Schuschnigg (and for which the Jews were in no sense to blame).[95] By May 1938, 7,000 out of 33,000 Jewish-owned businesses in Vienna had already been closed down; by August 1938, 23,000 more had gone. The remaining ones were Aryanized. Official action had in many cases been preceded by unofficial violence. Shortly after the takeover, a gang of stormtroopers threw Franz Rothenberg, chairman of the board of the Kreditanstalt, the most important Austrian bank, into a car and pushed him out at top speed, killing him instantly. Isidor Pollack, director-general of a dynamite factory, was beaten so badly by brownshirts in April that he died of his injuries; his firm was taken over by I. G. Farben, while the Kreditanstalt fell into the hands of the Deutsche Bank.[96]

Meanwhile, Austrian Nazis were breaking into Jewish premises, houses and apartments, looting the contents, and driving the inhabitants out onto the streets, where they were mustered under a hail of curses and blows and taken away to clean anti-Nazi graffiti off the city's buildings. Soon a new version of this sport was discovered: the Jews were made to kneel on the streets and clean away Austrian crosses and other signs painted or chalked on them by patriots amidst the derisive comments and applause of the onlookers. Frequently they were doused with cold water, pushed over, or kicked as they carried out their humiliating task. 'Day after day', wrote George Gedye, the Vienna correspondent of the London *Daily Telegraph*,

Nazi storm-troopers, surrounded by jostling, jeering and laughing mobs of 'golden Viennese hearts', dragged Jews from shops, offices and homes, men and women, put scrubbing-brushes in their hands, splashed them well with acid, and made them go down on their knees and scrub away for hours at the hopeless task of removing Schuschnigg propaganda. All this I could watch from my office window overlooking the Graben. (Where there was none available, I have seen Nazis painting it for the Jews to remove.) . . . Every morning in the Habsburgergasse the S. S. squads were told how many Jews to round up that day for menial tasks . . . The favourite task was that of cleaning the bowls of the w.c.s in the S. S. barracks, which the Jews were forced to do simply with their naked hands.[97]

Other Jews, going about their daily business on the streets, were assaulted with impunity, their wallets robbed and their fur coats taken before they were beaten up.[98]

By 17 March 1938 even Heydrich was proposing to get the Gestapo to arrest those Nazis who were responsible for such acts. It was not until 29 April, however, when stormtrooper leaders were threatened with dismissal if they allowed these outrages to continue, that the tide of violent incidents began to subside. Meanwhile, the Nazis had begun officially to confiscate Jewish-owned apartments in Vienna: 44,000 out of 70,000 had been Aryanized by the end of 1938. They also initiated the forced expulsion of Jewish populations in a manner far more direct than had so far occurred in the Old Reich. In the small eastern region of the Burgenland, bordering on Hungary, the new Nazi rulers confiscated the property of the 3,800 members of the old-established Jewish community there, closed down all Jewish businesses, arrested community leaders, then used the creation of a security zone on the border as an excuse to expel the entire Jewish population. Many Jews were hauled off to police stations, and beaten until they signed documents surrendering all their assets. The police took them to the border and forced them across. However, since neighbouring countries often refused to accept them, many Jews were left stranded in no-man's land. Fifty-one of them were dumped unceremoniously on a barren, sandy islet on the Danube, in an incident that aroused worldwide press condemnation. The majority fled to friends and relatives in Vienna. By the end of 1938 there were no Jews left in the Burgenland. Partly in response to this mass flight, the Gestapo in Vienna arrested 1,900 Jews who were known to have criminal convictions, however trivial, between 25 and 27 May 1938 and sent them to Dachau, where they were segregated and particularly brutally mistreated. The police also arrested and expelled all foreign Jews and even German Jews living in Vienna. Altogether, 5,000 Jews had been deported from Austria by November 1938. By this time, too, Jews who lived outside the capital were being forcibly removed to Vienna. All these events created a panic amongst Austria's Jewish population. Many hundreds committed suicide in despair. Thousands of others sought to leave the country by every means they could. In order to speed up this process, the Nazi authorities established a Central Agency for Jewish Emigration on 20 August 1938.[99]

It was run by Adolf Eichmann, a man who was subsequently to become notorious for his role in the wartime extermination of Europe's Jews. His career, therefore, deserves closer scrutiny at the moment, in 1938, when he first acquired a degree of prominence, not least because the procedures he set up in the Central Agency were to have a far wider application later. Eichmann was originally a Rhinelander. Born in 1906, he had lived in Austria since his family moved to Linz the year before the outbreak of the First World War. Middle-class by background and upbringing, Eichmann did not have a university qualification, but had worked as a sales representative for a petroleum company during the

1920s. As a member of Austria's small Protestant minority, he identified strongly with pan-German nationalism, joined the independent youth movement and hobnobbed with right-wing nationalists, most notably the Kaltenbrunners, a family of middle-class pan-Germans. He joined the Austrian Nazi Party in 1932 and fell under the influence of Ernst Kaltenbrunner, a 29-year-old law graduate and former student fraternity activist. Kaltenbrunner was an active antisemite who had joined the Austrian SS in 1930, and in 1932 he persuaded Eichmann to become a member of the SS as well. Losing his job in the Depression, Eichmann moved to Germany in August 1933 and underwent intensive physical and ideological training in the SS. Soon he had joined Heydrich's SS Security Service to compile information about Freemasons in Germany. His diligence and efficiency secured his rapid promotion through the ranks. By 1936 he was working in the Security Service's Jewish Department, writing briefing papers on Zionism, emigration and similar topics and imbibing the Department's ethos of radical, 'rational' anti-semitism.[100]

Eichmann arrived in Vienna on 16 March 1938 as part of a special unit, already kitted out with an arrest list of prominent Jews. The Security Service realized that the orderly conduct of forced emigration required the collaboration of Jewish leaders, especially if the poorest Jews, who lacked the means to leave and start a new life elsewhere, were to be included in the plan. Eichmann ordered leading members of the Jewish community up from their cells for interview and selected Josef Löwenherz, a respected lawyer, as the most suitable for his purpose. He sent him back to his cell with orders that he was not to be released until he had produced a plan for the mass emigration of Austria's Jews. Löwenherz's request for a streamlined system of processing applications that did away with the chicanery and deliberate delays common up to then met with a ready response. Eichmann instituted an orderly method of processing applications and arranged for the confiscated assets of the Jewish community and its members to be used by the Central Agency for subsidizing the emigration of poor Jews. Prodded by horror stories spread about the maltreatment of the Austrian Jews held in Dachau, by systematic abuse and insults from Agency officials, and by the continuing terror on the streets, Austria's Jews queued in their thousands to obtain exit visas. Löwenherz and other Jews co-opted into the Agency's work were repeatedly threatened with deportation to Dachau if they did not fill their quotas. The result, Eichmann later bragged, was that some 100,000 Austrian Jews had emigrated legally by May 1939, and several thousands more had crossed the border illegally, many of them eventually reaching Palestine. Newly promoted as a reward, and revelling in his new power, Eichmann became coarse and brutal in his dealings with individual Jews. His Agency, with its assembly-line processing, its plundering of Jewish assets to subsidize the emigration of the poor, its application of terror and its use of Jewish collaborators, became a model for the SS Security Service in its subsequent dealings with the Jews.[101]

V

The incorporation of Austria into the Third Reich, with its accompanying anti-Jewish excesses, gave a tremendous boost to antisemitism across the whole of Germany. Apart from anything else, the addition of 200,000 Jews to the population of the Third Reich more than balanced out the numbers of Jews whom the Nazis had succeeded in forcing out of Germany between March 1933 and March 1938.[102] It almost made the effort seem in vain. So the Nazis redoubled their determination to speed up the process of forced emigration. Without the Austrian example, and the feelings of triumph and invulnerability it engendered in Nazi Party activists, it is impossible to understand the upsurge of violence towards Jews that swept across Germany in the summer of 1938 and culminated in the pogrom of 9–10 November. The full force of the pogrom was felt in Austria as well. Forty-two synagogues were burned down in Vienna, most of the remaining Jewish-owned shops were destroyed, and nearly 2,000 Jewish families were summarily ejected from their houses and apartments. A detachment of SS men trashed the Jewish community headquarters and the Zionist offices on 10 November. Eichmann complained that the pogrom disrupted the orderly conduct of emigration, but in fact he was well aware that its basic intention was to speed up the whole process through the sudden application of a spectacular degree of mass terror, and this indeed was its affect in Austria as elsewhere.[103]

Just as striking was the impulse the annexation of Austria and the expropriation of its Jewish community gave to the cultural ambitions of leading Nazis. They confiscated many major art collections, including those of the Rothschilds, which the Reich Finance Ministry eventually began selling off to meet newly imposed tax bills. The Mayor of Nuremberg succeeded in having the crown jewels of the Holy Roman Empire, taken from his city to Vienna in 1794, transferred back in preparation for the 1938 Party Rally. Art dealers began to gather round the looted collections like vultures round a carcass. Hermann Göring vetoed further sales and exports with an eye to acquiring some of the artworks for himself. But it was Hitler who led the plunder. A visit to Rome in May 1938 convinced him that Greater Germany too needed a major artistic capital, and his eye lighted upon Linz, where he had spent his childhood. On 26 June 1939 he ordered the art historian and Dresden museum director Hans Posse to create a collection for a planned art museum in Linz. On 24 July the Austrian administration under Bürckel was informed by Bormann that all confiscated collections were to be made available to Posse or Hitler personally; by October, Posse had managed to get the Rothschild collections included as well. The looting of the cultural heritage of Europe had begun.[104]

These acts of plunder were not widely known among Germans. Their immediate reactions to the annexation were mixed. The same pattern was evident as on previous occasions, such as the remilitarization of the Rhineland in 1936: national pride was mingled with nervousness, even panic, born out of fear of a general war. According to some reports, the latter was the first response to the Austrian crisis, giving way fairly quickly to nationalistic enthusiasm as the passivity of the other European powers made it clear that war would not come, at least not on this occasion. 'Hitler is a master of politics,' was one widespread view; 'yes, he's truly a great statesman, he's greater than Napoleon, because he's conquering the world without war.' The peaceful nature of the annexation was the key factor here. Workers may have been depressed by the absence of Socialist opposition ('where was Red Vienna?'), but many were also hugely impressed by Hitler's bloodless coup: 'He's really a good chap,' remembered one.[105]

Hitler's Vienna speech on 15 March 1938 was greeted by what one Social Democratic agent admitted was

a massive enthusiasm and joy at this success . . . The jubilation knew almost no
bounds any more . . . Even sections of society that had been cool towards Hitler
up to this point, or rejected him, were now carried along by the event and
admitted that Hitler was after all a great and clever statesman who would lead
Germany upwards again to greatness and esteem from the defeat of 1918.[106]

The annexation of Austria brought Hitler's popularity to unprecedented
heights. Middle-class nationalists were ecstatic, whatever their reservations on other points of the Third Reich's policies.[107] The reunification
of Germany and Austria was, wrote Luise Solmitz in her diary, 'world
history, the fulfilment of my old German dream, a truly united Germany,
through a man who fears nothing, knows no compromises, hindrances
or difficulties'. In mounting excitement she listened to the radio as it
broadcast the unfolding events, recording every move, every speech in
a spirit of mounting ecstasy despite all the problems from which her
family suffered because of their racially mixed status. 'It's all like a
dream,' she wrote, 'one is completely torn away from one's own world
and from oneself . . . One must recall that one is excluded from the
people's community oneself like a criminal or degraded person.'[108] Victor
Klemperer was in despair: 'We shall not live to see the end of the Third
Reich,' he wrote on 20 March 1938. He also noted that 'since yesterday
a broad yellow bill with the Star of David has been stuck to every post
of our fence: *Jew*'.[109]

For Hitler himself, the success of the annexation brought a further
increase in self-confidence, the certainty that he had been chosen by
Providence, the belief that he could do no wrong. His speeches at this
time are full of references to his own, divinely ordained status as the
architect of Germany's rebirth. There was now no one left to restrain
him. The army, still in a state of shock and, in parts of the officer corps,
disillusion after the Blomberg-Fritsch affair, had no answer to this major
success. Even those officers who were now convinced that Hitler would
lead them into the abyss in the long run felt unable to take any direct
action in the light of the huge popularity the Nazi Leader had now
attained. Already, Hitler was looking to Czechoslovakia, egged on by
Ribbentrop, who assured him blithely that Britain would not intervene.
So feeble had been the reaction of the other European powers to the
annexation of Austria that there seemed no reason why the takeover of

Czechoslovakia, announced as an intermediate aim by Hitler at the meeting recorded by Colonel Hossbach in 1937, should not go ahead.[110]

In his speech to the Reichstag on 18 March 1938, Hitler already referred in emotional terms to the 'brutal violation of countless millions of German racial comrades' across Europe. On 28 March, in the middle of a campaign of public speeches and rallies for the combined election and plebiscite to be held on 10 April, Hitler held a secret meeting with the leader of the Sudeten German Party, a Nazi-backed organization that claimed to represent the German minority in Czechoslovakia. The Party, Hitler said, had to avoid collaboration with the Czech government and instead embark on a campaign for 'total freedom for the Sudeten Germans'.[111] The subversion of Czechoslovakia was under way. Its ultimate end was the complete destruction of the Czechoslovak state and its absorption into the German Reich in one form or another. Only in this way could the boundaries of Germany be reordered in such a manner as to create a springboard for the invasion of Poland and Russia and the creation of the racially reconstituted 'living-space' for the Germans in Eastern Europe that Hitler had long desired. Hitler told his generals and Foreign Ministry officials on 28 May that he was 'utterly determined that Czechoslovakia should disappear from the map'. Two days later, revised military plans were presented for implementing his 'unalterable decision to smash Czechoslovakia by military action in the foreseeable future'.[112] For the first time, therefore, Hitler was now embarking on a course that could not be represented as the adjustment of unfair and punitive territorial provisions arrived at in the Peace Settlement of 1919. The consequences of this step were to be momentous.

THE RAPE OF CZECHOSLOVAKIA

I

The Republic of Czechoslovakia was one of Europe's few remaining democracies in 1938. Bolstered by deep-seated liberal traditions, Czech representatives at the peace negotiations in 1919 had succeeded in obtaining independence from the Habsburg monarchy, to which the states of Bohemia and Moravia had formerly belonged. The new state, unlike its Austrian neighbour to the south, began its life with excellent prospects, including a strong industrial base. Like other successor states to the old Habsburg monarchy, however, Czechoslovakia contained substantial national minorities, the largest of which consisted of some 3 million Germans, mostly clustered around the western, north-western and south-western border areas of the country. Although Czech was the official national language, nearly nine out of ten ethnic Germans were able to continue using their mother tongue when dealing with officialdom, German was used in schools in the relevant districts, and the German minority was represented in the Czech parliament. German parties participated in coalition governments, and German-speakers were able to pursue their own careers, although they needed Czech if they were to enter the civil service. Ethnic Germans, increasingly referred to as Sudeten Germans, after the area in which many of them lived, had full individual rights as citizens, in a country where civil freedoms were more respected than in most other parts of Europe. There was no guarantee of collective rights to the German-speaking minority, but the idea of granting it the status of a second 'state people' alongside the Czechs was widely discussed in the later 1920s.[113]

Two factors destroyed the relatively peaceful coexistence between

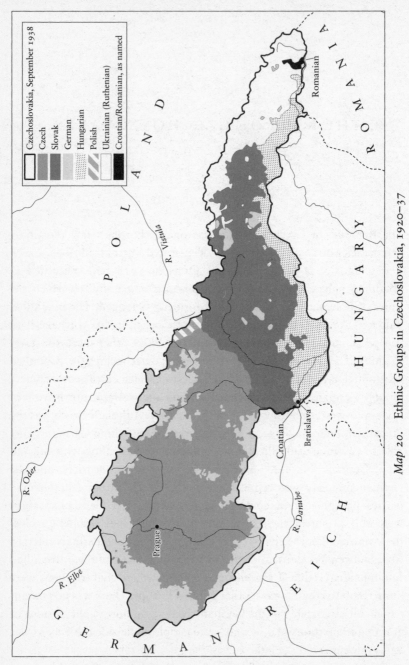

Map 20. Ethnic Groups in Czechoslovakia, 1920–37

Map 20. Ethnic Groups in Czechoslovakia, 1920–37

Czechs and Germans at the beginning of the 1930s. The first was the worldwide economic Depression, which affected the German-speaking population particularly badly. Consumer-oriented light industries such as glass and textiles, heavily concentrated in German-speaking areas, collapsed. By 1933, ethnic Germans constituted two-thirds of the Republic's unemployed. The state's overburdened social welfare system consigned many of them to poverty and destitution. At this point, the second factor, the Nazi seizure of power in Germany, came into play, causing growing numbers of desperate Sudeten Germans to look to the Third Reich as the German economy began to recover under the impact of rearmament, while its Czech counterpart still languished in the doldrums. In these circumstances, German-speakers rallied to the Sudeten German Party, which demanded economic improvements based on regional autonomy while protesting its loyalty to the Czechoslovak state and maintaining a discreet distance from the Nazis across the border in Germany. The Party's leader, the schoolteacher Konrad Henlein, came under increasing pressure from ex-members of banned German-nationalist extremist groups who joined his organization early in 1933. By 1937, Hitler's foreign policy successes had given them the upper hand. In the 1936 elections the Party gained 63 per cent of the ethnic German vote. Early in 1937 the Czech government, realizing the danger, made a series of important economic concessions, admitting German-speakers to the civil service and issuing government contracts to Sudeten German firms. But it was already too late. Funds were now flowing into the Party's coffers from Berlin, and with this financial leverage, the German government was able to bring Henlein into line behind a policy of detaching the Sudetenland from the rest of the Czechoslovak state.[114]

By the spring of 1938, its impatience sharply increased by the German annexation of Austria, the Sudeten German Party was becoming violent. Mass intimidation of its opponents in local elections helped to increase its vote to 75 per cent.[115] As pressure from Berlin mounted, the Czech government conceded the principle of Sudeten German autonomy and offered additional economic relief. But it was all to no avail.[116] Henlein was bent on secession, and Hitler was bent on war. But the invasion of Czechoslovakia, where the vast majority of the population was implacably opposed to Hitler, Nazism and the idea of a German takeover, was a vastly different prospect from the invasion of Austria, where the vast majority of the population was in favour of all or most of these things in one degree or another. Czechoslovakia was a bigger, wealthier and more powerful country than Austria, with a major armaments industry, including the Skoda works, one of Europe's leading arms manufacturers. Unlike the Austrian army, which was small, poorly prepared for action, and deeply divided in its attitudes towards Germany, the Czech army was a substantial, well-disciplined and well-equipped fighting force, united in its determination to resist a German invasion. German generals had already been nervous before the remilitarization of the Rhineland and the annexation of Austria. They were virtually panic-stricken when they learned of Hitler's intention to destroy Czechoslovakia. Not only were military preparations inadequate and rearmament short of target, but the likelihood of foreign intervention and a general war was far greater than before. Czechoslovakia was formally allied to France, after all; and the invasion could not really be presented as anything other than an act of aggression against a sovereign state upon which Germany – unlike in the case of Austria – had no claim to suzerainty in the eyes of the world.[117]

To be sure, the generals had few objections in principle to a takeover of Czechoslovakia, which obtruded geographically into the newly created Greater Germany in a strategically dangerous manner. Hatred and contempt for Slavs and democrats fused in their minds with a broader belief in the eventual creation of a German empire in East-Central Europe. Moreover, the acquisition of the Czech arms industry, skilled labour and plentiful raw materials would alleviate the Third Reich's increasingly dire supply situation in these fields. All of this added to the general strategic importance of Czechoslovakia in the eyes of Hermann Göring, whose prestige had been notably boosted by the annexation of Austria. Yet Göring and the generals were unconvinced that the moment was right for a move against the Czechs. It seemed to be a reckless and foolhardy act, running a real risk of a general war for which Germany in their view was quite unprepared. It would, they thought, be far more prudent to wait, pile on the pressure and secure piecemeal concessions. Their doubts grew as it began to become clear that Britain would not stand aside this time. As Goebbels unleashed a massive propaganda campaign full of horror stories about the supposed mistreatment of the Sudeten Germans by the Czechs, a sense of crisis started to grip the senior army commanders.[118]

On 5 May, the Chief of the Army General Staff, Ludwig Beck, informed Hitler that Germany was in no position to win a war should, as he thought likely, Britain intervene to protect the Czechs. Later in the month he repeated his warnings with greater insistence, and on 16 July he issued a memorandum to senior generals warning of dire consequences should the invasion go ahead. He even canvassed the idea of getting the top generals to resign *en masse* in protest against Hitler's plans. The other generals, however, were still demoralized by the Blomberg-Fritsch scandal. They were locked in a tradition of belief that the duty of soldiers was to obey orders and not involve themselves in politics. They feared that breaking their personal oath of loyalty to Hitler would be an act of dishonour. They were all too aware of Hitler's increased prestige and power after the annexation of Austria. And they did not in any case disagree with Hitler's aim of attacking Czechoslovakia, only with its timing. So although they shared many of Beck's concerns, they refused to back him this time. Nevertheless, Hitler still felt it necessary to appeal for the officers' support at meetings on 13 June and 10 August 1938. He was backed by the head of the army, General Brauchitsch, after subjecting him to a lengthy tirade when he submitted to him Beck's memorandum of 16 July 1938. Meanwhile, some of the ground had been cut from under Beck's feet by war games ordered by his own General Staff in June, which showed that Czechoslovakia could be conquered within eleven days, allowing the rapid transfer of troops to the West to mount a defence against any possible Franco-British military action. Objections that the defensive West Wall was not yet ready met with another tirade from Hitler. The British and French would not intervene, he said. And Fritz Todt, whom he had put in over the army's head in May to push on the building the West Wall, would have the fortifications ready by the onset of winter anyway.[119]

Feeling totally isolated, Beck resigned as Chief of the Army General Staff on 18 August 1938, to be succeeded by General Franz Halder, his deputy. The choice was an obvious one, but Halder was in fact not at all what he seemed to be from the Nazi leadership's point of view. Born in 1884, he was an artillery officer who came from a Franconian military family with strongly conservative leanings. Far from being a reliable tool of Nazi aggression, he shared many of Beck's reservations about the risky nature of Hitler's policy. In these, he was joined by a number of other conservative officers and diplomats, notably Admiral Wilhelm Canaris, head of military intelligence, and Erwin von Witzleben, a senior infantry general and commander of the Berlin military district. So deep was their disapproval of Hitler's reckless drive to war that they began to make plans to overthrow him. They joined forces with a group of younger officers who had already been plotting Hitler's downfall, notably Hans Oster, a Brigadier-General in Canaris's intelligence department. And they extended the conspiracy to include civilians who, they knew, would be needed to staff a post-Nazi government, including conservative figures who had developed more or less serious reservations about the direction in which the regime was heading, such as Schacht and Goerdeler, Foreign Ministry officials such as State Secretary Ernst von Weizsäcker and his juniors Adam von Trott zu Solz and Hans-Bernd von Haeften, and senior civil servants, including Hans Bernd Gisevius, a former assistant secretary in the Interior Ministry, and Count Peter Yorck von Wartenburg from the Reich Price Commissioner's office. The conspirators put out feelers to other alarmed conservatives and started detailed planning for the coup, sketching out troop deployments and debating whether Hitler should be assassinated or merely put into custody. A number of them, notably Goerdeler, travelled to other countries, especially Britain, to issue private warnings to senior politicians, government ministers, civil servants and anyone else who would listen about Hitler's bellicose intentions. They were met with polite expressions of interest, but were unable to secure any concrete pledges of support, though it is difficult to see exactly what these might have involved in concrete terms at this stage.[120]

The fundamental weakness of the conspiracy was that its members, by and large, did not disapprove of Hitler's basic aim of dismembering Czechoslovakia; they only deplored what they considered his irresponsible haste in doing so while the German economy and the armed forces were still unprepared for the general European war to which they feared it would lead. Thus if Hitler succeeded in his aim without provoking a general war, the rug would be pulled from under their feet.[121] Moreover, the men involved in the conspiracy had no support in the Nazi Party or in the vast apparatus of organizations through which it ruled Germany. Both the officer corps and the Foreign Office, the two centres of the plot, had been repeatedly discredited in the previous months, particularly over

Austria. The War Ministry, Göring told the officers in the middle of the crisis, housed 'the spirit of faint-heartedness. This spirit', he added, 'must go!'[122] If Halder and his fellow conspirators had succeeded in arresting Hitler, the army's image, branded reactionary by Goebbels, would have had little popular appeal even supposing the other generals had rallied to their cause. Success was unlikely, therefore. But in any case it was soon put out of the question by developments on the diplomatic front.[123]

II

By early September, events were coming to a head. Unlike the annexation of Austria, the takeover of Czechoslovakia required a lengthy build-up in view of the far greater military and international obstacles that stood in Hitler's way. It took him several months to overcome the objections of the generals and to develop the military planning, in which he involved himself personally since he did not trust the generals to do it to his satisfaction. Throughout the summer, Goebbels's ceaseless stream of anti-Czech propaganda made it abundantly clear to the international community that an invasion was being prepared in Berlin. Day after day, banner headlines in the newspapers blared forth stories about alleged Czech atrocities, the shooting of innocent Sudeten Germans, 'women and children mowed down by Czech armoured cars', the terrorization of the population by the Czech police, threatened gas attacks on Sudeten German villages, and the machinations of the 'world arsonists' centre Prague', the Trojan horse of Bolshevism in Central Europe.[124] The Czechs did in fact have an alliance with the Soviet Union, but it meant very little in practice, as they were soon to find out. Far more important was the fact that the integrity of Czechoslovakia was guaranteed by treaty with France. If France came to the Czechs' aid, then Britain would be bound to intervene too, as it had over Belgium under comparable circumstances in 1914. The British Prime Minister Neville Chamberlain was aware that Britain, though now hurriedly rearming, was in no condition to wage a general European war. He felt that the strain on British public finances would be unsustainable. Moreover, a general war, he thought, would bring upon British cities aerial bombardments that would make Guernica look like a tea-party. Not only was there no defence against them, it was believed, but they would probably, like the Italian bombardment of the Ethiopians, involve the use of poison gas on the defenceless people below. At the height of the crisis, indeed, the British government issued gas-masks to the civilian population and ordered the evacuation of London. In any case, Britain's global strategy dictated that the Empire, by far the largest in the world, came first, and Europe, in which the United Kingdom had little direct interest, a distant second. 'How horrible, fantastic, incredible it is', Chamberlain told his listeners during a BBC Radio broadcast towards the end of September 1938, 'that we should be digging trenches and trying on gas-masks here because of a quarrel in a far-away country between people of whom we know nothing.'[125]

Czechoslovakia was clearly further away than India, South Africa or Australia in the mental map of the British people as well as in the imagination of their Prime Minister. Chamberlain knew above all that he would find little or no public support for a war against Germany over the Sudeten question, even though by this time voices were being raised in the British political world demanding that Hitler's march of European conquest had to be stopped.[126] It still seemed unclear to Chamberlain that Hitler was bent on European conquest rather than merely determined to right the wrongs of the Treaty of Versailles and protect beleaguered ethnic German minorities. If he could be appeased on the Sudeten question then maybe he would be satisfied and a general war could be avoided. Chamberlain determined to intervene decisively to prevent a war by forcing the Czechs to give way. When Hitler gave a speech at the Nuremberg Party Rally on 12 September 1938 threatening war if the Sudeten Germans were not granted self-determination, Chamberlain demanded a meeting. As Henlein's thugs, acting on orders from Hitler, staged a wave of violent incidents designed to provoke Czech police repression, thus providing the excuse for German intervention, Chamberlain boarded an airplane for the first time in his life – in a sharp contrast to Hitler's embrace of this most modern means of travel years before – and flew to Munich. During a lengthy one-to-one meeting, witnessed only by an interpreter, Chamberlain agreed to a revision of Czech boundaries to accommodate the Sudeten Germans' wishes. But this did not seem to satisfy the German Leader. Chamberlain reacted to Hitler's bluster by asking him why he had agreed to meet him if he would admit no alternative to war. Faced with such an ultimatum, Hitler reluctantly agreed to another meeting.[127]

On 22 September 1938, after consulting the British cabinet about his concessions, Chamberlain flew once more to Germany and met Hitler in the Hotel Dreesen, in Bad Godesberg, on the river Rhine. The French, he assured Hitler, had agreed to his terms. So there would be no problem in reaching a settlement. To his astonishment, however, Hitler presented him with a fresh set of demands. The recent violence in Czechoslovakia meant, he said, that he would have to occupy the Sudetenland almost at once. Moreover, Poland and Hungary, both led by military, authoritarian nationalist governments that had scented blood in the atmosphere surrounding the negotiations, had also put in claims on Czech territory bordering their own, and these too, said Hitler, had to be met. The fronts now began to harden. The Czech government, recognizing the realities of the situation, had accepted the Anglo-French terms. But at the same time, a military government came to power in Prague under the impact of the crisis, and it was clear that no more concessions would be made. The British cabinet rejected the Bad Godesberg proposals, worried that the British public would see them as a humiliation for the government. Chamberlain sent a high-level mission to Berlin to make it clear to Hitler that Britain would not tolerate unilateral action. Hitler, furious, invited Sir Horace Wilson, the delegation's leader, to a speech he was to give at the Sports Palace on the evening of 26 September. It culminated in a violent tirade against the Czechs. William L. Shirer, who was at the rally, noted that Hitler was 'shouting and shrieking in the worst state of excitement I've ever seen him in . . . with a fanatical fire in his eyes'. Working himself up into a frenzy, he declared, to the tumultuous applause of 20,000 Nazi supporters, that the Czech genocide of the German minority could not be tolerated. He himself would march into the country at the head of his troops. October 1 would be the date.[128]

While the British and the Czechs prepared for war, it was in the end Hitler who backed down. Surprisingly, perhaps, the decisive influence here was that of Hermann Göring, who had been so hawkish over Austria. Like the generals, he was appalled that a general war was being risked over an issue where the key concessions to Germany had been made already. So, behind Hitler's back, he brokered a conference with the British, the French and, crucially, the Italians, who asked Hitler to postpone the invasion until the conference had met. Persuaded by Göring's strong reservations about a war, and seeing in Mussolini's request a way out of the situation without being humiliated, Hitler agreed. The conference met in Munich on 29 September 1938, without the Czechs, who had not been invited. Göring had drafted an agreement in advance, and had it put into formal terms by Weizsäcker in the Foreign Ministry. Ribbentrop was all for war ('he has a blind hatred of England,' noted Goebbels in his diary).[129] So he was not informed about the draft document, which was given to the Italian ambassador, who presented it to Hitler on 28 September as the work of Mussolini. After thirteen hours of negotiations on the fine print, the Munich Agreement was signed by the four powers on 29 September 1938. The following day, Chamberlain presented Hitler with a declaration that Britain and Germany would never go to war again. Hitler signed it without demur. On his return to England, Chamberlain waved it at cheering crowds from the first-floor window of 10, Downing Street. 'I believe it is peace for our time,' he told them. He genuinely seems to have believed that he had achieved a settlement that was satisfactory to all, including the Czechs, who, he declared, had been saved for a happier future. Hitler, he had told his sister after first meeting the German leader, was a man whose word could be trusted. All his experiences during the to-and-fro of negotiation do not seem to have disillusioned him.[130]

The sense of relief was as palpable in Germany as it was in Britain. Since May, there had been widespread popular anxiety in Germany about the possibility of war, made more acute by the Czech government's military mobilization in the same month. On previous occasions, the panic had been short-lived. But this time, the crisis dragged on for months. Even the SS Security Service admitted that there was a 'war psychosis' among the population that had lasted until the Munich Agreement had been signed. 'With reference to the superiority of the opponent, a defeatism emerged, that escalated into the strongest criticism of the "adventurous policy of the Reich".' Many people thought that the incorporation of the crisis-ridden Sudetenland into Germany would impose a severe economic burden on the Reich. At the tensest moments of the crisis, people were withdrawing their savings from the banks in panic; inhabitants of the areas bordering Czechoslovakia were making preparations to flee westward. Many Germans, regrettably from the Security

Service point of view, preferred to get their information from foreign radio stations, and this further increased their pessimism. The Security Service blamed intellectuals above all for this trend.[131]

But it was not merely intellectuals who were worried. Hitherto, Hitler had won the plaudits of the great mass of Germans by securing foreign policy triumphs without bloodshed. Now that it looked as if blood really would be spilled, things seemed very different. The general anxiety, Social Democratic agents noted in May 1938, stood in sharp contrast to the enthusiasm of August 1914. To be sure, most people thought the demands of the Sudeten Germans justified. But they wanted them to be realized without war.[132] Nobody, it was reported in July, thought that Germany could win a war against Britain and France. Some embittered ex-Social Democrats even hoped it would happen because defeat was the best way to get rid of the Nazis. But amongst many workers, there was also a widespread fatalism. Young people were frequently swept away by the vision of a great Germany, bestriding a vanquished Continent. Many older people were confused and felt they lacked detailed information.[133] As preparations for war intensified, popular anxiety grew.[134] The 'war psychosis' in the population, reported Goebbels in his diary on 31 August, was growing.[135] In the Ruhr, Social Democratic observers reported shortly before the Munich Agreement,

There reigns a gigantic restlessness. People are afraid that it will come to war, and that Germany will go under in it. Nowhere is any enthusiasm for war to be found. People know that a war against the greater part of Europe and against America must end in defeat for Germany . . . If it comes to a war, this war will be as unpopular in Germany as possible.[136]

Even the young, for all their enthusiasm for a Greater Germany, were now anxious about the situation.[137]

It was not just the working classes or the interview partners of Social Democratic agents who were worried. 'War, war, war', wrote Luise Solmitz in her diary on 13 September 1938, '– wherever one goes, one hears nothing else.' For a while her fear of a general war outweighed her customary patriotism. Suddenly 1914 meant something other than a spirit of national union: '1914 is eerily reviving. Every Sudeten German killed is a Franz Ferdinand.'[138] Nevertheless, her patriotic Jewish husband Friedrich Solmitz still volunteered for military service in his country's hour of need. His application was refused.[139] Among the population at large, confidence in Hitler's ability to make foreign policy gains without bloodshed was dented far more than it had been on previous occasions such as the Rhineland remilitarization or the annexation of Austria, precisely because the Czech crisis went on for so long. In the late summer and early autumn of 1938 there was a marked increase in the number of people brought before the Special Courts for criticism of Hitler himself.[140]

Correspondingly, the wave of relief that swept over the country on the announcement of the Munich Agreement was enormous. 'All of us can live on,' wrote Luise Solmitz in her diary, 'relaxed, happy, a terrible pressure removed from us all . . . Now this wonderful, unique experience. The Sudetenland gained, in peace with England and France.'[141] In Danzig, as a Social Democratic agent reported, almost everyone saw the Munich Agreement 'as a hundred per cent success for Hitler'.[142] But this was hardly surprising given the town's situation. Among Catholic workers in the Ruhr, by contrast, there were, reports of worries that Hitler's success would lead to an even more ruthless campaign against the Church. Nevertheless everyone was relieved that Hitler had obtained new territory for Germany without bloodshed. No wonder that Chamberlain was cheered as he passed through the streets of Munich after signing the Agreement. Everyone agreed that the Agreement had greatly strengthened Hitler's power and prestige. Only die-hard opponents of the regime were embittered by what they saw as the betrayal of the Czechs by the Western democracies. Only the gloomiest concluded 'that it'll go further'.[143]

Hitler himself was far from triumphant over the outcome. He had been cheated of the war for which he had been planning. He felt resentful at Göring's intervention. From this point on, relations between the two men cooled, leaving Ribbentrop, effectively excluded from the Munich negotiations, in a stronger position, as it did Himmler, who had also stood by Hitler in his desire for war. The army generals and their co-conspirators had to abandon their plans for a coup in the light of the peaceful outcome of the crisis, but they too were left weakened in their standing with Hitler, and in addition the more radical amongst them felt cheated by Chamberlain's intervention. Moreover, Hitler was only too aware of the fact that the majority of Germans did not want war, for all the efforts of the Third Reich to persuade them of its desirability. On

27 September 1938, he had organized a military parade through Berlin just at the time when Berliners were pouring out of their offices on their way home and could be expected to pause to cheer as the lorries and tanks rolled past. But, reported William L. Shirer,

They ducked into subways, refused to look on, and the handful that did stood at the curb in utter silence unable to find a word of cheer for the flower of their youth going away to the glorious war. It has been the most striking demonstration against war I've ever seen. Hitler himself reported furious. I had not been standing long at the corner when a policeman came up the Wilhelmstrasse from the direction of the Chancellery and shouted to the few of us standing at the curb that the Führer was on his balcony reviewing the troops. Few moved. I went down to have a look. Hitler stood there, and there weren't two hundred people in the street . . .[144]

Angry and dismayed, Hitler went inside.

On 10 November 1938 (immediately after the antisemitic pogrom, when Jewish men were being arrested all over Germany), Hitler expressed his dismay to a closed meeting of German press representatives:

Only by constantly emphasizing the German desire for peace and peaceful intentions was I able to gain the German people's freedom step by step and thus give it the armament necessary as a prerequisite for accomplishing the next step. It is self-evident that such a peace propaganda, carried on throughout the decades, also has its questionable aspect, for it can all too well lead to the impression in the minds of many people that the present regime is identified with the resolution and the willingness to preserve peace under all circumstances. This would, however, above all, lead to the German nation, instead of being prepared for events, being filled by a spirit of defeatism in the long run, and this would take away the successful achievements of the present regime.[145]

Hitler went on to rant against 'intellectuals' who were undermining the will to war. It was the role of the press, he said, to convince the people that war was necessary. They had to be brought to believe blindly in the correctness of the leadership's policies, even when these included war. Doubt only made them unhappy. 'Now it has become necessary gradually to reorient the German people psychologically, and to make it clear to them that there are things that cannot be achieved by peaceful means but must be carried through by force.'[146] That more than five years of indoctrination and preparation at every level had not achieved this aim already was an astonishing admission of failure. It showed that the vast majority of Germans, in Hitler's view, were falling far short of giving the regime the popular support it demanded, even in the area – foreign policy – where its aims supposedly had their broadest appeal.[147]

III

On 1 October 1938 German troops marched across the border into Czechoslovakia as the well-equipped Czech army withdrew from the strong positions it occupied in the mountainous and easily defensible border regions. The scenes that had greeted the German annexation of Austria were repeated in the Sudetenland. Ecstatic supporters of Henlein's Sudeten German Party lined the streets, cheering the German soldiers as they marched by, strewing flowers in their path and raising their arms in the Hitler salute. Amongst those who did not sympathize with the Nazis, a very different mood prevailed. Over 25,000 people, mostly Czech, had already fled from the Sudetenland into predominantly Czech areas in September. Now they were followed by another 150,000 from the same territory and other border areas between the signature of the Munich Agreement and the end of 1938, and almost 50,000 more in the following few months. The refugees included Czechs and Germans who qualified as Jewish under the Nuremberg Laws; they knew only too well what awaited them if they stayed. By May 1939 the number of Jews in the Sudetenland had fallen from 22,000 to fewer than 2,000 in all. A fifth of the Czech population of the border areas fled. Almost a quarter of the Sudeten German population had opposed Henlein's party, and 35,000 of them fled too, mostly German Social Democrats and Communists. The fate of those who remained showed that they had been wise to leave. The Gestapo and the SS Security Service moved in behind the German troops, and they arrested about 8,000 ethnic German and 2,000 Czech opponents of Nazism, putting the majority of them into concentration camps, a minority in state prisons following formal trials. Little over a month later, the violence of the pogrom of 9–10 November was extended to the Sudetenland too, and those Jews who remained there were subject to widespread violence, looting and destruction of their property. Fifty thousand employees of the Czechoslovak state, in the railways, the post office, the schools and local administration, were dismissed to make way for Germans, and also left for the rump Czecho-Slovak Republic, as it was now called.[148]

The predominantly German-speaking areas of western and northern Bohemia, northern Moravia and southern Silesia were incorporated into the Third Reich as the Reich Region Sudetenland, while southern Bohemia became part of Bavaria and southern Moravia was assigned to the former Austria. Henlein was made Reich Commissioner of the new region under the Reich Interior Ministry, and civil servants were drafted in from other parts of Germany to fill the posts in regional and local administration vacated by Czechs, Jews and leftists. Nevertheless, most administrators at all levels were Sudeten Germans, and – in sharp contrast to Austria – the Nazi regime took great care to perpetuate a distinctive sense of identity for the Sudetenland, leaving only the Gestapo and the SS (including its Security Service) in the hands of men from the Old Reich. Sudeten Germans themselves flocked to join the Nazi Party and enrol in the SA. Yet they were soon to be disillusioned. Long-standing local voluntary associations and clubs were dissolved or incorporated into Nazi Party organizations run from Berlin. Resentment against carpetbaggers from the Old Reich, limited though their numbers were, was soon widespread. Unemployment fell sharply, but industrial workers had to live with the long hours and poor pay that had become the norm in the Old Reich. Twenty-two per cent of Czech industrial production was located in the annexed areas, and it was rapidly incorporated into the German war economy, with German firms moving quickly in to take advantage of the Germanization and Aryanization of Czech and Jewish businesses. I.G. Farben, Carl Zeiss Jena and major German banks and insurance companies made significant acquisitions, though Sudeten German companies benefited from the loot as well. The 410,000 Czechs who remained in the annexed areas found their language banned for official use, their secondary schools closed and their voluntary associations and clubs shut down. They had now become second-class citizens.[149]

The Munich Agreement also gave the signal to smaller powers to take their slice of the Czechoslovak cake. On 30 September 1938 the Polish military government demanded the cession of the strip of land around

Teschen on the northern border of Czechoslovakia, which had a substantial Polish-speaking population; the Czechs had little option but to agree, and Polish troops marched in on 2 October 1938. The Czech general who handed over the region remarked to his Polish counterpart that he would not enjoy its possession for long: Poland was surely next in line itself. But the principle of maintaining the boundaries drawn by the 1919 Peace Settlement counted little in the face of the aggrandizing nationalism of the Polish colonels, who subjected the conquered region to the same policies of Polonization and authoritarian rule that they had already applied at home.[150] Along the southern frontier of Czechoslovakia, the authoritarian government of Hungary, under Admiral Horthy, also made its claim to a long strip of land in which the Magyar minority predominated. Its armed forces were poorly prepared for an invasion, however, and so the Hungarians had to resort to negotiation. The position was complicated by the fact that tensions between Czechs and Slovaks now came to the surface, reflecting long-standing economic, social, religious and cultural differences between the two main constituent groups of the Republic. On 7 October 1938, leaders of the Slovak political parties established an autonomous region with its own government, but nominally at least within the rump state left after the Munich Agreement. Competing claims by the Slovaks and Hungarians were eventually settled by the intervention of the Italians, who imposed a settlement (with German agreement) on 2 November 1938. It gave the Hungarians additional territory of 12,000 square kilometres of land with over a million inhabitants, including a sizeable minority of more than 200,000 Slovaks. This was less than they had originally demanded, but enough to satisfy them for the moment, and Hitler made it clear that he would not tolerate any military action on their part to secure further gains. The complete absence of Britain and France from the negotiations demonstrated with startling clarity the degree to which Axis powers now controlled affairs in this part of Europe.[151]

In recognition of this brutal fact of life, the governments of the region now did their best to accommodate themselves to German wishes. In the new tripartite rump state governed from Prague, right-wing governments suppressed the Communists and cracked down on Social Democrats. The military government in the Czech area did its best not to offend the Germans who now surrounded much of its territory. The autonomous

Slovak authorities in Bratislava created a one-party state and enforced its policies through a paramilitary force, the Hlinka Guard, which soon earned a justified reputation for brutality. In a third, newly created autonomous region in the east, known at the time as Carpatho-Ukraine, where the German consul exercised a dominant influence, national minorities were rigorously suppressed and Ukrainian was made the sole official language. On 7 December 1938 a treaty of economic co-operation was signed with Germany, giving the Third Reich control over the area's mineral resources. The Hungarians joined the Anti-Comintern Pact and the Romanian government offered Germany its friendship; in both countries the governments moved sharply to the right, with King Carol of Romania carrying out a coup against his own cabinet. In Hungary, Poland and Romania, anti-Jewish measures were stepped up. All these measures testified to something of a panic amongst the smaller nations of East-Central Europe. For many years, France had been trying to cement them together as a bulwark against German expansion. The Munich Agreement put paid to all that.[152]

Hitler had regarded Munich as no more than a temporary setback to his plans for invading and taking over the whole of Czechoslovakia, whatever the Western powers might think. Strategically, possession of the rest of the country would provide an additional jumping-off point for moving against Poland, whose military government steadfastly rejected Hitler's overtures to come into the Anti-Comintern Pact. The Polish government also refused to make concessions to Germany over Danzig, a Free City under League of Nations suzerainty, and the Corridor that gave Poland access to the Baltic but cut off West and East Prussia from the rest of the Reich. The largely German population of Danzig had rallied to the Nazi cause, as had that of another city on the borders of East Prussia and Lithuania, Memel, which had been given to the Lithuanians at the end of the First World War: Hitler now wanted both towns to return to Germany, and after the final collapse of negotiations with the Polish government, he decided to start piling on the pressure. Occupying the rest of the rump Czecho-Slovak state would also bring major economic resources into the Reich, since the bulk of the Czech arms industry was located there, along with very significant mineral resources, engineering, iron and steel, textiles, glass and other industries and the skilled workers who manned them. As the economic situation of the Reich deteriorated in the winter of 1938–9, the acquisition of these resources became an ever more tempting prospect. The Czecho-Slovak army's large stocks of advanced military equipment would help alleviate bottlenecks in German military supplies. Czech foreign currency reserves would be extremely useful too. Already on 21 October 1938 Hitler ordered the armed forces to prepare for the liquidation of the Czecho-Slovak state and the occupation of Memel and its surrounding territory. In the first two months of 1939 he gave three speeches to different, large groups of army officers, meeting in closed session, reiterating his vision for a Germany that was the dominant power in Europe, his belief that the problem of living-space in Eastern Europe had to be solved and his conviction that military force had to be used to achieve these goals.[153]

The opportunity to make good the enforced compromises of the Munich Agreement was provided by the rapid deterioration of relations between Czechs and Slovaks in the rump Republic over the issue of financial resources. As the squabble grew into a crisis, the mistaken belief that the Slovaks were about to declare full independence prompted the Czech government to send in troops to occupy Bratislava on 10 March 1939. A flurry of negotiations led to the Slovak leaders being flown to Berlin, where they were given the stark choice of either declaring complete independence under German protection or being taken over by the Hungarians, who had already been made aware of the opportunity. They decided on the former course. On 14 March 1939 the Slovak parliament proclaimed the country's independence, and the following day its leaders reluctantly asked the Third Reich for protection against the Czechs, after German gunboats on the Danube had targeted their guns on government buildings in Bratislava. Confronted with the imminent dissolution of his state, the President of Czecho-Slovakia, Emil Hácha, travelled with his Foreign Minister, Franzisek Chvalkovsky, to Berlin to meet Hitler. Just like Schuschnigg before him, Hácha was kept waiting far into the night (while Hitler watched a popular film), then was mercilessly bullied by the German Leader in the presence of senior civil servants, military officers and others, including Göring and Ribbentrop. German troops were already on the move, said Hitler. When Göring added that German bombers would be dropping their payloads on Prague within a few hours, the elderly, sick Czech President fainted. Revived by Hitler's personal physician, Hácha phoned Prague, ordering his troops not to fire on the invading Germans, then signed a document agreeing to the establishment of a German protectorate over his country shortly before four in the morning on 15 March 1939. 'I shall enter history as the greatest German of them all,' Hitler told his secretaries ecstatically as he emerged from the negotiations.[154]

IV

At six in the morning German troops crossed the Czech border. They reached Prague by nine. This time there were no crowds strewing flowers in their path, only groups of sullen and resentful Czechs who did nothing except raise their fists in the occasional gesture of defiance. That was only to be expected, Hitler later remarked; one could not expect them to be enthusiastic. During the afternoon, Hitler went by train to the border, then drove in an open-topped car through the snow, saluting the German troops as he passed them by. Prague was empty by the time he got there. The Czech troops were in their barracks, surrendering their arms and equipment to the invading Germans; civilians were staying at home. Hitler spent the night in the Hradschin Castle, the symbolic seat of Czech sovereignty, where he had a frugal meal – nothing had been prepared for his arrival – and worked out the terms of the decree establishing the German Protectorate, together with Interior Minister Frick and State Secretary Wilhelm Stuckart, who had already drafted the details of the post-annexation administration of Austria.[155]

Read out by Ribbentrop on Prague radio on the morning of 16 March 1939, the decree declared that the remaining Czech lands were henceforth to be known as the Reich Protectorate of Bohemia and Moravia, recalling their names under the old Habsburg monarchy. Democratic institutions, including the parliament, were abolished, but a nominal Czech administration remained in place, headed by Hácha as President, with a Prime Minister and an appointed, fifty-member Committee of National Solidarity under him. Altogether some 400,000 Czech state employees and civil servants remained in post, alongside, or subordinate to, a mere 2,000 administrators imported from Germany. Other Czech institutions, including the courts, were also preserved; but Czech law remained valid only where it dealt with matters not covered by the laws

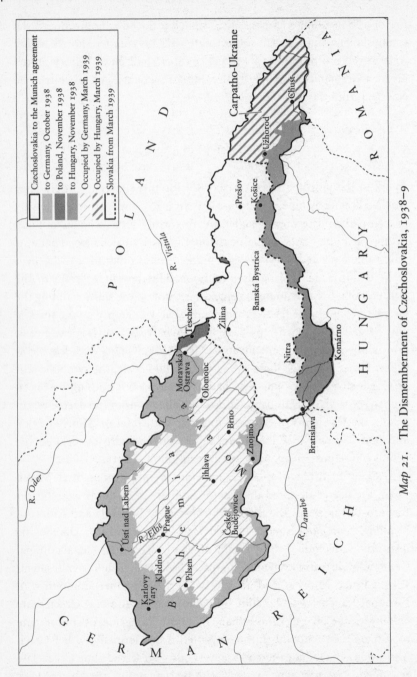

Czechoslovakia to the Munich agreement

☐ to Germany, October 1938
▨ to Poland, November 1938
▨ to Hungary, November 1938
▨ Occupied by Germany, March 1939
▨ Occupied by Hungary, March 1939
▨ Slovakia from March 1939

Map 21. The Dismemberment of Czechoslovakia, 1938–9

of the German Reich, which were now extended across the whole of the Protectorate and took precedence in every respect. Czechs and other nationalities were subject to all these laws, and to decrees issued by the Protectorate, but all Germans living in the Protectorate, including ethnic Germans already resident there, were German citizens and subject only to German law. Crucially, Czechs were not granted German citizenship. This introduced a difference in rights that was to become far more extensive, and touch far larger groups of people, later on.[156]

Real power lay in the hands of the Reich Protector. The man Hitler appointed to fill this post was Konstantin von Neurath, the former Foreign Minister, an old conservative to whom Hitler felt grateful for his role in resolving the Munich crisis the previous September. Neurath, together with German army officers such as the commanding general in Bohemia, Johannes Blaskowitz, attempted to steer a relatively moderate course, maintain discipline amongst the occupiers, and act with restraint towards the Czechs. Gradually, however, the mask of moderation began to slip. His resolve stiffened by Karl Hermann Frank, his deputy, who ran the SS and the police in the Protectorate, Neurath ordered the arrest of thousands of Communists, who were interrogated by the Gestapo and mostly released, and of the many German exiles, including Social Democrats, who had been caught by the German invasion in Prague. Most of these were sent to concentration camps in Germany. On 8 June 1939, the Gestapo arrested the entire town council of the mining community of Kladno after a German policeman was murdered; they were badly beaten, and some died. At the same time, six municipal councils elsewhere were dismissed, to be replaced by German administrators. More repressive laws followed, and steps were taken to identify the Jewish population of the Protectorate with a view to applying the Nuremberg Laws to them.[157]

Meanwhile, special units had moved into the occupied area to seize huge quantities of military equipment, arms and ammunition, including over 1,000 airplanes, 2,000 field artillery pieces, more than 800 tanks and much more besides. All of this, however, amounted to only a tiny fraction of Germany's military requirements; some was sold abroad in any case to earn much-needed foreign currency. Jewish firms were immediately expropriated and their assets transferred to German firms. The gold reserves of the Czech state were seized (the Bank of England, somewhat to the irritation of the British government, allowed over 800,000 ounces of gold to be shipped from the Czech government's London account to the new occupying authorities in Prague in June 1939). Nevertheless, representatives of the Four-Year Plan and the Reich Economics Ministry who arrived in Prague on 15 March were careful not to undermine the Czech economy or alienate non-Jewish Czech businessmen. Czech-owned international companies like the Bata shoe empire, for instance, brought in valuable profits, and were not seriously restricted by the German occupiers. The Skoda and other heavy industry and manufacturing enterprises continued to produce goods mainly for export to countries other than Germany. At the same time, however, the Germans rapidly introduced measures, already in place at home, for the conscription and direction of labour. Jobless Czech agricultural workers had already tried to escape unemployment at home by taking temporary jobs in the expanding German economy – over 105,000 in 1938 – and now German agents moved in to recruit still more. Thirty thousand new workers, most of them skilled industrial operatives, were persuaded to go to the Old Reich within the first month of the occupation.[158]

Building on the experience of the annexation of Austria, and extending it for the first time to a country which the Nazis regarded as a conquered foreign land, the occupation of Czechoslovakia created a number of institutions that formed a model for other countries later on. Native industry was left to get on with things under German direction, and with expanded German involvement through takeovers by German firms, especially of expropriated Jewish businesses. A native bureaucracy and a nominal native government was left in place under the control of a German administrator, the Reich Commissioner. The economy was integrated into the larger German sphere of influence, involving a division of labour with Germany – in this case, Czech industry was encouraged to export to South-east Europe, Germany to the West. Assets of the state, and of the Jewish population, were ruthlessly plundered (the Czech crown jewels went to Germany, and much more was soon to follow).[159]

Czech workers drafted into the Old Reich were given a special, inferior legal status. Previously, because of the need to maintain good relations with their states of origin, foreign labourers in Germany had been threatened mainly with deportation if they contravened the law. Now, however, such a threat was considered not only unnecessary but counter-productive. New regulations issued on 26 June and 4 July 1939 ordered protective custody in a concentration camp for Czech labourers in Germany who stole, looted, engaged in political activity, showed an attitude hostile to the National Socialist state, or refused to work. This placed them effectively outside the law. Despite this, 18,000 Czech workers migrated voluntarily to jobs in other parts of the Reich in March 1939, and over 16,000 in each of the following two months. Thereafter, numbers fell off rapidly. They were nowhere near enough to plug the gap in the Reich's labour supply. Coercion seemed increasingly likely. On 23 June 1939, looking forward to the coming European conflict, Göring remarked: 'During the war, hundreds of thousands will be deployed in Germany, in barracks and under supervision, from plants in the Protectorate not engaged in the war economy, and put to work especially in agriculture.'[160] The way to the systematic deportation and exploitation of millions of Europeans for the purposes of the German war economy had been opened.

This pattern was also foreshadowed in Slovakia, which was similarly incorporated into the German economic empire. Encouraged by Hitler, the Hungarians, who had ruled Slovakia for several centuries before the Treaty of Versailles had taken it away from them, had originally hoped to get the territory back. They were irritated by the decision of the Slovaks, backed by the German government, to declare independence under German protection. Hitler attempted to placate the Hungarian Regent Admiral Horthy by announcing on 12 March that he had a free hand to annex the Carpatho-Ukrainian region of Czecho-Slovakia, on which Hungary had long had a claim. Both governments justified this course of action by pointing out that on 6 March 1939 the Czecho-Slovak government had effectively brought Carpatho-Ukrainian autonomy to an end, citing the widespread abuse of power by the authorities; occupation could now plausibly be presented as another case of Czech oppression requiring intervention from outside. Only just over 12 per cent of the region's 552,000 inhabitants were Magyar, but the government in Budapest believed that the area belonged to Hungary by historic right. It sent in troops on 16 March 1939, also moving units across the Slovak border until the Germans ordered them to stop.[161] Finally, as a last act in this rapid series of events, Ribbentrop told the Lithuanian Foreign

Minister, summoned to Berlin on 20 March, that German planes would bomb their capital city, Kovno (Kaunas), if his government did not agree to cede Memel to Germany, as demanded by the town's Nazi-dominated German community. The fate of Czecho-Slovakia and Carpatho-Ukraine was enough to persuade the Lithuanians to agree, and the transfer document was signed on 23 March 1938. German troops entered the Memelland the same day, and early in the afternoon Hitler himself arrived on a German warship to address the jubilant local German crowds; he departed for Berlin the same evening.[162]

Once more, he had succeeded in annexing large amounts of territory without bloodshed. The crisis of March 1939 was a brief one, and it did not allow time for the build-up of the kind of 'war psychosis' that had dominated the summer months of the previous year. Approval of the incorporation of Memel into the Reich was almost universal, even amongst former Social Democrats. Nevertheless, Social Democratic agents reported widespread anxiety about the consequences of the invasion of Czecho-Slovakia, not least because it could not be justified as the rescue of a German minority from oppression despite the fact that Goebbels's propaganda claimed that the Czechs had been abusing the German minority in their midst. 'I think', one worker was reported as saying, 'they should have left the Czechs in peace amongst themselves, it won't end well.' It was not until the announcement that the occupation had taken place without loss of life that people began to applaud Hitler's latest success. Many people were reported as being indifferent, their nationalist sensibilities dulled by previous successes in Austria and the Sudetenland. Amongst the middle classes, there was a widespread feeling that it did not really matter so long as war was avoided. But doubts on this score were reported as being more widespread than ever. It was Hitler's least popular victory to date. 'We were always winning once before,' said one worker cynically, looking back to the propaganda claims of the First World War, 'and it came to a bad end.'[163]

MARCH INTO THE EAST

I

The anxiety that many ordinary Germans felt about war was, if anything, increased by the international reaction to the destruction of Czecho-Slovakia. The British government, led by Prime Minister Neville Chamberlain, had regarded the hard-fought Munich Agreement as sacrosanct, a great diplomatic achievement that settled all remaining problems in Central Europe. Chamberlain had believed Hitler's assurances that he had no more territorial demands to make. Now the piece of paper that Chamberlain had waved at his ecstatic supporters as evidence that he had secured 'peace for our time' had been torn to shreds. British opinion, reflected on the back benches of the House of Commons, shifted dramatically against the Germans. Hesitantly, following the advice of the Foreign Office, Chamberlain gave public voice in a speech on 17 March to the suspicion that Hitler was seeking not to right the wrongs of the 1919 Peace Settlement but 'to dominate the world by force'.[164]

The next day, the British cabinet agreed to open talks with the Polish government to see how best to stop the Germans threatening their country next. While Britain and France redoubled their efforts to rearm, and feverish negotiations continued with the Poles, news of the German threat to Poland was made public in reports from Berlin carried in the British press on 29 March. Chamberlain immediately issued a public guarantee that if Poland's independence were threatened, Britain would step in to defend it. The guarantee was intended to deter the Germans. However, it was hedged about with secret qualifications that left the door open for the policy of appeasement to continue. The British cabinet agreed that the guarantee would only come into effect if the Poles did not show 'provocative or stupid obstinacy' in the face of German demands for the return of Danzig and the Polish Corridor. Chamberlain, therefore, was still thinking of a negotiated settlement: one which would have left Poland as vulnerable as the Munich Agreement had left Czechoslovakia. Poland, after all, was a far-away country too. Moreover, the guarantee would be effective only if the Polish national forces were mobilized to resist a German invasion by force. The British coupled this condition with dire – and entirely justified – warnings to the Poles about the consequences to them should they actually do this. Chamberlain still continued to hope for peace, therefore, while shifting his ground from outright appeasement to a mixture of appeasement and containment.[165]

From the German point of view, Chamberlain's guarantee lacked credibility on a number of grounds. How, to begin with, was Britain actually going to come to the aid of Poland if war really did break out? How could the geographical and logistical problems be overcome? The vagueness of the guarantee, and Chamberlain's continued equivocations, only served to reinforce these questions. Above all, the experience of the previous years, from the Rhineland to Austria to the Munich Agreement, had implanted in Hitler's mind the firm conviction that Britain and France would shy away from taking action. Their leaders were spineless nonentities, he thought.[166] Moreover, unlike the situation of the previous year, the German army and its leadership had no hesitation about taking on the Poles, who – in contrast to the modern and well-armed Czechs – they regarded as backward, poorly led and poorly equipped. Already at the end of March 1939, Brauchitsch, informed by Hitler that military action would be required against Poland if negotiations over Danzig and the Corridor failed, had drafted a plan of invasion, codenamed 'Case White'. Hitler approved it, wrote the introduction, in which he declared that he would aim to localize the conflict, and ordered it to be ready for action by the beginning of September 1939. Just as in the previous year, a propaganda campaign now began in Berlin against the object of Germany's hostile attentions. A five-hour military parade through the city on Hitler's fiftieth birthday, on 20 April 1939, provided, as Goebbels wrote in his diary, 'a brilliant representation of German power and strength. Our heaviest artillery', he added, 'is being displayed for the first time.' Just over a week later, on 28 April 1939, Hitler formally announced to the Reichstag the abrogation of the Non-Aggression Pact with Poland signed in 1934 and the Naval Agreement with Britain signed the following year. Early in April 1939, Weizsäcker informed the Poles that the time for negotiation over Danzig and the Corridor was now at an end.[167]

On 23 May 1939 Hitler told military leaders, including Göring, Halder and Raeder, that 'further successes cannot be won without bloodshed'. 'It is not Danzig that is at stake,' he went on. 'For us it is a matter of expanding our living-space in the East and making food supplies secure . . . If fate forces us into a showdown with the West it is a good idea to possess a largish area in the East.' It was necessary therefore to attack Poland at the first suitable opportunity. Hitler conceded that Britain and France might come to Poland's aid. 'England is therefore our enemy and the showdown with England is a matter of life and death.' If possible, Poland would perish alone and unaided. But in the longer run, war with England and France was inevitable. 'England is the motive force driving against Germany.' It was to be hoped that such a war would be short. But it was as well to prepare, he said, for a war lasting ten or fifteen years. 'Time will decide against England.' If Holland, Belgium and France were occupied, English cities bombed and overseas supplies cut off by a maritime and airborne blockade, England would bleed to death. However, Germany would probably not be ready for the conflict for another five years, he added. German policy in 1939 therefore had to isolate Poland as far as possible and to ensure that the coming military action did not lead immediately to a general European war.[168] These rambling and in places even incoherent remarks betrayed Hitler's uncertainty about the consequences of invading Poland. However, they were accompanied by a concerted diplomatic campaign to cut the Poles off from any possible support. On 22 May the German alliance with Italy was upgraded to a 'Pact of Steel', while non-aggression agreements were concluded successfully with Latvia, Estonia and Denmark. A treaty signed in March 1939 gave Germany access to Romanian oil supplies in the event of a war, while similar, if less one-sided, trade links were also negotiated with Sweden and Norway, important sources of iron ore. However, negotiations with Turkey, Yugoslavia and Hungary proved less successful, leading to expressions of goodwill, especially on the economic front, but to few really concrete results.[169] The most startling opening was made in the direction of Moscow. Already in May, Hitler was beginning to realize that securing the benevolent neutrality of the Soviet Union, whose long border with Poland was of central strategic importance, would be vital for the success of the invasion. There was a danger that Britain and France would secure Soviet backing for the attempt to contain German aggression. By 6 June 1939, Hitler was no longer including in his speeches his customary diatribes against the menace of world Bolshevism. Instead, he began directing his fire against the Western democracies.[170] Behind the scenes, Ribbentrop began pushing for a formal pact with the Soviets. He was encouraged by a speech given by Stalin on 10 March 1939, in which he declared that he would not be willing to come to the rescue of the Western capitalist powers if they got into a conflict with Germany, since their policy of appeasing Hitler's demands had obviously strengthened Hitler's long-term aim of attacking the Soviet Union. On 3 May 1939, Stalin sent an unmistakable signal to Berlin by dismissing Maxim Litvinov, his long-term Foreign Minister and a proponent of collective security and civilized relations with the West. He replaced him with his hard-line henchman Vyacheslav Molotov. It escaped nobody's attention that Litvinov was a Jew, and Molotov was not.[171]

Stalin was in a difficult position in 1939. Over the previous few years he had carried out violent purges of his top generals, munitions factory managers and senior army officers. There were few left in the higher echelons of the regime with any direct experience of warfare. Competent technical experts had been arrested and killed in their thousands. Soviet military preparedness was lamentable.[172] Stalin was aware from June 1939 onwards of Hitler's intention to invade Poland in late August or early September.[173] More than anything else, he needed to ensure that the invasion went no further. He needed time to regroup and rebuild the Red Army, refashion his arms and equipment production, and get ready for the assault he was sure would follow some time after the German conquest of Poland. To some extent, he left open the option of forging an alliance with the Western powers; but they were hesitant, regarding him as unreliable, and Ribbentrop and the German Foreign Office were eager, despite Hitler's own personal reservations. As the hints from Moscow grew stronger, Ribbentrop saw an opportunity to shock the British, whom he still hated intensely after the humiliations of his time as ambassador in London, and deliver a coup that would win Hitler's undying gratitude and approval. Negotiations on improving Soviet–German trade relations started, faltered, and started again. Molotov and Ribbentrop both indicated that an economic agreement should have a political dimension. This was not long in taking shape. By early August 1939, Ribbentrop and Weizsäcker, with Hitler's approval, had drawn up plans for a joint partition of Poland with the Soviets. Still Stalin hesitated. Finally, however, on 21 August he agreed to Hitler's increasingly urgent requests for a formal pact. Sidelining half-hearted British attempts to reach an agreement, the Soviet dictator invited Ribbentrop to Moscow. By 23 August, Ribbentrop had arrived. By the early hours of the following morning, the Non-Aggression Pact had been signed.[174]

A formal alliance between two powers that had spent the previous six years mutually vilifying each other in public, and had been the major backers of the two opposing sides in the Spanish Civil War, was unexpected, to say the least.[175] However, there were strong reasons for the agreement on both sides. From Hitler's point of view, it was necessary to secure Soviet acquiescence in the German invasion of Poland, otherwise the nightmare scenario of the invasion broadening out into a European war on two fronts began to look a distinct possibility. From Stalin's perspective, it provided a respite and opened up the enticing prospect of Europe's capitalist powers, Germany, France and Britain, fighting a war of mutual destruction between themselves. Moreover, while the published version of the Pact committed both states not to make war on each other for ten years, to settle disputes by negotiation or third-party arbitration, and to increase their trade with one another, its secret clauses allocated spheres of influence in East-Central Europe to Germany and the Soviet Union, under which Stalin would take over the eastern part of Poland, together with Latvia, Lithuania and Estonia, and Hitler the western part. The significance of these clauses was enormous. Both Hitler and Stalin realized that the Pact was unlikely to last the stipulated ten years. Indeed, it did not even last two. But in the longer run, the boundary it drew in Poland between the German and Soviet spheres was to prove permanent, while the Soviet occupation of the Baltic states was to last until near the end of the twentieth century.[176]

There were other consequences of the Pact too. During the detailed negotiations, the German side raised the question of German political refugees in the Soviet Union. Stalin had no interest in protecting them;

indeed he was deeply suspicious of foreigners of any kind who had found a home in Russia, and of many of the Russians who came into contact with them. So he agreed to send them back to the Third Reich. Some 4,000 German citizens were duly rounded up and handed over to the Gestapo by the Soviet authorities after the Pact had been signed. Between 1,000 and 1,200 were German Communists. Some, like Margarete Buber-Neumann, had already been imprisoned by Stalin's secret police before being sent to a German concentration camp; her husband, Heinz Neumann, had been purged from the German Party leadership in 1932 for urging a united front with the Social Democrats against the Nazi threat; sent first to Spain, then Moscow, he had been arrested in 1937 and executed. His widow was deported directly from a Soviet labour camp to Ravensbrück concentration camp in 1940. For those German Communist exiles who were Jewish, an even worse fate was in store. The conductor and composer Hans Walter David was one of their number. Born in 1893, he had fled to Paris in 1933 then Moscow in 1935. He fell victim to Stalin's great purge in 1937, and was sentenced to a labour camp in 1939 for allegedly spying for the Germans, an example of Stalin's paranoid suspicion of foreigners in the Soviet Union. In April 1940, David was informed that his sentence had been commuted into one of deportation. He was handed over to the Germans on 2 May 1940, and murdered by the SS. In February 1940 a grateful German Embassy in Moscow thanked the Soviet authorities for their co-operation in locating and surrendering a large number of exiles like him.[177]

Meanwhile, Communist parties all over Europe struggled to sell the Pact to their members, many of whom had joined in the first place because the party seemed to offer the best guarantee of carrying the fight against fascism to the enemy. Disorientation followed disbelief. Many felt betrayed. Yet before long, most Communists had come round to the idea that the Pact might not be such a bad thing after all. Years of schooling in party discipline, of supporting every twist and turn in party doctrine and policy, made it easy in the end to accept even this startling U-turn. Some thought it might even lead to the legalization of the Communist Party in Germany; many believed that a war between the capitalist powers was none of their business anyway; all revered Stalin as a great thinker and master of political tactics, a world genius who always knew best and whose decisions were always right.[178] Some Nazis, too, were doubtful about the wisdom of the Pact. Anti-Communism was a central tenet of Nazi ideology, and now Hitler seemed to be betraying it. The morning after the Pact's announcement, the front garden of the Brown House, the Nazi Party headquarters in Munich, was covered in Party badges thrown there in disgust by disgruntled Party members. Alfred Rosenberg, the arch-anti-Communist, blamed Ribbentrop's ambition for the Pact. An alliance with Britain would have been preferable, he thought. Nevertheless, like most other Nazis, he was so inured to accepting Hitler's every decision as above discussion that he acquiesced anyway. Many realized the *rapprochement* with the Soviet Union was purely tactical. 'The Leader has made a brilliant move,' wrote Goebbels admiringly in his diary.[179]

II

Hitler's growing sense of urgency in the last days and weeks before the signing of the Pact derived not least from the fact that the invasion of Poland had already been fixed for 26 August 1939.[180] In the meantime, Hitler had taken steps to avoid a build-up of the kind of 'war psychosis' that had made the mass of ordinary Germans so uneasy during the Czechoslovak crisis the previous summer. He made a point of carrying on in public as if nothing out of the ordinary was going on, going on a tour of his childhood haunts in Austria, visiting the Bayreuth Festival, taking part in a massive street parade of German art and culture in Munich and whiling away several weeks at his mountain retreat on the Obersalzberg. He announced that the annual Party Rally in Nuremberg would be a 'Rally of Peace' and would begin early in September (by which time he in fact envisaged that German armies would be marching across Poland). And he made a point of focusing public references to Poland on the position of Danzig. In reality this was a side-issue, no more than a pretext, if that. But from May onwards, Goebbels's daily press instructions unfolded a hate campaign against Poland that made it seem as if the ethnic German inhabitants of the country, and above all of Danzig, were in constant, mortal and growing danger from violence meted out to them by Poles. 'Ethnic Germans flee from Polish terror', screamed the headlines. 'German houses broken into with axes –

Terrorized by Poles for weeks – Hundreds of refugees are arrested by the Poles'. Poles were allegedly murdering ethnic Germans, shooting at German passers-by in Danzig, and generally threatening to make their lives unbearable. Although the Polish government's policy towards the ethnic German minority had been considerably less liberal and tolerant than that of its Czech counterpart, these stories were grotesque exaggerations if not pure invention. For their part, the Nazis who dominated the political scene in Danzig kept up the pressure by provoking the Poles and staging incidents for the German press to exploit, such as mounting violent attacks on Polish customs officers and spreading atrocity stories when the officers defended themselves.[181]

But the barrage of propaganda let fly by Goebbels made it seem as if it was the Sudetenland all over again, and that the incorporation of Danzig into the Reich, coupled with some as yet undefined arrangement over the Polish Corridor, and perhaps brokered again by Britain and France, was what Hitler was after. Even the Social Democrats conceded that the Poles were despised and disliked by the vast majority of the German population, including workers, who saw them as dirty, backward, and cheap competition in the labour market. The clashes that had taken place in Silesia at the end of the First World War had lost none of their bitter resonances twenty years on. Yet the hope was general that the issue would be settled peacefully. 'Danzig', Social Democratic sympathizers were reported as thinking, '. . . is a purely German city after all. Who can have anything against Germany gathering it to itself again? The Danzig matter is basically much simpler than things were with Czechoslovakia.' Surely England and France would understand that.[182]

Such sentiments were common amongst supporters of the Nazis too. 'None of us', Melita Maschmann later recalled, 'doubted that Hitler would avoid war if he could possibly contrive to do so.'[183] He had, after all, done it so many times before. Hitler was a diplomatic genius, and they believed his assurances that he was a man of peace.[184] Reporting on the attitude towards the crisis shown by the rural population in the Bavarian district of Ebermannstadt, a local official concluded bluntly on 30 June 1939: 'The desire for peace is stronger than the desire for war. Amongst the overwhelming majority of the population a solution to the Danzig question will therefore only find agreement if this happens in the same bloodless way as the previous annexations in the East have.'[185]

The idea that Hitler wanted a peaceful solution to the Danzig problem was not just intended to keep the anxieties of the domestic population at a minimum; on 11 August 1939 Hitler met the League of Nations High Commissioner in Danzig, the Swiss diplomat Carl Burckhardt, at the Obersalzberg, at his own request, to indicate his readiness to negotiate with the British. At the same time, he managed to spoil this calculated pose of reasonableness by shouting that he would destroy Poland completely if its government failed to comply with his demands.[186]

None of Hitler's diplomatic moves had much of an effect on the stance taken by the other international players in this deadly game, not even his announcement of the Nazi–Soviet Pact. The Polish government had always been suspicious and resentful of the Soviet Union, with which Poland had fought a bitter war in the early 1920s, so from this point of view the Pact made little difference. The events in Danzig and similar disturbances in Silesia only stiffened the Poles' resolve to resist any kind of deal, given the fact that it would deliver them up to Germany just as the Munich Agreement had delivered up the Czechs. But in any case a deal seemed unlikely. Both the British and the French governments insisted that the Nazi–Soviet Pact could not alter their decision to stand by Poland, as Chamberlain told Hitler in a letter couriered to him at the Obersalzberg by the generally pro-German British Ambassador Sir Nevile Henderson on 23 August 1939. Receiving the letter, Hitler subjected Henderson to a wild tirade against the British, who were, he shouted accusingly, determined to exterminate Germany altogether in the interests of inferior races. On 25 August 1939, however, back in Berlin, Hitler took a different tack, offering Henderson in sweeping if rather vague terms a general settlement with Britain once the Polish question was solved. While Henderson flew back to London for consultations, Hitler learned that the British had just signed a military alliance with Poland. Ribbentrop's poor reputation in Britain was clearly frustrating his attempt to win Chamberlain round. Sidelining his Foreign Minister for the moment, Hitler turned to Göring, who had always enjoyed a better reputation in London. Göring's Swedish friend Birger Dahlerus was sent to take further soundings in the British capital. They elicited the response, delivered by Henderson on 28 August 1939, that the British government was willing to guarantee peacefully negotiated German–Polish boundaries and to support the return of the German overseas colonies mandated to the League of Nations in the 1919 Peace Settlement, but that the British were still committed to back Poland by force of arms should the Germans invade.[187]

On 22 August 1939, Hitler summoned top commanders of the armed forces to the Obersalzberg to tell them the invasion was going ahead. They arrived in civilian clothing so as to avoid suspicion. The Pact with Stalin was about to be signed, and he was in a confident mood. He had already decided in the spring that he was going to invade Poland, he said. 'I first thought I would turn against the West in a few years, and only after that against the East. But the sequence of these things cannot be fixed.' The Polish situation had become intolerable. The moment to strike had come. 'England and France have undertaken obligations which neither is in a position to fulfil. There is no real rearmament in England, but only propaganda.' Thus there would be no general war if he invaded Poland. The risks for the Western democracies were too great. At the same time, the conquest of the East would open up supplies of grain and raw materials which would frustrate any future attempt at a blockade. 'A start has been made on the destruction of England's hegemony.' 'Our enemies', he added, 'are tiny little worms. I came to know them in Munich.'[188] Over lunch, a number of the officers present had let their disquiet at these sentiments become apparent. Many of them felt that Hitler was deceiving himself when he claimed that Britain and France would not intervene. To stiffen their resolve, Hitler addressed them again in the afternoon. 'Everyone', he told them, 'must hold the view that we have been determined to fight the western Powers from the start. A life and death struggle.' The Western leaders were 'weaker men'. Even if they declared war, there was little they could do in the short run. 'The destruction of Poland remains the priority,' he concluded.[189]

Hitler in fact continued to believe that the British would not intervene; the long-term threat of American power, he thought, would drive them towards an alliance with Germany.[190] But the intention, which he made clear to the generals at this time, of launching the invasion on 26 August was unexpectedly frustrated by Mussolini, who felt affronted that despite all the assurances contained in the Pact of Steel, Hitler had chosen not to take him fully into his confidence over Poland. The news of the planned invasion, communicated to Ciano by Ribbentrop earlier in the month, had come as a complete surprise to the Italians. On 24 August

1939 Hitler had written to Mussolini personally asking for Italian backing. The troops had already been given their marching orders on 25 August 1939, when Mussolini's reply arrived at the Reich Chancellery: German airports had already been closed, the annual Nuremberg Rally cancelled, and food rationing introduced with effect from 27 August 1939. Mussolini told Hitler that Italy was not in a position to offer any military assistance in the event of a war. 'The Italians are behaving just like they did in 1914,' fumed Hitler. He cancelled the marching orders, and the invasion ground to a halt just before it reached the Polish border.[191]

The endgame was now under way. Overcoming his fury at the Italians, who compounded their offence by offering to call a conference with the British and the French to impose a settlement on the lines of the Munich Agreement, Hitler made a last effort to secure Anglo-French neutrality. Further meetings with Henderson failed to budge the British on the crucial issue of their guarantee to Poland in the event of armed conflict. Much of what Hitler had to say, including the offer of a plebiscite in the Corridor coupled with the return of Danzig to Germany, was no more than window-dressing designed to assure the German public that he had made every effort to maintain peace. When Ribbentrop communicated the offer to Henderson in the Reich Chancellery at midnight on 29 August 1939, he read it out at a speed too great for the ambassador to make proper notes, then flung it on the table saying it was out of date anyway. The interpreter at the meeting later reported that the atmosphere had been so bad he thought the two men would come to blows. Hitler had his offer broadcast on German radio on the evening of 30 August 1939, blaming the British and the Poles, who had been asked at the last minute to send an emissary to Berlin, for its failure. By this time, the army had been given a fresh set of orders to march into Poland in the early hours of 1 September 1939.[192]

Acting according to plans arranged some time before by Heydrich, SS men in civilian clothing staged a mock assault on the German radio station at Gleiwitz, in Upper Silesia. Its staff were replaced by another detachment from the SS. Evidence of the Poles' supposedly murderous assault was provided by two concentration camp inmates from Sachsenhausen, killed by lethal injections and dumped at the radio station to be photographed by the German media. The orders, approved by Hitler personally, referred to the bodies as 'canned goods'. A third man, Franz Honiok, a pro-Polish German citizen, was arrested on 30 August 1939 as someone who could be plausibly identified as a Polish irregular, and taken out of the police gaol by the SS at Gleiwitz the next day. He was put to sleep with an injection, placed inside the radio station, and, still unconscious, shot dead. To lend further authenticity to the action, the Polish-speaking SS men shouted anti-German slogans into the microphone before leaving. Normally the radio station was only used for emergency weather forecasts, so hardly anybody was listening. Elsewhere, two other border incidents were staged by SS men dressed in Polish army uniforms. As one SS man came out of a German customs house that he had just helped smash to pieces, he stumbled over several dead bodies wearing Polish uniforms. Their heads, he reported later, were shaven, their faces had been beaten to make them unrecognizable, and their bodies were completely rigid.[193]

At a quarter to five on the morning of 1 September 1939 the German battleship *Schleswig-Holstein* opened fire on the Polish garrison and ammunition depot at the Westerplatte, a peninsula off the Vistula estuary which commanded the entrance to Danzig's harbour, and Stuka dive-bombers passed low over the city. Polish railway and postal officials were attacked by local German police units and shooting broke out in a number of places. Albert Forster, the Nazi Party Regional Leader in Danzig, put the League of Nations commissioner Burckhardt under house arrest and then gave him two hours to leave. Burckhardt packed his bags and drove off to Lithuania. All along the border between Poland and Germany, units of the German armed forces raised the customs barriers and drove through into Polish territory, while planes of the German air force flew into Polish airspace laden with bombs to drop on Poland's railways, roads and bridges, army bases, towns and cities. At ten in the morning, Hitler addressed a hastily summoned Reichstag. Exhausted and overwrought by the frantic negotiations of the previous days, Hitler was nervous and confused, stumbling over his words several times and making an unusually hesitant impression. The Poles had committed no fewer than fourteen serious violations of the border the previous night, he said (alluding to the incidents staged by Heydrich's men). Retaliation was necessary for these and other outrages. 'Henceforth, bomb will be avenged with bomb. He who fights with poison shall be fought with poison gas. He who distances himself from the rules of a humane conduct of warfare can only expect us to take the same step.' After the speech was over, the deputies solemnly voted to incorporate Danzig into the Reich. But not before Hitler had sounded a note that was not only full of foreboding but also replete with prophecy. He was ready to make any sacrifice, he said. 'I now wish to be nothing other than the first soldier of the German Reich. Therefore I have put on that tunic which has always been the most holy and dear to me. I shall not take it off again until after victory is ours, or – I shall not live to see the day!' Suicide in the event of defeat was already at the back of his mind.[194]

III

In Britain and France, as in Poland, the armed forces had been preparing for war since the beginning of the crisis. The British government ordered full mobilization on 31 August and, fearing air attacks, began to evacuate women and children from the cities. Sandbags were piled up outside government buildings, orders were given for nightly blackouts, and Chamberlain began discussing the formation of a war cabinet including such opponents of appeasement as Winston Churchill. But the feverish comings and goings of late August had begun to convince Chamberlain that a peaceful solution might be possible. Furious arguments broke out within the British cabinet. While Chamberlain dithered, his Foreign Secretary Lord Halifax continued to negotiate with the French, the Italians and the Germans. The negotiations got nowhere. A majority of the cabinet, brushing aside arguments for a delay, backed the issuing of a 'final warning' to Hitler. On the evening of 1 September 1939, Henderson told the German government that the conference proposed by the Italians on the Polish situation, based on Hitler's offer of 29 August, could only take place if German forces ceased fire and withdrew.[195]

On 2 September 1939, after more hours of telephone conversations between the British Foreign Office, the French and the Italians, Chamberlain faced a packed House of Commons shortly before eight o'clock in the evening. He began by telling members that he had received no reply from Hitler to the final warning delivered the previous day. 'It may be', he went on, 'that the delay is caused by consideration of a proposal which, meanwhile, had been put forward by the Italian Government, that hostilities should cease and that there should then immediately be a conference between the Five Powers, Great Britain, France, Poland, Germany and Italy.' He made no mention of a time-limit for a response, no reference to the carnage and devastation now in progress as Polish troops and civilians were being slaughtered by German ground and air attacks. His equivocal words made it look like Munich all over again. But the mood in the political elite, as in the country, had changed since March 1939. The great majority were now convinced that the Third Reich was aiming at European if not world domination, and that the time had come to stop it. A wave of fury swept across the House. As Arthur Greenwood stood up to deliver the opposition's reply, he was rudely interrupted. 'Speaking for the Labour Party,' Greenwood began. 'Speak for England!' shouted a Tory backbencher, Leo Amery. It was a sentiment widely felt across the House.[196]

Greenwood rose to the occasion. 'I am greatly disturbed', he said. 'An act of aggression took place thirty-eight hours ago . . . I wonder how long we are prepared to vacillate at a time when Britain, and all that Britain stands for, and human civilization are in peril.' Chamberlain was shattered by the hostility his words had aroused. A visitor in the public gallery later described him as 'a dithering old dodderer with shaking voice and hands'. A majority of the cabinet met informally immediately afterwards without him, appalled at his backsliding. He would have to issue an ultimatum to the Germans, they decided. Halifax and Chamberlain feared that if they did not issue it, the government would fall. Public opinion in Britain was behind firm action. As a huge thunderstorm broke over London, the cabinet met at 11.20 in the evening and took its decision. The next morning, at nine o'clock on 3 September 1939, Henderson handed a formal ultimatum to the German Foreign Ministry. Unless the Germans agreed to a ceasefire and withdrawal within two hours, Britain and Germany would be at war.[197]

The Germans replied in a lengthy, pre-prepared document handed over to Henderson shortly after the ultimatum expired at 11 a.m. It asserted that all Germany wanted to do was to correct the injustices of the Treaty of Versailles and blamed Britain for encouraging Polish aggression. At noon the French presented a similar, if somewhat lengthier ultimatum. It too was rejected, amidst assurances that Germany had no intention of invading France. By this time, Chamberlain had already broadcast to the British people that in the absence of a satisfactory reply to the ultimatum, 'this country is now at war with Germany'. 'Everything that I have worked for,' he told the House of Commons shortly afterwards, 'everything that I have hoped for, everything that I have believed in in my public life has crashed into ruins.' In the early afternoon, the news was broadcast to the German nation in a series of proclamations issued by Hitler. He had done everything he could to preserve peace, he told them, but British warmongering had made it impossible. The British people were not to blame, only their Jewish-plutocratic leaders. To the Nazi Party and its members he was more forthright. 'Our Jewish democratic global enemy has succeeded in placing the English people in a state of war with Germany,' he told them, and added: 'The year 1918 will not repeat itself.'[198]

Others were not so sure. The conservatives who had come together during the Munich crisis of the previous year to oppose Hitler's drive towards war were even more appalled as he turned his attention to Poland. In various ways they tried to make contact with the British and French governments, but their messages were mixed – some urged greater firmness, others a general European settlement – and they were not taken very seriously.[199] When Hitler rescinded his initial orders for the invasion of Poland, a few, including Schacht, Oster and Canaris, thought briefly that the blow to his prestige would bring him down. But they had no backing from the generals this time. The senior officers' greater, and wholly justified, military confidence in the face of Polish opposition, their long-nurtured ambitions to deal a blow to the Poles, their further months of being browbeaten and intimidated by the Nazi Leader, and their surprise and relief at the successful dismemberment of Czechoslovakia had overcome any reservations they still had about the overall thrust of Hitler's policy. A year on from the Munich crisis, the armed forces were in a far greater state of readiness; the Soviet Union had been neutralized; and there was in reality nothing the British or the French could do to rescue Poland from oblivion. Hitler had wanted to go to war in September 1938 and been frustrated at the last minute by Anglo-French intervention. This time, his resolve was far greater. For all the tergiversations of the last days of August 1939, his determination to invade Poland, even at the risk of a general European war, could not be shaken. When Göring, still trying to avoid a conflict with the British, suggested to him on 29 August 1939 that it was not necessary to 'gamble everything', Hitler replied: 'In my life, I've always put my whole stake on the table.'[200]

Going for broke was not something that appealed immediately to the mass of the German people. By 29 August 1939 they were becoming seriously alarmed. The mood in the rural Bavarian district of Ebermann-stadt, reported an official, was 'considerably depressed ... Although signs of a fear of war are nowhere to be found ... there can be no question of enthusiasm for war either. The memory of the world war and its consequences is still much too fresh to allow space for a jingoistic mood.' The outbreak of war, added another report filed a few weeks later, caused a general 'despondency' amongst the population.[201] Social Democratic observers concurred: there was 'no enthusiasm for war'.[202] Standing on the Wilhelmplatz around noon on 3 September, William L. Shirer joined a crowd of about 250 people who heard the loudspeakers announce the British declaration of war. 'When it was finished,' he reported, 'there was not a murmur.' He decided to sample the mood a little further: 'I walked in the streets,' he went on. 'On the faces of the people astonishment, depression ... In 1914, I believe, the excitement in Berlin on the first day of the World War was tremendous. To-day, no excitement, no hurrahs, no cheering, no throwing of flowers, no war fever, no war hysteria.' There was no rebirth of the legendary spirit of 1914 in September 1939. The propaganda war to fill Germans with hate for their new enemies had failed.[203]

Apprehension and anxiety were the commonest emotions as Germany entered a state of war. In Hamburg, Luise Solmitz was in despair. 'Who is going to carry off the miracle?' she asked on 29 August 1939. 'Who is going to help tortured humanity away from war to peace? Easy to answer: nothing and no one ... A butchery is beginning such as the world has not yet experienced.'[204] It was, above all, fear of bombing raids on German cities that spread despondency. If anything, it was made worse by the elaborate air-raid precautions people were now enjoined by their Block Wardens to undertake. ' "Air-raids," ' said an acquaintance to Luise Solmitz's husband on 31 August 1939, ' "well, it's not so terrible if we really do cop it a bit. It will take the pressure off the front." Is the front relieved, said Fr[iedrich], if the soldiers' parents, wives, children and homes are annihilated?'[205] Without expecting much protection from them, Luise Solmitz sewed sandbags to put in front of her windows. 'A world full of blood and atrocity,' she noted as the war broke out. 'And so we enter a time that has been so dreaded and feared, a time in comparison to which the 30 Years' War was a Sunday School outing . . . Now that Europe's wounds have been healed after 21 years, the West will be annihilated.'[206]

IV

War had been the objective of the Third Reich and its leaders from the moment they came to power in 1933. From that point up to the actual outbreak of hostilities in September 1939, they had focused relentlessly on preparing the nation for a conflict that would bring European, and eventually world, domination for Germany. The megalomania of these ambitions had been apparent in the gigantism of the plans developed by Hitler and Speer for Berlin, which was to become Germania, the new world capital. And the limitless scale of the Nazi drive for conquest and dominion over the rest of the world entailed a correspondingly thoroughgoing attempt to remould the minds, spirits and bodies of the German people to make them capable and worthy of the role of the new master-race that awaited them. The ruthlessly thorough co-ordination of German social institutions that gave the Nazi Party a near-monopoly over the organization of daily life from 1933 onwards was only a beginning. To be sure, Hitler and the leading Nazis had proclaimed in 1933-4 that they wanted to combine the best of the old and the new Germany in the creation of the Third Reich, to synthesize tradition and revolution and to reassure conservative elites as much as they channelled the élan of their own movement into the building of a new Germany. At the end of June 1934, indeed, the demands of the more radical Nazis for permanent revolution were ruthlessly quashed in the 'Night of the Long Knives' at the same time as conservatives were given a bloody reminder that the Third Reich was not going to go back to anything like the old order of the Kaiser's day.

Yet the synthesis of the old and the new that the bloodshed of 30 June 1934 seemed to restore was in reality already being undermined.

Unevenly, but unmistakeably, the balance was shifting in favour of the new. Unlike other regimes founded on the defeat of a Marxist revolution, such as Hungary, the Third Reich brought with it far more than a mere counter-revolution. Its ambitions extended far beyond the restoration of any real, imagined, sanitized or improved *status quo*. Almost immediately, the Nazi regime began attempting to co-ordinate all the major institutions that, for tactical reasons, it had not tried to bring under its aegis at the beginning of the Third Reich: the army, the Churches and business. This proved a difficult task, since the priorities of rearmament required circumspection where business and the military were concerned, while the assault on people's most deeply held religious beliefs aroused perhaps the most open and outspoken opposition that the Nazis encountered following the suppression of the labour movement. Yet by 1939 a good deal of headway had been made. Business, initially enthusiastic about the profits to be made from recovery and rearmament, had proved insufficiently patriotic from the Nazi point of view, and from 1936 onwards it was increasingly dragooned, regimented and outflanked in a state-led drive for military preparedness that relegated the profit motive to an issue of secondary importance. Schacht's bold, imaginative but ultimately conventional economic management was thrown overboard in 1937-8 when it began to impose limits on the drive to all-out war. The armed forces had been brought willingly under Hitler's control from 1934, and happily co-operated with rearmament for the next three years. But as senior officers like Beck, Blomberg and Fritsch began to drag their feet as the pace of events quickened early in 1938, they were replaced, along with Foreign Minister Neurath; the remaining doubters were silenced for the moment by Hitler's successful annexation of the Sudetenland in September 1938.

By this time, too, the regime had imposed itself unambiguously in the sphere of cultural policy, making its views on modernist art patently clear in the Degenerate Art exhibition staged in Munich in July 1937. And it had begun to impose a ruthlessly eugenic social policy that swept traditional Christian morality aside in the search to produce a physically and spiritually perfect Aryan race. Here, radical policies were introduced from the very beginning, with the forcible sterilization of the allegedly degenerate and the beginnings of the removal of Jews from the civil service, the professions, economic life, and, with the promulgation of the Nuremberg Laws of 1935, the sexual life of the Germans as well. Here too, however, the pace quickened noticeably in 1938, with new laws on marriage and divorce designed to ensure that only hereditarily fit Germans were allowed to procreate, and childless couples were encouraged to split up in the interests of the race. The antisemitic violence of the pogrom of 9–10 November 1938, the subsequent final expropriation of Germany's Jewish community, and their removal from the remaining areas of social and cultural life shared with the rest of the population, were only the most dramatic expressions of this quickening of pace. Less widely noticed, but for those it affected no less serious in its consequences, was the transformation of the concentration camps in 1937–8 from places of confinement and coercion for the remnants of the Social Democratic and Communist political opposition, now thoroughly defeated, to dumping-grounds for the eugenically undesirable, who were increasingly employed as slave labourers in heavy quarrying and other jobs designed, ultimately, to kill them.

In none of this were the Nazis attempting to turn the clock back. On the contrary, in every sphere, their infatuation with modernity quickly became apparent. It was present not just in the design rooms of arms factories, shipyards, aircraft construction companies, munitions production lines, medical research laboratories and chemical companies. Eugenics, including forced sterilization, was itself commonly accepted by scientists and commentators across the world as the modern face of social policy. For those who espoused it, belief in the centrality of race in human affairs also derived its legitimacy from what they regarded as the latest discoveries of modern science. Modernity also took on a concrete, physical form in the Third Reich. New drugs, synthetic substitutes for petrol, rubber and natural fibres, new means of communication such as television, new kinds of metal alloy, rockets that could be fired into space – all of these and much more were enthusiastically backed by the state, through government-financed research institutes and subsidies to big companies for research and development. The public face of Nazi modernism was evident in the motorways, carving imperiously through hills and spanning deep valleys in gleaming-white, clean and modern constructions; in Nazi buildings like the Order Castles or the site of the Nuremberg Party Rally or the new Reich Chancellery in Berlin, where the latest techniques were clothed in a neo-Classical garb that was the latest fashion in public architecture across the globe. Even in art, where Hitler ensured that every product of the leading modernist movements of the day was swept off the walls of German galleries and museums, the massive, muscular figures sculpted by Arno Breker and his imitators spoke not of traditional human forms but of a new type of man, physically perfect and ready for violent action. Even the idyllic country scenes painted by the 'blood-and-soil' school of German artists spoke not of a return to a rural world mired in the hierarchical and hidebound past, but rather of a new order where the peasant would be independent, prosperous and proud, delivering the food that would sustain Germany in the conflicts to come. For millions of Germans, the Third Reich, with its real or planned mass distribution of technological wonders such as the People's Receiver or the People's Car, meant modernity and progress available to all.[207]

Modernity was linked in the minds of the leading Nazis to conflict and war. Social Darwinism, the scientifically sanctioned principle that underlay so much Nazi thinking, postulated a world in which nations and races were engaged in a perpetual struggle for survival. Thus there was a paramount need, as Hitler and the leading Nazis saw it, to make Germany and the Germans fit for combat. As the urgency of this need grew rapidly, above all from late 1937 onwards, so the radicalism and the ruthlessness of the regime grew with it.[208] Traditional restraints were cast aside. The thoroughness and ruthlessness of the Nazi attempt to remould Germany and the Germans were virtually unparalleled elsewhere. Every part of intellectual and cultural life was bent to serve the purposes of preparing the people's minds for war. Schools and universities were increasingly turned into training-camps, to the detriment of scholarship and learning. Training camps, indeed, sprang up everywhere and affected almost every area of life, and not just for the young. The Third Reich was engaged in a vast experiment in human engineering, both physical and spiritual, that recognized no limits in its penetration of the individual's body and soul, as it tried to reconfigure them into a co-ordinated mass, moving and feeling as one. From the outset, coercion and fear were as much a part of this process as propaganda and persuasion. If ever a state merited being called totalitarian, then it was the Third Reich.

In all these spheres, the Third Reich moved appreciably closer to its goals in the six and a half years that elapsed between its beginnings in the spring of 1933 and the outbreak of war in the autumn of 1939. And yet, six and a half years is not a long time; scarcely long enough to achieve the scale and depth of the transformations the Nazis sought. In one area after another, the totalitarian impulse was forced to compromise with the intractability of human nature. The scale and severity of repression drove people into the private sphere, where they felt relatively safe in talking freely about politics; in public they paid the regime its necessary dues, but for most of them, that was all. The regime's most popular domestic policies and institutions were those that catered for people's private aspirations and desires: Strength Through Joy, National Socialist Welfare, job creation, the reduction of unemployment, a general feeling of stability and order after the alarms and excursions of the Weimar years. The overwhelming majority of adults, whose minds and beliefs had been formed before the onset of the Third Reich, kept their own values more or less intact; sometimes they overlapped strongly with those of the Nazis, sometimes they did not. It was above all the younger generation whom the Nazis targeted. In the long term, as the Third Reich moved steadily through its projected thousand years, the reservations of the older generations would not matter. The future lay with the young, and the future would be Nazi.

The young too, of course, like their elders, wanted their private pleasures, and the more they felt cheated of them by their perpetual mobilization in the Hitler Youth, the schools and the universities, the more they grumbled about life under the Third Reich. Some teachers and university professors managed to distance themselves from Nazi ideology, though the alternatives they had to offer were seldom dramatically different from the ideas the Nazis purveyed. The entertainment content of the media, film, radio, magazines, theatre and the rest, grew over time as boredom with outright propaganda amongst young and old became apparent. Education and culture did manage to survive, though only in a compromised form. Yet despite all this, six and a half years of incessant, unremitting propaganda had their effect. All commentators, whatever their point of view, were united in their belief that the younger generations, those born from the mid-1920s onwards, were on the whole more thoroughly imbued with the ideas and beliefs of National Socialism than their elders were. It was for example above all young people, even

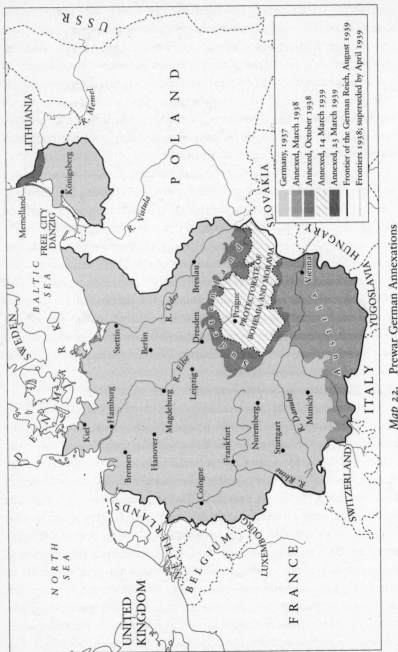

Map 22. Prewar German Annexations

children, who took part in the pogrom of November 1938 in the wake of the stormtroopers and SS who began the violence, while their elders in many places stood aside, aghast at the mayhem on the streets. But even the older generations were far from completely immune: antisemitism in particular was so insistently propagated that people began to use its language almost without thinking, and to think of the Jews as a race apart, however much they might have deplored the open violence of the November pogrom in 1938 or sympathized with individual Jews with whom they were personally acquainted.

Above all, however, it was the Nazis' nationalism that won people's support. However concerned they were at the threat of a general war, there was no mistaking the pride and satisfaction of the great majority of Germans, including many former Social Democrats and in all likelihood not a few ex-Communists as well, at Hitler's achievement in throwing off the universally hated yoke of Versailles. Resignation from the League of Nations, the plebiscite in the Saar, the remilitarization of the Rhineland, the annexation of Austria, the incorporation of the Sudetenland, the regaining of Memel, the takeover of Danzig – all of this seemed to Germans to be wiping out the shame of the 1919 Peace Settlement, restoring Germany to its rightful place in the world, claiming for Germans the right to self-determination granted to so many other nations at the end of the First World War.

All of this also appeared to Germans as the work above all of one man, Adolf Hitler, Leader of the Third Reich. The propaganda image of Hitler as the world statesman who had given back Germans pride in their country almost single-handedly did not, of course, entirely correspond to reality. Even in the area of foreign policy there were occasions, notably the annexation of Austria, where he had followed the lead of others (in this case Göring), or, as in the Munich crisis, been forced against his inclination to yield to international pressure. Others, notably Ribbentrop, had also wielded considerable influence on the decision-making process at key moments. Nevertheless, it had indeed been Hitler above all others who, sometimes encouraged by his immediate entourage, sometimes not, drove Germany down the road to war between 1933 and 1939. He laid down the broad parameters of policy and ideology for others to apply in detail. At crucial junctures he took personal command, often uncertainly and hesitantly at particular moments of crisis, but always pushing on towards his ultimate goal: war. The story of the Third Reich from 1933 to 1939 was not a story of ceaseless radicalization driven on by inherent instabilities in its system of rule, or by a constant competition for power between its satraps and minions, in which the most radical policy was always the most likely to be implemented. Irrational and unstable though it was, the Third Reich was driven in the first place from above, by Hitler and his key henchmen, above all Göring and Goebbels, later on joined by Ribbentrop. When Hitler was determined to slow down the implementation of a particular policy, for example in the case of antisemitism in the run-up to the 1936 Olympic Games, he had little difficulty in doing so. This does not mean that everything that happened in the Third Reich was ordained by Hitler; but it does mean that he was in the driving-seat, determining the general direction in which things moved.

Hitler himself of course had no doubts of his central importance to everything that happened in Nazi Germany. As time went on, his foreign policy successes began to convince him that he was indeed, as he said on more than one occasion towards the end of the 1930s, the greatest German who had ever lived: a man ordained by destiny, a gambler who won every throw, a sleepwalker guided by Providence. Well before 1939 he had come to believe in his own myth. Anyone who tried to restrain him was pushed aside. So far, his increasingly unshakeable faith in himself had proved more than justified. In September 1939, however, he made his first serious miscalculation. Despite all his efforts, despite Ribbentrop's assurances, despite Göring's intervention, despite Chamberlain's last-minute equivocations, the British had declared war. For the moment, however, Hitler was not concerned with them. In the West, the first few months of the conflict saw so little action that they quickly came to be known as the 'twilight war' or the 'drôle de guerre'. It was in the East that the real war was taking place. The war launched against Poland on 1 September 1939 was from the outset a war of racial conquest, subjugation and extermination. 'Close your hearts to pity,' Hitler told his generals on 22 August 1939. 'Act brutally! The stronger man is right! Eighty million people must obtain what is their right. Their existence must be made secure. The greatest harshness!'[209] Brutality and harshness, death and destruction were what the war would mean for millions of people in the conflict that had now begun.

Notes

Chapter 1. THE POLICE STATE

1. Karl-Heinz Minuth (ed.), *Akten der Reichskanzlei: Die Regierung Hitler, 1933–1934* (2 vols., Boppard, 1983), I. 630–31 (the above quotation combined two different sources for this speech).

2. Kurt Werner and Karl-Heinz Biernat, *Die Köpenicker Blutwoche, Juni 1933* (Berlin, 1958).

3. Quoted in Martin Broszat, *Der Staat Hitlers: Grundlegung und Entwicklung seiner inneren Verfassung* (Munich, 1969), 251–2.

4. Richard J. Evans, *The Coming of the Third Reich* (London, 2003), 344–9.

5. Richard Bessel, *Political Violence and the Rise of Nazism: The Storm Troopers in Eastern Germany 1925–1934* (London, 1984), 97; Peter Longerich, *Die braunen Bataillone: Geschichte der SA* (Munich, 1989), 184.

6. Bessel, *Political Violence*, 119–22; for the general background, see Wolfgang Sauer, *Die Mobilmachung der Gewalt* (Karl Dietrich Bracher *et al.*, *Die national-sozialistische Machtergreifung: Studien zur Errichtung des totalitären Herr-schaftssystems in Deutschland 1933/34* (3 vols., Frankfurt am Main, 1974 [1960] III. 255–324).

7. Peter H. Merkl, *Political Violence under the Swastika: 581 Early Nazis* (Princeton, 1975), 472–3, quoting Abel testimony no. 58.

8. Norbert Frei, *National Socialist Rule in Germany: The Führer State 1933–1945* (Oxford, 1993 [1987]), 13.

9. Ibid., 126.

10. Longerich, *Die braunen Bataillone*, 179–88.

11. Heinz Höhne, *Mordsache Röhm: Hitlers Durchbruch zur Alleinherrschaft, 1933–1934* (Reinbek, 1984), 127–8.

12. John W. Wheeler-Bennett, *The Nemesis of Power: The German Army in Politics 1918–1945* (London, 1953), 761.

13. Immo von Fallois, *Kalkül und Illusion: Der Machtkampf zwischen Reichswehr und SA während der Röhm-Krise 1934* (Berlin, 1994), 105–8.

14. Höhne, *Mordsache Röhm*, 59–122, for Röhm's growing ambition, and

177–206, for the growing unease of the army leadership. See also Evans, *The Coming of the Third Reich*, 316–17.

15. Fallois, *Kalkül*, 131; Robert J. O'Neill, *The German Army and the Nazi Party 1933–1939* (London, 1966), 38–42.

16. Minuth (ed.), *Akten der Reichskanzlei: Die Regierung Hitler, 1933–1934*, I. 1,156–8.

17. Bessel, *Political Violence*, 130–32, quoting the file on Max Heydebreck in the former Berlin Document Centre, now in the Bundesarchiv Berlin.

18. Heinrich Bennecke, *Die Reichswehr und der 'Röhm-Putsch'* (Munich, 1964), 43–4; Sauer, *Die Mobilmachung*, underlines the vagueness and lack of serious political content in Röhm's concept of revolution (338–9); see also Höhne, *Mordsache Röhm*, 207–26.

19. Minuth (ed.), *Akten der Reichskanzlei: Die Regierung Hitler, 1933–1934*, II. 1,393.

20. Frei, *National Socialist Rule*, 15–16; Edmund Forschbach, *Edgar J. Jung: Ein konservativer Revolutionär 30. Juni 1934* (Pfullingen, 1984).

21. Elke Fröhlich (ed.), *Die Tagebücher von Joseph Goebbels: Sämtliche Fragmente*, part I: *Aufzeichnungen 1924–1941* (Munich, 1987–96), II. 472 (21 May 1934).

22. Höhne, *Mordsache Röhm*, 227–38.

23. Klaus Behnken (ed.), *Deutschland-Berichte der Sozialdemokratischen Partei Deutschlands (Sopade) 1934–1940* (7 vols., Frankfurt am Main, 1980), I (1934), 99–117, 187.

24. Minuth (ed.), *Akten der Reichskanzlei: Die Regierung Hitler, 1933–1934* II. 1, 197–200; Max Domarus (ed.), *Hitler: Speeches and Proclamations 1932–1945: The Chronicle of a Dictatorship* (4 vols., London, 1990– [1962–3]), I. 442–6.

25. Höhne, *Mordsache Röhm*, 218–24.

26. Domarus, *Hitler*, I. 447.

27. Fröhlich (ed.), *Die Tagebücher*, I/II. 472–3 (29 June 1934).

28. Franz von Papen, *Memoirs* (London, 1952), 307–11; Hans-Adolf Jacobsen and Werner Jochmann (eds.), *Ausgewählte Dokumente zur Geschichte des National-sozialismus* (3 vols., Bielefeld, 1961).

29. Domarus, *Hitler*, I. 463–4.

30. Papen, *Memoirs*, 310–11.

31. Wheeler-Bennett, *Nemesis*, 319–20; Höhne, *Mordsache Röhm*, 239–46.

32. Longerich, *Die braunen Bataillone*, 215–16.

33. Domarus, *Hitler*, I. 466.

34. O'Neill, *The German Army*, 72–6; Longerich, *Die braunen Bataillone*, 215–17; Ian Kershaw, *Hitler*, I: *1889–1936: Hubris* (London, 1998), 510–12; Domarus, *Hitler*, I. 466–7; Bessel, *Political Violence*, 131–3; Höhne, *Mordsache Röhm*, 239–46.

35. Ralf Georg Reuth, *Goebbels: Eine Biographie* (Munich, 1990), 313.

36. Domarus, *Hitler*, I. 468–9.

37. Herbert Michaelis and Ernst Schraepler (eds.), *Ursachen und Folgen: Vom*

deutschen Zusammenbruch 1918 und 1945 bis zur staatlichen Neuordnung Deutschlands in der Gegenwart, X: *Das Dritte Reich: Die Errichtung des Führerstaates, die Abwendung von dem System der kollektiven Sicherheit* (Berlin, 1965), 168–72, document no. 2378 (reminiscences of Erich Kempka, first published in the German illustrated magazine *Quick*, 1954, no. 24).

38. Longerich, *Die braunen Bataillone*, 216–17; Domarus, *Hitler*, I. 470–71.

39. Longerich, *Die braunen Bataillone*, 217–18; Domarus, *Hitler*, I. 472–7; Kershaw, *Hitler*, I. 513–14; Behnken (ed.), *Deutschland-Berichte*, I. 194–5; Hitler's orders to the SA in *Völkischer Beobachter*, Sondernummer, 1 July 1934, front page; Röhm's murder in Karl Buchheim and Karl Otmar von Aretin (eds.), *Krone und Ketten: Erinnerungen eines bayerischen Edelmannes* (Munich, 1955), 365–6, excerpted and translated in Noakes and Pridham (eds.), *Nazism*, I. 10.

40. Detailed narrative in Höhne, *Mordsache Röhm*, 247–96.

41. Report on Schleicher in *Erste Beilage der Germania*, 180, 2 July 1934: 'Schleicher und sieben SA-Führer erschossen'; details in Höhne, *Mordsache Röhm*, 247–96, also for the following paragraphs.

42. Höhne, *Mordsache Röhm*, 247–96.

43. Bessel, *Political Violence*, 133–7.

44. Göring later declared that he had 'extended my task by striking a blow against these malcontents too'. That he did this spontaneously and on his own initiative on hearing of the events in Munich, as some historians have maintained, must be doubted in view of the care with which the rest of the action had been prepared, and the vehemence with which Hitler had denounced Papen and his associates a few days before. For the view that the action was 'improvised', see Longerich, *Die braunen Bataillone*, 218 (though his principal evidence, the statement by Göring, does not in fact demonstrate that he decided to 'extend' his task spontaneously and without consultation; the need to explain himself was obvious given the fact that the justification for the purge was provided by the supposed activities of Röhm, not those of Schleicher and Papen); for evidence of careful advance planning, see Bessel, *Political Violence*, 133–7. Further details in Kershaw, *Hitler*, I. 512–15; and Heinz Höhne, *The Order of the Death's Head: The Story of Hitler's SS* (London, 1972 [1966]), 85–121. Sauer, *Die Mobilmachung*, 334–64, notes the systematic work of preparation carried out by Hitler and the Party leadership from April onwards, stressing the importance of the propaganda offensive against Röhm and the SA, particularly within the Party. For Ballerstedt, see Evans, *The Coming of the Third Reich*, 181. For Ludendorff, see Harald Peuschel, *Die Männer um Hitler: Braune Biographien, Martin Bormann, Joseph Goebbels, Hermann Göring, Reinhard Heydrich, Heinrich Himmler und andere* (Düsseldorf, 1982).

45. 'Goebbels erstattet Bericht: Die grosse Rede des Reichspropagandaministers', *Berliner Tageblatt*, 307, 2 July 1934, 3.

46. Minuth (ed.), *Akten der Reichskanzlei: Die Regierung Hitler, 1933–1934*, I. 1,354–8; press report in *Berliner Tageblatt*, 310, 4 July 1934, front page.

47. *Erste Beilage der Germania*, 180, 2 July 1934; ibid., 181, 3 July 1934; *Berliner*

Tageblatt, 306, 1 July 1934, 2; for the 'purge' see particularly Göring's declaration, as reported in ibid., page 3, and *Völkischer Beobachter*, 182/183, 1/2 July 1934, front page.

48. Domarus, *Hitler*, I. 498.

49. Kershaw, *Hitler*, I. 517–22. Postwar attempts to bring the surviving killers to justice are documented in Otto Gritschneider, *'Der Führer hat Sie zum Tode verurteilt' . . .' : Hitlers 'Röhm-Putsch' – Morde vor Gericht* (Munich, 1993).

50. Bernd Stöver (ed.), *Berichte über die Lage in Deutschland: Die Meldungen der Gruppe Neu Beginnen aus dem Dritten Reich 1933–1936* (Bonn, 1996), 169–85, for some samples.

51. Behnken (ed.), *Deutschland-Berichte*, I. 197–203; Martin Broszat *et al.* (eds.), *Bayern in der NS-Zeit* (6 vols., Munich, 1977–83), I. 71 (Bekirksamt Eber-mannstadt, Halbmonatsbericht, 14 July 1934); Thomas Klein (ed.), *Die Lagebe-richte der Geheimen Staatspolizei über die Provinz Hessen-Nassau 1933–1936* (Cologne, 1986), 117; Wolfgang Ribbe (ed.), *Die Lageberichte der Geheimen Staatspolizei über die Provinz Brandenburg und die Reichshauptstadt Berlin 1933 bis 1936*, I: *Der Regierungsbezirk Potsdam* (Cologne, 1998), 141–2; *Berliner Illustrierte Nachtausgabe*, 151, 2 July 1934, front page, for the crowd; ibid., 153, 4 July 1934, front page, for the police warning; for the Propaganda Ministry, see Gabriele Toepser-Ziegert (ed.), *NS-Presseanweisungen der Vorkriegszeit: Edition und Dokumentation*, II: *1934* (Munich, 1985), 264 (3 July 1934).

52. Ian Kershaw, *The 'Hitler Myth': Image and Reality in the Third Reich* (Oxford, 1987), 83–95.

53. Jochen Klepper, *Unter dem Schatten deiner Flügel: Aus den Tagebüchern der Jahre 1932–1942* (Stuttgart, 1955), 194.

54. Staatsarchiv Hamburg 622–1, 11/511–13: Familie Solmitz: Luise Solmitz geb. Stephan, 1889–1973, Tagebuch: vols. 28 and 29, entries for 21 March 1933, 3 April 1933, 30 June 1934 (transcripts are held in the Forschungsstelle für Zeitgeschichte in Hamburg).

55. See the list in Höhne, *Mordsache Röhm*, 319–21.

56. Longerich, *Die braunen Bataillone*, 223; Bessel, *Political Violence*, 147–8.

57. Longerich, *Die braunen Bataillone*, 227–30.

58. Höhne, *The Order*, 113, 118, citing *Der Spiegel*, 15 May 1957, page 29, and Bennecke, *Die Reichswehr und der 'Röhm-Putsch'*, 65, 87–8; Peter Hoffmann, *Claus Schenk Graf von Stauffenberg und seine Brüder* (Stuttgart, 1992), 132; Hermann Foertsch, *Schuld und Verhängnis: Die Fritsch-Krise im Frühjahr 1938 als Wendepunkt in der Geschichte der nationalsozialistischen Zeit* (Stuttgart, 1951), 57–8.

59. Ferdinand Sauerbruch, *Das war mein Leben* (Bad Wörishofen, 1951), 519–20; for the dating of the visit, see Kershaw, *Hitler*, I. 748, n. 144. Papen, *Memoirs*, 334, denies this.

60. Tagebuch Luise Solmitz, 2 August 1934; Minuth (ed.), *Akten der Reich-skanzlei: Die Regierung Hitler, 1933–1934*, II. 1,384–90. In fact, Hitler did use

the title 'Reich President' again, when appointing Dönitz his successor in his 'Political Testament'. This illustrated the hypocrisy of his reference to the title's 'indissoluble' connection with Hindenburg; the reality was that the title of 'Leader' was indissolubly connected with Hitler and derived purely from his own person. See Hans Buchheim, 'The SS – Instrument of Domination', in Helmut Krausnick et al., Anatomy of the SS State (London, 1968 [1965]), 127–301, at 137.

61. Minuth (ed.), Akten der Reichskanzlei: Die Regierung Hitler, 1933–1934, I. 1,385 n. 6.

62. O'Neill, The German Army, 85–91.

63. Ibid., 85–91; for Beck, see Gert Buchheit, Ludwig Beck, ein preussischer General (Munich, 1964), 46.

64. O'Neill, The German Army, 87.

65. Buchheim, 'The SS', 127–32, quoting Ernst Rudolf Huber, Verfassungsrecht des Grossdeutschen Reiches (Hamburg, 1939). For the Boxheim putsch plans, see The Coming of the Third Reich, 274.

66. Ibid., 454–6.

67. Ernst Fraenkel, The Dual State: Law and Justice in National Socialism (New York, 1941).

68. Minuth (ed.), Akten der Reichskanzlei: Die Regierung Hitler, 1933–1934, I. 648 (Lammers to Hess, 11 July 1933).

69. Victor Klemperer, Tagebücher 1933–1934 (Ich will Zeugnis ablegen bis zum letzten: Tagebücher 1933–1945, I) (Berlin, 1999 [1995]), 42–3 (20 July 1933).

70. Reprinted and translated in Noakes and Pridham (eds.), Nazism, II. 39–40; see also the following commentary and documents, ibid., 41–64.

71. Ibid., 39–51; Broszat, Der Staat Hitlers, 244–73, 301–25; for Bormann and Hess, see Evans, The Coming of the Third Reich, 219–20, 176–7.

72. Noakes and Pridham (eds.), Nazism, II. 52–64.

73. Ibid., 57.

74. Alfred Kube, 'Hermann Göring: Second Man in the Third Reich', in Ronald Smelser and Rainer Zitelmann (eds.), The Nazi Elite (Basingstoke, 1993 [1989]), 62–73, at 65–6; also more generally Alfred Kube, Pour le mérite und Hakenkreuz: Hermann Göring im Dritten Reich (Munich, 1987 [1986]), and Stefan Martens, Hermann Göring: 'Erster Paladin des Führers' und 'Zweiter Mann im Reich' (Paderborn, 1985).

75. Buchheim, 'The SS', 142–3; Höhne, The Order, 70–76; Evans, The Coming of the Third Reich, 226–30.

76. Höhne, The Order, 124–8.

77. Ibid. 121–32.

78. Ibid., 131–6; Josef Ackermann, Heinrich Himmler als Ideologe (Göttingen, 1970), 253–4.

79. Hans Peter Bleuel, Strength Through Joy: Sex and Society in Nazi Germany (London, 1973 [1972]), 199.

80. Gunnar C. Böhnert, 'An Analysis of the Age and Education of the SS

Führerkorps 1925–1939', *Historical Social Research*, 12 (1979), 4–17; Friedrich Zipfel, 'Gestapo and SD: A Sociographic Profile of the Organisers of the Terror', in Stein U. Larsen *et al.* (eds.), *Who Were the Fascists? Social Roots of European Fascism* (Bergen, 1980), 301–11.

81. Hanno Sowade, 'Otto Ohlendorf: Non-conformist, SS Leader and Economic Functionary', in Smelser and Zitelmann (eds.), *The Nazi Elite*, 155–64, here 155–8. For the wider background, see Michael Wildt, *Generation des Unbedingten: Das Führungskorps des Reichssicherheitshauptamtes* (Hamburg, 2002), 41–208.

82. Joachim C. Fest, *The Face of the Third Reich* (London, 1979 [1963]), 152–70, and Günther Deschner, 'Reinhard Heydrich: Security Technocrat', in Smelser and Zitelmann (eds.), *The Nazi Elite*, 85–96, provide contrasting character sketches.

83. Höhne, *The Order*, 147–57.

84. Shlomo Aronson, *Reinhard Heydrich und die Frühgeschichte von Gestapo und SD* (Stuttgart, 1971).

85. For his own account of his resignation, see Rudolf Diels, *Lucifer ante Portas: Es spricht der erste Chef der Gestapo* (Stuttgart, 1950). For the complicated history of all these developments, see Christoph Graf, 'Kontinuitäten und Brüche. Von der Politischen Polizei der Weimarer Republik zur Geheimen Staatspolizei', in Gerhard Paul and Klaus-Michael Mallmann (eds.), *Die Gestapo – Mythos und Realität* (Darmstadt, 1995), 73–83, and Johannes Tuchel, 'Gestapa und Reichssicherheitshauptamt. Die Berliner Zentralinstitutionen der Gestapo', in ibid., 84–100.

86. George C. Browder, *Foundations of the Nazi Police State: The Formation of Sipo and SD* (Lexington, Ky., 1990); idem, *Hitler's Enforcers: The Gestapo and the SS Security Service in the Nazi Revolution* (New York and Oxford, 1996); and Peter Nitschke, 'Polizei und Gestapo. Vorauseilender Gehorsam oder polykratischer Konflikt?', in Paul and Mallmann (eds.), *Die Gestapo*, 306–22.

87. The best recent account of these events is Michael Schneider, *Unterm Hakenkreuz: Arbeiter und Arbeiterbewegung 1933 bis 1939* (Bonn, 1999), 34–120; see also Evans, *The Coming of the Third Reich*, 316–49, 355–61.

88. For a brief general introduction, see Detlev J. K. Peukert, 'Working-Class Resistance: Problems and Options', in David Clay Large (ed.), *Contending with Hitler: Varieties of German Resistance in the Third Reich* (Washington, D.C., 1991), 35–48.

89. Werner Blumenberg, *Kämpfer für die Freiheit* (Berlin, 1959).

90. Details in Gerhard Hetzer, 'Die Industriestadt Augsburg. Eine Sozialgeschichte der Arbeiteropposition', in Martin Broszat *et al.* (eds.), *Bayern*, III. 1–234, esp. 182–200; Helmut Beer, *Widerstand gegen den Nationalsozialismus in Nürnberg 1933–1945* (Nuremberg, 1976); Heike Breitschneider, *Der Widerstand gegen den Nationalsozialismus in München 1933 bis 1945* (Munich, 1968); Kurt Klotzbach, *Gegen den Nationalsozialismus: Widerstand und Verfolgung in Dortmund 1930–1945: Eine historisch-politische Studie* (Hanover, 1969); Hans-Josef

Steinberg, *Widerstand und Verfolgung in Essen 1933–1945* (Hanover, 1969); Karl Ditt, *Sozialdemokraten im Widerstand: Hamburg in der Anfangsphase des Dritten Reiches* (Hamburg, 1984), and numerous other local or regional studies; more generally, Schneider, *Unterm Hakenkreuz*, 928–62.

91. Otto Buchwitz, *50 Jahre Funktionär der deutschen Arbeiterbewegung* (Stuttgart, 1949), 156–63.

92. Erich Matthias, *Mit dem Gesicht nach Deutschland* (Düsseldorf, 1968), 215–25; English translation of the salient parts in Susanne Miller and Heinrich Potthoff, *A History of German Social Democracy: From 1848 to the Present* (Leamington Spa, 1986), 265–7.

93. Gerd-Rainer Horn, 'Radicalism and Moderation within German Social Democracy in Underground and Exile, 1933–1936', *German History*, 15 (1997), 200–220; Detlef Lehnert, *Sozialdemokratie zwischen Protestbewegung und Regierungspartei 1848 bis 1983* (Frankfurt am Main, 1983), 155–64.

94. Hetzer, 'Die Industriestadt Augsburg', gives a vivid impression of these disagreements. See also Lewis J. Edinger, *German Exile Politics: The Social Democratic Executive Committee in the Nazi Era* (Berkeley, Calif., 1956).

95. William Sheridan Allen, 'Social Democratic Resistance against Hitler and the European Tradition of Underground Movements', in Francis R. Nicosia and Lawrence D. Stokes (eds.), *Germans Against Nazism: Nonconformity, Opposition and Resistance in the Third Reich: Essays in Honour of Peter Hoffmann* (Oxford, 1990), 191–204.

96. Hans Gerd Schumann, *Nationalsozialismus und Gewerkschaftsbewegung: Die Vernichtung der deutschen Gewerkschaften und der Aufbau der Deutschen Arbeitsfront* (Hanover, 1958), 128–30.

97. Franz Osterroth and Dieter Schuster, *Chronik der deutschen Sozialdemokratie* (Hanover, 1963), 389; Ditt, *Sozialdemokraten*, 87–8; Allen, 'Social Democratic Resistance', 191–2; Schneider, *Unterm Hakenkreuz*, 1,065–9.

98. Francis L. Carsten, *The German Workers and the Nazis* (London, 1995); Schneider, *Unterm Hakenkreuz*, 866, 887–9, 1,004–8; Richard Löwenthal, *Die Widerstandsgruppe 'Neu Beginnen'* (Berlin, 1982); Jan Foitzik, *Zwischen den Fronten: Zur Politik, Organisation und Funktion linker politischer Kleinorganisationen im Widerstand 1933 bis 1939/40* (Bonn, 1986); Stöver (ed.), *Berichte*, xix–xxxix.

99. Hermann Weber, *Die Wandlung des deutschen Kommunismus: Die Stalinisierung der KPD in der Weimarer Republik* (abridged edn, Frankfurt am Main, 1971 [1969]), 245–6.

100. Eric D. Weitz, *Creating German Communism, 1890–1990: From Popular Protests to Socialist State* (Princeton, 1997), 286–9.

101. Horst Duhnke, *Die KPD von 1933 bis 1945* (Cologne, 1972); Schneider, *Unterm Hakenkreuz*, 902–26; more generally, Margot Pikarski and Günter Uebel (eds.), *Gestapo-Berichte: Über den antifaschistischen Widerstandskampf der KPD 1933 bis 1945* (3 vols., Berlin, 1989–90). For the leaflets, see Peter Dohms (ed.),

Flugschriften in Gestapo-Akten: Nachweis und Analyse der Flugschriften in den Gestapo-Akten des Hauptstaatsarchivs Düsseldorf (Siegburg, 1977) and Margot Pikarski and Günter Uebel (eds.), *Die KPD lebt! Flugblätter aus dem antifaschistischen Widerstandskampf der KPD, 1933–1945* (Berlin, 1980).

102. Detlev J. K. Peukert, *Die KPD im Widerstand: Verfolgung und Untergrundarbeit an Rhein und Ruhr, 1933 bis 1945* (Wuppertal, 1980), 106–9.

103. Allan Merson, *Communist Resistance in Nazi Germany* (London, 1985), 127.

104. See the pessimistic reports in Stöver (ed.), *Berichte*, 34–5, 87–90.

105. Edward H. Carr, *Twilight of the Comintern, 1930–1935* (London, 1982); Beatrix Herlemann, *Die Emigration als Kampfposten: Die Anleitung des kommunistischen Widerstandes in Deutschland aus Frankreich, Belgien und den Niederlanden* (Königstein im Taunus, 1982); Hermann Weber, 'Die KPD in der Illegalität', in Richard Löwenthal and Patrick von zur Mühlen (eds.), *Widerstand und Verweigerung in Deutschland 1933 bis 1945* (Berlin, 1982), 83–101.

106. Weitz, *Creating German Communism*, 292–300.

107. Merson, *Communist Resistance*, 124–52; Peukert, *Die KPD im Widerstand*; Eric A. Johnson, *Nazi Terror: The Gestapo, Jews, and Ordinary Germans* (New York, 1999), 161–94.

108. Weitz, *Creating German Communism*, 289–91.

109. See for example Hetzer, 'Die Industriestadt Augsburg', 150–78.

110. Schneider, *Unterm Hakenkreuz*, 1,061–4.

111. Anne Applebaum, *Gulag: A History of the Soviet Camps* (London, 2003), and Robert Conquest's classic *The Great Terror: A Reassessment* (London, 1992 [1968]); Simon Sebag Montefiore, *Stalin: The Court of the Red Tsar* (London, 2003) (121–38 for the murder of Kirov).

112. Weber, *Die Wandlung*, 357–8; idem, 'Weisse Flecken' in der Geschichte: Die KPD-Opfer der Stalinistischen Säuberungen und ihre Rehabilitierung* (Frankfurt am Main, 1990); and Institut für die Geschichte der Arbeiterbewegung (ed.), *In den Fängen des NKWD: Deutsche Opfer des stalinistischen Terrors in der UdSSR* (Berlin, 1991).

113. Richard J. Evans, *Rituals of Retribution: Capital Punishment in Germany 1600–1987* (Oxford, 1996), 620–23. The principle in question is known to jurists as *nulla poena sine lege*.

114. Günther Wieland, *Das war der Volksgerichtshof: Ermittlungen, Fakten, Dokumente* (Pfaffenweiler, 1989), 15–18; Evans, *Rituals*, 622–4, 576–7.

115. Hans Joachim Bernhard *et al.* (eds.), *Der Reichstagsbrandprozess und Georgi Dimitroff: Dokumente* (2 vols., Berlin, 1981–9); Georgi Dimitroff, *Reichstagsbrandprozess: Dokumente, Briefe und Aufzeichnungen* (Berlin, 1946).

116. *Völkischer Beobachter*, 24 December 1934, quoted in Wieland, *Das war der Volksgerichtshof*, 15.

117. Gerhard Fieberg (ed.), *Im Namen des deutschen Volkes: Justiz und Nationalsozialismus: Katalog zur Ausstellung des Bundesministers der Justiz* (Cologne, 1989), 267.

118. Wieland, *Das war der Volksgerichtshof*, 22–9; Hannes Heer, *Ernst Thälmann in Selbszeugnissen und Bilddokumenten* (Reinbek, 1975), 119–27.

119. Wieland, *Das war der Volksgerichtshof*, 45; see also especially Klaus Marxen, *Das Volk und sein Gerichtshof: Eine Studie zum nationalsozialistischen Volksgerichtshof* (Frankfurt am Main, 1994), and Walter Wagner, *Der Volksgerichtshof im nationalsozialistischen Staat* (Stuttgart, 1974).

120. Marxen, *Das Volk*, 57–61, 79–87; Holger Schlüter, *Die Urteilspraxis des nationalsozialistischen Volksgerichtshofs* (Berlin, 1995).

121. Ingo Müller, 'Nationalsozialistische Sondergerichte. Ihre Stellung im System des deutschen Strafverfahrens', in Martin Bennhold (ed.), *Spuren des Unrechts: Recht und Nationalsozialismus. Beiträge zur historischen Kontinuität* (Cologne, 1989), 17–34; Hans Wüllenweber, *Sondergerichte im Dritten Reich: Vergessene Verbrechen der Justiz* (Frankfurt am Main, 1990). Among numerous local studies, see especially Robert Bohn and Uwe Danker (eds.), *'Standgericht der inneren Front': Das Sondergericht Altona/Kiel 1932–1945* (Hamburg, 1998); Karl-Dieter Bornscheuer (ed.), *Justiz im Dritten Reich: NS-Sondergerichtsverfahren in Rheinland-Pfalz: Eine Dokumentation* (3 vols., Frankfurt am Main, 1994, an exemplary documentary collection); Gisela Diewald-Kerkmann *et al.*, *Vor braunen Richtern: Die Verfolgung von Widerstandshandlungen, Resistenz und sogenannter Heimtücke durch die Justiz in Bielefeld 1933–1945* (Bielefeld, 1992); Christiane Oehler, *Die Rechtsprechung des Sondergerichts Mannheim 1933–1945* (Berlin, 1997); Herbert Schmidt, *'Beabsichtige ich die Todesstrafe zu beantragen': Die nationalsozialistische Sondergerichtsbarkeit im Oberlandesgerichtsbezirk Düsseldorf 1933 bis 1945* (Essen, 1998); Gerd Weckbecker, *Zwischen Freispruch und Todesstrafe: Die Rechtsprechung der nationalsozialistischen Sondergerichte Frankfurt a.M. und Bromberg* (Baden-Baden, 1998).

122. Evans, *Rituals*, 643–4, 659, 662; Bernhard Düsing, *Die Geschichte der Abschaffung der Todesstrafe in der Bundesrepublik Deutschland unter besonderer Berücksichtigung ihres parlamentarischen Zustandekommens* (Schwenningen/Neckar, 1952), 210–11.

123. Quoted in Anthony McElligott, 'Das Altonaer Sondergericht und der Prozess vom Blutsonntag' (Vortrag im Rahmen der Veranstaltung des Stadtteilarchivs Ottensen, der Bezirksversammlung und der Kulturbehörde, Hamburg-Altona, 3 June 1992), 20–21. These sentences, on the twenty-year-old Bruno Tesch and three others, were finally retrospectively annulled in November 1992.

124. Evans, *Rituals*, 644–5.

125. Jan Valtin (pseudonym of Richard Krebs), *Out of the Night* (London, 1941, reprinted with postscript by Lyn Walsh *et al.*, London, 1988), 318–20.

126. Lothar Gruchmann, *Justiz im Dritten Reich, 1933–1940: Anpassung und Unterwerfung in der Ära Gürtner* (Munich, 1988), 897–8; Martin Hirsch *et al.* (eds.), *Recht, Verwaltung und Justiz im Nationalsozialismus: Ausgewählte Schriften, Gesetze und Gerichtsentscheidungen von 1933 bis 1945* (Cologne, 1984), 421–556; Eduard Kohlrausch (ed.), *Deutsche Strafgesetze vom 19.*

Dezember 1932 bis 12. Juni 1934 (Berlin, 1934); Evans, *Rituals*, 624–50; and especially Bernward Dörner, *'Heimtücke': Das Gesetz als Waffe: Kontrolle, Abschreckung und Verfolgung in Deutschland, 1933–1945* (Paderborn, 1998). For the judges, see Ralph Angermund, *Deutsche Richterschaft 1919–1945: Krisenerfahrung, Illusion, politische Rechtssprechung* (Frankurt am Main, 1990).

127. Edmund Mezger, *Kriminalpolitik auf kriminologischer Grundlage* (Stuttgart, 1934), v.

128. Gruchmann, *Justiz*, 822–924; Jürgen Regge and Werner Schubert (eds.), *Quellen zur Reform des Straf- und Strafprozessrechts, 2. Abteilung: NS-Zeit (1933–1939) – Strafgesetzbuch*, I: *Entwürfe eines Strafgesetzbuchs*; II: *Protokolle der Strafrechtskommission des Reichsjustizministeriums* (2 vols., Berlin, 1988–9).

129. 'Rede des Reichsrechtsführers Reichsminister Dr. Frank auf dem zweiten Empfangsabend des Wirtschaftsrates der Deutschen Akademie in Berlin über die Grundlagen der nationalsozialistischen Rechtsauffassung', 21 January 1936: document no. 59, in Paul Meier-Benneckenstein (ed.), *Dokument der deutschen Politik* (6 vols., Berlin, 1935–9), IV: *Deutschlands Aufstieg zur Grossmacht 1936*, 337–46.

130. Klaus Drobisch, 'Alltag im Zuchthaus Luckau 1933 bis 1939', in Dietrich Eichholtz (ed.), *Verfolgung, Alltag, Widerstand: Brandenburg in der NS-Zeit: Studien und Dokumente* (Berlin, 1993), 247–72, at 269–70.

131. Cited in Nikolaus Wachsmann, *Hitler's Prisons: Legal Terror in Nazi Germany* (New Haven, 2004), 179.

132. Ibid., 165–83.

133. Ibid., the minutes of the 1937 meeting are reprinted in Fieberg (ed.), *Justiz*, 160–61.

134. Düsing, *Die Geschichte*, 10–11; Evans, *Rituals*, 915–16; see also Wilfried Knauer (ed.), *Nationalsozialistische Justiz und Todesstrafe: Eine Dokumentation zur Gedenkstätte in der Justizvollzugsanstalt Wolfenbüttel* (Braunschweig, 1991).

135. For an exhaustive survey of the varieties of hereditarian and partial or qualified hereditarian theories of criminality in this period, see Richard Wetzell, *Inventing the Criminal: A History of German Criminology 1880–1945* (Chapel Hill, N.C., 2000), 179–232.

136. Christian Müller, *Das Gewohnheitsverbrechergesetz vom 24. November 1933: Kriminalpolitik als Rassenpolitik* (Baden-Baden, 1997); idem, ' "Modernes" Strafrecht im Nationalsozialismus: Das Gewohnheitsverbrechergesetz vom 24. 11. 1933', in Franz-Josef Düwell and Thomas Bormbaum (eds.), *Themen juristischer Zeitgeschichte*, III (Baden-Baden, 1999), 46–70.

137. Nikolaus Wachsmann, 'From Indefinite Confinement to Extermination: "Habitual Criminals" in the Third Reich', in Robert Gellately and Nathan Stoltzfus (eds.), *Social Outsiders in Nazi Germany* (Princeton, 2001), 165–91, esp. 171–2; Wachsmann, *Hitler's Prisons*, 128–35.

138. Ibid., 67.

139. Ibid., 90–114; Erich Kosthorst and Bernd Walter, *Konzentrations- und Straf-*

gefangenenlager im Dritten Reich: Beispiel Emsland (3 vols., Düsseldorf, 1983); Elke Suhr, *Die Emslandlager: Die politische und wirtschaftliche Bedeutung der emsländischen Konzentrations- und Strafgefangenenlager 1933–1945* (Bremen, 1985).

140. Friedrich Schlotterbeck, *The Darker the Night, The Brighter the Stars! A German Worker Remembers (1933–1945)* (London, 1947), 61–2.

141. Ibid.

142. Wachsmann, *Hitler's Prisons*, 78–88.

143. Wachsmann, 'From Indefinite Confinement', 174.

144. Wachsmann, *Hitler's Prisons*, 69–71 and figure 1.

145. Ibid., 70.

146. Gruchmann, *Justiz*, 897–8.

147. Michael Haerdter (ed.), *Wohnsitz: Nirgendwo: Vom Leben und Überleben auf der Strasse* (Berlin, 1982); Wolfgang Ayass, *'Asoziale' im Nationalsozialismus* (Stuttgart, 1995); Klaus Scherer, *'Asoziale' im Dritten Reich: Die vergessenen Verfolgten* (Münster, 1990); Gellately and Stoltzfus (eds.), *Social Outsiders*.

148. Quoted in Patrick Wagner, ' "Vernichtung der Berufsverbrecher". Die vorbeugende Verbrechensbekämpfung der Kriminalpolizei bis 1937', in Herbert *et al.* (eds.), *Die nationalsozialistischen Konzentrationslager: Entwicklung und Struktur* (2 vols., Göttingen, 1998), I. 87–110, at 101.

149. Ibid. (useful survey of the literature in vol. I, 17–40); Johannes Tuchel, *Konzentrationslager: Organisationsgeschichte und Funktion der 'Inspektion der Konzentrationslager' 1934–1938* (Boppard, 1991) and Karin Orth, *Das System der nationalsozialistischen Konzentrationslager: Eine politische Organisationsgeschichte* (Hamburg, 1999).

150. Ibid., 23–6; Klaus Drobisch and Günther Wieland, *System der NS-Konzentrationslager 1933–1939* (Berlin, 1993), 71–5; Klaus Drobisch, 'Frühe Konzentrationslager', in Karl Giebeler *et al.* (eds.), *Die frühen Konzentrationslager in Deutschland: Austausch zum Forschungsstand und zur pädagogischen Praxis in Gedenkstätten* (Bad Boll, 1996), 41–60; Falk Pingel, *Häftlinge unter SS-Herrschaft: Widerstand, Selbstbehauptung und Vernichtung im Konzentrationslager* (Hamburg, 1978), 30–49.

151. Evans, *The Coming of the Third Reich*, 345.

152. Martin Broszat, 'The Concentration Camps 1933–1945', in Krausnick *et al.*, *Anatomy of the SS State*, 397–496, at 408–31.

153. Rudolf Höss, *Commandant of Auschwitz: The Autobiography of Rudolf Hoess* (London, 1959 [1951]), 263; see also Klaus Drobisch, 'Theodor Eicke. Verkörperung des KZ-Systems', in Helmut Bock *et al.* (eds.), *Sturz ins Dritte Reich: Historische Miniaturen und Porträts 1933/35* (Leipzig, 1983), 283–9; Charles W. Sydnor, *Soldiers of Destruction: The SS Death's Head Division, 1933–1945* (Princeton, N.J., 1990 [1977]), 3–36; and, more generally, Hans-Günter Richardi, *Schule der Gewalt: Das Konzentrationslager Dachau, 1933–1934* (Munich, 1983), esp. 119–26, for Eicke.

154. See Barbara Distel and Ruth Jakusch, *Konzentrationslager Dachau, 1933–1945* (Munich, 1978), 68–9; for the replacement of the early camps by an organized system, see also Johannes Tuchel, 'Planung und Realität des Systems der Konzentrationslager 1934–1938', in Herbert *et al.* (eds.), *Die nationalsozialistischen Konzentrationslager*, 43–59; and Giebeler *et al.* (eds.), *Die frühen Konzentrationslager*.

155. Höss, *Commandant*, 83–4.

156. Ibid., 74–5.

157. Broszat, 'Concentration Camps', 429–45.

158. Ibid., 436; Pingel, *Häftlinge*, 50; more generally, Tuchel, *Konzentrationslager*, 121–58.

159. Wachsmann, *Hitler's Prisons*, 113; Noakes and Pridham (eds.), *Nazism*, II. 326.

160. Wachsmann, *Hitler's Prisons*, 128.

161. Günther Kimmel, 'Das Konzentrationslager Dachau: Eine Studie zu den nationalsozialistischen Gewaltverbrechen', in Broszat *et al.* (eds.), *Bayern*, II. 349–413, *esp.* 351–72; Orth, *Das System*, 33–5; Ulrich Herbert, 'Von der Gegenerbekämpfung zur "rassischen Generalprävention". "Schutzhaft" und Konzentrationslager in der Konzeption der Gestapo-Führung 1933–1939', in idem *et al.* (eds.), *Die nationalsozialistischen Konzentrationslager*, 60–81.

162. Tuchel, 'Planung und Realität'; Herbert, 'Von der Gegnerbekämpfung zur "rassischen Generalprävention"', 60–86.

163. Günter Morsch, 'Oranienburg-Sachsenhausen, Sachsenhausen-Oranienburg', in Herbert *et al.* (eds.), *Die nationalsozialistischen Konzentrationslager*, 111–34, at 127–9.

164. Pingel, *Häftlinge*, 80–87; Orth, *Das System*, 53.

165. Evans, *The Coming of the Third Reich*, 378–80.

166. Ayass, 'Asoziale', 22–4; Pingel, *Häftlinge*, 27.

167. Patrick Wagner, *Volksgemeinschaft ohne Verbrecher: Konzeptionen und Praxis der Kriminalpolizei in der Zeit der Weimarer Republik und des Nationalsozialismus* (Hamburg, 1996), 271.

168. Ayass, 'Asoziale', 140–65.

169. Quoted in ibid., 153.

170. Ibid.

171. Paul B. Jaskot, *The Architecture of Oppression: The SS, Forced Labor and the Nazi Monumental Building Economy* (London, 2000), 21–4.

172. Ayass, 'Asoziale', 169–72; Orth, *Das System*, 46–54.

173. Broszat, 'Concentration Camps', 446–59; Toni Siegert, 'Das Konzentrationslager Flossenbürg, gegründet für sogenannte Asoziale und Kriminelle', in Broszat *et al.* (eds.), *Bayern*, II. 429–93; Michael Burleigh and Wolfgang Wippermann, *The Racial State: Germany 1933–1945*, 167–73; Jeremy Noakes, 'Social Outcasts in the Third Reich', in Richard Bessel (ed.), *Life in the Third Reich* (Oxford, 1987), 183–96.

174. Orth, *Das System*, 48–9; Pingel, *Häftlinge*, 35–9; Hermann Kaienburg, 'Funktionswandel des KZ-Kosmos? Das Konzentrationslager Neuengamme 1938–1945', in Herbert *et al.* (eds.), *Konzentrationslager*, 259–84; idem, *'Vernichtung durch Arbeit': Der Fall Neuengamme: Die Wirtschaftsbestrebungen des SS und ihre Auswirkungen auf die Existenzbedingungen der KZ-Gefangenen* (Bonn, 1990).

175. Orth, *Das System*, 56–9. For these laws and regulations that landed these various categories in the camps, see also below, Chapter 6; for the categories, see also Paul Martin Neurath, *Die Gesellschaft des Terrors: Innenansichten der Konzentrationslager Dachau und Buchenwald* (Frankfurt am Main, 2004), 86–112. Neurath's book was originally presented as a doctoral dissertation to Columbia University, New York, in 1951.

176. Walter Poller, *Arztschreiber in Buchenwald: Bericht des Häftlings 996 aus Block 39* (Hamburg, 1946), 9–22; quote on 21–2.

177. Orth, *Das System*, 59–61; Poller, *Arztschreiber*, 23–74; more generally, Wolfgang Sofsky, *Die Ordnung des Terrors: Das Konzentrationslager* (Frankfurt am Main, 1993), 27–40.

178. Poller, *Arztschreiber*, 75–105; for camp music, see Guido Fackler, *'Des Lagers Stimme': Musik im KZ: Alltag und Häftlingskultur in den Konzentrationslagern 1933 bis 1936* (Bremen, 2000).

179. Leo Stein, *I Was in Hell with Niemöller* (London, 1942), 113–47.

180. Neurath, *Die Gesellschaft*, 44–86.

181. Ibid., 113–32; Hans Buchheim, 'Command and Compliance', in Krausnick *et al., Anatomy*, 303–96.

182. Poller, *Arztschreiber*, 227.

183. Lothar Gruchmann, 'Die bayerische Justiz im politischen Machtkampf 1933/34: Ihr Scheitern bei der Strafverfolgung von Mordfällen in Dachau', in Broszat *et al.* (eds.), *Bayern*, II. 415–28.

184. See the various press reports reproduced in Kimmel, 'Das Konzentrationslager', 356–8.

185. Sybil Milton, 'Die Konzentrationslager der dreissiger Jahre im Bild der in- und ausländischen Presse', in Herbert *et al.* (eds.), *Die nationalsozialistischen Konzentrationslager*, 135–47; Falk Pingel, 'Konzeption und Praxis der national-sozialistischen Konzentrationslager 1933 bis 1938. Kommentierende Bemerkungen', in ibid., 148–66, esp. 157–60.

186. Quoted from a variety of contemporary sources in Klaus-Michael Mallmann and Gerhard Paul, 'Omniscient, Omnipotent, Omnipresent? Gestapo, Society and Resistance', in David F. Crew (ed.), *Nazism and German Society 1933–1945* (London, 1994), 166–96, esp. 167–9; and Robert Gellately, *The Gestapo and German Society: Enforcing Racial Policy 1933–1945* (Oxford, 1990), esp. 4–8.

187. Mallmann and Paul, 'Omniscient, Omnipotent, Omnipresent?', 174–7.

188. Höhne, *The Order*, 162–3; Andreas Seeger, 'Vom bayerischen "System-beamten" zum Chef der Gestapo. Zur Person und Tätigkeit Heinrich Müllers (1900–1945)', in Paul and Mallmann (eds.), *Die Gestapo*, 255–67.

189. Höhne, *The Order*, 167–9; Volker Eichler, 'De Frankfurter Gestapo-Kartei. Entstehung, Struktur, Funktion, Überlieferungsgeschichte und Quellenwert', in Paul and Mallmann (eds.), *Die Gestapo*, 178–99; Rainer Eckert, 'Gestapo-Berichte. Abbildungen der Realität oder reine Spekulation?', in ibid., 200–218.

190. Melita Maschmann, *Account Rendered: A Dossier on My Former Self* (London, 1964), 43–5.

191. Valtin, *Out of the Night*, 448–73. For the historical realities behind Krebs's imaginative account of his own life, see Ernst von Waldenfels, *Der Spion, der aus Deutschland kam: Das geheime Leben des Seemanns Richard Krebs* (Berlin, 2003), for these events 179–209.

192. Valtin, *Out of the Night*, 487.

193. Waldenfels, *Der Spion*, 210–58.

194. Valtin, *Out of the Night*, 512–51; Dieter Nelles, 'Jan Valtins "Tagebuch der Hölle" – Legende und Wirklichkeit eines Schlüsselromans der Totalitärismustheorie', *1999: Zeitschrift für Sozialgeschichte des 20. und 21. Jahrhunderts*, 9 (1994), 11–45, provides a hostile account which corrects Krebs's narrative in many details, but is itself corrected on the larger picture in Waldenfels's more balanced approach.

195. For a full account, see Waldenfels, *Der Spion*, 209–58, esp. 214, 220, 237; see also the detailed but not entirely convincing critical review of this book by Dieter Nelles, 'Die Rehabilitation eines Gestapo-Agenten: Richard Krebs/Jan Valtin', *Sozial-Geschichte*, 18 (2003), 148–58.

196. Mallmann and Paul, 'Omniscient, Omnipotent, Omnipresent?'.

197. Ibid.; Gellately, *The Gestapo*, 144–58; Robert Gellately, 'The Gestapo and German Society: Political Denunciation in the Gestapo Case Files', *Journal of Modern History*, 6 (1988), 654–94; Martin Broszat, 'Politische Denunziationen in der NS-Zeit: Aus Forschungserfahrungen im Staatsarchiv München', *Archivalische Zeitschrift*, 73 (1977), 221–38; percentage analysis in Reinhard Mann, *Protest und Kontrolle im Dritten Reich: Nationalsozialistische Herrschaft in Alltag einer rheinischen Grossstadt* (Frankfurt am Main, 1987), 295; see also Gisela Diewald-Kerkmann, *Politische Denunziation im NS-Regime oder die kleine Macht der 'Volksgenossen'* (Bonn, 1995), and eadem, 'Denunziantentum und Gestapo. Die freiwilligen "Helfer" aus der Bevölkerung', in Paul and Mallmann (eds.), *Die Gestapo*, 288–305 (for the Gestapo's distaste for those who sent in denunciations for personal motives).

198. Weckbecker, *Zwischen Freispruch und Todesstrafe*, 77, 388, 779–800; Manfred Zeidler, *Das Sondergericht Freiberg: Zu Justiz und Repression in Sachsen, 1933–1940* (Dresden, 1998); Oehler, *Die Rechtsprechung*; Hans-Ulrich Ludewig and Dietrich Kuessner, *'Es sei also jeder gewarnt': Das Sondergericht Braunschweig 1933–1945* (Braunschweig, 2000); Klaus Bästlein, 'Sondergerichte in Norddeutschland als Verfolgungsinstanz', in Frank Bajohr (ed.), *Norddeutschland im Nationalsozialismus* (Hamburg, 1993), 218–38.

199. Peter Hüttenberger, 'Heimtückefälle vor dem Sondergericht München 1933–1939', in Broszat *et al.* (eds.), *Bayern*, IV. 435–526.

200. Ibid., esp. 452–57, 473–92.

201. Helmut Prantl (ed.), *Die kirchliche Lage in Bayern nach den Regierungspräsidentenberichten 1933–1943*, V: *Regierungsbezirk Pfalz 1933–1940* (Mainz, 1978), 157–8 (Monatsbericht der Regierung Speyer, 6 March 1937); Klaus-Michael Mallmann and Gerhard Paul, *Herrschaft und Alltag: Ein Industrierevier im Dritten Reich* (Bonn, 1991), 327–53.

202. Hüttenberger, 'Heimtückefälle', 512; Mallmann and Paul, *Herrschaft*, 175–245.

203. Bernward Dörner, 'NS-Herrschaft und Denunziation. Anmerkungen zu Defiziten in der Denunziationsforschung', *Historical Social Research*, 26 (2001), 55–69, at 58–61.

204. Mann, *Protest und Kontrolle*, 292; the source of the Gestapo's information could not be found in 13 per cent of the cases.

205. Hetzer, 'Die Industriestadt Augsburg', 146–50.

206. Ibid., 146–50. For pubs as centres of communication and socialization, see Richard J. Evans (ed.), *Kneipengespräche im Kaiserreich: Die Stimmungsberichte der Hamburger Politischen Polizei 1892–1914* (Reinbek, 1989).

207. Victor Klemperer, *I Shall Bear Witness: The Diaries of Victor Klemperer 1933–1941* (London, 1998 [1995]), 29.

208. Friedrich Reck-Malleczewen, *Diary of a Man in Despair* (London, 2000 [1947]), 52–3.

209. Hans-Jochen Gamm, *Der Flüsterwitz im Dritten Reich: Mündliche Dokumente zur Lage der Deutschen während des Nationalsozialismus* (Munich, 1990 [1963]), 41, 52.

210. Ibid., 37.

211. Ibid., 42.

212. Cited in Meike Wöhlert, *Der politische Witz in der NS-Zeit am Beispiel ausgesuchter SD-Berichte und Gestapo-Akten* (Frankfurt am Main, 1997), 150–51. Wöhlert's claim that most jokes were told in public is open to doubt, however, since those told in private seldom came to the attention of the Gestapo and the SS Security Service, whose reports form the basis for her work.

213. Klepper, *Unter dem Schatten*, 194.

214. Wöhlert, *Der politische Witz*, 156–63.

215. Ibid., 44.

216. Klemperer, *Tagebücher 1933–34*, 9 (10 March 1933).

217. Ibid., 19 (2 April 1933).

218. Charlotte Beradt, *Das Dritte Reich des Traums* (Frankfurt am Main, 1981 [1966]); 7 for this particular dream.

219. Ibid., 19–22, 40, 74.

220. Ibid., 5. Ley's statement can be found in Robert Ley, *Soldaten der Arbeit* (Munich, 1938), 71.

221. Detlef Schmiechen-Ackermann, 'Der "Blockwart". Die unteren Parteifunktionäre im nationalsozialistischen Terror- und Überwachungsapparat', *Viertel-*

jahrshefte für Zeitgeschichte (VfZ) 48 (2000), 575–602; also Dieter Rebentisch, 'Die "politische Beurteilung" als Herrschaftsinstrument der NSDAP', in Detlev Peukert and Jürgen Reulecke (eds.), *Die Reihen fast geschlossen: Beiträge zur Geschichte des Alltags unterm Nationalsozialismus* (Wuppertal, 1981), 107–28, on local party groups as instruments of surveillance and control.

222. Bernward Dörner, 'Alltagsterror und Denunziation. Zur Bedeutung von Anzeigen aus der Bevölkerung für die Verfolgungswirkung des nationalsozialistischen "Heimtücke-Gesetzes" in Krefeld', in Berliner Geschichtswerkstatt (ed.), *Alltagskultur, Subjektivität und Geschichte: Zur Theorie und Praxis der Alltagsgeschichte* (Münster, 1994), 254–71.

223. Ulrich Herbert, ' "Die guten und die schlechten Zeiten". Überlegungen zur diachronen Analyse lebensgeschichtlicher Interviews', in Lutz Niethammer (ed.), *'Die Jahre weiss man nicht, wo man die heute hinsetzen soll': Faschismuserfahrungen im Ruhrgebiet* (Berlin, 1983), 67–96, interview with Willi Erbach on 73–6.

224. Karl Dietrich Bracher, *Stufen der Machtergreifung* (vol. I of Bracher *et al.*, *Die nationalsozialistische Machtergreifung*), 475–7; Otmar Jung, *Plebiszit und Diktatur: Die Volksabstimmungen der Nationalsozialisten. Die Fälle 'Austritt aus dem Völkerbund' (1933), 'Staatsoberhaupt' (1934) und 'Anschluss Österreichs' (1938)* (Tübingen, 1995).

225. Klemperer, *I Shall Bear Witness*, 36 (23 October 1933).

226. Bracher, *Stufen*, 475–85. For the plebiscite, see below, 618–19.

227. Behnken (ed.), *Deutschland-Berichte*, II (1934), 347–9; Bracher, *Stufen* 485–98. Jews were still allowed to vote in this election. Robert Gellately, *Backing Hitler: Consent and Coercion in Nazi Germany* (Oxford, 2001), 14–16, takes these fabricated results as 'remarkable' evidence of 'popular backing' for the Nazi regime. Hans-Ulrich Wehler, *Deutsche Gesellschaftsgeschichte*, IV: *Vom Beginn des ersten Weltkriegs bis zur Gründung der beiden deutschen Staaten 1914–1949* (Munich, 2003), 614, goes so far as to claim, without considering the evidence, that the plebiscites reflected the real views of the German people, 'since a systematic strategy of manipulation was not pursued', a claim made with reference to the 1933 plebiscite but also (e.g. 652) implicitly to later 'elections' as well. For Wehler's drastic underplaying of the terroristic component of Nazi rule, see Rüdiger Hachtmann, 'Bürgertum, Revolution, Diktatur – zum vierten Band von Hans-Ulrich Wehlers "Gesellschaftsgeschichte" ', *Sozial-Geschichte*, 19 (2004), 60–87, at 77–83.

228. Tagebuch Luise Solmitz, 19 August 1934.

229. Klemperer, *I Shall Bear Witness*, 79 (21 August 1934). Klemperer and his wife both voted 'no', as in the previous plebiscite.

230. Behnken (ed.), *Deutschland-Berichte*, V (1938), 415–26; Theodor Eschenburg, 'Streiflichter zur Geschichte der Wahlen im Dritten Reich', *VfZ* 3 (1955), 311–6; the skimmed milk story is recounted in Höhne, *The Order*, 201; for the bishop, see Paul Kopf and Max Miller (eds.), *Die Vertreibung von Bischof Joannes Baptista Sproll von Rottenburg 1938–1945: Dokumente zur Geschichte des kirchlichen Widerstands* (Mainz, 1971). For a good local study of the elections and

plebiscites from 1933 to 1938, see Hetzer, 'Die Industriestadt Augsburg', 137–46. A vote of 98 per cent had already been achieved in 1936.

231. Tagebuch Luise Solmitz, 29 March 1936. For details of the unprecedented terror and chicanery in these elections, see Behnken (ed.), *Deutschland-Berichte*, III (1936), 407–60.

232. Jeremy Noakes, 'The Origins, Structure and Function of Nazi Terror', in Noel O'Sullivan (ed.), *Terrorism, Ideology and Revolution* (Brighton, 1986), 67–87, makes the point that after 1933 terror was threatened more often than used; for the argument that this was because most Germans had learned to show outward conformity with the dictates of the regime, see below, 495–7.

233. Robert G. Gellately, 'Die Gestapo und die deutsche Gesellschaft: Zur Entstehungsgeschichte einer selbstüberwachenden Gesellschaft', in Detlef Schmiechen-Ackermann (ed.), *Anpassung, Verweigerung, Widerstand: Soziale Milieus, Politische Kultur und der Widerstand gegen den Nationalsozialismus in Deutschland im regionalen Vergleich* (Berlin, 1997), 109–21; idem, 'Allwissend und allgegenwärtig? Entstehung, Funktion und Wandel des Gestapo-Mythos', in Paul and Mallmann (eds.), *Die Gestapo*, 47–72, at 67.

234. Werner Röhr, 'Über die Initiative zur terroristischen Gewalt der Gestapo – Fragen und Einwände zu Gerhard Paul', in idem and Brigitte Berlekamp (eds.), *Terror, Herrschaft und Alltag im Nationalsozialismus: Probleme der Sozialgeschichte des deutschen Faschismus* (Münster, 1995), 211–24.

235. Diewald-Kerkmann, *Politische Denunziation*, 63.

236. For an example of the recent tendency to trivialize the brutality and ideological commitment of the Gestapo, see Gerhard Paul and Klaus-Michael Mallmann, 'Auf dem Wege zu einer Sozialgeschichte des Terrors: Eine Zwischenbilanz', in idem (eds.), *Die Gestapo*, 3–18 (attacking 'the image of the Gestapo officer as a brutal, criminal-psychopathic demon in a black leather overcoat', 11). Examples of the willingness of some Gestapo officers to employ physical violence and torture are provided in Hans-Dieter Schmid, ' "Anständige Beamte" und "üble Schläger". Die Staatspolizeileitstelle Hannover', in ibid., 133–60.

237. Dörner, 'NS-Herrschaft', 61–8.

238. Gellately, 'Allwissend und Allgegenwärtig?'.

239. For a powerful statement of these, and similar points, see Michael Burleigh, *The Third Reich. A New History* (London, 2000), 149–215.

240. Bernward Dörner, 'Gestapo und "Heimtücke". Zur Praxis der Geheimen Staatspolizei bei der Verfolgung von Verstössen gegen das "Heimtücke-Gesetz" ', in Paul and Mallmann (eds.), *Die Gestapo*, 325–43, at 341.

241. Charles Townshend, *Terrorism: A Very Short Introduction* (Oxford, 2002), 36–52.

242. Dieter Nelles, 'Organisation des Terrors im Nationalsozialismus', *Sozialwissenschaftliche Literatur-Rundschau*, 25 (2002), 5–28; Karl-Heinz Reuband, 'Denunziation im Dritten Reich. Die Bedeutung von Systemunterstützung und Gelegenheitsstrukturen', *Historical Social Research*, 26 (2001), 219–34.

243. Herbert, ' "Die guten und die schlechten Zeiten" ', interview with Willi Erbach, at 73–6.

Chapter 2. THE MOBILIZATION OF THE SPIRIT

1. Helmut Heiber (ed.), *Goebbels-Reden* (2 vols., Düsseldorf, 1971–2), I: *1932–39*, 131–41 (Berlin, Grosser Saal der Philharmonie – Eröffnung der Reichs-kulturkammer, 15. 11. 33) and 82–107 (Berlin, Haus des Rundfunks – Ansprache an die Intendanten und Direktoren der Rundfunkgesellschaften, 25. 3. 33), at 82, 88, 131–4.

2. Ibid., 92–3.

3. Josef Wulf, *Die bildenden Künste im Dritten Reich: Eine Dokumentation* (Gütersloh, 1963), 94, reproduces the decree.

4. Evans, *The Coming of the Third Reich*, 392–461, for the cultural revolution of 1933.

5. Quoted in Zbynek Zeman, *Nazi Propaganda* (Oxford, 1973), 38, citing Karl-heinz Schmeer, *Die Regie des öffentlichen Lebens im Dritten Reich* (Munich, 1956), 28.

6. Werner Skrentny, 'Terrassen, Hochhäuser und die 13 Läden: Hoheluft und Eimsbüttel', in idem (ed.), *Hamburg zu Fuss: 20 Stadtteilrundgänge durch Ge-schichte und Gegenwart* (Hamburg 1986), 133. For the creation of Adolf-Hitler-Platz in Mittlerweilersbach, in Bavaria, for example, see Broszat *et al.* (eds.), *Bayern*, I. 69. More generally, see Richard Grunberger, *A Social History of the Third Reich* (Harmondsworth, 1974 [1971]), 101–22.

7. Ernest Kohn Bramsted, *Goebbels and National Socialist Propaganda 1925–1945* (East Lansing, Mich., 1965), 203–18.

8. Speech of Bavarian Education Minister Hans Schemm, quoted in *Münchner Neueste Nachrichten*, 21 April 1933, cited and translated in Kershaw, *The 'Hitler Myth'*, 58–9.

9. Tagebuch Luise Solmitz, 17 August 1934.

10. Kershaw, *The 'Hitler Myth'*, 60.

11. Ibid., 48–60.

12. Ibid., 67–9, 84–95; Peter Reichel, *Der schöne Schein des Dritten Reiches: Faszination und Gewalt des Faschismus* (Munich, 1991), 138–56.

13. Peter Reichel, ' "Volksgemeinschaft" und Führer-Mythos', in Bernd Ogan and Wolfgang W. Weiss (eds.), *Faszination und Gewalt: Zur politischen Ästhetik des Nationalsozialismus* (Nuremberg, 1992), 137–50, at 138–42.

14. Frederic Spotts, *Hitler and the Power of Aesthetics* (London, 2002), 56–72. See more generally Wolfgang Benz, 'The Ritual and Stage Management of National Socialism. Techniques of Domination and the Public Sphere', in John Milfull (ed.), *The Attractions of Fascism: Social Psychology and the Aesthetics of the 'Triumph of the Right'* (New York, 1990), 273–88. For flags, standards and other symbols,

see Horst Ueberhorst, 'Feste, Fahnen, Feiern: Die Bedeutung politischer Symbole und Rituale im Nationalsozialismus', in Rüdiger Voigt (ed.), *Symbole der Politik, Politik der Symbole* (Opladen, 1989), 157–78. For the cult of sacrifice, see Jay W. Baird, *To Die for Germany: Heroes in the Nazi Pantheon* (Bloomington, Ind., 1990).

15. William L. Shirer, *Berlin Diary: The Journal of a Foreign Correspondent 1934–1941* (London, 1970 [1941]), 22–7.

16. Hilmar Hoffmann, *The Triumph of Propaganda: Film and National Socialism 1933–1945* (Providence, R.I., 1996), 151–7; Reichel, *Der schöne Schein*, 116–38; Yvonne Karow, *Deutsches Opfer: Kultische Selbstauslöschung auf den Reichspart-eitagen der NSDAP* (Berlin, 1997); Siegfried Zelnhefer, *Die Reichsparteitage der NSDAP: Geschichte, Struktur und Bedeutung der grössten Propagandafeste im nationalsozialistischen Feierjahr* (Neustadt an der Aisch, 1991); idem, 'Die Reichs-parteitage der NSDAP', in Ogan and Weiss (eds.), *Faszination und Gewalt*, 79–94; Hans-Ulrich Thamer, 'Von der "Ästhetisierung der Politik": Die Nürnberger Parte-itage der NSDAP', in ibid., 95–103.

17. For a good analysis, see David Welch, *Propaganda and the German Cinema 1933–1945* (Oxford, 1983), 147–59.

18. Longerich, *Die braunen Bataillone*, 227–30; Zelnhefer, 'Die Reichsparteitage', points out that the SS sealed off Nuremberg's red-light district during the Rally. See also above, p. 40.

19. For a detailed analysis, emphasizing the pseudo-religious aspects of the Rally, see Herbert Heinzelmann, 'Die Heilige Messe des Reichsparteitages. Zur Zeichen-sprache von Leni Riefenstahls "Triumph des Willens"', in Ogan and Weiss (eds.), *Faszination und Gewalt*, 163–8.

20. Welch, *Propaganda*, 158–9; Kershaw, *The 'Hitler Myth'*, 69–70; see also Siegfried Kracauer, *From Caligari to Hitler: A Psychological History of the Ger-man Film* (Princeton, 1947), 300–303.

21. Leni Riefenstahl, *Memoiren 1902–1945* (Berlin, 1990 [1987]), esp. 185–231. For a celebrated critical essay on Riefenstahl's work, see Susan Sontag, 'Fascinating Fascism', in Brandon Taylor and Wilfried van der Will (eds.), *The Nazification of Art: Art, Design, Music, Architecture and Film in the Third Reich* (Winchester, 1990), 204–18; more generally, Glenn B. Infield, *Leni Riefenstahl: The Fallen Film Goddess* (New York, 1976).

22. Speech at the Kaiserhof, 28 March 1933, reprinted in Gerd Albrecht (ed.), *Der Film im Dritten Reich: Eine Dokumentation* (Karlsruhe, 1979), 26–31, unabridged translation in David Welch (ed.), *The Third Reich: Politics and Propa-ganda* (London, 2002), 185–9.

23. Heiber (ed.), *Goebbels-Reden*, I. 82–107, at 95 (speech of 25 March 1933).

24. Goebbels's interview with the magazine *Licht-Bild-Bühne*, 13 October 1933, repeating a phrase first used in a speech of 19 May 1933, cited in *Völkischer Beobachter*, 20 May 1933, both quoted in Welch, *Propaganda*, 76–7.

25. Ibid., 75–88.

26. Ibid., 88–93. For the analysis of a similar film, *Hitler Youth Quex*, see Eric Rentschler, *The Ministry of Illusion: Nazi Cinema and its Afterlife* (Cambridge, Mass., 1996), 53–69; Jay W. Baird, 'From Berlin to Neubabelsberg: Nazi Film Propaganda and Hitler Youth Quex', *Journal of Contemporary History*, 18 (1983), 495–515, and the interesting discussion by a distinguished anthropologist, Gregory Bateson, 'An Analysis of the Nazi Film *Hitlerjunge Quex*', in Margaret Mead and Rhoda Métraux (eds.), *The Study of Culture at a Distance* (Chicago, 1953), 302–14.

27. Welch, *Propaganda*, 31; Boguslaw Drewniak, *Der deutsche Film 1938–45: Ein Gesamtüberblick* (Düsseldorf, 1987), 621 and *passim* for statistics on the film industry.

28. Welch, *Propaganda*, 159–64; Marcus S. Phillips, 'The Nazi Control of the German Film Industry', *Journal of European Studies*, 1 (1971), 37–68, at 53; also Baird, *To Die For Germany*, 172–201.

29. Welch, *Propaganda*, 11–14; Andrea Winkler-Mayerhöpfer, *Starkult als Propagandamittel: Studien zum Unterhaltungsfilm im Dritten Reich* (Munich, 1992).

30. Carsten Laqua, *Wie Micky unter die Nazis fiel: Walt Disney und Deutschland* (Reinbek, 1992), 15–35, 45, 56–61. The 'e' was dropped from Mickey's name in German because this would have altered the original pronunciation.

31. Ibid., 65–71, 81, 86–7, 93–6.

32. Welch, *Propaganda*, 11–13; also Wolfgang Becker, *Film und Herrschaft: Organisationsprinzipien und Organisationsstrukturen der nationalsozialistischen Filmpropaganda* (Berlin, 1973), esp. 32–67, and 67–98 on censorship; see also Kraft Wetzel and Peter Hagemann, *Zensur: verbotene deutsche Filme 1933–1945* (Berlin, 1978), and Klaus-Jürgen Maiwald, *Filmzensur im NS-Staat* (Dortmund, 1983).

33. Jürgen Spiker, *Film und Kapital: Der Weg der deutschen Filmwirtschaft zum nationalsozialistischen Einheitskonzern* (Berlin, 1975), esp. 168–82; Klaus Kreimeier, *The UFA Story: A History of Germany's Greatest Film Company 1918–1945* (New York, 1996), 205–65.

34. Welch, *Propaganda*, 17–24, 30–38; Reichel, *Der schöne Schein*, 180–207.

35. Welch, *Propaganda*, 43; Karsten Witte, 'Die Filmkomödie im Dritten Reich', in Horst Denkler and Karl Prümm (eds.), *Die deutsche Literatur im Dritten Reich: Themen, Traditionen, Wirkungen* (Stuttgart, 1976), 347–65; see also Erwin Leiser, *Nazi Cinema* (London, 1974 [1968]).

36. Joseph Wulf, *Theater und Film im Dritten Reich: Eine Dokumentation* (Gütersloh, 1963), 329, quoting *Film-Kurier*, 29 September 1933; see also ibid., 330; also more generally, Felix Moeller, *Der Filmminister: Goebbels und der Film im Dritten Reich* (Berlin, 1998), and Stephen Lowry, *Pathos und Politik: Ideologie in Spielfilmen des Nationalsozialismus* (Tübingen, 1991).

37. See generally David S. Hull, *Film in the Third Reich: A Study of the German Cinema 1933–1945* (Berkeley, Calif., 1969); Gerd Albrecht, *Nationalsozialistische*

Filmpolitik: Eine soziologische Untersuchung über die Spielfilme des Dritten Reichs (Stuttgart, 1969), esp. 284–311; Karsten Witte, *Lachende Erben, Toller Tag: Filmkomödie im Dritten Reich* (Berlin, 1995); and Linda Schulte-Saase, *Entertaining the Third Reich: Illusions of Wholeness in Nazi Cinema* (Durham, N.C., 1996), arguing for the political significance of Nazi entertainment cinema.

38. Welch, *Propaganda*, 191–203, Hoffmann, *The Triumph*, 192–210.

39. Welch, *The Third Reich*, 38–41; Joseph Wulf, *Presse und Funk im Dritten Reich: Eine Dokumentation* (Gütersloh, 1963), 315–18; Grunberger, *A Social History*, 506–11; Inge Marssolek, 'Radio in Deutschland 1923–1960: Zur Sozial-geschichte eines Mediums', *Geschichte und Gesellschaft*, 27 (2001), 207–39, at 217; manufacturers were removed from the Reich Radio Chamber in 1934 and passed into the domain of the Reich Ministry of Economics (ibid., 40–41). The Chamber was merged in November 1939 into the Reich Radio Company (Wulf, *Presse und Funk*, 299–304). See also Inge Marssolek and Adelheid von Saldern (eds.), *Zuhören und Gehörtwerden*, I: *Radio im Nationalsozialismus: Zwischen Lenkung und Ablenkung* (Tübingen, 1998), and Florian Cebulla, *Rundfunk und ländliche Gesellschaft 1924–1945* (Göttingen, 2004), esp. 209–46.

40. Klepper, *Unter dem Schatten*, 59 (25 May 1933), 65–6 (7 June 1933), 85 (10 July 1933); see also Evans, *The Coming of the Third Reich*, 408–9. The German Publishing Institution (*Deutsche Verlags-Anstalt*) was his publisher.

41. Heiber (ed.), *Goebbels-Reden*, I. 91–4.

42. Marssolek, 'Radio', 217.

43. Heiber (ed.), *Goebbels-Reden*, I. 91–4.

44. Welch, *The Third Reich*, 40–42; Ribbe (ed.), *Die Lageberichte*, I. 144–5, 162, 189; Grunberger, *A Social History*, 507; Norbert Frei and Johannes Schmitz, *Journalismus im Dritten Reich* (Munich, 1989), 86–7; figures from Hans Pohle, *Der Rundfunk als Instrument der Politik: Zur Geschichte des Rundfunks von 1923 bis 1928* (Hamburg, 1955), 327–9; more generally, Ansgar Diller, *Rund-funkpolitik im Dritten Reich* (Munich, 1980); Nanny Drechsler, *Die Funktion der Musik im deutschen Rundfunk 1933–1945* (Pfaffenweiler, 1988); Reichel, *Der schöne Schein*, 159–79; Gerhard Hay, 'Rundfunk und Hörspiel als "Führungsmit-tel" des Nationalsozialismus', in Denkler and Prümm (eds.), *Die deutsche Litera-tur*, 366–81; Hans-Jörg Koch, *Das Wunschkonzert im NS-Rundfunk* (Cologne, 2003), 168–271; Uta C. Schmidt, 'Der Volksempfänger: Tabernakel moderner Massenkultur', in Inge Marssolek and Adelheid von Saldern (eds.), *Radiozeiten: Herrschaft, Alltag, Gesellschaft (1924–1960)* (Potsdam, 1999), 136–59. Tele-vision was only at an experimental stage in the 1930s; broadcasts were made to receivers located in shop windows: see Klaus Winker, *Fernsehen unterm Hakenk-reuz: Organisation, Programm, Personal* (Cologne, 1994).

45. Heinz Boberach (ed.), *Meldungen aus dem Reich, 1938–1945: Die geheimen Lageberichte des Sicherheitsdienstes der SS* (17 vols., Herrsching, 1984), II. 277–8.

46. Alan E. Steinweis, 'Weimar Culture and the Rise of National Socialism: The *Kampfbund für deutsche Kultur*', *Central European History*, 24 (1991), 402–23.

47. See Reinhard Bollmus, *Das Amt Rosenberg und seine Gegner: Studien zum Machtkampf im nationalsozialistischen Herrschaftssystem* (Stuttgart, 1970).

48. Hildegard Brenner, *Die Kunstpolitik des Nationalsozialismus* (Reinbek, 1963), 7–21, 73–86, provides a good narrative.

49. Reuth, *Goebbels*, 226.

50. Spotts, *Hitler*, 3–9, 74–5; Reichel, *Der schöne Schein*, 83–100.

51. Welch, *The Third Reich*, 30–32; Alan E. Steinweis, 'Cultural Eugenics: Social Policy, Economic Reform, and the Purge of Jews from German Cultural Life', in Glenn R. Cuomo (ed.), *National Socialist Cultural Policy* (New York, 1995), 23–37; Jonathan Petropoulos, 'A Guide through the Visual Arts Administration of the Third Reich', in ibid., 121–53; Brenner, *Die Kunstpolitik*, 53–63.

52. Spotts, *Hitler*, 76–7; Alan E. Steinweis, *Art, Ideology, and Economics in Nazi Germany: The Reich Chambers of Music, Theater, and the Visual Arts* (Chapel Hill, N.C., 1993), 4–6, 34–49, 83–102; Jonathan Petropoulos, *Art as Politics in the Third Reich* (Chapel Hill, N.C., 1996), 34–8, 64–70.

53. Ibid., 51–6.

54. Erik Levi, *Music in the Third Reich* (New York, 1994), 14–23; Spotts, *Hitler*, 74; Petropolous, *Art*, 38–40.

55. Steinweis, 'Cultural Eugenics', 28–9.

56. Modris Eksteins, *The Limits of Reason: The German Democratic Press and the Collapse of Weimar Democracy* (Oxford, 1975), 25–8, 125–33, 167–72, 215, 251–4.

57. Ibid., 260, 268–9, 272–3, 275, 277–9, 283–6, 290, 303; Günther Gillessen, *Auf verlorenem Posten: Die Frankfurter Zeitung im Dritten Reich* (Berlin, 1986), 44–63.

58. Ibid., 329–69, 537; Frei and Schmitz, *Journalismus*, 51–2; for Nazi hostility to the *Feuilleton*, see Wulf, *Presse und Funk*, 197–208.

59. Numerous examples in Gillessen, *Auf verlorenem Posten*.

60. Klein (ed.), *Die Lageberichte*, 525 (November, 1935), 551–3 (December, 1935); Gillessen, *Auf verlorenem Posten*, 342–3.

61. Ibid., 383.

62. Klein (ed.), *Die Lageberichte*, 574 (January, 1936).

63. Quoted in Eksteins, *The Limits of Reason*, 291.

64. Gillessen, *Auf verlorenem Posten*, 146; Gillessen's powerfully argued defence of the paper and its staff (527–38) cannot conceal the extent of the compromises they had to make with the regime; see the balanced but generally pessimistic verdict in Frei and Schmitz, *Journalismus*, 51–3. For a parallel case, the liberal quality daily the *Berlin Daily News-Sheet* (*Berliner Tageblatt*), see the documentary edition, mixed with personal reminiscences, by Margret Boveri, *Wir lügen alle: Eine Hauptstadtzeitung unter Hitler* (Olten, 1965).

65. Eksteins, *The Limits of Reason*, 202–4; Oron J. Hale, *The Captive Press in the Third Reich* (Princeton, N.J., 1964), 289–99; Bramsted, *Goebbels*, 124–42.

66. Welch, *The Third Reich*, 43–6; Hale, *The Captive Press*, 143–68; Eksteins,

The Limits of Reason, 281–311; Wulf, *Presse und Funk*, 39. The continued ownership of the *Frankfurt Newspaper* by I.G. Farben up to 1938 was a notable testimony to the vast influence wielded by the corporation in the Third Reich. See below, 370–71, 375–6.

67. Welch, *The Third Reich*, 46; Noakes and Pridham (eds.), *Nazism*, II. 193–5; text of the law in Wulf, *Presse und Funk*, 72–6. For Nazi concern not to offend 'religious sensibilities' in 1933, see below.

68. Norbert Frei, *Nationalsozialistische Eroberung der Provinzpresse: Gleichschaltung, Selbsanpassung und Resistenz in Bayern* (Stuttgart, 1980), esp. 164–7, 322–4; Hale, *The Captive Press*, 102–42, for the Party and the publishing industry at national and *Gau* level.

69. Grunberger, *A Social History*, 492–506; Hermann Froschauer and Renate Geyer, *Quellen des Hasses: Aus dem Archiv des 'Stürmer' 1933–1945* (Nuremberg, 1988); Fred Hahn (ed.), *Lieber Stürmer! Leserbriefe an das NS-Kampfblatt 1924–1945* (Stuttgart, 1978).

70. Wulf, *Presse und Funk*, 87–99. For a recent edition, see Gabriele Toepser-Ziegert (ed.), *NS-Presseanweisungen der Vorkriegszeit. Edition und Dokumentation*, I: *1933*; II: *1934*; III: *1935*; IV: *1936*; and the following volumes: V: *1937*; VI: *1938*, ed. Karen Peter (Munich, 1985–98). For background on policy, Karl-Dietrich Abel, *Presselenkung im NS-Staat: Eine Studie zur Geschichte der Publizistik in der nationalsozialistischen Zeit* (Berlin, 1990 [1968]).

71. See more generally Jürgen Hagemann, *Die Presselenkung im Dritten Reich* (Bonn, 1970), esp. 25–60; Fritz Sänger, *Politik der Täuschungen: Missbrauch der Presse im Dritten Reich: Weisungen, Informationen, Notizen, 1933–1939* (Vienna, 1975); and Henning Storek, *Dirigierte Öffentlichkeit: Die Zeitung als Herrschaftsmittel in den Anfangsjahren der nationalsozialistischen Regierung* (Opladen, 1972).

72. Gillessen, *Auf verlorenem Posten*, 224; for the regime's campaign against the Catholic press, see Hale, *The Captive Press*, 169–89, and below, 235.

73. Welch, *The Third Reich*, 47; Grunberger, *A Social History*, 504.

74. Klein (ed.), *Die Lageberichte*, 244–5; Ribbe (ed.), *Die Lageberichte*, I. 144–5 (Regierungspräsident Potsdam, August 1934).

75. Wulf, *Presse und Funk*, 84 and 279, quoted and translated in Noakes and Pridham (eds.), *Nazism*, II. 202.

76. David Bankier, *The Germans and the Final Solution: Public Opinion under Nazism* (Oxford, 1992), 20–27; Hale, *The Captive Press*, 57, 145–63, 231.

77. Heiber (ed.), *Goebbels-Reden*, I. 174–205 (Berlin: Sitzungssaal des ehemaligen Preussischen Herrenhauses – 1. Reichspressetag des Reichsverbandes der Deutschen Presse, 18. 11. 34), at 184–6.

78. Fröhlich (ed.), *Die Tagebücher*, I/II: *Diktate*, VIII. 101 (14 April 1943).

79. Hans Fallada, *Kleiner Mann – was nun?* (Reinbek, 1978 [1932]); English translation by Susan Bennett, *Little Man – What Now?* (London, 1996).

80. Jenny Williams, *More Lives than One: A Biography of Hans Fallada* (London,

1998), esp. 107–9, 127. More generally, see Cecilia von Studnitz, *Es war wie ein Rausch: Fallada und sein Leben* (Düsseldorf, 1997), and the incisive essay by Henry Ashby Turner, Jr, 'Fallada for Historians', *German Studies Review*, 26 (2003), 477–92.

81. Williams, *More Lives*, 135–49; Hans Fallada, *Wer einmal aus dem Blechknapf frisst* (Reinbek, 1980 [1934]).

82. Williams, *More Lives*, 149, 175–6, 188. Paul Mayer (ed.), *Ernst Rowohlt in Selbstzeugnissen und Bilddokumenten* (Reinbek, 1968); Walter Kiaulehn, *Mein Freund der Verleger – Ernst Rowohlt und seine Zeit* (Reinbek, 1967); Rowohlt survived the war and became a leading publisher in postwar West Germany.

83. Ibid., 150–62; Hans Fallada, *Wir hatten mal ein Kind: Eine Geschichte und Geschichten* (Reinbek, 1980 [1934]).

84. Williams, *More Lives*, 173–267 and 284 n. 18 (Rudolf Ditzen to Elizabeth Ditzen, 22 December 1946); Fröhlich (ed.), *Die Tagebücher*, I/V. 15, 126 (31 January 1938); Hans Fallada, *Altes Herz geht auf die Reise* (Munich, 1981 [1936]); *Wolf unter Wölfen* (Reinbek, 1991 [1937]); *Der eiserne Gustav: Roman* (Berlin, 1984 [1938]); *Der Trinker/Der Alpdruck* (Berlin, 1987 [1950]). See also Gunnar Müller-Waldeck and Roland Ulrich (eds.), *Hans Fallada: Sein Leben in Bildern und Briefen* (Berlin, 1997). For the chequered history of Fallada/Ditzen's brief postwar career, see Sabine Lange, '. . . *wir haben nicht nur das Chaos, sondern wir stehen an einem Beginn*' . . . *Hans Fallada 1945–1946* (Neubrandenburg, 1988).

85. Evans, *The Coming of the Third Reich*, 409–12.

86. Kurt R. Grossmann, *Ossietzky. Ein deutscher Patriot* (Frankfurt am Main, 1973 [1963]), 278–318; Josef Wulf, *Literatur und Dichtung im Dritten Reich: Eine Dokumentation* (Gütersloh, 1963), 259–61; Evans, *The Coming of the Third Reich*, 120, 136, 409, 429.

87. Wolfgang Emmerich, 'Die Literatur des antifaschistischen Widerstandes in Deutschland', in Denkler and Prümm (eds.), *Die deutsche Literatur*, 427–58.

88. James M. Ritchie, *German Literature under National Socialism* (London, 1983), 111–22; Ralf Schnell, *Literarische innere Emigration: 1933–1945* (Stuttgart, 1976), 113–32, at 121 for quote; Peter Barbian, 'Literary Policy in the Third Reich', in Cuomo (ed.), *National Socialist Cultural Policy*, 155–96; Reinhold Grimm, 'Im Dickicht der inneren Emigration', in Denkler and Prümm (eds.), *Die deutsche Literatur*, 406–26.

89. Ritchie, *German Literature*, 123–9; Friedrich P. Reck-Malleczewen, *Bockelson: Geschichte eines Massenwahns* (Stuttgart, 1968 [1937]); see also below, 414–16; and more generally, Heidrun Ehrke-Rotermund and Erwin Rotermund, *Zwischenreiche und Gegenwelten: Texte und Vorstudien zur 'Verdeckten Schreibweise' im 'Dritten Reich'* (Munich, 1999), 315–93, 527–46, on Reck and Jünger.

90. Klaus Vondung, 'Der literarische Nationalsozialismus. Ideologische, politische und sozialhistorische Wirkungszusammenhänge', in Denkler and Prümm (eds.), *Die deutsche Literatur*, 44–65; Karl Prümm, 'Das Erbe der Front. Der anti-

demokratische Kriegsroman der Weimarer Republik und seine nationalsozialistische Fortsetzung', in ibid., 138–64 (and other contributions in the same volume).

91. Heiber (ed.), *Goebbels-Reden*, I. 131–41, at 137.

92. Kurt Eggers, *Deutsche Gedichte* (Munich, 1934), 8, in Wulf, *Literatur*, 286; Alexander von Bormann, 'Das nationalsozialistische Gemeinschaftslied', in Denkler and Prümm (eds.), *Die deutsche Literatur*, 256–80; Gottfried Niedhart and George Broderick (eds.), *Lieder in Politik und Alltag des Nationalsozialismus* (Frankfurt am Main, 1999); and Eberhard Frommann, *Die Lieder der NS-Zeit: Untersuchungen zur nationalsozialistischen Liedpropaganda von den Anfängen bis zum Zweiten Weltkrieg* (Cologne, 1999).

93. Wulf, *Literatur*, 366, reprinting Fritz Sotke, 'So ist es', in *Wille und Macht* (15 January 1934), 1.

94. Reichel, *Der schöne Schein*, 323–35; more generally, Sebastian Graeb-Könneker, *Autochthone Modernität: Eine Untersuchung der vom Nationalsozialismus geforderten Literatur* (Opladen, 1996) and Uwe-Karsten Ketelsen, *Literatur und Drittes Reich* (Schernfeld, 1992); see also Baird, *To Die For Germany*, 130–54, on the poet Gerhard Schumann.

95. Evans, *The Coming of the Third Reich*, 417–18.

96. Wulf, *Literatur*, 113–23; Ritchie, *German Literature*, 48–54; idem, *Gottfried Benn: The Unreconstructed Expressionist* (London, 1972) – see especially his translation of Benn's 'To the Literary Emigrés: A Reply', 89–96; Reinhard Alter, *Gottfried Benn: The Artist and Politics (1910–1934)* (Frankfurt am Main, 1976), esp. 86–144

97. Wolfgang Willirich to Gottfried Benn, 27 August 1937, reprinted in Wulf, *Literatur*, 120–22.

98. Glenn R. Cuomo, 'Purging an "Art-Bolshevist": The Persecution of Gottfried Benn in the Years 1933–1938', *German Studies Review*, 9 (1986), 85–105; see also Gottfried Benn, *Gesammelte Werke*, ed. Dieter Wellershoff (4 vols., Wiesbaden, 1961), I. 440–52, 'Der neue Staat und die Intellektuellen', defending the Nazi seizure of power.

99. Jan-Pieter Barbian, *Literaturpolitik im 'Dritten Reich': Institutionen, Kompetenzen, Betätigungsfelder* (Munich, 1995 [1993]), 54–66 for the initial purges; 66–156 for a comprehensively detailed survey of censorship institutions. See also Dietrich Strothmann's survey, *Nationalsozialistische Literaturpolitik: Ein Beitrag zur Publizistik im Dritten Reich* (Bonn, 1960), with details of banned works; and Evans, *The Coming of the Third Reich*, 426–31.

100. Wulf, *Literatur*, 160–64; Ritchie, *German Literature*, 71–4. See also Siegfried Schliebs, 'Verboten, verbrannt, verfolgt ... Wolfgang Herrmann und seine "Schwarze Liste: Schöne Literatur" vom Mai 1933. Der Fall des Volksbibliothekars Dr Wolfgang Hermann', in Hermann Haarmann *et al.* (eds.), *'Das war ein Vorspiel nur ...': Bücherverbrennung in Deutschland 1933: Voraussetzungen und Folgen. Ausstellung der Akademie der Künste vom 8. Mai bis 3. Juli 1983*

(Berlin, 1983), 442–54; Barbian, *Literaturpolitik*, 217–319 for the book trade, 319–63 for libraries; Engelbrecht Boese, *Das öffentliche Bibliothekswesen im Dritten Reich* (Bad Honnef, 1987); and Margaret F. Stieg, *Public Libraries in Nazi Germany* (Tuscaloosa, Ala., 1992); Strothmann, *Nationalsozialistische Literaturpolitik*, 222–4, and Grunberger, *A Social History*, 452–3, for foreign authors.

101. Brenner, *Die Kunstpolitik*, 51.

102. Reichel, *Der schöne Schein*, 336–45; Boguslaw Drewniak, 'The Foundations of Theater Policy in Nazi Germany', in Cuomo (ed.), *National Socialist Cultural Policy*, 67–94; more details of the theatre business in the same author's *Das Theater im NS-Staat: Szenarium deutscher Zeitgeschichte 1933–1945* (Düsseldorf, 1983), with a discussion of the fate of the classics on 167–89; more still in the compendium by Thomas Eicher *et al.*, *Theater im 'Dritten Reich': Theaterpolitik, Spielplanstruktur, NS-Dramatik* (Seelze–Velber, 2000); documentary extracts in Wulf, *Theater und Film*; essays on specific aspects in Glen W. Gadberry (ed.), *Theater in the Third Reich, the Prewar Years: Essays on Theater in Nazi Germany* (Westport, Conn., 1995).

103. Steinweis, *Art*, 134–7.

104. See Wulf, *Theater und Film*, for details.

105. Friederike Euler, 'Theater zwischen Anpassung und Widerstand: Die Münchner Kammerspiele im Dritten Reich', in Broszat *et al.* (eds.), *Bayern*, II. 91–173; Grunberger, *A Social History*, 457–74.

106. William Niven, 'The Birth of Nazi drama?: *Thing* Plays', in John London (ed.), *Theatre under the Nazis* (Manchester, 2000), 54–95, esp. 73; more detail in Rainer Stommer, *Die inszenierte Volksgemeinschaft: Die 'Thing-Bewegung' im Dritten Reich* (Marburg, 1985), and the brief study by Johannes M. Reichl, *Das Thingspiel: Über den Versuch eines nationalsozialistischen Lehrstück-Theaters (Euringer – Heynick – Möller)* (Frankfurt, 1998), esp. 14–33; the origins of the movement are covered in Egon Menz, 'Sprechchor und Aufmarsch. Zur Entstehung des Thingspiels', in Denkler and Prümm (eds.), *Die deutsche Literatur*, 330–46; Brenner, *Die Kunstpolitik*, 95–106, and Rainer Stommer, '"Da oben versinkt einem der Alltag…"'. Thingstätten im Dritten Reich als Demonstration der Volksgemeinschaftsideologie', in Peukert and Reulecke (eds.), *Die Reihen fast geschlossen*, 149–73.

107. Heiber (ed.), *Goebbels-Reden*, I. 168–72 (Berlin, Sportpalast, Eröffnung der 'Woche des deutschen Buches', 5. 11. 34), at 177.

108. Donald R. Richards, *The German Bestseller in the Twentieth Century: A Complete Bibliography and Analysis 1915–1940* (Berne, 1968) (entries under individual authors in table B, best-seller lists in table A); revised figures in Tobias Schneider, 'Bestseller im Dritten Reich. Ermittlung und Analyse der meistverkauften Romane in Deutschland 1933–1944', *VfZ* 52 (2004), 77–97.

109. Hans Hagemeyer, speech to the Reichsarbeitsgemeinschaft für deutsche Buchwerbung on 28 August 1935, in Wulf, *Literatur*, 243–4; see also Goebbels's speech on 5 November 1934 (n. 107, above).

110. Wilhelm Baur, cited in ibid., plate 8, opp. 145; also 274–7.

111. Schneider, 'Bestseller', 80–85.

112. Kershaw, *Hitler*, I. 15–17.

113. Hans Dieter Schäfer, *Das gespaltene Bewusstsein: Über deutsche Kultur und Lebenswirklichkeit 1933–1945* (Munich, 1982), esp. 7–54; Thymian Bussemer, *Propaganda und Populärkultur. Konstruierte Erlebniswelten im Nationalsozialismus* (Wiesbaden, 2000), esp. 76–115.

114. Evans, *The Coming of the Third Reich*, 122–4, 413–16.

115. Fröhlich (ed.), *Die Tagebücher* (Munich, 2004), I/I. 293 (29 August 1924).

116. Peter Paret, *An Artist against the Third Reich: Ernst Barlach, 1933–1938* (Cambridge, 2003), 17–18, 23–69; Shearer West, *The Visual Arts in Germany 1890–1937: Utopia and Despair* (Manchester, 2000), 93–9; Brenner, *Die Kunstpolitik*, 65–71; Wolfgang Tarnowski, *Ernst Barlach und der Nationalsozialismus: Ein Abendvortrag, gehalten am 20. Oktober 1988 in der Katholischen Akademie Hamburg* (Hamburg, 1989), 41–5; Joseph Wulf, *Die bildenden Künste im Dritten Reich: Eine Dokumentation* (Gütersloh, 1963), 32. See also Akademie der Künste, Berlin (ed.), *Zwischen Anpassung und Widerstand: Kunst in Deutschland 1933–1945* (Berlin, 1978).

117. Paret, *An Artist*, 23–5, 38–43, 59; a better title for Paret's excellent book would perhaps have been *The Third Reich against an Artist*.

118. Ernst Barlach, *Die Briefe*, ed. Friedrich Dross (2 vols., Munich, 1968–9), II. 414 (Barlach to Leo Kestenberg, 13 November 1933).

119. Ibid., II. 374 (Ernst Barlach to Hans Barlach, 2 May 1933).

120. Cited in Paret, *An Artist*, 171 n. 33, and reprinted in Alfred Rosenberg, *Blut und Ehre: Ein Kampf für deutsche Wiedergeburt: Reden und Aufsätze von 1919–1933* (Munich, 1934), 250.

121. Paret, *An Artist*, 78–9, citing Barlach, *Die Briefe*, II. 388–9 (Barlach to Alois Schardt, 23 July 1933) and 425 (Barlach to Carl Albert Lange, 25 December 1933).

122. It survived the war and is now back in the cathedral.

123. Maschmann, *Account Rendered*, p. 25.

124. Fröhlich (ed.), *Die Tagebücher*, I/III. 56 (4 April 1936).

125. Barlach, *Briefe*, II. 735 (Barlach to Heinz Priebatsch, 23 October 1937).

126. Paret, *An Artist*, 137.

127. Peter Adam, *The Arts of the Third Reich* (London, 1992), 196–201.

128. Jonathan Petropoulos, *The Faustian Bargain: The Art World in Nazi Germany* (New York, 2000), 218–53; idem, 'From Seduction to Denial: Arno Breker's Engagement with National Socialism', in Richard A. Etlin (ed.), *Art, Culture, and Media under the Third Reich* (Chicago, 2002), 205–29; Wulf, *Die bildenden Künste*, 252; Volker Probst, *Der Bildhauer Arno Breker* (Bonn, 1978). Breker defended himself and his art in his memoirs published after the war: see Arno Breker, *Im Strahlungsfeld der Ereignisse, 1925–1965* (Preussisch Oldendorf, 1972).

129. Klaus Backes, *Hitler und die bildenden Künste: Kulturverständnis und Kunstpolitik im Dritten Reich* (Cologne, 1988), 10–56.

130. Erhard Klöss (ed.), *Reden des Führers: Politik und Propaganda Adolf Hitlers 1922–1945* (Munich, 1967), 108–20.

131. Evans, *The Coming of the Third Reich*, 413–16.

132. Lynn H. Nicholas, *The Rape of Europa: The Fate of Europe's Treasures in the Third Reich and the Second World War* (New York, 1994), 9–15.

133. Petropoulos, *The Faustian Bargain*, 13–25; more generally, Reichel, *Der schöne Schein*, 356–70.

134. Adam, *Arts*, 121–3; West, *The Visual Arts*, 188–9. For a survey of the work of the banned artists, see Werner Haftmann, *Verfemte Kunst: Bildende Künstler der inneren und äusseren Emigration in der Zeit des Nationalsozialismus* (Cologne, 1986) (esp. Beckmann, 47–67, Klee, 1,112–25, Kirchner 126–32, and Schlemmer, 37–13).

135. Petropoulos, *Art*, 57.

136. Spotts, *Hitler*, 151–64. Fröhlich (ed.), *Die Tagebücher*, I/II (5 June 1936); Backes, *Hitler*, 57–70; for the precursor exhibitions, see Christoph Zuschlag, 'An "Educational Exhibition". The Precursors of *Entartete Kunst* and its Individual Venues', in Stephanie Barron (ed.), *'Degenerate Art': The Fate of the Avant-Garde in Nazi Germany* (Los Angeles, 1991), 83–103, and in more detail, in Christoph Zuschlag, *'Entartete Kunst': Ausstellungsstrategien in Nazi-Deutschland* (Worms, 1995), 58–168 (protests in 1933 noted on 329).

137. Wulf, *Die bildenden Künste*, 140–44.

138. Petropoulos, *The Faustian Bargain*, 25; Reinhard Merker, *Die bildenden Künste im Nationalsozialismus: Kulturideologie, Kulturpolitik, Kulturproduktion* (Cologne, 1983), 143–5; Annegret Janda, The Fight for Modern Art: The Berlin Nationalgalerie after 1933', in Barron (ed.), *'Degenerate Art'*, 105–18.

139. Annegret Janda (ed.), *Das Schicksal einer Sammlung: Aufbau und Zerstörung der Neuen Abteilung der Nationalgalerie im ehemaligen Kronprinzen-Palais Unter den Linden 1918–1945* (Berlin, 1986), 16.

140. Inge Jádi *et al.*, *Beyond Reason: Art and Psychosis: Works from the Prinzhorn Collection* (London, 1996), and Hans Prinzhorn, *Bildnerei der Geisteskranken: Ein Beitrag zur Psychologie und Psychopathologie der Gestaltung* (Berlin, 1922).

141. Fritz Kaiser, *Führer durch die Ausstellung Entartete Kunst* (Berlin, 1937), 24–8.

142. Merker, *Die bildenden Künste*, 148–52. The instruction does not appear to have been carried out.

143. Kaiser, *Führer*, 2–22. The brochure is reproduced in Barron (ed.), *'Degenerate Art'*, 359–90; see also Mario-Andreas von Lüttichau, ' "*Entartete Kunst*", Munich, 1937: A Reconstruction', in ibid., 45–81, and the detailed account in Zuschlag, *'Entartete Kunst'*, 169–204 and 222–99.

144. Robert Böttcher, *Kunst und Kunsterziehung im neuen Reich* (Breslau, 1933), 41; Wolfgang Willrich, *Säuberung des Kunsttempels: Eine kunstpolitische*

Kampfschrift zur Gesundung deutscher Kunst im Geiste nordischer Art (Munich, 1937), 6.

145. Wulf, *Die bildenden Künste*, 319-20, 324, 327-33; for the orchestration of press publicity, see Karen Peter (ed.), *NS-Presseanweisungen der Vorkriegszeit: Edition und Dokumentation*, V: *1937* (Munich, 1998), 579, 587, 590, 631, 701.

146. *Berliner Morgenpost*, 172, 20 July 1937, front page; *Berliner Illustrierte Nachtausgabe*, 25 February 1938.

147. Peter Guenther, 'Three Days in Munich, July 1937', in Barron (ed.), *'Degenerate Art'*, 33-43; reactions of Carola Roth and others in Paul Ortwin Rave, *Kunstdiktatur in Dritten Reich* (Hamburg, 1949); telegram in Zuschlag, *'Entartete Kunst'*, 331; price-tag information in Peter-Klaus Schuster (ed.), *Die 'Kunststadt' München 1937: Nationalsozialismus und 'Entartete Kunst'* (Munich, 1987), 103-4; this also has a facsimile reproduction of the exhibition brochure (183-216).

148. Sean Rainbird (ed.), *Max Beckmann* (London, 2003), 274-7.

149. Backes, *Hitler*, 71-7, for a good brief survey.

150. Norbert Wolf, *Ernst Ludwig Kirchner 1880-1938: On the Edge of the Abyss of Time* (Cologne, 2003), 86-90.

151. Kaiser, *Führer*, 24-8.

152. Wulf, *Die bildenden Künste*, 118-27. Literary criticism suffered a similar fate (Strothmann, *Nationalsozialistische Literaturpolitik*, 258-300).

153. Quoted and translated in Adam, *The Arts*, 123.

154. Wulf, *Die bildenden Künste*, 337 (copy of the Law).

155. Adam, *The Arts*, 121-2; Merker, *Die bildenden Künste*, 155-6 (also for the quotations above).

156. Brenner, *Die Kunstpolitik*, 159.

157. Adam, *The Arts*, 122-7.

158. Merker, *Die bildenden Künste*, 155-6; Zuschlag, *'Entartete Kunst'*, 205-21; Petropoulos, *Art*, 76-81. Wulf, *Die bildenden Künste*, 340-41 for press reporting and the auction announcement.

159. Stephanie Barron, 'The Galerie Fischer Auction', in Barron (ed.), *'Degenerate Art'*, 135-69.

160. Angelika Königseder and Juliane Wetzel, 'Die "Bilderverbrennung" 1939 – ein Pendant?', *Zeitschrift für Geschichtswissenschaft*, 51(2003), 439-46, point out that while there is abundant documentary evidence for the proposal to burn the artworks, there is no written evidence that it was actually carried out, and no eyewitness accounts have come to light. There is only one source for the story, namely Rave, *Kunstdiktatur*. However, not one of the works on the list of those proposed for burning has ever been seen since 20 March 1939. See also Andreas Hüneke, 'On the Trail of Missing Masterpieces: Modern Art from German Galleries', in Barron (ed.), *'Degenerate Art'*, 121-33; Petropoulos, *Art*, 82-3 and 338 n. 50; and Georg Bussmann, *German Art of the Twentieth Century* (Munich, 1985), 113-24.

161. Wulf, *Die bildenden Künste*, 325-6.

162. Boberach (ed.), *Meldungen*, II. 275.

163. Ibid., 115.

164. Wulf, *Die bildenden Künste*, 96–110.

165. Nicholas, *The Rape*, 13.

166. Wulf, *Die bildenden Künste*, 113–7.

167. Ibid., 172–4, 181–4, 190–94.

168. Backes, *Hitler*, 77–83.

169. Klaus Wolbert, *Die Nackten und die Toten des 'Dritten Reiches': Folgen einer politischen Geschichte des Körpers in der Plastik des deutschen Faschismus* (Giessen, 1982), 34–60, 188–92, 235–6.

170. Merker, *Die bildenden Künste*, 163–6. For a digest of press reports, see Otto Thomae, *Die Propaganda-Maschinerie: Bildende Kunst und Öffentlichkeitsarbeit im Dritten Reich* (Berlin, 1978), 37–69.

171. Merker, *Die bildenden Künste*, 165 (with different figures); Petropoulos, *Art*, 57.

172. Guenther, 'Three Days in Munich', 33–43, at 33–4; see also Mario-Andreas von Lüttichau, '"Deutsche Kunst" und "Entartete Kunst": Die Münchner Ausstellungen 1937', in Schuster (ed.), *Die 'Kunststadt' München*, 83–118.

173. Adelheid von Saldern, '"Art for the People": From Cultural Conservatism to Nazi Cultural Policies', in eadem, *The Challenge of Modernity: German Social and Cultural Studies, 1890–1960* (Ann Arbor, Mich., 2002), 299–347.

174. Karl Arndt, 'Das "Haus der deutschen Kunst" – ein Symbol der neuen Machtverhältnisse', in Schuster (ed.), *Die 'Kunststadt' München*, 61–82; idem, 'Paul Ludwig Troost als Leitfigur der nationalsozialistischen Räpresentationsarchitektur', in Iris Lauterbach (ed.), *Bürokratie und Kult: Das Parteizentrum der NSDAP am Königsplatz in München: Geschichte und Rezeption* (Munich, 1995), 147–56; for the background to the building's commissioning, design and construction, see Karl Arndt, 'Die Münchener Architekturszene 1933/34 als ästhetisch-politisches Konfliktfeld', in Broszat *et al.* (eds.), *Bayern*, III. 443–512, esp. 443–84.

175. Quoted in Wulf, *Die bildenden Künste*, 220.

176. Rolf Badenhausen, 'Betrachtungen zum Bauwillen des Dritten Reiches', *Zeitschrift für Deutschkunde* 1937, 222–3, excerpted in Wulf, *Die bildenden Künste*, 223–4; Hans Lehmbruch, 'Acropolis Germaniae. Der Königsplatz – Forum der NSDAP', in Lauterbach (ed.), *Bürokratie und Kult*, 17–46; more generally, Reichel, *Der schöne Schein*, 287–311; for the indebtedness to Classicism, see Alex Scobie, *Hitler's State Architecture: The Impact of Classical Antiquity* (Philadelphia, Pa., 1990), esp. 56–68; for the Nazi cult of the dead, see Sabine Behrenbeck, *Der Kult um die toten Helden: Nationalsozialistische Mythen: Riten und Symbole 1923 bis 1945* (Vierow bei Greifswald, 1996), esp. 343–446; for the ceremonies accompanying the translation of the martyrs' bodies, see Baird, *To Die for Germany*, 41–72.

177. Barbara Miller Lane, *Architecture and Politics in Germany, 1918–1945* (Cambridge, Mass., 1968), 169–84.

178. Norbert Borrmann, *Paul Schultze-Naumburg, 1869–1949. Maler – Publizist – Architekt: Vom Kulturreformer der Jahrhundertwende zum Kulturpolitiker im Dritten Reich* (Essen, 1989), esp. 198–220; more generally, Joachim Petsch, 'Architektur und Städtebau im Dritten Reich – Anspruch und Wirklichkeit', in Peukert and Reulecke (eds.), *Die Reihen fast geschlossen*, 175–98, and Elke Pahl-Weber and Dirk Schubert, 'Myth and Reality in National Socialist Town Planning and Architecture: Housing and Urban Development in Hamburg, 1933–45', *Planning Perspectives*, 6 (1991), 161–88.

179. Jochen Thies, 'Nazi Architecture – A Blueprint for World Domination: The Last Aims of Adolf Hitler', in David Welch (ed.), *Nazi Propaganda: The Power and the Limitations* (London, 1983), 45–64, at 52; documentation for Berlin, Hamburg, Linz, Munich and Nuremberg in Jost Dülffer *et al.* (eds.), *Hitlers Städte: Baupolitik im Dritten Reich* (Cologne, 1978); see also Dirk Schubert, '. . . Ein neues Hamburg entsteht . . . Planungen in der "Führerstadt" Hamburg zwischen 1933–1945', in Hartmut Frank (ed.), *Faschistische Architekturen: Planen und Bauen in Europa 1930 bis 1945* (Hamburg, 1985), 299–318; Backes, *Hitler*, 117–93.

180. Adam, *The Arts*, 245–59; also Dieter Bartetzko, *Zwischen Zucht und Ekstase: Zur Theatralik von NS-Architektur* (Berlin, 1985); Robert R. Taylor, *The Word in Stone: The Role of Architecture in the National Socialist Ideology* (Berkeley, Calif., 1974), 250–69; Anna Teut, *Architektur im Dritten Reich 1933–1945* (Frankfurt am Main, 1967); Jochen Thies, *Architekt der Weltherrschaft: Die 'Endziele' Hitlers* (Düsseldorf, 1976), 62–164; Merker, *Die bildenden Künste*, 186–238.

181. Paul Giesler, 'Bauen im Dritten Reich', *Die Kunst im Dritten Reich*, September 1939, quoted in Adam, *The Arts*, 256; detailed illustrated survey in Angela Schönberger, *Die neue Reichskanzlei von Albert Speer: Zum Zusammenhang von nationalsozialistischer Ideologie und Architektur* (Berlin, 1981), 37–173.

182. Thies, *Architekt*, 62–104.

183. Albert Speer, *Inside the Third Reich: Memoirs* (London 1971 [1970]), 45–6.

184. Jost Dülffer, 'Albert Speer: Cultural and Economic Management', in Ronald Smelser and Rainer Zitelmann (eds.), *The Nazi Elite* (London, 1993 [1989]), 212–23; for Goebbels's vandalism, see Evans, *The Coming of the Third Reich*, 398. A counter-claim for inventing the 'cathedral of light' was made, however, by Walter Frentz and Leni Riefenstahl (Gitta Sereny, *Albert Speer: His Battle with Truth* (London, 1995), 129).

185. Siegfried Zelnhefer and Rudolf Käs (eds.), *Kulissen der Gewalt: Das Reichsparteitagsgelände in Nürnberg* (Munich, 1992), esp. 31–48 (Siegfried Zelnhefer, 'Bauen als Vorgriff auf den Sieg. Zur Geschichte des Reichsparteitagsgeländes').

186. Karen A. Fiss, 'In Hitler's Salon: The German Pavilion at the 1937 Paris Exposition Internationale', in Etlin (ed.), *Art*, 316–42, at 318–19, quoting Paul Westheim, *Paul Westheim: Kunstkritik aus dem Exil*, ed. Tanja Frank (Hanau, 1985), 151; see also Kurt Winkler, 'Inszenierung der Macht: Weltausstellung 1937.

Das "Deutsche Haus" als Standarte', in Klaus Behnken and Frank Wagner (eds.), *Inszenierung der Macht: Ästhetische Faszination in Faschismus* (Berlin, 1987), 217–25. The greater height of the German pavilion against its Soviet opposite number was deliberate; Speer had obtained plans of the Soviet structure in advance (Fies, 'In Hitler's Salon', 321–3).

187. Speer, *Inside*, 117–22, 195–220.

188. Dülffer, 'Albert Speer', 213–15; Joachim Petach, 'Architektur als Weltanschauung: Die Staats- und Parteiarchitektur im Nationalsozialismus', in Ogan and Weiss (eds.), *Faszination und Gewalt*, 197–204.

189. Speer, *Inside*, 197; Sereny, *Albert Speer*, 126–31.

190. Gerhard Splitt, *Richard Strauss 1933–1935: Ästhetik und Musikpolitik zu Beginn der nationalsozialistischen Herrschaft* (Pfaffenweiler, 1987), 42–59, discusses Strauss's possible motivations in a detailed examination of the evidence that is marred by an unnecessarily angry tone of moral condemnation; for a more balanced view, see Michael H. Kater, *Composers of the Nazi Era: Eight Portraits* (New York, 2000), 220–23.

191. Kater, *Composers*, 225–7.

192. Ibid., 211–12; Franz Grasberger (ed.), *Der Strom der Töne trug mich fort: Die Welt um Richard Strauss in Briefen* (Tutzing, 1967), 171–2; Walter Thomas, *Richard Strauss und seine Zeitgenossen* (Munich, 1964), 218.

193. Harry Graf Kessler, *Tagebücher 1918–1937*, ed. Wolfgang Pfeiffer-Belli (Frankfurt am Main, 1982 [1961]), 563 (14 June 1928); Kater, *Composers*, 213–16.

194. Ibid., 217–25.

195. Ibid., 229–46; Fred K. Prieberg, *Trial of Strength: Wilhelm Furtwängler and the Third Reich* (London, 1991 [1986]), 166–9.

196. Fred K. Prieberg, *Musik im NS-Staat* (Frankfurt am Main, 1982), 207–8; Josef Wulf, *Musik im Dritten Reich: Eine Dokumentation* (Gütersloh, 1963), 182–3; Saul Friedländer, *Nazi Germany and the Jews*, I: *The Years of Persecution 1933–1939* (London, 1997), 130–35; Albrecht Riethmüller, 'Stefan Zweig and the Fall of the Reich Music Chamber President, Richard Strauss', in Michael H. Kater and Albrecht Riethmüller (eds.), *Music and Nazism: Art under Tyranny, 1933–1945* (Laaber, 2003), 269–91. For Stefan Zweig's best-sellers, see Richards, *The German Bestseller*, 252–3; one of Zweig's books sold 300,000 copies from 1927 to 1931, and two others 170,000 each from 1922 to 1933 and 1931 to 1933 respectively.

197. Strauss, 'Geschichte der schweigsamen Frau', and Strauss to Hitler, 13 July 1935, both in Wulf, *Musik*, 183–4.

198. Kater, *Composers*, 247–59; Prieberg, *Musik*, 208–15; Lothar Gall, 'Richard Strauss und das "Dritte Reich" oder: Wie der Künstler Strauss sich missbrauchen liess', in Hanspeter Krellmann (ed.), *Wer war Richard Strauss? Neunzehn Antworten* (Frankfurt am Main, 1999), 123–36.

199. Levi, *Music*, 57–70, 94–8; Michael H. Kater, *The Twisted Muse: Musicians*

and Their Music in the Third Reich (New York, 1997), 77–9; Prieberg, *Musik*, 277–82; Wulf, *Musik*, 414–23 (extracts from the *Lexikon* and similar antisemitic works on 386–91).

200. Dirk Blasius, 'Die Ausstellung "Entartete Musik" von 1938. Ein Beitrag zum Kontinuitätsproblem der deutschen Geschichte', in Othmar N. Haberl and Tobias Korenke (eds.), *Politische Deutungskulturen: Festschrift für Karl Rohe* (Baden-Baden, 1999), 199–211. There was no time to produce a catalogue for the *Entartete Musik* exhibition, but on the fiftieth anniversary, a commemorative exhibition staged a reconstruction: see Albrecht Dümling and Peter Girth (eds.), *Entartete Musik: Eine kommentierte Rekonstruktion zur Düsseldorfer Ausstellung von 1938* (Düsseldorf, 1988); Ziegler's opening address is on 128–43; also Albrecht Dümling, 'The Target of Racial Purity: The "Degenerate Music" Exhibition in Düsseldorf, 1938', in Etlin (ed.), *Art*, 43–72; idem (ed.), *Banned by the Nazis: Entartete Musik: The Exhibition of Düsseldorf 1938/88 in Texts and Documents* (London, 1995); Eckhard John, *Musikbolschewismus: Die Politisierung der Musik in Deutschland 1918–1938* (Stuttgart, 1994), 367–81; and, arguing for the unpopularity of modern music in the Weimar Republic, Pamela M. Potter, 'The Nazi "Seizure" of the Berlin Philharmonic, or the Decline of a Bourgeois Musical Institution', in Cuomo (ed.), *Nazi Cultural Policy*, 39–65. See also Hans Severus Ziegler, *Entartete Musik: Eine Abrechnung* (Düsseldorf, 1938).

201. Fröhlich (ed.), *Die Tagebücher*, I/V. 323 (29 May 1938).

202. Zuschlag, *'Entartete Kunst'*, 315–20.

203. Levi, *Music*, 70–73; Prieberg, *Musik*, 144–64; Wulf, *Musik*, 407; Potter, 'The Nazi "Seizure"', 54.

204. Levi, *Music*, 74–81.

205. Ibid., 98–102.

206. Levi, *Music*, 104–5; Prieberg, *Musik*, 225–34. Berg's Piano Sonata opus 1 was performed on 29 November 1944 at a poetry reading in Vienna, with musical intermezzi organized by Anton von Webern (ibid., 299).

207. Ibid., 104–7; Prieberg, *Musik*, 137–8.

208. Levi, *Music*, 107–11; Kater, *Composers*, 31–6.

209. Levi, *Music*, 111–14; Wulf, *Musik*, 337–40 (for the quotes). See also Giselher Schubert, 'The Aesthetic Premises of a Nazi Conception of Music', in Kater and Riethmüller (eds.), *Music and Nazism*, 64–74.

210. Wulf, *Musik*, 341

211. Fröhlich (ed.), *Die Tagebücher*, I/III. 140 (27 July 1936). Wahnfried was the Wagner family home in Bayreuth.

212. Kater, *The Twisted Muse*, 197–201; Levi, *Music*, 199–201; Potter, 'The Nazi "Seizure"', 39–65. See also more generally Michael Meyer, *The Politics of Music in the Third Reich* (New York, 1991).

213. Levi, *Music*, 114–16.

214. Bernd Sponheuer, 'The National Socialist Discussion on the "German Quality" in Music', in Kater and Riethmüller (eds.), *Music and Nazism*, 32–42;

Reinhold Brinkmann, 'The Distorted Sublime: Music and National Socialist Ideology – A Sketch', in ibid., 43–63.

215. Kater, *Composers*, 3–30. Egk's real name was Mayer; he disliked its ordinariness so much that he used a pseudonym based on his wife's name, 'Elisabeth, geborene Karl' ('Elisabeth, née Karl'). Those who disliked him alleged that he really meant it to stand for 'Ein grosser Komponist' ('a great composer'). See also Michael Walter, *Hitler in der Oper: Deutsches Musikleben 1919–1945* (Stuttgart, 1995), 175–212.

216. Ibid., 111–43; see also the autobiography of Orff's wife, Luise Rinser, *Saturn auf der Sonne* (Frankfurt am Main, 1994), 94–5.

217. Frederic Spotts, *Bayreuth: A History of the Wagner Festival* (New Haven, 1994), esp. 159–88; Brigitte Hamann, *Winifred Wagner oder Hitlers Bayreuth* (Munich, 2002); Hans Rudolf Vaget, 'Hitler's Wagner: Musical Discourse as Cultural Space', in Kater and Riethmüller (eds.), *Music and Nazism*, 15–31.

218. Spotts, *Hitler*, 223–63; idem, *Bayreuth*, 165–75.

219. Speer, *Inside*, 103–5.

220. Levi, *Music*, 192–3.

221. Levi, *Music*, 217–18; more generally, Volker Dahm, 'Nationale Einheit und partikulare Vielfalt. Zur Frage der kulturpolitischen Gleichschaltung im Dritten Reich', *VfZ* 43 (1995), 221–65. For Pfitzner's complicated relationship with the Nazi leadership, see Kater, *Composers*, 144–82. Pfitzner was enraged at the favour shown to some modernist composers by the regime. Asked what he thought of modern music, he replied contemptuously: 'Egk mich am Orff!' (Berndt W. Wessling, *Wieland Wagner: Der Enkel* (Cologne, 1997), 257); see also John, *Musikbolschewismus*, 58–89, for Pfitzner's role in crystallizing right-wing hostility to 'musical Bolshevism' in the Weimar Republic.

222. Wulf, *Musik*, 403, quoting Karl Grunsky, 'Gedanken über Mendelssohn', *Westdeutscher Beobachter*, 10 March 1935.

223. Celia Applegate, 'The Past and Present of *Hausmusik* in the Third Reich', in Kater and Riethmüller (eds.), *Music and Nazism*, 136–49.

224. Steinweis, *Art*, 141–2.

225. For Nazi theories of music, see Pamela M. Potter, *Most German of the Arts: Musicology and Society from the Weimar Republic to the End of Hitler's Reich* (New Haven, 1998), esp. 200–234.

226. Walter Thomas, *Bis der Vorhang fiel: Berichtet nach Aufzeichnungen aus den Jahren 1940 bis 1945* (Dortmund, 1947), 241.

227. Kater, *Composers*, 86–110; idem, *Different Drummers: Jazz in the Culture of Nazi Germany* (New York, 1992), 29–56; idem, *The Twisted Muse*, 233–9; Wulf, *Musik*, 346–58; also Bernd Polster (ed.), *Swing Heil: Jazz im Nationalsozialismus* (Berlin, 1989).

228. Kater, *Different Drummers*, 90–95; Fröhlich (ed.), *Die Tagebücher*, I/III. 161–2 (2 June 1937), 165–6 (5 June 1937), 293 (7 Oct. 1937), 326 (5 Nov. 1937), 346 (26 Nov. 1937).

229. Kater, *Different Drummers*, 101–10; Arno Klönne, *Jugend im Dritten Reich: Die Hitler-Jugend und ihre Gegner* (Düsseldorf, 1982), 241–6.

230. Hartmut Berghoff, *Zwischen Kleinstadt und Weltmarkt: Hohner und die Harmonika 1857–1961. Unternehmensgeschichte als Gesellschaftsgeschichte* (Paderborn, 1997), 311, 360–61, 375, 615.

231. Ibid., 375, 412–19, 445–6.

232. Reichel, *Der schöne Schein*, 371.

233. Gerhard Paul, *Aufstand der Bilder: Die NS-Propaganda vor 1933* (Bonn, 1990); Peter Zimmermann, 'Die Bildsprache des Nationalsozialismus im Plakat', in Maria Rüger (ed.), *Kunst und Kunstkritik der dreissiger Jahre: 29 Standpunkte zu künstlerischen und ästhetischen Prozessen und Kontroversen* (Dresden, 1990), 223–36; Evans, *The Coming of the Third Reich*, 289–91.

234. See for example Marla S. Stone, *The Patron State: Culture and Politics in Fascist Italy* (Princeton, N.J., 1998); Edward Tannenbaum, *The Fascist Experience: Italian Society and Culture, 1922–1945* (New York, 1972), esp. 213–302; Orlando Figes and Boris Kolonitskii, *Interpreting the Russian Revolution: The Language and Symbols of 1917* (New Haven, 1999), esp. 30–103, 153–86, and Richard Stites, *Russian Popular Culture: Entertainment and Society since 1900* (Cambridge, 1992); summary in Richard J. Overy, *The Dictators: Hitler's Germany and Stalin's Russia* (New York, 2004), 349–91. For Nazi comment on the Futurist exhibition, see Willrich, *Säuberung*, 32.

235. As is the tendency in, for example, Spotts, *Hitler*, or Ehrhard Bahr, 'Nazi Cultural Politics: Intentionalism v. Functionalism', in Cuomo (ed.), *National Socialist Cultural Policy*, 5–22.

236. Dahm, 'Nationale Einheit', regards the growing prevalence of entertainment over outright propaganda as evidence of a growing freedom on the part of cultural producers, particularly at the local or regional level; but it was of course thoroughly consonant with the overall cultural purposes of the regime.

237. Jutta Sywottek, *Mobilmachung für den totalen Krieg: Die propagandistische Vorbereitung der deutschen Bevölkerung auf den Zweiten Weltkrieg* (Opladen, 1976).

238. See also below, 465–7, for the cultural programme of the Strength Through Joy organization, and 563–5 for Jewish culture in the Third Reich.

239. Heiber (ed.), *Goebbels-Reden*, I. 219–28 (Hamburg: Musikhalle – Eröffnung der 2. Reichs-Theaterfestwoche, 17. 4. 35), 219–28, at 220.

240. Rainer Stollmann, 'Faschistische Politik als Gesamtkunstwerk. Tendenzen der Ästhetisierung des politischen Lebens im Nationalsozialismus', in Denkler and Prümm (eds.), *Die deutsche Literatur*, 83–101 (somewhat over-theorized); the original concept of the aestheticization of politics comes from the Afterword to Walter Benjamin's celebrated essay 'Das Kunstwerk im Zeitalter seiner technischen Reproduzierbarkeit', in idem, *Gesammelte Schriften* I/II, ed. Rolf Tiedemann and Hermann Schweenhäuser (Frankfurt am Main, 1974), 508.

241. Heiber (ed.), *Goebbels-Reden*, I. 219–28 (Hamburg, Musikhalle – Eröffnung der 2. Reichs-Theaterfestwoche, 17. 6. 35), at 220, 224, 227.

242. Klemperer, *I Shall Bear Witness*, 109 (27 February 1935); Tagebuch Luise Solmitz, vol. 30 (5 July 1935–16 June 1937), *passim*.

243. John Heskett, 'Modernism and Archaism in Design in the Third Reich', in Taylor and van der Will (eds.), *The Nazification of Art*, 110–27.

244. Uwe Westphal, *Werbung im Dritten Reich* (Berlin, 1989), esp. 50–72. But see also Hans Deischmann, *Objects: A Chronicle of Subversion in Nazi Germany* (New York, 1995).

245. Victor Klemperer, *Tagebücher*, 14 (22 March 1933).

246. Rolf Steinberg (ed.), *Nazi-Kitsch* (Darmstadt, 1975) (a short catalogue of illustrations of these objects); for the puzzle, see 23.

247. Marion Godau, 'Anti-Moderne?', in Sabine Weissler (ed.), *Design in Deutschland 1933–45: Ästhetik und Organisation des Deutschen Werkbundes im 'Dritten Reich'* (Giessen, 1990), 74–87.

248. Joachim Wolschke-Bulmahn and Gert Gröning, 'The National Socialist Garden and Landscape Ideal: *Bodenständigkeit* (Rootedness in the Soil)', in Etlin (ed.), *Art*, 73–97; and Vroni Heinrich-Hampf, 'Über Gartenidylle und Gartenarchitektur im Dritten Reich', in Frank (ed.), *Faschistische Architekturen*, 271–81.

249. Leopold von Schenkendorf and Heinrich Hoffmann (ed.), *Kampf um's Dritte Reich: Eine Historische Bilderfolge* (Altona-Bahrenfeld, 1933).

250. *Die Kunst im Dritten Reich* 1937, 160, quoted in Britta Lammers, *Werbung im Nationalsozialismus: Die Kataloge der 'Grossen Deutschen Kunstausstellung'*, 1937–1944 (Weimar, 1999), 9.

251. Reichel, *Der schöne Schein*, 373–5; for the concealment of modern constructions by pseudo-archaic façades, see Lothar Suhling, 'Deutsche Baukunst. Technologie und Ideologie im Industriebau des "Dritten Reiches"', in Herbert Mehrtens and Steffen Richter (eds.), *Naturwissenschaft, Technik und NS-Ideologie: Beiträge zur Wissenschaftsgeschichte des Dritten Reichs* (Frankfurt am Main, 1980), 243–81.

252. Zeman, *Nazi Propaganda*, 177; Robert E. Herzstein, *The War that Hitler Won: The Most Infamous Propaganda Campaign in History* (London, 1979); Alexander D. Hardy, *Hitler's Secret Weapon: The 'Managed' Press and Propaganda Machine of Nazi Germany* (New York, 1967).

253. Victor Klemperer, *LTI. Notizbuch eines Philologen* (Leipzig, 1975 [1947]); see also Gerhard Bauer, *Sprache und Sprachlosigkeit im 'Dritten Reich'* (Cologne, 1990 [1988]); Wolfgang Bergsdorf, 'Sprachlenkung im Nationalsozialismus', in Martin Greiffenhagen (ed.), *Kampf um Wörter? Politische Begriffe im Meinungsstreit* (Munich, 1980), 65–74; Werner Bohleber and Jörg Drews (ed.), *'Gift, das du unbewusst eintrinkst...' Der Nationalsozialismus und die deutsche Sprache* (Bielefeld, 1994 [1991]); Siegfried Bork, *Missbrauch der Sprache: Tendenzen nationalsozialistischer Sprachregelung* (Munich, 1970); Karl-Heinz Brackmann and Renate Birkenhauer, *NS-Deutsch: 'Selbstverständliche' Begriffe und Schlagwörter aus der Zeit des Nationalsozialismus* (Straelen, 1988); Dolf Sternberger et al., *Aus dem Wörterbuch des Unmenschen* (Düsseldorf, 1968 [1957]).

254. Ribbe (ed.), *Die Lageberichte*, 162.

255. Ibid., 189, also 246.

256. Behnken (ed.), *Deutschland-Berichte*, IV (1937), 1,224–5 (14 October 1937). Similarly, already, in ibid., III (1936), 1,109–10.

257. Bankier, *The Germans*, 14–20, 28–34.

258. Kershaw, *The 'Hitler Myth'*, esp. 48–147.

259. Ian Kershaw, 'How Effective was Nazi Propaganda?', in David Welch (ed.), *Nazi Propaganda: The Power and the Limitations* (London, 1983), 180–205; more generally, Peter Longerich, 'Nationalsozialistische Propaganda', in Karl Dietrich Bracher *et al.* (eds.), *Deutschland 1933–1945: Neue Studien zur nationalsozialistischen Herrschaft* (Düsseldorf, 1992), 291–314.

Chapter 3. CONVERTING THE SOUL

1. Doris L. Bergen, *Twisted Cross: The German Christian Movement in the Third Reich* (Chapel Hill, N.C., 1996), 101–18; Manfred Kittel, 'Konfessioneller Konflikt und politische Kultur in der Weimarer Republik', in Olaf Blaschke (ed.), *Konfessionen im Konflikt: Deutschland zwischen 1800 und 1970: ein zweites konfessionelles Zeitalter* (Göttingen, 2002), 243–97.

2. For general overviews, see Thomas Nipperdey, *Deutsche Geschichte 1866–1918* (2 vols., Munich 1990), I: *Arbeitswelt und Bürgergeist*, 468–507. More detail in Wolfgang Altgeld, *Katholizismus, Protestantismus, Judentum: Über religiös begründete Gegensätze und nationalreligiöse Ideen in der Geschichte des deutschen Nationalismus* (Mainz, 1992); idem, 'Religion, Denomination and Nationalism in Nineteenth-Century Germany', in Helmut Walser Smith (ed.), *Protestants, Catholics and Jews in Germany, 1800–1913* (Oxford, 2001), 49–65; Helmut Walser Smith, *German Nationalism and Religious Conflict: Culture, Ideology, Politics, 1870–1914* (Princeton, N.J., 1995); John Horne and Alan Kramer, *German Atrocities 1914: A History of Denial* (New Haven, 2001), 157–8; Manfred Gailus, *Protestantismus und Nationalsozialismus: Studien zur nationalsozialistischen Durchdringung des protestantischen Sozialmilieus in Berlin* (Cologne, 2001), 40–51. For religious divisions and politics in the Weimar Republic, see Georges Castellan, *L'Allemagne de Weimar 1918–1933* (Paris, 1969), 209–40, still one of the few general histories of the Weimar Republic to take religion seriously. For the Day of Potsdam, see Evans, *The Coming of the Third Reich*, 350–51.

3. Martin Niemöller, *From U-Boat to Pulpit* (London, 1936 [1934]), 143.

4. Ibid., 180–83, 187; James Bentley, *Martin Niemöller* (Oxford, 1984), 20–30, 39–40.

5. Ibid., 42–68.

6. Nipperdey, *Deutsche Geschichte 1866–1918*, I. 507–28, for secularization in the nineteenth century; Hugh McLeod, *Religion and the People of Western Europe 1789–1989* (Oxford, 1997 [1981]), esp. 118–31, offers a good general survey;

idem, *Piety and Poverty: Working-Class Religion in Berlin, London, and New York 1870–1914* (New York, 1996) is a detailed comparative account.

7. Richard Steigmann-Gall, *The Holy Reich: Nazi Conceptions of Christianity 1919–1945* (Cambridge, 2003), 13–19, 68; Gailus, *Protestantismus*, 29–40, 643–4; see also Günter Brakelmann, 'Hoffnungen und Illusionen evangelischer Prediger zu Beginn des Dritten Reiches: Gottesdienstliche Feiern aus politischen Anlässen', in Peukert and Reulecke (eds.), *Die Reihen fast geschlossen*, 129–48.

8. Steigmann-Gall, *The Holy Reich*, 134–40.

9. Günter Brakelmann, 'Nationalprotestantismus und Nationalsozialismus', in Christian Jansen et al. (eds.), *Von der Aufgabe der Freiheit: Politische Verantwortung und bürgerliche Gesellschaft im 19. und 20. Jahrhundert: Festschrift für Hans Mommsen zum 5. November 1995* (Berlin, 1995), 337–50.

10. Detlef Schmiechen-Ackermann, *Kooperation und Abgrenzung: Bürgerliche Gruppen, evangelische Kirchengemeinden und katholisches Sozialmilieu in der Auseinandersetzung mit dem Nationalsozialismus in Hannover* (Hanover, 1999), esp. 138–60; Ernst Klee, *'Die SA Jesu Christi': Die Kirche im Banne Hitlers* (Frankfurt am Main, 1989), esp. 11–81; Björn Mensing, *Pfarrer und Nationalsozialismus: Geschichte einer Verstrickung am Beispiel der Evangelisch-Lutherischen Kirche in Bayern* (Göttingen, 1998), esp. 147–79; Robert P. Ericksen, *Theologians under Hitler: Gerhard Kittel, Paul Althaus, and Emanuel Hirsch* (New Haven, 1985).

11. Rainer Lächele, *Ein Volk, ein Reich, ein Glaube: Die Deutschen Christen in Württemberg 1925–60* (Stuttgart, 1993); Thomas M. Schneider, *Reichsbischof L. Müller: Eine Untersuchung zu Leben, Werk und Persönlichkeit* (Göttingen, 1993); Reijo E. Heinonen, *Anpassung und Identität: Theologie und Kirchenpolitik der Bremer Deutschen Christen 1933–1945* (Göttingen, 1978), esp. 19–47; Kurt Meier, *Die Deutschen Christen: Das Bild einer Bewegung im Kirchenkampf des Dritten Reiches* (Göttingen, 1964), esp. 1–37; James A. Zabel, *Nazism and the Pastors: A Study of the Ideas of Three Deutsche Christen Groups* (Missoula, Mont., 1976).

12. Quoted in Bracher, *Stufen*, 448.

13. Gailus, *Protestantismus*, 139–95.

14. Cited in Bracher, *Stufen*, 451.

15. Klaus Scholder, *Die Kirchen und das Dritte Reich*, I: *Vorgeschichte und Zeit der Illusionen 1918–1934* (Frankfurt am Main, 1977), Part 2, chapters 4–7, 10 and 12, provides a magisterially detailed narrative of these events.

16. Gailus, *Protestantismus*, 640–46. Bergen, *Twisted Cross*, 61–81.

17. Ibid., 103, 145, 166; Scholder, *Die Kirchen*, 702–5.

18. Eberhard Bethge, *Dietrich Bonhoeffer: Theologe, Christ, Zeitgenosse* (Munich, 1967), 321–6, 363–5; Jürgen Schmidt, *Martin Niemöller im Kirchenkampf* (Hamburg, 1971), 121–78; more generally on Protestantism and antisemitism in this period, Jochen-Christoph Kaiser, 'Protestantismus, Diakonie und "Judenfrage" 1933–41', *VfZ* 37 (1989), 673–714.

19. Gailus, *Protestantismus*, 647–53. These figures derive from the Confessing Church in the mid-to-late 1930s (see next paragraph).

20. Eberhard Busch, *Karl Barths Lebenslauf: Nach seinen Briefen und autobiographischen Texten* (Munich, 1975). Barth's writings on the Confessing Church are available in *Karl Barth zum Kirchenkampf: Beteiligung – Mahnung – Zuspruch* (Munich, 1956), esp. 213–36; see also Karl Barth, *The German Church Conflict* (London, 1965).

21. Bracher, *Stufen*, 441–62; John S. Conway, *The Nazi Persecution of the Churches 1933–1945* (London, 1968), 191; Bergen, *Twisted Cross*, 17–18.

22. Ribbe (ed.), *Die Lageberichte*, I. 385 (Lagebericht, Dec. 1935); Helmut Witetschek (ed.), *Die kirchliche Lage in Bayern nach den Regierungspräsidentenberichten 1933–1945*, II: *Regierungsbezirk Ober- und Mittelfranken* (Mainz, 1967), 66 (Lagesonderbericht der Regierung 9 December 1935, no. 54); for Niemöller, see Gailus, *Protestantismus*, 327–31, and Martin Niemöller, *Dahlemer Predigten 1936/37* (Munich, 1981).

23. Ribbe (ed.), *Die Lageberichte*, 231.

24. Klein (ed.), *Die Lageberichte*, 365 (Lagebericht, Dec. 1935).

25. For a detailed account of these events to the autumn of 1934, see Scholder, *Die Kirchen*, II: *Das Jahre der Ernüchterung 1934. Barmen und Rom* (Berlin, 1985), 11–118, 159–220, 269–356.

26. For Meiser, see Witetschek (ed.), *Die kirchliche Lage*, II. 34–59.

27. Bonhoeffer to Sutz, 28 April 1934, in Dietrich Bonhoeffer, *Gesammelte Schriften*, ed. Eberhard Bethge (Munich, 1958), I. 39–40 (quoted in Bergen, *Twisted Cross*, 140).

28. Gailus, *Protestantismus*, 654–6, 661–2.

29. Bentley, *Martin Niemöller*, 67–9; Gailus, *Protestantismus*, 656–8. Wolfgang Gerlach, *Als die Zeugen schwiegen: Bekennende Kirche und die Juden* (Berlin, 1993).

30. Gailus, *Protestantismus*, 658.

31. Klepper, *Unter dem Schatten*, 41 (8 March 1933, 11 March 1933), 46–7 (30 March 1933); Christopher Clark, *The Politics of Conversion: Missionary Protestantism and the Jews in Prussia, 1728–1941* (Oxford, 1995), esp. 285–98.

32. Robert P. Ericksen, 'A Radical Minority: Resistance in the German Protestant Church', in Nicosia and Stokes (eds.), *Germans Against Nazism*, 115–36; Shelley Baranowski, *The Confessing Church, Conservative Elites, and the Nazi State* (New York, 1986); Scholder, *Die Kirchen*, I. 701–42; Steigmann-Gall, *The Holy Reich*, 184–5; Ruth Zerner, 'German Protestant Responses to Nazi Persecution of the Jews', in Randolph Braham (ed.), *Perspectives on the Holocaust* (Boston, 1983), 57–68, quoting Niemöller's sermon at 63; Victoria Barnett, *For the Soul of the People: Protestant Protest against Hitler* (Oxford, 1992), esp. 60–103; for the Aryan Paragraph, Bergen, *Twisted Cross*, 57; for the Confessing Church and antisemitism, see Friedländer, *Nazi Germany*, 44–5; for a striking example of a confrontation between pastors of the German Christian and Confessing per-

suasions over the Aryan Paragraph, see Broszat *et al.* (eds.), *Bayern*, I. 110–11 (Aus Monatsbericht der Gendarmerie-Station Heiligenstadt, 25 Nov. 1937).

33. Ribbe (ed.), *Die Lageberichte*, 231.

34. Ibid., 230.

35. Bracher, *Stufen*, 458–62.

36. Bergen, *Twisted Cross*, 189–90.

37. Conway, *The Nazi Persecution*, 116–39.

38. Ibid., 202–214; Ribbe (ed.), *Die Lageberichte*, 243–4; Bentley, *Martin Niemöller*, 92–130.

39. Steigmann-Gall, *The Holy Reich*, 185–7 (an unsympathetic account, omitting all details of Niemöller's maltreatment); Conway, *The Nazi Persecution*, 212–13 and 433 n. 24; Bentley, *Martin Niemöller*, 143–7. Niemöller was tried alongside Otto Dibelius, another significant, if less well-known figure in the Confessing Church, who was also acquitted.

40. Stein, *I Was in Hell*, 147–51, quotes at 148, 151.

41. Bentley, *Martin Niemöller*, 147–57.

42. Gailus, *Protestantismus*, 329–31, 333–44.

43. Peter Novick, *The Holocaust and Collective Memory: The American Experience* (London, 2000), 221; the text authorized by Niemöller's widow Sibylle Niemöller, is quoted in full (in German) in Ruth Zerner, 'Martin Niemöller, Activist as Bystander: The Oft-Quoted Reflection', in Marvin Perry and Frederick M. Schweitzer (eds.), *Jewish-Christian Encounters over the Centuries: Symbiosis, Prejudice, Holocaust, Dialogue* (New York, 1994), 327–40, at 336 n. 7

44. Subsequent manipulations of Niemöller's statement, in the *Encylopedia of the Holocaust* and elsewhere, moved the Jews to first place in the list; others, including the US Holocaust Memorial Museum in Washington, D.C., omitted the Communists altogether. See Lionel Kochan, 'Martin Niemöller', in Yisrael Gutman (ed.), *Encyclopedia of the Holocaust* (4 vols., New York, 1990), III. 1,061; Jeshajahu Weinberg and Rina Elieli, *The Holocaust Museum in Washington* (New York, 1995), 163. In 1946, Niemöller remarked in a sermon after the war that if he had recognized in 1933 that in the Communists who were being thrown into concentration camps, Jesus Christ himself was being imprisoned, and stood by them, things might have been different (Bentley, *Martin Niemöller*, 165).

45. Adolf Hitler, *Mein Kampf*, translated by Ralph Manheim (London, 1969 [1925–7]), 393; more generally, see Steigmann-Gall, *The Holy Reich*, 29–46, 51–84.

46. Ibid., 133–4.

47. For some qualifications, see Oded Heilbronner, *Die Achillesferse des deutschen Katholizismus* (Gerlingen, 1998). For Catholic criticism of the Nazis, see Guenter Lewy, *The Catholic Church and Nazi Germany* (New York, 1964), 3–24.

48. Alfons Kupper (ed.), *Staatliche Akten über die Reichskonkordatsverhandlungen 1933* (Mainz, 1969), provides extensive documentation of the Church's concerns.

49. Scholder, *Die Kirchen*, I. 627–62, quotes at 630, 632; Lewy, *The Catholic Church*, 115–50. For details of the variety of positions within the Church on these tactics, see Ludwig Volk, *Bayerns Episkopat und Klerus in der Auseinandersetzung mit dem Nationalsozialismus 1930–1934* (Mainz, 1965); and Saul Friedländer, *Pius XII and the Third Reich* (London, 1966).

50. Conway, *The Nazi Persecution*, 67–71, 89–90.

51. Ibid., 78–81.

52. Ibid., 90–94; Lewy, *The Catholic Church*, 168–75; see above, 32–6, for the events of 1934.

53. Alfred Rosenberg, *Der Mythus des 20. Jahrhunderts: Eine Wertung der seelisch-geistigen Gestaltenkämpfe unserer Zeit* (Munich, 1935), esp. 607–36; Robert Cecil, *The Myth of the Master Race: Alfred Rosenberg and Nazi Ideology* (London, 1972), esp. 82–104, is still the best account of Rosenberg's ideas.

54. Klein (ed.), *Die Lageberichte*, 270 (Lagebericht, May 1935); Lewy, *The Catholic Church*, 151–68.

55. Bernhard Stasiewski (ed.), *Akten deutscher Bischöfe über die Lage der Kirche 1933–1945*, II: *1934–1935* (Mainz, 1976), 299–300 (Hirtenwort des deutschen Episkopats, 23 August 1935).

56. Peter Löffler (ed.), *Bischof Clemens August Graf von Galen: Akten, Briefe und Predigten 1933–1946*, I: *1933–1939* (Mainz, 1988), lxiv–lxvii, 168–84.

57. Ibid., 188–9 (Galen to Hitler, 7 April 1935).

58. Conway, *The Nazi Persecution*, 107–12; Klein (ed.), *Die Lageberichte*, 193, 207–8, 235, 246–8, 270, 282.

59. Ibid., 319; Conway, *The Nazi Persecution*, 157–60.

60. Klein (ed.), *Die Lageberichte*, 364.

61. Ibid., 208, 222–3.

62. Witetschek (ed.), *Die kirchliche Lage*, I: *Regierungsbezirk Oberbayern* (Mainz, 1966), 145, 150, 153 (reports of 9 June and 7–10 July 1936).

63. Ibid., 251 (Monatsbericht der Regierung Oberbayern, 10 July 1937).

64. Fröhlich (ed.), *Die Tagebücher*, I/III. 353–4 (31 January 1937); see more generally Hans Günter Hockerts, 'Die Goebbels-Tagebücher 1932–1941: Eine neue Hauptquelle zur Erforschung der nationalsozialistischen Kirchenpolitik', in Dieter Albrecht *et al.* (eds.), *Politik und Konfession: Festschrift für Konrad Repgen zum 60. Geburtstag* (Berlin, 1983), 359–92.

65. Jeremy Noakes, 'The Oldenburg Crucifix Struggle of November 1936: A Case Study of Opposition in the Third Reich', in Peter D. Stachura (ed.), *The Shaping of the Nazi State* (London, 1978), 210–33. For a similar incident in Cham, Bavaria, see Walter Ziegler (ed.), *Die kirchliche Lage in Bayern nach den Regierungspräsidentenberichten 1933–1943*, IV: *Regierungsbezirk Niederbayern und Oberpfalz 1933–1945* (Mainz, 1973), 229 (Monatsbericht der Regierung Regensburg, 8 May 1939); for documents on the state of the Church in Aachen, see Bernhard Vollmer (ed.), *Volksopposition im Polizeistaat: Gestapo und Regierungsberichte 1934 bis 1936* (Stuttgart, 1957); for Baden, see Jörg Schadt (ed.), *Verfolgung und Wider-*

stand unter dem Nationalsozialismus in Baden: Die Lageberichte der Gestapo und des Generalstaatsanwalts Karlsruhe 1933–1940 (Stuttgart, 1975).

66. Heinz Boberach (ed.), *Berichte des SD und der Gestapo über Kirchen und Kirchenvolk in Deutschland 1934–1944* (Mainz, 1971): 'Lageberichte des Chefs des Sicherheitsamtes des Reichsführers SS, Mai/Juni 1934', 3–63, at 25–31; ibid.: 'Das katholische Vereinswesen: Die Organisation der katholischen Jugendvereine. Sonderbericht des Chefs des Sicherheitshauptamtes des Reichsführers SS, September 1935', 118–51 (quote at 125); ibid.: 'Lagebericht der Zentralabteilung II/1 des Sicherheitshauptamtes des Reichsführers SS für Januar 1938', 274–8.

67. Steinweis, *Art*, 137–8.

68. Dieter Albrecht (ed.), *Der Notenwechsel zwischen dem Heiligen Stuhl und der deutschen Reichsregierung* (3 vols., Mainz, 1965–80), I: *Von der Ratifizierung des Reichskonkordats bis zur Enzyklika 'Mit brennender Sorge'*, esp. 6 (Denkschrift des erzbischöflichen Ordinariats München-Freising, 2 October 1933), 3–8, 37–44 and reply by German government 15 January 1934, (Promemoria des Heiligen Stuhls an die deutsche Reichsregierung 31 January 1934), 47–72, etc..

69. Ibid., 61.

70. Witetschek (ed.), *Die kirchliche Lage*, III: *Regierungsbezirk Schwaben* (Mainz, 1971), gives a particularly good impression of these myriad local struggles; see also Ziegler (ed.), *Die kirchliche Lage*, IV. xxxv; Edward N. Peterson, *The Limits of Hitler's Power* (Princeton, N.J., 1969), 301–4; and Ian Kershaw, *Popular Opinion and Political Dissent in the Third Reich: Bavaria 1933–1945* (Oxford, 1983), 185–223.

71. Both drafts of the Encyclical reprinted in Albrecht (ed.), *Der Notenwechsel*, I. 404–43.

72. Ibid., 410; contemporary English translation in *On the Condition of the Church in Germany* (London, 1937); see also Ernst C. Helmreich, *The German Churches under Hitler: Background, Struggle and Epilogue* (Detroit, Mich., 1979), 279–83; Conway, *The Nazi Persecution*, 164–7.

73. Albrecht (ed.), *Der Notenwechsel*, I. 421.

74. Ibid., II: *1937–1945*, response of German Aambassador to Pacelli, 12 April 1937 (1–5) and following correspondence; also Witetschek, *Die kirchliche Lage*, II. 166–71 (Monatsbericht der Regierung Ansbach, 6 April 1937).

75. Boberach (ed.), *Berichte* (Lagebericht der Zentralabteilung II/1 des Sicherheitshauptamtes des Reichsführers SS für Januar 1938), 274–8.

76. Edward D. R. Harrison, 'The Nazi Dissolution of the Monasteries: A Case-Study', *English Historical Review*, 109 (1994), 323–55; Witetschek (ed.), *Die Kirchliche Lage*, I. 244–6, 252–3, 299 (reports of Polizeidirektion 7 July 1937, 7 Aug. 1937, report of Regierung, 10 Nov. 1938).

77. Ulrich von Hehl *et al.* (eds.), *Priester unter Hitlers Terror: Eine biographische und statistische Erhebung* (2 vols., Mainz, 1996 [1984]).

78. *Völkischer Beobachter*, 212 (31 July 1935), 2; ibid., 337, Ausgabe A/Norddeutsche Ausgabe, Berlin, 3 December 1935, front page.

79. Ibid., 345, 11 December 1935, page 2; *Nachtausgabe*, 121, 26 May 1936.

80. *Berliner Morgenpost*, 102, 29 April 1937, front page; for priests and monks accused of sexual offences against young girls, see Ziegler (ed.), *Die kirchliche Lage*, IV. 173–5 (Monatsbericht der Regierung Regensburg, 8 December 1937).

81. *12-Uhr-Blatt*, Berlin, 102, 29 April 1937, front page.

82. Ibid., 128, 29 May 1937, front page.

83. Hans Günter Hockerts, *Die Sittlichkeitsprozesse gegen katholische Ordensangehörige und Priester 1936/37: Eine Studie zur nationalsozialistischen Herrschaftstechnik und zum Kirchenkampf* (Mainz, 1971), 78–112; quote from *Völkischer Beobachter*, 12 June 1936, at 91.

84. Quoted in Reuth, *Goebbels*, 361.

85. *12-Uhr-Blatt*, Berlin, 128, 29 May 1937, pages 1–2; *Nachtausgabe*, 122, 29 May 1937, page 3; *Völkischer Beobachter*, 159, 30 May 1937, pages 3–4; Hockerts, *Die Sittlichkeitsprozesse*, 113–18.

86. Conway, *The Nazi Persecution*, 168–91; Bertram quote at 179; Hockerts, *Die Sittlichkeitsprozesse*, 132–46. Broszat *et al.* (eds.), *Bayern*, I. 107.

87. *Völkischer Beobachter*, 145, 25 May 1937, page 3.

88. Conway, *The Nazi Persecution*, 168–95; Witetschek (ed.), *Die kirchliche Lage*, II. 300 n.2; George L. Mosse (ed.), *Nazi Culture: Intellectual, Cultural and Social Life in the Third Reich* (New York, 1975), 250–55, citing a list of complaints by the Confessing Church Bishop Theophil Wurm in Württemberg from June 1939, in Joachim Beckmann (ed.), *Kirchliches Jahrbuch für die evangelische Kirche in Deutschland 1933–1944* (Gütersloh, 1948), 343–7; Rolf Eilers, *Die nationalsozialistische Schulpolitik: Eine Studie zur Funktion der Erziehung im totalitären Staat* (Cologne, 1963), 22–8, 85–92 for statistics; good regional study by Franz Sonnenberger, 'Der neue "Kulturkampf". Die Gemeinschaftsschule und ihre historischen Voraussetzungen', in Broszat *et al.* (eds.), *Bayern*, III. 235–327.

89. Witetschek (ed.), *Die kirchliche Lage*, I: 283 (Monatsbericht der Regierung Oberbayern, 9 Dec. 1937).

90. Helmut Prantl (ed.), *Die kirchliche Lage in Bayern nach den Regierungspräsidentenberichten 1933–1945*, V: *Regierungsbezirk Pfalz 1933–1940* (Mainz, 1978), lv.

91. Ziegler (ed.), *Die kirchliche Lage*, IV, 201 (Monatsbericht der Regierung Regensburg, 8 June 1938).

92. Albrecht (ed.), *Der Notenwechsel*, II. *passim*.

93. Quoted in Conway, *The Nazi Persecution*, 216–17.

94. Ibid., 218–19; Kershaw, *The 'Hitler Myth'*, 105–20. For the village school-teacher as the leading force in the fight against the Church, led by the village priest, see the illuminating contemporary reports by the Nazi teachers' organization in Broszat *et al.* (eds.), *Bayern*, 1. 549–51.

95. Evans, *The Coming of the Third Reich*, 13–14; Denis Mack Smith, *Modern Italy: A Political History* (New Haven, 1997 [1959]), 83–5, 91–2, 200–201; Theodore Zeldin (ed.), *Conflicts in French Society: Anticlericalism, Education and Morals in the Nineteenth Century* (London, 1970).

96. Steigmann-Gall, *The Holy Reich*, 91–101.

97. For exaggerated claims of Rosenberg's influence, see for example Robert A. Pois, *National Socialism and the Religion of Nature* (London, 1986), esp. 42

98. Henry Picker, *Hitlers Tischgespräche im Führerhauptquartier 1941–42* (Bonn, 1951), 275 (11 April 1942); Fest, *The Face*, 254–5.

99. Reinhard Bollmus, 'Alfred Rosenberg: National Socialism's "Chief Ideologue"?' in Smelser and Zitelmann (eds.), *The Nazi Elite*, 183–93, at 187; and more generally, Harald Iber, *Christlicher Glaube oder rassischer Mythus: Die Auseinandersetzung der Bekennenden Kirche mit Alfred Rosenbergs 'Der Mythus des 20. Jahrhunderts'* (Frankfurt am Main, 1987), esp. 170–81; and Raimund Baumgärtner, *Weltanschauungskampf im Dritten Reich: Die Auseinandersetzung der Kirchen mit Alfred Rosenberg* (Mainz, 1977), esp. 106–34, 153.

100. Promemoria des Heiligen Stuhls an die Deutsche Reichsregierung, 13 May 1934, in Albrecht (ed.), *Der Notenwechsel*, 125–64, at 134–7, also quoted and translated in Conway, *The Nazi Persecution*, 109.

101. Johann Neuhäusler, *Kreuz und Hakenkreuz: Der Kampf des Nationalsozialismus gegen die katholische Kirche und der kirchliche Widerstand* (Munich, 1946), 251, cited in Mosse (ed.), *Nazi Culture*, 241.

102. Nuremberg document PS-3751, in Wulf, *Literatur*, 299–300. For further examples, see Gilmer W. Blackburn, *Education in the Third Reich: A Study of Race and History in Nazi Textbooks* (Albany, N.Y., 1985), 75–92, at 85.

103. Reck-Malleczewen, *Diary*, 33. For the somewhat questionable reliability of Reck's anecdotes, however, see below, 416.

104. Steigmann-Gall, *The Holy Reich*, 126–7; Albrecht (ed.), *Der Notenwechsel*, I. 134–7

105. Steigmann-Gall, *The Holy Reich*, 101–4.

106. Ackermann, *Heinrich Himmler*, 253–4; Bradley F. Smith and Agnes F. Peterson (eds.), *Heinrich Himmler-Geheimreden 1933–1945 und andere Ansprachen* (Frankfurt am Main, 1974), 160–61; Hans-Jochen Gamm, *Der braune Kult: Das Dritte Reich und seine Ersatzreligion: Ein Beitrag zur politischen Bildung* (Hamburg, 1962), esp. 78–89, 156–90; Manfred Ach and Clemens Pentrop (eds.), *Hitlers 'Religion': Pseudoreligiöse Elemente im nationalsozialistischen Sprachgebrauch* (Munich, 1991 [1979]).

107. Klein (ed.), *Die Lageberichte*, I. 195; (Übersicht der Staatspolizeistelle Kassel über die politische Lage im November 1934); Steigmann-Gall, *The Holy Reich*, 222.

108. Ibid., 87–91.

109. Ibid., 219–28.

110. Ibid., 230–40.

111. Conway, *The Nazi Persecution*, 213–22; Heike Kreutzer, *Das Reichskirchenministerium im Gefüge der nationalsozialistischen Herrschaft* (Düsseldorf, 2000), esp. 100–130.

112. Gailus, *Protestantismus*, 664–6.

113. Detlef Garbe, *Zwischen Widerstand und Martyrium: Die Zeugen Jehovas im 'Dritten Reich'* (Munich, 1993); Michael H. Kater, 'Die ernsten Bibelforscher im Dritten Reich', *VfZ* 17 (1969), 181–218; Zeidler, *Das Sondergericht Freiberg*, 49–55; Gerhard Hetzer, 'Ernste Bibelforscher in Augsburg', in Broszat *et al.* (eds.), *Bayern*, IV. 621–43. There is a good local study in Walter Struve, *Aufstieg und Herrschaft des Nationalsozialismus in einer industriellen Kleinstadt: Osterode am Harz 1918–1945* (Essen, 1992), 242–74.

114. Wachsmann, *Hitler's Prisons*, 125–8; Hans-Ulrich Ludewig and Dietrich Kuessner, *'Es sei also jeder gewarnt': Das Sondergericht Braunschweig 1933–1945* (Braunschweig, 2000), 89–90.

115. Hans-Eckhard Niermann, *Die Durchsetzung politischer und politisierter Strafjustiz im Dritten Reich* (Düsseldorf, 1995), 295–305; Schmidt, *'Beabsichtige ich, die Todesstrafe zu beantragen'*, 105–7; Wachsmann, *Hitler's Prisons*, 180–83.

116. Höss, *Commandant*, 94–8, 151–2.

117. Ribbe (ed.), *Die Lageberichte*, 230 (Lagebericht der Staatspolizeistelle Potsdam für Februar 1935).

118. Höhne, *The Order*, 131–6; Ackermann, *Heinrich Himmler*, 253–4; Steigmann-Gall, *The Holy Reich*, 120, 122, 132, 149–53. For Hitler's views on Himmler's religious ideas, see Speer, *Inside*, 94–5, 122. For public disquiet over the 'SS's alleged hostility to Christianity', see Ribbe (ed.), *Die Lageberichte*, 429 (Lagebericht der Staatspolizeistelle Potsdam für den Monat Februar 1936). See also Wolfgang Dierker, ' "Niema's Jesuiten, Niema's Sektierer": Die Religionspolitik des SD 1933–1941', in Michael Wildt (ed.), *Nachrichtendienst, politische Elite, Mordeinheit: Der Sicherheitsdienst des Reichsführers SS* (Hamburg, 2003), 86–117.

119. Domarus, *Hitler*, III. 1,145–7 (translation amended).

120. Klaus Vondung, *Magie und Manipulation: Ideologischer Kult und politische Religion des Nationalsozialismus* (Göttingen, 1971); Eric Voegelin, *The New Science of Politics: An Introduction* (Chicago, 1952); James M. Rhodes, *The Hitler Movement: A Modern Millenarian Revolution* (Stanford, 1980); Uriel Tal, *Structures of German 'Political Theology' in the Nazi Era* (Tel Aviv, 1979); Claus-Ekkehard Bärsch, *Die politische Religion des Nationalsozialismus: Die religiöse Dimension der NS-Ideologie in den Schriften von Dietrich Eckart, Joseph Goebbels, Alfred Rosenberg und Adolf Hitler* (Munich, 1998); Michael Ley and Julius H. Schoeps (eds.), *Der Nationalsozialismus als politische Religion* (Bodenheim, 1997); Hans Maier, *Politische Religionen: Die totalitären Regime und das Christentum* (Freiburg, 1995).

121. Numerous examples in Blackburn, *Education*, chapter 4 ('The Secular Religious Character of National Socialist History', 75–92); for a contemporary comment on the use of religious language in relation to Hitler, see Klemperer, *I Shall Bear Witness*, 39 (11 November 1933).

122. Domarus (ed.), *Hitler*, II. 833.

123. Gailus, *Protestantismus*, 664–5; Kershaw, *The 'Hitler Myth'*, 106–8.

124. Philippe Burrin, 'Political Religion. The Relevance of a Concept', *History and Memory*, 9 (1997), 321–49, provides more examples of religious language in Nazi rhetoric, but passes over too easily Hitler's hostility to the revival of pseudo-Germanic paganism: Richard Steigmann-Gall, 'Was National Socialism a Political Religion or a Religious Politics?', in Michael Geyer and Hartmut Lehmann (eds.), *Religion und Nation: Nation und Religion. Beiträge zu einer unbewältigten Geschichte* (Göttingen, 2004), 386–408, provides further examples of the hostility of many leading Nazis to paganist pseudo-religion.

125. George L. Mosse, *The Nationalization of the Masses: Political Symbolism and Mass Movements in Germany from the Napoleonic Wars through the Third Reich* (New York, 1975), esp. 207–17.

126. Blackburn, *Education*, 87.

127. Detlev J. K. Peukert, 'The Genesis of the "Final Solution" from the Spirit of Science', in Thomas Childers and Jane Caplan (eds.), *Reevaluating the Third Reich* (New York, 1993), 234–52.

128. 'Aus dem Jahresbericht des Direktors der Grossen Stadtschule (Gymnasium und Oberrealschule) zu Wismar über das Schuljahr 1933/34', no. 105 in Joachim S. Hohmann and Hermann Langer (eds.), *'Stolz, ein Deutscher zu sein...' Nationales Selbstverständnis in Schulaufsätzen 1914–1945* (Frankfurt am Main, 1995), 208.

129. Ibid., 226, no. 118: 'Adolf Hitler als Knabe: Aus dem Schreibheft von A. Sch., Weingarten, o.J.'.

130. Ibid., 257, no. 142: 'Waren unsere germanischen Vorfahren Barbaren? Aufsatz des Schülers M. K., Volksschule Tiefensee, 22. September 1937'.

131. Ibid., 276–7, no. 156: 'Totengedenken. Aufsatzentwurf des 14jährigen Schülers M. K., Volksschule Tiefensee, vom November 1938'.

132. Behnken (ed.), *Deutschland-Berichte*, II (1935), 203.

133. Hohmann and Langer (eds.), *'Stolz'*, 270–71, no. 153: 'Die Judenfrage ist eine Rassenfrage. Aufsatzentwurf von M. K., Schüler der 8. Klasse an der Volksschule in Tiefensee, Kreis Eilenburg, 1938'; further examples of schoolwork from this period in Dieter Rossmeissl, *'Ganz Deutschland wird zum Führer halten...' Zur politischen Erziehung in den Schulen des Dritten Reiches* (Frankfurt am Main, 1985), 110–66.

134. Blackburn, *Education*, 34–74; Mosse (ed.), *Nazi Culture* 283–4, citing *The Times* (London), 29 January 1935. See also Kurt-Ingo Flessau, *Schule der Diktatur: Lehrpläne und Schulbücher des Nationalsozialismus* (Munich, 1977), 59–62, 76–82.

135. Hohmann and Langer, *'Stolz'*, 209; Eilers, *Die nationalsozialistische Schulpolitik*, 13–15.

136. Illustration reproduced in Lisa Pine, *Nazi Family Policy, 1933–1945* (Oxford, 1997), 59; see more generally Rossmeissl, *'Ganz Deutschland'*, 171–80.

137. *Deutsches Lesebuch für Volksschulen: Fünftes und sechstes Schuljahr* (Braunschweig, n.d.), 365–6, quoted in Mosse (ed.), *Nazi Culture*, 291–3.

138. Franz Pöggeler, 'Politische Inhalte in Fibeln und Lesebüchern des "Dritten

Reiches"', in Joachim S. Hohmann (ed.), *Erster Weltkrieg und Nationalsozialistische 'Bewegung' im deutschen Lesebuch 1933–1945* (Frankfurt am Main, 1988), 75–104.

139. For an example of such an illustration from a schoolbook, see Hohmann and Langer, *'Stolz'*, 234; also Lisa Pine, 'The Dissemination of Nazi Ideology and Family Values through School Textbooks', *History of Education*, 25 (1996), 91–110; and illustrations in eadem, *Nazi Family Policy*, 61–3.

140. Sylvelin Wissmann, *Es war eben unsere Schulzeit: Das Bremer Volksschulwesen unter dem Nationalsozialismus* (Bremen, 1993), 52; more generally, see Eilers, *Die nationalsozialistische Schulpolitik*, 28–30, and Flessau, *Schule der Diktatur*, 66–73.

141. Behnken (ed.), *Deutschland-Berichte*, III (1936), 197–8. For official directives, see Margarete Götz, *Die Grundschule in der Zeit des Nationalsozialismus: Eine Untersuchung der inneren Ausgestaltung der vier unteren Jahrgänge der Volksschule auf der Grundlage amtlicher Massnahmen* (Bad Heilbrunn, 1997), esp. 40–140. For the use of unofficial Nazi pamphlets and teaching materials distributed in schools before officially revised textbooks were issued, see Benjamin Ortmeyer, *Schulzeit unterm Hitlerbild. Analysen, Berichte, Dokumente* (Frankfurt am Main, 1996), 50–54; more generally, see Joachim Trapp, *Kölner Schulen in der NS-Zeit* (Cologne, 1994), 1–112.

142. Kurt-Ingo Flessau, 'Schulen der Partei(lichkeit)? Notizen zum allgemeinbildenden Schulwesen des Dritten Reichs', in idem *et al.* (eds.), *Erziehung im Nationalsozialismus: '. . . und sie werden nicht mehr frei ihr ganzes Leben!'* (Cologne, 1987), 65–82; idem, *Schule der Diktatur*, 13–20; Wissmann, *Es war eben unsere Schulzeit*, 162, 193, for posters and noticeboards; Eilers, *Die nationalsozialistische Schulpolitik*, 31–7: the showing of films in schools became the subject of a typical Nazi power-struggle between the Propaganda Ministry and the Education Ministry (ibid., 32). School radio had little importance at this time (ibid., 32–33). For festivals, see Rossmeissl, *'Ganz Deutschland'*, 69–76.

143. Wolfgang Keim, *Erziehung unter der Nazi-Diktatur*, II: *Kriegsvorbereitung, Krieg und Holocaust* (Darmstadt, 1997), 34–56; Reinhard Dithmar, 'Literaturunterricht und Kriegserlebnis im Spiegel der nationalsozialistischen Programmatik', in Hohmann (ed.), *Erster Weltkrieg*, 54–74; Roland Schopf, 'Von Nibelungentreue, Märtyrertod und verschwörerischer Verschwiegenheit', in ibid., 194–214; Eilers, *Die nationalsozialistische Schulpolitik*, 85–98.

144. Norbert Hopster and Ulrich Nassen, *Literatur und Erziehung im Nationalsozialismus: Deutschunterricht als Körperkultur* (Paderborn, 1983), 31–40; Flessau, *Schule der Diktatur*, 58–9.

145. Ibid., 140–43.

146. Ortmeyer, *Schulzeit*, 55–78, for the Nazification of a variety of subjects; also Geert Platner (ed.), *Schule im Dritten Reich: Erziehung zum Tod? Eine Dokumentation* (Munich, 1983), 42–54 and 246–55, for racism, and 55–62 and 203–45, for militarism.

147. Flessau, *Schule der Diktatur*, 82–4, 143–54.

148. Cited in Behnken (ed.), *Deutschland-Berichte*, VI (1939), 329; examples also in Wissmann, *Es war eben unsere Schulzeit*, 59–69.

149. Franz Schnass, *Nationalpolitische Heimat- und Erdkunde* (Osterwieck am Harz, 1938), esp. 54–5; Bruno Plache, *Das Raumgefüge der Welt. Erdkundebuch für Schulen mit höheren Lehrzielen*, I: *Deutschland* (Göttingen, 1939), esp. 2. Hans-Günther Bracht, *Das höhere Schulwesen im Spannungsfeld von Demokratie und Nationalsozialismus: Ein Beitrag zur Kontinuitätsdebatte am Beispiel der preussischen Aufbauschule* (Frankfurt am Main, 1998), 603–17, overstresses the resistance of this subject to reframing in terms of Nazi ideology.

150. Flessau, *Schule der Diktatur*, 82–3.

151. Henning Heske, '... *und morgen die ganze Welt ...' Erdkundeunterricht im Nationalsozialismus* (Giessen, 1988), 188–250; examples include Ekkehart Staritz, *Deutsches Volk und deutscher Raum: Vom alten Germanien zum Dritten Reich* (Berlin, 1938), and Friedrich W. Schaafhausen, *Das Auslandsdeutschtum* (Cologne, 1934). For a good summary of Nazi teaching, see Margret Kraul, *Das deutsche Gymnasium 1780–1980* (Frankfurt am Main, 1984), 157–65.

152. Flessau, *Schule der Diktatur*, 99, 138–9.

153. Karl August Eckhardt, *Die Grundschulausbildung* (Dortmund, 1938), 90.

154. Platner (ed.), *Schule*, 121–3. However, the reminiscences of many well-known Germans printed in this collection, such as the later Federal Chancellor Helmut Kohl (82–3), underestimate in retrospect the extent to which the schools became permeated by racism and militarism in this period; the textbook extracts reproduced later in the book (203–65) provide an implicit corrective.

155. Trapp, *Kölner Schulen*, 39–40, 51–5.

156. 'Six Years Education in Nazi Germany', by an anonymous author, written in 1945 or 1946; typescript in the Leonard Nachlass, Box 12, Folder 'Englische Untersuchungen ueber die Deutschen zu verschiedenen Fragen der Schulpolitik', Georg-Eckert Institut für Schulbuchforschung, Braunschweig. I am grateful to Riccarda Torriani for supplying me with a copy of this document.

157. See Bracht, *Das höhere Schulwesen*, for a good account of the balance of freedom and compulsion in the teaching situation in one larger school. Hermann Schnorbach (ed.), *Lehrer und Schule unterm Hakenkreuz: Dokumente des Widerstands von 1930 bis 1945* (Königstein im Taunus, 1983), is remarkable for its lack of any documents on resistance by schoolteachers and their pupils in the Third Reich. See also Michael H. Kater, *Hitler Youth* (Cambridge, Mass., 2004), 42–4, about the growing politicization and compliance of teachers. For Jewish pupils, see below, 562–3.

158. Eilers, *Die nationalsozialistische Schulpolitik*, 66–9 (numbers at 68 n. 140).

159. Wolfgang Wippermann, 'Das Berliner Schulwesen in der NS-Zeit. Fragen, Thesen und methodische Bemerkungen', in Benno Schmoldt (ed.), *Schule in Berlin: Gestern und heute* (Berlin, 1989), 57–73, at 61–3; and Michael Burleigh and

Wolfgang Wippermann, *The Racial State: Germany 1933–1945* (Cambridge, 1991), 208, drawing on this article and other local history sources.

160. Eilers, *Die nationalsozialistische Schulpolitik*, 98–9.

161. Ibid., 3–6, 69–75.

162. Ibid., 6, 72–5, 76–85; Willi Feiten, *Der nationalsozialistische Lehrerbund: Entwicklung und Organisation: Ein Beitrag zum Aufbau und zur Organisationsstruktur des nationalsozialistischen Herrschaftssystems* (Weinheim, 1981), 177–84 (numbers at 181); Wolfgang Keim, *Erziehung unter der Nazi-Diktatur*, I: *Antidemokratische Potentiale, Machtantritt und Machtdurchsetzung* (Darmstadt, 1995), 97–112. Schemm died in 1935 and his successor Wächtler amended the foundation date retrospectively from 1927 to 1929, since it was only at the latter time that he himself had joined. See Schnorbach (ed.), *Lehrer und Schule*, 26–7; Behnken (ed.), *Deutschland-Berichte*, IV (1937), 874–5; and Trapp, *Kölner Schulen*, 28–47.

163. Behnken (ed.), *Deutschland-Berichte*, II (1935), 203; Wilfried Breyvogel and Thomas Lohmann, 'Schulalltag im Nationalsozialismus', in Peukert and Reulecke (eds.), *Die Reihen fast geschlossen* 199–221, at 215–16.

164. Breyvogel and Lohmann, 'Schulalltag', 216–18; examples of corporal punishment in Behnken (ed.), *Deutschland-Berichte*, II (1935), 208–9.

165. Broszat *et al.*, *Bayern* I. 543 ('Bericht NSLB, Kreis Garmisch-Partenkirchen, Gau München-Oberbayern', 2 June 1938); Trapp, *Kölner Schulen*, 39.

166. Broszat *et al.* (eds.), *Bayern*, II. 531–2.

167. Behnken (ed.), *Deutschland-Berichte*, II (1935), 205–12, and III (1936), 205–7, probably overestimating the extent of principled teacher opposition to the regime. Further comments on declining teacher numbers in ibid., VI (1939), 322–6.

168. Official statistics, excerpted and commented, in ibid., VI (1939), 319–20;

169. Ibid., I (1934), 580.

170. Ibid., III (1936), 190–2

171. Ibid., VI (1939), 321.

172. Ibid., I (1934), 568.

173. Ibid., II (1935), 202; Wissmann, *Es war eben unsere Schulzeit*, 173.

174. Behnken (ed.) *Deutschland-Berichte*, IV (1937), 1,048–9; Rossmeissl, *'Ganz Deutschland'*, 47–50.

175. Eilers, *Die nationalsozialistische Schulpolitik*, 54–66.

176. Behnken (ed.), *Deutschland-Berichte*, I (1934), 567–74.

177. Ibid., III (1936), 192.

178. Kater, *Hitler Youth*, 16; Arno Klönne, *Jugend im Dritten Reich: Die Hitler-Jugend und ihre Gegner* (Cologne, 1999 [1982]), 33–4. For an example of an essay on the subject of 'Warum bin ich nicht in der Hitlerjugend?' from 25 April 1934, see Hohmann and Langer (eds.), *'Stolz'*, 222–3 (no. 113: Aufsatz von M.S.: the student promised to join forthwith).

179. Klönne, *Jugend*, 15–42, table of membership on 33 (figures for 1939 include

Austria and the Sudetenland). For days off school, see Behnken (ed.), *Deutschland-Berichte*, I (1934), 552, and Trapp, *Kölner Schulen*, 67–72 (also for refusal of leaving certificate). On the Hitler Youth, see most recently Kater, *Hitler Youth*.

180. See Hubert Steinhaus, *Hitlers pädagogische Maximen: 'Mein Kampf' und die Destruktion der Erziehung im Nationalsozialismus* (Frankfurt am Main, 1981), 65–75, and Flessau, *Schule der Diktatur*, 22–31.

181. Hitler, *Mein Kampf*, 380, 383, 389.

182. Karl Christoph Lingelbach, *Erziehung und Erziehungstheorien im national-sozialistischen Deutschland: Ursprünge und Wandlungen der 1933–1945 in Deutschland vorherrschenden erziehungstheoretischen Strömungen; ihre polit-ischen Funktionen und ihr Verhältnis zur ausserschulischen Erziehungspraxis des 'Dritten Reiches'* (Frankfurt am Main, 1987 [1970]), 25–33, 65–80, 162–87; Ernst Hojer, *Nationalsozialismus und Pädagogik: Umfeld und Entwicklung der Pädagogik Ernst Kriecks* (Würzburg, 1996), 5–33 (on Hitler).

183. Domarus (ed.), *Hitler*, II. 701 (14 Sept. 1935); additional lines.

184. Behnken (ed.), *Deutschland-Berichte*, III (1936), 1,316.

185. Klönne, *Jugend*, 57–62.

186. Quoted in Behnken (ed.), *Deutschland-Berichte*, V (1938), 1,361.

187. Ibid., 1,362

188. Ibid., I (1934), 554.

189. Klönne, *Jugend* 133–4; for a good example; see also Hermann Graml, 'Integration und Entfremdung: Inanspruchnahme durch Staatsjugend und Dienstp-flicht', in Ute Benz and Wolfgang Benz (eds.), *Sozialisation und Traumatisierung: Kinder in der Zeit des Nationalsozialismus* (Frankfurt am Main, 1992), 70–79, at 74–9.

190. Maschmann, *Account Rendered*, 19–20.

191. Ibid., 27–8; see more generally Dagmar Resse, 'Bund Deutscher Mädel – Zur Geschichte der weiblichen deutschen Jugend im Dritten Reich', in Frauengruppe Faschismusforschung (ed.), *Mutterkreuz und Arbeitsbuch: Zur Geschichte der Frauen in der Weimarer Republik und im Nationalsozialismus* (Frankfurt am Main, 1981), 163–87.

192. Behnken (ed.), *Deutschland-Berichte*, I (1934), 554; more generally, see Klönne, *Jugend*, 121–7.

193. Behnken (ed.), *Deutschland-Berichte*, I (1934), 555.

194. Ibid., III (1936), 1,313–4; personal reminiscences to the same effect in Hans Siemsen, *Die Geschichte des Hitlerjungen Adolf Goer* (Düsseldorf, 1947), 49.

195. Behnken (ed.), *Deutschland-Berichte*, IV (1937), 842–4.

196. Klönne, *Jugend*, 57; Rossmeissl, '*Ganz Deutschland*', 77–89 (for collections).

197. Behnken (ed.), *Deutschland-Berichte*, I (1934), 556–7.

198. See already Reichsjugendführung (ed.), *HJ im Dienst: Ausbildungsvorschrift für die Ertüchtigung der deutschen Jugend* (Berlin, 1935).

199. Baldur von Schirach, *Die Hitler-Jugend: Idee und Gestalt* (Leipzig, 1938 [1934]), 57–65.

200. Behnken (ed.), *Deutschland-Berichte*, I (1934), 559–60; ibid., II (1935), 219–20; ibid., III (1936), 1,314–16, 1,323; more examples in ibid., IV (1937), 839–42; more examples of brutality in Kater, *Hitler Youth*, 30–31.

201. Behnken (ed.), *Deutschland-Berichte*, V (1938), 1,366.

202. Ibid., 1,378, 1,391–2.

203. Ibid.; also ibid., III (1936), 1,324–6; and 'Six Years Education in Nazi Germany', 4 (n. 156, above).

204. Behnken (ed.), *Deutschland-Berichte*, V (1938), 1,379.

205. Kurt Hass (ed.), *Jugend unterm Schicksal – Lebensberichte junger Deutscher 1946–1949* (Hamburg, 1950), 61–2, cited in Klönne, *Jugend*, 142–3.

206. Karl-Heinz Janssen, 'Eine Welt brach zusammen', in Hermann Glaser and Axel Silenius (eds.), *Jugend im Dritten Reich* (Frankfurt am Main, 1975), 88–90.

207. Behnken (ed.), *Deutschland-Berichte*, V (1938), 1,391.

208. Ibid., V (1938), 1,403.

209. Ibid., III (1936) 1,320–22; Kater, *Hitler Youth*, 38, for an example of a Hitler Youth member denouncing his father to the Gestapo for criticizing Hitler.

210. Schirach, *Die Hitler-Jugend*, 104.

211. Behnken (ed.), *Deutschland-Berichte*, V (1938), 1,403–5.

212. Ibid., III (1936), 1,322–3; for a similar example, see Klemperer, *I Shall Bear Witness*, 195 (31 December 1936).

213. Behnken (ed.), *Deutschland-Berichte*, I (1934), 564–6.

214. Ibid., V (1938), 1,392, 1,395, 1,398–1,400; further examples in ibid., II (1935), 692–4.

215. Ibid., V (1938), 1,396; ibid., III (1936) 1,317–19, for further sexual scandals; also Siemsen, *Die Geschichte*, 172–3.

216. Kater, *Hitler Youth*, 61–2, 151–2.

217. Behnken (ed.), *Deutschland-Berichte*, IV (1937), 845.

218. Ibid., IV (1937), 836, also 876–7; more generally, Daniel B. Horn, 'The Hitler Youth and Educational Decline in the Third Reich', *History of Education Quarterly*, 16 (1976), 425–47.

219. Wissmann, *Es war eben unsere Schulzeit*, 52.

220. Michael Zimmermann, 'Ausbruchshoffnungen: Junge Bergleute in den dreissiger Jahren', in Niethammer (ed.), *'Die Jahre weiss man nicht'*, 97–132, at 99–100.

221. Boberach (ed.), *Meldungen*, II. 286 (Vierteljahreslagebericht 1939 des Sicherheitshauptamtes).

222. Behnken (ed.), *Deutschland-Berichte*, I (1934), 574; Eilers, *Die nationalsozialistische Schulpolitik*, 121–6. See also, more generally, Ortmeyer, *Schulzeit*, 61–4, and Rossmeissl, *'Ganz Deutschland'*, 54–7.

223. Trapp, *Kölner Schulen*, 39.

224. Eilers, *Die nationalsozialistische Schulpolitik*, 50–54, 111–14; Behnken (ed.), *Deutschland-Berichte*, VI (1939), 332.

225. Ibid., 313–14; Trapp, *Kölner Schulen*, 113–15.

226. Harald Scholtz, *NS-Ausleseschulen: Internatsschulen als Herrschaftsmittel des Führerstaates* (Göttingen, 1973), 29–49, 57–69; Eilers, *Die nationalsozialistische Schulpolitik*, 41–2.

227. Elke Fröhlich, 'Die drei Typen der nationalsozialistischen Ausleseschulen', in Johannes Leeb (ed.), *'Wir waren Hitlers Eliteschüler': Ehemalige Zöglinge der NS-Ausleseschulen brechen ihr Schweigen* (Hamburg, 1998), 192–210, at 194–6 and 200.

228. Ibid., 201; Behnken (ed.), *Deutschland-Berichte*, V (1938), 1,386.

229. Fröhlich, 'Die drei Typen', 196–7.

230. Scholtz, *NS-Ausleseschulen*, 69; Horst Ueberhorst (ed.), *Elite für die Diktatur: Die Nationalpolitischen Erziehungsanstalten 1933–1945: Ein Dokumentarbericht* (Düsseldorf, 1969); see also the reminiscences in Leeb (ed.), *'Wir waren'*, 19–21, 76–7.

231. Fröhlich, 'Die drei Typen', 202–3; Kraul, *Das deutsche Gymnasium*, 173–6, emphasizes the ambivalent situation of the Napolas, between elite school and indoctrination centre. See also Stefan Baumeister, *NS-Führungskader. Rekrutierung und Ausbildung bis zum Beginn des Zweiten Weltkriegs 1933–1939* (Konstanz, 1997), 22–47. Kater, *Hitler Youth*, 52, somewhat exaggerates their effectiveness; on this, see also Christian Schneider *et al.*, *Das Erbe der NAPOLA: Versuch einer Generationengeschichte des Nationalsozialismus* (Hamburg, 1996), esp. 33–91, 189–92.

232. Eilers, *Die nationalsozialistische Schulpolitik*, 112.

233. Scholtz, *NS-Ausleseschulen*, 162–80; Kraul, *Das deutsche Gymnasium*, 176–8.

234. Behnken (ed.), *Deutschland-Berichte*, V (1938), 1,387; Eilers, *Die nationalsozialistische Schulpolitik*, 46–7.

235. Scholtz, *NS-Ausleseschulen*, 245.

236. Eilers, *Die nationalsozialistische Schulpolitik*, 47; Fröhlich, 'Die drei Typen', 203–7; Baumeister, *NS-Führungskader*, 48–66; see also Kater, *Hitler Youth*, 48–51.

237. Behnken (ed.), *Deutschland-Berichte*, V (1938), 1,387–8.

238. Eilers, *Die nationalsozialistische Schulpolitik*, 48–9; Baumeister, *NS-Führungskader*, 67–76.

239. Hans-Dieter Arntz, *Ordensburg Vogelsang 1934–1945: Erziehung zur politischen Führung im Dritten Reich* (Euskirchen, 1986), 104, 180–82.

240. Hardy Krüger, 'Von der Ordensburg nach Babelsberg', in Leeb (ed.), *'Wir waren'*, 49–55.

241. Fröhlich, 'Die drei Typen', 208–10; Baumeister, *NS-Führungskader*, 81–5; Scholtz, *NS-Ausleseschulen*, 299–324.

242. Baumeister, *NS-Führungskader*, 88–90; Scholtz, *NS-Ausleseschulen*, 288.

243. Eilers, *Die nationalsozialistische Schulpolitik*, 21–2.

244. Industrie- und Handelskammer Saarbrücken, cited in Behnken (ed.), *Deutschland-Berichte*, VI (1939), 317, with further examples.

245. Hans Schemm, *Hans Schemm spricht: Seine Reden und sein Werk* (Bayreuth, 1941 [1945]), 243–7, cited in Mosse (ed.), *Nazi Culture*, 282–3; also Behnken (ed.), *Deutschland-Berichte*, IV (1937), 868–9; ibid., 1,051–4.

246. Ibid., I (1934), 575.

247. Trapp, *Kölner Schulen*, 67, 12–23.

248. Behnken (ed.), *Deutschland-Berichte*, IV (1937), 866.

249. Ibid., IV (1937), 878.

250. 'Aus Tätigkeitsbericht des NSLB, Gau Mainfranken, Fachschaft II (Höhere Schulen), für das 2. und 3. Vierteljahr 1937', in Broszat *et al.* (eds.), *Bayern*, I. 542–3.

251. Behnken (ed.), *Deutschland-Berichte*, IV (1937), 834. See also Georg Schwingl, *Die Pervertierung der Schule im Nationalsozialismus: Ein Beitrag zum Begriff 'Totalitäre Erziehung'* (Regensburg, 1993), 159–64 ('Schule als vormilitärische Institution').

252. Michael Grüttner, *Studenten im Dritten Reich* (Paderborn, 1995), 87–92; Hellmut Seier, 'Der Rektor als Führer. Zur Hochschulpolitik des Reichserziehungsministeriums 1934–1945', *VfZ* 12 (1964), 105–46. For Hitler's speech, see Domarus (ed.), *Hitler*, II. 744. Traditionally, the Rectorship had been more a ceremonial than an executive office: see for example Frank Golczewski, *Kölner Universitätslehrer und der Nationalsozialismus: Personengeschichtliche Ansätze* (Cologne, 1988), 248–60.

253. Quoted in Grüttner, *Studenten*, 93.

254. Ibid., 94–100. For the earlier history of the National Socialist German Students' League, see Evans, *The Coming of the Third Reich*, 214–15, 429–31.

255. Grüttner, *Studenten*, 1–2; see also, more generally, Michael S. Steinberg, *Sabers and Brown Shirts: The German Students' Path to National Socialism, 1918–1935* (Chicago, 1977), 72–103.

256. Grüttner, *Studenten*, 245–59, quote on 254; see also Geoffrey J. Giles, *Students and National Socialism in Germany* (Princeton, N.J., 1985), 136–50.

257. Grüttner, *Studenten*, 259–60, 324.

258. Ibid., 287–316, quote on 307; Helma Brunck, *Die Deutsche Burschenschaft in der Weimarer Republik und im Nationalsozialismus* (Munich, 1999), esp. 330–59; Friedhelm Golücke (ed.), *Korporationen und Nationalsozialismus* (Schernfeld, 1989); Michael Grüttner, 'Die Korporationen und der Nationalsozialismus', in Harm-Hinrich Brandt and Matthias Stickler (eds.), 'Der Burschen Herrlichkeit'. *Geschichte und Gegenwart des studentischen Korporationswesens* (Würzburg, 1998), 125–43; Steinberg, *Sabers*, 154–72; Giles, *Students*, 175–86; Rosco G. S. Weber, *The German Student Corps in the Third Reich* (London, 1986), 102–69 (informative, but somewhat exaggerating the dimensions of the fraternities' resistance to Nazism). The fraternities dissolved also included non-duelling Catholic groups: see Hans Jürgen Rösgen, *Die Auflösung der katholischen Studentenverbände im Dritten Reich* (Bochum, 1995), esp. 105–46.

259. Grüttner, *Studenten*, 101–2, 487. In these and the following statistics, the 1939 figures are for the *Altreich*, i.e. not including Austria and the annexed part of Czechoslovakia, and are rounded off to the nearest thousand, or whole percentage.

260. Ibid., 126–35, 490.

261. Eilers, *Nationalsozialistische Schulpolitik*, 18–21.

262. Grüttner, *Studenten*, 491 and 109–26; Irmgard Weyrather, 'Numerus Clausus für Frauen – Studentinnen im Nationalsozialismus', in Frauengruppe Faschismusforschung (ed.), *Mutterkreuz*, 131–62; Jill Stephenson, *Women in Nazi Society* (London, 1975), 130–46.

263. Grüttner, *Studenten*, 102–3; Norbert Wenning, 'Das Gesetz gegen die Über-füllung deutscher Schulen und Hochschulen vom 25. April 1933 – ein erfolgreicher Versuch der Bildungsbegrenzung?', *Die deutsche Schule*, 78 (1986), 141–60.

264. Domarus, *Hitler*, II. 1, 251–2; see also Wilhelm Treue, 'Rede Hitlers vor der deutschen Presse (10. November 1938)', *VfZ* 6 (1958), 175–91, reprinting the entire speech; *Völkischer Beobachter*, 10 November 1938 ('Adolf Hitlers Rede an Grossdeutschland').

265. See for a good example Peter Chroust, *Giessener Universität und Faschismus. Studenten und Hochschullehrer 1918–1945* (2 vols., Münster, 1994), I. 187.

266. Grüttner, *Studenten*, 104–9.

267. Ibid., 227–9, quote on 227–8.

268. Gerhard Szczesny, *Als die Vergangenheit Gegenwart war: Lebensanlauf eines Ostpreussen* (Berlin, 1990), 90, cited along with other, similar, reminiscences in Grüttner, *Studenten*, 230–31.

269. Ibid., 229–37.

270. Ibid., 260–71, 341–8.

271. Ibid., 317–31, quotes on 329 and 331; similar conclusions in Konrad H. Jarausch, *Deutsche Studenten 1800–1970* (Frankfurt am Main 1984), 197–8; and Geoffrey J. Giles, 'The Rise of the National Socialist Students' Association and the Failure of Political Education in the Third Reich', in Stachura (ed.), *The Shaping*, 160–85, at 180–81; see also Steinberg, *Sabers*, 141–53, and Giles, *Students*, 186–201.

272. 'Eine nötig gewordene Klarstellung', *Der Student in Mecklenburg-Lübeck*, 15 December 1936, 9, quoted in Grüttner, *Studenten*, 156.

273. Ibid., 155–67.

274. Ibid., 168–78, quote on 174, n. 99.

275. Ibid., 331–40.

276. Ibid. 178–93; quote on 174 n. 99.

277. For the view that Nazification was both wide and deep in German universities, see Steven P. Remy, *The Heidelberg Myth: The Nazification and Denazification of a German University* (Cambridge, Mass., 2002), 50–84; but his argument is based on a selective sample of the most Nazi professors and their research, an account of aspects of university life such as nominations for honorary degrees, the foundation of new research institutes, the editorship of journals and similar, ultimately secondary matters, and almost completely neglects teaching. It also treats widespread pre-Nazi conservative ideas as if they were imported into the

universities by the Nazis. See also Christian Jansen, *Professoren und Politik: Politisches Denken und Handeln der Heidelberger Hochschullehrer 1914–1935* (Göttingen, 1992), esp. 230–36, demonstrating the turn of Heidelberg's professors to the anti-Weimar but non-Nazi right in the period 1930–35.

278. Léon Poliakov and Josef Wulf, *Das Dritte Reich und seine Denker: Dokumente* (Berlin, 1959), 73; Wilhelm Ribhegge, *Geschichte der Universität Münster: Europa in Westfalen* (Münster, 1985), 194.

279. Golczewski, *Kölner Universitätslehrer*, 338–49.

280. Grüttner, *Studenten*, 198–205; Krieck quote on 204; Giles, *Students*, 151–62; see the attempt to draw a balance by Hellmut Seier, 'Nationalsozialistisches Wissenschaftsverständnis und Hochschulpolitik', in Leonore Siegele-Wenschkewitz and Gerda Stuchlik (eds.), *Hochschule und Nationalsozialismus: Wissenschaftsgeschichte und Wissenschaftsbetrieb als Thema der Zeitgeschichte* (Frankfurt am Main, 1990), 5–21.

281. Hans-Paul Höpfner, *Die Universität Bonn in Dritten Reich: Akademische Biographien unter nationalsocialistischer Herrschaft* (Bonn, 1999), 540–44.

282. Boberach (ed.), *Meldungen*, II. 83 (Jahreslagebericht 1938 des Sicherheitshauptamtes).

283. Alan D. Beyerchen, *Scientists under Hitler. Politics and the Physics Community in the Third Reich* (New Haven, Conn., 1977), 79–85.

284. Ibid., 85–102; quote (93) from Lenard's unpublished memoirs, cited in Charlotte Schmidt-Schönbeck, *300 Jahre Physik und Astronomie an der Kieler Universität* (Kiel, 1965), 119.

285. Beyerchen, *Scientists*, 103–16.

286. Grüttner, *Studenten*, 194–8; Beyerchen, *Scientists*, 116–40, 63–4; Werner Heisenberg, *Der Teil und das Ganze: Gespräche im Umkreis der Atomphysik* (Munich, 1969), 206–12; but see also Paul Forman, 'Physics and Beyond: Historiographic Doubts: Encounters and Conversations with Werner Heisenberg', *Science*, 172 (14 May, 1971), 687–8; and Steffen Richter, 'Die "Deutsche Physik"', in Herbert Mehrtens and Steffan Richter (eds.), *Naturwissenschaft, Technik und NS-Ideologie: Beiträge zur Wissenschaftsgeschichte des Dritten Reichs* (Frankfurt am Main, 1980), 116–41, emphasizes the political nature of Aryan physics and its failure to make any real contribution to scientific theory or experimentation.

287. Beyerchen, *Scientists*, 141–67.

288. Helmut Lindner, '"Deutsche" und "gegentypische" Mathematik. Zur Begründung einer "arteigenen Mathematik" im "Dritten Reich" durch Ludwig Bieberbach', in Mehrtens and Richter (eds.), *Naturwissenschaft*, 88–115, esp. 105–8.

289. Martin Bechstedt, '"Gestalthafte Atomlehre" – Zur "Deutschen Chemie" im NS-Staat', in ibid., 142–65; also Horst Remane, 'Conrad Weygand und die "Deutsche Chemie"', in Christoph Meinel and Peter Voswinckel (eds.), *Medizin, Naturwissenschaft, Technik und Nationalsozialismus. Kontinuitäten und Diskontinuitäten* (Stuttgart, 1994), 183–91.

290. Herbert Mehrtens, 'Entartete Wissenschaft? Naturwissenschaften und

Nationalsozialismus', in Siegele-Wenschkewitz and Stuchlik (eds.), *Hochschule und Nationalsozialismus*, 113–28.

291. Beyerchen, *Scientists*, 71–8; Remy, *The Heidelberg Myth*, 55–6; Horst Möller, 'Nationalsozialistische Wissenschaftsideologie', in Jörg Tröger (ed.), *Hochschule und Wissenschaft im Dritten Reich* (Frankfurt am Main, 1984), 65–76, esp. 74–6; and Klaus Hentschel (ed.), *Physics and National Socialism: An Anthology of Primary Sources* (Basle, 1996), 116–18 (reprinting an anonymous article from *Nature*, 136 (14 December 1935), 927–8, on 'Nazi-Socialism and International Science'.

292. Helmut Maier (ed.), *Rüstungsforschung im Nationalsozialismus: Organisation, Mobilisierung und Entgrenzung der Technikwissenschaften* (Göttingen, 2002), particularly useful on company research and development; idem, *Forschung als Waffe: Rüstungsforschung in der Kaiser-Wilhelm-Gesellschaft und das KWI für Metallforschung 1900 bis 1947* (Göttingen, 2005); Susanne Heim, *Kalorien, Kautschuk, Karrieren. Pflanzenzüchtung und landwirtschaftliche Forschung in Kaiser-Wilhelm-Instituten 1933–1945* (Göttingen, 2003); Herbert Mehrtens, 'Kollaborationsverhältnisse: Natur- und Technikwissenschaften im NS-Staat und ihre Historie', in Meinel and Voswinckel (eds.), *Medizin*, 13–32.

293. Kristie Macrakis, *Surviving the Swastika: Scientific Research in Nazi Germany* (New York, 1993), esp. 84–186, 199–205; John Gimbel, *Science, Technology and Reparations: Exploitation and Plunder in Postwar Germany* (Stanford, Calif., 1990), 22.

294. See in general Hartmut Lehmann and Otto Gerhard Oexle (eds.), *Nationalsozialismus in den Kulturwissenschaften* (2 vols., Göttingen, 2004).

295. Karen Schönwälder, *Historiker und Politik: Geschichtswissenschaft im Nationalsozialismus* (Frankfurt am Main, 1992), 75–88, quote at 77 and 311 n.85; Helmut Heiber, *Walter Frank und sein Reichsinstitut für Geschichte des neuen Deutschlands* (Stuttgart, 1966) for an extremely detailed account; Winfried Schulze, 'German Historiography from the 1930s to the 1950s', in Hartmut Lehmann and James Van Horn Melton (eds.), *Paths of Continuity: Central European Historiography from the 1930s to the 1950s* (Cambridge, 1994), 19–42, at 24–5; more detail in idem, *Deutsche Geschichtswissenschaft nach 1945* (Munich, 1989), esp. 31–45; see also Bernd Faulenbach, 'Tendenzen der Geschichtswissenschaft im "Dritten Reich"', in Renate Knigge-Tesche (ed.), *Berater der braunen Macht: Wissenschaft und Wissenschaftler im NS-Staat* (Frankfurt am Main, 1999), 26–52, esp. 36–7 and 45–7; Peter Lambert, 'From Antifascist to *Volkshistoriker*: *Demos* and *Ethnos* in the Political Thought of Fritz Rörig, 1921–45', in Stefan Berger *et al.* (eds.), *Writing National Histories: Western Europe Since 1800* (London, 1999), 137–49.

296. Schönwälder, *Historiker*, 87; see also the useful East German study (to be used with the usual reservations) by Hans Schleier, 'Die *Historische Zeitschrift* 1918–1943', in Joachim Streisand (ed.), *Studien über die deutsche Geschichtswissenschaft von 1871 bis 1945* (2 vols., Berlin, 1965, 1969), II. 251–302, and the

same author's more recent brief account, 'German Historiography under National Socialism: Dreams of a Powerful Nation-state and German *Volkstum* Come True', in Berger *et al.* (eds.), *Writing National Histories*, 176–88.

297. Schönwälder, *Historiker*, 85–6; Gerhard Ritter, 'Die deutschen Historikertage', *Geschichte in Wissenschaft und Unterricht*, 4 (1953), 513–21, at 517.

298. Boberach (ed.), *Meldungen*, II. 86 (Jahreslagebericht 1938 des Sicherheitshauptamtes).

299. See generally Ingo Haar, *Historiker im Nationalsozialismus: Deutsche Geschichtswissenschaft und der 'Volkstumskampf' im Osten* (Göttingen, 2002); Michael Burleigh, *Germany Turns Eastwards. A Study of* Ostforschung *in the Third Reich* (Cambridge, 1988); Christoph Klessmann, 'Osteuropaforschung und Lebensraumpolitik im Dritten Reich', in Peter Lundgreen (ed.), *Wissenschaft im Dritten Reich* (Frankfurt am Main, 1985), 350–83; Karl Ferdinand Werner, *Das NS-Geschichtsbild und die deutsche Geschichtswissenschaft* (Stuttgart, 1967), esp. 9–23.

300. James Van Horn Melton, 'Continuities in German Historical Scholarship, 1933–1960', in Lehmann and Melton (eds.), *Paths*, 1–18, at 5; Georg G. Iggers, 'Introduction', in idem (ed.), *The Social History of Politics: Critical Perspectives in West German Historical Writing since 1945* (Leamington Spa, 1985), 1–48, at 17. One of the very few to be dismissed in 1933 was Franz Schnabel, a liberal Catholic historian and author of a great, multi-volume history of nineteenth-century Germany (Lothar Gall, 'Franz Schnabel (1887–1966)', in Lehmann and Melton (eds.), *Paths*, 155–65).

301. Hans Rothfels, *Ostraum, Preussentum und Reichsgedenke: Historische Abhandlungen. Vorträge und Reden* (Leipzig, 1935), vi; Schönwälder, *Historiker*, 78–9, 91–104.

302. Ibid., 77–80. See also Peter Schöttler (ed.), *Geschichtsschreibung als Legitimationswissenschaft 1918–1945* (Frankfurt am Main, 1997); Willi Oberkrome, *Volksgeschichter: Methodische Innovation und völkische Ideologisierung in der deutschen Geschichtswissenschaft 1918–1945* (Göttingen, 1992), esp. 102–70; and Reinhard Kühnl, 'Reichsdeutsche Geschichtswissenschaft', in Tröger (ed.), *Hochschule*, 92–104.

303. Christoph Cornelissen, *Gerhard Ritter: Geschichtswissenschaft und Politik im 20. Jahrhundert* (Düsseldorf, 2001), 230–46 (quote on 245, from Gerhard Ritter, *Friedrich der Grosse. Ein historisches Profil* (Leipzig, 1936), 252–3); see also Klaus Schwabe, 'Change and Continuity in German Historiography from 1933 into the Early 1950s: Gerhard Ritter (1888–1967)', in Lehmann and Melton (eds.), *Paths*, 82–108

304. Carsten Klingemann, *Soziologie im Dritten Reich* (Baden-Baden, 1996) for case-studies of different German institutes and universities; see also idem, 'Social-Scientific Experts – No Ideologues: Sociology and Social Research in the Third Reich', in Stephen P. Turner and Dirk Käsler (eds.), *Sociology Responds to Fascism* (London, 1992), 127–54; Otthein Rammstedt, 'Theorie und Empirie des

Volksfeindes. Zur Entwicklung einer "deutschen Soziologie"', in Lundgreen (ed.), *Wissenschaft*, 253–313; also Klaus Brintzinger, *Die Nationalökonomie an den Universitäten Freiburg, Heidelberg und Tübingen 1918–1945: Eine institutionshistorische, vergleichende Studie der wirtschaftswissenschaftlichen Fakultäten und Abteilungen südwestdeutscher Universitäten* (Frankfurt am Main, 1996).

305. Wilhelm Vosskamp, 'Kontinuität und Diskontinuität: Zur deutschen Literaturwissenschaft im Dritten Reich', in Lundgreen (ed.), *Wissenschaft*, 140–62.

306. Höpfner, *Die Universität Bonn*, 34–8, 146–217. See more generally the essays in Lehmann and Oexle (eds.), *Nationalsozialismus*.

307. Michael H. Kater, *Doctors under Hitler* (Chapel Hill, 1989), 111–20.

308. Ibid., 22–5, 120–21.

309. Ibid., 120–26, 147. Höpfner, *Die Universität Bonn*, 271–330. According to Kater, 17 per cent of doctors in Germany in 1933 were Jewish, and the proportion of university teachers of medicine was undoubtedly higher (Kater, *Doctors*, 139).

310. Klemperer, *I Shall Bear Witness*, 35 (9 October 1933).

311. Kater, *Doctors*, 172–3.

312. Robert N. Proctor, *The Nazi War on Cancer* (Princeton, N.J., 1999), 4, 198–203.

313. Ibid., 6–7.

314. Kater, *Doctors*, 174–6.

Chapter 4. PROSPERITY AND PLUNDER

1. Spotts, *Hitler*, 386–9; Martin Kornrumpf, *HAFRABA e.V.: Deutsche Autobahn-Planung 1926–1934* (Bonn, 1990); Kurt Gustav Kaftan, *Der Kampf um die Autobahnen: Geschichte der Autobahnen in Deutschland 1907–1935* (Berlin, 1955).

2. Franz Wilhelm Seidler, 'Fritz Todt: From Motorway Builder to Minister of State', in Smelser and Zitelmann (eds.), *The Nazi Elite*, 245–56, at 245–9; more detail in idem, *Fritz Todt: Baumeister Dritten Reiches* (Berlin, 1987 [1986]).

3. Fritz Todt, 'Der Strassenbau in nationalsozialistischen Staat', in Hans Heinrich Lammers and Hans Pfundtner (eds.) *Grundlagen, Aufbau und Wirtschaftsordnung des nationalsozialistischen Staates*, (3 vols., Berlin, 1937), III: *Die Wirtschaftsordnung des nationalsozialistischen Staates*; see also James Shand, 'The *Reichsautobahn*: Symbol for the Third Reich', *Journal of Contemporary History*, 19 (1984), 189–200; and Erhard Schütz and Eckhard Gruber, *Mythos Reichsautobahn: Bau und Inszenierung der 'Strassen des Führers' 1933–1941* (Berlin, 1996).

4. Spotts, *Hitler*, 391–3; Rainer Stommer (ed.), *Reichsautobahn: Pyramiden des Dritten Reiches* (Marburg, 1982), 107; Thomas Zeller, '"The Landscape's Crown": Landscape, Perception, and Modernizing Effects of the German Autobahn System, 1934–1941', in David E. Nye (ed.), *Technologies of Landscape: From Reaping to Recycling* (Amherst, Mass., 1999), 218–40);

5. Spotts, *Hitler*, 393–4; Ludolf Herbst, *Das nationalsozialistische Deutschland 1933–1945: Die Entfesselung der Gewalt: Rassismus und Krieg* (Frankfurt am Main, 1996), 97–8; Hans-Joachim Winkler, *Legenden um Hitler* (Berlin, 1963), 7–14; Dan P. Silverman, *Hitler's Economy: Nazi Work Creation Programs 1933–1936* (Cambridge, Mass., 1998), 147–57.

6. Richard J. Overy, 'Cars, Roads, and Economic Recovery in Germany, 1932–1938', *Economic History Review*, 2nd series, 28 (1975), 466–83, reprinted in idem, *War and Economy in the Third Reich* (Oxford, 1994), 68–89.

7. Domarus (ed.), *Hitler*, I. 250–51.

8. Overy, 'Cars, Roads, and Economic Recovery'; *Weekly Report of the German Institute for Business Research* (Institut für Konjunkturforschung, Berlin), vol. 7, no. 10 (7 March 1934), 53–5.

9. Gerhard Kroll, *Von der Weltwirtschaftskrise zur Staatskonjunktur* (Berlin, 1958), 462, 505; also Harry Niemann and Armin Hermann (eds.), *Die Entwicklung der Motorisierung im Deutschen Reich und den Nachfolgestaaten* (Stuttgart, 1995).

10. Klemperer, *I Shall Bear Witness*, 153 (translation corrected).

11. Ibid., 158 (translation corrected).

12. Geoffrey Spencely, 'R. J. Overy and the Motorisierung: A comment', *Economic History Review*, 32 (1979), 100–106; Richard J. Overy, 'The German *Motorisierung* and Rearmament. A Reply', *Economic History Review* 32 (1978), 207–13.

13. Heinz Wehner, 'Die Rolle des faschistischen Verkehrswesens in der ersten Periode des zweiten Weltkrieges', *Bulletin des Arbeitskreises Zweiter Weltkrieg*, 2 (1966), 37–61, at 41–2, cited in Hans-Erich Volkmann, 'The National Socialist Economy in Preparation for War', in Militärgeschichtliches Forschungsamt (ed.), *Germany and the Second World War* (10 vols., Oxford, 1990– [1979–]), I: *The Build-up of German Aggression* (Oxford, 1990), 157–372, at 228–9.

14. Klaus Hildebrand, 'Die Deutsche Reichsbahn in der nationalsozialistischen Diktatur 1933–1945', in Lothar Gall and Manfred Pohl (eds.), *Die Eisenbahn in Deutschland. Von den Anfängen bis zur Gegenwart* (Munich, 1999), 165–243, at 176–7; see also Stefan Arold, *Die technische Entwicklung und rüstungswirtschaftliche Bedeutung des Lokomotivbaus der Deutschen Reichsbahn im Dritten Reich (1933–1945)* (Stuttgart, 1997). Hitler's characteristic conceptual gigantism even made itself felt here, with his proposal to create new, bigger railways on a broader gauge than the existing one (ibid., 97).

15. Fritz Blaich, *Wirtschaft und Rüstung im 'Dritten Reich'* (Düsseldorf, 1987), 15–20; Simon Reich, *The Fruits of Fascism: Postwar Prosperity in Historical Perspective* (Ithaca, N.Y., 1990), 151.

16. Hans Mommsen and Manfred Grieger, *Das Volkswagenwerk und seine Arbeiter im Dritten Reich* (Düsseldorf, 1996), 52–113; for the Strength Through Joy organization, see below, 465–75.

17. Behnken (ed.), *Deutschland-Berichte*, VI (1939), 488.

18. Shelley Baranowski, *Strength Through Joy: Consumerism and Mass Tourism*

in the Third Reich (New York, 2004), 240–41; Reich, *The Fruits*, 147–201; in 1938 Ford and Opel produced 52 per cent of all vehicles made and sold in Germany (ibid., 159).

19. Karl Lärmer, *Autobahnbau in Deutschland 1933 bis 1945: Zu den Hintergründen* (Berlin, 1975), 54–7; Silverman, *Hitler's Economy*, 261.

20. Richard J. Overy, 'Unemployment in the Third Reich', in idem, *War and Economy*, 37–67, at 37–42 (originally published under the same title in *Business History*, 29 (1987), 253–82); Dietmar Petzina, 'The Extent and Causes of Unemployment in the Weimar Republic', in Peter D. Stachura (ed.), *Unemployment and the Great Depression in Weimar Germany* (London, 1986), 29–48.

21. Domarus (ed.), *Hitler*, I. 234.

22. Willi A. Boelcke, *Die deutsche Wirtschaft 1930–1945: Interna des Reichswirtschaftsministeriums* (Düsseldorf, 1983), 13–29.

23. Avraham Barkai, *Nazi Economics: Ideology, Theory, and Policy* (Oxford, 1990 [1988]), 28–35; Boelcke, *Die deutsche Wirtschaft*, 29–38; Wolfram Fischer, *Deutsche Wirtschaftspolitik 1918–1945* (Opladen, 1968), 52–5.

24. Michael Schneider, 'The Development of State Work Creation Policy in Germany, 1930–1933', in Stachura (ed.), *Unemployment*, 163–86; Helmut Marcon, *Arbeitsbeschaffungspolitik der Regierungen Papen und Schleicher. Grundsteinlegung für die Beschäftigungspolitik im Dritten Reich* (Bern, 1974).

25. Herbst, *Das nationalsozialistische Deutschland*, 95–6; Schneider, *Unterm Hakenkreuz*, 256–62.

26. Overy, 'Unemployment', 63–5; *Weekly Report of the German Institute for Business Research*, vol. 7, no. 17 (3 May 1934), 77–82.

27. Extract from the Law translated in Noakes and Pridham (eds.), *Nazism*, II. 257; Pine, *Nazi Family Policy*, 17.

28. Helen L. Boak, 'The State as an Employer of Women in the Weimar Republic', in William Robert Lee and Eve Rosenhaft (eds.), *The State and Social Change in Germany, 1880–1980* (Oxford, 1990), 61–98; more generally, Renate Bridenthal and Claudia Koonz, 'Beyond *Kinder, Küche, Kirche*: Weimar Women in Politics and Work', in Renate Bridenthal *et al.* (eds.), *When Biology Became Destiny: Women in Weimar and Nazi Germany* (New York, 1984), 33–65.

29. Julia Sneeringer, *Winning Women's Votes: Propaganda and Politics in Weimar Germany* (Chapel Hill, N.C., 2002).

30. *Frankfurter Zeitung*, 9 September 1934, quoted in Noakes and Pridham (eds.), *Nazism*, II. 255–6.

31. Goebbels, *Michael*, 41 (1934 edn), quoted in Mosse (ed.), *Nazi Culture*, 41.

32. Engelbert Huber, *Das ist Nationalsozialismus* (Stuttgart, 1933), 121–2, quoted in Mosse (ed.), *Nazi Culture*, 47.

33. Clifford Kirkpatrick, *Women in Nazi Germany* (London, 1939), 121.

34. Helgard Kramer, 'Frankfurt's Working Women: Scapegoats or Winners of the Great Depression?', in Richard J. Evans and Dick Geary (eds.), *The German*

Unemployed: Experiences and Consequences of Mass Unemployment from the Weimar Republic to the Third Reich (London, 1987), 108–41.

35. Herbst, *Das nationalsozialistische Deutschland*, 89–91; Kershaw, *The 'Hitler Myth'*, 59–64.

36. Werner Abelshauser, 'Kriegswirtschaft und Wirtschaftswunder. Deutschlands wirtschaftliche Mobilisierung für den Zweiten Weltkrieg und die Folgen für die Nachkriegszeit', *VfZg* 47 (1999), 503–38; English version, at greater length, in idem, 'Germany: Guns, Butter, and Economic Miracles', in Mark Harrison (ed.), *The Economics of World War II: Six Great Powers in International Comparison* (Cambridge, 1998), 122–76.

37. Harold James, 'Innovation and Conservatism in Economic Recovery: The Alleged "Nazi Recovery" of the 1930s', in Childers and Caplan (eds.), *Reevaluating the Third Reich*, 114–38; Peter Marschalck, *Bevölkerungsgeschichte Deutschlands im 19. und 20. Jahrhundert* (Frankfurt am Main, 1984), 67–71, 148.

38. Silverman, *Hitler's Economy*, 244, and 359 n. 68, criticizing the statistics provided by Overy, 'Unemployment', 65; however, the Weimar Republic figures were not that impressive either: see also Dan P. Silverman, 'A Pledge Unredeemed: The Housing Crisis in Weimar Germany', *Central European History*, 3 (March 1970), 112–39, at 119–20. See also Blaich, *Wirtschaft*, 15–21.

39. 'Germany's Economic Recovery', *The Economist*, 10 August 1935, 271–2.

40. Willi Hemmer, *Die 'unsichtbaren' Arbeitslosen. Statistische Methoden – Soziale Tatsachen* (Zeulenroda, 1935), 189; also Christoph Buchheim, 'Zur Natur des Wirtschaftsaufschwungs in der NS-Zeit', in idem *et al.* (eds.), *Zerrissene Zwischenkriegszeit: Wirtschaftshistorische Beiträge: Knut Borchardt zum 65. Geburtstag* (Baden-Baden, 1994), 97–119, at 105–7.

41. Birgit Wulff, 'The Third Reich and the Unemployed: National Socialist Work-creation Schemes in Hamburg, 1933–4', in Evans and Geary (eds.), *The German Unemployed*, 281–302; Timothy W. Mason, *Social Policy in the Third Reich: The Working Class and the 'National Community'* (Providence, R.I., 1993 [1977]), 109–28; Fritz Petrick, 'Eine Untersuchung zur Beseitigung der Arbeitslosigkeit unter der deutschen Jugend in den Jahren von 1933 bis 1935', *Jahrbuch für Wirtschaftsgeschichte* (1967), 287–300; Claudia Brunner, *Arbeitslosigkeit im NS-Staat: Das Beispiel München* (Pfaffenweiler, 1997), 337–40.

42. Birgit Wulff, *Arbeitslosigkeit und Arbeitsbeschaffungsmassnahmen in Hamburg 1933–1939: Eine Untersuchung zur nationalsozialistischen Wirtschafts- und Sozialpolitik* (Frankfurt am Main, 1987), esp. 269–82; details of other areas in Behnken (ed.), *Deutschland-Berichte*, I (1934), 123–9, 214–25.

43. Behnken (ed.), *Deutschland-Berichte*, II (1935), 786–7; Silverman, *Hitler's Economy*, 10–27 and 164–74; Bernhard Vollmer (ed.), *Volksopposition im Polizeistaat*, 96–7.

44. Christoph Buchheim, 'Die Wirtschaftsentwicklung im Dritten Reich – mehr

Desaster als Wunder. Eine Erwiderung auf Werner Abelshauser', *VfZ* 49 (2001), 653–4; at greater length in idem, 'Zur Natur'.

45. 'Germany's Economic Recovery', *The Economist*, 10 August 1935, 271–2, and 17 August 1935, 316–17; *Weekly Report of the German Institute for Business Research*, vol. 8, no. 22/23 (8 June 1935), 45–7; ibid., 32/33 (22 August 1935), 64–6; 'Unemployment in Germany', *The Economist*, 31 August 1935, 421.

46. Karl-Heinz Minuth (ed.), *Akten der Reichskanzlei: Die Regierung Hitler, 1933–1934*, I. 49–51; also in Blaich, *Wirtschaft*, 55–6 (Ministerbesprechung vom 8. 2. 1933).

47. Volkmann, 'The National Socialist Economy', 221–2; Dietmar Petzina, 'Hauptprobleme der deutschen Wirtschaftspolitik 1932/33', *VfZg* 15 (1967), 18–55, at 40; Günther Gereke, *Ich war königlich-preussischer Landrat* (Berlin, 1970), 157–8.

48. Spotts, *Hitler*, 393–4.

49. Domarus (ed.), *Hitler*, I. 250–51.

50. Blaich, *Wirtschaft*, 15–26.

51. Neil Gregor, *Daimler-Benz in the Third Reich* (London, 1998), 54; Fritz Blaich, 'Why Did the Pioneer Fall Behind? Motorization in Germany between the Wars', in Theo Barker (ed.), *The Economic and Social Effects of the Spread of Motor Vehicles: An International Centenary Tribute* (London, 1988), 148–64; Behnken (ed.), *Deutschland-Berichte*, VI (1939), 480–85; Mommsen and Grieger, *Das Volkswagenwerk*, 179–202 (figures on 197).

52. Volkmann, 'The National Socialist Economy', 228–9.

53. Robert J. O'Neill, *The German Army and the Nazi Party, 1933–1939* (London, 1968 [1966]), 65–6, citing the unpublished memoirs of Field-Marshal von Weichs.

54. 'Sitzung des Ausschusses der Reichsregierung für Arbeitsbeschaffung vom 9. 2. 1933, in Minuth (ed.), *Akten der Reichskanzlei: Die Regierung Hitler, 1933–1934*, I. 58–69, and Blaich, *Wirtschaft*, 56–8. The dissimulation did not long escape the notice of foreign observers. By 1935 a British correspondent was noting of a report issued by the Reich Bureau of Statistics: ' "Work-creation" expenditure, it is expressly shown in the new report, *includes* rearmament expenditure' (*The Economist*, 10 August 1935, 280; italics in original).

55. Volkmann, 'The National Socialist Economy', 223–4; Michael Geyer, *Deutsche Rüstungspolitik 1860–1980* (Frankfurt am Main, 1984), 139–40; idem, 'Das Zweite Rüstungsprogramm (1930–1934): Eine Dokumentation', *Militärgeschichtliche Mitteilungen*, 17 (1975), 125–72, at 134 and 158; see also Boelcke, *Die deutsche Wirtschaft*, 29–33.

56. Volkmann, 'The National Socialist Economy', 228–34; also Peter Kirchberg, 'Typisierung in der Kraftfahrzeugindustrie und der Generalbevollmächtigte für das Kraftfahrwesen', *Jahrbuch für Wirtschaftsgeschichte* (1969), 117–42; see also Edward L. Homze, *Arming the Luftwaffe: The Reich Air Ministry and the German Aircraft Industry, 1919–1939* (Lincoln, Nebr., 1976). Some of the literature in

this area underestimates the extent of rearmament from the beginning of the Third Reich and the state's role in driving it forward, and neglects the military imperative behind many apparently civil measures of job creation: see for example Overy, 'Cars, Roads and Economic Recovery'; idem, 'Hitler's War Plans and the German Economy, 1933–1939', in idem, *War and Economy*, 177–204; Michael Wolffsohn, 'Arbeitsbeschaffung und Rüstung im nationalsozialistischen Deutschland 1933', *Militärgeschichtliche Mitteilungen*, 22 (1978), 9–22; or Burton H. Klein, *Germany's Economic Preparations for War* (Cambridge, Mass., 1959); for critical comments, see Barkai, *Nazi Economics*, 217–24, and Berenice A. Carroll, *Design for Total War: Arms and Economics in the Third Reich* (The Hague, 1968). The primacy of rearmament was stressed already by Sauer, *Die Mobilmachung*, 140–64.

57. Wilhelm Deist, 'The Rearmament of the Wehrmacht', in Militärgeschichtliches Forschungsamt (ed.), *Germany*, I. 373–540, at 487.

58. Ibid., 456–7; O'Neill, *The German Army*, 134–5.

59. Boelcke, *Die deutsche Wirtschaft*, 171.

60. Volkmann, 'The National Socialist Economy', 234–8; Hans Luther, *Vor dem Abgrund 1930–1933: Reichsbankpräsident in Krisenzeiten* (Frankfurt am Main, 1964), especially the final chapter, 302–8.

61. Hjalmar Schacht, *My First Seventy-Six Years: The Autobiography of Hjalmar Schacht* (London, 1955), 10–154.

62. Ibid., 155–306.

63. Volkmann, 'The National Socialist Economy', 234–41; see also Willi A. Boelcke, *Die Kosten von Hitlers Krieg: Kriegsfinanzierung und finanzielles Kriegserbe in Deutschland 1933–1948* (Paderborn, 1985); Fischer, *Deutsche Wirtschaftspolitik*, 66–71; Dietmar Petzina, *Die deutsche Wirtschaft in der Zwischenkriegszeit* (Wiesbaden, 1977), 117–24.

64. Volkmann, 'The National Socialist Economy', 173–200; Blaich, *Wirtschaft*, 28.

65. Gustavo Corni and Horst Gies, *Brot, Butter, Kanonen. Die Ernährungswirtschaft in Deutschland unter der Diktatur Hitlers* (Berlin, 1997), 75–250, is now the most thorough account of the Reich Food Estate. See also Horst Gies, 'Der Reichsnährstand: Organ berufsständischer Selbstverwaltung oder Instrument staatlicher Wirtschaftslenkung?', *Zeitschrift für Agrargeschichte und Agrarsoziologie*, 21 (1973), 216–33; and idem, 'Die Rolle des Reichsnährstandes im Nationalsozialistischen Herrschaftssystem', in Gerhard Hirschfeld and Lothar Kettenacker (eds.), *The 'Führer State': Myth and Reality: Studies on the Structure and Politics of the Third Reich* (Stuttgart, 1981), 270–304.

66. Horst Gies, 'Aufgaben und Probleme der nationalsozialistischen Ernährungswirtschaft 1933–1939', *Vierteljahrschrift für Sozial- und Wirtschaftsgeschichte*, 22 (1979), 466–99.

67. Blaich, *Wirtschaft*, 27; Volkmann, 'The National Socialist Economy', 245–72.

68. Blaich, *Wirtschaft*, 23–4, 27; Volkmann, 'The National Socialist Economy', 258–62; Michael Krüger-Charlé, 'Carl Goerdelers Versuche der Durchsetzung

einer alternativen Politik 1933 bis 1937', in Jürgen Schmädeke and Peter Steinbach (eds.), *Der Widerstand gegen den Nationalsozialismus: Die deutsche Gesellschaft und der Widerstand gegen Hitler* (Munich, 1986), 383–404.

69. Gies, 'Die Rolle'; see also idem, 'Der Reichsnährstand'; idem, 'Revolution oder Kontinuität? Die personelle Struktur des Reichsnährstandes', in Günther Franz (ed.), *Bauernschaft und Bauernstand 1500–1970: Büdinger Vorträge 1911–1972* (Limburg, 1975), 323–30; John E. Farquharson, *The Plough and the Swastika: The NSDAP and Agriculture in Germany 1928–45* (London, 1976), 161–82.

70. Gies, 'Die Rolle'; Jürgen von Krudener, 'Zielkonflikte in der nationalsozialistischen Agrarpolitik: Ein Beitrag zur Diskussion des Leistungsproblems in zentralgelenkten Wirtschaftssystemen', *Zeitschrift für Wirtschafts- und Sozialwissenschaften*, 94 (1974), 335–61; Behnken (ed.), *Deutschland-Berichte*, V (1938), 488–98; Gustavo Corni, *Hitler and the Peasants: Agrarian Policy of the Third Reich, 1930–1939* (Princeton, N.J., 1990 [1989]), 245–68; Beatrix Herlemann, *'Der Bauer klebt am Hergebrachten': Bäuerliche Verhaltensweisen unterm Nationalsozialismus auf dem Gebiet des heutigen Landes Niedersachsen* (Hanover, 1993), 74–7 and 145–53; Farquharson, *The Plough*, 71–106.

71. See Corni, *Hitler and the Peasants*, 220–44; Farquharson, *The Plough*, 183–202; Herlemann, *'Der Bauer'*, 154–71.

72. Volkmann, 'The National Socialist Economy', 293–300, 350–54.

73. John H. Farquharson, *The Plough*, 169–70; for a good example of the successful transition to autarky in one area, see John Perkins, 'Nazi Autarchic Aspirations and the Beet-Sugar Industry, 1933–39', *European History Quarterly*, 20 (1990), 497–518; more generally, see Corni, *Hitler and the Peasants* 156–83.

74. Behnken (ed.), *Deutschland-Berichte* VI (1939), 624–42; for a thorough account of food production and market regulation, see Corni and Gies, *Brot*, 251–395.

75. The view of Peter Temin, *Lessons from the Great Depression* (Cambridge, Mass., 1989), 109–11, that the economy of the Third Reich was a socialist economy because it was steered by the state, which intervened continually and also devoted substantial resources to welfare projects, does not persuade; on these criteria almost all modern economies could be classified as socialist (Buchheim, 'Zur Natur', 99–100).

76. For the background to this, see Peter Hayes, *Industry and Ideology: IG Farben in the Nazi Era* (New York, 1987), 36–47, 114–20.

77. Homze, *Arming the Luftwaffe*, 192–3.

78. Dieter Swatek, *Unternehmenskonzentration als Ergebnis und Mittel nationalsozialistischer Wirtschaftspolitik* (Berlin, 1972); Ingeborg Esenwein-Rothe, *Die Wirtschaftsverbände von 1933 bis 1945* (Berlin, 1965).

79. For Hugenberg's tenure of the Ministry, see Boelcke, *Die deutsche Wirtschaft*, 47–65.

80. Gerald D. Feldman, *Allianz and the German Insurance Business, 1933–1945* (Cambridge, 2001), 1–50.

81. Ibid., 51–78.

82. Ibid., 78–105; Boelcke, *Die deutsche Wirtschaft*, 65–76.

83. Volkmann, 'The National Socialist Economy', 204–15; Noakes and Pridham, *Nazism*, II. 72–8.

84. Volkmann, 'The National Socialist Economy', 242–4; 'The Balance of Trade in Germany', Supplement to the *Weekly Report of the German Institute for Business Research* (Berlin, 11 April 1934).

85. 'The Transfer Problem and Germany's Foreign Exchange Reserves', *Weekly Report of the German Institute for Business Research*, 7 (Berlin, 6 June 1934); 'German Foreign Exchange Control and Foreign Trade', Supplement to the *Weekly Report of the German Institute for Business Research* (Berlin, 31 October 1934); Herbst, *Das nationalsozialistische Deutschland*, 160–62.

86. 'A Review of the First Year of German Foreign Trade Under the "New Plan"', *Weekly Report of the German Institute for Business Research*, 8 (Berlin, 2 October 1935).

87. 'The German Moratorium', *The Economist*, 23 June 1934, 1,378–9; more generally on Schacht's first period in office, see Boelcke, *Die deutsche Wirtschaft*, 77–82.

88. Volkmann, 'The National Socialist Economy', 245–7, citing a memorandum of 3 May 1935 by Schacht.

89. Blaich, *Wirtschaft*, 27; Boelcke, *Die deutsche Wirtschaft*, 100–117.

90. Volkmann, 'The National Socialist Economy', 262–72; Fischer, *Deutsche Wirtschaftspolitik*, 71–6.

91. The Four-Year Plan memorandum is reprinted in Blaich, *Wirtschaft*, 60–67, and Wilhelm Treue (ed.), 'Hitlers Denkschrift zum Vierjahresplan 1936', *VfZ* 3 (1955), 184–210, and translated in full in Noakes and Pridham (eds.), *Nazism*, II. 86–93. See also Arthur Schweitzer, 'Der ursprüngliche Vierjahresplan', *Jahrbücher für Nationalökonomie und Statistik*, 160 (1956), 348–96; and Dietmar Petzina, *Autarkiepolitik im Dritten Reich: Der nationalsozialistische Vierjahresplan (1936–42)* (Stuttgart, 1968).

92. Schacht, *My First Seventy-Six Years*, 362–77 (apologetic in tendency, with many omissions and misleading claims).

93. Friedrich Hossbach, *Zwischen Wehrmacht und Hitler 1934–1938* (Göttingen, 1965 [1949]), 217–20, and Hermann Gackenholz, 'Reichskanzlei 5. November 1937: Bemerkungen über "Politik und Kriegführung" im Dritten Reich', in Richard Dietrich and Gerhard Oestreich (ed.), *Forschungen zu Staat und Verfassung: Festgabe für Fritz Hartung* (Berlin, 1958), 459–84.

94. Hossbach, *Zwischen Wehrmacht und Hitler*, 186; Walter Bussmann, 'Zur Entstehung und Überlieferung der "Hossbach-Niederschrift"', *VfZ* 16 (1968), 373–84; Bradley F. Smith, 'Die Überlieferung der Hossbach-Niederschrift im Lichte neuer Quellen', *VfZ* 38 (1990), 329–36; Jonathan Wright and Paul Stafford, 'Hitler, Britain and the Hossbach Memorandum', *Militärgeschichtliche Mitteilungen*, 42 (1987), 77–123. These studies make it clear that the scepticism

about the document's authenticity expressed by Alan J. P. Taylor, *The Origins of the Second World War* (London, 1964 [1961]), 21–2 and 131–4, is unjustified.

95. Schacht, *My First Seventy-Six Years*, 362–77 (to be treated with the usual caution); Noakes and Pridham (eds.), *Nazism*, II. 95–8, 357–8.

96. Blaich, *Wirtschaft*, 26, 83, 91–4; Schacht, *My First Seventy-Six Years*, 386–94. Budgetary balances in Albrecht Ritschl, *Deutschlands Krise und Konjunktur 1924–1934: Binnenkonjunktur, Auslandsverschuldung und Reparationsproblem zwischen Dawes-Plan und Transfersperre* (Berlin, 2002), table A9; national income figures in ibid., table A12.

97. O'Neill, *The German Army*, 63–6, citing the unpublished memoirs of Field-Marshal von Weichs; Schacht, *My First Seventy-Six Years*, 395–414; more generally, Volkmann, 'The National Socialist Economy', 273–86.

98. Ibid., 300–309, 356; Fischer, *Deutsche Wirtschaftspolitik*, 77–82; Petzina, *Die deutsche Wirtschaft*, 124–39. For the 'organizational jungle', see Hans Kehrl, *Krisenmanager im Dritten Reich. 6 Jahre Frieden – 6 Jahre Krieg: Erinnerungen* (Düsseldorf, 1973), 74–86, 98–117. On the failure of planning and the inability of the regime to collect and process adequate statistics, see J. Adam Tooze, *Statistics and the German State, 1900–1945: The Making of Modern Economic Knowledge* (Cambridge, 2001), 215–45.

99. Volkmann, 'The National Socialist Economy', 309–15.

100. Ibid., 354–72.

101. Wilhelm Deist, 'The Rearmament of the Wehrmacht', 374–540, at 456–504; Homze, *Arming the Luftwaffe*; Michael Salewski, *Die deutsche Seekriegsleitung 1935–1945* (3 vols., Frankfurt am Main, 1970–75); Jost Dülffer, *Weimar, Hitler und die Marine: Reichspolitik und Flottenbau 1920–1939* (Düsseldorf, 1973); Lutz Budrass, *Flugzeugindustrie und Luftrüstung in Deutschland 1918–1945* (Düsseldorf, 1998) is the most recent comprehensive study.

102. Volkmann, 'The National Socialist Economy', 300–309.

103. Richard J. Overy, 'The German Pre-war Production Plans: November 1936–April 1939', *English Historical Review*, 90 (1975), 778–97.

104. Behnken (ed.), *Deutschland-Berichte*, VI (1939), 614–24.

105. 'Schreiben des Stellvertreters des Führers, Entscheidung, dass Frauen weder Richter noch Anwalt werden sollen, 24 August 1936', reprinted as document 108 in Ursula von Gersdorff, *Frauen im Kriegsdienst 1914–1945* (Stuttgart, 1969), 282.

106. Matthew Stibbe, *Women in the Third Reich* (London, 2003), 84–91; Tim Mason, 'Women in Germany, 1925–1940: Family, Welfare and Work', in idem, *Nazism, Fascism and the Working Class* (Cambridge, 1995), 131–211 (essay originally published in *History Workshop Journal*, 1 (1976), 74–133, and 2 (1976), 5–32); Dörte Winkler, *Frauenarbeit im 'Dritten Reich'* (Hamburg, 1977); Annemarie Tröger, 'The Creation of a Female Assembly-Line Proletariat', in Bridenthal *et al.* (eds.), *When Biology Became Destiny*, 237–70; Carola Sachse, *Industrial Housewives: Women's Social Work in the Factories of Nazi*

Germany (London, 1987); Stephenson, *Women in Nazi Society*, 75–115 (statistics of doctors on 166).

107. Lore Kleiber, ' "Wo ihr seid, da soll die Sonne scheinen!" – Der Frauenarbeitsdienst am Ende der Weimarer Republik und im Nationalsozialismus', in Frauengruppe Faschismusforschung (ed.), *Mutterkreuz*, 188–214; Jill Stephenson, 'Women's Labor Service in Nazi Germany', *Central European History*, 15 (1982), 241–65; Stefan Bajohr, 'Weiblicher Arbeitsdienst im "Dritten Reich". Ein Konflikt zwischen Ideologie und Ökonomie', *VfZ* 28 (1980), 331–57.

108. Maschmann, *Account Rendered*, 31–6.

109. Elizabeth D. Heineman, *What Difference Does a Husband Make? Women and Marital Status in Nazi and Postwar Germany* (London, 1999), 40–41, also for the following details.

110. Stibbe, *Women*, 88; Annemarie Tröger, 'Die Frau im wesensgemässen Einsatz', in Frauengruppe Faschismusforschung (ed.), *Mutterkreuz*, 246–72.

111. Timothy W. Mason, 'The Legacy of 1918 for National Socialism', in Anthony Nicholls and Erich Matthias (eds.), *German Democracy and the Triumph of Hitler: Essays in Recent German History* (London, 1971), 215–39.

112. Ulrich Herbert, *Hitler's Foreign Workers: Enforced Foreign Labor in Germany under the Third Reich* (Cambridge, 1997 [1985]), 27–60; see also below, 686–7.

113. Herbst, *Das nationalsozialistische Deutschland*, 160–77.

114. Hossbach, *Zwischen Wehrmacht und Hitler*, 186.

115. Josiah E. DuBois, Jr, *The Devil's Chemists: 24 Conspirators of the International Farben Cartel who Manufacture Wars* (Boston, Mass., 1952); Joseph Borkin, *The Crime and Punishment of I. G. Farben* (New York, 1978); Richard Sasuly, *IG Farben* (New York, 1947); Dietrich Eichholtz, 'Zum Anteil des IG Farben Konzerns an der Vorbereitung des Zweiten Weltkrieges', *Jahrbuch für Wirtschaftsgeschichte* (1969), 83–105; Ferdinand Grocek, 'Ein Staat im Staate – der IG-Farben Konzern', *Marxistische Blätter*, 4 (1966), 41–8; Willi Kling, *Kleine Geschichte der IG Farben – der Grossfabrikant des Todes* (Berlin, 1957); more generally, Arthur Schweitzer, *Big Business in the Third Reich* (Bloomington, Ind., 1964).

116. For good surveys of this literature, see Pierre Ayçoberry, *The Nazi Question: An Essay on the Interpretations of National Socialism (1922–1975)* (New York, 1981); A. James Gregor, *Fascism: The Classic Interpretations of the Interwar Period* (Morristown, N.J., 1983); Wolfgang Wippermann, *Zur Analyse des Faschismus: Die sozialistischen und kommunistischen Faschismustheorien, 1921–1945* (Frankfurt am Main, 1981); and Anson G. Rabinbach, 'Toward a Marxist Theory of Fascism and National Socialism', *New German Critique*, 1 (1974), 127–53.

117. Timothy Mason, 'The Primacy of Politics – Politics and Economics in National Socialist Germany', in Stuart J. Woolf (ed.), *The Nature of Fascism* (London, 1968), 165–95.

118. Alan S. Milward, 'Fascism and the Economy', in Walter Laqueur (ed.),

Fascism: A Reader's Guide: Analyses, Interpretations, Bibliography (New York, 1976), 409–53.

119. Fritz Thyssen's ghost-written memoir, *I Paid Hitler* (London, 1941), is unreliable; see Henry Ashby Turner, Jr, 'Fritz Thyssen und "I Paid Hitler"', *VfZ* 19 (1971), 225–44; see also Horst A. Wessel, *Thyssen & Co., Mülheim an der Ruhr: Die Geschichte einer Familie und ihrer Unternehmung* (Stuttgart, 1991), 48, 171.

120. Richard J. Overy, 'Heavy Industry in the Third Reich: The Reichswerke Crisis', in idem, *War and Economy in the Third Reich*, 93–118 (first published in *European History Quarterly*, 15 (1985), 313–39).

121. Richard J. Overy, ' "Primacy Always Belongs to Politics": Gustav Krupp and the Third Reich', in idem, *War and Economy in the Third Reich*, 119–43, at 119–25.

122. Felix Somary, *The Raven of Zürich: The Memoirs of Felix Somary* (London, 1986), 175; more generally, Overy, ' "Primacy"', 126–34; Henry Ashby Turner, Jr, *German Big Business and the Rise of Hitler* (New York, 1985), 338–9.

123. Overy, ' "Primacy"', 135–43; Lothar Gall, *Krupp: Der Aufstieg eines Industriemperiums* (Berlin, 2000); William Manchester, *The Arms of Krupp 1587–1968* (New York, 1970 [1968]), 499–511, 645–7, 743.

124. Hayes, *Industry and Ideology*, 125–211.

125. Ibid., 158–9, 180–83; Raymond G. Stokes, 'From the IG Farben Fusion to the Establishment of BASF AG (1925–1952)', in Werner Abelshauser *et al., German Industry and Global Enterprise. BASF: The History of a Company* (Cambridge, 2004), 206–361, at 262–3, 273–89. Gottfried Plumpe, *Die I.G. Farbenindustrie AG. Wirtschaft, Technik und Politik 1904–1945* (Berlin, 1990), largely follows Hayes, though in some respects it is less critical: see Peter Hayes, 'Zur umstrittenen Geschichte der I.G. Farbenindustrie AG', *Geschichte und Gesellschaft*, 18 (1992), 405–17; Plumpe's riposte does not convince: see Gottfried Plumpe, 'Antwort auf Peter Hayes', *Geschichte und Gesellschaft*, 18 (1992), 526–32.

126. Harold James, 'Die Deutsche Bank und die Diktatur 1933–1945', in Lothar Gall *et al., Die Deutsche Bank 1870–1995* (Munich, 1993), 315–408; see also Harold James, *The Nazi Dictatorship and the Deutsche Bank* (Cambridge, 2004).

127. Details in Behnken (ed.), *Deutschland-Berichte*, VI (1939), 511–16.

128. Ibid., 611–13.

129. Simone Ladwig-Winters, 'The Attack on Berlin Department Stores (*Warenhäuser*) after 1933', in David Bankier (ed.), *Probing the Depths of German Antisemitism: German Society and the Persecution of the Jews, 1933–1941* (Jerusalem, 2000), 246–67, at 246–50; eadem, *Wertheim – Ein Warenhausunternehmen und seine Eigentümer: Ein Beispiel der Entwicklung der Berliner Warenhäuser bis zur 'Arisierung'* (Münster, 1997); Klaus Strohmeyer, *Warenhäuser: Geschichte, Blüte und Untergang in Warenmeer* (Berlin, 1980); Heidrun Homburg, 'Warenhausunternehmen und ihre Gründer in Frankreich und Deutschland oder: eine diskrete Elite und mancherlei Mythen', *Jahrbuch für Wirtschaftsgeschichte* (1992), 183–

219. Rudolf Lenz, *Karstadt. Ein deutscher Warenhauskonzern 1920–1950* (Stuttgart, 1995); Werner E. Mosse, *The German-Jewish Economic Elite 1820–1935: A Socio-Cultural Profile* (Oxford, 1989), 18–20, 29–31, 70–78, 103–5, 111–13, 140–42; see also Konrad Fuchs, *Ein Konzern aus Sachsen: Das Kaufhaus Schocken als Spiegelbild deutscher Wirtschaft und Politik, 1901 bis 1953* (Stuttgart, 1990).

130. Ladwig-Winters, 'The Attack', 251.

131. Robert J. Gellately, *The Politics of Economic Despair. Shopkeepers and German Politics, 1890–1914* (London, 1974), 141–3.

132. Albrecht Tyrell (ed.), *Führer befiehl . . . Selbstzeugnisse aus der 'Kampfzeif' der NSDAP: Dokumentation und Analyse* (Düsseldorf, 1969), 24.

133. Translated and reprinted in Noakes and Pridham (eds.), *Nazism*, I. 76.

134. Heinrich Uhlig, *Die Warenhäuser im Dritten Reich* (Cologne, 1956), 78–9, 88–127.

135. Uhlig, *Warenhäuser*, 115–19; Ladwig-Winters, 'The Attack', 255–6; Johannes Ludwig, *Boykott – Enteignung – Mord: Die 'Entjuding' der deutschen Wirtschaft* (Hamburg 1989), 104–27.

136. Ladwig-Winters, 'The Attack', 25–62 (quote on 262). For the Factory Cell Organization, see below, 456–60.

137. Ladwig-Winters, 'The Attack', 263–7; for a good local example of the campaign against department stores, see Franz Fichtl *et al.*, *'Bambergs Wirtschaft Judenfrei': Die Verdrängung der jüdischen Geschäftsleute in den Jahren 1933 bis 1939* (Bamberg, 1998), 66–72.

138. Peter Longerich, *Politik der Vernichtung: Eine Gesamtdarstellung der nationalsozialistischen Judenverfolgung* (Munich, 1998), 46–54; Helmut Genschel, *Die Verdrängung der Juden aus der Wirtschaft im Dritten Reich* (Göttingen, 1966), 78–87; Gerhard Kratzsch, *Der Gauwirtschaftsapparat der NSDAP: Menschenführung – 'Arisierung' – Wehrwirtschaft im Gau Westfalen-Süd* (Münster, 1989), 117; Fichtl *et al.*, *'Bambergs Wirtschaft'*, 101–10; the best general survey is still Avraham Barkai, *From Boycott to Annihilation: The Economic Struggle of German Jews 1933–1943* (Hanover, N.H., 1989 [1988]).

139. Klemperer, *I Shall Bear Witness*, 65 (13 June 1934).

140. Friedländer, *Nazi Germany*, 234–5.

141. Joachim Meynert, *Was vor der 'Endlösung' geschah. Antisemitische Ausgrenzung und Verfolgung in Minden-Ravensburg, 1933–1945* (Münster, 1988), 82–99.

142. Quoted in Longerich, *Politik*, 55.

143. Ibid.

144. Ibid., 55–6, 70–88.

145. All quoted in ibid., 97–8; report and translation in *The Economist*, 24 August 1935, 36–6. For Schacht's claim to have opposed antisemitism, see Schacht, *My First Seventy-Six Years*, 467–8; it was largely swallowed by his first serious biographer, Heinz Pentzlin, *Hjalmar Schacht: Leben und Wirken einer umstrittenen Persönlichkeit* (Berlin, 1980). Boelcke, *Die deutsche Wirtschaft*, 117–28 and

210–17, provides a useful introduction to Aryanization, but is too kind to Schacht.

146. Schacht, *My First Seventy-Six Years*, 357.

147. Albert Fischer, 'The Minister of Economics and the Expulsion of the Jews from the German Economy', in Bankier (ed.), *Probing*, 213–25; see also idem, *Hjalmar Schacht und Deutschlands 'Judenfrage': Der 'Wirtschaftsdiktator' und die Vertreibung der Juden aus der deutschen Wirtschaft* (Cologne, 1995).

148. Petra Bräutigam, *Mittelständische Unternehmer im Nationalsozialismus: Wirtschaftliche Entwicklungen und soziale Verhaltensweisen in der Schuh- und Lederindustrie Badens und Württembergs* (Munich, 1997), 167–73, 297–336.

149. Frank Bajohr, 'The "Aryanization" of Jewish Companies and German Society: The Example of Hamburg', in Bankier (ed.), *Probing*, 226–45, at 227–34. For traditional mercantile attitudes, see Richard J. Evans, *Death in Hamburg: Society and Politics in the Cholera Years 1830–1910* (Oxford, 1987), esp. 33–9, 392–4; and Niall Ferguson, *Paper and Iron: Hamburg Business and German Politics in the Era of Inflation 1897–1927* (Cambridge, 1995), 60–64.

150. Bajohr, 'The "Aryanization"', 235–8; more detail in idem, *'Aryanization' in Hamburg: The Economic Exclusion of Jews and the Confiscation of their Property in Nazi Germany* (New York, 2002 [1997]), chapter 4.

151. Bajohr, 'The "Aryanization"', 234–41; more senior businessmen staffed the equivalent office in the Party Regional headquarters of Southern Westphalia: see Gerhard Kratzsch, 'Die "Entjudung" der mittelständischen Wirtschaft im Regierungsbezirk Arnsberg', in Arno Herzig *et al.* (eds.), *Verdrängung und Vernichtung der Juden in Westfalen* (Münster, 1994), 91–114, at 97. State offices asserted themselves more vigorously, by contrast, in some other areas: see for example Hans-Joachim Fliedner, *Die Judenverfolgung in Mannheim 1933–1945* (Stuttgart, 1971), 114, and Kratzsch, *Der Gauwirtschaftsapparat*, 151 and 180; also Dirk van Laak, 'Die Mitwirkenden bei der "Arisierung". Dargestellt am Beispiel der rheinisch-westfälischen Industrieregion, 1933–1940', in Ursula Büttner (ed.), *Die Deutschen und die Judenverfolgung im Dritten Reich* (Hamburg, 1992), 231–57.

152. Bajohr, 'The "Aryanization"', 237, criticizing Fraenkel, *The Dual State* (see above, 45), and Uwe Dietrich Adam, *Judenpolitik im Dritten Reich* (Düsseldorf, 1972), 359.

153. Fischer, *Hjalmar Schacht*, 187; Longerich, *Politik* 124; Stefan Mehl, *Das Reichsfinanzministerium und die Verfolgung der deutschen Juden, 1933–1943* (Berlin, 1990); Behnken (ed.), *Deutschland-Berichte*, V (1938), 1,291.

154. Fichtl *et al.*, *'Bambergs Wirtschaft'* 63–97, 111–32.

155. Treue (ed.), 'Hitlers Denkschrift', 204, 210.

156. Longerich, *Politik*, 124–6; Bajohr, *'Aryanization'*, 185–221; Dorothee Mussgnug, *Die Reichsfluchtsteuer 1931–1933* (Berlin, 1993).

157. Hans Nothnagel and Ewald Dähn, *Juden in Suhl: Ein geschichtlicher Überblick* (Konstanz, 1995), 129–31.

158. Albert Fischer, 'Jüdische Privatbanken im "Dritten Reich"', *Scripta Mercaturae. Zeitschrift für Wirtschafts- und Sozialgeschichte*, 28 (1994), 1–54; Chris-

topher Kopper, 'Die "Arisierung" jüdischer Privatbanken im Nationalsozialismus', *Sozialwissenschaftliche Informationen für Unterricht und Studium*, 20 (1991), 11–16.

159. See Christopher Kopper, 'Privates Bankwesen im Nationalsozialismus. Das Bankhaus M. M. Warburg & Co.', in Werner Plumpe and Christian Kleinschmidt (eds.), *Unternehmen zwischen Markt und Macht: Aspekte deutscher Unternehmens- und Industriegeschichte im 20 Jahrhundert* (Essen, 1992), 61–73; and A. Joshua Sherman, 'A Jewish Bank during the Schacht Era: M. M. Warburg & Co., 1933–1938', in Arnold Paucker (ed.), *The Jews in Nazi Germany 1933–1943* (Tübingen, 1986), 167–72.

160. Barkai, *From Boycott*, 70.

161. Longerich, *Politik*, 126–7; Avraham Barkai, 'The Fateful Year 1938: The Continuation and Acceleration of Plunder', in Walter H. Pehle (ed.), *November 1938: From 'Reichskristallnacht' to Genocide* (New York, 1991 [1988]), 95–122, at 97–9. Figures apply to the *Altreich*.

162. Genschel, *Die Verdrängung*, 126; see more generally Günter Plum, 'Wirtschaft und Erwerbsleben', in Wolfgang Benz (ed.), *Die Juden in Deutschland 1933–1945: Leben unter nationalsozialistischer Herrschaft* (Munich, 1988), 268–313, at 292–304; for a local study, see Meynert, *Was vor der 'Endlösung' geschah*, 156–77.

163. Longerich, *Politik*, 128; Barbara Händler-Lachmann and Thomas Werther, *Vergessene Geschäfte, verlorene Geschichte: Jüdisches Wirtschaftsleben in Marburg und seine Vernichtung im Nationalsozialismus* (Marburg, 1992); Axel Bruns-Wüstefeld, *Lohnende Geschäfte. Die 'Entjudung' der Wirtschaft am Beispiel Göttingens* (Hanover, 1997); also Benigna Schönhagen, *Tübingen unterm Hakenkreuz: Eine Universitätsstadt in der Zeit des Nationalsozialismus* (Tübingen, 1991).

164. Barkai, 'The Fateful Year', 97–113; Longerich, *Politik*, 126–30, 159–61, 165–9. Unless otherwise noted, these statistics include only the *Altreich*; the 1938 Aryanization statistics also include Austria. Further details in Plum, 'Wirtschaft', 304–13. See also more generally Peter Hayes and Irmtrud Wojak (eds.), *'Arisierung' im Nationalsozialismus: Volksgemeinschaft, Raub und Gedächtnis* (Frankfurt am Main, 2000). Among many other useful local studies, see also in particular Dirk van Laak, ' "Wenn einer ein Herz im Leibe hat, der lässt sich von einem deutschen Arzt behandeln" – Die "Entjudung" der Essener Wirtschaft von 1933 bis 1941', in Alte Synagoge (ed.), *Entrechtung und Selbsthilfe: Zur Geschichte der Juden in Essen unter dem Nationalsozialismus* (Essen, 1994), 12–30.

165. Barkai, 'The Fateful Year', citing Peter Hanke, *Zur Geschichte der Juden in München zwischen 1933 und 1945* (Munich, 1967), 154–5.

166. Avraham Barkai, 'Die deutschen Unternehmer und die Judenpolitik im "Dritten Reich"', *Geschichte und Gesellschaft*, 15 (1989), 227–47. Bajohr, 'The "Aryanization"', 241–2; for a local study revealing the huge range of different types and sizes of enterprise involved, see Angelika Baumann and Andreas Heusler

(eds.), *München 'arisiert': Entrechtung und Enteignung der Juden in der NS-Zeit* (Munich, 2004).

167. Behnken (ed.), *Deutschland-Berichte*, V (1938), 750.

168. Ibid., VI (1939), 599; echoed in Genschel, *Die Verdrängung*, 213.

169. Harold James, *The Deutsche Bank and the Nazi Economic War against the Jews: The Expropriation of Jewish-owned Property* (Cambridge, 2001), 36–48.

170. Dieter Ziegler, 'Die Verdrängung der Juden aus der Dresdner Bank 1933–1938', *VfZ* 47 (1999), 187–216; Stokes, 'From the IG Farben Fusion', 291–2. For banks, see more generally Christopher Kopper, *Zwischen Marktwirtschaft und Dirigismus: Bankenpolitik im 'Dritten Reich' 1933–1939* (Bonn, 1995).

171. Paul Erker, *Industrieeliten in der NS-Zeit: Anpassungsbereitschaft und Eigeninteresse von Unternehmern in der Rüstungs- und Kriegswirtschaft 1936–1945* (Passau, 1993), 7–14.

172. Feldman, *Allianz*, 125–39.

173. Friedländer, *Nazi Germany*, 234–6.

174. Kratzsch, *Der Gauwirtschaftsapparat*, 217–18, 506.

175. James, *The Deutsche Bank*, 36–48.

176. Barkai, *From Boycott*, 75.

177. Behnken (ed.), *Deutschland-Berichte*, V (1938), 176–9.

178. Bräutigam, *Mittelständische Unternehmer*, 332–6; for the Tack shoe business, see Ludwig, *Boykott*, 128–53.

179. Feldman, *Allianz*, 147–9.

180. James, *The Deutsche Bank*, 49–50; Peter Hayes, 'Big Business and "Aryanization" in Germany 1933–1939', *Jahrbuch für Antisemitismusforschung* 3 (1994), 254–81, at 267. I.G. Farben seems to have played little or no part in such acquisitions: see Stokes, 'From the IG Farben Fusion', 291.

181. Bernhard Lorentz, 'Die Commerzbank und die "Arisierung" im Altreich. Ein Vergleich der Netzwerkstrukturen und Handlungsspielräume von Grossbanken in der NS-Zeit', *VfZ* 50 (2002), 237–68; Ludolf Herbst and Thomas Weihe (eds.), *Die Commerzbank und die Juden 1933–1945* (Munich, 2004).

182. Ludwig, *Boykott*, 154–74.

183. Bajohr, 'The "Aryanization"', 242–5; Peter Hayes, 'Fritz Roessler and Nazism: The Observations of a German Industrialist, 1930–37', *Central European History*, 20 (1987), 58–83; at greater length, see also now Peter Hayes, *From Cooperation to Complicity. Degussa in the Third Reich* (New York, 2005).

184. Frank Bajohr and Joachim Szodrzynski, '"Keine jüdische Hautcreme mehr benutzen." Die antisemitische Kampagne gegen die Hamburger Firma Beiersdorf', in Arno Herzig (ed.), *Die Juden in Hamburg 1590–1990* (Hamburg, 1991), 515–26.

185. Longerich, *Politik*, 127; Bajohr, 'The "Aryanization"', 242–7.

186. Rainer Karlsch and Raymond G. Stokes, *Faktor Öl: Die Geschichte der Mineralölwirtschaft in Deutschland, 1859–1974* (Munich, 2003), 161–3; Lukas

Straumann and Daniel Wildmann, *Schweizer Chemieunternehmen im 'Dritten Reich'* (Zürich, 2001), 68–9.

187. Reinhold Billstein *et al.*, *Working for the Enemy: Ford, General Motors and Forced Labor in Germany during the Second World War* (New York, 2000).

188. Frank Bajohr, *Parvenüs und Profiteure: Korruption in der NS-Zeit* (Frankfurt am Main, 2001), 99–105.

189. Ibid., 104–18; idem, 'Gauleiter in Hamburg. Zur Person und Tätigkeit Karl Kaufmanns', *VfZ* 43 (1995), 27–95.

190. Bajohr, *Parvenüs*, 117–21; Saul K. Padover, *Experiment in Germany: The Story of an American Intelligence Officer* (New York, 1946), 57.

191. Gerd R. Ueberschär and Winfried Vogel, *Dienen und Verdienen: Hitlers Geschenke an seine Eliten* (Frankfurt am Main, 1999), 35–55; Bajohr, *Parvenüs*, 17–21.

192. Ueberschär and Vogel, *Dienen und Verdienen*, 55–69.

193. Ibid., 77–8.

194. Ibid., 90–93; Bajohr, *Parvenüs*, 34–6; see also Wulf C. Schwarzwäller, *The Unknown Hitler: His Private Life and Fortune* (Bethesda, Md., 1989 [1986]), and 'Der Nazi-Diktator zahlte nicht mal Steuern', *Die Welt*, 17 December 2004.

195. Bajohr, *Parvenüs*, 21–6. This system inspired the joke that NSDAP stood for 'Na, suchst du auch Pöstchen?' ('So you're also looking for little positions in the state?') (Gamm, *Der Flüsterwitz*, 77).

196. Bajohr, *Parvenüs*, 27–33.

197. Herbert, ' "Die guten und die schlechten Zeiten" ', interview with Willi Erbach.

198. Steinberg, *Sabers*, 142–4.

199. Bajohr, *Parvenüs*, 49–55.

200. Ibid., 63–8.

201. Ibid., 69–70.

202. Ibid., 71–4.

203. Ibid., 75–94; Behnken (ed.), *Deutschland-Berichte*, IV (1937), 549–53.

204. Ibid., 514–18.

205. Klemperer, *I Shall Bear Witness*, 84–5 (27 September 1934).

206. Grunberger, *A Social History*, 419–25, 468–9; Gamm, *Der Flüsterwitz*, 88, 90; Kershaw, *The 'Hitler Myth'*, 96–104. Finck was subsequently released but was expelled from the Reich Culture Chamber and barred from working, though he made a reappearance in troop entertainment during the war (Grunberger, *A Social History*, 469).

207. Richard J. Overy, 'Germany, "Domestic Crisis", and War in 1939', in idem, *War and Economy*, 205–32, at 214–15.

208. Peter Hayes, 'Polycracy and Policy in the Third Reich: The Case of the Economy', in Childers and Caplan (eds.), *Reevaluating*, 190–210. On the remaining room for manoeuvre of businessmen and industrialists in 1939, see Fritz Blaich, 'Die bayerische Industrie 1933–1939. Elemente von Gleichschaltung, Konfor-

mismus und Selbstbehauptung', in Broszat *et al.* (eds.), *Bayern*, II. 237–80.

209. Tim Mason, 'The Domestic Dynamics of Nazi Conquests: A Response to Critics', in Childers and Caplan (eds.), *Reevaluating the Third Reich*, 161–89.

210. Benhken (ed.), *Deutschland-Berichte*, VI (1939), 643–9; Overy, '"Domestic Crisis"', 216, table 7.1.

Chapter 5. BUILDING THE PEOPLE'S COMMUNITY

1. Friedrich Reck-Malleczewen, *Diary of a Man in Despair* (London, 1995 [1966]), 36–9, 59, 36, 95, 85–6.

2. Ibid., 63.

3. Ibid., 78.

4. Ibid., 52.

5. Ibid., 84–5.

6. Ibid., 85.

7. Christine Zeile, 'Ein biographischer Essay', in Friedrich Reck, *Tagebuch eines Verzweifelten* (Frankfurt am Main, 1994), 251–98. Norman Stone, in his Introduction to the English edition, does not question Reck's title (*Diary*, 5–15, at 12); nor does his translator (Translator's Preface, 17–20, at 18). Burleigh, *The Third Reich*, 5, also describes him as an 'aristocrat'; Gellately, *The Gestapo*, 131, calls him a 'noble from southern Germany'. For a detailed dissection of his fantasies, see Alphons Kappeler, *Ein Fall von 'Pseudologia phantastica' in der deutschen Literatur: Fritz Reck-Malleczewen* (2 vols., Göppingen, 1975), I. 5–179.

8. Kappeler, *Ein Fall*, II. 482–92.

9. Heinz Reif, *Adel im 19. und 20. Jahrhundert* (Munich, 1999), 54, 112, 117; Georg H. Kleine, 'Adelsgenossenschaft und Nationalsozialismus', *VfZ* 26 (1978), 100–143; Shelley Baranowski, 'East Elbian Landed Elites and Germany's Turn to Fascism: The *Sonderweg* Controversy Revisited', *European History Quarterly*, 26 (1996), 209–40; Willibald Gutsche and Joachim Petzold, 'Das Verhältnis der Hohenzollern zum Faschismus', *Zeitschrift für Geschichtswissenschaft*, 29 (1981), 917–39; Wolfgang Zollitsch, 'Adel und adlige Machteliten in der Endphase der Weimarer Republik. Standespolitik und agrarische Interessen', in Heinrich August Winkler (ed.), *Die deutsche Staatskrise 1930–1933: Handlungsspielräume und Alternativen* (Munich, 1992), 239–62; Karl Otmar von Aretin, 'Der bayerische Adel von der Monarchie zum Dritten Reich', in Broszat *et al.* (eds.), *Bayern*, III. 513–68, at 525, 542, 554–6. Stephan Malinowski, *Vom König zum Führer. Sozialer Niedergang und politische Radikalisierung im deutschen Adel zwischen Kaiserreich und NS-Staat* (Berlin, 2003), 321–475, provides a comprehensive and readable survey of aristocratic clubs and pressure-groups.

10. Höhne, *The Order*, 142–8; Gutsche and Petzold, 'Das Verhältnis'; Reif, *Adel*, 54; more generally, Martin Broszat and Klaus Schwabe (eds.), *Die deutschen Eliten und der Weg in den Zweiten Weltkrieg* (Munich, 1989).

11. Malinowski, *Vom König*, 560–78. See also the studies in Heinz Reif (ed.), *Adel und Bürgertum in Deutschland*, II: *Entwicklungslinien und Wendepunkte im 20. Jahrhundert* (Berlin, 2001) and the detailed examples presented in Friedrich Keinemann, *Vom Krummstab zur Republik: Westfälischer Adel unter preussischer Herrschaft 1802–1945* (Bochum, 1997) and Eckart Conze, *Von deutschem Adel: Die Grafen von Bernstorff im zwanzigsten Jahrhundert* (Stuttgart, 2000).

12. Tyrell, *Führer befiehl . . .* , 24; Noakes and Pridham (eds.), *Nazism*, I. 61.

13. Evans, *The Coming of the Third Reich*, 369–73; Corni, *Hitler and the Peasants*, 39–65; Petzina, *Die deutsche Wirtschaft*, 115–16.

14. Matthias Eidenbenz, *'Blut und Boden': Zu Funktion und Genese der Metaphern des Agrarismus und Biologismus in der nationalsozialistischen Bauernpropaganda R. W. Darrés* (Bern, 1993); Oswald Spengler was the first to bring the two words into the same context, though setting them in opposition to one another (ibid., 2–3).

15. Evans, *The Coming of the Third Reich*, 228, 334; Gustavo Corni, 'Richard Walther Darré: The Blood and Soil Ideologue', in Smelser and Zitelmann (eds.), *The Nazi Elite*, 18–27; Horst Gies, *R. Walther Darré und die nationalsozialistische Bauernpolitik 1930 bis 1933* (Frankfurt am Main, 1966); idem, 'Die nationalsozialistische Machtergreifung auf dem agrarpolitischen Sektor', *Zeitschrift für Agrargeschichte und Agrarsoziologie*, 16 (1968), 210–32; Horst Gies, 'NSDAP und landwirtschaftliche Organisationen in der Endphase der Weimarer Republik', *VfZ* 15 (1967), 341–67; Farquharson, *The Plough* 13–73; Herlemann, 'Der Bauer', 53–73.

16. Horst Gies, 'Die nationalsozialistische Machtergreifung', 210–32; idem, 'Landbvevölkerung und Nationalsozialismus. Der Weg in den Reichsnährstand', *Zeitgeschichte*, 13 (1986), 123–41.

17. Farquharson, *The Plough*, 107–40.

18. Corni, *Hitler and the Peasants*, 121; Minuth (ed.), *Akten der Reichskanzlei: Die Regierung Hitler, 1933–1934*, I. 399–401.

19. Corni, *Hitler and the Peasants*, 116–42; Farquharson, *The Plough*, 141–60.

20. Behnken (ed.), *Deutschland-Berichte*, I (1934), 52 (April/May).

21. Ibid., 52.

22. Ibid., 741 (November/December, report from southern Bavaria); more generally, Friedrich Grundmann, *Agrarpolitik im 'Dritten Reich': Anspruch und Wirklichkeit des Reichserbhofgesetzes* (Hamburg, 1979); Herlemann, 'Der Bauer', 127–45.

23. Behnken (ed.), *Deutschland-Berichte*, I (1934), 741–2.

24. Ibid., 232 (also for the preceding passage); more generally, see the account in Corni, *Hitler and the Peasants*, 143–55.

25. Behnken (ed.), *Deutschland-Berichte*, I (1934), 232–3; see also Michael Schwartz, 'Bauern vor dem Sondergericht. Resistenz und Verfolgung im bäuerlichen Milieu Westfalens', in Anselm Faust (ed.), *Verfolgung und Widerstand im Rheinland und in Westfalen 1933–1945* (Cologne, 1992), 113–23.

26. See for example Herlemann, 'Der Bauer', 226-9.

27. Behnken (ed.), Deutschland-Berichte, IV (1937), 1,098-140; examples on 1,100 and 1,103.

28. Wolfram Pyta, Dorfgemeinschaft und Parteipolitik 1918-1933: Die Verschränkung von Milieu und Parteien in der protestantischen Landgebieten Deutschlands in der Weimarer Republik (Düsseldorf, 1996), 470-73.

29. Zdenek Zofka, Die Ausbreitung des Nationalsozialismus auf dem Lande: Eine regionale Fallstudie zur politischen Einstellung der Landbevölkerung in der Zeit des Aufstiegs und der Machtergreifung der NSDAP 1928-1936 (Munich, 1979); Herlemann, 'Der Bauer', 77-88.

30. Zdenek Zofka, 'Dorfeliten und NSDAP. Fallbeispiele der Gleichschaltung aus dem Kreis Günzburg', in Broszat et al. (eds.), Bayern, IV. 383-434, at 429 (Aus dem Schreiben des Landrats von Bad Aibling an die zuständige Behörde der US-Militärregierung vom 12. Dezember 1945).

31. Ibid., 431 (Aus einem Schreiben des Bezirksamts Erding an die Kreisleitung Erding vom 5. März 1937).

32. Ibid., 432 (Aus der Stellungnahme des Bezirksamtes München vom 27. September 1938).

33. Caroline Wagner, Die NSDAP auf dem Dorf: Eine Sozialgeschichte der NS-Machtergreifung in Lippe (Münster, 1998).

34. Gerhard Wilke, 'Village Life in Nazi Germany', in Richard Bessel (ed.), Life in the Third Reich (Oxford, 1987), 17-24. See also the full-length study by Kurt Wagner, Leben auf dem Lande im Wandel der Industrialisierung: 'Das Dorf war früher auch keine heile Welt': Veränderung der dörflichen Lebensweise und der politischen Kultur vor dem Hintergrund der Industrialisierung am Beispiel des nordhessischen Dorfes Körle (1800-1970) (Frankfurt am Main, 1986).

35. Gerhard Wilke and Kurt Wagner, 'Family and Household: Social Structures in a German Village Between the Two World Wars', in Richard J. Evans and William Robert Lee (eds.), The German Family: Essays on the Social History of the Family in Nineteenth- and Twentieth-century Germany (London, 1981), 120-47; Grunberger, A Social History, 200, citing Hans Müller, Deutsches Bauerntum zwischen Gestern und Morgen (Witzburg, 1940), 28.

36. Gerhard Wilke, 'The Sins of the Fathers: Village Society and Social Control in the Weimar Republic', in Richard J. Evans and W. R. Lee (eds.), The German Peasantry: Conflict and Community in Rural Society from the Eighteenth to the Twentieth Centuries (London, 1986), 174-204.

37. For similar findings for Lippe, see Wagner, Die NSDAP, passim.

38. Kurt Wagner and Gerhard Wilke, 'Dorfleben im Dritten Reich: Körle in Hessen', in Peukert and Reulecke (eds.), Die Reihen fast geschlossen, 85-106. For another, comparable study, see Wolfgang Kaschuba and Carola Lipp, 'Kein Volk steht auf, kein Sturm bricht los. Stationen dörflichen Lebens auf dem Weg in den Faschismus', in Johannes Beck et al. (eds.), Terror und Hoffnung in Deutschland 1933-1945: Leben im Faschismus (Reinbek, 1980), 111-55, and idem, Dörfliches

Überleben: Zur Geschichte materieller und sozialer Reproduktion ländlicher Gesellschaft im 19. und frühen 20. Jahrhundert (Tübingen, 1982), 232–59. For a more general assessment, see also Wolfgang Kaschuba, *Lebenswelt und Kultur der unterbürgerlichen Schichten im 19. und 20. Jahrhundert* (Munich, 1990), 47–9.

39. Daniela Münkel, *Nationalsozialistiche Agrarpolitik und Bauernalltag* (Frankfurt am Main, 1996), 192–320; see also eadem, *Bauern und Nationalsozialismus: Der Landkreis Celle im Dritten Reich* (Bielefeld, 1991); and eadem, 'Hakenkreuz und "Blut und Boden": Bäuerliches Leben im Landkreis Celle 1933–1939', *Zeitschrift für Agrargeschichte und Agrarsoziologie*, 40 (1992), 206–47.

40. See also the discussion in Herlemann, *'Der Bauer'*, 88–119.

41. Münkel, *Nationalsozialistische Agrarpolitik*, 278–80, 319–20, 466–81; Wagner, *Die NSDAP*, however, emphasizes the relatively high level of denunciations in some villages in Lippe. For the failure of agricultural modernization, see Peter Exner, *Ländliche Gesellschaft und Landwirtschaft in Westfalen, 1919–1969* (Paderborn, 1997); Joachim Lehmann, 'Mecklenburgische Landwirtschaft und "Modernisierung" in den dreissiger Jahren', in Frank Bajohr (ed.), *Norddeutschland*, 335–46; and Daniela Münkel (ed.), *Der lange Abschied vom Agrarland: Agrarpolitik, Landwirtschaft und ländliche Gesellschaft zwischen Weimar und Bonn* (Göttingen, 2000). For a brief assessment of the Harvest Thanksgiving Festival, see Herlemann, *'Der Bauer'*, 223.

42. From a large literature, see in particular Heinz-Gerhard Haupt (ed.), *Die radikale Mitte: Lebensweisen und Politik von Kleinhändlern und Handwerkern in Deutschland seit 1848* (Munich, 1985); David Blackbourn, 'Between Resignation and Volatility: The German Petty Bourgeoisie in the Nineteenth Century', in idem, *Populists and Patricians: Essays in Modern German History* (London, 1987), 84–113; Heinrich August Winkler, *Mittelstand, Demokratie und Nationalsozialismus: Die politische Entwicklung von Handwerk und Kleinhandel in der Weimarer Republik* (Cologne, 1972); Adelheid von Saldern, *Mittelstand im 'Dritten Reich': Handwerker – Einzelhändler – Bauern* (Frankfurt am Main, 1979).

43. David Schoenbaum, *Hitler's Social Revolution: Class and Status in Nazi Germany, 1933–1939* (London, 1967), 136–7; Saldern, *Mittelstand, passim*; Behnken (ed.), *Deutschland-Berichte*, VI (1939), 228–32.

44. Friedrich Lenger, *Sozialgeschichte der deutschen Handwerker seit 1800* (Frankfurt am Main, 1988), 195–203. For the Labour Front, see below, 459–65.

45. Blaich, *Wirtschaft*, 19–20; Petzina, *Die deutsche Wirtschaft*, 142.

46. Lenger, *Sozialgeschichte*, 132–7 and 163–202; Bernhard Keller, *Das Handwerk im faschistischen Deutschland: Zum Problem der Massenbasis* (Cologne, 1980), 68–84 (some useful information despite Marxist-Leninist approach).

47. Schoenbaum, *Hitler's Social Revolution*, 136–43, 147–50; Behnken (ed.), *Deutschland-Berichte*, VI (1939), 251–4.

48. Lenger, *Sozialgeschichte*, 195–203; Schoenbaum, *Hitler's Social Revolution*, 136–43, 147–50. The contention of Adelheid von Saldern that artisanal trades

achieved much of what they wanted in the Third Reich is only partially convincing even for the period 1933–6 and not at all for the period thereafter: see Heinrich August Winkler, 'Der entbehrliche Stand. Zur Mittelstandspolitik im "Dritten Reich"', *Archiv für Sozialgeschichte*, 17 (1977), 1–4; Adelheid von Saldern, *Mittelstand*; eadem, '"Alter Mittelstand" im "Dritten Reich". Anmerkungen zu einer Kontroverse', *Geschichte und Gesellschaft*, 12 (1986), 235–43; Heinrich August Winkler, 'Ein neuer Mythos vom alten Mittelstand. Antwort auf eine Antikritik', *Geschichte und Gesellschaft*, 12 (1986), 548–57.

49. Gerald Schröder, 'Die "Wiedergeburt" der Pharmazie – 1933 bis 1934', in Mehrtens and Richter (eds.), *Naturwissenschaft*, 166–88; Franz Leimkugel, 'Antisemitische Gesetzgebung in der Pharmazie, 1933–1939', in Meinel and Voswinckel (eds.), *Medizin*, 230–35.

50. Martin F. Brumme, '"Prachtvoll fegt der eiserne Besen durch die deutschen Lande." Die Tierärzte und das Jahr 1933', in Meinel and Voswinckel (eds.), *Medizin*, 173–82.

51. Schoenbaum, *Hitler's Social Revolution*, 144–6.

52. Behnken (ed.), *Deutschland-Berichte*, I (1934), 49–50.

53. Ibid., 111–12.

54. Ibid., II (1935), 453–60.

55. Ibid., 1,334–54.

56. Ibid., VI (1939), 868–98.

57. Günther Schulz, *Die Angestellten seit dem 19. Jahrhundert* (Munich, 2000), 36–7; Michael Prinz, *Vom neuen Mittelstand zum Volksgenossen: Die Entwicklung des sozialen Status der Angestellten von der Weimarer Republik bis zum Ende der NS-Zeit* (Munich, 1986), 92–143, 229.

58. Prinz, *Vom neuen Mittelstand*, 334–5.

59. Behnken (ed.), *Deutschland-Berichte*, III (1936), 732–3.

60. Konrad H. Jarausch, *The Unfree Professions: German Lawyers, Teachers, and Engineers, 1900–1950* (New York, 1990), 142–69.

61. Kater, *Doctors*, 35–6.

62. See above, 317–18.

63. Kater, *Doctors*, 35–40.

64. Ibid., 25–34, 54–74; see also idem, 'Medizin und Mediziner im Dritten Reich', *Historische Zeitschrift*, 244 (1987), 299–352.

65. Domarus, *Hitler*, II. 692.

66. Boberach (ed.), *Meldungen*, II. 281 (Vierteljahrslagebericht 1939 des Sicherheitshauptamtes Band 2).

67. Jane Caplan, *Government without Administration: State and Civil Service in Weimar and Nazi Germany* (Oxford, 1988), 215–59.

68. Document printed in Hans Mommsen, *Beamtentum im Dritten Reich: Mit ausgewählten Quellen zur nationalsozialistischen Beamtenpolitik* (Stuttgart, 1976) 146–8.

69. Caplan, *Government*, 321–5.

70. Jane Caplan, ' "The Imaginary Unity of Particular Interests": The "Tradition" of the Civil Service in German History', *Social History*, 4 (1978), 299–317; eadem, 'Bureaucracy, Politics and the National Socialist State', in Stachura (ed.), *The Shaping*, 234–56.

71. Hedda Kalshoven, *Ich denk so viel an Euch: Ein deutsch-holländischer Briefwechsel 1920–1949* (Munich, 1995 [1991]), 151–2.

72. Ibid., 152.

73. Ibid., 161 (3 February 1933).

74. Ibid., 169 (10 March 1933).

75. Ibid., 177–8 (14 March 1933).

76. Ibid., 182–4 (22 March 1933).

77. Ibid., 187 (30 March 1933).

78. Ibid., 189 (6 April 1933).

79. Ibid., 199 (17 May 1933).

80. Ibid., also 198 (12 May 1933).

81. Ibid., 202–3 (25 May 1933).

82. Ibid., 202 (25 May 1933).

83. Ibid., 175–6 (14 March 1933).

84. Ibid., 180 (14 March 1933).

85. Ibid., 189 (6 April 1933).

86. Ibid., 189–90 (6 April 1933).

87. Ibid., 216 (18 October 1933).

88. Ibid., 212–13 (*Braunschweigische Landeszeitung*, 19 October 1933).

89. Ibid., 236 (14 July 1934); also her daughter's letter of 7 July on the same page.

90. Evans, *The Coming of the Third Reich*, 425.

91. Kalshoven, *Ich denk*, 17–31. There is no reason to suppose that the family stopped mentioning politics in their letters out of fear that they were being intercepted by the Gestapo, although this must remain a possibility.

92. Hanna Haack, 'Arbeitslose in Deutschland. Ergebnisse und Analyse der Berufszählung vom 16. Juni 1933', *Jahrbuch für Wirtschaftsgeschichte* (1986), 36–69; useful brief summary in Heinrich August Winkler, *Der Weg in die Katastrophe: Arbeiter und Arbeiterbewegung in der Weimarer Republik 1930 bis 1933* (Berlin, 1987), 93–9; see also the classic study by Thedor Julius Geiger, *Die soziale Schichtung des deutschen Volkes* (Stuttgart, 1967 [1932]). The category of the 'economically active' (*Erwerbspersonen*) includes registered unemployed in these sectors as well as persons still in employment (*Erwerbstätige*).

93. Evans, *The Coming of the Third Reich*, 333–49, 355–61.

94. Boelcke, *Die deutsche Wirtschaft*, 68–9. Hans-Gerd Schumann, *Nationalsozialismus und Gewerkschaftsbewegung: Die Vernichtung der deutschen Gewerkschaften und der Aufbau der 'Deutschen Arbeitsfront'* (Hanover, 1958), 63; Ronald Smelser, *Robert Ley: Hitler's Labor Front Leader* (Oxford, 1988), 117–25; Mason, *Social Policy*, 63–108.

95. Smelser, *Robert Ley*, 126–34.

96. Schumann, *Nationalsozialismus und Gewerkschaftsbewegung*, 63–5.

97. Ronald Smelser, 'Robert Ley: The Brown Collectivist', in idem and Zitelmann (eds.), *The Nazi Elite*, 144–54, at 144–5; also, at greater length, Smelser, *Robert Ley*, 6–16.

98. Ibid., 17–69.

99. Ibid. 125–34.

100. Ibid., 135–9.

101. Timothy W. Mason, 'The Workers' Opposition in Nazi Germany', *History Workshop Journal*, 11 (1987), 120–37.

102. Smelser, *Robert Ley*, 140–42; Noakes and Pridham (eds.), *Nazism*, II. 149; Schoenbaum, *Hitler's Social Revolution*, 91–8.

103. Quoted in Broszat, *Der Staat Hitlers*, 190 (note).

104. Heidrun Homburg, *Rationalisierung und Industriearbeit. Arbeitsmarkt – Management – Arbeiterschaft im Siemens-Konzern Berlin 1900–1939* (Berlin, 1991), 681–2.

105. Smelser, *Robert Ley*, 98–116; Speer, *Inside*, 217; Felix Kersten, *The Kersten Memoirs 1940–1945* (London, 1956 [1952]) (not always reliable); Hans-Peter Bleuel, *Strength Through Joy: Sex and Society in Nazi Germany* (London, 1973 [1972]), 3.

106. Bajohr, *Parvenüs*, 55–62.

107. Behnken (ed.), *Deutschland-Berichte*, IV (1937), 538–40.

108. Shelley Baranowski, *Strength Through Joy*, 11–51; see also Hermann Weiss, 'Ideologie der Freizeit im Dritten Reich: Die NS-Gemeinschaft "Kraft durch Freude"', *Archiv für Sozialgeschichte*, 33 (1993), 289–303.

109. Quoted in Behnken (ed.), *Deutschland-Berichte*, VI (1939), 463.

110. Baranowski, *Strength Through Joy*, 51–66; also von Saldern, '"Art for the People"', 322–9; Schneider, *Unterm Hakenkreuz*, 228–9.

111. Behnken (ed.), *Deutschland-Berichte*, V (1938), 158.

112. Baranowski, *Strength Through Joy*, 118–42; Schneider, *Unterm Hakenkreuz*, 230–34.

113. Baranowski, *Strength Through Joy*, 142–54.

114. Behnken (ed.), *Deutschland-Berichte*, II (1935), 176; similar reports in ibid., 846–7.

115. Ibid., VI (1939), 468.

116. Baranowski, *Strength Through Joy*, 165–7; Behnken (ed.), *Deutschland-Berichte*, VI (1939), 464–8.

117. Jürgen Rostock and Franz Zadnicek, *Paradiesruinen: Das KdF-Seebad der Zwanzigtausend auf Rügen* (Berlin, 1997 [1992]); Baranowski, *Strength Through Joy*, 155–61, 231; Hasso Spode, 'Ein Seebad für zwanzigtausend Volksgenossen: Zur Grammatik und Geschichte des Fordistischen Urlaubs', in Peter J. Brenner (ed.), *Reisekultur in Deutschland: Von der Weimarer Republic zum 'Dritten Reich'* (Tübingen, 1997), 7–47; for comparison, John K. Walton, *The British Seaside: Holidays and Resorts in the Twentieth Century* (Manchester, 2000). The resort

had an everyday parallel in 'Strength-Through-Joy Town', built to accommodate the workers at the new Volkswagen plant: see Mommsen and Grieger, *Das Volkswagenwerk*, 250–82.

118. Baranowski, *Strength Through Joy*, 66–74; Behnken (ed.), *Deutschland-Berichte*, II (1935), 175; further reports in ibid., V (1938), 165–75, and VI (1939), 468–85 and 879–87.

119. Baranowski, *Strength Through Joy*, 166–75.

120. Ibid., 162–75; Mason, *Social Policy*, 160 and n. 20; William D. Bayles, *Caesars in Goosestep* (New York, 1940); Behnken (ed.), *Deutschland-Berichte*, I (1934), 524; ibid., VI (1939), 479.

121. Ibid., (1936), 884.

122. Hasso Spode, '"Der deutsche Arbeiter reist": Massentourismus im Dritten Reich', in Gerhard Huck (ed.), *Sozialgeschichte der Freizeit: Untersuchungen zum Wandel der Alltagskultur in Deutschland* (Wuppertal, 1980), 281–306; Schneider, *Unterm Hakenkreuz*, 670–78; Behnken (ed.), *Deutschland-Berichte*, I (1934), 523–7.

123. Mason, *Social Policy*, 159.

124. Behnken (ed.), *Deutschland-Berichte*, VI (1939), 474.

125. Ibid., V (1938), 172.

126. Mason, *Social Policy*, 158–64.

127. Behnken (ed.), *Deutschland-Berichte*, VI (1939), 468.

128. Herbert, '"Die guten und die schlechten Zeiten"', 67–96.

129. Schneider, *Unterm Hakenkreuz*, 676; Behnken (ed.), *Deutschland-Berichte*, VI (1939), 474.

130. Ibid., II (1935), 1,455–6.

131. Ibid., 849.

132. For an important study of this process, see Lynn Abrams, *Workers' Culture in Imperial Germany: Leisure and Recreation in the Rhineland and Westphalia* (London, 1992); for the labour movement's cultural traditions see, among many other studies, Vernon L. Lidtke, *The Alternative Culture: Socialist Labor in Imperial Germany* (New York, 1985), and W. L. Guttsman, *Workers' Culture in Weimar Germany: Between Tradition and Commitment* (Oxford, 1990).

133. Baranowski, *Strength Through Joy*, 165.

134. Schneider, *Unterm Hakenkreuz*, 672; Christine Keitz, 'Die Anfänge des modernen Massentourismus in der Weimarer Republik', *Archiv für Sozialgeschichte*, 33 (1993), 179–209, at 192.

135. See Kristin A. Semmens, *Seeing Hitler's Germany: Tourism in the Third Reich* (London, 2005).

136. Baranowski, *Strength Through Joy*, 75–117; Chup Friemert, *Schönheit der Arbeit: Produktionsästhetik im Faschismus* (Munich, 1980); and Anson G. Rabinbach, 'The Aesthetics of Production in the Third Reich', in George L. Mosse (ed.), *International Fascism: New Thoughts and New Approaches* (London, 1979), 189–222. For one example, see Matthias Frese, *Betriebspolitik im 'Dritten Reich'*:

Deutsche Arbeitsfront, Unternehmer und Staatsbürokratie in der westdeutschen Grossindustrie, 1933–1939 (Paderborn, 1991), 383–95; further reports in Behnken (ed.), *Deutschland-Berichte*, III (1936), 886–7, and V (1938), 173–5.

137. Ibid., VI (1939), 463.

138. Ibid., II (1935), 846.

139. Cited in Schneider, *Unterm Hakenkreuz*, 678.

140. Blaich, *Wirtschaft*, 19–20.

141. 'Upswing Without Prosperity? Some Notes on the Development in the Lower Income Classes in Germany', *Supplement to the Weekly Report of the German Institute for Business Research* (Berlin, 24 February 1937).

142. Rüdiger Hachtmann, *Industriearbeit im 'Dritten Reich': Untersuchungen zu den Lohn- und Arbeitsbedingungen in Deutschland 1933–1945* (Göttingen, 1989), 156–9; Dietmar Petzina et al. (eds.), *Sozialgeschichtliches Arbeitsbuch*, III: *Materialien zur Statistik des Reiches 1914–1945* (Munich, 1978), 98; Mason, *Social Policy*, 128–33.

143. Schneider, *Unterm Hakenkreuz*, 546–52.

144. Petzina et al. (eds.), *Sozialgeschichtliches Arbeitsbuch*, III. 103.

145. Klaus Wisotzky, *Der Ruhrbergbau im Dritten Reich: Studien zur Sozialpolitik im Ruhrbergbau und zum sozialen Verhalten der Bergleute in den Jahren 1933 bis 1939* (Düsseldorf, 1983), 81–7; Behnken (ed.), *Deutschland-Berichte*, V (1938), 311–12.

146. See, for example, Michael Stahlmann, *Die erste Revolution in der Autoindustrie: Management und Arbeitspolitik von 1900–1940* (Frankfurt am Main, 1993), 85–8 (on the Opel car factory); Magnus Tessner, *Die deutsche Automobilindustrie im Strukturwandel von 1919 bis 1938* (Cologne, 1994), 205–6; and Homburg, *Rationalisierung, passim*.

147. Timothy Mason, *Arbeiterklasse und Volkgemeinschaft: Dokumente und Materialien zur deutschen Arbeiterpolitik 1936–1939* (Opladen, 1975), 669–70; Behnken (ed.), *Deutschland-Berichte*, VI (1939), 163–7; for the disciplining of the workforce in the automobile industry, see Ernst Kaiser and Michael Knorn, '*Wir lebten und schliefen zwischen den Toten': Rüstungsproduktion, Zwangsarbeit und Vernichtung in den Frankfurter Adlerwerken* (Frankfurt am Main, 1994), 39–48.

148. Behnken (ed.), *Deutschland-Berichte*, VI (1939), 159–60.

149. Mason, *Arbeiterklasse*, 198–203.

150. Bernard P. Bellon, *Mercedes in Peace and War: German Automobile Workers, 1903–1945* (New York, 1990), 227.

151. Mason, *Social Policy*, 181–94.

152. Behnken (ed.), *Deutschland-Berichte*, VI (1939), 167–8, 338–46.

153. Mason, *Social Policy*, 266–74; Behnken (ed.), *Deutschland-Berichte*, V (1938), 1,086–94; VI (1939), 352–6; see also, for a detailed example, Andreas Meyhoff, *Blohm und Voss im 'Dritten Reich': Eine Hamburger Grosswerft zwischen Geschäft und Politik* (Hamburg, 2001).

154. Herbert, ' "Die guten und die schlechten Zeiten" ', 93; for the thesis that class conflict of this kind contributed towards a prewar crisis, see Timothy Mason, 'Arbeiteropposition im nationalsozialistischen Deutschland', in Peukert and Reulecke (eds.), *Die Reihen fast geschlossen*, 293–314; second thoughts in Mason, *Social Policy*, 275–331; balanced assessment in Schneider, *Unterm Hakenkreuz*, 752–65; detailed local study of a mining community in Klaus Tenfelde, 'Proletarische Provinz: Radikalisierung und Widerstand in Penzberg/Oberbayern 1900 bis 1945', in Broszat *et al.* (eds.), *Bayern*, IV: 1–382, at 320–37.

155. Hitler, *Mein Kampf*, 27–8.

156. Evans, *The Coming of the Third Reich*, 140–45, 378–80; David F. Crew, *Germans on Welfare: From Weimar to Hitler* (New York, 1998), 6, 212–15.

157. Florian Tennstedt, 'Wohltat und Interesse. Das Winterhilfswerk des Deutschen Volkes. Die Weimarer Vorgeschichte und ihre Instrumentalisierung durch das NS-Regime', *Geschichte und Gesellschaft*, 13 (1987), 157–80.

158. Thomas E. de Witt, ' "The Struggle Against Hunger and Cold": Winter Relief in Nazi Germany, 1933–1939', *Canadian Journal of History*, 12 (1978), 361–81.

159. Herwart Vorländer, *Die NSV: Darstellung und Dokumentation einer nationalsozialistischen Organisation* (Boppard, 1988), 4–5, 44–62.

160. Behnken (ed.), *Deutschland-Berichte*, II (1935), 1,430, and V (1938), 77–115; De Witt, 'The Struggle'.

161. De Witt, 'The Struggle'; also Herwart Vorländer, 'NS-Volkswohlfahrt und Winterhilfswerk des deutschen Volkes', *VfZ* 34 (1986), 341–80; and idem, *Die NSV*, 230, 53–4.

162. De Witt, ' "The Struggle" '; Speer, *Inside*, 179–80; Vorländer, *Die NSV*, 51–2.

163. Ibid., 6–37.

164. Ibid., 214.

165. Quoted in Adelheid Gräfin zu Castell Rüdenhausen, ' "Nicht mitzuleiden, mitzukämpfen sind wir da!" Nationalsozialistische Volkswohlfahrt im Gau Westfalen-Nord', in Peukert and Reulecke (eds.), *Die Reihen fast geschlossen*, 223–44, at 224–5.

166. Gamm, *Der Flüsterwitz*, 90; Behnken (ed.), *Deutschland-Berichte*, II (1935), 1,421–47; Castell Rüdenhausen, ' "Nicht mitzuleiden" '; see also Peter Zolling, *Zwischen Integration und Segregation: Sozialpolitik im 'Dritten Reich' am Beispiel der 'Nationalsozialistischen Volkswohlfahrt' (NSV) in Hamburg* (Frankfurt am Main, 1986).

167. Behnken (ed.), *Deutschland-Berichte*, II (1935), 1,447–55; see also ibid., I (1934), 42–8.

168. Maschmann, *Account Rendered*, 13.

169. Ibid., 10–18.

170. Kershaw, *The 'Hitler Myth'*, 64–5, 73–7.

171. William Sheridan Allen, *The Nazi Seizure of Power: The Experience of a Single German Town 1922–1945* (New York, 1984 [1965]), 266–73.

172. Ibid.

173. Ibid.

174. Ibid., 274–91. See also the richly detailed though more politically oriented local study by Struve, *Aufstieg*, and the documentary collection edited by Lawrence D. Stokes, *Kleinstadt und Nationalsozialismus: Ausgewählte Dokumente zur Geschichte von Eutin, 1918–1945* (Neumünster, 1984) (both North Germany).

175. Bernd Stöver, *Volksgemeinschaft im Dritten Reich: Die Konsensbereitschaft der Deutschen aus der Sicht sozialistischer Exilberichte* (Düsseldorf, 1993), 115–203, 421.

176. Domarus (ed.), *Hitler*, I. 415–17.

177. Ibid., II. 892.

178. *Völkischer Beobachter*, 29 September 1935, cited in Schoenbaum, *Hitler's Social Revolution*, 67.

179. See above, 268, 300–301; for Reck's views, see *Diary*, 63–4.

180. Tagebuch Luise Solmitz, 28 April 1933.

181. For a selective comparison, see Overy, *The Dictators*, 218–64; for the argument that the Third Reich modernized German society through Keynesian economic policies and the destruction of traditional social institutions like the trade unions, see Werner Abelshauser and Anselm Faust, *Wirtschafts- und Sozialpolitik: Eine nationalsozialistische Revolution?* (Tübingen, 1983).

182. Henry Ashby Turner, Jr, 'Fascism and Modernization', in idem (ed.), *Reappraisals of Fascism* (New York, 1975), 117–39.

183. See the useful discussion in Ian Kershaw, *The Nazi Dictatorship: Problems and Perspectives of Interpretation* (4th edn, London, 2000 [1985]), 161–82; Horst Matzerath and Heinrich Volkmann, 'Modernisierungstheorie und Nationalsozialismus', in Jürgen Kocka (ed.), *Theorien in der Praxis des Historikers* (Göttingen, 1977), 86–116; Jeremy Noakes, 'Nazism and Revolution', in Noel O'Sullivan (ed.), *Revolutionary Theory and Political Reality* (London, 1983), 73–100. For the view that Nazism deliberately sought to modernize German society, see Rainer Zitelmann, *Hitler: The Politics of Seduction* (London, 1999 [1987]). This has not been widely accepted, at least, not in the form put by Zitelmann.

Chapter 6. TOWARDS THE RACIAL UTOPIA

1. Paul Weindling, *Health, Race and German Politics between National Unification and Nazism, 1870–1945* (Cambridge, 1989), 60–84; Evans, *The Coming of the Third Reich*, 35–6; Robert N. Proctor, *Racial Hygiene: Medicine under the Nazis*, (London, 1988), 47.

2. Evans, *The Coming of the Third Reich*, 34–8, 377–8; Hans-Walter Schmuhl, *Rassenhygiene, Nationalsozialismus, Euthanasie: Von der Verhütung zur Vernichtung 'lebensunwerten Lebens', 1890–1945* (Göttingen, 1987), 49–105.

3. Weindling, *Health*, 489–503.

4. Longerich, *Politik*, 47–50.

5. Evans, *The Coming of the Third Reich* 37, 145, 377–80; Proctor, *Racial Hygiene*, 10–104 (95 for Frick's committee); Schmuhl, *Rassenhygiene*, 154–68; Christian Ganssmüller, *Die Erbgesundheitspolitik des dritten Reiches: Planung, Durchführung und Durchsetzung* (Cologne, 1987), 34–115; Jeremy Noakes, 'Nazism and Eugenics: The Background to the Nazi Sterilization Law of 14 July 1933', in Roger Bullen *et al.* (eds.), *Ideas into Politics: Aspects of European History 1880–1950* (London, 1984), 75–94.

6. Gisela Bock, *Zwangssterilisation im Nationalsozialismus: Studien zur Frauen- politik und Rassenpolitik* (Opladen, 1986), 230–32.

7. Ganssmüller, *Die Erbgesundheitspolitik*, 45–6: another 40,000 were sterilized in areas annexed by Germany in 1938–9.

8. Michael Burleigh, *Death and Deliverance: 'Euthanasia' in Germany c.1900– 1945* (Cambridge, 1994), 56–66.

9. Quoted in Andrea Brücks, 'Zwangssterilisation gegen "Ballastexistenzen"', in Klaus Frahm *et al.* (eds.), *Verachtet – verfolgt – vernichtet: Zu den 'vergessenen' Opfern des NS-Regimes* (Hamburg, 1986), 103–8.

10. Longerich, *Politik*, 61–2.

11. Joachim Müller, *Sterilisation und Gesetzgebung bis 1933* (Husum, 1985); Wachsmann, *Hitler's Prisons*, 151.

12. Michael Schwartz, *Sozialistische Eugenik: Eugenische Sozialtechnologien in Debatten und Politik der Deutschen Sozialdemokratie 1890–1933* (Bonn, 1995).

13. Wachsmann, *Hitler's Prisons*, 149–56.

14. Klaus-Dieter Thomann, '"Krüppel sind nicht minderwertig." Körperbehind- erte im Nationalsozialismus', in Meinel and Voswinckel (eds.), *Medizin*, 208–20, at 208–12, citing Wilhelm Frick, 'Bevölkerungs- und Rassepolitik', in Elsbeth Unverricht (eds.), *Unsere Zeit und Wir: Das Buch der deutschen Frau* (Gauting, 1933), 97–109, at 103.

15. Thomann, '"Krüppel"', 213–16.

16. Rossmeissl, *'Ganz Deutschland'*, 134.

17. Proctor, *Racial Hygiene*, 95–101; Stefan Kühl, *The Nazi Connection: Eugen- ics, American Racism, and German National Socialism* (New York, 1994).

18. Alberto Spektorowski and Elisabeth Mizrachi, 'Eugenics and the Welfare State in Sweden: The Politics of Social Margins and the Idea of a Productive Society', *Journal of Contemporary History*, 39 (2004), 333–52; Alex Duval Smith and Maciej Zeremba, 'Outcasts from Nordic Super-Race', *Observer*, 24 August 1997, 6.

19. Proctor, *Racial Hygiene*, 171; for Protestant welfare policy, see Sabine Schleier- macher, *Sozialethik im Spannungsfeld von Sozial- und Rassenhygiene Der Mediz- iner Hans Harmsen im Centralausschuss für die Innere Mission* (Husum, 1998).

20. Proctor, *Racial Hygiene*, 123.

21. James Woycke, *Birth Control in Germany 1871–1933* (London, 1988), 154;

Evans, *The Coming of the Third Reich*, 375–8; Stibbe, *Women*, 43; Henry P. David *et al.*, 'Abortion and Eugenics in Nazi Germany', *Population and Development Review*, 14 (1988), 81–112.

22. Quoted in Proctor, *Racial Hygiene*, 124.

23. Richard J. Evans, *The Feminist Movement in Germany 1894–1933* (London, 1976), 255–60; idem, *The Coming of the Third Reich*, 185–6.

24. Stibbe, *Women*, 34–40; Jill Stephenson, *The Nazi Organization of Women* (London, 1981), 97–125; eadem, 'The Nazi Organisation of Women, 1933–1939', in Stachura (ed.), *The Shaping*, 186–209. Some of Scholtz-Klink's eleven children did not survive infancy.

25. Irmgard Weyrather, *Muttertag und Mutterkreuz: Die Kult um die 'deutsche Mutter' im Nationalsozialismus* (Frankfurt am Main, 1993); Susanna Dammer, 'Kinder, Küche, Kriegsarbeit – Die Schulung der Frauen durch die NS-Frauenschaft', in Frauengruppe Faschismusforschung (ed.), *Mutterkreuz*, 215–45; Karin Hausen, 'Mother's Day in the Weimar Republic', in Renate Bridenthal *et al.* (eds.), *When Biology Became Destiny*, 131–52; eadem, 'The "German Mother's Day" 1923–1933', in Hans Medick and David Sabean (eds.), *Interest and Emotion: Essays in the Study of Family and Kinship* (Cambridge, 1984), 371–413.

26. Stibbe, *Women*, 34–40; Claudia Koonz, *Mothers in the Fatherland: Women, the Family and Nazi Politics* (London, 1988 [1987]), 177–219; Stephenson, *The Nazi Organization*, 130–77; Pine, *Nazi Family Policy*, 47–81; Michael Kater, 'Die deutsche Elternschaft im nationalsozialistischen Erziehungssystem. Ein Beitrag zur Sozialgeschichte der Familie', *Vierteljahrschrift für Sozial- und Wirtschaftsgeschichte*, 67 (1980), 484–512; Dammer, 'Kinder, Küche, Kriegsarbeit'.

27. Pine, *Nazi Family Policy*, 88–116; Dorothee Klinksiek, *Die Frau im NS-Staat* (Stuttgart, 1982), 93; Jill Stephenson, '*Reichsbund der Kinderreichen*: The League of Large Families in the Population Policy of Nazi Germany', *European Studies Review*, 9 (1979), 350–75.

28. Marschalck, *Bevölkerungsgeschichte*, 158.

29. Gisela Bock, 'Antinatalism, Maternity and Paternity in National Socialist Realism', in Crew (ed.), *Nazism*, 110–40, at 124.

30. Marschalck, *Bevölkerungsgeschichte*, 159.

31. Proctor, *Racial Hygiene*, 126.

32. Stibbe, *Women*, 53–4; Bock, *Zwangssterilisation*, 166–7.

33. Pine, *Nazi Family Policy*, 16–18; Gabriele Czarnowski, ' "The Value of Marriage for the *Volksgemeinschaft*": Policies towards Women and Marriage under National Socialism', in Richard Bessel (ed.), *Fascist Italy and Nazi Germany: Comparisons and Contrasts* (Cambridge, 1996), 94–112, at 107–8; Stephenson, *Women in Nazi Society*, 41–3.

34. Gansmüller, *Die Erbgesundheitspolitik*, 132–47.

35. Höhne, *The Order*, 130–46; Pine, *Nazi Family Policy*, 38–46; Catrine Clay and Michael Leapman, *Master Race: The Lebensborn Experiment in Nazi Germany* (London, 1995).

36. Irene Guenther, *Nazi Chic? Fashioning Women in the Third Reich* (Oxford, 2004), 91–141.

37. Ibid., 91–141, 167–201.

38. Thus the major debate of the 1980s, between Claudia Koonz, *Mothers in the Fatherland*, emphasizing the creation of a sheltered domestic sphere and thus women's complicity in, perhaps even encouragement of, the violence and hatred perpetrated by men in the public sphere, and Bock, 'Anti-Natalism', stressing the victimization of women through the state's increasingly directive, violent and negative policies towards women as mothers, is largely based on a misapprehension: see Adelheid von Saldern, 'Victims or Perpetrators? Controversies about the Role of Women in the Nazi State', in Crew (ed.), *Nazism*, 141–65; and Dagmar Reese and Carola Sachse, 'Frauenforschung zum Nationalsozialismus. Eine Bilanz', in Lerke Gravenhorst and Carmen Tatschmurat (eds.), *Töchter-Fragen: NS-Frauengeschichte* (Freiburg, 1990), 73–106.

39. Maria S. Quine, *Population Politics in Twentieth-Century Europe: Fascist Dictatorships and Liberal Democracies* (London, 1996); Richard Stites, *The Women's Liberation Movement in Russia: Feminism, Nihilism, and Bolshevism, 1860–1930* (Princeton, N.J., 1978).

40. Sybil H. Milton, '"Gypsies" as Social Outsiders in Nazi Germany', in Gellately and Stoltzfus (eds.), *Social Outsiders*, 212–32, puts their number much higher, at 35,000 (212). As Guenter Lewy, *The Nazi Persecution of the Gypsies* (New York, 2000), 1–14, points out, it has become conventional in Germany to refer to the Gypsies by their tribal names (Sinti and Roma, though the smallest group, the Lalleri, are usually, inexplicably, omitted), because the Nazis used the term *Zigeuner* (Gypsy) to refer to them collectively. The arguments against using the term are rehearsed in Burleigh and Wippermann, *The Racial State*, 113. However, the fact that the Nazis used this term does not itself make it pejorative, and indeed, as Lewy notes, 'several Gypsy writers have insisted on the uninterrupted use of the term in order to maintain historical continuity and express solidarity with those who were persecuted under this name' (ix). Following Lewy, the term 'Gypsy' is used in what follows.

41. Evans, 'Social Outsiders'; Michael Zimmermann, *Verfolgt, vertrieben, vernichtet: Die nationalsozialistische Vernichtungspolitik gegen Sinti und Roma* (Essen, 1989), 14–42; idem, *Rassenutopie und Genozid: Die nationalsozialistische 'Lösung der Zigeunerfrage'* (Hamburg, 1996); Rainer Hehemann, *Die 'Bekämpfung des Zigeunerunwesens' im Wilhelminischen Deutschland und in der Weimarer Republik, 1871–1933* (Frankfurt am Main, 1987); Joachim S. Hohmann, *Geschichte der Zigeunerverfolgung in Deutschland* (Frankfurt am Main, 1981); Leo Lucassen, *Zigeuner: Die Geschichte eines polizeilichen Ordnungsbegriffes in Deutschland, 1700–1945* (Cologne, 1996); Joachim S. Hohmann, *Verfolgte ohne Heimat: Die Geschichte der Zigeuner in Deutschland* (Frankfurt am Main, 1990). The Bavarian law is reprinted in part in Burleigh and Wippermann, *The Racial State*, 114–15.

42. Wolfgang Wippermann and Ute Brucker-Boroujerdi, 'Nationalsozialistische Zwangslager in Berlin, III: Das "Zigeunerlager Marzahn" ', *Berliner Forschungen*, 2 (1987), 189–201; Eva von Hase-Mihalik and Doris Kreuzkamp, '*Du kriegst auch einen schönen Wohnwagen*': *Zwangslager für Sinti und Roma während des Nationalsozialismus in Frankfurt am Main* (Frankfurt am Main, 1990); Karola Fings and Frank Sparing, '*z. Zt. Zigeunerlager*': *Die Verfolgung der Düsseldorfer Sinti und Roma im Nationalsozialismus* (Cologne, 1992); Frank Sparing, 'The Gypsy Camps: The Creation, Character and Meaning of an Instrument for the Persecution of Sinti and Romanies under National Socialism', in Karola Fings *et al.*, *From 'Race Science' to the Camps: The Gypsies during the Second World War* (Hatfield, 1997), 39–70.

43. Lewy, *The Nazi Persecution*, 24–49; Joachim S. Hohmann, *Robert Ritter und die Erben der Kriminalbiologie*: *'Zigeunerforschung' im Nationalsozialismus und in Westdeutschland im Zeichen des Rassismus* (Fankfurt am Main, 1991). The decree is reprinted in Burleigh and Wippermann, *The Racial State*, 120–21.

44. Lewy, *The Nazi Persecution*, 47–55; Proctor, *Racial Hygiene*, 214–15; Herbert Heuss, 'German Policies of Gypsy Persecution', in Fings *et al.*, *From 'Race Science'*, 15–37; Karola Fings, 'Romanies and Sinti in the Concentration Camps', in ibid., 71–109; see also Ulrich König, *Sinti und Roma unter dem Nationalsozialismus*: *Verfolgung und Widerstand* (Bochum, 1989), 75–82, and Wolfgang Wippermann, *Das Leben in Frankfurt am Main zur NS-Zeit*, II: *Die nationalsozialistische Zigeunerverfolgung* (Frankfurt am Main, 1986), 19–27.

45. Evans, *The Coming of the Third Reich*, 186–7.

46. Reiner Pommerin, '*Sterilisierung der Rheinlandbastarde*': *Das Schicksal einer farbigen deutschen Minderheit 1918–1937* (Düsseldorf, 1979), 56–77; Proctor, *Racial Hygiene*, 112–14.

47. Pommerin, '*Sterilisierung*', 77–84.

48. Evans, *The Coming of the Third Reich*, 127–8, 375–6.

49. Burkhard Jellonek, *Homosexuelle unter dem Hakenkreuz: Die Verfolgung von Homosexuellen in Dritten Reich* (Paderborn, 1990), 19–50; Richard Plant, *The Pink Triangle: The Nazi War Against Homosexuals* (Edinburgh, 1987 [1986]), 72–104; Smith and Peterson (eds.), *Heinrich Himmler: Geheimreden 1933–1945*, 90–91, 115–23; Geoffrey J. Giles, 'The Institutionalization of Homosexual Panic in the Third Reich', in Gellately and Stoltzfus (eds.), *Social Outsiders*, 233–55.

50. Claudia Schoppmann, *Days of Masquerade: Life Stories of Lesbian Women During the Third Reich* (New York, 1996 [1993]).

51. Jellonek, *Homosexuelle*, 51–94; Proctor, *Racial Hygiene*, 212–14.

52. Jellonek, *Homosexuelle*, 95–110; Hans-Georg Stümke, 'Vom "unausgeglichenen Geschlechtshaushalt". Zur Verfolgung Homosexueller', in Frahm *et al.* (eds.), *Verachtet – verfolgt – vernichtet*, 46–63.

53. Quoted at length in Hans-Georg Stümke and Rudi Finkler, *Rosa Winkel, rosa Listen: Homosexuelle und 'Gesundes Volksempfinden' von Auschwitz bis heute* (Reinbek, 1981), 217–21.

54. Jürgen Baumann, *Paragraph 175: Über die Möglichkeit, die einfache, nicht-jugendgefährdende und nichtöffentliche Homosexualität unter Erwachsenen straffrei zu lassen (zugleich ein Beitrag zur Säkularisierung des Strafrechts)* (Berlin, 1968), 66.

55. Jellonnek, *Homosexuelle*, 12–13.

56. Jeffrey Weeks, *Sex, Politics and Society: The Regulation of Sexuality since 1800* (London, 1981), 239–40; Joachim S. Hohmann (ed.), *Keine Zeit für gute Freunde: Homosexuelle in Deutschland 1933–1969 – Ein Lese- und Bilderbuch* (Berlin, 1982).

57. Rüdiger Lautmann, *et al.*, 'Der rosa Winkel in den nationalsozialistischen Konzentrationslager', in idem (ed.), *Seminar: Gesellschaft und Homosexualität* (Frankfurt am Main, 1977), 325–65, at 332–3.

58. Rüdiger Lautmann, 'Gay Prisoners in Concentration Camps as Compared with Jehovah's Witnesses and Political Prisoners', in Michael Berenbaum (ed.), *A Mosaic of Victims: Non-Jews Persecuted and Murdered by the Nazis* (London, 1990), 200–206.

59. Albrecht Langelüddecke, *Die Entmannung von Sittlichkeitsverbrechern* (Berlin, 1963); Wachsmann, *Hitler's Prisons*, 140–41; Geoffrey Giles, '"The Most Unkindest Cut of All". Castration, Homosexuality and Nazi Justice', *Journal of Contemporary History*, 27 (1992), 41–61; Jellonnek, *Homosexuelle*, 140–71.

60. Wachsmann, *Hitler's Prisons*, 139–49, 368. The total reached 2,300 by 1945 (Longerich, *Politik*, 62).

61. Wachsmann, *Hitler's Prisons*, 400–401; Frank Sparing, 'Zwangskastration im Nationalsozialismus. Das Beispiel der Kriminalbiologischen Sammelstelle Köln', in Peter Busse and Klaus Schreiber (eds.), *Kriminalbiologie* (Düsseldorf, 1997), 169–212.

62. Burkhard Jellonnek, 'Staatspolizeiliche Fahndungs- und Ermittlungsmethoden gegen Homosexuelle. Regionale Differenzen und Gemeinsamkeiten', in Paul and Mallmann (eds.), *Die Gestapo*, 343–56.

63. For a good introduction to the situation of Jews in Germany in 1933–45, see Michael A. Meyer (ed.), *German-Jewish History in Modern Times*, IV: *Renewal and Destruction, 1918–1945* (New York, 1998), 195–388; Marion A. Kaplan, *Between Dignity and Despair: Jewish Life in Nazi Germany* (New York, 1998). For Nazi antisemitism and its antecedents, see also Evans, *The Coming of the Third Reich*, 21–34, 164–5, 431–40.

64. Longerich, *Politik*, 59.

65. For the economic boycotts, see above, 382–6.

66. Hermann Froschauer, 'Streicher und "Der Stürmer"', in Ogan and Weiss (eds.), *Faszination und Gewalt*, 41–8; Hahn (ed.), *Lieber Stürmer!*

67. Bankier, *The Germans*, 28–37.

68. Longerich, *Politik*, 70–74; Bankier, *The Germans*, 14–20.

69. Bankier, *The Germans*, 28–9; Longerich, *Politik*, 74–8, 94–5; Longerich argues persuasively against the view of many historians that the antisemitic outrages of 1935 were spontaneous attempts by the party basis to pressure the

leadership into taking legislative action (e.g. Adam, *Judenpolitik*, 114–16; Herbst, *Das nationalsozialistische Deutschland*, 153–5; Ian Kershaw, 'The Persecution of the Jews and German Popular Opinion in the Third Reich', *Leo Baeck Institute Year Book*, 26 (1981), 261–89, at 265; Hermann Graml, *Reichskristallnacht: Antisemitismus und Judenverfolgung im Dritten Reich* (Munich 1988), 143. For the argument that the antisemitic actions of 1935 were mainly instrumental, see Hans Mommsen and Dieter Obst, 'Die Reaktion der deutschen Bevölkerung auf die Verfolgung der Juden 1933–1943', in Hans Mommsen and Susanne Willems (eds.), *Herrschaftsalltag im Dritten Reich: Studien und Texte* (Düsseldorf, 1988), 374–421, at 385.

70. Illustrations in Ian Kershaw, 'Antisemitismus und Volksmeinung. Reaktionen auf die Judenverfolgung', in Broszat *et al.* (eds.), *Bayern*, II. 281–348, at 302–8.

71. Longerich, *Politik*, 86–90; Behnken (ed.), *Deutschland-Berichte*, II (1935), 920–33.

72. Ibid., 933–7; Longerich, *Politik*, 86–90, 100; Friedländer, *Nazi Germany*, 137–9.

73. Longerich, *Politik*, 85–94; Behnken (ed.), *Deutschland-Berichte*, II (1935), 923 (August 1935).

74. Ibid., 922 (August 1935), cited in Longerich, *Politik*, 93.

75. Ibid., 94–101; Lothar Gruchmann, ' "Blutschutzgesetz" und Justiz: Entstehung und Anwendung des Nürnberger Gesetzes von 15. September 1935', in Ogan and Weiss (eds.), *Faszination und Gewalt*, 49–60. For details of further violent antisemitic outrages in the last weeks of August, see Behnken (ed.), *Deutschland-Berichte*, II (1935), 1,026–45, and early September, Longerich, *Politik*, 107. For discussions adumbrating the Nuremberg Laws from 1933 onwards, see Friedländer, *Nazi Germany*, 118–23.

76. 'Die Reichstagsrede des Führers', *Berliner Tageblatt*, 438, 16 September 1935, 2. Longerich, *Politik*, 102–5, and Bankier, *The Germans*, 41–66, make it clear that the Nuremberg Laws were not a last-minute improvisation; see also Werner Strauss, ' "Das Reichsministerium des Innern und die Judengesetzgebung": Aufzeichnungen von Dr. Bernhard Lösener', *VfZ* 9 (1961), 264–313; Friedländer, *Nazi Germany*, 141–50; and Hermann Graml, *Reichskristallnacht*, 133–56.

77. 'Göring begründet die Gesetze', *Berliner Tageblatt*, 438, 16 September 1935, 2.

78. Longerich, *Politik*, 105–6.

79. Beate Meyer, 'The Mixed Marriage: A Guarantee of Survival or a Reflection of German Society during the Nazi Regime?', in Bankier (ed.), *Probing*, 54–77; Friedländer, *Nazi Germany*, 151, for the statistics, and also Beate Meyer's fundamental study, *'Jüdische Mischlinge': Rassenpolitik und Verfolgungserfahrung 1933–1945* (Hamburg, 1999), 25, 162–5. The first head-count of Jews on the racial basis provided by the Nuremberg Laws was in the Census of 1939 (*Statistisches Jahrbuch für das Deutsche Reich*, 59 (Berlin, 1941–2), 27: 'Die Juden und jüdische Mischlinge in den Reichsteilen und nach Gemeindegrössenklassen 1939').

80. Jeremy Noakes, 'The Development of Nazi Policy towards the German-Jewish

'Mischlinge', 1933–1945', *Leo Baeck Institute Year Book*, 34 (1989), 291–354; idem, 'Wohin gehören die "Judenmischlinge"? Die Entstehung der ersten Durchführungsverordnungen zu den Nürnberger Gesetzen', in Ursula Büttner (ed.), *Das Unrechtsrregime: Internationale Forschung über der Nationalsozialismus: Festschrift für Werner Jochmann zum 65. Geburtstag* (2 vols., Hamburg, 1986), II. 69–89; Longerich, *Politik*, 112–15; Friedländer, *Nazi Germany*, 151–67; Meynert, *Was vor der 'Endlösung' geschah*, 247–51; Meyer, *'Jüdische Mischlinge'*, 29–31 and 96–104; Kaplan, *Between Dignity and Despair*, 74–93.

81. Toepser-Ziegert (ed.), *NS-Presseanweisungen*, II: 1935, 586 (16 September 1935).

82. Meyer, *'Jüdische Mischlinge'*, 230–37.

83. Bryan M. Rigg, *Hitler's Jewish Soldiers: The Untold Story of Nazi Racial Laws and Men of Jewish Descent in the German Military* (Lawrence, Kans., 2002), 51–109. The title is a misnomer: these were not 'Jewish' soldiers at all; the fact that they were half-Jewish or quarter-Jewish made them more German than Jewish as far as the armed forces were concerned. Rigg's estimates of 150,000 mixed-race German soldiers serving between 1933 and 1945 seems a considerable exaggeration, given the fact that the 1939 Census reckoned the total number of people of all ages and both sexes who counted as mixed-race under the Nuremberg Laws in 1935 to be no more than 114,000 in Germany and Austria combined.

84. Summarized in Longerich, *Politik*, 106–11; originals in Behnken (ed.), *Deutschland-Berichte*, II (1935), 1,026–1,045, and III (1936), 20–55; see also Otto Dov Kulka, 'Die Nürnberger Rassengesetze und die deutsche Bevölkerung im Lichte geheimer NS-Lage- und Stimmungsberichte', *VfZ* 32 (1964), 582–624.

85. Behnken (ed.), *Deutschland-Berichte*, III (1936), 26–7.

86. Maschmann, *Account Rendered*, 40–41.

87. Ibid., 30.

88. Ibid., 30, 40–41, 45–7, 49–51, 56.

89. Longerich, *Politik*, 108–9, argues persuasively against Bankier's view (*The Germans*, 76–80) that 'the vast majority of the population approved of the Nuremberg Laws because they identified with the racialist policy' and that 'in most cases . . . the objections stemmed from self-interest'.

90. Wachsmann, *Hitler's Prisons*, 158; Ernst Noam and Wolf-Arno Kropat (eds.), *Justiz und Judenverfolgung* (2 vols., Wiesbaden, 1975), I. *Juden vor Gericht 1933–1945*, 109–68; Inge Marssolek, ' "Die Zeichen an der Wand". Denunziation aus der Perspektive des jüdischen Alltags im "Dritten Reich" ', *Historical Social Research*, 26 (2001), 204–18.

91. Gruchmann, ' "Blutschutzgesetz" ', 53.

92. Wachsmann, *Hitler's Prisons*, 162, 180.

93. Walter Poller, *Medical Block Buchenwald: The Personal Testimony of Inmate 996, Block 36* (London, 1988 [1946]), 128–36.

94. Behnken (ed.), *Deutschland-Berichte*, III (1936), 36, 40–41.

95. Gellately, *The Gestapo*, 165–79; see also Christl Wickert, 'Popular Attitudes

to National Socialist Antisemitism: Denunciations for "Insidious Offenses" and "Racial Ignominy"', in Bankier (ed.), *Probing*, 282–95, and Wolfgang Wippermann, *Das Leben in Frankfurt zur NS-Zeit*, I: *Die nationalsozialistische Judenverfolgung* (Frankfurt am Main, 1986), 68–83.

96. Gellately, *The Gestapo*, 197–8, persuasively rejecting the argument of Sarah Gordon, *Hitler, Germans and the 'Jewish Question'* (Princeton, N.J., 1984), that behaviour of this kind amounted to resistance to the Nuremberg Laws. See also Alexandra Przyrembel, *'Rassenschande': Reinheitsmythos und Vernichtungslegitimation im Nationalsozialismus* (Göttingen, 2003).

97. Oliver Pretzel, Afterword, in Sebastian Haffner, *Defying Hitler: A Memoir* (London, 2002 [2000]), 241–50.

98. Werner Rosenstock, 'Exodus 1933–1939: A Survey of Jewish Emigration from Germany', *Leo Baeck Institute Yearbook*, 1 (1956), 373–90; Herbert A. Strauss, 'Jewish Emigration from Germany: Nazi Policies and Jewish Responses', *Leo Baeck Institute Yearbook*, 25 (1980), 313–61, and 26 (1981), 343–409; Avraham Barkai, 'German Interests in the Haavara-Transfer Agreement 1933–1939', *Leo Baeck Institute Yearbook*, 35 (1990), 254–66; Friedländer, *Nazi Germany*, 60–65; 'Jüdische Bevölkerungsstatistik', in Wolfgang Benz (ed.), *Die Juden in Deutschland 1933–1945: Leben unter nationalsozialistischer Herrschaft* (Munich, 1988), 733, according to which there were roughly 100,000 non-German Jews in Germany in 1933 in addition to the 437,000 German members of the Jewish faith counted in the official statistics. In May 1939 there were still more than 25,000 non-German Jews living in Germany. The 1939 figures include Austria; the 1938 ones do not. For emigration taxes, see above, 389–90. For a local study, see Meynert, *Was vor der 'Endlösung' geschah*, 178–207.

99. Francis R. Nicosia, *The Third Reich and the Palestine Question* (London, 1985), 29–49; also idem, 'Ein nützlicher Feind: Zionismus im nationalsozialistischen Deutschland 1933–1939', *VfZ* 37 (1989), 367–400; Graml, *Reichskristallnacht*, 131–2; Juliane Wetzel, 'Auswanderung aus Deutschland', in Benz (ed.), *Die Juden*, 413–98, at 446–77; the Agreement is reprinted with other relevant material in Rolf Vogel, *Ein Stempel hat gefehlt: Dokumente zur Emigration deutscher Juden* (Munich, 1977), 107–53. For the considerable difficulties facing German Jews who arrived in Palestine, see Wolfgang Benz, *Flucht aus Deutschland: Zum Exil im 20. Jahrhundert* (Munich, 2001), 120–50, and Werner Feilchenfeld et al., *Haavara-Transfer nach Palästina und Einwanderung deutscher Juden 1933–1939* (Tübingen, 1972).

100. Friedländer, *Nazi Germany*, 60–62, 65; Jacob Boas, 'German-Jewish Internal Politics under Hitler 1933–1939', *Leo Baeck Institute Yearbook*, 29 (1984), 2–25; Longerich, *Politik*, 56–8.

101. Yehuda Bauer, *My Brother's Keeper: A History of the American Jewish Joint Distribution Committee 1929–1939* (Philadelphia, Pa., 1974); Louise London, 'Jewish Refugees, Anglo-Jewry and British Government Policy', in David Cesarani (ed.), *The Making of Modern Anglo-Jewry* (Oxford, 1990), 163–90; Bernard

Wasserstein, 'Patterns of Jewish Leadership in Great Britain during the Nazi Era', in Randolph L. Braham (ed.), *Jewish Leadership during the Nazi Era: Patterns of Behavior in the Free World* (New York, 1985), 29–43. Richard Bolchover, *British Jewry and the Holocaust* (Cambridge, 1993), is a passionate but one-sided indictment.

102. Louise London, *Whitehall and the Jews 1933–1948: British Immigration Policy and the Holocaust* (Cambridge, 2000), 16–57; A. Joshua Sherman, *Island Refuge: Britain and Refugees from the Third Reich, 1933–1939* (London, 1973); Bernard Wasserstein, *Britain and the Jews of Europe, 1939–1945* (Oxford, 1979); Vicki Caron, *Uneasy Asylum: France and the Jewish Refugee Crisis, 1933–1942* (Stanford, Calif., 1999); Fritz Kieffer, *Judenverfolgung in Deutschland – eine innere Angelegenheit? Internationale Reaktionen auf die Flüchtlingsproblematik 1933–1939* (Stuttgart, 2002). For Poland and Romania, see below, 606–10.

103. Quoted in Wetzel, 'Auswanderung', 428.

104. Paul Sauer, *Die Schicksale der jüdischen Bürger Baden-Württembergs während der nationalsozialistischen Verfolgungszeit, 1933–1945* (Stuttgart, 1969), 138–9; see more generally Salomon Adler-Rudel, *Jüdische Selbsthilfe unter dem Naziregime 1933–1939 im Spiegel der Berichte der Reichvertretung der Juden in Deutschland* (Tübingen, 1974), 72–120.

105. David Kramer, 'Jewish Welfare Work under the Impact of Pauperization', in Arnold Paucker (ed.), *The Jews in Nazi Germany* (Tübingen, 1986), 173–88; Beate Gohl, *Jüdische Wohlfahrtspflege im Nationalsozialismus: Frankfurt am Main 1933–1943* (Frankfurt am Main, 1997); Avraham Barkai, 'Jewish Life under Persecution', in Meyer (ed.), *German-Jewish History*, 231–57; and idem, 'Shifting Organizational Relationships', in ibid., 259–82.

106. Clemens Vollnhals, 'Jüdische Selbsthilfe bis 1938', in Benz (ed.), *Die Juden in Deutschland*, 314–411, at 330–41, also for the preceding paragraph.

107. Ibid., 341–63; see also Wolf Gruner, 'Public Welfare and the German Jews under National Socialism', in Bankier (ed.), *Probing*, 78–105; and Adler-Rudel, *Jüdische Selbsthilfe*, 19–46, 121–82.

108. Vollnhals, 'Jüdische Selbsthilfe'; Volker Dahm, 'Kulturelles und geistiges Leben', in Benz (ed.), *Die Juden*, 75–267, at 83–124; Esriel Hildesheimer, *Jüdische Selbstverwaltung unter dem NS-Regime: Der Existenzkampf der Reichsvertretung und Reichsvereinigung der Juden in Deutschland* (Tübingen, 1994); Longerich, *Politik*, 44, 133; Dorothea Bessen, 'Der Jüdische Kulturbund Rhein-Ruhr 1933–1938', in Alte Synagoge (ed.), *Entrechtung und Selbsthilfe*, 43–65; and Paul Mendes-Flohr, 'Jewish Cultural Life under National Socialism', in Meyer (ed.), *German-Jewish History*, IV. 283–312.

109. Henryk M. Broder and Heike Geisel, *Premiere und Pogrom: Der Jüdische Kulturbund 1933–1941. Texte und Bilder* (Berlin, 1992); Hajo Bernett, *Der jüdische Sport im nationalsozialistischen Deutschland 1933–1938* (Schorndorf, 1978); Kurt Düwell, 'Jewish Cultural Centers in Nazi Germany: Expectations and Accomplishments', in Jehuda Reinharz and Walter Schatzberg (eds.), *The Jewish Response*

to German Culture: From the Enlightenment to the Second World War (Hanover, N.H., 1985), 294–316; Wetzel, 'Auswanderung', 438–41; good summary in Friedländer, *Nazi Germany*, 65–8.

110. Michael Meyer, 1941, quoted in Wetzel, 'Auswanderung', 418, after his illegal emigration to Palestine the previous year.

111. Ibid., 413–98, and Statistical Appendix at 733. These figures are all for the so-called '*Altreich*', i.e. not including Austria or the Sudetenland.

112. Quoted in Monika Richarz (ed.), *Jüdisches Leben in Deutschland: Selbstzeugnisse zur Sozialgeschichte 1918–1945*, III (Stuttgart, 1982), 339.

113. Meyer, 'The Mixed Marriage', 54–61; eadem, '*Jüdische Mischlinge*', 68–76; Nathan Stoltzfus, *Resistance of the Heart: Intermarriage and the Rosenstrasse Protest in Nazi Germany* (New York, 1996), 43–9.

114. Meyer, 'The Mixed Marriage'.

115. Stoltzfus, *Resistance*, 106–8.

116. Klemperer, *Tagebücher 1933/34*, 38–9 (9 July 1933); the quotation is not in the English edition.

117. Klemperer, *I Shall Bear Witness*, 33 (9 October 1933), 60 (5 April 1934), 66 (13 June 1933), 71 (14 July 1933), 77 (4 August 1934).

118. Ibid., 111 (23 March 1935).

119. Ibid., 114 (30 April 1935), 114–16 (2 May 1935), 117 (7 May 1935), 119 (30 May 1935), 124 (11 August 1935), 126 (16 September 1935), 128 (17 September 1935), 129 (6 October 1935, *recte* 5 October); also 179 (29 August 1936) and 191 (24 November 1936).

120. Ibid., 260 (9 October 1938).

121. Tagebuch Luise Solmitz, 1934, (manuscript version), fol. 120–21.

122. Ibid., 25 March 1933.

123. Ibid., 31 March, 1 April 1933.

124. Ibid., 8 March 1934.

125. Ibid., 15 September, 19 September 1935.

126. Ibid., 8 March, 9 March, 17 September 1936.

127. Ibid., 9 February, 12 February 1937.

128. Heinz Höhne, *Die Zeit der Illusionen: Hitler und die Anfänge des Dritten Reiches 1933–1936* (Düsseldorf, 1991), 333–51.

129. Quoted via the *New York Times*, 6 July 1936, 6, in Richard D. Mandell, *The Nazi Olympics* (London, 1972 [1971]), 140.

130. Ibid., 122–58.

131. Speer, *Inside*, 119, 129; Mandell, *The Nazi Olympics*, 227–9.

132. Shirer, *Berlin Diary*, 44–5, 57–8. Shirer put 'pensions' for bed-and-breakfast establishments.

133. Friedländer, *Nazi Germany*, 125.

134. Kershaw, *The 'Hitler Myth'*, 236–7.

135. Klemperer, *Tagebücher 1935–1936*, 123; see also idem, *I Shall Bear Witness*, 293.

136. Longerich, *Politik*, 116–21.

137. Quoted in Wetzel, 'Auswanderung', 498.

138. Ibid., 420.

139. Falk Wiesemann, 'Juden auf dem Lande: Die wirtschaftliche Ausgrenzung der jüdischen Viehhändler in Bayern', in Peukert and Reulecke (eds.), *Die Reihen fast geschlossen*, 381–96; Longerich, *Politik*, 122–3.

140. Longerich, *Politik*, 155–9; Domarus, *Hitler*, II. 939–40; Peter Longerich, *Der ungeschriebene Befehl: Hitler und der Weg zur Endlösung* (Munich, 2001), 53–6; Fröhlich (ed.), *Die Tagebücher*, I/IV, 429 (29 November 1937).

141. Longerich, *Politik*, 159–60, 170–87; Tagebuch Luise Solmitz, 14 September 1938.

142. Longerich, *Politik*, 170–80; see also Wolf Gruner, 'Die Reichshauptstadt und die Verfolgung der Berliner Juden 1933–1945', in Reinhard Rürup (ed.), *Jüdische Geschichte in Berlin: Bilder und Dokumente* (Berlin, 1995), 229–66, at 229–42; and Fröhlich (ed.), *Die Tagebücher* I/V. 340 (11 June 1938).

143. See below, 657–61.

144. Fröhlich (ed.), *Die Tagebücher* I/V. 393 (25 July 1938).

145. Michael Wildt, 'Violence against Jews in Germany, 1933–1939', in Bankier (ed.), *Probing*, 191–4.

146. Longerich, *Politik*, 181–95; Wolf-Arno Kropat, *'Reichskristallnacht': Der Judenpogrom vom 7. bis 10. November 1938 – Urheber, Täter, Hintergründe* (Wiesbaden, 1997), 36–49.

147. Longerich, *Politik*, 161–2.

148. Ibid., 116, 195–7; Trude Maurer, 'The Background for Kristallnacht: The Expulsion of Polish Jews', in Pehle (ed.), *November 1938*, 44–72; Sybil Milton, 'The Expulsion of Polish Jews from Germany October 1938 to July 1939: A Documentation', *Leo Baeck Institute Yearbook*, 29 (1984), 169–200; contemporary reports in Behnken (ed.), *Deutschland-Berichte*, V (1938), 1,181–6.

149. Helmut Heiber, 'Der Fall Grünspan', *VfZ*, 5 (1957), 134–72; Graml, *Reichskristallnacht*, 9–16; Kropat, *'Reichskristallnacht'*, 50–55; Hans-Jürgen Döscher, *'Reichskristallnacht': Die November-Pogrome 1938* (Frankfurt am Main, 1988), 57–76, with documents and photographs. For the press campaign, see Wolfgang Benz, 'The Relapse into Barbarism', in Pehle (ed.), *November 1938*, 1–43, at 3–8; Hagemann, *Die Presselenkung*, 148; and Peter (ed.), *NS-Presseanweisungen*, VI: *1938* (Munich, 1999), 1,047, 1,050–54. For events in Hesse, see Kropat, *'Reichskristallnacht'*, 56–78, and idem, *Kristallnacht in Hessen: Der Judenpogrom vom November 1938: Eine Dokumentation* (Wiesbaden, 1997 [1988]), 19–50. For the general argument, Longerich, *Der ungeschriebene Befehl*, 60–61.

150. There are solid accounts in Wolfgang Benz, 'The Relapse into Barbarism', 3–15; also idem, 'Der Novemberpogrom 1938', in Benz (ed.), *Die Juden*, 499–544; Hitler's role is outlined in Longerich, *Der ungeschriebene Befehl*, 61–4; the evidence on the origins of the pogrom is carefully sifted in Longerich, *Politik*, 198–202 and the accompanying endnotes; see also Kropat, *'Reichskristallnacht'*, 79–89

and 172–81. For Hitler's purposes in unleashing the pogrom, see Domarus (ed.), *Hitler*, II. 1,235–42. The many accounts that portray the pogrom as improvised at the last minute, or that attribute it to Goebbels alone, correspond neither to the evidence nor to the context of the events of the preceding months and weeks: for such arguments, see for example Dieter Obst, *'Reichskristallnacht': Ursachen und Verlauf des antisemitischen Pogroms vom November 1938* (Frankfurt am Main, 1991); Uwe Dietrich Adam, 'How Spontaneous Was the Pogrom?', in Pehle (ed.), *November 1938*, 73–94; Döscher, *'Reichskristallnacht'*, 77–80. See also, with varying accents, Hermann Graml, *Reichskristallnacht*, 17–19; Ulrich Herbert, 'Von der "Reichskristallnacht" zum "Holocaust". Der 9. November und das Ende des "Radau-Antisemitismus"', in idem, *Arbeit, Volkstum, Weltanschauung: Über Fremde und Deutsche im 20. Jahrhundert* (Frankfurt am Main, 1995), 59–78; Barkai, *From Boycott to Annihilation*, 133–8; Kurt Pätzold and Irene Runge, *Pogromnacht 1938* (Berlin, 1988); Kaplan, *Between Dignity and Despair*, 119–44; and Kropat, *'Reichskristallnacht'*, for a selection of key documents.

151. Nuremberg Document PS 3063 (Report of the Supreme Party Tribunal, 13 February 1939), in *Trial of the Major War Criminals before the International Military Tribunal, Nuremberg, 14 November 1945–1 October 1946* (Nuremberg, 1948), XXXII. 20–29.

152. Müller to all Stapostellen and Stapoleitstellen, 9 November 1939, in *Trial of the Major War Criminals*, XXV. 376–80, at 377 (ND 374–PS); Hermann Graml, *Anti-Semitism in the Third Reich* (Cambridge, Mass., 1992), 13; for Hitler's meeting with Himmler, see Kershaw, *Hitler*, II. 883 n. 56.

153. Quoted and discussed, with other documents, in Richard J. Evans, *Lying About Hitler. History, Holocaust and the David Irving Trial* (New York, 2001), 52–61; see also Longerich, *Politik*, 198–202; Graml, *Reichskristallnacht*, 20–22; and Kropat, *'Reichskristallnacht'*, 89–108.

154. Quoted in Longerich, *Politik*, 199–200.

155. Saskia Lorenz, 'Die Zerstörung der Synagogen unter dem Nationalsozialismus', in Arno Herzig (ed.), *Verdrängung*, 153–72; Behnken (ed.), *Deutschland-Berichte*, V (1938), 187.

156. For good evidence of the full participation of the SS, see Michael Zimmermann, 'Die "Reichskristallnacht" 1938 in Essen', in Alte Synagoge (ed.), *Entrechtung und Selbsthilfe*, 66–97.

157. Behnken (ed.), *Deutschland-Berichte*, V (1938), 1,188.

158. Sauer, *Die Schicksale*, 420.

159. Avraham Barkai, 'The Fateful Year', 95–122; Longerich, *Politik*, 203. For further details see for example Karl H. Debus, 'Die Reichskristallnacht in der Pfalz', *Zeitschrift für die Geschichte des Oberrheins*, 129 (1981), 445–515; Joachim Meynert, *Was vor der 'Endlösung' geschah*, 208–22; Graml, *Reichskristallnacht*, 22–49; Fichtl *et al.*, *'Bambergs Wirtschaft'*, 135–89; Kropat, *'Reichskristallnacht'*, 109–18; idem, *Kristallnacht in Hessen*, 51–136; and Wippermann, *Das Leben*, 1. 97–107. Herbert Schultheis, *Die Reichskristallnacht*

in Deutschland nach Augenzeugenberichten (Bad Neustadt an der Saale, 1985), reprints a contemporary collection of eyewitness reports.

160. Wildt, 'Violence', 191–200.

161. Longerich, *Politik*, 203–5 and 642–3, n. 231; Friedländer, *Nazi Germany*, 269–79.

162. Tagebuch Luise Solmitz, 10 November 1938.

163. Behnken (ed.), *Deutschland-Berichte*, V (1938), 1,191.

164. Ibid.

165. Ibid., 1,208.

166. Reck-Malleczewen, *Diary*, 80.

167. Behnken (ed.), *Deutschland-Berichte*, V (1938), 1,207.

168. Klepper, *Unter den Schatten*, 675.

169. Maschmann, *Account Rendered*, 56–7. Further, varied reactions from non-Jewish Germans are quoted and discussed in Benz, 'Der Novemberpogrom', 525–8; Bankier, *The Germans*, 85–8; Kropat, *'Reichskristallnacht'*, 153–69; idem, *Kristallnacht in Hessen*, 241–6; and Helmut Gatzen, *Novemberpogrom 1938 in Gütersloh: Nachts Orgie der Gewalt, tags organisierte Vernichtung* (Gütersloh, 1993), 63–7. Jörg Wollenberg (ed.), *The German Public and the Persecution of the Jews 1933–1945: 'No One Participated, No One Knew'* (Atlantic Highlands, N. J., 1996 [1989]) contains documents and essays, of varying quality.

170. Friedländer, *Nazi Germany*, 297.

171. Witetschek (ed.), *Die kirchliche Lage*, I. 300 (no. 122, Regierung Oberbayern, 10 December 1938).

172. Michael Faulhaber, *Judaism, Christianity, and Germany: Advent Sermons Preached in St Michael's, Munich in 1933* (London, 1934), 1–6, 13–16, 107–10, reprinted in Mosse (ed.), *Nazi Culture*, 256–61; Friedländer, *Nazi Germany*, 297; Walter Zwi Bacharach, 'The Catholic Anti-Jewish Prejudice, Hitler and the Jews', in Bankier (ed.), *Probing*, 415–30.

173. Horst Matzerath (ed.), '. . . *vergessen kann man die Zeit nicht, das ist nicht möglich* . . .' *Kölner erinnern sich an die Jahre 1929–1945* (Cologne, 1985), 172; see also Ursula Büttner, '"The Jewish Problem becomes a Christian Problem": German Protestants and the Persecution of the Jews in the Third Reich', in Bankier (ed.), *Probing*, 431–59.

174. Longerich, *Politik*, 206.

175. Fröhlich (ed.), *Die Tagebücher*, I/VI. 180–81 (10 November 1938).

176. *Trial of the Major War Criminals*, XXXII. 29 (ND 3063–PS).

177. Fröhlich (ed.), *Die Tagebücher*, I/VI. 181 (10 November 1938).

178. Ibid., 182 (11 November 1938); for the call to bring the action to an end, see 'Keine weiteren Aktionen mehr', *Berliner Volks-Zeitung*, 534, 11 November 1938, front page; 'Keine Einzel-Aktionen gegen das Judentum', *Berliner Morgenpost*, 270, 11 November 1938, front page; etc.

179. Longerich, *Politik*, 204; for suicides, see Konrad Kuriet and Helmut Eschwege

(eds.), *Selbstbehauptung und Widerstand: Deutsche Juden im Kampf um Existenz und Menschenwürde 1933–1945* (Hamburg, 1984), 202.

180. Obst, *Reichskristallnacht*, 284–5, 297–307; Wildt, 'Violence', 201–2; Zimmermann, 'Die "Reichskristallnacht"', 77.

181. Wildt, 'Violence', 204; Pingel, *Häftlinge*, 94; Anthony Read and David Fisher, *Kristallnacht: Unleashing the Holocaust* (London, 1989), 121–35; Kropat, '*Reichskristallnacht*', 138–41; idem, *Kristallnacht in Hessen*, 167–79.

182. Quoted in Benz, 'The Relapse', 17.

183. *Völkischer Beobachter*, 11 November 1938 (North German edition), 2; Benz, 'The Relapse', 18.

184. Peter (ed.), *NS-Presseanweisungen*, VI: *1938*, 1,060–61.

185. Reprinted in *Berliner Morgenpost*, 271, 12 November 1938, front page. For a broader analysis, see Herbert Obenaus, 'The Germans: "An Antisemitic People". The Press Camapaign after 9 November 1938', in Bankier (ed.), *Probing*, 147–80.

186. Read and Fisher, *Kristallnacht*, 166–79.

187. Treue (ed.), 'Hitlers Denkschrift', 210.

188. Fröhlich (ed.), *Die Tagebücher* I/VI. 182 (11 November 1938).

189. Barkai, 'The Fateful Year', 119–20; lengthy extracts from the minutes in Wilfried Mairgünther, *Reichkristallnacht* (Kiel, 1987), 90–130.

190. *Trial of the Major War Criminals*, XXVIII. 499–540, at 509–10.

191. Bruno Blau (ed.), *Das Ausnahmerecht für die Juden in Deutschland, 1933–1945* (Düsseldorf, 1954 [1952]), 54–62; 'Dr. Goebbels: Theater, Kinos, Konzerte für Juden verboten', *Berliner Illustrierte Nachtausgabe*, 266, 12 November 1938, front page; Longerich, *Politik*, 208–9; Kropat, '*Reichskristallnacht*', 127–34. For cogent criticism of the legend that Göring and Himmler disapproved of the pogrom in principle, see Graml, *Reichskristallnacht*, 177, and Kropat, '*Reichskristallnacht*', 119–27.

192. Jonny Moser, 'Depriving Jews of Their Legal Rights in the Third Reich', in Pehle (ed.), *November 1938*, 123–38; see also, more generally, Kropat, '*Reichskristallnacht*', 134–8.

193. Barkai, 'The Fateful Year', 119–20; 'Beratung über die Massnahmen gegen Juden: Die Aufbringung der Sühne von 1 Milliarde', *Berliner Illustrierte Nachtausgabe*, 267, 14 November 1935, front page.

194. Genschel, *Die Verdrängung*, 206; local examples in Fichtl *et. al.*, 'Bambergs Wirtschaft', 183–97.

195. 'Dr. Goebbels über die Lösung der Judenfrage', *Berliner Illustrierte Nachtausgabe*, 267, 14 November 1938, 2; for a full list of the measures themselves, see Longerich, *Politik*, 208–19; also Friedländer, *Nazi Germany*, 280–305.

196. Barkai, 'The Fateful Year', 121–2; Moser, 'Depriving Jews', 123–38, at 126–34; Konrad Kwiet, 'Nach dem Pogrom: Stufen der Ausgrenzung', in Benz (ed.), *Die Juden*, 545–659; Longerich, *Politik*, 218–19; Wolf Gruner, *Der geschlossene Arbeitseinsatz deutscher Juden: Zur Zwangsarbeit als Element der Verfolgung, 1938–1943* (Berlin, 1997); for local examples, see Uwe Lohalm,

'Local Administration and Nazi Anti-Jewish Policy', in Bankier (ed.), *Probing*, 109–46, and Meynert, *Was vor der 'Endlösung' geschah*, 230–33. For the Reich Association, see Otto Dov Kulka (ed.), *Deutsches Judentum unter dem Nationalsozialismus*, I: *Dokumente zur Geschichte der Reichsvertretung der deutschen Juden 1933–1939* (Tübingen, 1997), 410–28.

197. Wildt, 'Violence', 204–8.

198. Boberach (ed.), *Meldungen*, II. 21–6, 221–2.

199. Wetzel, 'Auswanderung', 420.

200. Quoted in Hannah Arendt, *The Origins of Totalitarianism* (London, 1973 [1955]), 269, n. 2; see also Wetzel, 'Auswanderung', 426, 429; and Avraham Barkai, 'Self-Help in the Dilemma: "To Leave or to Stay?"', in Meyer (ed.), *German-Jewish History*, IV. 313–32. For the origins of the Reich Centre, see below, 659–61.

201. Not counting Austria and the Sudetenland, which when added made 330,539 (*Statistisches Jahrbuch für das deutsche Reich*, 59 (1941/42), 27: 'Die Juden und jüdischen Mischlinge in den Reichsteilen und nach Gemeindegrössenklassen 1939').

202. 'Jüdische Bevölkerungsstatistik', in Benz (ed.), *Die Juden*, 733. These figures are obtained by subtracting the total of roughly 26,000 Jews of foreign nationality from Wetzel's total for each year. Further statistics are supplied in Konrad Kwiet, 'To Leave or Not to Leave: The German Jews at the Crossroads', in Pehle (ed.), *November 1938*, 139–53.

203. Wetzel, 'Auswanderung', 423–5; Arthur D. Morse, *While Six Million Died: A Chronicle of American Apathy* (New York, 1967); David Wyman, *Paper Walls: America and the Refugee Crisis, 1938–1941* (Amherst, Mass., 1968); Richard Breitman and Alan Kraut, *American Refugee Policy and European Jewry, 1933–1945* (Bloomingtom 1987); see also Irving Abella and Harold Troper, *None Is Too Many: Canada and the Jews of Europe, 1933–1948* (Toronto, 1983).

204. Klemperer, *I Shall Bear Witness*, 241 (20 March 1938), 247 (23 May 1938), 251 (12 July 1938), 252–3 (10 August 1938), 263–4 (27 November 1938), 266 (3 December 1938).

205. Ibid., 267–8 (6 December 1938), 269 (15 December 1938), 279 (10 January 1939). See also Susanne Heim, 'The German–Jewish Relationship in the Diaries of Victor Klemperer', in Bankier (ed.), *Probing*, 312–25; and, more generally, Meynert, *Was vor der 'Endlösung' geschah*, 223–9.

206. Tagebuch Luise Solmitz, 12 November 1938, 13 November 1938, 15 November 1938, 22 November 1938, 1 December 1938, 14 March 1939, 29 August 1939.

207. *Trial of the Major War Criminals*, XXVIII. 534 (ND 1816–PS). For the meeting on 6 December, see Longerich, *Politik*, 210–12.

208. Longerich, *Politik*, 206; Friedländer, *Nazi Germany*, 288–92 and 298–9.

209. Kershaw, *The 'Hitler Myth'*, 235–9.

210. Longerich, *Der ungeschriebene Befehl*, 55–7.

211. Ibid., 67; James Marshall-Cornwell *et al.* (eds.), *Akten zur deutschen auswär-tigen Politik, 1918–1945: Aus den Akten des Deutschen Auswärtigen Amtes* (Series A-E, Baden-Baden, 1951–95), Series D, IV. 291–5, at 293 ('Aufzeichnung des Legationsrats Hewel, Berchtesgaden', 24 November 1938).

212. 'Aufzeichnung des Legationsrats Hewel', 21 January 1939, in Marshall-Cornwell *et al.* (eds.), *Akten*, Series D, IV, 167–71, at 170.

213. Domarus, *Hitler*, II. 1,055–8.

214. Herbert A. Strauss, 'The Drive for War and the Pogroms of November 1938: Testing Explanatory Models', *Leo Baeck Institute Yearbook*, 35 (1990), 267–78.

215. Longerich, *Politik*, 220–21; Philippe Burrin, *Hitler and the Jews: The Genesis of the Holocaust* (London, 1994 [1989]), 61–3. For the view that Hitler's threat was not to be taken seriously, and was not followed up by any approach on his part to the United States, see Graml, *Reichskristallnacht*, 105–6.

216. Friedländer, *Nazi Germany*, 211–24; William W. Hagen, 'Before the "Final Solution": Toward a Comparative Analysis of Political Anti-Semitism in Interwar Germany and Poland', *Journal of Modern History*, 68 (1996), 351–81; Joseph Marcus, *Social and Political History of the Jews in Poland, 1919–1939* (Berlin, 1983) – not always accurate in detail; Celia S. Heller, *On the Edge of Destruction: Jews of Poland between the two World Wars* (New York, 1977); Yisrael Gutman, *The Jews of Poland between Two World Wars* (Hanover, N.H., 1989); James D. Wynot, Jr, '"A Necessary Cruelty": The Emergence of Official Anti-Semitism in Poland, 1935–39', *American Historical Review*, 76 (1971), 1,035–58.

217. Emanuel Melzer, 'The Polish Authorities and the Jewish Question, 1930–1939', in Alfred A. Greenbaum (ed.), *Minority Problems in Eastern Europe between the World Wars, with Emphasis on the Jewish Minority* (Hebrew University of Jerusalem, Institute for Advanced Studies, typescript, Jerusalem, 1988), 77–81; Jerzy Tomascewski, 'Economic and Social Situation of Jews in Poland, 1918–1939', in ibid., 101–6; Ezra Mendelsohn, *The Jews of East Central Europe between the World Wars* (Bloomington, Ind., 1983), 11–83.

218. Magnus Brechtken, *'Madagaskar für die Juden': Antisemitische Idee und politische Praxis 1885–1945* (Munich, 1997), 81–164.

219. Mendelsohn, *The Jews*; Bela Vago, *The Shadow of the Swastika: The Rise of Fascism and Anti-Semitism in the Danube Basin, 1936–1939* (London, 1975).

220. Mendelsohn, *The Jews*, 171–211; David Schaary, 'The Romanian Authorities and the Jewish Communities in Romania between the Two World Wars', in Greenbaum (ed.), *Minority Problems*, 89–95; Paul A. Shapiro, 'Prelude to Dictatorship in Romania: The National Christian Party in Power, December 1937–February 1938', *Canadian-American Slavic Studies*, 8 (1974), 45–88.

221. Mendelsohn, *The Jews*, 85–128; see also the introductory sections of Randolph H. Braham, *The Politics of Genocide: The Holocaust in Hungary* (2 vols., New York, 1980).

Chapter 7. THE ROAD TO WAR

1. Kershaw, *Hitler* I: 484–6, 531–6.

2. Anton Joachimsthaler, *Hitlers Liste: Ein Dokument persönlicher Beziehungen* (Munich, 2003); Semmery, *Seeing Hitler's Germany*, 56.

3. Kershaw, *Hitler*, I. 537.

4. Speer, *Inside*, 194–5.

5. Evans, *The Coming of the Third Reich*, 434; above, 168, 172, 177, 180, 581–2.

6. *Völkischer Beobachter*, 25 May 1928, quoted in Gerhard L. Weinberg, *The Foreign Policy of Hitler's Germany*, I: *Diplomatic Revolution in Europe 1933– 1936* (London, 1970), 22 (translation adjusted); original in Bärbel Dusik (ed.), *Hitler: Reden, Schriften, Anordnungen: Februar 1925 bis Januar 1933* (5 vols., Munich 1992–8), II. 845–9, at 856 (italics in original).

7. Quoted in Weinberg, *The Foreign Policy*, I. 163; for background, see Anthony Komjathy and Rebecca Stockwell, *German Minorities and the Third Reich: Ethnic Germans of East Central Europe between the Wars* (New York, 1980).

8. See the general argument in Thies, *Architekt der Weltherrschaft*; more directly, see Milan Hauner, 'Did Hitler Want a World Dominion?', *Journal of Contemporary History*, 13 (1978), 15–32; Günter Moltmann, 'Weltherrschaftsideen Hitlers', in Otto Brunner and Dietrich Gerhard (eds.), *Europa und Übersee: Festschrift für Egmont Zechlin* (Hamburg, 1961), 197–240; and Geoffrey Stoakes, *Hitler and the Quest for World Dominion* (Leamington Spa, 1986).

9. For useful introductory discussions, see Hermann Graml, 'Grundzüge national-sozialistische Aussenpolitik', in Martin Broszat and Horst Möller (eds.), *Das Dritte Reich: Herrschaftsstruktur und Geschichte* (Munich, 1986 [1983]), 104–26; idem, 'Wer bestimmte die Aussenpolitik des Dritten Reiches? Ein Beitrag zur Kontroverse um Polykratie und Monokratie im NS-Herrschaftssystem', in Manfred Funke *et al.* (eds.), *Demokratie und Diktatur: Geist und Gestalt politischer Herrschaft in Deutschland und Europa: Festschrift für Karl Dietrich Bracher* (Düsseldorf, 1987), 223–36; Wolfgang Michalka, 'Conflicts within the German Leadership on the Objectives and Tactics of German Foreign Policy 1933–9', in Wolfgang J. Mommsen and Lothar Kettenacker (eds.), *The Fascist Challenge and the Policy of Appeasement* (London, 1983), 48–60; and Andreas Hillgruber, 'Grundzüge der nationalsozialistischen Aussenpolitik 1933–1945', *Saeculum*, 24 (1973), 328–45.

10. For a range of views on British and French foreign policy in the 1930s, see David Dilks, ' "We Must Hope for the Best and Prepare for the Worst" ': The Prime Minister, the Cabinet and Hitler's Germany, 1937–1939', in Patrick Finney (ed.), *The Origins of the Second World War* (London, 1997) 43–61; Sidney Aster, ' "Guilty Men": The Case of Neville Chamberlain', in ibid., 62–77; Anthony Adamthwaite, 'France and the Coming of War', in ibid., 78–89; Robert A. C. Parker, 'Alterative to Apeasment', in ibid., 206–21.

11. Günter Wollstein, 'Eine Denkschrift des Staatssekretärs Bernhard von Bülow vom März 1933', *Militärgeschichtliche Mitteilungen*, 1 (1973), 77–94; for the background, see Peter Krüger, *Die Aussenpolitik der Republik von Weimar* (Darmstadt, 1985); Hans-Adolf Jacobsen, *Nationalsozialistische Aussenpolitik 1933–1939* (Frankfurt am Main, 1968), 20–89 and 319–47; Jost Dülffer, 'Grundbedingungen der nationalsozialistischen Aussenpolitik', in Leo Haupts and Georg Mölich (eds.), *Strukturelemente des Nationalsozialismus. Rasseideologie, Unterdrückungsmaschinerie, Aussenpolitik* (Cologne, 1981), 61–88; idem, 'Zum "decision-making process" in der deutschen Aussenpolitik 1933–1939', in Manfred Funke (ed.), *Hitler, Deutschland und die Mächte: Materialien zur Aussenpolitik des Dritten Reiches* (Düsseldorf, 1976), 186–204.

12. Kershaw, *Hitler*, I. 490–95; Weinberg, *The Foreign Policy*, I. 159–79; for continuities and discontinuities in the early 1930s, see Günter Wollstein, *Vom Weimarer Revisionismus zu Hitler: Das Deutsche Reich und die Grossmächte in der Anfangsphase der nationalsozialistischen Herrschaft in Deutschland* (Bonn, 1973).

13. Domarus (ed.), *Hitler* I. 364–75.

14. See above, 109–10.

15. Herbert S. Levine, *Hitler's Free City. A History of the Nazi Party in Danzig, 1925–39* (Chicago, 1973), Weinberg, *The Foreign Policy*, I. 184–94; Klaus Hildebrand, *The Foreign Policy of the Third Reich* (London, 1973 [1970]), 24–33 (stressing the coherence of Hitler's long-term, step-by-step approach); Manfred Messerschmidt, 'Foreign Policy and Preparation for War', in Militärgeschichtliches Forschungsamt (ed.), *Germany*, 541–717, at 590–93; Klaus Hildebrand, *Das vergangene Reich: Deutsche Aussenpolitik von Bismarck bis Hitler, 1871–1945* (Stuttgart, 1995), 586–92.

16. Martin Kitchen, *The Coming of Austrian Fascism* (London, 1980), 36–110; Bruce F. Pauley, *Hitler and the Forgotten Nazis. A History of Austrian National Socialism* (Chapel Hill, N.C., 1981), 3–15; George E. R. Gedye, *Fallen Bastions: The Central European Tragedy* (London, 1939), 9–126. Charles A. Gulick, *Austria from Habsburg to Hitler* (2 vols., Berkeley, Calif., 1948), is a very detailed narrative, now rather outdated.

17. Francis L. Carsten, *Fascist Movements in Austria: From Schönerer to Hitler* (London, 1977), 229–70, still the authoritative account; Kitchen, *The Coming*, 173–262; Pauley, *Hitler and the Forgotten Nazis*, 16–103, stressing the internal disunity of the party; for Schönerer, see Evans, *The Coming of the Third Reich*, 42–4, 163–4; also more generally Bruce F. Pauley, *From Prejudice to Persecution: A History of Austrian Anti-Semitism* (Chapel Hill, N.C., 1992).

18. Carsten, *Fascist Movements*, 254–92 (254 for the quote); Gedye, *Fallen Bastions*, 101–43; Pauley, *Hitler and the Forgotten Nazis*, 104–54; Hildebrand, *Das vergangene Reich*, 593–9.

19. Kershaw, *Hitler*, I. 522–4; among older works, see also Dieter Ross, *Hitler und Dollfuss: Die deutsche Österreich-Politik, 1933–1934* (Hamburg, 1966).

20. Domarus (ed.), *Hitler*, I. 504–7.

21. Hildebrand, *Das vergangene Reich*, 578–86.

22. Patrick von zur Mühlen, *'Schlagt Hitler an der Saar!' Abstimmungskampf, Emigration und Widerstand im Saargebiet, 1933–1945* (Bonn, 1979), 230–32; Gerhard Paul, *'Deutsche Mutter – heim zu Dir!' Warum es misslang, Hitler an der Saar zu schlagen: Der Saarkampf 1933 bis 1935* (Cologne, 1984), 376–401.

23. Mühlen, *'Schlagt Hitler'*, 73–4, 195, 229; Paul, *'Deutsche Mutter'*, 102–32; Markus Gestier, *Die christlichen Parteien an der Saar und ihr Verhältnis zum deutschen Nationalstaat in den Abstimmungskämpfen 1935 und 1955* (St Ingbert, 1991), 48–69; Ludwig Linsmayer, *Politische Kultur im Saargebiet 1920–1932: Symbolische Politik, verhinderte Demokratisierung, nationalisiertes Kulturleben in einer abgetrennten Region* (St Ingbert, 1992), 447; Klaus-Michael Mallmann and Gerhard Paul, *Milieus und Widerstand: Eine Verhaltensgeschichte der Gesellschaft im Nationalsozialismus* (Bonn 1995), 203–23; Dieter Muskalla, *NS-Politik an der Saar unter Josef Bürckel: Gleichschaltung – Neuordnung – Verwaltung* (Saarbrücken, 1995), 71.

24. Mühlen, *'Schlagt Hitler'*, 204–7, 230–31; Paul, *'Deutsche Mutter'*, 214–32; Linsmayer, *Politische Kultur*, 447.

25. Behnken (ed.), *Deutschland-Berichte*, II (1935), 9–15 (quote on 10).

26. Mallmann, and Paul, *Herrschaft*, 26–32.

27. Klaus-Michael Mallmann and Gerhard Paul, *Das zersplitterte Nein: Saarländer gegen Hitler* (Bonn, 1989), vi–vii; idem, *Herrschaft*, 39–54; idem, *Milieus*, 530–35; Muskalla, *NS-Politik*, 187, 551–96, 600–601.

28. Mallmann and Paul, *Herrschaft*, 55–64, 114–34.

29. Domarus (ed.), *Hitler*, II. 643–8, at 644; Behnken (ed.), *Deutschland-Berichte*, II (1935), 117–20, 154–7.

30. Tagebuch Luise Solmitz, 1 March 1935.

31. Stöver (ed.), *Berichte*, 336.

32. Weinberg, *The Foreign Policy*, I. 203–6.

33. Tagebuch Luise Solmitz 1935: 16 March 1935.

34. Ibid.

35. Behnken (ed.), *Deutschland-Berichte*, II (1935), 409–14. William L. Shirer's account (*Berlin Diary*, 32–4), which recorded universal and unqualified enthusiasm, was strongly coloured by his deeply held belief, expressed again in his *The Rise and Fall of the Third Reich*, that all Germans were 'militarists at heart'.

36. Kershaw, *Hitler*, I. 556–8; Dülffer, *Weimar*, 256–67, 325–54; Geoffrey T. Waddington, 'Hitler, Ribbentrop, die NSDAP und der Niedergang des Britischen Empire 1935–1938', *VfZ* 40 (1992), 274–306; Hildebrand, *Das vergangene Reich*, 600–604.

37. Fest, *The Face*, 265–82; Wolfgang Michalka, 'Joachim von Ribbentrop: From Wine Merchant to Foreign Minister', in Smelser and Zitelmann (eds.), *The Nazi Elite*, 165–72.

38. Jacobsen, *Nationalsozialistische Aussenpolitik*, 298–318.

39. Fest, *The Face*, 271–6; Michalka, 'Joachim von Ribbentrop', 166–8; Jacobsen,

Nationalsozialistische Aussenpolitik, 252–318; at greater length, Wolfgang Michalka, *Ribbentrop und die deutsche Weltpolitik 1933–1940: Aussenpolitische Konzeptionen und Entscheidungsprozesse im Dritten Reich* (Munich, 1989 [1980]); recent reassessment in Stefan Kley, *Hitler, Ribbentrop und die Entfesselung des Zweiten Weltkrieges* (Paderborn, 1996).

40. For the Ethiopian war see George L. Steer, *Caesar in Abyssinia* (London, 1936), Alberto Sbacchi, *Legacy of Bitterness: Ethiopia and Fascist Italy, 1935–1941* (Laurenceville, N.J., 1997), and Anthony Mockler, *Haile Selassie's War* (Oxford, 1984); background in Denis Mack Smith, *Mussolini's Roman Empire* (London, 1976).

41. Evans, *The Coming of the Third Reich*, 184–5.

42. 'Memorandum by the Ambassador in Italy (20 January 1936)', in John W. Wheeler-Bennett *et al.* (eds.), *Documents on German Foreign Policy 1918–1945* (13 vols., London, 1950–70), series C, IV: *The Third Reich: First Phase* (London, 1962), 1,013–16.

43. Weinberg, *The Foreign Policy*, I. 207–38.

44. Ibid., 239–63.

45. Shirer, *Berlin Diary*, 49–51.

46. Ibid., 54–6; Domarus (ed.), *Hitler*, II, 787–90.

47. Tagebuch Luise Solmitz, 1936: 7 March.

48. Behnken (ed.), *Deutschland-Berichte*, III (1936), 303.

49. Ibid., 468.

50. Ibid., 300–320, 460–78 ('Rheinlandbesetzung und Kriegs-Angst').

51. Stöver, *Volksgemeinschaft*, 418–19.

52. Behnken (ed.), *Deutschland-Berichte*, III (1936), 302; see also Kershaw, *The 'Hitler Myth'*, 124–9.

53. Weinberg, *The Foreign Policy*, I. 239–63; Donald Cameron Watt, 'German Plans for the Reoccupation of the Rhineland: A Note', *Journal of Contemporary History*, 1 (1966), 193–9; Hildebrand, *Das vergangene Reich*, 604–17; James T. Emmerson, *The Rhineland Crisis, 7 March 1936: A Critical Study in Multilateral Diplomacy* (London, 1977).

54. Domarus, *Hitler*, II. 790; Kershaw, *Hitler*, I. 590–91.

55. Weinberg, *The Foreign Policy*, I. 264–84. The question, much debated by historians, of when the right moment would have been to have stopped Hitler is a non-issue, since virtually no European government wanted to before 1939. It is only this imaginary scenario that informs the conclusion of Stephen A. Schuker, 'France and the Remilitarization of the Rhineland, 1936', *French Historical Studies*, 14 (1986), 299–338, that 1936 was not a turning-point (also in Finney (ed.) *The Origins of the Second World War*, 222–44).

56. Weinberg, *The Foreign Policy*, I. 284–93, somewhat overplaying economic considerations; further details in idem, *The Foreign Policy of Nazi Germany*, II: *Starting World War II, 1937–1939* (Chicago, 1980), 142–66; see also Paul Preston, *The Spanish Civil War 1936–69* (London, 1986), 80–81.

57. Paul Preston, *Franco: A Biography* (London, 1993), 158–61; Hugh Thomas, *The Spanish Civil War* (3rd edn, London, 1986 [1961]), 579–80; Christian Leitz, 'Nazi Germany's Intervention in the Spanish Civil War and the Foundation of HISMA/ROWAK', in Paul Preston and Ann L. Mackenzie (eds.), *The Republic Besieged: Civil War in Spain, 1936–1939* (Edinburgh, 1996), 53–85; Hans-Henning Abendroth, 'Deutschlands Rolle im Spanischen Bürgerkrieg', in Manfred Funke (ed.), *Hitler, Deutschland und die Mächte*, 471–88.

58. Preston, *Franco*, 203–9; more generally Hans-Henning Abendroth, *Hitler in der spanischen Arena: Die deutsch-spanischen Beziehungen im Spannungsfeld der europäischen Interessenpolitik vom Ausbruch des Bürgerkrieges bis zum Ausbruch des Weltkrieges (1936–1939)* (Paderborn, 1973); Robert H. Whealey, *Hitler and Spain: The Nazi Role in the Spanish Civil War, 1936–1939* (Lexington, Ky., 1989).

59. Preston, *Franco*, 243–4.

60. Thomas, *The Spanish Civil War*, 623–31.

61. Herbert R. Southworth, *Guernica! Guernica! A Study of Journalism, Propaganda and History* (Berkeley, Calif., 1977).

62. Preston, *Franco*, 246.

63. Ibid., 303, 329–30.

64. Willard C. Frank, 'The Spanish Civil War and the Coming of the Second World War', *International History Review*, 9 (1987), 368–409.

65. Hildebrand, *The Foreign Policy*, 45; Herbst, *Das nationalsozialistische Deutschland*, 177–83; Elizabeth Wiskemann, *The Rome–Berlin Axis: A History of the Relations between Hitler and Mussolini* (London, 1949); John P. Fox, *Germany and the Far Eastern Crisis, 1931–1938: A Study in Diplomacy and Ideology* (Oxford, 1982); Theo Sommer, *Deutschland und Japan zwischen den Mächten 1935–1940: Vom Antikominternpakt zum Dreimächtepakt: Eine Studie zur diplomatischen Vorgeschichte des Zweiten Weltkrieges* (Tübingen, 1962); Weinberg, *The Foreign Policy*, II. 167–91.

66. Hildebrand, *The Foreign Policy*, 38–50; Josef Henke, *England in Hitlers politischem Kalkül, 1935–1939* (Boppard, 1973); Klaus Hildebrand, *Vom Reich zum Weltreich: Hitler, NSDAP und koloniale Frage 1919–1945* (Munich, 1969), 491–348; more generally, Wolfgang Michalka, *Ribbentrop*.

67. See above, 358–60.

68. O'Neill, *The German Army*, 178–95; Kershaw, *Hitler*, II. 49–51; Klaus-Jürgen Müller, *Das Heer und Hitler: Armee und nationalsozialistisches Regime 1933–1940* (Stuttgart, 1988 [1969]), 244.

69. The standard work on these events is Karl-Heinz Janssen and Fritz Tobias, *Der Sturz der Generäle: Hitler und die Blomberg-Fritsch Krise 1938* (Munich, 1994). For a vivid brief account, of these and following events, see Kershaw, *Hitler*, II. 51–7. Goebbels quotes in Fröhlich (ed.), *Die Tagebücher*, I/V. 117 (27 January 1938) and 118–20 (28 January 1938).

70. Janssen and Tobias, *Der Sturz*, 140.

71. Ibid., 173–84 on Fritsch's trial, 245–51 on his death, and 253–8 on Blomberg's fate after the war; see also O'Neill, *The German Army*, 196–204.

72. Janssen and Tobias, *Der Sturz*, 197–233, at 197–9.

73. Domarus, *Hitler*, II. 1,025 (the whole speech is partly reproduced, partly summarized, on 1,019–340).

74. David G. Maxwell, 'Ernst Hanfstaengl: Des "Führers" Klavierspieler', in Ronald Smelser *et al.* (eds.), *Die braune Elite*, II: *21 weitere biographische Skizzen* (Darmstadt, 1993), 137–49, a distillation of the author's Ph.D. dissertation, 'Unwanted Exile: A Biography of Dr Ernst "Putzi" Hanfstaengl' (SUNY, Binghampton, 1988). See also the useful popular account by Peter Conradi, *Hitler's Piano Player: The Rise and Fall of Ernst Hanfstaengl, Confidant of Hitler, Ally of FDR* (New York, 2004).

75. Kershaw, *Hitler*, II. 63–6; Gerhard L. Weinberg, 'Hitler's Private Testament of May 2, 1938', *Journal of Modern History*, 27 (1955), 415–19; Gerhard Botz, *Der 13. März und die Anschluss-Bewegung: Selbstaufgabe, Okkupation und Selbstfindung Österreichs 1918–1945* (Vienna, 1978), 5–14; Carsten, *Fascist Movements*, 299–301.

76. Ibid., 293–314; Gedye, *Fallen Bastions*, 144–216.

77. Alfred Kube, *Pour le mérite und Hakenkreuz: Hermann Göring im Dritten Reich* (Munich, 1986), 233–43; Hildebrand, *Das vergangene Reich*, 618–51, also for the following; Stefan Martens, 'Die Rolle Hermann Görings in der deutschen Aussenpolitik 1937/38', in Franz Knipping and Klaus-Jürgen Müller (eds.), *Machtbewusstsein in Deutschland am Vorabend des Zweiten Weltkrieges* (Paderborn, 1984), 75–82, for Göring's role; Kley, *Hitler*, 35–49, for Ribbentrop's.

78. Kershaw, *Hitler*, II. 63–4; also Weinberg, *The Foreign Policy*, II. 261–312; Weinberg, 'Hitler's Private Testament'.

79. Carsten, *Fascist Movements*, 271–88; Barbara Jelavich, *Modern Austria: Empire and Republic 1800–1986* (Cambridge, 1987), 192–216; Behnken (ed.) *Deutschland-Berichte*, V (1938), 236–49.

80. Domarus, *Hitler*, II. 1,013–14; Kurt von Schuschnigg, *Austrian Requiem* (London, 1947), 13–32, at 21, 25; Jelavich, *Modern Austria*, 217–18. For Papen, see Franz Müller, *Ein 'Rechtskatholik' zwischen Kreuz und Hakenkreuz: Franz von Papen als Sonderbevollmächtigter in Wien 1934–1938* (Frankfurt am Main, 1990); and Joachim Petzold, *Franz von Papen: Ein deutsches Verhängnis* (Munich, 1995), 239–51.

81. Kershaw, *Hitler*, II. 70–72; Gedye, *Fallen Bastions*, 217–35; Erwin A. Schmidl, *März 38: Der deutsche Einmarsch in Österreich* (Vienna, 1987), 31–42, for German military preparations.

82. Carsten, *Fascist Movements*, 315–23; Schmidl, *März 38*, 1–29, 43–68.

83. 'Generalfeldmarschall Göring mit Seyss-Inquart, 11.3.1938', in *International Military Tribunal*, XXXI. 360–2; also, Jelavich, *Modern Austria*, 218–21; Gedye, *Fallen Bastions*, 236–77; and Ralf Georg Reuth (ed.), *Die Tagebücher*, I/5, 197–201 (10–11 March 1938); Schmidl, *März 38*, 69–109; Pauley, *Hitler and the Forgotten Nazis*, 155–92.

84. Kershaw, *Hitler*, II. 76–8; Carsten, *Fascist Movements*, 323; Shirer, *Berlin Diary*, 80–85; Gedye, *Fallen Bastions*, 278–99; Fröhlich (ed.), *Die Tagebücher*, I/5, 202–6 (12–13 March 1938); Schmidl, *März 38*, 111–34, for the seizure of power in the provinces; Pauley, *Hitler and the Forgotten Nazis*, 193–215.

85. Shirer, *Berlin Diary*, 84–6, for one example.

86. Domarus, *Hitler*, II. 1,049–50; Kershaw, *Hitler*, II. 79–82.

87. Domarus, *Hitler*, II. 1,051 (interview with Ward Price, 12 March 1938); Schmidl, *März 38*, 211–38; Fröhlich (ed.), *Die Tagebücher*, I/5, 204–12 (13–16 March 1938); Gerhard Botz, *Die Eingliederung Österreichs in das deutsche Reich: Planung und Verwirklichung des politisch-administrativen Anschlusses (1938–1940)* (Linz, 1972), 22–39, for early ideas and proposals. For the reasons for Hitler's delay in moving on to Vienna, wrongly attributed at the time to the blockage of the roads by broken-down German tanks and lorries, see Kershaw, *Hitler*, II. 868, n. 115.

88. Domarus (ed.), *Hitler*, II. 1,052–5; Botz, *Die Eingliederung*, 61–72, for the Law of 13 February 1938; 73–115 for later developments.

89. Domarus (ed.), *Hitler*, II. 1,055–7; Pauley, *Hitler and the Forgotten Nazis*, 216–22.

90. Domarus (ed.), *Hitler*, II. 1,059; Pauley, *Hitler and the Forgotten Nazis*, 217; Gerhard Botz, *Wien vom 'Anschluss' zum Krieg: Nationalsozialistische Machtübernahme und politisch-soziale Umgestaltung am Beispiel der Stadt Wien 1938/39* (Vienna, 1978), 117–46.

91. Botz, *Wien*, 175–85. In some electoral areas the number of 'yes' votes was higher than the number of electors. For the methods customarily applied in such votes in the Third Reich, see above, 109–13. See also Evan B. Bukey, 'Popular Opinion in Vienna after the Anschluss', in Fred Parkinson (ed.), *Conquering the Past: Austrian Nazism Yesterday and Today* (Detroit, Mich., 1989), 151–64.

92. Hans-Erich Volkmann, 'The National Socialist Economy in Preparation for War', in Militärgeschichtliches Forschungsamt (eds.), *Germany*, 157–372, at 323–7; Norbert Schausberger, 'Wirtschaftliche Aspekte des Anschlusses Österreichs an das Deutsche Reich (Dokumentation)', *Militärgeschichtliche Mitteilungen*, 8 (1970), 133–64; idem, *Der Griff nach Österreich: Der Anschluss* (Vienna, 1978).

93. Gordon Brook-Shepherd, *The Austrians: A Thousand-Year Odyssey* (London, 1996), 341–3; Botz, *Wien*, 55–8, 255–9; Schmidl, *März 38*, 232–7; Florian Freund, 'Mauthausen – zu Strukturen von Haupt- und Aussenlagern', in Wolfgang Benz (ed.), *KZ-Aussenlager – Geschichte und Erinnerung* (Dachau, 1999), 254–72.

94. Robert Körber, *Rassesieg in Wien, der Grenzfeste des Reiches* (Vienna, 1939), 271, 281.

95. Longerich, *Politik*, 162–5. See also Herbert Rosenkranz, *Verfolgung und Selbstbehauptung: Die Juden in Österreich 1938–1945* (Vienna, 1978).

96. Friedländer, *Nazi Germany*, 241–4.

97. Gedye, *Fallen Bastions*, 308–9.

98. Ibid.; Botz, *Wien*, 93–105.

99. Longerich, *Politik*, 163–4; Wolfgang Neugebauer (ed.), *Widerstand und Verfolgung im Burgenland: Eine Dokumentation* (Vienna, 1979); Gerhard Botz, *Wohnungspolitik und Judendeportation in Wien, 1938 bis 1945: Zur Funktion des Antisemitismus als Ersatz nationalsozialistischer Sozialpolitik* (Vienna, 1975); Gedye, *Fallen Bastions*, 300–306, 360–62; Eckart Früh, 'Terror und Selbstmord in Wien nach der Annexion Österreichs', in Felix Kreissler (ed.), *Fünfzig Jahre danach – Der 'Anschluss' von innen geschen* (Vienna, 1989), 216–26.

100. David Cesarani, *Eichmann: His Life and Crimes* (London, 2004), 18–60; see also Peter Black, 'Ernst Kaltenbrunner: Chief of the Reich Security Main Office', in Smelser and Zitelmann (eds.), *The Nazi Elite*, 133–43, and idem, *Ernst Kaltenbrunner: Vassall Himmlers: Eine SS-Karriere* (Paderborn, 1991).

101. Ibid., 61–76; Doron Rabinovici, *Instanzen der Ohnmacht: Wien 1938–1945: Der Weg zum Judenrat* (Frankfurt am Main, 2000); Hans Safrian, *Die Eichmann-Männer* (Vienna, 1993); idem, 'Expediting Expropriation and Expulsion: The Impact of the "Vienna Model" on Anti-Jewish Policies in Nazi Gemany, 1938', *Holocaust and Genocide Studies*, 14 (2000), 390–414; Gabriele Anderl and Dirk Rupnow, *Die Zentralstelle für jüdische Auswanderung als Beraubungsinstitution* (Vienna, 2004); Friedländer, *Nazi Germany*, 243–8; Debórah Dwork and Robert Jan Van Pelt, *Holocaust: A History* (London, 2002), 95–8, 121–5; Botz, *Wien*, 243–54.

102. Behnken (ed.), *Deutschland-Berichte*, VI (1939), 381.

103. Cesarani, *Eichmann*, 70–71; Botz, *Wien*, 397–411.

104. Nicholas, *The Rape*, 37–46; Petropoulos, *The Faustian Bargain*, 170–85.

105. Behnken (ed.), *Deutschland-Berichte*, V (1938), 260.

106. Ibid., 264.

107. Kershaw, *The 'Hitler Myth'*, 129–32.

108. Tagebuch Luise Solmitz, 11 March 1938, 12 March 1938, 13 March 1938.

109. Klemperer, *I Shall Bear Witness*, 241 (20 March 1938).

110. Kershaw, *Hitler*, II. 90–91.

111. Domarus (ed.), *Hitler*, II. 1,061–76.

112. Quoted in ibid., 100–101.

113. Jürgen Tampke, *Czech-German Relations and the Politics of Central Europe: From Bohemia to the EU* (London, 2003), 25–44; Rudolf Jaworski, *Vorposten oder Minderheit? Der Sudetendeutsche Volkstumskampf in den Beziehungen zwischen der Weimarer Republik und der CSR* (Stuttgart, 1977); Jaroslav Kucera, *Minderheit im Nationalstaat: Die Sprachenfrage in den tschechisch-deutschen Beziehungen 1918–1938* (Munich, 1999).

114. Tampke, *Czech-German Relations*, 45–53; Hugh Seton-Watson, *Eastern Europe between the Wars 1918–1941* (New York, 1967 [1945]), 277–83; Carlile A. Macartney and Alan W. Palmer, *Independent Eastern Europe: A History* (London, 1966), 156–9, 190–98, 363–6; Christoph Boyer, *Nationale Kontrahenten oder Partner? Studien zu den Beziehungen zwischen Deutschen und Tschechen in der Wirtschaft der CSR* (Munich, 1999); Ronald M. Smelser, *The*

Sudeten Problem 1933–1938: Volkstumpolitik and the Formulation of Nazi Foreign Policy (Folkestone, 1975); Gedye, *Fallen Bastions*, 363–450; Jörg Kracik, *Die Politik des deutschen Aktivismus in der Tschechoslowakei 1920–1938* (Frankfurt am Main, 1999).

115. Nancy M. Wingfield, *Minority Politics in a Multinational State: The German Social Democratic Party 1918–1938* (New York, 1989), 169, but see also Reinhard Schmutzer, 'Der Wahlsieg der Sudetendeutschen Partei: Die Legende von der faschistischen Bekenntniswahl', *Zeitschrift für Ostforschung*, 41 (1992), 345–85.

116. Tampke, *Czech-German Relations*, 53–4.

117. Kershaw, *Hitler*, II. 87–108; Klaus-Jürgen Müller, *General Ludwig Beck: Studien und Dokumente zur politisch-militärischen. Vorstellungswelt und Tätigkeit des Generalstabschefs des deutschen Heeres 1933–1938* (Boppard, 1980); criticized by Peter Hoffmann, 'Generaloberst Ludwig Becks militärpolitisches Denken', *Historische Zeitschrift*, 234 (1981), 101–21; convincing response in Klaus-Jürgen Müller, 'Militärpolitik nicht Militäropposition!', *Historische Zeitschrift*, 235 (1982), 355–71.

118. O'Neill, *The German Army*, 211–22; Müller, *Das Heer*, 300–344.

119. Müller (ed.), *General Ludwig Beck*, 287.

120. Joachim Fest, *Plotting Hitler's Death: The Story of the German Resistance* (London, 1996 [1994]), 71–101, provides a dramatic narrative of the plot; Klemens von Klemperer, *German Resistance against Hitler: The Search for Allies Abroad 1938–1945* (Oxford, 1992), 86–110, and Patricia Meehan, *The Unnecessary War: Whitehall and the German Resistance to Hitler* (London, 1992), chart attempts to enlist foreign support. Among numerous older accounts, see Harold C. Deutsch, *The Conspiracy against Hitler in the Twilight War* (Minneapolis, 1968), and Peter Hoffmann, *Widerstand – Staatsstreich – Attentat: Der Kampf der Opposition gegen Hitler* (4th edn, Munich, 1985 [1969]).

121. Attempts to argue that the opposition at this stage was driven by more fundamental principles have not met with widespread acceptance amongst historians. See Müller, 'Militärpolitik', for the controversy over Beck's motives, and Rainer A. Blasius, *Für Grossdeutschland – gegen den grossen Krieg: Staatssekretär Ernst Frhr. von Weizsäcker in den Krisen um die Tschechoslowakei und Polen 1938/39* (Cologne, 1981), for Weizsäcker's motives. For Halder, see O'Neill, *The German Army*, 224–31.

122. Cited from the memoirs of General Weichs, in ibid., 226.

123. For the following, see the narratives in Hildebrand, *Das vergangene Reich*, 651–66, and Weinberg, *The Foreign Policy*, II. 313–464.

124. Behnken (ed.), *Deutschland-Berichte*, V (1938), 559, 823–5; Shirer, *Berlin Diary*, 111; Fröhlich (ed.), *Die Tagebücher*, I/VI. 80–81 (10 September 1938), 95 (17 September 1938) *et seq.*

125. *The Times*, 28 September 1938. Chamberlain's policy of appeasement has generated a vast, controversial literature. Martin Gilbert, *The Roots of Appeasement* (London, 1966), is an early attempt at a balanced approach; Robert A. C.

Parker, *Chamberlain and Appeasement: British Policy and the Coming of the Second World War* (London, 1993) is a good detailed survey; Keith Robbins, *Munich 1938* (London, 1968) remains the best overall account of the crisis.

126. Robert A. C. Parker, *Churchill and Appeasement* (London, 2000), 167–89; David Reynolds, *In Command of History: Churchill Fighting and Writing the Second World War* (London, 2004), 91–110.

127. Kershaw, *Hitler*, II. 108–13; Robbins, *Munich 1938*, 268–80.

128. Domarus (ed.), *Hitler*, II. 1,181–94; Shirer, *Berlin Diary*, 116; Robbins, *Munich 1938*, 288–302; Fröhlich (ed.), *Die Tagebücher*, I/VI. 94–116 (17–27 September 1938).

129. Ibid., 119 (29 September 1938).

130. Robbins, *Munich 1938*, 303–19; *The Times*, 1 October 1938; Kershaw, *Hitler*, II. 113–23; also Kley, *Hitler*, 49–146.

131. Boberach (ed.), *Meldungen*, II. 72–3.

132. Behnken (ed.), *Deutschland-Berichte*, V (1938), 367–90.

133. Ibid., 681–99.

134. Ibid., 809–41.

135. Fröhlich (ed.), *Die Tagebücher*, I/VI. 65 (31 August 1938).

136. Behnken (ed.), *Deutschland-Berichte*, V (1938), 915–18.

137. Ibid., 913–39.

138. Tagebuch Luise Solmitz, 13 September, 14 September 1938.

139. Ibid., 16 September 1938.

140. Kershaw, *The 'Hitler Myth'*, 132–9.

141. Tagebuch Luise Solmitz, 1939; 30 September.

142. Behnken (ed.), *Deutschland-Berichte*, V (1938), 944–6.

143. Ibid., 947.

144. Shirer, *Berlin Diary*, 117.

145. Domarus, *Hitler*, II. 1,245 (translation adjusted).

146. Ibid., 1,244–55 (translation adjusted).

147. Kershaw, *The 'Hitler Myth'*, 123–4.

148. Tampke, *Czech-German Relations*, 57; Volker Zimmermann, *Die Sudetendeutschen im NS-Staat. Politik und Stimmung der Bevölkerung im Reichsgau Sudetenland (1938–1945)* (Essen, 1999), 79–82; Peter Heumos, *Die Emigration aus der Tschechoslowakei nach Westeuropa und dem Nahen Osten 1938–1945* (Munich, 1989), 15–27; Detlef Brandes *et al.* (eds.), *Erzwungene Trennung: Vertreibungen und Aussiedlungen in und aus der Tschechoslowakei 1938–1947 im Vergleich mit Polen, Ungarn und Jugoslawien* (Essen, 1999). Many refugees subsequently emigrated to Britain and other countries outside the region.

149. Tampke, *Czech-German Relations*, 57–9; Zimmermann, *Die Sudetendeutschen*, 183–209; Hayes, *Industry and Ideology*, 232–43; Feldman, *Allianz*, 302–4; Alice Teichova, 'The Protectorate of Bohemia and Moravia (1939–1945): The Economic Dimension', in Mikuláš Teich (ed.), *Bohemia in History* (Cambridge, 1998), 267–305, at 267–9.

150. Hans Roos, *A History of Modern Poland from the Foundation of the State in the First World War to the Present Day* (London, 1966 [1961]), 154–6; Macartney and Palmer, *Independent Eastern Europe*, 387–8.

151. Ibid., 388–9; Jörg K. Hoensch, *A History of Modern Hungary 1867–1986* (London, 1988 [1984]), 131–41.

152. Macartney and Palmer, *Independent Eastern Europe*, 388–97.

153. Kershaw, *Hitler*, II. 157–68.

154. Ibid., 168–71; Macartney and Palmer, *Independent Eastern Europe*, 398–9; Donald Cameron Watt, *How War Came: The Immediate Origins of the Second World War, 1938–1939* (London, 1989), 141–54; Hildebrand, *Das vergangene Reich*, 666–78; Weinberg, *The Foreign Policy*, II. 465–534; Fröhlich (ed.), *Die Tagebücher* I/6, 285–7 (15 March 1939).

155. Vojtech Mastny, *The Czechs under Nazi Rule: The Failure of National Resistance, 1939–42* (London, 1971), 45–64; Fröhlich (ed.), *Die Tagebücher*, I/VI. 289 (17 March 1939).

156. Teichova, 'The Protectorate', 274–5.

157. Fröhlich (ed.), *Die Tagebücher*, I/VI. 125 (2 October 1928); Mastny, *The Czechs*, 56; Detlef Brandes, *Die Tschechen unter deutschem Protektorat*, I: *Besatzungspolitik, Kollaboration und Widerstand im Protektorat Böhmen und Mähren bis Heydrichs Tod* (Munich, 1968); idem, 'Die Politik des Dritten Reiches gegenüber der Tschechoslowakei', in Funke (ed.), *Hitler, Deutschland und die Mächte*, 508–23; idem, 'Nationalsozialistische Tschechenpolitik im Protektorat Böhmen und Mähren', in idem and Vaclav Kural (eds.), *Der Weg in die Katastrophe: Deutsch-tschechoslowakische Beziehungen 1938–1947* (Essen, 1994), 39–56.

158. Brandes, *Die Tschechen*, 154–5; Mastny, *The Czechs*, 65–85; Teichova, 'The Protectorate', 277–80; David Blaazer, 'Finance and the End of Appeasement: The Bank of England, the National Government and the Czech Gold', *Journal of Contemporary History*, 40 (2005), 25–40.

159. Nicholas, *The Rape*, 43–4; Mastny, *The Czechs*, 80–82.

160. Details, including Göring quote (translation adjusted), in Herbert, *Hitler's Foreign Workers*, 57; see 'Sitzungsbericht zur 2. Sitzung des Reichsverteidigungsrabes', in *International Military Tribunal*, XXXIII. 147–60, at 153–4.

161. Hoensch, *Modern Hungary*, 142–3; Macartney and Palmer, *Independent Eastern Europe*, 400–401.

162. Watt, *How War Came*, 156–7; Kershaw, *Hitler*, II. 175–6; see also Martin Broszat, 'Die memeldeutschen Organisationen und der Nationalsozialismus 1933–1939', *VfZ* 5 (1957), 273–8.

163. Behnken (ed.), *Deutschland-Berichte*, VI (1939), 275–93; quotes on 283; Kershaw, *The 'Hitler Myth'*, 139–40.

164. Neville Chamberlain, *The Struggle for Peace* (London, 1939), 418; Fröhlich (ed.), *Die Tagebücher*, VI/VI. 291–2 (19 March 1939).

165. Anna M. Cienciala, 'Poland in British and French Policy in 1939: Determination to Fight – or Avoid War?', *Polish Review*, 34 (1989), 199–226; Watt,

How War Came, 162–87; Parker, *Chamberlain and Appeasement*, 204–6; Simon Newman, *March 1939: The British Guarantee to Poland: A Study in the Continuity of British Foreign Policy* (Oxford, 1976); Philip M. H. Bell, *The Origins of the Second World War in Europe* (London, 1986), 250–55.

166. See in general Andreas Hillgruber, *Deutsche Grossmacht- und Weltpolitik im 19. und 20. Jahrhundert* (Düsseldorf, 1979 [1977]), 180–97.

167. Kershaw, *Hitler*, II. 177–90; Christian Hartmann and Sergej Slutsch, 'Franz Halder und die Kriegsvorbereitungen im Frühjahr 1939: Eine Ansprache des Generalstabschefs des Heers', *VfZ* 45 (1997), 467–95; Fröhlich (ed.), *Die Tagebücher*, I/VI. 323 (21 April 1939); Watt, *How War Came*, 188–98; Domarus (ed.), *Hitler*, III. 1,519–96.

168. Ibid., 1,616–24.

169. Weinberg, *The Foreign Policy*, II. 192–248.

170. Domarus (ed.), *Hitler*, III. 1,633.

171. Watt, *How War Came*, 232–4; Joachim von Ribbentrop, *The Ribbentrop Memoirs* (London, 1954 [1953]), 109–15.

172. David M. Glantz, *Stumbling Colossus: The Red Army on the Eve of World War* (Lawrence, Kans., 1998); John Erickson, *The Soviet High Command: A Military-Political History, 1918–1941* (London, 2001 [1962]).

173. Dmitri Volkogonov, *Stalin: Triumph and Tragedy* (London, 1995 [1989]), 357.

174. Watt, *How War Came*, 447–61; Kershaw, *Hitler*, II. 189–205; Weinberg, *The Foreign Policy*, II. 601–11; Fröhlich (ed.), *Die Tagebücher*, I/VII. 73 (23 August 1939); more detail in Anthony Read and David Fisher, *The Deadly Embrace: Hitler, Stalin, and the Nazi-Soviet Pact, 1939–1941* (London, 1988); Geoffrey K. Roberts, *The Unholy Alliance: Stalin's Pact with Hitler* (London, 1991), 221–6.

175. See Hans-Erich Volkmann (ed.), *Das Russlandbild im Dritten Reich* (Cologne, 1994).

176. Robert Service, *Stalin: A Biography* (London, 2004), 395–403; Roberts, *The Unholy Alliance*, 267–8, for the secret additional protocols.

177. Weber, '*Weisse Flecken*', 36–7; Institut für Geschichte der Arbeiterbewegung (ed.), *In den Fängen des NKWD: Deutsche Opfer des stalinistischen Terrors in der UdSSR* (Berlin, 1991); Margarete Buber-Neumann, *Under Two Dictators* (London, 1949), 159–75.

178. Peukert, *Die KPD im Widerstand*, 326–33.

179. Kershaw, *Hitler*, II. 205–6; Fröhlich (ed.), *Die Tagebücher*, I/VII. 73 (23 August 1939).

180. Kley, *Hitler*, 201–24.

181. Behnken (ed.), *Deutschland-Berichte*, VI (1939), 546–60; Kershaw, *Hitler*, II. 197–201; Levine, *Hitler's Free City*; Rüdiger Ruhnau, *Die Freie Stadt Danzig, 1919–1939* (Berg am See, 1979); Weinberg, *The Foreign Policy*, II. 525–627, for a wide-ranging narrative of the crisis; Albert S. Kowowski, *Polens Politik gegenüber*

seiner deutschen Minderheit 1919–1939 (Wiesbaden, 1998); and Martin Broszat, *Zweihundert Jahre deutsche Polenpolitik* (Frankfurt am Main, 1972 [1963]), 173–233, for sober assessments of the condition of ethnic Germans in independent Poland; Christian Raitz von Frentz, *A Lesson Forgotten: Minority Protection under the League of Nations: The Case of the German Minority in Poland, 1920–1934* (Münster, 2000), for the international dimension.

182. Behnken (ed.), *Deutschland-Berichte*, VI (1939), 561.

183. Maschmann, *Account Rendered*, 58.

184. Ilse McKee, *Tomorrow the World* (London, 1960), 27; more generally, Ian Kershaw, 'Der Überfall auf Polen und die öffentliche Meinung in Deutschland', in Ernst W. Hansen *et al.* (eds.), *Politischer Wandel, organisierter Gewalt und nationale Sicherheit: Beiträge zur neueren Geschichte Deutschlands und Frankreichs: Festschrift für Klaus-Jürgen Müller* (Munich, 1995), 237–50.

185. Broszat *et al.* (eds.), *Bayern*, I. 131 (Aus Monatsbericht des Bezirksamts, 30. 6. 1939); see also Kershaw, *The 'Hitler Myth'*, 142.

186. Carl J. Burckhardt, *Meine Danziger Mission 1937–1939* (Munich, 1960), 337–53; Watt, *How War Came*, 322–7, 433–40; Herbert S. Levine, 'The Mediator: Carl J. Burckhardt's Efforts to Avert a Second World War', *Journal of Modern History*, 45 (1973), 439–53; and Paul Stauffer, *Zwischen Hofmannsthal und Hitler: Carl J. Burckhardt: Facetten einer aussergewöhnlichen Existenz* (Zurich, 1991).

187. Watt, *How War Came*, 462–78; Kershaw, *Hitler*, II. 211–14; for Henderson, see Neville, *Appeasing Hitler*.

188. Domarus (ed.), *Hitler*, III. 1,663–7; for Hitler's continuing hopes of British neutrality, see e.g. Fröhlich (ed.), *Die Tagebücher*, I/VII. 75 (24 August 1939).

189. Domarus (ed.), *Hitler*, III. 1,668–9; Kershaw, *Hitler*, II. 206–10; see also Winfried Baumgart, 'Zur Ansprache Hitlers vor den Führern der Wehrmacht am 22. August 1939. Eine quellenkritische Untersuchung', *VfZ* 16 (1968), 120–49; Hermann Böhm, 'Zur Ansprache Hitlers vor den Führern der Wehrmacht am 22. August 1939', *VfZ* 19 (1971), 294–300; and Winfried Baumgart, 'Zur Ansprache Hitlers vor den Führern der Wehrmacht am 22. August 1939: Eine Erwiderung', *VfZ* 19 (1971), 301–4.

190. Gerwin Strobl, *The Germanic Isle: Nazi Perceptions of Britain* (Cambridge, 2000), 202–16.

191. Watt, *How War Came*, 479–528.

192. Kershaw, *Hitler*, II. 218–23; Domarus (ed.), *Hitler*, III. 1,700–42; Hildebrand, *Das vergangene Reich*, 678–704.

193. Höhne, *The Order*, 238–44; Jürgen Runzheimer, 'Der Überfall auf den Sender Gleiwitz im Jahre 1939', *VfZ* 10 (1962), 408–26; Watt, *How War Came*, 530–34; Alfred Spiess and Heiner Lichtenstein, *Das Unternehmen Tannenberg: Der Anlass zum Zweiten Welturieg* (Wiesbaden, 1979), 74–84, 132–5.

194. Domarus (ed.), *Hitler*, III. 1,744–57 (translation adjusted); military-political narrative in Horst Rohde, 'Hitler's First Blitzkrieg and Its Consequences for North-

eastern Europe', in Militärgeschichtliches Forschungsamt (ed.), *Germany and the Second World War*, II: *Germany's Initial Conquests in Europe* (Oxford, 2000 [1991]), 67–150; Polish narrative in Janusz Piekalkiewicz, *Polenfeldzug: Hitler und Stalin zerschlagen die Polnische Republik* (Bergisch-Gladbach, 1982); detailed accounts of the final crisis in Weinberg, *The Foreign Policy*, II. 628–55; and Kley, *Hitler*, 225–320.

195. Watt, *How War Came*, 530–89; Fröhlich (ed.), *Die Tagebücher*, I/VII. 82–8 (29 August–1 September 1939).

196. Parker, *Churchill and Appeasement*, 253–7.

197. Watt, *How War Came*, 590–604.

198. Ibid.; Domarus (ed.), *Hitler*, III. 1,758–91; Fröhlich (ed.), *Die Tagebücher*, I/VII. 90–2 (3–4 September 1939).

199. Klemperer, *German Resistance*, 110–34.

200. Kershaw, *Hitler*, II. 224–30; Leonidas E. Hill (ed.), *Die Weizsäcker-Papiere 1933–1950* (Frankfurt am Main, 1974), 162.

201. Broszat *et al.* (eds.), *Bayern*, I. 133–4 (Aus Monatsbericht des Gendarmerie-Kreisführers, 29. 8. 1939; Aus Monatsbericht des Bezirksamts, 30. 9. 1939).

202. Behnken (ed.), *Deutschland-Berichte*, VI (1939), 980.

203. Sywottek, *Mobilmachung*, 238–41; Shirer, *Berlin Diary*, 158–60.

204. Tagebuch Luise Solmitz, 1939: 29 August.

205. Ibid., 31 August 1939.

206. Ibid., 1 September 1939.

207. See in general Peter Fritzsche, 'Nazi Modern', *Modernism/Modernity*, 3 (1996), 1–21.

208. Richard Bessel, *Nazism and War* (London, 2004), esp. 32–89.

209. Domarus (ed.), *Hitler*, III. 1,668–9.

Bibliography

Abel, Karl-Dietrich, *Presselenkung im NS-Staat: Eine Studie zur Geschichte der Publizistik in der nationalsozialistischen Zeit* (Berlin, 1990 [1968]).

Abella, Irving M., and Troper, Harold, *None Is Too Many: Canada and the Jews of Europe, 1933–1948* (New York, 1983).

Abelshauser, Werner, 'Germany: Guns, Butter, and Economic Miracles', in Harrison (ed.), *The Economics of World War II*, 122–76.

——, 'Kriegswirtschaft und Wirtschaftswunder. Deutschlands wirtschaftliche Mobilisierung für den Zweiten Weltkrieg und die Folgen für die Nachkriegszeit', *VfZ* 47 (1999), 503–38.

——, *The Dynamics of German Industry: The German Road Towards the New Economy and the American Challenge* (New York, 2005).

——, and Faust, Anselm (eds.), *Wirtschafts- und Sozialpolitik: Eine nationalsozialistische Revolution?* (Tübingen, 1983).

——, et al., *German Industry and Global Enterprise: BASF: The History of a Company* (Cambridge, 2004).

Abendroth, Hans-Henning, *Hitler in der spanischen Arena: Die deutsch-spanischen Beziehungen im Spannungsfeld der europäischen Interessenpolitik vom Ausbruch des Bürgerkrieges bis zum Ausbruch des Weltkrieges, 1936–1939* (Paderborn, 1973).

——, 'Deutschlands Rolle im Spanischen Bürgerkrieg', in Funke (ed.), *Hitler, Deutschland und die Mächte*, 471–88.

Abrams, Lynn, *Workers' Culture in Imperial Germany: Leisure and Recreation in the Rhineland and Westphalia* (London, 1992).

Ach, Manfred, and Pentrop, Clemens (eds.), *Hitlers 'Religion': Pseudoreligiöse Elemente im nationalsozialistischen Sprachgebrauch* (Munich, 1991 [1979]).

Ackermann, Josef, *Heinrich Himmler als Ideologe* (Göttingen, 1970).

Adam, Peter, *The Arts of the Third Reich* (London, 1992).

Adam, Uwe Dietrich, *Judenpolitik im Dritten Reich* (Düsseldorf, 1972).

——, 'How Spontaneous Was the Pogrom?', in Pehle (ed.), *November 1938*, 73–94.

Adamthwaite, Anthony, 'France and the Coming of War', in Finney (ed.), *The Origins of the Second World War*, 78–89.

Adler-Rudel, Salomon, *Jüdische Selbsthilfe unter dem Naziregime 1933–1939, im Spiegel der Berichte der Reichsvertretung der Juden in Deutschland* (Tübingen, 1974).

Akademie der Künste, Berlin (ed.), *Zwischen Anpassung und Widerstand: Kunst in Deutschland 1933–1945* (Berlin, 1978).

Albrecht, Dieter (ed.), *Der Notenwechsel zwischen dem Heiligen Stuhl und der Deutschen Reichsregierung* (3 vols., Mainz, 1965–80).

——, *et al.* (eds.), *Politik und Konfession: Festschrift für Konrad Repgen zum 60. Geburtstag* (Berlin, 1983).

Albrecht, Gerd, *Nationalsozialistische Filmpolitik: Eine soziologische Untersuchung über die Spielfilme des Dritten Reichs* (Stuttgart, 1969).

——, *Der Film im Dritten Reich: Eine Dokumentation* (Karlsruhe, 1979).

Allen, William Sheridan, *The Nazi Seizure of Power: The Experience of a Single German Town, 1922–1945* (New York, 1984 [1965]).

——, 'Social Democratic Resistance against Hitler and the European Tradition of Underground Movements', in Nicosia and Stokes (eds.), *Germans Against Nazism*, 191–204.

Alter, Reinhard, *Gottfried Benn: The Artist and Politics (1910–1934)* (Frankfurt am Main, 1976).

Alte Synagoge, (ed.), *Entrechtung und Selbsthilfe: Zur Geschichte der Juden in Essen unter dem Nationalsozialismus* (Essen, 1994).

Altgeld, Wolfgang, *Katholizismus, Protestantismus, Judentum: Über religiös begründete Gegensätze und nationalreligiöse Ideen in der Geschichte des deutschen Nationalismus* (Mainz, 1992).

——, 'Religion, Denomination and Nationalism in Nineteenth-Century Germany', in Smith (ed.), *Protestants, Catholics, and Jews*, 49–65.

Anderl, Gabriele, and Rupnow, Dirk, *Die Zentralstelle für jüdische Auswanderung als Beraubungsinstitution* (Vienna, 2004).

Angermund, Ralph, *Deutsche Richterschaft 1919–1945: Krisenerfahrung, Illusion, politische Rechtsprechung* (Frankfurt am Main, 1990).

Applebaum, Anne, *Gulag: A History of the Soviet Camps* (London, 2003).

Applegate, Celia, 'The Past and Present of *Hausmusik* in the Third Reich', in Kater and Riethmüller (eds.), *Music and Nazism*, 136–49.

Arendt, Hannah, *The Origins of Totalitarianism* (London, 1973 [1955]).

Aretin, Karl Otmar von, 'Der bayerische Adel von der Monarchie zum Dritten Reich', in Broszat *et al.* (eds.), *Bayern*, III. 513–68.

——, and Buchheim, Karl (eds.), *Krone und Ketten: Erinnerungen eines bayerischen Edelmannes* (Munich, 1955).

Arndt, Karl, 'Die Münchener Architekturszene 1933/34 als ästhetisch-politisches Konfliktfeld', in Broszat *et al.* (eds.), *Bayern*, III. 443–512.

——, 'Das "Haus der deutschen Kunst" – ein Symbol der neuen Machtverhältnisse', in Schuster (ed.), *Die 'Kunststadt' München*, 61–82.

——, *Nationalsozialismus und 'Entartete Kunst': Die 'Kunststadt' München 1937* (Munich, 1988).

——, 'Paul Ludwig Troost als Leitfigur der nationalsozialistischen Räpresentationsarchitektur', in Lauterbach (ed.), *Bürokratie und Kult*, 147–56.

Arntz, H. Dieter, *Ordensburg Vogelsang 1934–1945: Erziehung zur politischen Führung im Dritten Reich* (Euskirchen, 1986).

Arold, Stefan, *Die technische Entwicklung und rüstungswirtschaftliche Bedeutung des Lokomotivbaus der Deutschen Reichsbahn im Dritten Reich (1933–1945)* (Stuttgart, 1997).

Aronson, Shlomo, *Reinhard Heydrich und die Frühgeschichte von Gestapo und SD* (Stuttgart, 1971).

Aster, Sidney, ' "Guilty Men": The Case of Neville Chamberlain', in Finney (ed.), *The Origins of the Second World War*, 62–77.

Ayass, Wolfgang, *'Asoziale' im Nationalsozialismus* (Stuttgart, 1995).

Ayçoberry, Pierre, *The Nazi Question: An Essay on the Interpretations of National Socialism (1922–1975)* (New York, 1981).

Bacharach, Walter Zwi, 'The Catholic Anti-Jewish Prejudice, Hitler and the Jews', in Bankier (ed.), *Probing*, 415–30.

Backes, Klaus, *Hitler und die bildenden Künste: Kulturverständnis und Kunstpolitik im Dritten Reich* (Cologne, 1988).

Bahr, Ehrhard, 'Nazi Cultural Politics: Intentionalism v. Functionalism', in Cuomo (ed.), *National Socialist Cultural Policy*, 5–22.

Baird, Jay W., 'From Berlin to Neubabelsberg: Nazi Film Propaganda and Hitler Youth Quex', *Journal of Contemporary History*, 18 (1983), 495–515.

——, *To Die for Germany: Heroes in the Nazi Pantheon* (Bloomington, Ind., 1990).

Bajohr, Frank, 'Gauleiter in Hamburg. Zur Person und Tätigkeit Karl Kaufmanns', *VfZ* 43 (1995), 27–95.

——, 'The "Aryanization" of Jewish Companies and German Society: The Example of Hamburg', in Bankier (ed.), *Probing*, 226–45.

——, *Parvenüs und Profiteure: Korruption in der NS-Zeit* (Frankfurt am Main, 2001).

——, *'Aryanization' in Hamburg: The Economic Exclusion of Jews and the Confiscation of their Property in Nazi Germany* (New York, 2002 [1997]).

——, (ed.), *Norddeutschland im Nationalsozialismus* (Hamburg, 1993).

——, and Szodrzynski, Joachim, ' "Keine jüdische Hautcreme mehr benutzen." Die antisemitische Kampagne gegen die Hamburger Firma Beiersdorf', in Herzig (ed.), *Die Juden in Hamburg*, 15–26.

Bajohr, Stefan, 'Weiblicher Arbeitsdienst im "Dritten Reich". Ein Konflikt zwischen Ideologie und Ökonomie', *VfZ* 28 (1980), 331–57.

Bankier, David, *The Germans and The Final Solution: Public Opinion under Nazism* (Oxford, 1992).

—— (ed.), *Probing the Depths of German Antisemitism: German Society and the Persecution of the Jews, 1933–1941* (Jerusalem, 2000).

Baranowski, Shelley, *The Confessing Church, Conservative Elites, and the Nazi State* (New York, 1986).

——, 'East Elbian Landed Elites and Germany's Turn to Fascism: The *Sonderweg* Controversy Revisited', *European History Quarterly*, 26 (1996), 209–40.

——, *Strength Through Joy: Consumerism and Mass Tourism in the Third Reich* (New York, 2004).

Barbian, Jan-Pieter, *Literaturpolitik im 'Dritten Reich': Institutionen, Kompetenzen, Betätigungsfelder.* (Munich, 1995 [1993]).

Barbian, Peter, 'Literary Policy in the Third Reich', in Cuomo (ed.), *National Socialist Cultural Policy*, 155–96.

Barkai, Avraham, *From Boycott to Annihilation: The Economic Struggle of German Jews 1933–1943* (Hanover, N.H., 1989 [1988]).

——, 'Die deutschen Unternehmer und die Judenpolitik im "Dritten Reich"', *Geschichte und Gesellschaft*, 15 (1989), 235–7.

——, *Nazi Economics: Ideology, Theory, and Policy* (Oxford, 1990 [1988]).

——, 'German Interests in the Haavara-Transfer Agreement 1933–1939', *Leo Baeck Institute Yearbook* 35 (1990), 254–66.

——, 'The Fateful Year 1938: The Continuation and Acceleration of Plunder', in Pehle (ed.), *November 1938*, 95–122.

——, 'Jewish Life under Persecution', in Meyer (ed.), *German-Jewish History*, 231–57.

——, 'Shifting Organizational Relationships' in Meyer (ed.), *German-Jewish History*, 259–82.

——, 'Self-Help in the Dilemma: "To Leave or to Stay?"', in Meyer (ed.), *German-Jewish History*, 313–32.

Barker, Theo (ed.), *The Economic and Social Effects of the Spread of Motor Vehicles: An International Centenary Tribute* (London, 1988).

Barlach, Ernst, *Die Briefe*, ed. Friedrich Dross (2 vols., Munich, 1968–9).

Barnett, Victoria, *For the Soul of the People: Protestant Protest against Hitler* (Oxford 1992).

Barron, Stephanie (ed.), *Degenerate Art: The Fate of the Avant-Garde in Nazi Germany* (Los Angeles, 1991).

——, 'The Galerie Fischer Auction', in eadem (ed.), *Degenerate Art*, 135–71.

Bärsch, Claus-Ekkehard, *Die politische Religion des Nationalsozialismus: Die religiöse Dimension der NS-Ideologie in der Schriften von Dietrich Eckhard, Joseph Goebbels, Alfred Rosenberg und Adolf Hitler* (Munich, 1998).

Bartetzko, Dieter, *Zwischen Zucht und Ekstase: Zur Theatralik von NS-Architektur* (Berlin, 1985).

Barth, Karl, *Karl Barth zum Kirchenkampf: Beteiligung, Mahnung, Zuspruch* (Munich, 1956).

——, *The German Church Conflict* (London, 1965).

Bästlein, Klaus, 'Sondergerichte in Norddeutschland als Verfolgungsinstanz', in Bajohr (ed.), *Norddeutschland im Nationalsozialismus*, 218–38.

Bateson, Gregory, 'An Analysis of the Nazi Film *Hitlerjunge Quex*', in Mead and Métraux (eds.), *The Study of Culture at a Distance*, 302–14.

Bauer, Gerhard, *Sprache und Sprachlosigkeit im 'Dritten Reich'* (Cologne, 1990 [1988]).

Bauer, Yehuda, *My Brother's Keeper: A History of the American Jewish Joint Distribution Committee, 1929–1939* (Philadelphia, 1974).

Baumann, Angelika, and Heusler, Andreas (eds.), *München 'arisiert': Entrechtung und Enteignung der Juden in der NS-Zeit* (Munich, 2004).

Baumann, Jürgen, *Paragraph 175: Über die Möglichkeit, die einfache, nicht-jugendgefährdende und nichtöffentliche Homosexualität unter Erwachsenen straffrei zu lassen* (Berlin, 1968).

Baumeister, Stefan, *NS-Führungskader: Rekrutierung und Ausbildung bis zum Beginn des Zweiten Weltkriegs, 1933–1939* (Konstanz, 1997).

Baumgart, Winfried, 'Zur Ansprache Hitlers vor den Führern der Wehrmacht am 22. August 1939. Eine quellenkritische Untersuchung', *VfZ* 16 (1968), 120–49.

——, 'Zur Ansprache Hitlers vor den Führern der Wehrmacht am 22. August 1939: Eine Erwiderung', *VfZ* 19 (1971), 301–4.

Baumgärtner, Raimund, *Weltanschauungskampf im Dritten Reich: Die Auseinandersetzung der Kirchen mit Alfred Rosenberg* (Mainz, 1977).

Bayles, William D., *Caesars in Goosestep* (New York, 1940).

Bechstedt, Martin, '"Gestalthafte Atomlehre" – Zur "Deutschen Chemie" im NS-Staat', in Mehrtens and Richter (eds.), *Naturwissenschaft*, 142–65.

Beck, Johannes, *et al.* (eds.), *Terror und Hoffnung in Deutschland, 1933–1945: Leben im Faschismus* (Reinbek, 1980).

Becker, Wolfgang, *Film und Herrschaft; Organisationsprinzipien und Organisationsstrukturen der nationalsozialistischen Filmpropaganda* (Berlin, 1973).

Beer, Helmut, *Widerstand gegen den Nationalsozialismus in Nürnberg 1933–1945* (Nuremberg, 1976).

Behnken, Klaus (ed.), *Deutschland-Berichte der Sozialdemokratischen Partei Deutschlands (Sopade) 1934–1940* (7 vols., Frankfurt am Main, 1980).

——, and Wagner, Frank, *Inszenierung der Macht: Ästhetische Faszination im Faschismus* (Berlin, 1987).

Behrenbeck, Sabine, *Der Kult um die toten Helden: Nationalsozialistische Mythen, Riten und Symbole 1923 bis 1945* (Vierow bei Greifswald, 1996).

Bell, Philip M. H., *The Origins of the Second World War in Europe* (London, 1986).

Bellon, Bernard P., *Mercedes in Peace and War: German Automobile Workers, 1903–1945* (New York, 1990).

Benjamin, Walter, 'Das Kunstwerk im Zeitalter seiner technischen Reproduzierbarkeit', in idem, *Gesammelte Schriften*, I/II, ed. Rolf Tiedemann and Hermann Schweppenhäuser (Frankfurt am Main, 1974).

Benn, Gottfried, *Gesammelte Werke*, ed. Dieter Wellershoff (4 vols., Wiesbaden, 1961).

Bennecke, Heinrich, *Die Reichswehr und der 'Röhm-Putsch'* (Munich, 1964).

Bennhold, Martin (ed.), *Spuren des Unrechts: Recht und Nationalsozialismus. Beiträge zur historischen Kontinuität* (Cologne, 1989).

Bentley, James, *Martin Niemöller, 1892–1984* (Oxford, 1984).

Benz, Ute, and Benz, Wolfgang, *Sozialisation und Traumatisierung: Kinder in der Zeit des Nationalsozialismus* (Frankfurt am Main, 1992).

Benz, Wolfgang (ed.), *Die Juden in Deutschland 1933–1945. Leben unter nationalsozialistischer Herrschaft* (Munich, 1988).

——, 'The Ritual and Stage Management of National Socialism. Techniques of Domination and the Public Sphere', in Milfull (ed.), *The Attractions of Fascism*, 273–88.

——, 'The Relapse into Barbarism', in Pehle (ed.), *November 1938*.

—— (ed.), *KZ-Aussenlager – Geschichte und Errinerung* (Dachau, 1999).

——, *Flucht aus Deutschland: Zum Exil im 20. Jahrhundert* (Munich, 2001).

Beradt, Charlotte, *Das Dritte Reich des Traums* (Frankfurt am Main, 1981 [1966]).

Berenbaum, Michael, *A Mosaic of Victims: Non-Jews Persecuted and Murdered by the Nazis* (New York, 1990).

Bergen, Doris L., *Twisted Cross: The German Christian Movement in the Third Reich* (Chapel Hill, N.C., 1996).

Berger, Stefan, *et al.* (eds.), *Writing National Histories: Western Europe since 1800* (London, 1999).

Berghoff, Hartmut, *Zwischen Kleinstadt und Weltmarkt: Hohner und die Harmonika 1857–1961: Unternehmensgeschichte als Gesellschaftsgeschichte* (Paderborn, 1997).

Bergsdorf, Wolfgang, 'Sprachlenkung im Nationalsozialismus', in Greiffenhagen (ed.), *Kampf um Wörter?*, 65–74.

Berliner Geschichtswerkstatt (ed.), *Alltagskultur, Subjektivität und Geschichte: zur Theorie und Praxis von Alltagsgeschichte* (Münster, 1994).

Berliner Illustrierte Nachtausgabe (1933–9).

Bernett, Hajo, *Der jüdische Sport im nationalsozialistischen Deutschland 1933–1938* (Schorndorf, 1978).

Bernhard, Hans Joachim, *et al.* (eds.), *Der Reichstagsbrandprozess und Georgi Dimitroff: Dokumente* (2 vols., Berlin, 1981–9).

Bessel, Richard, *Political Violence and the Rise of Nazism: The Storm Troopers in Eastern Germany 1925–1934* (London, 1984).

—— (ed.), *Life in the Third Reich* (Oxford, 1987).

—— (ed.), *Fascist Italy and Nazi Germany: Comparisons and Contrasts* (Cambridge, 1996).

——, *Nazism and War* (London, 2004).

Bessen, Dorothea, 'Der Jüdische Kulturbund Rhein-Ruhr 1933–1938', in Alte Synagoge (ed.), *Entrechtung und Selbsthilfe*, 43–65.

Bethge, Eberhard, *Dietrich Bonhoeffer: Theologe, Christ, Zeitgenosse* (Munich, 1967).

Beyerchen, Alan D., *Scientists under Hitler: Politics and the Physics Community in the Third Reich* (New Haven, Conn., 1977).

Billstein, Reinhold, *et al.*, *Working for the Enemy: Ford, General Motors, and Forced Labor in Germany during the Second World War* (New York, 2000).

Blaazer, David, 'Finance and the End of Appeasement: The Bank of England, the National Government and the Czech Gold', *Journal of Contemporary History*, 40 (2005), 25–40.

Black, Peter, 'Ernst Kaltenbrunner: Chief of the Reich Security Main Office', in Smelser and Zitelmann (eds.), *The Nazi Elite*, 133–43.

——, *Ernst Kaltenbrunner: Vassall Himmlers: Eine SS-Karriere* (Paderborn, 1991).

Blackbourn, David, *Populists and Patricians: Essays in Modern German History* (London, 1987).

Blackburn, Gilmer W., *Education in the Third Reich: A Study of Race and History in Nazi Textbooks* (Albany, N. Y., 1985).

Blaich, Fritz, 'Die bayerische Industrie 1933–1939. Elemente von Gleichschaltung, Konformismus und Selbstbehauptung', in Broszat *et al.* (eds.), *Bayern*, II. 237–80.

——, *Wirtschaft und Rüstung im 'Dritten Reich'* (Düsseldorf, 1987).

——, 'Why Did the Pioneer Fall Behind? Motorization in Germany between the Wars', in Barker (ed.), *The Economic and Social Effects of the Spread of Motor Vehicles*, 149–55.

Blaschke, Olaf (ed.), *Konfessionen im Konflikt: Deutschland zwischen 1800 und 1970: Ein zweites konfessionelles Zeitalter* (Göttingen, 2002).

Blasius, Dirk, 'Die Ausstellung "Entartete Musik" von 1938. Ein Beitrag zum Kontinuitätsproblem der deutschen Geschichte', in Haberl and Korenke (eds.), *Politische Deutungskulturen*, 199–211.

Blasius, Rainer A., *Für Grossdeutschland – gegen den grossen Krieg: Staatssekretär Ernst Frhr. von Weizsäcker in den Krisen um die Tschechoslowakei und Polen 1938/39* (Cologne, 1981).

Blau, Bruno, *Das Ausnahmerecht für die Juden in Deutschland 1933–1945* (Düsseldorf, 1954 [1952]).

Bleuel, Hans Peter, *Strength Through Joy: Sex and Society in Nazi Germany* (London, 1973 [1972]).

Blumenberg, Werner, *Kämpfer für die Freiheit* (Berlin, 1959).

Boak, Helen L., 'The State as an Employer of Women in the Weimar Republic', in Lee and Rosenhaft (eds.), *The State and Social Change in Germany*, 61–98.

Boas, Jacob, 'German-Jewish Internal Politics under Hitler 1933–1939', *Leo Baeck Institute Yearbook*, 29 (1984), 2–25.

Boberach, Heinz (ed.), *Berichte des SD und der Gestapo über Kirchen und Kirchenvolk in Deutschland 1934–1944* (Mainz, 1971).

——, *Meldungen aus dem Reich, 1938–1945: Die geheimen Lageberichte des Sicherheitsdienstes der SS* (17 vols., Herrsching, 1984).

Bock, Gisela, *Zwangssterilisation im Nationalsozialismus: Studien zur Rassenpolitik und Frauenpolitik* (Opladen, 1986).

——, 'Antinatalism, Maternity and Paternity in National Socialist Realism', in Crew (ed.), *Nazism*, 110–40.

Bock, Helmut, *et al.* (eds.), *Sturz ins Dritte Reich: Historische Miniaturen und Porträts 1933/35* (Leipzig, 1983).

Boelcke, Willi A., *Die deutsche Wirtschaft 1930–1945: Interna des Reichswirtschaftsministeriums* (Düsseldorf, 1983).

——, *Die Kosten von Hitlers Krieg: Kriegsfinanzierung und finanzielles Kriegserbe in Deutschland 1933–1948* (Paderborn, 1985).

Boese, Engelbrecht, *Das öffentliche Bibliothekswesen im Dritten Reich* (Bad Honnef, 1987).

Bohleber, Werner, and Drew, Jörg, *'Gift, das du unbewusst eintrinkst . . .' Der Nationalsozialismus und die deutsche Sprache* (Bielefeld, 1994 [1991]).

Böhm, Hermann, 'Zur Ansprache Hitlers vor den Führern der Wehrmacht am 22. August 1939', *VfZ* 19 (1971), 294–300.

Bohn, Robert, and Danker, Uwe *'Standgericht der inneren Front': Das Sondergericht Altona/Kiel 1932–1945* (Hamburg, 1998).

Böhnert, Gunnar C., 'An Analysis of the Age and Education of the SS *Führerkorps* 1925–1939', *Historical Social Research*, 12 (1979), 4–17.

Bolchover, Richard, *British Jewry and the Holocaust* (Cambridge, 1993).

Bollmus, Reinhard, *Das Amt Rosenberg und seine Gegner: Studien zum Machtkampf im nationalsozialistischen Herrschaftssystem* (Stuttgart, 1970).

——, 'Alfred Rosenberg: National Socialism's "Chief Ideologue"?', in Smelser and Zitelman (eds.), *The Nazi Elite*, 183–93.

Bonhoeffer, Dietrich, *Gesammelte Schriften* (Munich, 1958).

Bork, Siegfried, *Missbrauch der Sprache: Tendenzen nationalsozialistischer Sprachregelung* (Munich, 1970).

Borkin, Joseph, *The Crime and Punishment of I. G. Farben* (New York, 1978).

Bormann, Alexander von, 'Das nationalsozialistische Gemeinschaftslied', in Denkler and Prümm (eds.), *Die deutsche Literatur*, 256–80.

Bornscheuer, Karl-Dieter (ed.), *Justiz im Dritten Reich: NS-Sondergerichtsverfahren in Rheinland-Pfalz: Eine Dokumentation* (3 vols., Frankfurt am Main, 1994).

Borrmann, Norbert, *Paul Schultze-Naumburg, 1869–1949: Maler, Publizist, Architekt: Vom Kulturreformer der Jahrhundertwende zum Kulturpolitiker im Dritten Reich* (Essen, 1989).

Böttcher, Robert, *Kunst und Kunsterziehung im neuen Reich* (Breslau, 1933).

Botz, Gerhard, *Die Eingliederung Österreichs in das deutsche Reich: Planung und Verwirklichung des politisch-administrativen Anschlusses (1938–1940)* (Linz, 1972).

——, *Wohnungspolitik und Judendeportation in Wien 1938 bis 1945: Zur Funktion des Antisemitismus als Ersatz nationalsozialistischer Sozialpolitik* (Vienna, 1975).

——, *Der 13. März 38 und die Anschlussbewegung: Selbstaufgabe, Okkupation und Selbstfindung Osterreichs 1908–1945* (Vienna, 1978).

——, *Wien, vom 'Anschluss' zum Krieg: Nationalsozialistische Machtübernahme und politisch-soziale Umgestaltung am Beispiel der Stadt Wien 1938/39* (Vienna, 1978).

Boveri, Margret, *Wir lügen alle: Eine Hauptstadtzeitung unter Hitler* (Olten, 1965).

Boyer, Christoph, *Nationale Kontrahenten oder Partner? Studien zu den Beziehungen zwischen Tschechen und Deutschen in der Wirtschaft der CSR* (Munich, 1999).

Bracher, Karl Dietrich, *et al.*, *Die nationalsozialistische Machtergreifung: Studien zur Errichtung des totalitären Herrschaftssystems in Deutschland 1933/34* (3 vols., Frankfurt am Main, 1974 [1960]).

——, *et al.* (eds.), *Deutschland 1933–1945: Neue Studien zur nationalsozialistischen Herrschaft* (Bonn, 1993 [1992]).

Bracht, Hans-Günther, *Das höhere Schulwesen im Spannungsfeld von Demokratie und Nationalsozialismus: Ein Beitrag zur Kontinuitätsdebatte am Beispiel der preussischen Aufbauschule* (Frankfurt am Main, 1998).

Brackmann, Karl-Heinz, and Birkenhauer, Renate, *NS-Deutsch: Selbstverständliche Begriffe und Schlagwörter aus der Zeit des Nationalsozialismus* (Straelen, 1988).

Braham Randolph L., *The Politics of Genocide: The Holocaust in Hungary* (2 vols., New York, 1980).

——, *Perspectives on the Holocaust* (Boston, 1983).

—— (ed.), *Jewish Leadership during the Nazi Era: Patterns of Behavior in the Free World* (New York, 1985).

Brakelmann, Günter, 'Hoffnungen und Illusionen evangelischer Prediger zu Beginn des Dritten Reiches: gottesdienstliche Feiern aus politischen Anlässen', in Peukert and Reulecke (eds.), *Die Reihen fast geschlossen*, 129–48.

——, 'Nationalprotestantismus und Nationalsozialismus', in Jansen *et al.* (eds.), *Von der Aufgabe der Freiheit*, 337–50.

Bramsted, Ernest Kohn, *Goebbels and National Socialist Propaganda, 1925–1945* (East Lansing, Mich., 1965).

Brand-Claussen, Bettina (ed.), *Beyond Reason: Art and Psychosis: Works from the Prinzhorn Collection* (London, 1996).

Brandes, Detlef, 'Die Politik des Dritten Reiches gegenüber der Tschechoslowakei', in Funke (ed.), *Hitler, Deutschland und die Mächte*, 508–23.

——, *Die Tschechen unter deutschem Protektorat* (2 vols., Munich, 1967–75).

——, and Kural, Vaclav (eds.), *Der Weg in die Katastrophe: Deutsch-tschechoslowakische Beziehungen 1938–1947* (Essen, 1994).

——, *et al.*, *Erzwungene Trennung: Vertreibungen und Aussiedlungen in und aus der Tschechoslowakei, 1938–1947 im Vergleich mit Polen, Ungarn und Jugoslawien* (Essen, 1999).

Brandt, Harm-Hinrich, and Stickler, Mattiàs (eds.), *'Der Burschen Herrlichkeit': Geschichte und Gegenwart des studentischen Korporationswesens* (Würzburg, 1998).

Bräutigam, Petra, *Mittelständische Unternehmer im Nationalsozialismus: Wirtschaftliche Entwicklungen und soziale Verhaltensweisen in der Schuh- und Lederindustrie Badens und Württembergs* (Munich, 1997).

Brechtken, Magnus, *'Madagaskar für die Juden': Antisemitische Idee und politische Praxis 1885–1945* (Munich, 1997).

Breitman, Richard, and Kraut, Alan, *American Refugee Policy and European Jewry, 1933–1945* (Bloomington, Ind., 1987).

Breitschneider, Heike, *Der Widerstand gegen den Nationalsozialismus in München 1933 bis 1945* (Munich, 1968).

Breker, Arno, *Im Strahlungsfeld der Ereignisse 1925–1965* (Preussisch Oldendorf, 1972).

Brenner, Hildegard, *Die Kunstpolitik des Nationalsozialismus* (Reinbek, 1963).

Brenner, Peter J., *Reisekultur in Deutschland: Von der Weimarer Republik zum 'Dritten Reich'* (Tübingen, 1997).

Breyvogel, Wilfried, and Lohmann, Thomas, 'Schulalltag im Nationalsozialismus', in Peukert and Reulecke (eds.), *Die Reihen fast geschlossen*, 199–221.

Bridenthal, Renate, and Koonz, Claudia, 'Beyond *Kinder, Küche, Kirche*: Weimar Women in Politics and Work', in Bridenthal *et al.* (eds.), *When Biology Became Destiny*, 33–65.

Bridenthal, Renate, *et al.* (eds.), *When Biology Became Destiny: Women in Weimar and Nazi Germany* (New York, 1984).

Brinkmann, Reinhold, 'The Distorted Sublime: Music and National Socialist Ideology – A Sketch', in Kater and Riethmüller (eds.), *Music and Nazism*, 42–63.

Brintzinger, Klaus-Rainer, *Die Nationalökonomie an den Universitäten Freiburg, Heidelberg und Tübingen 1918–1945: Eine institutionenhistorische, vergleichende Studie der wirtschaftswissenschaftlichen Fakultäten und Abteilungen südwestdeutscher Universitäten* (Frankfurt am Main, 1996).

Broder, Henryk M., and Geisel, Eike (eds.), *Premiere und Pogrom: Der Jüdische Kulturbund 1933–1941: Texte und Bilder* (Berlin, 1992).

Brook-Shepherd, Gordon, *The Austrians: A Thousand-year Odyssey* (London, 1996).

Broszat, Martin, 'Die memeldeutschen Organisationen und der Nationalsozialismus 1933–1939', *VfZ* 5 (1957), 273–8.

——, *Der Staat Hitlers: Grundlegung und Entwicklung seiner inneren Verfassung* (Munich, 1969).

——, 'The Concentration Camps 1933–1945', in Krausnick *et al.*, *Anatomy*, 397–496.

——, *Zweihundert Jahre deutsche Polenpolitik* (Frankfurt am Main, 1972 [1963]).

——, 'Politische Denunziationen in der NS-Zeit: Aus Forschungserfahrungen im Staatsarchiv München', *Archivalische Zeitschrift*, 73 (1977), 221–38.

——, and Möller, Horst (eds.), *Das Dritte Reich: Herrschaftsstruktur und Geschichte* (Munich, 1986 [1983]).

——, and Schwabe, Klaus (eds.), *Die Deutschen Eliten und der Weg in den Zweiten Weltkrieg* (Munich, 1989).

——, *et al.* (eds.), *Bayern in der NS-Zeit* (6 vols., Munich, 1977–83).

Browder, George C., *Foundations of the Nazi Police State: The Formation of Sipo and SD* (Lexington, Ky., 1990).

——, *Hitler's Enforcers: The Gestapo and the SS Security Service in the Nazi Revolution* (New York and Oxford, 1996).

Brücks, Andrea, 'Zwangssterilisation gegen "Ballastexistenzen"', in Frahm *et al.* (eds.), *Verachtet – verfolgt – vernichtet*, 103–8.

Brumme, Martin F., '"Prachtvoll fegt der eiserne Besen durch die deutschen Lande." Die Tierärzte und das Jahr 1933', in Meinel and Voswinckel (eds.), *Medizin*, 173–82.

Brunck, Helma, *Die Deutsche Burschenschaft in der Weimarer Republik und im Nationalsozialismus* (Munich, 1999).

Brunner, Claudia, *Arbeitslosigkeit im NS-Staat: Das Beispiel München* (Pfaffenweiler, 1997).

Brunner, Otto, and Gerhard, Dietrich (eds.), *Europa und Übersee: Festschrift für Egmont Zechlin* (Hamburg, 1961).

Bruns-Wüstefeld, Alex, *Lohnende Geschäfte: Die 'Entjudung' der Wirtschaft am Beispiel Göttingens* (Hanover, 1997).

Buber-Neumann, Margarete, *Under Two Dictators* (London, 1949).

Buchheim, Christoph, 'Zur Natur des Wirtschaftsaufschwungs in der NS-Zeit', in idem *et al.* (eds.), *Zerrissene Zwischenkriegszeit: Wirtschaftshistorische Beiträge: Knut Borchardt zum 65. Geburtstag* (Baden-Baden, 1994), 97–119.

——, 'Die Wirtschaftsentwicklung im Dritten Reich – mehr Desaster als Wunder. Eine Erwiderung auf Werner Abelshauser', *VfZ* 49 (2001), 653–4.

Buchheim, Hans, 'Command and Compliance', in Krausnick *et al.*, *Anatomy*, 303–96.

——, 'The SS: Instrument of Domination', in Krausnick *et al.*, *Anatomy*, 127–301.

Buchheit, Gert, *Ludwig Beck, ein preussischer General* (Munich, 1964).

Buchwitz, Otto, *50 Jahre Funktionär der deutschen Arbeiterbewegung* (Stuttgart, 1949).

Budrass, Lutz, *Flugzeugindustrie und Luftrüstung in Deutschland 1918–1945* (Düsseldorf, 1998).

Bukey, Evan B., 'Popular Opinion in Vienna after the Anschluss', in Parkinson (ed.), *Conquering the Past*, 151–64.

Bullen, R. J., *et al.* (eds.), *Ideas into Politics: Aspects of European History 1880–1950* (London, 1984).

Burckhardt, Carl Jacob, *Meine Danziger Mission, 1937–1939* (Munich, 1960).

Burleigh, Michael, *Germany Turns Eastwards: A Study of Ostforschung in the Third Reich* (Cambridge, 1988).

——, *Death and Deliverance: 'Euthanasia' in Germany c.1900–1945* (Cambridge, 1994).

——, *The Third Reich: A New History* (London, 2000).

——, and Wippermann, Wolfgang, *The Racial State: Germany 1933–1945* (Cambridge, 1991).

Burrin, Philippe, *Hitler and the Jews: The Genesis of the Holocaust* (London, 1994 [1989]).

——, 'Political Religion. The Relevance of a Concept', *History and Memory*, 9 (1997), 321–49.

Busch, Eberhard, *Karl Barths Lebenslauf: Nach seinen Briefen und autobiographischen Texten* (Munich, 1975).

Bussemer, Thymian, *Propaganda und Populärkultur: Konstruierte Erlebniswelten im Nationalsozialismus* (Wiesbaden, 2000).

Bussmann, Georg, *German Art of the Twentieth Century* (Munich, 1985).

Bussmann, Walter, 'Zur Entstehung und Überlieferung der "Hossbach-Niederschrift"', *VfZ* 16 (1968), 373–8.

Büttner, Ursula (ed.), *Die Deutschen und die Judenverfolgung im Dritten Reich* (Hamburg, 1992).

——, '"The Jewish Problem becomes a Christian Problem": German Protestants and the Persecution of the Jews in the Third Reich', in Bankier (ed.), *Probing*, 431–59.

—— (ed.), *Das Unrechtsregime: Internationale Forschung über den Nationalsozialismus: Festschrift für Werner Jochmann zum 65. Geburtstag* (2 vols., Hamburg, 1986).

Caplan, Jane, 'Bureaucracy, Politics and the National Socialist State', in Stachura (ed.), *The Shaping*, 234–56.

——, '"The Imaginary Unity of Particular Interests": The "Tradition" of the Civil Service in German History', *Social History*, 4 (1978), 299–317.

——, *Government Without Administration: State and Civil Service in Weimar and Nazi Germany* (Oxford, 1988).

Caron, Vicki, *Uneasy Asylum: France and the Jewish Refugee Crisis, 1933–1942* (Stanford, 1999).

Carr, Edward Hallett, *The Twilight of Comintern, 1930–1935* (London, 1982).

Carroll, Berenice A., *Design for Total War: Arms and Economics in the Third Reich* (The Hague, 1968).

Carsten, F. L., *Fascist Movements in Austria: From Schönerer to Hitler* (London, 1977).

——, *The German Workers and the Nazis* (London, 1995).

Castellan, Georges, *L'Allemagne de Weimar, 1918–1933* (Paris, 1969).

Castell Rüdenhausen, Adelheid Gräfin zu, '"Nicht mitzuleiden, mitzukämpfen sind wir da!" Nationalsozialistische Volkswohlfahrt im Gau Westfalen-Nord', in Peukert and Reulecke (eds.), *Die Reihen fast geschlossen*, 223–44.

Cebulla, Florian, *Rundfunk und ländliche Gesellschaft 1924–1945* (Göttingen, 2004).

Cecil, Robert, *The Myth of the Master Race: Alfred Rosenberg and Nazi Ideology* (London, 1972).

Cesarani, David, *The Making of Modern Anglo-Jewry* (Oxford, 1990).

——, *Eichmann: His Life and Crimes* (London, 2004).

Chamberlain, Neville, *The Struggle for Peace* (London, 1939).

Childers, Thomas, and Caplan, Jane (eds.), *Reevaluating the Third Reich* (New York, 1993).

Chroust, Peter, *Giessener Universität und Faschismus: Studenten und Hochschullehrer, 1918–1945* (2 vols., Münster, 1994).

Cienciala, Anna M., 'Poland in British and French Policy in 1939: Determination to Fight – or Avoid War?', *Polish Review*, 34 (1989), 199–226.

Clark, Christopher, *The Politics of Conversion: Missionary Protestantism and the Jews in Prussia, 1728–1941* (Oxford, 1995).

Clay, Catrine, and Leapmahn, Michael, *Master Race: The Lebensborn Experiment in Nazi Germany* (London, 1995).

Conquest, Robert, *The Great Terror: A Reassessment* (London, 1992 [1968]).

Conradi, Peter, *Hitler's Piano Player: The Rise and Fall of Ernst Hanfstaengl, Confidant of Hitler, Ally of FDR* (New York, 2004).

Conway, John S., *The Nazi Persecution of the Churches 1933–1945* (London, 1968).

Conze, Eckart, *Von deutschem Adel: Die Grafen von Bernstorff im zwanzigsten Jahrhundert* (Stuttgart, 2000).

Cornelissen, Christoph, *Gerhard Ritter: Geschichtswissenschaft und Politik im 20. Jahrhundert* (Düsseldorf, 2001).

Corni, Gustavo, *Hitler and the Peasants: Agrarian Policy of the Third Reich, 1930–1939* (Princeton, N.J., 1990 [1989]).

——, 'Richard Walther Darré: The Blood and Soil Ideologue', in Smelser and Zitelmann (eds.), *The Nazi Elite*, 18–27.

Corni, Gustavo, and Gies, Horst, *Brot, Butter, Kanonen: Die Ernährungswirtschaft in Deutschland unter der Diktatur Hitlers* (Berlin, 1997).

Crew, David F., *Germans on Welfare: From Weimar to Hitler* (New York, 1998).

—— (ed.), *Nazism and German Society, 1933–1945* (London, 1994).

Cuomo, Glenn R., 'Purging an "Art-Bolshevist": The Persecution of Gottfried Benn in the Years 1933–1938', *German Studies Review*, 9 (1986), 85–105.

—— (ed.), *National Socialist Cultural Policy* (New York, 1995).

Czarnowski, Gabriele, '"The Value of Marriage for the *Volksgemeinschaft*": Policies towards Women and Marriage under National Socialism', in Bessel (ed.), *Fascist Italy*, 94–112.

Dahm, Volker, 'Kulturelles und geistiges Leben', in Benz (ed.), *Die Juden*, 75–267.

——, 'Nationale Einheit und partikulare Vielfalt. Zur Frage der kulturpolitischen Gleichschaltung im Dritten Reich', *VfZ* 43 (1995), 221–65.

Dammer, Susanna, 'Kinder, Küche, Kriegsarbeit – Die Schulung der Frauen durch die NS-Frauenschaft', in Frauengruppe Faschismusforschung (ed.), *Mutterkreuz*, 215–45.

David, Henry P., *et al.*, 'Abortion and Eugenics in Nazi Germany', *Population and Development Review*, 14 (1988), 81–112.

Debus, Karl H., 'Die Reichskristallnacht in der Pfalz', *Zeitschrift für die Geschichte des Oberrheins*, 129 (1981), 445–515.

Deischmann, Hans, *Objects: A Chronicle of Subversion in Nazi Germany* (New York, 1995).

Deist, Wilhelm, 'The Rearmament of the Wehrmacht', in Militärgeschichtliches Forschungsamt (ed.), *Germany*, I: *The Build-up of German Aggression*, 373–540.

Denkler, Horst, and Prümm, Karl (eds.), *Die deutsche Literatur im Dritten Reich: Themen, Traditionen, Wirkungen* (Stuttgart, 1976).

Deschner, Günther, 'Reinhard Heydrich: Security Technocrat', in Smelser and Zitelmann (eds.), *The Nazi Elite*, 85–96.

Deutsch, Harold C., *The Conspiracy Against Hitler in the Twilight War* (Minneapolis, 1968).

De Witt, Thomas E., ' "The Struggle Against Hunger and Cold": Winter Relief in Nazi Germany, 1933–1939', *Canadian Journal of History*, 12 (1978), 361–81.

Diels, Rudolf, *Lucifer ante Portas: Es spricht der erste Chef der Gestapo* (Stuttgart, 1950).

Dierker, Wolfgang, ' "Niema's Jesuiten, Niema's Sektierer": Die Religionspolitik des SD 1933–1941', in Wildt (ed.), *Nachrichtendienst*, 86–117.

Dietrich, Richard, and Oestreich, Gerhard (eds.), *Forschungen zu Staat und Verfassung: Festgabe für Fritz Hartung* (Berlin, 1958).

Diewald-Kerkmann, Gisela, *Politische Denunziation im NS-Regime oder die kleine Macht der 'Volksgenossen'* (Bonn, 1995).

——, 'Denunziantentum und Gestapo. Die freiwilligen "Helfer" aus der Bevölkerung', in Paul and Mallmann (eds.), *Die Gestapo*, 288–305.

——, *et al.*, *Vor braunen Richtern: Die Verfolgung von Widerstandshandlungen, Resistenz und Sogenannter Heimtücke durch die Justiz in Bielefeld 1933–1945* (Bielefeld, 1992).

Dilks, David, ' "We Must Hope for the Best and Prepare for the Worst": the Prime Minister, the Cabinet and Hitler's Germany 1937–1939', in Finney (ed.), *The Origins of the Second World War*, 43–61.

Diller, Ansgar, *Rundfunkpolitik im Dritten Reich* (Munich, 1980).

Dimitroff, Georgi, *Reichstagsbrandprozess: Dokumente, Briefe und Aufzeichnungen* (Berlin, 1946).

Distel, Barbara, and Jakusch, Ruth, *Konzentrationslager Dachau, 1933–1945* (Munich, 1978).

Dithmar, Reinhard, 'Literaturunterricht und Kriegserlebnis im Spiegel der national-sozialistischen Programmatik', in Hohmann (ed.), *Erster Weltkrieg*, 54–74.

Ditt, Karl, *Sozialdemokraten im Widerstand: Hamburg in der Anfangsphase des Dritten Reiches* (Hamburg, 1984).

Dohms, Peter, *Flugschriften in Gestapo-Akten: Nachweis und Analyse der Flugschriften in den Gestapo-Akten des Hauptstaatsarchivs* (Siegburg, 1977).

Domarus, Max (ed.), *Hitler: Speeches and Proclamations, 1932–1945: The Chronicle of a Dictatorship* (4 vols., London, 1990– [1962–3]).

Dörner, Bernward, 'Alltagsterror und Denunziation. Zur Bedeutung von Anzeigen aus der Bevölkerung für die Verfolgungswirkung des nationalsozialistischen "Heimtücke-Gesetzes" in Krefeld', in Berliner Geschichtswerkstatt (ed.), *Alltagskultur, Subjektivität und Geschichte: Zur Theorie und Praxis der Alltagsgeschichte* (Münster, 1994), 254–71.

——, 'Gestapo und "Heimtücke". Zur Praxis der Geheimen Staatspolizei bei der Verfolgung von Verstössen gegen das "Heimtücke-Gesetz"', in Paul and Mallmann (eds.), *Die Gestapo*, 325–43.

——, *'Heimtücke': Das Gesetz als Waffe: Kontrolle, Abschreckung und Verfolgung in Deutschland, 1933–1945* (Paderborn, 1998).

——, 'NS-Herrschaft und Denunziation. Anmerkungen zu Defiziten in der Denunziationsforschung', *Historical Social Research*, 26 (2001), 55–69.

Döscher, Hans-Jürgen, *'Reichskristallnacht': Die November-Pogrome 1938* (Frankfurt am Main, 1988), 57–76.

Drechsler, Nanny, *Die Funktion der Musik im deutschen Rundfunk, 1933–1945* (Pfaffenweiler, 1988).

Drewniak, Boguslaw, *Das Theater im NS-Staat: Szenarium deutscher Zeitgeschichte, 1933–1945* (Düsseldorf, 1983).

——, *Der deutsche Film 1938–1945: Ein Gesamtüberblick* (Düsseldorf, 1987).

——, 'The Foundations of Theater Policy in Nazi Germany', in Cuomo (ed.), *National Socialist Cultural Policy*, 67–94.

Drobisch, Klaus, 'Theodor Eicke. Verkörperung des KZ-Systems', in Bock *et al.* (eds.), *Sturz ins Dritte Reich*, 283–9.

——, 'Alltag im Zuchthaus Luckau 1933 bis 1939', in Eichholtz (ed.), *Verfolgung, Alltag, Widerstand*, 242–72.

——, 'Frühe Konzentrationslager', in Giebeler *et al.* (eds.), *Die frühen Konzentrationslager in Deutschland*, 41–60.

——, and Wieland, Günther, *System der NS-Konzentrationslager 1933–1939* (Berlin, 1993).

Du Bois, Josiah E., Jr, *The Devil's Chemists: 24 Conspirators of the International Farben Cartel Who Manufacture Wars* (Boston, Mass., 1952).

Duhnke, Horst, *Die KPD von 1933 bis 1945* (Cologne, 1972).

Dülffer, Jost, *Weimar, Hitler und die Marine: Reichspolitik und Flottenbau, 1920–1939* (Düsseldorf, 1973).

——, 'Zum "decision-making process" in der deutschen Aussenpolitik 1933–1939', in Funke (ed.), *Hitler, Deutschland und die Mächte*, 186–204.

——, 'Grundbedingungen der nationalsozialistischen Aussenpolitik', in Haupts and Mölich (eds.), *Strukturelemente*, 61–88.

——, 'Albert Speer: Cultural and Economic Management', in Smelser and Zitelmann (eds.), *The Nazi Elite*, 212–23.

——, *et al.*, *Hitlers Städte: Baupolitik im Dritten Reich* (Cologne, 1978).

Dümling, Albrecht, 'The Target of Racial Purity: The "Degenerate Music" Exhibition in Düsseldorf, 1938', in Etlin (ed.), *Art*, 43–72.

——, and Girth, Peter (eds.), *Entartete Musik: Eine kommentierte Rekonstruktion zur Düsseldorfer Ausstellung von 1938* (Düsseldorf, 1988).

—— (ed.), *Banned by the Nazis: Entartete Musik: The Exhibition of Düsseldorf, 1938 in Texts and Documents* (London, 1995 [1988]).

Dusik, Bärbel (ed.), *Hitler: Reden, Schriften, Anordnungen: Februar 1925 bis Januar 1933* (5 vols., Munich, 1992–8).

Düsing, Bernhard, *Die Geschichte der Abschaffung der Todesstrafe in der Bundesrepublik Deutschland unter besonderer Berücksichtigung ihres parlamentarischen Zustandekommens* (Schwenningen/Neckar, 1952).

Düwell, Kurt, 'Jewish Cultural Centers in Nazi Germany: Expectations and Accomplishments', in Reinharz and Schatzberg (eds.), *The Jewish Response*, 294–316.

Dwork, Deborah, and Van Pelt, Robert Jan, *Holocaust: A History* (New York, 2002).

Eckert, Rainer, 'Gestapo-Berichte. Abbildungen der Realität oder reine Spekulation?', in Paul and Mallmann (eds.), *Die Gestapo*, 200–218.

Eckhardt, Karl August, *Die Grundschulbildung* (Dortmund, 1938).

Edinger, Lewis Joachim, *German Exile Politics: The Social Democratic Executive Committee in the Nazi Era* (Berkeley, Calif., 1956).

Eggers, Kurt, *Deutsche Gedichte* (Munich, 1938).

Ehrke-Rotermund, Heidrun, and Rotermund, Erwin, *Zwischenreiche und Gegenwelten: Texte und Vorstudien zur 'Verdeckten Schreibweise' im 'Dritten Reich'* (Munich, 1999).

Eicher, Thomas, *et al.*, *Theater im 'Dritten Reich': Theaterpolitik, Spielplanstruktur, NS-Dramatik* (Seelze-Velber, 2000).

Eichholtz, Dietrich, 'Zum Anteil des IG Farben Konzerns an der Vorbereitung des Zweiten Weltkrieges', *Jahrbuch für Wirtschaftsgeschichte* (1969), 83–105.

—— (ed.), *Verfolgung, Alltag, Widerstand: Brandenburg in der NS-Zeit: Studien und Dokumente* (Berlin, 1993).

Eichhorn, Ernst, *et al.*, *Kulissen der Gewalt: Das Reichsparteitagsgelände in Nürnberg* (Munich, 1992).

Eichler, Volker, 'Die Frankfurter Gestapo-Kartei. Entstehung, Struktur, Funktion,

Überlieferungsgeschichte und Quellenwert', in Paul and Mallmann (eds.), *Die Gestapo*, 178–99.

Eidenbenz, Mathias, *'Blut und Boden': Zu Funktion und Genese der Metaphern des Agrarismus und Biologismus in der nationalsozialistischen Bauernpropaganda R. W. Darrés* (Bern, 1993).

Eilers, Rolf, *Die nationalsozialistische Schulpolitik: Eine Studie zur Funktion der Erziehung im totalitären Staat* (Cologne, 1963).

Eksteins, Modris, *The Limits of Reason: The German Democratic Press and the Collapse of Weimar Democracy* (Oxford, 1975).

Emmerich, Wolfgang, 'Die Literatur des antifaschistischen Widerstandes in Deutschland', in Denkler and Prümm (eds.), *Die deutsche Literatur*, 427–58.

Emmerson, James Thomas, *The Rhineland Crisis, 7 March 1936: A Critical Study in Multilateral Diplomacy* (London, 1977).

Ericksen, Robert P., *Theologians under Hitler: Gerhard Kittel, Paul Althaus, and Emanuel Hirsch* (New Haven, Conn., 1985).

——, 'A Radical Minority: Resistance in the German Protestant Church', in Nicosia and Stokes (eds.), *Germans Against Nazism*, 115–36.

Erickson, John, *The Soviet High Command: A Military-Political History, 1918–1941* (London, 2001 [1962]).

Erker, Paul, *Industrieeliten in der NS-Zeit: Anpassungsbereitschaft und Eigeninteresse von Unternehmen in der Rüstungs- und Kriegswirtschaft, 1936–1945* (Passau, 1993).

Eschenburg, Theodor, 'Streiflichter zur Geschichte der Wahlen im Dritten Reich', *VfZ* 3 (1955), 311–16.

Esenwein-Rothe, Ingeborg, *Die Wirtschaftsverbände von 1933 bis 1945* (Berlin, 1965).

Etlin, Richard A. (ed.), *Art, Culture, and Media under the Third Reich* (Chicago, 2002).

Euler, Friederike, 'Theater zwischen Anpassung und Widerstand. Die Münchner Kammerspiele im Dritten Reich', in Broszat *et al.* (eds.), *Bayern*, II. 91–173.

Evans, Richard J., *The Feminist Movement in Germany, 1894–1933* (London, 1976).

——, *Death in Hamburg: Society and Politics in the Cholera Years, 1830–1910* (Oxford, 1987).

—— (ed.), *Kneipengespräche im Kaiserreich: Die Stimmungsberichte der Hamburger politischen Polizei 1892–1914* (Reinbek, 1989).

——, *Rituals of Retribution: Capital Punishment in Germany 1600–1987* (Oxford, 1996).

——, *Lying About Hitler: History, Holocaust, and the David Irving Trial* (New York, 2001).

——, *The Coming of the Third Reich* (London, 2003).

——, and Geary, Dick (eds.), *The German Unemployed: Experiences and Conse-*

quences of Mass Unemployment from the Weimar Republic to the Third Reich (London, 1987).

——, and Lee, William Robert (eds.), *The German Family: Essays on the Social History of the Family in Nineteenth- and Twentieth-Century Germany* (London, 1981).

——, *The German Peasantry: Conflict and Community in Rural Society from the Eighteenth to the Twentieth Centuries* (London, 1986).

Exner, Peter, *Ländliche Gesellschaft und Landwirtschaft in Westfalen, 1919–1969* (Paderborn, 1997).

Fackler, Guido, *'Des Lagers Stimme': Musik im KZ: Alltag und Häftlingskultur in den Konzentrationslagern 1933 bis 1936* (Bremen, 2000).

Fallada, Hans, *Kleiner Mann – was nun?* (Reinbek, 1978 [1932]).

——, *Wer einmal aus dem Blechnapf frisst* (Reinbek, 1980 [1934]).

——, *Wir hatten mal ein Kind: Eine Geschichte und Geschichten* (Reinbek, 1980 [1934]).

——, *Altes Herz geht auf die Reise* (Munich, 1981 [1936]).

——, *Der eiserne Gustav: Roman* (Berlin, 1984 [1938]).

——, *Der Trinker/Der Alpdruck* (Berlin, 1987 [1950]).

——, *Wolf unter Wölfen* (Reinbek, 1991 [1937]).

——, *Little Man – What Now?*, translated by Susan Bennett (London, 1996).

Fallois, Immo von, *Kalkül und Illusion: Der Machtkampf zwischen Reichswehr und SA während der Röhm-Krise 1934* (Berlin, 1994).

Farquharson, John E., *The Plough and the Swastika: The NSDAP and Agriculture in Germany 1928–45* (London, 1976).

Faulenbach, Bernd, 'Tendenzen der Geschichtswissenschaft im "Dritten Reich"', in Knigge-Tesche (ed.), *Berater der Braunen Macht*, 26–52.

Faulhaber, Michael von, *Judaism, Christianity and Germany: Advent Sermons Preached in St Michael's, Munich, in 1933* (London, 1934).

Faust, Anselm (ed.), *Verfolgung und Widerstand im Rheinland und in Westfalen, 1933–1945* (Cologne, 1992).

Feilchenfeld, Werner, *et al.*, *Haavara-Transfer nach Palästina und Einwanderung deutscher Juden 1933–1939* (Tübingen, 1972).

Feiten, Willi, *Der Nationalsozialistische Lehrerbund: Entwicklung und Organisation: Ein Beitrag zum Aufbau und zur Organisationsstruktur des nationalsozialistischen Herrschaftssystems* (Weinheim, 1981).

Feldman, Gerald D., *Allianz and the German Insurance Business, 1933–1945* (Cambridge, 2001).

Ferguson, Niall, *Paper and Iron: Hamburg Business and German Politics in the Era of Inflation, 1897–1927* (Cambridge, 1995).

Fest, Joachim C., *The Face of the Third Reich* (London, 1979 [1963]).

——, *Plotting Hitler's Death: The Story of the German Resistance* (London, 1996 [1994]).

Fichtl, Franz, *et al.*, *'Bambergs Wirtschaft Judenfrei': Die Verdrängung der jüdischen Geschäftsleute in den Jahren 1933 bis 1939* (Bamberg, 1998).

Fieberg, Gerhard (ed.), *Im Namen des deutschen Volkes: Justiz und National-sozialismus: Katalog zur Ausstellung des Bundesministers der Justiz* (Cologne, 1989).

Figes, Orlando, and Kolinitskii, Boris, *Interpreting the Russian Revolution: The Language and Symbols of 1917* (New Haven, Conn., 1999).

Fings, Karola, and Sparing, Frank, z. Zt. *Zigeunerlager: Die Verfolgung der Düsseldorfer Sinti und Roma im Nationalsozialismus* (Cologne, 1992).

——, et al., *From 'Race Science' to the Camps: The Gypsies during the Second World War* (Hatfield, 1997).

Finney, Patrick (ed.), *The Origins of the Second World War* (London, 1997).

Fischer, Albert, 'Jüdische Privatbanken im "Dritten Reich" ', *Scripta Mercaturae: Zeitschrift für Wirtschafts- und Sozialgeschichte*, 28 (1994), 1–54.

——, *Hjalmar Schacht und Deutschlands 'Judenfrage': Der 'Wirtschafts-diktator' und die Vertreibung der Juden aus der deutschen Wirtschaft* (Cologne, 1995).

——, 'The Minister of Economics and the Expulsion of the Jews from the German Economy', in Bankier (ed.), *Probing*, 213–25.

Fischer, Wolfram, *Deutsche Wirtschaftspolitik 1918–1945* (Opladen, 1968).

Fiss, Karen A., 'In Hitler's Salon: The German Pavilion at the 1937 Paris Exposition Internationale', in Etlin (ed.), *Art*, 316–42.

Flessau, Kurt-Ingo, *Schule der Diktatur: Lehrpläne und Schulbücher des Nationalsozialismus* (Munich, 1977).

——, et al. (eds.), *Erziehung im Nationalsozialismus: '... und sie werden nicht mehr frei ihr ganzes Leben!'* (Cologne, 1987).

Fliedner, Hans-Joachim, *Die Judenverfolgung in Mannheim 1933–1945* (Stuttgart, 1971).

Foertsch, Hermann, *Schuld und Verhängnis: Die Fritsch-Krise im Frühjahr 1938 als Wendepunkt in der Geschichte der nationalsozialistischen Zeit* (Stuttgart, 1951).

Foitzik, Jan, *Zwischen den Fronten: Zur Politik, Organisation und Funktion linker politischer Kleinorganisationen im Widerstand 1933 bis 1939/40* (Bonn, 1986).

Forman, Paul, 'Physics and Beyond: Historiographic Doubts: Encounters and Conversations with Werner Heisenberg', *Science*, 172 (14 May 1971), 687–8.

Forschbach, Edmund, *Edgar J. Jung: Ein konservativer Revolutionär. 30. Juni 1934* (Pfullingen, 1984).

Fox, John P., *Germany and the Far Eastern Crisis, 1931–1938: A Study in Diplomacy and Ideology* (Oxford, 1982).

Fraenkel, Ernst, *The Dual State: Law and Justice in National Socialism* (New York, 1941).

Frahm, Klaus, et al. (eds.), *Verachtet – verfolgt – vernichtet: Zu den vergessenen Opfern des NS-Regimes* (Hamburg, 1986).

Frank, Hartmut (ed.), *Faschistische Architekturen: Planen und Bauen in Europa, 1930 bis 1945* (Hamburg, 1985).

Frank, Willard C., 'The Spanish Civil War and the Coming of the Second World War', *International History Review*, 9 (1987), 368–409.

Franz, Günther (ed.), *Bauernschaft und Bauernstand 1500–1970: Büdinger Vorträge 1911–1972* (Limburg, 1975).

Frauengruppe Faschismusforschung (ed.), *Mutterkreuz und Arbeitsbuch: Zur Geschichte der Frauen in der Weimarer Republik und im Nationalsozialismus* (Frankfurt am Main, 1981).

Frei, Norbert, *Nationalsozialistische Eroberung der Provinzpresse: Gleichschaltung, Selbstanpassung und Resistenz in Bayern* (Stuttgart, 1980).

——, and Schmitz, Johannes, *Journalismus im Dritten Reich* (Munich, 1989).

——, *National Socialist Rule in Germany: The Führer State 1933–1945* (Oxford, 1993 [1987]).

Frese, Matthias, *Betriebspolitik im 'Dritten Reich': Deutsche Arbeitsfront, Unternehmer und Staatsbürokratie in der westdeutschen Grossindustrie, 1933–1939* (Paderborn, 1991).

Freund, Florian, 'Mauthausen – zu Strukturen von Haupt- und Aussenlagern', in Benz (ed.), *KZ-Aussenlager*, 254–72.

Friedländer, Saul, *Pius XII and the Third Reich* (London, 1966).

——, *Nazi Germany and the Jews: The Years of Persecution 1933–1939* (New York, 1997).

Friemert, Chup, *Schönheit der Arbeit: Produktionsästhetik im Faschismus* (Munich, 1980).

Fritzsche, Peter, 'Nazi Modern', *Modernism/Modernity*, 3 (1996), 1–21.

Fröhlich, Elke (ed.), *Die Tagebücher von Joseph Goebbels*, I: *Aufzeichnungen 1923–1941* (9 vols.); II: *Diktate 1941–1945* (15 vols.) (Munich, 1993–2000).

——, 'Die drei Typen der nationalsozialistischen Ausleseschulen', in Leeb (ed.), *'Wir waren'*, 192–210.

Frommann, Eberhard, *Die Lieder der NS-Zeit: Untersuchungen zur nationalsozialistischen Liedpropaganda von den Anfängen bis zum Zweiten Weltkrieg* (Cologne, 1999).

Froschauer, Hermann, 'Streicher und "Der Stürmer"', in Ogan and Weiss (eds.), *Faszination und Gewalt*, 41–8.

——, and Geyer, Renate, *Quellen des Hasses: Aus dem Archiv des 'Stürmer' 1933–1945* (Nuremberg, 1988).

Früh, Eckhart, 'Terror und Selbstmord in Wien nach der Annexion Österreichs', in Kreissler (ed.), *Fünfzig Jahre danach*, 216–26.

Fuchs, Konrad, *Ein Konzern aus Sachsen: Das Kaufhaus Schocken als Spiegelbild deutscher Wirtschaft und Politik 1901 bis 1953* (Stuttgart, 1990).

Funke, Manfred (ed.), *Hitler, Deutschland und die Mächte: Materialien zur Aussenpolitik des Dritten Reiches* (Düsseldorf, 1976).

——, 'Nationalsozialistische Tschechenpolitik im Protektorat Böhmen und Mähren', in idem and Vaclav Kural (eds.), *Der Weg in die Katastrophe: Deutschtschechoslowakische Beziehungen 1938–1947* (Essen, 1994).

——, *et al.* (eds.), *Demokratie und Diktatur: Geist und Gestalt politischer Herrschaft in Deutschland und Europa: Festschrift für Karl Dietrich Bracher* (Düsseldorf, 1987).

Gackenholz, Hermann, 'Reichskanzlei 5. November 1937: Bemerkungen über "Politik und Kriegführung" im Dritten Reich', in Dietrich and Oestreich (ed.), *Forschungen zu Staat und Verfassung*, 459–84.

Gadberry, Glen W., *Theatre in the Third Reich, the Prewar Years: Essays on Theatre in Nazi Germany* (Westport, Conn., 1995).

Gailus, Manfred, *Protestantismus und Nationalsozialismus: Studien zur nationalsozialistischen Durchdringung des protestantischen Sozialmilieus in Berlin* (Cologne, 2001).

Gall, Lothar, 'Franz Schnabel (1887–1966)', in Lehmann and Melton (eds.), *Paths*, 155–65.

——, *Krupp: Der Aufstieg eines Industrieimperiums* (Berlin, 2000).

——, 'Richard Strauss und das "Dritte Reich" oder: Wie der Künstler Strauss sich missbrauchen liess', in Krellmann (ed.), *Wer war Richard Strauss?*, 123–36.

——, and Pohl, Manfred (eds.), *Die Eisenbahn in Deutschland: Von den Anfängen bis zur Gegenwart* (Munich, 1999).

Gamm, Hans-Jochen, *Der braune Kult: Das Dritte Reich und seine Ersatzreligion. Ein Beitrag zur politischen Bildung* (Hamburg, 1962).

——, *Der Flüsterwitz im Dritten Reich: Mündliche Dokumente zur Lage der Deutschen während des Nationalsozialismus* (Munich, 1990 [1963]).

Ganssmüller, Christian, *Die Erbgesundheitspolitik des Dritten Reiches: Planung, Durchführung und Durchsetzung* (Cologne, 1987).

Garbe, Detlef, *Zwischen Widerstand und Martyrium: Die Zeugen Jehovas im 'Dritten Reich'* (Munich, 1993).

Gatzen, Helmut, *Novemberpogrom 1938 in Gütersloh: Nachts Orgie der Gewalt, tags organisierte Vernichtung* (Gütersloh, 1993).

Gedye, George E. R., *Fallen Bastions: The Central European Tragedy* (London, 1939).

Geiger, Theodor Julius, *Die soziale Schichtung des deutschen Volkes* (Stuttgart, 1967 [1932]).

Gellately, Robert, *The Politics of Economic Despair: Shopkeepers and German Politics 1890–1914* (London, 1974).

——, 'The Gestapo and German Society: Political Denunciation in the Gestapo Case Files', *Journal of Modern History*, 60 (1988), 654–94.

——, *The Gestapo and German Society: Enforcing Racial Policy 1933–1945* (Oxford, 1990).

——, 'Allwissend und allgegenwärtig? Entstehung, Funktion und Wandel des Gestapo-Mythos', in Paul and Mallmann (eds.), *Die Gestapo*, 47–72.

——, 'Die Gestapo und die deutsche Gesellschaft: Zur Entstehungsgeschichte einer selbstüberwachenden Gesellschaft', in Schmiechen-Ackermann (ed.), *Anpassung, Verweigerung, Widerstand*, 109–21.

——, *Backing Hitler: Consent and Coercion in Nazi Germany* (Oxford, 2001).

——, and Nathan Stoltzfus (eds.), *Social Outsiders in Nazi Germany* (Princeton, N.J., 2001).

Genschel, Helmut, *Die Verdrängung der Juden aus der Wirtschaft im Dritten Reich* (Göttingen, 1966).

Gereke, Günther, *Ich war königlich-preussischer Landrat* (Berlin, 1970).

Gerlach, Wolfgang, *Als die Zeugen schwiegen: Bekennende Kirche und die Juden* (Berlin, 1993 [1987]).

'Germany's Economic Recovery', *The Economist*, 10 August 1935, 271–2.

Gersdorff, Ursula von, *Frauen im Kriegsdienst 1914–1945* (Stuttgart, 1969).

Gestier, Markus, *Die christlichen Parteien an der Saar und ihr Verhältnis zum deutschen Nationalstaat in den Abstimmungskämpfen 1935 und 1955* (St Ingbert, 1991).

Geyer, Michael, 'Das Zweite Rüstungsprogramm (1930–1934): Eine Dokumentation', *Militärgeschichtliche Mitteilungen*, 17 (1975), 125–72.

——, *Deutsche Rüstungspolitik 1860–1980.* (Frankfurt am Main, 1984).

——, and Lehmann, Hartmut (eds.), *Religion und Nation: Nation und Religion: Beiträge zu einer unbewältigten Geschichte* (Göttingen, 2004).

Giebeler, Karl, *et al.* (eds.), *Die frühen Konzentrationslager in Deutschland: Austausch zum Forschungsstand und zur pädagogischen Praxis in Gedenkstätten* (Bad Boll, 1996).

Gies, Horst, R. *Walther Darré und die nationalsozialistische Bauernpolitik in den Jahren 1930 bis 1933* (Frankfurt am Main, 1966).

——, 'NSDAP und landwirtschaftliche Organisationen in der Endphase der Weimarer Republik', *VfZ* 15 (1967), 341–67.

——, 'Die nationalsozialistische Machtergreifung auf dem agrarpolitischen Sektor', *Zeitschrift für Agrargeschichte und Agrarsoziologie*, 16 (1968), 210–32.

——, 'Der Reichsnährstand: Organ berufsständischer Selbstverwaltung oder Instrument staatlicher Wirtschaftslenkung?' *Zeitschrift für Agrargeschichte und Agrarsoziologie*, 21 (1973), 216–33.

——, 'Revolution oder Kontinuität? Die personelle Struktur des Reichsnährstandes', in Franz (ed.), *Bauernschaft und Bauernstand*, 323–30.

——, 'Aufgaben und Probleme der nationalsozialistischen Ernährungswirtschaft 1933–1939', *Vierteljahrschrift für Sozial- und Wirtschaftsgeschichte*, 22 (1979), 466–99.

——, 'Die Rolle des Reichsnährstandes im Nationalsozialistischen Herrschaftssystem', in Hirschfeld and Kettenacker (eds.), *The 'Führer State'*, 270–304.

——, 'Landbevölkerung und Nationalsozialismus. Der Weg in den Reichsnährstand', *Zeitgeschichte*, 13 (1986), 123–41.

Gilbert, Martin, *The Roots of Appeasement* (London, 1966).

Giles, Geoffrey J., 'The Rise of the National Socialist Students' Association and the Failure of Political Education in the Third Reich', in Stachura (ed.), *The Shaping*, 160–85.

——, *Students and National Socialism in Germany* (Princeton, N.J., 1985).

——, '"The Most Unkindest Cut of All": Castration, Homosexuality and Nazi Justice', *Journal of Contemporary History*, 27 (1992), 41–61.

——, 'The Institutionalization of Homosexual Panic in the Third Reich', in Gellately and Stoltzfus (eds.), *Social Outsiders*, 233–55.

Gillessen, Günther, *Auf verlorenem Posten: Die Frankfurter Zeitung im Dritten Reich* (Berlin, 1986).

Gimbel, John, *Science, Technology, and Reparations: Exploitation and Plunder in Postwar Germany* (Stanford, Calif., 1990).

Glantz, David M., *Stumbling Colossus: The Red Army on the Eve of World War* (Lawrence, Kans., 1998).

Glaser, Hermann, and Silenius, Axel (eds.), *Jugend im Dritten Reich* (Frankfurt am Main, 1975).

Godau, Marion, 'Anti-Moderne?', in Weissler (ed.), *Design in Deutschland, 1933–1945*, 74–87.

Gohl, Beate, *Jüdische Wohlfahrtspflege im Nationalsozialismus: Frankfurt am Main 1933–1943* (Frankfurt am Main, 1997).

Golczewski, Frank, *Kölner Universitätslehrer und der Nationalsozialismus: Personengeschichtliche Ansätze* (Cologne, 1988).

Golücke, Friedhelm, *Korporationen und Nationalsozialismus* (Schernfeld, 1989).

Gordon, Sarah Ann, *Hitler, Germans, and the 'Jewish Question'* (Princeton, 1984).

Götz, Margarete, *Die Grundschule in der Zeit des Nationalsozialismus: Eine Untersuchung der inneren Ausgestaltung der vier unteren Jahrgänge der Volksschule auf der Grundlage amtlicher Massnahmen* (Bad Heilbrunn, 1997).

Graeb-Könneker, Sebastian, *Autochthone Modernität: Eine Untersuchung der vom Nationalsozialismus geförderten Literatur* (Opladen, 1996).

Graf, Christoph, 'Kontinuitäten und Brüche. Von der Politischen Polizei der Weimarer Republik zur Geheimen Staatspolizei', in Paul and Mallmann (eds.), *Die Gestapo*, 73–83.

Graml, Hermann, 'Wer bestimmte die Aussenpolitik des Dritten Reiches? Ein Beitrag zur Kontroverse um Polykratie und Monokratie im NS-Herrschaftssystem', in Funke *et al.* (eds.), *Demokratie und Diktatur*, 223–36.

——, 'Grundzüge nationalsozialistische Aussenpolitik', in Broszat and Möller (eds.), *Das Dritte Reich*, 104–26.

——, *Reichskristallnacht: Antisemitismus und Judenverfolgung im Dritten Reich* (Munich, 1988). Translated as *Anti-Semitism in the Third Reich* (Cambridge, Mass., 1992).

——, 'Integration und Entfremdung: Inanspruchnahme durch Staatsjugend und Dienstpflicht', in Benz and Benz (eds.), *Sozialisation und Traumatisierung*, 74–9.

Grasberger, Franz (ed.), *Der Strom der Töne trug mich fort: Die Welt um Richard Strauss in Briefen* (Tutzing, 1967).

Gravenhorst, Lerke, and Tatschmurat, Carmen (eds.), *Töchter-Fragen: NS-Frauengeschichte* (Freiburg, 1990).

Greenbaum, Alfred A. (ed.), *Minority Problems in Eastern Europe between the World Wars with Emphasis on the Jewish Minority* (Hebrew University of Jerusalem, Institute for Advanced Studies, typescript, Jerusalem, 1988).

Gregor, A. James, *Fascism: The Classic Interpretations of the Interwar Period* (Morristown, N.J., 1983).

Gregor, Neil, *Daimler-Benz in the Third Reich* (London, 1998).

Greiffenhagen, Martin (ed.), *Kampf um Wörter? Politische Begriffe im Meinungsstreit* (Munich, 1980).

Grimm, Reinhold, 'Im Dickicht der inneren Emigration', in Denkler and Prümm (eds.), *Die deutsche Literatur*, 406–26.

Gritschneider, Otto, *'Der Führer hat Sie zum Tode verurteilt . . .': Hitlers 'Röhm-Putsch'-Morde vor Gericht* (Munich, 1993).

Grocek, Ferdinand, 'Ein Staat im Staate – der IG-Farben Konzern', *Marxistische Blätter*, 4 (1966), 41–8.

Grossmann, Kurt Richard, *Ossietzky, ein deutscher Patriot* (Frankfurt, 1973 [1963]).

Gruchmann, Lothar, 'Die bayerische Justiz im politischen Machtkampf 1933/34: Ihr Scheitern bei der Strafverfolgung von Mordfällen in Dachau', in Broszat *et al.* (eds.), *Bayern*, II. 415–28.

——, *Justiz im Dritten Reich, 1933–1940: Anpassung und Unterwerfung in der Ära Gürtner* (Munich, 1988).

——, ' "Blutschutzgesetz" und Justiz: Entstehung und Anwerdurg des Nürnberger Gesetzes vom 15 September 1935', in Ogan and Weiss (eds.), *Faszination und Gewalt*, 49–60.

Grunberger, Richard, *A Social History of the Third Reich* (Harmondsworth, 1974 [1971]).

Grundmann, Friedrich, *Agrarpolitik im 'Dritten Reich': Anspruch und Wirklichkeit des Reichserbhofgesetzes* (Hamburg, 1979).

Gruner, Wolf, 'Die Reichshauptstadt und die Verfolgung der Berliner Juden 1933–1945', in Rürup *et al.* (ed.), *Jüdische Geschichte*, 229–66.

——, *Der geschlossene Arbeitseinsatz deutscher Juden: Zur Zwangsarbeit als Element der Verfolgung 1938–1943* (Berlin, 1997).

——, 'Public Welfare and the German Jews under National Socialism', in Bankier (ed.), *Probing*, 78–105.

Grüttner, Michael, *Studenten im Dritten Reich* (Paderborn, 1995).

——, 'Die Korporationen und der Nationalsozialismus', in Brandt and Stickler (eds.), *'Der Burschen Herrlichkeit'*, 125–43.

Guenther, Irene, *Nazi Chic?: Fashioning Women in the Third Reich* (Oxford, 2004).

Guenther, Peter, 'Three Days in Munich, July 1937', in Barron (ed.), *Degenerate Art*, 33–43.

Gulick, Charles Adams, *Austria from Habsburg to Hitler* (Berkeley, Calif., 1948).

Gutman, Yisrael (ed.), *Encyclopedia of the Holocaust* (4 vols., New York, 1990).

——, *The Jews of Poland between Two World Wars* (Hanover, N.H., 1989).

Gutsche, Willibald, and Petzold, Joachim, 'Das Verhältnis der Hohenzollern zum Faschismus', *Zeitschrift für Geschichtswissenschaft*, 29 (1981), 917–39.

Guttsman, W. L., *Workers' Culture in Weimar Germany: Between Tradition and Commitment* (Oxford, 1990).

Haack, Hanna, 'Arbeitslose in Deutschland. Ergebnisse und Analyse der Berufszählung vom 16. Juni 1933', *Jahrbuch für Wirtschaftsgeschichte* (1986), 36–69.

Haar, Ingo, *Historiker im Nationalsozialismus: Deutsche Geschichtswissenschaft und der 'Volkstumskampf' im Osten* (Göttingen, 2002).

Haarmann, Hermann, *et al.* (eds.), *'Das war ein Vorspiel nur – ': Bücherverbrennung in Deutschland 1933: Voraussetzungen und Folgen. Ausstellung der Akademie der Künste vom 8. Mai bis 3. Juli 1983* (Berlin, 1983).

Haberl, Othmar N., and Korenke, Tobias (eds.), *Politische Deutungskulturen: Festschrift für Karl Rohe* (Baden-Baden, 1999).

Hachtmann, Rüdiger, *Industriearbeit im 'Dritten Reich': Untersuchungen zu den Lohn- und Arbeitsbedingungen in Deutschland, 1933–1945* (Göttingen, 1989).

——, 'Bürgertum, Revolution, Diktatur – zum vierten Band von Hans-Ulrich Wehlers "Gesellschaftsgeschichte"', *Sozial-Geschichte*, 19 (2004), 60–87.

Haerdter, Michael (ed.), *Wohnsitz: Nirgendwo: Vom Leben und vom Überleben auf der Strasse* (Berlin, 1982).

Haffner, Sebastian, *Defying Hitler: A Memoir* (London, 2002 [2000]).

Haftmann, Werner, *Verfemte Kunst: Bildende Künstler der inneren und äusseren Emigration in der Zeit des Nationalsozialismus* (Cologne, 1986).

Hagemann, Jürgen, *Die Presselenkung im Dritten Reich* (Bonn, 1970).

Hagen, William W., 'Before the "Final Solution": Toward a Comparative Analysis of Political Anti-Semitism in Interwar Germany and Poland', *Journal of Modern History*, 68 (1996), 351–81.

Hahn, Fred (ed.), *Lieber Stürmer! Leserbriefe an das NS-Kampfblatt 1924–1945* (Stuttgart, 1978).

Hale, Oron J., *The Captive Press in the Third Reich* (Princeton, N.J., 1964).

Hamann, Brigitte, *Winifred Wagner oder Hitlers Bayreuth* (Munich, 2002).

Händler-Lachmann, Barbara and Werther, Thomas, *Vergessene Geschäfte, verlorene Geschichte: Jüdisches Wirtschaftsleben in Marburg und seine Vernichtung im Nationalsozialismus* (Marburg, 1992).

Hanke, Peter, *Zur Geschichte der Juden in München zwischen 1933 und 1945* (Munich, 1967).

Hansen, Ernst W., *et al.* (eds.), *Politischer Wandel, organisierte Gewalt und nationale Sicherheit: Beiträge zur neueren Geschichte Deutschlands und Frankreichs: Festschrift für Klaus-Jürgen Müller* (Munich, 1995).

Hardy, Alexander G., *Hitler's Secret Weapon: The 'Managed' Press and Propaganda Machine of Nazi Germany* (New York, 1968).

Harrison, Edward D. R., 'The Nazi Dissolution of the Monasteries: A Case-Study', *English Historical Review*, 109 (1994), 323–55.

Harrison, Mark (ed.), *The Economics of World War II: Six Great Powers in International Comparison* (Cambridge, 1998).

Hartmann, Christian, and Slutsch, Sergej, 'Franz Halder und die Kriegsvorbereitungen im Frühjahr 1939. Eine Ansprache des Generalstabschefs des Heers', *VfZ* 45 (1997), 467–95.

Hase-Mihalik, Eva von, and Kreuzkamp, Doris, *Du kriegst auch einen schönen Wohnwagen: Zwangslager für Sinti und Roma während des Nationalsozialismus in Frankfurt am Main* (Frankfurt am Main, 1990).

Hass, Kurt, *Jugend unterm Schicksal: Lebensberichte junger Deutscher 1946–1949* (Hamburg, 1950).

Hauner, Milan, 'Did Hitler Want a World Dominion?', *Journal of Contemporary History*, 13 (1978), 15–32.

Haupt, Heinz-Gerhard (ed.), *Die radikale Mitte: Lebensweisen und Politik von Kleinhändlern und Handwerkern in Deutschland seit 1848* (Munich, 1985).

Haupts, Leo, and Möhlich, Georg (eds.), *Strukturelemente des Nationalsozialismus: Rassenideologie, Unterdrückungsmaschinerie, Aussenpolitik* (Cologne, 1981).

Hausen, Karin, 'Mother's Day in the Weimar Republic', in Bridenthal *et al.* (eds.), *When Biology Became Destiny*, 131–52.

——, 'The "German Mother's Day" 1923–1933', in Medick and Sabean (eds.), *Interest and Emotion*, 371–413.

Hay, Gerhard, 'Rundfunk und Hörspiel als "Führungsmittel" des Nationalsozialismus', in Denkler and Prümm (eds.), *Die deutsche Literatur*, 366–81.

Hayes, Peter, 'Fritz Roessler and Nazism: The Observations of a German Industrialist, 1930–37', *Central European History*, 20 (1987), 58–83.

——, *Industry and Ideology: IG Farben in the Nazi Era* (New York, 1987).

——, 'Zur umstrittenen Geschichte der I. G. Farbenindustrie AG', *Geschichte und Gesellschaft*, 18 (1992), 405–17.

——, 'Polycracy and Policy in the Third Reich: The Case of the Economy', in Childers and Caplan (eds.), *Reevaluating the Third Reich*, 190–210.

——, 'Big Business and "Aryanization" in Germany 1933–1939', *Jahrbuch für Antisemitismusforschung*, 3 (1994), 254–81.

——, *From Cooperation to Complicity: Degussa in the Third Reich* (New York, 2005).

——, and Wojak, Irmtrud (eds.), *'Arisierung' im Nationalsozialismus: Volksgemeinschaft, Raub und Gedächtnis* (Frankfurt am Main, 2000).

Heer, Hannes, *Ernst Thälmann in Selbstzeugnissen und Bilddokumenten* (Reinbek, 1975).

Hehemann, Rainer, *Die 'Bekämpfung des Zigeunerunwesens' im Wilhelminischen Deutschland und in der Weimarer Republik, 1871–1933* (Frankfurt am Main, 1987).

Hehl, Ulrich von, *et al.* (eds.), *Priester unter Hitlers Terror: Eine biographische und statistische Erhebung* (2 vols., Mainz, 1996 [1984]).

Heiber, Helmut, 'Der Fall Grünspan', *VfZ* 5 (1957), 134–72.

——, *Walter Frank und sein Reichsinstitut für Geschichte des neuen Deutschlands* (Stuttgart, 1966).

—— (ed.), *Goebbels-Reden* (2 vols., Düsseldorf, 1971–2).

Heilbronner, Oded, *Die Achillesferse des deutschen Katholizismus* (Gerlingen, 1998).

Heim, Susanne, 'The German-Jewish Relationship in the Diaries of Victor Klemperer', in Bankier (ed.), *Probing*, 312–25.

——, *Kalorien, Kautschuk, Karrieren: Pflanzenzüchtung und landwirtschaftliche Forschung in Kaiser-Wilhelm-Instituten 1933–1945* (Göttingen, 2003).

Heineman, Elizabeth D., *What Difference Does a Husband Make? Women and Marital Status in Nazi and Postwar Germany* (London, 1999).

Heinonen, Reijo E., *Anpassung und Identität: Theologie und Kirchenpolitik der Bremer Deutschen Christen 1933–1945* (Göttingen, 1978).

Heinrich-Hampf, Vroni, 'Über Gartenidylle und Gartenarchitektur im Dritten Reich', in Frank (ed.), *Faschistische Architekturen*, 271–81.

Heinzelmann, Herbert, 'Die Heilige Messe des Reichsparteitage. Zur Zeichensprache von Leni Riefenstahls "Triumph des Willens"', in Ogan and Weiss (eds.), *Faszination und Gewalt*, 163–8.

Heisenberg, Werner, *Der Teil und das Ganze: Gespräche im Umkreis der Atomphysik* (Munich, 1969).

Heller, Celia S., *On the Edge of Destruction: Jews of Poland between the Two World Wars* (New York, 1977).

Helmreich, Ernst C., *The German Churches under Hitler: Background, Struggle, and Epilogue* (Detroit, Mich., 1979).

Hemmer, Willi, *Die 'unsichtbaren' Arbeitslosen: Statistische Methoden, soziale Tatsachen* (Zeulenroda, 1935).

Henke, Josef, *England in Hitlers politischem Kalkül 1935–1939* (Boppard, 1973).

Hentschel, Klaus (ed.), *Physics and National Socialism: An Anthology of Primary Sources* (Basle, 1996).

Herbert, Ulrich, ' "Die guten und die schlechten Zeiten". Überlegungen zur diachronen Analyse lebensgeschichtlicher Interviews', in Niethammer (ed.), *'Die Jahre weiss man nicht'*, 67–96.

——, *Arbeit, Volkstum, Weltanschauung: Über Fremde und Deutsche im 20. Jahrhundert* (Frankfurt am Main, 1995).

——, *Hitler's Foreign Workers: Enforced Foreign Labor in Germany under the Third Reich* (Cambridge, 1997 [1985]).

——, *et al.* (eds.), *Die nationalsozialistischen Konzentrationslager: Entwicklung und Struktur* (2 vols., Göttingen, 1998).

——, 'Von der Gegenerbekämpfung zur "rassischen Generalprävention". "Schutzhaft" und Konzentrationslager in der Konzeption der Gestapo-Führung 1933–1939', in idem (eds.), *Die nationalsozialistischen Konzentrationslager*, I. 60–81.

——, 'Die nationalsozialllistischen Konzentrationslager: Geschichte, Erinnerung, Forschung', in idem (eds.), *Die nationalsozialistischen Konzentrationslager*, I. 17–40.

Herbst, Ludolf, *Das nationalsozialistische Deutschland 1933–1945: Die Entfesselung der Gewalt: Rassimus und Krieg* (Frankfurt am Main, 1996).

——, and Weihe, Thomas (eds.), *Die Commerzbank und die Juden 1933–1945* (Munich, 2004).

Herlemann, Beatrix, *Die Emigration als Kampfposten: Die Anleitung des kommunistischen Widerstandes in Deutschland aus Frankreich, Belgien und den Niederlanden* (Königstein im Taunus, 1982).

——, *'Der Bauer klebt am Hergebrachten': Bäuerliche Verhaltensweisen unterm Nationalsozialismus auf dem Gebiet des heutigen Landes Niedersachsen* (Hanover, 1993).

Herzig, Arno (ed.), *Die Juden in Hamburg 1590 bis 1990: Wissenschaftliche Beiträge der Universität Hamburg zur Ausstellung 'Vierhundert Jahre Juden in Hamburg'* (Hamburg, 1991).

—— and Lorenz, Ina (eds.), *Verdrängung und Vernichtung der Juden unter dem Nationalsozialismus* (Hamburg, 1992).

—— et al. (eds.), *Verdrängung und Vernichtung der Juden in Westfalen* (Münster, 1994).

Herzstein, Robert Edwin, *The War that Hitler Won: The Most Infamous Propaganda Campaign in History* (London, 1979).

Heske, Henning, '. . . und morgen die ganze Welt': Erdkundeunterricht im Nationalsozialismus* (Giessen, 1988).

Heskett, John, 'Modernism and Archaism in Design in the Third Reich', in Taylor and van der Will (eds.), *The Nazification of Art*, 110–27.

Hetzer, Gerhard, 'Die Industriestadt Augsburg. Eine Sozialgeschichte der Arbeiteropposition', in Broszat et al. (eds.), *Bayern*, III. 1–234.

——, 'Ernste Bibelforscher in Augsburg', in Broszat et al. (eds.), *Bayern*, IV. 621–44.

Heumos, Peter, *Die Emigration aus der Tschechoslowakei nach Westeuropa und dem Nahen Osten 1938* (Munich, 1989).

Hildebrand, Klaus, *Vom Reich zum Weltreich: Hitler, NSDAP und koloniale Frage 1919–1945* (Munich, 1969).

——, *The Foreign Policy of the Third Reich* (London, 1973 [1970]).

——, *Das vergangene Reich: Deutsche Aussenpolitik von Bismarck bis Hitler, 1871–1945* (Stuttgart, 1995).

——, 'Die Deutsche Reichsbahn in der nationalsozialistischen Diktatur 1933–1945', in Gall and Pohl (eds.), *Die Eisenbahn in Deutschland*, 163–243.

Hildesheimer, Esriel, *Jüdische Selbstverwaltung unter dem NS-Regime: Der Existenzkampf der Reichsvertretung und Reichsvereinigung der Juden in Deutschland* (Tübingen, 1994).

Hill, Leonidas E. (ed.), *Die Weizsäcker-Papiere 1933–1950* (Frankfurt am Main, 1974).

Hillgruber, Andreas, 'Grundzüge der nationalsozialistischen Aussenpolitik 1933–1945', *Saeculum*, 24 (1973), 328–45.

——, *Deutsche Grossmacht- und Weltpolitik im 19. und 20. Jahrhundert* (Düsseldorf, 1979).

Hirsch, Martin, *et al.* (eds.), *Recht, Verwaltung und Justiz im Nationalsozialismus: ausgewählte Schriften, Gesetze und Gerichtsentscheidungen von 1933 bis 1945* (Cologne, 1984).

Hirschfeld, Gerhard, and Kettenacker, Lothar (eds.), *The 'Führer State': Myth and Reality: Studies on the Structure and Politics of the Third Reich* (Stuttgart, 1981).

Hitler, Adolf, *Mein Kampf* (London, 1969 [1925–7]).

——, *The Speeches of Adolf Hitler, April 1922–August 1939: An English Translation of Representative Passages* (New York, 1981).

Hockerts, Hans Günter, *Die Sittlichkeitsprozesse gegen katholische Ordensangehörige und Priester 1936/37: Eine Studie zur nationalsozialistischen Herrschaftstechnik und zum Kirchenkampf* (Mainz, 1971).

——, 'Die Goebbels-Tagebücher 1932–1941: Eine neue Hauptquelle zur Erforschung der nationalsozialistischen Kirchenpolitik', in Albrecht *et al.* (eds.), *Politik und Konfession: Festschrift für Konrad Repgen zum 60. Geburtstag* (Berlin, 1983), 359–92.

Hoensch, Jörg K., *A History of Modern Hungary, 1867–1986* (London, 1988 [1984]).

Hoffmann, Hilmar, (ed.), *The Triumph of Propaganda: Film and National Socialism, 1933–1945* (Providence, R.I., 1996).

Hoffmann, Peter, 'Generaloberst Ludwig Becks militärpolitisches Denken', *Historische Zeitschrift*, 234 (1981), 101–21.

——, *Widerstand – Staatsstreich – Attentat: Der Kampf der Opposition gegen Hitler* (4th edn, Munich, 1985).

——, *Claus Schenk Graf von Stauffenberg und seine Brüder* (Stuttgart, 1992).

Hohmann, Joachim S., *Geschichte der Zigeunerverfolgung in Deutschland* (Frankfurt am Main, 1981).

—— (ed.), *Erster Weltkrieg und nationalsozialistische 'Bewegung' im deutschen Lesebuch 1933–1945* (Frankfurt am Main, 1988).

——, *Verfolgte ohne Heimat: Die Geschichte der Zigeuner in Deutschland* (Frankfurt am Main, 1990).

——, *Robert Ritter und die Erben der Kriminalbiologie: 'Zigeunerforschung' im Nationalsozialismus und in Westdeutschland im Zeichen des Rassismus* (Frankfurt am Main, 1991).

—— (ed.), *Keine Zeit für gute Freunde: Homosexuelle in Deutschland 1933–1969 – Ein Lese- und Bilderbuch* (Berlin, 1982).

——, and Larger, Hermann, '*Stolz, ein Deutscher zu sein...*': *Nationales Selbstverständnis in Schulaufsätzen, 1914–1945* (Frankfurt am Main, 1995).

Höhne, Heinz, *The Order of the Death's Head: The Story of Hitler's SS* (London, 1972 [1966]).

——, *Mordsache Röhm: Hitlers Durchbruch zur Alleinherrschaft, 1933–1934* (Reinbek, 1984).

——, *Die Zeit der Illusionen: Hitler und die Anfänge des Dritten Reiches 1933–1936* (Düsseldorf, 1991)

Hojer, Ernst, *Nationalsozialismus und Pädagogik: Umfeld und Entwicklung der Pädagogik Ernst Kriecks* (Würzburg, 1996).

Homburg, Heidrun, *Rationalisierung und Industriearbeit: Arbeitsmarkt – Management – Arbeiterschaft im Siemens-Konzern Berlin 1900–1939* (Berlin, 1991).

——, 'Warenhausunternehmen und ihre Gründer in Frankreich und Deutschland oder: eine diskrete Elite und mancherlei Mythen', *Jahrbuch für Wirtschaftsgeschichte* (1992), 183–219.

Homze, Edward L., *Arming the Luftwaffe: The Reich Air Ministry and the German Aircraft Industry, 1919–39* (Lincoln, Nebr. 1976).

Hopster, Norbert, and Nassen, Ulrich, *Literatur und Erziehung im Nationalsozialismus: Deutschunterricht als Körperkultur* (Paderborn, 1983).

Horn, Daniel B., 'The Hitler Youth and Educational Decline in the Third Reich', *History of Education Quarterly*, 16 (1976), 425–47.

Horn, Gerd-Rainer, 'Radicalism and Moderation within German Social Democracy in Underground and Exile, 1933–1936', *German History*, 15 (1997), 200–220.

Horne, John N., and Kramer, Alan, *German Atrocities, 1914: A History of Denial* (New Haven, Conn. 2001).

Höpfner, Hans-Paul, *Die Universität Bonn im Dritten Reich: Akademische Biographien unter nationalsozialistischer Herrschaft* (Bonn, 1999).

Höss, Rudolf, *Commandant of Auschwitz: The Autobiography of Rudolf Hoess* (London, 1959 [1951]).

Hossbach, Friedrich, *Zwischen Wehrmacht und Hitler, 1934–1938* (Göttingen, 1965 [1949]).

Huber, Engelbert, *Das ist Nationalsozialismus* (Stuttgart, 1933).

Huber, Ernst Rudolf, *Verfassungsrecht des Grossdeutschen Reiches* (Hamburg, 1939).

Huck, Gerhard (ed.), *Sozialgeschichte der Freizeit: Untersuchungen zum Wandel der Alltagskultur in Deutschland* (Wuppertal, 1980).

Hull, David Stewart, *Film in the Third Reich: A Study of the German Cinema, 1933–1945* (Berkeley, Calif., 1969).

——, 'On the Trail of Missing Masterpieces: Modern Art from German Galleries', in Barron (ed.), *Degenerate Art*, 121–33.

Hüttenberger, Peter, 'Heimtückefälle vor dem Sondergericht München 1933–1939', in Broszat *et al.* (eds.), *Bayern*, IV. 435–526.

Iber, Harald, *Christlicher Glaube oder rassischer Mythus: Die Auseinandersetzung der Bekennenden Kirche mit Alfred Rosenbergs 'Der Mythus des 20. Jahrhunderts'* (Frankfurt am Main, 1987).

Iggers, Georg G. (ed.), *The Social History of Politics: Critical Perspectives in West German Historical Writing since 1945* (Leamington Spa, 1985).

——, 'Introduction', in idem (ed.), *The Social History of Politics*, 1–48.

Infield, Glenn B., *Leni Riefenstahl: The Fallen Film Goddess* (New York, 1976).

Institut für die Geschichte der Arbeiterbewegung (ed.), *In den Fängen des NKWD: Deutsche Opfer des stalinistischen Terrors in der UdSSR* (Berlin, 1991).

Jacobsen, Hans Adolf, *Nationalsozialistische Aussenpolitik, 1933–1938* (Frankfurt am Main, 1968).

——, *et al. (eds.), Ausgewählte Dokumente zur Geschichte des Nationalsozialismus, 1933–1945* (3 vols., Bielefeld, 1961).

Jádi, Inge, *et al. Beyond Reason: Art and Psychosis. Works from the Prinzhorn Collection* (London, 1996).

James, Harold, 'Die Deutsche Bank und die Diktatur 1933–1945', in Lothar Gall et al., *Die Deutsche Bank 1870–1995* (Munich, 1993), 315–408.

——, 'Innovation and Conservatism in Economic Recovery: The Alleged "Nazi Recovery" of the 1930s', in Childers and Caplan (eds.), *Reevaluating the Third Reich*, 114–38.

——, *The Deutsche Bank and the Nazi Economic War against the Jews: The Expropriation of Jewish-owned Property* (Cambridge, 2001).

——, *The Nazi Dictatorship and the Deutsche Bank* (Cambridge, 2004).

Janda, Annegret, 'The Fight for Modern Art: The Berlin Nationalgalerie after 1933', in Barron (ed.), *Degenerate Art*, 105–18.

——, (ed.), *Das Schicksal einer Sammlung: Aufbau und Zerstörung der Neuen Abteilung der Nationalgalerie im ehemaligen Kronprinzen-Palais: Unter den Linden 1918–1945* (Berlin, 1986).

Jansen, Christian, *Professoren und Politik: Politisches Denken und Handeln der Heidelberger Hochschullehrer 1914–1935* (Göttingen, 1992).

——, *et al. (eds.), Von der Aufgabe der Freiheit: Politische Verantwortung und bürgerliche Gesellschaft im 19. und 20. Jahrhundert: Festschrift für Hans Mommsen zum 5. November 1995* (Berlin, 1995).

Janssen, Karl-Heinz, 'Eine Welt brach zusammen', in Glaser and Silenius (eds.), *Jugend im Dritten Reich*, 88–90.

——, and Tobias, Fritz, *Der Sturz der Generäle: Hitler und die Blomberg-Fritsch Krise 1938* (Munich, 1994 [1938]).

Jarausch, Konrad H., *Deutsche Studenten 1800–1970* (Frankfurt am Main, 1984).

——, *The Unfree Professions: German Lawyers, Teachers, and Engineers, 1900–1950* (New York, 1990).

Jaskot, Paul B., *The Architecture of Oppression: The SS, Forced Labor and the Nazi Monumental Building Economy* (London, 2000).

Jaworski, Rudolf, *Vorposten oder Minderheit?: Der sudetendeutsche Volkstums-*

kampf in den Beziehungen zwischen der Weimarer Republik und der CSR (Stuttgart, 1977).

Jelavich, Barbara, *Modern Austria: Empire and Republic, 1815–1986* (Cambridge, 1987).

Jellonnek, Burkhard, *Homosexuelle unter dem Hakenkreuz: Die Verfolgung von Homosexuellen in Dritten Reich* (Paderborn, 1990).

——, 'Staatspolizeiliche Fahndungs- und Ermittlungsmethoden gegen Homosexuelle. Regionale Differenzen und Gemeinsamkeiten', in Paul and Mallmann (eds.), *Die Gestapo*, 343–56.

Joachimsthaler, Anton, *Hitlers Liste: Ein Dokument persönlicher Beziehungen* (Munich, 2003).

John, Eckhard, *Musikbolschewismus: Die Politisierung der Musik in Deutschland, 1918–1938* (Stuttgart, 1994).

Johnson, Eric A., *Nazi Terror: The Gestapo, Jews, and Ordinary Germans* (New York, 1999).

Jung, Otmar, *Plebiszit und Diktatur: Die Volksabstimmungen der Nationalsozialisten: Die Fälle 'Austritt aus dem Völkerbund' (1933), 'Staatsoberhaupt' (1934) und 'Anschluss Österreichs' (1938)* (Tübingen, 1995).

Jupper, Alfons (ed.), *Staatliche Akten über die Reichskonkordatsverhandlungen 1933* (Mainz, 1969).

Kaftan, Kurt Gustav, *Der Kampf um die Autobahnen: Geschichte der Autobahnen in Deutschland 1907–1935* (Berlin, 1955).

Kaienburg, Hermann, 'Funktionswandel des KZ-Kosmos? Das Konzentrationslager Neuengamme 1938–1945', in Herbert *et al.* (eds.), *Die nationalsozialistischen Konzentrationslager*, 259–84.

——, '*Vernichtung durch Arbeit': Der Fall Neuengamme: Die Wirtschaftsbestrebungen der SS und ihre Auswirkungen auf die Existenzbedingungen der KZ-Gefangenen* (Bonn, 1990).

Kaiser, Ernst, and Knorn, Michael, '*Wir lebten und schliefen zwischen den Toten': Rüstungsproduktion, Zwangsarbeit und Vernichtung in den Frankfurter Adlerwerken* (Frankfurt am Main, 1994).

Kaiser, Fritz, *Führer durch die Ausstellung Entartete Kunst* (Berlin, 1937).

Kaiser, Jochen-Christoph, 'Protestantismus, Diakonie und "Judenfrage" 1933–41', *VfZ* 37 (1989), 673–714.

Kalshoven, Hedda (ed.), *Ich denk so viel an Euch: Ein deutsch-holländischer Briefwechsel 1920–1949* (Munich, 1995 [1991]).

Kaplan, Marion A., *Between Dignity and Despair: Jewish Life in Nazi Germany* (New York, 1998).

Kappeler, Alphons, *Ein Fall von 'Pseudologia phantastica' in der deutschen Literatur: Fritz Reck-Malleczewen* (2 vols., Göppingen, 1975).

Karlsch, Rainer, and Stokes, Raymond G., *Faktor Öl: Die Geschichte der Mineralölwirtschaft in Deutschland 1859–1974* (Munich, 2003).

Karow, Yvonne, *Deutsches Opfer: Kultische Selbstauslöschung auf den Reichs-parteitagen der NSDAP* (Berlin, 1997).

Kaschuba, Wolfgang, *Lebenswelt und Kultur der unterbürgerlichen Schichten im 19. und 20. Jahrhunderi* (Munich, 1990).

——, and Lipp, Carola, 'Kein Volk steht auf, kein Sturm bricht los. Stationen dörflichen Lebens auf dem Weg in den Faschismus', in Beck *et al.* (eds.), *Terror und Hoffnung*, 111–55.

——, *Dörfliches Überleben: Zur Geschichte materieller und sozialer Reproduktion ländlicher Gesellschaft im 19. und frühen 20. Jahrhundert* (Tübingen, 1982).

Kater, Michael H., 'Die ernsten Bibelforscher im Dritten Reich', *VfZ* 17 (1969), 181–218.

——, 'Die deutsche Elternschaft im nationalsozialistischen Erziehungssystem. Ein Beitrag zur Sozialgeschichte der Familie', *Vierteljahrsschrift für Sozial- und Wirtschaftsgeschichte*, 67 (1980), 484–512.

——, 'Medizin und Mediziner im Dritten Reich', *Historische Zeitschrift*, 244 (1987), 299–352.

——, *Doctors under Hitler* (Chapel Hill, N.C., 1989).

——, *Different Drummers: Jazz in the Culture of Nazi Germany* (New York, 1992).

——, *The Twisted Muse: Musicians and their Music in the Third Reich* (New York, 1997).

——, *Composers of the Nazi Era: Eight Portraits* (New York, 2000).

——, *Hitler Youth* (Cambridge, Mass., 2004).

——, and Riethmüller, Albrecht (eds.), *Music and Nazism: Art under Tyranny, 1933–1945* (Laaber, 2003).

Kehrl, Hans, *Krisenmanager im Dritten Reich: 6 Jahre Frieden, 6 Jahre Krieg: Erinnerungen* (Düsseldorf, 1973).

Keim, Wolfgang, *Erziehung unter der Nazi-Diktatur* (2 vols., Darmstadt, 1995–7).

Keinemann, Friedrich, *Vom Krummstab zur Republik: Westfälischer Adel unter preussischer Herrschaft 1802–1945* (Bochum, 1997).

Keitz, Christine, 'Die Anfänge des modernen Massentourismus in der Weimarer Republik', *Archiv für Sozialgeschichte*, 33 (1993), 179–209.

Keller, Bernhard, *Das Handwerk im faschistischen Deutschland: Zum Problem der Massenbasis* (Cologne, 1980).

Kershaw, Ian, 'Antisemitismus und Volksmeinung. Reaktionen auf die Juden-verfolgung', in Broszat *et al.* (eds.), *Bayern*, II. 280–348.

——, 'The Persecution of the Jews and German Popular Opinion in the Third Reich', *Leo Baeck Institute Year Book*, 26 (1981), 261–89.

——, *Popular Opinion and Political Dissent in the Third Reich: Bavaria 1933–1945* (Oxford, 1983).

——, 'How Effective Was Nazi Propaganda?', in Welch (ed.), *Nazi Propaganda*, 180–205.

——, The 'Hitler Myth': Image and Reality in the Third Reich (Oxford, 1987).

——, 'Der Überfall auf Polen und die öffentliche Meinung in Deutschland', in Hansen *et al.* (eds.), *Politischer Wandel*, 237–50.

——, Hitler, 1889–1936: I Hubris (London, 1998).

——, Hitler, 1936–1945: II Nemesis (London, 2000).

——, The Nazi Dictatorship: Problems and Perspectives of Interpretation (4th edn, London, 2000 [1985]).

Kersten, Felix, *The Kersten Memoirs, 1940–1945* (London, 1956 [1952]).

Kessler, Harry Graf, *Tagebücher, 1918–1937*, ed. Wolfgang Pfeiffer-Belli (Frankfurt am Main, 1982 [1961]).

Ketelsen, Uwe-Karsten, *Literatur und Drittes Reich* (Schernfeld, 1992).

Kiaulehn, Walther, *Mein Freund der Verleger – Ernst Rowohlt und seine Zeit* (Reinbek, 1967).

Kieffer, Fritz, *Judenverfolgung in Deutschland – eine innere Angelegenheit? Internationale Reaktionen auf die Flüchtlingsproblematik 1933–1939* (Stuttgart, 2002).

Kiemeier, Klaus, *The Ufa Story: A History of Germany's Greatest Film Company 1918–1945* (New York, 1996).

Kimmel, Günther, 'Das Konzentrationslager Dachau: Eine Studie zu den nationalsozialistischen Gewaltverbrechen', in Broszat *et al.* (eds.), *Bayern*, II. 349–413.

Kirchberg, Peter, 'Typisierung in der Kraftfahrzeugindustrie und der Generalbevollmächtigte für das Kraftfahrwesen', *Jahrbuch für Wirtschaftsgeschichte* (1969), 117–42.

Kirchliches Jahrbuch für die Evangelische Kirche in Deutschland 1933–1944 (Gütersloh, 1948).

Kirkpatrick, Clifford, *Women in Nazi Germany* (London, 1939).

Kitchen, Martin, *The Coming of Austrian Fascism* (London, 1980).

Kittel, Manfred, 'Konfessioneller Konflikt und politische Kultur in der Weimarer Republik', in Blaschke (ed.), *Konfessionen im Konflikt*, 243–98.

Klee, Ernst, *Die SA Jesu Christi: Die Kirchen im Banne Hitlers* (Frankfurt am Main, 1989).

Kleiber, Lore, ' "Wo ihr seid, da soll die Sonne scheinen!" – Der Frauenarbeitsdienst am Ende der Weimarer Republik und im Nationalsozialismus', in Frauengruppe Faschismusforschung (ed.), *Mutterkreuz*, 188–214.

Klein, Burton H., *Germany's Economic Preparations for War* (Cambridge, Mass., 1959).

Klein, Thomas (ed.), *Die Lageberichte der Geheimen Staatspolizei über die Provinz Hessen-Nassau, 1933–1936* (Cologne, 1986).

Kleine, George H., 'Adelsgenossenschaft und Nationalsozialismus', *VfZ* 26 (1978), 100–143.

Klemperer, Klemens von, *German Resistance Against Hitler: The Search for Allies Abroad, 1938–1945* (Oxford, 1992).

Klemperer, Victor, *LTI: Notizbuch eines Philologen* (Leipzig, 1975 [1947]).

——, *I Shall Bear Witness: The Diaries of Victor Klemperer 1933–1941* (London, 1998 [1995]).

——, *Tagebücher 1933–1934 (Ich will Zeugnis ablegen bis zum letzten: Tagebücher 1933–1945*, I) (Berlin, 1999 [1995]).

Klepper, Jochen, *Unter dem Schatten Deiner Flügel: Aus den Tagebüchern der Jahre 1932–1942* (Stuttgart, 1956).

Klessmann, Christoph, 'Osteuropaforschung und Lebensraumpolitik im Dritten Reich', in Lundgreen (ed.), *Wissenschaft im Dritten Reich*, 350–83.

Kley, Stefan, *Hitler, Ribbentrop und die Entfesselung des Zweiten Weltkriegs* (Paderborn, 1996).

Kling, Willi, *Kleine Geschichte der IG Farben – der Grossfabrikant des Todes* (Berlin, 1957).

Klingemann, Carsten, 'Social-scientific Experts – No Ideologues: Sociology and Social Research in the Third Reich', in Turner and Käsler (eds.), *Sociology Responds to Fascism*, 127–54.

——, *Soziologie im Dritten Reich* (Baden-Baden, 1996).

Klinksiek, Dorothee, *Die Frau im NS-Staat* (Stuttgart, 1982).

Klönne, Arno, *Jugend im Dritten Reich: Die Hitler-Jugend und ihre Gegner* (Cologne, 1999 [1982]).

Klöss, Erhard (ed.), *Reden des Führers: Politik und Propaganda Adolf Hitlers, 1922–1945* (Munich, 1967).

Klotzbach, Kurt, *Gegen den Nationalsozialismus: Widerstand und Verfolgung in Dortmund 1930–1945: Eine historisch-politische Studie* (Hanover, 1969).

Knauer, Wilfried (ed.), *Nationalsozialistische Justiz und Todesstrafe: Eine Dokumentation zur Gedenkstätte in der Justizvollzugsanstalt Wolfenbüttel* (Braunschweig, 1991).

Knigge-Tesche, Renate (ed.), *Berater der Braunen Macht: Wissenschaft und Wissenschaftler im NS-Staat* (Frankfurt am Main, 1999).

Knipping, Franz, and Müller, Klaus-Jürgen, *Machtbewusstsein in Deutschland am Vorabend des Zweiten Weltkrieges* (Paderborn, 1984).

Koch, Hans-Jörg, *Das Wunschkonzert im NS-Rundfunk* (Cologne, 2003).

Kochan, Lionel, 'Martin Niemöller', in Gutman (ed.), *Encyclopedia of the Holocaust*, III. 1,061.

Kocka, Jürgen (ed.), *Theorien in der Praxis des Historikers* (Göttingen, 1977).

Kohlrausch, Eduard (ed.), *Deutsche Strafgesetze vom 19. Dezember 1932 bis 12. Juni 1934* (Berlin, 1934).

Komjathy, Anthony T., and Stockwell, Rebecca, *German Minorities and the Third Reich: Ethnic Germans of East Central Europe between the Wars* (New York, 1980).

König, Ulrich, *Sinti und Roma unter dem Nationalsozialismus: Verfolgung und Widerstand* (Bochum, 1989).

Königseder, Angelika, and Wetzel, Juliane, 'Die "Bilderverbrennung" 1939 – ein Pendant?', in *Zeitschrift für Geschichtswissenschaft*, 5 (2003), 439–46.

Koonz, Claudia, *Mothers in the Fatherland: Women, the Family, and Nazi Politics* (London, 1988 [1987]).

Kopf, Paul, and Miller, Max (eds.), *Die Vertreibung von Bischof Joannes Baptista Sproll von Rottenburg, 1938–1945: Dokumente zur Geschichte des kirchlichen Widerstands* (Mainz, 1971).

Kopper, Christopher, 'Die "Arisierung" jüdischer Privatbanken im Nationalsozialismus', *Sozialwissenschaftliche Information für Unterricht und Studium*, 20 (1991), 11–16.

——, 'Privates Bankwesen im Nationalsozialismus. Das Bankhaus M. M. Warburg & Co.', in Werner Plumpe and Christian Kleinschmidt (eds.), *Unternehmen zwischen Markt und Macht: Aspekte deutscher Unternehmens- und Industriegeschichte im 20 Jahrhundert* (Essen, 1992), 61–73.

——, *Zwischen Marktwirtschaft und Dirigismus: Bankenpolitik im 'Dritten Reich', 1933–1939* (Bonn, 1995).

Körber, Robert, *Rassensieg in Wien, der Grenzfeste des Reiches* (Vienna, 1939).

Kornrumpf, Martin, *HAFRABA e.V.: Deutsche Autobahn-Planung 1926–1934* (Bonn, 1990).

Kosthorst, Erich, and Walter, Bernd, *Konzentrations und Strafgefangenenlager im Dritten Reich: Beispiel Emsland* (3 vols., Düsseldorf, 1983).

Kowowski, Albert S., *Polens Politik gegenüber seiner deutschen Minderheit, 1919–1939* (Wiesbaden, 1998).

Kracauer, Siegfried, *From Caligari to Hitler: A Psychological History of the German Film* (Princeton, N.J., 1947).

Kracik, Jörg, *Die Politik des deutschen Aktivismus in der Tschechoslowakei, 1920–1938* (Frankfurt am Main, 1999).

Kramer, David, 'Jewish Welfare Work under the Impact of Pauperization', in Paucker *et al.* (eds.), *The Jews in Nazi Germany*, 173–88.

Kramer, Helgard, 'Frankfurt's Working Women: Scapegoats or Winners of the Great Depression?', in Evans and Geary (eds.), *The German Unemployed* 108–41.

Kratzsch, Gerhard, *Der Gauwirtschaftsapparat der NSDAP: Menschenführung – 'Arisierung' – Wehrwirtschaft im Gau Westfalen-Süd: Eine Studie zur Herrschaftspraxis im totalitären Staat* (Münster, 1989).

——, 'Die "Entjudung" der mittelständischen Wirtschaft im Regierungsbezirk Arnsberg', in Herzig *et al.* (eds.), *Verdrängung und Vernichtung*, 91–114.

Kraul, Margret, *Das deutsche Gymnasium 1780–1980* (Frankfurt am Main, 1984).

Krausnick, Helmut, *et al.*, *Anatomy of the SS State* (London, 1968 [1965]).

Kreimeier, Klaus, *The Ufa Story: A History of Germany's Greatest Film Company, 1918–1945* (New York, 1996).

Kreisster, Felix (ed.), *Fünfzig Jahre danach – der 'Anschluss' von innen gesehen* (Vienna, 1989).

Krellmann, Hanspeter (ed.), *Wer war Richard Strauss?: Neunzehn Antworten* (Frankfurt am Main, 1999).

Kreutzer, Heike, *Das Reichskirchenministerium im Gefüge der nationalsozial-istischen Herrschaft* (Düsseldorf, 2000).

Kroll, Gerhard, *Von der Weltwirtschaftskrise zur Staatskonjunktur* (Berlin, 1958).

Kropat, Wolf-Arno, *Kristallnacht in Hessen: Der Judenpogrom vom November 1938: Eine Dokumentation* (Wiesbaden, 1997 [1988]).

——, *'Reichskristallnacht': Der Judenpogrom vom 7. bis 10. November 1938- Urheber, Täter, Hintergründe* (Wiesbaden, 1997).

—— (ed.), *Justiz und Judenverfolgung* (2 vols., Wiesbaden, 1975).

Krudener, Jürgen von, 'Zielkonflikte in der nationalsozialistischen Agrarpolitik: Ein Beitrag zur Diskussion des Leistungsproblems in zentralgelenkten Wirtschaftssystemen', *Zeitschrift für Wirtschafts- und Sozialwissenschaften*, 94 (1974), 335–61.

Krüger, Hardy, 'Von der Ordensburg nach Babelsberg', in Leeb (ed.), *'Wir waren'*, 49–55.

Krüger, Peter, *Die Aussenpolitik der Republik von Weimar* (Darmstadt, 1985).

Krüger-Charlé, Michael, 'Carl Goerdelers Versuche der Durchsetzung einer alternativen Politik 1933 bis 1937', in Schmädeke and Steinback (eds.), *Der Widerstand*, 383–404.

Kucera, Jaroslav, *Minderheit im Nationalstaat: Die Sprachenfrage in den tschechisch-deutschen Beziehungen 1918–1938* (Munich, 1999).

Kube, Alfred, *Pour le mérite und Hakenkreuz: Hermann Göring im Dritten Reich* (Munich, 1987 [1986]).

——, 'Hermann Goering: Second Man in the Third Reich', in Smelser and Zitelmann (eds.), *The Nazi Elite*, 62–73.

Kühl, Stefan, *The Nazi Connection: Eugenics, American Racism, and German National Socialism* (New York, 1994).

Kühnl, Reinhard, 'Reichsdeutsche Geschichtswissenschaft', in Tröger (ed.), *Hochschule*, 92–104.

Kulka, Otto Dov, 'Die Nürnberger Rassengesetze und die deutsche Bevölkerung im Lichte geheimer NS-Lage- und Stimmungsberichte', *VfZ* 32 (1984), 582–624.

—— (ed.) *Deutsches Judentum unter dem Nationalsozialismus*, I: *Dokumente zur Geschichte der Reichsvertretung der deutschen Juden 1933–1939* (Tübingen, 1997).

Kupper, Alfons (ed.), *Staatliche Akten über die Reichskonkordatsverhandlungen 1933* (Mainz, 1969).

Kwiet, Konrad, 'Nach dem Pogrom: Stufen der Ausgrenzung', in Benz (ed.), *Die Juden*, 545–659.

——, 'To Leave or Not to Leave: The German Jews at the Crossroads', in Pehle (ed.), *November 1938*, 139–53.

——, and Eschwege, Helmut (eds.), *Selbstbehauptung und Widerstand: Deutsche Juden im Kampf um Existenz und Menschenwürde 1933–1945* (Hamburg, 1984).

Laak, Dirk van, 'Die Mitwirkenden bei der "Arisierung". Dargestellt am Beispiel der rheinisch-westfälischen Industrieregion, 1933–1940', in Büttner (ed.), *Die Deutschen*, 231–57.

——, '"Wenn einer ein Herz im Leibe hat, der lässt sich von einem deutschen Arzt behandeln" – Die "Entjudung" der Essener Wirtschaft von 1933 bis 1941', in Alte Synagoge (ed.), *Entrechtung und Selbsthilfe*, 12–30.

Lächele, Rainer, *Ein Volk, ein Reich, ein Glaube: Die Deutschen Christen in Württemberg 1925–1960* (Stuttgart, 1993).

Ladwig-Winters, Simone, *Wertheim, ein Warenhausunternehmen und seine Eigentümer: Ein Beispiel der Entwicklung der Berliner Warenhäuser bis zur 'Arisierung'* (Münster, 1997).

——, 'The Attack on Berlin Department Stores (*Warenhäuser*) after 1933', in Bankier (ed.), *Probing*, 246–67.

Lambert, Peter, 'From Antifascist to Volkshistoriker: *Demos* and *Etnos* in the Political Thought of Fritz Rörig, 1921–45', in Berger *et al.* (eds.), *Writing National Histories*, 137–49.

Lammers, Britta, *Werbung im Nationalsozialismus: Die Kataloge der 'Grossen Deutschen Kunstausstellung'*, 1937–1944 (Weimar, 1999).

Lane, Barbara Miller, *Architecture and Politics in Germany, 1918–1945* (Cambridge, Mass., 1968).

Lange, Sabine, '. . . wir haben nicht nur das Chaos, sondern wir stehen an einem Beginn . . .' Hans Fallada 1945–1946 (Neubrandenburg, 1988).

Langelüddeke, Albrecht, *Die Entmannung von Sittlichkeitsverbrechern* (Berlin, 1963).

Laqua, Carsten, *Wie Micky unter die Nazis fiel: Walt Disney und Deutschland* (Reinbek, 1992).

Laqueur, Walter, *Fascism: A Reader's Guide: Analyses, Interpretations, Bibliography* (New York, 1976).

Large, David Clay (ed.), *Contending with Hitler: Varieties of German Resistance in the Third Reich* (Washington, D.C., 1991).

Lärmer, Karl, *Autobahnbau in Deutschland 1933 bis 1945: Zu den Hintergründen* (Berlin, 1975).

Larsen, Stein U. *et al.* (eds.), *Who Were the Fascists? Social Roots of European Fascism* (Bergen, 1980).

Lauterbach, Iris (ed.), *Bürokratie und Kult: Das Parteizentrum der NSDAP am Königsplatz in München: Geschichte und Rezeption* (Munich, 1995).

Lautmann, Rüdiger, *Seminar: Gesellschaft und Homosexualität* (Frankfurt am Main, 1977).

——, 'Gay Prisoners in Concentration Camps as Compared with Jehovah's Witnesses and Political Prisoners', in Berenbaum (ed.), *A Mosaic of Victims*, 200–206.

Lee, W. Robert, and Rosenhaft, Eve (eds.), *The State and Social Change in Germany 1880–1980* (Oxford, 1990).

Leeb, Johannes (ed.), 'Wir waren Hitlers Eliteschüler': Ehemalige Zöglinge der NS-Ausleseschulen brechen ihr Schweigen (Hamburg, 1998).

Lehmann, Hartmut, and Melton, James Van Horn (eds.), Paths of Continuity: Central European Historiography from the 1930s to the 1950s (Cambridge, 1994).

——, and Oexle, Otto Gerhard (eds.), Nationalsozialismus in den Kulturwissenschaften (2 vols., Göttingen, 2004–5).

Lehmann, Joachim, 'Mecklenburgische Landwirtschaft und "Modernisierung"' in den dreissiger Jahren', in Bajohr (ed.), Norddeutschland im Nationalsozialismus, 335–46.

Lehmbruch, Hans, 'Acropolis Germaniae. Der Königsplatz-Forum der NSDAP', in Lauterbach (ed.), Bürokratie und Kult, 17–46.

Lehnert, Detlef, Sozialdemokratie zwischen Protestbewegung und Regierungspartei 1848 bis 1983 (Frankfurt am Main, 1983).

Leimkugel, Franz, 'Antisemitische Gesetzgebung in der Pharmazie, 1933–1939', in Meinel and Voswinckel (eds.), Medizin, 230–35.

Leiser, Erwin, Nazi Cinema (London, 1974 [1968]).

Leitz, Christian, 'Nazi Germany's Intervention in the Spanish Civil War and the Foundation of HISMA/ROWAK', in Preston and Mackenzie (eds.), The Republic Besieged, 53–85.

Lenger, Friedrich, Sozialgeschichte der deutschen Handwerker seit 1800 (Frankfurt am Main, 1988).

Lenz, Rudolf, Karstadt: Ein deutscher Warenhauskonzern 1920–1950 (Stuttgart, 1995).

Levi, Erik, Music in the Third Reich (New York, 1994).

Levine, Herbert S., Hitler's Free City: A History of the Nazi Party in Danzig, 1925–39 (Chicago, 1973).

——, 'The Mediator: Carl J. Burckhardt's Efforts to Avert a Second World War', Journal of Modern History, 45 (1973), 439–53.

Lewy, Guenter, The Catholic Church and Nazi Germany (New York, 1964).

——, The Nazi Persecution of the Gypsies (New York, 2000).

Ley, Michael, and Schoeps, Julian H., Der Nationalsozialismus als politische Religion (Bodenheim, 1997).

Ley, Robert, Soldaten der Arbeit (Munich, 1938).

Lidtke, Vernon L., The Alternative Culture: Socialist Labor in Imperial Germany (New York, 1985).

Lindner, Helmut, '"Deutsche" und "gegentypische" Mathematik. Zur Begründung einer "arteigenen Mathematik" im "Dritten Reich" durch Ludwig Bieberbach', in Mehrtens and Richter (eds.), Naturwissenschaft, 88–115.

Lingelbach, Karl Christoph, Erziehung und Erziehungstheorien im nationalsozialistischen Deutschland: Ursprünge und Wandlungen der 1933–1945 in Deutschlands vorherrschenden erziehungstheoretischen Strömungen: Ihre politischen

Funktionen und ihr Verhältnis zur ausserschulischen Erziehungspraxis des 'Dritten Reiches' (Frankfurt am Main, 1987 [1970]).

Linsmayer, Ludwig, *Politische Kultur im Saargebiet 1920–1932: Symbolische Politik, verhinderte Demokratisierung, nationalisiertes Kulturleben in einer abgetrennten Region* (St Ingbert, 1992).

Löffler, Peter (ed.), *Bischof Clemens August Graf von Galen: Akten, Briefe und Predigten 1933–1946*, I: *1933–1939* (Mainz, 1988).

Lohalm, Uwe, 'Local Administration and Nazi Anti-Jewish Policy', in Bankier (ed.), *Probing*, 109–46.

London, John, *Theatre under the Nazis* (Manchester, 2000).

London, Louise, 'Jewish Refugees, Anglo-Jewry and British Government Policy', in Cesarani (ed.), *The Making of Modern Anglo-Jewry*, 163–90.

——, *Whitehall and the Jews, 1933–1948: British Immigration Policy, Jewish Refugees, and the Holocaust* (Cambridge, 2000).

Longerich, Peter, *Die braunen Bataillone: Geschichte der SA* (Munich, 1989).

——, 'Nationalsozialistische Propaganda', in Bracher *et al.* (eds.), *Deutschland 1933–1945*, 291–314.

——, *Politik der Vernichtung: Eine Gesamtdarstellung der nationalsozialistischen Judenverfolgung* (Munich, 1998).

——, *Der ungeschriebene Befehl: Hitler und der Weg zur 'Endlösung'* (Munich, 2001).

Lorentz, Bernhard, 'Die Commerzbank und die "Arisierung" im Altreich. Ein Vergleich der Netzwerkstrukturen und Handlungsspielräume von Grossbanken in der NS-Zeit', *VfZ* 50 (2002), 237–68.

Lorenz, Saskia, 'Die Zerstörung der Synagogen unter dem Nationalsozialismus', in Herzig (ed.), *Verdrängung und Vernichtung*, 153–72.

Löwenthal, Richard, *Die Widerstandsgruppe 'Neu Beginnen'* (Berlin, 1982).

——, and von zur Mühlen, Patrick (eds.), *Widerstand und Verweigerung in Deutschland 1933 bis 1945* (Berlin, 1982).

Lowry, Stephen, *Pathos und Politik: Ideologie in Spielfilmen des Nationalsozialismus* (Tübingen, 1991).

Lucassen, Leo, *Zigeuner: Die Geschichte eines polizeilichen Ordnungsbegriffes in Deutschland, 1700–1945* (Cologne, 1996).

Ludewig, Hans-Ulrich, and Kuessner, David, *'Es sei also jeder gewarnt': Das Sondergericht Braunschweig 1933–1945* (Braunschweig, 2000).

Ludwig, Johannes, *Boykott – Enteignung – Mord: Die 'Entjudung' der deutschen Wirtschaft* (Hamburg, 1989).

Lundgreen, Peter (ed.), *Wissenschaft im Dritten Reich* (Frankfurt am Main, 1985).

Luther, Hans, *Vor dem Abgrund, 1930–1933: Reichsbankpräsident in Krisenzeiten* (Berlin, 1964).

Lüttichau, Mario-Andreas von, ' "Deutsche Kunst" and "Entartete Kunst": Die Münchner Ausstellungen 1937', in Schuster (ed.), *Die 'Kunststadt' München*, 12–36.

——, '"*Entartete Kunst*"', Munich, 1937: A Reconstruction', in Barron (ed.), *Degenerate Art*, 45–81.

Macartney, Carlile A., and Palmer, Alan, *Independent Eastern Europe: A History* (London, 1966).

Mack Smith, Denis, *Mussolini's Roman Empire* (London, 1976).

——, *Modern Italy: A Political History* (New Haven, Conn., 1997 [1959]).

Macrakis, Kristie, *Surviving the Swastika: Scientific Research in Nazi Germany* (New York, 1993).

Maier, Hans, *Politische Religionen: Die totalitären Regime und das Christentum* (Freiburg, 1995).

Maier, Helmut (ed.), *Rüstungsforschung im Nationalsozialismus: Organisation, Mobilisierung und Entgrenzung der Technikwissenschaften* (Göttingen, 2002).

Mairgünther, Wilfred, *Reichskristallnacht* (Kiel, 1987).

Maiwald, Klaus-Jürgen, *Filmzensur im NS-Staat* (Dortmund, 1983).

Malinowski, Stephan, *Vom König zum Führer: Sozialer Niedergang und politische Radikalisierung im deutschen Adel zwischen Kaiserreich und NS-Staat* (Berlin, 2003).

Mallmann, Klaus-Michael, and Gerhard, Paul, *Das zersplitterte Nein: Saarländer gegen Hitler* (Bonn, 1989).

——, *Herrschaft und Alltag: Ein Industrierevier im Dritten Reich* (Bonn, 1991).

——, 'Omniscient, Omnipotent, Omnipresent? Gestapo, Society and Resistance', in Crew (ed.), *Nazism*, 166–96.

——, *Milieus und Widerstand. Eine Verhaltensgeschichte der Gesellschaft im Nationalsozialismus* (Bonn, 1995).

Manchester, William, *The Arms of Krupp, 1587–1968* (New York, 1970 [1968]).

Mandell, Richard D., *The Nazi Olympics* (London, 1972 [1971]).

Mann, Reinhard, *Protest und Kontrolle im Dritten Reich: Nationalsozialistische Herrschaft im Alltag einer rheinischen Grossstadt* (Frankfurt am Main, 1987).

Marcon, Helmut, *Arbeitsbeschaffungspolitik der Regierungen Papen und Schleicher: Grundsteinlegung für die Beschäftigungspolitik im Dritten Reich* (Bern, 1974).

Marcus, Joseph, *Social and Political History of the Jews in Poland, 1919–1939* (Berlin, 1983).

Marschalck, Peter, *Bevölkerungsgeschichte Deutschlands im 19. und 20. Jahrhundert* (Frankfurt am Main, 1984).

Marshall-Cornwell, James *et al.* (eds.), *Akten zur deutschen auswärtigen Politik, 1918–1945: Aus den Akten des Deutschen Auswärtigen Amtes* (series A-E, Baden-Baden, 1951–95).

Marssolek, Inge, 'Radio in Deutschland 1923–1960: Zur Sozialgeschichte eines Mediums', *Geschichte und Gesellschaft*, 27 (2001), 207–39.

——, ' "Die Zeichen an der Wand". Denunziation aus der Persective des jüdischen Alltags im "Dritten Reich" ', *Historical Social Research*, 26 (2001), 204–18.

——, and Saldern, Adelheid von (eds.), *Zuhören und Gehörtwerden*, I: *Radio im Nationalsozialismus: Zwischen Lenkung und Ablenkung* (Tübingen, 1998).

——, *Radiozeiten: Herrschaft, Alltag, Gesellschaft (1924–1960).* (Potsdam, 1999).

Martens, Stefan, 'Die Rolle Hermann Görings in der deutschen Aussenpolitik 1937/38', in Knipping and Müller (eds.), *Machtbewusstsein*, 75–82.

——, *Hermann Göring: 'Erster Paladin des Führers' und 'Zweiter Mann im Reich'* (Paderborn, 1985).

Marxen, Klaus, *Das Volk und sein Gerichtshof: Eine Studie zum nationalsozialistischen Volksgerichtshof* (Frankfurt am Main, 1994).

Maschmann, Melita, *Account Rendered: A Dossier on My Former Self* (London, 1964).

Mason, Timothy W., 'The Primacy of Politics – Politics and Economics in National Socialist Germany', in Woolf (ed.), *The Nature of Fascism*, 165–95.

——, 'The Legacy of 1918 for National Socialism', in Nicholls and Matthias (eds.), *German Democracy*, 215–40.

—— (ed.), *Arbeiterklasse und Volksgemeinschaft: Dokumente und Materialien zur deutschen Arbeiterpolitik 1936–1939* (Opladen, 1975).

——, 'The Workers' Opposition in Nazi Germany', *History Workshop Journal*, 11 (1987), 120–37.

——, *Social Policy in the Third Reich: The Working Class and the 'National Community'* (Providence, R.I., 1993 [1977]).

——, 'The Domestic Dynamics of Nazi Conquests: A Response to Critics', in Childers and Caplan (eds.), *Reevaluating the Third Reich*, 161–89.

——, *Nazism, Fascism and the Working Class* (Cambridge, 1995).

——, 'Women in Germany, 1925–1940: Family, Welfare and Work', in idem, *Nazism, Fascism and the Working Class*, 131–211.

Mastny, Vojtech, *The Czechs under Nazi Rule: The Failure of National Resistance, 1939–1942* (London, 1971).

Matthias, Erich, *Mit dem Gesicht nach Deutschland* (Düsseldorf, 1968).

Matzerath, Horst (ed.), '. . . vergessen kann man die Zeit nicht, das ist nicht möglich . . .': Kölner erinnern sich an die Jahre 1929–1945* (Cologne, 1985).

——, and Volkmann, Heinrich, 'Modernisierungstheorie und Nationalsozialismus', in Kocka (ed.), *Theorien*, 86–116.

Maurer, Trude, 'The Background for Kristallnacht: The Expulsion of Polish Jews', in Pehle (ed.), *November 1938*, 44–72.

Maxwell, David G., 'Ernst Hanfstaengl: Des "Führers" Klavierspieler', in Smelser *et al.* (eds.), *Die braune Elite*, II: *21 weitere biographische Skizzen*, 137–49.

Mayer, Paul (ed.), *Ernst Rowohlt in Selbstzeugnissen und Bilddokumenten* (Reinbeck, 1968).

McKee, Ilse, *Tomorrow the World* (London, 1960).

McLeod, Hugh, *Piety and Poverty: Working-Class Religion in Berlin, London, and New York, 1870–1914* (New York, 1996).

——, *Religion and the People of Western Europe, 1789–1989* (Oxford, 1997 [1981]).

Mead, Margaret, and Métraux, Rhoda (eds.), *The Study of Culture at a Distance* (Chicago, 1953).

Medick, Hans, and Sabean, David (eds.), *Interest and Emotion: Essays in the Study of Family and Kinship* (Cambridge, 1984).

Meehan, Patricia, *The Unnecessary War: Whitehall and the German Resistance to Hitler* (London, 1992).

Mehl, Stefan, *Das Reichsfinanzministerium und die Verfolgung der deutschen Juden, 1933–1943* (Berlin, 1990).

Mehrtens, Herbert, 'Entartete Wissenschaft? Naturwissenschaften und National-sozialismus', in Siegele-Wenschkewitz and Stuchlik (eds.), *Hochschule*, 113–28.

——, 'Kollaborationsverhältnisse: Natur- und Technikwissenschaften im NS-Staat und ihre Historie', in Meinel and Voswinckel (eds.), *Medizin*, 13–32.

——, and Richter, Steffen (eds.), *Naturwissenschaft, Technik und NS-Ideologie: Beiträge zur Wissenschaftsgeschichte des Dritten Reichs* (Frankfurt am Main, 1980).

Meier, Kurt, *Die Deutschen Christen: Das Bild einer Bewegung im Kirchenkampf des Dritten Reiches* (Göttingen, 1964).

Meier-Benneckenstein, Paul (ed.), *Dokumente der deutschen Politik*, IV: *Deutsch-lands Aufstieg zur Grossmacht 1936* (Berlin, 1937).

Meinel, Christoph, and Voswinckel, Peter (eds.), *Medizin, Naturwissenschaft, Technik und Nationalsozialismus: Kontinuitäten und Diskontinuitäten* (Stuttgart, 1994).

Melton, James Van Horn, 'Continuities in German Historical Scholarship, 1933–1960', in Lehmann and Melton (eds.), *Paths*, 1–18.

Melzer, Emanuel, 'The Polish Authorities and the Jewish Question, 1930–1939', in Greenbaum (ed.), *Minority Problems*, 77–81.

Mendelsohn, Ezra, *The Jews of East Central Europe Between the World Wars* (Bloomington, Ind., 1983).

Mendes-Flohr, Paul, 'Jewish Cultural Life under National Socialism', in Meyer (ed.), *German-Jewish History*, 283–312.

Mensing, Björn, *Pfarrer und Nationalsozialismus: Geschichte einer Verstrickung am Beispiel der Evangelisch-Lutherischen Kirche in Bayern* (Göttingen, 1998).

Menz, Egon, 'Sprechchor und Aufmarsch. Zur Entstehung des Thingspiels', in Denkler and Prümm (eds.), *Die deutsche Literatur*, 330–46.

Merker, Reinhard, *Die bildenden Künste im Nationalsozialismus: Kulturideologie, Kulturpolitik, Kulturproduktion* (Cologne, 1983).

Merkl, Peter H., *Political Violence under the Swastika: 581 Early Nazis* (Princeton, N.J., 1975).

Merson, Allan, *Communist Resistance in Nazi Germany* (London, 1985).

Messerschmidt, Manfred, 'Foreign Policy and Preparation for War', in Militärges-chichtliches Forschungsamt (ed.), *Germany*, 541–717.

Meyer, Beate, *'Jüdische Mischlinge': Rassenpolitik und Verfolgungserfahrung 1933–1945* (Hamburg, 1999).

——, 'The Mixed Marriage: A Guarantee of Survival or a Reflection of German Society during the Nazi Regime?', in Bankier (ed.), *Probing*, 54–77.

Meyer, Michael, *The Politics of Music in the Third Reich* (New York, 1991).

Meyer, Michael A. (ed.), *German-Jewish History in Modern Times* (4 vols., New York, 1998 [1996]).

Meyhoff, Andreas, *Blohm und Voss im 'Dritten Reich': Eine Hamburger Grossfwerft zwischen Geschäft und Politik* (Hamburg, 2001).

Meynert, Joachim, *Was vor der 'Endlösung' geschah: Antisemitische Ausgrenzung und Verfolgung in Minden-Ravensberg, 1933–1945* (Münster, 1988).

Mezger, Edmund, *Kriminalpolitik auf kriminologischer Grundlage* (Stuttgart, 1934).

Michaelis, Herbert, and Schraepler, Ernst (eds.), *Ursachen und Folgen: Vom deutschen Zusammenbruch 1918 und 1945 bis zur staatlichen Neuordnung Deutschlands in der Gegenwart* (25 vols., Berlin, 1965–79).

Michalka, Wolfgang, 'Conflicts within the German Leadership on the Objectives and Tactics of German Foreign Policy 1933–9', in Mommsen and Kettenacker (eds.), *The Fascist Challenge and the Policy of Appeasement*, 48–60.

——, *Ribbentrop und die deutsche Weltpolitik, 1933–1940: Aussenpolitische Konzeptionen und Entscheidungsprozesse im Dritten Reich* (Munich, 1989 [1980]).

——, 'Joachim von Ribbentrop: From Wine Merchant to Foreign Minister', in Smelser and Zitelmann (eds.), *The Nazi Elite*, 165–72.

Milfull, John (ed.), *The Attractions of Fascism: Social Psychology and Aesthetics of the 'Triumph of the Right'* (New York, 1990).

Militärgeschichtliches Forschungsamt (ed.), *Germany and the Second World War* (10 vols., Oxford 1990–[1979–]).

Miller, Susanne, and Polthoff, Heinrich, *A History of German Social Democracy: From 1848 to the Present* (Leamington Spa, 1986).

Milton, Sybil, 'The Expulsion of Polish Jews from Germany October 1938 to July 1939: A Documentation', *Leo Baeck Institute Yearbook*, 29 (1984), 169–200.

——, 'Die Konzentrationslager der dreissiger Jahre im Bild der in- und ausländischen Presse', in Herbert *et al.* (eds.), *Die nationalsozialistischen Konzentrationslager*, 135–47.

——, ' "Gypsies" as Social Outsiders in Nazi Germany', in Gellately and Stoltzfus (eds.), *Social Outsiders*, 212–32.

Milward, Alan S., 'Fascism and the Economy', in Laqueur (ed.), *Fascism: A Reader's Guide*, 409–53.

Minuth, Karl-Heinz (ed.), *Akten der Reichskanzlei: Die Regierung Hitler, 1933–1934* (2 vols., Boppard, 1983).

Mockler, Anthony, *Haile Selassie's War* (Oxford, 1984).

Moeller, Felix, *Der Filmminister: Goebbels und der Film im Dritten Reich* (Berlin, 1998).

Möller, Horst, 'Nationalsozialistische Wissenschaftsideologie', in Tröger (ed.), *Hochschule*, 65–76.

Moltmann, Günter, 'Weltherrschaftsideen Hitlers', in Brunner and Gerhard (eds.), *Europa und Übersee*, 197–240.

Mommsen, Hans, *Beamtentum im Dritten Reich: Mit ausgewählten Quellen zur nationalsozialistischen Beamtenpolitik* (Stuttgart, 1976).

——, and Grieger, Manfred, *Das Volkswagenwerk und seine Arbeiter im Dritten Reich* (Düsseldorf, 1996).

——, and Willems, Susanne (eds.), *Herrschaftsalltag im Dritten Reich: Studien und Texte* (Düsseldorf, 1988).

Mommsen, Wolfgang J., and Kettenacker, Lothar (eds.), *The Fascist Challenge and the Policy of Appeasement* (London, 1983).

Montefiore, Simon Sebag, *Stalin: The Court of The Red Tsar* (London, 2003).

Morsch, Günter, 'Oranienburg-Sachsenhausen, Sachsenhausen-Oranienburg', in Herbert *et al.* (eds.), *Die nationalsozialistischen Konzentrationslager*, 111–34.

Morse, Arthur D., *While Six Million Died: A Chronicle of American Apathy* (New York, 1967).

Moser, Jonny, 'Depriving Jews of Their Legal Rights in The Third Reich', in Pehle (ed.), *November 1938*, 127–32.

Mosse, George L. (ed.), *Nazi Culture: Intellectual, Cultural and Social Life in the Third Reich* (London, 1966).

——, *The Nationalization of the Masses: Political Symbolism and Mass Movements in Germany from the Napoleonic Wars through the Third Reich* (New York, 1975).

—— (ed.), *International Fascism: New Thoughts and New Approaches* (London, 1979).

Mosse, Werner E., *The German-Jewish Economic Elite, 1820–1935: A Socio-Cultural Profile* (Oxford, 1989).

Mühlen, Patrick von zur, *'Schlagt Hitler an der Saar!': Abstimmungskampf, Emigration und Widerstand im Saargebiet, 1933–1935* (Bonn, 1979).

Müller, Christian, *Das Gewohnheitsverbrechergesetz vom 24. November 1933. Kriminalpolitik als Rassenpolitik* (Baden-Baden, 1997).

——, ' "Modernes" Strafrecht im Nationalsozialismus: Das Gewohnheitsverbrechergesetz vom 24. 11. 1933', in Franz-Josef Düwell and Thomas Bormbaum (eds.), *Themen juristischer Zeitgeschichte*, III (Baden-Baden, 1999), 46–70.

Müller, Franz, *Ein 'Rechtskatholik' zwischen Kreuz und Hakenkreuz: Franz von Papen als Sonderbevollmächtigter Hitlers in Wien 1934–1938* (Frankfurt am Main, 1990).

Müller, Hans, *Deutsches Bauerntum zwischen Gestern und Morgen* (Witzburg, 1940).

Müller, Ingo, 'Nationalsozialistische Sondergerichte. Ihre Stellung im System des deutschen Strafverfahrens', in Bennhold (ed.), *Spuren des Unrechts*, 17–34.

Müller, Joachim, *Sterilisation und Gesetzgebung bis 1933* (Husum, 1985).

Müller, Klaus-Jürgen, *Das Heer und Hitler: Armee und nationalsozialistisches Regime 1933–1940* (Stuttgart, 1969).

—— (ed.), *General Ludwig Beck: Studien und Dokumente zur politisch-militärischen Vorstellungswelt und Tätigkeit des Generalstabschefs des deutschen Heeres 1933–1938* (Boppard, 1980).

——, 'Militärpolitik nicht Militäropposition!', *Historische Zeitschrift*, 235 (1982), 355–71.

Müller-Waldeck, Gunnar, and Ulrich, Roland, *Hans Fallada: Sein Leben in Bildern und Briefen* (Berlin, 1997).

Münkel, Daniela, *Bauern und Nationalsozialismus: Der Landkreis Celle im Dritten Reich* (Bielefeld, 1991).

——, 'Hakenkreuz und "Blut und Boden". Bäuerliches Leben im Landkreis Celle 1933–1939', *Zeitschrift für Agrargeschichte und Agrarsoziologie*, 40 (1992), 206–47.

——, *Nationalsozialistische Agrarpolitik und Bauernalltag* (Frankfurt am Main, 1996).

——, *Der lange Abschied vom Agrarland: Agrarpolitik, Landwirtschaft und ländliche Gesellschaft zwischen Weimar und Bonn* (Göttingen, 2000).

Muskalla, Dieter, *NS-Politik an der Saar unter Josef Bürckel: Gleichschaltung – Neuordnung – Verwaltung* (Saarbrücken, 1995).

Mussgnug, Dorothee, *Die Reichsfluchtsteuer 1931–1933* (Berlin, 1993).

Nelles, Dieter, 'Jan Valtins "Tagebuch der Hölle – Legende und Wirklichkeit eines Schlüsselromans der Totalitarismustheorie', *1999: Zeitschrift für Sozialgeschichte des 20. und 21. Jahrhunderts*, 9 (1994), 11–45.

——, 'Organisation des Terrors im Nationalsozialismus', *Sozialwissenschaftliche Literatur-Rundschau*, 25 (2002), 5–28.

——, 'Die Rehabilitation eines Gestapo-Agenten: Richard Krebs/Jan Valtin', *Sozial-Geschichte*, 18 (2003), 148–58.

Neugebauer, Wolfgang, (ed.), *Widerstand und Verfolgung im Burgenland: Eine Dokumentation* (Vienna, 1979).

Neuhäusler, Johann, *Kreuz und Hakenkreuz: Der Kampf des Nationalsozialismus gegen die katholische Kirche und der kirchliche Widerstand* (Munich, 1946).

Neurath, Paul Martin, *Die Gesellschaft des Terrors: Innenansichten der Konzentrationslager Dachau und Buchenwald* (Frankfurt am Main, 2004).

Neville, Peter, *Appeasing Hitler: The Diplomacy of Sir Nevile Henderson, 1937–39* (Basingstoke, 1999).

Newman, Simon, *March 1939: The British Guarantee to Poland: A Study in the Continuity of British Foreign Policy* (Oxford, 1976).

Nicholas, Lynn H., *The Rape of Europa: The Fate of Europe's Treasures in the Third Reich and the Second World War* (New York, 1994).

Nicholls, Anthony J., and Matthias, Erich (eds.), *German Democracy and the Triumph of Hitler: Essays in Recent German History* (London, 1971).

Nicosia, Francis R., *The Third Reich and the Palestine Question* (London, 1985).

——, 'Ein nützlicher Feind: Zionismus im nationalsozialistischen Deutschland 1933–1939', *VfZ* 37 (1989), 367–400.

——, and Lawrence D. Stokes (eds.), *Germans Against Nazism: Nonconformity, Opposition and Resistance in the Third Reich: Essays in Honour of Peter Hoffmann* (Oxford, 1990).

Niedhart, Gottfried, and Broderick, George, *Lieder in Politik und Alltag des Nationalsozialismus* (Frankfurt am Main, 1999).

Niemann, Harry, and Herman, Armin (eds.), *Die Entwicklung der Motorisierung im Deutschen Reich und den Nachfolgestaaten* (Stuttgart, 1995).

Niemöller, Martin, *From U-boat to Pulpit* (London, 1936 [1934]).

——, *Dahlemer Predigten 1936/37* (Munich, 1981).

Niermann, Hans-Eckhard, *Die Durchsetzung politischer und politisierter Strafjustiz im Dritten Reich* (Düsseldorf, 1995).

Niethammer, Lutz (ed.), *'Die Jahre weiss man nicht, wo man die heute hinsetzen soll': Faschismuserfahrungen im Ruhrgebiet: Lebensgeschichte und Sozialkultur im Ruhrgebiet 1930 bis 1960* (Berlin, 1983).

Nipperdey, Thomas, *Deutsche Geschichte 1866–1918* (2 vols., Munich, 1990).

Niven, William, 'The Birth of Nazi Drama? *Thing* Plays', in London (ed.), *Theatre under the Nazis*, 54–95.

Noakes, Jeremy, 'The Oldenburg Crucifix Struggle of November 1936: A Case Study of Opposition in the Third Reich', in Stachura (ed.), *The Shaping*, 210–33.

——, 'Nazism and Revolution', in Noel O'Sullivan (ed.), *Revolutionary Theory and Political Reality* (London, 1983), 73–100.

——, 'Nazism and Eugenics: The Background to the Nazi Sterilization Law of 14 July 1933', in Bullen *et al.* (eds.), *Ideas into Politics*, 75–94.

——, 'Wohin gehören die "Judenmischlinge"? Die Entstehung der ersten Durchführungsverordnungen zu den Nürnberger Gesetzen', in Büttner (ed.), *Das Unrechtsregime*, II. 69–89.

——, 'The Origins, Structure and Function of Nazi Terror', in O'Sullivan (ed.), *Terrorism, Ideology and Revolution*, 67–87.

——, 'Social Outcasts in the Third Reich', in Bessel (ed.), *Life in the Third Reich*, 183–96.

——, 'The Development of Nazi Policy towards the German-Jewish "Mischlinge", 1933–1945', *Leo Baeck Institute Year Book*, 34 (1989), 291–354.

——, and Geoffrey Pridham (eds.), *Nazism 1919–1945* (4 vols., Exeter, 1983–98 [1974]).

Nitschke, Peter, 'Polizei und Gestapo. Vorauseilender Gehorsam oder polykratischer Konflikt?', in Paul and Mallmann (eds.), *Die Gestapo*, 306–22.

Noam, Ernst, and Kropat, Wolf-Arno (eds.), *Justiz und Judenverfolgung* (2 vols., Wiesbaden, 1975).

Nothnagel, Hans, and Dähn, Ewald, *Juden in Suhl: Ein geschichtlicher Überblick* (Konstanz, 1995).

Novick, Peter, *The Holocaust and Collective Memory: The American Experience* (London, 2000).

Nye, David E. (ed.), *Technologies of Landscape: From Reaping to Recycling* (Amherst, Mass., 1999).

Obenaus, Herbert, 'The Germans: "An Antisemitic People". The Press Campaign after 9 November 1938', in Bankier (ed.), *Probing*, 147–80.

Oberkrome, Willi, *Volksgeschichte: Methodische Innovation und völkische Ideologisierung in der deutschen Geschichtswissenschaft 1918–1945* (Göttingen, 1992).

Obst, Dieter, *Reichskristallnacht: Ursachen und Verlauf des antisemitischen Pogroms vom November 1938* (Frankfurt am Main, 1991).

Oehler, Christiane, *Die Rechtsprechung des Sondergerichts Mannheim 1933–1945* (Berlin, 1997).

Ogan, Bernd, and Weiss, Wolfgang W., *Faszination und Gewalt: Zur politischen Ästhetik des Nationalsozialismus* (Nuremberg, 1992).

O'Neill, Robert J., *The German Army and the Nazi Party 1933–1939* (London, 1968 [1966]).

Orth, Karin, *Das System der nationalsozialistischen Konzentrationslager: Eine politische Organisationsgeschichte* (Hamburg, 1999).

Ortmeyer, Benjamin, *Schulzeit unterm Hitlerbild: Analysen, Berichte, Dokumente* (Frankfurt am Main, 1996).

Osterroth, Franz, and Schuster, Dieter, *Chronik der deutschen Sozialdemokratie* (Hanover, 1963).

O'Sullivan, Noel (ed.), *Terrorism, Ideology and Revolution* (Brighton, 1986).

Overy, Richard J., 'Cars, Roads, and Economic Recovery in Germany, 1932–1938', *Economic History Review*, 2nd Series, 28 (1975), 466–83.

——, 'The German Pre-war Production Plans: November 1936–April 1939', *English Historical Review*, 90 (1975), 778–97.

——, 'The German *Motorisierung* and Rearmament: A Reply', *Economic History Review*, 32 (1979), 107–13.

——, 'Heavy Industry in the Third Reich: The Reichswerke Crisis', *European History Quarterly*, 15 (1985), 313–39.

——, 'Unemployment in the Third Reich', *Business History*, 29 (1987), 253–82.

——, *War and Economy in the Third Reich* (Oxford, 1994).

——, *The Dictators: Hitler's Germany and Stalin's Russia* (New York, 2004).

Padover, Saul K., *Experiment in Germany: The Story of an American Intelligence Officer* (New York, 1946).

Pahl-Weber, Elke, and Schubert, Dirk, 'Myth and Reality in National Socialist Town Planning and Architecture: Housing and Urban Development in Hamburg, 1933–45', *Planning Perspectives*, 6 (1991), 161–88.

Papen, Franz von, *Memoirs* (London, 1952).

Paret, Peter, *An Artist Against the Third Reich: Ernst Barlach, 1933–1938* (Cambridge, 2003).

Parker, Robert A. C., *Chamberlain and Appeasement: British Policy and the Coming of the Second World War* (London, 1993).

——, 'Alternatives to Appeasement', in Finney (ed.), *The Origins of the Second World War*, 206–21.

——, *Churchill and Appeasement* (London, 2000).

Parkinson, Fred (ed.), *Conquering the Past: Austrian Nazism Yesterday and Today* (Detroit, Mich., 1959).

Pätzold, Kurt, and Runge, Irene, *Pogromnacht 1938* (Berlin, 1988).

Paucker, Arnold *et al.* (eds.), *The Jews in Nazi Germany, 1933–1945* (Tübingen, 1986).

Paul, Gerhard, *'Deutsche Mutter – heim zu Dir!': Warum es misslang, Hitler an der Saar zu schlagen: Der Saarkampf 1933–1935* (Cologne, 1984).

——, *Aufstand der Bilder: Die NS-Propaganda vor 1933* (Bonn, 1990).

——, and Mallmann, Klaus-Michael, 'Auf dem Wege zu einer Sozialgeschichte des Terrors: Eine Zwischenbilanz', in idem (eds.), *Die Gestapo*, 3–18.

——, *Milieus und Widerstand: Eine Verhaltensgeschichte der Gesellschaft im Nationalsozialismus* (Bonn, 1995).

—— (eds.), *Die Gestapo: Mythos und Realität* (Darmstadt, 1995).

Pauley, Bruce F., *Hitler and the Forgotten Nazis: A History of Austrian National Socialism* (Chapel Hill, N.C., 1981).

——, *From Prejudice to Persecution: A History of Austrian Anti-Semitism* (Chapel Hill, N.C., 1992).

Pehle, Walter H., *November 1938: From 'Reichskristallnacht' to Genocide* (New York, 1991).

Pentzlin, Heinz, *Hjalmar Schacht: Leben und Wirken einer umstrittenen Persönlichkeit* (Berlin, 1980).

Perkins, John, 'Nazi Autarchic Aspirations and the Beet-Sugar Industry, 1933–39', *European History Quarterly*, 29 (1990), 497–518.

Perry, Marvin, and Schweitzer, Frederick M., *Jewish-Christian Encounters over the Centuries: Symbiosis, Prejudice, Holocaust, Dialogue* (New York, 1994).

Petach, Joachim, 'Architektur als Weltanschauung: Die Staats- und Parteiarchitektur im Nationalsozialismus', in Ogan and Weiss (eds.), *Faszination und Gewalt*, 197–204.

Peter, Karen (ed.), *NS-Presseanweisungen der Vorkriegszeit: Edition und Dokumentation*, V: *1937* (Munich, 1998); VI: *1938* (Munich, 1999).

Peterson, Agnes. F., *et al.* (eds.), *Himmler: Geheimreden 1933 bis 1945* (Frankfurt am Main, 1974).

Peterson, Edward N., *The Limits of Hitler's Power* (Princeton, N.J., 1969).

Petrick, Fritz, 'Eine Untersuchung zur Beseitigung der Arbeitslosigkeit unter der deutschen Jugend in den Jahren von 1933 bis 1935', *Jahrbuch für Wirtschaftsgeschichte* (1967), 287–300.

Petropoulos, Jonathan, 'A Guide through the Visual Arts Administration of the Third Reich', in Cuomo (ed.), *National Socialist Cultural Policy*, 121–53.

——, *Art as Politics in the Third Reich* (Chapel Hill, N.C., 1996).

——, *The Faustian Bargain: The Art World in Nazi Germany* (New York, 2000).

——, 'From Seduction to Denial: Arno Breker's Engagement with National Socialism', in Etlin (ed.), *Art*, 205–29.

Petsch, Joachim, 'Architektur und Städtebau im Dritten Reich – Anspruch und Wirklichkeit', in Peukert and Reulecke (eds.), *Die Reihen fast geschlossen*, 175–98.

Petzina, Dietmar, 'Hauptprobleme der deutschen Wirtschaftspolitik 1932/33', *VfZ* 15 (1967), 18–55.

——, *Autarkiepolitik im Dritten Reich: Der nationalsozialistische Vierjahresplan (1936–42)* (Stuttgart, 1968).

——, *Die deutsche Wirtschaft in der Zwischenkriegszeit* (Wiesbaden, 1977).

——, 'The Extent and Causes of Unemployment in the Weimar Republic', in Stachura (ed.), *Unemployment*, 29–48.

—— et al. (eds.), *Sozialgeschichtliches Arbeitsbuch*, III: *Materialien zur Statistik des Deutschen Reiches 1914–1945* (Munich, 1978).

Petzold, Joachim, *Franz von Papen: Ein deutsches Verhängnis* (Munich, 1995).

Peukert, Detlev J. K., *Die KPD im Widerstand: Verfolgung und Untergrundarbeit an Rhein und Ruhr 1933 bis 1945* (Wuppertal, 1980).

——, 'Working-Class Resistance: Problems and Options', in Large (ed.), *Contending with Hitler*, 35–48.

——, 'The Genesis of the "Final Solution" from the Spirit of Science', in Childers and Caplan (eds.), *Reevaluating the Third Reich*, 234–52.

——, and Reulecke, Jürgen (eds.), *Die Reihen fast geschlossen: Beiträge zur Geschichte des Alltags unterm Nationalsozialismus* (Wuppertal, 1981).

Peuschel, Harald, *Die Männer um Hitler: Braune Biographien – Martin Bormann, Joseph Goebbels, Hermann Göring, Reinhard Heydrich, Heinrich Himmler und andere* (Düsseldorf, 1982).

Phillips, Marcus S., 'The Nazi Control of the German Film Industry', *Journal of European Studies*, 1 (1971), 37–68.

Picker, Henry (ed.), *Hitlers Tischgespräche im Führerhauptquartier 1941–42* (Bonn, 1951).

Piekalkiewicz, Janusz, *Polenfeldzug: Hitler und Stalin zerschlagen die Polnische Republik* (Bergisch Gladbach, 1982).

Pikarski, Margot, and Uebel, Günter (eds.), *Die KPD lebt! Flugblätter aus dem antifaschistischen Widerstandskampf der KPD 1933–1945* (3 vols., Berlin, 1980–89).

——, *Gestapo-Berichte über den antifaschistischen Widerstandskampf der KPD 1933 bis 1945* (3 vols., Berlin, 1989–90).

Pine, Lisa, 'The Dissemination of Nazi Ideology and Family Virtues through School Textbooks', *History of Education*, 25 (1996), 91–110.

——, *Nazi Family Policy, 1933–1945* (Oxford, 1997).

Pingel, Falk, *Häftlinge unter SS-Herrschaft: Widerstand, Selbstbehauptung und Vernichtung im Konzentrationslager* (Hamburg, 1978).

——, 'Konzeption und Praxis der nationalsozialistischen Konzentrationslager 1933 bis 1938. Kommentierende Bemerkungen', in Herbert *et al.* (eds.), *Die nationalsozialistischen Konzentrationslager*, 148–66.

Plache, Bruno, *Das Raumgefüge der Welt: Erdkundebuch für Schulen mit höheren Lehrzielen*, I: *Deutschland* (Göttingen, 1939).

Plant, Richard, *The Pink Triangle: The Nazi War against Homosexuals* (Edinburgh, 1987 [1986]).

Platner, Geert (ed.), *Schule im Dritten Reich, Erziehung zum Tod? Eine Dokumentation* (Munich, 1983).

Plum, Günter, 'Wirtschaft und Erwerbsleben', in Benz (ed.), *Die Juden in Deutschland 1933–1945*, 268–313.

Plumpe, Gottfried, *Die I.G. Farbenindustrie AG: Wirtschaft, Technik und Politik 1904–1945* (Berlin, 1990).

——, 'Antwort auf Peter Hayes', *Geschichte und Gesellschaft*, 18 (1992), 526–32.

Plumpe, Werner, and Kleinschmidt, Christian (eds.) *Unternehmen zwischen Markt und Macht: Aspekte deutscher Unternehmens- und Industriegeschichte im 20. Jahrhundert* (Essen, 1992).

Pöggeler, Franz, 'Politische Inhalte in Fibeln und Lesebüchern des "Dritten Reiches"', in Hohmann (ed.), *Erster Weltkrieg*, 75–104.

Pohle, Heinz, *Der Rundfunk als Instrument der Politik: Zur Geschichte des Rundfunks von 1923 bis 1928* (Hamburg, 1955).

Pois, Robert A., *National Socialism and the Religion of Nature* (London, 1986).

Poliakov, Léon, and Wulf, Josef (eds.), *Das Dritte Reich und seine Denker: Dokumente* (Berlin, 1959).

Poller, Walter, *Arztschreiber in Buchenwald: Bericht des Häftlings 996 aus Block 36* (Hamburg, 1946).

Polster, Bernd, *Swing Heil: Jazz im Nationalsozialismus* (Berlin, 1989).

Pommerin, Reiner, *'Sterilisierung der Rheinlandbastarde': Das Schicksal einer farbigen deutschen Minderheit 1918–1937* (Düsseldorf, 1979).

Potter, Pamela M., 'The Nazi "Seizure" of the Berlin Philharmonic, or the Decline of a Bourgeois Musical Institution', in Cuomo (ed.), *National Socialist Cultural Policy*, 39–65.

——, *Most German of the Arts: Musicology and Society from the Weimar Republic to the End of Hitler's Reich* (New Haven, Conn., 1998).

Prantl, Helmut (ed.), *Die kirchliche Lage in Bayern nach den Regierungspräsidentenberichten 1933–1943*, V: *Regierungsbezirk Pfalz 1933–1940* (Mainz, 1978).

Preston, Paul, *The Spanish Civil War, 1936–39* (London, 1986).

——, *Franco: A Biography* (London, 1993).

——, and Mackenzie, Anne L. (eds.), *The Republic Besieged: Civil War in Spain 1936–1939* (Edinburgh, 1996).

Prieberg, Fred K., *Musik im NS-Staat* (Frankfurt am Main, 1982).

——, *Trial of Strength: Wilhelm Furtwängler in the Third Reich* (London, 1991 [1986]).

Prinz, Michael, *Vom neuen Mittelstand zum Volksgenossen: Die Entwicklung des sozialen Status der Angestellten von der Weimarer Republik bis zum Ende der NS-Zeit* (Munich, 1986).

Prinzhorn, Hans, *Bildnerei der Geisteskranken: Ein Beitrag zur Psychologie und Psychopathologie der Gestaltung* (Berlin, 1922).

Probst, Volker, *Der Bildhauer Arno Breker* (Bonn, 1978).

Proctor, Robert N., *Racial Hygiene: Medicine under the Nazis* (London, 1988).

——, *The Nazi War on Cancer* (Princeton, N.J., 1999).

Prümm, Karl, 'Das Erbe der Front. Der antidemokratische Kriegsroman der Weimarer Republik und seine nationalsozialistische Fortsetzung', in Denkler and Prümm (eds.), *Die deutsche Literatur*, 138–64.

Przyrembel, Alexandra, *'Rassenschande': Reinheitsmythos und Vernichtungslegitimation im Nationalsozialismus* (Göttingen, 2003).

Pyta, Wolfram, *Dorfgemeinschaft und Parteipolitik, 1918–1933: Die Verschränkung von Milieu und Parteien in den protestantischen Landgebieten Deutschlands in der Weimarer Republik* (Düsseldorf, 1996).

Quine, Maria S., *Population Politics in Twentieth-Century Europe: Fascist Dictatorships and Liberal Democracies* (London, 1996).

Rabinbach, Anson G., 'Toward a Marxist Theory of Fascism and National Socialism', *New German Critique*, 1 (1974), 127–53.

——, 'The Aesthetics of Production in the Third Reich', in Mosse (ed.), *International Fascism*, 189–222.

Rabinovici, Doron, 'Expediting Expropriation and Expulsion: The Impact of the "Vienna Model" on Anti-Jewish Policies in Nazi Gemany, 1938', *Holocaust and Genocide Studies*, 14 (2000), 390–414.

——, *Instanzen der Ohnmacht: Wien 1938–1945: Der Weg zum Judenrat* (Frankfurt am Main, 2000).

Rainbird, Sean (ed.), *Max Beckmann* (New York, 2003).

Raitz von Frentz, Christian, *A Lesson Forgotten: Minority Protection under the League of Nations: The Case of the German Minority in Poland, 1920–1934* (Münster, 2000).

Rammstedt, Otthein, 'Theorie und Empirie des Volksfeindes. Zur Entwicklung einer "deutschen Soziologie"', in Lundgreen (ed.), *Wissenschaft*, 253–313.

Rave, Paul Ortwin, *Kunstdiktatur im Dritten Reich* (Hamburg, 1949).

Read, Anthony, and Fisher, David, *The Deadly Embrace: Hitler, Stalin, and the Nazi-Soviet Pact, 1939–1941* (London, 1988).

——, *Kristallnacht: Unleashing the Holocaust* (London, 1989).

Rebentisch, Dieter, 'Die "politische Beurteilung" als Herrschaftsinstrument der NSDAP', in Peukert and Reulecke (eds.), *Die Reihen fast geschlossen*, 107–28.

Reck, Friedrich, *Bockelson: Geschichte eines Messenwahns* (Stuttgart, 1968 [1937]).

——, *Diary of a Man in Despair* (London, 2000 [1966]).

Reese, Dagmar, and Sachse, Carola, 'Frauenforschung zum Nationalsozialismus. Eine Bilanz', in Gravenhorst and Tatschmurat (eds.), *Töchter-Fragen*, 73–106.

Regge, Jürgen, and Schubert, Werner (eds.), *Quellen zur Reform des Straf- und Strafprozessrechts, 2. Abteilung: NS-Zeit (1933–1939) – Strafgesetzbuch*, I: *Entwürfe eines Strafgesetzbuchs*; II: *Protokolle der Strafrechtskommission des Reichsjustizministeriums* (2 vols., Berlin, 1988–9).

Reich, Simon, *The Fruits of Fascism: Postwar Prosperity in Historical Perspective* (Ithaca, N.Y., 1990).

Reichel, Peter, *Der schöne Schein des Dritten Reiches: Faszination und Gewalt des Faschismus* (Munich, 1992).

——, ' "Volksgemeinschaft" und Führer-Mythos', in Ogan and Weiss (eds.), *Faszination und Gewalt*, 137–50.

Reichl, Johannes M., *Das Thingspiel. Über den Versuch eines nationalsozialistischen Lehrstück-Theaters (Euringer – Heynick – Möller)* (Frankfurt, 1998).

Reichsjugendführung, *HJ im Dienst, Ausbildungsvorschrift für die Ertüchtigung der deutschen Jugend* (Berlin, 1935).

Reif, Heinz, *Adel im 19. und 20. Jahrhundert* (Munich, 1999).

—— (ed.), *Adel und Bürgertum in Deutschland*, II: *Entwicklergslinien und Wendepunkte im 20. Jahrhundert* (Berlin, 2001).

Reinharz, Jehuda, and Schatzberg, Walter (eds.), *The Jewish Response to German Culture: From the Enlightenment to the Second World War* (Hanover, N.H., 1985).

Remane, Horst, 'Conrad Weygand und die "Deutsche Chemie" ', in Meinel and Voswinckel (eds.), *Medizin*, 183–91.

Remy, Steven P., *The Heidelberg Myth: The Nazification and Denazification of a German University* (Cambridge, Mass., 2002).

Rentschler, Eric, *The Ministry of Illusion: Nazi Cinema and its Afterlife* (Cambridge, Mass., 1996).

Resse, Dagmar, 'Bund Deutscher Mädel. Zur Geschichte der weiblichen deutschen Jugend im Dritten Reich', in Frauengruppe Faschismusforschung (ed.), *Mutterkreuz*, 163–87.

Reuband, Karl-Heinz, 'Denunziation im Dritten Reich. Die Bedeutung von Systemunterstützung und Gelegenheitsstrukturen', *Historical Social Research*, 26 (2001), 219–34.

Reuth, Ralf Georg, *Goebbels: Eine Biographie* (Munich, 1990).

Reynolds, David, *In Command of History: Churchill Fighting and Writing the Second World War* (London, 2004).

Rheinland-Pfalz, Ministerium der Justiz (ed.), *Justiz im Dritten Reich: NS-Sondergerichtsverfahren in Rheinland-Pfalz: Eine Dokumentation* (3 vols., Frankfurt am Main, 1994).

Rhodes, James M., *The Hitler Movement: A Modern Millenarian Revolution* (Stanford, 1980).

Ribbe, Wolfgang (ed.), *Die Lageberichte der Geheimen Staatspolizei über die Provinz Brandenburg und die Reichshauptstadt Berlin 1933 bis 1936*, I: *Der Regerierungsbezirk Potsdam* (Cologne, 1998).

Ribbentrop, Joachim von, *The Ribbentrop Memoirs* (London, 1954 [1953]).

Ribhegge, Wilhelm, *Geschichte der Universität Münster: Europa in Westfalen* (Münster, 1985).

Richardi, Hans-Günter, *Schule der Gewalt: Das Konzentrationslager Dachau 1933–1934* (Munich, 1983).

Richards, Donald Ray, *The German Bestseller in the Twentieth Century: A Complete Bibliography and Analysis, 1915–1940* (Berne, 1968).

Richarz, Monika, *Jüdisches Leben in Deutschland: Selbstzeugnisse zur Sozialgeschichte 1918–1945* (3 vols., Stuttgart, 1982).

Richter, Steffen, 'Die "Deutsche Physik"', in Mehrtens and Richter (eds.), *Naturwissenschaft*, 116–41.

Riefenstahl, Leni, *Memoiren 1902–1945* (Berlin, 1990 [1987]).

Riethmüller, Albrecht, 'Stefan Zweig and the Fall of the Reich Music Chamber President Richard Strauss', in Kater and Riethmüller (eds.), *Music and Nazism*, 269–91.

Rigg, Bryan Mark, *Hitler's Jewish Soldiers: The Untold Story of Nazi Racial Laws and Men of Jewish Descent in the German Military* (Lawrence, Kans., 2002).

Rinser, Luise, *Saturn auf der Sonne* (Frankfurt am Main, 1994).

Ritchie, James M., *Gottfried Benn: The Unreconstructed Expressionist* (London, 1972).

——, *German Literature under National Socialism* (London, 1983).

Ritschl, Albrecht, *Deutschlands Krise und Konjunktur 1924–1934: Binnenkonjunktur, Auslandsverschuldung und Reparationsproblem zwischen Dawes-Plan und Transfersperre* (Berlin, 2002).

Ritter, Gerhard, 'Die deutschen Historikertage', *Geschichte in Wissenschaft und Unterricht*, 4 (1953), 513–21.

Robbins, Keith, *Munich 1938* (London, 1968).

Roberts, Geoffrey K., *The Unholy Alliance: Stalin's Pact with Hitler* (London, 1991).

Rohde, Horst, 'Hitler's First Blitzkrieg and Its Consequences for North-eastern Europe', in Militärgeschichtliches Forschungsamt (ed.), *Germany*, II. 67–150.

Röhr, Werner, 'Über die Initiative zur terroristischen Gewalt der Gestapo – Fragen und Einwände zu Gerhard Paul', in idem and Brigitte Berlekamp (eds.), *Terror, Herrschaft und Alltag im Nationalsozialismus. Probleme der Sozialgeschichte des deutschen Faschismus* (Münster, 1995), 211–24.

Roos, Hans, *A History of Modern Poland: From the Foundation of the State in the First World War to the Present Day* (London, 1966 [1961]).

Rosenberg, Alfred, *Blut und Ehre: Ein Kampf für deutsche Wiedergeburt: Reden und Aufsätze von 1919–1933* (Munich, 1934).

——, *Der Mythos des 20. Jahrhunderts: Eine Wertung der seelisch-geistigen Gestaltenkämpfe unserer Zeit* (Munich, 1935).

Rosenkranz, Herbert, *Verfolgung und Selbstbehauptung: Die Juden in Österreich 1938–1945* (Vienna, 1978).

Rosenstock, Werner, 'Exodus 1933–1939: A Survey of Jewish Emigration from Germany', *Leo Baeck Institute Yearbook*, 1 (1956), 373–90.

Rösgen, Hans Jürgen, *Die Auflösung der katholischen Studentenverbände im Dritten Reich* (Bochum, 1995).

Ross, Dieter, *Hitler und Dollfuss. Die deutsche Österreich-Politik, 1933–1934* (Hamburg, 1966).

Rossmeissl, Dieter, *'Ganz Deutschland wird zum Führer halten . . .' Zur politischen Erziehung in den Schulen des Dritten Reiches* (Frankfurt am Main, 1985).

Rostock, Jürgen, and Zadnicek, Franz, *Paradiesruinen: Das KdF-Seebad der Zwanzigtausend auf Rügen* (Berlin, 1997 [1992]).

Rothfels, Hans, *Ostraum Preussentum und Reichsgedanke: Historische Abhandlungen, Vorträge und Reden* (Leipzig, 1935).

Rüger, Maria (ed.), *Kunst und Kunstkritik der dreissiger Jahre: 29 Standpunkte zu künstlerischen und ästhetischen Prozessen und Kontroversen* (Dresden, 1990).

Ruhnau, Rüdiger, *Die Freie Stadt Danzig, 1919–1939* (Berg am See, 1979).

Runzheimer, Jürgen, 'Der Überfall auf den Sender Gleiwitz im Jahre 1939', *VfZ* 10 (1962), 408–26.

Rürup, Reinhard (ed.), *Jüdische Geschichte in Berlin* (Berlin, 1995).

Sachse, Carola, *Industrial Housewives: Women's Social Work in the Factories in Nazi Germany* (London, 1987).

Safrian, Hans, *Die Eichmann-Männer* (Vienna, 1992).

——, 'Expediting Expropriation and Expulsion: The Impact of the "Vienna Model" on Anti-Jewish Policies in Nazi Germany, 1938', *Holocaust and Genocide Studies*, 14 (2000), 390–414.

Saldern, Adelheid von, *Mittelstand im 'Dritten Reich': Handwerker – Einzelhändler – Bauern* (Frankfurt am Main, 1985 [1979]).

——, '"Alter Mittelstand" im "Dritten Reich". Anmerkungen zu einer Kontroverse', *Geschichte und Gesellschaft*, 12 (1986), 235–43.

——, 'Victims or Perpetrators? Controversies about the Role of Women in the Nazi State', in Crew (ed.), *Nazism*, 141–65.

——, '"Art for the People": From Cultural Conservatism to Nazi Cultural Policies', in idem, *The Challenge of Modernity*, 299–347.

——, *The Challenge of Modernity: German Social and Cultural Studies, 1890–1960* (Ann Arbor, 2002).

Salewski, Michael, *Die deutsche Seekriegsleitung 1935–1945* (3 vols., Frankfurt am Main, 1970–75).

Sänger, Fritz, *Politik der Täuschungen. Missbrauch der Presse im Dritten Reich. Weisungen, Informationen, Notizen, 1933–1939* (Vienna, 1975).

Sasuly, Richard, *IG Farben* (New York, 1947).

Sauer, Paul, (ed.), *Die Schicksale der jüdischen Bürger Baden-Württembergs während der nationalsozialistischen Verfolgungszeit 1933–1945* (Stuttgart, 1969).

Sauerbruch, Ferdinand, *Das war mein Leben* (Bad Wörishofen, 1951).

Sbacchi, Alberto, *Legacy of Bitterness: Ethiopia and Fascist Italy, 1935–1941* (Lawrenceville, N.J., 1997).

Schaafhausen, Frederick W., *Das Auslandsdeutschtum* (Cologne, 1934).

Schaary, David, 'The Romanian Authorities and the Jewish Communities in Romania between the Two World Wars', in Greenbaum (ed.), *Minority Problems*, 89–95.

Schacht, Hjalmar H. G., *My First Seventy-Six Years: The Autobiography of Hjalmar Schacht* (London, 1955).

Schadt, Jörg (ed.), *Verfolgung und Widerstand unter dem Nationalsozialismus in Baden: Die Lageberichte der Gestapo und des Generalstaatsanwalts Karlsruhe, 1933–1940* (Stuttgart, 1976).

Schäfer, Hans Dieter, *Das gespaltene Bewusstsein: Über deutsche Kultur und Lebenswirklichkeit 1933–1945* (Munich, 1982).

Schausberger, Norbert, *Der Griff nach Österreich: Der Anschluss* (Vienna, 1978).

——, 'Wirtschaftliche Aspekte des Anschlusses Österreichs an das Deutsche Reich (Dokumentation)', *Militärgeschichtliche Mitteilungen*, 8 (1970), 133–64.

Schemm, Hans, *Hans Schemm spricht: Seine Reden und sein Werk* (Bayreuth, 1941 [1935]).

Schenkendorf, Leopold von, and Hoffmann, Heinrich, *Kampf um's dritte Reich: Eine historische Bilderfolge* (Altona-Bahrenfeld, 1933).

Scherer, Klaus, *'Asoziale' im Dritten Reich: Die vergessenen Verfolgten* (Münster, 1990).

Schirach, Baldur von, *Die Hitler-Jugend: Idee und Gestalt* (Leipzig, 1938 [1934]).

Schleier, Hans, 'Die *Historische Zeitschrift* 1918–1943', in Streisand (ed.), *Studien über die deutsche Geschichtswissenschaft*, II. 51–302.

——, 'German Historiography under National Socialism: Dreams of a Powerful Nation-state and German Volkstum Come True', in Berger *et al.* (eds.), *Writing National Histories*, 176–88.

Schleiermacher, Sabine, *Sozialethik im Spannungsfeld von Sozial- und Rassenhygiene: Der Mediziner Hans Harmsen im Centralausschuss für die Innere Mission* (Husum, 1998).

Schliebs, Siegfried, 'Verboten, verbrannt, verfolgt . . . Wolfgang Herrmann und seine "Schwarze Liste: Schöne Literatur" vom Mai 1933. Der Fall des Volksbibliothekars Dr Wolfgang Herrmann', in Haarmann *et al.* (eds.), *"Das war ein Vorspiel nur . . ."*, 442–54.

Schlotterbeck, Friedrich, *The Darker the Night, The Brighter The Stars: A German Worker Remembers (1933–1945)* (London, 1947).

Schlüter, Holger, *Die Urteilspraxis des nationalsozialistischen Volksgerichtshofs* (Berlin, 1995).

Schmädeke, Jürgen, and Steinbach, Peter (eds.), *Der Widerstand gegen den Nationalsozialismus: Die deutsche Gesellschaft und der Widerstand gegen Hitler* (Munich, 1986).

Schmeer, Karlheinz, *Die Regie des öffentlichen Lebens im Dritten Reich* (Munich, 1956).

Schmid, Hans-Dieter, '"Anständige Beamte" und "üble Schläger". Die Staatspolizeileitstelle Hannover', in Paul and Mallmann (eds.), *Die Gestapo*, 133–60.

Schmidl, Erwin A., *März 38: Der deutsche Einmarsch in Österreich* (Vienna, 1987).

Schmidt, Herbert, *'Beabsichtige ich die Todesstrafe zu beantragen': Die nationalsozialistische Sondergerichtsbarkeit im Oberlandesgerichtsbezirk Düsseldorf 1933–1945* (Essen, 1998).

Schmidt, Jürgen, *Martin Niemöller im Kirchenkampf* (Hamburg, 1971).

Schmidt, Uta C., 'Der Volksempfänger: Tabernakel moderner Massenkultur', in Marssolek and von Saldern (eds.), *Radiozeiten*, 136–59.

Schmidt-Schönbeck, Charlotte, *300 Jahre Physik und Astronomie an der Kieler Universität* (Kiel, 1965).

Schmiechen-Ackermann, Detlef, *Anpassung, Verweigerung, Widerstand: Soziale Milieus, politische Kultur und der Widerstand gegen den Nationalsozialismus in Deutschland im regionalen Vergleich* (Berlin, 1997).

——, *Kooperation und Abgrenzung: Bürgerliche Gruppen, evangelische Kirchengemeinden und katholisches Sozialmilieu in der Auseinandersetzung mit dem Nationalsozialismus in Hannover* (Hanover, 1999).

——, 'Der "Blockwart". Die unteren Parteifunktionäre im nationalsozialistischen Terror- und Überwachungsapparat', *VfZ* 48 (2000), 575–602.

Schmoldt, Benno (ed.), *Schule in Berlin: Gestern und heute* (Berlin, 1989).

Schmuhl, Hans-Walter, *Rassenhygiene, Nationalsozialismus, Euthanasie: Von der Verhütung zur Vernichtung 'lebensunwerten Lebens', 1890–1945* (Göttingen, 1987).

Schmutzer, Reinhard, 'Der Wahlsieg der Sudetendeutsche Partei: Die Legende von der faschistischen Bekenntniswahl', *Zeitschrift für Ostforschung*, 41 (1992), 345–84.

Schnass, Franz, *Nationalpolitische Heimat- und Erdkunde, eine lebensnahe Methodik* (Osterwieck am Harz, 1938).

Schneider, Christian, *et al.*, *Das Erbe der NAPOLA: Versuch einer Generationengeschichte des Nationalsozialismus* (Hamburg, 1996).

Schneider, Michael, 'The Development of State Work Creation Policy in Germany, 1930–1933', in Stachura (ed.), *Unemployment*, 163–86.

——, *'Unterm Hakenkreuz': Arbeiter und Arbeiterbewegung 1933 bis 1939* (Bonn, 1999).

Schneider, Thomas Martin, *Reichsbischof Ludwig Müller: Eine Untersuchung zu Leben, Werk und Persönlichkeit* (Göttingen, 1993).

Schneider, Tobias, 'Bestseller im Dritten Reich. Ermittlung und Analyse der meistverkauften Romane in Deutschland 1933–1944', *VfZ* 52 (2004), 77–97.

Schnell, Ralf, *Literarische innere Emigration: 1933–1945* (Stuttgart, 1976).

Schnorbach, Hermann, *Lehrer und Schule unterm Hakenkreuz: Dokumente des Widerstands von 1930 bis 1945* (Königstein im Taunus, 1983).

Schoenbaum, David, *Hitler's Social Revolution: Class and Status in Nazi Germany, 1933–1939* (London, 1967).

Scholder, Klaus, *Die Kirchen und das Dritte Reich*, I: *Vorgeschichte und Zeit der Illusionen 1918–1934* (Frankfurt am Main, 1977).

——, *Die Kirchen und das Dritte Reich*, II: *Das Jahr der Ernüchterung 1934: Barmen und Rom* (Berlin, 1985).

Scholtz, Harald, *NS-Ausleseschulen: Internatsschulen als Herrschaftsmittel des Führerstaates* (Göttingen, 1973).

Schönberger, Angela, *Die neue Reichskanzlei von Albert Speer: Zum Zusammenhang von nationalsozialistischer Ideologie und Architektur* (Berlin, 1981).

Schönhagen, Benigna, *Tübingen unterm Hakenkreuz: Eine Universitätsstadt in der Zeit des Nationalsozialismus* (Tübingen, 1991).

Schönwälder, Karen, *Historiker und Politik. Geschichtswissenschaft im Nationalsozialismus* (Frankfurt am Main, 1992).

Schopf, Roland, 'Von Nibelungentreue, Märtyrertod und verschwörerischer Verschwiegenheit', in Hohmann (ed.), *Erster Weltkrieg*, 194–214.

Schoppmann, Claudia, *Days of Masquerade: Life Stories of Lesbian Women during the Third Reich* (New York, 1996 [1993]).

Schöttler, Peter, *Geschichtsschreibung als Legitimationswissenschaft 1918–1945* (Frankfurt am Main, 1997).

Schröder, Gerald, 'Die "Wiedergeburt" der Pharmazie – 1933 bis 1934', in Mehrtens and Richter (eds.), *Naturwissenschaft*, 166–88.

Schubert, Dirk, ' "... Ein neues Hamburg entsteht ...". Planungen in der "Führerstadt" Hamburg zwischen 1933–1945', in Hartmut Frank (ed.), *Faschistische Architekturen*, 299–318.

Schubert, Giselher, 'The Aesthetic Premises of a Nazi Conception of Music', in Kater and Riethmüller (eds.), *Music and Nazism*, 64–74.

Schuker, Stephen A., 'France and the Remilitarization of the Rhineland, 1936', *French Historical Studies*, 14 (1986), 299–338. (Also in Finney (ed.), *The Origins of the Second World War*, 222–44).

Schulte-Sasse, Linda, *Entertaining the Third Reich: Illusions of Wholeness in Nazi Cinema* (Durham, N.C., 1996).

Schultheis, Herbert, *Die Reichskristallnacht in Deutschland nach Augenzeugenberichten* (Bad Neustadt an der Saale, 1985).

Schulz, Günther, *Die Angestellten seit dem 19. Jahrhundert* (Munich, 2000).

Schulze, Winfried, *Deutsche Geschichtswissenschaft nach 1945* (Munich, 1989).

——, 'German Historiography from the 1930s to the 1950s', in Lehmann and Melton (eds.), *Paths*, 19–42.

Schumann, Hans Gerd, *Nationalsozialismus und Gewerkschaftsbewegung: Die Vernichtung der deutschen Gewerkschaften und der Aufbau der 'Deutschen Arbeitsfront'* (Hanover, 1958).

Schuschnigg, Kurt, *et al.*, *Austrian Requiem* (London, 1947).

Schuster, Peter-Klaus (ed.), *Die 'Kunststadt' München 1937: Nationalsozialismus und 'entartete Kunst'* (Munich, 1988).

Schütz, Erhard H., and Gruber, Eckard, *Mythos Reichsautobahn: Bau und Inszenierung der 'Strassen des Führers' 1933–1941* (Berlin, 1996).

Schwabe, Klaus, 'Change and Continuity in German Historiography from 1933 into the Early 1950s: Gerhard Ritter (1888–1967)', in Lehmann and Melton (eds.), *Paths*, 82–108.

Schwartz, Michael, 'Bauern vor dem Sondergericht. Resistenz und Verfolgung im bäuerlichen Milieu Westfalens', in Faust (ed.), *Verfolgung und Widerstand*, 113–23.

——, *Sozialistische Eugenik: Eugenische Sozialtechnologien in Debatten und Politik der deutschen Sozialdemokratie 1890–1933* (Bonn, 1995).

Schwarzwäller, Wulf C., *The Unknown Hitler: His Private Life and Fortune* (Bethesda, Md., 1989 [1986]).

Schweitzer, Arthur, 'Der ursprüngliche Vierjahresplan', *Jahrbücher für Nationalökonomie und Statistik*, 160 (1956), 348–96.

——, *Big Business in the Third Reich* (Bloomington, Ind., 1964).

Schwingl, Georg, *Die Pervertierung der Schule im Nationalsozialismus: Ein Beitrag zum Begriff 'Totalitäre Erziehung'* (Regensburg, 1993).

Scobie, Alex, *Hitler's State Architecture: The Impact of Classical Antiquity* (Philadelphia, Pa., 1990).

Seeger, Andreas, 'Vom bayerischen "Systembeamten" zum Chef der Gestapo. Zur Person und Tätigkeit Heinrich Müllers (1900–1945)', in Paul and Mallmann (eds.), *Die Gestapo*, 255–67.

Seidler, Franz Wilhelm, *Fritz Todt: Baumeister des Dritten Reiches* (Munich, 1986).

——, 'Fritz Todt: From Motorway Builder to Minister of State', in Smelser and Zitelmann (eds.), *The Nazi Elite*, 245–56.

Seier, Hellmut, 'Der Rektor als Führer. Zur Hochschulpolitik des Reichserziehungsministeriums 1934–1945', *VfZ* 12 (1964), 105–46.

Seier, Hellmut, 'Nationalsozialistisches Wissenschaftsverständnis und Hochschulpolitik', in Siegele-Wenschkewitz and Stuchlik (eds.), *Hochschule*, 5–21.

Semmens, Kristin A., *Seeing Hitler's Germany: Tourism in The Third Reich* (London, 2005).

Sereny, Gitta, *Albert Speer: His Battle with Truth* (London, 1995).

Service, Robert, *Stalin: A Biography* (London, 2004).

Seton-Watson, Hugh, *Eastern Europe between the Wars, 1918–1941* (New York, 1967 [1945]).

Shand, James, 'The *Reichsautobahn*: Symbol for the Third Reich', *Journal of Contemporary History*, 19 (1984), 189–200.

Shapiro, Paul A., 'Prelude to Dictatorship in Romania: The National Christian Party in Power, December 1937–February 1938', *Canadian-American Slavic Studies*, 8 (1974), 45–88.

Sherman, A. Joshua, *Island Refuge: Britain and Refugees from the Third Reich, 1933–1939* (London, 1973).

——, 'A Jewish Bank during the Schacht Era: M. M. Warburg & Co., 1933–1938', in Paucker (ed.), *The Jews in Nazi Germany 1933–1943*, 16–76.

Shirer, William L., *Berlin Diary: The Journal of a Foreign Correspondent, 1934–1941* (London, 1970 [1941]).

Siegele-Wenschkewitz, Leonore, and Stuchlik, Gerda, *Hochschule und Nationalsozialismus: Wissenschaftsgeschichte und Wissenschaftsbetrieb als Thema der Zeitgeschichte* (Frankfurt am Main, 1990).

Siegert, Toni, 'Das Konzentrationslager Flossenbürg, gegründet für sogenannte Asoziale und Kriminelle', in Broszat *et al.* (eds.), *Bayern*, II. 429–93.

Siemsen, Hans, *Die Geschichte des Hitlerjungen Adolf Goers* (Düsseldorf, 1947).

Silverman, Dan P., 'A Pledge Unredeemed: The Housing Crisis in Weimar Germany', *Central European History*, 3 (1970), 119–20.

——, *Hitler's Economy: Nazi Work Creation Programs, 1933–1936* (London, 1998).

Skrentny, Werner, *Hamburg zu Fuss: 20 Stadtteilrundgänge durch Geschichte und Gegenwart* (Hamburg, 1986).

Smelser, Ronald M., *The Sudeten Problem, 1933–1938: Volkstumspolitik and the Formulation of Nazi Foreign Policy* (Folkestone, 1975).

——, *Robert Ley: Hitler's Labor Front Leader* (Oxford, 1988).

——, 'Robert Ley: The Brown Collectivist', in idem and Zitelmann (eds.), *The Nazi Elite*, 144–54.

——, and Zitelmann, Rainer (eds.), *The Nazi Elite* (Basingstoke, 1993 [1989]).

——, *et al.* (eds.), *Die Braune Elite*, II: *21 weitere biographische Skizzen* (Darmstadt, 1993).

Smith, Bradley F., 'Die Überlieferung der Hossbach-Niederschrift im Lichte neuer Quellen', *VfZ* 38 (1990), 329–36.

——, and Peterson, Agnes F. (eds.), *Heinrich Himmler: Geheimreden 1933–1945* (Frankfurt am Main, 1974).

Smith, Helmut Walser, *German Nationalism and Religious Conflict: Culture, Ideology, Politics, 1870–1914* (Princeton, N.J., 1995).

—— (ed.), *Protestants, Catholics, and Jews in Germany, 1800–1914* (Oxford, 2001).

Sneeringer, Julia, *Winning Women's Votes: Propaganda and Politics in Weimar Germany* (Chapel Hill, N.C., 2002).

Sofsky, Wolfgang, *Die Ordnung des Terrors: Das Konzentrationslager* (Frankfurt am Main, 1993).

Solmitz, Luise, *Tagebach* (Staatsarchiv der Freien- und Hansestadt Hamburg, 622–1, 111511–13: Familie Solmitz; transcripts in Forschungsstelle für Zeitgemschichte, Hamburg).

Somary, Felix, *The Raven of Zürich: The Memoirs of Felix Somary* (London, 1986).

Sommer, Theo, *Deutschland und Japan zwischen den Mächten, 1935–1940: Vom Antikominternpakt zum Dreimächtepakt: Eine Studie zur diplomatischen Vorgeschichte des Zweiten Weltkriegs* (Tübingen, 1962).

Sontag, Susan, 'Fascinating Fascism', in Taylor and van der Will (eds.), *The Nazification of Art*, 204–18.

Southworth, Herbert R., *Guernica! Guernica!: A Study of Journalism, Diplomacy, Propaganda, and History* (Berkeley, Calif., 1977).

Sowade, Hanno, 'Otto Ohlendorf: Non-conformist, SS Leader and Economic Functionary', in Smelser and Zitelmann (eds.), *The Nazi Elite*, 155–64.

Sparing, Frank, 'The Gypsy Camps: The Creation, Character and Meaning of an Instrument for the Persecution of Sinti and Romanies under National Socialism' in Fings *et al., From 'Race Science' to the Camps*, 39–70.

——, 'Zwangskastration im Nationalsozialismus. Das Beispiel der Kriminalbiologischen Sammelstelle Köln', in Peter Busse and Klaus Schreiber (eds.), *Kriminalbiologie* (Düsseldorf, 1997).

Speer, Albert, *Inside the Third Reich: Memoirs* (London, 1971 [1970]).

Spektorowski, Alberto, and Mizrachi, Elisabeth, 'Eugenics and the Welfare State in Sweden: The Politics of Social Margins and the Idea of a Productive Society', *Journal of Contemporary History*, 39 (2004), 333–52.

Spenceley, Geoffrey, 'R. J. Overy and the Motorisierung: A Comment', *Economic History Review*, 32 (1979), 100–106.

Spiess, Alfred, and Lichtenstein, Heiner, *Das Unternehmen Tannenberg: Der Anlass zum Zweiten Weitkrieg* (Wiesbaden, 1979).

Spiker, Jürgen, *Film und Kapital: Der Weg der deutschen Filmwirtschaft zum nationalsozialistischen Einheitskonzern* (Berlin, 1975).

Splitt, Gerhard, *Richard Strauss 1933–1935: Ästhetik und Musikpolitik zu Beginn der nationalsozialistischen Herrschaft* (Pfaffenweiler, 1987).

Spode, Hasso, ' "Der deutsche Arbeiter reist": Massentourismus im Dritten Reich', in Huck (ed.), *Sozialgeschichte der Freizeit*, 281–306.

——, 'Ein Seebad für zwanzigtausend Volksgenossen: Zur Grammatik und Geschichte des Fordistischen Urlaubs', in Brenner (ed.), *Reisekultur in Deutschland*, 7–47.

Sponheuer, Bernd, 'The National Socialist Discussion on the "German Quality" in Music', in Kater and Riethmüller (eds.), *Music and Nazism*, 32–42.

Spotts, Frederic, *Bayreuth: A History of the Wagner Festival* (New Haven, Conn. 1994).

——, *Hitler and the Power of Aesthetics* (London, 2002)

Stachura, Peter D. (ed.), *The Shaping of the Nazi State* (London, 1978).

—— (ed.), *Unemployment and the Great Depression in Weimar Germany* (London, 1986).

Stahlmann, Michael, *Die erste Revolution in der Autoindustrie: Management und Arbeitspolitik von 1900–1940* (Frankfurt am Main, 1993).

Staritz, Ekkehart, *Deutsches Volk und deutscher Raum: Vom alten Germanien zum Dritten Reich: Vom after Germanien zum Dritten Reich* (Berlin, 1938).

Stasiewski, Bernhard (ed.), *Akten deutscher Bischöfe über die Lage der Kirche, 1933–1945* (6 vols., Mainz, 1968–85).

Statistisches Jahrbuch für das Deutsche Reich, 59 (Berlin, 1941–2).

Stauffer, Paul, *Zwischen Hofmannsthal und Hitler: Carl J. Burckhardt: Facetten einer aussergewöhnlichen Existenz* (Zürich, 1991).

Steer, George L., *Caesar in Abyssinia* (London, 1936).

Steigmann-Gall, Richard, *The Holy Reich: Nazi Conceptions of Christianity, 1919–1945* (Cambridge, 2003).

——, 'Was National Socialism a Political Religion or a Religious Politics?', in Geyer and Lehmann (eds.), *Religion und Nation: Nation und Religion*, 386–408.

Stein, Leo, *I Was in Hell with Niemoeller* (London, 1942).

Steinberg, Hans-Josef, *Widerstand und Verfolgung in Essen, 1933–1945* (Hanover, 1969).

Steinberg, Michael Stephen, *Sabers and Brown Shirts: The German Students' Path to National Socialism, 1918–1935* (Chicago, 1977).

Steinberg, Rolf, *Nazi-Kitsch* (Darmstadt, 1975).

Steinhaus, Hubert, *Hitlers pädagogische Maximen: 'Mein Kampf' und die Destruktion der Erziehung im Nationalsozialismus* (Frankfurt am Main, 1981).

Steinweis, Alan E., 'Weimar Culture and the Rise of National Socialism: The Kampfbund für deutsche Kultur', *Central European History*, 24 (1991), 402–23.

——, *Art, Ideology and Economics in Nazi Germany: The Reich Chambers of Music, Theater, and the Visual Arts* (Chapel Hill, N.C., 1993).

——, 'Cultural Eugenics: Social Policy, Economic Reform, and the Purge of Jews from German Cultural life', in Cuomo (ed.), *National Socialist Cultural Policy*, 23–37.

Stephenson, Jill, *Women in Nazi Society* (London, 1975).

——, 'The Nazi Organisation of Women, 1933–1939', in Stachura (ed.), *The Shaping*, 186–209.

——, '*Reichsbund der Kinderreichen*: The League of Large Families in the Population Policy of Nazi Germany', *European Studies Review*, 9 (1979), 350–75.

——, *The Nazi Organization of Women* (London, 1981).

——, 'Women's Labor Service in Nazi Germany', *Central European History*, 15 (1982), 241–65.

Sternberger, Dolf, *Aus dem Wörterbuch des Unmenschen* (Düsseldorf, 1968 [1957]).

Stibbe, Matthew, *Women in the Third Reich* (London, 2003).

Stieg, Margaret F., *Public Libraries in Nazi Germany* (Tuscaloosa, Ala., 1992).

Stites, Richard, *The Women's Liberation Movement in Russia: Feminism, Nihilism, and Bolshevism 1860–1930* (Princeton, N.J., 1978).

——, *Russian Popular Culture: Entertainment and Society since 1900* (Cambridge, 1992).

Stoakes, Geoffrey, *Hitler and the Quest for World Dominion* (Leamington Spa, 1986).

Stokes, Lawrence D., *Kleinstadt und Nationalsozialismus: Ausgewählte Dokumente zur Geschichte von Eutin, 1918–1945* (Neumünster, 1984).

Stokes, Raymond G., 'From the IG Farben Fusion to the Establishment of BASF AG (1925–1952)', in Abelshauser *et al., German Industry*, 206–361.

Stollmann, Rainer, 'Faschistische Politik als Gesamtkunstwerk. Tendenzen der Ästhetisierung des politischen Lebens im Nationalsozialismus', in Denkler and Prümm (eds.), *Die deutsche Literatur*, 83–101.

Stoltzfus, Nathan, *Resistance of the Heart: Intermarriage and the Rosenstrasse Protest in Nazi Germany* (New York, 1996).

Stommer, Rainer, ' "Da oben versinkt einem der Alltag . . .". Thingstätten im Dritten Reich als Demonstration der Volksgemeinschaftsideologie', in Peukert and Reulecke (eds.), *Die Reihen fast geschlossen*, 149–73.

—— (ed.), *Reichsautobahn: Pyramiden des Dritten Reichs: Analysen zur Ästhetik eines unbewältigten Mythos* (Marburg, 1982).

——, *Die inszenierte Volksgemeinschaft: Die 'Thing-Bewegung' im Dritten Reich* (Marburg, 1985).

Stone, Marla, *The Patron State: Culture and Politics in Fascist Italy* (Princeton, N.J., 1998).

Storek, Henning, *Dirigierte Öffentlichkeit: Die Zeitung als Herrschaftsmittel in den Anfangsjahren der nationalsozialistischen Regierung* (Opladen, 1972).

Stöver, Bernd, *Volksgemeinschaft im Dritten Reich: Die Konsensbereitschaft der Deutschen aus der Sicht sozialistischer Exilberichte* (Düsseldorf, 1993).

—— (ed.), *Berichte über die Lage in Deutschland: Die Meldungen der Gruppe Neu Beginnen aus dem Dritten Reich 1933–1936* (Bonn, 1996).

Straumann, Lukas, and Wildmann, Daniel, Schweizer Chemieunternehmen im 'Dritten Reich' (Zürich, 2001).

Strauss, Herbert A., 'Jewish Emigration from Germany: Nazi Policies and Jewish Responses', *Leo Baeck Institute Yearbook*, 25 (1980), 313–61, and 26 (1981), 343–409.

——, 'The Drive for War and the Pogroms of November 1938: Testing Explanatory Models', *Leo Baeck Institute Yearbook*, 35 (1990), 267–78.

Strauss, Werner, ' "Das Reichsministerium des Innern und die Judengesetzgebung": Aufzeichnungen von Dr. Bernhard Lösener', *VfZ* 9 (1961), 264–313.

Streisand, Joachim (ed.), *Studien über die deutsche Geschichtswissenschaft von 1871 bis 1945* (2 vols., Berlin, 1965, 1969).

Strobl, Gerwin, *The Germanic Isle: Nazi Perceptions of Britain* (Cambridge, 2000).

Strohmeyer, Klaus, *Warenhäuser: Geschichte, Blüte und Untergang im Warenmeer* (Berlin, 1980).

Strothmann, Dietrich, *Nationalsozialistische Literaturpolitik: Ein Beitrag zur Publizistik im Dritten Reich* (Bonn, 1960).

Struve, Walter, *Aufsteig und Herrschaft des Nationalsozialismus in einer industriellen Kleinstadt: Osterode am Harz 1918–1945* (Essen, 1992).

Studnitz, Cecilia von, *Es war wie ein Rausch: Fallada und sein Leben* (Düsseldorf, 1997).

Stümke, Hans-Georg, 'Vom "unausgeglichenen Geschlechtshaushalt"': Zur Verfolgung Homosexueller', in Frahm *et al.* (eds.), *Verachtet*, 46–63.

——, and Finkler, Rudi, *Rosa Winkel, rosa Listen: Homosexuelle und 'Gesundes Volksempfinden' von Auschwitz bis heute* (Reinbek, 1981).

Suhling, Lothar, 'Deutsche Baukunst. Technologie und Ideologie im Industriebau des "Dritten Reiches"', in Mehrtens and Richter (eds.), *Naturwissenschaft*, 243–81.

Suhr, Elke, *Die Emslandlager: Die politische und wirtschaftliche Bedeutung der emsländischen Konzentrations- und Strafgefangenlager, 1933–1945* (Bremen, 1985).

Swatek, Dieter, *Unternehmenskonzentration als Ergebnis und Mittel nationalsozialistischer Wirtschaftspolitik* (Berlin, 1972).

Sydnor, Charles W., *Soldiers of Destruction: The SS Death's Head Division, 1933–1945* (Princeton, N.J., 1990 [1977]).

Sywottek, Jutta, *Mobilmachung für den totalen Krieg: Die propagandistische Vorbereitung der deutschen Bevölkerung auf den Zweiten Weltkrieg* (Opladen, 1976).

Szczesny, Gerhard, *Als die Vergangenheit Gegenwart war: Lebensanlauf eines Ostpreussen* (Berlin, 1990).

Tal, Uriel, *Structures of German 'Political Theology' in the Nazi Era* (Tel Aviv, 1979).

Tampke, Jürgen, *Czech-German Relations and the Politics of Central Europe: From Bohemia to the EU* (London, 2003).

Tannenbaum, Edward R., *The Fascist Experience: Italian Society and Culture, 1922–1945* (New York, 1972).

Tarnowski, Wolfgang, *Ernst Barlach und der Nationalsozialismus: Ein Abendvortrag, gehalten am 20. Oktober 1988 in der Katholischen Akademie Hamburg* (Hamburg, 1989).

Taylor, Alan J. P., *The Origins of the Second World War* (Harmondsworth, 1964 [1961]).

Taylor, Brandon, and van der Will, Wilfried (eds.), *The Nazification of Art: Art, Design, Music, Architecture, and Film in the Third Reich* (Winchester, 1990).

Taylor, Robert R., *The Word in Stone: The Role of Architecture in the National Socialist Ideology* (Berkeley, Calif., 1974).

Teich, Mikulás (ed.), *Bohemia in History* (Cambridge, 1998).

Teichova, Alice, 'The Protectorate of Bohemia and Moravia (1939–1945): The Economic Dimension', in Teich (ed.), *Bohemia in History*, 267–305.

Temin, Peter, *Lessons from the Great Depression* (Cambridge, Mass., 1989).

Tenfelde, Klaus, 'Proletarische Provinz: Radikalisierung und Widerstand in Penzberg/Oberbayern 1900 bis 1945', in Broszat et al. (eds.), *Bayern*, IV. 320–37.

Tennstedt, Florian, 'Wohltat und Interesse. Das Winterhilfswerk des Deutschen Volkes. Die Weimarer Vorgeschichte und ihre Instrumentalisierung durch das NS-Regime', *Geschichte und Gesellschaft*, 13 (1987), 157–80.

Tessner, Magnus, *Die deutsche Automobilindustrie im Strukturwandel von 1919 bis 1938* (Cologne, 1994).

Teut, Anna, *Architektur im Dritten Reich, 1933–1945* (Frankfurt am Main, 1967).

Thamer, Hans-Ulrich, 'Von der "Ästhetisierung der Politik": Die Nürnberger Parteitage der NSDAP', in Ogan and Weiss (eds.), *Faszination und Gewalt*, 95–103.

Thies, Jochen, *Architekt der Weltherrschaft: Die 'Endziele' Hitlers* (Düsseldorf, 1976).

——, 'Nazi Architecture – A Blueprint for World Domination: The Last Aims of Adolf Hitler', in Welch (ed.), *Nazi Propaganda*, 45–64.

Thomae, Otto, *Die Propaganda-Maschinerie: Bildende Kunst und Öffentlichkeitsarbeit im Dritten Reich* (Berlin, 1978).

Thomann, Klaus-Dieter, '"Krüppel sind nicht minderwertig." Körperbehinderte im Nationalsozialismus', in Meinel and Voswinckel (eds.), *Medizin*, 208–20.

Thomas, Hugh, *The Spanish Civil War* (3rd edn, London, 1986 [1961]).

Thomas, Walter, *Bis der Vorhang fiel* (Dortmund, 1947).

——, *Richard Strauss und seine Zeitgenossen* (Munich, 1964).

Thyssen, Fritz, *I Paid Hitler* (London, 1941).

Todt, Fritz, 'Der Strassenbau im nationalsozialistischen Staat', in Hans Heinrich Lammers and Hans Pfundtner (eds.), *Grundlagen, Aufbau und Wirtschaftsordnung des national sozialistischen Staates* (Berlin, 1937), III: *Die Wirtschaftsordnung des nationalsozialistischen Staates*.

Toepser-Ziegert, Gabriele (ed.), *NS-Presseanweisungen der Vorkriegszeit: Edition und Dokumentation*, I: *1933*; II: *1934*; III: *1935*; IV: *1936* (Munich, 1984–93).

Tomascewski, Jerzy, 'Economic and Social Situation of Jews in Poland, 1918–1939', Greenbaum (ed.), *Minority Problems*, 101–6.

Tooze, J. Adam, *Statistics and the German State, 1900–1945: The Making of Modern Economic Knowledge* (Cambridge, 2001).

Townshend, Charles, *Terrorism: A Very Short Introduction* (Oxford, 2002).

Trapp, Joachim, *Kölner Schulen in der NS-Zeit* (Cologne, 1994).

Treue, Wilhelm, 'Rede Hitlers vor der deutschen Presse (10 November 1938)', *VfZ* 6 (1958), 175–91.

—— (ed.), 'Hitlers Denkschrift zum Vierjahresplan 1936', *VfZ* 3 (1955), 184–203.

Trial of the Major War Criminals before the International Military Tribunal, Nuremberg, 14 November 1945–1 October 1946 (Nuremberg, 1948).

Tröger, Annemarie, 'Die Frau im wesensgemässen Einsatz', in Frauengruppe Faschismusforschung (ed.), *Mutterkreuz*, 246–72.

——, 'The Creation of a Female Assembly-Line Proletariat', in Bridenthal *et al.* (eds.), *When Biology Became Destiny*, 237–70.

Tröger, Jörg, *Forschung als Waffe: Rüstungsforschung in der Kaiser-Wilhelm-Gesellschaft und das KWI für Metallforschung 1900 bis 1947* (Göttingen, 2005).

—— (ed.), *Hochschule und Wissenschaft im Dritten Reich* (Frankfurt am Main, 1984).

Tuchel, Johannes, *Konzentrationslager: Organisationsgeschichte und Funktion der 'Inspektion der Konzentrationslager', 1934–1938* (Boppard, 1991).

——, 'Gestapa und Reichssicherheitshauptamt. Die Berliner Zentralinstitutionen der Gestapo', in Paul and Mallmann (eds.), *Die Gestapo*, 84–100.

——, 'Planung und Realität des Systems der Konzentrationslager 1934–1938', in Herbert *et al.* (eds.), *Die nationalsozialistischen Konzentrationslager*, 43–59.

Turner, Henry Ashby, Jr, 'Fritz Thyssen and "I Paid Hitler"', *VfZ* 19 (1971), 225–44.

——, *German Big Business and the Rise of Hitler* (New York, 1985).

——, 'Fallada for Historians', *German Studies Review*, 36 (2003), 477–92.

——, 'Fascism and Modernization', in idem (ed.), *Reappraisals of Fascism*, 117–39.

—— (ed.), *Reappraisals of Fascism* (New York, 1975).

Turner, Stephen P., and Käsler, Dirk (eds.), *Sociology Responds to Fascism* (London, 1992).

Tyrell, Albrecht (ed.), *Führer befiehl . . . Selbstzeugnisse aus der 'Kampfzeit' des NSDAP: Dokumentation und Analyse* (Düsseldorf, 1969).

Ueberhorst, Horst (ed.), *Elite für die Diktatur: Die Nationalpolitischen Erziehungsanstalten 1933–1945: Ein Dokumentarbericht* (Düsseldorf, 1969).

——, 'Feste, Fahnen, Feiern: Die Bedeutung politischer Symbole und Rituale im Nationalsozialismus', in Voigt (ed.), *Symbole der Politik*, 157–78.

Ueberschär, Gerd R., and Vogel, Winfried, *Dienen und Verdienen: Hitlers Geschenke an seine Eliten* (Frankfurt, 1999).

Uhlig, Heinrich, *Die Warenhäuser im Dritten Reich* (Cologne, 1956).

Unverricht, Elsbeth, *Unsere Zeit und Wir: Das Buch der deutschen Frau* (Gauting, 1932).

Vaget, Hans Rudolf, 'Hitler's Wagner: Musical Discourse as Cultural Space', in Kater and Riethmüller (eds.), *Music and Nazism*, 15–31.

Vago, Bela, *The Shadow of the Swastika: The Rise of Fascism and Anti-Semitism in the Danube Basin, 1936–1939* (London, 1975).

Valtin, Jan (pseud. Richard Krebs), *Out of the Night* (London, 1941, reprinted with postscript by Lyn Walsh *et al.*, London, 1988).

Voegelin, Eric, *The New Science of Politics: An Introduction* (Chicago, 1952).

Vogel, Rolf, *Ein Stempel hat gefehlt: Dokumente zur Emigration deutscher Juden* (Munich, 1977).

Voigt, Rüdiger (ed.), *Symbole der Politik: Politik der Symbole* (Opladen, 1989).

Volk, Ludwig, *Bayerns Episkopat und Klerus in der Auseinandersetzung mit dem Nationalsozialismus 1930–1934* (Mainz, 1965).

Völkischer Beobachter, 1933–9.

Volkmann, Hans-Erich, *Das Russlandbild im Dritten Reich* (Cologne, 1994).

——, 'The National Socialist Economy in Preparation for War', in Militärgeschichtliches Forschungsant (ed.), *Germany and the Second World War*, 157–372.

Volkogonov, Dmitri, *Stalin: Triumph and Tragedy* (London, 1995 [1989]).

Vollmer, Bernhard (ed.), *Volksopposition im Polizeistaat: Gestapo- und Regierungsberichte 1934–1936* (Stuttgart, 1957).

Vollnhals, Clemens, 'Jüdische Selbsthilfe bis 1938', in Benz (ed.), *Die Juden in Deutschland*, 314–411.

Vondung, Klaus, *Magie und Manipulation: Ideologischer Kult und politische Religion des Nationalsozialismus* (Göttingen, 1971).

——, 'Der literarische Nationalsozialismus. Ideologische, politische und sozialhistorische Wirkungszusammenhänge', in Denkler and Prümm (eds.), *Die deutsche Literatur*, 44–65.

Vorländer, Herwart, 'NS-Volkswohlfahrt und Winterhilfswerk des deutschen Volkes', *VfZ* 34 (1986), 341–80.

——, *Die NSV: Darstellung und Dokumentation einer nationalsozialistischen Organisation* (Boppard, 1988).

Vosskamp, Wilhelm, 'Kontinuität und Diskontinuität: Zur deutschen Literaturwissenschaft im Dritten Reich', in Lundgreen (ed.), *Wissenschaft*, 140–62.

Wachsmann, Nikolaus, 'From Indefinite Confinement to Extermination: "Habitual Criminals" in the Third Reich', in Gellately and Stoltzfus (eds.), *Social Outsiders in Nazi Germany*, 165–91.

——, *Hitler's Prisons: Legal Terror in Nazi Germany* (New Haven, Conn., 2004).

Waddington, Geoffrey T., 'Hitler, Ribbentrop, die NSDAP und der Niedergang des Britischen Empire 1935–1938', *VfZ* 40 (1992), 273–306.

Wagner, Caroline, *Die NSDAP auf dem Dorf: Eine Sozialgeschichte der NS-Machtergreifung in Lippe* (Münster, 1998).

Wagner, Kurt, *Leben auf dem Lande im Wandel des Industrialisierung: 'Das Dorf war früher auch keine heile Welt': Die Veränderung der dörflichen Lebensweise und der politischen Kultur vor dem Hintergrund der Industrialisierung, am Beispiel des nordhessischen Dorfes Körle* (Frankfurt am Main, 1986).

——, and Wilke, Gerhard, 'Dorfleben im Dritten Reich: Körle in Hessen', in Peukert and Reulecke (eds.), *Die Reihen fast geschlossen*, 85–106.

Wagner, Patrick, ' "Vernichtung der Berufsverbrecher". Die vorbeugende Verbrechensbekämpfung der Kriminalpolizei bis 1937', in Herbert *et al.* (eds.), *Die nationalsozialistischen Konzentrationslager*, 87–110.

——, *Volksgemeinschaft ohne Verbrecher: Konzeptionen und Praxis der Kriminalpolizei in der Zeit der Weimarer Republik und des Nationalsozialismus* (Hamburg, 1996).

Wagner, Walter F., *Der Volksgerichtshof im nationalsozialistischen Staat* (Stuttgart, 1974).

Waiwald, Klaus-Jürgen, *Filmzensur im NS-Staat* (Dortmund, 1983).

Waldenfels, Ernst von, *Der Spion, der aus Deutschland kam: Das geheime Leben des Seemanns Richard Krebs* (Berlin, 2003).

Walter, Michael, *Hitler in der Oper: Deutsches Musikleben 1919–1945* (Stuttgart, 1995).

Walton, John K., *The British Seaside: Holidays and Resorts in the Twentieth Century* (Manchester, 2000).

Wasserstein, Bernard, *Britain and the Jews of Europe, 1939–1945* (Oxford, 1979).

——, 'Patterns of Jewish Leadership in Great Britain during the Nazi Era', in Braham (ed.), *Jewish Leadership during the Nazi Era*, 29–43.

Watt, Donald Cameron, 'German Plans for the Reoccupation of the Rhineland: A Note', *Journal of Contemporary History*, 1 (1966), 193–9.

——, *How War Came: The Immediate Origins of the Second World War, 1938–1939* (London, 1989).

Weber, Hermann, *Die Wandlung des deutschen Kommunismus: Die Stalinisierung der KPD in der Weimarer Republik* (abridged edn, Frankfurt am Main, 1971 [1969]).

——, 'Die KPD in der Illegalität', in Löwenthal and von zur Mühlen (eds.), *Widerstand*, 83–101.

——, 'Weisse Flecken' in der Geschichte: Die KPD-Opfer der Stalinistischen Säuberungen und ihre Rehabilitierung* (Frankfurt am Main, 1990).

Weber, Rosco G. S., *The German Student Corps in the Third Reich* (New York, 1986)

Weckbecker, Gerd, *Zwischen Freispruch und Todesstrafe: Die Rechtsprechung der nationalsozialistischen Sondergerichte Frankfurt a.M. und Bromberg* (Baden-Baden, 1998).

Weekly Report of the German Institute for Business Research (with Supplements), (Institut für Konjunkturforschung, Berlin, 1933–9).

Weeks, Jeffrey, *Sex, Politics, and Society: The Regulation of Sexuality since 1800* (London, 1981).

Wehler, Hans-Ulrich, *Deutsche Gesellschaftsgeschichte*, IV: *Vom Beginn des ersten Weltkriegs bis zur Gründung der beiden deutschen Staaten 1914–1949* (Munich, 2003).

Wehner, Heinz, 'Die Rolle des faschistischen Verkehrswesens in der ersten Periode des zweiten Weltkrieges', *Bulletin des Arbeitskreises Zweiter Weltkrieg*, 2 (1966), 37–61.

Weinberg, Gerhard L., 'Hitler's Private Testament of May 2, 1938', *Journal of Modern History*, 27 (1955), 415–19.

——, *The Foreign Policy of Hitler's Germany*, I: *Diplomatic Revolution in Europe, 1933–36* (London, 1970).

——, *The Foreign Policy of Hitler's Germany*, II: *Starting World War II, 1937–1939* (Chicago, 1980).

Weinberg, Jeshajahu, *et al.*, *The Holocaust Museum in Washington* (New York, 1995).

Weindling, Paul, *Health, Race and German Politics Between National Unification and Nazism, 1870–1945* (Cambridge, 1989)

Weiss, Hermann, 'Ideologie der Freizeit im Dritten Reich: Die NS-Gemeinschaft "Kraft durch Freude" ', *Archiv für Sozialgeschichte*, 33 (1993), 289–303.

Weissler, Sabine (ed.), *Design in Deutschland, 1933–45: Ästhetik und Organisation des Deutschen Werkbundes im 'Dritten Reich'* (Giessen, 1990).

Weitz, Eric D., *Creating German Communism, 1890–1990: From Popular Protests to Socialist State* (Princeton, 1997).

Welch, David (ed.), *Nazi Propaganda: The Power and the Limitations* (London, 1983).

——, *Propaganda and the German Cinema, 1933–1945* (Oxford, 1983).

——, *The Third Reich: Politics and Propaganda* (London, 2002).

Wenning, Norbert, 'Das Gesetz gegen die Überfüllung deutscher Schulen und Hochschulen vom 25. April 1933 – ein erfolgreicher Versuch der Bildungsbegrenzung?' *Die deutsche Schule*, 78 (1986), 141–60.

Werner, Karl Ferdinand, *Das NS-Geschichtsbild und die deutsche Geschichtswissenschaft* (Stuttgart, 1967).

Werner, Kurt, and Biernat, Karl-Heinz, *Die Köpenicker Blutwoche, Juni, 1933* (Berlin, 1958).

Wessel, Horst A., *Thyssen & Co., Mülheim an der Ruhr: Die Geschichte einer Familie und ihrer Unternehmung* (Stuttgart, 1991).

Wessling, Berndt Wilhelm, *Wieland Wagner, der Enkel: Eine Biographie* (Cologne, 1997).

West, Shearer, *The Visual Arts in Germany 1890–1937: Utopia and Despair* (Manchester, 2000).

Westheim, Paul, *Paul Westheim: Kunstkritik aus den Exil*, ed. Tanja Frank (Hanau, 1985).

Westphal, Uwe, *Werbung im Dritten Reich* (Berlin, 1989).

Wetzel, Juliane, 'Auswanderung aus Deutschland', in Benz (ed.), *Die Juden in Deutschland*, 413–98.

Wetzel, Kraft, and Hagemann, Peter, *Zensur: Verbotene deutsche Filme 1933–1945* (Berlin, 1978).

Wetzell, Richard F., *Inventing the Criminal: A History of German Criminology, 1880–1945* (Chapel Hill, N.C., 2000).

Weyrather, Irmgard, 'Numerus Clausus für Frauen – Studentinnen im National-sozialismus', in Frauengruppe Faschismusforschung (ed.), *Mutterkreuz*, 131–62.

——, *Muttertag und Mutterkreuz: Der Kult um die 'deutsche Mutter' im Nationalsozialismus* (Frankfurt am Main, 1993).

Whealey, Robert H., *Hitler and Spain: The Nazi Role in the Spanish Civil War, 1936–1939* (Lexington, Ky., 1989).

Wheeler-Bennett, John W., *The Nemesis of Power: The German Army in Politics, 1918–1945* (London and New York, 1953).

——, *et al.* (eds.), *Documents on German Foreign Policy 1918–1945* (13 vols., London, 1950–70).

Wickert, Christl, 'Popular Attitudes to National Socialist Antisemitism: Denun-ciations for "Insidious Offenses" and "Racial Ignominy"', in Bankier (ed.), *Probing*, 282–95.

Wieland, Günther, *Das war der Volksgerichtshof: Ermittlungen, Fakten, Doku-mente* (Pfaffenweiler, 1989).

Wiesemann, Falk, 'Juden auf dem Lande: die wirtschaftliche Ausgrenzung der jüdischen Viehhändler in Bayern', in Peukert and Reulecke (eds.), *Die Reihen fast geschlossen*, 381–96.

Wildt, Michael, 'Violence against Jews in Germany, 1933–1939', in Bankier (ed.), *Probing*, 181–212.

——, *Generation des Unbedingten: Das Führungskorps des Reichssicherheits-hauptamtes* (Hamburg, 2002).

—— (ed.), *Nachrichtendienst, politische Elite, Mordeinheit: Der Sicherheitsdienst des Reichsführers-SS* (Hamburg, 2003).

Wilke, Gerhard, 'The Sins of the Fathers: Village Society and Social Control in the Weimar Republic', in Evans and Lee (eds.), *The German Peasantry* 174–204.

——, 'Village Life in Nazi Germany', in Bessel (ed.), *Life in the Third Reich*, 17–24.

——, and Wagner, Kurt, 'Family and Household: Social Structures in a German Village Between the Two World Wars', in Evans and Lee (eds.), *The German Family*, 120–47.

Williams, Jenny, *More Lives Than One: A Biography of Hans Fallada* (London, 1998).

Willrich, Wolfgang, *Säuberung des Kunsttempels: Eine kunstpolitische Kampf-schrift zur Gesundung deutscher Kunst im Geiste nordischer Art* (Munich, 1937).

Wingfield, Nancy M., *Minority Politics in a Multinational State: The German Social Democratic Party 1918–1938* (New York, 1989).

Winkler, Dörte, *Frauenarbeit im 'Dritten Reich'* (Hamburg, 1977).

Winkler, Hans Joachim, *Legenden um Hitler: Schöpfer der Autobahnen* (Berlin, 1963).

Winkler, Heinrich August, *Mittelstand, Demokratie und Nationalsozialismus: Die politische Entwicklung von Handwerk und Kleinhandel in der Weimarer Republik* (Cologne, 1972).

——, 'Der entbehrliche Stand. Zur Mittelstandspolitik im "Dritten Reich"', *Archiv für Sozialgeschichte*, 17 (1977), 1–40.

——, 'Ein neuer Mythos vom alten Mittelstand. Antwort auf eine Antikritik', *Geschichte und Gesellschaft*, 12 (1986), 548–57.

——, *Der Weg in die Katastrophe: Arbeiter und Arbeiterbewegung in der Weimarer Republik 1930 bis 1933* (Berlin, 1987).

—— (ed.), *Die deutsche Staatskrise 1930–1933: Handlungsspielräume und Alternativen* (Munich, 1992).

Winkler, Klaus, *Fernsehen unterm Hakenkreuz: Organisation – Programm – Personal* (Cologne, 1994).

Winkler, Kurt, 'Inszenierung der Macht: Weltausstellung 1937. Das "Deutsche Haus" als Standarte', in Behnken and Wagner (eds.), *Inszenierung*, 217–25.

Winkler-Mayerhöfer, Andrea, *Starkult als Propagandamittel? Studien zum Unterhaltungsfilm im Dritten Reich* (Munich, 1992).

Wippermann, Wolfgang, *Zur Analyse des Faschismus: Die sozialistischen und kommunistischen Faschismustheorien 1921–1945* (Frankfurt am Main, 1981).

——, *Das Leben in Frankfurt zur NS-Zeit* (4 vols., Frankfurt am Main, 1986).

——, 'Das Berliner Schulwesen in der NS-Zeit. Fragen, Thesen und methodische Bemerkungen', in Schmoldt (ed.), *Schule in Berlin*, 57–73.

——, and Brucker-Boroujerdi, Ute, 'Nationalsozialistische Zwangslager in Berlin III: Das "Zigeunerlager Marzahn"', *Berliner Forschungen*, 2 (1987), 189–94.

Wiskemann, Elizabeth, *The Rome–Berlin Axis: A History of the Relations Between Hitler and Mussolini* (London, 1949).

Wisotzky, Klaus, *Der Ruhrbergbau im Dritten Reich: Studien zur Sozialpolitik im Ruhrbergbau und zum sozialen Verhalten der Bergleute in den Jahren 1933 bis 1939* (Düsseldorf, 1983).

Wissmann, Sylvelin, *Es war eben unsere Schulzeit: Das Bremer Volksschulwesen unter dem Nationalsozialismus* (Bremen, 1993).

Witetschek, Helmut (ed.), *Die kirchliche Lage in Bayern nach den Regierungspräsidentenberichten 1933–1945* (7 vols., Mainz, 1966–71).

Witte, Karsten, 'Die Filmkomödie im Dritten Reich', in Denkler and Prümm (eds.), *Die deutsche Literatur*, 347–65.

——, *Lachende Erben, toller Tag: Filmkomödie im Dritten Reich* (Berlin, 1995).

Wöhlert, Meike, *Der politische Witz in der NS-Zeit am Beispiel ausgesuchter SD-Berichte und Gestapo-Akten* (Frankfurt am Main, 1997).

Wojak, Irmtrud, et al., *'Arisierung' im Nationalsozialismus: Volksgemeinschaft, Raub und Gedächtnis* (Frankfurt, 2000).

Wolbert, Klaus, *Die Nackten und die Toten des 'Dritten Reiches': Folgen einer politischen Geschichte des Körpers in der Plastik des deutschen Faschismus* (Giessen, 1982).

Wolf, Norbert, *Ernst Ludwig Kirchner 1880–1938: On the Edge of the Abyss of Time* (Cologne, 2003).

Wolffsohn, Michael, 'Arbeitsbeschaffung und Rüstung im nationalsozialistischen Deutschland 1933', *Militärgeschichtliche Mitteilungen*, 22 (1977), 9–19.

Wollenberg, Jörg (ed.), *The German Public and the Persecution of Jews, 1933–1945: 'No One Participated, No One Knew'* (Atlantic Highlands, N.J., 1996 [1989]).

Wollstein, Günter, 'Eine Denkschrift des Staatssekretärs Bernhard von Bülow vom März 1933', *Militärgeschichtliche Mitteilungen*, 1 (1973), 77–94.

——, *Vom Weimarer Revisionismus zu Hitler: Das Deutsche Reich und die Grossmächte in der Anfangsphase der nationalsozialistischen Herrschaft in Deutschland* (Bonn, 1973).

Wolschke-Bulmahn, Joachim, and Gröning, Gert, 'The National Socialist Garden and Landscape Ideal: Bodenständigkeit (Rootedness in the Soil)', in Etlin (ed.), *Art*, 73–97.

Woolf, Stuart J. (ed.), *The Nature of Fascism* (London, 1968).

Woycke, James, *Birth Control in Germany, 1871–1933* (London, 1988).

Wright, Jonathan, and Stafford, Paul, 'Hitler, Britain and the Hossbach Memorandum', *Militärgeschichtliche Mitteilungen*, 42 (1987), 77–123.

Wulf, Joseph, *Die bildenden Künste im Dritten Reich: Eine Dokumentation* (Gütersloh, 1963).

——, *Literatur und Dichtung im Dritten Reich: Eine Dokumentation* (Gütersloh, 1963).

——, *Presse und Funk im Dritten Reich: Eine Dokumentation* (Gütersloh, 1963).

——, *Musik im Dritten Reich: Eine Dokumentation* (Gütersloh, 1963).

——, *Theater und Film im Dritten Reich: Eine Dokumentation* (Gütersloh, 1963).

Wulff, Birgit, *Arbeitslosigkeit und Arbeitsbeschaffungsmassnahmen in Hamburg 1933–1939: Eine Untersuchung zur nationalsozialistischen Wirtschafts- und Sozialpolitik* (Frankfurt am Main, 1987).

——, 'The Third Reich and the Unemployed: National Socialist Work-creation Schemes in Hamburg, 1933–4', in Evans and Geary (eds.), *The German Unemployed*, 281–302.

Wüllenweber, Hans, *Sondergerichte im Dritten Reich: Vergessene Verbrechen der Justiz* (Frankfurt am Main, 1990).

Wyman, David S., *Paper Walls; America and the Refugee Crisis, 1938–1941* (Amherst, Mass., 1968).

Wynot, James D., Jr, '"A Necessary Cruelty": The Emergence of Official Anti-Semitism in Poland, 1935–39', *American Historical Review*, 76 (1971), 1,035–58.

Zabel, James A., *Nazism and the Pastors: A Study of the Ideas of Three Deutsche Christen Groups* (Missoula, Mont., 1976).

Zeidler, Manfred, *Das Sondergericht Freiberg: Zu Justiz und Repression in Sachsen, 1933–1940* (Dresden, 1998).

Zeile, Christine, 'Ein biographischer Essay', in Friedrich R. Reck-Malleczewen, *Tagebuch eines Verzweifelten* (Frankfurt am Main, 1994), 251–98.

Zeinhefer, Siegfried, 'Die Reichsparteitage der NSDAP', in Ogan and Weiss (eds.), *Faszination und Gewalt*, 79–94.

Zeldin, Theodore (ed.), *Conflicts in French Society: Anticlericalism, Education and Morals in the Nineteenth Century: Essays* (London, 1970).

Zeller, Thomas, ' "The Landscape's Crown": Landscape, Perception, and Modernizing Effects of the German Autobahn System, 1934–1941', in Nye (ed.), *Technologies of Landscape*, 218–40.

Zelnhefer, Siegfried, *Die Reichsparteitage der NSDAP: Geschichte, Struktur und Bedeutung der grössten Propagandafeste im nationalsozialistischen Feierjahr* (Neustadt an der Aisch, 1991).

——, and Käs, Rudolf (eds.), *Kulissen der Gewalt: Das Reichsparteitagsgelände in Nürnberg* (Munich, 1992).

Zeman, Zbynek. A. B., *Nazi Propaganda* (Oxford, 1973).

Zerner, Ruth, 'German Protestant Responses to Nazi Persecution of the Jews', in Braham (ed.), *Perspectives on the Holocaust*, 57–68.

——, 'Martin Niemöller, Activist as Bystander: The Oft-Quoted Reflection', in Perry and Schweitzer (eds.), *Jewish-Christian Encounters over the Centuries*, 327–40.

Ziegler, Dieter, 'Die Verdrängung der Juden aus der Dresdner Bank 1933–1938', *VfZ* 47 (1999), 187–216.

Ziegler, Hans Severus, *Entartete Musik: Eine Abrechnung* (Düsseldorf, 1938).

Ziegler, Walter (ed.), *Die kirchliche Lage in Bayern nach den Regierungspräsidentenberichten 1933–1943, IV: Regierungsbezirk Niederbayern und Oberpfalz 1933–1945* (Mainz, 1973).

Zimmermann, Michael, 'Ausbruchshoffnungen: Junge Bergleute in den dreissigen Jahren', in Niethammer (ed.), *Die Jahre weiss man nicht*, 97–132.

——, *Verfolgt, vertrieben, vernichtet: Die nationalsozialistische Vernichtungspolitik gegen Sinti und Roma* (Essen, 1989).

——, *Rassenutopie und Genozid: Die nationalsozialistische 'Lösung der Zigeunerfrage'* (Hamburg, 1996).

Zimmermann, Peter, 'Die Bildsprache des Nationalsozialismus im Plakat', in Rüger (ed.), *Kunst*, 223–36.

Zimmermann, Volker, *Die Sudetendeutschen im NS-Staat: Politik und Stimmung der Bevölkerung im Reichsgau Sudetenland (1938–1945)* (Essen, 1999).

Zipfel, Friedrich, 'Gestapo and SD: A Sociographic Profile of the Organisers of the Terror', in Larsen *et al.* (eds.), *Who Were the Fascists?*, 301–11.

Zitelmann, Rainer, *Hitler: The Policies of Seduction* (London, 1999 [1987]).

Zofka, Zdenek, *Die Ausbreitung des Nationalsozialismus auf dem Lande: Eine regionale Fallstudie zur politischen Einstellung der Landbevölkerung in der Zeit des Aufstiegs und der Machtergreifung der NSDAP 1928–1936* (Munich, 1979).

——, 'Dorfeliten und NSDAP. Fallbeispiele der Gleichschaltung aus dem Kreis Günzburg', in Broszat *et al.* (eds.), *Bayern*, IV. 383–434.

Zolling, Peter, *Zwischen Integration und Segregation: Sozialpolitik im 'Dritten Reich' am Beispiel der 'Nationalsozialistischen Volkswohlfahrt' (NSV) in Hamburg* (Frankfurt am Main, 1986).

Zollitsch, Wolfgang, 'Adel und adlige Machteliten in der Endphase der Weimarer Republik. Standespolitik und agrarische Interessen', in Winkler (ed.), *Die deutsche Staatskrise*, 239–56.

Zuschlag, Christoph, 'An "Educational Exhibition". The Precursors of Entartete Kunst and Its Individual Venues', in Barron (ed.), *Degenerate Art*, 83–103.

——, *'Entartete Kunst': Ausstellungsstrategien in Nazi-Deutschland* (Worms, 1995).

Index

Numbers in bold indicate maps.

The Coming of the Third Reich

There is no story in twentieth-century history more important to understand than Hitler's rise to power and the collapse of civilization in Nazi Germany. A masterful synthesis of a vast body of scholarly work integrated with important new research and interpretations, Evans's history restores drama and contingency to the rise to power of Hitler and the Nazis, even as it shows how ready Germany was by the early 1930s for such a takeover to occur. *The Coming of the Third Reich* is a masterwork of the historian's art and the book by which all others on the subject will be judged.

"Will long remain the definitive English-language account. . . . An impressive achievement."—*The Atlantic Monthly*

ISBN 0-14-303469-3

Death in Hamburg

Society and Politics in the Cholera Years, 1830–1910

Why were nearly 10,000 people killed in six weeks in Hamburg while most of Europe was left almost unscathed? In his acclaimed study of the great cholera epidemic of 1892, Richard J. Evans explains that it was largely because the town was a "free city" within Germany, governed by the "English" ideals of laissez-faire. The absence of an effective public-health policy combined with ill-founded medical theories and the miserable living conditions of the poor to create a scene ripe for tragedy. The story of the cholera years is, in Richard Evans's hands, tragically revealing of the age's social inequalities and governmental pitilessness and incompetence; it also offers disquieting parallels with the world's public-health landscape today.

ISBN 0-14-303636-X